lonely planet

W9-AUT-071

Middle East

Turkey
p413

Syria
p406

Iraq
p186

Iran
p138

**Israel and the
Palestinian
Territories**
p210

Lebanon
p357

Jordan
p291

Egypt
p50

THIS EDITION WRITTEN AND RESEARCHED BY

Anthony Ham,

Sofia Barbarani, Jessica Lee, Virginia Maxwell, Daniel Robinson,

Anthony Sattin, Andy Symington, Jenny Walker

Contents

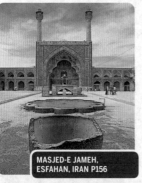

ROB VERHOEVEN & ALESSANDRA MAGNI / GETTY IMAGES ©

**MASJED-E JAMEH,
ESFAHAN, IRAN P156**

OLIVIER CIRENDINI / GETTY IMAGES ©

**MEDITERRANEAN COAST,
TURKEY P457**

ON THE ROAD

Contents

ON THE ROAD

NEMRUT DAĞI, TURKEY P489

HOT-AIR BALLOONS OVER CAPPADOCIA, TURKEY P474

Contents

SPECIAL FEATURES

Welcome to the Middle East

The Middle East is one of history's grand epics – a cradle of civilisations and a beautiful, complicated land that's home to some of the most hospitable people on the planet.

History Writ Large

In the Middle East, history is not something you read about in books. Here, it's a story written on the stones that litter the region, from the flagstones of old Roman roads to the building blocks of ancient Egypt, and the delicately carved tombs and temples from Petra to Baalbek. This is where humankind first built cities and learned to write, and it was from here that Judaism, Christianity and Islam all arose. Wherever you find yourself, the past is always present because here, perhaps more than anywhere else on earth, history is the heart and soul of the land.

Home of Hospitality

At some point on your visit to the Middle East, you'll be sitting in a coffeehouse or looking lost in a labyrinth of narrow lanes when someone will strike up a conversation and, within minutes, invite you home to meet their family and share a meal. Or someone will simply approach and say with unmistakable warmth, 'Welcome'. These spontaneous, disarming and utterly genuine words of welcome can occur anywhere. And when they do, they can suddenly (and forever) change the way you see the Middle East.

Cities

The Middle East's cities read like a roll-call of historical heavyweights: Jerusalem, Damascus, Beirut, Cairo, İstanbul, Erbil, Esfahan. Aside from ranking among the oldest continuously inhabited cities on earth, these ancient-modern metropolises are places to take the pulse of a region. It is in the region's cities, too, that you find the stirring, aspirational architecture that so distinguishes the three great monotheistic faiths. There they sit alongside the more secular charms of bazaars and coffeehouses that seem to embody all the mystery and storytelling magic of a land that gave us *The Thousand and One Nights*.

Wilderness

Beyond city limits, the Middle East is a land of mighty rivers (the Nile, Euphrates), even mightier deserts (the Sahara and peerless Wadi Rum) and green landscapes of exceptional beauty. Exploring these wilderness areas – from snowcapped summits in Turkey, Iran and Lebanon to the kaleidoscopic waters of the Red Sea – lies at the heart of the region's appeal. The message is simple: Forget the clichés that masquerade as Middle Eastern truth – a visit here is one of the most varied and soulful travel experiences on earth.

Why I Love the Middle East

By Anthony Ham, Writer

It was in Damascus that I first fell for the Middle East. Here was a city of storytellers, of warm and welcoming people, of history brought alive at every turn. Ten years later (a decade in which I had marvelled at the peerless beauty of Esfahan and struck out into the Sahara at Siwa, among many Middle Eastern journeys), I returned to Damascus and fell in love all over again. War may since have engulfed the country, but Damascus, and the Middle East, has seen it all before – nowhere else on earth is life lived with such an awareness of history.

For more about our writers, see page 608

Above: İstanbul's Blue Mosque (p417)

Middle East

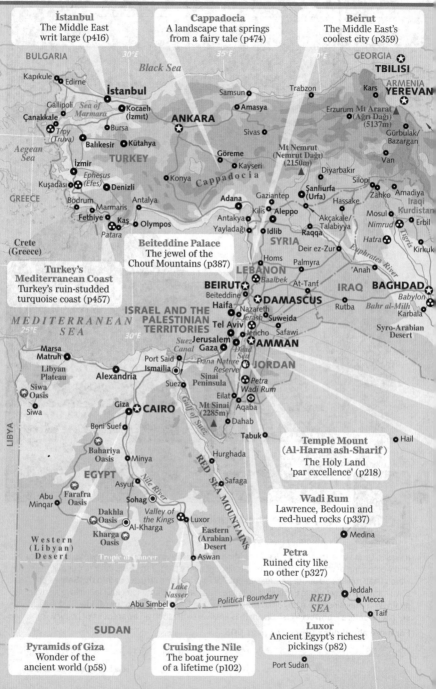

İstanbul
The Middle East
writ large (p416)

Cappadocia
A landscape that springs
from a fairy tale (p474)

Beirut
The Middle East's
coolest city (p359)

BULGARIA

Black Sea

GEORGIA

TBILISI

Kapıkule
Edirne

Samsun

Trabzon

Kars

ARMENIA
YEREVAN

İstanbul

Kocaeli
(İzmit)

Amasya

Erzurum Mt Ararat
(Ağrı Dağı)
(5137m)

Gallipoli
Çanakkale
Sea of
Marmara

ANKARA

Gürbulak/
Bazargan

Troy
(Truva)
Bursa

Sivas

Balıkesir
Kütahya

Van

İzmir
Ephesus
(Efes)

Göreme

Mt Nemrut
(Nemrut Dağı)
(2150m)

Diyarbakır

Silopi

TURKEY

Kayseri

Cappadocia

Şanlıurfa
(Urfa)

Zakho
Amadiya

Kuşadası
Denizli

Konya

Iraqi
Kurdistan

GREECE

Bodrum

Antalya

Adana

Gaziantep

Hassake

Akçakale/
Talabiyya

Mosul
Nimrud
Erbil

Marmaris

Kilis
Aleppo

Fethiye
Kaş
Olympos

Antakya
Yayladağı
Idlib

Raqqa

Hatra

Kirkuk

Patara

SYRIA

Deir ez-Zur

Euphrates River

Beiteddine Palace
The jewel of the
Chouf Mountains (p387)

Homs

Palmyra

'Anah

Crete
(Greece)

**Turkey's
Mediterranean Coast**
Turkey's ruin-studded
turquoise coast (p457)

LEBANON
Baalbek
At-Taft

IRAQ
BAGHDAD

Babylon

BEIRUT
Beiteddine
DAMASCUS

Rutba
Bahr al-Milh

MEDITERRANEAN
SEA

Haifa
Nazareth

ISRAEL AND THE
PALESTINIAN
TERRITORIES

Jerash
Suweida

Karbala

Tel Aviv

Jericho
Safawi

Syro-Arabian
Desert

Suez
Canal
Gaza

Jerusalem

AMMAN

Marsa
Matruh

Port Said

Dana Nature
Reserve

JORDAN

Libyan
Plateau

Alexandria
Ismailia

Sinai
Peninsula

Petra
Wadi Rum

Siwa
Oasis

Suez

Mt Sinai
(2285m)

Eilat
Aqaba

**Temple Mount
(Al-Haram ash-Sharif)**
The Holy Land
'par excellence' (p218)

Hail

Siwa

Giza
CAIRO

Dahab

Beni Suef

Tabuk

LIBYA

Bahariya
Oasis
Minya

Hurghada

Wadi Rum
Lawrence, Bedouin and
red-hued rocks (p337)

EGYPT

Safaga

Asyut

Abu
Minqar
Farafra
Oasis

Sohag

Medina

Dakhla
Oasis

Valley of
the Kings
Luxor

Al-Kharga

Eastern
(Arabian)
Desert

Petra
Ruined city like
no other (p327)

Western
(Libyan)
Desert

Kharga
Oasis

Tropic of Cancer

Aswan

Lake
Nasser

Political Boundary

RED
SEA

Jeddah
Mecca

Abu Simbel

Taif

SUDAN

Pyramids of Giza
Wonder of the
ancient world (p58)

Cruising the Nile
The boat journey
of a lifetime (p102)

Luxor
Ancient Egypt's richest
pickings (p82)

Port Sudan

0 ————— 300 km
0 ————— 180 miles

Tabriz
World Heritage-
listed bazaar (p149)

UZBEKISTAN

Charjou ○   ○ Qarshi

TURKMENISTAN

BAKU
✪

Turkmenbashi ○

ASHGHABAT
✪

○ Mary

AZERBAIJAN

*Caspian
Sea*

Sarakhs

AZERBAIJAN

Gorgan ○   Mashhad ○

○ Tabriz

Rasht ○

○ Herat

TEHRAN
✪

AFGHANISTAN

○ Qom

Sulaymaniyah ○   ○ Hamadan

IRAN

ELEVATION

| 5000m |
| 2000m |
| 500m |
| 200m |
| 0 |

○ Esfahan

Zahedan ○

PAKISTAN

Zagros Mountains

○ Kerman

River

Ahvaz ○

Persepolis

Ur ✪   Basra ○   ○ Abadan

○ Shiraz

KUWAIT
✪

Bushehr ○

Busehr ○   Bandar-e Abbas ○

Chabahar ○

KUWAIT CITY

The Gulf

Tel Aviv Beaches
Mediterranean sand along
Israel's shore (p234)

OMAN   25°N

Dammam ○

BAHRAIN
✪ MANAMA

Dubai ○

Floating in the Dead Sea
Your most buoyant,
otherworldly moment (p258)

✪ DOHA

ABU DHABI
✪

✪ MUSCAT

QATAR

Hofuf ○

UNITED ARAB
EMIRATES

○ Sur

RIYADH
✪

Al-Ashkarah ○

Esfahan
Blue-tiled architectural
perfection (p156)

*Masirah
Island*

T h e   E m p t y
Q u a r t e r
(Rub'al-Khali)

OMAN   20°N

Persepolis
Ancient Persia's vivid
showpiece (p170)

*ARABIAN
SEA*

YEMEN   Salalah ○

15°N

The Middle East's
Top 20

Petra, Jordan

1 Ever since Swiss explorer Johann Ludwig Burckhardt rediscovered this spectacular site in 1812, the ancient Nabataean city of Petra (p327) has been drawing the crowds, and with good reason. This is one of the Middle East's most treasured attractions and when the sun sets over the honeycombed landscape of tombs, carved facades, pillars and golden sandstone cliffs, it's a hard-hearted visitor who's left unaffected by its magic. Allow a couple of days to do the site justice and to visit the main monuments at optimum times of the day.

Pyramids of Giza, Egypt

2 Towering over both the urban sprawl of Cairo and the desert plains beyond, the Pyramids of Giza and the Sphinx (p58) are at the top of every traveller's itinerary. Bring plenty of water, an empty memory card and a lot of patience! You'll have to fend off hordes of people pushing horse rides and Bedouin headdresses in order to enjoy this ancient funerary complex, but no trip to Egypt is complete without a photo of you in front of the last surviving ancient wonder of the world.

REYNOLD MAINSE / GETTY IMAGES ©

BLAINE HARRINGTON III / ALAMY ©

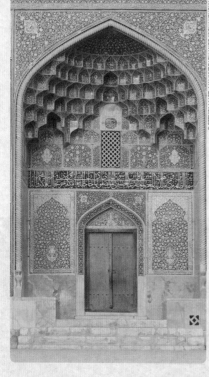

ANDREA THOMPSON PHOTOGRAPHY / GETTY IMAGES ©

Esfahan, Iran

3 There are are few more beautiful places on the planet than Esfahan's be-jewelled core (p156). The city's blue-tiled mosques, intricate and exquisite, share the city centre with refined pleasure palaces and elegant arched bridg-es, all within sight of ex-pansive gardens, tree-lined boulevards and a central square that brims with life in all its Persian complex-ity. Tea houses, hidden away beneath the arches or littered throughout the splendid bazaar, are anoth-er wonderful entry point into this most beguiling of cities. Above left: Masjed-e Sheikh Lotfollah (p156)

Temple Mount, Israel & the Palestinian Territories

4 Few places on earth excite emotions to the same extent as Jerusalem's Dome of the Rock (p218). Sacred to Muslims, Jews and Christians alike – it was said to be here that Abra-ham showed his readiness to sacrifice his son to God, and from here that Moham-med ascended to heaven – it's an epicentre of religious convergence and conflict. It's also home to a gold-plated mosque of singular beauty, built to represent humankind's yearning for God. Top right: Dome of the Rock (p218)

Wadi Rum, Jordan

5 It wasn't just the sublime vista of Wadi Rum (p337) – with its burnished sandstone cliffs and fire-coloured dunes – that impressed Lawrence of Arabia as he paced through the land of the Bedouin. He was also impressed by the stoicism of the people who endured unimaginable hardships associated with a life in the desert. Today, it's possible to get a glimpse of that tra-ditional way of life, albeit with a few more creature comforts, by staying in one of the Bedouin camps scattered across this de-sert wilderness.

5

Cruising the Nile, Egypt

6 The Nile (p102) is Egypt's lifeline, an artery that feeds the entire country, from south to north. Only by setting adrift on it can you appreciate its importance and its beauty, and more practically, only by boat, preferably a wind-propelled felucca, can you see some archaeological sites as they were meant to be seen. Sailing is the slowest and most relaxing way to go, but even from the deck of a multistorey floating hotel you're likely to glimpse the magic.

DANITA DELIMONT / GETTY IMAGES ©

6

Cappadocia, Turkey

7 Cappadocia (p474) was Mother Nature in her surrealism phase. This lunarscape of wacky rock, sculpted by wind and rain, could have been ripped right off the pages of a geological fantasy. Humans have also left their mark, honeycombing the hillsides with cave dwellings and underground cities, and hollowing out Byzantine churches decorated with vibrant frescos. Today troglodyte living has been shaken up for the 21st century with hot-air ballooning from above, trail-hiking on the ground and seriously cool cave-hotels below.

Beiteddine Palace, Lebanon

8 Home to picturesque Druze villages set amid ancient cedar forests, the mountainous Chouf district is justly famous as the home of this magnificent 19th-century palace (p387). It incorporates many traditional features of Arab architecture, including opulently decorated reception rooms, elegant private apartments, a hammam lined with intricately inlaid marble, and an extensive collection of perfectly preserved Byzantine mosaics housed in the vaulted former stables.

CELIA PETERSON / GETTY IMAGES ©

BRIAN LAWRENCE / GETTY IMAGES ©

Persepolis, Iran

9 The Middle East may be strewn with landmarks left by the ancients, but few carry the raw, emotional power of Persepolis (p170). It's the combination of scale (monumental staircases dominate), detail (the bas-reliefs are extraordinary) and setting (the site rises from the sands against a backdrop of pretty hills) that gives this Unesco site its appeal. Begun by Darius the Great at the height of the Achaemenid Empire's powers in the 6th century BC, it's one of the region's most memorable ruined cities. Above: horse sculpture, ruins of Persepolis

İstanbul, Turkey

10 In İstanbul (p416), you can board a commuter ferry to flit between continents and be rewarded at sunset with the city's most magical sight, when the taper-ing minarets of the Old City are thrown into relief against a dusky pink sky. Elsewhere, history reso-nates with profound force amid the Ottoman and Byzantine glories of the Blue Mosque, Aya Sofya and Topkapı Palace. Such is İstanbul, a collision of continents and a glorious accumulation of civilisa-tions. Little wonder, then, that locals call their city the greatest in the world. Top right: Blue Mosque (p417)

Beirut, Lebanon

11 Few cities have the cachet of Beirut (p359) and few have earned it quite so tough. Battle-scarred yet ever-buoyant, this is a city that rises magnificently to the challenge of balancing the cultures of the West and the Middle East. Beirut is both the sophisticated and hedonistic place that once partied under the sobriquet of the 'Paris of the Middle East', and a demographi-cally diverse city that's rife with contradictions. Never is this more true than at sunset along the waterfront Corniche, where miniskirted rollerbladers dodge veiled Shiite families intent on escaping the heat. Bottom right: downtown Beirut

Luxor, Egypt

12 With the greatest concentration of ancient Egyptian monuments anywhere in Egypt, Luxor (p82) repays time. You can spend days or weeks around this town, walking through the columned halls of the great temples on the east bank of the Nile, such as the Ramesseum, or climbing down into the tombs of pharaohs in the Valley of the Kings on the west bank. Just watching the sun rise over the Nile or set behind the Theban hills count as two of Egypt's most unforgettable moments.

Top: Temple of Karnak (p83)

Floating in the Dead Sea, Jordan

13 Floating in the Dead Sea (p314) is one of the world's great natural experiences. Floating is the right word for it: thanks to an eye-stingingly high salt content, it is virtually impossible to swim in the viscous waters of a sea that is 1000ft lower than sea level. The experience is usually accompanied by a mud bath, a bake in the sun and a health-giving spa treatment at one of the modern pleasure palaces lined up along the Dead Sea's shores.

Tel Aviv Beaches, Israel & the Palestinian Territories

14 Just over 100 years ago, Tel Aviv (p231) was little more than sand dunes. Nowadays it's a sprawling, cosmopolitan city bursting with bars, bistros and boutiques, though the beach is still the epicentre of life. Each beach along the coast of Tel Aviv has its own personality – sporty, party, alternative, gay or religious – all set against the Mediterranean's deep blue backdrop.

Mediterranean Coast, Turkey

15 Long before the beachgoers discovered Turkey's Mediterranean coast (p457), the Empire builders descended in their droves, leaving the remnants of once-grand cities in their wake. Backed by rugged cliffs that tumble down to a turquoise sea, this famed sun-and-sand destination is a whole lot more than its resorts. Quaint villages snuggle into hillsides, ruins lay scattered across craggy mountain slopes and those white strips of beach beckon all who visit.

MICHAEL HONOR / GETTY IMAGES ©

Mt Sinai, Egypt

16 It may not be the highest of Sinai's craggy peaks, but Mt Sinai (p126) is the peninsula's most sacred. A place of pilgrimage for Jews, Christians and Muslims alike, the summit affords the magnificent spectacle of light washing over the sea of surrounding mountain tops. Down below, tucked into the mountain's base, is St Katherine's Monastery. Its sturdy Byzantine fortifications are built over the spot where Moses is believed to have witnessed the burning bush. Above: St Katherine's Monastery (p126)

Grand Bazaar, Tabriz, Iran

17 The sensory overload that comes from visiting a Middle Eastern souq is nowhere more memorable than in the main market of Tabriz (p149). Recently restored to its former glories, this thousand-year-old souq, a Unesco World Heritage site, covers 7 sq km and is a true labyrinth of alleyways, vaulted ceilings and glorious domed halls. Each corner of the bazaar has its speciality, but wander to get lost, follow the enticing smells and explore without hurrying through this world where tourists are rarely seen.

Ramallah & Bethlehem, Israel & the Palestinian Territories

18 Ramallah (p264), in the West Bank, is a fine place to take the pulse of Palestinian life. It's a city that struggles daily with its status as a not-quite Palestinian state but does so with remarkable energy. Not far away, Bethlehem (p267), the place of Christ's birth, is a far cry from its humble origins as the birthplace of Christianity but this clamorous city has numerous churches, a fine bazaar and the exceptional former palace of King Herod of biblical infamy. Bottom right: Bethlehem

Ruins of Empire, Jordan

19 For a country so small, Jordan punches well above its weight in world-class monuments, boasting some of the finest Roman ruins outside Rome. Most countries would be pleased to have attractions like the Citadel or the Roman Theatre in Amman, but these pale into insignificance compared with the superbly preserved ruins at Jerash (p307). Visit during a chariot race when commentary from a red-plumed centurion will help bring this ancient outpost of Rome alive.

Below top: South Gate (p307), Jerash

Park Life, Iraq

20 Nobody loves a picnic like an Iraqi Kurd and come summer weekends it can seem as if the entire population has descended on the nearest park. Some of these parks have to be seen to be believed: boating lakes and dancing fountains, enormous children's playgrounds, horse riding and amusement parks, plastic caves, glow-in-the-dark trees and even the odd cable car all feature. Throw in masses of picnicking locals, dozens of noisy wedding parties and coyly courting couples and you get the most fun in Iraq.

Below bottom: Shanadar Park (p191), Erbil

19

20

Need to Know

For more information, see Survival Guide (p561)

Currency

Egyptian pound, Iranian rial, Iraqi dinar, new Israeli shekel, Jordanian dinar, Lebanese pound, Turkish lira.

Language

Arabic, Hebrew and Turkish; English & French widely spoken

Visas

Most visas available on arrival; an Israeli stamp will mean no entry to Iran, Iraq, Lebanon or Syria.

Money

ATMs and credit-card use widespread, except in Iraq; US dollars universally accepted, followed by euros and British pounds.

Mobile Phones

SIM cards widely available. Coverage generally widespread.

Time

All countries in the region are GMT/UTC plus two hours, except Iraq (GMT/UTC plus three hours) and Iran (GMT/UTC plus 31/2 hours). All countries operate on daylight saving hours from around April to September.

When to Go

İstanbul
GO Year-round

Beirut
GO Year-round.

Jerusalem
GO Oct–May

Erbil
GO Oct–May

Tehran
GO Mar–Jun

Cairo
GO Oct–Apr

Desert, dry climate
Dry climate
Warm to hot summers, mild winters
Warm to hot summers, cold winters

High Season
(Jun-Aug & Dec-Jan)

➡ Med beaches and Turkish sites extremely crowded.

➡ Religious holidays (including Christmas–New Year) are mini high seasons.

➡ Prices are sky high and transport crowded; book accommodation well in advance.

Shoulder
(May-Mar & Sep-Nov)

➡ Religious festivals aside, spring and autumn represent shoulder seasons in most countries.

➡ Weather is often agreeable and crowds are generally smaller at main sites.

Low Season
(Jun-Aug & Dec-Feb)

➡ Egypt's Nile Valley and desert can be unbearably hot in summer.

➡ Turkey's Med and Aegean beaches are almost deserted in winter.

Useful Websites

➡ **Lonely Planet** (www. lonelyplanet.com/middle-east) Destination information, hotel bookings, traveller forum and more.

➡ **Al-Ahram Weekly** (http:// weekly.ahram.org.eg) Egypt's English-language newspaper.

➡ **Al-Bab** (www.al-bab.com) Portal covering the entire Arab world.

➡ **Al-Jazeera** (www.aljazeera. com/news/middleeast) CNN of the Arab world.

➡ **Bible Places** (www. bibleplaces.com) Biblical sites.

➡ **Haaretz** (www.haaretz. com) News from an Israeli perspective.

Country Codes

Egypt	☑20
Iran	☑98
Iraq	☑964
Israel & the Palestinian Territories	☑972
Jordan	☑962
Lebanon	☑961
Syria	☑963
Turkey	☑90

Exchange Rates

See individual chapters for exchange rates at the time of publication; see also www. xe.com.

Opening Hours

➡ With a few exceptions, the end-of-week holiday throughout the Middle East is Friday. In Israel and the Palestinian Territories it's Saturday (Shabbat), while in Lebanon and Turkey it's Sunday. In countries where Friday is the holiday, many embassies and offices are also closed on Thursday, although in areas where there are lots of tourists, many private businesses and shops are open on Thursday and many stores will reopen in the evening on Friday.

➡ It's worth remembering that shops and businesses may have different opening hours for different times of the year – they tend to work shorter hours in winter and open earlier in summer to allow for a longer lunchtime siesta. During Ramadan (the month-long fast for Muslims), almost everything shuts down in the afternoon.

Arriving in the Middle East

Cairo International Airport, Egypt Prearrange taxi pickup (E£120 to E£150) or bargain on arrival (E£100); one hour to centre. Buses E£3; up to two hours to centre.

Ben-Gurion International Airport, Tel Aviv, Israel A taxi costs 280NIS/150NIS to Jerusalem/Tel Aviv, a sherut (shared taxi) costs 64NIS to Jerusalem, while a train to Tel Aviv costs 18NIS.

Queen Alia International Airport, Amman, Jordan Airport Express bus (JD3, 45 minutes) runs hourly to the North Bus Station. A taxi costs JD20 to JD25 from the airport.

İstanbul Atatürk International Airport, Turkey Havataş (Havaş) airport buses run to Taksim Meydanı every 30 minutes (₺10, one hour); a taxi to Sultanahmet/Taksim Meydanı costs ₺45/55.

Getting Around

Getting around requires careful planning to circumvent the roadblocks (Iraq and, possibly, Israel). The Middle East has a reasonable transport network, although distances are long and standards vary from country to country.

Air Decent air connections between most countries, allowing you to hop over the war zones. Only Turkey, Jordan and Egypt have flights to/from Israel.

Bus Extensive domestic and international bus services.

Car Road conditions generally good but poor driving and speeding can be a problem; consider paying extra for a local driver.

Ferry Connects Jordan with Egypt.

Train Turkey, Israel, Iran and Egypt have domestic train networks; there are no cross-border train services.

For much more on **getting around**, see p574

If You Like

Ancient Cities

The cradle of civilisation, the crossroads of ancient empires...however you want to describe the region, the Middle East has ruins in abundance.

Petra Extraordinary tombs hewn from the rock by the Nabataeans. (p327)

Luxor Ancient Egypt in all its glory, from the Temple of Karnak to the west bank temples. (p82)

Ephesus An astonishing theatre and some wonderfully preserved temples. (p450)

Persepolis Iran's landmark from pre-Islamic Persia, famous for its bas-reliefs. (p170)

Caesarea An aqueduct, an amphitheatre and other Roman ruins spread out along the Mediterranean Coast. (p241)

Jerash Temples, arches, a distinctive oval plaza and an outstanding colonnaded way in Jordan's north. (p307)

Temple of Echmoun Intact outpost of Phoenician culture in southern Lebanon. (p385)

Pyramids of Giza Not exactly a city but worthy of one. (p58)

Deserts & Oases

It was from the desert that the great monotheistic faiths emerged, and the Middle East is still home to some of the most beautiful and soulful desert landscapes on earth.

Wadi Rum Exceptional rock formations, extraordinary colours, Bedouin companions and echoes of Lawrence of Arabia. (p337)

Western oases Egypt's remote oasis towns and gateways to the Sahara's White and Black Deserts. (p104)

Ein Gedi Israel's canyon oases are home to a profusion of plant and animal life. (p258)

Eastern Desert Jordan's eastern wastes are home to a surprising collection of castles and wildlife sanctuaries. (p317)

Sinai Peninsula The southern peninsula remains one of the Middle East's finest coastal playgrounds with a fascinating hinterland. (p116)

Mosques

Mosques stand at the very heart of Middle Eastern life. In many cases, the architecture speaks to the aesthetic aspirations of a people, with symmetrical forms and exquisite decorative features.

Dome of the Rock, Jerusalem Not technically a mosque, but rather a shrine, and one of Islam's holiest sites, with a graceful octagonal plan, gorgeous mosaic tiles and a gleaming gold dome. (p218)

Blue Mosque, İstanbul The personification of Islamic architectural grace and perfect proportions. (p417)

Masjed-e Jameh, Esfahan One of the high points of Persian Islamic architecture, both in scale and exquisite detail. (p156)

Masjed-e Shah, Esfahan Magnificent blue-tiled mosque in the heart of Esfahan. (p156)

Süleymaniye Mosque, İstanbul The highpoint of 16th-century Ottoman mosque design and İstanbul's grandest. (p417)

Al-Azhar Mosque, Cairo One of the oldest mosques in Egypt and the world's oldest surviving university. (p55)

Masjed-e Nasir-al-Molk, Shiraz Stunning example of Iranian mosque architecture, with dazzling detail and magnificent tilework at every turn. (p166)

Souqs & Bazaars

The souqs and bazaars that snake through so many Middle Eastern towns provide many visitors with their most memorable experiences of the region.

Khan al-Khalili, Cairo Cairo's Byzantine-era bazaar is a tourist cliché, but with very good reason. (p58)

Top: Masjed-e Jameh (p156), Esfahan, Iran
Bottom: Khan al-Khalili market (p58), Cairo, Egypt

PLAN YOUR TRIP IF YOU LIKE

Castles & Fortresses

During the Crusades in particular, seemingly every conceivable hilltop was colonised by a defensive fortress. Many remain, in some cases beautifully preserved.

Biblical Landmarks

The Bible – and the Torah, and the Quran – live and breathe in the cities and soil of the Middle East, particularly the Levantine arc.

Jerusalem Jerusalem is the Bible writ large. (p212)

Bethlehem The Church of the Nativity stands on the site where Jesus is believed to have been born. (p267)

Mt Sinai Said to be where Moses received the Ten Commandments from God atop the summit, in Egypt. (p126)

Bethany-Beyond-the-Jordan Jordanian site where Jesus was baptised. (p313)

Machaerus Herod the Great's castle in Jordan, where John the Baptist was martyred. (p323)

Mt Nebo Where Moses looked over the Promised Land. (p322)

Antakya Saints Peter and Paul both preached at this site in Turkey, and there's a church to prove it. (p469)

Hammams

The hammam (hamam in Turkey and Iran) is a wonderful sensual indulgence. You'll never forget the massage on tiled slabs, sweltering steam-rooms and scalding tea.

Çemberlitaş Hamamı, İstanbul Sixteenth-century Ottoman hamam with an atmosphere to match in İstanbul. (p423)

Ayasofya Hürrem Sultan Hamamı, İstanbul İstanbul's most beautiful hamam. (p423)

Hammam Al Shifa This local place has a hot room, a sauna and a steam room. (p272)

Hiking

The Middle East is – perhaps surprisingly – a top hiking destination, with Jordan and Israel in particular offering rewarding trails from short day hikes to longer, multiday expeditions.

Lycian Way, Turkey One of the world's most beautiful walks, along the Mediterranean rim from Fethiye to Antalya. (p460)

Dana Biosphere Reserve, Jordan Trek through one of the Middle East's most intact ecosystems. (p325)

Makhtesh Ramon, Israel Hike through this vast desert crater, famous for its multicoloured sandstone. (p260)

Petra, Jordan Hike through the main site, with intriguing trails leading further to little-known tombs. (p327)

Qadisha Valley, Lebanon The starting point of hikes along the spine of Lebanon. (p381)

Diving & Snorkelling

The Red Sea could be the finest place to dive and snorkel on earth, with varied underwater topography in one of the richest and most varied marine ecosystems you'll find.

Sharm el-Sheikh, Egypt Base for the *Thistlegorm*, a sunken WWII cargo ship that's the world's best wreck dive. (p117)

Dahab, Egypt A place of snorkelling legend and home to the famous Blue Hole. (p120)

Ras Mohammed National Park, Egypt A national marine park teeming with more fish life than you can poke a regulator at. (p117)

Aqaba, Jordan Jordan's wedge of the Red Sea has hundreds of coral species and around 1000 fish species. (p339)

Marsa Alam, Egypt A remote and virgin reef offshore and the perfect place for shark spotting. (p116)

Eilat, Israel Israel's best snorkelling, plus a chance to commune with fish without getting wet... (p261)

Urban Vibes

The Middle East is not just about religion, old stones and history lessons at every turn. The region's cities can be vibrant, exciting places racing headlong towards the future.

Beirut One of the most resilient cities on earth, Beirut can be sassy and sophisticated in equal measure. (p359)

Tel Aviv Jerusalem's alter ego is secular, international and more than a little hedonistic. (p231)

Erbil Few places capture the hope and excitement of the new Iraq quite like this irresistible Kurdish city. (p188)

Amman Jordan's capital has some of the most enduring oases of urban cool in the region. (p294)

Alexandria A culturally rich city as much Mediterranean as Egyptian. (p76)

İstanbul One of the world's great cities: European, Middle Eastern and Turkish all at once. (p416)

Beaches

The Middle East has some superb places to lay out your towel. You're most likely to feel comfortable doing so in Turkey, Israel and some parts of Egypt.

Windsurfing (p44) on the Red Sea, Egypt

Çıralı, Turkey Right alongside that old traveller favourite hangout of Olympos. (p463)

Patara, Turkey Twenty kilometres of unbroken and largely unspoiled sand. (p460)

Nuweiba, Egypt One of the quieter Egyptian Red Sea shores with plenty to do or lovely beaches on which to do nothing. (p126)

Dahab, Egypt Yes, it's a scene, but the location is dramatic and you haven't lazed on a Middle Eastern beach unless you've done so at Dahab. (p120)

Tel Aviv, Israel Long stretches of soft sand, with all the amenities of Israel's liveliest city right nearby. (p231)

Coral Beach Nature Reserve, Israel Eilat's best beach is ideal for snorkellers. (p261)

Dead Sea, Jordan Float (swimming is near impossible) in the buoyant salt sea. (p314)

Berenice and Tala Bay Beaches, Jordan Learn to dive without the vibe on Jordan's laid-back South Coast. (p341)

Wildlife

Ecotourism projects and wildlife reserves now protect some of the Middle East's most charismatic fauna.

Ras Mohammed National Park, Egypt One of the Red Sea's few protected areas teems with marine life. (p117)

Shaumari Wildlife Reserve, Jordan Arabian oryx, ostrich, gazelles and Persian onagers are bred in large enclosures in preparation for reintroduction to the wild. (p318)

Mujib Biosphere Reserve, Jordan An enclosure for the Nubian ibex and the chance to see caracals. (p316)

Chouf Cedar Reserve, Lebanon If you're (extremely) lucky, you might see wolves, wild cats, ibexes and gazelles. (p389)

Month By Month

January

Much of the region, including desert regions at night, can be bitterly cold and there can be snow on the high peaks. Egypt and the Red Sea have relatively balmy temperatures.

✯✯ Christmas (Orthodox)

Orthodox Christians commemorate the birth of Jesus (it's celebrated by Eastern Orthodox churches on 6 and 7 January and by Armenians in the Holy Land on 18 and 19 January). Important among Christian communities in Lebanon, Egypt and Syria.

February

The winter chill continues throughout much of the region, though it's the perfect time of year in the south. Egypt's beaches and Nile Valley can be busy, while Turkish mountain passes may be impassable.

✯✯ Ascension of Ramses II

The sun penetrates the inner sanctuary of the temple at Abu Simbel in southern Egypt, illuminating the statues of the gods within, on 22 February and 22 October.

✯✯ Purim

Purim celebrates the foiling of a plot to wipe out the Jews of ancient Persia. Children and adults put on costumes for an evening of revelry.

March

In Egypt intense sandstorms can darken the horizon, but the hillsides and valleys of the Levant, Turkey and northern Iraq are green – it's a great time for hiking. Low-season room prices in most areas.

✯✯ Nevruz

Kurds and Alevis celebrate the ancient Middle Eastern spring festival on 21 March with much jumping over bonfires and general jollity.

Banned until a few years ago in Turkey, Nevruz is now an official holiday with huge parties, particularly in Diyarbakır. It's called No Ruz in Iran, and most Iranians go on holiday at this time.

April

A shoulder season for much of the Middle East, April is a wonderful time to visit: the wildflowers are in bloom in the Levant, tourist numbers at Egyptian archaeological sites drop off and there is good beach weather in southwest Turkey.

✯✯ Passover

Known as Pesach, this weeklong festival celebrates the liberation of the Israelites from slavery in Egypt with ritual family dinners and Shabbat-like closures on the first and seventh days. Lots of Israelis go on holiday, so it's high season in Israel.

✯✯ Easter

During Holy Week, Catholic pilgrims throng Jerusalem's Via Dolorosa and the Church of the Holy Sepulchre, and many Protestants gather at the Garden Tomb.

Dates for Orthodox celebrations differ slightly.

✰✰ Dahab Festival

A mash-up of a windsurfing contest, divers' meet, DJ party and Bedouin culture show, this weeklong get-together is as groovy as its host town of Dahab. Oh, and camel races too! Details at bedouinfestival.com.

✰✰ Fajr Film Festival

Iran's premier film festival features Iranian and international films and red-carpet events in more than 20 cinemas across Tehran; see www.fajrfilmfestival.com.

May

It's still peak tourist season in the Levant with warm weather on the way. High season prices in coastal areas are yet to kick in, but it's good beach weather from the Red Sea to the Mediterranean.

✰✰ Dance with the Sufis

In Luxor, in the third week of the Islamic month of Sha'aban, the Sufi festival of Moulid of Abu al-Haggag offers a taste of rural religious tradition. Several smaller villages have *moulids* (religious festivals) around the same time.

June

You'll encounter long days and sunny, warm weather all across the region. The tourist high season draws large crowds and higher

room prices in many areas. It's unbearably hot in Egypt by the end of the month.

✰ Israel Festival

Four weeks of music, theatre and dance performances (some of them free) in and around Jerusalem add a real spring to the step of the city in early summer. Check out www.israel-festival.org.il for dates and programs.

✰✰ Ramadan

The holy month of dawn-to-dusk fasting by Muslims (called Ramazan in Iran) is offset by celebratory breakfast meals after sunset. Offices may have shorter hours, and restaurants may close during daylight hours. Foodies will love this time; ambitious sightseers may be frustrated.

✰✰ Eid al-Fitr

The Festival of Fast-Breaking that marks the end of Ramadan is celebrated with entirely understandable gusto throughout Muslim areas. It's generally a family-centric festival, but travellers will find themselves caught up in it all.

July

A great time for festivals, but the weather can be unpleasantly hot in most areas. It is, however, high season along Turkey's Aegean and Mediterranean coasts, while holidaying Europeans can push prices up anywhere.

✰ Byblos International Festival

Lebanon kicks off the Levantine summer with pop,

classic, opera and world-music performances, many of which are staged among the ruins of Byblos' ancient harbour. It can start in late June and continue on into August; check www.byblos-festival.org for details.

✰ Jerash Festival

Hosted within world-class ruins, Jordan's much-loved Jerash Festival of Culture & Arts brings ancient Jerash to life with plays, poetry recitals, opera and concerts. Held annually since 1981, the festival (www.jerashfestival.jo) is held over 17 days from mid-July to mid-August.

✰ Beiteddine Festival

Lebanon's full program of summer events continues with this terrific arts festival (www.beiteddine.org) with music, dance and theatre held in the beautiful courtyard of the Beiteddine Palace. It usually spills over into August.

August

The heat takes its toll everywhere; unless you're by the beach in Turkey, it's a month to avoid. High-season rates (and overbooking) apply in many coastal areas.

✰ Red Sea Jazz

Eilat in August gives you the chance to combine long days by the water with some terrific jazz (www.redseajazzeilat.com). It draws international acts, takes place in the last week of August and it's probably the best jazz festival in the region.

September

Two of the most important Jewish holidays make for mini high seasons. Elsewhere, temperatures are starting to fall (only slightly in Egypt) and high-season crowds and prices start to ebb in Turkey.

✯✯ Rosh Hashanah

The Jewish New Year causes Shabbat-like closures that last for two days. Some Israelis go on holiday, so accommodation is scarce and room prices rise. Unless you're here for the ambience or for religious reasons, avoid this one.

✯✯ Yom Kippur

The Jewish Day of Atonement is a solemn day of reflection and fasting – and cycling on the empty roads. In Jewish areas, all businesses shut and transportation (including by private car) completely ceases; Israel's airports and land borders close. Eerie.

☆ International İstanbul Biennial

The city's major visual-arts shindig, considered to be one of the world's most prestigious biennials, takes place from mid-September to mid-November in odd-numbered years, with artists and performers from around the world.

✯✯ Eid al-Adha

For the Feast of the Sacrifice, a four-day Muslim holiday, families slaughter sheep and goats at home, even in large cities. There's literally blood in the streets, and the air smells of roasting meat. In short, not for vegetarians.

Top: Ascension of Ramses II (p26)
Bottom: Preparations for Sukkot in Jerusalem

October

As the summer heat finally breaks, Egypt comes back into play and the crowds have tapered off in Turkey. Elsewhere, it's a pleasant month with mild temperatures, although rain is possible. A great month for festivals.

☆ Akbank Jazz Festival

From late September to mid-October, İstanbul celebrates its love of jazz with this eclectic line-up of local and international performers. The festival (www.akbanksanat.com) marked its 25th anniversary in 2015, and gains in prestige every year.

☆ Antalya Golden Orange Film Festival

Held in early October, Turkey's foremost film event (www.altinportakal.org.tr) features screenings, a parade of stars in cars and the obligatory controversy. At the award ceremony in Aspendos, the Golden Orange, nicknamed the Turkish Oscar, is awarded to film-makers.

☆ Beirut International Film Festival

Beirut's contribution to the cinematic calendar is an increasingly high-profile film festival (www.beirutfilmfestival.org) with a growing reputation as one of the best in the Middle East.

☆ Sukkot

The week-long Feast of the Tabernacles holiday recollects the Israelites' 40 years of wandering in the desert. Families build *sukkot* (foliage-roofed booths) in which they dine and sometimes sleep. The first and seventh day are Shabbat-like public holidays.

☆ Ashura

Ashura marks the martyrdom of Imam Hossein and is the most intense, passionate date on the Shia Muslim calendar. It is celebrated with religious theatre and sombre parades in which men self-flagellate. It's especially big in Iran and in parts of Lebanon and Iraq.

November

Good for sightseeing with surprisingly chilly weather and smallish crowds even at the more popular sights. Rain possibilities may deter hikers, but Saharan expeditions in Egypt are again possible after the summer break.

☆ Cairo International Film Festival

From the last weekend in November into December, this 10-day event shows recent films from all over the world.

☆ Arab Music Festival

In November, 10 days of classical, traditional and orchestral Arabic music are held at the Cairo Opera House and other venues. See www.cairoopera.org.

December

The Middle East's winter begins in earnest, and low-season prices apply in most areas, except Christian areas at Christmas, ski resorts and in Egypt where Europeans flood in search of winter sun.

☆ Hanukkah

The Jewish Festival of Lights celebrates the rededication of the Temple after the Maccabean revolt. Families light candles over eight nights using a nine-branched candelabra and waistlines bulge due to jelly doughnuts.

☆ Christmas

Midnight Catholic Mass is celebrated in the Church of the Nativity in Bethlehem. Christmas is a public holiday in the West Bank but not in many other areas. Orthodox Christians must wait until early January for their Christmas.

☆ Prophet's Birthday

Moulid al-Nabi is a region-wide celebration with sweets and new clothes for kids and general merriment in all Muslim areas. In Cairo, the week before is an intense Sufi scene at Midan al-Hussein.

Itineraries

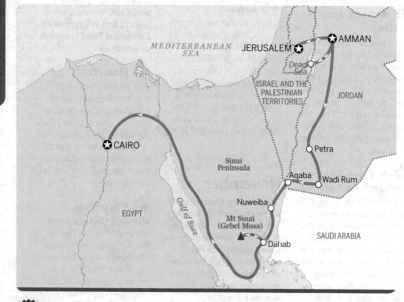

Amman to Cairo

This journey represents a shorter version of the old İstanbul-to-Cairo traveller favourite (no longer possible due to the war in Syria) and includes some of the Middle East's premier attractions.

Your journey starts in **Amman**, a cosmopolitan city with Roman ruins and brilliant restaurants. After visit to the **Dead Sea** (an easy day trip from the capital), detour to **Jerusalem**, the Middle East's spiritual heart. Returning to Jordan, spend some time exploring fabulous **Petra**, the Middle East's most beguiling ancient city. Further south, Petra's rival to the title of Jordan's most spectacular site is **Wadi Rum**, a soulful red-hued desert landscape that rewards those who spend a couple of days exploring. From here, leave Jordan behind and cross the Red Sea at **Aqaba** to **Nueweiba** in Egypt. Where you go from here depends on the prevailing security situation, with much of the Sinai Peninsula considered risky at the time of research. Assuming all is well, continue on from Nuweiba to **Dahab**, for Red Sea snorkelling and an excursion to catch sunrise from atop **Mt Sinai**. From Dahab (or from Nuweiba if security is uncertain) make for clamorous, attraction-rich **Cairo**.

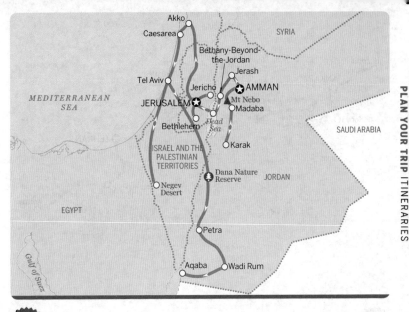

3 WEEKS Jordan, Israel & the Palestinian Territories

Welcome to the Middle Eastern heartland for a trip through the best that Jordan, Israel and the Palestinian Territories have to offer. Although distances can be small, there's a lot to pack in. Most of this trip is best accomplished using public transport.

Amman may lack the cachet of other Middle Eastern cities, but most travellers end up staying longer than planned. From here, it's easy to make side trips to many of Jordan's must-see destinations; the echoes of Moses at **Mt Nebo**, the mosaics of **Madaba** and the Crusader castle of **Karak** all deserve your time. When you're ready to move on, head to **Jerash**, a quiet yet rewarding ancient site with a wonderful colonnaded way running through its heart. Travelling south, **Bethany-Beyond-the-Jordan**, the place where Christ was baptised, resonates strongly with pilgrims, while floating in the buoyant waters of the **Dead Sea** is a signature Middle Eastern experience.

Across the Jordan River, roiling **Jerusalem** is the starting point of so much Middle Eastern history. From Jerusalem, your ability to visit the biblical towns of **Bethlehem** and **Jericho** will depend on the security situation. In the country's north, timeless **Akko** and the world-class ruins of **Caesarea** are worth as much time as you can give them. On your way back, don't miss **Tel Aviv**, a lively place to let your hair down and discover the hedonistic side of Israeli life. Its antithesis, the **Negev Desert**, is a wilderness area that you simply don't expect to find in this ever-crowded corner of the earth.

Crossing back into Jordan, the spectacular scenery of **Dana Nature Reserve** shouldn't be missed, while **Petra** is an astonishing place, where reality outstrips even the most lofty expectations. If time allows, spend at least a couple of days here, so you can savour the main tombs as well as visit the site's more outlying areas. The same applies to **Wadi Rum** – you could get a taste of this soulful place in a day, but you'll gain a deeper understanding of its gravitas if you sleep out under the stars for at least one night. The laid-back Red Sea port of **Aqaba**, with world-class diving and snorkelling, provides the perfect place to rest at journey's end.

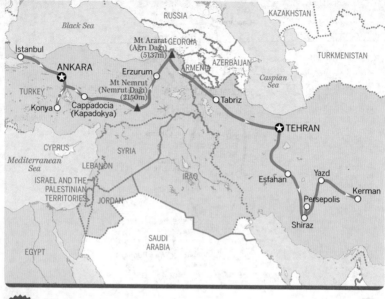

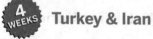

Turkey & Iran

4 WEEKS

From marvellous İstanbul to the fascinating cities of central Iran, this itinerary takes you from the Middle East's most Western-oriented corner to its least. Neither, however, conforms to stereotypes and the journey between the two is like traversing the region's complicated soul. Allow two weeks for each country.

İstanbul is at once a destination in its own right and the starting point of so many Turkish journeys. After a few days, make for **Ankara**, the country's underrated capital, and then take a detour to conservative but welcoming **Konya**, the spiritual home of the Sufis. Perhaps returning via Ankara, make for the otherworldly landscapes of **Cappadocia (Kapadokya)** that seem to have sprung from a wonderfully childlike imagination. Linger as long as you can here – it's a landscape that really gets under skin the longer you stay. When you can finally tear yourself away, begin the long journey east to the brooding statues of **Mt Nemrut**, surely one of Turkey's most thought-provoking sights. By the time you reach **Erzurum**, you'll have left the last remnants of tourist Turkey, and your reward in this eastern city is a fine open-air gallery of Seljuk- and Mongol-era monuments. Consider climbing **Mt Ararat** (although you need to plan well in advance to do so), before crossing the border into Iran.

Your first stop in Iran should be **Tabriz**, not least because its bazaar is one of the finest, most evocative of all Middle Eastern markets. Spend a day or two in **Tehran**, itself home to an overwhelming market as well as fine museums. But after a couple of days, stop resisting the temptation and head on to **Esfahan**, one of the Middle East's most beautiful, most bejewelled cities (at least in the centre), with its utterly exquisite gardens, arched bridges and tiled mosques. **Shiraz** is a cultured, appealing city, not to mention the gateway to **Persepolis**, that towering monument to all that was good about ancient Persia. Continue to **Yazd** and check into an atmospheric traditional hotel in the old town. Spend two days exploring the old city, the Zoroastrian Towers of Silence and perhaps making a trek into the desert. Finish up in **Kerman**, from where you can take a tour to the remarkable 'sand castles' of the Kaluts.

Above: Nemrut Dağı
(Mt Nemrut; p489),
Turkey

Right: Aramgah-e
Shah-e Cheragh
(p165), Shiraz, Iran

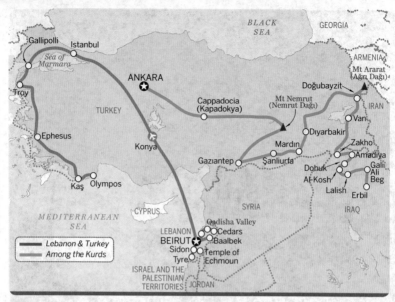

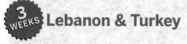

Lebanon & Turkey
Among the Kurds

3 WEEKS Lebanon & Turkey

4 WEEKS Among the Kurds

For this Mediterranean sojourn, count on a week to 10 days in Lebanon and two weeks in Turkey.

Begin in **Beirut**, a glamorous metropolis, the Middle East in complicated microcosm and filled with Mediterranean joie de vivre. If it's safe, head south to the Phoenician heartland – **Sidon**, the **Temple of Echmoun** and **Tyre**. East of Beirut, **Baalbek** is one of the Middle East's premier Roman sites, though you will need to check the security situation before you set off. Head north, to the pretty fishing port of **Byblos**, then finish up with some hiking through the **Qadisha Valley**, finally putting on your skis at the **Cedars**.

From Beirut, fly to **İstanbul** for a few days in that most glorious of cities. Three days should give you a taste before you move on to visit **Gallipoli**, with its poignant echoes of WWI, and **Troy**, where altogether more ancient battles took place. Work your way around the coast, pausing at the mighty ruins of **Ephesus**, which rank among the Middle East's most imposing, and lingering in the delightful Mediterranean villages of **Kaş** or **Olympos**, where you'll wonder why life can't always be like this.

Begin in **Ankara**, the heart of Turkey's secularist Atatürk cult of personality, where you'll find a splendid museum and a fine citadel. On your way southeast into the Kurdish heartland, make the obligatory stop in **Cappadocia (Kapadokya)** and **Mt Nemrut** before exploring the rarely visited but always fascinating cities of **Gaziantep** and **Şanliurfa**. Nearby **Mardın** combines a beautiful setting with equally beautiful architecture and a fascinating cultural mix. By the time you reach **Dıyarbakir**, with its intriguing architecture, you're deep in Kurdish territory. Head for **Doğubayzit**, one of eastern Turkey's most extraordinary sights, with a legendary castle and stunning views of **Mt Ararat**; the mountain can be climbed, although most travellers content themselves with not-so-distant views from the town. Further south, **Van** is home to the lovely Armenian church on Akdamar Island. If you've come this far, it's likely you're en route to Iraq. If it's safe, cross into **Zakho** with its iconic bridge, then spend as long as they'll let you getting to know **Amadiya**, **Dohuk**, **Al-Kosh**, **Lalish** and **Gali Ali Beg**, before finishing up in **Erbil**, one of the oldest cities on earth, but one rushing headlong towards the future.

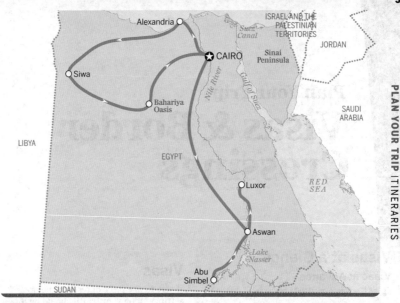

Land of the Pharaohs

There's so much to see in Egypt that it deserves its own itinerary. Count on a week for Cairo and Alexandria, a week for the Western Oases, and another week for the country's south. When security returns to the Sinai Peninsula, you could spend an extra week there.

So many Egyptian journeys revolve around **Cairo**, and you'll return here again and again. Apart from being the Middle East's largest and most clamorous metropolis, Cairo is also home to the iconic Pyramids of Giza, the Egyptian Museum and a wonderful coffeehouse culture. Return to Cairo, then head north to **Alexandria**, Egypt's sophisticated and quintessentially Mediterranean city. It feels like nowhere else in the country, and a combination of terrific museums and great food gives you futher reason to visit. A *really* long journey west is worth it for your first sight of **Siwa**, one of the Sahara's great oasis outposts and home to an ancient temple in the sands. It's the sort of place where you can stand on the outskirts of the village, just as Alexander the Great did, and contemplate eternity. Dusty desert trails lead to the **Bahariya Oasis**; you'll need to rent a private 4WD to reach Bahariya, but why not make it part of a deep desert expedition from Bahariya into the White and Black Deserts.

It's back to Cairo to enjoy the pleasures of civilisation for a day or two, then jump on a train south to **Aswan**, one of Africa's loveliest riverside spots. There's a monastery and museum to anchor your explorations of the city, but its real charm is its proximity to the Nile. Take the detour south into Nubia to **Abu Simbel**, one of Egypt's most extraordinary temples, then from Aswan sail slowly up the Nile aboard a felucca, savouring the slow rhythms of life along this, the world's longest river all the way to **Luxor**, home to the richest collection of Pharaonic sites in the country. Here you'll find so much of what drew you to Egypt in the first place, including the Temples of Karnak, the Valley of the Kings and the Valley of the Queens.

Plan Your Trip
Visas & Border Crossings

Visas at a Glance

Visas in Advance

Egypt If entering overland from Israel

Iran Safest option is to obtain in advance

Arab Iraq Tourist visas not possible

Jordan If you need a multiple-entry visa

Turkey Purchase online before travel

Visas Available on Arrival

Egypt Except if crossing from Israel

Iran Possibly available at Iranian international airports but risk of rejection – best to obtain in advance

Iraqi Kurdistan

Israel and the Palestinian Territories

Jordan Single-entry visas except if first entry on King Hussein/Allenby Bridge

Lebanon

Israeli Passport Stamps

OK for entry Egypt, Jordan, Turkey

Will be denied entry Iraq, Iran, Lebanon, Syria

Visas

If you do one piece of research before setting out on your trip, it should be to familiarise yourself with the requirements for obtaining visas for the countries that you intend to visit. For the unwary, it can be a minefield. For the well informed, it shouldn't pose too many difficulties.

The major issue arises if you plan to visit Israel and the Palestinian Territories. If you do, then you may need to think carefully about the order in which you visit the countries of the Middle East, or prepare for a little sleight of hand to ensure there is no trace of you having visited Israel and therefore avoid limiting the other countries that you're able visit.

Egypt

Most Egyptian tourist visas can be obtained on arrival. It couldn't be easier if you're arriving by air, while those travelling from Jordan can obtain a visa at the port in Aqaba before boarding the ferry. Visa fees vary by nationality and can usually be paid in Egyptian pounds, US dollars, UK pounds or euros. Visas granted on arrival allow you to stay in Egypt for one month.

The only exception to these general rules is if you plan to enter Egypt from Israel via the Taba border crossing. In this case, we recommend that you apply for your Egyptian visa in advance in Tel Aviv or Eilat. If you just turn up at this border crossing without a visa in your passport, your visa must be guaranteed by an Egyptian travel agency – more trouble than it's worth.

Iran

Iranian visas can be a pain to organise. The process is slow (start at least two months prior to your planned travel), somewhat unpredictable, and rules can change without warning. But the vast majority of people do get a visa within two or three weeks. Note that all applications stall over the No Ruz holiday period (late March); submit before 8 March to be sure.

There are three kinds of visas:

➡ **Tourist visa** Issued for up to 30 days and extendable. Must be obtained before coming to Iran from Iranian embassy or consulate.

➡ **Tourist visa on arrival (VOA)** Issued for 15 days on arrival at any Iranian international airport. Convenient but risky, as you may be denied entry.

➡ **Transit visa** Issued for five to seven days. You must enter and exit via different countries, and have a visa or a ticket to an onward country. Not available to US passport holders.

Iraq

Most nationalities can obtain a free, 15-day visa for Iraqi Kurdistan at the point of entry. This visa, which is not valid for the rest of the country, can be extended for a further 30 days in Erbil.

For everywhere outside of Iraqi Kurdistan, Iraqi embassies in your home country will only issue visas for those with official business in the country. Tourist visas are not available.

Israel & the Palestinian Territories

Tourist visas are issued to nationals of most Western countries at airports and land border crossings. Although most visas are for three-month periods, travellers arriving overland from Egypt or Jordan are sometimes given two-week or one-month visas. Some visas may also come with restrictions relating to travel inside the Palestinian Territories.

Jordan

Visitors to Jordan can obtain a one-month tourist visa at airports and *most* land borders. Such visas are single entry and cost JD40.

There are two exceptions. First, the only border crossing where visas are not available on arrival is the King Hussein/Allenby Bridge, which connects Jordan with Israel and the Palestinian Territories. This applies if you are entering Jordan for the first time. If, however, you are *returning* to Jordan

---

BANNED: ISRAELI PASSPORT STAMPS

Arab countries have widely varying policies on admitting travellers whose passports show evidence of a visit to Israel. Jordan and Egypt, with which Israel has peace treaties, have no problem at all, and the same goes for Tunisia, Morocco and many of the Gulf emirates (but not Saudi Arabia).

If there's any chance you'll be heading to Arab or Muslim countries during the life of your passport, your best bet is to make sure that it shows no indication that you've been to Israel. Fortunately, Israeli passport inspectors no longer stamp tourists' passports and instead issue a small loose-leaf entry card to serve as proof of lawful entry. Keep this with you at all times until you leave Israel.

Unfortunately, Egyptian and Jordanian officials are not so obliging about their own stamps, even though having a stamp from one of those countries' land crossings to Israel or the West Bank can be no less 'incriminating' than having an Israeli one. This is especially true of Lebanon, Iran and Syria, which have been known to put travellers on the next plane out if they find even the slightest evidence of travel to Israel. Such evidence can include a longer stay in Jordan or Egypt than is allowed under that country's visa rules with no evidence of a visa extension.

Some countries, including the United States, allow their citizens to carry more than one passport, but it can still be difficult to make this work without leaving unexplained gaps in the entry/exit paper trail.

after visiting Israel and the Palestinian Territories and you do so within the one-month validity of your original Jordanian visa, you may re-enter Jordan at this crossing without the need for a second visa.

The second exception applies if you are arriving in Aqaba. Because the city is located within a free-trade zone, arrivals are issued with a free, 15-day visa. If you wish to stay longer than this, you must register with the local authorities.

Lebanon

One-month Lebanese tourist visas are available for most nationalities on arrival at airports and land borders. They should be issued free of charge, but charges of LL50,000 have in the past sometimes been levied by immigration officials at land borders. Given, however, that Lebanon's only land borders are those with Syria (too dangerous to visit) and Israel (the latter hasn't been open in decades), the issue is unlikely to arise for the foreseeable future.

Syria

It is currently not safe to visit Syria. Prior to the conflict in Syria, tourist visas were available at Syrian airports and land borders to travellers with no Syrian embassy or consulate in their country of nationality or residence. For everyone else, one-month tourist visas were available from Syrian embassies or consulates. It is impossible to say whether these rules will apply when Syria returns to peace.

Turkey

It's important to note that Turkish visa rules have changed significantly in recent years and that visas are no longer available at the point of entry for most nationalities.

If you come from Denmark, Finland, France, Germany, Israel, Italy, Japan, New Zealand, Sweden and Switzerland, you don't need a Turkish visa for stays of up to 90 days.

For most other nationalities, three-month, multiple-entry tourist visas must be purchased online at www.evisa.gov.tr/en prior to arrival. Payment can be made by credit card and fees range from free (for South Africans) up to US$60 (for Canadians and Australians). You then print out the visa and present it on arrival in Turkey. Purchase at least two days before you plan to travel.

Border Crossings

Border crossings in the Middle East can be slow and it can take hours to pass through immigration and customs formalities, especially if you bring your own car. Showing patience, politeness and good humour *may* speed up the process.

If travelling overland to or from the Middle East, you can approach the region from Africa, the Caucasus, Iran or Europe.

Egypt
Sudan

The only border crossing between Egypt and Sudan is the ferry crossing between Aswan and Wadi Halfa. Before setting out, check the security situation in Sudan; many East African overlanders fly from Egypt to Addis Ababa in Ethiopia.

Libya

Egypt's only border crossing with Libya is at Amsaad, on the Mediterranean coast 12km west of Sallum. With the situation in Libya still in a state of flux at the time of writing, you should check the visa situation with the Libyan embassy in Cairo, and the security situation generally, before setting out.

Iran
Afghanistan

The border at Dogharon, 20km east of Taybad, is open and straightforward, although security is a major concern on the Afghan side of the border. Daily buses between Herat and Mashhad make the trip simpler still. Visas are not issued here.

Armenia

The border between Iran and Armenia is only 35km long, with one crossing point in Iran at Norduz. Armenian visas are issued at the border, though sometimes the bus leaves before you have your visa – apart from that it's pretty smooth.

Azerbaijan

The Azeri border has two recognised crossings: between Azerbaijan (Astara) and Iran (Astara), and Azerbaijan (Culfa) and Iran (Jolfa), the latter leading to the exclave of Nakhchivan, from where you cannot enter Armenia and must fly to get to Baku. Visas are not issued here.

MIDDLE EAST BORDER CROSSINGS AT A GLANCE

TO/FROM	FROM/TO	BORDER CROSSINGS
Egypt	Israel and the Palestinian Territories	Taba
Egypt	Jordan	Connected by ferry; entry points at Nuweiba and Aqaba
Jordan	Israel and the Palestinian Territories	Crossings at: King Hussein Bridge/Allenby Bridge (close to Jerusalem); Jordan River Bridge/Sheikh Hussein Bridge (close to Beit She'an/Irbid); Wadi Arabia/Yitzhak Rabin (close to Eilat/Aqaba)
Jordan	Iraq	Not recommended; Karama/Tarbil crossing, 330km east of Amman
Iran	Iraqi Kurdistan	Of five crossings, the only crossing possibly open to foreign travellers is Haji Omaran (180km northeast of Erbin and Panjwin)
Turkey	Iran	Crossings at Gürbulak-Bazargan, near Doğubayazıt (Turkey) and Şahabat (Iran), and the Esendere-Sero border southeast of Van (Turkey)
Turkey	Iraqi Kurdistan	In Turkey it's known as Habur Gate or Silopi while in Iraq it's Ibrahim Khalil, near the city of Zakho

Pakistan

Along the 830km border with Pakistan, the only recognised crossing for foreigners is between Mirjaveh (Iran) and Taftan (Pakistan). As always in this part of the world, check the security situation on both sides of the border before setting out.

Turkmenistan

There are three border posts along this 1206km-long frontier. From west to east, there is inconvenient and little-used Incheh Borun/Gyzyl-Etrek; Bajgiran linking Mashhad and the Turkmen capital Ashgabat; and Sarakhs and Saraghs for those heading east. You must change transport at all three crossings. The paperwork and organisation involved in travelling to Turkmenistan is a hassle.

Iraq

Note that overland travel is not possible across Iraq's borders with Kuwait and Saudi Arabia.

Turkey
Armenia

Turkey's border with Armenia has been closed for many years and appears unlikely to open any time soon. To reach Armenia, you'll need to travel via Georgia.

Bulgaria

There are three border crossings between Bulgaria and Turkey. The main border crossing is the busy Kapitan-Andreevo/Kapıkule, 18km west of Edirne on the E5. The closest town on the Bulgarian side is Svilengrad, some 10km from the border. This crossing is open 24 hours daily.

There's a second crossing at Lesovo-Hamzabeyli, some 25km north of Edirne; it's a quieter option during the busy summer months than Kapitan-Andreevo/Kapıkule, but takes a little longer to get to and there's no public transport.

The third crossing is at Malko Târnovo-Kırıkkale, some 70km northeast of Edirne and 92km south of Burgas.

Georgia

The main border crossing is at Sarp on the Black Sea coast, between Hopa (Turkey) and Batum (Georgia). You can also cross inland at the Türkgözü border crossing near Posof, north of Kars (Turkey) and southwest of Akhaltsikhe (Georgia). The Sarp border crossing is open 24 hours a day; Türkgözü is open from 8am to 8pm, although in winter you might want to double check that it's open at all.

Greece

The most popular ways of getting to Turkey from Europe are to make your way to Alexandroupolis in Greece and cross at Kipi-İpsala, 43km northeast of Alexandroupolis, or Kastanies-Pazarkule, 139km northeast, near the Turkish city of Edirne. Both borders are open 24 hours.

Plan Your Trip
Activities

Top Activities

Best Desert Safaris
Wadi Rum, Jordan; October–May

Best Diving & Snorkelling
Red Sea, Egypt and Jordan; year-round

Best Hiking
Dana Biosphere Reserve, Jordan; March–May and September–November

Best Sailing
Felucca trip, Aswan to Luxor; year-round

Best Skiing
The Cedars, Lebanon; December–April

Best Sea Kayaking
Kaş, Turkey; May–September

Other Activities

Archaeological Digs
For details on archaeological digs in Israel that welcome paying volunteers, try the Biblical Archaeology Society (http://digs.bib-arch.org/digs) or the Hebrew University of Jerusalem (http://archaeology.huji.ac.il/news/excavations.asp).

Hot-Air ballooning
Cappadocia, Turkey and Luxor, Egypt

Canyoning
Mujib Biosphere Reserve, Jordan

Planning Your Trip

When to Go?

The Middle East is an excellent year-round activities destination, although some activities will require planning to make sure you're here at the right time.

Summer (especially from June to September) the ideal time to enjoy diving, snorkelling and other water sports.

Unless you're near or in the water, the rest of the year is likely to be better for most other activities. From June to September, and especially in July and August, desert expeditions in the Sahara and Wadi Rum may be too hot for comfort (and, particularly in the case of the Sahara, may even be impossible). The best time to be in the desert also happens to be your best bet for finding snow in Lebanon and Iran: December to March is the best period if you're here to go snow skiing.

Hiking is possible year round, although punishing daytime temperatures mean you should avoid the middle of the day if hiking in summer. The most comfortable hiking conditions are September to November and March to May.

What to Take?

There are few requirements for most activities and those operators who organise activities (such as diving and snorkelling) will provide the necessary equipment. Bicycles and mountain bikes can be rented in the Middle East, but serious cyclists and bikers may want to bring their own bicycles. Most hikers head out onto the trail under their own steam, but even those who plan on joining an organised hike in the region with a guide will usually need to bring their own equipment.

Getting Active

From deep-desert safaris in the Sahara to snow-skiing in Lebanon, from hiking the high valleys of central Jordan to diving and snorkelling the Red Sea, there aren't too many activities that you *can't* do in the Middle East.

Cycling & Mountain Biking

The Middle East offers some fantastic, if largely undeveloped, opportunities for cyclists. Unlike in Europe, you're likely to have many of the trails to yourself. However, the heat can be a killer (avoid June to September) and you'll need to be pretty self-sufficient, as spare parts can be extremely scarce. One of the highlights of travelling in this way is that locals in more out-of-the-way places will wonder what on earth you're doing – an ideal way to break the ice and meet new friends.

The Arava region in Israel is popular for mountain biking, while mountain biking also has great potential in Jordan, but there's very little in the way of organised expeditions. In Iran, Esfahan to Yazd is an increasingly popular route for European cyclists. In Iran, consider avoiding the main highways and taking the secondary routes, which are much better suited to cycle touring. Cycling traffic is light and few locals ride, but a steady stream of overlanders brave the traffic en route between Europe and Asia.

Desert Safaris

An expedition into the deserts of the Middle East will rank among your most memorable experiences of the region – the solitude, the gravitas of an empty landscape, the interplay of light and shadow on the sands. Various kinds of expeditions are possible, although they represent very different experiences. Camel trekking is environmentally friendly and slows you down to the pace of the deserts' traditional Bedouin inhabitants, but you'll be restricted to a fairly small corner of the desert. Travelling by 4WD allows you to cover greater distances but is usually more expensive.

Where to Go on a Desert Safari

Wadi Rum in Jordan has many calling cards: the orange sand, the improbable rocky mountains, the soulful Bedouin inhabitants who are the ideal companions around a desert campfire, and the haunting echoes of Lawrence of Arabia. When you add to this the ease of getting here and exploring – it's accessible from major travel routes and is compact enough to visit within short time frames – and the professional operators that run expeditions here, it's hardly surprising that Wadi Rum is the desert experience that travellers to the Middle East love most. Everything is possible here, from afternoon camel treks to 4WD safaris and hikes lasting several days.

Other deserts where expeditions are possible include Egypt's Western Oases, for 4WD safaris into the Sahara from **Bahariya Oasis** and **Siwa Oasis**. If the security situation permits, Egypt's **Sinai Peninsula** is good for overnight, two- or three-day camel treks.

Israel is another possibility, with the **Negev Desert** a wonderful place to explore, as are the wild wadis and untamed mountains around the southern end of the **Dead Sea** on the Israeli side of the border.

Diving & Snorkelling

The Red Sea is one of the world's premier diving sites. Snorkellers heading out for the first time will be blown away by this dazzling underwater world of colourful coral and fish life, extensive reef systems and the occasional shipwreck. For experienced divers, there are plenty of sites to escape the wide-eyed newbies and see underwater landscapes that are both challenging and exceptionally beautiful.

Most dive centres offer every possible kind of dive course. The average open-water certification course for beginners, either with CMAS, PADI or NAUI, takes about five days and usually includes several dives. The total cost starts from around US$300; prices depend on the operator and location. A day's diving (two dives), including equipment and air fills, costs US$75 to US$150. An introductory dive is around US$80. Full equipment can be hired for about US$30 per day.

The best bases for diving and snorkelling are in **Sharm el-Sheikh**, **Dahab**, **Nuweiba** or **Hurghada** in Egypt; **Aqaba** in Jordan; or **Eilat** in Israel.

Top: Skiing at Uludağ National Park (p437), Turkey

Bottom: Hiker, Cappadocia (p474), Turkey

SCOTT HAILSTONE / GETTY IMAGES ©

Snorkelling and scuba diving is also possible at many points along Turkey's Mediterranean coast, although what's on offer doesn't come close to the Red Sea.

Hiking

Israel & the Palestinian Territories

Israel in particular has some fabulous trekking possibilities, many of them in the **Upper Galilee** and **Golan** regions. In the Negev Desert, two spots stand out: the **Makhtesh Ramon**, which is the Middle East's largest crater, and **Ein Avdat National Park**, where you can trek through canyons and pools.

Jordan

Jordan is perhaps the Middle East's premier trekking destination, most notably in the spectacular landscapes of **Wadi Rum**, **Dana Biosphere Reserve**, **Wadi Mujib** and **Petra**.

Lebanon

In Lebanon, the **Qadisha Valley** offers the pick of the hiking possibilities, although insecurity can be an issue – make careful enquiries about the prevailing situation before setting out.

Turkey

In Turkey, some fine trails pass through the **Kaçkar Mountains**, the **Taurus Mountains** (near Niğde), the mountains **Cappadocia**, and **Mt Ararat** (5137m) near Doğubayazıt. But our pick of the long-distance walks is the **Lycian Way**, a stunning, world-class coastal walk between Fethiye and Antalya on the Mediterranean coast.

Iran

Solo trekking is possible but taking a guide is a good idea as much for their translation skills along the route as the actual navigation. In remote regions, especially near borders, you may stumble across military/police/security areas; an Iranian guide or a few phrases of Farsi should hopefully smooth over any misunderstandings.

One- and two-day walks are possible in many areas, particularly the northwest and around Tehran. Day and overnight desert treks can be easily arranged from **Yazd**. But perhaps the most popular and rewarding route (in spring and summer) is through the historic **Alamut** area, once home to the Assassins, including a trek taking you across the Alborz Mountains and down to the Caspian.

Horse Riding

The rocky trails of the Middle East lend themselves to exploration by horseback. There aren't many operators out here, least of all ones whom we recommend, but it is possible to visit some of the region's iconic attractions in this way. These include:

➡ Wadi Rum (p337), Jordan
➡ Cappadocia (p474), Turkey
➡ West Bank tombs (p88), Luxor, Egypt
➡ Pyramids of Giza (p58), Cairo, Egypt
➡ Makhtesh Ramon (p260), Israel

HIKING PERSONAL EQUIPMENT CHECKLIST

☐ Sturdy hiking boots

☐ A high-quality sleeping bag – any time from October through to March can see overnight temperatures plummet in desert areas

☐ Warm clothing, including a jacket, jumper (sweater) or anorak (windbreaker) that can be added or removed

☐ A sturdy but lightweight tent

☐ Mosquito repellent

☐ A lightweight stove

☐ Trousers for walking, preferably made from breathable waterproof (and windproof) material such as Gore-Tex

☐ An air-filled sleeping pad

☐ Swiss army knife

☐ Torch (flashlight) or headlamp, with extra batteries

Sailing & Boat Trips

From the Nile to the Mediterranean, cruising the waters is a wonderfully laid-back way to travel.

Egypt

Drifting down the **Nile** aboard a felucca (traditional sailing boat) is one of the quintessential Middle Eastern experiences. Although trips are possible elsewhere, most take place **between Aswan and Luxor** and possibilities range from day trips to five-day expeditions with stops at some lesser-visited riverside temples en route. **Cairo** is also possible for sunset trips.

Turkey

Turkey's Mediterranean and Aegean coasts are ideal for yacht cruising, especially given its proximity to the Greek islands.

The most romantic option is to sail along the coast in a *gület* (traditional wooden yacht). The most popular excursion is a four-day, three-night trip from **Fethiye to Kale**. Other possibilities include everything from day trips to two-week luxury charters, and you can hire crewless bareboats or flotilla boats, or take a cabin on a boat hired by an agency. Ask anywhere near the docks for details; the following towns have the largest number of options: **Kuşadası**, **Bodrum**, **Fethiye** and **Marmaris**.

Skiing

'Snow sports in the Middle East' probably sounds like it belongs in the tall-tales-told-to-gullible-travellers category, but the skiing can be excellent, if highly localised.

Lebanon

In the 1970s, Beirut was famous for the fact that you could swim in the Mediterranean waters of the Lebanese capital in the morning, then ski on the slopes of Jebel Makmel, northeast of Beirut, in the afternoon. No sooner had the guns of civil war fallen silent than the Lebanese once again reclaimed the slopes from the militias, and their infectious optimism has seen the ski resorts going from strength to strength.

The Cedars is Lebanon's premier ski resort. The ski season takes place here from around December to April, depending on snow conditions. Equipment can be rented from a number of small ski shops at the base of the lifts.

For more on skiing in Lebanon, contact **Ski Lebanon** (www.skileb.com) for information, packages, trips and accommodation bookings.

Iran

There are more than 20 functioning ski fields in Iran. The season is long, the snow is often powdery and untracked and, compared with Western fields, skiing in Iran is a bargain.

The season in the **Alborz Mountains** (where most slopes are located) starts as early as November and lasts until just after No Ruz (ie late March); **around Tabriz** and at **Dizin** (close to Tehran) it can last until mid-May. Skiing is also possible in the Zagros Mountains, with smallish fields at **Sepidan** north of Shiraz, and **Chelgerd**, west of Esfahan.

All the resorts have lodges, chalets and hotels, which charge from about US$50 to US$150 for a room. Ski lifts cost as little as US$8 a day. You can hire skis, poles and boots, but not clothes, at the resorts.

Contact or visit the very helpful Iran Ski Federation (www.skifed.ir) for details of all the slopes.

Turkey

Uludağ National Park, centred on the Great Mountain (2543m), is Turkey's most popular ski resort. The season runs from December to April in most years.

Water Sports

Any Red Sea resort worth its salt will let you indulge your passion for water sports from windsurfing to waterskiing. Many of Turkey's Mediterranean beach resorts also offer ample opportunities for waterskiing, windsurfing, tandem paragliding or parasailing.

More specifically, important water sports locations include:

Eilat, Israel Arguably the Middle East's water-sports capital with waterskiing, parasailing and a host of other water-borne thrills on offer.

Moon Beach, Sharm el-Sheikh, Egypt The region's best windsurfing spot.

Hurghada, Egypt Good for kitesurfing.

Aqaba, Jordan Offers a good range of sports.

Kaş, Turkey The region's best spot for sea kayaking.

Plan Your Trip

Travel with Children

We have a simple message for those of you considering travelling with your children to the Middle East: go for it. If you don't believe us, look around – you won't see many families of travellers, but the ones you do see will probably be having a pretty-good time.

Middle East for Kids

Health & Safety

All travellers with children should know how to treat minor ailments and when to seek medical treatment. Make sure the children are up to date with routine vaccinations, and discuss possible travel vaccines well before departure as some vaccines are not suitable for children aged under one year.

On the all-important question of security, there are plenty of places in the Middle East that are extremely safe and any place that's safe for you to visit will generally be safe for your children.

Public transport is rarely easy with children: car sickness is a problem, they'll usually end up on your lap, functional seat belts are rare, even in taxis, and accidents are common.

Eating Out

It's common for locals to eat out as a family. As a result, waiters are welcoming, or at least accepting of children. Best of all, the region's cuisine is generally child friendly, being simple and varied, although you should always make sure the meat is well cooked. On the downside, Middle Eastern ice creams may be too much of a risk for tender young stomachs and, although some places have high chairs, they're very

Best Regions for Kids

Turkey

For the most part, travelling in Turkey is no different than anywhere else in Europe. The beach resorts of the Aegean and Mediterranean probably hold the greatest appeal, but don't forget the fairy-chimney landscape of Cappadocia. Public transport and road infrastructure is generally excellent, although distances between destinations can be long.

Jordan & Israel & the Palestinian Territories

Israel has terrific beaches, while Jordan boasts fabulous castles, camel trekking and the chance to float in the Dead Sea. An additional plus to travelling in these two compact countries is the short distances to get anywhere, while standards of food hygiene are relatively high.

Egypt

Train rides and sailing boats down the Nile go some way towards compensating for the long distances between destinations. Throw in beaches, Red Sea snorkelling and Tintin & the Pharaohs come to life, and kids could easily fall in love with the country.

much in the minority. Kids' menus are rare except in Western-style hotel restaurants in larger cities.

Beach Holidays

The beaches of the Middle East are ideal for families and factoring in some beach time to go with the region's more adult attractions can be an extremely wise move. The safest and most easily accessible place to begin is Turkey's Mediterranean coast. Egypt, Jordan and Israel all have excellent beaches, many of which have a range of activities on offer, from boat rides to diving and snorkelling.

Cultures

Unlike any vaguely news-savvy adult, most children have yet to have their perceptions of the Middle East distorted by stereotypes. Discovering for themselves just how friendly the people of the Middle East can be is a lesson that will last a lifetime. More than that, your own chances of meeting locals (especially local families) is greatly enhanced if you're travelling as a family.

Children's Highlights

Temples & Castles

Temple of Karnak Sound-and-light show that's a great alternative to history books.

Petra If they've seen *Indiana Jones*, watch them go wide-eyed with recognition.

Karak and Shobak Jordanian castles filled with legends of knights and damsels in distress.

Cappadocia Fairy-tale landscape made for a child's fertile imagination.

Cities

Jerusalem Child-friendly activities; brings Sunday-school lessons to life.

Esfahan Welcoming open spaces with plenty of families enjoying them.

İstanbul Make geography interesting by visiting two continents in one day.

Beaches & Activities

Snorkelling the Red Sea A whole new world to make *Nemo* look tame.

Spending time on Turkey's beaches Gentle waters and family-friendly facilities.

Sailing a felucca up the Nile from Aswan to Luxor An unforgettable journey.

Floating in the Dead Sea Yes, even Dad floats!

Riding a camel through Wadi Rum Be Lawrence of Arabia for a day.

Horse riding in Luxor An original way to experience west-bank temples.

Planning

What to Bring

Disposable nappies, powdered milk, formula and bottled water are widely available throughout the region in most large supermarkets, although don't expect to find your favourite brands; stock up in larger towns as some items won't be available elsewhere.

If you'll be travelling by taxi or minibus, you may consider bringing a child's seatbelt adjuster and/or a car seat; very few vehicles have the latter.

Other useful items to bring include child-friendly insect repellent and a blanket to spread out to use as a makeshift nappy-changing area.

When to Go

The best times to visit the Middle East are in autumn (September to November) or spring (March to May). Travel is certainly possible at other times, but winter (December to February) can be bitterly cold in the evenings and rain can be frequent. And unless you'll be spending all of your time in the water, avoid travel in the summer (especially in July and August) as the extreme heat can be quite uncomfortable and energy sapping.

Accommodation

Your chances of finding what you need (such as cots) increase the more you're willing to pay. And you'll almost certainly want something with a private bathroom and hot water, thereby precluding most budget accommodation. Hygiene standards at many budget establishments can also be poor.

Children under two usually stay for free in most hotels. There's often a supplementary charge for squeezing in extra beds. Large family rooms or adjoining rooms with connecting doors are occasionally available.

Countries at a Glance

Every country in the region promises stirring historical landmarks and provide attractions worth anchoring your visit around. A choice of spectacular landscapes could similarly determine your route through the region, with Turkey, Jordan and Egypt the highlights. If Red Sea diving and snorkelling appeal, it has to be Egypt (and, to a lesser extent, Jordan and Israel), while camel trekking is possible in both Jordan and Egypt. Turkey has the most beautiful beaches, while travellers for whom food is the main event will want to spend most of their time in Turkey and Lebanon.

Egypt

Ruins
Diving
Landscapes

The country's Nile Valley is an extraordinary open-air museum to Egypt's glorious past, while the waters off Egypt's Red Sea coast rank among the premier diving and snorkelling destinations on earth. Elsewhere, Egypt's landscapes have epic qualities.

p50

Iran

History
Architecture
Cities

Iran is the antithesis of media stereotypes, a friendly, hospitable country with some of the Middle East's most decorated mosques and other religious architecture, the magnificent ruins of Persepolis and engaging, bazaar-filled cities like Shiraz, Yazd and Esfahan.

p138

Iraq

Landscapes
Novelty
Urban Life

Most of Iraq remains downright dangerous to travellers although some regions of the Kurdish northeast, including Erbil and Sulaymaniyah, were safe at the time of writing. Travellers here report lively, friendly cities and earn considerable traveller cachet in the process.

p186

Israel & the Palestinian Territories

History
Cities
Activities

Sacred ground to the three great faiths, Israel and the Palestinian Territories are modern countries grafted onto a deeply spiritual land. It's the land of peerless Jerusalem, brash Tel Aviv and vibrant Ramallah.

p210

Jordan

Ruins
Landscapes
Activities

Surrounded by conflict, Jordan is something of a travellers' oasis, home to the Middle East's most extraordinary ancient city (Petra), the best desert scenery (Wadi Rum) and splendid snorkelling off-shore from the country's thin sliver of Red Sea coast.

p291

Lebanon

Ruins
Landscapes
Food

From Phoenician ruins to the fantastic Roman temples at Baalbek, from a rugged Mediterranean coast to the interior's snow-capped mountains, Leba-non packs a lot into a very small area. It also happens to be a world-class culinary destination.

p357

Syria

Inaccessible

Before the war, Syria was a traveller favourite of ancient cities, astonishing ruins, exceptional food and hospitable locals. While conflict ravages most of the country and the country is extremely dangerous to visit, a disrupted version of everyday life continues.

p406

Turkey

Cities
Beaches
Ruins

Turkey is where the Middle East meets Europe, literally so in İstanbul, one of the most beautiful cities on earth. Elsewhere, expect an array of first-rate attractions including breathtaking Cappadocia, an exquisite turquoise-hued coast, Roman Ephesus and soulful Mt Nemrut.

p413

On the
Road

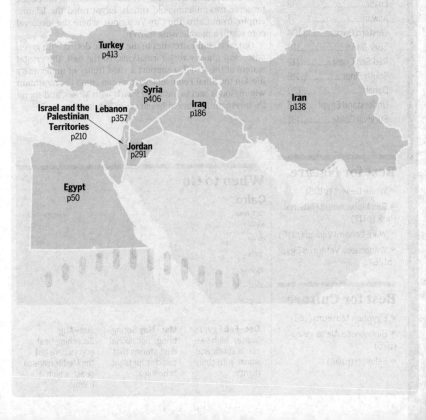

Egypt

Includes ➜

Best for Nature

➜ White Desert (p105)

➜ Ras Mohammed National Park (p117)

➜ Wadi Lahami Village (p116)

➜ Wilderness Ventures Egypt (p126)

Best for Culture

➜ Egyptian Museum (p51)

➜ Bibliotheca Alexandrina (p76)

➜ Eskaleh (p104)

Why Go?

As Herodotus wrote in the 5th century BC, Egypt 'has more wonders in it than any other country in the world'. But the Pharaonic temples and pyramids that awed the Greek historian are just the beginning.

In desert monasteries, Egypt's native Christians, the Copts, preserve two-millennia-old rituals. Egypt ruled the Islamic empire from Cairo, the City Victorious, where the medieval core is still a mesmerising warren.

Out west, sand stretches to the Sahara, dotted with green oases and ghostly rock formations. To the east, the crystal waters of the Red Sea support a vivid frenzy of underwater life. On the Sinai Peninsula, visitors can climb the mountain where God is said to have had words with Moses, and spend their remaining days at beach camp Shangri-Las.

When to Go

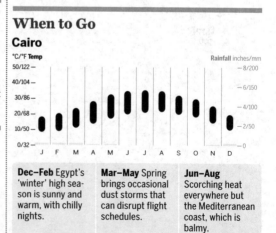

Cairo

Dec–Feb Egypt's 'winter' high season is sunny and warm, with chilly nights.

Mar–May Spring brings occasional dust storms that can disrupt flight schedules.

Jun–Aug Scorching heat everywhere but the Mediterranean coast, which is balmy.

CAIRO

القاهرة

02 / POP 22 MILLION

Known to its residents as Umm al-Dunya (Mother of the World), modern Cairo is a hotchpotch of recent growth barely covering a dense bed of history. Wander down to Islamic Cairo to tread on medieval stones. Head out west to Giza's famed pyramids and the time warp sets you back a full 4500 years. Meanwhile, the city's main museum bursts at the seams with its priceless wealth of antiquities. But the real allure of Cairo lies in the quiet moments in between: sipping a sugary tea or puffing leisurely on a sheesha while watching the city whirl past you.

History

Cairo is not ancient, though the presence of the Pyramids leads many to believe otherwise. Its foundations were laid in AD 969 by the early Islamic Fatimid dynasty. Under the rule of subsequent dynasties, Cairo swelled and burst its walls, but at heart it remained a medieval city for 900 years. It wasn't until the mid-19th century that Cairo started to change in any significant way.

The site of modern Downtown Cairo, west of what is now Midan Opera, was then a swampy plain subject to the annual flooding of the Nile. In 1863, when the French-educated Ismail Pasha came to power, he was determined to upgrade the image of his capital, which he believed could only be done by starting afresh. For 10 years the former marsh became one vast building site as Ismail invited architects from Belgium, France and Italy to create a brand-new European-style district, which earned the nickname 'Paris on the Nile'. This building boom has continued until the present day, if with somewhat less aesthetic cohesion, with the city's boundaries constantly expanding into the surrounding desert.

Sights

Downtown

Midan Tahrir   SQUARE

(Map p62) Midan Tahrir (Liberation Sq) gained world renown in early 2011, when millions of Egyptians converged there to oust then-president Hosni Mubarak. On a regular day, it's just your average giant traffic circle, albeit one where half-a-dozen major arteries converge, and one that's still occasionally taken over by demonstrations. However, the main reason for visiting this square is the lurid pink bulk of the Egyptian Museum.

Egyptian Museum   MUSEUM

(Map p62; 2579 6948; www.egyptianmuseum-cairo.org; Midan Tahrir; adult/student E£75/40, mummy room E£100; 9am-5pm Sat-Thu, to 4pm Fri) One of the world's most important

---

EGYPT CAIRO

NEED TO KNOW

Fast Facts

➡ **Capital** Cairo

➡ **Country code** 20

➡ **Language** Arabic

➡ **Official name** Arab Republic of Egypt

➡ **Population** 87 million

➡ **Currency** Egyptian pound (E£)

➡ **Mobile phones** GSM phone network widespread.

➡ **Money** ATMs are common.

➡ **Visas** Available on arrival for many nationalities.

Exchange Rates

Australia	A$1	E£6.6
Euro zone	€1	E£9.6
Israel	1NIS	E£2
Jordan	JD1	E£10
UK	£1	E£11.9
USA	US$1	E£7.1

For current exchange rates see www.xe.com.

Resources

➡ **Lonely Planet** (www.lonelyplanet.com/egypt) Destination info, hotel booking and forum.

➡ **Egypt Tourism** (www.egypt.travel) Official tourism-ministry site.

➡ **Daily News Egypt** (www.thedailynewsegypt.com) Best English newspaper.

➡ **Mada Masr** (www.madamasr.com) Independent progressive online reporting in English.

➡ **Theban Mapping Project** (www.thebanmappingproject.com) Archaeological database and news.

Egypt Highlights

1 Tip your head back and gape at the **Pyramids of Giza** (p58).

2 Give your regards to Tutankhamun in the mazelike **Egyptian Museum** (p51) in Cairo.

3 Explore ancient tombs and temples in the open-air museum that is **Luxor** (p82).

4 Enjoy the ultimate 'away from it all' in western oases like **Siwa** (p108).

5 Revel in the underwater wonderland that flourishes in **Ras Mohammed National Park** (p117).

6 Sail on the waters of history on a **Nile** cruise (p102).

7 Marvel at Ramses II's colossal temple at far flung **Abu Simbel** (p103).

8 Watch the sun set over tranquil **Aswan** (p97), the heart of Nubia.

9 Go Mediterranean in **Alexandria** (p76), Egypt's cultural port city.

10 Kick back for a day or a week in **Al-Quseir** (p115) or elsewhere on the Red Sea.

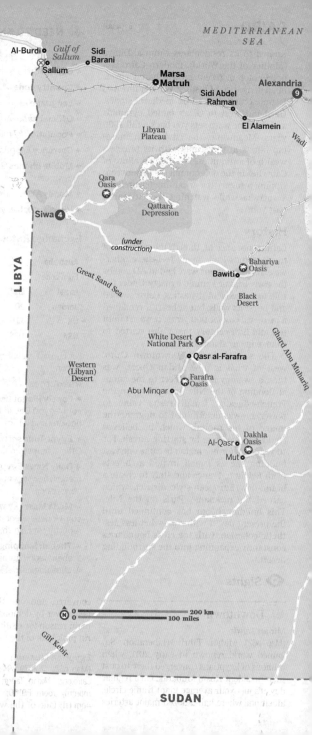

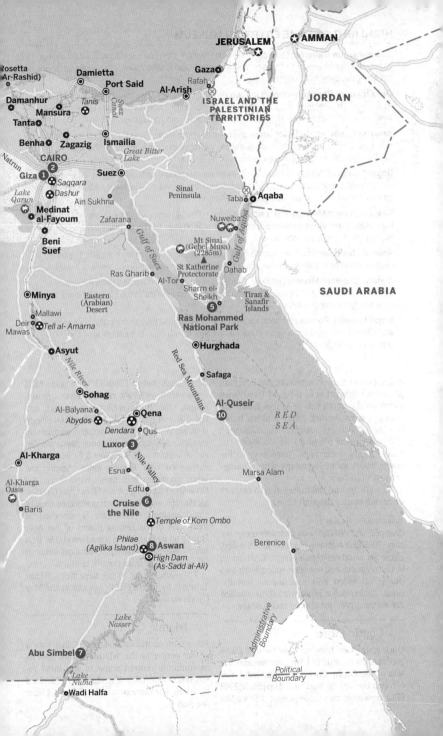

HIGHLIGHTS OF THE EGYPTIAN MUSEUM

Tutankhamun Galleries (1st floor, east side) Top on everyone's list, King Tut's treasures occupy a large chunk of the museum's upper floor. Go first to room 3 to see his sarcophagi while the crowds are light.

Old Kingdom Rooms (ground floor, rooms 42, 37 and 32) After peeking at Tutankhamun, return to the ground floor for a chronological tour. Look out for the statue of well-muscled Khafre – you may also recognise him from the Sphinx.

Amarna Room (ground floor, room 3) The artwork commissioned by Akhenaten for his new capital at Tell al-Amarna is dramatically different in style from his predecessors. Say hi to his wife, Nefertiti, while you're here.

Royal Tombs of Tanis (1st floor, room 2) While everyone else is gawking at Tutankhamun's treasure down the hall, this room of gem-encrusted gold jewellery, found at the largest ruined city in the Nile Delta, is often empty.

Graeco-Roman Mummy Portraits (1st floor, room 14) From very late in ancient Egyptian history, these wood-panel portraits were placed over the faces of embalmed dead, staring up in vividly realistic style.

Animal Mummies (1st floor, rooms 53 and 54) This long, dim room contains the bundled remains of the ancients' beloved pets, honoured gods and even their last meals.

Middle Kingdom Models (1st floor, rooms 32 and 27) Pop in here to get a picture of common life in ancient Egypt, depicted in miniature dioramas made to accompany the pharaoh to the other world.

Royal Mummy Rooms (1st floor, rooms 56 and 46) These mummies put a human face on all the stunning objects you've seen. The ticket booth is on the east side of the museum, near room 56.

---

collections of ancient artefacts, the Egyptian Museum takes pride of place in Downtown Cairo, on the north side of Midan Tahrir. Inside the great domed, oddly pinkish building, the glittering treasures of Tutankhamun and other great pharaohs lie alongside the grave goods, mummies, jewellery, eating bowls and toys of Egyptians whose names are lost to history.

To walk around the museum is to embark on an adventure through time.

Townhouse Gallery　　　　　GALLERY
(Map p62; ☑ 2576 8086; www.thetownhousegallery. com; 10 Sharia Nabrawy; ☉ noon-9pm Sat-Wed) **FREE** Set amid car-repair shops, Townhouse is Cairo's most cutting-edge space, with emphasis on video and multimedia installations. It also has a large workshop situated across the street, for classes and confabs.

◉ Coptic Cairo

Once known as Babylon, this part of Cairo predates the coming of Islam and remains the seat of the Coptic Christian community. You can visit the **Coptic Museum** (Map p56; ☑ 2363 9742; www.coptic-cairo.com/museum; 3 Sharia Mar Girgis; adult/student E£60/30, audio guide E£10; ☉ 9am-4pm), with its gorgeous mosaics, manuscripts, tapestries and Christian artwork, and the 9th-century **Hanging Church** (Al-Kineesa al-Mu'allaqa; Map p56; www.coptic-cairo.com/old cairo/church/mollaqa/mollaqa.html; Sharia Mar Girgis; ☉ Coptic mass 8-11am Wed & Fri, 9-11am Sun), suspended over Roman gates. Among the other churches and monasteries here, the **Church of St Sergius and Bacchus** (Abu Sarga; Map p56; www.coptic-cairo.com/oldcairo/church/ sarga/sarga.html; ☉ 8am-4pm) is supposed to mark one of the resting places of the Holy Family on its flight from King Herod. The **Ben Ezra Synagogue** (Map p56; donations welcome) **FREE** also dates from the 9th century.

The easiest way to get here from Midan Tahrir is by metro (E£1); get out at the Mar Girgis station.

◉ Islamic Cairo

For many centuries, 'Islamic' Cairo was a power centre of the Islamic world, and its monuments remain some of the most resplendent examples of architecture inspired by Islam. For more on visiting Islamic Cairo, see p68.

Egyptian Museum

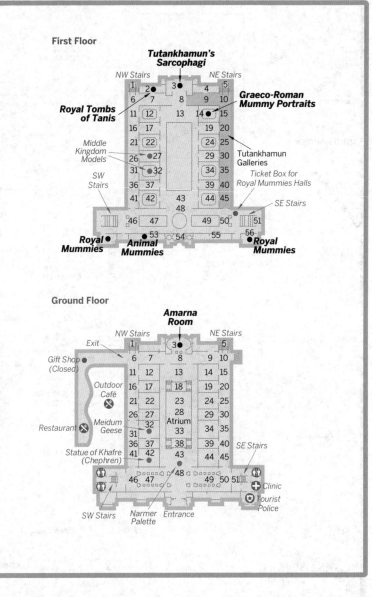

First Floor

Tutankhamun's Sarcophagi

NW Stairs

NE Stairs

Graeco-Roman Mummy Portraits

Royal Tombs of Tanis

Middle Kingdom Models

Tutankhamun Galleries

Ticket Box for Royal Mummies Halls

SW Stairs

SE Stairs

Royal Mummies

Animal Mummies

Royal Mummies

Ground Floor

Amarna Room

NW Stairs

NE Stairs

Exit

Gift Shop (Closed)

Outdoor Café

Atrium

Restaurant

Meidum Geese

Statue of Khafre (Chephren)

SE Stairs

Clinic

Tourist Police

SW Stairs

Narmer Palette

Entrance

★ **Al-Azhar Mosque** MOSQUE
(Gami' al-Azhar; Map p66; Sharia al-Azhar; ⊙24hr)
FREE Founded in AD 970 as the centrepiece of the newly created Fatimid city, Al-Azhar is one of Cairo's earlier mosques, and its sheikh is considered the highest theological authority for Egyptian Muslims. The building is a harmonious blend of architectural styles, the result of numerous enlargements over a thousand years. The tomb chamber, located through a doorway on the left just inside the entrance, has a beautiful mihrab

Cairo

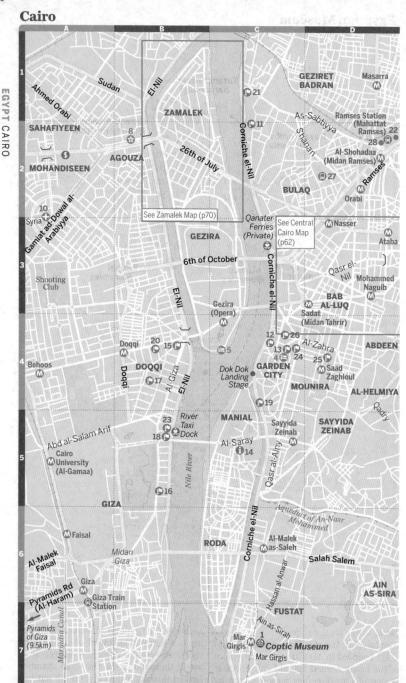

Ahmed Orabi

Sudan

El-Nil

GEZIRET BADRAN

Masarra

As-Sabtiyya

Ramses Station (Mahattat Ramses)

ZAMALEK

SAHAFIYEEN

8

26th of July

Corniche el-Nil

Shanan

Al-Shohadaa (Midan Ramses)

28

AGOUZA

MOHANDISEEN

21

11

27

BULAQ

Ramses

Orabi

Gamiat ad-Dowal al-Arabiyya

10

Syria

See Zamalek Map (p70)

GEZIRA

Qanater Ferries (Private)

See Central Cairo Map (p62)

Nasser

Ataba

6th of October

Corniche el-Nil

Qasr el-Nil

Mohammed Naguib

Shooting Club

El-Nil

Gezira (Opera)

BAB AL-LUQ

Sadat (Midan Tahrir)

Doqqi

20

15

Al-Giza El-Nil

5

12

13

26

Al-Zahra

24

ABDEEN

Behoos

DOQQI

17

Dok Dok Landing Stage

GARDEN CITY

25

4

Saad Zaghloul

MOUNIRA

AL-HELMIYA

Qadry

19

Abd al-Salam Arif

23

River Taxi Dock

MANIAL

Sayyida Zeinab

SAYYIDA ZEINAB

18

Al-Saray

14

Cairo University (Al-Gamaa)

Nile River

Qasr al-Ainy

GIZA

16

Aqueduct of An-Nasr Mohammed

Faisal

Midan Giza

RODA

Corniche el-Nil

Al-Malek as-Saleh

Salah Salem

AIN AS-SIRA

Al-Malek Faisal

Giza

Hassan al-Anwar

Pyramids Rd (Al-Haram)

Giza Train Station

FUSTAT

Ain as-Sirah

Pyramids of Giza (9.5km)

Mar Girgis

Coptic Museum

Mar Girgis

1

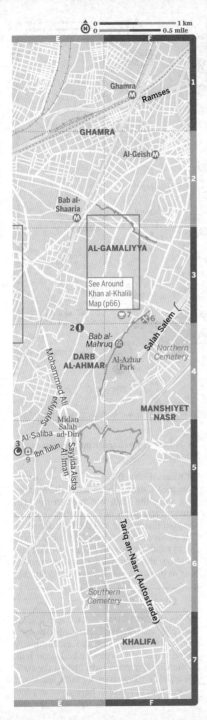

Cairo

(a niche indicating the direction of Mecca) and should not be missed.

Mausoleum of Al-Ghouri MOSQUE, TOMB
(Map p66; Sharia al-Muizz li-Din Allah; adult/student E£30/20; ◷9am-5pm) The penultimate Mamluk sultan al-Ghouri built his funerary complex in 1504, on both sides of

Giza Plateau

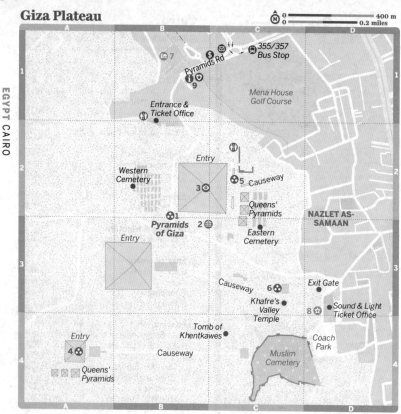

Sharia al-Muizz. At the age of 78, Al-Ghouri was beheaded in Syria, and his body was never recovered. The elegant mausoleum actually contains the body of Tumanbey, his successor, hanged by the Turks in 1517. There is a weekly musical event on Sundays at 9pm, not to be confused with the Sufi dancing at the Wikala of al-Ghouri (Map p66; ☑ 2511 0472; Sharia Mohammed Abduh; adult/student E£25/15; ☺ 9am-5pm Sat-Thu) up the street.

Mosque of Ibn Tulun   MOSQUE
(Map p56; Sharia al-Saliba; ☺ 8am-4pm) **FREE**
The city's oldest intact, functioning Islamic monument is easily identified by its high walls topped with neat crenulations that resemble a string of paper dolls. It was built between AD 876 and 879 by Ibn Tulun, who was sent to rule the outpost of Al-Fustat in the 9th century by the Abbasid caliph of Baghdad. It's also one of the most beautiful mosques in Cairo, and its geometric simplic-

ity is best appreciated from the top of the minaret.

★ Khan al-Khalili   MARKET
(Map p66) Cairenes have plied their trades here since the khan was built in the 14th century, and parts of the market, such as the gold district, are still the first choice for thousands of locals. Open from early morning to sundown (except Friday morning and Sunday), although many shops are open as long as there are customers, even on Sunday.

◉ Giza

★ Pyramids of Giza   ARCHAEOLOGICAL SITE
(Map p58; adult/student E£80/40; ☺ 8am-4pm)
For nearly 4000 years, the extraordinary shape, impeccable geometry and sheer bulk of the Giza Pyramids have invited the obvious question: 'How were we built, and why?'

Centuries of research have given us parts of the answer. We know they were massive

Giza Plateau

tombs constructed on the orders of the pharaohs by teams of workers tens-of-thousands strong. This is supported by the discovery of a pyramid-builders' settlement, complete with areas for large-scale food production and medical facilities.

➡ **Great Pyramid of Khufu**   ARCHAEOLOGICAL SITE
(Great Pyramid of Cheops; Map p58; admission E£200; ⊘8am-4pm) The oldest pyramid in Giza and the largest in Egypt, Khufu's Great Pyramid stood 146m high when it was completed around 2570 BC. After 46 windy centuries, its height has been reduced by 9m.

There isn't much to see inside the pyramid, but the experience of climbing through the ancient structure is unforgettable – though impossible if you suffer the tiniest degree of claustrophobia. The elderly and unfit should not attempt the climb, as it is very steep.

➡ **Cheops Boat Museum**   MUSEUM
(Map p58; adult/student E£50/25; ⊘9am-4pm Oct-May, to 5pm Jun-Sep) Immediately south of the Great Pyramid is this fascinating museum with exactly one object on display: one of Cheops' five solar barques (boats), buried near his pyramid, and unearthed in 1954. This huge, stunning ancient wood vessel, possibly the oldest boat in existence, was carefully restored from 1200 pieces of Lebanese cedar and encased in this museum to protect it from the elements. Visitors to the museum must help this process by donning protective footwear to keep sand out.

➡ **Pyramid of Menkaure**   ARCHAEOLOGICAL SITE
(Pyramid of Mycerinus; Map p58; adult/student E£40/20; ⊘8am-4pm) At 62m (originally 66.5m), this pyramid is the smallest of the trio, only about one-tenth the bulk of the Great Pyramid. The pharaoh Menkaure died before the structure was finished – around the bottom are several courses of granite

EGYPT CAIRO

ℹ **PYRAMIDS PRACTICALITIES**

Entrance & Tickets
The main entrance is at the end of Pyramids Rd (Sharia al-Haram). Additional tickets are required for the Cheops Boat Museum and the pyramid interiors. A limited number of tickets to get inside the Great Pyramid are sold at the main ticket booth in two lots, starting at 8am and 1pm. Cameras are not allowed inside pyramids and tombs.

Facilities & Food
Toilets are at the main entrance, in the Cheops Boat Museum and in a trailer near the Great Pyramid. For food, there's an expensive cafe (drinks E£20, sandwiches E£25–55) by the Sphinx, but for the same amount, you can refresh at the nearby Pizza Hut or at the cafe at the opulent Mena House Oberoi (Map p58; ☎02-3377 3222; www.menahouse-hotel.com; Pyramids Rd). For cheap eats, walk northeast on the main road through Nazlet as-Samaan. A short taxi ride away (around E£15), about 2km north on the Maryutia Canal, is the extremely popular Andrea's (☎02-3383 1133; 59 Tir'at al-Maryutia; mains E£35-50; ⊘noon-midnight), famed for its succulent spit-roast chicken in a garden setting.

Getting There & Away
Take the metro to Giza then go by taxi (about E£15), microbus (E£3) or bus (E£1 or E£2). Microbuses cluster outside the metro (drivers yell 'Haram'); get off where the van turns off Pyramids Rd and walk 1km straight to the entrance. Buses stop on the north side of Pyramids Rd; 355 and 357 (white with blue-and-red stripes) terminate in front of Mena House Oberoi, about 250m from the site entrance.

The Pyramids of Giza

Constructed more than 4000 years ago, the Pyramids are the last remaining wonder of the ancient world.

The giant structures – the **Great Pyramid of Khufu ❶**, the smaller **Pyramid of Khafre ❷** and the **Pyramid of Menkaure ❸** – deservedly sit at the top of many travellers' to-do lists. But the site is challenging to explore, with everything, including the smaller **Queens' Pyramids ❹** and assorted tombs such as the **Tomb of Senegemib-Inti ❺**, spread out in the desert under the hot sun. And it all looks, at fi rst glance, a bit smaller than you might have thought.

It helps to imagine them as they were: originally, the Pyramids gleamed in the sun, covered in a smooth white limestone casing. These enormous mausoleums, each devoted to a single pharaoh, were part of larger complexes. At the east base of each was a 'funerary temple', where the pharaoh was worshipped after his demise, with daily rounds of offerings to sustain his soul. In the ground around the pyramids, wooden boats – so-called solar barques – were buried with more supplies to transport the pharaoh's soul to the afterlife (one of these has been reconstructed and sits in the **Cheops Boat Museum ❻**). From each funerary temple, a long stone-paved causeway extended down the hill.

At the base of the plateau, a lake covered the land where the village of Nazlet as-Samaan is now – this was fed by a canal and enlarged with fl ood waters each year. At the end of each causeway, a 'valley temple' stood at the water's edge to greet visitors. Next to Khafre's valley temple, the lion-bodied **Sphinx ❼** stands guard.

So much about the Pyramids remains mysterious – including the whereabouts of the bodies of the pharaohs themselves. But there's still plenty for visitors to see. Here we show you both the big picture and the little details to look out for, starting with the **ticket booth and entrance ❽**.

ZORA O'NEILL

Pyramid of Khafre
Khufu's son built this pyramid, which has some surviving limestone casing at the top. Scattered around the base are enormous granite stones that once added a snappy black stripe to the lowest level of the structure.

Khafre's Valley Temple

Eastern Cemetery

❼

The Sphinx
This human-headed beast, thought to be a portrait of Khafre, guards the base of the plateau. The entrance is only through Khafre's valley temple. Come early or late in the day to avoid the long queue.

ZORA O'NEILL

Cheops Boat Museum
Preserved in its own modern tomb, this 4500-year-old cedar barge was dug up from in front of the Great Pyramid and reassembled by expert craftsmen like a 1224-piece jigsaw puzzle.

ZORA O'NEILL

Pyramid of Menkaure (Mycerinus)
This pyramid opens alternately with the Pyramid of Khafre. The gash in the exterior is the folly of Sultan al-Aziz Uthman, who tried to dismantle the pyramid in 1196.

Tomb of Senegemib-Inti
The Giza Plateau is dotted with small tombs like this one. Opening schedules vary each year. Duck inside to look for delicate wall carvings and enjoy a bit of shade.

Western Cemetery

Khafre's Funerary Temple

Ticket Booth & Entrance
Buy tickets, marked with a hologram sticker, here and only here. All other options are counterfeit. Clean bathrooms, the only good facilities, are in a building just to the east.

Queens' Pyramids
These smaller piles were built as the tombs of Khufu's sister, mother and wife. They're in bad shape, but some show the original limestone casing at the base – feel how smoothly the stones are fitted.

Great Pyramid of Khufu (Cheops)
Clamber inside the corridors to marvel at the precision engineering of the seamless stone blocks, each weighing 2.5 tonnes. Pause to consider the full weight of 2.3 million of them.

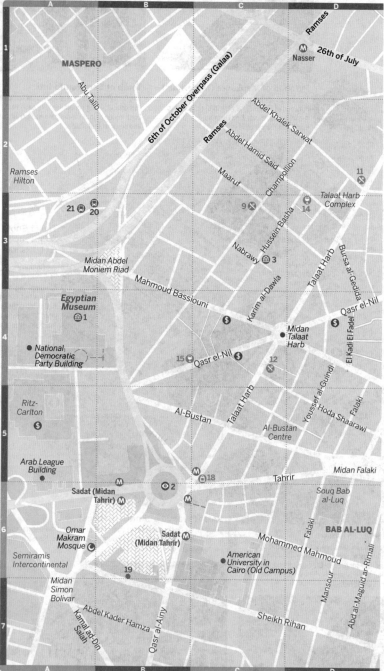

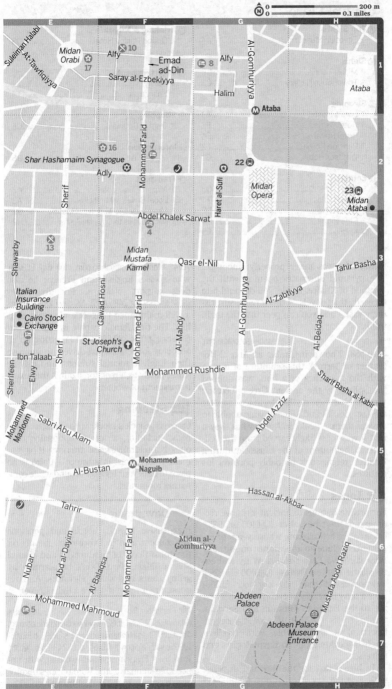

0   200 m
0   0.1 miles

Suleiman Halabi
At-Tawfiqiyya
Midan Orabi 17
Alfy 10
Emad ad-Din
Saray al-Ezbekiyya
8
Alfy
Halim
Al-Gomhuriyya
Ataba
Ataba

Shar Hashamaim Synagogue 16
Adly
Mohammed Farid 7
22
Sherif
Haret al-Sufi
Midan Opera
23 Midan Ataba

Abdel Khalek Sarwat 4
13
Shawarby
Midan Mustafa Kamel
Qasr el-Nil
Tahir Basha

Italian Insurance Building
Cairo Stock Exchange
6
Gawad Hosni
St Joseph's Church
Mohammed Farid
Al-Mahdy
Al-Gomhuriyya
Al-Zabtiyya
Al-Beidaq

Ibn Talaab
Sherif
Elwy
Sherifeen
Mohammed Rushdie
Abdel Azziz
Sharif Basha al-Kabir

Mohammed Mazloom
Sabri Abu Alam
Al-Bustan
Mohammed Naguib
Hassan al-Akbar

Tahrir
Nubar
Abd al-Dayim
Al-Balaqsa
Mohammed Farid
Midan al-Gomhuriyya

Mohammed Mahmoud
5
Abdeen Palace
Mustafa Abdel Raziq
Abdeen Palace Museum Entrance

Central Cairo

facing that was never properly smoothed. The pyramid alternates opening with the Pyramid of Khafre. Inside, you descend into three distinct levels – the largest surprisingly vast – and you can peer into the main tomb.

➜ **Sphinx** ARCHAEOLOGICAL SITE
(Map p58) Known in Arabic as Abu al-Hol (Father of Terror), this sculpture of a man with the haunches of a lion, was dubbed the Sphinx by the ancient Greeks because it resembled their mythical winged monster who set riddles and killed anyone unable to answer them. A geological survey has shown that it was most likely carved from the bedrock at the bottom of the causeway, during Khafre's reign, so it probably portrays his features.

👣 Tours

For private outings to ancient sites, we recommend Hassan Saber (☏0100 515 9857; hassansaber@hotmail.com), whose years of experience include an appearance on Anthony Bourdain's *No Reservations*. Witty and enthusiastic Ahmed Seddik (☏0100 676 8269; www.ahmedseddik.com; day-long tour E£200) runs a busy itinerary of group tours; his best are to the Egyptian Museum and Saqqara. Samo Tours (☏2299 1155; www.samoegypttours.com) is also reliable, with excellent English-speaking guides, Egyptologists and drivers.

To hire a taxi for the day and dispense with a guide, try Aton Amon (☏0100 621

7674; aton_manos@yahoo.com; full day E£320), who speaks English and French; he also does airport pick-ups. Friendly Fathy el-Menesy (☏2486 4251; full day E£320) owns a well-maintained Peugeot and speaks English. The first female cabbie in Cairo, Nour Gaber (☏0114 888 5561; 🚗) is setting up an academy for female taxi drivers to improve their English, mental strength and driving skills, partly as a reaction against the sexual harassment of women.

🛏 Sleeping

Cairo is chock-a-block with budget crash pads, including a few exceptionally good ones, but midrange gems are rarer. It pays to make reservations in advance – Cairo is no place to haul your luggage around while comparing room rates.

🛏 Downtown

Inexpensive hostels, hotels and pensions are concentrated in Downtown, mainly on the upper floors of buildings on and around Sharia Talaat Harb. Don't be alarmed by grimy stairs and shaky elevators. And request a rear room if you're a light sleeper.

⭐ **Pension Roma** PENSION $
(Map p62; ☏2391 1088; www.pensionroma.com.eg; 4th fl, 169 Sharia Mohammed Farid; s E£109, d E£155-199.75, with air-con s E£164, d E£249-258; 🌀🛜) Run by a French-Egyptian woman with impeccable standards, the Roma brings dignity, even elegance, to the budget-travel scene. The

towering ceilings, antique furniture and filmy white curtains create a feeling of timeless calm. Most rooms have shared bathrooms, and some rooms have showers. Rooms in the new extension on a higher floor have en suite bathrooms and air-con, and are quieter.

Dina's Hostel
HOSTEL $

(Map p62; ☑ 2396 3902; www.dinashostel.com; 5th fl, 42 Sharia Abdel Khalek Sarwat; d E£210, dm/ s/d without bathroom E£50/125/160; ❋ ☏) Tranquil and tidy, Dina's is a good hostel option, not least because it's woman-owned and low on pressure tactics. It's also easy on the eyes, with warm colours, Egyptian appliqué pillows and soaring ceilings. The place has more private rooms than dorm beds, but it stays true to hostel roots with a gleaming shared kitchen.

★ Hotel Royal
BOUTIQUE HOTEL $$

(Map p62; ☑ 2391 7203; cairohotelroyal.com; 1st fl, 10 Sharia Elwy; s/d/ste US$35/45/65; ❋ ☏) The Royal's owner brought back a minimalist all-white Scandinavian sensibility after living in Norway, all brightened with a touch of Egyptian glitz. All rooms have niceties like minifridges, comfy office-style desk chairs and bunches of flowers on bedside tables. It's smack in the middle of a lively late-night cafe scene, but away from main-street traffic noise.

Hotel Osiris
HOTEL $$

(Map p62; ☑ 0100 531 1822, 2794 5728; www. hotelosiris.fr; 12th fl, 49 Sharia Nubar; s/d/tr from €25/40/50; ❋ ☏) On the top floor of a commercial building, the Osiris' rooms enjoy views across the city. The French-Egyptian couple who run the place keep the tile floors and white walls spotless, and the pretty hand-sewn appliqué bedspreads tidily arranged on the plush mattresses. Breakfast involves fresh juice, crêpes and omelettes. Its location in Bab al-Luq is quiet at night.

🛏 Garden City

Mandarin Hotel
HOTEL $$

(Map p56; ☑ 2115 1145; Al-Sabah tower, 8 Sharia Ibrahim Naguib; s/d E£20/26; ❋ ☏) Not quite as sleek as its website suggests, but still showing a bit of style, with a red-and-gold colour scheme and balconies off every room. Perks include fridges and a small but functional shared kitchen. With only 18 rooms, it fills up fast – book ahead.

🛏 Islamic Cairo

The negatives: no immediate metro access, touts like locusts, nowhere to get a beer and more than the usual number of mosques with loudspeakers. But this is the place to plunge in at Cairo's deep end.

A STROLL THROUGH HISTORY

One of the best walks in Islamic Cairo is a loop through the district north of Khan al-Khalili, which is undergoing massive restoration. From Midan Hussein, walk north up Sharia al-Gamaliyya, a major medieval thoroughfare for traders. After about 300m, on your left you will see the Wikala al-Bazara (Map p66; Sharia al-Tombakshiyya; adult/student E£20/10; ☺8am-5pm), a beautifully restored caravanserai. Continue heading north until you hit the T-intersection of Sharia Al-Galal, marking the old northern wall. Pass through the square-towered Bab an-Nasr (Map p66), or Gate of Victory, and walk left to the rounded Bab al-Futuh (Gate of Conquests; Map p66). Both were built in 1087 as the two northern entrances to the new walled Fatimid city of Al-Qahira. Bab Zuweila (Map p56; Sharia al-Muizz li-Din Allah; adult/student E£20/10; ☺9am-5pm), the southern gate and once a place of execution, can be climbed for a fee.

From Bab al-Futuh, walk back south via Sharia al-Muizz li-Din Allah. Don't miss the spectacular Beit el-Suhaymi (Map p66; Darb al-Asfar; adult/student E£35/15; ☺9am-5pm), a complex of three houses tucked down a small alley on your left.

Just before you reach Khan al-Khalili again, you pass through the stretch known as Bein al-Qasreen (Palace Walk; Map p66; Sharia al-Muizz li-Din Allah), the main drag of Fatimid Egypt. Here, the Madrassa and Mausoleum of Barquq (Map p66; Sharia al-Muizz li-Din Allah; adult/student E£100/50, 1 ticket covers all the sights from Bein al-Qasreen to Bab al-Futuh; ☺9am-5pm), with its black-and-white marble portal, is lavish inside, and the Madrassa and Mausoleum of An-Nasir Mohammed (Map p66; Sharia al-Muizz li-Din Allah; adult/student E£100/50, 1 ticket covers all the sights from Bein al-Qasreen to Bab al-Futuh; ☺9am-5pm) sports a plundered Gothic doorway from a church in Akko (Acre).

Around Khan al-Khalili

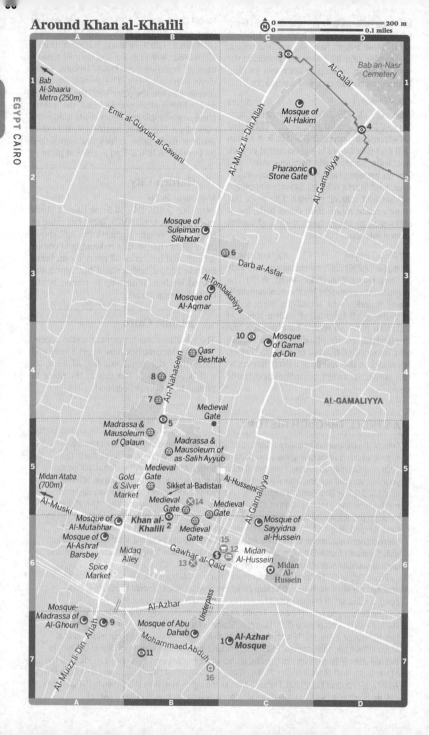

N 0 ————————————— 200 m
0 ————————————— 0.1 miles

Bab Al-Shaaria Metro (250m)

Emir al-Guyush al-Gawani

Al-Muizz li-Din Allah

Al-Galal

Bab an-Nasr Cemetery

3

Mosque of Al-Hakim

4

Pharaonic Stone Gate

Al-Gamaliyya

Mosque of Suleiman Silahdar

6

Darb al-Asfar

Al-Tombakshiyya

Mosque of Al-Aqmar

10

Mosque of Gamal ad-Din

Qasr Beshtak

AL-GAMALIYYA

8

7

An-Nahaseen

5

Medieval Gate

Madrassa & Mausoleum of Qalaun

Madrassa & Mausoleum of as-Salih Ayyub

Midan Ataba (700m)

Al-Muski

Gold & Silver Market

Medieval Gate

Sikket al-Badistan

Medieval Gate

Al-Husseini

Medieval Gate

14

Medieval Gate

Al-Gamaliyya

Mosque of Al-Mutahhar

Khan al-Khalili

2

Medieval Gate

Mosque of Sayyidna al-Hussein

Mosque of Al-Ashraf Barsbey

Midaq Alley

15

12

Midan Al-Hussein

Spice Market

Gawhar al-Qaid

13

Midan Al-Hussein

Mosque-Madrassa of Al-Ghouri

Al-Azhar

Underpass

Al-Muizz li-Din Allah

9

Mosque of Abu Dahab

Mohammaed Abduh

1

Al-Azhar Mosque

11

16

Around Khan al-Khalili

El Hussein HOTEL $
(Map p66; ☎ 2591 8089; Midan al-Hussein; s/d E£155/180; ✳) Off either side of an open-ended hallway where street noise reverberates, the rooms here are dreary and service surly. But the view from the front-facing ones with balconies affords mesmerising people-watching on the square below. There's a top-floor restaurant too. Entrance is in the back alley, one block off the square.

🛏 Zamalek & Gezira

Relatively quiet Zamalek offers the best night's sleep in the city, if not the cheapest. Good restaurants, shops, bars and coffeehouses are nearby, but most sights are a taxi ride away over traffic-jammed bridges.

Mayfair Hotel HOTEL $
(Map p70; ☎ 2735 7315; www.mayfaircairo.com; 2nd fl, 9 Sharia Aziz Osman; s/d from E£275/320, without bathroom E£190/215; ✳🖥) The cheapest sleep in the neighbourhood, on a quiet street, with a fine large terrace. Double rooms are clean and a good size, with balconies, TVs and fridges. Some single rooms are cramped, and the young staff perfectly

nice but perhaps a tad too attentive to female guests.

★Hotel Longchamps HOTEL $$
(Map p70; ☎ 2735 2311; http://hotellongchamps. com; 5th fl, 21 Sharia Ismail Mohammed; s/d/tr from US$80/106/126; ✳🖥) The old-style Hotel Longchamps is very much a favourite of returning visitors to Cairo, a home away from home – it's like staying in a smart Cairene apartment – with a friendly and extremely helpful owner. The comfortable, stylish rooms are spacious and well maintained; if you want your own balcony and a small bathtub, get an 'executive' room.

Golden Tulip Flamenco Hotel HOTEL $$
(Map p70; ☎ 2735 0815; www.flamencohotels. com; 2 Sharia Gezirat al-Wusta; s/d/tr from US$87/97/128; ✳🖥) This popular place is a reasonable alternative to five-star heavyweights. Rooms are comfortable and well equipped, if slightly cramped in standard configuration. The extra US$10 for 'superior' class gives you interior space and a balcony overlooking the houseboats on the Nile.

Sofitel El Gezirah LUXURY HOTEL $$$
(Map p56; ☎ 2737 3737; www.sofitel.com; Sharia al-Orman; r from US$150; ✳🖥✳) Tired from long travels? Rest up here in a sumptuous room with superb views, and let the staff look after you. This hotel, on the tip of Gezira island, is delightfully quiet compared to other hotels in the area, but it can be hard to get a cab out. There are several good restaurants, one of them a favourite of ours, and the Buddha Bar.

🍴 Eating

🍴 Downtown

The best area for budget eats.

Abu Tarek EGYPTIAN $
(Map p62; 40 Sharia Champollion; dishes E£5-12; ⊙8am-midnight; 🍴) 'We have no other branches!' proclaims this temple of *kushari* (mix of noodles, rice, black lentils, fried onions and tomato sauce). No, the place has just expanded, decade by decade, into the upper storeys of its building, even as it has held onto the unofficial 'Best Kushari' title. It's worth eating in to check out the elaborate decor upstairs. You must pay in advance, either at the till downstairs (for takeaway) or with your waiter.

(i) VISITING ISLAMIC CAIRO

→ Dress modestly, with legs and shoulders covered. Wear sturdy shoes that are easily slipped off for entering mosques.

→ Caretakers (who should be tipped) are usually around from 9am until early evening. Mosques are often closed to visitors during prayer times.

→ The closest metro stops are Ataba, about 1km away, and Bab al-Shaaria, 300m west of Bab al-Futuh. By taxi, ask for 'Al-Hussein', the name of the main square and mosque next to Khan al-Khalili.

Akher Sa'a   EGYPTIAN FAST FOOD $
(Map p62; ☑ 2575 1668; 14 Sharia Abdel Khalek, Sarwat; dishes E£2-10; ⊙24hr) A frantically busy fuul and ta'amiyya takeaway joint with a no-frills cafeteria next door, Akher Sa'a has a limited menu but its food is fresh and good. It has a fast-food-style set-up downstairs (note the genius giant-ta'amiyya 'burger') but glacial table service upstairs. There is also a branch on **Sharia Alfy** (Map p62; 8 Sharia Alfy; dishes E£2-10; ⊙24hr).

★ Café Riche   EGYPTIAN, EUROPEAN $$
(Map p62; ☑ 2392 9793; 17 Sharia Talaat Harb; dishes E£30-50; ⊙10am-midnight; ☑) This narrow restaurant, allegedly the oldest in Cairo, was the favoured drinking spot of the intelligentsia. A certain old guard still sits under the ceiling fans, along with tourists who like the historic ambience. It's a reliable and nostalgic spot to enjoy a cold beer (E£12) and a meal of slightly Frenchified Egyptian dishes.

Kafein   EUROPEAN, VEGETARIAN $$
(Map p62; ☑ 0100 302 5346; 28 Sharia Sherif; sandwiches E£24-30, salads E£25; ⊙7am-1.30am; ✴☏☑) A great addition to Downtown eateries is this air-conditioned cafe-restaurant on two floors, with a small terrace in the little alley off Sharia Sherif. Many a foreign journalist enjoys the cool, free wi-fi and good coffee (E£8) here. On offer are delicious sandwiches, fresh salads, milk shakes, teas served in a pot (E£15) and fresh juices.

✕ Islamic Cairo

There are plenty of fast-food joints around Midan al-Hussein but the restaurants in this part of town are limited – you really have to like grilled meat, and not be too squeamish about hygiene.

Al-Halwagy   EGYPTIAN $
(Map p66; ☑ 2591 7055; Midan al-Hussein; dishes E£6-30; ⊙24hr) Not directly on the square, but just behind a row of buildings, this good ta'amiyya, fuul and salad place has been around for nearly a century. You can eat at pavement tables or hide away upstairs.

Khan el-Khalili Restaurant &
Mahfouz Coffee Shop   EGYPTIAN $$
(Map p66; ☑ 2590 3788; 5 Sikket al-Badistan; snacks E£15-40, mains E£35-105; ⊙10am-2am) The luxurious Moorish-style interiors of this restaurant and adjoining cafe are a popular haven from the khan's bustle. The place may be geared to tourists but the food is good, the air-con is strong and the toilets are clean. Look for the metal detector in the lane, immediately west of the medieval gate.

Citadel View   MIDDLE EASTERN $$
(Map p56; ☑ 2510 9151; Al-Azhar Park; mains E£42-130; ⊙noon-midnight; ☑) Eating at this gorgeous restaurant in Al-Azhar Park – on a vast multilevel terrace, with the whole city sprawled below – feels great. Fortunately the prices are not so stratospheric, and the food is good, with dishes like spicy sausage with pomegranate syrup and grilled fish with tahini. On Friday, only a buffet (E£150) is on offer. No alcohol.

✕ Zamalek

Cheap dining is not one of the island's fortes but hip hang-outs are.

★ Zööba   EGYPTIAN $$
(Map p70; ☑ 02-3345 3980; www.ZoobaEats.com; Sharia 26th of July; salads E£12-15, mains E£13-19, desserts E£3-15; ⊙8am-1am) Small eatery serving fresh street food prepared with a gourmet twist; the delicious dishes can also be taken away - ideal for a picnic. Fresh juices, salads, whole-wheat *kushari* and fabulous salads. Keep space for the more-ish desserts like rice pudding with sweet potatoes and cinnamon. All is served at a zinc-clad table in the funkiest and most eclectic of decors.

Cairo Kitchen
EGYPTIAN **$$**

(Map p70; ☑ 2735 4000; www.cairokitchen.com; 118 Sharia 26th of July; salads E£9-25, mains E£23-55; ⊙ 10am-midnight) Cairo Kitchen is a contemporary restaurant serving up traditional wholesome Egyptian home cooking. Order from the counter – a salad plate, a brown-rice *kushari* or a typical Egyptian stew of the day. The decor is colourful, prices are good and the place is popular with Cairenes. The cookbook is already out too. Entrance on Sharia Aziz Osman.

L'Aubergine
BISTRO **$$**

(Map p70; ☑ 2738 0080; 5 Sharia Sayyed al-Bakry; mains E£39-95; ⊙ noon-2am; ☑) This snug, white-walled, candlelit restaurant devotes half its menu to global vegetarian dishes, such as Turkish stewed aubergine and gnocchi with blue cheese. You can't go wrong with most of the cheesier, creamier items, and the chill-out soundtrack is a nice respite from Cairo street noise. At 10pm the DJ turns up the music, and a younger crowd arrives.

🍷 Drinking & Nightlife

Cairo isn't a 'dry' city, but locals tend to run on caffeine by day, available at both traditional ahwas (coffeehouses) and European-style cafes.

Downtown

Vent
BAR, CULTURAL CENTRE

(Map p62; ☑ 2574 7898; 6 Sharia Qasr el-Nil; ⊙ noon-2am) Cairo's most happening and coolest art-space-cum-bar with live -music sessions by international and local hip-hop and grime artists. Screenings of experimental films and other events. This was formerly the Arabesque restaurant.

Odeon Palace Hotel
BAR

(Map p62; ☑ 2577 6637; www.hodeon.com; 6 Sharia Abdel Hamid Said; ⊙ 24hr) Its fake turf singed from sheesha coals, this slightly dilapidated rooftop bar is favoured by Cairo's heavy-drinking theatre and cinema clique, and is a great place to watch the sun go down (or even better come up).

Islamic Cairo

Fishawi's
COFFEEHOUSE

(Map p66; Khan al-Khalili; ⊙ 24hr, during Ramadan 5pm-3am) Probably the oldest ahwa in the city, and certainly the most celebrated, Fishawi's has been a great place to watch

the world go by since 1773. Despite being swamped by foreign tourists and equally wide-eyed out-of-town Egyptians, it is a regular ahwa, serving up *shai* (tea) and sheesha to stallholders and shoppers alike. Prices vary so confirm with your waiter.

Coffeeshop Al-Khatoun
COFFEEHOUSE

(Map p56; Midan Al-Khatoun; tea & sheesha E£15; ⊙ 3pm-1am) Tucked away in a quiet square behind Al-Azhar, this modern outdoor ahwa is a great place to rest up after a walk, with tea and snacks and comfortable pillow-strewn benches. In the evenings it attracts an arty crowd – students from the Arabic Oud House school on the square and others.

Zamalek

Sequoia
LOUNGE

(Map p70; ☑ 2576 8086; www.sequoiaonline. ne; 3 Sharia Abu al-Feda, Zamalek; beer E£34, minimum charge Sun-Wed E£125, Thu-Sat E£150; ⊙ 1pm-1am) At the very northern tip of Zamalek, this sprawling Nile-side lounge is a swanky scene, with low cushions for nursing a sheesha, snacking on everything from Egyptian-style mezze (E£25-60) to sushi and sipping a cocktail (E£48-83). We don't recommend it for main meals. Bring an extra layer – evenings right on the water can be surprisingly cool.

☆ Entertainment

For free fun after dark, street life can be entertainment enough. Stroll the pedestrian area around Midan Orabi, and also check out the Nile Corniche Downtown and Qasr el-Nil bridge.

Live Music

Many venues are eclectic, changing musical styles and scenes every night. Many also start as restaurants and shift into club mode after midnight, at which point the door policy gets stricter. Big packs of men (and sometimes even single men) are always a no-no – go in a mixed group if you can, and ideally make reservations.

Cairo Jazz Club
JAZZ, DJ

(Map p56; ☑ 02-3345 9939; www.cairojazzclub. com; 197 Sharia 26th of July, Agouza; ⊙ 5pm-3am) The Cairo Jazz Club has kept up with the beat, and it has one of the city's liveliest stages, with modern Egyptian folk, electronica, fusion and more, seven nights a week, usually starting around 10pm. You must book a

Zamalek

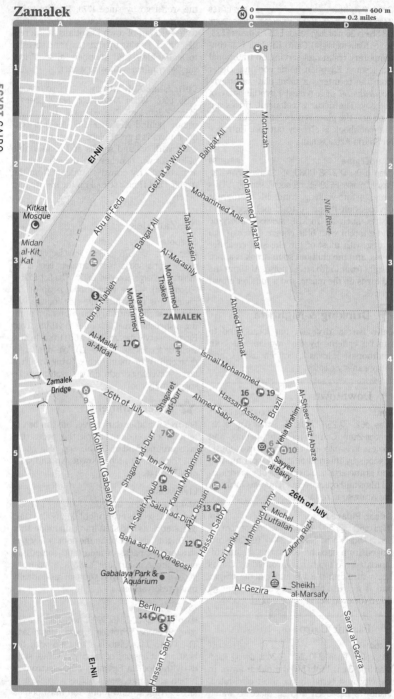

Zamalek

table ahead (online is easiest), and no one under 25 is admitted.

El Sawy Culture Wheel LIVE MUSIC
(El Sakia; Map p70; ☎2736 8881; www.culturewheel.com; Sharia 26th of July, Zamalek; ⊕8am-midnight) The most popular young Egyptian rock and jazz bands play at this lively and very active complex of a dozen performance spaces and galleries tucked under a bridge overpass. The main entrance is on the south side of 26th of July; there's a nice outdoor cafe by the Nile too.

Belly Dancing

If you see only one belly dancer in your life, it had better be in Cairo, the art form's true home. Many of them are Russian rather than Egyptian these days, but it doesn't mean they can't shake it. The best perform at Cairo's five-star hotels; at the other end are the dive halls where it's more about the seedy scene than dancing prowess. **Shahrazad** (Map p62; 1 Sharia Alfy, Downtown; admission E£5; ⊕10pm-2am) and **Palmyra** (Map p62; off Sharia 26th of July, Downtown; cover charge E£10, minimum charge E£30; ⊕10pm-2am) are two of the best Downtown venues.

🔒 Shopping

Egypt's best shopping is in Cairo, though you wouldn't know it on a first stroll through Khan al-Khalili, stocked with made-in-China tat – the trick is knowing where to look. For general gear, Downtown along Sharia Qasr el-Nil has cheap, mass-market fashion. Sharia al-Marashly and Sharia Mansour Mohammed in Zamalek have some gem boutiques, and not all of them are as expensive as you'd expect. For everything else, head to Citystars, Cairo's best mall, out east near the suburb of Heliopolis.

🔒 Downtown & Garden City

★Oum El Dounia HANDICRAFTS
(Map p62; ☎2393 8273; 1st fl, 3 Sharia Talaat Harb; ⊕10am-9pm) At a great central location, Oum El Dounia sells an exceptionally tasteful and good-value selection of locally made crafts. These include glassware, ceramics, jewellery, cotton clothes made in Akhmim, and other interesting trinkets. Illustrated postcards by cartoonist Golo make a nice change. One room is dedicated to books on Egypt, in French and in English.

🔒 Islamic Cairo

★Abd El Zaher GIFTS
(Map p66; 31 Sharia Mohammed Abduh; ⊕9am-11pm) Cairo's last working bookbinder also makes beautiful leather- and oil-paper-bound blank books, photo albums and diaries. Gold monogramming is included in the prices, which are heartbreakingly low considering the work that goes into them. Getting your own books bound starts around E£30 and takes a few days.

Khan Misr Touloun HANDICRAFTS
(Map p56; ☎2365 2227; Midan ibn Tulun; ⊕10am-5pm Mon-Sat) This shop opposite the Mosque of Ibn Tulun is stacked with a desirable jumble of reasonably priced crafts, wooden chests, jewellery, pottery, puppets and scarves. Closes for vacation in August.

🔒 Zamalek

Fair Trade Egypt HANDICRAFTS
(Map p70; ☎2736 5123; fairtradeegypt.org/; 1st fl, 27 Sharia Yehia Ibrahim; ⊕9am-8pm) Crafts sold

CAIRO CRAFTS: WHAT & WHERE

In addition to shops, these are the best districts for certain goods.

Gold and silver Head to the gold district on the west end of Khan al-Khalili.

Backgammon and sheesha pipes Shops on Sharia al-Muizz, near Bein al-Qasreen, sell these and other cafe gear to local ahwa owners.

Appliqué Best buys are at the Tentmakers Bazaar (Sharia al-Khayamiyya), south of Bab Zuweila.

Spices Most dealers in the Khan are more trouble than they're worth. Try shops around Midan Falaki.

Perfume In addition to the southwest corner of Khan al-Khalili, try shops around Midan Falaki.

Inlay Artisans in Darb al-Ahmar sell out of their workshops.

Muski glass Available everywhere, but interesting to see the glassblowing studios in the district north of Bab al-Futuh.

here are produced in income-generating projects throughout the country. Items for sale include Bedouin rugs, hand-woven cotton, pottery from Al-Fayoum and beaded jewellery from Aswan. The cotton bedcovers and shawls are particularly lovely, and prices are very reasonable.

❶ Orientation

Midan Tahrir is the centre. Northeast of Tahrir is Downtown, a noisy, busy commercial district centred on Sharia Talaat Harb. This is where you'll find many cheap eateries and most budget hotels. Midan Ramses, location of the city's main train station, marks the northernmost extent of Downtown. Heading east leads to Midan Ataba, the threshold of Islamic Cairo.

Sitting in the middle of the Nile is the island neighbourhood of Zamalek, historically favoured by ruling elites, with a few midrange hotels and plenty of restaurants and bars.

The west bank of the Nile is newer and more residential. The primary districts, north to south, are Mohandiseen, Doqqi and Giza, all heavy on concrete and light on charm. The city stretches some 20km west to the Pyramids.

❶ Information

EMERGENCY
Ambulance (☑123)
Police (☑122)
Main Tourist Police Office (Map p62; ☑216, 2395 9116; Sharia Adly) Next door to the main tourist office

MEDICAL SERVICES
Many of Cairo's hospitals suffer from antiquated equipment and a cavalier attitude to hygiene, but there are exceptions, including the Ma'adi branch of **As-Salam International Hospital** (Map p56; ☑2524 0250, emergency 19885; www.assih.com; Corniche el-Nil, Ma'adi).

Pharmacies abound in Cairo and almost anything can be obtained without a prescription. Al-Ezaby is a pharmacy that operates 24 hours and delivers; it has numerous branches.

MONEY
Banks and forex bureaux are all over town, especially on Sharia Adly Downtown and Sharia 26th of July in Zamalek – forex offices give slightly better rates on cash and are typically open till 8pm. There are oodles of ATMs throughout the city.
American Express (Map p62; ☑2574 7991; 15 Sharia Qasr el-Nil, Downtown; ◷9am-3pm Sat-Thu)
Thomas Cook (Map p62; ☑2574 3955, emergency 0100 140 1367; www.thomascookegypt.com; 17 Sharia Mahmoud Bassiouni, Downtown; ◷8am-4.30pm Sat-Thu) Other branches are located at Heliopolis (☑2416 4000; 7 Sharia Baghdad, Korba; ◷8am-4.30pm Sat-Thu), the airport (☑emergency 2265 3147; Airport; ◷24hr) and Zamalek (Map p70; ☑2696 2101, emergency 0100 538 9968; 3A Sharia Ismail Mohammed; ◷8am-4.30pm Sat-Thu).

TOURIST INFORMATION
Ministry of Tourism (Main tourist office; ☑2391 3454; 5 Sharia Adly; ◷9am-6pm) Branches also at the Pyramids (Map p58; ☑02-3383 8823; Pyramids Rd; ◷8.30am-5pm) and Ramses Station (Tourist Office and Police; Map p56; ☑2492 5985; Ramses Station; ◷9am-7pm).

TRAVEL AGENCIES
The streets around Midan Tahrir teem with travel agencies, but watch out for dodgy operators. Along with Amex and Thomas Cook, the following are reliable:
Backpacker Concierge (☑0106 350 7118; www.backpackerconcierge.com) Culturally and environmentally responsible desert trips and Nile cruises, plus more focused custom trips such as food tours. No walk-in office, but can

communicate via phone, email, Facebook and Twitter.

Egypt Panorama Tours (☎ 2359 0200; www. eptours.com; 4 Rd 79, Ma'adi; ⊙ 9am-5pm) Opposite Ma'adi metro station, this is one of the best-established agencies in town. It will book tickets, tours and hotel rooms and courier the documents to you, if necessary. It's good for four- and five-star hotel deals and tours within Egypt and around the Mediterranean. Note that separate departments handle flights and excursions.

❶ Getting There & Away

AIR

Cairo is the hub for all flights within Egypt. For flight information call ☎ 0900 77777 from a landline in Egypt or ☎ 27777 from a mobile phone.

BUS

The main bus station for all destinations in the Suez Canal area, Sinai, the deserts, Alexandria and Upper Egypt, is **Cairo Gateway** (Turgoman Garage; Map p56; Sharia al-Gisr, Bulaq), 400m west of the Orabi metro stop. Tickets are sold at different windows according to company and destination.

Companies operating here are **East Delta Travel Co** (☎ 2419 8533) for Suez and the Sinai; **West & Mid Delta Bus Co** (☎ 2432 0049; http://westmidbus-eg.com) for Alexandria, Marsa Matruh and Siwa; **Super Jet** (☎ 3572 5032, 2290 9017) for some Sinai resort towns; and **Upper Egypt Travel Co** (☎ 2576 0261) to Western Desert oases and Luxor (though for the latter, the train is better).

At the time of research, some smaller bus operators were setting up at Ramses Railway Station. Head here if the Cairo Gateway departure times aren't ideal.

Some buses from Sinai still stop at the Abbassiyya Garage (there is a nearby metro) and some from the Delta at Abboud, some 800m from Mezallat metro.

MICROBUS

You can get a seat in a microbus or taxi to most destinations from the blocks between Ramses Station and Midan Ulali, just to the southwest. For the Western Oases, head to Moneib, on

BUSES FROM CAIRO GATEWAY

DESTINATION	COMPANY	PRICE (E£)	DURATION (HR)	TIMES
Alexandria	West & Mid Delta	30-50	3	hourly 5am-12.05am
Al-Kharga	Upper Egypt Travel Co	70	8-10	9.30pm, 10.30pm
Al-Quseir	Upper Egypt Travel Co	70-80	10	5.30am, 11pm, 1.30am
Bahariya (Bawiti)	Upper Egypt Travel Co	35	4-5	6.30am, 8am
Dahab	East Delta	90	9	8am, 1.30pm, 7.30pm, 11.45pm
Dakhla	Upper Egypt Travel Co	75-90	8-10	7pm, 8.30pm
Farafra	Upper Egypt Travel Co	45-55	8-10	7am, 8am
Hurghada	Super Jet	68	6	7.30am, 2.30pm, 11.10pm
Luxor	Upper Egypt Travel Co	100-120	11	9pm
Marsa Matruh	West & Mid Delta	65-75	5	6.15am, 8.30am, 11am, 4.30pm, 7.30pm, 10pm, 11.30pm
Port Said	East Delta	25	4	hourly 6.30am-9.30pm
Sharm el-Sheikh	East Delta	65-80	7	10.30am, 4.30pm, 11pm, 1am
Sharm el-Sheikh	Super Jet	85-98	7	7.30am, 1.15pm, 10.45pm
Siwa	West Delta	80	11	7.30pm, 11.30pm
St Katherine's	East Delta	50	7	11am
Suez	East Delta	15-20	2	every 30min 6am-7pm
Taba & Nuweiba	East Delta	80-100	8	9.30am, 11.30pm

Sharia el-Nil in Giza, under the ring-road overpass (take a taxi or walk 800m east from the Sakkiat Mekki metro stop).

TRAIN

Ramses Station (Mahattat Ramses; ☎ 2575 3555; Midan Ramses, Downtown; Ⓜ Al-Shohadaa) is Cairo's main train station. It was under renovation at the time of research, but should have a **left luggage office** (Map p56; per piece per day E£5; ⊙ 24hr), a post office, ATMs and a tourist-information office (p72). Confirm times and train numbers first at the information desk, then head to the appropriate windows: Alexandra tickets are in the main building, while Upper Egypt tickets are across the tracks to the north. First-class tickets for Alexandria and destinations to Aswan can be bought online at www.enr.gov.eg.

Secondary stations include Giza, for the sleeper to Upper Egypt, and Ain Shams, in the northeast part of the city, for Suez.

Alexandria

There are two types of express trains to Alexandria (you will want to avoid the non-express): Spanish (*esbani*) and French (*faransawi*). Special and Spanish trains make fewer stops than the French ones. First class (*ula*) gets you a roomier, assigned seat and usually a much cleaner bathroom.

Luxor & Aswan

Tourists can theoretically take any train to Upper Egypt, but in practice you are likely to be pointed towards the sleeping car (especially while many foreign governments discourage visits to places between Cairo and Luxor). If you do encounter this problem you can purchase a ticket for a seat on board for a small additional fee, or in advance online.

The overnight wagon service to Luxor and Aswan is operated by a private company, **Watania Sleeping Trains** (Map p56; ☎ 02-3748 9488; www.wataniasleepingtrains.com; ⊙ 9am-8pm). You can purchase tickets at the point of departure, Giza Station, at Ramses and online. In high season (October to April), book several days in advance.

Marsa Matruh

Watania runs a train to the Mediterranean coast three times a week during the summer season.

Suez Canal

Delays on this route are common; going by bus is more efficient. If you're determined to travel by train, the best option is to Ismailia.

❶ Getting Around

TO/FROM THE AIRPORT

Cairo International Airport (www.cairo-airport.com) is 20km northeast of Cairo.

MAJOR TRAINS FROM CAIRO

DESTINATION	STATION	PRICE	DURATION (HR)	TIMES
Alexandria (direct)	Ramses	E£50	2½	8am, 9am, 11am, noon, 2pm, 6pm, 7pm, 9pm, 10.30pm
Alexandria (stopping)	Ramses	E£35	3-3½	8 daily, 6am-8.15pm
Ismailia	Ramses	E£15	3	6.15am, 1pm, 1.45pm, 2.45pm, 5.45pm, 7.50pm, 10pm
Luxor & Aswan (sleeper)	Giza	US$100	10 (Luxor), 14 (Aswan)	8pm, 9.35pm
Luxor & Aswan (sleeper)	Ramses	US$100	10 (Luxor), 14 (Aswan)	8.15pm
Luxor	Ramses	E£90	10½	8am, noon, 7pm, 8pm, 1am
Marsa Matruh (sleeper)	Giza	E£252	7	11pm Sat, Mon, Wed mid-Jun–mid-Sep
Port Said	Ramses	E£21	4	6.15am, 1.45pm, 7.50pm
Suez (2nd class, fan only)	Ain Shams	E£15-18	2¼	6.15am, 9.20am, 1.10pm, 4.15pm, 6.45pm, 9.45pm
Tanta	Ramses	E£35-50	1-1½	6am, 8.15am, 10am, 11am, noon, 2.10pm, 3.10pm, 4pm, 5.15pm
Zagazig	Ramses	E£15	1½	5.15am, 6.15am, 1pm, 1.45pm, 3.40pm, 7.50pm, 10pm

TOP EGYPTIAN ITINERARIES

One Week

If you only have a week, focus on the attractions of **Cairo**, such as the Egyptian Museum and the Coptic Museum, plus great coffeehouses, funky bars and live-music venues. Midweek, fly or take the train to **Luxor**, to admire the ancient ruins of Thebes. From there, you can hop over to **Sharm el-Sheikh** in the Sinai – there are great snorkelling and diving options on either side of the Red Sea.

Two Weeks

In two weeks, you can cover Egypt's main sights. Head out from Cairo on the sleeper train to **Aswan**, where you can soak up Nubian culture. Sail back down the Nile to **Luxor** on a felucca or cruise boat. Train (or fly) back to Cairo, where you can spend two days seeing the Pyramids of Giza, the Egyptian Museum and the medieval souq of Khan al-Khalili. If you're heading west, **Siwa Oasis** is the obvious destination. If you're heading east, fly or take a bus to **Sharm el-Sheikh** and recharge on the Red Sea. From there, it is possible to cross into Jordan.

Terminal 3 (☑16707; al-Matar al-Gideed) handles all of EgyptAir and Star Alliance flights. **Terminal 1** (☑2265 5000), 2km away, handles all other flights. A blue-and-white shuttle bus connects Terminals 1 and 3, though a shuttle train (called the APM) was scheduled to go into service soon. All buildings have ATMs after customs. There is no left-luggage service. For transport to the city, you have a few options.

Bus

Air-con bus 27 or 356 (E£4, plus E£2 per large luggage item, one hour) runs every 20 minutes, 7am to midnight, to Midan Abdel Moniem Riad (behind the Egyptian Museum). After hours, the only option is bus 400 (E£1). You must take a blue-and-white shuttle bus from the terminals to the bus station; if the shuttle is headed for Terminal 3 (ie, has left Terminal 1), it will stop across the street from the bus station, not in it.

Taxi

The going rate to central Cairo is around E£95; you'll need to negotiate. (To the airport from the centre, you can easily get a meter taxi; you'll also pay the E£5 to enter the airport grounds.) Limousines (from car desks in the terminals) cost about E£110, and **Cairo Airport Shuttle Bus** (☑19970; www.cairoshuttlebus.com; to Downtown E£110) runs cars and small vans and has a desk at Terminal 1, arrivals 1 (though it can pick you up anywhere).

BUS & MINIBUS

Cairo's main local bus and minibus stations are at Midan Abdel Moniem Riad and Midan Ataba. Fares range from 75pt to E£2. There is no known system map; buses are labelled in Arabic numerals only.

METRO

The metro system, now comprising three lines and expanding, is efficient, inexpensive (E£1 for any distance) and, outside rush hours, not too crowded. Given Cairo's traffic jams, if you can make even a portion of your journey on the metro, you'll save time. The two centre cars are typically reserved for women. Keep your ticket to feed into the machine on the way out.

MICROBUS

Private microbuses are hard to use unless you're familiar with their routes; you can flag them down anywhere by yelling out your destination. The most useful route for visitors is the one from the Giza metro stop to near the Pyramids. Fares range between 75pt and E£4 depending on distance, paid after you take your seat.

RIVER BUS

Of limited utility, but scenic, the river bus runs from the Maspero river bus terminal, north of the Ramses Hilton, to Giza by the zoo and Cairo University. Boats depart every 15 minutes; the trip takes 30 minutes and the fare is E£1.

TAXI

By far the easiest way of getting anywhere is by white taxi. They're easily flagged down at any time, and they use meters, starting at E£2.50, plus E£1.25 per kilometre and E£0.25 waiting. A tip of 10% or so is much appreciated. A few unmetered black-and-white taxis still ply the streets, but they're gradually aging out of the system.

Hiring a taxi for a longer period runs from E£30 to E£40 per hour, depending on your bargaining skills; E£300–400 for a full day is typical.

MEDITERRANEAN COAST

Alexandria الإسكندرية

♪ 03

Although Alexandria today has barely an ancient stone to show for its glorious past, it is in its cosmopolitan allure and Mediterranean pace of life that the magic lies. Sprawling necklacelike along a curving bay, this city offers a splendid cluster of restaurants, some moody, antediluvian cafes and a vibrant youth scene.

History

Established in 331 BC by Alexander the Great, the city became a major trade centre and focal point of learning for the entire Mediterranean world. Its ancient library held 500,000 volumes and the Pharos lighthouse was one of the seven wonders of the world. Alexandria continued as the capital of Egypt under the Roman Empire and its eastern offshoot, the Byzantine Empire. From the 7th century AD onwards, the city declined into insignificance. In 1798, Napoleon's arrival and Alexandria's subsequent redevelopment as a major port attracted people from all over the world, but Nasser's 1952 revolution put an end to much of the city's pluralistic charm. The 2011 revolution started here after 28-year-old Khaled Said's beating death by police sparked a protest movement on Facebook, then in the streets.

◉ Sights

One of the main sights, the Graeco-Roman Museum, remains closed for restoration.

★ **Bibliotheca Alexandrina**　MUSEUM
(Map p78; ♪483 9999; www.bibalex.org; Al-Corniche, Shatby; adult/student combined ticket E£70/5; ⊙10am-4pm Sun-Thu) Alexandria's ancient library was one of the greatest of all classical institutions, and while replacing it might seem a Herculean task, the new Bibliotheca Alexandrina manages it with aplomb. Opened in 2002, this impressive piece of modern architecture is a deliberate attempt to rekindle the brilliance of the original centre of learning and culture. The complex has become one of Egypt's major cultural venues, a stage for numerous international performers, and is home to a collection of brilliant museums.

★ **Alexandria National Museum**　MUSEUM
(Map p78; 110 Sharia Tariq al-Horreyya; adult/student E£40/25; ⊙9am-4.30pm) This excellent museum sets a high benchmark for summing up Alexandria's past. With a small, thoughtfully selected and well-labelled collection singled out from Alexandria's other museums, it does a sterling job of relating

---

WORTH A TRIP

MEMPHIS, SAQQARA & DAHSHUR　ممفس سقارة & دهشور

There's little left of the former Pharaonic capital of Memphis, 24km south of Cairo. It's worth visiting, however, for the open-air **Mit Rahina Museum** (Memphis; adult/student E£40/20, parking E£5; ⊙8am-4pm, to 3pm during Ramadan), centred on a gigantic fallen statue of Ramses II, which gives a rare opportunity to inspect carving up close.

A few kilometres away is **Saqqara** (adult/student E£80/40, parking E£5; ⊙8am-4pm, to 3pm during Ramadan), a massive necropolis covering 7 sq km of desert and strewn with pyramids, temples and tombs. Deceased pharaohs and their families, administrators, generals and sacred animals were interred here. The star attractions here are the **Step Pyramid of Zoser**, the world's oldest stone monument and the first decent attempt at a pyramid; the excellent small **Imhotep Museum**, showcasing the best finds from the site; and the **Serapeum**, catacomb tombs of sacred bulls.

Ten kilometres south of Saqqara is **Dahshur** (adult/student E£60/30, parking E£5; ⊙8am-4pm, to 3pm during Ramadan), an impressive field of 4th- and 12th-dynasty pyramids, including the **Bent Pyramid** (off limits to visitors) and the wonderful **Red Pyramid**, the oldest true pyramid in Egypt. It's arguably a better experience to clamber down into this than the Great Pyramid at Giza, because you'll almost certainly be alone here. And the ticket is far more reasonably priced.

Visit the three sites by taxi (E£250 to E£300) or join a day tour. In winter, visit Dahshur first, as it's furthest away; in warmer weather, start with Saqqara to avoid the worst heat.

the city's history from antiquity until the modern period.

Housed in a beautifully restored Italianate villa, it stocks several thousand years of Alexandrian history, arranged chronologically over three floors. Well-written information panels throughout provide useful insights into the life and beliefs of Alexandrians through the centuries.

Catacombs of Kom ash-Suqqafa
ARCHAEOLOGICAL SITE

(Carmous; adult/student E£40/25; ⊙9am-5pm) Discovered accidentally in 1900 when a donkey disappeared through the ground, these catacombs are the largest known Roman burial site in Egypt and one of the last major works of construction dedicated to the religion of ancient Egypt.

Demonstrating Alexandria's hallmark fusion of Pharaonic and Greek styles, the architects used a Graeco-Roman approach. The catacombs consist of three tiers of tombs and chambers cut into bedrock to a depth of 35m (the bottom level is flooded and inaccessible).

Roman Amphitheatre
RUIN

(Kom al-Dikka; Map p78; Sharia Yousri; adult/student E£30/15) While the 13 white-marble terraces of the only Roman amphitheatre in Egypt may not be impressive in scale, they remain a superbly preserved ode to the days of the centurion. This site was discovered when foundations were being laid for an apartment building on a site known unceremoniously as Kom al-Dikka (Mound of Rubble). In Ptolemaic times this area was known as the Park of Pan, a pleasure garden where citizens of Alexandria could indulge in various lazy pursuits.

🛏 Sleeping

June to September is Alexandria's high season, when you'll need to book in advance.

Hotel Union
HOTEL $

(Map p80; ☑480 7312; 5th fl, 164 Al-Corniche; s E£120-230, d E£180-250, s/d without bathroom E£80/100; ❄🖥) The Union is one of Alexandria's best budget options in the city centre and is always bustling with a mix of Egyptian holidaymakers and foreign travellers. The simple rooms (which come in a bewildering mix of bathroom/view/air-con rates) are well maintained, and cleanliness here far exceeds the city's usual haphazard hotel standards. It's a safe and solid backpacker choice.

WORTH A TRIP

EL ALAMEIN

In June 1942, El Alamein became the site of the great showdown between the German Afrika Korps, headed by Field Marshal Erwin Rommel, the celebrated 'Desert Fox', and an Allied army under General Bernard Montgomery. More than 80,000 soldiers were killed or wounded at El Alamein and in subsequent battles for North Africa.

El Alamein is now noted for its fine beaches, which make a good day trip from Alexandria. A **war museum** (☑410 0021; adult/student E£20/10; ⊙9am-2pm) and the Commonwealth, German and Italian **war cemeteries** (⊙7am-2.30pm) mark the scene of one of the biggest tank battles in history.

The easiest way to visit is to organise a private taxi, which will cost between E£350 and E£440, taking in the museum, cemeteries, a beach and bringing you back to Alexandria. Alternatively, catch any of the Marsa Matruh buses from Al-Mo'af Al-Gedid station in Alexandria.

Triomphe Hotel
HOTEL $

(Map p80; ☑480 7585; adalabaza@hotmail.com; 3rd fl, Sharia Gamal ad-Din Yassin; d/tr E£150/180, s/d without bathroom E£75/130) The homely Triumph has a leafy lobby that makes you feel like you've wandered into someone's living room. Spacious rooms cling to shreds of former elegance, with high ceilings and dark-wood furniture, though some are ageing more gracefully than others. It's worth paying extra for the en suite doubles (which have balconies with side sea views) even if you're travelling solo.

★ Egypt Hotel
HOTEL $$

(Map p80; ☑481 4483; 1 Sharia Degla; s/d/tr US$65/70/80; ❄🖥) The Egypt fills a desperate need for decent midrange digs. A noticeable step up from the budget choices, it's set in a renovated 100-year-old Italian building right on the Corniche. Smallish rooms have old-school-style high beds with crisp white linen, wood floors, lovely dark-wood furniture, clean bathrooms, powerful air-con and small balconies with sea or street views.

Windsor Palace Hotel
HISTORIC HOTEL $$$

(Map p80; ☑480 8123; www.paradiseinnegypt. com; 17 Sharia ash-Shohada; r with sea/street view

Central Alexandria

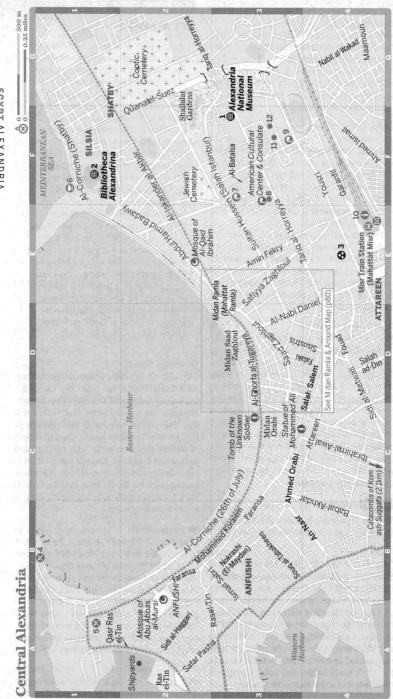

500 m
0.25 miles

EGYPT ALEXANDRIA

Central Alexandria

US$120/100, ste from US$140) This bejewelled Edwardian gem has been keeping a watchful eye on the Med since 1907. In the 1990s the Windsor was given a much-needed nip and tuck. Thankfully the wonderful old elevators and grand lobby were retained, and rooms still boast the sort of old-world, green-and-gold pizazz that wouldn't be out of place on the *Orient Express*.

✴ Eating

The main place for cheap eats – fuul, ta'amiyya, sandwiches – is around where Sharia Safiyya Zaghloul meets Midan Ramla.

Anfushi has some of Alexandria's best and freshest seafood.

★ **Mohammed Ahmed** EGYPTIAN FAST FOOD $
(Map p80; ☏ 483 3576; 17 Sharia Shakor Pasha; dishes E£2-8; ⊙24hr; 🖉) Looking for us at lunchtime in Alex? We're usually scoffing fuul and felafel here. Mohammed Ahmed is the undisputed king of spectacularly good and cheap Egyptian standards. Select your fuul (we recommend *iskandarani*), add some felafel, choose a few accompanying salads, and let the feasting begin. Note that the street sign on the corner of Saad Zaghloul calls this Abdel Fattah el-Hadary St.

Taverna EGYPTIAN FAST FOOD $
(Map p80; ☏ 487 8591; Mahattat Ramla; mains E£9-35; ⊙7am-1am; 🖉) This deservedly popular establishment serves up some of the best shwarma in town plus excellent hand-thrown sweet or savoury *fiteer* (Egyptian flaky pizza) – we're rather partial to the chocolate and banana one. It also does a fine Western-style pizza if you're hankering for Italian. Eat in or take away.

★ **Kadoura** SEAFOOD $$
(Map p78; ☏ 480 0405; 33 Sharia Bairam at-Tonsi; mains E£35-80) Pronounced 'Adora', this is one of Alexandria's most authentic fish restaurants, where food is served at tables in the narrow street. Pick your fish from a huge ice-packed selection, usually including sea bass, red and grey mullet, bluefish, sole, squid, crab and prawns. A selection of mezze is served with all orders (don't hope for a menu).

CAFE CULTURE

Alexandria is a cafe town – and since the first half of the 20th century, the city's diverse population has congregated to live out life's dramas over pastries and a cup of tea or coffee. Many of these old haunts are definitely worth a visit for historical associations and grand decor, but not always for the food.

Athineos (Map p80; ☏ 486 8131; 21 Midan Saad Zaghloul) lives and breathes nostalgia. The cafe part on Midan Ramla still has its original '40s fittings, period character, and quite possibly some of its original customers. Also facing Midan Ramla is **Trianon** (Map p80; 56 Midan Saad Zaghloul; ⊙9am-midnight), a favourite haunt of the Greek poet Cavafy, who worked in offices above. Stroll around the corner to check out **Délices** (Map p80; 46 Sharia Saad Zaghloul; ⊙9am-late; 🕾). This enormous old tearoom drips with atmosphere and can actually whip up a decent breakfast.

Vinous (Map p80; ☏ 486 0956; cnr Sharia al-Nabi Daniel & Tariq al-Horreyya) is an old-school patisserie with more grand deco styling than you can poke a puff pastry at. For one last pick-me-up coffee, head over to Sharia Saad Zaghloul and **Sofianopoulos Coffee Store** (Map p80; ☏ 484 5469; 21 Sharia Saad Zaghloul), a gorgeous coffee retailer that would be in a museum anywhere else in the world.

★ Greek Club
GREEK $$

(White and Blue Restaurant; Map p78; ☑ 480 2690; Top fl, Greek Nautical Club, Al-Corniche; mains E£20-70; ☑) The Greek Club's wide terrace is just the ticket for catching the evening breeze and watching the lights along Alex's legendary bay. The moussaka and the souvlaki are both easy menu winners, and the seafood selection (priced by weight) is excellent, too. Order your fish Greek-style – oven baked with lemon, olive oil and oregano.

🍷 Drinking & Nightlife

Alexandria's Corniche becomes one long ahwa in summertime, though many places tend to overcharge summer tourists. The city isn't much of a boozing town, but there are notable exceptions.

★ Selsela Cafe
CAFE

(Map p78; Chatby Beach, Al-Corniche) At this fantastic cafe across from the Bibliotheca Alexandrina you can sip tea and smoke sheesha to the sound of waves rolling in, and smell sea air instead of petrol fumes (yay). Directly on the water, it has rustic palm-frond shaded tables replete with twinkling coloured lights, set on a small curving beach where you can hardly hear the traffic.

★ Cap d'Or
BAR

(Map p80; ☑ 487 5177; 4 Sharia Adbi Bek Ishak; ☺10am-3am) The Cap d'Or, just off Sharia Saad Zaghloul, is one of the only surviving typical Alexandrian bars. With beer flowing generously, stained-glass windows, a long marble-topped bar, plenty of ancient memorabilia decorating the walls and crackling tapes of old French chanson (a type of traditional folk music) or Egyptian hits, it feels like a throwback to Alex's cosmopolitan past.

Midan Ramla & Around

Sleeping
1 Egypt Hotel D1
2 Hotel Union B2
3 Triomphe Hotel B2
4 Windsor Palace Hotel B2

Eating
5 Mohammed Ahmed C2
6 Taverna D2

Drinking & Nightlife
7 Athineos D1
8 Cap d'Or A3
9 Delices C2
10 Sofianopoulos Coffee Store A3
11 Spitfire A3
12 Trianon C2
13 Vinous D4

Information
14 French Consulate A2
15 Italian Consulate C1
16 Main Tourist Office C2
17 Passport Office B4

Transport
18 EgyptAir D1
19 No 1 Minibus to Sidi Gaber C2
20 West & Mid Delta Bus Co C2

Spitfire BAR
(Map p80; 7 Sharia L'Ancienne Bourse; ⊙2pm-1.30am Mon-Sat) Just north of Sharia Saad Zaghloul, Spitfire has a rough-and-ready feel and a reputation as a sailors' hang-out. Walls are plastered with shipping-line stickers, rock-and-roll memorabilia and photos of drunk regulars. It's a great place for a fun evening out drinking with a mixed clientele of locals, expats, and passers-through.

ℹ Orientation

Alexandria is a waterfront city, nearly 20km long from east to west and only about 3km wide. Its focal points are Midan Ramla (where the train terminates) and adjacent Midan Saad Zaghloul, around which are the main tourist office, restaurants, cafes and most of the cheaper hotels. To the west are the older quarters, such as Anfushi. To the east are newer, swisher suburbs stretching 15km along the coastline to easternmost Montazah.

ℹ Information

For changing cash, the simplest option is to use one of the many exchange bureaux on the side streets between Midan Ramla and the Corniche.

Al-Madina at-Tibiya (Alexandria Medical City Hospital; ✆543 7402, 543 2150; Sharia Ahmed Shawky, Rushdy; ⊙24hr) Well-equipped private hospital.

American Express (Amex; ✆420 2288; www.americanexpress.com.eg; Elsaladya Bldg, Sharia 14th Mai, Smouha; ⊙9am-4pm Sun-Thu) Changes cash and travellers cheques, and is also a travel agency.

Mahattat Misr Tourist Office (Map p78; ✆392 5985; Platform 1, Misr Train Station; ⊙8.30am-6pm) The staff are eager to help, even if they don't have much actual information.

Main Tourist Office (Map p80; ✆485 1556; Midan Saad Zaghloul; ⊙8.30am-6pm) Hands out a good brochure (with map) of Alexandria sights and has friendly staff.

Thomas Cook (Map p80; ✆484 7830; Midan Ramla; ⊙8am-5pm) Money exchange and also changes travellers cheques.

Tourist Police (Map p80; ✆485 0507; Midan Saad Zaghloul) Upstairs from the main tourist office.

ℹ Getting There & Away

AIR
EgyptAir (Map p80; ✆487 3357; 19 Midan Ramla) has several daily flights to Cairo (from E£150).

BUS
All long-distance buses leave from Al-Mo'af al-Gedid (New Garage), several kilometres south of Midan Saad Zaghloul; to get there either catch a microbus from Misr Train Station (E£2), or grab a taxi from the city centre (E£25).

West & Mid Delta Bus Co (Map p80; ✆480 9685; Midan Saad Zaghloul; ⊙9am-9pm), on the southwest corner of Midan Saad Zaghloul in the city centre, and considerably nicer **Super Jet** (✆543 5222; Sidi Gaber Train Station; ⊙8am-10pm), opposite Sidi Gaber Train Station, next to the fountain, operate from here.

Cairo
Super Jet and West & Mid Delta both have hourly buses to Cairo (E£35–40, 2½ hours), also stopping at Cairo airport (E£35), from early morning.

North Coast & Siwa
West & Mid Delta has hourly departures to Marsa Matruh (E£30, four hours); a few continue on to Sallum (E£35–45, nine hours) on the border with Libya. For Siwa (E£55, nine hours), buses go at 8.30am, 11am and 10pm; or just take any Marsa Matruh bus and change to a microbus there.

Super Jet runs five buses to Marsa Matruh (E£35) daily during summer (June to September), the last leaving in the late afternoon. Most Marsa Matruh buses stop in El Alamein

EGYPT ALEXANDRIA

(one hour), and will stop at Sidi Abdel Rahman on request, though you will have to pay the full Marsa Matruh fare.

Sinai

West & Mid Delta has one daily service to Sharm el-Sheikh (E£100, eight to 10 hours) at 9pm.

Suez Canal & Red Sea Coast

Super Jet has a daily evening service to Hurghada (E£100, nine hours). West & Mid Delta has four services a day to Port Said (E£30, four to five hours) and four to Suez (E£45, five hours). It also has two buses to Hurghada and Port Safaga (E£95).

SERVEES & MICROBUS

Servees (service taxis) and microbuses for Cairo (E£25) depart from outside Misr Train Station. All others go from Al-Mo'af al-Gedid (New Garage) bus station at Moharrem Bey.

TRAIN

The main terminal is **Mahattat Misr** (☑ 426 3207; Sharia Al-Nabi Daniel), about 1km south of Midan Ramla in the city centre. **Mahattat Sidi Gaber** (☑ 426 3953) serves the eastern suburbs. Trains from Cairo stop at Sidi Gaber first, and most locals get off here.

There are 10 trains daily between Cairo and Alexandria, from 8am to 10pm. There are two train types: Spanish (*esbani*) and French (*faransawi*). Spanish trains (1st/2nd class E£50/35, 2½ hours) are better and make fewer stops. The French train (1st/2nd class E£41/25, 3½ to four hours) makes multiple stops. There are two daily trains to Luxor at 5pm and 10pm (1st/2nd class E£129/69), with the 5pm train continuing to Aswan (1st/2nd class E£148/77).

At Mahattat Misr, 1st- and 2nd-class tickets to Cairo are sold at the ticket office along platform 1; 3rd- and 2nd-class ordinary tickets are sold in the front hall.

❶ Getting Around

TO/FROM THE AIRPORT

All flights to Alexandria arrive at Burg al-Arab (HBE) airport, about 45km southwest of the city. Smaller Nouzha (ALY) airport, 7km southeast, was being renovated at the time of research.

For Burg al-Arab, an air-conditioned bus (one way E£6 plus E£1 per bag, one hour) leaves from the Sofitel Cecil hotel, three hours before all departures; confirm the exact time at the Cecil. A taxi to/from the airport should cost between E£100 and E£150. You can also catch bus 475 (one hour) from Misr Train Station.

If you do need to get to/from Nouzha, a taxi should cost no more than E£20.

MICROBUS

The most useful are the ones zooming along the Corniche. There are no set departure points or stops, so when one passes, wave and shout your destination; if it's heading that way it will stop. It's anywhere from 50pt for a short trip to E£1.50 to Montazah.

RED BUS

An air-conditioned, red, double-decker bus (E£3) plies the Corniche every 15 to 30 minutes between Ras el-Tin and the Sheraton in Montazah. It's worth riding the length of the Corniche on the upper deck, just for the views.

TAXI

There are no working taxi meters in Alexandria, though the possibility was being discussed at the time of research. Sample fares:

➡ Midan Ramla to Misr Train Station E£5

➡ Midan Saad Zaghloul to Fort Qaitbey (west edge of the harbour) E£5

➡ Midan Saad Zaghloul to the Bibliotheca Alexandrina (east end) E£5

➡ Cecil Hotel to Montazah (eastern suburbs) E£25

TRAM

Alexandria's old trams are fun to ride, but very slow. Midan Ramla is the main station. Lime-yellow-coloured trams go west and blue-coloured ones travel east. The fare is 25pt.

Tram 14 goes to Misr Train Station; tram 15 goes through Anfushi; trams 1 and 25 go to Sidi Gaber.

NILE VALLEY   وادي النيل

In this part of the country, the life-giving Nile snakes its way through Egypt's desolate belly. An abundance of ancient riches lines its green shores.

Luxor   الأقصر

☑ 095 / POP 484,132

Built on ruins of the once-brilliant, 4000-year-old city of Ta Ipet (the Sanctuary), which the ancient Greeks called Thebes, modern-day Luxor was capital of one of history's most prosperous and powerful empires. Many of the relics seem to mushroom directly from the sprawl of this bustling modern Egyptian town. For most visitors, the opulent cache of tombs and funerary temples scattered across the west bank make this Egypt's must-see destination.

History

Thebes emerged as the main power in Upper Egypt under the 11th- and 12th-dynasty pharaohs. Rising against the northern capital of Heracleopolis, Thebes reunited the country under its political, religious and administrative control. After a period of decline, the Theban princes liberated the country from foreign rule and created the New Kingdom. At the height of their glory and opulence, from 1550 to 1069 BC, all the New Kingdom pharaohs (with the exception of Akhenaten, who moved to Tell al-Amarna) made Thebes their capital. The city had a population of nearly a million, and the architectural activity was astounding.

◉ Sights

Luxor consists of three separate areas: the town of Luxor itself on the east bank of the Nile; the village of Karnak, 2km to the northeast; and the towns of Gurna, New Gurna and Al-Gezira near the monuments and necropolis of ancient Thebes, all on the west bank of the Nile.

◉ East Bank

★ Karnak TEMPLE
(☑ 238 0270; Sharia Maabad al-Karnak; adult/student E£65/40; ☉ 6am-6pm; Ⓟ) Karnak is an extraordinary complex of sanctuaries, kiosks, pylons and obelisks, dedicated to the Theban triad (the Egyptian gods of Amun, Mut and Khonsu) but also to the greater glory of pharaohs. Constructed over more than 1500 years, it has at its heart the temple of Amun, 'home' of the local god who became the most powerful deity in Egypt and the wider region. Be sure to allow enough time: wandering through this gigantic complex is one of the highlights of any visit to Egypt.

Everything is on a gigantic scale: the site covers over 2 sq km, large enough to contain about 10 cathedrals, while its main structure, the Temple of Amun, is one of the world's largest religious complexes. This was where the god lived on earth, surrounded by the houses of his wife Mut and their son Khonsu, two other huge temple complexes on this site. Built, added to, dismantled, restored, enlarged and decorated over nearly 1500 years, Karnak was the most important place of worship in Egypt during the New Kingdom, when it was called Ipet-Sut, meaning 'The Most Esteemed of Places'.

The great **Temple of Amun-Ra**, with its famous hypostyle hall, has a spectacular forest of giant papyrus-shaped columns. On its southern side is the **Mut Temple Enclosure**, once linked to the main temple by an avenue of ram-headed sphinxes. To the north is the **Montu Temple Enclosure**, which honoured the local Theban war god. The 3km paved avenue of human-headed sphinxes that once linked the great Temple of Amun at Karnak with Luxor Temple is now again being cleared. Most of what you can see was built by the powerful pharaohs of the 18th to 20th dynasties (1570–1090 BC), who spent fortunes on making their mark in this most sacred of places. Later pharaohs extended and rebuilt the complex, as did the Ptolemies and early Christians. The further into the complex you venture, the older the structures.

The light is most beautiful in the early morning or later afternoon, and the temple is quieter then, as later in the morning tour buses bring day trippers from Hurghada. It pays to visit more than once, to make sense of the overwhelming jumble of ancient remains.

Luxor Temple TEMPLE
(Map p86; ☑ 237 2408; Corniche an-Nil; adult/student E£60/30; ☉ 6am-9pm) Largely built by the New Kingdom pharaohs Amenhotep III (1390–1352 BC) and Ramses II (1279–1213 BC), this temple is a strikingly graceful monument in the heart of the modern town. Also known as the Southern Sanctuary, it was largely built for the Opet celebrations, when the statues of Amun, Mut and Khonsu

Luxor's West Bank

Sometimes there is no way around the crowds of visitors and hawkers in the Valley of the Kings, but try to go early, before it gets hot. Stop off at the **Colossi of Memnon ❶** as you pass them, taking a look at the ongoing excavation of the ruins of the Temple of Amenhotep III, whose entrance they once flanked. From the royal tombs, drive around the hillside to visit the massive terraced **Temple of Hatshepsut ❷**, almost entirely reconstructed but still good to see as it is the best surviving example of classical-style Egyptian architecture in Luxor.

The Theban hillside further to the south is pitted with thousands of tomb openings. The Tombs of the Nobles in what was **Gurna Village ❸** and the nearby **Workers' Tombs ❹** at Deir al-Medina are very different in style and construction from the royal burials. In some ways, their views of everyday life are more impressive than the more orthodox scenes on the walls of the royal tombs.

In the afternoon, drop down towards the line between desert and agriculture to see two royal temples. The Ramesseum is dedicated to the memory of Ramses II and contains the upper half of a massive statue of the pharaoh. In midafternoon, when the light starts to soften, head over to **Medinat Habu ❺**, the temple of Ramses III. The last of the great imperial temples built during the New Kingdom, the temple has retained much of its grandeur, as well as extensive (and often exaggerated) records of the king's reign.

TOP TIPS

» **Allow** at least one day.

» **Tickets** for everything except the Valley of the Kings must be bought at the ticket office.

» **Bring** a hat, sunscreen and plenty of water.

» **Photography** is not allowed inside the tombs, but there is plenty to see – and photograph – outside.

Medinat Habu
Original paintwork, applied more than 3000 years ago, can still be seen on lintels and inner columns. Some of this was preserved by the mudbrick houses and chapels of early Christians (since destroyed).

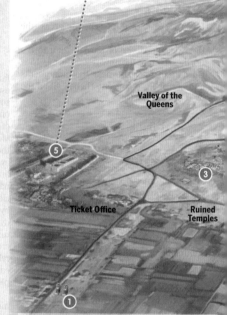

Valley of the Queens

❺

❸

Ticket Office

Ruined Temples

❶

Colossi of Memnon
Although the Greeks called him Memnon, the colossi were built for Pharaoh Amenhotep III, who built the largest of all funerary temples here on the west bank (its ruins are only now being excavated).

Workers' Tombs (Deir al-Medina)

What to do with your spare time if you were an ancient Egyptian tomb worker? Cut a tomb and decorate it with things you didn't have in this life, including ceilings decorated with rug patterns.

Temple of Hatshepsut

Hatshepsut's funerary temple is unlike any other in Luxor. Built on three terraces with its back to the hill that contains the Valley of the Kings, it was once as grand as the pharaoh-queen.

Valley of the Kings

②

④

Tombs of the Nobles (all this hillside)

Ramesseum (Temple of Ramses II)

Gurna Village

Rumours of treasure beneath houses in Gurna led the government to move the villagers and demolish their houses in the early 2000s. Some Gurna houses dated back to at least the beginning of the 19th century.

Luxor – East Bank

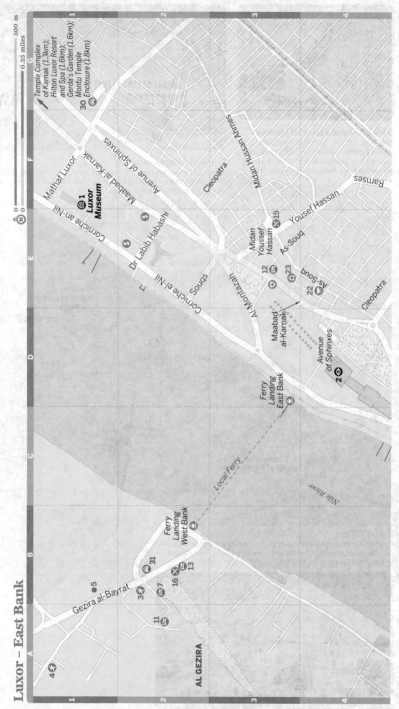

Temple Complex
of Karnak (1.3km);
Hilton Luxor Resort
and Spa (1.6km);
Gerda's Garden (1.6km);
Montu Temple
Enclosure (1.8km)

500 m
0.25 miles

Mathaf Luxor

Corniche an-Nil

Maabad al-Karnak

Avenue of Sphinxes

1 Luxor Museum

Dr Labib Habashi

Sphinxes

Corniche el-Nil

Cleopatra

Midan Hussan Ahmes

Ramses

Midan
Youssef
Hassan

Yousef Hassan

As-Souq

Al-Montazah

As-Souq

Cleopatra

Maabad
al-Karnak

Avenue
of Sphinxes

2

Ferry Landing
East Bank

Local Ferry

Nile River

Ferry
Landing
West Bank

Gezira al-Bayrat

AL GEZIRA

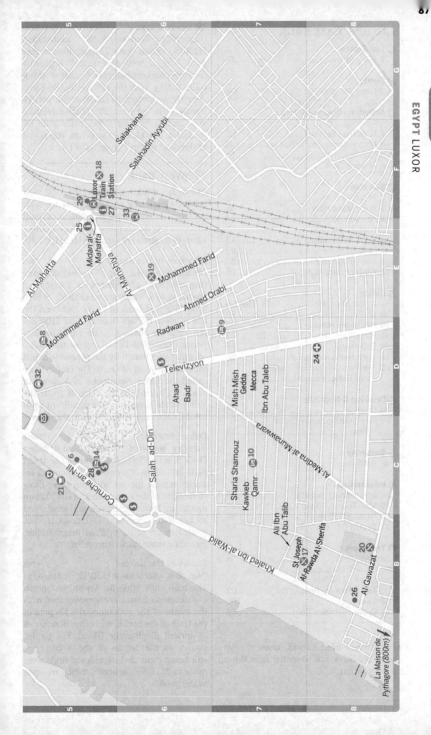

Luxor – East Bank

were brought from Karnak, along the Avenue of Sphinxes, and reunited here during the inundation.

★ Luxor Museum   MUSEUM
(Map p86; Corniche an-Nil; adult/student E£100/50; ⏱9am-5pm) This wonderful museum has a well-chosen and brilliantly displayed and explained collection of antiquities dating from the end of the Old Kingdom right through to the Mamluk period, mostly gathered from the Theban temples and necropolis. The ticket price puts off many, but don't let that stop you: this is one of the most rewarding sights in Luxor.

◎ West Bank

The lush Egyptian countryside of the west bank conceals the world's largest open-air museum. It was here that pharaohs built their memorial temples and where thousands of tombs were excavated into the hills.

★ Valley of the Kings   TOMB
(Wadi Biban al-Muluk; Map p90; www.thebanmappingproject.com; adult/student for 3 tombs excl Ramses VI, Ay & Tutankhamun E£100/50; ⏱6am-4pm) The west bank of Luxor had been the site of royal burials since around 2100 BC, but it was the pharaohs of the New Kingdom period (1550–1069 BC) who chose this isolated valley dominated by the pyramid-shaped mountain peak of Al-Qurn (The Horn). Once called the Great Necropolis of Millions of Years of Pharaoh, or the Place of Truth, the Valley of the Kings has 63 magnificent royal tombs, each quite different from the other.

Deir al-Bahri   TEMPLE
(Funerary Temple of Hatshepsut; adult/student E£30/15; ⏱6am-5pm) Rising out of the desert plain in a series of terraces, Hatshepsut's funerary temple merges with the sheer limestone cliffs of the eastern face of the Theban mountain. It was desecrated and vandalised by her bitter successor, Tuthmosis III, but retains much of its original magnificence, including some fascinating reliefs.

Tombs of the Nobles   TOMB
(Map p98; adult/student E£30/15; ⏱8am-4pm) The high cliffs opposite Aswan, just north of Kitchener's Island, are honeycombed with the tombs of the governors, the Keepers of the Gate of the South, and other dignitaries of ancient Elephantine Island. The tombs, known as the Tombs of the Nobles, are still being excavated: significant finds were made in 2014. Six decorated tombs are open to the public.

Carter's House & the Replica Tomb of Tutankhamun   MUSEUM

(Map p90; adult/student E£50/25; ⊙9am-5pm; P ♿) The domed house where Howard Carter lived during his search for Tutankhamun's tomb is surrounded by a garden on what is otherwise a barren slope above the road from Deir al-Bahri to the Valley of the Kings. The house has been restored and decorated with pictures and tools of the excavation. An exact replica of Tutankhamun's burial chamber has been constructed on the edge of the garden along with an exhibition relating to the discovery of the tomb.

★ Medinat Habu   TEMPLE

(Map p90; adult/student E£40/20; ⊙6am-5pm) Ramses III's magnificent memorial temple of Medinat Habu is perhaps one of the most underrated sites on the west bank. With the Theban mountains as a backdrop and the sleepy village of Kom Lolah in front, it is a wonderful place to visit, especially in the late afternoon when the light softens.

Ramesseum   TEMPLE

(Map p90; adult/student E£40/20; ⊙6am-5pm) Ramses II called his massive memorial temple 'the Temple of Millions of Years of User-Maat-Ra'; classical visitors called it the tomb of Ozymandias; and Jean-François Champollion, who deciphered hieroglyphics, called it the Ramesseum. Like other memorial temples it was part of Ramses II's funerary complex. His tomb was built deep in the hills, but his memorial temple was on the edge of the cultivation on a canal that connected with the Nile and with other memorial temples.

Colossi of Memnon   MONUMENT

(Map p90) FREE The two faceless Colossi of Memnon, originally representing Pharaoh Amenhotep III and rising majestically about 18m from the plain, are the first monuments tourists see when they visit the west bank. Yet few visitors have any idea that these giant enthroned figures are set in front of the main entrance to an equally impressive funerary temple, the largest in Egypt, the remains of which are slowly being brought to light.

🏃 Activities

Felucca Rides

Feluccas cruise the Nile throughout the day, and cost between E£30 and E£40 per hour per boat, depending on your bargaining skills. The most popular trip is to Banana Island, a tiny, palm-dotted isle about 5km upriver. The trip takes between two and three hours, ideally timed to watch the sunset from the boat.

Horse Riding

A sunset ride around the west-bank temples is an unforgettable experience. Two stables offer guided horse rides, the better being Nobi's Arabian Horse Stables (Map p86; ☑0100 504 8558, 231 0024; www.luxorstables. com; approx per hr with helmet E£35 for camel or horse, LE£25 for donkey; ⊙7am-sunset), which is

EGYPT LUXOR

ℹ WEST BANK PRACTICALITIES

⇒ Pace yourself – it's impossible to see everything.

⇒ All sites are open 6am to 5pm daily.

⇒ Tickets for Deir al-Bahri (Temple of Hatshepsut), the Assassif Tombs, the Valley of the Kings and the Valley of the Queens are sold at the sites.

⇒ All other tickets are sold at the Antiquities Inspectorate Ticket Office (Map p90; main road, 3km inland from ferry landing; ⊙6am-5pm).

⇒ Tickets are valid only on the day of purchase and no refunds are given.

⇒ Photography is strictly forbidden in tombs, and guards may confiscate film or memory cards.

⇒ Distances are large: 3km to the antiquities office, and another 1km to the Valley of the Queens, and 5km to the Valley of the Kings.

⇒ Tour groups visit Deir al-Bahri and the Valley of the Kings in the morning. Hit exceptionally hot Deir al-Bahri as early as possible, to beat the heat and crowds, but you can leave the tombs till the afternoon.

⇒ Carry plenty of water, a hat, small change and a torch.

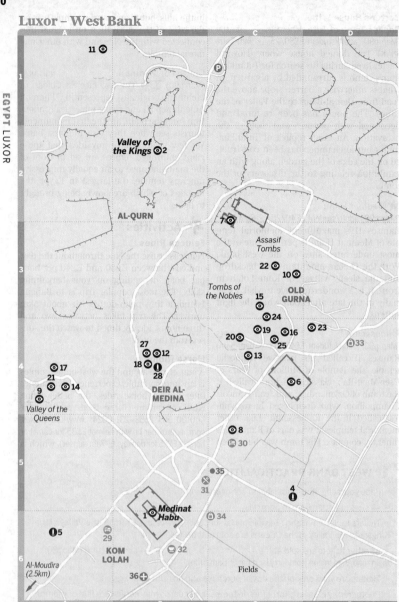

Valley of
the Kings ⊙2

AL-QURN

7⊙

*Assasif
Tombs*

22⊙

10⊙

*Tombs of
the Nobles*

15⊙

OLD
GURNA

⊙24

⊙19 ⊙16

20⊙

⊙25

⊙23

📇33

⊙13

27⊙ ⊙12

18⊙ ❶

28

DEIR AL-
MEDINA

⊙6

⊙17

21⊙

9⊙ ⊙14

*Valley of the
Queens*

⊙8

📇30

●35

✗31

❶4

❶5

KOM
LOLAH

❶ *Medinat
Habu*

📇29

📇34

🍴32

*Al-Moudira
(2.5km)*

36✚

Fields

11⊙

known for its well-kept horses. If you phone ahead to book, Nobi's staff will collect you from the east bank in a launch. Rides usually take three hours. He also offers camel and donkey rides.

🏃 Tours

Most small budget hotels aggressively promote their own tours (E£75 to E£100 is the going rate), but often they lead only to papyrus shops and alabaster factories. On the upper end, American Express and Thomas Cook

Agency (Map p86; ☑ 0100 294 3169; http://quest-foregyptianadventure.com; Gezira al-Bayrat).

🛏 Sleeping

The cost of Luxor accommodation is a roller coaster driven by demand. May to September is the low season, when some hotels drop their charges by nearly 50%. At peak season (October to April, and particularly around the school-holiday periods of Christmas and Easter), you are advised to book ahead.

The west bank is quieter, has fewer touts and is closer to Luxor's main tombs and temples. There is a great selection of mid-range accommodation but eating options are limited. The east bank has most of the shopping and entertainment action, as well as most of Luxor's budget hotels and cheap eateries. It's home to the Karnak and Luxor temples, and Luxor Museum.

East Bank

★ Nefertiti Hotel
HOTEL **$**

(Map p86; ☑ 237 2386; www.nefertitihotel.com; Sharia as-Sahabi, btwn Sharia Maabad al-Karnak & Sharia as-Souq; s/d/tr E£160/200/270; ☻❄️🛜) Aladin as-Sahabi runs his family's hotel with care and passion, offering recently renovated, midrange facilities at budget prices. No wonder this hotel is popular with our readers: rooms are simple but very cosy and come with kettles and tea/coffee, the small private bathrooms are spotless, and an excellent breakfast is served on the roof terrace. One of the best midrange options.

★ Boomerang Hotel
HOTEL **$**

(Map p86; ☑ 228 0981; www.boomerangluxor.com; Mohamed Farid; dm E£25, d E£45-120; ❄️🛜) If the 1970s exist in Luxor it is in the Boomerang (although it was not actually here in the '70s) – a happy mix of Australia and Egypt with a range of budget rooms, some with air-con and en suite bathrooms, lounge and terrace, Aussie BBQ, tour booking, free wi-fi and just about everything else you could need.

Happy Land Hotel
HOSTEL **$**

(Map p86; ☑ 227 1828; www.luxorhappyland.com; Sharia Qamr; s/d E£85/90, without bathroom E£75/80; ❄️@🛜) The Happy Land, a backpackers' favourite, offers clean rooms and spotless bathrooms, as well as very friendly service, a copious breakfast with fruit and cornflakes and a rooftop terrace. Competition among Luxor's budget hotels is fierce,

arrange tours from E£250 per half-day. Two local agencies are partcularly recommended: Aladin Tours (Map p86; ☑ 237 2386, 0100 601 6132; http://nefertitihotel.com/tours; Nefertiti Hotel, Sharia as-Sahbi; ⏰ 10am-6pm) and QEA Travel

Luxor – West Bank

and the Happy Land comes out well almost every time. It doesn't need to send touts to the station!

Fontana Hotel   HOSTEL $
(Map p86; ☑228 0663, 0100 733 3238; www.fontanaluxorhotel.net; Sharia Radwan, off Sharia Televizyon; s/d/tr E£40/60/75, without bathroom E£30/50/65; ❋🕸📶) An old stalwart of the city's budget-hotel scene, this 25-room hotel has clean rooms, a washing machine for guest use, a luggage-storage room, a rooftop terrace and a kitchen. Bathrooms are generally large and clean, and toilet paper and towels are provided. The owner, Magdi Soliman, is helpful. Beware extra breakfast charges.

★ **La Maison de Pythagore**   GUESTHOUSE $$
(☑0100 535 0532; www.louxor-egypte.com; Al-Awamiya; s/d/tr €35/50/60; ❋📶) This small guesthouse with seven rooms in a traditional Egyptian house is tucked away in the village behind the Sheraton Hotel, close to the tourist facilities and the Nile, but a world away from Luxor's hustle. Run by the Belgian Anne and her son Thomas, it's a great place to stay for a few days.

★ **Hilton Luxor Resort and Spa**   LUXURY HOTEL $$$
(☑239 9999; www.hiltonluxor.com; New Karnak; r from US$220; ❋🕸📶☀) The Luxor Hilton is the slickest, most luxurious resort in Luxor. Located 2km north of Luxor centre, past the Karnak temples, the large Nile-side rooms are elegant and tastefully decorated in a warm Asian-inspired style with lots of neutral colours and wood. Communal areas exude calm and tranquillity and the spa is impressive, more Thailand than Egypt.

The large grounds include two Nile-view infinity swimming pools with submerged sun loungers, a Technogym, and several top-class restaurants, including the Mediterranean Olives and a chic Asian bistro, Silk Road. The staff and management are young and very hands-on. This hotel is almost a destination in itself, albeit not very family oriented.

Winter Palace Hotel   HISTORIC HOTEL $$$
(Map p86; ☑237 1197; www.sofitel.com; Corniche an-Nil; old wing r from $160, ste from $450; ◗❋@📶☀) The Winter Palace was built to attract the aristocracy of Europe and is one of Egypt's most famous historic hotels. A wonderfully atmospheric Victorian pile,

it has high ceilings, lots of gorgeous textiles, fabulous views over the Nile, an enormous garden with exotic trees and shrubs, a huge swimming pool and a tennis court.

West Bank

Marsam Hotel
HISTORIC HOTEL $

(Map p90; ☑ 237 2403, 231 1603; www.marsamluxor.com; Old Gurna; s/d €15/25, without bathroom €12/20; P ❋ ☎) The oldest hotel on the west bank, the Marsam was originally built in the 1920s as a house for archaeologists from the University of Chicago, but was later turned into a hotel by Sheikh Ali of the local Abd el Rasoul family. The family have run it ever since. Work in 2013 left the hotel looking its best.

Al-Gezira Hotel
HOTEL $

(Map p86; ☑ 231 2505; www.el-geziras.com; Gezira al-Bayrat; s/d/tr E£100/150/210; ❋ ☎) This hotel, in a modern building, is very much a home away from home – literally so for quite a few archaeologists during the winter season. The charming owners make everyone feel welcome, so that the hotel is often full. The 11 homey rooms are pristine, all with private bathrooms, overlooking the lake or a dried-up branch of the Nile.

★ Beit Sabée
BOUTIQUE HOTEL $$

(Map p90; ☑ 0111 837 5604; www.beitsabee.com; Bairat; d €30-80; ❂ ❋ ☎) More like a house than a hotel, Beit Sabée has appeared in design magazines for its cool use of Nubian colours and local furnishings with a twist. Near the farms around Medinat Habu, it offers quiet accommodation, a closer contact with rural Egypt and fabulous views of the desert and Medina Habu from the rooftop.

Nile Valley Hotel
HOTEL $$

(Map p86; ☑ 231 1477, 0122 796 4473; www.nilevalley.nl; Al-Gezira; s/d/tr/ste E£195/255/310/330; ❂ ❋ ☎ ❋) A delightful Dutch-Egyptian-run hotel in a modern block right near the ferry landing. The comfortable rooms almost all have ultraclean private bathrooms, satellite TV and air-con. Upstairs is a good rooftop bar-restaurant with fantastic views of the Nile and Luxor Temple, and there is a pool and children's pool in the garden.

Hotel Sheherazade
HOTEL $$

(Map p86; ☑ 0100 611 5939, 231 1228; www.hotelsheherazade.com; Al-Gezira; s/d/tr E£200/280 /350, flat E£400, 3-course meals per person E£45; ❋ ☎) Mohamed El Sanuoy's dream of build-

ing a hotel has culminated in one of the most welcoming of west bank hotels and somewhere he takes great pride in. The 28 comfortable and spacious rooms are decorated with local colour and furnishings and all have ensuite bathrooms with water heated by solar panels. The Moorish-style building is surrounded by a garden.

★ Al-Moudira
LUXURY HOTEL $$$

(☑ 0122 392 8332, 095 255 1440; www.moudira.com; Daba'iyya; r US$285, ste US$355; ❂ ❋ @ ☎ ❋) Al-Moudira is a luxury hotel with a style and individuality so often lacking in Egypt. A Moorish fantasy of pointed arches and soaring domes, surrounded by lush green and birdsong, the hotel has 54 rooms grouped around a small garden courtyard, a large pool and hammam (bathhouse). It has a tranquil courtyard restaurant and vibrant bar, and excellent and friendly service.

✕ Eating

East Bank

Sharia al-Mahatta has a number of fine sandwich stands, juice stands and other cheap-eat possibilities, as well as an off-licence selling alcohol. The fruit-and-veg market on Sharia as-Souq is best in the early morning.

★ Wenkie's German Ice Cream & Iced Coffee Parlour
ICE CREAM $

(Map p86; ☑ 0128 894 7380; www.facebook.com/wenkies; Sharia al-Gawazat, opposite the Nile Palace; ice creams from E£2; ❂ 2-8pm Sat-Thu) For people who only opened a shop in February 2014, Ernst and Babette Wenk have quickly become legends, serving the finest, freshest most delicious ice cream in Luxor – some are saying even in the world. Using organic buffalo milk and local fresh fruits, they make and sell ices and sorbets from a small shop/parlour near the passport office.

Koshari Alzaeem
EGYPTIAN FAST FOOD $

(Map p86; Midan Youssef Hassan; kushari E£5-15; ❂ 24hr) Probably the best *kushari* in town. The few tables tend to fill up fast. There is a second, larger branch near the junction of Televizyon and Al-Manshiya streets.

★ Sofra Restaurant & Café
EGYPTIAN $$

(Map p86; ☑ 235 9752; www.sofra.com.eg; 90 Sharia Mohamed Farid; mains E£20-60; ❂ 11am-midnight) Sofra remains our favourite restaurant in Luxor. Located in a 1930s house, away from all the tourist tat, it is as Egyptian as can be, in menu, decor and even in price. The large menu features all the traditional Egyptian dishes, such as stuffed pigeon and excellent duck, as well as a large selection of salads, dips (E£4) and mezze.

As-Sahaby Lane   EGYPTIAN $$
(Map p86; ☎095 236 5509; www.nefertitihotel. com/sahabi.htm; Sharia as-Sahaby, off Sharia as-Souq; mains E£45-70; ⊙9am-11.30pm) Great easygoing alfresco restaurant in the lane running between the souq and the street to the Karnak temples. Fresh and well-prepared Egyptian dishes like *fiteer* (flaky pizza) and *tagen* (stew cooked in earthenware pots) are served alongside good pizzas and salads, although the chef is constantly expanding his range: look out for the new camel with couscous.

Pizza Roma.It   ITALIAN $$
(Map p86; ☎0111 879 9559; Sharia St Joseph; dishes E£40-60) The most popular Italian restaurant in Luxor. Run by an Italian woman and her Egyptian partner, the small orange-painted restaurant serves a long list of pastas and pizzas, as well as some classic Italian meat dishes. All are reliable, made as closely as possible to the Italian way.

The restaurant attracts a mix of locals, tourists, expats and visiting Cairenes. It doesn't serve alcohol, but you can bring your own. For dessert, head around the corner for ice cream from Wenkie's.

Salahadeen   EGYPTIAN $$
(Map p86; ☎0100 757 1855; www.salahadeen. com; Mara Hotel, Sharia Salahadin Ayyubi, off Sharia Salakhana; dishes E£18-60; ⊙6pm-midnight; ✷) Salahadeen offers a set three-course menu of fresh home-cooked Egyptian food. Most dishes consist of vegetables, and the vegetarian options are not cooked in a meat broth as in so many other places. It is essential to book ahead. Alcohol is served.

Gerda's Garden   EGYPTIAN, EUROPEAN $$
(☎235 8688, 0122 5348 326; www.luxor-german-restaurant.com; opp Hilton Luxor, New Karnak; dishes E£15-45; ⊙6.30-11pm; ✷) Gerda is one half of a German-Egyptian couple whose restaurant has built a strong following with European residents and regular visitors to Luxor. The decor is homely provincial European bistro, but the menu features both Egyptian specials like kebab and delicious grilled pigeon, and very European comfort food for

those slightly homesick, such as goulash and potato salad.

✖ West Bank

Restaurant Mohammed   EGYPTIAN $
(Map p90; ☎0120 325 1307; Kom Lolah; set meals E£35-60) Mohammed's is a blast of old-time Luxor, a simple, family-run restaurant attached to the owner's mud-brick house, where charming Mohammed Abdel Lahi serves with his son Azab, while his wife cooks. The small menu includes meat grills, delicious chicken and duck as well as stuffed pigeon, a local speciality. Stella beer is usually available as well as Egyptian wine.

Nile Valley Hotel   INTERNATIONAL $$
(Map p86; Al-Gezira; meals E£40-60; ⊙8am-11pm) A popular rooftop restaurant with a bird's-eye view of the west-bank's waterfront, the river and Luxor Temple, the Nile Valley has a wide-ranging menu of Egyptian and international specialities. It is also a good place to relax with a cold beer (E£16).

★ Al-Moudira   MEDITERRANEAN $$$
(☎0120 325 1307; Daba'iyya; mains E£75-110; ⊙8am-midnight) In keeping with its flamboyant decor, Al-Moudira has the most sophisticated and most expensive food on the west bank, with great salads and grills at lunchtime. The more elaborate dinner menu, which changes daily, has delicious Mediterranean-Lebanese cuisine. This is a great place for a romantic dinner in the courtyard, or by the fire in the winter. Reserve ahead.

🍷 Drinking & Nightlife

Cilantro   CAFE
(Map p86; lower level, Corniche an-Nil) A pleasant, popular outdoor cafe, right on the Nile, in front of the Winter Palace Hotel. The former Metropolitan is now part of the Egyptian coffee chain Cilantro, serving dull though usually reliable snacks and good coffee. Away from the hassle of the Corniche, right by the waterline, it is a good place to while away a moment.

New Oum Koulsoum Coffee Shop   CAFE
(Map p86; oumkolsoumcaffe.com; Sharia as-Souq; ⊙24hr) Pleasant ahwa right in the heart of the souq, on a large terrace with welcoming mist machines, where you can recover from shopping and haggling and watch the crowds without any hassle. On the menu are fresh juices (E£10 to E£20), hot and

cold drinks and a good sheesha (E£15), as well as 'professional Nespresso' coffee (E£15).

Marsam Hotel
CAFE

(Map p90; www.marsamluxor.com; Old Gurna; ☎) The old hotel has a beautiful, shaded garden courtyard, a very pleasant place for a drink, day or night.

Maratonga Cafeteria
CAFE

(Map p90; ☑231 0233; Kom Lolah; ⊙6am-11pm) This friendly outdoor cafe-restaurant, in front of Medinat Habu, is the best place to sip a cold drink under a big tree after wandering through Ramses III's magnificent temple, or to have a delicious *tagen* (E£40) or salad for lunch.The view is superlative and the atmosphere is relaxing.

🛍 Shopping

All the usual souvenirs can be had in Luxor, but alabaster is ubiquitous although it is mined halfway back to Cairo. Head for the west bank, where factories near the Ramesseum and Deir al-Bahri sell a range of products. Abo el Hassan Alabaster Factory (Map p90; ☑0106 733 3081; West Bank, opposite Tombs of the Nobles ; ⊙8am-4pm) is recommended. Just off the souq, Habiba (Map p86; ☑0100 124 2026, 235 7305; www.habibagallery. com; Sharia Sidi Mahmoud, off Sharia as-Souq; ⊙10am-10pm) has the most interesting handicrafts on the east bank and Caravanserai (Map p90; ☑0122 327 8771; www.caravanserailuxor.com; Kom Lolah; ⊙8am-10pm) on the west bank.

ⓘ Information

DANGERS & ANNOYANCES

Luxor is perhaps the hassle capital of Egypt. If you're a man, breathe deep and smile. If you're a woman, be reserved. Because there is some female sex tourism in Luxor, women can be seen as possible customers of another sort.

MEDICAL SERVICES

Dr Boutros (Map p90; ☑231 0851; Kom Lolah) Excellent English- and French-speaking doctor, who works on the west bank.

International Hospital (Map p86; ☑228 0192, 228 0194; Sharia Televizyon) The best place in town.

MONEY

Many banks have branches in Luxor offering ATMs and foreign-exchange services. Money can be changed at a slew of forex offices around

town and at **American Express** (Map p86; ☑237 8333; Corniche an-Nil; ⊙9am-4.30pm) and **Thomas Cook** (Map p86; ☑237 2196; www.thomascookegypt.com; ⊙8am-8pm), both beside the Winter Palace.

TOURIST INFORMATION

Main Tourist Office (Map p86; ☑237 3294, 237 2215; Midan al-Mahatta; ⊙9am-8pm) Very helpful and well-informed tourist information opposite the train station, run by Taher Eladesy. There is also an office for hotel bookings, tours and tickets for the sound and light show in Karnak. There's a branch (Map p86; ☑237 0259; Train Station; ⊙8am-8pm) in the train station too.

ⓘ Getting There & Away

AIR

EgyptAir (Map p86; ☑238 0581; www.egyptair. com; Winter Palace Hotel, Corniche an-Nil; ⊙8am-8pm) EgyptAir operates flights to Cairo, Abu Simbel (via Aswan) and Sharm el-Sheikh. A one-way ticket to Cairo costs between E£370 and E£720. The staff here are efficient and friendly.

BUS

Zanakta Bus Station (☑0128 436 663) is out of town on the road to the airport – about 1km before it. A taxi from the town to the bus station will cost around E£25 to E£35, but it's a good idea to check as some **Upper Egypt Bus Co** (Map p86; ☑232 3218, 237 2118; Midan al-Mahatta) services leave from the office near the train station. Another operator is **Super Jet** (☑236 7732).

CRUISES

The best times of the year for cruising are October/November and April/May. During the high season (November to March), an armada of cruise boats travels the Nile between Aswan and Esna (for Luxor), stopping at Edfu and Kom Ombo en route. You can often make deals directly with the boat captains in Esna, rather than through a travel agency. Feluccas can also be organised from Esna, but most travellers prefer to go the other way (Aswan to Luxor), as this is how the current runs.

MICROBUS

The microbus station is behind the train station. Minivans run from Luxor to Aswan (E£20) via Esna (E£5), Edfu (E£9) and Kom Ombo (E£15), as well as to Hurghada (E£20) via Qena (E£4). There is no service to Asyut.

The drivers are always ready to privatise the car to make special trips up the Nile to Aswan, stopping at the sights on the way; expect to pay about E£500. To Asyut or to Hurghada, the

BUSES FROM LUXOR

For Al-Quseir and Marsa Alam, change at Safaga. For Qena, it's cheaper to take a *servees*. At the time of writing, there were no buses between Luxor and Aswan. For the Western Desert, take a train to Asyut, then one of several daily buses to Al-Kharga (E£18) and Dakhla (E£30).

DESTINATION	PRICE (E£)	DURATION (HR)	TIMES
Cairo	100	10-12	7pm
Cairo (Super Jet)	110	10-12	8pm
Dahab	140	16-17	4.30pm
Hurghada	35-40	4	5 daily, 8.30am-8pm
Hurghada (Super Jet)	45	4	8pm
Ismailia	75	10	7.30pm
Nuweiba	15	1	10.30am
Port Said	80	12	7.30pm
Qena	8	1-2	frequent, 6.30am-8pm
Safaga	30-35	4½	5 daily, 8.30am-8pm
Sharm el-Sheikh	130	12	4.30pm

going rate is about E£500. It is possible to take a private *servees* to Al-Kharga via the direct road, avoiding Asyut, at E£700 for the car (maximum seven people).

TRAIN

Luxor Station (Map p86; ☏ 237 2018; Midan al-Mahatta) has left-luggage, a tourist office and a post office.

The **Watania Sleeping Trains** (☏ 02-2574 9474, 237 2015; www.wataniasleepingtrains. com) go daily to Cairo at 7.15pm and 10.30pm (single/double including dinner and breakfast US$100/120, child four to nine years US$85, nine hours).

For day trains headed north to Cairo (1st/2nd class E£25/15), the best is 981, at 8.25am, stopping at Qena (for Dendara; 1st/2nd class E£28/19) and Asyut (for the Western Desert; E£53/30). The slower 983 leaves at 10.30am, and the 935 at noon.

There are several trains to Aswan (adult 1st/2nd class E£41/25, three hours) including the 1902 at 9.30am and the 980 at 6pm. All train tickets are better bought in advance, but if you buy your ticket on the train there is a charge of E£6.

ⓘ Getting Around

TO/FROM THE AIRPORT

Luxor International Airport is 7km east of town. A taxi will cost between E£70 to E£100 to east-bank destinations. There is no bus.

BICYCLE

Easily the most pleasant way to get around, bicycles can be rented on the west bank and from most hotels for around E£12 to E£15 per day. You can take a bicycle on the ferry connecting the

east and west banks, or pick one up on the west bank at **Mohamed Setouhy** (Gezira Bike Rental; Map p86; ☏ 0100 223 9710; per hour E£10).

FERRY & BOAT

The *baladi* (municipal) ferry (E£1) runs to the west bank from the dock in front of Luxor Temple. Private launches charge E£10 to E£20 per boat each way for the same trip.

HANTOUR

The most interesting way to get around town is by horse and carriage, also called a *calèche*. Rates range from E£20 to E£100 per hour depending on your haggling skills. Expect to pay about E£30 to Karnak.

PICK-UP TAXIS

Kabout (pick-up trucks) and microbuses can be the quickest and easiest way to get about in Luxor. They ply fixed routes and will stop whenever flagged down. To get to the Karnak temples take a microbus from Luxor station or from behind Luxor Temple for 50pt. Other routes run inside the town. On the west bank, trucks wait in the lot by the ferry landing, with drivers shouting out the villages they're headed for; the Gurna route passes the antiquities ticket office.

Dendara   دندرة

☏ 096

The wonderfully preserved Temple of Hathor (adult/student E£35/20; ⏱8am-5pm) at Dendara is one of the most impressive temples in Egypt. Built at the very end of the Pharaonic period, its main building is still virtually intact, with a great stone roof and columns, dark chambers, underground crypts and twisting stairways, all carved with hieroglyphs. The head of Hathor, the goddess of pleasure and love, is carved on six of the 24 columns of the outer hypostyle hall, and on the walls are scenes of Roman emperors as pharaohs.

Dendara is 4km southwest of Qena on the west side of the Nile and an easy day trip from Luxor. A return taxi will cost about E£400. If tourism picks up, there will also be day boat trips to Dendara and nearby Abydos, best arranged through a tour agency in Luxor. If you arrive in Qena by train, you will need to take a taxi to the temple (around E£50 to the temple and back with some waiting time).

Esna إسنا

The hypostyle hall, with its 24 columns still supporting a roof, is all that remains of the **Temple of Khnum** (adult/student E£30/15; ⏰ 6am-5pm), constructed by Egypt's Ptolemaic rulers. Dedicated to the ram-headed creator god who fashioned humankind on his potter's wheel using Nile clay, its pillars are decorated with hieroglyphic accounts of temple ceremonies.

Trains between Luxor and Aswan stop here, but the station is on the opposite side of the Nile; so is the drop-off point if you arrive in a microbus. Hop a *kabout* from by the canal. It's much easier to take a day tour or travel in a private taxi (E£150 return from Luxor or E£450 to Aswan with stops en route).

Edfu إدفو

The **Temple of Horus** (adult/student E£60/30; ⏰ 7am-7pm) is the star attraction here. It is the best-preserved temple in Egypt, 53km south of Esna. One of the last great Egyptian attempts at monument building on a grand scale (it took about 200 years to complete), it was dedicated to the falcon-headed son of Osiris. Walking through the half-lit halls, many filled with detailed inscriptions of temple rituals and priesthood rites, is both mesmerising and eerie.

Trains running between Luxor and Aswan stop here, but the station is approximately 4km from the temple. Pick-ups travel between the station and town for E£8 (for the whole truck). Again, it's easier to take a day tour or travel in a private taxi from

DON'T MISS

ANIMALIA

Mohamed Sobhi, a passionate and knowledgeable Nubian guide, and his family maintain a sort of unofficial Nubian Museum called **Animalia** (Map p98; 📞 097-231 4152, 0100 545 6420; main street, Siou, Elephantine Island, Aswan; admission E£5, incl guided tour E£10; ⏰ 8am-7pm). They have dedicated part of their large house to the traditions, flora and fauna and the history of Nubia. Sobhi also has a small shop selling crafts at fixed prices and a lovely roof terrace for drinks and lunch.

Luxor (E£200 return or E£450 to Aswan with stops en route and depending on your bargaining skills).

Kom Ombo كوم أمبو

The **Temple of Kom Ombo** (adult/student E£40/20; ⏰ 7am-7pm), spectacularly crowning an outcrop on a bend in the Nile, is unique for its dual dedication to the crocodile and falcon gods Sobek and Haroeris. The symmetrical main temple dates from the Ptolemaic times. The newly opened Crocodile Museum beautifully displays mummified crocodiles, once plentiful here as they basked on the Nile's shores.

The easiest way to visit Kom Ombo is to take a day tour or travel by private taxi, from about E£450 round trip from Luxor, with a stop at Edfu, or onward to Aswan.

Aswan أسوان

📞 097

With a pace of life as slow as the meandering Nile in this part of Egypt, picturesque Aswan will have you reaching for your point-and-shoot every few minutes. Just north of the first cataract and the southernmost boundary of ancient Egypt's empire, contemporary Aswan is a sleepy Nile-side town fringed by palms and sandy expanses and the river is dotted with flocks of graceful feluccas. Outside the summer months, when daily temperatures soar to 50°C, Aswan is an ideal place to see the Nile the ancient way, on a sailboat, or to base yourself as you explore the fantastic ruins of nearby Abu Simbel.

Aswan

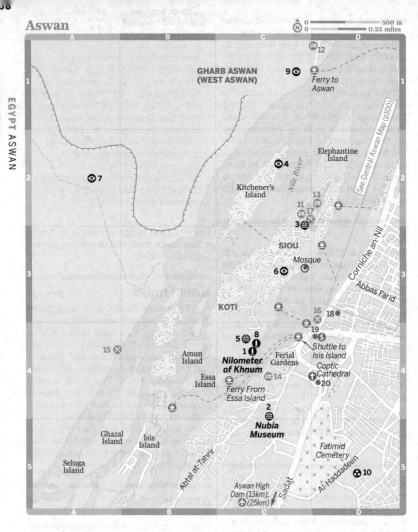

N
0 ———————————— 500 m
0 ———————————— 0.25 miles

GHARB ASWAN
(WEST ASWAN)

9

Ferry to
Aswan

12

See Central Aswan Map (p100)

Elephantine
Island

4

Kitchener's
Island

Nile River

13
11 17
3

SIOU

Mosque

6

Corniche an-Nil

Abbas Farid

KOTI

16 18
19

5 8
1
**Nilometer
of Khnum**

Amun
Island

Ferial
Gardens

Shuttle to
Isis Island

Coptic
Cathedral
20

Essa
Island

Ferry From
Essa Island

14

15

2

**Nubia
Museum**

Ghazal
Island

Isis
Island

Fatimid
Cemetery

10

Seluga
Island

Abtal at-Tahrir

Aswan High
Dam (13km);
(25km)

Sadat

Al-Haddadeen

⊙ Sights

Aswan's sights are spread out, mostly to the south and west of the town. The souq cuts right through the centre of town, parallel to the Nile. The Nubia Museum is within walking distance, just, but all other sights require transport. The sites on the islands and on the west bank involve a short boat trip. The biggest of the islands, Elephantine (Map p98), has the remains of the ancient frontier town of Abu and a small museum with local finds.

★ Nubia Museum   MUSEUM
(Map p98; ☏ 319333; www.numibia.net/nubia/intro.htm; el Fanadek St; adult/student E£60/30; ◷ 9am-1pm & 5-9pm winter, 6-10pm summer) The little-visited Nubia Museum, opposite Basma Hotel, is a treat, a showcase of the history, art and culture of Nubia. Established in 1997, in cooperation with Unesco, the museum is a reminder of what was lost beneath Lake Nasser. Exhibits are beautifully displayed in huge halls, where clearly written explanations take you from 4500 BC through to the present day.

Aswan

EGYPT ASWAN

Unfinished Obelisk ARCHAEOLOGICAL SITE
(Map p98; adult/student E£40/20; ⊙8am-5pm)
Aswan was the source of Egypt's finest granite, the hard stone ancient Egyptians used to make statues, and to embellish temples, pyramids and obelisks. In the Northern Quarries, about 1.5km from town opposite the Fatimid Cemetery, is a huge discarded obelisk, which would have been the largest of all, but was abandoned before it was completely extracted.

Microbuses will drop you within a few minutes' walk. Private taxis will charge about E£15.

Aswan Botanical Gardens GARDENS
(Map p98; admission E£20; ⊙8am-6pm) Kitchener's Island, to the west of Elephantine Island, was given to Lord Horatio Kitchener in the 1890s when he was commander of the Egyptian army. Indulging his passion for beautiful palms and plants, Kitchener turned the entire island into the stunning Aswan Botanical Gardens, importing plants from the Far East, India and parts of Africa.

Monastery of St Simeon MONASTERY
(Deir Amba Samaan; Map p98; adult/student E£30/15; ⊙8am-4pm) The fortresslike 7th-century Monastery of St Simeon was first dedicated to the local saint Anba Hedra, who renounced the world on his wedding day. It was rebuilt in the 10th century and dedicated to St Simeon. From here the monks travelled into Nubia, in the hope of converting the Nubians to Christianity. To get there, take a private boat across the Nile, scramble up the desert track on foot (about 25 minutes) or hire a camel to take you up (expect to pay about E£30).

🏃 Activities

Top of the priority list for most visitors is a quick trip between Aswan's many islands on a felucca. The afternoon is the ideal time to do this, as the fiery sun plonks itself down over Aswan's dunes. The trustworthy Gelal (☎0122 415 4902), who hangs out near Panorama Restaurant and the ferry landing, offers hassle-free tours on his family's feluccas at a fixed price (E£35 per boat for an hour, E£50 for a motor boat). According to the tourist office, sailing-boat rates are E£70 and motor boats E£80 an hour. Alternatively, take a day trip (fishing or not) on Lake Nasser with African Angler (☎230 9748; www.african-angler.net; per person from $185 incl rods & lunch).

🛏 Sleeping

Aswan's accommodation scene isn't nearly as good value as Luxor's. Be warned that hotels in the centre of town, particularly those on the Corniche, can be noisy at night.

Baaba Dool GUESTHOUSE $
(Map p98; ☎0100 497 2608; Siou, Elephantine Island; r without bathroom per person €10) A great place to unwind for a few days. A few rooms in this beautiful mud-brick house are painted in Nubian style, and have superb views over the Nile and the botanical gardens. Rooms are very basic but clean (bring a sleeping bag) and there are shared hot showers. Mustapha can arrange meals. Book ahead.

⭐**Philae Hotel** HOTEL $$
(Map p100; ☎0100 222 9628, 231 2090; www.philae-hotel.com; Corniche an-Nil; s/d/tr US$80/100/120; ❄🛜) The well-established

Central Aswan

Philae Hotel is by far the best midrange hotel in town. The tasteful and cosy rooms are decorated in fabrics with Arabic calligraphy and elegant local furnishings. The hotel restaurant serves mainly vegetarian organic food from its own gardens, and at very reasonable prices for the quality (mains from E£55 to E£70). The Philae is no longer a secret, so book ahead.

Bet al-Kerem   GUESTHOUSE $$

(Map p98; ☎ 012 391 1052, 012 384 2218; www. betelkerem.com; Gharb Aswan, West Bank; s/d with shared bathroom €30/40; ❄) This modern hotel on the west side of the Nile overlooking the desert and the Tomb of the Nobles is a great find, offering nine quiet and comfortable rooms with very clean shared bathrooms. The hotel boasts a wonderful rooftop terrace overlooking the Nile and Nubian village, and the staff are both friendly and proud to be Nubian.

Call ahead and Shaaban will come and fetch you or explain how to get there. The restaurant serves delicious meals (from €7 to €10).

Keylany Hotel   HOTEL $$

(Map p100; ☎ 231 7332; www.keylanyhotel.com; 25 Sharia Keylany; s/d/tr US$23/34/45; ❄@🛜❄) This great little hotel used to come at budget prices, but costs have gone up and some find it expensive for what is on offer. The simple but comfortable rooms are furnished with pine furniture, and have spotless bathrooms with proper showers and hot water. The management and staff are friendly and helpful.

★ Sofitel Old
Cataract Hotel & Spa   HISTORIC HOTEL $$$

(Map p98; ☎ 231 6000; www.sofitel-legend.com; Sharia Abtal at-Tahrir; s/d from US$295/320; ❄❄) The grande dame of Aswan hotels, the Cataract is a destination in itself and brings you back to the days of Agatha Christie, who is said to have written part of her novel *Death on the Nile* here (the hotel certainly featured in the movie). The splendid buildings and well-tended gardens command fantastic views of the Nile and the desert.

Mövenpick Resort Aswan RESORT $$$

(Map p98; ☑ 230 3455; www.moevenpick-aswan.com; Elephantine Island; s/d from US$90/144; ❄ @ ≋) Hidden in a large, lush garden but dominated by an eyesore tower, the Mövenpick sits on the northern end of Elephantine Island. The hotel recently had a total makeover and has very comfortable rooms, decorated in Nubian style and colours. The swimming pool is great, as is the tower-top restaurant and bar.

✖ Eating

Along Sharia as-Souq and Sharia Abtal at-Tahrir there are plenty of small restaurants and cafes, good for taking in the lively souq atmosphere.

Panorama EGYPTIAN $

(Map p98; ☑ 231 6169; Corniche an-Nil; dishes E£10-30) With its pleasant Nile-side terrace, this is a great place to chill and sip a herbal tea or fresh juice. It also serves simple Egyptian stews cooked in clay pots, with salad, mezze (a selection of starters) and rice or chips, or an all-day breakfast. Not to be confused with the restaurant of the same name in the Mövenpick Resort.

Al-Makka GRILL $$

(Map p100; ☑ 230 3232; Sharia Abtal at-Tahrir; mains E£35-50; ⊙ noon-2am) Popular with meat-eating local families, this place is famous for its excellent fresh kebabs and *kofta* (mincemeat and spices grilled on a skewer), as well as pigeon and chicken. Everything comes with bread, salad, tahini and TV. It's opposite the Ramses Hotel.

Its sister-restaurant Al-Madina (Map p100; ☑ 230 5696; Sharia as-Souq) serves a similar menu.

Salah Ad-Din INTERNATIONAL $$

(Map p100; ☑ 231 0361; Corniche an-Nil; mains E£40-80; ⊙ noon-late) One of the best of the Nile-side restaurants, with several terraces and a freezing air-conditioned dining room. The menu has Egyptian, Nubian and international dishes, a notch better than most restaurants in Aswan. The service is efficient and the beers are cool (E£18). There is also a terrace to smoke a sheesha.

Nubian Beach EGYPTIAN $$

(Map p98; west bank; set menu per person E£65) Nubian cafe-restaurant set in a quiet garden on the west bank of the Nile, against the backdrop of a towering sand dune and near a popular swimming spot. During the heat of the day or on cold winter nights, there is a beautifully painted room indoors. The food is simple but good, and beer is sometimes served.

★ Panorama
Restaurant & Bar INTERNATIONAL $$$

(Map p98; ☑ 230 3455; www.moevenpick-hotels.com; Mövenpick Resort Aswan, Elephantine Island; mains E£90-160) The Panorama is the best thing to open in Aswan, and in the Mövenpick's eyesore tower, in a long time. The food is good, service friendly and efficient, the room is elegant; but the real draw is the 360-degree view of Aswan, the river and the desert, spectacular at sunset, glittering at night.

ⓘ Information

The main banks all have branches (with ATMs) on the Corniche.

American Express (Map p98; ☑ 230 6983; Corniche an-Nil; ⊙ 9am-5pm)

Main Tourist Office (Map p100; ☑ 231 2811; Midan al-Mahatta; ⊙ 8am-3pm & 7-9pm Sat-Thu) This tourist office has little material, and little access to any, but staff can advise on timetables, and give an idea of prices for taxis and feluccas.

Thomas Cook (Map p100; ☑ 230 4011; Corniche an-Nil; ⊙ 8am-2pm & 5-9pm)

ⓘ Getting There & Away

AIR

EgyptAir (Map p98; ☑ 231 5000; Corniche an-Nil; ⊙ 8am-3pm & 7-9pm Sat-Thu) offers several daily flights between Aswan and Cairo (E£320 to E£896, 1¼ hours). If tourist demand increases, the 30-minute flight to Luxor may be reinstated. Flights to Abu Simbel were also on hold at the time of writing.

BUS

The bus station is 3.5km north of the train station. At the time of research, there were no buses to Luxor and travel to Abu Simbel was restricted to four foreigners per bus. Upper Egypt Bus Co has two buses to Abu Simbel (E£25, four hours), departing 8am and 5pm. A direct bus to Cairo (E£110, 14 hours) leaves at 3.30pm and 4pm daily.

CRUISING THE NILE FELUCCA STYLE

An Egyptian proverb advises, 'The one who voyages the Nile must have sails made of patience' and that's exactly the appeal of a felucca, the single-sailed boat. At the leisurely pace of the wind, you pass within arm's reach of river-bank villages, fishers plying their trade and palms swaying leisurely as the desert sunset burns bright.

Feluccas are decked out in comfy cushions and usually hold six to eight passengers, making for a more intimate experience than large cruise boats, especially as there are no private spaces. Trips can be arranged from Aswan to the temples at Kom Ombo, Edfu or Esna and last between two and five days. Each evening, feluccas moor and set up camp either on the shore or on the boat. Food is prepared on the boat, and often captains and crew burst into song and dance at the slightest provocation.

FELUCCA

Aswan is the best place to arrange overnight felucca trips. The most popular trips are to Kom Ombo (one night, two days, from E£100 per person) or Edfu (up to three nights, four days, at least E£130), but some people go on to Esna (four nights, five days, from E£160). Feluccas don't go beyond, to Luxor, due to the locks at Esna.

You can get boats for less, but you might have a resentful captain and crew, or be eating bread and beans. Keep some of the fee until you reach your destination in case you stop prematurely due to 'breakdowns'.

Many of the better felucca captains can be found in Nile-side restaurants such as the Aswan Moon or Emy, or on Elephantine Island. Be sure to meet a few – and inspect boats – before choosing.

MICROBUS

Microbuses depart from the bus station, which is located 3.5km north of the train station. A taxi there will cost E£15, or 50pt in a communal taxi. To Luxor costs E£20, to Kom Ombo E£3 and to Edfu E£10.

TRAIN

From **Aswan Train Station** (☑ 231 4754; Midan al-Mahatta) a number of daily trains run north to Cairo from 5am to 9.10pm (E£120, 14 hours). Tickets should be bought in advance, but can be bought on the train for an additional fee. Student discounts are available. All trains heading north to Luxor (E£25, three hours) stop at Kom Ombo, Edfu and Esna.

Watania Sleeping Trains (☑ 230 2124; www. wataniasleepingtrains.com; s/d cabin per person incl dinner & breakfast US$120/100, per child US$85) has two daily services to Cairo at the hours of 4pm and 7pm. The trip takes 14 hours in total.

ⓘ Getting Around

TO/FROM THE AIRPORT

Aswan International Airport (☑ 248 0333) lies about 25km southwest of town; a taxi into town costs about E£50 to E£70.

FERRY

Two public ferries (E£1) run to Elephantine Island; the one across from EgyptAir goes to the Aswan Museum, while the one across from Thomas Cook goes to Siou. A third ferry (E£1) goes from the landing across from the train station to West Aswan and the Tombs of the Nobles.

TAXI

A taxi tour that includes Philae, the High Dam and the Unfinished Obelisk costs around E£200 to E£300 for the car. Taxis can also take you on day trips to Kom Ombo for about E£250 to E£350. A taxi anywhere in town costs E£5 to E£15.

Philae (Agilika Island)   فيلة معبد

The dreamy Temple of Isis (adult/child E£60/30; ☉ 7am-4pm Oct-May, to 5pm Jun-Sep), just south of Aswan, was dedicated to Isis, who found the heart of her slain brother, Osiris, on Philae Island. The temple was built and added to between the 4th century BC and 3rd century AD. Early Christians later turned the hypostyle hall into a chapel – this, in turn, was vandalised by early Muslims. From 1902, with the opening of the old Aswan Dam, Philae was submerged for several months each year. During the 1960s, the temple was relocated stone by stone to nearby Agilika Island.

The ticket office is on the mainland, just before the boat landing. You'll pay around E£60 for a taxi to bring you here, wait for an hour or so and then bring you back to town. You'll need to negotiate a price for a boat; theoretically, it shouldn't be more than E£10 per person return. Regardless, tip your boatman a couple of pounds.

A nightly sound-and-light show (www.soundandlight.com.eg; adult/child E£70/50; ☉ shows 6.30pm, 7.45pm & 9pm Oct-May, 7pm, 8.15pm & 9.30pm May-Sep), lasting 1½ hours, is held at the temple. Check the website or the tourist office in Aswan for performance times and languages.

High Dam السد العالي

The controversial Aswan High Dam (as-Sadd al-Ali; adult/child E£20/10; Ⓟ), 13km south of town, contains 18 times the amount of material used in the Great Pyramid of Khufu and created Lake Nasser, the world's largest artificial lake. Displays detail the dimensions and the construction of the dam, and a monument honours Soviet-Egyptian friendship. Most people visit as part of an organised trip, but a taxi from Aswan is about E£25 each way.

Abu Simbel أبو سمبل

 097

Laid-back and quiet, the town of Abu Simbel lies 280km south of Aswan and only 40km north of the Sudanese border. Abu Simbel's temples alone are certainly worth the trip, for themselves and for their recent history: between 1964 and 1968, both temples were relocated above the High Dam flood. Anyone interested in peace and tranquility, and Nubian culture, might hang around for a few days. There are banks in town, but no ATMs.

◉ Sights & Activities

The two temples of Abu Simbel are reached by road or, if you are on a cruise boat, from one of the jetties leading directly into the fenced temple compound.

Great Temple of Ramses II   MONUMENT

Carved out of the mountain on the west bank of the Nile between 1274 and 1244 BC, Ramses II's imposing temple was as much dedicated to the deified pharaoh himself as to Ra-Horakhty, Amun and Ptah. The four colossal statues of the pharoah, which front the temple, are like gigantic sentinels watching over the incoming traffic from the south,

undoubtedly designed as a warning of the strength of the pharaoh.

Over the centuries both the Nile and the desert sands shifted, and this temple was lost to the world until 1813, when it was rediscovered by chance by the Swiss explorer Jean-Louis Burckhardt. Only one of the heads was completely showing above the sand, the next head was broken off and, of the remaining two, only the crowns could be seen. Enough sand was cleared away in 1817 by Giovanni Belzoni for the temple to be entered.

From the temple's forecourt, a short flight of steps leads up to the terrace in front of the massive rock-cut facade, which is about 30m high and 35m wide. Guarding the entrance, three of the four famous colossal statues stare out across the water into eternity – the inner left statue collapsed in antiquity and its upper body still lies on the ground. The statues, more than 20m high, are accompanied by smaller statues of the pharaoh's mother, Queen Tuya, his wife Nefertari and some of his favourite children. Above the entrance, between the central throned colossi, is the figure of the falcon-headed sun god Ra-Horakhty.

The roof of the large hall is decorated with vultures, symbolising the protective goddess Nekhbet, and is supported by eight columns, each fronted by an Osiride statue of Ramses II. Reliefs on the walls depict the pharaoh's prowess in battle, trampling over his enemies and slaughtering them in front of the gods. On the north wall is a depiction of the famous Battle of Kadesh (c 1274 BC), in what is now Syria, where Ramses inspired his demoralised army, so that they won the battle against the Hittites. The scene is dominated by a famous relief of Ramses in his chariot, shooting arrows at his fleeing enemies. Also visible is the Egyptian camp, walled off by its soldiers' round-topped shields, and the fortified Hittite town, surrounded by the Orontes River.

The next hall, the four-columned vestibule where Ramses and Nefertari are shown in front of the gods and the solar barques, leads to the sacred sanctuary, where Ramses and the triad of gods of the Great Temple sit on their thrones.

The original temple was aligned in such a way that each 21 February and 21 October, Ramses' birthday and coronation day, the first rays of the rising sun moved across the hypostyle hall, through the vestibule and into the sanctuary, where they illuminate the figures of Ra-Horakhty, Ramses II and Amun. Ptah, to the left, was never supposed to be illuminated. Since the temples were moved, this phenomenon happens one day later.

Temple of Hathor   MONUMENT

Next to the Great Temple of Ramses II is the much smaller Temple of Hathor, with a rock-cut facade fronted by six 10m-high standing statues of Ramses and Nefertari, with some of their many children by their side. Nefertari here wears the costume of the goddess Hathor, and is, unusually, portrayed as the same height as her husband (instead of knee-height, as most consorts were depicted).

Inside, the six pillars of the hypostyle hall are crowned with capitals in the bovine shape of Hathor. On the walls the queen appears in front of the gods very much equal to Ramses II, and she is seen honouring her husband. The vestibule and adjoining chambers, which have colourful scenes of the goddess and her sacred barque, lead to the sanctuary, which has a weathered statue of Hathor as a cow emerging from the rock. The art here is softer and more graceful than in the Great Temple.

🛏 Sleeping & Eating

Abu Simbel Village   HOTEL $

(☑340 0092; s/d E£80/100) The only reason to recommend the Abu Simbel Village is its price: its basic, vaulted rooms are tired and not always clean, but it is the cheapest option for staying in Abu Simbel, which you have to do if you want to get to the temples at dawn or see the Sound and Light show. Take meals in town.

★ Eskaleh   GUESTHOUSE $$

(Beit an-Nubi; ☑340 1288, 0122 368 0521; www.eskaleh.net; d €60-70; ❄@🛜) ✎ Part Nubian cultural centre with a library dedicated to Nubian history and culture, part ecolodge in a traditional Nubian mud-brick house, Eskaleh is known locally as the Nubian house (Beit an-Nubi). By far the most interesting place to eat or stay in Abu Simbel, it's also a destination in its own right and a perfect base for a visit to the temples.

ℹ Getting There & Away

AIR

EgyptAir flies to Abu Simbel from Cairo via Aswan.

BUS

From Abu Simbel to Aswan (four hours), buses leave at 8am, 9.30am, 1pm and 4pm from the Wadi el-Nil Restaurant on the main road. There is no advance booking, and tickets (E£25) are purchased on board. Microbuses make the same journey in three hours (E£30).

WESTERN OASES

الواحات الغربية

The vast sandy expanses west of the Nile, all the way to the Great Sand Sea, make up the Western Desert, a natural wonder as unfathomable as it is inhospitable. Five major oases lie in this formidable khaki ocean. In these islands of fresh water and greenery, you can explore crumbling Roman forts, flourishing palm plantations and medieval fortified towns. It's also here that you'll find the eerie rock formations of the White and Black Deserts, a dreamscape of pinnacles eroded into surreal shapes, as well as the exceptionally tranquil oasis of Siwa.

Travel in this region takes time, but the Western Desert vaunts some of the most jaw-dropping scenery in all of Egypt.

Al-Kharga Oasis   الواحات الخارجة

☑092

The largest of the oases and the closest to the Nile Valley, Al-Kharga hides its attractions under a drab veneer of provincial busyness. A trade-route waypoint since ancient times, it has one sight in particular that merits a stopover.

◉ Sights

If you really dig archaeology, be sure to visit the small Museum of Antiquities (Sharia Gamal Abdel Nasser; adult/student E£25/15; ☺8am-3pm). and the Qasr al-Ghueita (adult/student E£25/15; ☺8am-5pm), an imposing ancient mud-brick fortress with a stone temple inside. If you want a guide, Sameh Abdel Rihem (☑0100 296 2192) is an expert on Kharga's antiquities.

★ Necropolis of Al-Bagawat   ARCHAEOLOGICAL SITE

(adult/student incl Monastery of Al-Kashef E£35/15; ☺8am-5pm) It may not look like much from afar, but this necropolis is one of the earliest surviving and best-preserved Christian cem-

WHITE & BLACK DESERTS

Upon first glimpse of the White Desert (Sahra al-Beida), you'll feel like Alice fallen through the desert looking glass. Beginning 20km northeast of Farafra, the yellow desert sands are pierced by chalky rock formations, sprouting almost supernaturally from the ground. Blindingly white spires reach for the sky, like frost-coloured lollipops licked into shapes – some surreal, some familiar as chickens or camels – by the dry desert winds. A few kilometres north, the desert is littered with quartz crystals, best viewed at the famous Crystal Mountain. Further north, closer to Bawiti, the change in the desert floor from beige to black signals the beginning of the Black Desert (Sahara Suda). Here, layers of black powder and rubble, eroded from former mountains, lie strewn all over the sandy earth.

You need a 4WD to enter deep into the deserts. Bahariya Oasis is the more popular starting point for tours, though they can be less expensive from Farafra. For an overnight camping trip, expect to pay between E£400 and E£800 per vehicle, plus US$5 national-park fee per person, plus E£10 per person for each night slept out.

---

eteries in the world. About 1km north of the Temple of Hibis, it's built on the site of an earlier Egyptian necropolis, with most of the 263 mud-brick chapel-tombs appearing to date from the 4th to the 6th centuries AD. Some have interiors decorated with vivid murals of biblical scenes and boast ornate facades.

🛏 Sleeping & Eating

There's nothing particularly wonderful about Kharga's hotels, but these are the best of the bunch. There's a smattering of basic eateries around Midan Sho'ala, Sharia al-Adel and near Midan Basateen.

Kharga Oasis Hotel HOTEL $
(☑792 1206, 0126 866 6299; Midan Nasser; r/bungalow €10/15; ❇) This homage to the 1960s' love of concrete blocks is your best bet for bedding down for the night in Al-Kharga. The main building sports large rooms with decent beds and bathrooms, but opt for one of the traditionally styled domed bungalows out back, set around a tranquil and lush palm-filled garden (beware the mosquitoes) for a bit more style.

The hotel is run by the government, so service and maintenance is haphazard at best. If you can't get through to the hotel on either of the contact numbers when booking, ring **Mohsen Abd Al Moneam** (☑0100 180 6127) of the tourist office to book on your behalf. Breakfast is not included.

El-Radwan Hotel HOTEL $
(☑792 1716; off Sharia Gamal Abdel Nasser; s/d E£90/120; ❇) One of the only decent (and we use that word loosely) budget hotels in Al-Kharga. The air-con mostly works, the

water runs and the rooms pass muster if you need a cheap sleep. The facade looks like it's about to fall down but, oh, well, it does get better on the inside. Breakfast is not included.

ⓘ Information

New Valley Tourist Office (☑792 1206; Midan Nasser; ⊙9am-2pm Sat-Thu) Speak to Mohsen Abd Al Moneam, a motherlode of knowledge about Al-Kharga Oasis. He can arrange private transport to sights and also to Luxor. Call his mobile.

ⓘ Getting There & Away

AIR

The airport is 5km north of town. The Petroleum Service Company (usually) has Monday and Thursday flights on a 15-seat plane, leaving Cairo at 8am and returning from Al-Kharga at 3pm (E£600 one way, 1½ hours). Contact the tourist office for schedules and bookings.

BUS

Upper Egypt Bus Co (☑792 4587; Sharia Mohammed Farid) operates buses to Cairo (E£65, eight to 10 hours) at 9pm and 10pm. There are three departures to Asyut (E£25, three to four hours, 6am, 7am, 9am) and one to Dakhla Oasis (E£25, three hours, 2pm). For Luxor, either change in Asyut or hire a private taxi.

MICROBUS

The most convenient way to get to Dakhla (E£25, three hours) or Asyut (E£25, three to four hours), minivans leave from the microbus station at Midan Sho'ala.

TAXI

Taxis can get you to Luxor (via Jaja) in four hours, but will set you back about E£50. Cairo (seven hours) costs E£1350 for the whole car.

Dakhla Oasis الواحات الداخلة

🔊 092

Shaded by swaying palms and studded with traditional villages and ancient mud-brick forts, Dakhla exemplifies oasis life.

👁 Sights

The main town is modern Mut, with most of the hotels and other services, but medieval Al-Qasr is more enchanting, a brilliantly preserved desert caravan town with a small museum and enough sights for several hours of exploring.

🛏 Sleeping

El Forsan Hotel HOTEL $

(📞 782 1343; Sharia al-Wadi; s/d E£135/180, bungalow without air-con E£90/135; ❄️ 🛜) Ignore the creepy horror-movie corridor as you enter because El Forsan is the best budget deal in town. A recent paint job and new bed linen (including duvets) has smartened up the air-con rooms, while out the back within the garden there are domed mud-brick (rather worn) bungalows. Friendly manager Zaqaria whips up great breakfasts.

Al-Qasr Hotel HOSTEL $

(📞 787 6013; Main Highway, Al-Qasr; r without bathroom E£30) This old backpacker favourite sits above a cafe-restaurant on the main highway through Al-Qasr. Rooms are as basic as they get but there's a breezy upstairs communal sitting area where you can play games or relax, and for E£5 you can sleep on a mattress on the roof. Owner Mohamed has a long history of fine hospitality.

⭐ **Al Tarfa Desert Sanctuary** BOUTIQUE HOTEL $$$

(📞 910 5007; www.altarfa.net; r full board s/d €360/440; ❄️ 🛜 🏊) Taking the high end to unheard-of heights in Dakhla, Al Tarfa is flat-out desert-fabulous. The traditionally inspired decor is superbly tasteful and impeccably rendered, down to the smallest detail – from the embroidered bedspreads that look like museum-quality pieces to the mud-plastered walls that don't show a single crack. Private transfers to the hotel's isolated site, north of Al-Qasr, can be arranged.

Even the golden dunes that flow behind the resort seem like they've been landscaped to undulating perfection. Each suite is unique; the pool is like a liquid sapphire; and the spa features massage therapists brought in from Thailand.

🍴 Eating

Said Shihad EGYPTIAN $$

(Sharia as-Sawra al-Khadra; meals E£20-35) Owner Said is on to a good thing here: grilling up a meat-centric feast nightly to a dedicated following of hungry locals. The shish kebab is the thing to go for – perfectly succulent and served with potatoes in a tomato sauce, rice and beans.

Ahmed Hamdy's Restaurant EGYPTIAN $$

(📞 782 0767; Sharia as-Sawra al-Khadra; meals E£20-30) On the main road into town is Ahmed Hamdy's popular place serving delicious chicken, kebabs, vegetables and a few other small dishes inside or on the terrace. The freshly squeezed lime juice is excellent and you can request beer (E£12) and sheesha.

ℹ Information

Tourist Office (📞 782 1685, 0122 179 6467; Sharia as-Sawra al-Khadra; ⏰ 8am-3pm) Friendly tourist-office director Omar Ahmad can help with all your oasis queries. He can be contacted anytime on his mobile.

ℹ Getting There & Around

BUS

Upper Egypt Bus Co (📞 782 4366; Sharia al-Wadi) runs buses to Cairo (E£90, 10 hours) via Al-Kharga Oasis (E£25, two to three hours) and Asyut (E£50, five hours) at 7pm and 7.30pm. You can also travel to Cairo via Farafra Oasis (E£35, four hours) and Bahariya Oasis (E£60, seven hours) at 6am and 6pm.

MICROBUS

Microbuses to Al-Kharga (E£25), Farafra (E£40) and Cairo (E£90, night runs only) leave when full – which isn't often – from the old part of Mut, near the mosque.

Farafra Oasis واحة الفرافرة

🔊 092

Blink and you'll miss the smallest, and probably dustiest, of the oases. Farafra can be an alternative setting-off point for trips into the spectacular White Desert.

👁 Sights & Activities

Badr's Museum (📞 751 0091; off Sharia al-Mardasa; suggested donation E£10; ⏰ 8.30am-sunset) is the only attraction in town. We salute the effort put into this place by self-taught local artist Badr Abdel Moghny. Desert tours are arranged through the few hotels.

🍴 Sleeping & Eating

Dining choices are limited to hotels (Al-Badawiya is solid) and a trio of grill joints in the centre of town. Alcohol isn't available.

Sunrise Hotel & Safari HOTEL $
(☑ 0122 720 1387; wahafarafra@yahoo.com; Bahariya–Dakhla rd; r E£150) The Sunrise has gone for the Bedouin domed motif, and has installed refrigerators and TVs in brick bungalows that surround a rectangular courtyard. Some of the rooms have a strong septic stench, so check out a few. The family who run this place also run Farafra's other cheapie hotel option – the Al-Waha Hotel.

Al-Badawiya Safari & Hotel HOTEL $$
(☑ 751 0060; www.badawiya.com; Bahariya–Dakhla rd; s/d US$25/35, ste with air-con US$35/50; ❄🛜🏊) Al-Badawiya dominates Farafra tourism with its hotel and safari outfit. Comfortable domed rooms have plenty of traditional Bedouin style, though they could do with a lick of maintenance. There's a refreshing (albeit small) pool and a restaurant. The White and Western Desert tours are thoroughly professional.

ℹ Getting There & Away

BUS
Upper Egypt Bus Co goes from Farafra to Cairo (E£45, eight to 10 hours) via Bahariya (E£25, three hours) at 10am and 10pm. Buses from Farafra to Dakhla (E£25, four hours) originate in Cairo and leave around 2pm to 3pm and around 2am. Tickets are bought from the conductor.

MICROBUS
Microbuses to Dakhla (E£20, three to four hours) and Bahariya (E£20, three hours) leave from the town's main intersection when full (not often).

Bahariya Oasis الواحات البحرية
☑ 02

Just 365km from Cairo, Bahariya is the Western Desert's most bustling and visited oasis. Set among hills and thick with date palms and springs, Bahariya is also the most convenient jumping-off point for the White and Black Deserts. Buses drop you at Bawiti, the dusty main village.

◉ Sights & Activities

Attractions in and around Bawiti include the Temple of Alexander, the 26th-dynasty tombs at Qarat Qasr Salim and the 10 famous Graeco-Roman mummies in the Golden Mummies Museum (al-Mathaf; Sharia al-Mathaf; Bawiti joint site ticket adult/student E£60/30; ⊙8am-2pm), just south of the main road in Bawiti.

☞ Tours

There is ferocious competition among tour guides offering trips into the deserts. Visit the helpful tourist office if you feel overwhelmed. Well-established local safari outfits include Eden Garden Tours (☑0100 071 0707; www.edengardentours.com; Eden Garden Camp); Helal Travel (☑0122 423 6580; www.helaltravel.com; Under the Moon Camp); and White Desert Tours (☑0122 321 2179; www.whitedeserttours.com; International Hot Spring Hotel). Some freelance guides are also good, and slightly less expensive.

🍴 Sleeping & Eating

Sort out accommodation in Bawiti before you arrive, especially in high season (September to November and February to April), to avoid dealing with the frenzy of touts that swarm each arriving bus.

Food options are limited to the hotels, roast chicken in the market area and the aptly named Popular Restaurant (☑847 2239; Sharia Safaya; set meals E£45), which serves set meals and cold beer.

🛏 Bawiti

Old Oasis Hotel HOTEL $
(☑3847 3028; www.oldoasis.hostel.com; s/d/tr E£120/180/220, without air-con E£90/120/180; ❄🛜🏊) One of the most charming places to stay in Bawiti town sits among a pretty garden of palm and olive trees. It has 13 simple but impeccable fan rooms, plus a few fancier stone-wall air-con rooms. A large pool receives steaming hot water from the nearby spring; the run-off waters the garden, where there's a shady restaurant-cafe. The hotel is located by El-Beshmo spring.

New Oasis Hotel HOTEL $
(☑0122 847 4171; max_rfs@hotmail.com; s/d E£100/200, without air-con E£65/150; ❄) A study in curvaceous construction, this small, homey hotel has several teardrop-shaped rooms, some with balconies overlooking the expansive palm groves nearby. Inside, the rooms are in good shape, though someone seems to have been a little overzealous with the powder blue paint. It's one of the

nicer budget options in town, located next to El-Beshmo spring.

Alpenblick Hotel
HOTEL **$$**

(☑ 3847 2184; www.alpenblick-hotel-oasis.com; s/d €13/22, d without air-con €16; ✱) This grandaddy of the Bahariya hotel scene keeps getting dragged out of retirement by its consecutive owners; the current ones give a warm welcome. The rooms are spick-and-span though simple, and there's a large shaded courtyard where you can hang out and meet other travellers.

To find it, follow the signs from the turn-off opposite the tourist information building.

🛏 Around Bawiti

Badr's Sahara Camp
HUT **$**

(☑ 0122 792 2728; www.badrysaharacamp.com; s/d E£60/100) A couple of kilometres from Bawiti, Badr's Sahara Camp has a handful of bucolic, African-influenced huts, each with two beds and small patios out front. Hot water and electricity can't always be counted on, but cool desert breezes and knockout views of the oasis valley can. Pick-ups are available.

★ Under the Moon Camp
BUNGALOW **$$**

(☑ 0122 423 6580; www.helaltravel.com; El-Hayz; huts s/d half board E£200/250, bungalows s/d half board E£300/350) Isolated in the small oasis hamlet of El-Hayz, 45km south of Bawiti, this beautiful camp features several round, stone huts (no electricity) and some new mud-brick bungalows (with lights) scattered around a garden compound. The accommodation is as simple as it gets, but the hospitality and the setting can't be beat.

Nature Camp
BUNGALOW **$$**

(☑ 0127 718 8476; naturecamps@hotmail.com; Bir al-Ghaba; r half board per person E£150) 🌿 At the foot of Gebel Dist, 17km north of Bawiti, Nature Camp sets new standards for environmentally focused budget accommodation. The peaceful cluster of candlelit and intricately designed thatch huts looks out onto the expansive desert beside Bir al-Ghaba. The food is very good (meals E£25) and the owner, Ashraf Lotfe, is a skilled desert hand.

ℹ Information

Tourist Office (☑ 3847 3039; Sharia Misr; ⊙ 8am-2pm & 7-9pm Sat-Thu) Run by helpful Mohamed Abd el-Kader, who can also be contacted on ☑ 0122 373 6567.

ℹ Getting There & Away

BUS

Upper Egypt Bus Co (☑ 3847 3610; Sharia Misr; ⊙ roughly 9am-1pm & 7-11pm) runs to Cairo (E£40, four to five hours) at 6.30am, 10am and 3pm from the kiosk near the post office. Buy tickets the day before travelling. Two more Cairo-bound buses originate in Dakhla and pass through Bawiti around noon and midnight, stopping at the Hilal Coffeehouse at the western end of town.

For Farafra (E£20, two hours) and Dakhla (E£40, four to five hours), hop on one of the buses that leave Bahariya around noon and 11.30pm from the Upper Egypt Bus Co kiosk and Hilal Coffeehouse.

FOUR-WHEEL DRIVE

There is no public transport to Siwa, so you will have to hire a private 4WD for the journey. If there's a 4WD from Siwa that's returning empty, you might be able to ride with it for half the usual E£1500. Permits (US$5 per person) are required and easy to get from the bank.

MICROBUS

Minibuses run from Bawiti to Cairo (E£40), near the Moneib metro station in Giza. Minibuses to Farafra (E£25) and Dakhla (E£45) are rare, best caught an hour or so before the night bus departs. All leave from Hilal Coffeehouse.

Siwa Oasis
واحة سيوة

☑ 046

Easily the prettiest, and most remote, of Egypt's oases, sleepy Siwa is the perfect antidote to the commotion of bustling Egyptian cities. Isolated for centuries from the rest of the country, Siwa today hasn't strayed from its traditional roots – donkeys work alongside combustion engines, and Siwi, the local Berber language, dominates. A long detour from the Nile Valley, Siwa rewards those who trek out here with gorgeous freshwater springs, a dash of ancient history and generous helpings of tranquillity among palm-shaded streets.

◉ Sights & Activities

The town centre is marked by the jagged remnants of the medieval mud-brick **Fortress of Shali**, and the only proper attraction is the **House of Siwa Museum** (adult/student E£10/5; ⊙ 9am-2.30pm Sun-Thu), worth a peek for the embroidered wedding dresses. Beyond these are acres of date-palm groves and a profusion of dazzling, freshwater **springs**. The remains of the **Temple**

of the Oracle (adult/student E£25/15; ⊙ 9am-5pm), which once housed the famed oracle of Amun, and some Graeco-Roman **tombs** can easily be visited on a day trip. At the edge of town are the towering dunes of the **Great Sand Sea**.

☞ Tours

Many safari companies in Siwa organise half- and full-day tours of town and various springs (from E£150). We highly recommend **Ghazal Safari** (☑ 0100 277 1234); driver/guide Abd El-Rahman Azmy has a kick-ass vehicle and a contagious love for Siwa.

⌁ Sleeping

Make sure your hotel room has screened windows; the mosquitoes in Siwa are insatiable.

Kelany Hotel   HOTEL $
(☑ 0102 336 9627; Sharia Azmi Kilani; s/d/tr E£80/120/150; ❖ ⌁) Kelany's small rooms may be showing their age but they're still a step above other budget places in Siwa; if you're looking for a cheap sleep with air-con and working wi-fi, this is your best bet. The rooftop restaurant (meals E£35) features views of the Fortress of Shali, Gebel Dakrur and everything in between. Breakfast is not included.

Palm Trees Hotel   HOTEL $
(☑ 460 1703, 0122 104 6652; m_s_siwa@yahoo.com; Sharia Torrar; s/d E£35/50, without bathroom E£25/35, bungalow s/d E£50/70, r with air-con E£75; ❖) If you can handle the mosquitoes (seriously, bring bug-spray), then this popular budget hotel is a lovely place to stay. It has sufficiently tidy rooms boasting screened windows, fans and balconies. The shady garden with date-palm furniture is delightful and the few ground-level bungalows have porches spilling onto the greenery.

★ Shali Lodge   BOUTIQUE HOTEL $$
(☑ 0101 118 5820; www.siwa.com/accommodations.html; Sharia Subukha; s/d/tr/ste E£285/375/475/550; ⊙ Sep-Jun; ⌁) ⊘ This tiny, beautiful mud-brick hotel, owned by environmentalist Mounir Neamatallah, nestles in a lush palm grove about 100m from Siwa's main square. The large, extremely comfortable rooms have lots of curvacious mud-brick goodness, exposed palm beams, rock-walled bathrooms and cushioned sitting nooks. Tasteful and quiet, this is how small hotels should be.

RESPECTING LOCAL CUSTOMS

Siwa may seem more laid-back than other parts of Egypt, but modesty is perhaps even more serious business here. When Western women (or men, for that matter) wear shorts and tank tops, it's about the same as walking naked around a stranger's home. Keep your skin covered – as with anywhere in the country, showing respect earns respect.

★ Al-Babinshal   BOUTIQUE HOTEL $$
(☑ 460 1499; www.siwa.com/accommodations.html; s/d E£285/365; ⊙ Sep-Jun) ⊘ This gorgeous, curvy mud-brick hotel is seamlessly grafted onto Shali fortress with its labyrinthine architecture all built from kershef bricks like the original fort. A maze of tunnels and stairways connects the spacious and cool rooms. Decor is distinctly desert-style with date-palm furniture, local textiles and traditional wooden-shuttered windows used in abundance to add to the local vibe.

✖ Eating & Drinking

No alcohol is served in Siwa restaurants.

★ Abdu's Restaurant   INTERNATIONAL $
(☑ 460 1243; Central Market Sq; dishes E£5-30; ⊙ 8.30am-midnight) Before wi-fi and smartphones, there were places like this – a village hub where people gathered nightly to meet, catch up and swap stories. The longest-running restaurant in town remains the best eating option thanks to its friendly, on-the-ball staff and a huge menu of breakfast dishes, pasta, traditional dishes, vegetable stews, couscous, roasted chickens and pizza.

Kenooz Siwa   EGYPTIAN $$
(☑ 046 460 1299; Shali Lodge, Sharia Subukha; mains E£15-25; ⊙ 8am-midnight Sep-Jun) On the roof terrace of Shali Lodge, this cafe-restaurant is a great place to hang out while enjoying a mint tea or a cold drink. Mains include some unique Siwan specialities, such as baked lentils and eggplant with pomegranate sauce.

Abo Ayman Restaurant   GRILL $$
(off Sharia Sadat; meals E£13-23; ⊙ 11am-midnight) Roasted on a hand-turned spit over coals in an old oil drum, the chickens at Abo Ayman are the juiciest in Siwa. They're well

seasoned, and served with salad, tahini and bread. You can sit inside at low tables, but we like the tables outside with street views.

ℹ️ Information

Tourist Office (☑ 460 1338; mahdi_hweiti@ yahoo.com; Siwa Town; ⏰ 9am-2pm Sat-Thu, plus 5-8pm Oct-Apr) Siwa's tourist officer, Mahdi Hweiti, is extremely knowledgable about the oasis and can help arrange desert safaris or trips to surrounding villages. His mobile number is ☑ 0100 546 1992. The office is opposite the bus station.

ℹ️ Getting There & Away

BUS

West & Mid Delta Bus Co operates and sells tickets from the bus stop opposite the tourist police station, although when you arrive you'll be let off near the central market square. Buy your ticket ahead, as buses are often full.

There are three daily buses to Alexandria (E£55, eight hours), stopping at Marsa Matruh (E£30, four hours); these leave at 7am, 10am and 10pm. There's one daily departure to Cairo (E£120); it was suspended when we visited, but should be reinstated.

FOUR-WHEEL DRIVE

A new road linking Siwa and Bahariya is about half-finished, and the whole distance (about 400km) can be crossed in five hours. A 4WD is necessary (there is no bus or *servees*), and drivers and the required permits are easy to arrange on either end. You'll pay about E£1500 per car.

MICROBUS

Microbuses going to Marsa Matruh leave from the main square near the King Fuad Mosque. They are more frequent and much more comfortable than the West & Mid Delta bus; tickets cost the same.

ℹ️ Getting Around

BICYCLE

One of the best ways to get around, bikes can be rented from several sources; bicycle repair shops are best. The going rate is E£15 to E£20 per day.

DONKEY CARTS

Otherwise known as *careta*s, donkey carts are a much-used mode of transport for Siwans and can be a more amusing, if slower, way to get around. After haggling, expect to pay about E£30 for two to three hours or E£10 for a short trip.

SERVEES

Pick-up trucks (50pt to E£1) link Siwa town with the surrounding villages.

SUEZ CANAL قناة السويس

An engineering marvel by any measure, the 1869-built canal that severs Africa from Asia is darned impressive. Though the region is hardly geared for tourists, intrepid travellers are rewarded not only with a couple of picturesque colonial-built cities, but also the unforgettable sight of behemoth supertankers virtually gliding through the deserts that make up the Isthmus of Suez.

Port Said بورسعيد
☑ 066

At the mouth of the Suez Canal's Mediterranean entrance, Port Said tips its hat to a prosperous past. At the heart of a lively port city, its muddle of grand but faded wooden buildings still manages to cling to some colonial charm. Visit for the yesteryear allure and the modern canal. A boardwalk provides up-close views of this manmade marvel.

⊙ Sights & Activities

The easiest way to explore the canal is to take the **free public ferry** from near the tourist office across the canal to Port Fuad and back. Main attractions include the 19th-century **Suez Canal House** (Commercial Basin) and the market street of **Sharia al-Muski**.

Military Museum   MUSEUM
(☑ 322 4657; Sharia 23rd of July; admission E£5; ⏰ 10am-3pm Sat-Thu) This little museum is worth a peek for its information on the canal and also for some rather bizarre exhibits (complete with toy soldiers) documenting the 1956 Suez Crisis and the 1967 and 1973 wars with Israel. In the museum gardens you can view a few captured US tanks with

---

ℹ️ SUEZ CANAL: FAST FACTS

Construction Begun 1859, completed 1869

Length 190km

Surface width 280–345m

Depth 22.5m

Speed limit 11–14km/h

World trade passing through canal 14%

Vessels passing annually Over 20,000

BUSES FROM PORT SAID

DESTINATION	PRICE (E£)	DURATION (HR)	TIMES
Alexandria (East Delta)	30	4-5	7am, 11am, 2pm, 4pm, 6pm, 8pm
Alexandria (Super Jet)	30	4	4.30pm
Cairo (Super Jet)	25	4	every 30min
Cairo (East Delta)	25	4	hourly 5am-9pm
Ismailia (East Delta)	10	1½	hourly 6am-6pm
Suez (East Delta)	15	2½-3	6am, 10am, 2pm, 4pm

the Star of David painted on them, as well as an odd collection of unexploded ordnance (UXOs).

🛏 Sleeping

New Continental   HOTEL $
(☏ 322 5024; 30 Sharia al-Gomhuriyya; s/d E£150/220; ❄) Friendly management makes this typical Egyptian budget hotel stand out from the crowd. Light-filled rooms have teensy balconies and come in a range of sizes, so ask to see a few. All come with TV and an astounding clutter of furniture. We particularly love the hilarious gold palm-tree-mural decor in the hallways.

★ **Holiday Hotel**   HOTEL $$
(☏ 322 0711; Sharia al-Gomhuriyya; s/d E£235/320; ❄ 🛜) The Holiday has had a rather swish makeover that includes a new cafe fronting the entrance and smallish, refitted rooms freshly decked out in soothing shades of beige and boasting Ikea-style furniture. It's all surprisingly modern and tasteful. Plenty of company employees from the ships stay here, so the friendly staff are used to foreigners.

🍴 Eating

Self-caterers will find all the groceries they need at Metro Supermarket on Sharia al-Geish. For fruit and vegetables, try the lively market on Sharia Souq, three blocks north of Sharia al-Gomhuriyya.

★ **El Borg**   SEAFOOD $$
(☏ 332 3442; Beach Plaza, off Sharia Atef as-Sadat; mains E£20-50; ⏱ 10am-3am) This massive Port Said institution is always buzzing with families on a night out. There's a small menu of grills if you don't feel like fish, but the good-value fresh seafood is really what the crowds flock here for. Eat on the shorefront terrace in the evening for superb beach-promenade people-watching.

★ **Pizza Pino**   ITALIAN $$
(Sharia al-Gomhuriyya; mains E£20-50) This art deco–style bistro has plenty of cosy appeal and attentive staff. Pizza Pino is a local favourite for its hearty portions of pasta, good pizzas and decently priced grills. If only the background music didn't make you feel like you're stuck in an elevator with Kenny G.

ℹ Information

The main banks all have branches with ATMs in town, mostly along Sharia al-Gomhuriyya. There is a good **tourist office** (☏ 323 5289; 8 Sharia Palestine; ⏱ 10am-7pm Sat-Thu).

ℹ Getting There & Away

BOAT
In theory there are boats from Port Said across to Turkey, but in practice the service is very unreliable.

BUS
The bus station is about 3km from the town centre at the beginning of the road to Cairo (about E£10 in a taxi). **Super Jet** (☏ 372 1779) and **East Delta Travel Co** (☏ 372 9883) run services from here. Bookings are advisable.

MICROBUS & SERVEES
The microbus and *servees* station is next door to the train station. Sample fares: Cairo (E£25), Ismailia (E£10), Suez (E£15).

TRAIN
Services to Cairo (1st-/2nd-class E£21/11, five hours), via Ismailia (E£11/4) run at 5.30am, 1pm and 5.30pm. There's also a 2nd-class-only service at 7.30pm. Delays are common and buses are, generally speaking, quicker and more comfortable.

Suez   السويس
☏ 062

Poor Suez. Thanks to a heavy thumping delivered during the 1967 and 1973 wars, it has none of the nostalgic appeal of Port Said or Ismailia, and overzealous security measures have made viewing the canal here a no-go. But the town remains a transit hub.

The town is in two parts: Suez proper, the chaotic main settlement, and Port Tawfiq, a catatonic suburb at the mouth of the canal.

Sleeping & Eating

If you do get stuck here, **Medina Hotel** (☑ 322 4056; Sharia Talaat Harb; s/d E£75/125; ✴) and, at the top end, **Hotel Green House** (☑ 319 1553, 319 1554; greenhouse-suez@hotmail.com; Sharia al-Geish; s/d from E£500/628; ✴ @ ☒) are your best bets. For inexpensive food, wander around the Sharia Talaat Harb area.

Getting There & Away

BUS

The bus station is 5km out of town along the road to Cairo. **East Delta Travel Co** (☑ 356 4853) services the Sinai, and **Upper Egypt Bus Co** (☑ 356 4258) handles the Red Sea coast and the Nile Valley.

SERVEES

The *servees* station is beside the bus station and prices are similar to the buses. The only place in the Sinai they serve is Al-Tor (E£15).

TRAIN

Six uncomfortable, 2nd-class Cairo-bound trains depart Suez daily (E£15 to E£18, three hours) going only as far as Ain Shams, 10km northeast of central Cairo; the first Cairo-bound train leaves at 5.30am. There are also eight slow trains to Ismailia.

RED SEA COAST

ساحل البحر لاحمر

The long stretch of Egyptian coastline that meets the Red Sea, extending from Suez to Sudan, is fringed by world-class coral reefs and clear aqua waters. It is said that Moses parted the waters here and early Christians established the first monasteries. These days, however, the legions are holidaymakers, keener on sunbathing than Bible locations.

Ravenous development has steamrolled its way through Hurghada, heart of the European package-tourist scene, while the political unrest in Egypt has stalled further plans, leaving the concrete husks of unfinished future resorts. Further south, Marsa Alam, so close to the Red Sea's most beautiful reefs, has received a bit of the 'developer's touch', but the time-warp town of Al-Quseir remains a picturesque, if not very lively, waypoint.

Hurghada
الغردقة

☑ 065

Hurghada is a poster child for everything that can go wrong with mass tourism. Uninhibited growth over the years has disfigured this part of the Red Sea coast, with relentless concrete spread destroying much of the fringing-reef ecosystems along the way. Nevertheless, there are a few low-key resorts that manage to retain shreds of calm, and for many touring the Nile Valley it remains the most accessible part of the Red Sea. At press time, boats were set to begin running between Hurghada and Sharm el-Sheikh in the Sinai, a convenient short cut.

A main road connects Ad-Dahar, the main town area, with Sigala, where the port is. South of Sigala, a road winds 15km through the 'resort strip', the upmarket tourism enclave.

BUSES FROM SUEZ

DESTINATION	PRICE (E£)	DURATION (HR)	TIMES
Cairo	15-20	2	every 30min 6am-9pm
Dahab	60	7	11am
Hurghada	35-40	4	hourly 5am-11pm
Ismailia	10	1½	every 30min 6am-4pm
Luxor via Qena	60-70	9-10	8am, 2pm, 8pm
Port Said	20	2½	7am, 9am, 11am, 12.15pm, 3.30pm
Sharm el-Sheikh	50	6	8.30am, 11am, 1.30pm, 3pm, 4.30pm, 5.15pm, 6pm
St Katherine	35	4	2pm

◉ Sights & Activities

There's little to do in Hurghada itself other than sit on a beach and dream of other places. The **public beach** in Sigala is less than appealing, though many resorts offer preferable sun-and-sand options (nonguest-access charges range from E£25 to E£75).

If you go diving or snorkelling, arrange with a specific operator, rather than through your hotel, as those trips often go to the closest, overdived reefs. **Jasmin Diving Centre** (✆ 346 0334; www.jasmin-diving.com; Grand Seas Resort Hostmark, Resort Strip; 3 days (3 dives) €87, 2-day PADI Scuba Diver course from €175) has an excellent reputation.

🛏 Sleeping

Most budget hotels are in Ad-Dahar, at the northern end of a long stretch of resorts. Don't immediately rule out higher-end resorts – fantastic deals can be had in low seasons (April to August), so long as you book ahead online.

El-Arosa Hotel

HOTEL **$**

(✆ 0106 667 8765, 354 8434; elarosahotel@yahoo. com; off Corniche; s/d/tr E£100/120/180; ❄ ☀) El-Arosa overlooks the sea from the inland side of the Corniche. Few of the quaintly old-fashioned rooms have ocean views but they boast decent amenities and there's even a pool (albeit located in the dining room). Staff are extremely sweet and the whole place has a homely feel. Guests get beach day-use at a hotel across the road.

Seaview

HOTEL **$**

(✆ 0127 200 0968; www.seaviewhotel.com.eg; Corniche; s/d/tr E£120/180/230; ❄ 🛜) You may need sunglasses to deal with the garish yellow and orange hallways but this place is a great budget deal. Neat, bright rooms are painted an easier-on-the-eye white and green, and all have balconies and some superweird sci-fi-style paintings on the walls. Guests can use the beach at a hotel close by for a small fee.

Steigenberger Al Dau Beach Hotel

RESORT **$$**

(✆ 346 5400; www.steigenbergeraldaubeach.com; Resort Strip; r half board from €67; ❄ 🛜 ☀) Large, tastefully decorated rooms, a mind-boggling amount of activities on offer and an absolutely mammoth pool make the Steigenberger a long-running favourite for a family holiday. The private beach is kept beautiful-

TOP RED SEA DIVE SITES

Thistlegorm Closest to Sharm el-Sheikh, this WWII cargo ship is, arguably, the best wreck dive in the world.

Ras Mohammed National Park (p117) Teeming with more fish life than you can poke a regulator at.

Blue Hole (p122) The famed sinkhole near Dahab is as dangerous as it is gorgeous.

Elphinstone A remote reef off the shore of Marsa Alam, good for shark spotting.

Lighthouse Reef (Map p121; Assalah) Great for beginners, a colourful world of darting, curious fish only a few steps from Dahab's shore.

ly clean and the manicured gardens offer a shady retreat after a day in the sun.

🍴 Eating

Ad-Dahar and Sigala have dozens of inexpensive local-style restaurants.

Gad

EGYPTIAN FAST FOOD **$**

(Sharia Sheraton, Sigala; dishes E£5-45; 🍴) If you're looking for cheap, filling and tasty Egyptian staples, you can't go wrong with Egypt's favourite fast-food restaurant. The sprawling menu covers everything from felafel and shwarma to *fiteer* (Egyptian flaky pizza) and full kebab meals. There's another **branch** (Sharia an-Nasr) in Ad-Dahar.

Abu Khadigah

EGYPTIAN **$**

(Sharia Sheraton, Sigala; meals E£10-20) For authentic Egyptian kebabs and other local staples, Abu Khadigah is just the ticket. It's known for its *kofta* (mincemeat and spices grilled on a skewer) and stuffed cabbage leaves.

Moby Dick

INTERNATIONAL **$$**

(Sharia Sheraton, Sigala; mains E£35-100) People rave about Moby Dick's succulent steaks but it also does pasta and seafood as well, and has a fine line in crispy, fresh salads. There's a really nice vibe here and the helpful, chatty staff seem to really care about the food. Beer is also well priced at just E£10 per bottle.

🍷 Drinking & Entertainment

Thanks to its large community of resident dive instructors, tour guides, hotel employees and other foreigners, Hurghada has some of Egypt's liveliest nightlife.

South Beach
BAR

(Sharia Sheraton, Sigala; ⊙10am-2pm) This beach bar has a lovely patch of sand, a good restaurant and plenty of live music to dance to in the evening. It's also home to Egypt's first ice-bar. Yep, you don't get much more bizarre than walking out of blistering heat to don a coat and drink cocktails at -5°C.

El Mashrabia
CAFE

(Sharia Sheraton, Sigala; hot drinks E£4-14, juice E£12-14, sheesha E£2.50-10) This is our favourite pit stop in Hurghada for a juice, tea or sheesha. El Mashrabia is slap on Sigala's main road, with shady outdoor seating and a dimly lit cafe decorated in a mishmash of Chinese lanterns and Pharaonic art. It's easy to spot – the facade is decorated with fake *mashrabiyya* (wooden lattice screens) windows.

ℹ Information

There are internet cafes all over the city and in many hotels, most charging between E£5 and E£10 per hour. Banks are scattered all over Hurghada: most have ATMs. Many upmarket hotels also have ATMs in their lobbies. There is a **Tourist Office** (☑ 344 4420; Resort Strip; ⊙8am-8pm Sat-Thu, 2-10pm Fri) kiosk in the middle of the resort strip.

ℹ Getting There & Away

AIR
EgyptAir (☑ 344 3592, 344 3593; www.egyptair.com; Resort Strip) has daily flights to Cairo and several charter companies fly in from Europe.

BOAT
The ferry between Hurghada and Sharm el-Sheikh has been suspended, but not yet cancelled.

BUS
Upper Egypt Bus Co (☑ 354 7582; off Sharia an-Nasr, Ad-Dahar) has a station at the southern end of Ad-Dahar. Super Jet is 500m further south. Ideally, book ahead for long-distance services such as to Luxor and Cairo.

SERVEES
The *servees* station, off Sharia an-Nasr in Ad-Dahar, has cars to Cairo (E£55 to E£70, six hours), Safaga (E£10, one hour) and Al-Quseir (E£10, 1½ hours). It is also possible to take one to Luxor (E£25, five hours).

ℹ Getting Around

TO/FROM THE AIRPORT
Hurghada International Airport is located 6km southwest of town. A taxi to downtown Ad-Dahar costs between E£25 and E£35.

MICROBUS
Microbuses run throughout the day from central Ad-Dahar south along the resort strip and along Sharia an-Nasr and other major routes. Rides cost between E£1 and E£3.

TAXI
Taxis from Ad-Dahar to the start of the resort strip (around the Marriott hotel) charge about E£15. Travelling from the bus station to the centre of Ad-Dahar, expect to pay E£10.

BUSES FROM HURGHADA

DESTINATION	PRICE (E£)	DURATION (HR)	TIMES
Al-Quseir (Upper Egypt Bus)	15	1½	5.30am, 9.30am, 4pm, 1.30am
Alexandria (Super Jet)	100	9	2.30pm
Aswan (Upper Egypt Bus)	45-50	7	10.30pm, 12.30am
Cairo (Super Jet)	70	6	noon, 2.30pm, 5pm, midnight
Cairo (Upper Egypt Bus)	65	6	8 departures daily
Luxor (Super Jet)	40	4	8.30am
Luxor (Upper Egypt Bus)	30	5	8pm, 10.30pm, 12.30am, 3.30am
Marsa Alam (Upper Egypt Bus)	25	4	9.30am, 4pm, 1.30am
Suez (Upper Egypt Bus)	50	4-5	7am, 11am, 12.30pm, 3pm, 4pm, 5.30pm, 11.30pm

CHOOSING A DIVE SCHOOL

Here's some advice for when you're considering donning flippers for the first time.

➡ Do your homework. You're about to spend a chunk of money and put your life in a stranger's hands, so it pays to visit several outfits.

➡ Check to see how well the equipment is treated and stored. Stay away from shops with buoyancy control devices (BCDs) and regulators left out in the sun or strewn about their equipment room.

➡ Big schools have lots of instructors and shiny equipment, but they can feel like impersonal diving factories. Some smaller outfits can offer a more personal touch.

➡ Try to find an instructor who speaks your native language. Ask other travellers for recommendations, talk to several instructors and go with the one you feel most comfortable with.

➡ Check whether your travel insurance covers diving accidents. If not, see what sort of insurance the school provides. Find the location of the nearest hyperbaric chamber, just in case.

Al-Quseir   القصير
☑ 065

It's hard not to fall in love with this sleepy Red Sea port, passed by most tourists. Beautiful Ottoman-era, coral-block buildings line the waterfront, and a maze of dusty laneways snake inland. It's worth a stopover to soak up some oceanside serenity and get a glimpse of the region before tourism took over.

In Pharaonic times, the port was the departure point for boats heading south to the fabled East African kingdom of Punt, and until the 10th century, Al-Quseir was one of the most important exit points for pilgrims to Mecca. Later, it became an important import channel for Indian spices destined for Europe.

◉ Sights

Ottoman Fortress   FORTRESS
(Sharia al-Gomhurriyya; admission E£15; ⊙ 9am-5pm) Much of the original exterior wall of this small fortress remains intact, although it was modified several times by the French, as well as the British, who permanently altered the fortress by firing some 6000 cannonballs upon it during a heated battle in the 19th century. Inside some of the rooms there are interesting information boards documenting the history of Al-Quseir.

⌂ Sleeping & Eating

Dining options are limited to **Restaurant Marianne** (☑ 065 333 4386; Sharia Port Said; mains E£20-40) and the ta'amiyya and fish stands at the seafront and the bus station.

★ **Al-Quseir Hotel**   HISTORIC HOTEL **$**
(☑ 333 2301; www.alquseirhotel.com; Sharia Port Said; r without bathroom E£138-158, with air-con E£198; ❋) If you're looking for atmosphere rather than amenities, this renovated 1920s merchant's house is a delightful place to stay. Sitting right on the seafront, Al-Quseir Hotel has just six simple but spacious rooms and is brimming full of character with its original narrow wooden staircase, high wooden ceilings and latticework on the windows.

Rocky Valley Beach Camp   BEACH CAMP **$$**
(☑ 333 5247; www.rockyvalleydiverscamp.com; 1 week full board incl diving per person €350) About 10km north of Al-Quseir, this camp is a veritable paradise for shoestringing scuba aficionados. Rocky Valley lures in divers by offering a variety of cheap all-inclusive packages, which include Bedouin-style tents, beachside barbecues, late-night beach parties and some incredible reefs right off the shore. It's a fun place where management works hard to foster a communal atmosphere.

Mövenpick Sirena Beach   RESORT **$$$**
(☑ 335 0410; www.moevenpick-quseir.com; s/d US$130/185; ❋@🛜🏊) This low-set, domed ensemble 7km north of Al-Quseir centre is one of the most laid-back resorts along the coast. Its amenities include excellent food and the usual five-star facilities, diving centre, quiet evenings and a refreshing absence of glitz. The management is known for its environmentally conscious approach.

ℹ Information

The town has a 24-hour telephone centrale, a National Bank of Egypt branch with an ATM, and a post office.

ℹ Getting There & Around

The bus and *servees* stations are next to each other about 3km northwest of the Safaga road. A taxi from the bus station to the waterfront costs E£5.

BUS

Buses run to Cairo (E£80, 10 hours) via Hurghada (E£20 to E£25, 1½ to two hours), departing at 8.30am, 1pm, 3.30pm and 10pm. Buses to Marsa Alam (E£15, two hours) are at 4am, 6pm and 10pm but the schedule changes frequently so check beforehand.

MICROBUS

Microbuses go along Sharia al-Gomhuriyya, with some also going to the bus and *servees* stations. Fares are between 50pt and E£1.

SERVEES

Sample fares: Hurghada (E£15 to E£20, 1½ hours) and Marsa Alam (E£15, two hours).

Marsa Alam مرسى علم

☑ 065

The Red Sea off the coast of Marsa Alam shelters some of the most impressive diving in the world. Not long ago these sites were accessible only by boat from Hurghada and Sharm el-Sheikh, but new development has made this area an easier jumping-off point. Despite a construction drive of slick resorts north and south of town, the area is still a diver's dream, and some long-standing beach camps here cater to those who want to spend most of their time underwater. Hossam Hassan's **Red Sea Diving Safari** (☑ 02-337 1833, 02-337 9942; www.redsea-divingsafari.com; Marsa Shagra; 5-day diving packages from €175) outfit at Marsa Shagra is recommended.

🛏 Sleeping & Eating

Most visitors to Marsa Alam eat at their resorts. In town, there's a small supermarket with the basics, and a couple of cafes at the junction where you can find ta'amiyya and similar fare.

Um Tondoba BEACH CAMP $$
(☑ 0111 181 2277; www.deep-south-diving.com; Marsa Alam; s/d full board hut €25/50, chalet €35/70) Stripping it right back to the basics of sun, sea and sand, Um Tondoba offers basic palm-thatch beach huts and domed concrete chalets (located across the road from the beach rather than on the shore), good diving packages and an exceptionally mellow atmosphere. It's 14km south of Marsa Alam along the main road.

★ **Wadi Lahami Village** BEACH CAMP $$$
(☑ 0122 391 3786, Cairo head office 02-3337 1833; www.redsea-divingsafari.com; Wadi Lahami; s/d full board tent €60/90, royal tent €65/100, chalet €80/120) 🖊 Tucked into a remote mangrove bay 120km south along the main road from Marsa Alam, this hideaway is worth the extra effort it takes to get here. Diving is the main activity – the pristine reefs of the Fury Shoals are easily reached by boat – but the lonely location, and nearby mangroves, are a perfect setting for nature lovers as well.

Marsa Shagra Village BEACH CAMP $$$
(☑ 0122 244 9073, Cairo head office 02-3337 1833; www.redsea-divingsafari.com; Marsa Shagra; s/d full board tent €65/100, royal tent €70/110, hut €75/110; 🛜) 🖊 This large-scale camp offers spectacular snorkelling and diving just offshore. Marsa Shagra was one of the first eco-minded places to open on the Red Sea and, despite the development that has gone on around it, has stayed true to its sustainable-tourism credentials. It's 24km north of Marsa Alam along the main road.

ℹ Getting There & Away

AIR

EgyptAir flies from Cairo to **Marsa Alam International Airport** (☑ 370 0021), 67km north of Marsa Alam along the Al-Quseir road. There is no public transport, so you'll need to arrange a transfer in advance with your hotel.

BUS

Marsa Alam bus station is just past the T-junction along the Edfu road. Buses to Cairo (E£85 to E£90, 10 to 11 hours) via Al-Quseir (E£15, two hours) and Hurghada (E£30 to E£35, 3½ to four hours) depart at 1.30pm and 8.30pm, but check beforehand as timetables change frequently.

SOUTH SINAI

The breathtaking region of Sinai (سيناء) is famed in the Bible as the place Moses received the Ten Commandments. It's also here that ancient and modern armies fought and continue to fight, and where Bedouin tribes established their homes. This striking desertscape rolls straight into the turquoise waters of the Red Sea, offering countless opportunities for exploration of both the mountainous desert and pristine underwater ecosystems. Visitors can take their pick of places to stay while exploring the peninsula: the glitzy resorts of Sharm el-Sheikh, the chilled-out vibes of Dahab or the remote and low-key Nuweiba and St Katherine Protectorate.

Northern Sinai has been a no-go area for some time as it is home to serveral violent groups. Their conflict with the Egyptian security services has spilled over into tourist areas in the south: three tourists and their driver were killed in a bombing at Taba in Feburary 2014. Security in Sharm el-Sheikh has been beefed up and the vast majority of holidaymakers have enjoyed their stay here without incident – but it is worth checking current warnings.

Ras Mohammed National Park محمية رأس محمد

Declared a **national marine park** (admission per person €6; ☉8am-5pm) in 1988, the headland of Ras Mohammed lies about 20km west of Sharm el-Sheikh. The waters surrounding the peninsula are considered the jewel in the crown of the Red Sea, and most of the Red Sea's 1000 fish species can be seen in what remains one of the world's most spectacular coral-reef ecosystems.

Camping (€6 per person) is allowed in designated areas. Take all supplies and your passport with you; it is not possible to enter the park if you have only a Sinai permit and not a full visa.

Many people visit the reefs to dive on dayboats or live-aboards, but walk-in snorkelling is excellent too (bring your own gear). You can hire a taxi from Sharm el-Sheikh for around E£200 for the day or join one of the many day tours by 4WD or bus from Sharm el-Sheikh. They will drop you at the best beaches and snorkelling sites. Tours may not include the €6 park-entry fee.

To move around the park you'll need a vehicle. Access is restricted to certain parts of the park and, for conservation reasons, it's forbidden to leave the official tracks.

Sharm el-Sheikh شرم الشيخ

☏069

The proudly brash resort destination of Sharm el-Sheikh is the main jumping-off point for spectacular, world-class diving.

Sharm today has little to do with the desert that surrounds it and has become an enclave for pleasure-seeking Westerners and a great getaway for families. Independent travellers who are looking for something more authentic would be wise to move up the coast to Dahab.

Na'ama Bay is the centre of the action, where most resorts are clustered. About 6km west, Sharm el-Sheikh, the centre of which is called Sharm al-Maya or Old Sharm, has a selection of inexpensive eateries. On a clifftop above is Hadaba, lined with primarily midrange resorts. Around 12km northeast of Na'ama Bay, Shark's Bay is home to the area's best budget accommodation.

◉ Sights & Activities

Any of the many **dive** operators in Sharm can give you a rundown on the superb underwater possibilities in the area. Going on a live-aboard enables you to visit several, and can cost less than staying on land in Sharm.

Snorkelling around Sharm is excellent, even in central Na'ama Bay, though it's better to make your way to the **Near and Middle Gardens**, the even more beautiful **Far Garden** or **Ras Um Sid Reef**, near the lighthouse at Sharm el-Sheikh, and best of all at Ras Mohammed National Park.

🛏 Sleeping

Budget digs are very thin on the ground in Sharm. In the midrange and up, prices fluctuate wildly depending on the number of tourists in town; book online for deals.

★**Sinai Old Spices**　　　　　　B&B $
(☏0120 222 0509; www.sinaioldspices.com; Roissat area; s/d €15/24; P❋☎) Hidden behind a terracotta wall, this charming B&B serves up quirky style using locally inspired architecture. The individually decorated rooms come with kitchenettes and fabulous modern bathrooms. It's a E£30 taxi ride from Sharm, so won't suit everyone, but offers a retreat from the bright lights of Na'ama Bay.

Phone beforehand to arrange a pick-up, or get directions; it's tricky to find.

Aida 2　　　　　　　　　　HOTEL $
(off Sultan Qabos St, Na'ama Bay; s/d US$20/28; ❋☎▩) Surprisingly quiet for being slap on the shopping drag, this cheapie hotel has decent-sized rooms set around a tiny pool. There's a strong smell of chlorine in the corridors (which also seem to be a prime

Sinai

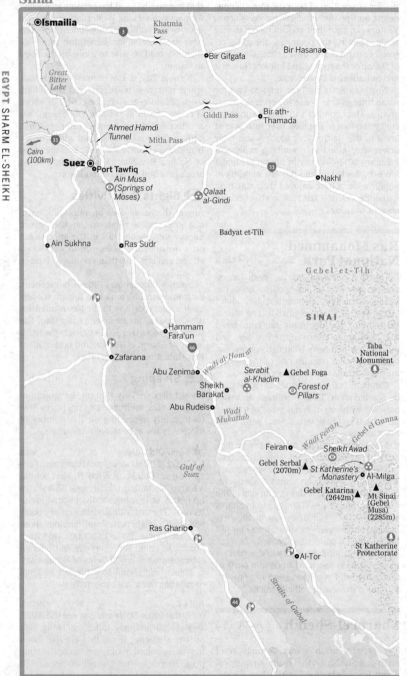

Ismailia

Khatmia Pass

Bir Gifgafa

Bir Hasana

Great Bitter Lake

Giddi Pass

Bir ath-Thamada

Ahmed Hamdi Tunnel

Mitla Pass

Cairo (100km)

Suez ⊙ Port Tawfiq

Ain Musa (Springs of Moses)

Qalaat al-Gindi

Nakhl

Badyat et-Tih

Ain Sukhna

Ras Sudr

Gebel-et-Tih

SINAI

Taba National Monument

Hammam Fara'un

Wadi al-Homur

Zafarana

Abu Zenima

Serabit al-Khadim

▲ Gebel Foga

Forest of Pillars

Sheikh Barakat

Abu Rudeis

Wadi Mukattab

Gebel el Gunna

Wadi Feiran

Feiran

Sheikh Awad

Gulf of Suez

Gebel Serbal (2070m) ▲

St Katherine's Monastery

Al-Milga

Gebel Katarina (2642m) ▲

▲ Mt Sinai (Gebel Musa) (2285m)

Ras Gharib

Al-Tor

St Katherine Protectorate

Straits of Gubal

cockroach party area) but the rooms themselves are a real budget find.

★ **Camel Hotel** HOTEL **$$**
(☑ 360 0700; www.cameldive.com; King of Bahrain St, Na'ama Bay; r from US$50; ✵ ☎ ☷) Attached to the dive centre of the same name, Camel Hotel is the smart choice to stay if diving is your main agenda in Sharm. Despite being in the heart of Na'ama Bay, the spacious, modern rooms, set around a lovely courtyard pool area, are gloriously quiet (thanks to soundproof windows), so you're guaranteed a good night's sleep.

Shark's Bay Umbi Diving Village HOTEL **$$**
(☑ 360 0942; www.sharksbay.com; Shark's Bay; s/d cabin €26/40, r €37/50, hut without bathroom €19/24; ℗ ✵ ☎) This long-standing Bedouin-owned place is a tumble of cute chalets flowing down to the beach. Pine beach cabins are spick and span, if a bit of a squeeze, and larger rooms are built into the cliff above. Cheaper, spartan huts (with mattresses, mosquito nets and fans) are up on the clifftop. To get here, ask the taxi driver for 'Shark's Bay Umbi'.

✗ Eating

Cheap eats are clustered around Sharm Old Market, while Na'ama Bay is graced with higher-end places. Approach the promenade here with caution – not all the food is as good as the view.

Koshary El-Sheikh EGYPTIAN FAST FOOD **$**
(King of Bahrain St, Sharm Old Market, Sharm al-Maya; meals E£5-10) Egypt's favourite carbohydrate-fuelled feast, *kushari* (mix of noodles, rice, black lentils, fried onions and tomato sauce), is dished up here.

★ **Fares Seafood** SEAFOOD **$$**
(City Council St, Hadaba; mains E£35-100; ☾ noon-late; ✵) Always crowded with locals, Fares is a Sharm el-Sheikh institution for good-value seafood. Order fish priced by weight or choose from one of the pasta or *tagen* (stew cooked in a deep clay pot) options on the menu. We're pretty partial to the mixed *tagen* of calamari and shrimp.

El-Masrien EGYPTIAN **$$**
(King of Bahrain St, Sharm Old Market, Sharm al-Maya; dishes E£8-40; ☾ noon-late) This old-fashioned restaurant is our top dining spot in Sharm Old Market. Its continued success is due to the simple fact it delivers succulent kebabs, *kofta* (mincemeat and spices grilled

on a skewer) and all the usual Egyptian staples without the prices of fancier Sharm restaurants. Service here is superfriendly, too.

Tandoori   INDIAN $$
(Camel Hotel, King of Bahrain St, Na'ama Bay; dishes E£40-125; ⊘ from 6.30pm; ☑) The courtyard of the Camel Hotel is home to what many consider Sharm's best Indian food. Granted, it leans towards Anglo-Indian (all the korma, butter chicken and madras dishes are there), but it's all executed brilliantly. There's a fantastic choice for vegetarians, too, with plenty of paneer (Indian cottage cheese) and palak (spinach) based curries.

★Fairuz   MIDDLE EASTERN $$$
(King of Bahrain St, Na'ama Bay; mezze dishes E£18-28, mains E£85-165; ☑) This Levantine restaurant is a mouth-watering journey through the subtle flavours of the Middle East. Choose *batingan bi laban* (aubergine in garlicky yoghurt), *makinek* (spicy sausages) and *loubieh* (a green-bean stew) to share with delicious fresh-from-the-oven bread. The mezze set menu (E£105 per person, minimum two people) is the best way to sample an array of flavours.

🍷 Drinking & Nightlife

Compared with the rest of relatively conservative Egypt, Sharm el-Sheikh nightlife can either be a shock to the senses or a welcome relief. All the action is in Na'ama Bay.

★Farsha Cafe   CAFE
(Sharia el-Bahr, Ras Um Sid) All nooks and crannies, floor cushions, Bedouin tents and swinging lamps, Farsha is the kind of place that travellers come to for a coffee and find themselves lingering four drinks and a sheesha pipe later. Great for a lazy day full of lounging or a night of chilled-out music and cocktails.

Pacha   CLUB
(www.pachasharm.com; King of Bahrain St, Na'ama Bay; tickets presale/at door E£140/180; ⊘ 11pm-late) The hub of Sharm's nightlife, Pacha goes wild pretty much every night of the week. Watch for advertising around town to find out about upcoming events. Women gain free entry into the club before midnight.

ℹ Information

Many restaurants offer wi-fi, and internet cafes dotted around town charge between E£5 and E£10 per hour. There are ATMs every few metres in Na'ama Bay.

Thomas Cook (☑ 360 1808; Gafy Mall, Peace Rd, Na'ama Bay; ⊘ 9am-2pm & 6-10pm) Just west of Sinai Star Hotel.

ℹ Getting There & Away

AIR
Egypt Air has several flights per day to Cairo. There are also many direct flights to Europe.

BOAT
The ferry between Sharm el-Sheikh and Hurghada stopped in 2010. Enquire at any of the hotels and travel agencies in Sharm el-Sheikh for up-to-date information or contact the **Sharm el-Sheikh Port Office** (☑ 366 0217).

BUS
The **East Delta Travel Co bus station** (☑ 366 0660) is just off Peace Rd behind the Mobil petrol station. It runs 11 buses to Cairo (E£60 to E£80, seven hours) daily. Heading north, there are buses to Dahab (E£15, 1½ hours) at 7am, 9am, 3pm, 5pm and 9pm; the 9am and 5pm services carry on to Nuweiba (E£30, three hours) and Taba (E£55, 4½ hours).

Super Jet (☑ 366 1622) buses leave from just behind the East Delta station. Buses run to Cairo (E£85, six to seven hours) at 11am, 1pm, 3pm and 11.30pm. The 3pm service continues on to Alexandria (E£110, eight to nine hours).

Seats on Cairo buses should be reserved in advance.

ℹ Getting Around

TO/FROM THE AIRPORT
Sharm el-Sheikh Airport (☑ 362 3304; www.sharm-el-sheikh.airport-authority.com; Peace Rd) is about 10km north of Na'ama Bay at Ras Nasrany; taxis generally charge from E£20 to E£25 to Sharm or Na'ama Bay. Prepare to bargain hard.

MICROBUS & TAXI
Blue-and-white microbuses (E£2) connect Na'ama Bay and Sharm el-Sheikh. Taxis charge a minimum of E£15 between the two centres. Many hotels also run free shuttle buses.

Dahab دهب

☑ 069

Dahab remains the Middle East's prime beach resort for independent travellers. There are two parts to it. Dahab City to the south has resort hotels, the bus station and other services. Beachfront Assalah, originally a Bedouin village and now the major tourist stretch, is further divided into three areas. The northernmost point, where most

Dahab

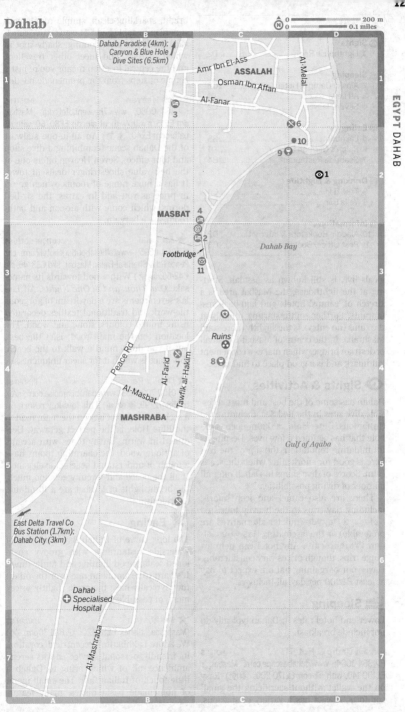

Dahab

locals live, is still known as Assalah. Starting at the lighthouse, the Masbat area is a stretch of 'camps', hotels and laid-back restaurants. Further south, starting roughly at the ruins (no entry), is the slightly more staid Mashraba. In the centre of Masbat is a small pedestrian bridge, which makes a convenient landmark and is a good place to find taxis.

◉ Sights & Activities

Dahab has some of the best and most accessible dive sites in the Red Sea, including the (in)famous Blue Hole, a 130m-deep sinkhole that has claimed a few lives. Despite its intimidating reputation, the top of the reef here is good for snorkelling when the sea is calm. Scores of dive shops in Dahab offer all manner of diving possibilities.

There are also camel and jeep safaris, including day trips to the heavily touristed Coloured Canyon (quieter alternatives are preferable) or the fascinating Ras Abu Gallum Protectorate. Any hotel can help arrange trips, though prices vary considerably. Have your bargaining hat on; expect to pay at least E£200 per day, all-inclusive.

🛏 Sleeping

Lower-end hotel rates in Dahab typically do not include breakfast.

Alaska Camp & Hotel　　　HOTEL $
(☑364 1004; www.dahabescape.com; Masbat; r E£100-140, with air-con E£170-200; ❄🛜) Easy on the wallet without sacrificing the small comforts, Alaska has a variety of spacious,

bright, sparkling-clean, simple rooms with supercomfortable beds. The attractive courtyard garden is a welcoming, shady spot in which to relax and meet other travellers, and the central location means you're just a couple of steps from the promenade bustle.

Seven Heaven　　　HOSTEL $
(☑364 0080; www.7heavenhotel.com; Masbat; dm E£15, r with/without air-con E£80/60, without bathroom E£40; ❄🛜) An all-in-one stalwart of the Dahab scene (combining a dive shop and tour office), Seven Heaven offers one of the best-value shoestringer deals in town. It has a huge range of rooms, which go up in price as you add in extras; the six-bed dorms, which come with air-con and bathroom, are a bargain.

★**Alf Leila**　　　BOUTIQUE HOTEL $$
(☑364 0595; www.alfleilaboutiquehotel.com; cnr Peace Rd & Sharia al-Fanar, Masbat; s/d €33/46, ste €42-65; ❄🛜) With a nod towards its namesake *One Thousand & One Nights*, Alf Leila's seven rooms are a daydream of gorgeous tile-work and traditional textiles decorated using muted colours, stone and wood. The location (on the main road) isn't the best, but if you don't mind a walk to the beach, this place is worth it for sheer uniqueness.

★**Dahab Paradise**　　　RESORT $$
(☑0100 700 4133; www.dahabparadise.com; s/d/tr €58/72/99; ❄🛜🏊) This low-key resort, on a secluded sweep of bay on the main road to the Blue Hole, is the perfect getaway. Decorated in warm, earthy tones with accents of antique wood, the charming rooms have a touch of understated beach-chic elegance. If all the peace and serenity gets too much, the bright lights of Masbat are a 10-minute taxiride away.

✖ Eating

The long curve of Dahab Bay is a string of waterside restaurants with groovy cushioned seats, mood lighting and funky tunes. It's hard to recommend one over the other: they typically have the same slightly pricey menu of passable food.

★**Lakhbatita**　　　ITALIAN $$
(Mashraba; dishes E£65-120; ⊙6-11.30pm; 🚗) We adore Lakhbatita's eccentric decoration, its friendly, personal service and its serene ambience, all of which bring to Dahab a little touch of Italian flair. The small menu of homemade pasta dishes, many featur-

BUSES FROM DAHAB

Be sure to check departure times with hotel staff, as they're subject to change, especially in the low season.

DESTINATION	PRICE (E£)	DURATION (HR)	TIMES
Cairo	90	9	9am, 12.30pm, 3pm, 10pm
Hurghada	105	10	4pm
Luxor	130	18	4pm
Nuweiba	15	1	10.30am
Sharm el-Sheikh	15-20	2	11 services daily
Taba	45	2	10.30am

ing seafood, is a cut above what's served up elsewhere. Try the mushroom ravioli or the garlic and chilli prawns. No alcohol is served but diners are welcome to bring their own.

Seabride Restaurant SEAFOOD $$
(Mashraba; meals E£40-60) Located away from the shorefront, this is the locals' favourite haunt for seafood. All meals come loaded with fish soup, rice, salad, baba ghanoosh (purée of grilled aubergines), a delectably tangy tahini and bread. Fish is priced by weight (choose from the display downstairs) or order cheaper options off the menu. The spicy Bedouin calamari is seafood Dahab-style.

Ralph's German Bakery CAFE $$
(Sharia al-Fanar, Mashrab; coffee E£10-18, pastries E£6-12, sandwiches & breakfasts E£20-30; ⊙ 7am-6pm; ⚲) Singlehandedly raising the bar for coffee in Dahab, this place is caffeine heaven and is also Dahab's top stop for breakfast. People who have the willpower to not add one of the delectable Danish pastries onto their order are doing better than us.

🍷 Drinking & Nightlife

Dahab is fairly quiet at night, but there is a good selection of lively bars, some of which turn into discos if the atmosphere is right.

Tree Bar BAR
(Mashraba; ⊙ 10pm-late) Two-for-one cocktail deals and a thumping soundtrack of urban, house and R&B make this open-air beachfront bar Dahab's top late-night party venue.

Yalla Bar BAR
(Masbat; beer E£10-12; 🕱) This hugely popular waterfront bar-restaurant has a winning formula of friendly staff and excellent happy-hour beer prices (from 5pm to 9pm).

ℹ️ Information

Free wi-fi is widely available at most hotels and many of the restaurants. There are plenty of ATMs scattered along the waterfront throughout Masbat, and a handy post office/bookshop on the waterfront in Masbat, next to Bamboo House Hotel, where you can also place calls.
Aladdin Bookstore & Internet (Masbat; per hr E£5) Also home to a secondhand bookshop.
Dr Haikal (🕿 0100 143 3325; Dahab City) Local doctor whose surgery near the lagoon also has a hyperbaric chamber.

ℹ️ Getting There & Around

BUS
From the bus station in Dahab City, **East Delta Travel Co** (🕿 364 1808) runs to other Sinai beach towns and elsewhere in Egypt. In addition, **Bedouin Bus** (🕿 0101 668 4274; www.bedouinbus.com) connects Dahab to St Katherine on Tuesday and Friday (E£50, two hours); confirm the schedule on the website.

TAXI
Taxi drivers at the bus station (and around town) charge E£100 to Sharm el-Sheikh and E£250 to St Katherine. A taxi (usually a pickup truck) between Assalah and Dahab City costs E£5.

St Katherine Protectorate
محمية كاترينا القديسة
🕿 069

The 4350-sq-km national park protects a unique high-desert ecosystem, as well as St Katherine's Monastery and the adjacent Mt Sinai, both sacred to the world's three main monotheistic religions. Although it can be difficult to pry yourself away from Sinai's beaches, a visit to the St Katherine Protectorate is not to be missed. Be sure to check the security situation before setting out. If it is quiet, hiking with guide in the desert is recommended

St Katherine's Monastery

A HISTORY OF THE MONASTERY

4th Century With hermetic communities congregating in the area, a chapel is established around the site of Moses' miraculous **Burning Bush ❶**.

6th Century In a show of might, Emperor Justinian adds the monastery **fortifications ❷** and orders the building of the basilica, which is graced by Byzantine art, including the **Mosaic of the Transfiguration ❸**.

7th Century The prophet Mohammed signs the **Ahtiname ❹**, a declaration of his protection of the monastery. When the Arab armies conquer Egypt in AD 641, the monastery is left untouched. Despite the era's tumultuous times, monastery abbot St John Klimakos writes his famed **Ladder of Divine Ascent ❺** treatise, depicted in the Sacred Sacristy.

9th Century Extraordinary happenings surround the monastery when, according to tradition, a monk discovers the body of St Katherine on a mountain summit.

11th Century To escape the wrath of Fatimid caliph Al-Hakim, wily monks build a mosque within the monastery grounds.

15th Century Frequent raids and attacks on the monastery lead the monks to build the **Ancient Gate ❻** to prevent the ransacking of church treasures and to keep the monastic community safe.

19th Century In 1859 biblical scholar Constantin von Tischendorf borrows 347 pages of the **Codex Sinaiticus ❼** from the monastery, but fails to get his library books back on time. Greek artisans travel from the island of Tinos in 1871 to help construct the **bell tower ❽**.

20th Century Renovations inside the monastery reveal 18 more missing parchment leaves from the Codex Sinaiticus, proving that all the secrets hidden within these ancient walls may not yet be revealed.

SIMON BALSON/ALAMY ©

Fortifications
The formidable walls are 2m thick and 11m high. Justinian sent a Balkan garrison to watch over the newly fortified monastery, and today's local Jabaleyya tribe are said to be their descendents.

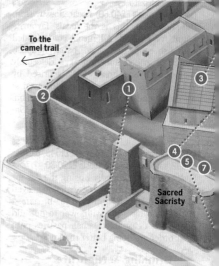

To the camel trail

Sacred Sacristy

The Burning Bush
This flourishing bramble (the endemic Sinai shrub *Rubus Sanctus*) was transplanted in the 10th century to its present location. Tradition states that cuttings of the plant refuse to grow outside the monastery walls.

JESSICA LEE

Mosaic of the Transfiguration

Lavishly made using thousands of pieces of glass, gold, silver and stone tesserae, this Byzantine mosaic (completed AD 551) recreates Christianity's Gospel accounts of Jesus' miraculous revelation as the son of God.

Ahtiname

A monastery delegation sought the protection of Mohammed, and he signed his guarantee by handprint. This document on display in the Sacred Sacrity is only a copy; the original is in Istanbul.

To Steps of Repentence

Library

Bell Tower

The nine bells that hang inside the tower were a present from Tsar Alexander II of Russia. While these are rung for Sunday services, an older semantron (wooden percussion instrument) signals vespers and matins.

8

Church of the Transfiguration

6

Ancient Gate

Look up at the high walls and you'll see a ramshackle wooden structure. In times of strife monks left via this primitive lift, lowered to the ground by a pulley.

Codex Sinaiticus

The world's oldest near-complete bible; 347 pages of the Codex were taken to Russia in 1859 and sold by Stalin to the UK in 1933. Remaining parchments are displayed in the manuscript room.

Ladder of Divine Ascent

This 12th-century icon is one of the monastery's most valuable. It depicts abbot St John Klimakos leading a band of monks up the ladder of salvation to heaven.

(from €50 per person per day). Mountain Tours and **Wilderness Ventures Egypt** (☑0128 282 7182; www.wilderness-ventures-egypt.com) are both recommended.

◉ Sights

St Katherine's Monastery is tucked at the foot of Mt Sinai (locally called Gebel Musa). Approximately 3.5km west from here is the small town of Al-Milga, also called Katreen, where most tourist services are available.

★**St Katherine's Monastery**   MONASTERY
(☑Cairo 02-2482 8513; ⊘9am-noon Mon-Thu & Sat, except religious holidays) FREE This ancient monastery traces its founding to about AD 330, when the Byzantine empress Helena had a small chapel and a fortified refuge for local hermits built beside what was believed to be the burning bush from which God spoke to Moses. Today St Katherine's is considered one of the oldest continually functioning monastic communities in the world, and its chapel is one of early Christianity's only surviving churches.

★**Mt Sinai**   MOUNTAIN
(Gebel Musa; compulsory guide E£125, camel rides one way E£125) Known locally as Gebel Musa, Mt Sinai is revered by Christians, Muslims and Jews, all of whom believe that God delivered his Ten Commandments to Moses at its summit. The mountain is easy and beautiful to climb, and offers a taste of the magnificence of southern Sinai's high mountain region. For pilgrims, it also offers a moving glimpse into biblical times. All hikers must be accompanied by a local Bedouin guide (hired from the monastery car park).

🛏 Sleeping & Eating

In Al-Milga there's a bakery opposite the mosque and a couple of well-stocked supermarkets in the shopping arcade. A few small restaurants are just behind the bakery.

★**Al-Karm Ecolodge**   LODGE $
(☑0100 132 4693; Sheikh Awaad; r without bathroom incl half/full board per person E£100/120) Surrounded by lush gardens in a remote wadi, this Bedouin-owned ecolodge is the perfect spot to sample the tranquillity and rugged beauty of southern Sinai. It deserves kudos for its environmental efforts: solar-powered showers; composting toilets; and beautifully designed, simple stone and palm-trunk rooms decorated with local textiles, which blend into the scenery. Transport

and lodge booking is easiest done through **Mountain Tours Office** (☑347 0457; www.sheikhmousa.com; El-Malga Bedouin Camp, Al-Miga, St Katherine Protectorate); minimal English is spoken at the lodge.

Monastery Guesthouse   GUESTHOUSE $$
(☑347 0353; St Katherine's Monastery; s/d US$35/60; ❄) A favourite of pilgrims the world over, this guesthouse right next to St Katherine's Monastery offers well-kept rooms surrounding a pleasant courtyard. Meals at the on-site cafeteria are filling and tasty, and lunches can be arranged for a few extra dollars per person. Make sure to ask for a mountain-view rather than a courtyard-view room.

ℹ Information

The **St Katherine Protectorate Office** (☑347 0032), near the entrance to Al-Milga, sometimes has informative guide booklets. In the village of Al-Milga, there's a post office, telephone centrale and an internet cafe. The Banque Misr here will change cash and give Visa and MasterCard advances. The only ATM is near the entrance to the monastery.

ℹ Getting There & Away

BUS

East Delta Travel Co (☑347 0250) has its station and ticket office just off the main road in Al-Milga, behind the mosque. There is a daily bus to Cairo (E£50, seven hours) at 6am, via Wadi Feiran and Suez (E£40, five hours). Local transport initiative **Bedouin Bus** (☑0101 668 4274; www.bedouinbus.com; one-way E£50) runs between Al-Milga and Dahab and Nuweiba. To Dahab the bus departs every Tuesday and Friday at 11am, and to Nuweiba at 8am every Wednesday and Sunday. Both cost E£50 and take two hours. The bus leaves from next to the bakery (opposite the mosque). There may also be a service to Cairo.

SERVEES

Taxis and pick-ups wait at the monastery car park for people coming down from Mt Sinai in the morning, and then again around noon when visiting hours end. A lift to the village costs E£10 to E£15. The rate per car to Dahab or Sharm el-Sheikh is E£250.

Nuweiba   نويبع

☑069

Like Dahab, the beaches here are golden, the water crystal clear, the desert mountains shimmering pink. And yet Nuweiba has the catatonic feel of a post-apocalyptic beach resort – perhaps because it's stretched randomly over about 15km, without a clear centre. If you want to avoid the scenes at Sharm and Dahab and just relax solo on a tranquil beach, it could well be the place for you, although the downturn in tourism since 2011 has left the place looking more ramshackle than ever.

◎ Sights & Activities

Apart from lazing on the beach and soaking in the plentiful peace, underwater delights are the feature attraction, with scuba diving and snorkelling keeping many visitors busy. Emperor Divers (www.emperordivers.com) has a solid reputation.

Nuweiba is the jumping-off point for 4WD or camel treks to sights such as Coloured Canyon, Ain Khudra, Ain Umm Ahmed (the largest oasis in eastern Sinai) and Ain al-Furtega (another palm-filled oasis). Most hotels and beach camps along the coast will be able to organise a trip for you, with all-inclusive camel treks costing around E£300 to E£400 per day.

🛏 Sleeping

Petra Camp
BEACH CAMP $

(☏ 0100 472 2001; mahmoud.sokhar@gmail.com; Tarabin; s/d hut E£44/88; ❈) One of the nicest camps in Tarabin. The centrepiece here is an atmospheric open-air restaurant that was constructed from recycled wood salvaged from a defunct Cairo theatre. Huts are simple but well cared for and most come with air-con. The communal bathrooms are clean, and the restaurant serves up a decent selection of Egyptian and international favourites.

★ Sawa Camp
BEACH CAMP $

(☏ 0100 272 2838; www.sawacamp.com; Mahash area; s/d hut E£95/160) A strip of perfect white beach, hammocks on every hut porch, solar-powered showers and a restaurant dishing up delicious meals: Sawa ticks all the boxes for a laid-back, family-friendly travel stop that's great for unwinding. Bedouin owner Salama has got all the little touches right. Simple *hoosha* (palm-thatch) huts all have electricity and the communal bathrooms are kept spotless.

★ Nakhil Inn
HOTEL $$

(☏ 350 0879; www.nakhil-inn.com; Tarabin; s/d €35/42; ❈ 🛜) The friendly Nakhil is a cosy compromise for those who want hotel comforts without the crowds. The charming studio-style wooden cabins exude simple beach chic. Guests can snorkel the reef just a few metres from the shore, go kayaking or diving, or simply unwind while lazing about in one of the hammocks or seating spots along the private beach.

Habiba Village
BEACH CAMP $$

(☏ 0122 217 6624; www.habibavillage.com; Nuweiba City; s/d/tr €29/39/49; ❈ 🛜) ✦ The rooms are a little rough around the edges for the price but are set around a quiet courtyard that's a hop, skip and jump from a nice beach with a good snorkelling reef. Management is engaged in a local permaculture project and has set up an organic farm where interested long-stayers (three month minimum commitment) can volunteer.

Basata
BEACH CAMP $$

(☏ 350 0481; www.basata.com; Ras Burgaa area; campsites per person €12, s/d hut €23/40, 3-person chalets €80) Basata (meaning 'simplicity' in Arabic) is an ecologically minded settlement that uses organically grown produce and recycles its rubbish. Self-catering is the norm – there's a communal kitchen and cooking ingredients are available to buy – but it does serve dinner for those feeling lazy. The ambience is laid-back and family friendly with a New Age twist.

🍴 Eating

Eating options in Nuweiba are limited. Fuul and ta'amiyya places cluster at the port. There's a supermarket in Nuweiba City, and a sprinkling of open-air eateries among the camps on Tarabin's promenade.

Cleopatra Restaurant
SEAFOOD $$

(Nuweiba City; dishes E£20-50) One of the more popular tourist restaurants in Nuweiba City, Cleopatra offers up the bounty of the sea along with a few Western fast-food favourites.

ℹ Information

The post and telephone offices are next to the tiny bus station in the Nuweiba Port area. Near the port and bus station, the Banque Misr, Banque du Caire and National Bank of Egypt branches have ATMs but will not change Jordanian dinars. In Nuweiba City, the **National Bank of Egypt** (Helnan Nuweiba) has an ATM. The **Almostakbal Internet Café** (Nuweiba City; per hr E£4; ☺ 9am-3am) is behind Dr Shishkebab in Nuweiba City.

BOAT

There are ferries to Aqaba in Jordan, but service is erratic.

BUS

Buses going to or from Taba stop at both the port and its nearby bus station. You can also request that they stop outside the hospital in Nuweiba City, but this is on the whim of the driver. Buses don't stop at Tarabin. **East Delta Travel Co** (☑ 352 0371; Nuweiba Port) has buses at 9am, noon and 3pm to Taba (E£15, one hour). The 9am and 3pm continue to Cairo, but foreigners are not allowed on the Taba–Cairo road. Buses to Sharm el-Sheikh (E£30, three to four hours) via Dahab (E£15, one hour) leave at 6.30am and 4pm.

SERVEES

Taxis and a couple of *servees* cars hang out by the port. Unless you get there when the ferry has arrived from Aqaba, you'll have to wait a long time for a *servees* to fill up. A taxi to Dahab costs about E£150 and roughly E£100 to the beach camps on the Nuweiba–Taba road.

Taba طابا

☑ 069

This busy border crossing between Egypt and Israel is open 24 hours but you should check your government's travel advisory before using it (at the time of writing, there were warnings against travelling in this part of Sinai). Just inside the border are an ATM and several foreign-exchange booths. Cash and travellers cheques can also be exchanged at the Taba Hilton. The town has a couple of banks, a small hospital and various shops.

Taxis and minibuses wait just past the border on the Egypt side. Per-person fares are about E£15 to Nuweiba, E£30 to Dahab and E£45 to Sharm el-Sheikh. But if business is slack, you may have a long wait for the vehicle to fill up. You could pay for the remaining seats, or head for the bus station, about 800m south of the border. **East Delta Travel Co** (☑ 353 0250) has buses to Nuweiba (E£15, one hour) at 3pm and 4pm; the 3pm bus carries on to Dahab (E£30, 2½ hours) and Sharm el-Sheikh (E£45, four hours). There is a bus to Cairo via Nakhl, but foreigners are not allowed to take it. The only road open to foreigners is via Sharm el-Sheikh.

NORTH SINAI

Rarely visited by tourists, northern Sinai has a barren desert interior, much of which is off limits to foreigners, and a palm-fringed Mediterranean coast backed by soft white sands sculpted into low dunes.

The region is home to several violent groups and the situation on the ground is extremely fluid, with outbreaks of violence and bombing campaigns occurring with no prior warning. Travellers should heed travel advisories before planning any journeys here.

UNDERSTAND EGYPT

Egypt Today

Egyptians seemed united in January 2011 when they forced President Hosni Mubarak from power, but they have been increasingly divided ever since. The Muslim Brotherhood made history when their candidate, Mohammed Morsi, became the first democratically elected president in an open election that pitched him against a former Mubarak minister. But within a year of Morsi's election, millions were back in the streets, this time protesting against his increasingly Islamist and exclusive agenda. The army intervened to remove him from power and crushed his supporters in months of bloodshed. With two presidents in prison awaiting trials, the former army chief, Abdel Fattah al-Sisi, won the presidential election and has overseen a clampdown on the Muslim Brotherhood and pro-democracy activitists. Parliamentary elections have been promised. Most Egyptians are significantly worse off than when they rose up against Mubarak and hope the future will bring a more stable and prosperous life.

History

Ancient Egypt

For centuries before 3000 BC, the fertility and regularity of the annual Nile floods supported communities along the Nile valley. These small kingdoms eventually coalesced into two important states, one covering the valley, the other consisting of the Delta itself.

The pharaoh Menes' (Narmer's) unification of these two states in about 3100 BC set the scene for the greatest civilisation of ancient times.

Little is known of the immediate successors of Menes except that, attributed with divine ancestry, they promoted the development of a highly stratified society, patronised the arts and built numerous temples and public works. In the 27th century BC, Egypt's pyramids began to materialise. Ruling from nearby Memphis, the Pharaoh Zoser and his chief architect, Imhotep, built what may have been the first – the Step Pyramid at Saqqara.

For the next three dynasties and 500 years (a period called the Old Kingdom), the power of Egypt's pharaohs, and the size and scale of their pyramids and temples increased dramatically. The immense dimensions of these buildings served as a reminder of the pharaoh's importance and power over his people. The last three pharaohs of the 4th dynasty, Khufu (Cheops), Khafre (Chephren) and Menkaure (Mycerinus), left their legendary mark by commissioning the three Great Pyramids of Giza.

The New Kingdom, its capital at Thebes and later Memphis, represented a renaissance of art and empire in Pharaonic Egypt. For almost 400 years, from the 18th to the 20th dynasties (1550–1069 BC), Egypt was a formidable power in northeast Africa and the eastern Mediterranean. But by the time Ramses III came to power (1184 BC) as the second pharaoh of the 20th dynasty, disunity had again become the norm. Taking advantage of this, the army of Alexander the Great took control of Egypt in the 4th century BC.

Alexander founded a new capital, Alexandria, on the Mediterranean coast, and for the next 300 years the land of the Nile was ruled by a dynasty established by one of the Macedonian's generals, Ptolemy. Romans followed the Ptolemaic dynasty, during which time Christianity took hold. Then came Islam and the Arabs, conquering Egypt in AD 640. In due course, rule by the Ottoman Turks and the Europeans followed (the French under Napoleon, then the British) – shifts of power common to much of the Middle East.

Modern Egypt

Egyptian self-rule was restored through the Revolution of 1952, led by the Free Officers. Colonel Gamal Abdel Nasser, the coalition's leader, was confirmed as president in elections in 1956 and successfully faced down Britain, France and Israel to reclaim the Suez Canal. Nasser was unsuccessful, however, in the 1967 war with Israel, and died shortly after of heart failure. Anwar Sadat, his successor, also fought Israel, in 1973. The eventual outcome of the so-called October War was the 1979 Camp David Agreement, which established peace with Israel. In certain quarters, Camp David was viewed as treacherous abandonment of Nasser's pan-Arab principles; it ultimately cost Sadat his life at the hands of an assassin in 1981.

Sadat's murderer was a member of the terrorist organisation Islamic Jihad. Sadat's successor, Hosni Mubarak, reinstated emergency law and cracked down on Islamist groups. For almost three decades, Mubarak managed to control the domestic political situation – and the Muslim Brotherhood.

LIFE AFTER DEATH

Ancient Egyptians developed an intricate belief system around death and the afterlife. Life in the beyond was believed to be a vast improvement on life on earth, and you literally could take everything with you. Burial chambers were packed with life's necessities: household goods, riches and even family members and slaves – anything that might come in handy for a long and comfy life ever after. Corpses were ritually cleaned, hollowed out and mummified to create a body that would be useful for an eternity on the other side.

Belief had it that after death the deceased would travel along a treacherous river to the Hall of Final Judgement, where one's life would be reviewed by Anubis, god of mummification. A scale was used to measure the weight of one's heart against the 'feather of truth'. The heart was thought to hold a record of all the deeds of one's life, and if a heart was lighter than the feather (and thus chaste), eternal life with the gods was granted. If the heart was heavy with guilt and outweighed the feather, the deceased was consumed by Ammit, a hybrid crocodile, lion and hippopotamus creature, to disappear forever.

But discontent brewed among the poorer sections of society as the country's economic situation worsened. Frequent attempts were made on the life of the president and his ministers. In 1997 another Islamist group, Gama'a al-Islamiyya, carried out a bloody massacre of 58 holidaymakers and four Egyptians at the Temple of Hatshepsut in Luxor. The massacre crippled the economy and destroyed grassroots support for militant groups. The Muslim Brotherhood declared a ceasefire the following year and entered the political process. It won the 2012 presidential election, following the overthrow of Mubarak, but its lack of experience in running a government quickly alientated it from the majority of Egyptians, especially when President Morsi pushed through an Islamist constitution without sufficient consultation. Since his overthrow in the summer of 2013, the military has ruled, either directly, or through the election of former field marshal, now President Sisi.

People

With 87 million people, Egypt has the third-largest population in Africa (after Nigeria and Ethiopia) and is also the most populous country in the Arab world.

The blood of the pharaohs flows in the veins of many Egyptians today, but centuries of invading Libyans, Persians, Greeks, Romans, Arabs and Turks have added to the mix. Some independent indigenous groups persist: the nomadic Bedouin tribes, now for the most part settled in Sinai and Egypt's deserts; the Berbers of Siwa Oasis; and dark-skinned Nubians from the regions south of Aswan that were swallowed up by the High Dam.

About 90% of Egypt's population is Muslim; much of the remainder is Coptic Christian. Most of the time, the two communities peacefully coexist, although sectarian divisions come to the fore periodically. Islam permeates most aspects of Egypt's culture, from social norms and mores to laws, but Egypt does not follow Sharia law and Islamic fundamentalism is supported only by a minority.

Arts

Literature

Egypt's literary pride is Naguib Mahfouz (1911–2006), awarded the Nobel Prize for literature in 1988; his Cairo Trilogy was some of the first work to sympathetically portray working-class Egyptians. Other notable Egyptian writers include feminist Nawal al-Saadawi, an outspoken critic on behalf of women; her nonfiction book *The Hidden Face of Eve* is still banned in Egypt. As interested with workaday Egyptians as Mahfouz and as outspoken as Al-Saadawi, Alaa al-Aswany is best known for his meldodramatic but enthralling novel *The Yacoubian Building*, the world's best-selling novel in Arabic.

Cinema

Egypt's golden years were the 1940s and 1950s, when Cairo studios turned out more than 100 movies a year, filling cinemas throughout the Arab world with charming musicals that are still classics of regional cinema. Egypt's best-known director is Youssef Chahine (1926–2008), honoured at Cannes in 1997 with a lifetime achievement award. The political upheavals of recent years has seen a revival of Egypt's filmmakers: *The Square*, a documentary by Jehane Noujaim about Cairo's Tahrir Square during the antiMubarak protests was nominated for an Oscar and won several other awards in 2014.

ESSENTIAL EGYPTIAN FOOD & DRINK

Fiteer The Egyptian pizza, with a flaky pastry base and either sweet or savoury toppings.

Fuul Slow-cooked fava beans, mashed more than in neighbouring countries.

Hamam mahshi Roast pigeon stuffed with *fireek* (green wheat) and rice.

Kushari A vegetarian's best friend: noodles, rice, black lentils, chickpeas and fried onions, with a tangy tomato sauce.

Molokhiyya A slippery, garlicky leafy green soup, served with rabbit or chicken.

Ta'amiya What Egyptians call felafel, packed with herbs and shaped into flat patties.

Music

Alongside cinema, classical Arabic music peaked in the 1950s, the prime years of iconic diva Umm Kolthum. The country came to a standstill during her weekly live radio broadcast of lovelorn songs, some upwards of an hour long. Contemporary music is more lightweight, in the form of pop stars like Amr Diab, known across the Arab world for catchy choruses and loads of synthesisers. During the 2011 revolution, protest songs filled the air, and hip hop has also inspired many working-class performers.

Food & Drink

Egyptian food is an earthy variant of Middle Eastern cuisine – a mix of dishes from Turkish, Levantine, Greek and ancient Egyptian traditions. Compared with its neighbours, Egyptian cuisine might seem to lack refinement and diversity, but the food here is good, honest peasant fare that packs an occasional sensational punch. High points include seafood on the Mediterranean coast, pickled vegetables with loads of garlic, succulent mangoes in summer and fresh dates in autumn, and a dish called *kushari* (a mix of noodles, rice, black lentils, fried onions and tomato sauce) for a carbohydrate load. Wash it down with ubiquitous tea or an ice-cold beer.

SURVIVAL GUIDE

ⓘ Directory A–Z

ACCOMMODATION

Good hostels in Egypt are rare, but there are loads of excellent budget hotels. Decent midrange hotels are harder to find. At the top end, the major international chains are represented in the larger cities and there are a very few exceptional independently owned and run boutique hotels.

Winter (December to February) is high season, with higher hotel rates; June to August is the low season, except on the coasts, and to a lesser degree in Cairo.

Rates can usually be negotiated in off-peak seasons, during the middle of the week and if the downturn in tourism continues. Many hotels will take US dollars or euros in payment. Some higher-end places even request it. Lower-end hotels usually demand cash payment, though

---

ⓘ SLEEPING PRICE RANGES

Prices in reviews are for rooms in the winter high season (December to February), and include breakfast and taxes unless otherwise indicated.

$ less than E£250

$$ E£250 to E£750

$$$ more than E£750

---

it's not a given that all upmarket hotels accept credit cards.

CHILDREN

➡ Egyptians are extraordinarily welcoming to children, but Egypt's budget and midrange hotels rarely have child-friendly facilities. Cots, babysitting services and other amenities are usually available only in top-end hotels.

➡ Restaurants everywhere are very welcoming to families, and high chairs are sometimes available.

➡ Towns and cities have few parks with playground equipment. Fortunately, there are other things kids find cool: felucca and camel rides, exploring the interiors of pyramids and snorkelling on Sinai reefs are only a few.

➡ Formula is readily available in pharmacies, and supermarkets stock disposable nappies.

DISCOUNT CARDS

The International Student Identity Card (ISIC) gives significant discounts on some museum and site entries. Some travellers have also been able to get the discount with HI cards and Eurail cards.

To get an ISIC in Cairo, visit **Egyptian Student Travel Services** (Map p56; ☎ 02-2363 7251, 02-2531 0330; www.estsegypt.com; 23 Sharia al-Manial, Rhoda Island). You'll need a university ID card, a photocopy of your passport and one photo. Beware counterfeit operations in Downtown Cairo.

ⓘ MILITARY PERMITS

For extended wilderness trips, you may need military permits. They are required for the Eastern Desert south of Shams Allam (50km south of Marsa Allam), around Lake Nasser, between Bahariyya and Siwa and off-road in the Western Desert. Safari companies can usually obtain them but may need two weeks' notice.

EMBASSIES & CONSULATES

Australian Embassy (Map p56; ☎02-2770 6600; www.egypt.embassy.gov.au; 11th fl, World Trade Centre, 1191 Corniche el-Nil, Cairo; ☉8am-4.15pm Sun-Wed, to-1.30pm Thu) Located 1km north of 26th of July Bridge, Cairo

Canadian Embassy (Map p56; ☎02-2791 8700; www.canadainternational.gc.ca/egypt-egypte; 26 Sharia Kamel ash-Shenawy, Garden City, Cairo; ☉8am-4.30pm Sun-Wed, 8am-1.30pm Thu)

Dutch Embassy (Map p70; ☎02-2739 5500; http://egypt.nlembassy.org; 18 Sharia Hassan Sabry, Zamalek, Cairo; ☉8am-4pm Sun-Thu) It's 1km north of 26th of July Bridge.

Ethiopian Embassy & Consulate Cairo Embassy (Map p56; ☎02-3335 3696; ethio@ethioembassy.org.eg; Villa 11, Midan Messaha, Doqqi) Cairo Consulate (21 Sharia Sheikh Mohamed al-Ghazali, Doqqi, Cairo Street; ☉Sun-Thu 8.30am-4pm)

French Embassy & Consulate (www.ambafrance-eg.org) Cairo Embassy (Map p56; ☎Embassy 02-35673200, 29 av. Sharia Charles de Gaulle, Giza, Cairo) Cairo Consulate (☎02-35673350; 7 Sharia Abi Shammar, Giza, Cairo) Alexandria Consulate (Map p80; ☎03-34847950; 2 Midan Ahmed Orabi, Mansheya, Alexandria; ☉Sun-Thu 9.30am-5pm)

German Embassy & Consulates (www.kairo.diplo.de) Cairo Embassy (Map p70; ☎02-27282000, 2 Sharia Berlin, off Sharia Hassan Sabry, Zamalek; ☉Sun-Thu 9am-noon) Alexandria Consulate (Map p78; ☎03-4867503; 9 Sharia el-Fawatem, Mazarita; ☉Mon-Thu 12.30pm-2pm) Hurghada Consulate (☎065-344 3605; 365 Sharia al-Gabal al-Shamali)

Iranian Embassy (Map p56; ☎02-3348 6492; 12 Sharia Refa'a, off Midan al-Misaha, Doqqi, Cairo; ☉7.30am-2.30pm Sat-Thu)

Irish Embassy (Map p70; ☎02-2735 8264; www.embassyofireland.org.eg; 22 Hassan Assem, Zamalek, Cairo; ☉9am-noon Sun-Thu)

Israeli Embassy & Consulate (embassies.gov.il; ☉10am-12.30pm Sun-Thu) Cairo Embassy (Map p56; ☎02-3332 1500; 6 Sharia Ibn Malek, Giza) Alexandria Consulate (☎03-544 9501; 15 Sharia Mena, Rushdy)

Italian Embassy & Consulate (ambasciata.cairo@esteri.it) Cairo Embassy (Map p56; ☎02-2794 3194; 15 Sharia Abd al-Rahman Fahmy, Garden City) Alexandria Consulate (Map p80; ☎03-487 9470; 25 Midan Saad Zaghloul)

Jordanian Embassy (Map p56; ☎02-3749 9912; 6 Sharia Gohainy, Cairo)

Lebanese Embassy & Consulate (www.lebembassyegypt.org) Cairo Embassy (Map p70; ☎02-2738 2823; 22 Sharia Mansour Mohammed, Zamalek; ☉9am-12pm Sun-Thu)

Alexandria Consulate (Map p78; ☎03-484 6589; 64 Sharia Tariq al-Horreyya)

Libyan Embassy & Consulate Cairo Embassy (Map p70; ☎02-735 1269; 7 Sharia el-Saleh Ayoub, Zamalek) Alexandria Consulate (Map p78; ☎494 0877; 4 Sharia Batris Lumomba)

New Zealand Embassy (Map p56; ☎02-2461 6000; www.nzembassy.com; Level 8, North Tower, Nile City Towers, 2005 Corniche el-Nil, Cairo; ☉9am-3pm Sun-Thu)

Saudi Arabian Embassy & Consulates (☎02-3774 9800; egemb@mofa.gov.sa) Cairo Embassy (Map p56; ☎02-3761 4308; 2 Sharia Ahmed Nessim, Giza; ☉8am-3pm Sat-Thu) Alexandria Consulate (Map p78; ☎03-497 7951; 12 Sharia Jabarti) Suez Consulate (☎062-333 4016; 10 Sharia Abbas al-Akkad, Port Tawfiq)

Spanish Embassy & Consulate (emb.elcairo@maec.es) Cairo Embassy (☎02-2735 6462; 41 Ismail Mohamed, Zamalek) Alexandria Consulate (☎0100 340 7177; 101 Sharia Tariq al-Horreyya)

Sudanese Embassy & Consulate Cairo Embassy (Map p56; ☎02-2794 9661; 3 El Ibrahimi, Garden City; ☉9am-3pm Sun-Thu) Aswan Consulate (☎097-230 7231; Bldg 20, Atlas)

Turkish Embassy & Consulate Cairo Embassy (Map p56; ☎02-2797 8400; 25 Sharia Falaki, Mounira) Alexandria Consulate (Map p78; ☎03-399 0700; 11 Sharia Kamel el-Kilany)

UK Embassy & Consulate (www.ukinegypt.fco.gov.uk, consular.cairo@fco.gov.uk) Cairo Embassy (Map p56; ☎02-2791 6000; 7 Sharia Ahmed Ragheb, Garden City; ☉8am-3.30pm Sun-Wed, 8am-2pm Thu) Alexandria Consulate (☎03-546 7001; Sharia Mena, Rushdy; ☉10am-1pm Sun-Thu)

US Embassy (Map p56; ☎02-2797 3300; www.egypt.usembassy.gov; 5 Sharia Tawfiq Diab, Garden City, Cairo; ☉9am-4pm Sun-Thu)

FOOD

Many restaurants do not quote taxes (10%) in the menu prices, and will also add 12% for 'service', but this is typically used to cover wait-staff salaries and is not strictly a bonus. So an additional cash tip, paid directly to your server, is nice.

ⓘ EATING PRICE RANGES

Prices in reviews represent the cost of a standard main-course dish.

$ less than E£20

$$ E£20 to E£80

$$$ more than E£80

GAY & LESBIAN TRAVELLERS

In early 2014 an Egyptian court convicted four men of the 'crime' of gay sex: they were sentenced to a total of 28 years in prison. Eighty more were arrested. The situation remains very tense. However, plenty of same-sex activity goes on, ever more discreetly.

MONEY

Change There is a sometimes a shortage of small change, which is invaluable for tips, taxi fares and more. Withdraw odd amounts from ATMs to avoid a stack of unwieldy E£200 notes, hoard small bills and always try to break big bills at fancier establishments.

Currency Egyptian pound (E£), *guinay* in Arabic, divided into 100 piastres (pt).

Exchange rate The government sets the exchange rate, which has moved significantly downwards since 2011.

Notes and coins 5pt, 10pt and 25pt coins are basically extinct; 50pt notes and coins are on their way. E£1 coins are the most commonly used small change, while E£5, E£10, E£20, E£50, E£100 and E£200 notes are commonly used.

Prices Produce markets and some other venues sometimes write prices in piastres: E£3.50 as 350pt, for example.

ATMs

Cash machines are common, except in Middle Egypt and the oases, where you may find only one. Then you'll be stuck if there's a technical problem, so load up before going somewhere remote. Banque Misr, CIB, Egyptian American Bank and HSBC are the most reliable.

Credit Cards

Major cards are accepted in most midrange-and-up establishments. In remote areas they remain useless. You may be charged a percentage of the sale (anywhere between 3% and 10%).

Moneychangers

Money can be changed at Amex and Thomas Cook offices, as well as commercial banks, foreign exchange (forex) bureaux and some hotels. Rates don't vary much, but forex bureaux usually don't charge commission. Don't accept bills that are badly defaced, shabby or torn because you'll have difficulty offloading them later.

Tipping & Bargaining

Bargaining is a part of everyday life in Egypt and people haggle for everything from hotel rooms to clothes. (The exceptions are places like supermarkets, and among friends.) Tipping, called baksheesh, is another fact of life. Salaries are extremely low and are supplemented by tips. In hotels and restaurants the 12% service charge goes into the till; an additional tip of between 10% and 15% is expected for the waiter. When in doubt, tip.

SERVICE	TIP
Ahwa or cafe	E£3-5
Hotel staff (collective)	E£15-20 per guest per day
Informal mosque or monument guide	E£10-20 (more if you climb a minaret)
Meter taxi	5%
Restaurant	10-15%
Shoe attendant in mosque	E£5-10
Toilet attendant	E£5-10

OPENING HOURS

The weekend is Friday and Saturday; some businesses close Sunday. During Ramadan, offices, museums and tourist sites keep shorter hours.

Banks 8.30am to 2.30pm Sunday to Thursday

Bars and clubs Early evening until 3am, often later (particularly in Cairo)

Cafes 7am to 1am

Government offices 8am to 2pm Sunday to Thursday. Tourist offices are generally open longer

Post offices 8.30am to 2pm Saturday to Thursday

Private offices 10am to 2pm and 4pm to 9pm Saturday to Thursday

Restaurants Noon to midnight

Shops 9am to 1pm and 5pm to 10pm June to September, 10am to 6pm October to May

PUBLIC HOLIDAYS

In addition to the main Islamic holidays, Egypt celebrates the following public holidays:

New Year's Day 1 January – Official holiday but many businesses stay open.

Coptic Christmas 7 January – Most government offices and all Coptic businesses close.

National Police Day 25 January – Now overshadowed by the 2011 uprising, which began on this day.

Sham an-Nessim March/April – First Monday after Coptic Easter, this tradition with

---

ESSENTIAL EGYPTIAN VOCAB

Mafeesh Mushkila No problem, dude!

Malish Whatever...don't worry about it.

Khalas It's over, finished, OK, understand?

Mumkin Possibly or please or maybe.

SHOPPING

So great is the quantity of junk souvenirs in Egypt that it can easily hide the good stuff – but if you persist, you'll find some treasures. Look out for modern housewares using traditional techniques, and Siwan, Bedouin and Nubian handicrafts. Followinghe most popular items, available in every tourist destination in the country:

Appliqué and fabric On geometric and figurative tablecloths, pillowcases and more, stitches should be barely visible. Printed fabric used for tents is inexpensive when sold by the metre (about E£10).

Gold and silver Gold and silver are sold by weight. Check the international market price before you buy, then add some extra for work.

Perfume Essential oils are often diluted with vegetable oil. Watch when your bottles are packed up – make sure they're filled from the stock you sampled.

Papyrus True papyrus is heavy and difficult to tear, and veins should be visible in the light. A small painting on faux papyrus (made from banana leaves) can go for just E£10; a good-quality piece can easily be 10 times as much.

Spices Buy whole spices, never ground, for freshness, and skip the 'saffron' – it's really safflower and tastes of little more than dust.

Pharaonic roots is celebrated by all Egyptians, with family picnics. Few businesses close.

Sinai Liberation Day 25 April

May Day 1 May – Labour Day

Revolution Day 23 July – Date of the 1952 coup

Armed Forces Day 6 October

SAFE TRAVEL

You're generally safe walking around Egypt day or night but security has been less sure since 2011. Women should take special care. Bag and wallet snatchings have increased, often as drive-bys on mopeds. Carry your bag across your body, and keep it looped around a chair leg in restaurants. Don't walk on empty streets late at night

More common theft, such as items stolen from locked hotel rooms and even from safes, is a possibility, so secure your belongings in a locked suitcase.

Generally, unwary visitors are parted from their money through scams.

TELEPHONE

Area codes Leave off the initial zero when calling from outside Egypt.

Country code ☑ 20

Directory assistance ☑ 140 or ☑ 141

International access code from Egypt ☑ 00

Mobile Phones

Egypt's GSM network (on the 900MHz/1800MHz band) has thorough coverage, at least in urban areas. SIM cards from any of the three carriers (Vodafone, the largest; Mobinil; Etisalat) cost E£15. You can buy them and top-up cards from most kiosks, and you may be asked to show a passport. For pay-as-you-go data service (about E£5 per day or E£50 per month), register at a company phone shop.

Public Phones

Pay phones (from yellow-and-green Menatel and red-and-blue Nile Tel) are card-operated. Cards are sold at shops and kiosks. After you insert the card into the telephone, press the flag in the top left corner to get instructions in English.

Alternatively, telephone centrales are offices where you book a call at the desk, pay in advance for three minutes, then take your call in a booth. Centrales also offer fax services.

TIME

Egypt is two hours ahead of GMT/UTC.

TOURIST INFORMATION

The **Egyptian Tourist Authority** (www.egypt. travel) has offices throughout the country. Individual staff members may be helpful, but often they're doling out rather dated maps and brochures. Smaller towns and oases tend to have better offices than big cities. In short, don't rely on these offices, but don't rule them out either.

TRAVELLERS WITH DISABILITIES

Egypt for All (☑ 0122-396 1991; www.egypt-forall.com; 334 Sharia Sudan, Mohandiseen, Cairo) This organisation specialises in organising travel arrangements for travellers who are mobility impaired.

VISAS

Visas are required for most foreigners, although travel in Sinai between Sharm el-Sheikh and Taba (including St Katherine's Monastery but not Ras Mohammed National Park) requires no visa, only a free entry stamp, good for a 15-day stay and only for citizens of the United Kingdom, the United States and European Union.

Places of Issue

Visas are available for most nationalities at the airport on arrival (though check before departure), and are typically valid for 30 days. If you want more time, apply in advance or get an extension once in Egypt. Payment is accepted in US dollars, UK pounds and euros.

If travelling overland from Jordan, visas are available at the port in Aqaba.

If travelling overland from Israel, visas at available at the border only if guaranteed by an Egyptian travel agency; otherwise, apply in advance in Tel Aviv or at the consulate in Eilat.

Extensions

Visa extensions used to be routine, but are now subject to scrutiny, especially after repeat extensions. There's a 14-day grace period for extension application, with E£100 late fee. If you leave during this time, you must pay a E£135 fine at the airport. Most large cities have passport offices for extensions.

Alexandria Passport office (Map p80; ☑ 03-482 7873; 2nd fl, 25 Sharia Talaat Harb; ⏰ 8.30am-2pm Mon-Thu, 10am-2pm Fri, 9am-11am Sat & Sun) Off Sharia Salah Salem.

Aswan Passport office (Map p98; ☑ 097-231 2238; 1st fl, Police Bldg, Corniche an-Nil; ⏰ 8.30am-1pm Sat-Thu)

Cairo Mogamma (Map p62; Mogamma Bldg, Midan Tahrir, Downtown; ⏰ 8am-1.30pm Sat-Wed) Get a form from window 12 on the 1st floor, then stamps from window 43 and file it all back at window 12; next-day pick-up is at window 38.

Luxor Passport office (Map p86; ☑ 095-238 0885; Sharia Khalid ibn al-Walid; ⏰ 8am-2pm Sat-Thu) Almost opposite the Isis Pyramisa Hotel, south of the centre. There's a branch in the west bank, near the Antiquities Inspectorate Ticket Office.

VISA COSTS

Australia	A$35
Canada	C$25
Euro zone	€25
Israel	65NIS
Japan	¥5500
New Zealand	NZ$45
UK	UK£15
USA	US$15

🛈 PRACTICALITIES

Alcohol Available, typically only at higher-end restaurants and tourist spots. Drinking on the street is taboo, as is public drunkenness.

Electricity 220V, using the European two round-pin plug.

Newspapers The independent English newspaper the *Daily News Egypt* is available online at www.dailynewsegypt.com.

Security Checkpoints are common on highways outside Cairo. Carry your passport with you.

Smoking Common in Egypt, including in restaurants and bars. Sheesha (hookah or water pipe) is a common social pastime. It delivers substantially more nicotine than a cigarette.

Water Tap water in Egypt is not considered safe to drink, with the exception of Cairo, where it's drinkable but not palatable.

Weights and measures Egypt uses the metric system.

WOMEN TRAVELLERS

In public at least, Egypt is a man's world, and solo women will certainly receive comments in the street – some polite, others less so – and possible groping. As small consolation, street harassment is a major problem for Egyptian women as well. With basic smarts, the constant male attention can be at least relegated to background irritation.

➡ Wear long sleeves and pants or skirts. Sunglasses also deflect attention.

➡ Carry a scarf to cover your head inside mosques.

➡ Outside of Red Sea resorts, swim in shorts and a T-shirt at least.

➡ A wedding ring sometimes helps, but it's more effective if your 'husband' (any male travel companion) is present. Most effective: travel with a child.

➡ Keep your distance. Even innocent, friendly talk can be misconstrued as flirtation, as can any physical contact.

➡ Ignore obnoxious comments – if you respond to every one, you'll wear yourself out, and public shaming seldom gets satisfying results.

➡ Avoid city buses at peak times; the crowds make them prime groping zones.

➡ Bring tampons and contraceptives with you; outside of Cairo, they can be expensive.

ℹ Getting There & Away

Egypt's borders are open to neighbouring countries, but at the time of writing, we do not recommend that you use them all. Travel in Libya and through northern Sinai is not safe. A ferry runs once a week between Aswan and Sudan. A ferry also operates from Nuweiba to Aqaba in Jordan. By air, Cairo is the obvious international hub, but Alexandria, Hughada, Luxor and Sharm el-Sheikh also receive direct flights.

ENTERING EGYPT

At Cairo and other international airports, the main formality is getting a visa, if you haven't arranged one in advance. Visas are sold at a row of bank booths in every arrivals terminal. Pay cash in foreign currency, then present the sticker with your arrival form and passport at the immigration desks. By land or sea, the process is similar. Your passport must be valid for at least six months from your date of entry.

Israeli stamps in your passport (and Israeli passports, for that matter) are not a problem.

AIR

Aswan, Hurghada and Marsa Alam handle international charter flights.

Alexandria Has become a viable alternate airport, especially for low-cost carriers **Air Arabia** (www.airarabia.com) and **flydubai** (www.flydubai.com).

Cairo Served by all the major international carriers, including good-value **EgyptAir** (www.egyptair.com). Air Sinai (really just EgyptAir in disguise) flies from Tel Aviv; buy tickets at the unmarked office at Ben Yehuda and Allenby.

Luxor Receives direct international flights from London (EgyptAir). **EasyJet** (www.easyjet.com) may resume its service from London Gatwick.

Sharm el-Sheikh Served by a number of European and Middle Eastern budget airlines. Arrive here only if you'll be spending time in the Sinai and Jordan; otherwise, it's an eight-hour bus ride to Cairo.

LAND

Border Crossings

The only land border shared by the rest of the Middle East is with Israel and the Palestinian Territories.

Rafah With a few exceptions, Egypt has kept the Rafah crossing between Sinai and Gaza closed since 2013. When and if it reopens, it is unlikely to be usable by leisure travellers.

Taba The border at Taba is open, but we do not recommend that you use it. North Sinai was not safe for travellers at the time of research. A bus was attacked at the Taba crossing in 2014, killing four people.

> ### ℹ PORT TAX
>
> All Egyptian international ferries charge US$10/E£50 port tax per person on top of the ticket price.

SEA

There are ferries between Egypt and Jordan, Saudi Arabia and Sudan.

Israel & the Palestinian Territories

There's been talk about resuming the boat service from Port Said to Haifa. At the time of writing, this service was still nonexistent. Contact **Varianos Travel** (www.varianostravel.com) in Cyprus.

Jordan

Public Ferries AB Maritime run both a fast and slow ferry connecting Nuweiba in Egypt and Aqaba in Jordan, but the service is erratic and delay times can be as much as 20 hours.

Visas Most nationalities are entitled to receive a free Jordanian visa upon arrival in Aqaba. You hand in your passport to the immigration officials onboard the ferry and collect it in the immigration building in Aqaba.

Saudi Arabia

Ferries run from Hurghada to Duba, though they are not recommended due to erratic schedules, which fluctuate according to work and hajj seasons. Note that tourist visas are not available for Saudi Arabia, though there is an elusive tourist transit visa, which you must apply for well in advance.

ℹ Getting Around

AIR

EgyptAir (www.egyptair.com) is the only domestic carrier, and fares can be surprisingly cheap, though they vary considerably depending on season. Domestic one-way fares can be less than US$100.

BICYCLE

Cairo-based club **Cycle Egypt** (www.cycle-egypt.com), and its very active Facebook group, is a good starting point for making local contacts and getting advice on shops and gear. Also check the Thorn Tree travel forum on www.lonelyplanet.com, where there's a dedicated section for cyclists.

BOAT

No trip to Egypt is complete without a trip down the Nile. You can take the trip on a felucca (a traditional sailboat) or opt for a modern steamer or cruise ship.

At the time of research, the boat service from Hurghada to Sharm el-Sheikh was still not running.

BUS

You can get to most cities, towns and villages in Egypt on a bus, at a very reasonable price. For many long-distance routes beyond the Nile Valley, it's the best option, and sometimes the only one. Buses aren't necessarily fast, though, and if you're going to or from Cairo, you'll lose at least an hour just in city traffic. Delays are common, especially later in the day as schedules get backed up. When buying tickets, it's a good idea to have a rough idea beforehand of costs, so you don't get sold a standard bus ticket at deluxe-bus prices.

CAR & MOTORCYCLE

Proceed with caution. Driving in Cairo is a crazy affair, and only slightly less nerve-racking in other parts of the country (night driving should be completely avoided). But some intrepid readers have reported that driving is a wonderful way to leave the tour buses in the dust.

A motorcycle would be a good way to travel around Egypt, but you must bring your own, and the red tape is extensive. Ask your country's automobile association and Egyptian embassy about regulations.

An International Driving Permit is required to drive in Egypt, and you risk a heavy fine if you're caught without one. Likewise, ensure that you always have all car registration papers with you while driving.

LOCAL TRANSPORT

Bus

Several of the biggest Egyptian cities have bus systems. Practically speaking, you might use them only in Cairo and Alexandria. They're often overcrowded and rarely roll to a complete stop. Buy your ticket from the conductor.

Microbus

These 14-seat minivans run informally alongside city bus systems, or sometimes in lieu of them. For the average traveller they can be difficult to use, as they are unmarked. Typically you pay the driver from your seat.

Pick-up Trucks

Toyota and Chevrolet pick-up trucks cover some routes between smaller towns and villages off the main roads, especially where passengers might have cargo. Trucks are also sometimes used within towns. To indicate that you want to get out, pound on the floor with your foot; pay your fare to the driver when you get out.

Taxi

Even the smallest cities in Cairo have taxis. They're inexpensive and efficient, even if the cars themselves have seen better days.

Fares In Cairo metered taxis are taking over, but everywhere else, locals know the accepted price and pay it without (much) negotiation. Check with locals for guidelines on taxi rates, as fares change as petrol prices rise.

Negotiating For short fares, setting a price beforehand reveals you don't know the system. But for long distances – from the airport to the city centre, for instance – you should agree on a price before getting in.

Paying In unmetered taxis, get out first, then hand money through the window. If a driver suspects you don't know the correct fare, you'll get an aghast 'How could you possibly pay me so little?' look, if not a full-on argument. Don't be drawn in if you're sure of your position, but remember E£5 makes a far greater difference to your driver than it does to you.

MICROBUS

The microbus ('meekrobas'), often also called a micro or a minibus, is a Toyota van with seats for 14 passengers. They run most of the same routes that buses do, for a bit cheaper. They also stop anywhere on request, and will pick up riders along the way if there's a free seat. You can usually find one headed where you want to go, no matter the time of day.

Microbuses run on no schedule – they just wait until they're full, then take off. If you're in a hurry or just want more room, you can buy an extra seat. They usually congregate outside bus and train stations, or at major highway intersections on the edges of cities. Drivers shout their destinations; just shout yours back, and eventually you'll wind up in the right zone.

Pay the driver once you're underway. This involves passing your money up hand-to-hand through the rows; your change will be returned the same way.

TRAIN

Egypt's British-built rail system comprises more than 5000km of track to almost every major city and town, but not to the Sinai. The system is antiquated, and cars are often grubby and battered. Aside from two main routes (Cairo–Alexandria and Cairo–Aswan), you have to be fond of trains to prefer them to a deluxe bus, though 1st class is usually fine and still inexpensive. For destinations near Cairo, however, trains win because they don't get stuck in traffic.

For specific schedules, consult the **Egyptian Railways** (www.enr.gov.eg) website, where you can also purchase tickets.

Iran

Includes ➔

Best Places to Stay

➔ Kandovan Laleh Rocky Hotel (p153)

➔ Dibai House (p157)

➔ Niayesh Boutique Hotel (p167)

➔ Escan Hotel (p145)

Best Places to Eat

➔ Haft Khan (p169)

➔ Alborz (p145)

➔ Talar Yazd (p164)

➔ Baliq (p152)

Why Go?

Rewarding doesn't begin to cover Iran as a destination. This exceptionally welcoming country has a multifaceted history and rich, artistic culture manifested in myriad ways. Hospitality is a way of life here and chatting with locals over tea or a meal will likely provide your most memorable moments.

Stunning mosques, palaces and ruins from different eras provide architectural wonder, while the shopping culture of the brilliant bazaars adds a colour beyond description. The outdoors, too, is captivating, with baking deserts and soaring mountain ranges providing a spectacular backdrop wherever you gaze.

Good, cheap transport makes getting around easy and Iran is also very safe for travellers. Though Iranian citizens are often subject to government repression, culturally sensitive and respectful foreigners are unlikely to encounter problems. In fact, many travellers rate Iran as their most-memorable-ever travel experience: come and see why.

When to Go
Tehran

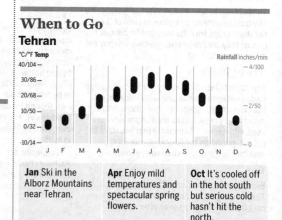

°C/°F Temp
Rainfall inches/mm

Jan Ski in the Alborz Mountains near Tehran.

Apr Enjoy mild temperatures and spectacular spring flowers.

Oct It's cooled off in the hot south but serious cold hasn't hit the north.

TEHRAN

تهران

📱 021 / POP 15.8 MILLION / ELEV 1184M

A sprawling metropolis and one of the world's 20 largest cities, Tehran is the beating heart of the nation. Iran's capital has a lovely natural setting, sloping down from the Alborz Mountains, through the boutiques and liberal atmosphere of the wealthy north to the poorer, lively south. Rapid growth has come at a cost: terrible traffic and constant pollution mean it's far from relaxing. Still, Tehran's immense cultural vitality, not to mention the impressive museums and galleries it's packed with, make it an intriguing place to visit.

History

Tehran wasn't particularly significant until it became the 19th-century centre of Qajar Persia and steadily expanded. By 1900 it had grown to 250,000 people, and in the 20th century it became one of the most populous cities on earth.

◉ Sights

◎ Central & Southern Tehran

Tehran Bazar　　　　　　　BAZAAR

(بازار تهران; Map p142; main entrance 15 Khordad Ave; ⊙7am-5pm Sat-Wed, to noon Thu; Ⓜ Panzdah-e Khordad) FREE This maze of bustling alleys makes for fascinating exploration. The warren of people and goods is a city within a city and includes guesthouses, restaurants and mosques. Most lanes specialise in a particular commodity: copper, paper, gold, spices and carpets, among others.

Golestan Palace　　　　　　PALACE

(کاخ گلستان; Map p142; www.golestanpalace.ir; Arg Sq; admission US$4.50, plus per sight US$1.50; ⊙9am-4.30pm Sun-Fri; Ⓜ Panzdah-e Khordad) This monument to the glories and excesses of the Qajar rulers is made up of several grand buildings set around a carefully manicured garden. Separate tickets cover each.

The **Negar Khane** (Art Gallery) displays a collection of Qajar-era paintings. Portraits of the shahs show dashing figures with catwalk poses and jewelled scabbards. The palace's centrepiece is the small but dazzling **Talar-e-Aineh** (Hall of Mirrors) and its enormous adjoining halls, with fine plaster moulding, mirrorwork, and gifts from European royals.

ⓘ NEED TO KNOW

➡ **Capital** Tehran

➡ **Country code** 📱98

➡ **Language** Farsi (Persian), Azari, Arabic, other ethnic languages

➡ **Official name** Islamic Republic of Iran

➡ **Population** 77.45 million

➡ **Currency** Iranian rial (IRR)

➡ **Mobile phones** Your foreign SIM may not work. Local SIMs easily obtained (p182).

➡ **Money** Foreign credit and debit cards don't work (p181). *Bring all you need in cash.*

➡ **Visas** Nearly all need a visa and US, UK and Canadian citizens will need a guide too (see p182).

Exchange Rates

Australia	A$1	IRR21,665
Canada	C$1	IRR22,444
Euro zone	€1	IRR29,914
Japan	¥100	IRR23,470
Turkey	1TKL	IRR10,735
UK	£1	IRR41,291
USA	US$1	IRR28,215

For official exchange rates, see Central Bank of Iran (www.cbi.ir).

➡ **Time** 3½ hours ahead of UTC/GMT. Daylight saving late March to late September.

➡ **Emergency** 📱115 (ambulance), 📱110 (police).

➡ **Dress** Women must conform to a dress code (p183).

➡ **Transport** Good network of buses, trains, shuttle taxis and domestic flights (p183).

➡ **Connections** Direct buses from Turkey, Azerbaijan, Armenia; trains from Turkey. Direct flights from Turkey, Europe, Central Asia and the Gulf (p183).

➡ **Alcohol** Banned (see p145).

➡ **Daily Costs** Budget hotel double room US$21, restaurant mains US$8, six-hour bus US$5.

Iran Highlights

1 Admiring Esfahan's enormous **square** (p156) and the stunning buildings that surround it.

2 Looking upon the works of the mighty Achaemenid Kings at ruined yet majestic **Persepolis** (p170).

3 Hiking the Alborz range in fabled, utterly picturesque **Alamut Valley** (p154).

4 Watching Shiite Islam in action at the spectacular shrine of Imam Reza at **Mashhad** (p172).

5 Pacing the ancient mud-brick centre of the enchanting desert town of **Yazd** (p162).

6 Diving into the sights, sounds and smells of the fabulous bazaar at **Tabriz** (p151).

7 Getting energised by the frantic buzz of Tehran and browsing its excellent **museums** (p144).

8 Exploring the poetic history and fine eating scene of liberal **Shiraz** (p165).

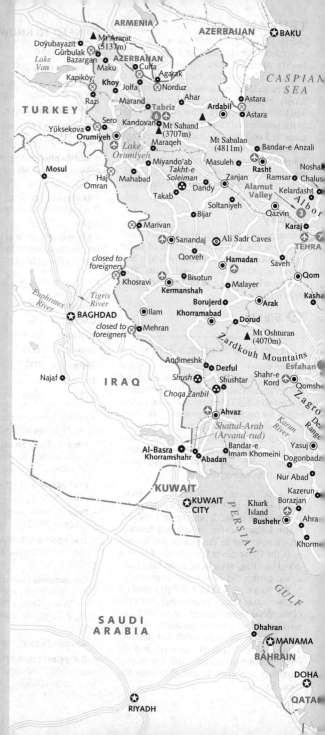

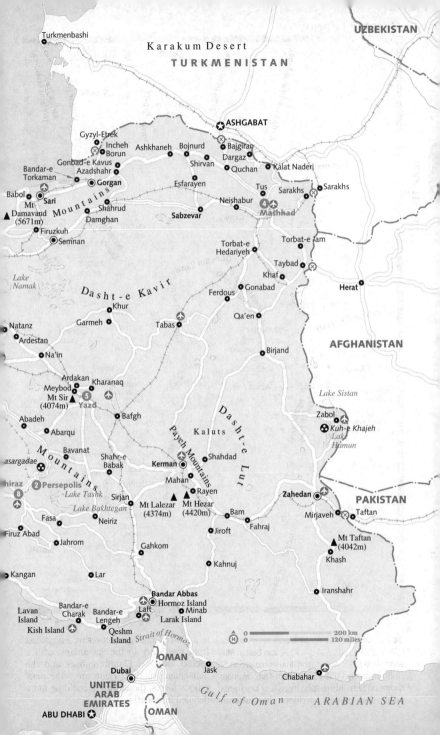

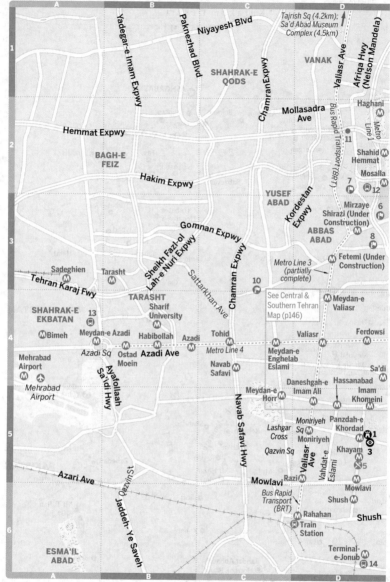

★ **National Museum of Iran**　MUSEUM
(موزه ملي ايران باستان), Iran Bastan Museum; Map p146; www.nationalmuseumofiran.ir; Si Tir St; admission US$4.50; ☉9am-4pm; M Imam Khomeini) Sensibly displaying a few key items rather than endless corridors, this museum is a Tehran highlight, covering everything from prehistory to the Sassanians, with a special focus on Elamite culture and the Achaemenid period. There are some marvellous pieces, though there could be more detailed information.

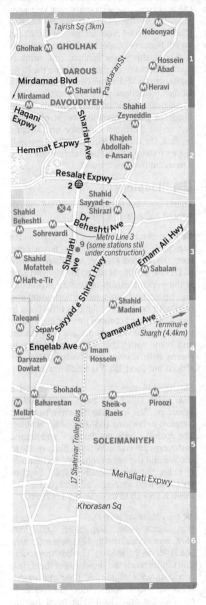

Greater Tehran

a stunning coronation frieze and a headless statue of Darius the Great whose base details all his subject peoples.

Ebrat Museum
MUSEUM

(موزه عبرت; Map p146; www.ebratmuseum.ir; off Kushik Mesri St; admission US$3; ⊙ tours 10am & 2pm Wed-Mon; Ⓜ Imam Khomeini) This one-time prison of the Shah's brutal secret police now exhibits that brutality with a healthy measure of propaganda. Visitors must follow the 1¾-hour tour, conducted in Farsi by a former prisoner. Gruesome waxwork dummies re-create prison life: some have brief explanations in English, and there are several subtitled audiovisuals.

The elephant in the room is that the abhorrence of torture expressed here is not shared by the ruling regime.

★ Treasury of National Jewels
MUSEUM

(موزه جواهرات ملی; Map p146; ☏ +98 21 6446 3785; www.cbi.ir; Ferdosi St; admission US$4.50, no under 12s; ⊙ 2-4.30pm Sat-Tue, to 3.30pm Nov-Mar; Ⓜ Sa'di) Accessed via repeated security screenings, this bank vault houses the incredible jewellery with which the Safavid and Qajar monarchs adorned themselves. Much of the collection dates back to Safavid times; pieces range from bling (a jewelled umbrella) to exquisite items with inlaid turquoise. Cameras, phones, bags and guidebooks must be left at reception.

The free multilingual guided tours are worthwhile, as there are no descriptions.

There are standout early ceramics, delicate stone cups, cylinder seals, a bull sculpture that guarded the ziggurat temple of Choqa Zanbil and fine Lorestan bronzes. Achaemenid finds – the majority from Persepolis – include cuneiform inscriptions,

Iranian Artists' Forum
CULTURAL CENTRE

(خانه هنرمندان; Map p146; www.iranartists.org; Park-e Honar, Mousavi St; ⊙1-8pm; Ⓜ Taleqani) FREE
One of several galleries around this part of Tehran, this is something of an art hub, with eight spaces over two levels exhibiting works in all media on a monthly rotation. There's also a cracking shop, a vegetarian restaurant and a cafe. A great place to meet locals.

Tehran Museum of Contemporary Art
GALLERY

(موزه هنرهای معاصر تهران; Map p146; Kargar Ave; admission US$1.50; ⊙10am-7pm Mon-Thu, 3-7pm Fri; Ⓜ Meydan-e Enghelab Eslami) This striking concrete modernist building was constructed during the shah's rush to build modern landmarks in the 1970s. As you spiral downwards, you pass through works of various 20th-century Iranian artistic movements. The Western art collection was locked in the vaults at time of our last visit. The cafe here is a pleasant spot, with courtyard seating.

⊙ Northern Tehran

★ Reza Abbasi Museum
MUSEUM

(موزه رضا عباسی; Map p142; www.rezaabbasimuseum.ir; 892 Shariati Ave; admission US$3; ⊙9am-5pm Tue-Sun) If you like Iranian art, this is a must-see. Exhibits are organised chronologically starting with the top-floor Pre-Islamic Gallery, where you'll find great Lorestan bronzes, as well as Achaemenid gold bowls, drinking vessels and decorative pieces, often with exquisite carvings of bulls and rams. The Islamic Gallery exhibits ceramics, fabrics and brassware, while the Painting Gallery shows samples of fine calligraphy from ancient Qurans and illustrated manuscripts.

DON'T MISS

CITY ESCAPE: DARBAND دربند

Where Tehran ends and mountains begin, this valley makes a great escape from city fumes. Three kilometres uphill from Tajrish Sq, the road ends, becoming a path winding up a narrow rocky valley, with water cascading down the slope. The trail passes a picturesque succession of teahouses, restaurants and fruit-conserve stalls: the most relaxing places in Tehran to kick back, with a mountain-village feel. Darband, which also has a ski lift, is most popular in the evening and on Thursdays and Fridays.

Sa'd Abad Museum Complex
PALACE, MUSEUMS

(مجموعه موزه سعد آباد; www.sadmu.com; Valiasr Ave, Taheri St; admission US$4.50, plus per museum US$1.50; ⊙9am-4.30pm Tue-Sun; Ⓜ Tajrish) Set on 110 hectares of spectacular mountainside parkland, this was a Pahlavi royal summer home. There are 19 museums here; the highlights are the White and Green palaces: both Pahlavi residences, plus the grounds.

All tickets must be bought in advance at the front gate (1.5km northwest of Tajrish Sq) or the northern entrance on Darband Sq: ask for the English map. The grounds slope up steeply from the main entrance, but a free minibus zips around.

🛏 Sleeping

There are many budget options on or around noisy Amir Kabir St.

★ Firouzeh Hotel
HOTEL $

(Map p146; ☏021-3311 3508; www.firouzehhotel.com; Dowlat Abad Alley, off Amir Kabir St; s/tw US$22/34; ❄@⊚; Ⓜ Mellat) Mr Mousavi here is the personification of Persian hospitality and his enthusiasm, useful information and help with bookings make this little hotel in an unlovely part of town into the city's backpacker centre. The rooms are very decent and come with cable TV, fridge and bathrooms with shower and basin; toilets are shared but good. Wi-fi is a dollar a day.

Mashhad Hostel
HOSTEL $

(Map p146; ☏021-3311 3062; mashhadhostel@yahoo.com; 388 Amir Kabir St; dm/s/tw without bathroom or breakfast US$6/9/12; ⊚; Ⓜ Mellat) The rooms – beds not bunks – and shared bathrooms are cramped, you'll likely queue to shower and the front rooms are horrendously noisy, but the generally helpful English-speaking management and backpacker vibe mean it appeals to those on tight budgets.

★ Iran Markazi Hotel
HOTEL $$

(Iran Central Hotel; Map p146; ☏021-3399 6577; www.markazihotel.ir; 419 Lalehzar St; s/tw US$31/45; ❄⊚; Ⓜ Sa'di) Though the rooms don't quite reach the standards of the stylish corridors with white-tiled floor and mood-lit, stone-faced walls, they are perfectly comfortable and clean. The hotel has an interesting central location on a lively little street and offers excellent value.

Golestan Hotel
HOTEL $$

(Map p146; ☏021-6671 1417; www.gollestanhotel.com; 14 Hafez St, Hassan Abad Sq; s/d US$31/44; ❄@⊚; Ⓜ Hassanabad) Among a bevy of furniture stores on a quiet section of Hafez St, fish-tank-filled Golestan is in an area around historic Hassan Abad Sq that is bright, open and more social than Amir Kabir St. Rooms are compact but clean and though management speaks little English, they are kindly and it's good value. The Metro is on the doorstep.

Hafez Hotel
HOTEL $$

(Map p146; ☑ 021-6674 3073; www.hafezhotel.net; Bank Alley, off Ferdosi St; s/d US$27/40, without bathroom US$18/28; ❋ @ 🛜; Ⓜ Sa'di) Gleaming lacquered floors, decent modern bathrooms and relative peace and quiet make this a fine option in a lane off Ferdosi St. Congenial management make this newly renovated place a standout at this price, if you bag one of the larger renovated rooms: some others are pretty tiny. There's a restaurant too.

★ Escan Hotel
HOTEL $$$

(Map p146; ☑ 021-8834 7385; www.escanhotel.com; 29 Mousavi St; s/d US$85/119; ❋ @ 🛜; Ⓜ Ferdowsi) The completely refurbished Escan has 42 sizeable, well-equipped, very clean and quiet rooms that remind of modern three-star hotels elsewhere but are unusually well finished by Iranian standards. Service is professional.

✕ Eating

The wealthy north has international flavours served in designer spaces.

★ Khoshbin
GILANI $

(Map p146; 510 North Sa'di St; meals US$3-7; ☉ 11.30am-3.30pm; Ⓜ Sa'di) Tiny, no-frills Khoshbin is an institution among Tehranis, who cram onto the fast-turnover tables for authentic Gilani (food from the Gilan region) lunches. Highlights include *mirza ghasemi* (mashed vegetables), *kuli* (carp roe) and particularly the fish (including trout, sturgeon and smoked salmon). Expect to queue.

Dizi
IRANIAN $

(Map p146; 52 Kalantari St; dizi US$4.50-6; ☉ noon-4.30pm Sat-Thu; Ⓜ Haft-e-Tir) The name gives a clue to the menu: that's right, it's Iran's favourite stew, and they do it damn well. Waiters or the cordial boss will show you how to eat it if in doubt. It's been going for decades, has outdoor tables and a characterful interior decked with paintings. Look for the bare-brick facade and prepare to queue.

Iran Tak
TEAHOUSE $$

(Map p146; Valiasr Ave; mains US$4-9; ☉ 10am-10pm; Ⓜ Valiasr) An appealing underground

---

ⓘ ALCOHOL

Alcohol in Iran is banned for Muslims, though Christian minorities are allowed to produce it for their own use. In fact, alcohol use is quite widespread behind closed doors and you may be offered it at Iranians' homes. Forget about hotel bars or nightclubs though: there's no such thing.

---

space set around a tinkling fountain with a modern-yet-traditional ambience, this is an inviting venue for a meal or just tea and a waterpipe. The short, good-value menu includes an excellent *abgusht* (stew), some traditional rice dishes and yoghurty starters. Look out for the tiled entrance near a newspaper kiosk.

Khayyam Restaurant
TEAHOUSE $$

(Map p142; Khayyam St; mains US$5-13; ☉ noon-11pm; Ⓜ Khayyam) Opposite the Imamzadeh Seyyed Nasreddin Mosque (look for the dome), this 300-year-old building was originally part of the mosque before being separated when Khayyam St intervened. The Iranian fare (mainly kabab, chicken and fish) is well prepared and plentiful, and the interior very appealing. For tea, *qalyans* (waterpipes) and sweets (US$2) after an outing in the bazaar, it's also hard to beat.

Armenian Club
IRANIAN $$

(Map p146; ☑ 021-6670 0521; Khark St; mains US$5-20; ☉ 7.30-11.30pm Sat-Wed, 7.30pm-midnight Thu-Fri; Ⓜ Valiasr) Almost a one-off in Tehran; a Christian establishment where women can wear whatever they want. The food varies – a range of kababs are accompanied by several fish options (grilled sturgeon is expensive but tasty) and a couple of mediocre Russian dishes. You can order wine with your meal. There's no sign. Guests welcome as long as you're not Muslim (by government order). It's near Nofl Loshato St.

★ Alborz
IRANIAN $$$

(Map p142; ☑ 021-8876 1907; www.alborzrest.com; cnr Nikou Khadam & Sohrevardi Sts; mains US$11-27; ☉ noon-midnight; Ⓜ Shahid Beheshti) This upstairs place is popular with well-heeled Iranians for business dinners and family celebrations. The kabab form is taken to great heights: beautifully presented platters with, especially, very toothsome lamb. The salad bar is brilliant – worth the trip in itself.

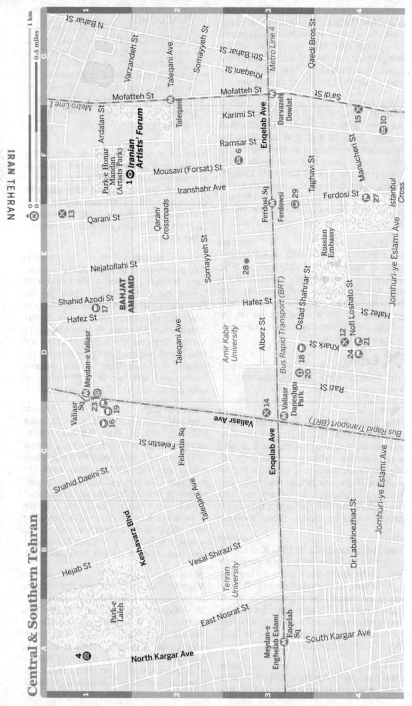

Central & Southern Tehran

IRAN TEHRAN

0.5 miles

1 km

Park-e Laleh

North Kargar Ave

Keshavarz Blvd

Hejab St

Shahid Daeini St

Vesal Shirazi St

Felestin Sq

Taleqani Ave

Valiasr Sq

Meydan-e Valiasr

Shahid Azodi St

Hafez St

BAHJAT AMBAMD

Nejatollahi St

Qarani St

Park-e Honar Mandan (Artists Park)

1 Iranian Artists' Forum

Ardalan St

Taleqani St

Varzandeh St

Taleqani Ave

Somayyeh St

Sth Bahar St

N Bahar St

Mofatteh St

Mofatteh St

Metro Line 1

Khagani St

Qaedi Bros St

Metro Line 4

Sa'di St

Enqelab Ave

Karimi St

Darvazeh Dowlat

Ramsar St

6

Mousavi (Forsat) St

Iranshahr Ave

Somayyeh St

Qarani Crossroads

13

Taghavi St

Ferdosi St

27

Manucher St

15

10

Ferdosi Sq

Ferdowsi

29

Russian Embassy

Ostad Shahriar St

Nofil Loshato St

Hafez St

Jomhuri-ye Eslami Ave

Istanbul Cross

28

Hafez St

Alborz St

Amir Kabir University

Taleqani Ave

Somayyeh St

Razi St

Bus Rapid Transport (BRT)

12

Khark St

24

21

18

20

14

Valiasr

Daneshgu Park

Valiasr Ave

Enqelab Ave

Bus Rapid Transport (BRT)

16

19

23

Dr Labatinezhad St

Jomhuri-ye Eslami Ave

Tehran University

East Nosrat St

Meydan-e Enghelab Eslami

Enqelab Sq

South Kargar Ave

North Kargar Ave

4

IRAN TEHRAN

Central & Southern Tehran

There are lots of nice touches, but the drinks and extras they bring are charged.

🍷 Drinking & Nightlife

Over the past decade Tehran has developed a modern cafe scene that contrasts with the more traditional teahouses. Meydan-e Valiasr is one of the livelier evening zones, with juice bars, ice-cream kiosks and good cafes.

Cafe Haftad-o Hasht CAFE
(Cafe 78; Map p146; www.facebook.com/cafe78iran; 38 South Shahid Azodi St, off Karim Khan-e Zand

WORTH A TRIP

SKIING

Skiing in the Alborz Mountains can be one of the most unexpected pleasures of a trip to Iran. There are several resorts within day-trip distance of Tehran. The slopes at **Tochal** (www.tochal.org) are accessed via the Tochal Telecabin in northern Tehran. The pick of the bunch, however, are **Shemshak** (day pass US$20) and **Dizin** (www.dizinskiresort. com; day pass US$20).

Ave; ⊘11am-11pm Sat-Thu, 4-11pm Fri; 🛜; M Meydan-e Valiasr) This cafe near several galleries is a good place to get in touch with Tehran's young artistic community. The coffee, wide range of teas, snacks, service and conversation are all worthwhile.

Un Cafe   CAFE
(Map p146; www.facebook.com/uncafeun; 145 North Mozaffar St; ⊘9am-11pm Sat-Thu, 4-10.30pm Fri; 🛜; M Meydan-e Valiasr) With its solid dark-wood tables and chairs, black-and-white portraits and gleaming espresso machine, this is an excellent cafe with an artsy feel. There's a range of sandwiches and mocktails: try the zingy house special, a palate-cleansing pint of lime, ginger and apple.

Agha Bozorg   TEAHOUSE
(Map p146; 28 Keshavarz Blvd; ⊘7am-midnight; M Meydan-e Valiasr) This atmosphere-packed underground place is full of young Iranians flirting, drinking tea, smoking *qalyans* and eating under attractive vaulted ceilings. The *dizi* (US$4.50) and kababs are reliably good, though at busy times it packs out.

Cafe Opera   CAFE
(Map p146; www.cafeopera.ir; cnr Khark & Ostad Shahrior Sts; ⊘8am-10pm Sat-Thu, 4-10pm Fri; M Valiasr) Cosy and attractively decked out like a hipster bar with old projectors, cameras and radios, this is a sweet little place to stop for coffee or hot chocolate.

🔒 Shopping

There are carpet stores all over Tehran but nowhere is the experience as memorable, and the price as negotiable, as in the bazaar, with its more than 4000 merchants.

ℹ️ Orientation

The whole city slopes down from the Alborz Mountains: if you're walking uphill you're usually going north. Differences between poorer, congested southern Tehran, where the major sights are, and the comparatively glitzy north are plain to see. Valiasr Ave runs 17km from south to north.

ℹ️ Information

Tehran has no tourist information office but you can buy city maps at some newspaper kiosks and **Gita Shenasi** (Map p146; 🖉 021-6670 3221; www.gitashenasi.com; 20 Ostad Shahrior St; ⊘8am-6.30pm Sat-Wed & 8am-1pm Thu; M Valiasr).

DANGERS & ANNOYANCES

The chaotic traffic and its ugly child, pollution, are the main Tehran annoyances.

EMERGENCY

If your emergency is not life threatening, ask your hotel for the most appropriate hospital or police station.

INTERNET ACCESS

Valiasr Commercial Centre (Map p146; Valiasr Sq; per hr US$1.20; ⊘8am-9pm) Several small, fast *coffeenets* on lower ground floor.

MONEY

There are dozens of exchange shops on Ferdosi St south of Ferdosi Sq.

TRAVEL AGENCIES

There are numerous travel agencies throughout the centre.

VISA EXTENSIONS

Foreign Intelligence Office (Map p142; Soroush St, near Shariati Ave; ⊘8am-1.30pm Sat-Wed, 8am-noon Thu)

ℹ️ Getting There & Away

Every town and city of any size is directly linked to Tehran by bus, and usually by air and train.

BUSES FROM TEHRAN

DESTINATION	FARE (US$; VIP/ MAHMOOLY)	DURATION (HR)
Esfahan	7/4	5-6
Kashan	4/3	3
Mashhad	14/9	13-14
Shiraz	14/9	10-13
Tabriz	10/6	8
Yazd	10/6	7-8

AIR

Imam Khomeini International Airport (www.
ikia.ir) Almost all international services use this
airport 35km south of Tehran.

Mehrabad Airport (Map p142; mehrabad.
airport.ir) Most domestic flights use this, on
the western edge of the city. The Metro is due
to reach here some time soon.

BUS

Tehran has four bus terminals.

Terminal-e Arzhantin (Central terminal,
Beyhaqi terminal; Map p142; ☎ 021-8873 2535;
Arzhantin Sq; Ⓜ Mosalla) is in northern Tehran
and has many VIP services. It's accessible by
bus, shuttle taxi, or a short cab from Mosalla
Metro.

Terminal-e Shargh (Eastern Terminal; ☎ 021-
7786 8080; Damavand Rd) serves eastern Iran.
Take the BRT east on Enqelab Ave.

Terminal-e Jonub (Southern Terminal; Map
p142; Ⓜ Terminal-e Jonub), accessible by
Metro, serves all points south and southeast.

Terminal-e Gharb (Terminal-e Azadi; Map
p142; ☎ 021-4465 9672; Ⓜ Meydan-e Azadi)
serves western Iran, the Caspian region and
international destinations including Ankara and
İstanbul (in Turkey), Baku (in Azerbaijan) and
Yerevan (Armenia). It's on the Metro.

Iran Peyma (Map p146; ☎ 021-6670 7148;
www.iranpeyma.info; Ferdosi St; ⊙10am-3pm
Sat-Thu; Ⓜ Ferdowsi) has a handy central
booking office.

TAXI

Savaris leave from the appropriate bus terminals. For example, for Kashan (US$8) and even
Esfahan (US$15) they leave by Terminal-e Jonub
and Qazvin or Tabriz from the western (Azadi)
terminal.

TRAIN

The impressive **train station** (Rah-Ahan Sq;
Ⓜ Rahahan) is at the south end of Valiasr Ave.
Ticket purchase is upstairs. Take the Metro to
Rahahan (Line 3), or BRT buses south along
Valiasr Ave, which terminate here.

ⓘ Getting Around

TO/FROM THE AIRPORT

Taxis from Imam Khomeini airport to Tehran
cost a fixed-price US$12; vice versa it's US$9–
18: allow at least 90 minutes in traffic. Shuttle
buses run to Metro stop Haram-e Motahar (Line
1) and to Mehrabad Airport.

Mehrabad Airport is more central. The Metro
will soon reach it; meanwhile taxis cost US$4–6
to central Tehran. Cheaper options include
shuttle taxi and public buses to Enqelab and
Vanak Sqs.

TRAINS FROM TEHRAN

DESTINATION	FARE (US$)	DURATION (HR)
Esfahan	10	7
Kashan	3-9	3
Mashhad	10-18	7-12
Shiraz	24	15
Tabriz	7.50-12	13
Yazd	7-12	5½-7

BUS

Tehran has an extensive local bus network; tickets cost 15–20¢ from booths near bus stops.

Bus Rapid Transport (BRT)

These are rapid buses along four routes with
dedicated lanes. Tickets cost 20¢. Two lines are
especially useful: along Valiasr Ave, and from
Azadi Sq in the west via the centre to Terminal-e
Shargh in the east.

METRO

Tehran's **Metro** (www.tehranmetro.com) is a major project and the city's only hope against pollution. Five lines are at least partially complete.

Tickets cost 15¢ per single trip, or 20¢ with a
change. Buy a chargeable card (Credit Ticket),
which costs 15¢, and gives much cheaper journeys. It works on some buses also.

Trains start at 5.30am and stop by 11pm. Services are crowded, crazily so during peak hours.
The first and last carriages are for women only,
though women are free to travel in any carriage.

TAXI

Adrenalin-boosting motorcycle taxis are available at major corners (short rides start from 30¢).

Private Taxi

Fares start around US$2; US$3 should get you
a fair way across town, and US$4.50 a long
distance.

Shuttle Taxi

Minimum fare is 30¢ for one or two *meydans*
(squares) of travel.

WESTERN IRAN   ایران غربی

Tabriz   تبریز

☎ 041 / POP 1.4 MILLION / ELEV 1351M

A fascinating bazaar and the buzz of commerce and mingling ethnicities make this
sprawling city a very positive introduction to
Iran for overlanders. It had a spell as capital

Central Tabriz

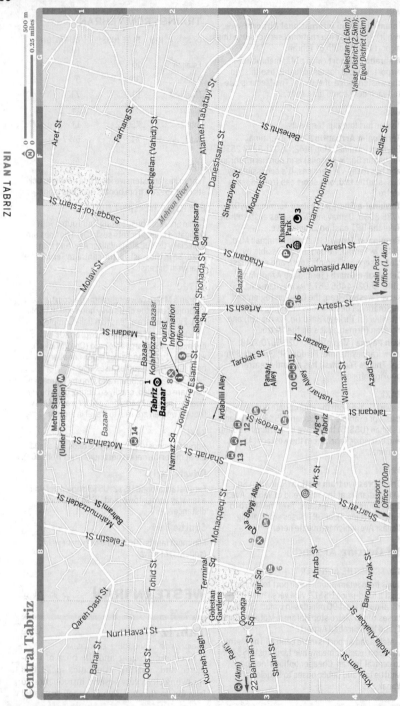

Delestan (1.6km);
Valiasr District (2.5km);
El'goil District (6km)

Main Post
Office (1.4km)

Passport
Office (700m)

Khaqani Park

Golestan Gardens

Metro Station
(Under Construction)

Tabriz Bazaar

Tourist Information Office

Arg-e Tabriz

500 m
0.25 miles

Central Tabriz

and has proven influential in the country's recent history, playing an important part in the constitutional revolution of the early 20th century and seeing major protests against both the Shah and post-revolution regime. It can be freezing cold in winter, but the Azari welcome is warm any time of year.

◎ Sights

★ Tabriz Bazaar
BAZAAR

(بازار تبریز; ⊘ roughly 8am-9pm Sat-Thu) The magnificent, labyrinthine covered bazaar covers some 7 sq km with numerous caravanserais and impressive *timchehs* (halls). Construction began over a millennium ago, though much of the fine brick vaulting is 18th century. Upon entering what was an important Silk Road trading station one feels like a launched pinball, bouncing around through an extraordinary colourful maze, only emerging when chance or carelessness dictates.

Azarbayjan Museum
MUSEUM

(موزه آذربایجان; Imam Khomeini St; admission US$3; ⊘ 8am-5.30pm Tue-Sun) The pre-Islamic ground floor at this archaeological museum – a small but standout display – includes obsidian blades, carved stone 'handbags' (perhaps authority symbols), great bronzes from Loristan, rhytons used for ceremoni-

al liquids, plus a re-created Iron Age burial found nearby. Upstairs are exquisite agate stamp seals and coins, Islamic-era pottery and reweaves of a pair of famous carpets. Reasonable info in English.

Kabud Mosque
MOSQUE

(Blue Mosque, مسجد کبود; Imam Khomeini St; admission US$3; ⊘ 8am-5.30pm Sat-Thu) When completed in the 15th century, every surface covered with intricate blue tiles, this was among the era's most majestic buildings. However, it collapsed in a 1779 earthquake and was rubble until reconstruction finally started in 1951. Only on the entrance portal (which survived) can you get an idea of the exterior's former magnificence. Inside is also blue with missing patterns added around patches of original tiles.

👉 Tours

Hossein Ravanyar
GUIDE

(☑ 0935-299 2296; www.iranoverland.com) Great for touring in the northwest, or around Iran in general.

Nasser Khan
GUIDE

(☑ 0914-116 0149; amicodelmondo@yahoo.com) Legendary multilingual pillar of the tourist information office. Huge knowledge, can arrange excursions and is great for Tabriz cultural itineraries and gastronomic experiences.

🛏 Sleeping

There are free, well-equipped, guarded campsites near the university and in Elgoli Park.

Park Hotel
HOTEL $

(☑ 041-3555 1852; www.hotelparktabriz.com; Imam Khomeini St; s/tw US$25/30; ❄ 🛜) The best of the hotels on this strip by some distance, the Park has friendly English-speaking management and rather nice rooms with blond-wood furniture, minibar and decent shower. There's a pleasant downstairs TV lounge, OK breakfast and a back patio. Rooms near the stairs have better wi-fi signal.

Bagh Guesthouse
MOSAFERKHANEH $

(Bargh Hotel; ☑ 041-3555 2762; Ferdosi St; s/d US$8/13) Brighter and cleaner than most *mosaferkhanehs* (budget places with shared facilities), rooms in this dignified tiled place are fairly small but five of the 12 have double beds, unusual at this price range. Showers cost a little extra.

IRAN TABRIZ

AZARIS

Although there's an independent republic of Azerbaijan, the majority of Azerbaijanis actually live in Iran, where they make up at least 25% of the population. Iranian Azerbaijanis (called Azaris), commonly called 'Turks' because of their Turkic dialect, are well integrated into Iranian society: current supreme leader Ali Khamenei is an ethnic Azari.

Hotel Sahand
HOTEL $$

(☑ 041-3553 4626; Imam Khomeini St; s/d US$34/50; Ⓟꙮ☎) Almost in the boutique class with a shiny lift featuring Persepolis engravings and some rough-stone effects on the walls, this is gleamingly clean and has covered parking. Rooms are spacious; some look over the mosque opposite. Despite the main-street location, the soundproofing works OK. Heavy discounts negotiable for multinight stays.

Hotel Sina
HOTEL $$

(☑ 041-3551 6211; Fajr Sq; s/tw US$27/37; Ⓟꙮ☎) Calm yet central, this relatively plush midrange option has bright corridors with strip carpets over clean tiled floors. Rooms are neat with colourful blankets and are fully equipped. Parking is limited.

Pars Elgoli Hotel
HOTEL $$$

(☑ 041-3380 7820; www.pars-hotels.com; Elgoli Park; s/d/ste US$66/116/182; Ⓟꙮ@☎🏊) This sleek-looking business hotel towers over the city's favourite park, Elgoli, 8km from the centre. Facilities, including a decent pool, are great. Rooms are spacious but very standard in feel. They have magnificent views though; as does the revolving restaurant.

🍴 Eating & Drinking

Good street-food options include tasty potato-and-boiled-egg wraps.

Ferdosi
TEAHOUSE $

(off North Ferdosi St; dizi US$3; ⊙6am-7pm) This traditional and characterful vaulted one-room basement starts off the day with breakfast omelettes, then around lunchtime produces what local experts rate as Tabriz's best *dizi* (stew). In the afternoon, go for tea, bubbling *qalyans* (waterpipes) and plump, moist dates.

★ Baliq
SEAFOOD $$

(☑ 041-3385 9294; Golshahr St; meals US$4-11; ⊙noon-11pm) Fresh whole fish, fish kababs, fish köfte balls in the salad bar, fishing nets on the ceiling, and aquariums between the tables. Standards are excellent, the enticing decor includes log-and-rope chairs and a cave-wall trickling with water. Get off a Rahnamae–Golshahr shuttle-taxi on 35m Sina St.

Delestan
AZARBAYJANI $$

(www.delestanfoods.com; 29 Bahman St; mains US$4-13; ⊙11am-11pm) Some 4km east of the centre, near the entrance to the university, this is divided into two parts. The bright fast-food section is popular with students but take the door to the right into the calmer, more traditional area, for notable Azarbayjani dishes. Take a phrasebook for the menu.

Tabriz Modern Restaurant
IRANIAN $$

(Imam Khomeini St; meals US$5-10; ⊙noon-11pm; ☎) This English-speaking favourite is handy for the central hotel strip and serves kababs and fried trout in a spacious basement dining hall. Meal prices include barley-and-barberry soup and mediocre serve-yourself salad.

ℹ Information

CONSULATES

Azerbaijani Consulate (☑ 041-3333 4802; Mokhaberat St, Valiasr; ⊙9am-noon Sun-Thu) Tourist visas available.

Turkish Consulate (☑ 041-3300 1070; http://tebriz.bk.mfa.gov.tr; Homafar Sq, Valiasr; ⊙9am-2pm Sun-Thu)

INTERNET

Deniz Coffeenet (Maghazeh Haye Sanqi Alley, off Shari'ati St; per hr 75¢; ⊙9.30am-9.30pm) Decent connection.

MONEY

Ramin Exchange (☑ 041-3526 2016; ramin.chalani@hotmail.co.uk; 69 Saraie Amir, Passage Farsh; ⊙9am-6pm Sat-Thu) In the southeast corner of the bazaar. Can be tricky to find: ask at the tourist office.

TOURIST INFORMATION

Tourist Information Office (☑ 041-3524 6235; www.tabriz.ir; North Ferdosi St; ⊙9am-2pm & 4-7pm Sat-Thu) Free maps, help with organising trips and a mine of information that will transform your appreciation of this city. Upstairs in the forecourt of the main bazaar entrance.

VISA EXTENSIONS

Passport Office (☑ 041-3477 6666; Saeb St; ⊙8am-1.30pm Sat-Wed, to 11.30pm Thu)

Helpful. You can get a one-day extension at the airport too.

ℹ Getting There & Away

AIR

Several airlines connect Tabriz with Tehran and Mashhad daily. Turkish Airlines flies direct to İstanbul, Azerbaijan Airlines to Baku.

BUS & TAXI

Most buses and savaris use the **main bus terminal** (📞 479 6091), 3km south of the centre.

International Buses

Buses to Yerevan, Armenia (US$55, 20 hours), Baku, Azerbaijan (US$27 to US$34, 13 to 17 hours), İstanbul (US$60, 30 hours) and other Turkish destinations typically leave around 10pm from outside their ticket offices on Imam Khomeini St but sometimes depart from a bus terminal: check.

Aram Safar (📞 041-3556 0597; Imam Khomeini St) For Baku, Azerbaijan.

Khosh Rah (📞 041-3556 6833; Imam Khomeini St) Destinations including İstanbul.

Mihan Safar International (📞 041-3475 0979; Imam Khomeini St) Several international bus services.

TRAIN

Overnight trains to Tehran (US$7.50 to US$12, 13 hours) run via Qazvin. There are also direct trains to Mashhad. The **train station** (📞 041-3444 4419; Rahohan Sq) is 5km west of central Tabriz.

There are two trains weekly to Van in Turkey.

ℹ Getting Around

TO/FROM THE AIRPORT

Bus 136 runs from Motahhari St every 40 minutes. Taxis should cost US$1 to US$2.

BUS

Useful city bus routes include 104 to the bus terminal and 110 to Valiasr. Pre-buy 10¢ tickets or pay the driver. Several services run the length of 22 Bahman St (for the train station) including 111. Bus 101 runs to Elgoli from near Saat Sq.

BUSES FROM TABRIZ

DESTINATION	FARE (US$)	DURATION (HR)
Esfahan	13	17
Mashhad	17	23
Qazvin	8	7 (Tehran bus)
Shiraz	21	22
Tehran	6/8 (VIP)	8

METRO

Tabriz metro is an ongoing project eventually due to link Elgoli in the southeast to the airport in the northwest via the central area. A handful of stations should be open by the time you read this.

SHUTTLE TAXI

A key route runs along Imam Khomeini St from Fajr Sq to Abaresan Crossing (60¢), but on returning diverts onto Jomhuri-e Eslami St passing the bazaar. Change at major intersections for Valiasr and Elgoli.

Kandovan كندوان

POP 600 / ELEV 1300M

Remarkable **Kandovan** (admission 60¢) is a photogenic settlement of troglodyte homes and barns carved out of curiously eroded rocks. These sit above the modern village like a conference of stone ice-cream cones. Scrambling along steep, narrow paths between them gives you ample idea of the place within a few minutes. However, staying overnight allows you to 'feel' the village without the crowds.

🛏 Sleeping & Eating

Non-troglodyte homes in the lower village offer **rooms**; these vary from US$3 to US$25 and differ wildly. Most are summer-only. Eateries cluster along the riverbank.

★**Kandovan Laleh
Rocky Hotel**   BOUTIQUE HOTEL $$$

(📞 041-3323 0191; www.irtdc.ir; r without/with Jacuzzi US$94/110, ste US$160-202; 🅿🛜) At the village entrance, these remarkable rooms are carved out of rock knolls. They are luxurious affairs with stylish lighting, oriental-style futon-beds, underfloor heating and (in many) deep-stepped Jacuzzis as well as fully equipped bathrooms. Delicious breakfast included.

ℹ Getting There & Away

Minibuses from Tabriz run regularly to Osku (30¢, 50 minutes), from where infrequent buses/minibuses go on to Kandovan (25km). A return taxi with waiting time will cost US$7 to US$10 from Osku, US$15 to US$24 from Tabriz.

Qazvin قزوین

📞 028 / POP 381,600 / ELEV 1301M

Gateway to majestic Alamut Valley, Qazvin is a pleasant place with good transport connections and a handful of minor sights. It was once capital of all Iran and is famed for carpets and seedless grapes.

Tours

All accommodation options can book Alamut Valley tours, best started early in the morning.

Yousef Shariyat GUIDE
(☑0919-180 7076; yousef.sh.khoo@gmail.com) For trips to the Alamut Valley and elsewhere in the region, Yousef's excellent English, interesting conversation, wide knowledge and calm driving make him a winner. Alamut day trips cost US$70 for up to four.

Sleeping

Taleghani Inn MOSAFERKHANEH $
(☑028-3322 4239; Khaleqi Alley, off Taleqani St; d without/with bathroom US$21/27) Spacious, spotless and central, this renovated guesthouse is run by a serious, cordial family. Rooms are spacious, and come with or without bathroom.

Alborz Hotel HOTEL $$
(☑028-3322 6631; Talegani St; s/tw US$33/54; P✳@☞) This appealing midrange option has fully equipped modern rooms ranging from compact to spacious. They come with solid wooden furniture and cable channels, though bathrooms are more basic. Downside: air-con is noisy. We recommend booking tours elsewhere.

Eating

Nemooneh IRANIAN $$
(☑028-3332 8448; cnr Buali & Ferdosi Sts; mains US$5-11; ☺noon-3.30pm & 7-10.30pm) With a uniformed doorman and army of waiters, this is Qazvin's best dining option. Browse the handy picture menu and choose from local specialities or a range of juicy kabab options. Salads are prepacked though.

PERSIAN GARDENS

A group of Iranian gardens, several in Central Iran, are on the World Heritage list, as the best existing examples of the classic Persian Garden form. Traditionally conceived to symbolise Paradise, these gardens are all divided into four sectors symbolising the Zoroastrian elements of sky, earth, water and plants and date to different periods from the 6th century BC on.

Drinking & Nightlife

Negarossaltaneh CAFE
(34 Vazir Bazaar; ☺10am-10pm Sat-Thu, 5-10pm Fri) In the posh, renovated brick-vaulted part of the bazaar, this boutique cafe (top cappuccino) has owners who delight in explaining their range of exquisite herbal teas and refreshing cool drinks.

Information

Tourist Information (☑028-3335 4708; Naderi St; ☺8am-6pm Sat-Thu, 9am-4pm Fri) Faces historic Rah Kushk Gate and offers free maps and brochures. Very helpful.

Getting There & Away

BUS, MINIBUS & TAXI
Mo'allem Kalayeh savaris (US$4.50, two hours) depart from Qaribqosh Sq, 2km east of Valiasr Sq. Tehran savaris (US$2.20) leave from outside the main bus terminal.

From the **main bus terminal** (Darvazeh Sq), there are frequent services to Tehran (US$1.50, two hours), and daily departures to:
Esfahan (US$5.50, 6½ hours)
Mashhad (US$8.50, 16 hours)
Tabriz (US$8, eight hours)

TRAIN
Trains run to Tehran (US$2, two hours), Tabriz (US$6 to US$10, 11 hours) and Mashhad.

Getting Around

For the bus terminal change shuttle taxi at Valiasr Sq. From the terminal to Azadi Sq loop around via the bazaar.

Alamut Valley الموت

Few places in Iran offer a more tempting invitation to hike, explore and reflect than the fabled Alamut Valley. Beneath soaring Alborz peaks, the inspiring landscapes are delightfully varied and spiced by a fascinating medieval history: the ruined fortresses that dot the valley were once home to the feared medieval religious cult of the Assassins.

Taking a tour, or savaris plus taxis, it's possible to visit Alamut Castle (the best of the fortresses) and other attractions in a long day from Qazvin. Hitching around the valley is also easy. But it's much more fun to take your time, staying at Gazor Khan and doing some hiking.

Mo'allem Kalayeh & Around

معلم کلایه

📞 028 / POP 2200 / ELEV 1817M

Sometimes called Alamut town, Mo'allem Kalayeh is the Alamut Valley's one-street district centre. It's a useful transport staging post for the region and has two of the valley's popular sights nearby.

⊙ Sights

Andej CANYON

(اندج) The 8km road-spur to Andej (elevation 1587m) passes beside three truly awesome red-rock side canyons, where you can cross the river on a rickety bridge and explore. Afterwards, fork left uphill in Andej village and double back around towards Mo'allem for a magnificent perspective from above.

Evan Lake LAKE

(دریاچه اوان; Ovan Lake) This small lake is accessed via an 8km side road between Razmiyan and Mo'allem. It's a pretty spot with its mountain backdrop, though views are marred by power lines.

🛏 Sleeping

Haddodi Restaurant MOSAFERKHANEH $

(📞 028-3321 6362; tw US$21) This restaurant on the main street just past the eagle statue has two simple rooms, with more on the way.

ℹ Getting There & Away

Savaris run to/from Qazvin (US$4, two hours); a dar baste (charter) costs around US$15. For Gazor Khan charters cost US$5, or US$10 including Andej en route.

Gazor Khan

گازر خان

📞 028 / ELEV 2062M

The pleasant, unpretentious little cherry-growing village of Gazor Khan goes about its business under the crag-top ruined castle that is the valley's major sight.

⊙ Sights & Activities

Several tempting mountain hikes start in Gazor Khan or Khoshkchal village, a steep, 15-minute 4WD ride beyond. Accommodation options can give route advice.

★ Alamut Castle RUIN

(قلعه الموت; admission US$3; ⊙ dawn-dusk) The region's greatest attraction is this fabled ruin of Hasan-e Sabbah's famous fortress on a dramatic crag rising abruptly above

OFF THE BEATEN TRACK

TREKKING TOWARDS THE CASPIAN

Crossing the Alborz on foot from the Alamut Valley to the Caspian hinterland is scenically stunning and culturally fascinating.

Start in pretty, canyon-framed Garmarud, 18km east of the Gazor Khan turning, then go via picturesque Pichebon hamlet and across 3200m Salambar Pass beside a small, partly renovated caravanserai. It's a slow descent to Salajanbar. Scenic Maran is next, then it's another downhill to pretty Yuj among flower-filled meadows.

Homestays are available in all villages. Garmarud, a US$9 taxi from Mo'allem Kelayeh, has guides and mules: recommended for keeping off the asphalt and avoiding wrong turns. From Yuj, the odd savari heads back to civilisation.

IRAN ALAMUT VALLEY

Gazor Khan. The access path requires a steep climb via an obvious stairway. On top, archaeological workings are shielded by unsightly corrugated metal sheeting. But the phenomenal views from the ramparts are unmissable.

🛏 Sleeping & Eating

Golestan Inn GUESTHOUSE $

(Golestan Garden; 📞 0912-582 2901, 028-3371 9289; www.tooralamoot.ir; s/d/tr US$12/18/21; 🅿) Just above the castle path, this is warmly family-run. 'Suites' are simple, modern en suite rooms with heating, fridge and TV: there are great views from the upstairs terrace. Cheaper rooms share a basic bathroom. Home-cooked meals are tasty and the resident myna bird speaks Farsi punctuated by evil laughter.

Hotel Koosaran HOSTEL $

(📞 028-3371 9218; dm US$7.50) Basic but likeable, this hotel is effectively just the guest room in Ali Samie's family home. It can sleep up to five, three in beds and two on mattresses. The flat roof facing Gazor Khan's village square makes a great people-watching perch.

ℹ Getting There & Away

Early morning savaris run to Qazvin (US$5, 2½ hours) from the square. For Mo'allem Kalayeh it's a US$5 taxi charter or an easy hitch.

CENTRAL IRAN ایران مرکزی

Esfahan اصفهان

♪ 031 / POP 1.76 MILLION / ELEV 1590M

Esfahan's profusion of tree-lined boulevards, Persian gardens and important Islamic buildings gives it a visual appeal unmatched by any other city. Artisans working here underpin its reputation as a living museum of traditional culture. Walking through the historic bazaar, over the picturesque bridges and around the magnificent square are Iranian highlights.

History

The Buyid period saw an explosion of construction here, then in 1047 the Seljuks made Esfahan their capital. The Mongols put an end to that; it wasn't until the Safavids that Esfahan once again became Iran's premier city. Taking the throne in 1587, Shah Abbas I transformed it into a city worthy of an empire.

⊙ Sights

Strolling along the Zayandeh River, crossing back and forth on the historic **bridges** (پلهای زاینده رود), is especially pleasant at sunset and in the early evening when most of the bridges are illuminated. Several of the bridges are historic, Safavid-era crossings and a spectacular sight. When there's water, there's a great social scene along the riverbanks, especially on Fridays, with boating, strolling and picnicking.

Masjed-e Jameh   MOSQUE
(مسجد جامع; Allameh Majlesi St; admission US$3; ⊙9-11am & 1.15-4.30pm) One of Iran's largest mosques, this is a veritable museum of Islamic architecture and a busy place of worship. The first mosque was built in the 8th century, but there have been numerous rebuildings and expansions. The main

---

IRAN'S NOMADS

Despite 20th-century resettlement programs, there are still about a million people living as nomads in Iran. They are mostly Turkic Qashqa'i and Bakhtiyari, but there are also Kurds, Lors, Baluchis and smaller groups. To visit them it's best to go with a specialist guide from Shiraz or Esfahan.

---

courtyard is surrounded by four contrasting *iwans* (vaulted halls). You can wander discreetly into the courtyard outside of opening times.

Bazar-e Bozorg   BAZAAR
(بازار بزرگ; ⊙around 9am-8pm Sat-Thu) One of Iran's most fascinating bazaars, this sprawling covered marketplace links Naqsh-e Jahan (Imam) Sq with the Masjed-e Jameh, 1.7km northeast. The bazaar is a maze of lanes, madrasehs, *khans* (caravanserais) and *timchehs* (halls). Among the prominent industries are the carpet sellers, off to the west.

★ Naqsh-e Jahan (Imam) Square   SQUARE
(میدان امام میدان نقش جهان) Begun in 1602 as the centrepiece of Abbas' capital, the square is home to the Safavid's finest architectural jewels. At 512m long and 163m wide, this immense space is one of the world's largest public squares and best visited in the late afternoon, when local families promenade, the light softens and splendid architecture is illuminated. Note the polo goalposts used in 17th-century matches.

Masjed-e Shah   MOSQUE
(مسجد امام; Masjed-e Imam; Naqsh-e Jahan Sq; admission US$3; ⊙9-11.30am & 1-4.15pm Sat-Thu, 1-4.15pm Fri) The richness of this mosque's blue-tiled mosaic designs and Safavid-era architecture form a visually stunning monument to Shah Abbas' reign. Although each part is a masterpiece, the unity of the overall design leaves a lasting impression. Contemplate the richness of the domed ceiling in the main sanctuary, with its golden rose pattern surrounded by concentric circles of mosaics on a deep-blue background. The hollow in the double-layered dome is responsible for the loud echoes under it.

★ Masjed-e Sheikh Lotfollah   MOSQUE
(مسجد شیخ لطف الله, Sheikh Lotfollah Mosque; Naqsh-e Jahan Sq; admission US$3; ⊙9-11.30am & 1-4.30pm) This exquisitely harmonious little mosque is breathtakingly beautiful. With no minaret or courtyard (it was probably used only by the shah's harem), it boasts a fine **portal**, with excellent Safavid-era mosaics. Inside the sanctuary, reached by a twisting hallway, marvel at the wall's complex mosaics and extraordinarily beautiful ceiling, with shrinking yellow motifs. High, latticed windows produce a constantly changing interplay of light and shadow.

Kakh-e Ali Qapu
PALACE

(کاخ عالی قاپو, Ali Qapu Palace; Naqsh-e Jahan Sq; admission US$4.50; ☺9am-4pm) This six-storey building served both as residence and monumental gateway to palaces in the parklands beyond. The **elevated terrace** has slender columns and will have magnificent views over the square (once restoration is finished). The **throne room** conserves much original decoration, while the stunning top-floor **music room** has stucco walls and ceiling cut-outs of vases and other utensils to enhance the acoustics. The audioguide (US$3) is worth considering due to the lack of printed information.

Kakh-e Chehel Sotun
PALACE

(کاخ چهلستون, Chehel Sotun Palace; Ostandari St; admission US$4.50; ☺9am-4.30pm) Part of the former Safavid-era precinct, this was built as pleasure pavilion and reception hall. The elegant Achaemenid-inspired columned terrace perfectly bridges the Persian love of interior splendour and gardens (the garden here is an excellent example of the classic Persian form). Its slender wooden pillars rise to a superb ceiling with exquisite inlay work.

The **Great Hall** contains a fine 9th-century Quran and rich frescos portraying court life and Safavid-era battles.

🛏 Sleeping

Book accommodation ahead from March to August. There's a free campground in Fadak Garden.

Esfahan Tourist Hotel
HOTEL $

(☎031-3220 4437; www.etouristhotel.com; Abbas Abad St; s/d US$19/29; ❄☎) On the back of a recent renovation, this has become a value-packed option in a pleasingly lively zone. The rooms have a great feel; bathrooms aren't quite as shiny but they're OK. Downstairs a stylish cafe-restaurant does American-style breakfasts and is a relaxing place for coffee.

Totia Hotel
HOTEL $

(☎031-3223 7535; www.totiahotel.com; Masjed-e Sayyed St; r US$24; P❄☎) This impeccably run place offers three-star quality at one-star prices. Service is courteous; renovated rooms are spacious and, if you get one at the back, quiet. All rooms are extremely clean and comfortable. Wi-fi costs 60¢ per 100MB.

JOLFA

Esfahan's Armenian quarter dates from Shah Abbas' time, when he transported a colony of Christians here for their entrepreneurial skills. Today it's an area of upmarket boutiques and historic churches; it's worth heading over here for the sights, especially the old gospels and rich wall paintings of the **Kelisa-ye Vank** (کلیسای وانک, Vank Cathedral, Church of St Joseph of Arimathea; Kelisa St; admission US$4.50; ☺8am-5.30pm Sat-Thu, 8.30am-12.30pm Fri), and atmosphere. The best cafes and eateries are around little Jolfa Sq. They include sleek modern-design **Hermes** (Jolfa Alley; meals US$3-7; ☺11am-11.30pm; ☎) for coffee, burgers or pizza, or romantic **Romanos** (☎031-3624 0094; off Jolfa Sq; mains US$4-10; ☺11am-midnight; ☎), with restaurant and teahouse sections in an attractively restored hammam.

Amir Kabir Hostel
HOSTEL $

(☎031-1222 7273; mrziaee@hotmail.com; Chahar Bagh Abbasi St; dm/s/tw US$9/10.50/18; ☎) Offering simple but reasonable dorms, some surrounding a courtyard, this is one of the cheapest options. Rooms and shared facilities were clean when we last visited, though travellers report that ain't always so. The place could do with a bit of a cheer-up.

★Dibai House
GUESTHOUSE $$

(☎031-3220 9787; www.dibaihouse.com; Farhangi Alley, off Moshir Alley; s/tw US$35/50; ☎) Hidden away deep in the bazaar district, this fabulously restored traditional house makes for a wonderfully relaxing base. It's delightful, with a chilled mother-and-daughter team creating a modern-yet-timeless Iranian tone. Larger, traditional rooms share a bathroom; or there are smaller en suite rooms in the newer (still beautiful) courtyard.

Take Farhangi Alley off Moshir St: the entrance is in the tunnel.

★Hasht Behesht
Apartment Hotel
APARTMENTS $$

(☎031-3221 4868; www.hbahotel.com; cnr Ostandari St & Aghili Alley; d/tr/q apt US$40/54/64; ❄☎) Centrally located and one of the best accommodation options in town, offering clean and well-maintained apartments with comfortable beds, equipped kitchenettes and satellite TV. It's very modern and

Central Esfahan

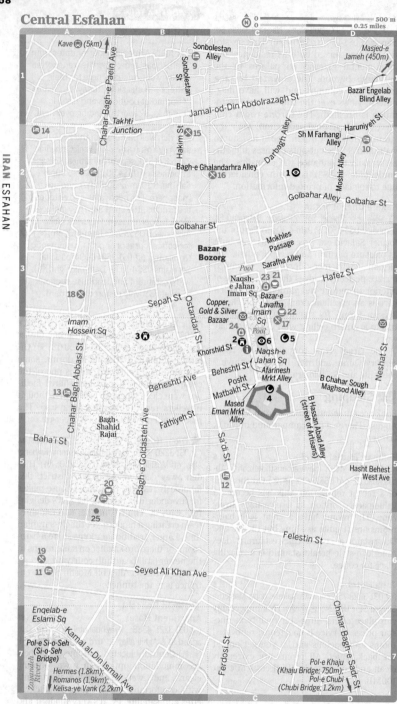

Central Esfahan

attractive. Breakfast is available (in-room) for an extra US$5.

Iran Hotel   HOTEL $$
(📞 031-3220 2740; www.iranhotel.biz; Chahar Bagh Abbasi St; s/d US$23/37; 🌀🏠) On a quiet lane but just off the main drag, this budget hotel offers commodious rooms with low beds, Persian rugs and a fridge. It would be a good option even if it weren't for the ultra-helpful, English-speaking management: they go out of their way to be welcoming.

Bekhradi's Historical Residence   HOTEL $$$
(📞 031-3448 2072; www.safavidinn.com; 56 Sonbolestan Alley, off Sonbolestan St; r from US$78; 🌀🏠) This quiet, modest-sized *khan-e sonati* (traditional house) is the real Safavid-style deal; elegantly restored rooms are set around two garden courtyards, and the larger suites upstairs can easily fit a

family. The owner is kind and gentlemanly. It's just off the roundabout on Sonbolestan St.

Abbasi Hotel   HOTEL $$$
(📞 031-3222 6010; www.abbasihotel.ir; Shahid Medani St; s/d US$64/98, deluxe d US$117-147, ste US$165-258; 🌀🏠@🏠🏠) The Abbasi's main building was once a caravanserai, and has atmosphere in spades. If you stay in one of the (utterly gorgeous) suites or in one of the deluxe doubles you'll no doubt be extremely happy, but rooms in the new building on the eastern side of the wonderful central garden courtyard lack the same ambience.

🍴 Eating

Specialities include *beryani* (ground mutton wrapped in flat bread), *khoresht-e mast* (a strange concoction of lamb, yoghurt, egg, saffron, sugar and orange peel) and *gaz*, a delicious nougat. Saffron or pistachio ice cream is also a must.

Chahar Bagh Abbasi St is wildly popular with locals for fast food.

Grandma's Table   IRANIAN $
(Hakim St; dishes US$2-3; ⊙noon-4pm) This diminutive family-run restaurant lives up to its name, offering a selection of traditional Iranian dishes – stews, meatballs and more – at local prices. It's a great place to try what Iranians eat at home and it's all delicious and authentic. Service was a bit abrupt when we passed by, but it was probably one of those days.

Nobahar   IRANIAN $
(Chahar Bagh Abbasi St; meals US$3-7; ⊙11am-3pm & 6-10pm) This basement restaurant has been around forever because it serves reliably good, reasonably priced soup, kababs and rice dishes. Clean, modern and cheerful, it's a solid choice.

Shahrzad   IRANIAN $$
(📞 031-3220 4490; www.shahrzad-restaurant.com; Abbas Abad St; mains US$5-12; ⊙11.30am-10.30pm) Opulent Qajar-style wall paintings, stained-glass windows and battalions of black-suited waiters contribute to Shahrzad's reputation as the best popular eatery in Esfahan. House specialities include lamb cutlets, quail and fish kababs. The lemon beer is on tap and comes in a chilled glass. Get there early or late for meals or prepare to queue.

Malek Soltan Jarchi Bashi   IRANIAN $$

(☎ 031-3220 7453; www.jarchibashi.com; Bagh-e Ghalandarha Alley, Hakim St; mains US$6-11; ⊘ noon-4pm & 7-11pm) A sumptuous, romantic renovation of a 400-year-old bathhouse; the vaulted interior is a delight with tinkling fountains and colourful decoration. The menu covers kabab options plus *beryani* (including a 'diet' version) and other dishes. Well-meaning staff whip out the reheated fare from the kitchen with indecent haste, but the space is worth it even for just tea and dates.

Naghsh-e-Jahan
Traditional Banquet Hall   IRANIAN $$

(☎ 031-3220 0729; Naqsh-e Jahan Sq; meals US$4-12; ⊘ noon-3pm & 7-10.30pm) The best of the 'traditional' restaurants around Naqsh-e Jahan Sq, this restaurant uses stained-glass, colourful tiles and *takhts* (daybeds) to create a Qajar-era ambience, and caters mainly for tourists. The food is decent, however, with plenty of choice.

🍷 Drinking & Nightlife

Roozegar   CAFE

(off Naqsh-e Jahan Sq; ⊘ 10am-11pm; 🛜) After a few laps around the square or bazaar, this little cafe is a lovely spot to come and unwind. Soothing music on the stereo, good coffee and a range of herbal teas served with *nabat* (crystallised sugar) will soon have you raring to go again. Head into a courtyard north of the Lotfollah mosque, then turn left into another courtyard.

Abbasi Hotel
Teahouse   TEAHOUSE

(www.abbasihotel.ir; Abbasi Hotel, Shahid Medani St; ⊘ 4-10.30pm; 🛜) The setting at the rear of this hotel's fruit-tree-packed courtyard is a delight. Locals flock here in the evening to eat *ash-e reshte* (noodle soup with beans and vegetables). There are several herbal teas available, with sweet snacks to accom-

pany them. Order and pay at the cash register, and then give your ticket to one of the waiters.

Azadegan Teahouse   TEAHOUSE

(Chaykhaneh-ye Azadegan; off Naqsh-e Jahan Sq; ⊘ 7am-midnight) Off the northeastern corner of Naqsh-e Jahan Sq, this popular place sports an astonishing collection of teahouse-junk hanging from walls and ceiling. Enter down the passageway lined with scooters, lamps and old radios.

🛍 Shopping

Esfahan has a wide selection of handicrafts, including carpets, hand-painted miniatures on camel bone, intricate metalwork and enamelware. Two reliable carpet dealers to get you started:

Aladdin Carpets   CARPETS

(☎ 031-3221 1461; aladdin_shop@yahoo.com; 160 Naqsh-e Jahan Sq; ⊘ 9am-1pm & 3-7pm Sat-Thu) Small shop, interesting range and a cordial English-speaking boss.

Paradise Handicrafts   CARPETS, HANDICRAFTS

(☎ 031-3220 4860; paradisecarpets@yahoo.com; 19 Afarinesh Bazaar, Naqsh-e Jahan Sq; ⊘ 9am-1pm & 3-7pm Sat-Thu) Friendly father-and-son team specialising in nomadic carpets. High-quality pieces, can arrange card payments and postage.

ℹ Orientation

Most sites are within easy walking distance of the main street, Chahar Bagh Abbasi, which has lots of accommodation options.

ℹ Information

INTERNET ACCESS

There are several *coffeenets* along Chahar Bagh Abbasi St.

MEDICAL SERVICES

Al-Zahra Hospital (☎ 031-3668 4444; Soffeh St) English-speaking doctors.

MONEY

On Sepah St just west of the junction with Ostandari St there are a number of exchange offices.

TOURIST INFORMATION

Tourist Office (☎ 031-3221 6831; Naqsh-e Jahan Sq; ⊘ 7.30am-2pm Sat-Thu) Roughly opposite the Ali Qapu Palace ticket office.

OFF THE BEATEN TRACK

DESERT VILLAGES

Rather than barrelling down the Esfahan–Yazd highway in a direct bus, take your time and stop off in villages in the Dasht-e Kavir desert on the way. Toudeshk, Na'in and further-flung Garmeh all have appealing sleeping options.

TRAINS FROM ESFAHAN

DESTINATION	FARE (US$)	DURATION (HR)	DEPARTURES
Kashan	5	4	daily (Tehran service)
Mashhad	22	17	daily
Shiraz	15	8	Sun-Tue nights
Tehran	10	7	daily
Yazd	4	3½	4 weekly

TRAVEL AGENCIES

Iran Travel & Tourism (☏ 031-3222 3010; irantravel1964@yahoo.com; Shahid Medani St; ⊘ 8.30am-7pm Sat-Thu) Book plane and train tickets here.

VISA EXTENSIONS

Department of Aliens Affairs (Rudaki St; ⊘ 8am-2pm Sat-Thu) In the Rudeki neighbourhood. Get there early for same-day extensions.

ⓘ Getting There & Away

AIR

Regular flights hit Tehran and Mashhad; a handful go to other cities. Turkish Airlines flies direct from İstanbul; Iran Air serves Kuwait and Dubai.

BUS

You're most likely to use Kave terminal in the north. To get there, take a bus (15¢) or shuttle taxi (60¢) north along Chahar Bagh Abbasi St. A taxi from downtown should cost around US$4.

Destinations include:

Mashhad (*mahmooly*/VIP US$11/14, 17 hours)
Shiraz (US$4/7.50, six to seven hours)
Tabriz (US$8/13, 15 hours)
Tehran (US$5/7, six to seven hours)
Yazd (US$4/6, four to five hours)

TRAIN

The train station is way south. To get there, catch a bus from outside Kowsar International Hotel on Mellat Blvd and leave at least an hour. A taxi costs US$6.

ⓘ Getting Around

TO/FROM THE AIRPORT

The airport is 25km northeast; taxis cost around US$6.

BUS & MINIBUS

Local buses and minibuses cost from 15¢; pay at ticket booths or direct to the driver.

METRO

Esfahan's new **metro** (www.esfahanmetro.org) was meant to open in 2005 but was still under construction last time we visited.

TAXI

Taxis around the centre cost US$1.50 to US$3. Long Chahar Bagh Abbas St is the city's main thoroughfare, and shuttle taxis ply it for about 10¢ per kilometre.

Yazd يزد

☏ 035 / POP 486.200 / ELEV 1216M

With its winding lanes, forest of *badgirs* (windtowers) and glorious mud-brick old town, desert Yazd is a scenic highlight of Iran. Wedged between two deserts, it doesn't have big-ticket sights but is enchanting; a place to wander in the maze of evocatively historic streets and lanes.

History

Yazd has a long history as an important trading post, with the main home-grown industries being silk, textiles and carpets. Marco Polo is known to have passed through in the 13th century.

QANATS

For at least 2000 years Iranians have been digging *qanats* (underground aqueducts) for irrigation and drinking water. Some of these impressive engineering feats are dozens of kilometres long. While modern irrigation projects now take priority, *qanats* are still important. For the lowdown, head for the **Yazd Water Museum** (Amir Chakhmaq Sq; admission US$1.50; ⊘ 8am-2.30pm & 3.30-7pm), in a mansion with a *qanat* underneath. Displays are clear, interesting and mostly in English.

Yazd

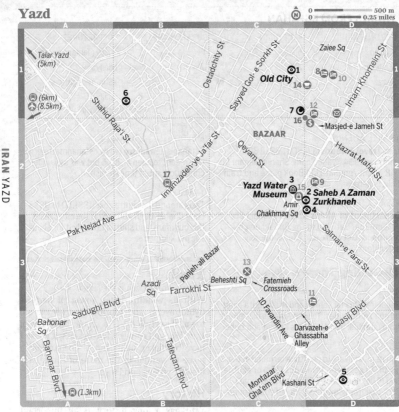

◉ Sights

★ Old City
NEIGHBOURHOOD

(بافت قدیم) With its *badgirs* (windtowers) poking from a baked-brown labyrinth, old Yazd feels, and is, ancient. Just about everything is made from sun-dried mud bricks, and houses are shielded behind high walls on narrow *kuches* (lanes) crisscrossing town. Wander to discover simple courtyards, ornate wooden doors and lovely adobe architecture. Ascend to the rooftops at some point for fine views over town and the desert beyond.

Masjed-e Jameh
MOSQUE

(مسجد جامع, Jameh Mosque; Masjed-e Jameh St; ⊙24hr) FREE Dominating the old city, this magnificent building has a tiled entrance portal that is one of Iran's tallest, flanked by impressive minarets and adorned with a 15th-century inscription. The exquisite mosaics on the dome and mihrab, and the tiles above the main western entrance to the courtyard, are particularly stunning.

Bagh-e Dolat Abad
PAVILION, GARDENS

(باغ دولت آباد; admission US$3; ⊙7.30am-5pm) Once belonging to a residence of regent Karim Khan Zand, these classic Persian gardens were built about 1750. The pavilion's interior is superb, with intricate latticework and exquisite stained glass. It also has Iran's loftiest *badgir*, standing nearly 34m. There's a restaurant and cafe. Reach it via a pleasant stroll along the dry canal on Shahid Raja St just west of Imamzadeh-ye Ja'far.

★ Saheb A Zaman Zurkhaneh
ZURKHANEH

(زور خانه صاحب الزمان; admission US$1.50; ⊙workouts Sat-Thu) Just off the north side of Amir Chakhmaq Sq, this traditional Iranian gym is an interesting cultural insight, part aerobics and weights class, part religious rite. The building is a cavernous 16th-century *ab anbar* (water reservoir). There

Yazd

are several hour-long workouts daily (except Fridays), with a fixed 6pm slot.

👉 Tours

Yazd is a base for tours, with the most popular being a half-day in the desert (including camel riding) or a trip to Kharanaq, Chak Chak and Meybod. You can get a driver-guide to do the latter circuit for under US$30 but better guides usually charge more. There are numerous worthwhile guides.

Amir Sharafat　　　　　　　　　　GUIDE
(☑ 0913-253 6370; amirsharafat@gmail.com) Amir speaks excellent English and is relaxed but very knowledgeable; he's been warmly recommended by several readers.

Mohsen Hajisaeid　　　　　　　　GUIDE
(☑ 0913-351 4460; www.iranpersiatour.com) Mohsen is great for organising things, and a mine of cultural and practical knowledge.

Mehran Toosizadeh　　　　　　　GUIDE
(☑ 0913-359 7003; www.mehran-2c.blogfa.com) Friendly and very helpful, Mehran speaks good English.

🛏 Sleeping

The old city is the most atmospheric area to stay. Several 'traditional hotels' make characterful lodgings, though service in many can be glib.

Kohan Traditional Hotel　　　　HOTEL $
(Kohan Kashaneh; ☑ 035-5621 2485; www.kohan-hotel.ir; Fahadan District; s/d US$21/30; ❄ @ 🕎)
A renovated, historic family home in old-town Yazd endowed with a relaxed, genu-inely welcoming ambience. Unadorned but comfortable rooms are set around a lush garden courtyard, and there's a restaurant serving local dishes plus a roof terrace. Discounts may be available off-season.

Hotel Kourosh　　　　　　HOTEL, HOSTEL $
(☑ 035-5620 3560; www.yazdhotelkourosh.com; Fahadan District; dm/s/d US$10/24/33; ❄ 🕎)
Deep in Yazd's mud-brick heart, this cordial place surrounds a pretty garden courtyard. Rooms are traditional in style: comfortable enough but don't expect luxury. Some are better than others, and there's an OK dorm. There's something appealingly relaxing about the vibe here and staff are genuinely friendly.

Silk Road Hotel　　　　　HOSTEL, HOTEL $
(☑ 035-5625 2730; www.silkroadhotelgroup.com; 5 Tal-e Khakestary Alley, off Masjed-e Jameh St; dm/s/d/tr US$6/25/35/45; ❄ @ 🕎) The mix of attractive courtyard, decent restaurant, laid-back vibe and fair prices have made this Yazd's backpacker centre. We get lots of criticism of it (they tend to overbook, then shunt

---

THE BADGIRS OF YAZD

Any summer visitor will understand immediately why the city's roofscape is a forest of badgirs (windtowers, pronounced 'bad-gears'). These ancient systems of natural air-conditioning are designed to catch even the lightest breeze and direct it to the rooms or water reservoir below. To appreciate the effect, just stand beneath one.

ⓘ WARNING

Yazd is a backpacker hub, and common problems are present: complacent hotel staff, shonky guides, and a declining quality of service from popular places and people. Ask fellow travellers for up-to-the-minute recommendations.

More seriously, solo female travellers have reported being harassed and sexually assaulted here. We recommend not walking alone around the old town.

you to a sister establishment) and rooms aren't anything special, but the atmosphere and social scene appeal.

Hotel Vali
HOTEL **$$**

(☑ 035-5622 8050; www.valihotel.com; off Imam Khomeini Ave; d with bathroom US$40-65; P ✳ 🛜) This restored caravanserai certainly looks the part: the large canvas-covered courtyard space is a fine sight. There's a bewildering range of rooms, some with exterior bathroom, and with sizes ranging from spacious to compact. The location is great and there's an on-site restaurant, but service is poor, sometimes comically so.

Laleh Hotel
HOTEL **$$$**

(☑ 035-5622 5048; www.yazdlalehhotel.com; off Darvazeh-e Ghassabha Alley, Basij Blvd; s/d US$46/71; P ✳ @ 🛜) Laleh is one of the prettiest of the restored homes, with slightly faded rooms set around three attractive courtyards in a working-class, old-town neighbourhood off the tourist beat but reasonably central. It also has an attractive restaurant-teahouse. From Basij, turn down Darvazeh and take the seventh left (including alleys) then first right.

🍴 Eating & Drinking

Traditional hotels have courtyard teahouse-restaurants: atmospheric places for a meal or drink, though the quality in most is mediocre. Camel meat is available in stews and at certain kabab stalls.

In the passage under the Amir Chakhmaq building kababis specialise in *jigar* (liver) and other meats (30¢ to US$1 per skewer).

Baharestan Restaurant
IRANIAN **$**

(Beheshti Sq; meals US$2-4; ⊙ 11.30am-4pm) Forget atmosphere and style: the Baharestan is about tasty staples at very tasty

prices; the *khoresht* (stew) and kababs are decent. No toilet.

⭐ Talar Yazd
IRANIAN **$$**

(☑ 035-5525 2019; www.talareyazd.ir; Ghandehaeri Alley, off Jomhuri-e Eslami Blvd; mains US$3-8; ⊙ noon-4pm & 7-11pm) It's an 8km ride from central Yazd (US$3 in a cab) but worth every metre. Elegant but uncomplicated, the Talar presents a short menu of classic Iranian dishes plus items like slow-roast lamb. It's all reliably delicious: kababs are succulent and flavoursome, service is attentive and prices more than fair. Go on your first night as you'll want to return.

Caesar
ITALIAN, IRANIAN **$$**

(☑ 035-5826 5600; 140 Saderat Bank St, off Abuzar Sq; mains US$4-10; ⊙ 11.30am-3.30pm & 7.30-11.30pm) Caesar, in vogue with a fashionable crowd, is a world away from old-town Yazd. Classic Italian dishes are worthwhile, though the Iranian dishes are better. Upstairs is quieter, the fresh lemonade delicious and the coffee tops. It's quite a way southeast; a US$3 cab ride from downtown.

Art Center
TEAHOUSE

(House of Mehdi Malek Zadeh; entry US$1.20; ⊙ 8am-9pm) This rooftop teahouse is a lovely place to relax with a cup of something. Climb further for brilliant views over Yazd's *badgirs* and courtyards. There are crafts for sale and they do light meals like omelettes and soups.

🛍 Shopping

Haj Khalifeh Ali Rahbar
CONFECTIONER

(www.hajkhalifehalirahbar.com; cnr Amir Chakhmaq Sq & Imam Khomeini St; ⊙ 9am-1pm & 5-9pm Sat-Thu) Yazd is famous for sweets and the most famous shop is this centenarian place. Look around, write down what you want, take it to the counter where your choice will be boxed, take the receipt and pay at the cash-

BUSES FROM YAZD

DESTINATION	FARE (US$; MAHMOOLY/ VIP)	DURATION (HR)
Esfahan	4/6	4-5
Kashan	4/6	4½
Kerman	4/7	3½-4½
Mashhad	8/13	11-13
Shiraz	4/7	5-6
Tehran	6/10	6-7

TRAINS FROM YAZD

DESTINATION	FARE (US$)	DURATION (HR)
Esfahan	4	3½
Kerman	5	6
Mashhad	17	14
Tehran via Kashan	7-12	5½-7

ier, then collect your sweets. And prepare for a major sugar high.

ℹ️ Information

MONEY

Kazemi Exchange (Masjed-e Jameh St; ⊘9am-1pm & 4-6pm Sat-Thu) Not the best rates but a very convenient central location.

TOURIST INFORMATION

Several tour companies run 'tourist information' offices around the old town.

Tourist Office (Amir Chakhmaq Sq; ⊘5-8pm Sat-Thu; 🐦) Located in the Amir Chakhmaq Complex, it supplies maps, books tours and offers free wi-fi. It plans to open mornings too.

TRAVEL AGENCIES

Starsland Tour & Travel (📋035-1827 0091; starsland91@yahoo.com; Masjed-e Jameh St; ⊘9am-2.30pm & 3.30-6pm) Upstairs office; helpful for arranging tours and onward travel on trains, planes or buses.

VISA EXTENSIONS

Tourist Police Office (📋035-5218 3867; Kashani St; ⊘8am-2pm Sat-Wed, 8am-noon Thu) Close to Abuzar Sq. Recent traveller reports have been positive.

ℹ️ Getting There & Away

AIR

There are daily flights to Tehran and Mashhad.

BUS

All buses leave from the **main bus terminal** (Rah Ahan Blvd).

ℹ️ Getting Around

The airport is on Yazd's western fringe. The main bus terminal is 7km west of the centre, and the train station about 3km southwest. Local buses (15¢) travel between the bus terminal and a stop near the corner of Imamzadeh-ye Ja'far and Shahid Raja'i Sts.

Taxis *dar baste* (charter) cost around US$2 to US$4 from transport terminals to the city centre.

Shiraz شیراز

📋071 / POP 1.46 MILLION / ELEV 1531M

Celebrated as the heartland of Persian culture for millennia, Shiraz has become synonymous with education, nightingales, poetry and wine. It's home to splendid gardens, poets' tombs, exquisite mosques and echoes of ancient sophistication that reward lingering. And Persepolis is just down the road.

History

The encouragement of enlightened rulers and the presence of artists and scholars helped make Shiraz one of the greatest cities in the Islamic world throughout the 13th and 14th centuries. Centuries of decline followed until Karim Khan of the short-lived Zand dynasty made it his capital in 1750.

⊙ Sights

Bazar-e Vakil   BAZAAR
(بازار وکیل; ⊘8am-9pm Sat-Thu) The city's ancient trading district is home to several bazaars dating from different periods. The finest and most famous is the Bazar-e Vakil, a cruciform structure commissioned by Karim Khan: part of his plan to make Shiraz into a great trading centre. The wide vaulted brick avenues are architectural masterpieces.

★**Aramgah-e Shah-e Cheragh**   SHRINE
(آرامگاه شاهچراغ; Ahmadi Sq; ⊘variable, often 24hr) **FREE** One of Iran's holiest Shiite sites, this shrine is where Sayyed Mir Ahmad, a brother of Imam Reza, was killed in 835. From the courtyard, admire the bulbous blue-tiled dome and gold-topped minarets; the attractive, well-kept **museum** houses an interesting archaeological collection and prized old Qurans.

Non-Muslims can usually enter the spectacular shrine itself, where countless mirror tiles reflect the faithful's passion, with a respectful attitude. Drop by the friendly International Affairs office for a chat, tea and free guided visit.

Check bags and cameras by the complex entrance. Women must grab a chador as they go in.

Arg-e Karim Khan   FORTRESS
(ارگ کریمخان, Citadel of Karim Khan; Shohada Sq; admission US$4.50; ⊘7.30am-8.30pm) Dominating the centre, this burly fortress formed part of Karim Khan's royal court. The high walls are punctuated by four attractive

THE CLASSIC YAZD DAY TRIP

Kharanaq

The virtually deserted and crumbling mud-brick village of Kharanaq (Kharanagh) is in a valley about 70km north of Yazd and a very picturesque spot for a wander, great for photography in the morning or late afternoon. The restored **caravanserai** is now a hotel.

Chak Chak

This isolated desert cliff-face **Ateshkadeh** (آتشکده, Sacred Eternal Flame; Kashani St; admission US$1; ☺8am-sunset) is Iran's most important Zoroastrian pilgrimage site. Legend has it that after the Arab invasion in AD 637, the Sassanian princess Nikbanuh fled to this site. Short of water, she threw her staff at the cliff and water began dripping out – *chak, chak* means 'drip, drip'. The setting is spectacular but the modern pilgrim buildings very ugly. The **fire temple** is home to the drip. The dramatic views make it worth the visit.

Meybod

Meybod is an ancient mud-brick town with several intriguing buildings. In the centre, crumbling **Narin castle** (admission US$3; ☺8am-sunset) dates from Sassanian times but has Achaemenid foundations and evidence of much earlier settlement beneath. It's open all day but the guard often slips off for lunch.

A cluster of sights in the west of town include a beautifully restored **caravanserai**, with craft shops, a restaurant and a *zeilo* (prayer rug) **museum** (admission incl icehouse 30¢; ☺9am-5pm Sat-Thu, to 7pm summer). Alongside is a 300-year-old **post house** (admission US$1.50; ☺9am-5pm Sat-Thu); ask at the caravanserai if it's closed. It's in front of a handsome *ab anbar* (reservoir) and opposite a huge, conical-roofed Safavid-era **icehouse** (same ticket as the *zeilo* museum).

As you leave town towards Yazd, stop at the impressive **pigeon house**, with 4000 niches.

14m-high circular towers, one with a noticeable lean. Inside is a large citrus-tree **courtyard** and dusty **museum**; the beautiful stucco work in the **bathhouse** is worth the price of admission.

★ **Masjed-e Vakil** MOSQUE
(مسجد وکیل, Regent's Mosque; admission US$1.50; ☺9am-sunset) Begun in Karim Khan's time, this mosque has an impressive tiled portal, a recessed entrance decorated with tiles and *muqarnas* (stone carvings), two vast *iwans*, a magnificent inner courtyard surrounded by beautifully tiled alcoves and porches, and a pleasingly proportioned vaulted prayer hall.

Masjed-e Nasir-al-Molk MOSQUE
(مسجد نصیرالملک, Nasir-al-Molk Mosque, Pink Mosque; off Lotf Ali Khan Blvd; admission US$1.50; ☺7.30am-noon, 3-6.30pm) This 19th-century mosque with exquisite tiling has some particularly fine *muqarnas* in the smallish outer portal and in the northern *iwan*, but the winter prayer hall, where, early in the morning, the sun shining through stained glass dapples the carved pillars with coloured light, is spectacular. The museum area

opens onto a well where cows walked downhill to raise the water.

Aramgah-e Hafez MAUSOLEUM
(آرامگاه حافظ, Tomb of Hafez; Golestan Blvd; admission US$4.50; ☺7.30am-9.30pm) Hafez the poet is a folk hero: loved, revered, popular as a pop star. Almost every Iranian can quote his work and people read fortunes by opening Hafez to a random page. There is no better place to try to understand Iran's relationship with poetry than here at his tomb set in a garden. After sunset, with sung poems broadcast, there's a great atmosphere.

Bagh-e Eram GARDENS
(باغ ارم, Garden of Paradise; Eram Blvd; admission US$4.50; ☺8am-12.30pm & 2.30-5pm) Famous for its tall cypresses, this Unesco-listed garden was laid out during the Qajar period but incorporates earlier elements. The many hidden corners are wildly popular with young Shirazis.

☞ Tours

Tours can also be arranged through almost every hotel in town.

Iran Travel Service TOURS
(📱 0917-300 3249; www.irantravelservice.com)
Helpful boss Mojtaba is a mine of information on Iran.

Morteza Mehrparvar DRIVING TOURS
(📱 0917-314 6124; www.mori-tours.com) Morteza knows central Iran intimately: a great choice for journeys to Yazd via Persepolis/Pasargadae or over the Zagros Mountains to Esfahan.

Pars Tours TOURS
(📱 071-3223 2428; www.key2persia.com; Zand Blvd; ⏰ 9am-9pm Sat-Thu, to 1pm Fri) Offers a huge range of tours, including popular, good-value half/full-day group trips to Persepolis for US$30/55 per person.

🛏 Sleeping

Golshan Hostel HOSTEL, HOTEL $
(📱 071-3222 0715; www.golshanhostel.com; Alley 38, Lotf Ali Khan Blvd; dm/s/d US$10/30/35; 🛜) Set around a traditional-style courtyard on a busy commercial street by the bazaar, this has a characterful location. The dorm and rooms can echo with noise, but they are comfortable: bathrooms in private rooms are tiny but OK.

Sasan Hotel HOTEL $
(📱 071-3230 2028; www.sasan-hotel.com; Anvari St; s/d US$24/35; ❄@🛜) This is a clean, well-maintained place in a good location. Some rooms have bathrooms with Western toilets, others squats; all are decent and commodious, though there's street noise at the front. Wi-fi costs extra and they sell their tours hard.

Anvari Hotel HOTEL $
(📱 071-3233 7591; Anvari St; s/d US$18/21, without bathroom US$15/18; ❄🛜) There's nothing fancy about this four-storey budget place, but it's clean and comfortable enough for the money. Rooms have hard beds, satellite TV and noisy air-conditioning units. Private bathrooms have squat toilets, but there are a couple of Western versions in the shared bathrooms. Breakfast costs an extra 30¢.

⭐ **Niayesh Boutique Hotel** HOTEL, HOSTEL $$
(📱 071-3223 3622; www.niayeshhotels.com; 10 Shahzadeh Jamaili Lane; dm/s/d US$9/25/40; 🅿❄🛜) This traditional hotel is tucked away and worth finding: it's got great character. Sleep in the clean and comfortable dorm or in private rooms; some arranged

around the central, sociable cafe-restaurant courtyard (noisy but appealing); others in an annexe. Staff are efficient rather than effusive but traveller-friendly facilities include laundry service and tours.

⭐ **Karim Khan Hotel** HOTEL $$
(📱 071-3223 5001; www.karimkhanhotel.com; Rudaki Ave; s/d/tr US$40/49/62; 🅿❄@🛜) Eye-catchingly decorated in period style, this newish hotel offers excellent value for what is, despite the odd defect, a handsome, ultra-central place. Rooms aren't quite opulent, but are attractive, with decent modern bathrooms. Breakfast is served in their sister hotel a few metres away.

Parhami Traditional House HOMESTAY $$
(📱 071-3223 2015; off Lotf Ali Khan Zand Blvd; s/d US$30/35; 🛜) Though it's overpriced for what it offers (try for a discount), there's something peaceful and authentic about this pretty, very friendly family home set around a little citrus-filled courtyard. Some rooms are poky, but others are substantially more spacious.

From the alley directly opposite the one leading to Nasir-al-Molk mosque, turn left, right, then left at the car park. Follow this lane: after a few twists, you'll see a big metal door with a buzzer on your left.

🍴 Eating

Local staples include ice-cream-and-noodle concoction *faludeh* and Shirazi salad, a refreshing melange of onion, tomato and cucumber. But the famous Shiraz (Syrah) grape is no longer made into the wine that inspired Hafez to poetry.

Seray-e Mehr Teahouse TEAHOUSE $
(Seray-e Mehr, Bazar-e Vakil; meals US$3-6, tea US$1; ⏰ 10am-8pm Sat-Thu) A fine stop after bazaar wandering, this two-level teahouse has a small menu of tasty favourites and a relaxed (when a tour group isn't in) atmosphere in which to sit, eat and sip tea. It also has a clean Western toilet.

Bell Passi IRANIAN, ITALIAN $$
(📱 071-3227 4924; www.bellpassi.ir; Khakshenasi St; mains US$5-9; ⏰ 8-11am, noon-3pm & 6.30-11pm) A lovely lunch option after a stroll in nearby Bagh-e Eram, this has a dark, stylish interior and does a nice line in risottos, pasta, pizza, enormous Caesar salads and very tasty Iranian fish and kabab dishes. Service is friendly and there are a few fresh juice options.

IRAN SHIRAZ

Shiraz

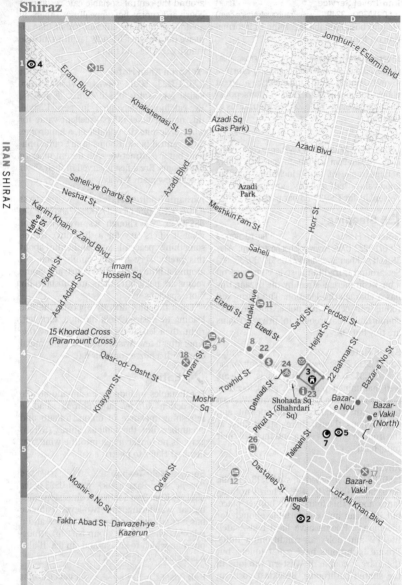

Shater Abbas   IRANIAN **$$**
(☎071-3227 1617; Khakshenasi St, off Azadi Blvd; mains US$4-13; ⏱11.30am-11.30pm; ☎) The bustling open kitchen and the hard-working waiters attest to the popularity of this long-standing favourite. Descend the stairs into the basement and claim a table for a salad buffet and excellent kababs or fish dishes accompanied by the delicious bread you see being baked as you enter.

Shiraz

◎ Sights

◎ Activities, Courses & Tours

◎ Sleeping

◎ Eating

◎ Drinking & Nightlife

◎ Information

◎ Transport

unfortunately the food, mostly kababs and fish, is pricey and doesn't quite live up to the surroundings. You may prefer coffee from the ground-floor cafe. It's 30¢ to visit outside of opening hours.

★ **Haft Khan**　　　　　　　IRANIAN $$$
(☏ 0917-787 8400; www.haftkhanco.com; cnr 17th Alley & Quran Jadid Blvd; buffet US$19, à la carte meals US$8-21; ◎ 10am-midnight; ☏ ✐) This stylish place has five levels of restaurants, including an all-you-can-eat lunchtime buffet (huge array, great for vegetarians). Even better is the modern-traditional basement, a beautiful white space with standout Iranian dishes including hard-to-find regional specials (and sheep's head). Mains comfortably serve two; try the exquisite cordials.

Shapouri Gardens　　　　　IRANIAN $$
(www.shapourigarden.com; Anvari St; mains US$5-12; ◎ noon-4pm & 7-11pm; ☏) On a street devoted to muscle-powder shops and fast food, this striking 1930s villa surprises. It's a romantic spot, with lovely balcony seating;

Surrounds are modern and elegant, service attentive.

🍷 Drinking & Nightlife

★ Ferdowsi Cafe
CAFE

(Ferdosi St; ⊙9am-11pm; 🛜) Our favourite cafe has a loyal local crowd of liberally minded young Shirazis, overseen by genial boss Mojtaba. Ask him about the range of brilliant flavoured teas (the sour one is a real jolt for the tastebuds) and the cake of the day, reliably sweet and delicious. They do generous plates of pasta, omelettes and the like too.

Kachar
TEAHOUSE

(Rudaki Ave; ⊙10am-11pm) This upstairs tea-house is welcoming and a good place to meet locals, as the Tetris-like shuffling of cushion stools and tables in the small rooms means you'll probably end up sharing with someone. It's good for tea and *qalyan,* or a limited but tasty menu of food. Prices are high-ish but it's atmospheric.

ℹ️ Information

MONEY

Zand Exchange (📱 071-3222 2854; Karim Khan-e Zand Blvd; ⊙8am-1pm & 4-7pm Sat-Wed, 8am-1pm Thu) One of several exchange places in this area.

TOURIST INFORMATION

Tourist Office (📱 071-3224 1985; Karim Khan-e Zand Blvd; ⊙9.30am-4.30pm Sat-Thu) Helpful English-speaking 'Shahram' Hamidi is a fixture here. He sometimes can't open until 11am or so.

TRAVEL AGENCIES

Hadavi Flying Group (📱 071-3222 2483; hadavifc@yahoo.com; Karim Khan-e Zand Blvd; ⊙8.30am-1pm & 4-8pm Sat-Thu) Helpful, central English-speaking office for flights, trains and some buses.

VISA EXTENSIONS

Department of Aliens Affairs (57 St, off Modarres Blvd; ⊙8am-1pm Sat-Wed, 8-11am Thu) Best place to extend in Iran.

ℹ️ Getting There & Away

AIR

There are daily flights to Tehran and Mashhad, less frequent ones to other cities.

Shiraz is served from İstanbul by Turkish Airlines and from Gulf cities by several carriers including budget airline Air Arabia.

BUSES FROM SHIRAZ

DESTINATION	FARE (US$; MAHMOOLY/ VIP)	DURATION (HR)
Esfahan	4/7.50	6-7
Kashan	5/8	8-9
Mashhad	11/20	16-19
Tabriz	21	22
Tehran	9/14	10-13
Yazd	4/7	5-6

BUS & TAXI

Most long-distance buses and savaris operate from **Karandish terminal** (Terminal-e Bozorg; Salman-e Farsi Blvd).

TRAIN

There are three weekly night trains to Tehran (US$24, 15 hours) via Esfahan and Kashan.

ℹ️ Getting Around

From bus terminal to central Shiraz is a flat US$2 fare.

The **Shiraz Urban Railway** (www.shirazmetro. ir) is being built. The limited stretch currently open isn't really useful for travellers.

Shuttle taxis cost 30¢ to 65¢. Taxis *dar baste* charge between US$1.50 and US$4.50 depending on distance.

Bike Station (Karim Khan-e Zand Blvd; per hr US$1.50; ⊙7.30am-8pm) Just west of Shohada Sq, grab a bike to explore Shiraz. You'll need a document as a deposit.

Persepolis
پرسپولیس

ELEV 1630M

Magnificent **Persepolis** (Takht-e Jamshid; admission US$4.50, parking US$1.50; ⊙8am-5pm Nov-Mar, to 7pm Apr-Oct) embodies the zenith of the Achaemenid empire, and its demise. The monumental staircases, exquisite reliefs and imposing gateways make it Iran's most impressive ancient site.

There is little shade: bring a hat, sunglasses and water. Backpacks and tripods must be deposited by the entrance.

History

Work here began with Darius I (the Great), who took the throne in 520 BC, and it was added to by subsequent kings. It was a ceremonial capital at the heart of an enormous empire, a showcase designed to awe visitors with its scale and beauty. During the annual No Ruz (New Year) celebration, subjects came from across the empire to pay homage and tribute to the ruler. Persepolis was burned to the ground during Alexander the Great's visit in 330 BC.

◉ Sights

Grand Stairway & Xerxes' Gateway GATEWAY
Entry to the complex is via the monumental **Grand Stairway**. Atop it, **Xerxes' Gateway** (also known as the Gate of All Nations) is still a wonderfully impressive monument, guarded by Assyrian-influenced, bull-like figures. A cuneiform inscription declares Xerxes I as the builder. Centuries of graffitists have also left their mark, including explorer Henry Morton Stanley.

Beyond are **column capitals** decorated with evocative double griffin heads, apparently buried without ever being used – a short-lived caprice of royalty, perhaps.

★ **Apadana Palace & Staircase** PALACE
The grandest palace at Persepolis has bas-reliefs along the northern wall evocatively depicting the scenes of splendour that accompanied the arrival of delegations to meet with the king. Most impressive of all, however, are the wonderful reliefs of the Apadana Staircase. The panels at the southern end are the most interesting, showing 23 delegations, a rich record of the nations of the time, bringing their gifts to the Achaemenid king.

Private Palaces PALACES
The southwestern corner of the site is dominated by palaces likely constructed during the reigns of Darius and Xerxes. The **Tachara** is easily the most striking, with monolithic doorjambs still standing, covered in bas-reliefs and cuneiform inscriptions. The southern stairs bear highly skilled, photogenic reliefs.

Persepolis Museum MUSEUM
What was perhaps once the royal harem now houses the museum, currently closed to the public.

Treasury & Tombs RUIN, TOMBS
Darius' Treasury is one of the site's earliest structures. When Alexander looted Persepolis it's reported he needed 3000 camels to cart off the contents. Foundations and column bases are all that remain. On the hill above are the striking rock-hewn tombs of **Artaxerxes II** and **Artaxerxes III**.

Palace of 100 Columns PALACE
With an extravagant hall supported by 100 stone columns, this was the second-largest building at Persepolis, built during the

IRAN PERSEPOLIS

Persepolis

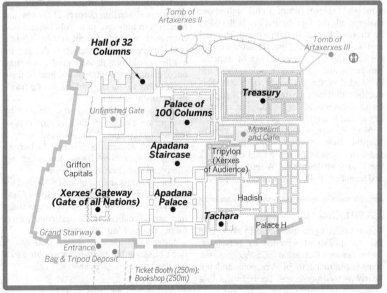

Tomb of
Artaxerxes II

Tomb of
Artaxerxes III

Hall of 32 Columns

Treasury

Unfinished Gate

Palace of 100 Columns

Museum and Cafe

Apadana Staircase

Tripylon (Xerxes of Audience)

Griffon Capitals

Xerxes' Gateway (Gate of all Nations)

Apadana Palace

Hadish

Tachara

Palace H

Grand Stairway

Entrance

Bag & Tripod Deposit

Ticket Booth (250m);
Bookshop (250m)

reigns of Xerxes and Artaxerxes I. Reliefs on the doorjambs at the back (south) depict a king, soldiers and representatives of subject nations.

☞ Tours

Every Shiraz hotel organises Persepolis tours. For trips including nearby Naqsh-e Rostam a driver-guide usually charges US$45 for a half-day tour. A full-day tour to those sights plus Pasargadae and lunch will cost US$75. Some full-day tours include an interesting traditional lunch. Visits are cheaper with a nonguiding driver or taxi.

Tours are worthwhile if hurried: the advantage of a private driver is that you can dictate what time is spent where.

Guides vary widely; some give out wildly inaccurate information. Official guides are available at the site.

❶ Getting There & Away

Persepolis is 53km northeast of Shiraz. Many travellers take tours or hire a driver, but you can get a minibus or savari to Marvdasht, from where a taxi should cost US$2 to US$3.

If you're coming from Yazd or Esfahan, you can jump off the bus at Marvdasht.

Naqsh-e Rostam

The spectacular rock tombs at **Naqsh-e Rostam** (admission US$3; ⊙8am-5pm) are a must-see. Hewn out of a cliff high above the ground, the four tombs are believed to be those of Darius II, Artaxerxes I, Darius I and Xerxes I. Below them, Sassanian reliefs cut into the cliff depict scenes of imperial conquests and royal ceremonies; there are detailed descriptions below each one. Facing the cliff the **Bun Khanak** was thought to be an Achaemenid fire temple, but scholars argue that it might have been a treasury.

Most Persepolis tours include a visit to Naqsh-e Rostam, 3km from the Shiraz–Esfahan highway. In winter you could walk the 6km from Persepolis. A return trip in a taxi from Persepolis will cost around US$4.50.

Pasargadae

Begun under Cyrus the Great in about 546 BC but quickly superseded by Persepolis, **Pasargadae** (admission US$4.50; ⊙8am-5pm) is 80km north of Persepolis and not nearly as well preserved. It's beautiful in a lonely, windswept way. The hard-to-discern remnants of **Darius' garden** are World Heritage; the austere and awesomely simple **Tomb of Cyrus** stands proudly on the Morghab Plain.

Visit Pasargadae on a tour or by jumping off a bus between Shiraz and Yazd/Esfahan (or vice versa). It's a 5.5km walk or cab from the turn-off.

NORTHEASTERN IRAN شمال شرقی ایران

Mashhad مشهد

☎ 051 / POP 2.75 MILLION / ELEV 985M

Mashhad is Iran's holiest and second-biggest city. Its *raison d'être* and main sight is the beautiful, massive shrine complex commemorating the AD 817 martyrdom of Shiite Islam's eighth Imam, Reza. Tens of millions converge here yearly to pay their respects; witnessing the emotion is profoundly moving. During major pilgrim periods, accommodation and transport books out.

◉ Sights

★ **Haram-e Razavi**   SHRINE
(رضوی حرام; Imam Reza Shrine; www.imamrezashrine.com; ⊙24hr) FREE Imam Reza's Holy Shrine is enveloped in a series of sacred precincts. This magical city-within-a-city sprouts dazzling clusters of domes and minarets in blue and pure gold behind vast courtyards and magnificent arcades. It's one of the marvels of the Islamic world, and its glories should be fully savoured more than once: compare the orderly overload of dusk prayer-time to the fairy-tale calm of a flood-lit nocturnal wander.

You have to check bags and cameras by the entrance, although discreet mobile photos are acceptable. Women must wear a chador: it's sometimes possible to borrow one from your hotel. Dress for either sex should be conservative and clean.

Non-Muslims are not officially allowed inside the Holy Shrine or Azim-e Gohar Shad mosque, though those who act respectfully may not be challenged. Be particularly careful not to upset Muslim sensibilities.

Entering vast **Razavi Grand Courtyard**: don't miss, on the far side, descending to a fabulous mirrored **prayer hall**.

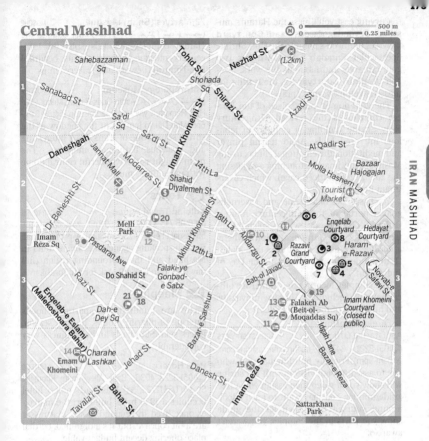

Central Mashhad

Curving east you'll pass the Haram's museums. Beyond, gorgeous **Azadi Courtyard** provides one access point to the Holy Shrine. Spectacular **Enqelab Courtyard** has two gold minarets and fabulous tile work. Sizeable **Jomhuri Courtyard** is the setting for massed evening *namaz* (prayers).

The gold-domed centrepiece of the Haram complex is the revered 17th-century **Holy Shrine** building, a complex of fabulous mirrored halls. Amid tearful prayer and meditation, the emotional climax to any Mashhad pilgrimage is touching and kissing the *zarih* (gold-latticed cage), which covers Imam Reza's tomb.

You'll see the blue dome and cavernous golden portal of the 15th-century **Azim-e Gohar Shad** mosque, whose splendid interior hosts the *minbar* (pulpit) where, according to Shiite tradition, the Mahdi (12th 'hidden' Imam) will sit on the Day of Judgement.

The complex incorporates numerous other features, including a library, university, and hundreds of rooms and halls.

➤ **Foreign Pilgrims Assistance Office**　　TOURIST SERVICES
(☑ 051-3221 3474; iro@imamrezashrine.com; ⊙6am-9pm) Friendly multilingual staff who live to assist foreign visitors with the shrine will show you a video then assign you a free guide/minder. You may want to have a look around yourself first, then let the guide show you parts of the complex you weren't aware of.

➤ **Central Museum**　　MUSEUM
(موزه مرکزی; Muze-ye Merkezi; admission incl Carpet Museum 30¢; ⊙8am-5.45pm Sat-Thu, 8am-noon Fri) Bequests and donations fill this eclectic museum, which includes old elements of shrine decor as well as stamps and coins, telescopes and globes, sporting medals presented by pious athletes, seashells, stuffed sharks and landscape paintings of Surrey. Notice Mahmood Farshchian's famous wood-and-mother-of-pearl classic *After-noon of Ashura,* a grief-stricken depiction of Imam Hossein's horse returning empty to camp after the Imam's killing.

➤ **Carpet Museum**　　MUSEUM
(موزه فرش; admission incl with Central Museum; ⊙8am-12.30pm Sat-Wed, to 11.30am Thu, to noon Fri) Rugs here range from beautiful classics (including three Safavid- and Mughal-era ones downstairs) through to garish coral gardens.

72-Martyrs (Shah) Mosque　　MOSQUE
(هفتاد و دو - شهدا (شاه) مسجد) Just outside the Haram complex sits this splendid 15th-century mosque, famous for its beautiful late-Timurid tilework and tracery lamps.

Anthropology Museum　　MUSEUM
(موزه انسان شناسی; Astan Quds Razavi, Mehdi Gholibek Hamam; www.aqm.ir; admission 15¢; ⊙8am-6pm Mon-Thu, to 1pm Fri) In the shadow of the shrine squats one of Iran's most interesting and spacious bathhouse museums. The main delight is the wonderful central dome with naive 1920s murals.

👉 Tours

Adibian Travel Agency　　CAR TOURS
(☑ 0915-735 9060, 051-3859 8151; www.adibian.com; 56 Pasdaran Ave; ⊙7.30am-8pm) A professional, English-speaking agency that offers tours in Mashhad and the surrounding region (full day US$30 to US$66). Ask for Mr Torabi.

🛏 Sleeping

There are hundreds of apartment-hotels catering to pilgrim groups. In peak season, prices soar. Standards and cleanliness vary considerably.

Pars Hotel　　HOTEL $
(☑ 051-3222 4030; Bank Alley, Imam Khomeini St; s/d US$12/22; 🕸) Mashhad's oldest hotel occupies a 1935 brick building; the manager once lived in England. Some mattresses are a bit concave, but it's a dignified, cordial place offering decent budget value.

Vali's Homestay　　HOSTEL $
(☑ 0939-250 1447, 051-3851 6980; www.valishomestay.com; 277, 38th Alley Malekoshoara Bahar; dm/s/d US$10/20/25; ⊖@🕸) Eccentric, enthusiastic multilingual Vali offers backpacker accommodation: a pleasant carpeted dorm in a converted garage with a nonlockable private room off it. The highlight is the delicious home-cooked dinner (US$5); breakfast is US$2. Solo female travellers have reported feeling uncomfortable. From the main road, take the lane signposted '38' and 'mosque'; Vali's is at the end on the left.

Taranom Apartment Hotel　　APARTMENTS $$
(☑ 051-3225 2517; Tavakoli Alley; s/d US$30/40; ❄@🕸) Handily located, this professional eight-storey tower has a cosy mini-atrium and well-appointed minisuites with fluffy towels and brilliant hot showers. Prices soar in pilgrim season.

A GUIDE TO KABABS

In any restaurant, most main-dish options will be kabab. These are served either with bread or with buttery rice (*chelo kabab*). Kababs are tasty, healthy and cooked shish-style over charcoal. Fish kababs are often available, and very tasty. Other common incarnations include:

Barg Pieces of lamb or beef

Bakhtiari *Barg* and *juje*

Juje Marinated chicken pieces

Kubideh Minced mutton, breadcrumbs and onion

Sheesh/Shishlik Grilled meat pieces with bone, often lamb chops

Soltani *Kubideh* and *barg*

Hotel Noor   HOTEL $$
(☎051-3223 2970; www.hotelnoor.ir; Andarzgu/Khosravino St; d US$41; P❋@☎) The gently trendy 1st-floor lobby is bright and open with English-speaking staff. Rooms are unfussy, unexciting but spacious and commodious affairs with bagged-towels, double beds and a choice of toilets. Splendid value in peak season. The in-house restaurant is decent too.

Javad Hotel   HOTEL $$$
(☎051-3222 4135; www.javadhotel.com; Imam Reza St; r US$115; P❋@☎) One of several upmarket hotels lining Imam Reza as it approaches the sanctuary, this appeals for its proximity, warmly decorated rooms, polite staff and good facilities. There's a downstairs cafe and upstairs restaurant serving good kababs and soup/salad bar at fair prices. Rooms have low, relaxing beds, with plenty of doubles available. A spa complex was in the works.

✕ Eating

Cheap eateries crowd the lanes off Imam Reza St. For something more upmarket, there are few options apart from hotels. Look out for *maajun,* a fabulous mush of crushed walnuts, pistachios, ice cream, cream, banana and honey.

Ghods   IRANIAN $
(Imam Reza St; mains US$3-8) Look for the bronze deer on the staircase to find this basement restaurant, overlit but attractive enough in black and white. The woodcut menu is a nice touch and runs to predictable kabab favourites. They come out dry-ish but with plenty of taste and decent fresh bread.

★ Hezardestan Traditional Teahouse   TEAHOUSE $$
(☎051-3222 2943; Jannat Mall; mains US$7.50-14, tea, fruit & dessert charge US$4.50; ⊙11am-4pm & 6-11pm) This discreet basement is one of Iran's most beautiful teahouse-restaurants. Carpets, samovars, antique *qalyans,* cushions and wooden benches are surrounded by walls adorned with scenes from Ferdosi's *Shahnameh.* The short menu of food is tasty; just be prepared for hefty 'service' and 'tea' charges that can double the bill.

🔒 Shopping

Mashhad is great for buying carpets in distinctive Khorasan styles. Other purchases include turquoise, saffron and shrine souvenirs of debatable taste.

Saroye Saeed   CARPETS
(Andarzgu St; ⊙8am-2pm & 4-7pm Sat-Wed, 8am-2pm Thu) A multi-unit carpet market mostly aiming at bulk dealers, so prices can be excellent. There's a top-floor repair workshop and little sales pressure. Near the red neon 'Hosseini' sign.

ℹ Information

CONSULATES

Afghan Consulate (☎051-3854 1653; www.cg-afg.com; Do Shahid St; ⊙8am-noon Sat-Wed) Friendly, but by no means guaranteed to issue visas. Apply early and, in principle, the 30-day tourist visa should be ready the same day for a flat €75 fee.

Pakistani Consulate (☎051-3222 9845; mofa.gov.pk; Imam Khomeini St; ⊙9am-noon Sat-Wed) No visas for non-Iranians.

Turkmen Consulate (☎051-3854 7066; Do Shahid St, off Dah-e Dey Sq; ⊙8.30am-noon Mon-Thu & Sat) Allow several days for a five-day transit visa (most nationalities US$55). Mondays and Thursdays are theoretically for truckers only. You'll need an onward visa (Uzbek best, Kazakhstan also accepted, Azerbaijan maybe) and you must be able to state the entry and exit points by which you'll transit Turkmenistan.

Vali's Homestay can help with the process for a US$20 fee if you forward Vali the paperwork beforehand.

MONEY

Abrishami Exchange (Imam Khomeini St; ⊙9.30am-1.30pm & 5.30-7.30pm Sat-Wed,

9.30am-1.30pm Thu) One of several currency-exchange places on this block.

TOURIST INFORMATION
Pilgrim information counters in the shrine complex and at the airport can supply you with maps.

VISA EXTENSIONS
Edareh-ye Gozarnameh (☎ 051-3218 3907; 45 Metri-ye Reza St, Piruzi Blvd; ⊙ 8am-1pm Sat-Wed, to 10.30am Thu) Not the best place to apply.

❶ Getting There & Away

AIR
There are daily connections to all of Iran's major cities. Internationally, there are services to several Central Asian capitals as well as Gulf cities, including budget connections to Sharjah with Air Arabia, Dubai with FlyDubai and Kuwait with Jazeera.

BUS
Destinations served daily from the **main bus terminal** (end of Imam Reza St) include:
Esfahan (normal/VIP US$10/14, 17 hours)
Shiraz (US$12, 18 hours)
Tabriz (US$23, 23 hours)
Tehran (normal/VIP US$8.50/14, 14 hours, very frequent)
Yazd (normal/VIP US$8/13.50, 12 hours)

❶ Getting Around

TO/FROM THE AIRPORT
The metro should have reached the airport by the time you read this; the most central stops are Imam Khomeini and Basij: from the latter it's an easy change on to the bus to get to the Haram area. Taxis from the airport to the centre cost US$4.50.

BUS
Buy 10¢ tickets at ticket booths. From stops near Falakeh Ab, southbound bus 84 runs to the bus terminal.

TAXI
Shuttle taxis usually cost 30¢ (60¢ for longer hops). Taxis *dar baste* cost US$1.50 to US$3.

TRAINS FROM MASHHAD

DESTINATION	FARE (US$)	DURATION (HR)
Esfahan	22	17
Shiraz	12-27	17-24
Tabriz	18-28	25
Tehran	10-18	7-12
Yazd	17	14

UNDERSTAND IRAN

Iran Today

Social Freedoms
Despite the violent crackdown on the Green Movement after Ahmadinejad's re-election in 2009, the years since have seen a gradual relaxation in on-street repression. Morality police have eased off and street fashions have become more daring. The election of reform-minded Hassan Rouhani as president has given this further impetus.

Human Rights
As a traveller among the friendly Iranians, it is tempting to begin to think of the country as a benign clerical democracy with headscarves. This is far from being the case. While there's latitude – the mullahs don't really care about people using banned social media, for example, as long as they're listening to One Direction and not using Twitter to criticise the state – those who cross the line are dealt with extremely harshly. Iran's human rights record is abysmal, with the death penalty applied hundreds of times yearly, including for things like homosexuality and insulting the Prophet, after trials that are often deeply unjust. Journalists are regularly silenced; Iran languishes close to the bottom of the World Press Freedom Index. Iran for Iranians and for visitors are two wholly distinct experiences.

Nuclear Tensions
Iran feels it has a right to nuclear energy and has a sophisticated program to deliver this. It insists it has no plan to build nuclear weapons (Khameini describes them as un-Islamic), yet it has been uncooperative with international monitors.

The results, fuelled by former president Ahmadinejad's aggressive pronouncements against Israel, have been a swath of Security Council resolutions and economic sanctions which have cut Iran off from the international banking system. At time of writing however, talks were slow but ongoing and hopes of eventual resolution remained.

Economic Issues

The sanctions, together with highly subsidised food and energy, are putting enormous strain on the economy. Inflation has been rampant in recent years, unemployment is high and, right at the worst moment for Iran, oil prices plummeted in 2014 as fracking in other countries reduced demand for Middle Eastern stocks. Times will be tough.

The Future

Radical change has been coming in Iran for some time now; it's a question of how and when. While Western governments' self-interested agenda has almost exclusively been about regime change in Iran over the last decades, the emergence of Isis has moved the goalposts to some degree. Iran is a powerful ally against violent Sunni fundamentalism and offers vital military support to the embattled Iraqi government. So Western leaders, given an illusory choice, would probably now prefer gradual change in Iran to prevent more instability in the region. Within Iran, with mosque attendances dwindling and domestic approval for rule-by-cleric low, something has to give. But people are quietly hopeful that Rouhani may be able to deliver real change and increased freedom. He will be watched with interest.

History

Elam & the Aryans

A prominent early civilisation was Elam, a kingdom influenced by Sumer and regularly at war with them. The Elamites' capital, Susa (Shush), is Iran's most important archaeological site.

In the late 2nd millennium BC, Indo-European Aryan tribes began arriving from the north. Persians settled in central Iran, bringing the teachings of Zoroaster and the worship of Ahuramazda, traditions that would coalesce into what we now know as Zoroastrianism.

Achaemenids

The Persians and northwesterly Medes were unified under Cyrus, who ascended the throne in 559 BC and within 20 years created the greatest empire the world had known.

Darius I expanded the empire and created the magnificent ceremonial complex at Persepolis to serve as the imperial showcase. The defeat of his son Xerxes at Salamis in Greece in 480 BC began a slow decline culminating in Alexander the Great's conquest 150 years later.

Parthians & Sassanians

After Alexander's death, Persia was controlled by the Seleucids, but the Parthians, expert horse riders and archers, took over in the 3rd century and ruled for five centuries, punctuated with regular skirmishes with the Romans.

The Sassanians (Sassanids) went one better. In AD 260 King Shapur defeated the Romans at Edessa and actually captured Emperor Valerian.

Arab Conquest, Seljuks & Mongols

The Arabs defeated the Sassanians twice in 637, effectively ending the dynasty. The Persians adopted Islam but Iranian culture and administration enormously influenced the Arabs as they spread across the Middle East.

As caliphate power waned in the 9th century, local tribes established their own dynasties, eventually ousted by the Seljuks, a Turkic people who captured Esfahan in 1051, making it the capital. Their rule heralded a new era in Persian art, architecture, literature and science but their political power soon fragmented.

In the early 13th century, they came to a bloody end when rampaging Mongols under Genghis Khan, and later his grandson, swept across the Iranian plateau, leaving devastation in their wake. Despite the destruction, they eventually became great arts patrons and endowed many fine monuments.

However, in a story repeated throughout Iranian history, the tough conquerors found that the seductive Persian culture with its poetry, wine and romance soon rendered them ripe for conquest by the next hardcase that showed up on their borders.

That was Tamerlane, who came from Central Asia and conquered Persia, becoming famous for both his penchant for the arts and his bloodthirstiness.

HOME COOKING

For proper Iranian cooking, the best result is to get invited into an Iranian home. There's a good chance that will happen and when it does, just say 'yes'. As a guest you will be honoured as a 'gift of God' and the fabulous food and humbling hospitality should make for a meal you'll remember for a lifetime.

Safavid Iran & the 18th century

Synonymous with the glory of Iran, the Safavids ruled from the early 16th century. They turned Persia Shiite and ushered in a great national revival, especially under Shah Abbas I (r 1587–1629) who made Esfahan a wondrous city.

Things fell apart again in the 18th century, but two notable figures were Nader Shah, a military genius whose wars finally bankrupted the country, and Karim Khan Zand, a more dove-ish figure responsible for a golden age in Shiraz.

Foreign Powers

Constant meddling in Iranian affairs by Britain and Russia characterises the 19th century and Qajar dynasty. The pattern continued through the 20th century, with the pro-democracy Constitutional movement put down partly by Russia, then British-backed Reza Shah staging a coup and founding the Pahlavi dynasty.

Meanwhile, oil was drilled by the Anglo-Persian company (now BP) but outdated original agreeements didn't fairly compensate Iran. When reforming prime minister Mohammad Mossadegh tried for a better deal in the 1950s, the British refused, so he nationalised the industry. The CIA, paranoid about the spread of socialism, helped orchestrate a coup and Mossadegh was toppled.

The Islamic Revolution

Under Pahlavi rule, resistance had smouldered. Secular, communist and Islamic groups had a common desire to remove the shah, whose reforms were too slow for some and too un-Islamic for others. Exiled Ayatollah Khomeini was an inspirational figure, but much of the organising was done by unionists, communists and ordinary middle-class citizens. On 16 January 1979, Shah Mohammad Reza Pahlavi and his third wife, Farah Diba fled. Khomeini took the reins and moved fast, eliminating opposition and establishing a theocracy under the principle of velayat-e faqih (rule of Islamic jurists).

A brutal war with Western-backed Saddam Hussein's Iraq followed, and the sacrifice, often religiously inspired, of the Iranians became legendary: these shuhada (martyrs) are revered nationwide.

Khomeini died in 1989 and the supreme leadership passed to Ali Khamenei. Under him, presidents have ranged from smooth operator Akbar Hashemi Rafsanjani to reformist cleric Mohammad Khatami (1997–2005) and populist, hardline Mahmoud Ahmadinejad (2005–13). The election of Hassan Rouhani, seen as a moderate and a reformer, in 2013 sparked hope for systemic change.

Food & Drink

Iran is home to a diverse cuisine with great regional variations. Restaurant menus are over dominated by kababs and fast food, so you'll sometimes have to make a bit of an effort to find other specialities.

Dishes to look out for include zereshk polo ba morgh (chicken on rice tangy with barberries), ghorme sabzi (meat, beans and vegetables, served with rice) and khoresht (thick stew) including fesenjan (a pomegranate and walnut stew, normally with chicken).

Teahouses are venues for tea and qalyan (waterpipes) but also characterful spots for eating. A classic dish is dizi (abgusht), a delicious meat and chickpea stew with broth.

Soups – usually barley-based, often with barberries – and salads are the traditional accompaniments to a meal. Upmarket restaurants may have a salad bar.

There are several vegetarian restaurants in Tehran; not many elsewhere. Solace can be found, however, in the felafels, samosas,

ⓘ EATING DIZI

Eating dizi is a bit of an art. First, tear up some bread then drain off the broth over it (you may need to use two bits of bread to hold the scalding pot). Eat. Then pour the solids into the bowl and mash them into a paste with the pestle provided. Eat with a spoon or bread.

beans and beetroot sold in street stalls, salad bars in restaurants and various omelette and aubergine dishes.

Iran produces a head-spinning array of freshly made *shirini* (sweets): every town has its local specialities.

In the absence of alcohol, fruit-flavoured soft drinks are popular. 'Lemon beer' is a sweet, malt-based tipple with a shandy-ish flavour.

Arts

Architecture

Iranian architecture has influenced building throughout much of the Islamic world. Marvelling at mosques such as the small but perfect Masjed-e Sheikh Lotfollah in Esfahan will be among the highlights of your trip.

The defining aspects of Persian architecture are its monumental simplicity and lavish use of ornamentation and colour. Standard elements include: a courtyard and arcades, lofty entrance porticoes and four *iwan* (barrel-vaulted halls opening onto the courtyard).

These basic features are often so densely covered with decoration that observers are led to imagine the architecture is far more complex than it actually is. The decorations are normally geometric, floral or calligraphic.

Carpets

The best-known Iranian cultural export, the Persian carpet, is far more than just a floor covering to an Iranian. A Persian carpet is a display of wealth, an investment, an integral aspect of religious and cultural festivals, and part of everyday life.

Carpets come in almost as many different designs as there are ethnic groups and major urban centres. Some are inspired by religion; other common motifs include amulets to avert the evil eye and other, pre-Islamic motifs, such as stylised trees of life. They may also be inspired by whatever surrounds the weaver, eg trees, animals and flowers, particularly the lotus, rose and chrysanthemum. Gardens are commonly depicted.

In general, designs are classified as either 'tribal' or 'city' carpets. Tribal designs vary greatly depending on their origin, but are typically less ornate. City carpets are the classic Persian rugs, usually highly ornate floral designs around one or more medallions.

Millions of Iranians work in the industry but maintaining the brand is increasingly difficult with cheaper 'Persian carpets' being produced in India and Pakistan, and fewer young Iranians interested in learning to weave.

Poetry

Iranians venerate their great poets, who are seen as guardians of Persian culture and have mausolea that are popular pilgrimage sites.

FERDOSI

Ferdosi (940–1020) developed the *ruba'i* (quatrain) style of 'epic' historic poems and is remembered primarily for the *Shahnameh* (Book of Kings), which took 33 years to write. Ferdosi is seen as the saviour of Farsi, which he wrote in at a time when the language was under threat from Arabic.

HAFEZ

Hafez (1325–89) is the best-loved and most-quoted poet. This Shirazi's regular references to wine, courtship and nightingales have been interpreted in different ways (is wine literal or a metaphor for God?). His collected works, known as the Divan, can be found in almost every home in Iran.

OMAR KHAYYAM

Omar Khayyam (1047–1123) is the best-known poet in the West because of the famous translation of his *Rubaiyat* by Edward Fitzgerald. In Iran he is more famous as a mathematician, philosopher, historian and astronomer.

RUMI

Rumi (1207–73) was inspired by a great dervish, Shams-e Tabrizi, and many of his poems of divine love are addressed to him. He is credited with founding the Maulavi Sufi order (the whirling dervishes).

SA'DI

Like Hafez, Sa'di (1207–91) was a Shirazi whose elegantly phrased verses are still commonly used in conversation. His most famous works are the *Golestan* (Rose Garden) and *Bustan* (Garden of Trees).

Cinema

Iranian filmmakers are hugely popular in the Western art-house scene, though you're unlikely to see much of their work while in Iran, where locally made action films and dubbed Bollywood flicks dominate. Worth looking for: *A Separation* by Asghar Farhadi, *10* by Abbas Kiarostami, *Time For Love*, *Kandahar* or *Gabbeh* by Mohsen Makhmalbaf; *Blackboards* or *The Apple* by his daughter Samira Makhmalbaf; *Children of Heaven* or *The Willow Tree* by Majid Majidi; *The White Balloon* by Jafar Panahi; or *The Lizard* (Marmulak) by Kamal Tabrizi.

SURVIVAL GUIDE

ℹ️ Directory A–Z

ACCOMMODATION

➤ The budget staple is the *mosaferkhaneh*, offering cheap rooms with shared facilities.

➤ There are few dedicated hostels, but cheap hotels sometimes offer dormitories.

ℹ️ SLEEPING PRICE RANGES

The following price ranges refer to a double room including tax and breakfast unless stated:

$ less than US$35

$$ US$36 to US$70

$$$ more than US$70

➤ Many midrange and top-end hotels charge foreigners 25% or so more than Iranians.

➤ Pay in rials as many hotels only offer the official exchange rate: you can do much better in exchange offices.

➤ Most accommodation hangs on to your passport until you check out.

➤ Checkout time is usually noon or 2pm.

➤ There are few official campgrounds – though several large cities have well-equipped, secure, free ones.

➤ Reserving hotels in advance is recommended during busy periods but can be an exercise in patience. Many hotels won't answer emails, and reception staff often don't speak English. Phoning in the morning is a good idea, as staff working checkout usually have the best language skills.

➤ Unmarried foreign couples can usually get a room with no questions asked; increasing numbers of double beds are available.

Couchsurfing

Iran has very active **Couchsurfing** (www.couchsurfing.org) and **Hospitality Club** (www.hospitalityclub.org) communities: an easy and popular way to get 'inside' Iranian culture.

DANGERS & ANNOYANCES

In general, Iran is one of the world's safest countries for travellers.

Crossing the road is a different story: Iranian traffic is a gloriously (but perilously) anarchic free-for-all. Watch how the locals cross, and then go: boldly but cautiously. And watch for contra-flow traffic lanes and motorcycles using the pavement.

Police won't usually give you any hassle unless you're breaking the law. A common way of doing this is taking photographs where you shouldn't: bridges, borders, airports etc. Don't take photos in sensitive areas.

EMBASSIES & CONSULATES

For Iranian embassies see the **Iranian Ministry of Foreign Affairs** (www.mfa.ir) site. Addresses here are in Tehran; consulates are listed under Tabriz and Mashhad.

Afghan Embassy (Map p142; ☎ 021-8873 0826; www.afghanembassy.ir; cnr 4th St & Pakistan St, off Beheshti Ave; ⊙8am-2pm Sat-Wed; Ⓜ Shahid Beheshti) Issue of tourist visas (most countries around US$100) is unpredictable.

Australian Embassy (Map p142; ☎ 021-8386 3666; www.iran.embassy.gov.au; 2, 23rd St, Khaled Eslamboli Ave; ⊙7.30am-noon & 12.30-3.30pm Sun-Wed, to 2.45pm Thu)

Azerbaijani Consulate (☎ 021-2267 3511; www.azembassy.ir; Afshin Mahmudiyan St, Geytariyeh Blvd; ⊙10am-1pm Sun, Tue & Thu)

> ## ⓘ EATING PRICE RANGES
>
> The following price ranges refer to an average main course, taxes and service included:
>
> **$** less than US$5
>
> **$$** US$5 to US$9
>
> **$$$** more than US$9

Head here, not the embassy, for visas. It costs €60 for a 30-day tourist visa for most; ready in a day – you can pick it up between 5pm and 6pm.

Canadian Embassy (Map p142; ☏ 021-8152 0000; www.canadainternational.gc.ca/iran; 4 Shahid Sarafraz St, Motahhari Ave) Closed at time of research; see website for emergency contacts.

Dutch Embassy (☏ 021-2366 0000; iran.nlembassy.org; 7 Farmanieh; ◷7.30am-4pm Sun-Wed, to 1.30pm Thu; Ⓜ Nobonyad Sq)

French Embassy (Map p146; ☏ 021-6409 4000; www.ambafrance-ir.org; 64 Nofl Loshato St; ◷8.30am-noon Mon-Thu; Ⓜ Valiasr)

German Embassy (Map p146; ☏ 021-3999 0000; www.teheran.diplo.de; 324 Ferdosi St; ◷7am-3.30pm Sun-Thu; Ⓜ Sa'di)

Iraqi Embassy (Map p146; ☏ 021-8893 8865; tehemb@mofa.gov.iq; Valiasr Ave; Ⓜ Meydan-e Valiasr)

Italian Embassy (Map p146; ☏ 021-6672 6955; www.ambteheran.esteri.it; 68 Nofl Loshato St; ◷9am-1pm Sun-Thu; Ⓜ Valiasr)

New Zealand Embassy (☏ 021-2612 2175; www.nzembassy.com/iran; cnr 2nd Park Alley, Sosan St, North Golestan Complex, Aghdasiyeh St; ◷8.30am-12.30pm & 1-3pm Sun-Thu)

Pakistani Embassy (Map p142; ☏ 021-6694 1388; www.mofa.gov.pk/iran; Block 1, Etemadzadeh Ave, Jamshidabad, Dr Hossein Fatemi Ave; ◷8.30am-1.30pm Sat-Wed) Only visas for Iranians.

Turkish Embassy (Map p146; ☏ 021-3595 1100; tehran.emb.mfa.gov.tr; 337 Ferdosi St; ◷9am-5pm Sun-Thu; Ⓜ Sa'di)

Turkmen Embassy (☏ 021-2220 6731; 5 Barati St, off Vatanpour St, off Lavasani St, Farmanieh; ◷9.30-11am Sun-Thu)

UK Embassy (Map p146; ☏ 021-6670 5011; www.gov.uk; 198 Ferdosi St; Ⓜ Sa'di) Still closed at time of research but rumoured to have been opening soon.

US Interests Section of Swiss Embassy (☏ 021-2200 6002; www.eda.admin.ch/tehran; 2 Yasaman St, Sharifi Manesh Ave; ◷8am-noon Sun-Thu; Ⓜ Sadr)

GAY & LESBIAN TRAVELLERS

Homosexuality is punishable in some cases by death.

Barbaric laws aside, there is no reason why gay and lesbian travellers shouldn't visit Iran. It makes sense not to advertise that you're part of a same-sex couple; discretion is the better part of valour.

HEALTH

➡ Iran has a good system of medical care, and it's usually easy to find an English-speaking doctor.

➡ Tap water is safe to drink.

➡ Pay for medical and health care then claim it back on insurance. Costs are very low.

INSURANCE

➡ Travel insurance is compulsory.

➡ Shop around: some insurers consider the region a 'danger zone' and exclude it or charge large premiums.

INTERNET ACCESS

➡ Wi-fi is widespread, though speeds are slow.

➡ It's easy to buy data: on our last visit you could get 5GB for US$6 with Irancell, for example.

➡ Internet cafes are known as *coffeenets*.

➡ Access to thousands of websites is blocked, from news sites to Twitter, Facebook and Skype. To get around this, most Iranians use a VPN client: set one up before leaving home.

LEGAL MATTERS

➡ All drug and alcohol use is illegal.

➡ Having unmarried sex with an Iranian can be very harshly dealt with.

➡ Deliberate refusal to wear correct hejab (woman's headscarf) is a crime.

MONEY

➡ Currency is the Iranian rial; with inflation high, we've converted prices into US dollars, using exchange-office rates, not the lower official rate.

➡ Iran for the visitor is a purely cash economy. No cards. Just cash: bring high-denomination euros or US dollars. Other currencies can be changed in Tehran and other big cities.

> ## ⓘ IRANIAN CALENDARS
>
> The Persian solar calendar is in official and everyday use; the Muslim lunar calendar is used for Islamic religious matters; and the Western (Gregorian) calendar is used in dealing with foreigners. For conversions, hit www.iranchamber.com/calendar/converter/iranian_calendar_converter.php

ⓘ TOMANS

No sooner have you arrived in Iran than you will come up against the idiosyncratic local practice of talking about prices in tomans rather than rials. One toman is 10 rials.

Worse, many people will knock off the thousands, so 'five' becomes shorthand for 5000 tomans, ie 50,000 rials.

However confusing this sounds, once you get a feel for what things cost, you'll get the hang of it quickly.

In the interim, get the price written down, and double-check whether it's in rials or tomans.

→ Getting your hands on money once you're inside Iran is expensive and a nightmare.

→ If the idea of carrying cash around doesn't do it for you (Iran is very safe though), various banks offer a prepaid card that can't be used in ATMs but can be used at most shops, restaurants and hotels.

→ The easiest way to change money is at exchange shops, which offer better rates than the banks and do the deal in seconds. No ID is usually needed. Changing money on the street is common but illegal.

→ The coins you'll see are IR250, IR500, IR1000, IR2000 and IR5000. The main notes are IR500, IR1000, IR2000, IR5000, IR10,000, IR20,000, IR50,000, IR100,000 and IR500,000.

Tipping

Tipping is not a big deal. In most restaurants a service charge is added to the bill anyway.

OPENING HOURS

Opening and closing times can be erratic, but you can rely on most businesses closing Thursday afternoons and Friday (the Iranian weekend). Businesses and sights typically open longer hours in the summer months.

POST

Post can take anything from a few days to several months to reach its destination.

TELEPHONE

→ To dial out call ⌨ 00; dialling in, drop the initial 0.

→ A pay-as-you-go SIM card is easily bought for around US$2 (a copy of your passport is needed).

→ The two big networks are MCI (Hamrah-e-Aval) and MTN (Irancell).

→ Top-ups can be bought at newspaper kiosks.

TOILETS

→ Almost all public toilets are squats: use the hose or carry toilet paper.

→ Hotels usually have a choice of squat or throne and have toilet paper, though sometimes you'll need to ask. Put your used sheets in the bin.

VISAS

→ Nearly all nationalities need a visa.

→ Apply well in advance (several weeks or more) of your trip, because a pre-authorisation is sought from Tehran before the actual visa application is processed.

→ The standard tourist visa is 30 days. It's usually no problem to extend it for another 30 days while in Iran; sometimes twice. Shiraz is widely reported to be the best place to do this.

→ Agencies can take the hassle out of the equation, but be aware that numerous travellers have reported problems with some companies. Reading online forums or asking other travellers for recommendations before choosing one is a good idea. Travel agencies specialising in Iran are normally reliable.

→ Costs vary by nationality; at the time of research most EU citizens paid €50 and €80, Australians, Brits and US citizens substantially more.

→ Israelis are banned and so is anyone with an Israeli stamp in their passport or a stamp from a border with Israel. Get a new passport if this applies to you.

→ Citizens of the USA (plus Canada and the UK at the time of research) must contract a ministry-approved driver/guide and submit a pre-planned itinerary.

→ Most international airports in Iran now issue an airport visa to certain nationalities (including Australia, New Zealand, most of the EU, China, Japan), valid for 15 days and extendable for another 15. In practice, some people get turned away, so it's worth using an agency to pre-authorise your airport visa.

→ Trabzon, Turkey, with a processing time of a couple of days, was one of the easiest places to get an Iranian visa at time of writing.

ⓘ BARGAINING

As a general rule the prices of groceries, food, sights, transport (except private taxis) and most things with a price tag attached are fixed. But virtually all prices in the bazaar are negotiable, particularly for souvenir-type products and always for carpets. In touristed areas, bargaining is essential.

WOMEN TRAVELLERS

➡ Women travelling alone regularly report groping on public transport: sit in the back of taxis and use women-only carriages on the metro.

➡ If you use them, take tampons for the whole trip; they're tough to find.

➡ Greet men by placing your hand over your heart rather than shaking hands.

➡ On intercity buses, sit next to another woman (your male companion is OK too). On city buses, you must sit in the women's area at the back.

What Should I Wear?

➡ All women, including foreigners, must wear figure-disguising clothing and cover their hair.

➡ There are basically two acceptable versions of this hejab: the chador, a head-to-toe black garment; or a manteau (coat) and *rusari* (scarf). In larger cities you'll see figure-hugging manteaus, skinny jeans, high heels and colourful *rusaris;* in towns and villages it's more conservative.

➡ All manteaus are worn over trousers; jeans are acceptable. Do not wear skirts. Loose-fitting cardigans going down to the mid-thigh are the most comfortable form of outerwear. In summer, you'll need something light – long peasant blouses and tunics work well.

➡ At shrines, chadors are sometimes compulsory and can be borrowed on-site.

ℹ Getting There & Away

It is fairly simple to reach Iran by plane, train from Turkey or across borders from neighbouring countries.

ENTERING THE COUNTRY

Assuming you have a visa, most border officials are efficient: tourists rarely get much hassle. Women need to be adequately covered from the moment they get off the plane or arrive at the border.

AIR

Most international flights hit Tehran, but Tabriz, Shiraz, Esfahan and Mashhad have options.

Airports & Airlines

Iranian airlines flying internationally don't appear on most flight searches. Due to sanctions, buying tickets is best done through a travel agent specialising in Iran. The two major airlines flying internationally are:

Iran Air (Map p146; www.iranair.com)
Mahan Air (Map p142; www.mahan.aero)

LAND

Bus

Buses run from Tabriz and Tehran to Ankara, İstanbul and other Turkish cities; to Baku, Azerbaijan and Yerevan, Armenia. These journeys

---

ℹ TA'AROF

Ta'arof is a system of formalised politeness ubiquitous in Iran. For example, an offer of food will be turned down several times, giving the person making the offer the chance to save face if in reality they don't have the ability to provide a meal. A good rule is to refuse any offer three times but, if they continue to insist, do accept. However, if a taxi driver or shopkeeper refuses payment, do remember that this is just *ta'arof* and insist on paying. Generally, Iranians realise that foreigners may not understand *ta'arof*, so you're unlikely to offend.

---

are easily accomplished in shorter hops, thus avoiding long delays at customs.

Train

The *Trans-Asia Express* runs weekly between Ankara and Tehran (at time of research the continuation to İstanbul was temporarily not operating), leaving Ankara at 10.25am on Wednesdays and running via Van (8pm Thursday) and Tabriz (6.30am Friday). The Ankara–Tehran journey takes around 56 hours and costs US$55. The return journey leaves Tehran 9.25pm Wednesday, arriving in Ankara on Saturday morning.

An extra train runs between Van and Tabriz on Tuesday nights (some websites erroneously have this train on a Wednesday). The Van–Tabriz leg costs US$18 on this service and takes nine hours. The return leaves Tabriz on Monday at 10.30pm.

Check www.raja.ir, www.iranrail.net or the Turkish railways website at www.tcdd.gov.tr for info.

SEA

There are relatively few ways to enter or leave Iran by sea. As services are infrequent, inconsistent and more expensive than flying, few people bother.

ℹ Getting Around

Transport is frequent, fairly modern and cheap. Travel agents will book planes, trains and, sometimes, buses, saving the trip to a transport terminal.

AIR

➡ Domestic airfares are low: US$30 to US$40. There are flights from nearly every city to Tehran and Mashhad, and fewer services connecting other places directly.

➡ Over a dozen airlines cover the country, few with much online info in English. Domestic prices are fixed, so it doesn't matter which airline you fly.

→ For tickets, the travel agencies give you all the flight options, but you'll pay a surcharge. Iran-specialised travel agents outside the country can book domestic tickets for a hefty mark-up. Tickets go on sale a few weeks before flights.

BUS

→ Buses are Iran's staple transport and are cheap, comfortable and frequent. There are two general types of bus: normal *(mahmooly)* and VIP, which has reclining seats and more space, costing around 50% more.

→ Some buses have toilets but many don't. Toilet stops aren't frequent so go easy on the tea.

→ Most services provide a meal or snack.

→ Bus terminals are filled with the offices of individual bus companies, though timetables are rarely in English. There's often an information desk which will point you to the right company, or listen for your destination being screamed out when a bus is about to leave.

→ Tickets are in Farsi, so learn the numerals.

CAR & MOTORCYCLE

You can hire cars in Iran, hire car-and-driver which doesn't cost much more, or bring your own car, which is exactly what a steady stream of travellers do en route between Europe and Asia. City driving is hair-raising but roads are generally in good condition.

HITCHING

Hitching is never completely safe in any country and we do not recommend it. In Iran, hitching is a novel concept. Occasionally drivers will offer foreigners a free ride in return for practising their English or out of simple hospitality. Like anywhere, you're most likely to find rides in more remote areas. Wave your hand palm down.

BORDER CROSSINGS

Afghanistan

The border between Taybad (Iran) and Islam Qala (Afghanistan) is straightforward. Transports run between Herat and Mashhad: expect long delays for drug searches. Visas not issued at border.

Armenia

One crossing point at Norduz. EU citizens don't need a visa; others can buy online or at the border (US$7 for 21 days).

Azerbaijan

Two recognised crossings: between Astara (Azerbaijan) and Astara (Iran), and Culfa (Azerbaijan) and Jolfa (Iran), the latter leading to the exclave of Nakhchivan, from where you must fly to get to Baku. Visas not issued at border.

Iraq

Southern border posts are open for locals only. Haji Omaran border near Piranshahr is the main gateway to Iraqi Kurdistan and at the time of research was open to foreigners. Many nationalities issued with visa on arrival.

Pakistan

Only recognised crossing for foreigners is between Mirjaveh (Iran) and Taftan (Pakistan). A rather unsafe zone at time of research.

Turkey

The main road crossing to/from Turkey is at Gürbulak (Turkey) and Bazargan (Iran). Another easy crossing is Kapiköy: minibuses run through here between Khoy (Iran) and Van (Turkey).

Turkmenistan

There are two main border crossings. Pay US$12 to US$15 in dollars to enter Turkmenistan; this is apart from your visa, which must be prearranged. The Sarakhs border post can be reached by train, bus or savari from Mashhad. Change buses in Quchan for the Bajgiran crossing, handy for Ashgabat.

LOCAL TRANSPORT

➡ Towns and cities have several options: local buses, shuttle taxis, private taxis and, in some cases, a metro.

➡ Bus numbers and destinations are usually only marked in Farsi. Tickets (around 15¢) usually have to be bought at booths before boarding. Women and small kids must board and sit at the back.

➡ Minibuses service local suburban routes and are often crammed: no room for segregation. Pay in cash when you get on.

➡ Metros are functioning in Tehran, Mashhad and Shiraz, with Tabriz and Esfahan on the way, but at time of research, only Tehran's was really useful to the traveller until more stations are opened.

Taxi

Shared shuttle taxis travel between major *meydans* (squares) and along main roads, so the key to using them is to learn the names of the *meydans* along your intended route. Shout your destination at the driver through the window, and they'll stop if they're going that way. Government-regulated fares start from 30¢ for a few blocks.

Any taxi without passengers can be chartered, as can many private cars, who will hoot if interested. Tell the driver where you want to go, and ask *'chand toman?'* Immediately offer about 60% but expect to end up paying about 75% or 80% of the originally quoted price.

Agency taxis, or 'telephone' taxis, are ordered by phone. Lone women are advised to do this after dark. Tehran has a women-only taxi company.

Private Taxi

Almost every car in the country is available for private hire. Needless to say, prices are open to negotiation. One way to avoid getting ripped off is to ask the driver of a savari for the price per person of a certain trip then multiply it by four.

> ### ℹ NA DAR BASTE!
>
> If you hail an empty taxi the driver will hope you are hiring it privately, which is known as *'dar baste'*, literally 'closed door'. If you want to share – cheaper for you, less money for the driver – say *'na dar baste'*, and they'll let you know if they're interested.

Savari

Savaris are shared taxis that run between towns up to a few hours apart. Speed is the main advantage because savaris are generally less comfortable than buses. A total of four passengers is normal: you wait for the savari to fill then depart. Passengers can agree to pay for empty seats between them.

Savaris usually leave from the relevant bus terminal. If in doubt, charter a private taxi and tell the driver *'savari'* and your destination.

TRAIN

➡ Iran's rail network is excellent, with largely modern trains running to many parts of the country.

➡ For routes and prices, see www.raja.ir, though the nonofficial www.iranrail.net is much easier if you don't read Farsi.

➡ The majority of trains have two classes. Some have bus-style seating, some compartments.

➡ On overnight trains (usually to/from Tehran) the 1st-class carriages have sleeper couchettes with four or six bunks. Solo women should strongly consider requesting a single-sex sleeper. On most 1st-class services meals are served in your compartment; long-distance trains also travel with a restaurant car.

➡ It's recommended you book ahead. This is often easier to do with a travel agent than at the station itself.

Iraq

Best for Nature

➡ The Hamilton Road (p195)

➡ Dukan (p197)

Best for Culture

➡ Kurdish Textile Museum (p191)

➡ Grand Bazaar (p199)

➡ Amna Suraka (p199)

Why Go?

Torn between its glorious past and its recent bloody history, Iraq is a country in turmoil. Following the 2003 US-led invasion and the problems that ensued, the country had little time to recover before a wave of violence swept through in June 2014, when jihadist group Isis took control of large swaths of north Iraq.

While the majority of the country is extremely dangerous, some parts of Iraq's semi-autonomous Kurdish region are still relatively stable. The security situation here can change rapidly, but much of the enclave has so far remained insulated from violence. Surrounded by imposing mountains and home to numerous archaeological sites, the region is largely untouched by tourism. Its future may be far from certain, but the warm and hospitable people here are inspiring nonetheless.

Iraq, including the Kurdish region, remains volatile, so be sure to keep up to date with the news and check with your foreign office for current advice before travelling.

When to Go
Erbil (Iraqi Kurdistan)

Mar Festivities are ongoing as the Kurds celebrate their new year, Newroz.

Apr Cool off at one of the many waterfalls and seek refuge from the growing heat.

Oct Milder temperatures and cool nights as the first signs of autumn appear.

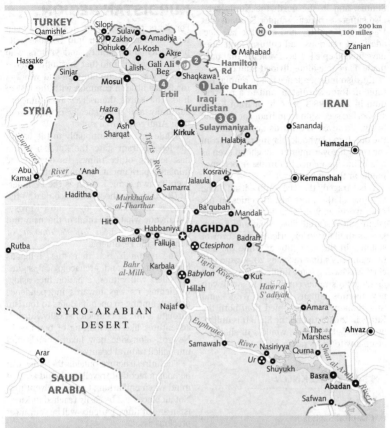

Iraq Highlights

1 Have a chai break at **Cafe Lara** (p197) and take in the view from the spacious balcony overlooking **Lake Dukan** (p197).

2 Travel through imposing gorges and mountains on the **Hamilton Road** (p196).

3 Travel back in history and learn about Kurdistan's tragic past in Sulaymaniyah's **Amna Suraka** (p199), a Saddam-era prison turned museum.

4 Visit the **textile museum** (p191) inside Erbil's Citadel for a colourful tour of Kurdish culture.

5 Pack a picnic, drive up Sulaymaniyah's **Goje Mountain** (p199) and wait for the sun to set and the city to light up.

A DIVIDED COUNTRY

For over a decade, Iraq has been synonymous with war. Since 2003, when the US-led invasion ended four decades of rule by Saddam Hussein, Iraq has witnessed only fleeting periods of calm, usually brought to an end by bloody terrorist attacks and bombings, frequently with massive civilian casualties.

In 2014, this situation was worse than ever. The brutal jihadi insurgency waged by Isis spread not only to the country's lawless western border regions with Syria, but also perilously close to Baghdad.

Analysts have long said that Iraq – created by foreign powers in the wake of WWII – was in fact three countries. In the east and south are the majority Shia, long repressed by Saddam, a Sunni leader; in the west the

Sunnis; and in the north the Kurds, who also suffered tragically under Saddam. But Iraq is one country, and over the last decade these religious and cultural fault lines have fuelled epic levels of violence that have made its people more divided than ever.

Kurdish independence is a perennial hot topic in Iraqi Kurdistan, and in a referendum in 2005, 98.8 per cent of Iraqi Kurds supported secession from Iraq. For the time being, however, the Kurds are sticking to the one-Iraq playbook, playing their part in the central government in Baghdad even as talk of independence in Kurdistan becomes public at the highest level.

It is a tragedy that the south – itself home to some of the most historic cities in the Arab world as well as at least two of Shia Islam's most scared sites, Najaf and Karbala – is unlikely to experience any form of stability in the near future. While the battle against Isis that raged as 2014 came to a close was having some limited successes, the jihadi army's ranks continued to swell with new recruits – many from the West – and they remained better armed than both the Kurds in the north and the Shia. It is unlikely, given that, that Iraq would – or should – be on any tourist's radar.

KURDISTAN REGION

For years the Kurdistan Region has been referred to as 'the other Iraq' because of its prosperity and stability, and visitors who venture here will find that this undiscovered land of jagged mountain tops and winding roads has little in common with the rest of Iraq. The Kurds themselves are ethnically, culturally and linguistically distinct from their Arab counterparts.

While tied constitutionally to the law of the federal Iraqi state, the Kurdish region has, among other things, its own prime minister, parliament, national anthem and even its own army. Known as the Peshmerga (Kurdish for 'those who face death') the army is the pride and joy of most Kurds – ask anyone what they think of the army and you are likely to hear *'biji Peshmerga'*, or 'long live the Peshmerga'.

The region is rich in castles, religious history, nature and archaeological sights. Travellers will witness a nation increasingly inching its way towards independence and attempting to open its doors to tourism through a mix of characteristically Kurdish adventures like the lighting of bonfires in Newroz, alongside new luxury hotels and unrivalled natural beauty.

The infrastructure outside the cities can be poor, a fact that travellers should keep in mind when embarking on their adventures. Not all places can be easily reached in Kurdistan and at times patience will be your most precious asset.

Erbil

أربيل

📞066 / POP 1.5 MILLION

Erbil (Irbil, Hawler, Hewler) is the capital of the Kurdistan Region and its largest city. Today it is also the fastest-growing city in Iraq, booming in ways that seemed impossible a decade ago.

While its modernity shines through in the shape of new glitzy hotels and American-style malls, the Kurdish capital has also retained a sense of authenticity, most visible in the imposing citadel in the centre of the city.

Often hailed as the oldest continuously inhabited city in the world, Erbil is a colourful mix of old and new, full of bustling bazaars, fascinating museums and lively nightlife on rooftop terraces.

In spite of its conservative nature, Erbil is a tolerant city with a variety of polarised

Iraqi Kurdistan

ethnicities and religions that have found ways to coexist in a part of the world where different cultures often struggle to exist side by side. This alone makes Kurdistan's capital an attractive destination.

History

Some archaeological findings suggest that the first sign of life in Erbil dates back to 6000 BC, while the first written evidence of the city itself dates back to 2000 BC, when it was referred to as Irbilium. Like most cities in the region Erbil has played host to an array of civilisations, including the Assyrians, the Medes, the Romans and more recently the Ottomans and the British, all of which have left a lasting impact on the city.

Although it has an eye on the future, Erbil is steeped in ancient history and has seen ongoing religious and cultural change, including the significant shift from being a centre of Christianity to a Muslim city in 642 AD. The city's Christian legacy is still present throughout the city.

In 1991, following the Gulf War and a number of Kurdish uprisings, Erbil came under complete control of the Kurds. The system temporarily broke down during the Kurdish Civil War (1994–97) between the region's two leading parties, the Patriotic Union of Kurdistan (PUK) and the Kurdistan Democratic Party (KDP).

The bloody war resulted in the then PUK-controlled capital being captured by the KDP, with the assistance of Saddam Hussein, a move that KDP critics have yet to forgive. In 1998 the parties signed a peace treaty under the watchful eye of the US, but friction between the two parties exists to this day. Travellers will note the difference in uniforms worn by soldiers in KDP areas and those in PUK areas, a visible sign of the lasting divisions between the two parties.

Following the 2003 US-led invasion, Erbil has been relatively stable with only a small number of attacks, including in August 2014 when a car bomb injured a number of people.

⊙ Sights

★ Citadel OLD TOWN

No one really knows who first built Erbil's citadel, but two things are (almost) certain: the imposing *qalat* (Kurdish for castle) is without a doubt the heart and soul of this bustling city and it has been continuously inhabited for 8000 years. Perched on a mound 32m above street level, it's Erbil's most precious historical asset, and in 2014

Erbil

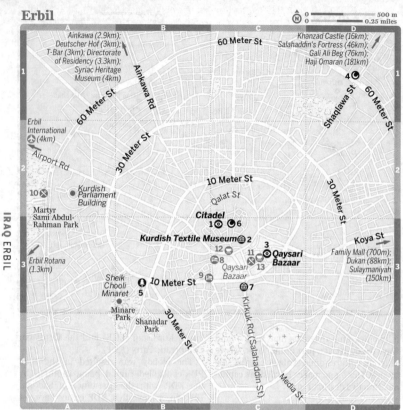

Erbil

⊙ Top Sights
1 Citadel	C3
2 Kurdish Textile Museum	C3
3 Qaysari Bazaar	C3

⊙ Sights
4 Jalil Khayat Mosque	D1
5 Minaret Park & Shanadar Park	B3
6 Mulla Afandi Mosque & Citadel Bath	C3
7 Museum and Archives of Education	C3

⊙ Sleeping
8 Bekhal Hotel	C3
9 Peace Pigeon Hotel	B3
Saira Miss Hotel	(see 8)

⊗ Eating
10 Dowa 2 Restaurant	A2
11 Najar Kebab	C3

⊙ Drinking & Nightlife
12 Machko Chai Khana	C3
13 Mam Khalil	C3

it was added to the Unesco World Heritage list.

In 2007 the citadel was partly closed for restoration and at the time of research its charming little alleyways and traditional courtyard houses were still shut off to the public. In order to carry out a major facelift, the Kurdish government compensated and relocated the families who lived in the citadel – only one family remains so as to not break the alleged 8000-year-old record. During its heyday the citadel was split into three neighbourhoods, the Serai, the Takya and the Topkhana, for the prominent families, the dervishes (religious people) and the farmers respectively.

Today visitors can walk the main street from north to south. The citadel's southern facade, which was reconstructed by Saddam's administration, was recently renovated and the huge statue of 12th-century Kurdish historian Mubarak Ahmad Sharafaddin relocated to Minaret Park.

Inside the citadel a single main road cuts straight through the 102,000 sq metres of the tell, leading visitors from the northern entrance to the south gate, through which you can peer down onto Erbil's main square and bazaar.

★ **Kurdish Textile Museum** MUSEUM
(www.kurdishtextilemuseum.com; ⊙9am-7pm Sat-Thu) FREE Recently renovated, this fascinating museum is a wonderful little place that's covered wall-to-wall in handmade Kurdish carpets. The exhibition also includes beautiful Kurdish hats from different tribes, traditional clothes and even kitchen utensils. Each item has a Kurdish and English description and most of the staff, including the owner, speak English. Take a tea break on the top floor, where you will find a cosy cafe. The museum is on the eastern side of the South Gate, just off the main road.

Mulla Afandi Mosque
& Citadel Bath MOSQUE
The Mulla Afandi Mosque is the only religious structure that remains in the citadel and was named after the Erbil-born Kurdish cleric and philosopher, Mulla Abu Bakr Effendi. The hammam next door was built in 1775. Both buildings are often closed, but if you are lucky you might bump into the custodian.

Museum and Archives of
Education MUSEUM
(Kirkuk Rd; ⊙8am-6pm Sun-Thu) FREE Tucked away in a little courtyard close to Erbil's main square, visitors can wander into what was once the capital's first school and is now a museum. This lovely little building feels somewhat out of place amid the more modern architecture surrounding it. Visitors will find quaint photographs of teachers and students from times gone by as well as archives, including teachers' pay slips from the 1920s.

★ **Qaysari Bazaar** BAZAAR
(⊙8am-late Sat-Thu) Sprawled out at the feet of the citadel and next to Erbil's main square, the Qaysari bazaar is one of the largest covered markets in the Kurdish region as well

as one of the oldest in the world. It is in the process of being renovated, but is still open to the public. The dark maze of narrow alleys can sometimes get a bit claustrophobic if you are there during its busiest hours. Visitors will find all sorts of different products, from Kurdish chewing gum to fresh cheese, kitchen utensils, jewellery and fabrics.

Minaret Park & Shanadar Park PARK
These two parks, known as the 'twin parks', are connected by the Erbil Teleferique and offer a green area in the heart of the city.

Minaret Park was named after the towering 36m-tall Mudhafaria Minaret (aka Chooli Minaret) thought to be the only remnant of what was once a large mosque built during the rule of Sultan kokburi, between 1190 and 1232.

Opposite Minaret Park is Shanadar Park, where lively Newroz celebrations are held in March. The park has fountains and an art gallery where you can sometimes stumble upon art exhibitions. Keep an eye out for live shows – if they are happening they are likely to happen at Shanadar.

Both parks are packed on Fridays.

Syriac Heritage Museum MUSEUM
(Ainkawa Museum; Ainkawa; ⊙9am-8pm Sun-Fri) FREE The first Syriac heritage museum in Iraq opened in 2011 in an attempt to recognise and highlight the importance of the Christian community in the country. The museum is located in the Christian quarter of Ainkawa, in the north of the city, and exhibits beautiful fabrics, farming appliances and photographs and works of prominent Syriac figures. The museum is a stone's throw from St George Church.

Jalil Khayat Mosque MOSQUE
(60 Meter St, opposite Royal Mall) Modelled after İstanbul's Blue Mosque, Erbil's largest mosque was comissioned by wealthy businessman Jalil Khayat and opened in 2007. The colourful building sits on 15,000 sq metres of land in Erbil's affluent Shoresh neighbourhood and is flanked by two 65m-tall minarets, easily seen from the citadel. The mosque can accomodate up to 2000 people; non-Muslims are welcomed outside prayer time.

Martyr Sami Abdul-Rahman Park PARK
(☑0750 490 4034; 60 Meter St; ⊙8am-midnight; ⓐ) FREE Across the road from the luxurious Divan Hotel is the equally beautiful Martyr Sami Abdul-Rahman Park, a sprawling green

oasis named after a prominent politician murdered in a terrorist attack. The urban space was built on what was once Saddam Hussein's 5th Corps Army military base and includes a running track, fountains, a lake, a stadium, a climbing gym and even a library. This is a favourite location for wedding parties and on warm spring evenings whole families will head out for evening strolls or a little jog around the running track.

🛏 Sleeping

Saira Miss Hotel
HOTEL $

(☑ 0750 4686 337; Bata Rd, Bazaar; s/d/tr without breakfast ID30,000/55,000/60,000; ❋ 🛜) The bedrooms are very small but clean and have the essentials, including a TV, fridge and aircon. The hotel owner was keen to point out that their generator works wonderfully and they don't have problems with power. The hotel is basically in the bazaar but the noise does not seem to make its way to the inside of the building.

Bekhal Hotel
HOTEL $

(☑ 066-251 05 38, 0750 4467 515; Bata Rd, Bazaar; per person without breakfast ID15,000; ❋) Spacious but otherwise fairly gloomy rooms which feel rather neglected. However, it's about as cheap as you'll find in Erbil. The owner speaks basic English.

★ Classy Hotel
HOTEL $$

(☑ 0750 639 7633, 0750 854 6663; www.classyhotel.net; Ainkawa Rd, next to police station; r from US$120) Classy is the perfect middle ground for those who aren't keen on spending a fortune but are looking for elegant decor and comfort. A journalists' favourite, you are likely to find international correspondents typing away on their laptops in the hotel bar. Opposite the lobby is the Greek Grill, a pleasant restaurant where you can also order alcoholic drinks. The room price includes breakfast and the gym, and you can pay by credit card, a rare treat in Kurdistan.

Peace Pigeon Hotel
HOTEL $$

(Kotri Salam Hotel; ☑ 0750 7754 949, 066-222 1776; www.kotrisalam.com; 10 Metre St, Choli St; s/d/tr incl breakfast US$60/75/100; ❋ 🛜) Named after the statue of the pigeon outside the hotel, the Peace Pigeon sits opposite what used to be Erbil's Jewish neighbourhood. The ample reception room exhibits photographs of Erbil and overlooks a bustling little street. The rooms are clean and include a fridge, TV and air-con. The friendly owner speaks English.

This is an ideal location for those keen to explore the city centre.

Divan Hotel
HOTEL $$$

(☑ 066-210 5000; www.divan.com.tr; Gulan St; r from US$400) If you're looking for a high-end hotel where you are likely to bump into wealthy CEOs and regional politicians, Divan is the place to go. Located across the road from Sami Abdul-Rahman Park, Divan is Erbil's newest addition to a growing list of five-star hotels. The hotel offers luxurious suites and a number of restaurants and bars with live music. Pop upstairs to sushi restaurant and bar Qi 21 on the hotel's 21st floor and get a breathtaking view of the city. The staff speak English and are very professional.

Erbil Rotana
HOTEL $$$

(☑ 066-210 5555, 066-210 5556; www.rotana.com; Gulan St; r from US$270; ❋ @ 🛜 ⛱) The Emirate hotel management company was the first to get its foot into Erbil's luxury hotel business, and this is a common choice for businessmen popping in and out of the city for work. From May to October its pricey swimming pool is open to the public and there are a number of bars and restaurants to choose from. The Italian one, however, is overpriced and does not live up to its name.

🍴 Eating

Erbil has a surprisingly varied array of restaurants on offer. From sushi to Lebanese dishes, all the way to American-style brunches, Erbil's diverse cuisine is a testament to the city's inclusive nature.

Najar Kebab
KEBAB $$

(Bazaar; mains ID12,000; ⏱ 7.30am-4pm Sat-Thu) This iconic kebab restaurant opened in 1936 and recently expanded to include a second building. Taste some of the best kebabs in town in the heart of the busy bazaar. As with most restaurants in Kurdistan, we recommend female travellers sit in the family section (reserved for women and families).

Moka & More
RESTAURANT, CAFE $$

(☑ 0751 051 0985; www.mokaandmore.com; 100 Meter St, opposite Italian Village; mains ID10,000-ID12,000; 🅿 ❋ 🛜 👶) Modern and welcoming, this restaurant offers a mix of Western and traditional dishes. Relax in the comfy sofas, smoke sheesha, and indulge yourself with one of the heavenly homemade oreo cakes.

IRAQ IN PEACETIME

There are many tragedies that have befallen Iraq, but one of the least-reported among them is the disruption to the country's vibrant social and cultural life.

The predominantly Shia south has traditionally been the country's most conservative corner; a deeply religious land, with one eye turned west towards the Arab world and the other looking east towards their coreligionists across the border in Iran. The sacred cities of Najaf and Karbala still attract Shia pilgrims from around the world, and the region is awash with legends of the past, from the Garden of Eden to the port city of Basra, from where Sinbad the Sailor set out on his epic journeys.

Central and western Iraq are the country's Sunni Arab heartland. More than anywhere else, it was the Sunni towns that prospered under Saddam Hussein. While this often came at the expense of other Iraqi regions and communities, these regions were, for much of the 20th century, some of the most liberal in Arab Iraq. The touchstones of Arab life in the Middle East, too, have always thrived here, from the big celebrations that once brought large extended families and even entire neighbourhoods together to the social life of coffee shops and bazaars as the meeting places of public life.

Connecting Sunni and Shia Iraq are a string of stirring historical sites, many of which flourished in ancient times in the fertile lands between the Tigris and Euphrates Rivers. The ancient Sumerian city of Ur, 15km south of Nasiriyya, is one of the most impressive archaeological sites in Iraq, dating back to at least 4000 BC. Little remains of ancient Babylon, except for several mounds and the famous Lion of Babylon, a basalt statue carved more than 2500 years ago.

It all comes together, as it always has, in Baghdad, one of the great meeting places and cultural powerhouses of the Middle East. Baghdad may be battered and suspicious, but it remains true to its roots as a city of storytellers and of streets lined with booksellers; a polyglot place ruled by cosmopolitan and conservative influences in equal measure.

Munch Restaurant & Cafe RESTAURANT, CAFE $$
(☑0750 817 9444; www.munchrestaurants.com; Gulan St, opposite Naz City; 🅿❄📶) Pop into Munch for an early breakfast before setting off for the day. This brunch-style restaurant offers a variety of breakfasts, including local and Western, as well as dinner. Clean and relaxed, and serving up a seriously substantial feed.

Marina Restaurant RESTAURANT $$$
(www.facebook.com/StarMarinaErbil; Ainkawa; mains ID20,000; ⊙1pm-late) Unlike most restaurants in Erbil, Marina serves alcohol and has some English-speaking waiters. This spacious restaurant serves a mixture of Lebanese and Syrian dishes. Grab a table in the garden and enjoy live music in this little oasis on the outskirts of Ainkawa. Good food, lively atmosphere and generally good service.

Dowa 2 Restaurant TURKISH $$$
(☑0750 4452 303; Martyr Sami Abdul-Rahman Park; set menu ID25,000; ⊙11am-midnight) A popular spot for Friday family lunch is at Dowa, with a mix of Turkish and Kurdish dishes. Visitors will welcome a leisurely stroll through the park after the massive portions.

🍷 Drinking & Nightlife

⭐ **Chaldean Cultural Center** BEER GARDEN
(Ainkawa Rd; mains ID4000) Find Erbil's cheapest beer and kebabs in a wonderful garden adjacent to the Chaldean Cultural Center. A popular destination in spring and summer, this place is always alive with chatter, Arab music and football games on the big screen.

T-Bar BAR
(Ainkawa; ⊙5pm-2am) Head to T-Bar on Monday night for Quiz Night, Erbil's most popular night among the expat community. This American-style sports bar has good service and is a good place to take refuge, with a warm dish and a beer, during Erbil's cold winter months.

Deutscher Hof BAR
(☑0750 488 3981; www.deutscher-hof-kabul.com; Ainkawa; mains ID15,000-20,000; ⊙noon-11pm) Wildly overpriced, this popular expat joint is the only restaurant in Erbil to serve pork. There are a selection of German dishes such

as bratwurst and beef stroganoff on offer and the vibrant beer garden is a pleasant location for an evening drink. If you're around in October, don't miss the annual Oktoberfest for a taste of Germany in Iraq.

Mamounia Sky Bar   BAR

(100 Meter St; ⊙noon-late) Situated on the 7th floor of the Noble Hotel, Sky Bar offers a wonderful view of Erbil by night. A restaurant by evening (mains ID20,000) and a club of sorts by night, it's a top destination for Erbil's wealthier clientele. Perhaps a little on the pretentious side, it is a good night out if you're looking for loud music and a mixed local/expat crowd. Enjoy cocktails, Western dishes and sheesha on the balcony.

Teahouses

★ **Mam Khalil**   TEAHOUSE

(Bazaar) Erbil's best-loved teahouse and teahouse owner, Mam Khalil (Uncle Khalil in Kurdish) is an institution. Elderly mam Khalil loves to welcome every single one of his guests with a hot glass of chai. The tiny room is usually jam-packed, and decorated with framed photographs of mam Khalil's famous customers. Unlike other teahouse in the city, Mam Khalil has retained a sense of genuine 'Kurdishness' to it. Pick from one of three options, tea, coffee or *mastao* (milk and water) and enjoy the bustling vibrant atmosphere around.

Machko Chai Khana   CAFE

(Citadel) Join Erbil's retired gentlemen as they sit in what is arguably the capital's most famous teahouse, albeit the most touristy one too. Relax in front of Machko's colourful facade and sip on sugary tea. The busy teahouse looks to have been built into the walls of the Citadel's southern wall and, as is the case with most teahouses in Kurdistan, it has long been a gathering place for Kurdish intellectuals and activists.

🛍 Shopping

Family Mall   MALL

(100 Metre St; ⊙9am-11pm) Take a quick peek if you're dying to know what Iraq's brand-new glossy malls might look like. Family Mall offers a cinema, arcade games, an ice-skating rink (admission ID6000) and a number of brand-name shops, including Mango and Levi's. A good place to keep in mind for electronics is Digital City on the 1st floor.

ℹ Information

There are ATMs in Noble Hotel, at the entrance of Ainkawa; Family Mall; Rotana Hotel and Majidi Mall. Transfer or receive money through Western Union at Family Mall.

The centre of Erbil is a moderately conservative area, where dressing modestly will avoid unwanted attention. Hotels around the bazaar are often run by families and are unlikely to rent rooms to unmarried couples. Tap water can be consumed, but it is not advisable. Always travel with bottled water, especially in the hotter months when the dry heat hits the city.

ℹ Getting There & Away

Erbil International Airport (www.erbilairport. net) is only 6km from the city centre and an increasing number of international airlines fly there.

You can take share taxis to Dohuk (ID15,000, 2½ hours) and to Shaqlawa (ID5000, one hour).

Direct shared taxis to Sulaymaniyah (ID15,000, 2½ hours) usually travel through the dangerous city of Kirkuk. While this shortens the journey by half an hour, we recommend that travellers ask the driver to take the Koya road instead. Not only is this second option safer, the route is incredibly scenic.

ℹ Getting Around

Erbil's many taxis start operating bright and early and don't stop until late at night. They don't use meters, but you shouldn't be paying more than ID5000 per trip – if you are it's likely you're being ripped off.

There are two taxi companies that operate inside the airport and both are unreasonably expensive. However, if you hop onto the free shuttle bus and go to the arrival terminal, you can grab one of the slightly cheaper taxis. It shouldn't cost more than ID23,000 ($20) to get anywhere in the city. Unfortunately, normal taxis with reasonable prices are not usually allowed to wait in the airport.

Around Erbil

⊙ Sights

Khanzad Castle   CASTLE

(Massif-Salahaddin Rd) Fifteen kilometres north of Erbil, perched on a tiny mound on the side of the road, is the very modern-looking Khanzad Castle. The two-floor military fort is made of stones and plaster and dates back to Sulaiman Beck, Prince of Soran, a former Kurdish emirate. The steps to the castle are steep and full of pebbles;

comfortable shoes are recommended. The castle is on the right-hand side when driving towards Shaqlawa from Erbil.

Salahaddin's Fortress CASTLE

(Deween Castle) Not much is left of Salahaddin's Fortress (also known as Deween Castle) but the view of the valleys sprawled out before it and the scenic drive through a more rural Kurdistan are worth the tiny detour.

The ruins are known as Salahaddin's Fortress because of a possible link between the founders of the castle – princes of the Zarzariya Tribe – and the famous 12th-century conqueror Salahaddin. The castle itself is thought to date back to the Soran Emirate.

The location is about 15km north of the city of Salahaddin, and is not that easy to get to, though most local drivers will know the way. Call it Deween Castle when asking.

Warning: the last 5km to the fortress is a gravel road lined by minefields, identified by piles of rocks that have been painted red. We recommend you never venture off hard surfaces.

Shaqlawa شقلاوة

With its cool temperatures and lush vegetation, Shaqlawa is every Hewleri's favourite weekend getaway. The city sits at the foot of Safeen Mountain, home to the ruins of 4th-century Rabban Beya Monastery. Only 50km northeast of Erbil, this Christian-majority city is an ideal day-trip destination and attracts Kurds and Iraqis alike.

In the Kore Valley, between Erbil and Shaqlawa, look out for a small exhibition of tanks on your left. The vehicles are there to commemorate the time in 1991 when an alleged 150 Peshmerga held off one of Saddam's divisions.

☉ Sights

★ Rabban Beya Monastery MONASTERY

On the way into the city on the main road, turn right just before the fire station onto a little dirt road. There you will find the starting point of the one-hour hike up to the 4th-century monastery. While the ruins themselves are not worth the strenuous trek, the views over the city and Beya Valley certainly are.

🛏 Sleeping & Eating

Hop over to Khanzad St to cool off in one of the many outdoor restaurants, and pop into the tiny shops for treats like *nana-qaysi*, a rubber-like tangy sweet made from fruits.

Stars Hotel and Swedish Village HOTEL $$

(✆0750 445 7230, 0750 746 6283; www.starshotelshaqlawa.com; Shaqlawa Rd; r/cabin incl breakfast US$100/120; ❄@☎) With a selection of rooms, cabins and suites, this hotel includes an indoor pool, sauna, gym and its own hiking trail. The rooms are clean and the staff welcoming, though the cabins are a bit dark and stuffy. Unlike most hotels in Kurdistan, the majority of the staff speak perfect English.

Safeen Restaurant KURDISH $$

(Khanzad St) This well-loved restaurant serves the usual range of kebabs and *masgouf* (grilled carp), Iraq's national dish.

❶ Getting There & Away

A place in a shared taxi from Erbil is ID5000 ($4). Grab a taxi anywhere in Shaqlawa to get back to Erbil – it shouldn't cost more than ID25,000 (US$21).

Gali Ali Beg & the Hamilton Road قلي علي بيك

Prepare yourself for one of the most amazing sights in the Middle East. The northeast corner of Iraqi Kurdistan is an unheralded area of beauty marked by cascading waterfalls, soaring snowcapped mountains, deep gorges cut by raging rivers, rolling green hills and lush valleys. It is, without a doubt, the most beautiful and awe-inspiring place in Iraq.

In 1928 New Zealand engineer Sir Archibald Milne Hamilton was commissioned to build a road from the Kurdish capital of Erbil to Haji Omaran on the Iranian border. This 'short cut' allowed the creation of a strategic and direct overland route from the Mediterranean cities of Beirut and Alexandretta (now Iskenderun) to the Caspian Sea, Tehran and on to India.

Named for its builder, the Hamilton Road remains a remarkable feat of engineering through some of the world's most impassable and inhospitable terrain. Kurds also call it the Haji Omaran road, and it crosses at least five mountain ranges, rising from Erbil's 409m to approximately 1850m on the Iran-Iraq border. The most scenic portion of the drive is the 55km stretch from Gali Ali Beg to Haji Omaran.

⦿ Sights

Leave behind the thick air of Erbil for quiet and peace – the only noise you should prepare yourself for is the rumbling cascades of water you will find along the Hamilton Road.

Not long after leaving the capital travellers will find an expanse of farmland on the right, most of which belongs to the Surchi tribe, one of Kurdistan's largest tribes. The area, called Dashti Harer or the Harer plains, is a beautiful sight in the spring.

Turn left after the town of Speelk if you need to stretch your legs and wander the protected Barzan area, the birthplace of Kurdish leader Mullah Mustafa Barzani, and venture into Shanidar, a cave that contains Neanderthal burial sites.

Back onto the Hamilton Road travellers will soon hit the 12km-long Gali Ali Beg Canyon and the adjacent Great Zab River, a 400km-long river that flows through Turkey and Iraq. This stretch of road feels like an open-air museum of the most stunning natural beauty.

The Lower Hamilton Road is where the famous Gali Ali Beg Waterfall is located, one of Kurdistan's most popular summer spots and the image on the ID5000 note. Carry on to the Upper Hamilton Road where the road meets Bekhal, a shady maze of restaurants and shops at the foot of cascading waterfalls.

After the town of Rawanduz – which was once the centre of the Soran Emirate – the road runs parallel to the Choman River, ascending towards the protected Sakran Valley and the town of Choman. En route towards the border you will also see Halgurd Mountain, the highest mountain in Iraq (3607m). The road's final destination is the border town of Haji Omaran, though there is little to see there.

Gali Ali Beg Waterfall   RESORT
(⌨ 0750 7750 750; Hamilton Rd) Bring your rubber flip-flops to Gali Ali Beg and cool off

LALISH

The quiet village of Lalish is the most sacred place on earth for the followers of the Yazidi faith – an ancient monotheistic religion that amalgamates different beliefs including Zoroastrianism, Judaism, Christianity and Islam. Estimates suggest there are fewer than one million Yazidis in the world, of which 600,000 are in Iraq.

Tucked away in a green valley in the Kurdish-controlled area of Ninawa Province, Lalish is one of the region's most precious sites. It's believed to be the earthly landing place of Tausi Melek, the venerated Peacock Angel who was created by God to complete the creation of the universe.

The pretty cluster of shrines and temples is also home to the tomb of Sheikh Adi ibn Musafir, a reformer of the Yazidi religion and a saint of sorts. His tomb is found inside the sanctuary, which is built in the characteristic way of Yazidi holy sites, featuring otherworldly sand-coloured conical roofs. A black stone snake guards the entrance to the sanctuary; visitors are asked to remove their shoes and not step on the thresholds. Dark rooms are covered in colourful silks that the faithful tie and untie while making wishes, and all around the remains of festive candles give off the smell of melted wax. The shrine's underground cave is reached by climbing down very narrow stairs. Yazidis go here to dampen their heads and wash their hands and feet in a holy spring.

Lalish is busiest in April, during the Yazidi new year, when hundreds of followers spill into the tiny site to light candles, make wishes and pray for a better year.

Routes to Lalish were increasingly unsafe at time of writing, so those considering a visit should bear in mind this might not be possible.

with your feet in the water. The tiny resort is located between the towns of Khelifan and Soran and is a popular tourist attraction for those looking to escape the searing summer temperatures. The fall is over 10m tall and overlooks a pond with small rubber row boats for rent. Unfortunately, the bathrooms are very dirty and the music very loud. If you choose to stay the night you can rent a space outdoors under a canopy for ID20,000 – bring your own mattress.

Bekhal Waterfall
RESORT

(Hamilton Rd) Descend into a parallel universe of cool, crisp, shady mazes at Bekhal Waterfall. The resort features a bazaar, a myriad of restaurants and cafes, individual food stalls selling fresh juices and pomegranates and its famous rumbling waterfalls. Bekhal also offers outdoor places you can rent for the day and night for ID25,000. Warning: if you're a light sleeper you may not appreciate the constant sound of cascading water.

Sakran Valley
NATURE

(Gally Sakran; Hamilton Rd) On your way to Haji Omaran, the protected area of Sakran Valley will appear on your right. Turn into the park after the sign for Sakran Valley and enjoy the untouched mountains and waterfalls. The area is quite remote and getting to the waterfalls is no easy feat; the roads are quite bad.

🛏 Sleeping & Eating

Both Gali Ali Beg and Bekhal are full of cafes and restaurants. Travellers can also rent outdoor spaces to sleep. Alternatively, there are a number of hotels on the road that runs through the falls.

Korek Mountain Resort & Spa
RESORT $$$

(☑0750 245 8888; www.thekorekmountain.com; chalets US$150-300; ❄🛜❄) Just up the road from Bekhal is the brand-new Korek Mountain Resort & Spa, the pride and joy of Kurdish tourism. Jump on a cable car for ID10,000 and glide up to 1800m as a vast panorama of mountains and villages, including Soran and Handren, unfolds beneath you.

ℹ Getting Around

Getting around the Hamilton Road without your own transport is problematic, with share taxis few and far between. The most convenient method of transport for the Hamilton Road is renting a car (ID230,000 to ID290,000 per day).

Try with either a taxi driver or a guide, but chances are that the guide will also speak English, which can be very helpful in an area where few speak English. An excellent, English-speaking Erbil-based driver is **Yaseen Ahmad** (☑0750 455 3687; https://www.facebook.com/alanyaseen).

Dukan
دوكان

About 60km northwest of Sulaymaniyah, endless rolling hills – that turn bright green in the spring months – encircle the largest man-made lake in Iraq.

In the warmer months families from all over the region flock to the banks to picnic. Hotels and cabins are available for those who wish to spend the night.

For a serene afternoon, hire a boat for a few hours and ask the captain to drop you off on one of the deserted islands in the lake – make sure to ask him to come back and pick you up later.

On the road to Sulaymaniyah, stop at Chami Rezan (look for the sign on the right if you're heading from Dukan). This tomb is thought by some to be the first human ceremonial burial site in the world.

🛏 Sleeping & Eating

Ashur Hotel
HOTEL $$

(☑0770 154 2159; d US$100) Offers family rooms for up to four people.

Lara Cafe
CAFE $

(Dukan) Look out onto Lake Dukan from Lara Cafe's balcony. Try their fresh *masgouf* or simply sit back with a glass of chai and smoke some sheesha. You will find this little cafe on your right, just before descending into Dukan from Erbil.

Sulaymaniyah
السليمانية

☑053 / POP 700,000

Cosmopolitan Sulaymaniyah (Kurdish: Slemani) is Iraqi Kurdistan's second-largest city, and the most liberal and Westernised city in Iraq. Founded in 1784, Sulaymaniyah is a young city by Mesopotamian standards, and that youthful vibrancy shows – by Iraqi standards this city is trendy, fashion forward, chic, sophisticated and free spirited. It has a strong arts and cultural scene with great museums and several universities.

IRAQ DUKAN

Sulaymaniyah

Sulaymaniyah

◉ Top Sights
1 Amna Suraka (Red Security)................A1
2 Grand Bazaar D2

◉ Sights
3 Azadi Park B1
4 Grand Mosque D2
5 Municipal Park C2
6 Slemani Museum.................................A2

⛺ Sleeping
7 Hotel Ashty B2

8 Hotel Mazy Plaza.................................D2

✖ Eating
9 Chalak's Cafe & Dining Galleria A1

◉ Drinking & Nightlife
10 Pasha's Coffee.................................D2
11 Sha'ab Chai Khana D2

ⓘ Information
12 Homa Travel C2

Suli, as it's often called, is the key protagonist of countless Kurdish love songs and poems. Known as Kurdistan's 'capital of culture', it is not only the region's cultural hub, but has also been the starting point of many revolutions and uprisings in Kurdish history. Unlike Duhok and Erbil, travellers are less likely to hear Arabic being spoken on the streets and will see a greater number of people in typical Kurdish dress. Sulaymaniyah will likely feel more open and relaxed to its visitors than other cities and towns in the region, characteristics that residents are very proud of.

The city has a much bigger, more organic feel than compact Erbil, and aside from the central core you'll probably want to take a taxi everywhere.

History

Sulaymaniyah was founded in 1784 by Kurdish Prince Ibrahim Pasha, who named it after his father, Sulaiman.

Since its founding, Sulaymaniyah has been considered a hub of Kurdish nationalism, revolutions and uprisings. The most recent was in 2011, when people took to the streets for 40 days to protest against alleged corruption in Kurdistan.

Between 1919 and 1923 the self-declared king of the failed Kingdom of Kurdistan, Mahmud Barzanji, sparked two uprisings against the British occupation. The Sulaymaniyah-born leader, whose huge portrait can be seen in the city centre, was eventually forced to sign a peace accord with the newly established state of Iraq.

In 1975 a number of disillusioned members of the KDP broke away and founded the PUK, a Sulaymaniyah-based party led by former Iraqi President Jalal Talabani. The party, its members and home city were brutally targeted by Saddam Hussein's Ba'ath regime until the infamous Kurdish uprisings of 1991 and the subsequent 'safe haven' of the Kurdish enclave.

The sense of calm that came with the 'safe haven' and de facto autonomy was broken in 1994 by the Kurds themselves, when a bloody civil war between the PUK and the KDP ensued. It continued until 1997, destroying much of Sulaymaniyah. In 1998 the two parties were forced by Washington to sign a peace treaty, but relations are fraught to this day.

◉ Sights

★ Amna Suraka (Red Security)   MUSEUM
(21st St; ⊙ 8.30am-noon & 1-4pm Sat-Thu) FREE
If walls could speak, the Amna Suraka museum would tell tales of unimaginable horrors at the hands of Saddam Hussein's intelligence services, the Mukhabarat. The 16,000- sq-metre compound encloses several buildings that were once used by Saddam Hussein's Ba'ath regime as offices, torturing chambers and cells. The first prisoners arrived in 1986 and were liberated in 1991, following a series of uprisings throughout the region – the vast majority of the prisoners were Kurds. In 2000 the haunting building was turned into a museum, a project spearheaded by Hero Talabani, PUK member and wife of former Iraqi president Jalal Talabani.

The imposing buildings have been left exactly as they were following the violent uprising – bulletholes and shattered windows dot the fading red facade. The courtyard has been turned into a garden of roses and is now home to a display of Iraqi weapons left behind by the invading army. Tanks, mortars and artillery weapons line the sides of the garden.

The first building hosts a colourful display of Kurdish culture. A long corridor leads to a number of rooms containing mannequins of Kurdish personalities, including Sheikh Mahmud Barzanji, as well as displays of traditional Kurdish clothes, tapestry, weaponry and jewellery.

In contrast, the second building contains the regime's torture chambers. Pain-stricken sculptures created by artist Kamaran Omer are displayed in dimly lit isolation cells and torture rooms. Strung from the ceiling, one sculpture is shown to be receiving electric shocks, a common form of torture. Another man grimaces as two guards beet his feet with wooden sticks. Blankets and water bowls have been left strewn across the cells, as if untouched. A statue of a young mother and her child is displayed in the last cell,

where the regime imprisoned women and often used rape as a method of tourture.

On the ground floor, photographs taken by an Iranian photojournalist expose the dire situation faced by the Kurds during the 1991 mass exodus to Iran and Turkey, when they were forced to flee Kurdistan because of the violence.

The Hall of Mirrors commemorates those who were killed during Saddam Hussein's genocide campaign (Al-Anfal) and the villages that were destroyed: 182,000 shards of mirrored glass line the wall of the 50m-long corridor, one for every victim of Al-Anfal, along with 4500 tiny light bulbs, for every Kurdish village destroyed. At the end of the pathway there is a replica of a traditional rural Kurdish home.

Guided tours are free and there are usually one or two guides who speak English.

★ Goyje Mountain   MOUNTAIN
The night view of the city from the northeastern Goyje Mountain is a beautiful sight and you'll be hard-pushed to find someone from Sulaymaniyah who does not own a photograph with the twinkling backdrop. In the warmer months you will find families barbecuing on the side of the road. Grab a cab and head up at night; it takes approximately 15 minutes from the city.

Slemani Museum   MUSEUM
(Sulaymaniyah Museum; Salim St; ⊙ 9am-2pm Sat-Thu) FREE This superb museum is a timeline of Mesopotamian history dating back to the Palaeolithic Age from 15,000 BC. The museum is divided into several galleries featuring an array of archaeological artefacts. Some of the more interesting finds include a ceramic coffin containing the skeleton of a 6000-year-old woman found near Dohuk, and a Greek statue of Hercules dating to 334 BC. There is also a fine display of Islamic ceramic arts from the Islamic Golden Age. Most of the exhibits have Kurdish and English signs. At the time of research some renovation work was under way which promised to make the museum even more visitor friendly.

★ Grand Bazaar   MARKET
(Malawi St; ⊙ 8am-6pm) Get lost (literally) in Sulaymaniyah's huge bazaar, said to be the largest in the Kurdish region. Give yourself a whole morning to wander the alleys and streets of this traditional market, where visitors can find just about anything they

IRAQ SULAYMANIYAH

look for, from beautiful jewellery to detailed maps of Iraq and Kurdistan, flags, instruments and a lot of food, including vegetables, fish and endless supplies of very sweet sweets.

Grand Mosque
MOSQUE

Built in 1784 and renovated in 2012 the Grand Mosque lost many of its original features during the renovations. It's a colourful sight nonetheless, packed with street vendors just outside the gate.

Sardam Gallery
GALLERY

(Salim St; ⊙9am-6pm Sun-Thu; **FREE**) Get a glimpse into what Sulaymaniyah's art scene is all about. This gallery features rotating exhibits by local Kurdish artists. Most of the work is modern abstract. The gallery is inside Sardam Publishing House, to the left of the tiny mall.

Parks of Sulaymaniyah

Sulaymaniyah is notably greener than Kurdistan's other cities. Time and money have been spent on creating green spaces in the city, and residents love spending their weekends at any one of the various parks.

Azadi Park
PARK

(Parki Azadi; park admission free, amusement park ID1000, rides ID500-1000; ⊙6am-midnight Apr-Oct) This is Sulaymaniyah's answer to Central Park and Coney Island all rolled into one. It's a huge place filled with gardens, playgrounds, restaurants, cafes and a small lake. It's a popular place for jogging, picnicking and people-watching. The best time to come is Friday night, when the park is packed with families and young people. The northwest corner of the park is a separate, fenced-in amusement park with a Ferris wheel, kiddie rides and plenty of junk-food vendors.

Municipal Park
PARK

(Salim St, at Sulaymaniyah Circle) Visitors are likely to pass by this sweet little park en route to the bazaar. Pop in for a stroll among green gardens and fountains.

🛏 Sleeping

From cheap hotels in the heart of the bustling bazaar to more luxurious ones on Salim St, Sulaymaniyah has an extensive array of places to sleep, the majority of which are in great locations.

Hotel Mazy Plaza
HOTEL $

(✉053-204 292, 0770 7772 165; mazyplaza@ yahoo.com; Beekas St; s/d without breakfast ID20,000/40,000; ❀) Large rooms and great prices on the outskirts of the bazaar. For those who don't like leaving their friends at home, Mazy can accommodate up to six people per room.

★ Hotel Ashty
HOTEL $$

(✉0320 7999, 0770 152 0539; hotel_ashti@hotmail.com; Salim St; d incl breakfast US$70-80) The best option for those with a midrange budget, Ashty is small, clean and elegantly decorated. It's located on Salim St, just a 10-minute walk from the bazaar and a number of other sights. The double rooms are not huge but include a TV, fridge and air-con. The beds are extremely comfortable and the hot shower is a treat after a day of sightseeing. The staff don't speak English but manage to communicate regardless and do so with a smile.

Grand Millennium Hotel
HOTEL $$

(✉0770 700 0000; www.millenniumhotels.com; Bakhtiary; d ID180,000) This brand-new hotel opened in March 2014 and has since hosted an array of celebrities. The rooms live up to its shiny exterior, with comfortable beds, soft carpeting, an ultra-technological bedside tablet to control lights, music etc, and the most glorious view of Sulaymaniyah. The 39-storey hotel has four bars, a steakhouse and spa – the only problem seems to be the lack of hot water, a definite issue in the winter.

🍴 Eating

If you're craving kebab, head on down to the bazaar where there are endless options. Look out for Omari Aje, the best-loved kebab shop in town, located behind the Sha'ab teahouse.

★ Shkar Restaurant 2
RESTAURANT $$

(✉053-319 5110, 0770 155 9873; Azady Hotel, opposite Talary Hunar Bldg; mains ID15,000) This restaurant is as typically Sulaymaniyan as you'll get. Open since 1986, Shkar is a long-standing favourite. Head on up to the family section on the 1st floor – much cleaner than the downstairs area – and you will be immediately served their soup of the day. Choose from a selection of rices, beautifully cooked vegetables and (of course) kebabs. Their warm bread is out of this world, the service quick and the staff polite. We highly recommend the okra and rice.

Nali's Cafe
CAFE $$

(☎053 322 2066; https://www.facebook.com/nalis.cafe; Sarchnar Hill; mains ID10,000-ID12,000; ⊙9am-11pm) A Western-style cafe reminiscent of Starbucks, with a wide range of Western dishes from breakfast omelettes to pizzas and salads. The service can be slow and the internet not particularly reliable, but if you need to catch your breath and relax on comfortable sofas, Nali's is just fine. The decor is modern, with redbrick walls and large glass windows. It also has an outside area with fountains, pleasant for evening coffees.

Caffe Barbera
CAFE $$

(http://caffebarbera.com; Baxtiari) Cafe Barbera presents itself as a genuine Italian cafe and if the coffee is anything to go by, then they aren't telling lies – it's great. There is also a selection of sandwiches, pastries and brunch options available.

★Chalak's Cafe & Dining Galleria
ITALIAN RESTAURANT $$$

(☎0770 151 2976; Salim St; mains ID10,000-ID17,000; ⊙10am-late; ❄🛜♿) Sulaymaniyah's watering hole is an Italian restaurant owned by arguably the region's most stylish Kurd, Chalak. The eponymous restaurant is cluttered with antiques, vintage posters and instruments. The low lighting and stained-glass window make for a relaxed atmosphere and the upstairs balcony is the perfect location for an evening drink. The pizza and pasta dishes are the closest you will get to Italian food in Kurdistan, and this is one of the few restaurants outside a hotel that serves alcohol. Pop in for a coffee, dinner or just a glass of wine; the service is good and most waiters speak perfect English.

Teahouses

★Sha'ab Chai Khana
CAFE

(Kawa St; ⊙6am-7pm) In the heart of the bazaar you will find Sulaymaniyah's most famous teahouse. Step into the loud, smoky room where the revolutionaries, intellectuals and artists of Sulaymaniyah still gather to discuss life. The large room is divided in two, with one area reserved for games of domino. Framed photographs carpet the walls and dozens of books line the shelves.

While teahouses are traditionally places for men, owner Omar is adamant that women are welcome to drop by for a glass of sweet tea too. Make sure you sign the guestbook on the way out.

★Pasha's Coffee
COFFEE SHOP

(Goran Quarter) In the Goran neighbourhood of Sulaymaniyah's city centre is one of the best coffee shops you will ever have the pleasure to know. Look for this little hole in-the-wall run by two Kurdish men and ask for a cold coffee (or hot, if you'd rather!). Brewed to perfection, this is a delightful surprise.

☆ Entertainment

Chavy Land
AMUSEMENT PARK

(☎0770 8972 424, 0750 7659 630; http://nali-agroup.com/chavi; admission ID1000; ⊙6pm-midnight Mon-Sun) This amusement park opened in 2013 and boasts one of the tallest Ferris wheels in the Middle East. Ideal for evening strolls, the park is well kept and has a number of rides, including a roller coaster, a house of horrors and a teleferic that takes visitors up to Goyje Mountain for a spectacular view.

ℹ Information

MONEY
Warka Bank (Salim St; ⊙9am-4pm, closed Fri) Offers Western Union services.

TRAVEL AGENCIES
Homa Travel (☎0770 1534 861; Mamostayan St; ⊙10am-6pm, closed Fri) Travel agent for Best Van bus tickets to Turkey.

ℹ Getting There & Away

Sulaymaniyah International Airport (www.sul-airport.com) is located about 15km out of the city. At the time of writing there were regular flights from London, İstanbul, Doha, Dubai and Amman, among others.

Taxis depart and arrive from various garages in the city, depending on your destination. Taxis to Erbil (ID20,000, 2½ hours) leave from the Erbil Garage, while taxis to Halabja (ID7000, one hour) depart from Halabja Garage.

ℹ Getting Around

Taxis are plentiful but operate without a meter, so be sure to negotiate your price before taking off. Most destinations within the city should cost between ID3000 and ID5000 (US$2 to US$4).

UNDERSTAND IRAQ

Iraq Today

In 2006, when Iraqis elected their first permanent democratic government led by Nouri al-Maliki, hope for stability was high. By the time the last US servicemen and women left Iraq at the end of 2011 violence had fallen dramatically, but problems between Maliki's party and Iraq's Sunni and Kurdish population were brewing under the surface.

The cracks in the government were already showing in 2012 when the fragile Shia majority coalition came close to collapse. By the end of that year, Sunni-led protests swept through Anbar Province – Iraqi Sunnis felt they were being marginalised and targeted by Maliki's government. Protests continued until violence escalated in January 2014 and the Iraqi government lost the city of Fallujah to Isis.

During that same month, Baghdad failed to transfer the Kurdish share of Iraq's federal budget to Erbil, angering the Kurdistan Regional Government. The lack of money gave the Kurds the perfect excuse to begin exporting their crude oil independently, putting further strain on Erbil-Baghdad relations. In August 2014 Maliki stepped down and was replaced by Haider al-Abadi, appointed by the new president, Kurdish Fuad Masum.

In June 2014 a greater threat materialised, in the form of Isis, presenting Baghdad and Erbil with a common enemy. An amalgamation of disillusioned civilians, former members of Saddam Hussein's Ba'ath Party and foreigners, Isis began operating in Iraq under an extreme version of sharia law, displacing over one million people and killing thousands. The group encouraged the Iraqi and Kurdish military to take up arms and foreign powers to intervene with air strikes.

During this time of chaos, 'disputed areas' like oil-rich Kirkuk were largely abandoned by an inefficient Iraqi army and swiftly filled by Kurdish soldiers. It is unlikely that the Kurds will agree to share control of Kirkuk again without a fight.

At the time of writing, the situation in Iraq was changing on a daily basis, cities falling and being retaken week in and week out. While there is really no saying in which direction Iraq is heading, Kurdistan does appear to be slowly edging its way towards a greater state of autonomy. There's no doubt the country has a steep upward road to climb before it can reach a sense of stability.

History

Ancient Mesopotamia

Iraq's story begins with the Sumerians, who flourished in the rich agricultural lands surrounding the Tigris and Euphrates Rivers from around 4000 BC. In 1750 BC, Hammurabi seized power and went on to dominate the annals of the Babylonian Empire. He developed the Code of Hammurabi, the first written codes of law in recorded history. Despite constant attacks from the Hittites and other neighbouring powers, Babylon would dominate the region until the 12th century BC, after which it went into a slow decline.

By the 7th century BC, the rival Assyrian civilisation had reached its high point under Ashurbanipal, whose capital at Nineveh was one of the great cities of the world with cuneiform libraries, luxurious royal courts and magnificent bas-reliefs. His expensive military campaigns against Babylonia and other neighbours, however, drained the kingdom of its wealth and manpower. In 612 BC, Nineveh and the Assyrian Empire fell to Babylonian King Nabopolassar.

The Neo-Babylonian Empire returned Babylon to its former glory. Nabopolassar's son, Nebuchadnezzar II, built the famous Hanging Gardens of Babylon and conquered Jerusalem. In 539 BC, Babylon finally fell to the Persian Empire of Cyrus the Great. The Persians were in turn defeated by Alexander the Great, who died in Babylon in 323 BC. For the next 1000 years, Mesopotamia was ruled by a string of empires, among them the Seleucid, Parthian and Sassanid.

Islamic Iraq

In AD 637 the Arab armies of Islam swept north from the Arabian Peninsula and occupied Iraq. Their most important centres became Al-Kufa, Baghdad and Mosul.

In 749 the first Abbasid caliph was proclaimed at Al-Kufa and the Abbasids would go on to make Iraq their own. The founding of Baghdad by Al-Mansur saw the city become, by some accounts, the greatest city in the world. In 1258 Hulagu – grandson of the feared Mongol ruler Genghis Khan – laid waste to Baghdad and killed the last Abbasid caliph. Political power in the Muslim world shifted elsewhere.

By 1638, Iraq had come under Ottoman rule. After a period of relative autonomy, the Ottomans centralised their rule in the 19th century, and Iraqi resentment against foreign occupation crystallised even as the Ottomans undertook a massive program of modernisation. The Ottomans held on until 1920, when the arrival of the British saw Iraq submit to yet another occupying force, which was first welcomed then resented by the Iraqis.

Independent Iraq

Iraq gained its independence from the British in 1932, in a decision-making process that left the Kurdish population with very little hope for their own independent state. By then the Kurdish independence movement had gained momentum and included a successful military branch, the Peshmerga (literal meaning: 'those who face death'). The Peshmerga were a key component in the Kurdish struggle for independence and eventually became the official armed forces of the Kurdistan Regional Government.

The period that followed was distinguished by a succession of coups and counter coups, and by the discovery of massive reserves of oil. During WWII, the British again occupied Iraq over fears that the pro-German government would cut oil supplies to Allied forces. On 14 July 1958, the pro-British monarchy was overthrown in a military coup and Iraq became a republic. In 1968 a bloodless coup brought the Ba'ath Party to power.

In 1961 the first Iraqi-Kurdish war began and lasted until 1970. During this period Mustafa Barzani – the father of current Kurdistan President Massoud Barzani – led the struggle to create an independent Kurdish state in Iraq.

The war ended in stalemate in 1970, leading to the Iraqi-Kurdish Autonomy Agreement in which a Kurdish autonomous region comprised of three governorates was created. In 1974 a second Iraqi-Kurdish war broke out, resulting in Baghdad taking back control of Kurdistan.

While the Kurds faced numerous struggles, the 1970s marked a glory decade for the rest of Iraq. The oil boom of the 1970s brought wealth and prosperity. Oil profits

WHAT'S IN A NAME?

Officially the Kurdish part of Iraq is known as the Kurdistan Region, but visitors will soon become aware of the sensitive topic that is the naming of Kurdistan.

Many Kurds reject the term Iraqi Kurdistan because of its association to Iraq and will instead refer to the region by its Kurdish name: Bashure Kurdistan, or South Kurdistan.

The term South Kurdistan is in relation to the other areas of the hypothetical Greater Kurdistan, which also includes parts of Syria, Turkey and Iran, known in Kurdish as Rojava, Bakur and Rojhelat respectively.

were heavily invested in education, health care and infrastructure.

Iraq's heyday ended on 16 July 1979, when an ambitious Ba'ath official named Saddam Hussein Abd al-Majid al-Tikriti worked his way into power. Saddam's first action as president was to secure his power by executing political and religious opponents.

Iran-Iraq War & Al-Anfal

Meanwhile, next door, the Islamic Revolution was busy toppling Iran's pro-Western government. Saddam – a secular Sunni Muslim – became increasingly concerned about the threat of a Shiite revolution in his own country. After several months of sabre rattling, Iraq invaded Iran on 22 September 1980 with the full support of the USA, the Soviet Union and several Arab and European states.

At first Iraq had the upper hand, but it soon found itself at an impasse. The eight years of war were characterised by Iranian human-wave infantry attacks and Iraq's use of chemical weapons against Iranian troops and civilians. The Iran-Iraq war ended as a stalemate on 20 August 1988. Each side suffered at least 200,000 deaths and incurred US$100 billion in war debts.

Even throughout the war with Iran, Saddam continued his systematic murder of Kurds. In 1983 over 8000 boys and men of the Barzani tribe were killed, in an attempt to get rid of all the men of military serving age.

In March 1988, Saddam's cousin and chief of Iraq's intelligence services, Ali Hassan al-Majid, ordered a chemical attack on the city of Halabja. Some 5000 civilians died as a result of the five-hour bombing and many more still bear physical and psychological scars. Some experts claim that Saddam attacked Halabja because both Kurdish and Iranian soldiers had sought shelter in the city.

In the closing months of the war, Saddam launched *Al-Anfal* ('the spoils of war'), a genocidal campaign against the Kurds and a small number of other minorities that lasted from February to September 1988. Dissident male Kurds were imprisoned in concentration camps and later killed in mass executions. The women were segregated and often died as a result of the prison's inhumane conditions.

The exact number of dead has never been fully ascertained but Iraqi prosecutors put the figure at 182,000 (other sources give a significantly higher figure). In addition, around 4500 Kurdish villages were destroyed.

Gulf War

The wounds of the Iran-Iraq war had barely healed when Saddam turned his attention to Kuwait. In July 1990 Saddam accused the Kuwaitis (with some justification) of waging 'economic warfare' against Iraq by attempting to artificially hold down the price of oil, and of stealing oil by slant-drilling into the Iraq side of the border. On 2 August 1990, Iraq invaded Kuwait, whose small armed forces were quickly overrun. Six days later, Iraq annexed Kuwait as its 19th province. It was a costly miscalculation.

Led by the US President George H W Bush, an international coalition of nearly one million troops from 34 countries amassed on Iraq's borders. On 17 January 1991, Operation Desert Storm began with a massive five-week bombing campaign, followed by a ground offensive that drove Iraqi forces from Kuwait. Widely varied figures estimate that between 20,000 and 100,000 Iraqis were killed. As part of the ceasefire agreement, the UN ordered Iraq to destroy all chemical, nuclear and biological weapons and long-range missile programs.

Shortly before the war ended, Iraqi Shiites and Kurds took up arms against Saddam, encouraged by the impending victory and promises of coalition support. But help never arrived. Saddam's forces quickly crushed the rebellion, leaving thousands more dead.

In Kurdistan a series of uprisings organised by the KDP and the PUK swept through the north, taking control of every town and city except for Mosul and Kirkuk. This was followed by fierce retaliation by Saddam and the exodus of Kurdish civilians to Iran and Turkey. Each year on 5 March, Kurdistan remembers and commemorates the uprisings.

Other opponents of Saddam were imprisoned, tortured or simply vanished. Coalition forces later established no-fly zones in southern and northern Iraq to protect the Shiites and Kurds. For the latter, this was the beginning of the end of their oppression.

In the meantime, the UN had imposed a stringent sanctions regime on Iraq. First enforced in August 1990, their original stated purpose was to compel Iraq to withdraw from Kuwait, pay reparations and disclose any weapons of mass destruction. The removal of Saddam, although never officially a goal, was believed by many to be a nonexpress aim of the sanctions. Whether this is true or not, the sanctions did little to undermine Saddam's regime; they did bring untold misery to the people of Iraq in the form of malnutrition, poverty, inadequate medical care and lack of clean water. The most hard hit group was children. Estimates of the number of children who died due to the effects of the sanctions and collateral effects of war vary hugely, but Unicef has estimated the figure to be around 500,000. When Madeleine Albright (at the time US ambassador to the UN) was questioned in 1996 about whether the death of so many children was too high a price for the removal of Saddam Hussein she replied, 'I think this is a very hard choice but the price, we think the price is worth it'.

2003 Iraq War

In a 12 September 2002 speech to the UN General Assembly, US President George W Bush set the stage for war by declaring that Iraq was manufacturing weapons of mass destruction (WMDs) and harbouring Al-Qaeda terrorists, among other claims. Saddam disputed the claims but reluctantly agreed to allow weapons inspectors back into the country. UN inspectors concluded that Iraq had failed to account for all its weapons, but insisted there was no evidence WMDs had existed. Meanwhile, a 'coalition of the willing' led by American and British troops was massing in Kuwait. On 20 March 2003 – without UN authority – the coalition launched its second war on Iraq. Allied forces easily overran Iraqi forces, with relatively few casualties. Baghdad fell on 9 April 2003, but Saddam escaped. On 1 May 2003, Bush declared victory under a banner that read 'Mission Accomplished'. But the war was just beginning.

While the initial optimism quickly vanished in Arab Iraq, the Kurds largely welcomed the allied forces as liberators and even co-operated with them in the overrunning of northern cities like Mosul and Kirkuk. An American-Kurdish joint operation also pushed members of extremist group Ansar al-Islam into Iran.

Throughout the rest of the country it soon became clear that planning for postwar Iraq had been woefully inadequate. The country descended into chaos and anarchy. The Iraqi army was disbanded in a process known as 'debathification' where former Ba'ath party members were excluded from the new Iraqi government, leaving millions of unemployed men on the street. The country was spiralling into a guerrilla war with a growing insurgency.

In December 2003, a dishevelled and bearded Saddam was found cowering in a spider hole near his hometown of Tikrit. Saddam was executed in December 2006 for crimes against humanity. This was the ultimate green light for the Kurds to start rebuilding their homeland.

In 2004 things went from bad to worse for Arab Iraq. The insurgency exploded, led by such groups as Al-Qaeda. That same year, photos emerged of American soldiers abusing Iraqi prisoners at Abu Ghraib prison, creating an international backlash against the occupation. Two major battles in the Sunni city of Fallujah did little to stem the bloodshed. On 22 February 2006, the holy Shiite shrine in Samarra was bombed, kicking off a wave of sectarian violence that pitched Iraqi Sunnis and Shiites against one another and left thousands dead. Kurds were reluctant to take military action in a sectarian war they did not see as their own.

The tide finally started to turn in 2007 when the US launched a troop surge that saw an extra 20,000 troops being sent to Iraq. Subsequently, the levels of violence began to fall, and foreign troops began to leave. Britain ended its combat operations in 2009 and the US in 2010, with the last US troops leaving at the end of 2011.

By the time of the final US withdrawal, the death toll from the war and subsequent insurgency in Iraq had reached an estimated 105,000 to 115,000 Iraqi civilians (based on figures provided by Iraq Body Count – other sources give a different figure), 10,125 Iraqi soldiers and police, 4800 coalition soldiers (mostly from the US) and 150 journalists. Tens of thousands more have been injured or maimed. The UN High Commissioner for Refugees estimates at least 3.4 million Iraqis have either fled the country or were internally displaced as a result of the war.

In a seemingly parallel universe the Kurds had quietly but quickly set out the foundations to build a state and by the time the US troops left, they were already considered a safe and modern region amid the chaos.

People & Society

National Psyche

Iraq is one of the most culturally and socially diverse countries in the Middle East. About 75% to 80% of the population is Arab, 15% to 20% Kurdish and the rest is made up of Turkomans, Assyrians, Persians, Chaldeans, Palestinians, Yazidis and nomadic Bedouins. Islam is the official religion of Iraq. Muslims make up 97% of the population – about 60% to 65% Shiite and 35% to 40% Sunni. There are also small but historically significant communities of Christians who belong to various sects including Chaldeans, Assyrians, Syrian and Roman Catholics. Other religious minorities are the Shabaks, Yazidis, Sabeans, the Mandeans (followers of John the Baptist) and a handful of Jews (a number of whom have ancestors who converted to Islam and no longer consider themselves Jewish).

Kurdish tradition has recently become intertwined with modernity, brought about by a wave of young returning diaspora Kurds – young men and women who were forced to flee Kurdistan during the '70s and '80s and were largely raised in the West. While the majority consider themselves Kurdish, they are strongly influenced by their Western upbringing, offering traditional Kurdistan a window into a different culture and at times clashing with Kurdish conservatism.

IRAQ PEOPLE & SOCIETY

ℹ SAFE TRAVEL

We've said it once and we'll say it again: Iraq is a war zone. In Kurdistan, violence and crime are rare, but not unheard of. Open hostility towards Western visitors – including Americans – is rare in Kurdistan. Checkpoints are common, so you should carry your passport with you at all times.

The security situation in Iraq, including the Kurdish region, is constantly changing. Be sure to check with your foreign office for current advice before travelling. Most countries strongly advise their citizens not to travel to anywhere in Iraq except Iraqi Kurdistan (though some also advise against this and if your country is one of these your travel insurance will be invalid – take out a special Iraq policy).

Arabic and Kurdish are the official languages of Iraq. Arabic is spoken by 80% of the population. The Kurds speak a language that is widely known as Kurdish, but in reality Kurds speak one of two Indo-European languages: Kurmanji and Sorani. In Iraqi Kurdistan, English education is now compulsory, so many young people understand at least a bit of English. Many young Kurds don't speak Arabic, while the older generations were forced to learn it at school as children.

Democracy has brought capitalism – and materialism – to the country. In Kurdistan the big cities have embraced a form of Western pop culture, but it only takes a quick drive to the outskirts to see that rural Kurdistan remains untouched by Western luxuries, and a sense of 'Kurdishness' prevails.

Daily Life

Arab and Kurdish Iraqi life revolves around the family and extended family, a bond that took on added significance during years of war, sanctions and international isolation. Family dominates all aspects of Iraqi life, with great importance on honour and reputation. It's a paternalistic, patriarchal and conservative society, especially in rural areas, although less so in Kurdish cities like Sulaymaniyah.

Iraq is primarily a tribal society. Allegiance to one's ethnic group often takes precedece over any party, provincial or national loyalties, and ethnic interests play an important role in the shaping of government and public policy.

The role of women is complex. Legally, men and women have the same rights. Women are commonplace in government, politics, media, private business and universities. Nevertheless, women are still expected to take on the traditional role as wife and mother. Arranged marriages are common, usually between first cousins – although less so in Kurdistan. So-called honour killings are not uncommon – the murder of 15-year-old Dunya at the hands of her 45-year-old polygamous husband in 2014 caused a large number of civilians and politicians to speak out against honour killings.

The sectarian violence that has swept through 'Arab Iraq' has forced many women back into the home and to adopt a more conservative style of dress. In the cities of Kurdistan things are more relaxed and women play a bigger part in daily street life.

Many an Iraqi's favourite pastime is picnicking. The Kurds in particular have turned the humble picnic into an art form and every Friday throughout the warmer months of the year Kurds descend en masse to the nearest park or beauty spot for a family picnic.

SURVIVAL GUIDE

ℹ Directory A–Z

ACCOMMODATION

For a developing country emerging from decades of war, Iraq is a surprisingly expensive place. Hotel rooms that went for US$5 before the war are now going for US$50. It all comes down to supply and demand.

We assume that readers are only travelling to Iraqi Kurdistan. The Kurdish Regional Government is focusing all its energies on building four- and five-star luxury hotels. Thankfully, family-run budget hotels are quite common, though they are unlikely to house unmarried couples. Older hotels usually have squat toilets, but Western toilets are increasingly common, especially in newer midrange and top-end establishments.

Prices in reviews are for double rooms in high season and include bathrooms, breakfast and taxes unless otherwise indicated.

$ less than ID70,000 (US$60)

$$ ID70,000 to ID174,000 (US$60 to US$150)

$$$ more than ID174,000 (US$150)

EMBASSIES & CONSULATES

Foreign embassies in Iraq can only provide limited consular services, if any.

International Offices in Kurdistan (www.dfr.krg.org; Erbil & Sulaymaniyah) For a list of international offices in Kurdistan, including consulates, visit the Department of Foreign Relations site.

Australian Embassy (☏ 01-538 2104; www.iraq.embassy.gov.au; Baghdad International Zone)

French Embassy (☏ 071 819 96; www.amba-france-iq.org; Baghdad)

German Embassy (☏ 01-543 1470; www.bagdad.diplo.de; al-Mansour district, Baghdad)

Netherlands Embassy (☏ 01-778 2571; iraq.nlembassy.org; Baghdad International Zone)

UK Embassy (☏ 0790 191 1684; http://ukiniraq.fco.gov.uk/en; Baghdad International Zone)

US Embassy (☏ 0760 030 3000; iraq.usembassy.gov; Baghdad International Zone)

FOOD

Prices in reviews represent the cost of a standard main-course dish unless otherwise noted.

$ less than ID10,000 (US$9)
$$ ID10,000 to ID15,000 (US$9 to US$12)
$$$ more than ID15,000 (US$12)

INTERNET ACCESS

Almost all hotels in Kurdistan now provide customers with wi-fi while most cafes in the big cities have free internet access.

MONEY

With a few rare exceptions, Iraq is a cash country. You should plan to bring enough cash – preferably US dollars – to last your entire trip. While ATMs do exist in Kurdistan, travellers should rely on them only in case of emergencies as they are rare and often out of service.

The official unit of currency is the Iraqi dinar (ID). Current banknotes in Kurdistan include 250, 500, 1000, 5000, 10,000 and 25,000 dinars. A 50 dinar note is in circulation in the rest of Iraq. Coins are no longer used. US dollars are also widely accepted; businesses often list prices in both dinars and dollars. US notes should be undamaged and printed after 2003.

In Iraqi Kurdistan, as in the rest of Iraq, dollars are king, but euros, British pounds and Turkish lira can usually be changed in larger centres. Money can be changed in banks, but for the best exchange rate, hit one of the street-corner exchange stands and look for the guys holding giant wads of cash.

Credit cards and travellers cheques are useless in Kurdistan. Many banks now offer international transfers. MoneyGram and Western Union money wire services can be found in Erbil and Sulaymaniyah.

Budget

Prices in Iraqi Kurdistan are on the rise. A basic room with attached bathroom can still be found for ID20,000 but not much less. Cheap meals consisting of various salads, kebabs, bread and tea can be had for ID7000 to ID9000. The one thing that isn't that cheap is transport, but as distances in Iraqi Kurdistan are short even this isn't going to break the bank. A seat in a share taxi between Erbil to Sulaymaniyah is ID15,000 to ID20,000.

OPENING HOURS

Officially, government offices, banks and private businesses are usually open 8am to 2pm Sunday to Wednesday and until 1.30pm on Thursday. Unofficially, business hours in Iraq are whenever the employees feel like showing up to work.

PUBLIC HOLIDAYS

In addition to the main Islamic holidays, Shiite Muslims also observe a number of other religious holidays. Iraq also observes the following:

Newroz (21 March) Kurdish New Year, Iraqi Kurdistan only.

Uprising against Saddam Hussein's regime (5 March)

Birthday of Mustafa Barzani, leader of Kurdistan's national democratic movement (14 March)

Commemoration of chemical attack on Halabja (16 March)

Commemoration of Al-Anfal genocide campaign against the Kurds (14 April)

Baghdad Liberation Day (9 April) Anniversary of the fall of Saddam Hussein's regime in 2003.

Ceasefire Day (8 August) End of Iran-Iraq war.

ℹ PRACTICALITIES

Electricity The electrical current is 230V AC, 50Hz. Wall sockets are unpredictable. Expect to find both two-pin European types and three-prong, British-type plugs.

Media For the news in English, check out Iraqi *Aswat al-Iraq* (www.aswatal-iraq.info) or Kurdish *Rudaw English* (rudaw.net/english). Of the international news broadcasters *Al-Jazeera* (www.al-jazeera.com) is the best for Iraqi-based news and features in English.

Weights and measures Iraq uses the metric system for weights and measures.

USEFUL WEBSITES

Thorn Tree (www.lonelyplanet.com/thorntree) This travel forum on Lonely Planet's website is easily the best place to go (even if we do say so ourselves!) for bang-up-to-date information on Iraqi travel.

Joe's Trippin': Iraq (http://joestrippin.blogspot.com/search/label/iraq) Blog of a ridiculously well-travelled Canadian living in Iraqi Kurdistan. Full of great ideas on things to see and do.

British Museum Iraq Project (www.britishmuseum.org/iraq) The British Museum's project to protect and preserve Iraq's cultural heritage.

Iraqi Kurdistan Tourism Ministry (http://tourismkurdistan.com) Concise answers to questions about the security situation, banking system and even gambling laws.

Iraqi Ministry of Foreign Affairs (http://mofa.gov.iq) Includes news and listings of Iraqi embassies abroad.

Kurdish Regional Government (http://krg.org) An overvierw of the governmental structure of the Kurdish region, up-to-date news and a brief history.

The Other Iraq (http://theotheriraq.com) Focusing on all things Kurdish.

UNAMI (www.uniraq.org) UN Assistance Mission for Iraq.

TELEPHONE

The country code for Iraq is ☑ 964, followed by the local area code (minus the zero), then the subscriber number. Due to the poor state of Iraq's landline telephones, most residents and businesses rely on mobile phones. Considering the mobile phone has only been around since 2003, Iraq has a surprisingly reliable and widespread network. The main service providers are Iraqna, AsiaCell and Korek. SIM cards and pay-as-you-go phones are widely available.

VISAS

The Kurdish Regional Government issues its own tourist visa, valid for travel within Iraqi Kurdistan only. Citizens of most countries, including Australia, the EU, New Zealand and USA, are automatically issued free, 15-day tourist visas at the point of entry. Thirty-day visa extensions can be obtained in Erbil at the **Directorate of Residency** (100 Metre St; ⊗ 8.30am-3pm, closed Fri) in the Ministry of Interior satellite building.

For information on visas, including whether you need to apply for one in advance, visit http://erbilresidency.com.

WOMEN TRAVELLERS

Kurdistan is safe for female travellers, and women are generally treated with courtesy and respect. Still, we recommend that it is best to always travel in pairs or groups. As in most parts of the Middle East, it's important to dress conservatively – no bare shoulders or legs, cleavage or other excessive skin should be on display. Kurdistan is a secular society, so there is no need to cover your hair. Western clothing is common throughout Iraq.

❶ Getting There & Away

AIR

Kurdistan has two international airports: Erbil and Sulaymaniyah. We do not recommend flying into Arab Iraq. Flying anywhere into Iraq and Kurdistan is very expensive due to high insurance costs and limited competition.

Austrian Airlines (www.aua.com) Flies from a number of cities via Vienna to Erbil.

Emirates (www.emirates.com) Flies from Dubai to Erbil and Sulaymaniyah.

Iraqi Airways (www.iraqiairways.co.uk) Connects Erbil and Sulaymaniyah to London Gatwick.

Lufthansa (www.lufthansa.com) Flies from Frankfurt and Vienna to Erbil.

Pegasus (www.flypgs.com) One of the cheapest ways of getting to Kurdistan by air is by flying first to İstanbul (Turkey) and then on to Erbil with this Turkish budget airline.

Royal Jordanian (www.rj.com) Flies from a number of cities via Amman to Erbil and Sulaymaniyah.

Turkish Airlines (www.thy.com) Flies between İstanbul, Erbil and Sulaymaniyah.

Zagros Jet (www.zagrosjet.com) A cheap way to get from İstanbul to Erbil and Sulaymaniyah.

LAND

Border Crossings

Iraq is bordered by six countries. At the time of writing, the only safe overland crossings are the Ibrahim Khalil border crossing between Silopi in Turkey and Zakho in Iraq, and the Iran-Iraq border crossings at Haji Omaran and Panjwin (note that you can only enter Iran with a prearranged visa). Of the Iranian border crossings (which are rarely used by foreign tourists), the Haji Omaran crossing is by far the easiest of the two in regards to transport connections, but whichever you use it's likely to involve some hitching (note that hitching is never completely safe in any country and we do not recommend it). All other borders are dangerous no-go zones.

Note that you cannot cross from Kurdistan into the rest of Iraq without a valid Iraqi visa, which independent travellers are highly unlikely to get – and even if you did, the overland crossing would be very dangerous.

Ibrahim Khalil This very busy border crossing can be quite slow to get across (allow an hour for crossing into Iraq and up to three hours crossing into Turkey – on bad days it can take up to six), but it's otherwise a breeze. Taxis in Silopi will take you to the Iraqi side of the border and handle all formalities for you. The price is set at US$50 per taxi. From the Iraqi side of the border taxis are available into Zakho.

It's also possible to travel direct from Erbil to Diyarbakir in southeast Turkey in one clean sweep by bus, via this crossing. **Best Van** (US$30) buses leave Erbil daily at 4pm. Tickets can be bought from a number of agents around Erbil, including from **İstanbul Iletisim** (10 Meter St) opposite the Peace Pigeon Hotel.

ⓘ Getting Around

LOCAL TRANSPORT

Taxis are the main mode of public transport in Kurdistan and the most reliable one. In cities, they are cheap and plentiful, usually costing no more than ID5000. For intercity travel within Iraqi Kurdistan, you have two choices: private taxi or cheaper, shared taxis. Shared taxis depart and arrive from a city 'garage', or large parking lot; drivers will be standing outside their vehicle, yelling the name of their destination. Shared taxis leave when they are full. Expect to pay between ID5000 to ID20,000, depending on your destination. When travelling between major cities in Iraqi Kurdistan, ensure you stay within Kurdish Peshmerga-controlled territory. Agree on price and route before getting in.

IRAQ GETTING AROUND

Israel & the Palestinian Territories

Why Go?

At the intersection of Asia, Europe and Africa, Israel and the Palestinian Territories have been a meeting place of cultures, empires and religions since the dawn of history. Cradle of Judaism and Christianity, and sacred to Muslims and Baha'is, the Holy Land offers visitors the opportunity both to immerse themselves in the richness and variety of their own religious traditions and to discover the beliefs, rituals and architecture of other faiths. Distances are short, so you can relax on a Mediterranean beach one day, spend the next rafting down the Jordan River or floating in the mineral-rich waters of the Dead Sea, and the day after that scuba diving in the Red Sea. Hikers can follow spring-fed tributaries of the Jordan, discover verdant oases tucked away in the arid bluffs above the Dead Sea, and explore the multicoloured sandstone formations of Makhtesh Ramon.

Best for Nature

➡ Ein Gedi Nature Reserve (p258)

➡ Makhtesh Ramon (p260)

➡ Hula Nature Reserve (p254)

➡ Red Sea Snorkelling (p261)

Best for Culture

➡ Israel Museum (p226)

➡ Tel Aviv's theatres and live music venues (p239)

➡ Tsfat's art galleries (p255)

➡ Ramallah (p264)

When to Go
Jerusalem

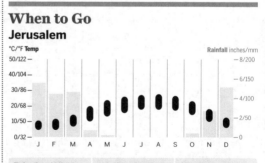

Feb–Apr Hillsides and valleys are carpeted with wildflowers; the ideal season for hiking.	**Jul–Aug** Warm and dry in Jerusalem, humid in Tel Aviv, infernal at the Dead Sea and Eilat.	**Sep–Oct** Jewish holidays generate a spike in domestic tourism – and room prices.

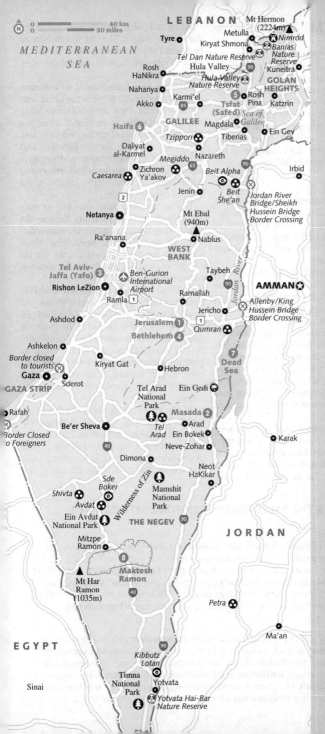

Israel & the Palestinian Territories Highlights

1 Admire the magnificence of Jerusalem's **Dome of the Rock** (p218), place a note between the ancient stones of the **Western Wall** (p219), and visit the **Church of the Holy Sepulchre** (p214), believed to be the site of Jesus's crucifixion.

2 Ascend the Snake Path before dawn and watch the sun rise from atop **Masada** (p259).

3 Take a dip in the warm Mediterranean and watch the bods at the beaches of **Tel Aviv-Jaffa** (Yafo; p231).

4 Explore the nooks and crannies of the **Church of the Nativity** (p268) in Bethlehem.

5 Wander the narrow alleyways of **Tsfat** (Safed; p255), a centre of Kabbalah (Jewish mysticism) since the 16th century.

6 Admire the breathtaking sea views from Haifa's spectacular **Baha'i Gardens** (p241).

7 Float in the briny, soothing waters of the **Dead Sea** (p258).

8 Hike amid the sheer cliffs and coloured sands of **Makhtesh Ramon** (p260).

JERUSALEM القدس ירושלים

□02 / POP 815,000

Holy to Jews, Christians and Muslims, Jerusalem is one of the world's foremost pilgrimage destinations – you can walk in the footsteps of prophets, pray in buildings built by order of kings and caliphs, and overnight in hospices where Crusaders and cardinals have slumbered. Even for the non-religious, it's hard not to be moved by the emotions and history that come alive in the narrow alleyways of the Old City.

History

According to the American historian Eric H Cline (in his 2004 book *Jerusalem Besieged*), Jerusalem has been destroyed at least twice, placed under siege 23 times, attacked another 52 times and captured and recaptured 44 times.

The first settlement on the site of Jerusalem was a small Jebusite village situated south of Mt Moriah (the Temple Mount), where the Bible says Abraham almost sacrificed his son Isaac. In 997 BC, King David captured the city and made it his capital. His son, King Solomon, built the First Temple, destroyed in 586 BC by Babylonian king Nebuchadnezzar, who exiled the Jews to Babylonia. In 538 BC they were allowed to return and almost immediately began construction of the Second Temple, consecrated in 516 BC.

Power in Jerusalem shifted between Jewish rulers, such as the Maccabees, and various regional empires, until the Romans took control in 63 BC, installing Herod the Great as king of Judea. He launched a massive building campaign, significantly expanding the Second Temple. The city was then ruled by a series of procurators; it was the fifth of these, Pontius Pilate, who ordered the crucifixion of Jesus.

Growing Jewish discontent with Roman rule exploded in AD 66 with the Great Jewish Revolt (the First Jewish-Roman War), which ended with the sacking of Jerusalem and the destruction of the Second Temple in AD 70. After the Bar Kochba Rebellion (AD 132–35), the Jews were banished from Jerusalem. Emperor Hadrian rebuilt the city as Aelia Capitolina, whose street grid forms the basis of today's Old City.

During the Byzantine era (4th to early 7th century AD), Christianity became the official state religion, forcing the conversion of many local Jews and Samaritans. Many Christian shrines were built; work on the Church of the Holy Sepulchre, for instance, commenced in AD 326.

In AD 638, Byzantine Jerusalem fell to the armies of Islam and came under the sway of Arab civilisation. The Dome of the Rock, instantly recognisable thanks to its gleaming gold dome, was completed in AD 691. But despite its significance to Islam, Jerusalem's political and economic fortunes fell into decline, in part because of the city's distance from the imperial capitals of Damascus and Cairo.

In the 11th century, Palestine fell to the Seljuk Turks, who stopped Christian pilgrims from visiting Jerusalem. The response of western European Christians was a series of Crusades – and Crusader kingdoms – that lasted from 1095 to 1270. The Crusaders took

---

TOP ISRAEL & THE PALESTINIAN TERRITORIES ITINERARIES

Ten Days

Spend three days exploring the wonders of **Jerusalem**, then take the slow train to **Tel Aviv** and spend a couple of days in cafes, at museums, cycling, and on the beach. Rent a car, if you can, and head north, spending two days at the **Sea of Galilee** and hiking at **Tel Dan** or **Banias**. Finally, drive west to **Haifa** to visit the gorgeous **Baha'i Gardens**, then down the coast to the ancient ruins of **Caesarea**. From Tel Aviv, fly home or head by bus to **Eilat** and, via the Yitzhak Rabin/Wadi Araba border crossing, to **Petra**, Jordan.

Two Weeks

Follow the 10-day itinerary but make additions. From **Jerusalem** take a day trip below sea level to **Qumran**, where the Essenes hid the Dead Sea Scrolls, and **Masada**, where Jewish Zealots defied the Roman legions. Take another day trip from Jerusalem, southward to friendly, engaging **Bethlehem** and the troubled city of **Hebron**. In the Lower Galilee, visit **Nazareth**, Jesus's boyhood stomping ground, and dine there. In the Upper Galilee, explore spiritual **Tsfat (Safed)**, centre of Kabbalah (Jewish mysticism).

Jerusalem in 1099, but lost it in 1187 to Saladin (Salah ad-Din), Kurdish founder of the Muslim Ayyubid dynasty.

In 1250 the city came under the influence of the Mamluks, successors to the Ayyubids, who ruled from Egypt and turned the city into a centre of Islamic learning. In 1517 the Ottoman Turks absorbed Jerusalem into their expanding empire, where it would remain, something of a backwater, for the next 400 years.

In the 19th century the first road linking Jerusalem with Jaffa was built, greatly increasing the number of Jewish and Christian pilgrims. By about 1850, Jews constituted the majority of the city's 25,000 residents. The first neighbourhood built outside the walls of the Old City was Yemin Moshe, established in 1860. Access to the city became quick and easy with the completion of the Jaffa–Jerusalem rail line in 1892.

The British captured Jerusalem from the Ottomans in December 1917 and later made it the capital of the British Mandate of Palestine. Tensions between Jews and Arabs flared in the 1920s and 1930s. After the British left Palestine in 1948, fighting between the new State of Israel and Jordan's Arab Legion resulted in the city partition. West Jerusalem became the capital of Israel; East Jerusalem, including the entire Old City, was annexed by Jordan.

Jerusalem was reunified after Israel captured the eastern part of the city during the 1967 Six Day War. Shortly after the war, Israel annexed East Jerusalem, declaring the entire city to be its 'eternal capital'. The Palestinians claim East Jerusalem as the capital of a future independent state of Palestine. Israel's separation wall – in many places around Jerusalem an 8m-high cement barrier – cuts mostly Arab East Jerusalem off from the West Bank.

⊙ Sights

Jerusalem is divided into three main areas: the walled Old City, with its four quarters; the predominantly Arab neighbourhoods of East Jerusalem; and mostly Jewish West Jerusalem.

⊙ Christian Quarter

The narrow streets of the Old City's 18.2-hectare Christian Quarter are lined with souvenir shops, artisans' workshops, hospices, hostels and religious institutions belonging to 20 different Christian denominations.

ℹ NEED TO KNOW

Fast Facts

➡ **Capitals** Jerusalem, Ramallah

➡ **Country codes** ☑ 972 (I), ☑ 972 or ☑ 970 (PT)

➡ **Languages** Hebrew and Arabic (I), Arabic (PT)

➡ **Populations** Israel 8.2 million, West Bank 2.7 million, Gaza 1.7 million

➡ **Currency** Israeli new shekel (NIS)

➡ **Mobile phones** Generally excellent 900/1800 MHz mobile-phone coverage

➡ **Money** ATMs widely available in Israel, less so in the Palestinian Territories

➡ **Visas** On-arrival visas available for most nationalities

Exchange Rates

Australia	A$1	3.26NIS
Egypt	E£10	5.45NIS
Euro zone	€1	4.75NIS
Jordan	JD1	5.26NIS
UK	£1	6.00NIS
USA	US$1	3.73NIS

For current exchange rates see www. xe.com.

Resources

➡ **Israel Nature & Parks Authority** (www.parks.org.il)

➡ **This Week in Palestine** (www. thisweekinpalestine.com)

➡ **Israel Ministry of Tourism** (www. goisrael.com)

Incorporating the final five Stations of the Cross (the other nine are along the Via Dolorosa, in the Muslim Quarter), the Church of the Holy Sepulchre stands on a site considered by most Christians to be the biblical Calvary or Golgotha, where Jesus was nailed to the cross, died and was resurrected. The destruction of the church in 1009 by the mad Fatimid caliph Al-Hakim helped spark the Crusades. The present-day church is more or less a Crusader structure of Byzantine origin.

To keep the peace between the Church of the Holy Sepulchre's notoriously fractious

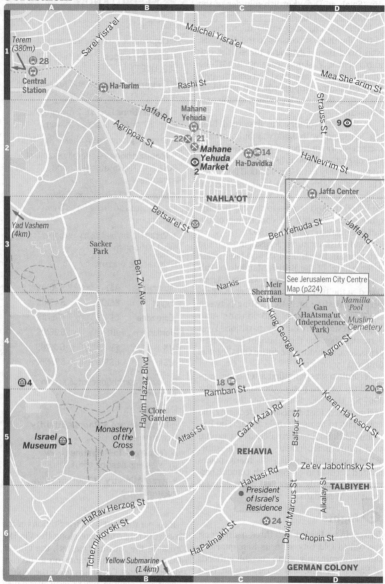

Christian denominations, a Muslim family, the Nusseibehs, keeps the keys, unlocking the doors each morning and securing them again at night. Visitors should dress modestly – the guards are very strict and refuse entry to those with bare legs, shoulders or backs.

★ **Church of the Holy Sepulchre** CHURCH
(Map p222; ☎ 02-626 7000; ⏰ 5am-9pm Easter-Sep, 4am-7pm Oct-Easter) Christendom's

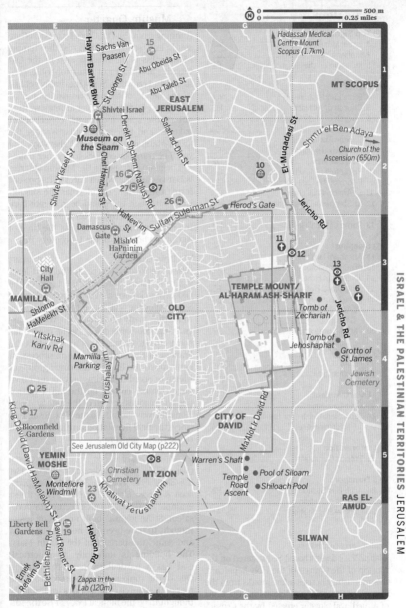

most important church huddles amid souqs on the edge of the Christian and Muslim Quarters. For the past 16 centuries Christian pilgrims have arrived at this spot from every corner of the globe, and while the church building itself may not look particularly regal or attractive, the tears, laments and prayers of the pilgrims have done much to sanctify it. Be aware that the church can be hard to locate – the easiest access is via Christian Quarter Rd.

Jerusalem

Ethiopian Monastery CHURCH
(Map p222; ☺ daylight hours) Sequestered on the rooftop of the Church of the Holy Sepulchre, this monastery houses a few monks from the Church of Ethiopia who live among the ruins of a medieval cloister erected by the Crusaders. The cupola in the middle of the roof section admits light to St Helena's crypt below. A door in the southeast corner leads through a chapel and downstairs to the courtyard of the Holy Sepulchre itself.

◎ Muslim Quarter

Running from the Old City's Damascus Gate south and southeast towards the Temple Mount, this is the liveliest area of the Old City; it's also the most claustrophobic, confusing and crowded. You'll inevitably get lost in the tangle of teeming humanity and be enchanted by the tempting aromas wafting out of the spice merchants, coffeehouses, bakeries and tiny restaurants. Wander the area's Mamluk and medieval alleyways and you'll be transported back to another time.

The main entrance to the Muslim Quarter is Damascus Gate, which dates in its present form from the time of Süleyman the Magnificent, although there had been a gate here long before the arrival of the Turks: this was the city's main gate as early as the time of Agrippa, who ruled in the 1st century BC.

Via Dolorosa RELIGIOUS SITE
(Way of the Sorrows; Map p222) The road leading from Lion's Gate into the heart of the Old City is known as Via Dolorosa (Way of Sorrows) or the Stations of the Cross. It's the route that many Christians believe was taken by the condemned Jesus as he carried his heavy cross to Calvary. At 3pm on Fridays, the Franciscan Fathers lead a solemn procession here; you're also likely to encounter groups of Italian or Spanish pilgrims lugging their own huge (rented) crosses up the hill. Explanations on plaques at each of the nine 'stations' along the way illuminate the New Testament story (the final five stations are in the Church of the Holy Sepulchre).

St Anne's Church CHURCH
(Map p214; adult/student/child under 13yr 8/6/3NIS; ☺8am-noon & 2-6pm Apr-Sep, 8am-noon & 2-5pm Mon-Sat Oct-Mar) The finest example of Crusader architecture in Jerusalem, St Anne's was built in 1138 on a site thought to have been the home of Joachim and Anne, the parents of the Virgin Mary. The building is unusually asymmetrical, and has a particularly beautiful interior. One of the sunken pools accessed from the rear of the church compound is traditionally thought to be the biblical **Pool of Bethesda** (Map p222) where Jesus is said to have healed a sick man (John 5:1–18).

Damascus Gate GATE
(Map p222) The scene in front of Damascus Gate is a colourful one – vendors heave goods in and out of the Old City, Israeli

ISRAEL & THE PALESTINIAN TERRITORIES JERUSALEM

THE OLD CITY & ITS GATES

The magical, mysterious Old City consists of the Temple Mount (Al-Haram ash-Sharif) and four quarters: Muslim, Christian, Jewish and Armenian, each with a distinct atmosphere. The sturdy walls (built 1553–42) are the legacy of Ottoman Sultan Süleyman the Magnificent.

Commanding a prominent elevated location overlooking the Old City, the **Citadel** (Tower of David; Map p222; ☑ 02-626 5333, 02-626 5325; www.towerofdavid.org.il; adult/ student/child 40/30/18NIS; ☺9am-4pm Sun-Thu, to 5pm Jul & Aug, 9am-2pm Fri & Sat, to 5pm Sat Jul & Aug) started life as the palace of Herod the Great. Also used as a palace by the Romans and Crusaders, the structure was extensively remodelled by the Mamluks and Ottomans and is now home to the impressive **Museum of the History of Jerusalem**, which tells the story of the city in a series of chronologically arranged exhibits starting in the second millenium BC and finishing in 1948.

Jaffa Gate (Map p222), the main entrance to the Old City from West Jerusalem, leads directly to the Christian and Armenian Quarters; it is so named because the old road to Jaffa started here. Moving clockwise, the **New Gate** (1887), built by Sultan Abdul Hamid, also gives access to the Christian Quarter. Down the hill, Damascus Gate, the most attractive and crowded of all the city gates, links the Muslim Quarter with the bustling centre of East Jerusalem.

It was near **Herod's Gate** in 1099 that the Crusaders first breached Jerusalem's walls. **Lions Gate** (Map p214), facing the Mount of Olives, is also called **St Stephen's Gate**, after the first Christian martyr, who was stoned to death nearby. It was from here that Israeli paratroops took the Old City in the 1967 Six Day War. **Dung Gate** links the Western Wall (the Jewish Quarter) with the City of David (p219) excavations, a bit down the slope to the south. **Zion Gate**, affording access to the Armenian and Jewish Quarters, is still pocked with reminders of the fierce fighting that took place here in 1948.

Truth be told, the idea of the 1km **walk** (Map p222; ☑ 02-627 7550; www.pami.co.il; adult/ child 16/8NIS; ☺9am-4pm Sat-Thu Oct-Mar, to 5pm Apr-Sep, 9am-2pm Fri) atop the ramparts is better than the reality. Views aren't all that impressive (they're better from the Citadel), and there's no shade, which makes it a real slog in high summer. Tickets are purchased from the 'Jerusalem Tourist Information Center' near Jaffa Gate. Because the ramparts in Temple Mount are off limits, there are two stretches: from Jaffa Gate south to Dung Gate, and from Jaffa Gate north to St Stephen's (Lions) Gate.

border police tap their truncheons, elderly Palestinian women from the villages squat on the pavement selling herbs, parents shepherd their young children through the crowds and tourists take it all in, appearing in turn bewildered and enchanted.

◉ Armenian Quarter & Mt Zion

Armenia became the first nation to officially embrace Christianity when their king converted in AD 303. After the Armenians' kingdom disappeared at the end of the 4th century, they adopted Jerusalem as their spiritual capital and have had an uninterrupted presence here ever since. The city's Armenian population, now numbered at about 1500, grew significantly in the early 1900s, when immigrants arrived – both to work on retiling the Dome of the Rock and to escape Ottoman Turkish persecution.

Mt Zion is situated out Zion Gate from the Old City's Armenian Quarter.

St James' (Jacques') Cathedral   CHURCH
(Map p222; Armenian Orthodox Patriarchate Rd; ☺morning prayers 6.30am, vespers 3pm, Mass 8.30am Sat & 9am Sun) Glowing lamps hang from the ceiling, glittering icons adorn every wall and richly patterned carpets are strewn across the floors, giving this 12th-century cathedral an aura of mystery lacking in many other Christian sites of Jerusalem. It's open only for services, the most impressive of which is held on Sunday when the Armenian Patriarch of Jerusalem presides. At other times, you can enter the courtyard to see the exterior, which is decorated with khatchkars (carved Armenian stone crosses).

Room of the Last Supper   RELIGIOUS SITE
(Cenacle, Coenaculum; Map p214; ☺8am-6pm) Considered to be the one of the most holy

TEMPLE MOUNT (AL-HARAM ASH-SHARIF)

There are few patches of ground as holy – or as disputed – as the Temple Mount (Map p222; ⊙ 7.30-11am & 1.30-2.30pm Sun-Thu Apr-Sep, 7.30-10am & 12.30-1.30pm Sun-Thu Oct-Mar), known to Muslims as Al-Haram ash-Sharif (the Noble Sanctuary) and Jews as Har HaBayit (the Temple Mount). This is Islam's third-holiest site, after Mecca and Medina.

The huge, open stone plaza, dotted with cypress trees, was built over the biblical Mt Moriah, the location, according to Jewish tradition, of the Foundation Stone of the world itself. It was here, says the Talmud, that Adam, Cain, Abel and Noah performed ritual sacrifices, and where Abraham offered his son Isaac to God in a supreme test of faith (Genesis 22:1–19). It was also the site of Solomon's First Temple, where the Ark of the Covenant was housed, and the Second Temple, destroyed by the Romans in AD 70. The Romans subsequently erected a temple to Zeus on the site, which later served as a Christian church.

The centrepiece of the Temple Mount today is the mosaic-adorned Dome of the Rock (Qubbet al-Sakhra; Map p222), completed in AD 691. Topped by a gold dome, it shelters the slab of stone from which Muslim tradition says Mohammed ascended to heaven on the Mi'raj (Night Journey).

Al-Aqsa Mosque is a functioning house of worship believed to be a partial conversion of a 6th-century Byzantine church. Some of the columns were donated, oddly enough, by Benito Mussolini.

The Temple Mount has nine gates but though you can leave the compound by most of them, non-Muslims are allowed to enter only at the Bab al-Maghariba/Sha'ar HaMugrabim (Gate of the Moors), reached from the Western Wall plaza. Line up early for security checks and bear in mind that the Mount closes on Muslim holidays. Modest dress is required. Non-Muslims can walk around the Temple Mount, but are barred from entering the Dome of the Rock.

places in the Christian world (up there with the Church of the Holy Sepulchre and the Church of the Nativity in Bethlehem), this austere and somewhat underwhelming space was part of the Holy Zion church built in AD 390. Retained in the 14th-century Crusader structure that replaced the original church, it was converted to a mosque during the Ottoman period and retains stained glass and a mihrab from that time.

King David's Tomb RELIGIOUS SITE
(Map p214; ⊙ 8am-6pm Sun-Thu, to 2pm Fri)
Erected by Crusaders two millennia after King David's death, this ground-floor tomb is of dubious authenticity but is nonetheless a Jewish holy place. The prayer hall is divided into sides for men and women, both leading to the velvet-draped tomb. Behind is an alcove believed to be a synagogue dating back to the AD 5th century.

⊙ Jewish Quarter

Unlike its bustling neighbours to the north, the Old City's Jewish Quarter is predominantly residential, with 4500 residents, modern stone buildings and a central square. The area was heavily shelled by the Arab Legion during the 1948 fighting and later demolished by the Jordanians, who expelled all the Jewish residents, so most of the area had to be rebuilt from scratch after 1967. Excavations have unearthed a number of archaeological sites.

The focal point of the Jewish Quarter is the Western Wall – Jews have long come here to mourn and lament the destruction of the Temple by the Romans in AD 70, which is why the site is also known as the Wailing Wall, a name that Jews tend to avoid.

Today, the area immediately in front of the wall serves as a great open-air synagogue, with a southern section for women and a larger northern section for men. Stuffed between the huge Herodian-era stones (identifiable by their indented edges) are prayers and petitions left by worshippers.

The wall plaza is open to members of all faiths 24 hours a day, 365 days a year. Modest dress is required, as is head covering for men (paper kippot are available). Photography is prohibited.

★ Western Wall
RELIGIOUS SITE

(Map p222) The builders of the Western Wall could never have fathomed that one day their massive creation would be an important religious shrine. Indeed, when it was built some 2000 years ago this most holy of all Jewish sites was merely a retaining wall supporting the outer portion of Temple Mount, upon which stood the Second Temple. Although the Temple was destroyed, its retaining structure remained and rabbinical texts maintain that the Shechina (divine presence) never deserted it.

Western Wall Tunnels
ARCHAEOLOGICAL SITE

(☑ 8.30am-5pm 02-627 1333; www.thekotel.org; adult/student & child 30/15NIS; ⊙ 7am-6pm Sun-Thu, to noon Fri) For a different perspective on the Western Wall, join a tour of the Western Wall Tunnels, a 488m passage that follows the northern extension of the wall. Dug out by archaeologists, the tunnel burrows down to the original street level (nicknamed Market St by tour guides because it was believed to have been a shopping area). The foundation stones here are enormous – one is a 570-ton monster the size of a small bus.

Jerusalem Archaeological Park & Davidson Centre
HISTORIC SITE

(Map p222; ☑ 02-627 7550; www.archpark.org.il; adult/student & child 30/16NIS, guided tours 160NIS, audioguide 5NIS; ⊙ 8am-5pm Sun-Thu, to 2pm Fri) Offering a peek into the history of the Temple Mount area, this archaeological site near Dung Gate incorporates the remains of streets, columns, gates, walls, plazas and mikvehs exposed during archaeological digs in the 1970s. There's also a modern visitor centre where two video presentations – an interesting one about the excavations and another reconstructing the site as it looked 2000 years ago – are presented in both Hebrew and English.

Cardo Maximus
HISTORIC SITE

(Map p222) Cutting a broad north–south swath, the sunken Cardo Maximus is the reconstructed main street of Roman and Byzantine Jerusalem. At one time it would have run the whole breadth of the city, up to what's now Damascus Gate, but in its present form it starts just south of David St, the tourist souq, serving as the main entry into the Jewish Quarter from the Muslim and Christian areas.

★ City of David
ARCHAEOLOGICAL SITE

(Map p222; ☑ *6033; www.cityofdavid.org.il; adult/child 29/15NIS, movie 13NIS, Enchanted Jerusalem tour adult/child 16-18yr 80/63NIS, Hebrew-language guided tour adult/child 60/45NIS; ⊙ 8am-5pm Sun-Thu, to 2pm Fri Oct-Mar, to 7pm Sun-Thu & to 4pm Fri Apr-Sep; 🚌 1, 2, 38) Excavations at this site started in the 1850s and are ongoing, proof of how rich an archaeological find it was. The oldest part of Jerusalem, it was a settlement during the Canaanite period and was captured by David, who is said to have brought the Ark of the Covenant here 3000 years ago. The main attraction is Hezekiah's Tunnel, a 500m-long passage of waist-deep water, but there is plenty more to see – allow at least three hours for your visit.

To get to the City of David from the Old City's Dung Gate (the gate nearest the Western Wall), head east (downhill) for 200m and take the road to the right; the entrance is then on the left. At the visitors centre you can watch a 3D movie about the city. If you'd like to walk through Hezekiah's Tunnel (highly recommended!), you can change into your swimsuit in the bathrooms and leave your gear in a locker (10NIS); alternatively, wear shorts. You will also need suitable footwear (flip-flops or waterproof shoes) and a torch (flashlight; sold at the ticket office for 4NIS).

◉ Mount of Olives

For Christians, this hillside is where Jesus took on the sins of the world, was arrested and later ascended to heaven. A half-dozen churches commemorate events in Jesus's life.

According to the Old Testament's Book of Zechariah, this is where God will redeem the dead on the Day of Judgement, which is why the Mount of Olives has served as a Jewish cemetery since the time of the First Temple.

The panorama of the Old City from the summit is spectacular – visit early in the morning for the clearest views.

Church of the Ascension
CHURCH

(☑ 02-628 7704; www.evangelisch-in-jerusalem.org; admission 5NIS; ⊙ 8am-1pm Mon-Sat; 🚌 75) In 1898, the Ottomans granted Germany 8 hectares of land on the Mount of Olives. This was set aside for a church and hospice, and the complex was named after Augusta Victoria, wife of Kaiser Wilhelm II. Completed in 1910, the church is decorated with mosaics and frescos, and has a 60m-high bell tower

Al-Haram ash-Sharif/ Temple Mount

A TOUR OF THE TEMPLE MOUNT

The Temple Mount encompasses multiple sites that span an area the size of one or two city blocks. A visit requires a little planning and may need to be accomplished over a couple of days.

Ascend the rickety wooden ramp at the Western Wall plaza to reach the Temple Mount at the Bab al-Maghariba (Gate of the Moors). Passing through the gate, continue ahead to view the understated facade of the **Al-Aqsa Mosque 1** and the sumptuous detail of the **Dome of the Rock 2**. Take a slow turn around the Dome to admire its surrounding structures, including the curious **Dome of the Chain 3** and the elegant **Sabil of Qaitbay 4**. Don't miss the stunning view of the Mount of Olives seen through the stone arches known as the **Scales of Souls 5**.

Exit the Temple Mount at the **Bab al-Qattanin (Gate of Cotton Merchants) 6**; and return to the Western Wall plaza where you can spend some time at the **Western Wall 7** and visit the **Jerusalem Archaeological Park & Davidson Centre 8**.

Scales of Souls
Muslims believe that scales will be hung from the column-supported arches to weigh the souls of the dead.

Bab al-Atim

Bab al-Ghawanima

Bab al-Nazir

Small Wall

Dome of the Ascension

Bab al-Hadad

5

6

Ba Sil

Bab al-Qattanin (Gate of Cotton Merchants)
This is the most imposing of the Haram's gates. Make a point of departing through here into the Mamluk-era arcaded market of the Cotton Merchants (Souq al-Qattanin).

Sabil of Qaitbay
This three-tiered, 13m-high structure is one of the finest pieces of architecture on the Temple Mount. It was built by Egyptians in 1482 as a charitable act to please Allah and features the only carved-stone dome outside Cairo.

TOP TIPS

» **Get in Early** Opening hours for the Temple Mount are limited and lines can be long during the busy summer season, so queue early (gates open at 7.30am).

» **Go Underground** An interesting way to reach the Jerusalem Archaeological Park is to take the underground tunnel that starts 600m away in the City of David (tickets for the park are sold at the City of David).

Dome of the Rock

The crown jewel of Jerusalem's architectural heritage, the Dome famously contains the enormous foundation stone that Jews believe is the centre of the earth and Muslims say is the spot where Mohammed made his ascent.

Dome of the Chain

Some believe this structure was built as a model for the Dome of the Rock. Legend has it that Solomon hung a chain from the dome and those who swore falsely while holding it were struck by lightning.

Al-Aqsa Mosque

One of the world's oldest mosques, Al-Aqsa (the Furthest Mosque) is 75m long and has a capacity for more than 5000 worshippers. The Crusaders called it Solomon's Temple and used it as a royal palace and stable for their horses.

Bab Hitta

Solomon's Throne

Summer Pulpit

Al-Kas Fountain

Musala Marwani Mosque (Solomon's Stables)

Mamluk Arcade

Dome of Learning

Bab al-Maghariba

Western Wall Plaza

Western Wall

Today it's the holiest place on earth for Jews and an important cultural nexus on Shabbat, when Jews from around the city come to sing, dance and pray by the Wall.

Coming Clean

Al-Kas Fountain, located between Al-Aqsa Mosque and the Dome of the Rock, is used for ritual washing before prayers.

Jerusalem Archaeological Park & Davidson Centre

This is the place to see Robinson's Arch, the steps that led up to the Temple Mount and ancient *mikveh* (Jewish ritual bath) where pilgrims washed prior to entering the holy temple.

Jerusalem Old City

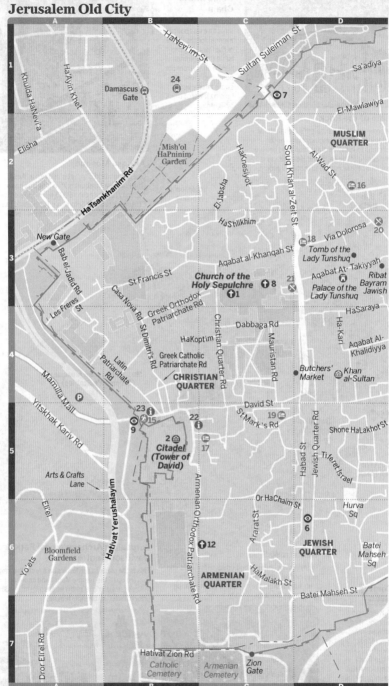

A

Khulda HaNevi'a

Ha'Ayin Khet

Elisha

Damascus Gate

New Gate

Ha Tsankhanim Rd

Bab el-Jadid Rd

Les Freres St

Mamilla Mall

Yitskhak Kariv Rd

Arts & Crafts Lane

El'rei

Yo'ets

Bloomfield Gardens

Dror El'rei Rd

B

HaNevi'im St

24

Mish'ol HaPninim Garden

St Francis St

Casa Nova Rd

Greek Orthodox Patriarchate Rd

St Dimitri's Rd

Latin Patriarchate Rd

HaKoptim

Greek Catholic Patriarchate Rd

CHRISTIAN QUARTER

23
15
9

2 Citadel (Tower of David)

22
17

Hativat Yerushalayim

Armenian Orthodox Patriarchate Rd

12

ARMENIAN QUARTER

Hativat Zion Rd

Catholic Cemetery

C

Sultan Suleiman St

7

Hakneslyot

El Jabsha

HaShlikhim

Aqabat al-Khanqah St

Church of the Holy Sepulchre
1
8

Christian Quarter Rd

Dabbaga Rd

Mauristan Rd

Souq Khan al-Zeit St
Al-Wad St

18

21

David St

St Mark's Rd

19

Or HaChaim St

Ararat St

6

JEWISH QUARTER

HaMalakh St

Armenian Cemetery

Zion Gate

Batei Mahseh St

D

Sa'adiya

El-Mawlawiya

MUSLIM QUARTER

16

Via Dolorosa
20

Tomb of the Lady Tunshuq

Aqabat At-Takiyyah
Ribat Bayram Jawish

Palace of the Lady Tunshuq

HaSaraya

Ha-Kari

Aqabat Al-Khalidiyya

Butchers' Market

Khan al-Sultan

Shone HaLakhot St

Habad St
Jewish Quarter Rd

Tiferet Israel

Hurva Sq

Batei Mahseh Sq

1

2

3

4

5

6

7

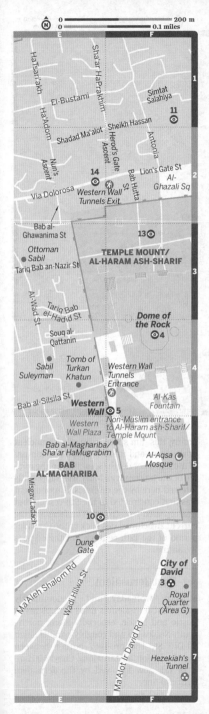

that can be climbed by visitors (203 steps). Unfortunately, views from the bell tower are underwhelming and obscured by a safety grille.

Church of All Nations   CHURCH
(Basilica of Gethsemene; Map p214; ⊘8am-5.50pm Apr-Sep, to 4.50pm Oct-Mar) Glistening golden mosaics mark the facade of this neo-classical Franciscan church built on the site of the Garden of Gethsemene and dedicated in 1924. The mosaic depicts Jesus assuming the suffering of the world, hence one of the church's alternative names – the Sanctuary of the Agony of Jesus Christ. More gold mosaics glint in the dim interior.

Garden of Gethsemane   GARDENS
(Map p214; ⊘8.30am-noon & 2.30-5pm, to 4pm Sun & Thu) Jesus is believed to have been

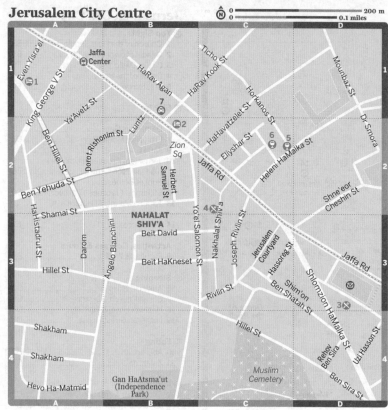

arrested in this garden (Mark 14:26, 32–50), which is attached to the Church of All Nations. It has some of the world's oldest olive trees (in Hebrew *gat shmanim* means 'oil press'), three of which have been scientifically dated as being over 2000 years old, making them witnesses to whatever biblical events may have occurred here. Enter from the narrow alleyway leading up the Mount of Olives.

Church of Mary Magdalene   CHURCH
(Map p214; ☺10am-noon Tue & Thu) The seven golden onion-shaped domes of the Russian Church of Mary Magdalene form one of Jerusalem's most attractive and surprising landmarks. Built in 1888 by Alexander III in memory of his mother, the church is now a convent and has one of the city's best choirs.

Tomb of the Virgin Mary   RELIGIOUS SITE
(Map p214; ☺5am-noon & 2.30-5pm Apr-Sep, from 6am Oct-Mar) One of the holiest sites in Chris-

tianity, this dim space is hung with ancient brass lamps and infused with a millennium of must. On her death (sometime in the middle of the 1st century), Mary was supposedly interred here by the disciples. A monument was first constructed in the 5th century but was repeatedly destroyed. The facade of the current structure dates back to the Crusader period of the 12th century, but the crypt is Byzantine.

◎ East Jerusalem

Modern, workaday and predominantly Arab, East Jerusalem is filled with plenty of hustle and bustle, especially along north–south Nablus Rd and roughly parallel Salah ad-Din St. The pre-1967 border between Israel and Jordan ran along Cheyl HaHandasa Rd, now followed by the Jerusalem light-rail line.

Jerusalem City Centre

Rockefeller Museum   MUSEUM
(Map p214; ☑02-628 2251; Sultan Suleiman St; ⊙10am-3pm Sun-Mon & Wed-Thu, to 2pm Sat; ⊡Damascus Gate) FREE Though overlooked by many visitors to the city, this archaeological museum is well worth a visit. Exhibits date from prehistoric times through to the Middle Ages and are presented chronologically. They include carved 12th-century lintels from the Church of the Holy Sepulchre, detailed 8th-century carvings and moldings recovered from Hisham's Palace near Jericho – don't miss the extraordinary stucco dome from the diwan (Muslim meeting place) – and an exquisite wooden model of the Church of the Holy Sepulchre inlaid with mother-of-pearl.

Garden Tomb   GARDENS
(Map p214; ☑02-627 2745; www.gardentomb.org; ⊙9am-noon & 2-5.30pm Mon-Sat; ⊡Damascus Gate) A tranquil patch of green in the middle of East Jerusalem's mayhem, this site is considered by its trustees to be both the garden and sepulchre of Joseph of Arimathea, and the place where Jesus was crucified, buried and resurrected. While enjoying little support for their claims, the trustees have provided a walled and attractively landscaped space that is more conducive to contemplation than the alternative site said to be that of the crucifixion, the Church of the Holy Sepulchre.

★Museum on the Seam   GALLERY
(Map p214; ☑02-628 1278; www.mots.org.il; 4 Chel Handasa St; adult/student/child under 14yr 30NIS/25NIS/free; ⊙10am-5pm Sun-Mon & Wed-Thu, to 2pm Fri, 2-9pm Tue; ⊡Shivtei Israel) Located on the 'seam' (border) between East and West Jerusalem, this gallery presents contemporary-art exhibitions that are challenging, controversial and satisfying in equal measure. The building itself served as a forward military position for the Israeli army from 1948 to 1967 and still bears the scars of war. Exhibitions change every six months, showcase work from regional artists and focus on issues of global conflict, prejudice, racism and human rights.

◉ City Centre

Jerusalem's city centre is northwest of the Old City. Its central axis is Jaffa Rd, which links Jaffa Gate (and the western tip of the Old City) with Mahane Yehuda Market (and, further west, the Central Bus Station). Midway between the Jaffa Gate and the market, about 1km from each, is Zion Square, a handy landmark and meeting point. Pedestrianised Ben Yehuda St connects Zion Sq – and adjacent, crafts-shop-lined Yoel Solomon St – with King George V St, creating a triangle.

The ultra-Orthodox neighbourhood of Mea She'arim is centred on Shabbat Square (Kikar HaShabbat), which – like the area's main drag, Mea She'arim St – is 600m north along Strauss St from the intersection of Jaffa St and King George V St. It's one of the world's most reluctant tourist attractions so comport yourself respectfully (eg don't take photos without permission) and dress conservatively (crucial if you're female – women should wear long skirts and long-sleeve shirts). Avoid the area during Shabbat – but Thursday night and Friday daytime, when residents are getting ready for Shabbat, are particularly lively times to visit.

★Mahane Yehuda Market   MARKET
(Map p214; www.machne.co.il; Jaffa Rd; ⊙8am-sunset Sun-Thu, 9am-2pm Fri; ⊡Mahane Yehuda) All walks of local life converge at this bustling market, a fascinating spectacle for the first-time visitor and a bargain food fair for the city's Jewish residents. Crammed with fresh fruit, olives, nuts, vegetables and just about anything else grown or picked from the Israeli soil, it's also a good place to purchase spices, teas, cheese, dried fruits, tahini, bread and pastries. At night, it reinvents itself as a restaurant and bar hub where local foodies, hipsters and tourists hang out.

Mea She'arim
AREA

(Map p214; 🚇 Jaffa Center) Walk north from Jaffa Rd along Strauss St and you'll soon enter a neighbourhood with squat, stone-fronted buildings, balconies adorned with drying laundry, bearded figures in black, and long-skirted mums trailed by a gaggle of formally dressed children. If you have the sense that you've stumbled upon an Eastern European *shtetl* (ghetto) of the 1880s then you are probably standing somewhere near Kikar Shabbat, the main intersection of Mea She'arim, Jerusalem's oldest ultra-Orthodox Jewish (Haredi) neighbourhood.

👁 Mount of Remembrance

The Mount of Remembrance (Har Ha-Zikaron) is 5km west of the city centre. The Jerusalem Light Rail's Mt Herzl stop is a 10-minute walk away.

★ Yad Vashem
MEMORIAL

(📞 02-644 3802; www.yadvashem.org; Hazikaron St; ⊙ 9am-5pm Sun-Wed, to 8pm Thu, to 2pm Fri; 🚇 Mt Herzl) FREE If there is a more moving and powerful museum experience in the world, we've yet to encounter it. This memorial to the six million Jews who died at the hands of the Nazis is sobering, of course, but it's also beautiful and uplifting. The museum's name was taken from Isaiah 56:5 and means 'A Memorial and a Name', and one of the highlights is the Hall of Names, where the names and personal details of millions of victims are recorded.

👁 Giv'at Ram

Home to the Knesset, Israel's Supreme Court and the Hebrew University's Faculty of Science, Giv'at Ram is about 2.5km southwest of the city centre.

★ Israel Museum
MUSEUM

(Map p214; 📞 02-670 8811; www.imj.org.il; 11 Ruppin Blvd, Museum Row; adult/student/child 5-17yr 50/37/25NIS; ⊙ 10am-5pm Sun, Mon, Wed, Thu & Sat, 4-9pm Tue, 10am-2pm Fri; 🚌 7, 9, 14, 35, 66) One of Israel's most impressive cultural assets, this splendid museum gives an excellent grounding in the region's 5000 years of history in its huge archaeological wing and has another equally impressive wing concentrating on Jewish art and life. But that's not all – the fine-arts wing has a significant collection of international and Israeli art, the museum's grounds feature an art garden, and there's a dedicated pavilion showcasing the museum's prize exhibit, the Dead Sea Scrolls.

Bible Lands Museum
MUSEUM

(Map p214; 📞 02-561 1066; www.blmj.org; 25 Stefan Wise St, Museum Row; adult/student & child 40/20NIS; ⊙ 9.30am-5.30pm Sun-Tue & Thu, to 9.30pm Wed, 10am-2pm Fri & Sat; 🚌 7, 9, 14, 35, 66) Exploring the people and civilisations who populate the Bible, this museum displays a wealth of artefacts showing how their different cultures were inter-related. The organisation of the exhibits can be a little confusing, so we recommend taking the free guided tour offered daily between Sunday and Friday at 10.30am (English) and 11am (Hebrew), on Wednesday at 5.30pm (English) and 6pm (Hebrew), and on Saturday at 11.30am (Hebrew only).

👉 Tours

The municipality's website (www.itraveljerusalem.com) offers free maps and apps for 15 self-guided audio walking tours of the Old City; go to Old City Jerusalem Essence/Old City Sites and Tours/Audio Walking Tours.

Green Olive Tours (📞 03-721 9540; www.greenolivetours.com), a well-regarded company with Israeli and Arab owners, offers a daily walking tour of the Old City (three hours, 130NIS), a twice-weekly walking and light-rail tour of West Jerusalem including Yad Vashem (three hours, 260NIS), and a twice-weekly walking tour of East Jerusalem (three hours, 140NIS). It also runs a number of tours into the West Bank.

Jerusalem-based **Abraham Tours** (📞 02-566 0045; www.abrahamtours.com; 67 HaNevi'im St) offers day tours into the West Bank; to Caesarea, Nazareth and Tiberias; and to the Dead Sea. It also runs trips to Petra and Wadi Rum in Jordan.

🛏 Sleeping

Most budget accommodation is located in the Old City's Muslim, Christian and Armenian Quarters, or in the city centre. Decent midrange options are thin on the ground, but there are plenty of choices in the top-end category, including atmospheric Christian hospices in the Old City and boutique hotels in the city centre. There are no hotels or guesthouses of note in the Old City's Jewish Quarter.

If you want atmosphere, by all means stay in the Old City – but note that the area is inconvenient if you have a car and/or lots of luggage. If you are after proximity to restaurants, bars, cafes and public transport, you are much better off staying in the city centre, Mamilla or Yemin Moshe.

Old City

Hashimi Hotel & Hostel
HOSTEL $

(Map p222; ☑ 02-628 4410; www.alhashimi-hotel-jerusalem.com; 73 Souq Khan al-Zeit St, Muslim Quarter; dm/s/d US$35/60/95; ❋◐☎) Slap bang in the middle of the souq, this Palestinian-owned hostel imposes a number of rules on its guests (no alcohol, no unmarried couples in the same room, no credit cards, no mixed dorms), but all is forgiven when the newly renovated rooms are inspected and the extraordinary view from the rooftop is admired.

★ Austrian Hospice
GUESTHOUSE $$

(Map p222; ☑ 02-626 5800; www.austrianhospice.com; 37 Via Dolorosa, Muslim Quarter; dm/s/d/tr €26/76/118/165; ◐☎) This castlelike guesthouse first opened in 1863 and has plenty of heritage features. Rooms are simply furnished but are large and have good beds; three have a balcony and two have air-con (€5 surcharge). Single-sex dorms are in the basement, where there are also squeaky-clean shared bathrooms. The cloistered garden cafe is a popular retreat for guests.

★ Lutheran Guest House
GUESTHOUSE $$

(Map p222; ☑ 02-626 6888; www.luth-guesthouse-jerusalem.com; St Mark's Rd, Armenian Quarter; call for prices; ❋☎) Beyond the heavy steel door are a welcoming lobby, a variety of rooms, a courtyard garden and rooftop reading room and a lounge. Guest rooms are simply furnished but comfortable, and there's a generous buffet breakfast. From Jaffa Gate, walk down David St, then take the first right up a narrow staircase; the guesthouse is 100m down on the left.

★ Christ Church
Guesthouse
GUESTHOUSE $$$

(Map p222; ☑ 02-627 7727; www.cmj-israel.org; Omar Ibn al-Khattab Sq, Jaffa Gate; s/d US$128/194; ℗❋◐☎) This wonderfully maintained guesthouse gets high marks for its period atmosphere, multilingual staff, prime location and garden setting. The simply furnished rooms have stone floors, domed ceilings and comfortable beds, and there are lounges where guests can relax over free tea and coffee. Breakfast (included), lunch (20NIS to

60NIS) and dinner (65NIS) are served in the on-site cafe.

East Jerusalem

★ American Colony Hotel
HISTORIC HOTEL $$$

(Map p214; ☑ 02-627 9777; www.americancolony.com; 1 Louis Vincent St; s US$265, d US$310-640, ste US$675-955; ℗❋◐☎⊠) This historic hotel, built in 1902 and now Swiss-run, was a popular lodging for wealthy Westerners in the early 20th century and is still is a destination of choice for many VIPs. There's a variety of rooms spread across three wings; all are elegant and comfortable, but those in the original building are definitely the best. The breakfast buffet is excellent.

Jerusalem Hotel
HOTEL $$$

(Map p214; ☑ 02-628 8982, 02-628 3282; www.jrshotel.com; Derekh Shchem/Nablus Rd; s/d US$160/240; ❋◐☎; ⊟ Shivtei Israel) With tile-clad stone walls, high ceilings and antique furnishings, this small and friendly hotel in an 1890s building opposite one of the East Jerusalem bus stations can rightfully claim boutique status. The vine-covered courtyard restaurant is a lovely spot for dinner in warm weather.

City Centre & Around

★ Abraham Hostel
HOSTEL $

(Map p214; ☑ 02-650 2200; https://abrahamhostels.com; 67 HaNevi'im St, Davidka Sq; dm/s/d 114/300/480NIS; ❋◐☎; ⊟Ha-Davidka) Put simply, the Abraham is an exemplar for hostels everywhere. The best backpacker option in the city (none of the others come close), it's conveniently located next to the Davidka tram stop, its en suite rooms are basic but clean, the convivial lounge-bar has an attached communal kitchen and – best of all – there's a huge entertainment and tours program.

Jerusalem Hostel & Guest House
HOSTEL $

(Map p224; ☑02-623 6102; www.jerusalem-hostel.com; 44 Jaffa Rd, Zion Sq; dm 90NIS, s 220-340NIS, d 270-360NIS; ✳@🛜; 🚇 Jaffa Center) A fine option for budget travellers keen to base themselves in the city centre, this hostel offers clean en suite rooms, single-sex dorms, a communal kitchen and a rooftop. There's a healthy traveller vibe, with loads of info tacked onto the walls as well as plenty of other guests willing to lend free advice.

Hotel Palatin
HOTEL $$

(Map p224; ☑02-623 1141; www.palatinhotel.com; 4 Agrippas St; s/d US$110/155; ✳🛜; 🚇 Jaffa Center) Located near the hub of Jerusalem's shopping and cafe district, the Palatin has small but reasonably comfortable rooms that are overpriced at the rack rates cited above but can be found at much better prices on booking sites. The friendly service almost (but not quite) compensates for the polyester sheets.

YMCA Three Arches Hotel
HOTEL $$$

(Map p214; ☑02-569 2692; www.ymca3arch.co.il; 26 King David St, Yemin Moshe; s/tw/tr/ste US$200/220/250/290; P✳@🛜🏊) This 1933 building is an important local landmark and a decent place to spend a few nights. The hotel's 56 rooms are simply furnished and could be cleaner; all have twin beds and cable TV. There's an on-site restaurant, a gym and a pool.

🛏 German Colony & Rechavia

St Andrew's Scottish Guesthouse
GUESTHOUSE $$

(Map p214; ☑02-673 2401; www.scotsguesthouse.com; 1 David Remez St, Yemin Moshe; s/d/tw/ste/apt US$135/180/200/240/380; P@🛜) St Andrew's feels like a bit of Scotland transported to the Middle East. Set on a hill overlooking the Old City, with leafy gardens and an imposing stone facade, it has simple rooms and one two-bedroom apartment sleeping four. The more expensive rooms include balconies with a view; others have access to a large sun deck. All have kettles.

Little House in Rehavia
HOTEL $$

(Map p214; ☑02-563 3344; www.jerusalem-hotel.co.il; 20 Ibn Ezra St, Rehavia; s 450NIS, d 600-690NIS; ✳🛜) There's a boutique feel to this hotel in a restored 1942 stone building. Located in one of Jerusalem's prettiest neighbourhoods (a 1.5km walk to the Old City), it has 28 rooms, a roof terrace, a garden and a strictly kosher dining room where a daily breakfast and Shabbat lunch and dinner are served.

🍴 Eating

A significant percentage of Jerusalem's restaurants are kosher and thus closed on Shabbat and Jewish holidays; when almost everything in the city's Jewish neighbourhoods shuts down, one option is to head to East Jerusalem.

For a self-catering extravaganza, visit the Mahane Yehuda Market, where stalls sell the city's finest produce – and innovative eateries offer grungy-chic gourmet.

🍴 Old City

Most Old City restaurants stick to hummus, kebabs, shwarma and other Middle Eastern fare. The only exceptions are around Jaffa Gate, where there are a few Mediterranean-style places, and at Hurva Sq in the Jewish Quarter, where there are American-style fast-food joints. Finding a meal after dark can be challenging as the Old City shuts down when the crowds go home.

Many places in the Muslim Quarter close during Ramadan.

⭐Abu Shukri
MIDDLE EASTERN $

(Map p222; ☑02-627 1538; 63 Al-Wad St, Muslim Quarter; hummus 20NIS; ⊘9am-4pm; 🍽) After the best hummus in the Old City? This local favourite gets our vote. The standard platter includes a bowl of fresh hummus with your choice of topping (chickpea, tahini, fuul or pine nuts), some pickles and a basket of pita bread. We recommend adding a side order of felafel (10NIS) and glass of freshly squeezed juice (10NIS).

⭐Zalatimo
SWEETS $

(Map p222; Souq Khan al-Zeit St, Muslim Quarter; mutabbaq 14NIS; ⊘variable) The Old City is home to many treasures: churches, mosques, synagogues and this pastry shop. Hidden in an arched vault underneath the Ethiopian Monastery, it is famous for its *mutabbaq* (filo pastry stuffed with clarified butter, cinnamon and walnuts or with un-salted sheep's cheese, baked in the oven un-til crisp and then drizzled with sugar syrup and rose water).

City Centre

The City Centre is jam-packed with restaurants, cafes, pizzerias, and hummus, felafel and shwarma joints.

Hamarakia SOUP $
(Map p224; ☑ 02-625 7797; 4 Koresh St; soups 30NIS, salads 28NIS; ☺ 12.30pm-midnight Sun-Thu, from 9pm Sat; ☑; ☒ City Hall) The name of the place (Soup Pot) pretty much sums up the vegan-friendly menu: choose from five soups, a few salads and dips. The long shared table, open kitchen and piano make for a very social atmosphere, so you may end up eating with new friends and listening to some impromptu live music (jazz jams and acoustic grunge).

Azura TURKISH $$
(Map p214; ☑ 02-623 5204; Iraqi Market, off Rehov HaEshkol St; hummus 22-40NIS, mains 22-100NIS; ☺ 9.30am-4pm, closed Shabbat; ☑; ☒ Mahane Yehuda) One of the city's best-loved eateries, Azura has been cooking up its Turkish-influenced comfort food since 1952. Its version of hummus scored well in our 'find the best hummus in Jerusalem' quest, and the signature dish – eggplant stuffed with cinnamon-scented minced beef and pine nuts – is delicious. On Friday, local shop-keepers head here for the oxtail special.

T'mol Shilshom CAFE $$
(Map p224; ☑ 02-623 2758; 5 Yo'el Salomon St; shakshukas 42-50NIS, mains 49-83NIS; ☺ 8.30am-11pm, closed Shabbat; ☞ ☑; ☒ Jaffa Center) Named after an SY Agnon novel, this old-school bohemian haunt has been attracting a literary-minded crowd for 20 years. The food's nothing to get excited about and the chairs are possibly the most uncomfortable you'll ever encounter, but it's a great place to visit when there's a concert or book reading (check the events calendar on the website).

★ Machneyuda ISRAELI $$$
(Map p214; ☑ 02-533 3442; www.machneyuda.co.il; 10 Beit Ya'akov St; mains 77-162NIS, tasting menu 265NIS; ☺ 12.30-4pm & 6.30-11pm Sun-Thu, to 3pm Fri; ☒ Mahane Yehuda) A trio of chefs has turned the local dining scene on its head at this fabulous restaurant near the market. It's not kosher, it's not staid (quite the opposite) and its menu travels the globe. Strangely enough, the locals adore it, so you'll need to book well in advance to score a table. The menu changes daily and through the seasons.

🍷 Drinking & Nightlife

Jerusalem's city centre is well endowed with bars. The best are in the Mahane Yehuda Market area and, in the vicinity of Zion Sq, on Rivlin, Ben Shatah, Helene HaMalka and Dorot Rishonim Sts. East Jerusalem bars tend to be inside hotels, while the Old City is almost as dry as the Negev.

★ Uganda BAR
(Map p224; ☑ 02-623 6087; http://ugandajlm.com/; 4 Aristobulos St; ☺ noon-late Sun-Fri, 2pm-late Sat; ☒ Jaffa Center) DJ sets, live gigs, exhibitions by local artists and political discussions are but some of the elements that make this alternative bar special. Named after the country once suggested as a location for the Jewish state, it doubles as a comics and record store, serves Palestinian beer (Taybeh), has comfortable seating and is a great place to spend a night.

★ Cassette Bar BAR
(HaCasetta; Map p224; 1 Horkanos St; ☺ 8pm-5am Sat-Thu, 2pm-6am Fri; ☒ Jaffa Center) Accessed from the street (look for the metal door covered with old cassette tapes) or through the rear of the Record Bar next door, this pint-sized bar is a long-standing hipster haunt. The crowd drinks well into the night, serenaded by alternative tracks.

Upstairs is **Videopub** (Map p224; 1st fl, 1 Horkanus St; ☺ 8pm-4am Mon-Thu, Sat & Sun, from 10pm Fri; ☒ Jaffa Center), a popular gay bar. Members of the local LGBT community flock to this teensy space to drink and dance (Thursday and Saturday are particularly busy).

☆ Entertainment

The Talpiot Industrial Area, home to a number of nightspots (including Yellow Submarine), is 3.5km southwest of Jaffa Gate; from the southern end of Emeq Refa'im St, head south on Pierre Koenig St for about 700m.

Cinematheque CINEMA
(Map p214; ☑ 02-565 4333, tickets ext 9377; www.jer-cin.org.il; 11 Hebron Rd) The Jerusalem Cinematheque, a favoured hang-out of secular,

ℹ DANGERS & ANNOYANCES

Demonstrations and marches by both Jews and Arabs are pretty common in Jerusalem, and while they are usually peaceful, it's still a good idea to remain vigilant in case things get rowdy (Damascus Gate and Temple Mount are regular flashpoints). The Mount of Olives has not always been the friendliest area to walk in and some female travellers strolling there alone have been hassled. If possible, visit the area in pairs. Ultra-Orthodox Jewish groups sometimes throw stone buses, burn garbage bins and confront the police at Shabbat Sq in Mea She'arim, which even on quiet days can turn hostile when tourists (especially immodestly dressed ones) saunter in.

left-leaning Jerusalemites, features quality foreign films and classics. This is also the home of the respected **Jerusalem Film Festival** (www.jff.org.il).

Jerusalem Centre for the Performing Arts CONCERT VENUE, THEATRE (Jerusalem Theatre; Map p214; ☎02-560 5755; www.jerusalem-theatre.co.il; 20 David Marcus St, Talbiyeh) This complex includes a concert hall, theatres and a cafe. Its Sherover Theatre has simultaneous English-language surtitles during certain performances. It's home to the Jerusalem Symphony Orchestra, and comedy, music, children's theatre and dance performances are also held here.

Zappa in the Lab LIVE MUSIC (☎*9080; www.zappa-club.co.il; 28 Hebron Rd) Crafted out of a disused railway warehouse, this small live-music venue stages jazz, folk, rock and pop. It's open most days of the week, but you need to check the website or call for upcoming events.

Yellow Submarine LIVE MUSIC (☎02-679 4040; www.yellowsubmarine.org.il; 13 HaRechavim St, Talpiot) Aiming to promote music and foster musical talent, this venue has a crowded program of live performances. Check the website for details.

ℹ Information

The best deals for changing money are at the private, commission-free exchange offices in the New City (around Zion Sq), East Jerusalem

(Salah ad-Din St) and in the Old City (Jaffa Gate). Note that many close early on Friday and remain closed all day Saturday.

ATMs are found across the city, including at Zion Sq in the city centre.

Christian Information Centre (Map p222; ☎02-627 2692; www.cicts.org; Omar ibn al-Khattab Sq; ☺8.30am-5.30pm Mon-Fri, to 12.30pm Sat) This office opposite the entrance to the Citadel is operated by the Franciscans and provides information on the city's Christian sites.

Hadassah Medical Centre Mount Scopus (☎02-584 4333; www.hadassah.org.il) The Mt Scopus campus of this nonprofit hospital has a 24-hour emergency department and a specialist pediatric emergency department that is also open 24 hours.

Jaffa Gate Tourist Office (Map p222; ☎02-627 1422; www.itraveljerusalem.com; Jaffa Gate; ☺8.30am-5pm Sat-Thu, to 1.30pm Fri) This is the main tourist office for Jerusalem. It supplies free maps, organises guides and provides information and advice. It's the second office after Jaffa Gate – don't confuse it with the 'Jerusalem Tourist Information Center', a private tourist company next door that sports an information icon above the door.

Main Post Office (Map p224; ☎02-624 4745; 23 Jaffa Rd; ☺8am-6pm Sun-Thu, to noon Fri)

Terem (☎1-599-520-520; www.terem.com; 80 Yirmiyahu St, Romema; ☺24hr; ⓖ Central Station) Efficient multilingual walk-in medical clinic that handles everything from minor ailments to emergencies. It's a five-minute walk from Central Bus Station.

ℹ Getting There & Away

BUS

Buses to major cities and towns across Israel leave from the **Central Bus Station** (Map p214; www.bus.co.il; Jaffa Rd; ⓖ Central Station). Destinations include Tel Aviv-Central Bus Station (bus 405; 19NIS, one hour, every 15 minutes), Tel Aviv-Arlozoroff Bus Terminal (bus 480; 19NIS, one hour, every 10 minutes), Haifa (buses 940, 947 and 960; 44NIS, two hours, every 15 minutes), Tiberias (bus 962; 44NIS, 2½ hours, hourly), Masada (bus 421, 444 or 486; 44NIS, 1¾ hours) and Eilat (bus 444; 82NIS, five hours, four daily).

If you are headed into northern areas of the West Bank such as Ramallah (bus 18, 7NIS), use the **Arab bus station** (Map p214; Derekh Shchem/Nablus Rd, East Jerusalem), on the street straight in front of Damascus Gate. The buses that leave from here are green and white.

For Bethlehem, take bus 21 (8NIS) from the **Arab bus station** (Map p222; Sultan Suleiman St, East Jerusalem) west of the Damascus Gate next to the tram stop. The buses that leave from here are blue and white. For Hebron, take bus 21, alight at Bab Al Zqaq and then take a Hebron bus (5NIS).

The general rule is that blue-and-white buses go to southern West Bank destinations and green- and-white buses go to northern West Bank destinations.

SHERUT

Sheruts (shared taxis; *servees* in Arabic) are much faster than buses and cost only a few shekels more; on Shabbat they're the only public transport to destinations in Israel.

Sheruts for Tel Aviv (24NIS per person on weekdays, 34NIS on Shabbat) depart from the corner of HaRav Kook St and Jaffa Rd, near Zion Sq; in Tel Aviv, they stop just outside the Central Bus Station.

TRAIN

Jerusalem's **railway station** (www.rail.co.il) is located in the southwest of the city, near the Jerusalem Mall. Scenic trains to Tel Aviv, including the Savidor/Center/Merkaz station (adult/child 22/17.50NIS, 1¾ hours), depart every hour or two between 5.43am and 9.43pm Sunday to Thursday; the last train on Friday is at 3pm. To get there from the Central Bus Station, take bus 6. Ring ☑5770 for more details.

ⓘ Getting Around

TO/FROM THE AIRPORT

Ben-Gurion airport is 52km west of Jerusalem, just off Rte 1 to Tel Aviv.

From just outside the airport's international arrivals hall, sheruts (24 hours, including Shabbat and Jewish holidays) leave when full and charge 41NIS per person for stops along a set route and 69NIS if you'd like to be dropped at a specific address in West Jerusalem. The service is operated by **Nesher service taxis** (☑1 599 500 205, 02-625 7227), which also offers transport from Jerusalem to the airport; book 24 hours in advance.

A private taxi costs 268NIS on weekdays, 320NIS at night (9pm to 5.30am) and on Shabbat and Jewish holidays.

BUS

Jerusalem is laced with a good network of city bus routes (6.90NIS per ride), some of them feeder lines for the light-rail system. To access information about routes, schedules and to download handy public-transport maps, see www.jet.gov.il.

To get to parts of East Jerusalem such as the Mount of Olives (bus 75; 5NIS), use the Arab bus station located on Sultan Suleiman St in East Jerusalem, near Herod's Gate. The buses that leave from here are blue and white.

LIGHT RAIL

Jerusalem Light Rail (JLR; ☑3686; www.citypass.co.il), inaugurated in 2011, consists of a single line that runs from Mt Herzl in the west of the city to Heyl HaAvir in Pisgat Ze'ev, in the city's far northeast. There are 23 stops along a 13.9km route including the Central Bus Station, Mahane Yehuda Market, Jaffa St in the city centre and Damascus Gate. Services run every 10 minutes or so from 5.30am to midnight daily except on Shabbat; on Saturdays services start one hour after Shabbat ends. Tickets (6.90NIS) can be purchased from the machines on tram stops but must be validated on board the tram.

TAXI

Plan on spending between 25NIS and 50NIS for trips anywhere within the central part of town. Always ask to use the meter. To order a taxi, options include **Hapalmach taxi** (☑02-679 2333).

Drivers at Jaffa Gate and next to the Tomb of the Virgin Mary on the Mount of Olives are notorious for refusing to use the meter and overcharging.

MEDITERRANEAN COAST

Stretching for 273km from Gaza to the Lebanese border, Israel's Mediterranean coastline has some fine beaches, first-rate archaeological sites, and many of the country's wealthiest and most innovative towns and cities.

Tel Aviv-Jaffa (Yafo)

תל אביב–יפו   تل ابيب-يافا

☑03 / POP 415,000

When the State of Israel hits the headlines, the state of Tel Aviv sits back with a cappuccino. Nicknamed 'the Bubble', Tel Aviv (or TLV) is a city of outdoor cafes, boutiques, bistros, leafy boulevards and long sandy beaches – and a favourite with Europeans looking for some year-round sun. All over the city, classic Bauhaus buildings are getting a well-needed facelift, while nearby skyscrapers rise towards the heavens. Yet the real Tel Aviv is best sought out in humble hummus joints, wine bars hidden down alleyways, fresh-fruit-shake stalls, quiet pocket parks and chaotic marketplaces.

◉ Sights

◉ City Centre

★**Tel Aviv Museum of Art**   GALLERY
(Map p232; ☑03-607 7020; www.tamuseum.com; 27 Shaul HaMelech Blvd; adult/student under 15yr

Central Tel Aviv

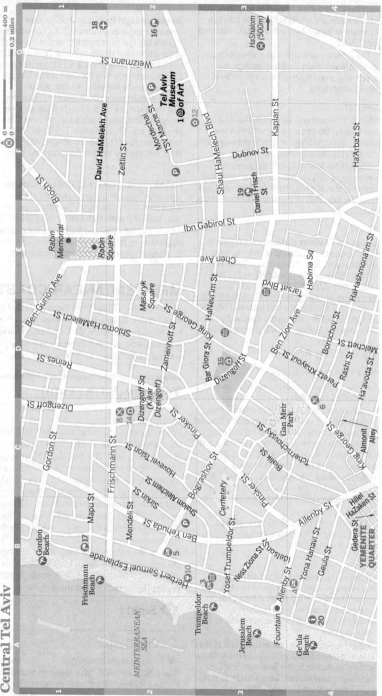

233

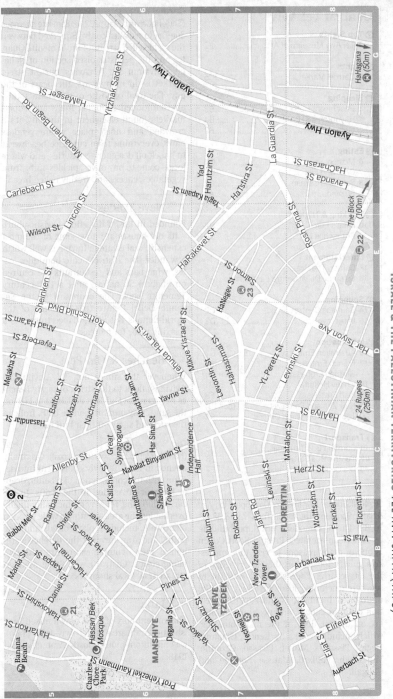

ISRAEL & THE PALESTINIAN TERRITORIES TEL AVIV-JAFFA (YAFO)

Central Tel Aviv

50/40NIS, under 15yr free; ⊙10am-6pm Mon-Wed & Sat, to 9pm Tue & Thu, to 2pm Fri; 🚌 7, 9, 18, 38, 42, 70, 82) The ultramodern 'envelope' building by American architect Preston Scott Cohen is one of many reasons to visit this impressive gallery located on the eastern edge of the city centre. There's a huge amount to see here (including loads for kids), but the undoubted highlight is the superb collection of impressionist and postimpressionist art on the 1st floor of the main building, which includes works by Renoir, Gauguin, Degas, Pissarro, Monet, Picasso, Cézanne, Van Gogh, Vuillard, Matisse, Soutine and Chagall.

Carmel Market   MARKET
(Shuk HaCarmel; Map p232; ⊙8am-late afternoon Sun-Thu, to mid-afternoon Fri) Squeezed between the dishevelled streets of the Yemenite Quarter and the pedestrianised section of Nahalat Binyamin St, Tel Aviv's busiest street market is, in many ways, the heart of the city. The total opposite of the characterless air-conditioned shopping malls and supermarkets found elsewhere in the city, it's a crowded and noisy place where vendors hawk everything from cut-price beachwear to knock-off designer accessories, and where locals come to buy olives, pickles, nuts, fruit, vegetables, cheese and freshly baked bread.

◉ Neve Tzedek

Founded in 1887, Jaffa's first Jewish suburb – its old houses are now some of the most expensive real estate in town – is well worth a wander. The district's cute boutiques, cafes, wine bars and restaurants are centred on Shabazi St, named after a 17th-century Yemenite poet. The courtyard of the Suzanne Dellal Centre (p243), home of the world-famous Bat Sheva dance troupe, is a relaxing place for a break.

◉ Beaches & Old Port

Whenever the sun is out, Tel Avivim (Tel Avivians) flock to the string of sandy beaches between the Old Port and Jaffa to laze on the sand, play *matkot* (paddle ball), frolic in the surf and show off their buff bods.

Old Port   PORT
(Namal; Map p236; www.namal.co.il) Originally opened in 1936, Tel Aviv's port went into decline with the construction of a better, deeper harbour at Ashdod in the 1960s. In the early 2000s the Tel Aviv municipality finally overhauled the area, creating a wide wooden boardwalk, including playgrounds and bike paths, and transforming the derelict warehouses into a commercial centre with big-name stores (Castro, Levi's, Steve Madden etc) to draw local shoppers

◉ Jaffa

The ancient port of Jaffa, now a mixed Jewish and Arab area of Tel Aviv-Jaffa (Yafo), was an autonomous, mostly Arab city until 1948.

★ **Old City** HISTORIC SITE
(Map p238; 🚌 Dan 10, 18, 25, 41) Centred on
Kikar Kedumim (Kedumim Sq), a paved
space edged by touristy shops and cafes, this
hilltop area overlooks the Mediterranean
Sea and is visually dominated by the Franciscan **St Peter's Church** (Map p238; ⊙ 8-
11.45am & 3-5pm Oct-Feb, to 6pm Mar-Sep). The
surrounding laneways are home to boutique
tourist accommodation, galleries and the occasional artisan's atelier.

To the east of the square, perched on Jaffa's highest point, **HaPisgah Gardens** (Map
p238) offers nice views north up the coast to
Tel Aviv.

★ **Flea Market** MARKET
(Map p238; ⊙ stalls 10am-3pm Sun-Fri; 🚌 Dan
10, 18, 25, 41) In recent years, lots of energy has gone into giving Jaffa's Old City a
tourism-triggered makeover, and the results
are undeniably attractive. However, the real
draw in this part of the city is considerably more dishevelled. Spread over a grid of
streets south of the clock tower, Jaffa's much-
loved *pishpeshuk* or *shuk ha-pishpeshim*
(flea market) is full of boutiques, laid-back
cafes, pop-up bars and colourful street stalls
selling vintage clothes and furniture, curios
and the occasional antique.

⊙ Northern Tel Aviv

Park HaYarkon's western tip is at the mouth
of the Yarkon River, situated at the northern
edge of the Old Port (Namal) area.

Beit Hatfutsot MUSEUM
(Museum of the Jewish People; 🕾 03-745 7800;
www.bh.org.il; Gate 2, Tel Aviv University, 2 Klausner

St, Ramat Aviv; adult/student & child 42/32NIS;
⊙ 10am-4pm Sun-Tue, to 7pm Wed & Thu, 9am-1pm
Fri; 🚌 Dan 7, 13, 25, 45) Beit Hatfutsot recounts
the epic story of Jewish exile and the global Jewish diaspora using objects, dioramas,
photographs, audiovisual presentations and
databases. Though its design and curatorial
approach were cutting edge when it opened
in 1978, the museum is looking dated these
days and will benefit from the major renovation and redevelopment that is currently
under way. This is scheduled to be completed in 2017.

Eretz Israel Museum MUSEUM
(Land of Israel Museum; 🕾 03-641 5244; www.
eretzmuseum.org.il; 2 Chaim Levanon St, Ramat
Aviv; adult/student 48/32NIS, child under 18yr free,
incl planetarium adult/child 80/32NIS; ⊙ 10am-
4pm Sun-Wed, to 8pm Thu, to 2pm Fri, to 3pm Sat,
planatarium shows 11.30am & 1.30pm Sun-Thu,
11am & noon Sat; 🚌 Dan 7, 13, 24, 25, 45, 127) Incorporating the archeological excavations of Tel
Qasile, an ancient port city dating from the
12th century BC, this museum sports a huge
and varied range of exhibits and deserves
at least half a day of your time. Sights include pavilions filled with glass and coins, a
reconstructed flour mill and olive-oil plant,
an ethnography and folklore collection, and
a garden built around a gorgeous Byzantine
bird mosaic. A planatarium is among the
other attractions.

🏃 Activities

Park HaYarkon OUTDOORS
(Ganei Yehoshua; Map p236; www.park.co.il; Rokach
Blvd) Joggers, cyclists, in-line skaters, foot-
ballers and frisbee-throwers should head
for this 3.5-sq-km stretch of grassy parkland

TEL AVIV'S BAUHAUS HERITAGE

Tel Aviv has more sleek, clean-lined Bauhaus (International Style) buildings than any other city in the world, which is why it was declared a Unesco World Heritage site in 2003.
The ideas and ideals of Bauhaus were brought from Germany to Palestine in the 1930s
by Jewish architects fleeing Nazi persecution.

Tel Aviv's Bauhaus heritage (www.white-city.co.il) is easy to spot, even through the
modifications and dilapidation of the past 70 years. Look for structures with horizontal
lines, curved corners (eg of balconies), 'thermometer stairwells' (stairwells with a row of
vertical windows to provide light), and a complete absence of ornamentation.

The **Bauhaus Center** (Map p232; 🕾 03-522 0249; www.bauhaus-center.com; 99 Dizengoff
St; ⊙ 10am-7.30pm Sun-Thu, to 2.30pm Fri) sells a variety of architecture-related books
and plans of the city and offers **mp3 tours** (60NIS) as well as a two-hour **walking
tour** (60NIS) every Friday at 10am. A better – and cheaper – alternative is the free
English-language **Bauhaus tour** run by the Tel Aviv Tourist Office (p240), which departs
from 46 Rothschild Blvd (corner Shadal St) every Saturday at 11am.

ISRAEL & THE PALESTINIAN TERRITORIES TEL AVIV-JAFFA (YAFO)

Northern Tel Aviv

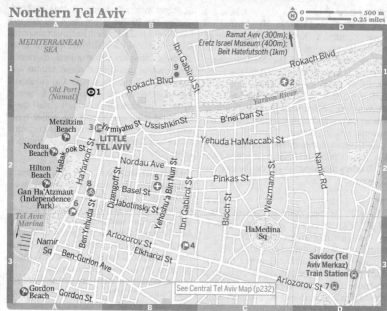

See Central Tel Aviv Map (p232)

along the Yarkon River, which makes up Tel Aviv's largest green space – its Central Park, if you will. The Sportek Centre, located here, has a climbing wall, basketball courts, a skate park and trampolines.

🛏 Sleeping

Many of Tel Aviv's accommodation options are in the city centre, so you can spend the day on the beach and pop back for a shower before heading out on foot for the night.

In all price categories, book ahead during July, August and the Jewish holidays of Sukkot, Rosh Hashanah, Hanukkah and Passover, when overseas tourists (especially from France) flock to the city.

★ Beachfront Hotel
HOSTEL **$**

(Map p232; ☑ 03-726 5230, 03-744 0347; www. telavivbeachfront.co.il; 78 Herbert Samuel Esplanade; dm/s US$30/80, d with/without bathroom US$99/79; ✳ @ ☎) The beach-party vibe is one of many reasons to stay at this hostel opposite Trumpeldor Beach. An array of clean, well-maintained dorms and rooms – some with views and private terraces – awaits, as does a rooftop bar serving free sangria nightly. Free wi-fi and beach towels are provided for guest use, but internet costs 60NIS per hour. No breakfast.

Hayarkon 48 Hostel
HOSTEL **$**

(Map p232; ☑ 03-516 8989; www.hayarkon48.com; 48 HaYarkon St; dm 113NIS, r with/without bathroom 385/330NIS; ✳ @ ☎) Just two blocks from the beach, this hostel has decent facilities including communal kitchen, rooftop terrace and lounge with pool table and TV/DVD. Dorms are mixed and female-only, and the simple private rooms have double bed and cable TV. All dorms and half of the private rooms have air-con.

Port Hotel
BOUTIQUE HOTEL **$$**

(Map p236; ☑03-544 5544; www.porthoteltelaviv.com; 4 Yirmiyahu St; s/d US$150/160; ✸✸☎) This self-titled 'mini hotel' near the Old Port offers something that is very rare in Tel Aviv – stylish accommodation for those on a budget. Though small and without views, rooms are clean and comfortable. The roof terrace and proximity to the beach are major assets.

Lusky Hotel
HOTEL **$$$**

(Map p232; ☑03-516 3030; www.luskysuites-htl.co.il; 84 HaYarkon St; s/d/ste US$140/200/315; ℙ✸☎) This family-run choice offers well-appointed rooms featuring large windows letting in lots of light. Most of these have kitchenettes, and a number have balconies with sea view – the pick of the bunch is undoubtedly the one-bedroom penthouse, which has a huge balcony overlooking the beach. Drivers will appreciate the free underground parking.

✗ Eating

Tel Aviv's dining scene is both varied and exciting. Coinciding with the boutique makeover that the city is undergoing, there is a rising crop of 'chef restaurants' (ie eateries run by celebrity chefs), as well as an ever-growing number of swanky brasseries. From Sunday to Friday, many restaurants offer good-value 'business lunch' deals.

Fast-food joints are never more than a few steps away, with a particularly good selection along Ben Yehuda, Allenby and Ibn Gabirol Sts.

★ Miznon
ISRAELI **$**

(Map p232; 30 King George St; pitas 23-44NIS; ☺noon-1am Sun-Thu, to 3pm Fri, from 7pm Sat; ☑) The vibe here is bustling, the prices are (very) reasonable and the staff are young, friendly and full of energy. And let's not forget the most important thing – the food is exceptionally delicious. Huge pitas stuffed with your choice of veggies, chicken, offal or meat await, as do fish and chips or roasted spiced yam and cauliflower (yum!).

Sabich Frishman
MIDDLE EASTERN **$**

(Map p232; 42 Frishman St; sabich 18NIS; ☺9am-11.30pm Sun-Thu, Fri before Shabbat, Sat after Shabbat; ☑) This tiny stall specialises in *sabich*, an Iraqi-derived snack consisting of fried aubergine, boiled egg, cabbage, salad, potato, hummus and spicy amba (mango) sauce, all stuffed into a pita. It's on the corner of Dizengoff and Frishman Sts – just look for the long lines and the felafel stall next door.

★ Orna and Ella
ISRAELI **$$**

(Map p232; ☑03-525 2085; www.ornaandella.com; 33 Sheinken St; breakfast 36-58NIS, mains 42-92NIS; ☺8.30am-midnight Sun-Thu, from 10am Fri & Sat; ☎☑) Effortlessly melding its serious gastronomic focus with a casual-chic decor and a neighbourhood vibe, this restaurant-cafe is beloved of locals for good reason. Seasonal, often organic, ingredients are used to excellent effect in hearty breakfasts and refined lunches and dinners. Vegans, vegetarians and anyone who appreciates good food will be very happy here. Dine inside, or in a rear courtyard.

ESSENTIAL FOOD & DRINK

Amba Iraqi-style mango chutney.

Bourekas Flaky Balkan pastries filled with Bulgarian cheese, spinach or mushrooms.

Challah Braided bread traditionally eaten by Jews on the Sabbath.

Cholent A heavy meat and potato stew simmered overnight and served for Sabbath lunch.

Labneh (labaneh) Thick, creamy yoghurt cheese, often smothered in olive oil and sprinkled with *zaatar*.

Sabich A pita pocket filled with fried aubergine (eggplant), boiled potato, hard-boiled egg, tahini, amba and freshly chopped vegies.

S'chug Yemenite hot chilli paste.

Shakshuka A spicy Moroccan egg and tomato stew, usually eaten for breakfast.

Zaatar A spice blend that includes hyssop, sumac and sesame seeds.

Jaffa (Yafo)

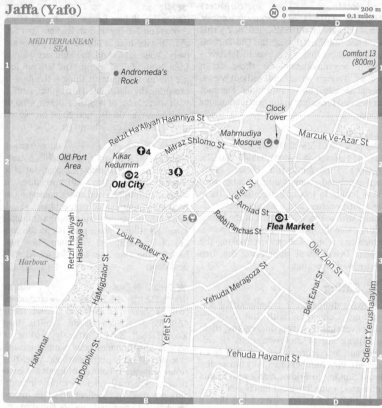

Suzanna   MIDDLE EASTERN **$$**

(Map p232; ☎03-944 3060; www.suzana.rest-e.co.il; 9 Shabazi St, Neve Tzedek; breakfast 49NIS, meals 55-86NIS; ☺10am-2am) A long-standing Neve Tzedek favourite, Suzanna offers a Middle Eastern mix of dishes. Some of these are more successful than others, so the 'I'll have what they're having' approach pays off here. Enjoy your meal during summer months on the large open courtyard in the shade of an enormous ficus tree.

🍷 Drinking & Nightlife

The city has a fantastic bar scene – there are drinking dens to suit every taste and budget. Some are hipster hot spots, others are neighbourhood joints so chilled they're almost co-matose. When it comes to clubbing, dance bars and bars hosting live gigs dominate the scene. Dress codes are relaxed.

★**Rothschild 12**   BAR, CAFE, CLUB

(Map p232; www.rothschild12.co.il; 12 Rothschild Blvd; ☺7am-late Sun-Thu, from 8am Fri & Sat) Be warned: it's all but impossible to restrict yourself to a single visit here. One of our favourite breakfast stops (pastries and bread are French-style and delicious), it's equally good for lunch (burgers, *sabich*, toasted sandwiches), afternoon coffee, aperitifs or late-night drinks. The soundtrack comes courtesy of jazz discs during the day and live bands and DJs at night.

★**Anna Loulou Bar**   BAR, CLUB

(Map p238; www.annalouloubar.com; 1 HaPninim St, Old Jaffa; ☺9pm-3am Mon-Sat; 🚍Dan 10, 18, 25, 41) Describing itself as a cross between underground bar and cultural center, this gay- and smoker-friendly hipster bar is perhaps the only joint in town where Arab and Jewish locals party together. The music is predominantly electro-Arab, African or Mid-

Jaffa (Yafo)

◎ **Top Sights**
1 Flea Market C3
2 Old City B2

◎ **Sights**
3 HaPisgah Gardens..............................B2
4 St Peter's Church B2
   St Peter's Monastery..................(see 4)

● **Drinking & Nightlife**
5 Anna Loulou Bar B3

---

dle Eastern, although there's the occasional wild-card event (country, hip-hop, drag shows). Wednesday is the night to party.

Comfort 13   CLUB
(13 Kompert St, Florentin; admission 60NIS; ⊙11pm-late) Down an alleyway in the grungy enclave of Florentin, Comfort 13 is one of the city's biggest and best clubs; nights span from trashy pop to trance to electronica, as well as occasional live rock bands. Check its Facebook page for updates.

Mike's Place   PUB
(Map p232; www.mikesplacebars.com; 86 Herbert Samuel Esplanade; ⊙11am-late; 🛜) On the beach next to the US Embassy, the original branch of this country-wide operation offers frothy pints, sport on the big screen, open-mic nights, jam sessions and live gigs (mainly rock and acoustic). The sizeable menu has grill-style meals, cocktails and beer.

☆ Entertainment

Theatre & Dance

Suzanne Dellal Centre   DANCE
(Map p232; 03-510 5656; www.suzannedellal.org.il; 5 Yechieli St) Stages a variety of performing arts including dance, music and ballet, and is home to the world-famous Bat Sheva dance company.

Cameri Theatre   THEATRE
(Map p232; 03-606 0960; www.cameri.co.il; 30 Leonardo da Vinci St) Hosts first-rate theatre performances in Hebrew, on some nights with simultaneous English translation or English-language surtitles.

Live Music

Goldstar Zappa Club   LIVE MUSIC
(03-762 6666; www.zappa-club.co.il; 24 Raoul Wallenberg St, Ramat HaChayal) Local and international music luminaries play at this intimate club, situated 8km northeast of central

Tel Aviv, so it's best accessed by car or taxi. Call or look out for listings to find out who's on while you're here.

Barby   LIVE MUSIC
(03-518 8123; www.barby.co.il; 52 Kibbutz Galuyot St) This Tel Aviv institution at the southernmost point of the city is a favourite venue for reggae, rock and random alternative bands.

🛍 Shopping

The most interesting boutiques are found in the Jaffa Flea Market, Shabazi St in Neve Tzedek and Sheinkin St in the city centre. At the **Nahalat Binyamin Crafts Market** (www.nachlat-binyamin.com; ⊙10am-5pm Tue, to 6pm or 7pm summer, 10am to 4.30pm Fri)t – a great place to walk around and soak up Tel Aviv's exuberant atmosphere – artists sell ceramics, jewellery, glasswork and Judaica they have made.

   Lametayel (Map p232; 077-333 4501; www.lametayel.co.il; top fl, 50 Dizengoff St, Dizengoff Center; ⊙10am-9pm Sun-Thu, to 2.30pm Fri), Israel's largest camping and travel-equipment shop, carries a full range of Lonely Planet guides and is a prime source of information for Israeli backpackers.

❶ Orientation

Tel Aviv is centred on five north–south streets that parallel the middle part of the city's 6km of seafront. Nearest the sand is Herbert Samuel Esplanade, while hotel-lined HaYarkon St – which heads north to the Yarkon River – lies a block inland. East of HaYarkon St is Ben Yehuda St, followed by once-chic Dizengoff St – the area between Dizengoff Sq and Dizengoff Centre serves as the focal point of the city centre. Restaurant-lined Ibn Gabirol St forms the eastern boundary of the city centre.

   The Neve Tzedek and Florentin districts mark the southernmost reaches of the city centre – south of there is Jaffa – while Park HaYarkon and, on the coast, the Old Port (Namal) mark the northernmost.

❶ Information

The best currency-exchange deals are at the private bureaus that don't charge commission, for example on Dizengoff, Allenby and Ben Yehuda Sts. Most post offices change cash and travellers cheques, commission free.

Ichilov Hospital (Tel Aviv Sourasky Medical Centre; Map p232; 03-697 4444; www.tasmc.org.il; 6 Weizmann St) Near the city centre, Ichilov is the city's big central hospital,

ℹ USEFUL TEL AVIV WEBSITES

DIY Tel Aviv (www.diytelavivguide.com/blog) Alternative guide to food, drink, nightlife, shopping and culture.

Midnight East (www.midnighteast.com/mag) Interesting arts- and culture-focused blog.

Secret Tel Aviv (www.secrettelaviv.com) Listings and advice from locals.

Tel Aviv City (www.telavivcity.com/eng) Local guide to Tel Aviv.

Tel Aviv Guide (www.telavivguide.net) Entertainment, hotels and restaurant reviews.

Time Out Israel (http://timeout.co.il/en) Plenty of Tel Aviv listings and features.

Visit TLV (www.visit-tlv.com) The municipality's excellent website.

with 24-hour emergency room and a travellers' clinic (the Malram Clinic) for immunisations.

Tel Aviv Doctor (Map p236; ☎ 054 941 4243, toll-free 1 800 201 999; www.telaviv-doctor.com; Room 106, 35 Basel St, Basel Heights Medical Centre; ⊙ daily) A medical clinic aimed at travellers and English speakers. For minor problems it's less expensive than Ichilov Hospital's emergency room.

Tourist Information Office (Map p232; ☎ 03-516 6188; www.visit-tlv.com; 46 Herbert Samuel Esplanade; ⊙ 9.30am-6.30pm Sun-Thu, to 2pm Fri Apr-Oct, to 5.30pm Sun-Thu & to 1pm Nov-Mar) Tel Aviv's main tourist-information office has super-helpful staff and can provide maps, brochures and plenty of advice.

ℹ Getting There & Away

During Shabbat and on Jewish holidays, sheruts (share taxis) offer the only public transport.

BUS

Most intercity buses depart from the 6th floor of Tel Aviv's enormous, confusing and filthy **central bus station** (Map p232; ☎ 03-638 3945), where there's also an efficient information desk. Suburban and city buses use the 4th and 7th floors. Tickets can be bought from the driver or from ticket booths.

Egged (☎ 03-694 8888; www.egged.co.il) buses leave for Jerusalem (bus 405; 19NIS, one hour, every 15 minutes), Haifa (bus 921; 25NIS, 1½ hours, frequent), Tiberias (bus 836, 44NIS, 2½ hours, hourly), Nazareth's Rte 75 ring road

(bus 826; 39.50NIS, 2¼ hours, several times an hour) and Eilat (buses 393, 394 and 790; 82NIS, 5½ hours, hourly).

Tel Aviv's second bus station, the open-air **Arlozorov Terminal** (Map p236), adjoins the Tel Aviv Savidor/Merkaz train station northeast of the city centre. If staying in the centre or north, Egged bus 480 (19NIS, one hour, every 10 minutes) is the most convenient service to Jerusalem.

CAR

Most car-rental companies have offices on Ha-Yarkon St.

SHERUT

Sheruts (in most cases yellow minibuses) depart from Tsemach David St outside the Central Bus Station. Destinations include Jerusalem (24NIS, on Shabbat 34NIS) and Haifa (30NIS, on Shabbat 45NIS).

TRAIN

Tel Aviv has four train stations: Savidor (Merkaz), HaHagana, HaShalom and University. Destinations include Haifa (30.50NIS, one hour, two or three hourly except Shabbat) and Akko (39NIS, 1½ hours).

ℹ Getting Around

Getting around the compact centre is easiest on foot or by bicycle – two wheels are a great way to avoid traffic snarls, packed buses and unscrupulous taxi drivers.

TO/FROM THE AIRPORT

Ben-Gurion Airport is 18km southeast of central Tel Aviv.

The fastest way to get to/from the airport is by train (16NIS, twice an hour, 24 hours a day except on Shabbat, ie Friday afternoon to Saturday night, and Jewish holidays). Airport trains serve all four Tel Aviv stations except between midnight and 5am, when they stop only at Savidor station (and run just once an hour).

At the airport, metered taxis leave from an orderly taxi rank and use government-controlled prices unless you ask to use the meter. Depending on traffic, the ride into central Tel Aviv takes about 20 minutes and costs 150NIS (200NIS from 9pm to 5.30am).

BICYCLE

The quickest and easiest way to get around Tel Aviv is on a bicycle, thanks in part to 120km of dedicated bike paths along thoroughfares such as Rothschild Blvd, Chen Ave, Ben Gurion Ave and Ibn Gabirol St. For epic rides, go to Park Ha-Yarkon and head east, or pedal along the 10km coastal promenade.

Tel-O-Fun (☎ 6070; www.tel-o-fun.co.il) is a citywide scheme which lets riders pick up and drop off the green bicycles at over 75 docking stations. A daily access card costs from 17NIS. The first 30 minutes of usage are free; after that there are fees that get progressively higher, starting at NIS5 per 30 minutes. To avoid fees, simply return your bike and, after waiting at least 10 minutes, take another one. Pay with your credit card at any Tel-O-Fun station, but be aware that instructions are in Hebrew only – ask a local to translate.

For longer rentals, try **O-Fun** (Map p236; ☑ 03-544 2292; www.rentabikeisrael.com; 197 Ben Yehuda St; per hour/24hr/weekend 25/75/130NIS; ☺ 9.30am-7pm Sun-Thu, to 2pm Fri).

BUS

Tel Aviv city buses are operated by the **Dan** (☑ 03-639 4444; www.dan.co.il; single fare 6.60NIS) cooperative from 5.30am to midnight, except Shabbat. A ticket for a single ride costs 6.90NIS and a one-day pass (*hofshi yomi*) allowing unlimited bus travel around Tel Aviv and its suburbs costs 15NIS (plus 5NIS for a Rav-Kav travel card).

TAXI

By law, all taxis – easy to flag down on major thoroughfares – must use their meter. Plan on 30NIS to 40NIS for trips within the central city.

Caesarea   קיסריה قيسارية

Caesarea (Qeysarya; pronounced kay-*sar*-ee-ya in Hebrew), gorgeously situated on the shores of the sparkling, turquoise Mediterranean, was one of the great ports of antiquity, rivalling storied harbours such as Alexandria and Carthage. Today, Caesarea National Park (www.parks.org.il; adult/child 40/24NIS, harbour only 14NIS; ☺ 8am-6pm Sat-Thu, to 4pm Fri Apr-Sep, 8am-4pm Sat-Thu, to 3pm Fri Oct-Mar, last entry 1hr before closing) is one of the Levant's most impressive Roman sites (rivalled, in Israel, only by Beit She'an). Roman highlights include a 4000-seat theatre and an amphitheatre once used for chariot races and bloody gladiatorial contests

Cafes and restaurants add to the scene – you can dine alfresco by the sea until late at night.

Caesarea National Park is 40km south of Haifa and 57km north of Tel Aviv.

Haifa   חיפה حيفا

☑ 04 / POP 272,000

Haifa is one of the world's most beautiful port cities. The views from the top of majes-

tic Mt Carmel (546m) are breathtaking, especially from the Baha'i Gardens, but almost everywhere you look in the city there are interesting, if not always beautiful, urban landscapes, many from the late Ottoman and Mandate (Bauhaus) periods.

⊙ Sights

To get from Carmel Centre (the Gan HaEm stop on the Carmelit funicular railway) to the start of the Baha'i Gardens' Upper Terrace Tour, walk 1km north along Yefe Nof St, which affords the city's finest bay views. The tour ends down on HaTziyonut Blvd; to get back up to Carmel Centre, take bus 136 (6.90NIS, every 15 minutes) or a sherut (line 136; 7NIS).

The bustling streets of Hadar, the city's mid-20th-century commercial centre, are lined with eateries and inexpensive shops.

★ **Baha'i Gardens**   GARDENS
(☑ 04-831 3131; www.ganbahai.org.il; 45 Yefe Nof St, Upper Terrace Tour, 80 HaTziyonut Blvd. Shrine of the Bab; ☺ lower gardens 9am-5pm, Shrine of the Bab 9am-noon, closed Baha'i holidays & Yom Kippur) FREE The best way to see these world famous gardens is to take a free, 45-minute Upper Terrace Tour from the top of the gardens. Except on Wednesday, an English-language tour starts at noon, with additional tours in Hebrew or Russian on most days at 11am and 2pm (see the website for the monthly schedule). It's first come, first served, so get there a half-hour ahead. Both men and women must wear clothing that covers their shoulders (a shawl is OK) and knees.

Tikotin Museum of Japanese Art   MUSEUM
(www.tmja.org.il; 89 HaNassi Ave; adult/child 30/20NIS; ☺ 10am-4pm Sun-Wed, to 7pm Thu, to 1pm Fri, to 3pm Sat) Founded by Felix Tikotin in 1957, this museum – unique in the Middle East – puts on superb exhibits of Japanese art.

★ **Hecht Museum**   MUSEUM
(http://mushecht.haifa.ac.il; 199 Abba Hushi Blvd; ☺ 10am-4pm Sun, Mon, Wed & Thu, to 7pm Tue, to 1pm Fri, to 2pm Sat) FREE One of Israel's most engaging museums, the Hecht's standout highlight is the extraordinary Ma'agan Mikhael Shipwreck, the remarkably well-preserved remains of a 13.5m-long merchant ship from 400 BC – that's four centuries older than the Ancient Galilee Ship on display at the Sea of Galilee! The archaeology section also features a whole room on the

Haifa

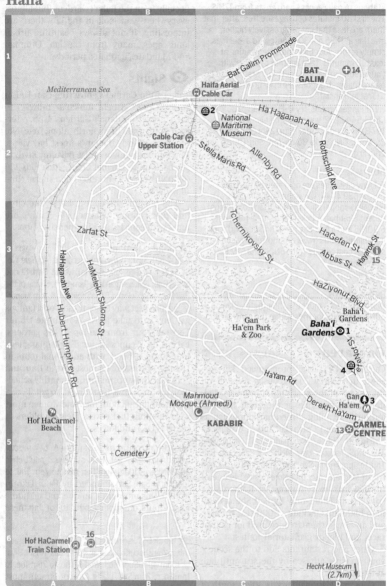

ISRAEL & THE PALESTINIAN TERRITORIES HAIFA

Mediterranean Sea

Bat Galim Promenade

BAT GALIM

⊕ 14

Haifa Aerial Cable Car

Ha Haganah Ave

🏛 **2**

National Maritime Museum

Cable Car Upper Station

Stella Maris Rd

Allenby Rd

Rothschild Ave

Zarfat St

Tchernikovsky St

HaGefen St

Hayarok St

Abbas St

i 15

HaZiyonut Blvd

Baha'i Gardens

Gan Ha'em Park & Zoo

Baha'i Gardens ◎ **1**

HaTzionut St

HaHaganah Ave

HaMelekh Shlomo St

Hubert Humphrey Rd

4 🏛

HaYam Rd

Mahmoud Mosque (Ahmedi)

Gan Ha'em 🚹 **3**
Ⓜ

KABABIR

Derekh HaYam

13 ⊕ **CARMEL CENTRE**

Hof HaCarmel Beach

Cemetery

Hof HaCarmel Train Station

16 🏛

Hecht Museum (2.7km) ↓

Phoenicians; Israelite, Moabite and Phoenician seals from the First Temple period; and an important collection of ancient coins, including some issued by revolt leader Bar Kochba.

Clandestine Immigration & Naval Museum MUSEUM
(www.amutayam.org.il; 204 Allenby Rd; adult/child incl National Maritime Museum 15/10NIS; ⊗10am-4pm Sun-Thu) A lot more evocative and dramatic than you might expect, this

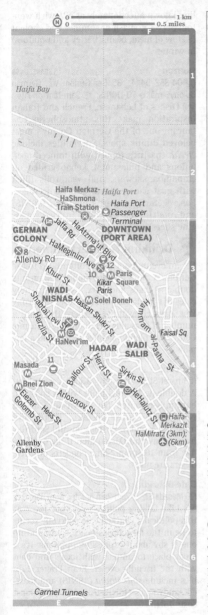

carried 434 refugees to Palestine in 1947; intercepted by the British, they were sent to internment camps on Cyprus. The museum is run by the Ministry of Defense, so you'll need your passport to get in.

🛏 Sleeping

★ **Port Inn** GUESTHOUSE **$**
(☑ 04-852 4401; www.portinn.co.il; 34 Jaffa Rd, Port Area; dm/s/d/tr/q 130/290/340/450/550NIS; dm without breakfast 90NIS; ❀ @ ☞) A magnet for budget travellers, this friendly guesthouse has helpful staff, a lovely back garden, a small kitchen and washing machines; the lounge and dining room are great for meeting other guests. The 16 rooms are spotless and colourfully, if simply, furnished; dorm rooms have four, five and nine beds. Apartments across the street cost 400/500/600NIS for three/four/five people (breakfast not included).

museum showcases the Zionist Movement's determined efforts to infiltrate Jewish refugees from Europe into British-blockaded Palestine from 1934 to 1948. The centrepiece is a WWII landing craft rechristened the *Af-Al-Pi-Chen* ('nevertheless' in Hebrew) that

St Charles Hospice
GUESTHOUSE $

(☑04-855 3705; www.pat-rosary.com; 105 Jaffa Rd, Port Area; s/d/q 180/300/390NIS; ✴@🛜) Operated by the Catholic Rosary Sisters, this guesthouse occupies a beautiful building (built 1880) with a lovely garden out back. Rooms are simple but comfortably furnished and come with private showers. The gate is often locked – just ring the bell. Curfew is generally 11pm. Payment must be made in cash.

Art Gallery Hotel
HOTEL $$

(☑04-861 6161; www.hotelgallery.co.il; 61 Herzl St, Hadar; s/d 450/500NIS; ✴@🛜) Original works by local artists adorn both the public spaces and the 40 rooms, which are smallish but otherwise pleasant and nicely outfitted. Opened as a small hotel in 1938, this creative hostelry has a small fitness room, massage and a 5th-floor deck with port views and picnic tables. Situated near the Metronit's Talpiyot Market stop.

✖ Eating

More than a dozen excellent restaurants, some owned by Arab celebrity chefs, line elegant Ben-Gurion Ave in the German Colony. Almost all are open seven days a week. Carmel Centre has a nice mix of upscale restaurants, sleek cafes and takeaway joints. In Hadar, there are places selling felafel, shwarma and other cheap eats along the northwestern part of Herzl St.

★ HaMis'ada shel Ima
ETHIOPIAN $

(Mother's Restaurant; 20 HaNevi'im St, Hadar; mains 35-40NIS; ⊘11am-11pm Sun-Fri, sundown-10pm or 11pm Sat night; ☑) Stepping into this utterly unpretentious eatery is like a quick trip to Addis Ababa. The spicy and lip-smackingly satisfying Ethiopian dishes are served – and eaten – with *injera* (spongy Ethiopian flatbread made with teff flour) and can be washed down with two kinds of Ethiopian beer (13NIS). It's hidden away in the courtyard of the Amisragas building.

★ Ma'ayan HaBira
JEWISH $$

(☑04-862 3193; 4 Nathanson St; mains 30-120NIS; ⊘10am-5pm Sun-Fri, to 11pm Tue, to 10pm Thu) Founded in 1950 as a butcher's shop and sausage factory, this old-timer is famous for serving beer (thus the name) and Eastern European Jewish 'soul food', including jellied calf's foot, gefilte fish, chopped liver and *kreplach,* a meat-stuffed dumpling known affectionately as a 'Jewish wonton'. Serves goulash in summer and cholent (a stew of meat, beans, barley and potatoes) in winter.

Douzan
LEBANESE $$$

(☑04-852 5444; 35 Ben-Gurion Ave, German Colony; mains 70-110NIS; ⊘9am-1am or later; ☑) Dishes of Lebanese, French and Italian inspiration make this atmospheric restaurant one of the German Colony's most beloved dining spots. Specialities include *sfeeha* (pastries topped with minced beef, onions and pine nuts), kebab grilled on cinnamon skewers, and veal rolls filled with goat cheese, pesto and garlic sauce. For vegetarians, there's tabouleh (38NIS) and *rolettini* (cheese rolled in fried aubergine slices).

🍷 Drinking & Entertainment

For an evening out, locals often head to the German Colony, where many restaurants double as cafes and bars; to the hip, lefty cafes of the Masada St area; or to the grimy Port Area (Downtown), where there are a number of bars along HaBankim St. Carmel Centre has plenty of coffeehouses and a few pubs.

Syncopa
BAR

(5 Khayat St, Downtown; ⊘8.30pm-2am or later) A double-decker nightspot with a softly lit, burgundy-coloured bar downstairs and a performance space upstairs. There's live music on Monday, Wednesday and Saturday from 10pm, and DJs do their thing on Tuesday from 10.30pm. Some concerts are free, others are not.

Cafe Masada
CAFE

(16 Masada St; ⊘7am-2am or later, from 9am Sat; 🛜) Like talking politics over your java? At this politically charged cafe everyone seems to be in the far-left pro-peace camp and no one is shy about expressing opinions. It's a great place to mingle with locals and chat with the friendly owner, Eran Prager. Edibles include *shakshuka* (28NIS) and toasted sandwiches (16NIS to 28NIS); breakfast costs 45NIS.

Haifa Cinematheque
CINEMA

(☑04-833 8888; www.ethos.co.il; 142 HaNassi Ave, Carmel Centre; ticket 33NIS) Screens avantgarde, offbeat and art films in two halls. Out front, bronze stars in the pavement honour major figures in Israeli cinema.

ⓘ Orientation

The higher up the slopes of Mt Carmel you go, the wealthier the neighbourhoods tend to be.

The gritty Downtown (Ir Tachtit) and adjacent Port Area (Ezor HaNamal), built during the late Ottoman period and the British Mandate, are on the flats adjacent to Haifa Port. Landmarks include the Haifa Merkaz-HaShmona train station, which affords easy access to Ben-Gurion airport, Tel Aviv and Akko; and Paris Sq (Kikar Pariz), the lower terminus of the Carmelit funicular railway (a steep, six-station metro). About 1km west of there, directly below the Baha'i Gardens, is Ben-Gurion Ave, the elegant main thoroughfare of the German Colony. The mostly Arab neighbourhood of Wadi Nisnas is in a little valley midway between Paris Sq and the German Colony.

About 1km south (up the slope) from Paris Sq is Herzl St, the heart of Hadar HaCarmel, universally known as Hadar. The HaNev'im stop on the Carmelit is 350m northwest of the corner of Herzl and Balfour Sts (the heart of Hadar) and 350m southeast of Wadi Nisnas' main drag, HaWadi St.

Around the Carmelit's upper terminus, Gan HaEm, is Carmel Centre (Merkaz HaCarmel), the commercial and dining heart of the affluent neighbourhoods that are strung out along the ridge of Mt Carmel.

Free street maps are available at most hotels and the Haifa tourist office.

ⓘ Information

Rambam Medical Centre (Rambam Health Care Campus; ☏1 700 505 150, emergency room 04-777 1300; www.rambam.org.il; 8 HaAliya HaShniya St, Bat Galim; ⊙24hr) One of Israel's largest and most-respected hospitals.

Tourist Office (Haifa Tourist Board; ☏1 800 305 090, 04-853 5606; www.tour-haifa.co.il; 48 Ben-Gurion Ave, German Colony; ⊙8.30am-6pm Sun-Thu, to 1pm Fri) Has useful publications, including *A Guide to Haifa Tourism* and a city map (4NIS) outlining four themed walking tours. Situated near the top of Ben-Gurion Ave.

ⓘ Getting There & Away

BUS

Haifa has two central bus stations. Linking the two is the 24/7 Metronit line 1 (30 minutes), which loops around via the German Colony and the Port Area; and bus 101 (15 minutes), which goes through the Carmel Tunnels, a toll-road tunnel under Mt Carmel.

Haifa-Hof HaCarmel, used by buses heading south along the coast (ie towards Tel Aviv), is on the Mediterranean (western) side of Mt Carmel. It's 8km around the base of Mt Carmel from the German Colony, near the Haifa-Hof HaCarmel train station. Destinations include Jerusalem (Egged bus 940; 44NIS, two hours, every 30 to 90 minutes except Friday evening to sundown Saturday). The quickest way to get to Tel Aviv is by train.

Haifa-Merkazit HaMifratz, on the Haifa Bay side of Mt Carmel, is used by most buses to destinations north and east of Haifa. It is 8km southeast of the German Colony, a few hundred metres – through the giant Lev HaMifratz shopping mall – from the Lev HaMifratz train station. Train is the fastest way to Akko.

Destinations include:

Jerusalem (Egged bus 960; 45.30NIS, 1¾ hours, one or two times an hour except Friday afternoon to sundown Saturday)

Nazareth (buses 331 and 339, shared by Nazareth Tourism & Transport and GB Tours; 19NIS, one hour, twice an hour Sunday to Friday, hourly all-day Saturday)

Tiberias (Egged bus 430; 25NIS, 1¼ hours, twice an hour except Friday afternoon to sundown Saturday)

Tsfat (Nateev Express bus 361; 1¾ hours, twice an hour) via Akko (45 minutes).

SHERUT

Seven-day-a-week **sheruts to Akko and Tel Aviv** (☏04-862 2115; weekday/Shabbat 30/45NIS) depart from Hadar, from various places around the intersection of Herzl and HaNevi'im Sts.

A sherut to the airport (77NIS from the sherut station, or 119NIS from your hotel) requires booking one day in advance; call ☏04-866 2324.

TRAIN

Trains do not run from Friday afternoon until sundown on Saturday. Haifa has four train stations: Haifa-Hof HaCarmel (near the Haifa-Hof HaCarmel bus station); Haifa Merkaz-HaShmona (Haifa Center-HaShmona; in the Downtown/Port area); Haifa-Bat Galim (near Ramban hospital); and Lev HaMifratz (near the Haifa-Merkazit HaMifratz bus station). Travel by train within Haifa, between any of the following stations (departing every 10 to 20 minutes), costs 6NIS.

Other rail destinations include the following:

Akko (16NIS, 30 minutes, three times an hour)
Ben-Gurion airport (41.50NIS, 1¾ hours, twice an hour)
Tel Aviv (32NIS, one hour, two or three times an hour)

ℹ Getting Around

The six-station **Carmelit** (🕿 04-837 6861; www.carmelithaifa.co.il; single trip 6.90NIS, daily pass 15NIS; ⊙ 6am-midnight Sun-Thu, to 3pm Fri, sundown-midnight Sat), Israel's only metro (technically it's a funicular railway), connects Paris Sq (Kikar Pariz) in the Downtown/Port Area with Hadar (HaNevi'im stop) and Carmel Centre (Gan HaEm stop).

For travel along and around Mt Carmel's flanks you'll need buses and the Metronit, a three-line bus service, inaugurated in 2013, that has its own dedicated lanes. Metronit line 1 links the two central bus stations, Haifa-Merkazit HaMifratz and Haifa-Hof HaCarmel, via the Downtown/Port Area and the German Colony at least twice an hour (every six minutes at peak times) 24 hours a day, seven days a week (yes, including Shabbat!).

Akko (Acre) עכו عكا

🕿 04 / POP 47,000

Marco Polo passed through Akko (Acre; Akka in Arabic) around 750 years ago and much of the place hasn't changed a lot since then. Today, Old Akko seduces visitors with towering ramparts, deep moats, green domes, slender minarets, church towers, secret passageways and subterranean vaults. It was awarded Unesco World Heritage status in 2001. Akko can easily be visited on a day trip from Haifa.

⊙ Sights

Step into the towering, stone-vaulted **Knight's Halls**, built 800 years ago by the Hospitallers (a monastic military order), and it's not hard to envision the medieval knights who once lived and dined here. A few blocks away, the extraordinary **Templars' Tunnel**, 350m long, was built by the Knights Templar (another military order) to connect their main fortress, just north of the black-and-white-striped **lighthouse** at Old Akko's southwestern tip, with **Khan al-Umdan**, next to the **Marina**.

Visitor Centre VISITOR CENTRE

(🕿 04-995 6706; www.akko.org.il; all sites adult/child 46/39NIS; ⊙ visitor centre & sites 8.30am-6.30pm daylight-saving time, to 4.30pm winter time, closes 2hr earlier Fri) Facing a shady park, the Visitor Centre is the best place to begin a visit to Akko's Crusader sites. Staff can help you plan your tour of the city, sell you an indispensable map (3NIS), show you a **scale model** of the city and screen an eight-

minute introductory **film** (available in nine languages). Tickets are sold at a kiosk out front (and at both entrances to the Templars' Tunnel); pick up your audioguide at a second kiosk (ID deposit required).

Souq MARKET

(⊙ to late afternoon daily) Fresh hummus is boiled in giant vats, while nearby fresh-caught fish flop off the tables. As carts trundle past, children shuck corn and vendors hawk fresh fruit, all to a soundtrack of Arabic music. At the lower end of the souq, visit **Kurdi & Berit** (⊙ 9.30am-6pm), a tourist-friendly shop that ships herbs and spices worldwide.

🛏 Sleeping

Akko Gate Hostel HOSTEL **$**

(🕿 04-991 0410; www.akkogate.com; 13/14 Salah ad-Din St; dm/s/d/tr/5-bed without breakfast US$25/60/85/120/160; ❉ @ 🛜) Run by the friendly Walid, this long-running hostel is just inside the old city, steps from the cheap eats of Salah ad-Din St. In an Ottoman-era building, the 12 rooms (12 more are planned) are simply furnished and a little dated but are clean and come with minifridges. The basic kitchen is out on a balcony. Breakfast costs 25NIS.

Akkotel HOTEL **$$$**

(🕿 04-987 7100; www.akkotel.com; Salah ad-Din St; s/d/q US$160/190/285; ❉ @ 🛜) Embedded in the old city ramparts, this family-run hotel has 16 rooms (including five for families) with vaulted ceilings, stone windowsills and walls 1m or or even 2m thick. The rooftop terrace affords fantastic views of the city and Haifa Bay. Wheelchair accessible. Has seven reserved parking places.

🍴 Eating

Old Akko has some excellent dining options, particularly if you're in the mood for fish or seafood. For cheap eats, there are quite a few places selling hummus, felafel and/or shwarma long Salah ad-Din St.

Hummus Said MIDDLE EASTERN **$**

(hummus 15NIS; ⊙ 6am-2.30pm Sun-Fri; 🖉) Deep inside the souq, this place is something of an institution, doling out plates of soft, creamy hummus to connoisseurs from around the country. For 17NIS you get salads, pickles, pita and hummus with fuul (fava-bean paste) or garlic.

Akko (Acre)

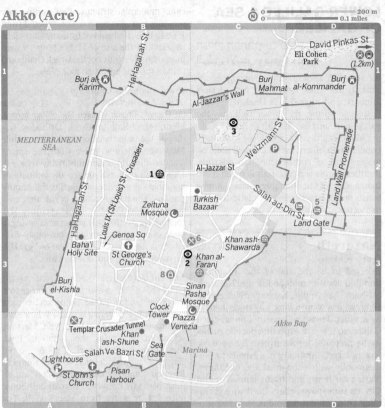

Akko (Acre)

★**Uri Buri**   SEAFOOD **$$$**

(☑04-955 2212; HaHaganah St; mains 65-114NIS; half portions 51-63NIS; ⊘noon-midnight; ☑) Uri Buri is a man of many talents who's done everything from spear fishing to defusing bombs to founding the luxurious Effendi Hotel. But he's best known for making award-winning fish and seafood dishes – recommended options include fish soup, crab with seaweed, creamy trout fast-cooked in a hot casserole, and sashimi served with wasabi-flavoured sorbet.

ℹ Getting There & Away

Akko's train and bus stations are about 1.5km northeast of the Old City.

Train is the fastest and most scenic way to travel to/from Haifa Merkaz-HaShmonah (16NIS, 30 minutes, three times an hour), Tel Aviv (41.50NIS, 1¾ hours, hourly) and Ben-Gurion airport (51.50NIS, two hours, hourly).

Akko (Acre)

◎ Sights

1 Hammam al-Pasha	B2
2 Souq	B3
3 Visitor Centre	C2

☐ Sleeping

4 Akko Gate Hostel	D2
5 Akkotel	D2

☒ Eating

6 Hummus Said	C3
7 Uri Buri	A4

☐ Shopping

8 Kurdi & Berit	B3

Sheruts (seven days a week) wait outside the Akko bus station (up the block from the train station) and depart when full to Haifa-Hadar and Nahariya.

LOWER GALILEE & SEA OF GALILEE

הגליל התחתון ים כנרת

الجليل الاسفل وبحيرة طبريا

Blessed with ancient stone synagogues, archaeological sites associated with Jesus's ministry, and rugged hills cloaked in wildflowers in spring, the Lower Galilee – the part of northern Israel south of Rte 85 (linking Akko with the Sea of Galilee) – is hugely popular with hikers, cyclists, Israeli holidaymakers and, of course, Christian pilgrims. But these days even Nazareth is much more than a place of Christian pilgrimage – it now boasts one of Israel's most sophisticated dining scenes.

Nazareth

נצרת الناصرة

🖉 04 / POP 74,000

Believed to be the site of the Annunciation and Jesus's childhood home, Nazareth (Al-Naasira in Arabic, Natzrat or Natzeret in Hebrew) has come a long way since its days as a quiet Jewish village in Roman-ruled Galilee, so if you're expecting bucolic rusticity be prepared for a surprise. These days, Israel's largest Arab city is a bustling minimetropolis with shop-lined thoroughfares, blaring car horns and traffic jams. The Old City, its stone-paved alleys lined with crumbling Ottoman-era mansions, is in the process of reinventing itself as a sophisticated cultural and culinary destination.

Everything in Nazareth is open for business on Shabbat (Friday night and Saturday). On Sunday, on the other hand, while attractions and pastry shops are open, stores and most restaurants are not.

◉ Sights

The peaceful rooftop gardens of the **Centre International Marie de Nazareth** (🖉04-646 1266; www.cimdn.org; Al-Bishara St; recommended donation 50NIS; ⊙9.30am-noon & 2.30-6pm Mon-Sat, last entry 5pm), landscaped with plants mentioned in the Bible, afford 360-degree panoramas of the city.

Basilica of the Annunciation   CHURCH
(🖉04-565 0001; www.basilicanazareth.org; Al-Bishara St; ⊙Upper Basilica 8am-6pm, Grotto of the Annunciation 5.45am-6pm, for silent prayer 6-9pm) FREE Dominating the Old City's skyline is the lantern-topped cupola of this Franciscan-run Roman Catholic basilica, an auda-

cious modernist structure that's unlike any building you've ever seen. Constructed from 1960 to 1969, it's believed by many Christians to stand on the site of Mary's home, where many churches (but not the Greek Orthodox) believe the Annunciation took place.

Greek Orthodox Church of the Annunciation   CHURCH
(St Gabriel's Church; Church Sq; ⊙7am-noon & 1-6pm) According to Greek Orthodox tradition, the Annunciation took place while Mary was fetching water from the spring situated directly under this richly frescoed, 17th-century church (other denominations hold that she was at home during the Annunciation). The barrel-vaulted crypt, first constructed under Constantine (4th century AD), shelters Nazareth's only year-round spring, a place everyone in the village obviously visited often. Check out the centuries-old graffiti carved around the outside doorway.

Ancient Bathhouse   ARCHAEOLOGICAL SITE
(🖉04-657 8539; www.nazarethbathhouse.com; Mary's Well Sq; tour 120NIS, per person 5 or more people 28NIS; ⊙9am-7pm Mon-Sat) When Elias Shama and his Belgian-born wife, Martina, set about renovating their shop in 1993, they uncovered a network of 2000-year-old clay pipes almost identical to ones found in Pompeii – and then, under the floor, an almost perfectly preserved Roman bathhouse once fed by water from Mary's Well. The 30-minute tour, which draws you into the excitement of serendipitous discovery, ends with refreshments.

🛏 Sleeping

Sisters of Nazareth Guest House   GUESTHOUSE $
(🖉04-655 4304; 6167 St; dm/s/d/tr without breakfast 75/220/260/330NIS) Set around a flowery courtyard with archaeological excavations underneath, this 46-room establishment, in a building that dates from 1855, is run by the Sisters of Nazareth, a French Catholic order. Dorm beds (16 for men, six for women) are in spotless, barrackslike rooms. The gate is locked for the night at 10.30pm sharp.

★ Fauzi Azar Inn   GUESTHOUSE $$
(🖉04-602 0469; www.fauziazarinn.com; dm 90NIS, d 350-500NIS; ❋@🛜) Hidden away in a gorgeous, two-century-old stone house in the Old City, this place has oodles of charm – and so do the staff. The 14 rooms are simple but tasteful, though they're no match for the

Lower Galilee & Sea of Galilee

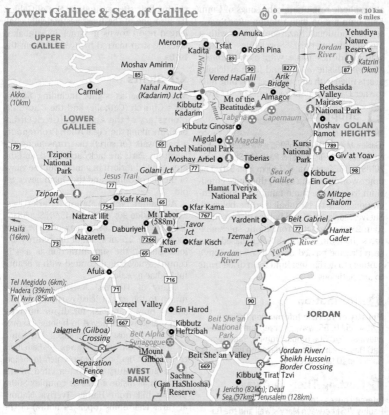

lounge's arched windows, marble floors and 5m-high frescoed ceiling. A great place to meet other travellers – or to volunteer (see website).

⭐ **Al-Mutran Guest House**   GUESTHOUSE **$$**
(☏ 04-645 7947; www.al-mutran.com; Bishop's Sq; d US$108-128, ste US$220; ❄ @ 🛜) Adjacent to the residence of Nazareth's Greek Orthodox *mutran* ('bishop' in Arabic), this family-run gem occupies a gorgeous, 200-year-old mansion with 4.5m-high ceilings, Ottoman arches and antique floor tiles. Nonguests are welcome to drop by the stylish lobby, with its Ottoman pillows and Bedouin textiles, for a coffee (7NIS).

✕ Eating

Nazareth's dining scene has recently become so drop-dead delicious that it's worth staying the night (or weekend) for. The buzzword is 'fusion', with European-inspired dishes infused with local seasonings and then served – with an extra helping of Arab hospitality – in atmospheric Old City mansions. Reservations are recommended on Friday and Saturday.

⭐ **Abu Ashraf**   HUMMUS **$**
(Diwan al-Saraya; 6134 St; mains 20NIS; ⏰ 8am-8pm Mon-Sat, noon-3pm or 4pm Sun; ✐) This old-time hummus joint and coffeehouse (the beans are roasted on the premises) is famous all over town for its *katayef* (sweet pancakes folded over Umm Ashraf's goat's cheese or cinnamon walnuts, then doused with geranium syrup; three for 12NIS, including coffee or tea 19NIS). Has excellent vegetable salads. Ebullient owner Abu Ashraf loves to share stories about Nazareth.

⭐ **AlReda**   FUSION **$$$**
(☏ 04-608 4404; 21 Al-Bishara St; mains 60-128NIS; ⏰ 1pm-2am Mon-Sat, 7pm-2am Sun; ✐) In a 200-year-old Ottoman-era mansion, this

atmospheric restaurant – the songs of Umm Kalthoum are on high rotation after 8pm – serves traditional Nazarene recipes with a Mediterranean twist. Specialities include seasonal dishes made with okra *(bamya)* and wild thistle *(akub)*, and fresh artichoke hearts filled with chopped beef and pine nuts (owner Daher Zeidani loves nuts of all sorts).

🛍 Shopping

★ Elbabour   FOOD

(Galilee Mill; ☑ 04-645 5596; www.elbabour.com; entrances on Al-Bishara St & Paulus VI St; per 100g 20NIS; ⊘ 8.30am-7pm or 7.30pm Mon-Sat) The other-worldly aroma inside this spice emporium, run by the same family for four generations, has to be inhaled to be believed. Shelves, sacks, bins and bottles display more than 2500 products, from exotic spice mixtures (including Pierina's Spice, based on a secret recipe passed down by owner Tony's mother) to herbal teas, and from dried fruits to aromatic oils.

ℹ Information

Ministry of Tourism Information Office
(☑ 04-657 0555; www.goisrael.com; 58 Casanova St; ⊘ 8.30am-5pm Mon-Fri, 9am-5pm Sat) Has brochures about Nazareth and the Galilee in 10 languages.

ℹ Getting There & Away

Intercity buses stop along traffic-plagued Paulus VI St between Mary's Well and the Basilica of the Annunciation; on the northbound side for Kafr Kana, Tiberias and Akko, on the southbound side for Haifa, Tel Aviv and Jerusalem. Nazarene Tours (p289) runs buses to Amman.

Akko (Egged bus 343; 31.50NIS, 1½ hours, hourly except Saturday)

Haifa (Merkazit HaMifratz and/or Merkaz HaShmona Train Station; buses 331 and 339, shared by Nazareth Tourism & Transport and GB Tours; 17.20NIS, one hour, twice an hour Sunday to Friday, hourly Saturday)

Tiberias (Nazareth Tourism & Transport bus 431; 19NIS, one hour, hourly except Friday evening and Saturday) Some buses stop on Nazareth's ring road, Rte 75, instead of on Paulus VI St.

Tiberias   טבריה طبريا

☑ 04 / POP 42,000

Tiberias is one of the four holy cities of Judaism, the burial place of venerated Jewish sages, and a very popular base for Christians visiting holy sites around the Sea of Galilee. It's also one of the most aesthetically challenged resort towns in Israel, its sunbaked lakeside strip marred by eyesores from the 1970s.

◉ Sights

Most of Tiberias' sights, including St Peter's Church (Catholic) and the Church & Monastery of the Apostles (Greek Orthodox), are along the Yigal Allon Promenade, a boardwalk (of sorts) that runs along the lakefront. Parts are tacky and faded, and the area can feel forlorn in winter, but the views of the Sea of Galilee and the Golan never get old.

At Hamat Tveriya National Park (Eliezer Kaplan Ave/Rte 90; adult/child 15/7NIS; ⊘ 8am-5pm daylight-saving time, to 4pm winter time, closes 1hr earlier Fri), 2.5km south of the centre (take local bus 5), the star attraction is a 4th-century synagogue decorated with a beautiful Zodiac mosaic.

Many of Tiberias' Jewish visitors are drawn to the city at least partly by the desire to pray – and ask for divine intercession – at graves believed to belong to some of Judaism's most eminent sages. The tomb of Rabbi Meir Ba'al Hanes (⊘ 6am-10pm or later Sun-Thu, in summer/winter to 5/3pm Fri), a 2nd-century sage often cited in the Mishnah, is inside a hillside complex 300m up the hill from Hamat Tveriya National Park. The tombs (open 24 hours) of the Rambam (1135–1204), a Cordova-born polymath famous for his rationalist approach to religion and life, and Yohanan ben Zakkai, Judaism's most eminent 1st-century sage, are on Ben Zakkai St four blocks northeast of the central bus station.

🛏 Sleeping

Tiberias has some of the Galilee's cheapest dorm beds. Camping is permitted at almost all of the beaches, both free and pay, that ring the Sea of Galilee, including the municipal Hof Ganim (Rte 90; per person 20NIS), 1.5km south of the centre of Tiberias.

Aviv Hostel   HOSTEL $

(☑ 04-672 0007; 66 HaGalil St; dm 80NIS, d without breakfast US$65; ❄ @ 🛜) Best thought of as a cheap hotel. Staff are indifferent, the 26 rooms are slightly scuffed and the sheets are polyester, but amenities include proper spring mattresses and fridges. Dorm beds are all nonbunk; women-only dorms are

Tiberias

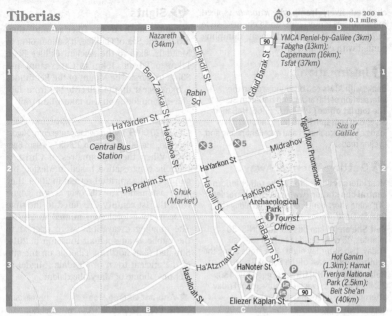

available. Lift-equipped. Breakfast costs US$11.

YMCA Peniel-by-Galilee GUESTHOUSE $$
(04-672 0685; www.ymca-galilee.co.il; Rte 90; s/d 450/550NIS; ❄🛜🐕) Built in the 1920s as a holiday home for the founder of the Jerusalem YMCA, this guesthouse is a gem. Set on a secluded, shady lakeshore, it has a clean pebbly beach, a natural pool fed by a warm spring and a richly decorated lobby with a distinctly Mandate-era vibe. The 14 rooms are forgivably simple; some have kitchenettes.

Aviv Holiday Flats HOTEL $$
(04-671 2272; http://aviv-hotel.xwx.co.il; 2 HaNoter St; s/d/tr/q US$78/98/113/128) The 30 handsome, modern studio apartments have at least 30 sq metres of space, balconies, kitchenettes and new sheets and mattresses. One of the best deals in town.

✕ Eating

The Yigal Allon Promenade has a number of places to grab a bite or sip a beer, as does the perpendicular Midrahov (pedestrian mall) and a nearby section of HaBanim St. Truly excellent meals-in-a-pita are served up by four rival Felafel & Shwarma Stalls (HaGalil St; felafel 15NIS, shwarma 24NIS; ☺6am or 7am-

8pm or 9pm Sun-Thu, 8am-1hr before sundown Fri; ✓). **Supersol Sheli** (HaBanim St; ☺8am-9pm Sun-Thu, to 2.30/3.30pm Fri winter/summer) has picnic supplies.

Only a handful of in-town eateries are open on Shabbat, making Friday night a great time to check out Nazareth's dazzling dining scene.

Guy ISRAELI $$
(04-672 3036; HaGalil St; mains 38-75NIS; ☺noon-9pm or 10pm Sun-Thu, to 1hr before sundown Fri; ✓) An unpretentious, old-time Mizrahi (oriental-Jewish) restaurant featuring home-style grilled meats, soups (winter only; 17NIS to 22NIS) and a delicious array of stuffed vegetables, as well as Ashkenazi-style

chopped liver, Iraqi-style *kubbeh* (spiced meat balls in tangy soup) and Lebanese-style *kubbeh* (a fried cracked-wheat dumpling stuffed with chopped meat).

ℹ️ Information

Banks with ATMs can be found around the intersection of HaYarden and HaBanim Sts. The **tourist office** (📋 04-672 5666; HaBanim St; ⊗ 8.30am-4pm Sun-Thu, to noon Fri) has loads of free brochures and excellent hiking and cycling maps.

ℹ️ Getting There & Away

Most intercity buses stop at the rather forlorn **central bus station** (www.bus.co.il; HaYarden St); some short-haul lines also stop along Ha-Galil St. Destinations include:

Beit She'an (Afikim bus 28; 16.50NIS, 30 minutes, 15 daily Sunday to Thursday, six Friday, two Saturday night) Has stops along the southwestern coast of the Sea of Galilee.

Haifa-Merkazit HaMifratz (Egged bus 430; 25NIS, 1¼ hours, twice an hour except Friday afternoon to sundown Saturday)

Jerusalem (Egged buses 959, 961 and 962; 40NIS, 2½ to three hours, every one or two hours except Friday evening to sundown Saturday) Goes via Beit She'an.

Nazareth (Nazareth Tourism & Transport bus 431; 19NIS, one hour, hourly except Friday evening and Saturday) Some buses stop on Rte 75 instead of in central Nazareth. Goes via Kafr Kana.

Tel Aviv (Egged bus 836; 40NIS, 2¾ hours, hourly except Friday afternoon to Saturday afternoon) Sheruts from outside the bus station are faster.

Tsfat (Afikim bus 450; 16.90NIS, 40 minutes, hourly Sunday to Friday afternoon, one Saturday night)

Sea of Galilee

بحيرة طبريا

ים כנרת

The shores of the Sea of Galilee (in Hebrew, Yam Kinneret or HaKinneret), by far Israel's largest freshwater lake, are lined with great places to relax: beaches, camping grounds, cycling trails and walking tracks.

Jesus spent most of his ministry around the Sea of Galilee. This is where he is believed to have performed some of his best-known miracles (the multiplication of the loaves and fishes, walking on water), and it was overlooking the Kinneret that he delivered the Sermon on the Mount.

◉ Sights

Heading north from Tiberias and then around the Sea of Galilee, it's about 6km to Magdala, 8km to the Ancient Galilee Boat, 13km to Tabgha, 16km to Capernaum and 33km to Kursi. The Mount of the Beatitudes is 3km by car up the hill (Rte 90) from Tabgha – or, on foot, you can take a 1km trail.

Magdala ARCHAEOLOGICAL SITE
(📋 04-620 0099; www.magdalacenter.com; Migdal Junction, Rte 90; admission 10NIS; ⊗ 9am-6pm daily) When the Legionnaires of Christ, a Catholic congregation based in Mexico, began to build a spiritual retreat in 2009, they were astonished to discover a synagogue from the 1st century CE, dated to the time of Jesus by a local coin minted in 29 CE. The ongoing excavations were opened to the public as an open-air museum in 2014. Situated 6km north of Tiberias on the site of the ancient town of Magdala (Migdal in Hebrew), home of Mary Magdalene.

★ **Ancient Galilee Boat** HISTORIC SITE
(Jesus Boat; 📋 04-672 7700; www.bet-alon.co.il; Kibbutz Ginosar, Rte 90; adult/child 20/15NIS; ⊗ 8am-5pm Sun-Thu, to 4pm Fri, to 5pm Sat) In 1986, when the level of the Sea of Galilee was particularly low, a local fisherman made an extraordinary discovery: the remains of a wooden boat later determined to have plied these waters in the time of Jesus's ministry. The 8.2m fishing vessel, made of 12 kinds of (apparently recycled) wood, can be seen inside Kibbutz Ginosar's **Yigal Alon Centre**. Wall panels and three short films tell the fascinating story of its discovery and preservation (so does the website).

Tabgha CHURCH
Two Catholic churches a few hundred metres apart occupy the stretch of Sea of Galilee lakefront known as Tabgha (an Arabic corruption of the Greek *hepta pega,* meaning 'seven springs'). An attractive walkway links Tabgha with Capernaum, a distance of about 3km.

★ **Mount of the Beatitudes** CHURCH
(Har HaOsher; 📋 04-671 1225; Rte 90; per car 10NIS; ⊗ 8-11.45am & 2-4.45pm) This breathtaking hillside Roman Catholic church, built in 1937, stands on a site believed since at least the 4th century to be where Jesus delivered his Sermon on the Mount – the eight Beatitudes (Matthew 5–7) – the opening lines of which begin with the phrase 'Blessed are...' The sermon also includes the Lord's Prayer

and oft-quoted phrases such as 'salt of the earth', 'light of the world' and 'judge not, lest ye be judged'.

Capernaum ARCHAEOLOGICAL SITE

(Kfar Nachum, Kfar Nahum; admission 3NIS; ⊙ 8am-5pm, last entry 4.30pm) The New Testament relates that the prosperous lakeside village of Capernaum (estimated population 1500), on the imperial highway from Tiberias to Damascus, was Jesus's base during the most influential period of his Galilean ministry (Matthew 4:13, Mark 2:1, John 6:59). It is mentioned by name 16 times: this is where Jesus is believed to have preached at the synagogue (Mark 1:21), healed the sick and recruited his first disciples, fishers Peter, Andrew, James and John and Matthew the tax collector.

Kursi National Park ARCHAEOLOGICAL SITE

(☑ 04-673 1983; www.parks.org.il; cnr Rte 92 & Rte 789; adult/child 15/7NIS; ⊙ 8am-4pm Oct-Mar, to 5pm Apr-Sep, closes 1hr earlier Fri, last entry 30min before closing) Mentioned in the Talmud as a place of idol worship, this Gentile fishing village – discovered by chance in the early 1970s – is where Jesus is believed to have cast a contingent of demon spirits out of two men and into a herd of swine (Mark 5:1–13, Luke 8:26–39). The beautifully conserved ruins feature an impressive 5th-century Byzantine monastery.

🛏 Sleeping

Camping is possible on almost all Sea of Galilee beaches.

Moshav Giv'at Yoav is 13km southeast of Kursi (Kursy) Junction (the intersection of Rte 92 and Rte 789).

★ Genghis Khan in the Golan HOSTEL $

(☑ 052 371 5687; www.gkhan.co.il; Giv'at Yoav; dm/6-person tents 100/600NIS, linen & towel per stay 20NIS; ✽) Hosts Sara and Bentzi Zafrir offer the warmest of welcomes and a fantastic independent-travel vibe here. Inspired by the yurts (gers) used by the nomads of Mongolia, they designed and handmade five colour-coded yurts, each of which sleeps six or 10 on comfortable foam mattresses. Powerful air-con makes sure you stay toasty warm in winter and cool in summer.

Sea of Galilee Guesthouse GUESTHOUSE $$

(☑ 04-693 0063; www.seaofgalileeguesthouse.com; Almagor, off Rte 8277; dm without breakfast 100NIS, d 550NIS, 5-bed apt 750NIS; ✽@🛜) Lovely gardens with panoramic views of

CYCLING AROUND THE SEA

The Sea of Galilee is great cycling territory. Completely circumnavigating the lake (60km) takes about six hours; for about 70% of the distance you can follow the Kinneret Trail. For a half-day ride, you can head to Yardenit, 8km south of Tiberias, from where an 8km circuit follows the Jordan River. **Aviv Hostel** (☑ 04-672 0007; 66 HaGalil St; per day 70NIS; ⊙ 7am or 8am-sundown, to 7pm summer) rents bicycles.

the Sea of Galilee surround the simple, cheery rooms and photo-adorned breakfast room of this 30-bed guesthouse, suffused with an old-time Israeli vibe. Serves great breakfasts (40NIS extra if you're in a dorm bed). Cooking facilities are available. If you've got a tent, you can camp. Wheelchair accessible.

★ Pilgerhaus Tabgha GUESTHOUSE $$$

(☑ 04-670 0100; www.heilig-land-verein.de; s/d Sat-Wed 100/680NIS, Thu & Fri 600/880NIS; ✽@🛜) Opened in 1889, this 70-room German Catholic guesthouse – geared to Christian pilgrims but open to all – is a tranquil place with glorious gardens, right on the shores of the Sea of Galilee. Sumptuously renovated in 2001, it's ideal for meditation and reflection amid exemplary Germanic cleanliness and order. Wheelchair accessible. Situated about 500m from Capernaum Junction.

ⓘ Getting There & Around

All the buses (Egged and Afikim) that link Tiberias with points north via Rte 90, including Tsfat and Kiryat Shmona, pass by Magdala (Migdal Junction; 6.60NIS), Kibbutz Ginosar (the Ancient Galilee Boat is about 1km from Rte 90), Capernaum Junction (Tzomet Kfar Nahum, which is a short walk from Tabgha but about 4km west of Capernaum) and Mount of the Beatitudes' 1km-long access road.

From Tiberias, Rama bus 52 to the Golan town of Katzrin (35 minutes, three or four daily except mid-afternoon Friday to sundown Saturday) serves the Sea of Galilee's northwestern and northern shore, including Magdala, Ginosar, Tabgha and Capernaum. Rama bus 57, also to Katzrin, (50 minutes, seven daily except mid-afternoon Friday and Saturday), follows the lake's southern and eastern shores, passing by Kursi National Park.

DON'T MISS

NATIONAL PARKS

The Galilee Panhandle and the Hula Valley are a crucial stopping point for many of the estimated 500-million birds that pass through Israel each year on their way from Europe to Africa, and vice versa. The area's most outstanding national parks include:

Hula Nature Reserve (☑04-693 7069; www.parks.org.il; adult/child 35/21NIS; ⊙8am-5pm Sun-Thu, to 4pm Fri, last entry 1hr before closing) Migrating birds flock to the wetlands of Israel's first nature reserve, founded in 1964. Situated 15km north of Rosh Pina, at a point 2km west of Rte 90.

Tel Dan Nature Reserve (☑04-695 1579; adult/child 29/15NIS; ⊙8am-4pm or 5pm Sat-Thu, to 3pm or 4pm Fri, last entry 1hr before closing) Has year-round springs, abundant vegetation and the remains of a grand city inhabited by the Canaanites in the 18th century BC and the Israelites during the First Temple period (from the 12th century BC). Situated 10km northeast of Kiryat Shmona.

Banias Nature Reserve (☑Banias Springs 04-690 2577, Banias Waterfall 04-695 0272; www.parks.org.il; Rte 99; adult/child 29/15NIS, incl Nimrod Fortress 40/20NIS; ⊙8am-4pm or 5pm Sat-Thu, to 3pm or 4pm Fri) The gushing springs, waterfalls and lushly shaded streams of Banias Nature Reserve form one of Israel's most beautiful – and popular – nature spots. Situated 15km northeast of Kiryat Shmona.

Nimrod Fortress (☑04-694 9277; www.parks.org.il; Rte 989; adult/child 22/10NIS; ⊙8am-4pm or 5pm Sat-Thu, to 3pm or 4pm Fri, last entry 1hr before closing) Towers fairy-tale-like on a long, narrow ridge (altitude 815m) on the southwestern slopes of Mt Hermon. If you're going to visit just one Crusader-era fortress during your trip, this should be it. Situated 21km northeast of Kiryat Shmona.

Beit She'an

بيت شأن بيسان

☑04 / POP 17,000

Founded sometime in the 5th millennium BC, Beit She'an – today a struggling modern town – has the most extensive Roman-era ruins in Israel.

⊙ Sights

Beit She'an National Park (☑04-658 7189; Rte 90; adult/child 40/24NIS; ⊙8am-4pm Oct–Mar, to 5pm Apr–Sep, closes 1hr earlier Fri, last entry 30min before closing) is the best place in the country to get a sense of what it might have been like to live, work and shop in the Roman Empire. Colonnaded streets, a 7000-seat theatre, two bathhouses and piles of columns crumpled by the AD 749 earthquake evoke the aesthetics, grandeur, self-confidence and decadence of Roman provincial life in the centuries after Jesus.

The extraordinarily well-preserved mosaics (including a 12-panel zodiac circle) at the **Beit Alpha Synagogue** (www.parks.org.il; Kibbutz Heftzibah; adult/child 22/10NIS; ⊙8am-5pm daylight-saving time, 8am-4pm winter time, closes 1hr earlier Fri, last entry 1hr before closing), 8km west of town, are among the most dazzling ever found in Israel. Served by Kavim bus 412 (at least hourly).

⎙ Sleeping

HI – Beit She'an Guest House HOSTEL $$ (☑02-594 5644; www.iyha.org.il; 129 Menahem Begin Ave/Rte 90; s/d 385/510NIS, additional adult/child 160/125NIS; @🌐🛜) Within easy walking distance of Beit She'an's antiquities, this 62-room hostel has attractive public areas, a great rooftop patio and a pool (open April to September). Rooms are practical and clean and have five beds; individual dorm beds are not available. Situated a bit south of the intercity bus stops. Wheelchair accessible.

ℹ Getting There & Away

Beit She'an does not have a proper bus station. Rather, buses stop along Menahem Begin Ave, aka Rte 90. To get to Nazareth and Tel Aviv, change buses in Afula. Travellers heading to Jordan can use the Jordan River/Sheikh Hussein Border Crossing, 8km east of town.

Jerusalem (Egged bus 961; 44NIS, two hours, six daily Sunday to Thursday, five Friday, three Saturday night) Via the Jordan Valley.

Tiberias (Afikim bus 28; 16.50NIS, 30 minutes, 15 daily Sunday to Thursday, six Friday, two Saturday night)

UPPER GALILEE & GOLAN HEIGHTS

הגליל העליון רמת הגולן

الجليل الاولى هضبة الجولان

The rolling, green hills of the Upper Galilee (the area north of Rte 85) and the wild plateaux and peaks of the Golan Heights offer an incredible variety of activities to challenge the body and the soul – and nourish the stomach and the mind. Domestic tourists flock to the area – some are looking for luxurious *tzimmerim* (B&Bs), boutique wineries and gourmet country restaurants, others come in search of superb hiking, cycling and horse riding, white-water rafting and even skiing. Yet other visitors are attracted by the dazzling carpets of spring wildflowers, some of the world's best bird-watching and the spiritual charms of Tsfat, long a hugely important centre of Kabbalah (Jewish mysticism). The entire region, its summits refreshingly cool in summer, is just a short drive from the Christian sites and refreshing beaches of the Sea of Galilee.

Tsfat (Safed)

צפת صفد

04 / POP 32,000

The mountaintop city of Tsfat is an ethereal place to get lost for a day or two. A centre of Kabbalah (Jewish mysticism) since the 16th century, it's home to an otherworldly mixture of Hasidic Jews, artists and devout-but-mellow former hippies, a surprising number of them American immigrants.

On Shabbat (Friday night and Saturday until sundown), commerce completely shuts down. While this may be inconvenient if you're looking for a bite to eat, the lack of traffic creates a meditative, spiritual Sabbath atmosphere through which joyful Hasidic tunes waft from hidden synagogues and unseen dining rooms.

○ Sights

Synagogue Quarter

Tsfat's long-time Jewish neighbourhood spills down the hillside from HaMaginim Sq (Kikar HaMaginim; Defenders' Sq), which dates from 1777. All of Tsfat's historic Kabbalist synagogues are a quick (if often confusing) walk from here.

The main alley in the Synagogue Quarter, called Alkabetz St and Beit Yosef St (Yo-sef Caro St), is lined with joyously colourful art galleries. The tombs of famous Kabbalists are in the cemetery down the slope from the Synagogue Quarter.

Synagogue hours tend to be irregular, especially in winter, and unannounced closings (eg for Monday- and Thursday-morning bar mitzvahs) are common. Visitors should wear modest clothing (no shorts or bare shoulders); kippas/yarmulkes are provided for men (or you can wear any hat). Caretakers appreciate a small donation (5NIS). Synagogues are closed to tourists on Shabbat and Jewish holidays.

Ashkenazi Ari Synagogue   SYNAGOGUE
(Najara St; ⊙ 9.30am-about 7pm Sun-Thu, 9.30am-1pm Fri, closed during prayers) Founded in the 16th century by Sephardic Jews from Greece, this synagogue was destroyed in the 1837 earthquake and rebuilt in the 1850s. It stands on the site where the great Kabbalist Yitzhak Luria (Isaac Luria; 1534–72; often known by the name Ari) used to greet the Sabbath. In the 18th century it came to serve Tsfat's Ashkenazim Hasidic community, hence the synagogue's name (the Jerusalem-born Ari had a Sephardic mother and an Ashkenazi father).

Caro Synagogue   SYNAGOGUE
(04-692 3284, Eyal 050 855 0462; Beit Yosef St; ⊙ 9am-5.30pm Sun-Thu, 9am-3pm or 4pm in winter, 9am-noon Fri) Named (like the street it's on) in honour of the author of the *Shulchan Aruch* (the most authoritative codification of Jewish law), Toledo-born Rabbi Yosef Caro (1488–1575), this synagogue was founded as a house of study in the 1500s but rebuilt after the earthquakes of 1759 and 1837 – and again in 1903. To the right as you face the ark, hanging in one of the windows, you can see the twisted remains of a Katyusha rocket from Lebanon that landed just outside in 2006.

Artists' Quarter

The neighbourhood south of the Ma'alot Olei HaGardom stairway used to be Tsfat's Arab quarter, as you can see from the minarets, but after the 1948 war the area was developed as an Israeli artists' colony. Most of the galleries and studios around the quarter are open to visitors, with many artists is happy to talk about their work and even happier to make a sale.

ISRAEL & THE PALESTINIAN TERRITORIES TSFAT (SAFED)

Upper Galilee & the Golan Heights

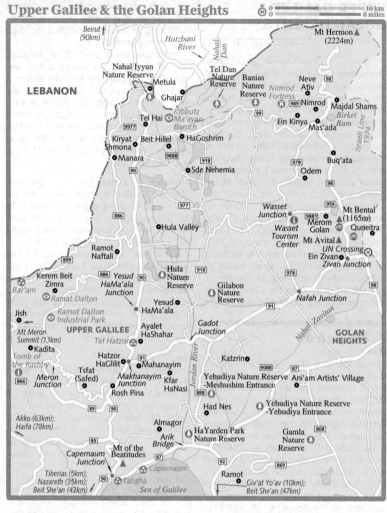

Courses

Tzfat Kabbalah Center KABBALAH
(International Center for Tzfat Kabbalah; 04-682 1771; www.tzfat-kabbalah.org; 1st fl, Fig Tree Courtyard, 28 Alkabetz St, Synagogue Quarter; 9am-6pm Sun-Thu, 9am-1pm Fri) Adherents of all religions, or none at all, are welcome to drop by for an introduction to Jewish mysticism and on-the-spot meditation. Hour-long personalised workshops with Eyal Riess, who lectures around the world on the Tsfat Kabbalah tradition, cost 150NIS to 250NIS. Screens films (18NIS) on Tsfat in Hebrew, English, Spanish and Russian.

Sleeping

The Mt Canaan area (elevation 950m) is about 4.5km northeast of the city centre. It is served by local bus 3 (4.80NIS, 22 minutes, twice an hour until 9pm Sunday to Thursday, to 2.30pm Friday) from the central bus station, or you can take a taxi (25NIS during the day).

Adler Apartments STUDIO APARTMENTS $
(052 344 7766; adler1.4u@gmail.com; office in Adler's Change, 88 Yerushalayim St; d without breakfast 300NIS, Fri night & all day Sat 350NIS, additional bed 100NIS;) Has 10 clean, practical,

simply furnished apartments with kitchenette, in or near the centre of town. If you're arriving on Saturday, easy-going Baruch can arrange key pick-up.

★**Safed Inn**   GUESTHOUSE $$
(Ruckenstein B&B; ☑04-697 1007; www.safedinn.com; 1 Merom Kna'an St, Mt Cannan; dm/s/d/q without breakfast US$29/100/129/158, additional person US$29; ☺reception 8am-8pm; ❀@☺) Opened in 1936, this garden guesthouse has comfortable rooms untouched by interior-design theories, a sauna, an outdoor hot tub (open 8pm to 11pm) and washing machines (15NIS). Riki and Dov get rave reviews for their local knowledge and tasty continental/Israeli breakfasts (30/60NIS). Call ahead if you'll be arriving after 8pm.

Carmel Hotel   HOTEL $$
(☑050 242 1092, 04-692 0053; 8 Ha'Ari St, ie 8 Ya'avetz St; s/d/q without breakfast US$75/100/150; ❀@☺) Thanks to owner Shlomo – who is likely to insist that you try his limoncello – staying here is like having the run of a big, old family house. Some of the 12 simply furnished rooms are romantic and some aren't but they're all clean and practical and some have fantastic views.

✖ Eating

Places selling pizza, felafel and shwarma can be found along Yerushalayim St and, on the edge of the Synagogue Quarter, at HaMaginim Sq.

All of central Tsfat's restaurants close on Shabbat. If you decide not to drive to nearby settlements such as Rosh Pina to dine, you can order ready-made food from several places on Yerushalayim St, with pick-up on Friday in the early afternoon – ask your accommodation for details. Another option is to self-cater at the **Coöp Shop Supermarket** (102 Arlozoroff St; ☺7.30am-9pm Sun-Wed, to 10pm Thu, to 1pm or 2pm Fri).

Lahuhe Original
Yemenite Food Bar   YEMENITE $
(22 Alkabetz St, Synagogue Quarter; mains 25-35NIS; ☺9am-7pm Sun-Thu, 9am to 2hr before sunset Fri) Decked out in a gown and kaftan that Abraham might have worn, Ronen flips pan-fried 'Yemenite pizza' called *lachuch* (35NIS).

★**HaAri 8**   ISRAELI $$
(☑04-692 0033; 8 Ha'Ari St; mains from 58NIS; ☺11am-11pm Sun-Thu, closed Fri, sometimes opens after sundown Sat; ☑) When the mayor has VIP guests, this is where he brings them. Specialities include steak, grilled meats, 'cigars' filled with chopped meat, fish and fresh salads. Vegetarians options include salads, soups and pasta. Has a playroom for kids.

ℹ Orientation

Central Tsfat's main thoroughfare, lined with shops and eateries, is north–south Yerushalayim St (Jerusalem St). West of there, a broad staircase called Ma'alot Olei HaGardom divides the Synagogue Quarter (to the north) from the Artists' Quarter (to the south).

ℹ Getting There & Away

The fastest way to get to Tel Aviv is to take Egged bus 361 to Akko and then hop on a train. The **central bus station** (www.bus.co.il; HaAtzma'ut St), situated about 700m west of the Synagogue Quarter, is linked to the following:

RAFTING THE JORDAN

First-time visitors are often surprised at the Jordan's creek-sized proportions, but first-time rafters are often bowled over – sometimes into the soup – by how powerful its flow can be. Several excellent outfits offer rafting and kayaking down the Jordan (from 90NIS) – competition is as fierce as the current, which means standards of service and safety are high. Discounts of 20% or more are often available on the internet if you book at least 24 hours ahead, and from locally distributed coupon books.

Kfar Blum Kayaks (☑04-690 2616; www.kayaks.co.il; ☺10am-3pm or 4pm, open late Mar or early Apr-Oct or Nov) To get there from Gomeh Junction on Hwy 90, follow the signs to Kfar Blum and go a bit past the kibbutz entrance.

Ma'ayan-HaGoshrim Kayaks (☑077-271 7500; www.kayak.co.il; Kibbutz Ma'ayan Baruch; ☺Apr-Oct) Based up near the Lebanese border at the entrance to Kibbutz Ma'ayan Baruch (a bit north of Rte 99).

Haifa-Mercazit HaMifratz (Nateev Express bus 361; 1¾ hours, twice an hour) Goes via Akko (one hour).

Jerusalem (Nateev Express bus 982; 40NIS; 3¼ hours, eight daily Sunday to Thursday, five Friday, at least three Saturday night)

Tiberias (Afikim bus 450; 16.50NIS, 40 minutes, hourly Sunday to Friday afternoon, one Saturday night)

DEAD SEA ים המלח البحر الميت

The lowest place on the face of the earth, the Dead Sea (elevation 429m below sea level) brings together breathtaking natural beauty and compelling ancient history.

ⓘ Getting There & Around

It's possible, though a bit fiddly, to explore the Dead Sea by public bus. To avoid hanging around wilting under the sun, it's a good idea to plan your itinerary in advance.

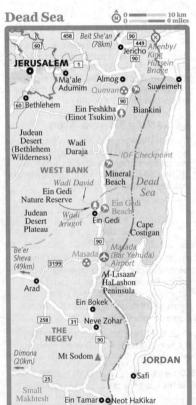

Dead Sea

Egged buses (www.bus.co.il) link sites along Rte 90 (including, from north to south, Qumran, Ein Gedi Nature Reserve, Ein Gedi Beach, Masada and Ein Bokek) with the following. All of the following lines can be used for local travel north and south along Rte 90, eg from Masada to Ein Gedi Beach:

Eilat (bus 444; 49.50NIS to 82NIS, 2½ to four hours, four daily Sunday to Thursday, three on Friday, one to three Saturday afternoon and night)

Jerusalem (buses 421, 444 and 486; 25NIS to 49.50NIS, one to two hours, about hourly 7am to 5pm daily Sunday to Thursday, hourly until about 2pm Friday, at least one Saturday night)

Tel Aviv (bus 421; 46NIS to 49.50NIS, 1¾ to 3¼ hours, departs Tel Aviv's Central (Arlozoroff/Savidor) train station at 8.45am and Neve Zohar at 2pm Sunday to Friday)

Ein Gedi עין גדי عين جدي

♩ 08 / POP 530

Nestled in two dramatic canyons that plunge from the arid moonscape of the Judean Desert to the shores of the Dead Sea, Ein Gedi is one of Israel's most magical desert oases.

The area stretches for 6km along Rte 90, with separate turn-offs and bus stops for (from north to south): Ein Gedi Nature Reserve (this is the turn-off to use for the oases of Wadi David and Wadi Arugot and the Ein Gedi Youth Hostel), Ein Gedi Beach (1km south of the reserve), Kibbutz Ein Gedi (3km south of the reserve) and Ein Gedi Spa (6km south of the reserve).

◉ Sights & Activities

A paradise of dramatic canyons, freshwater springs, waterfalls and lush tropical vegetation (wear your swimsuit), the **Ein Gedi Nature Reserve** (☏08-658 4285; www.parks.org.il) consists of two roughly parallel canyons, **Wadi David** and **Wadi Arugot**, each of which has its own entrance complex and ticket office. The key to a successful hike in the reserve is the excellent colour-coded map-brochure given out when you buy your tickets. Food is not allowed in the reserve.

Situated about midway between the Wadi David and Wadi Arugot ticket offices, a 5th-century-AD **synagogue** (Ein Gedi Antiquities National Park; adult with/without nature reserve 29/15NIS, child 15/7NIS; ⊗8am-4pm or 5pm) sports a superb mosaic floor.

Ein Gedi Beach (Rte 90) `FREE`, hugely popular but steep and unpleasantly stony

QUMRAN

קומראן قمران

World-famous for having hidden the Dead Sea Scrolls (documents written from 200 BC to AD 68 that include the oldest-known manuscripts of the Hebrew Bible), Qumran (☎02-994 2235; www.parks.org.il; Rte 90; adult/child 29/15NIS; ⊙8am-4pm or 5pm Sat-Thu, 8am-3pm or 4pm Fri, last entry 1hr before closing) was the site of a small Essene settlement destroyed by the Romans in AD 68. It's situated 35km east of Jerusalem and 35km north of Ein Gedi. All Jerusalem–Dead Sea buses pass by here.

(bring plastic flip-flops), fulfills the bare requirements of those seeking a Dead Sea float in that it has toilets and changing rooms (2NIS; 6am to 7pm or 8pm) and a 24-hour snack bar. It's situated 1km south (a 20-minute walk) along Rte 90 from the Ein Gedi Nature Reserve turn-off.

🛏 Sleeping & Eating

Don't show up without reservations. There are few dining options in the Ein Gedi area so arrive with picnic supplies and consider having dinner at your hostel.

Ein Gedi Youth Hostel HOSTEL $
(Beit Sarah; ☎02-594 5600, reservations 1-599 510 511; www.iyha.org.il; Rte 90, near Ein Gedi Nature Reserve; dm/s/d 124/301/381NIS, additional adult/child 2-17yr 110/85NIS; ✳@🛜) The sensational setting and contemporary rooms, with four or five beds and brand-new aircon units, make this 68-room hostel madly popular (more rooms are planned). Dinner is 58NIS (67NIS on Friday) and it offers discounts to various area attractions. It's situated 200m up the slope from the Rte 90 turn-off to Ein Gedi Nature Reserve. Reserve well ahead.

Masada

מצדה مسعدة
☎08

After the Romans conquered Jerusalem in AD 70, almost a thousand Jews – men, women and children – made a desperate last stand atop Masada, a desert mesa edged by sheer cliffs. From AD 72 the mesa was surrounded by a ring of military encampments belonging to Rome's feared 10th Legion. As a Roman battering ram was about to breach the walls of their fastness, Masada's defenders chose suicide over enslavement. When Roman soldiers swarmed onto the top of the flat-topped mountain, they were met with silence.

◉ Sights & Activities

The easy way to get to the top of Masada (Metzada; ☎08-658 4208; adult/child 29/15NIS) is to take the cable car (return/one way 76/57NIS, child 43/29NIS; ⊙every 15min 8am-4pm or 5pm Sat-Thu, 8am-3pm or 4pm Fri, last trip up 45min before closing), which whisks you from the Visitors Centre to the top in Swiss comfort in just three minutes.

But if you're up for it, hiking up the Snake Path will give you a much better appreciation of Masada's geography – and a good workout. This famously serpentine footpath winds its way up the mountain's eastern flank, starting from near the Visitors Centre. Walking up takes about 60 minutes; count on spending 30 minutes to come back down. If you'd like to watch sunrise from the summit (highly recommended!), get to the base an hour before the sun comes up, ie sometime between 4.30am (in June) and 5.30am (in December). Before 8am, access is from the separation wall near the youth hostel.

You can also ascend Masada from the west side, via the Roman-built Ramp Trail, which is accessible only from Arad (from the Visitors Centre, it's a 68km drive via Rte 31 and then Rte 3199).

The Masada Museum (Visitors Centre; admission incl audioguide atop Masada 20NIS; ⊙8.30am-4pm or 5pm Sat-Thu, to 3pm or 4pm Fri, last entry 30mn before closing), inside the Visitors Centre, offers a really excellent introduction to Masada's archaeology and history.

🛏 Sleeping

The only place to stay right at Masada is the Masada Guest House (☎02-594 5623/4; www.iyha.org.il; dm/s/d 145/305/424NIS; ⊙reservations 8am-6pm Sun-Fri; ✳@🛜🏊), a 350-bed hostel situated a few hundred metres below the Visitors Centre.

ℹ Getting There & Away

Masada's Visitors Centre, on the eastern side of the mountain, is 21km south of the Ein Gedi Nature Reserve (and 3km west of Rte 90). All intercity buses serving the Dead Sea stop a few hundred metres from the Visitors Centre; bus times are posted at the Visitors Centre ticket windows.

Ein Bokek   עין בוקק   عين بوقيق

Sandwiched between the turquoise waters of the southern Dead Sea and a dramatic tan bluff, Ein Bokek's strip of luxury hotels is the region's main tourist zone. Ein Bokek (also spelled En Boqeq) has the Dead Sea's nicest free beaches.

Unless you camp on the beach (free), there's no budget (or even midrange) accommodation in Ein Bokek's two hotel zones. But if you're up for a splurge there are loads of options – the area's dozen hotels offer crisply air-conditioned facilities, gorgeous swimming pools, state-of-the-art spas and buffet bonanzas. Good options include the 213-bed Hod HaMidbar (☑08-668 8222; www.hodhotel.co.il; d incl half-board US$280-340; ❋ @ ⊛ ☒).

NEGEV   הנגב   النقب

The Negev Desert, often bypassed by travellers hurrying to Eilat, is much more than just sand. Comprising 62% of Israel's land mass, it offers a world of adventure, including superb desert hikes. Perhaps the biggest secret of the Negev is Makhtesh Ramon, a crater-like wilderness that feels like another planet.

Mitzpe Ramon
מצפה רמון   متسبي رمون
☑08 / POP 5500

This small high desert town sits on the edge of Makhtesh Ramon, a dramatic makhtesh (erosion cirque, ie crater) that's home to a huge number of hiking, cycling and horse-riding trails, as well as cliffs offering rappelling opportunities. Despite being in the heart of the desert, Mitzpe Ramon (elevation 900m) is also one of the coldest places in Israel – snow falls here more often than in Jerusalem.

DON'T MISS

JUST ACROSS THE BORDER: PETRA, JORDAN

The stunning Nabataean city of Petra (p327) is an easy (day) trip through the Yitzhak Rabin–Wadi Araba border crossing.

◉ Sights

Israel is a small country but Makhtesh Ramon is one place where it feels vast. Featuring multicoloured sandstone, volcanic rock and fossils, this extraordinary geological marvel is 300m deep, 8km wide and 40km long.

Perched on the makhtesh rim, the Ramon Visitor Centre (☑08-658 8691; mm.ramon@npa.org.il; museum adult/student/child 5-18yr 29/25/15NIS, combined ticket museum & Bio Ramon adult/child 35/18NIS; ⊗8am-4pm Sat-Thu, to 3pm Fri Apr-Sep, to 3pm Sat-Thu, to 2pm Fri Oct-Mar) ✐ has an extremely helpful information desk providing information about the Makhtesh Ramon Nature Reserve, as well as a museum with four exhibition spaces, the most interesting of which is the hall with a 3D exhibition about the creation of the makhtesh and the audiovisual hall where a movie about desert animals is screened. Bookings are essential if you wish to visit the museum.

Located on the northern edge of town, the Spice Route Quarter – a cluster of hangars and warehouses once used by the military – houses artisanal factories, artists' studios, boutique hotels, cafes and a dance workshop, some with a distinct hippy vibe.

⊨ Sleeping

★ Desert Shade   DESERT LODGE $
(☑054 627 7413, 08-658 6229; http://desert-shade.com; dm 80-90NIS, s/d/tr tent 180/250/360NIS; Ⓟ⊛) Right on the edge of the makhtesh, with simply extraordinary views, this place offers accommodation in a Bedouin tent sleeping 20, in smaller dorms or in private 'ecotents'. Showers and toilets are in a clean barrackslike block. Communal areas include an attractive lounge/bar, a guest kitchen and a huge campfire area on the crater's edge. A light breakfast costs 30NIS.

Chez Eugène
BOUTIQUE HOTEL **$$$**

(☑ 052 664 6939, 08-653 9595; www.mitzper-amonhotel.co.il; 8 Har Ardon St, Spice Route Quarter; weekday/weekend d 670/840NIS, ste 840/1090NIS; P ❋ ☎) Mitzpe's only boutique hotel opened in 2010 and its designer-chic rooms are starting to look a bit worn. It's extremely well run, though, and charming manager Naomi Dvora is a font of information about the region. The on-site restaurant is a definite plus.

❶ Getting There & Away

Mitzpe Ramon is 103km south of Be'er Sheva and 150km north of Eilat. Metropoline buses 60 and 64 travel between Mitzpe and Be'er Sheva (17NIS, 1½ hours, frequent) from 5am to 9.30pm; bus 65 is a faster service that only stops on the highway. From Sunday to Thursday, Egged bus 392 travels from Be'er Sheva to Eilat via Mitzpe four times per day (49NIS, three hours).

Eilat
אילת ايلات

☑ 08 / POP 47,500

A thin wedge between Jordan and Egypt at the southern tip of Israel, the glitzy Red Sea resort of Eilat is where Israelis – singles and families – come to relax and have fun all year round. The average daily high is 21°C in January and 40°C in July.

The turquoise-tinted waters of the Red Sea offer snorkelling, diving and swimming opportunities galore, but for many visitors Eilat's real appeal is its proximity to desert mountains and canyons.

◉ Sights & Activities

The Red Sea offers some great diving opportunities and Eilat – despite some reef degradation over the years – has no shortage of dive clubs. Prices vary but average around 250NIS for a guided snorkel or introductory dive and 450NIS for a dive lesson (including equipment hire). Equipment hire costs around 60NIS for snorkel, mask and fins and 170NIS for a wetsuit, tank and breathing equipment. Eilat is a great place for beginners looking to do a PADI scuba course.

★ **Coral Beach Nature Reserve**
DIVE SITE

(Map p261; ☑ 057 855 2381; adult/student/child 35/30/21NIS; ☺9am-5pm Apr-Sep, to 4pm Oct-Mar; ☒15) The beach at this marine reserve overseen by the Israel Nature and Parks Authority is definitely the best on this part of the coast, and the protected waters are

a utopia for snorkellers. A wooden bridge leads from the shore to the beginning of the reef, which is over 1km in length and is home to a diverse array of coral and tropical fish. Underwater trails are marked by buoys, and snorkelling equipment can be hired for 19NIS.

Underwater Observatory Marine Park
AQUARIUM

(Map p261; ☑ 08-636 4200; www.coralworld.co.il; South Beach; adult/child 104/84NIS; ☺8.30am-4pm; ☒15) For as much aquatic action as you can get without entering the water, visit

Eilat Town Centre

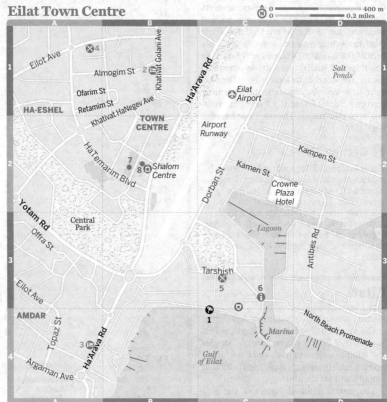

Eilat Town Centre

◎ Sights
1 North Beach C4

🛏 Sleeping
2 Arava Hostel B1
3 Eilat Youth Hostel & Guest
House A4

⊗ Eating
4 Eddie's Hide-A-Way A1
5 Pastory C3

ℹ Information
6 Tourist Information Office C3

ℹ Transport
7 Arkia B2
8 Israir B2

this marine park near Coral Beach. As well as standard aquarium features such as shark and sea-turtle pools, there are two glassed-in observation halls in an oceanarium 12m below the surface of the Red Sea, a children's adventure park where little ones can pet and feed koi, and a theme-park-style 'Journey into the World of Sharks' movie experience. Tickets are valid for three days.

North Beach   BEACH
(Map p262) The main stretch of beach in town, North Beach stretches from the Meridien Hotel past the lagoons and all the way to the Jordanian border. Its backdrop of high-rise hotels and a promenade of bars, cafes and restaurants means that it is perennially crowded and full of action.

🛏 Sleeping

The cost of rooms rises by about 25% at weekends and 50% (or more) during Israeli school holidays and in July/August; reserve ahead during these times.

Five-star chain hotels are plentiful around the lagoons at North Beach and along the road to Taba. Most have bland decor, fixed-price buffets and large pool areas. All are geared towards families and can be noisy.

Camping is illegal on most of Eilat's beaches. Exceptions are the areas east of Herod's Beach, towards the Jordanian border.

Arava Hostel
HOSTEL $

(Map p262; ☎08-637 4687; www.a55.co.il; 106 Almogim St; dm/s/d 70/200/220NIS; P ❄ @ ⬤) The only Eilat hostel with an authentic backpacker vibe, the Arava wouldn't win any awards for its dated rooms and dark, cramped dorms or for its location far from the beach. There are compensations, though: a front garden perfect for sunset beers, communal kitchen, laundry (15NIS per load) and free parking. Internet costs 16NIS per hour; wi-fi is free.

Eilat Youth Hostel & Guest House
HOSTEL $$

(Map p262; ☎02-594 5605; www.iyha.org.il; 7 Ha-Arava Rd; dm/s/d 130/292/400NIS; P ❄ @ ⬤) If it weren't for the ubiquitous groups of noisy schoolkids staying here, this huge hostel with its expansive front balcony overlooking the Gulf of Eilat would be one of our top accommodation picks. Even with the school-group factor in play, it's an extremely attractive option due to its modern, clean and comfortable rooms and dorms. Free parking and wi-fi; internet 1NIS per minute.

✗ Eating

Many of Eilat's eating options are spread along the hotel-packed North Beach promenade, with cheap eats in the New Tourism Centre (Merkaz Tayarut Chadash), 500m to the west.

★ Pastory
ITALIAN $$

(Map p262; ☎08-634 5111; 7 Tarshish St; pizza 48-68NIS, pasta 58-96NIS, mains 72-168NIS; ⊗1-11pm) *Mamma mia!* Who would have thought that an authentic Italian-style trattoria serving *molto delizioso* cuisine would be found in a North Beach back street? This family-friendly place behind the Leonardo Plaza Hotel serves antipasti platters packed with flavourful morsels, al dente pasta with rustic sauces, piping-hot pizza with quality toppings and an irresistible array of homemade desserts and gelato. Go.

Eddie's Hide-A-Way
INTERNATIONAL $$$

(Map p262; ☎08-637 1137; www.eddieshide-away.rest-e.co.il; 68 Aghmonim St; mains 46-125NIS; ⊗6-11.30pm Mon-Fri, 2-11.30pm Sat) The surrounds and menu have hardly changed since this ramshackle place opened back in 1979, so it's a testament to Eddie's abilities as a host that it's been packed most nights since. The food is hit-and-miss, but you're sure to be happy with a steak and a bottle from the unexpectedly impressive wine list. Enter off Eilot Ave.

▼ Drinking & Nightlife

The drinking scene in Eilat is largely confined to raucous pubs in the North Beach precinct. The club scene is healthy, but venues have short lifespans and hot spots change every season – staff at your hotel or at the tourist office on North Beach Promenade will be able to give you the low-down.

ⓘ Information

To change money, head to one of the many exchange bureaux in the old commercial centre off HaTmarim Blvd.

Tourist Information Office (Map p262; ☎08-630 9111; eilatinfo@tourism.gov.il; Bridge House, North Beach Promenade; ⊗8.30am-5pm Sun-Thu, 8am-1pm Fri) This extremely helpful office answers questions, supplies free maps and brochures and sells secondhand English, French and German books.

Tourist Police (Map p262; North Beach Promenade; ⊗hours vary) This station is near the tourist information office at North Beach.

Yoseftal Hospital (Map p261; ☎08-635 8015; cnr Yotam Rd & Argaman Ave; ⊗24hr emergency dept)

ⓘ Getting There & Away

The Yitzhak Rabin–Wadi Araba border crossing between Israel and Jordan is about 5km northeast of Eilat, while the Taba border crossing with Egypt is about 8.5km southwest of town.

AIR

Both **Arkia** (Map p262; ☎08-638 4888; www.arkia.com; Red Canyon Mall) and **Israir** (Map p262; ☎1 700 505 777; www.israirairlines.com; Shalom Centre) fly several times daily between Eilat's municipal **airport** (Map p262; ☎1 700 705 022; www.iaa.gov.il/Rashat/en-US/Airports/Eilat) – right in the heart of town – and Tel Aviv's Sde Dov and Ben-Gurion airports (from US$25, 35 minutes).

BUS

It's a good idea to reserve ahead for travel to/from Eilat via www.egged.co.il or by calling ⌨2800. Buses do not run from Friday afternoon until Saturday afternoon. There are no direct buses from the Taba border crossing to Cairo.

Jerusalem (Egged bus 444; 82NIS, five hours, three or four daily Sunday to Friday, two on Saturday night) Via the Dead Sea, including Ein Gedi (49.50NIS, three hours)

Mitzpe Ramon (Egged bus 392; 49NIS, 2¼ hours, four a day)

Tel Aviv-Central Bus Station (Egged buses 393, 394 or 790; 82NIS, five hours, departures every 90 minutes or two hours from 5am to 7pm, overnight service at 1am)

ⓘ Getting Around

Bus 15 (bus 16 when northbound) links the central bus station with Coral Beach (4.90NIS, 30 minutes) and the Taba border crossing every hour from 8am to 9pm Sunday to Thursday, 8am to 3pm Friday and 9am to 7pm Saturday. A taxi from the town centre to the border crossing costs around NIS60.

To reach the Yitzhak Rabin–Wadi Araba border crossing to Jordan, you'll have to take a taxi (45NIS).

WEST BANK

الضفة الغربية   הגדה המערבית

'Welcome' is a word you hear a lot in the West Bank. Whether it's shouted by a street trader in a bustling souq, expressed with a smile over a plate of felafel or roared from a taxi over booming Arabic music, Palestinians are forever wanting to make tourists feel appreciated.

This might surprise visitors, given the popular conception of the West Bank as a poster child for strife, violence and failed peace agreements. And it is true that dirt-poor refugee camps, barbed-wire checkpoints and the towering separation barrier are rarely far from the eye. But there is another Palestine too: one of bustling cities and chaotic souqs, rolling hills and traditional villages, olives groves and chalky desertscapes where biblical sites abound.

Perhaps most appealing is the chance to meet Palestinians who remain hopeful of peace and stability even under untold pressures. The West Bank may not be the easiest place in which to travel – but the effort is richly rewarded.

Ramallah & Al-Bireh

رام الله البيرة   רמאללה אל בירה

⌨02 / POP 65,000

Ramallah and Al-Bireh were once separate villages, but now make up one urban conglomerate. Though Al-Bireh's history can be traced back to the Canaanites, Ramallah was only settled in by Christians in the 1500s, and these days is a bustling, cosmopolitan city, with a thriving art scene and vibrant nightlife.

Ramallah is home to numerous restaurants, cafes and bars, English is widely spoken and transport links are superb. As such, it makes an excellent base for further forays into the West Bank.

◎ Sights

Muqata'a   HISTORIC BUILDING
(Al-Itha'a St; ⊙tomb 9am-9pm daily) Those interested in modern history might want to stop at the now-rebuilt Muqata'a, Yasser Arafat's large presidential compound, where he was based during the last days of the Second Intifada. He was evacuated from his base in 2004 while under Israeli siege and later died in a Paris hospital. In 2014 his body was briefly exhumed for tests after speculation that he had been poisoned. Arafat's enormous **cubicle tomb** is guarded by soldiers and adorned with wreaths.

Al-Kamandjati   CONCERT HALL
(⌨02-297 3101; www.alkamandjati.com; Old City) This small conservatory, which features an ancient arch with an edgy, modern copper entryway, offers intimate concerts and recitals.

🛏 Sleeping

★ Area D Hostel   HOSTEL $
(⌨056 934 9042; http://ramallahhostel.com; Vegetable Market St; dm 70NIS, d 160-200NIS) With cosy, spotless dorms and a number of private rooms, Area D makes a great hub for tourists – not least because its position on the top floor of Ramallah's service-taxi garage means you can get a ride to most parts of the West Bank without having to leave the building. Staff are helpful, the location is fantastic and the open-plan lounge is a lovely place to relax.

Royal Court Suites Hotel   HOTEL $$
(⌨02-296 4040; www.rcshotel.com; Jaffa St; s/d/ste 305/355/445NIS; ❋@☎) This is a reliable

midrange option 15 minutes' walk downhill from the centre of town. Many of the rooms come with kitchen facilities and balconies and all have wi-fi and breakfast. The suites are enormous. Consider asking for a room at the back of the hotel where it is much quieter.

Mövenpick Ramallah HOTEL $$$
(☎02-298 5888; www.moevenpick-hotels.com/en/middle-east; Al Masyoun; s/d US$180/200) One of only a handful of Western-branded hotels in the West Bank, the Mövenpick has become a hub for Palestine's great and good – as evidenced by the flashy cars that pull up outside its imposing glass-fronted lobby. It has huge rooms, excellent staff and great facilities, including a gym and pool (summer only). Book online for better rates.

✕ Eating

★La Vie Cafe RESTAURANT, BAR $$
(☎02-296 4115; info@lavie-cafe.com; Castel St; mains 35-70NIS; ⊙10am-midnight Sat-Thu, 4pm-midnight Fri) Tucked away on a quiet street just 10 minutes' walk from Al-Manara, this place has a diverse menu of pasta, pizza and sandwiches, with much of its produce grown in owners Saleh and Morgan's roof garden. On weekends, La Vie is a popular nightspot, serving a range of beers, wines and cocktails.

Pronto Resto-Café ITALIAN $$
(Al-Muntazah; mains 45-75NIS; ⊙7am-11pm) This dark and cosy little trattoria is a popular spot for musicians, film-makers, professionals and peacemakers. The pizzas are top notch and a handful of pasta options make it the only place for real Italian food in Ramallah. Pronto prides itself on local ingredients, from the fish (caught in Jaffa) to the wine (from Bethlehem).

Zamn CAFE $$
(Al-Tireh; coffee from 10NIS, mains 35-60NIS; ⊙7am-11pm; 🐸) The hippest spot in Ramallah and meeting ground for reporters and NGO workers, Zamn is a fun place for a morning croissant and cuppa or a lunchtime sandwich. Walk down Dar Ibrahim and bear right at the roundabout.

🍷 Drinking & Nightlife

★Al-Snobar CLUB
(Pine; ☎02-296 5571; www.al-snowbar.com; ⊙May-Oct) This entertainment complex has a flashy restaurant, a swimming pool and

TAYBEH تاييبه الطيبة

Taybeh has two claims to fame: it's the place where tradition holds that Jesus stayed with his disciples in his final hours (John 11:54); and it produces the Palestinian Territories' only beer, which you can sample yourself at the **Taybeh Beer Brewery** (☎02-289 8868; www.taybehbeer.net). Call to arrange a tour, or drop by for its annual two-day **Oktoberfest**, a must-visit if you are anywhere in the region. Taybeh is around 15km from Ramallah, on a remote and very picturesque hillside.

one of the hottest nightclubs in the city. Note that it's only open in high season. It's located 2km northwest of Al-Manara Sq. Take a taxi, everyone knows it.

Sangria's BAR
(☎02-295 6808; Jaffa Rd, Al-Muntazah; ⊙noon-midnight; 🐸) A veteran Ramallah hang-out, Sangria's beer garden is the place to be on Thursday and Saturday nights. The Mexican and international menu is ambitious, but you are here for the drinks menu – arguably one of the best in the city, with everything from local Taybeh beer (15NIS) to a range of cocktails (35NIS to 40NIS) to sangria, of course, at 80NIS a litre.

☆ Entertainment

Al-Kasaba Theater & Cinematheque CINEMA
(☎02-296 5292; www.alkasaba.org; Al-Manara) A magnet for artists, musicians and film and theatre buffs. It's well worth catching a performance or screening here while you're in town.

Khalil Sakakini Centre CULTURAL CENTRE
(☎02-298 7374; www.sakakini.org; Al-Muntazah) Hosts art exhibitions by the locally and internationally renowned, along with a whole host of other cultural pursuits. Check the website for upcoming events.

ℹ Getting There & Around

From the old Arab bus station in East Jerusalem take bus 18 (30 minutes) all the way to Ramallah, from 6am until 9pm (7pm in winter). After this you can take a service taxi from Ramallah to Qalandia checkpoint and then a taxi to Jerusalem.

JEWISH SETTLEMENTS

Israeli Jewish colonies set up in the Palestinian Territories are most often referred to as 'settlements'. Hundreds of thousands of Israeli settlers currently live in more than 100 Jewish settlements in the West Bank.

Settlements range in size from a collection of caravans on a remote hilltop to large urban areas. There are a variety of reasons cited by settlers for why they live on the West Bank: most commonly, cheaper housing prices than in Israel and, among the religious, the fulfilment of biblical prophecy and an extension of the will of God.

Under most interpretations of international law, which forbids the transfer of civilians to land under military occupation, all Israeli settlements on the West Bank and in East Jerusalem are illegal. The Israeli right disputes this interpretation of international law. Key complaints against Jewish settlements are that they often occupy private Palestinian land (as opposed to state-owned land), divert precious water resources from surrounding Palestinian cities, towns and villages, and, most significantly, fragment the territory of the West Bank, making the establishment of a coherent, contiguous and viable Palestinian state impossible. Violent clashes between Palestinians, settlers and Israeli soldiers are common.

The USA and EU have declared the settlements an obstacle to peace but Israeli Prime Minister Binyamin Netanyahu's right-wing coalition government has continued to construct housing in West Bank settlements and East Jerusalem, announcing plans throughout 2014 to build thousands of new settlement units.

To find out more, visit the websites of the Palestinian NGO Al-Haq (alhaq.mits.ps) or left-wing Israeli organisation B'Tselem (www.btselem.org). For a settler's perspective, the settlement of Gush Etzion, near Bethlehem, has a visitor centre and museum (www.gush-etzion.org.il).

On exiting the West Bank you will need to disembark at Qalandia to show your passport and return to the bus on the other side of the checkpoint, so hold onto your bus ticket.

Everything within the Ramallah area is 10 minutes or less by private taxi and should cost 10NIS to 20NIS.

The main bus station has services to Nablus and Hebron, and the service-taxi parking garage across the road (below Area D Hostel) has servees to almost everywhere else.

Jericho & Around   יריחו اریحا

📍 02 / POP 20,300

Jericho is said to be one of the world's oldest continuously inhabited cities and this is no idle boast – archaeological evidence traces the city's history back over 10,000 years.

The city has modernised somewhat since the Canaanite period, but not much. Small-scale farming still makes up a significant portion of the local economy, although tourism is making inroads. Most visitors just stay long enough to ascend the Mount of Temptation and marvel at the archaeological remains of Tel al-Sultan (Ancient Jericho).

Sights

The Tree of Zacchaeus, on Ein as-Sultan St, is said to be the very same sycamore that Zacchaeus, a wealthy publican, climbed 2000 years ago for a better view of the preaching Jesus (Luke 19:1–10).

The steep canyon of Wadi Qelt, situated between Jerusalem and Jericho, is a naturalist's treat, where you'll find a waterfall, wildlife and the remains of Roman-era aqueducts along the way. Among several monasteries established in this area, you'll find the spectacular 5th-century St George's Monastery blending into a rock face. Further towards Jericho and off the main road is Nabi Musa, a popular pilgrimage for Muslim visitors.

Tel al-Sultan (Ancient Jericho)   RUIN

(adult/child 10/5NIS; ⏰8am-5pm) It is impossible not feel a sense of history strolling around the mounds and ruins at Tel al-Sultan, where remains of dwellings and fortifications dating back some 10,000 years have been unearthed. You will see what look like sand dunes and stairways (the oldest-known stairways in the world); underneath, the layers of civilisation go back even further into the mists of history.

Mount of Temptation & Monastery of the Qurantul   RELIGIOUS SITE

(round trip 55NIS; ⊘8am-9pm) It was on the Mount of Temptation where, so we're told, Jesus resisted Satan after his 40-day fast in the desert. The Monastery of the Qurantul marks the spot where the Devil urged Jesus to make a loaf of bread out of a stone (Matthew 4:1–11). The monastery is an incredible feat of engineering, cut into the cliff face with dramatic views over the Dead Sea to Jordan.

Opening times for the monastery are sporadic but as with all tourist attractions in Palestine it is best to go early – or at least a couple of hours before sunset. Note that the caretaker may lock the door if he is showing big groups around, so it is worth hanging around a few minutes if you find it closed.

Cable cars (www.jericho-cablecar.com; 60NIS; ⊘8am-8pm) stop just before the monastery, and even the short climb up the stairs to the front gate can be a struggle in the midday heat. They sometimes stop running without notice, making for a sweaty 400m climb. The juice sellers and a couple of restaurants provide a good spot to catch your breath.

Hisham's Palace   RUIN

(Khirbet al-Mafjar; admission 10NIS; ⊘8am-6pm) A short drive north of Tel al-Sultan, this is a spot not to be missed. The sprawling winter hunting retreat of Caliph Hisham Ibn Abd al-Malik must have been magnificent on its creation in the 8th century, with its baths, mosaic floors and pillars – so much so that archaelogists have labelled it the 'Versaille of the Middle East'. It was not fated to last, however – it was destroyed by an earthquake soon after its creation.

🛏 Sleeping

★Sami Youth Hostel   GUESTHOUSE $

(✆02-232 4220; eyad_alalem@live.com; r 120NIS; 🖧) The best budget option in Jericho, this guesthouse is nestled deep in the ramshackle refugee camp, with a dozen private rooms in a clean, quiet and enigmatically furnished two-storey hostel. Coming into Jericho from Hwy 90, take a left at the first roundabout, then continue straight; the guesthouse will be on your right. Failing that, ask any local for 'Hotel Sami' and they will point the way.

Oasis Hotel   HOTEL $$$

(✆02-231 1200; www.intercontinental.com; d US$120-40, ste US$200; 🕸@🖧🏊) Until 2014 this cavernous hotel was the Intercontinental Jericho, and the logo is still visible on the side of the building, one of the tallest in the city. Much of the decor has remained the same, and rooms are clean and modern, with baths and TVs. The hotel also has two pools, a bar and helpful staff.

🍴 Eating

★Al Essawe   RESTAURANT $

(Main Sq; mains 15-45NIS; ⊘6am-11pm daily) On a corner overlooking Jericho's main square, Al Essawe's lovely 2nd-floor terrace is an excellent place to watch the world go by. The owner speaks English and the restaurant serves the usual Arabic fare, kebabs, felafel and mezze. Al Essawe's speciality is barbequed chicken in lemon sauce. Coffee and sheesha are served on the roof terrace.

Abu Omar   MIDDLE EASTERN $

(Ein al-Sultan St; mains 20-50NIS; ⊘6am-midnight) Next to the main square, this local favourite serves everything from felafel in pita (4NIS) to a half-chicken dinner for two people (50NIS).

ℹ Information

Staff at the new tourist-information centre in Jericho's main square are helpful and speak fluent English. It is open daily.

ℹ Getting There & Away

There are no direct *servees* from Jerusalem to Jericho. A private taxi ride from Jerusalem to Jericho (or vice versa) should cost around 400NIS.

The best way to reach Jericho via public transport is from Ramallah, where buses leave regularly throughout the day.

Remember to bring a passport; you'll need to show it on the way back to Jerusalem.

Bethlehem   בית לחם بيت لحم

✆02 / POP 27,800

Most visitors come to Bethlehem with a preconceived image – a small stone village, a manger and shepherds in their fields – thanks to memories of a childhood nativity, perhaps, or years of scenic Christmas cards.

The reality is actually quite different. Bethlehem positively hums with activity, its winding streets congested with traffic and its main square filled with snap-happy

ⓘ CHECKPOINTS

Checkpoints (in Hebrew, *machsomim*) control the flow of travellers between the West Bank and Israel. There are also some checkpoints inside the West Bank. Most checkpoints are run by the Israel Defense Forces (IDF), although some have been outsourced to private contractors. Operating hours of checkpoints vary and they range in size from small pedestrian-only checkpoints to larger ones that accommodate vehicles and resemble an international border crossing.

Foreign-passport holders are allowed to travel through IDF checkpoints and do not need any special documentation – just show your passport and visa and put your bags through an X-ray machine. Try to avoid passing through a checkpoint in the early morning (7am to 9am) or on Muslim or Jewish holidays due to long lines.

For more details on the conditions at individual checkpoints, visit the website of the left-wing Israeli group Machsom Watch (www.machsomwatch.org).

The following are some of the main checkpoints into and out of the West Bank:

Abu Dis This checkpoint connects East Jerusalem to Abu Dis, from where travellers can connect to Jericho.

Bethlehem 300 Located south of Jerusalem at the entrance to Rachel's Tomb.

Bethlehem (highway) You will go through this checkpoint if you take bus 21 from Bethlehem.

Jalameh Located 10km south of Afula, this checkpoint is one of the best in terms of ease and accessibility.

Qalandia Between Jerusalem and Ramallah.

---

tourists scrambling to keep up with their guides.

Churches now cover many of the holy sites but there is plenty to see and do, even for the nonreligious. There's a lively Old City and bazaar, plus sites around town including the incredible Herodium. At the numerous cultural centres you can critique local art, watch performances and talk politics.

◉ Sights

Manger Square & Old City HISTORIC SITE
The narrow limestone streets and exotic storefronts are a scene from another age, particularly Pope Paul VI St, Star St and the narrow alleys connecting the two. Visit on a Sunday to experience some church services. Most in attendance will be Palestinians and resident monks and nuns, but visitors are welcome to attend or stop in for a few moments of contemplation.

Spend a Sunday morning dropping discreetly in and out of the sights. Set out early to the 19th-century Lutheran Christmas Church (Pope Paul VI St, Madbasseh Sq) to experience a Lutheran service. Then head towards Manger Sq to the more modern St Mary's Syrian Orthodox Church (⊙9am-5pm), where Sunday Mass is held in Syriac. Descend the stairs to Manger Sq and enter the Church of the Nativity to find a Greek Orthodox service in session. Tiptoe through the cloisters around to the left and through a passage to St Catherine's Church for a Roman Catholic Mass.

And finally, don't miss a visit to the little souq, with its range of fruit and vegetables, meat and fish, junk, shoes and some mighty tasty snacks. Known to locals as the Green Market, the souq was established in 1929.

Church of the Nativity CHURCH
(⊙6.30am-7.30pm spring-autumn, to 6pm winter) Though many have argued over whether X (or, in this case, a star) really does mark the spot, the Church of the Nativity nevertheless makes an imposing marker for the birthplace of Jesus. Also called the Basilica of the Nativity, it's the oldest continuously operating church, commissioned in 326 AD by Emperor Constantine. To really get the most out of a visit, negotiate a price for a tour from one of the handful of tour guides you'll find milling outside (around 50NIS per hour is a decent price): they know all the nooks and crannies intimately, and may even introduce you to some of the resident priests and monks.

St Catherine's Church CHURCH
Midnight Mass at this pink-toned church, next door to the Church of the Nativity, is

broadcast across the world on Christmas Eve, but there's nothing like being there in person for an atmospheric – if rather lengthy – Christmas experience. Access the church via the Church of the Nativity to first wander through the Crusader-era Franciscan cloister with a statue of St Jerome.

Milk Grotto Chapel CHURCH
(Milk Grotto St; ⊙8am-6pm summer, to 5pm winter) A short walk from Manger Sq is the lesser-known Milk Grotto Chapel. The white rock inside this stony chapel is said to bring milk to a mother's bosom and enhance fertility in women who swallow a morsel of the chalky substance. Legend has it that Mary and Joseph stopped here to feed the baby during their flight to Egypt; a drop of milk touched the red rock, turning it white.

Old Bethlehem Museum MUSEUM
(☑02-274 2589; www.arabwomenunion.org; Star St; admission 8NIS; ⊙8am-noon Mon-Sat & 2-5pm Mon-Wed, Fri & Sat) This museum is located in a typical Palestinian home of the 19th century. See native costumes, peruse the collection of early-20th-century photos of Palestine, and purchase embroidery produced by the Bethlehem Arab Women's Union, at the embroidery centre upstairs.

🛏 Sleeping

Since most hotels in Bethlehem cater to a pilgrim crowd, expect to pay 30% to 50% more at Christmas or Easter time, and book your room well in advance.

Bethlehem Youth Hostel HOSTEL $
(☑02-274 8466, 059 964 6146; byh@ejepal.org; Anatreh St; dm 70NIS; @🕸) Once a backpacker staple in Bethlehem, this hostel has moved

to a smaller building next door and now has just one dorm for men and one for women. The former, bizarrely, looks over a prison yard, where armed guards watch inmates playing ping pong. Still, staff are helpful and it is great value.

Dar Annadwa GUESTHOUSE $$
(Abu Gubran; ☑02-277 0047; www.diyar.ps; 109 Pope Paul VI St, Old City; s/d US$66/92; 🕸) Students from the International Center's art school provide decor in this very comfortable, Lutheran-sponsored, boutique guesthouse with all the amenities. Each of its 13 tasteful rooms is named after a Palestinian village. Book ahead because reception is often closed.

★Casanova Orient Palace HOTEL $$
(☑02-274 3980; www.casanovapalace.com; s/d/tr from US$45/60/90; @🕸) The closest you'll get to sleeping in the manger itself, this perennially popular place offers reasonable rooms and a buzzing atmosphere, particularly around Christmas. The lobby, just off Manger Sq next to the Church of the Nativity, is as much a gathering place for transient tourists and devout dignitaries as it is for hotel guests. The hotel has two sections: a nicer wing closer to the square and a more basic wing around the corner (next to the church).

Arab Women's Union GUESTHOUSE $$
(☑02-277 5857; www.elbeit.org; Beit Sahour; s/d/tr US$30/60/80; @) 🌿 The women who run this guesthouse in beautiful Beit Sahour recycle paper, run community programs and produce olive-wood artefacts. The rooms are clean and modern although it is a little out of the way.

ISRAEL'S SEPARATION WALL

From 1967 until the Second Intifada (2000–05), most Palestinians were still able to cross into Israel from the West Bank with relative ease. But after scores of suicide bombers crossed over from the West Bank, killing hundreds of Israeli civilians, the government built a huge separation barrier.

Except in Jerusalem, most of the fence matches the Green Line (the 1949 armistice between Israel and Jordan) – but only roughly. The fence, or wall, is extremely controversial. Quite a few sections loop around Jewish settlements, separating Palestinians from their communities and businesses. Many Palestinians call it the 'Apartheid Wall' and see it as part of a concerted campaign to grab land wherever possible. Israel – where the barrier is seen as a security success – says that the route of the fence can always be modified, eg if there is a final-status accord on borders.

Demonstrations are periodically held in parts of the West Bank where the wall cuts through villages.

HEBRON (AL-KHALIL) & THE TOMB OF THE PATRIARCHS

For Jews, Christians and Muslims alike, Hebron (Al-Khalil in Arabic) is considered the cradle of organised religion. Sadly, the common thread of beliefs has done little to improve relations between the major monotheistic religions, and Hebron has long been the location of religious violence. Jewish settlements within the city centre have created palpable tension and the city remains fairly unstable.

The focal point of Hebron for most visitors is **Ibrahimi Mosque/Tomb of the Patriarchs** (☉8am-4pm Sun-Thu, except during prayers), or Cave of Machpelah, the collective tomb of Abraham, Isaac and Jacob, along with their wives (except Rachel). Be aware of the strict security and separate prayer spaces for Jews and Muslims.

When entering the mosque, you will be asked to remove your shoes, and women will be handed a head covering.

✖ Eating

For fast food, stroll along Manger St or head up to the small souq just off Pope Paul VI St. Here you'll find fist-size felafel and sizzling shwarmas. Many of the restaurants and midrange hotels in Bethlehem serve alcohol.

★ **Afteem**   MIDDLE EASTERN **$**
(Manger Sq; felafel 6NIS, hummus from 15NIS) A Bethlehem institution for decades. Top-notch hummus and *masabacha* (warm hummus with whole chickpeas) are dispensed to locals' delight, just down the ramp from Manger Sq. For something a little different, go for a delectable bowl of *fatteh* – a sort of soupy hummus topping submerged pieces of pita and finished with roasted pine nuts.

Square   MIDDLE EASTERN, WESTERN **$**
(Manger Sq; mains from 35NIS; ☉9am-midnight; 🔊) A swish lounge-style place right in the heart of Bethlehem, this makes a great respite from a long walking tour around the city. Sip a cappuccino or order a light lunch (salads and pastas) in the basement dining room. Also available are beers and wines,

cocktails and sheesha, best enjoyed on the terrace overlooking the square.

Peace Center Restaurant   SANDWICHES, ITALIAN **$**
(Manger Sq; mains 20-45NIS; ☉9am-6pm Mon-Sat) This spacious, central spot is great for a light snack or something more refined such as Mediterranean salmon or *shish tawooq* (chicken skewers). The restaurant has daily specials, including traditional Palestinian dishes such as *mansaf,* a joint of meat served on rice with fatty broth. Staff are friendly and helpful.

❶ Information

Peace Center (☎02-276 6677; ☉8am-3pm Mon-Thu & Sat) This information desk gives away city maps and provides helpful hints on accommodation and transport. It often holds art and photography exhibitions.

❶ Getting There & Away

Bus 21 from Jerusalem to Bethlehem (30 minutes) departs every 15 minutes between 6am and 9pm (until 6.30pm in winter) from the Damascus Gate bus station. Alternatively, take bus 24 from Jerusalem to the main Bethlehem checkpoint, from where there are taxis into Bethlehem.

The best way to get from Bethlehem to the sites that surround it is by taxi. Visits to multiple sites can be arranged for a fixed price (around 50NIS an hour is standard). Drivers congregate outside Checkpoint 300, Manger Sq or the 21 bus stop to Jerusalem.

Around Bethlehem

The easiest way to visit the sights around Bethlehem is to hire a taxi for a half or whole day.

◎ Sights

Situated at Beit Sahour, around 1km east of Bethlehem, **Shepherds' Fields** is where the shepherds who visited Jesus in his manger are said to have tended their flocks. It's a pleasant stroll up here to a little old church, a favourite photo-op destination for local brides. It's accessible by private taxi from Bethlehem (15NIS), or catch Beit Sahour-bound bus 47 (2NIS) from Shepherd's St, just below Manger Sq.

Herodium   PALACE
(adult/child 27/14NIS; ☉8am-5pm Apr-Sep, to 4pm Oct-Mar) King Herod's spectacular

fortress-palace, Herodium, built between 23 and 15 BC, was known through the centuries to Arab inhabitants as the Mountain of Paradise.

Even from a distance, you won't miss the site: it rises from the Judean Desert like a flat-topped caricature of a volcano (the top is actually an extension of the natural hill, hollowed out to hold Herod's palace), 9km south of Beit Sahour.

To get here, take a private taxi from Bethlehem (around 50NIS per hour), and negotiate at least an hour's waiting time. Try to avoid Fridays, when Herodium fills with tour buses from Israel.

Mar Saba Monastery   MONASTERY
(⊘ 8am-sunset Sat-Tue & Thu) A must-see on any journey through the Holy Land is Mar Saba Monastery, a bleak and beautiful 20km drive east of Bethlehem (beyond Beit Sahour). This phenomenal cliff-clinging copper-domed hermitage, founded in 439 AD, is best seen from the opposite slope, but men can exercise their privilege by going inside and getting a tour with one of the 15 monks still in residence. Women can get a bird's-eye view from the Women's Tower, a rather squat structure opposite the monastery itself.

Nablus   שכם نابلس

📱 09 / POP 126,000

Situated in and around a lush spring valley between Mt Gerizim (Jarzim in Arabic) and arid Mt Ebal, Nablus (known as Shechem in Hebrew) is a bustling, exciting and vibrant metropolis, with an Old City to rival Jerusalem's – not least because of the lack of tour groups clogging its narrow alleyways.

◎ Sights & Activities

Al-Qasaba   NEIGHBOURHOOD
The focal point for visitors to Nablus is Al-Qasaba (Casbah or Old City), where you'll find an Ottoman-era rabbit warren of shops, stalls and pastry stands, spice sacks and vegetable mounds. Amid the clamour, you'll find dozens of contemplative mosques, including the **Al-Kebir Mosque** (Great Mosque), which is built on the site of an earlier Crusader church and Byzantine and Roman basilicas. Bits and pieces of its earlier incarnations have survived; look out for the huge columns and capitals, traces of the Byzantine structure.

Jacob's Well   CHURCH
(donations appreciated; ⊘ 8am-noon & 2-4pm) Near the entrance to Balata (population 20,000), the largest United Nations Relief

ISRAEL & THE PALESTINIAN TERRITORIES NABLUS

Around Bethlehem, Ramallah & Jericho

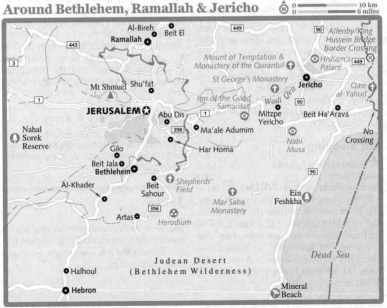

MT GERIZIM

One of the world's last communities of Samaritans, the ancient religion closely related to Judaism, lives on Mt Gerizim, one of the hills that overlooks Nablus. Learn more about them at the excellent Samaritan Museum (☑02-237 0249; samaritans-mu@hotmail.com; admission 15NIS; ⊘9am-3pm Sun-Fri, to 1pm Sat) and nearby Good Samaritan Center (⊘9am-4pm Sun-Fri, to 1pm Sat) FREE before walking the ruins of the Platform (adult/student 22/19NIS; ⊘9am-sunset daily) – the site of the ruined Samaritan Temple – built on land which the faithful believe was the first created by God. From Nablus, Mt Gerizim can be reached by taxi in around 10 minutes (50ils, return).

and Works Agency refugee camp in the West Bank, you'll find the spot where Christians believe a Samaritan woman offered Jesus a drink of water, and that he then revealed to her that he was the Messiah (John 4:13–14).

A Byzantine church destroyed in the Samaritan revolt of 529 CE was replaced by a Crusader church, which itself fell into ruins in the Middle Ages. The current church, St Photina the Samaritan, was built in the 1860s by the Greek Orthodox Patriarchate.

Hammam Al Shifa   BATHHOUSE

(35NIS; ⊘9am-11pm daily, Thu women-only) This can be hard to find but locals will point the way. Hand over your valuables before changing into a towel (or swimming costume, if you have one). The hammam has a hot room – a heated platform for lying on – a sauna and steam room. Massages (NIS10) are not for the faint-hearted.

🛏 Sleeping

★**International Friends Guesthouse**   HOTEL $

(www.guesthouse.ps; dm/d 85/200NIS; 🛜) Set in a leafy garden, this is a clean, smart hostel just 10 minutes' walk from the walls of the Old City. Manager Jihad is a local lad who returned from overseas a few years ago and is a wealth of knowledge on Nablus. The hostel has four large dorms and one double room. It is often booked by groups so be sure to call ahead.

Al-Yasmeen Hotel   HOTEL $$

(☑02-233 3555; www.alyasmeen.com; s/d/tr US$70/80/100; ✳🛜) Tucked away in the heart of the bustling Old City, this place has long been the preferred choice for journalists, diplomats and NGO types. Helpful and polite staff, clean rooms and traditional architecture make it a great midrange choice in the city. It is worth splashing out the extra US$10 for a double room.

🍴 Eating

The Nablus speciality is sweets, including Arabic pastries, halva, Turkish delight and especially *kunafa* (vermicelli-like pastry over a cheese base soaked in syrup).

★**Al Aqsa**   RESTAURANT $

(Old City; 4NIS; ⊘8am-sunset) This tiny eatery next door to the Al-Kebir Mosque in the kasbah is unanimously considered to produce the finest *kunafa* in Palestine, and every day the warm, elastic cheese and syrup-soaked wheat shreds (it works, trust us) is divvied up from huge circular trays and dispensed to a throng of hungry customers. Do as the locals do and eat standing in the street outside.

Assaraya   MIDDLE EASTERN $$

(Hitten St; mains 40-70NIS; ⊘10am-10pm) For a more formal sit-down meal, ascend Assaraya's wood-panelled staircase from the main gate into the Old City and take a seat in the restaurant's two-storey glass atrium, which overlooks Martyrs Sq. The tables are adorned with folded white napkins and wine glasses (although there is no wine, this being Nablus), and the restaurant serves a mixture of Western and Arabic fare.

ℹ Getting There & Away

There is no direct bus service to Nablus from Jerusalem. You will need to change at either Qalandia checkpoint or Ramallah, where a *servees* will cost 17NIS.

Jenin   ג'נין جنين

☑04 / POP 40,000

The West Bank's northernmost city, Jenin's bustling old town and thriving arts and theatre scene make it an essential stop on any Palestine itinerary.

⊙ Sights

Masjid Jenin al-Kabir & Downtown   MOSQUE, NEIGHBOURHOOD

With its unmissable green roof, Masjid Jenin al-Kabir (Jenin Great Mosque), was built in 1566 on the orders of Fatima Khatun, then wife of the governor of Damascus. Cross the street and enter a dense network of alleys that form the Old City, today largely occupied by furniture makers, barbers and machinists. Two blocks south of the mosque is King Talal St, which leads to Jerusalem Sq, the main bus station and the Jenin Cinema. It's fun to wander into the souq, North of King Talal St, which is absolutely bursting with activity.

Freedom Theatre   THEATRE

(☑04-250 3345; www.thefreedomtheatre.org; ⊙9am-4pm daily) This world-renowned theatre group has persevered in the face of difficult circumstances since it was founded in 2006. Its founder, Juliano Mar Khamis, was assassinated in 2011 by masked gunmen outside the theatre building in the heart of Jenin's refugee camp and his killer has never been idenitified. The Palestinian film-makers, actors, photographers and directors who have moved through the theatre have also had to put up with significant Israeli restrictions on movement.

Despite this, the Freedom Theatre holds regular performances in both Arabic and English, and foreign visitors are always warmly received whether there is a show on or not.

🛏 Sleeping & Eating

★ Cinema Guesthouse   GUESTHOUSE $

(☑059 931 7968; www.cinemajenin.org; 1 Azzaytoon St; dm/s/d 75/125/250NIS; @🖳) A quiet spot in the heart of chaotic Jenin, this is a great place to meet other travellers (or NGO workers, journalists, activists and the like) and unwind for a day or two. It has three spacious dorm rooms, a couple of tiny private rooms and a nice kitchen for cooking communal meals. Breakfast is an extra 10NIS. The English-speaking manager is a font of information on the area. It's opposite the central bus station.

Awtar   WESTERN, MIDDLE EASTERN $

(Cinema Circle; dishes 20-60NIS; ⊙8am-midnight) Head up to Awtar's spacious roof garden for a choice of Arabic and Western dishes under the stars. Even on cool evenings, the terrace is packed with groups of men and women drinking, eating and chatting over sheesha. Downstairs, the restaurant has bay windows overlooking the street and serves Arab staples as well as pizza, burgers and enormous salads.

THE GAZA STRIP

قطاع غزة   רצועת עזה

Gaza has been off the to-do list for travellers for some time – and for good reason. Israel has blockaded the tiny strip from land, air and sea since just after Islamist party Hamas took control in 2006, keeping Gaza's 1.8 million residents in and, with the exception of a handful of journalists, politicians and aid workers, the world out. Even if it were possible to visit Gaza, it would not be recommended: Hamas has fought three wars with Israel between 2006 and 2014 and the strip remains unstable and dangerous.

At 45km long and 10km wide, Gaza is one of the most densely populated places in the world – but it remains desperately poor, with hundreds of thousands of people living either in ramshackle refugee camps or heavily bombed towns and cities. It doesn't need to be: literacy levels are upwards of 97% and its seas hold untapped natural-gas reserves worth up to US$7 billion. Its historic sites go back three millennia and it is home to one of the most beautiful coastlines in the Mediterranean.

At the end of 2014, billions were pledged internationally to rebuild the strip, but it is difficult to see how any serious change can take place while the blockade continues and while many Palestinian militants remain committed to establishing a Palestine 'from the river to the sea' (the Jordan to the Mediterranean) – leaving little room for their Israeli neighbours.

UNDERSTAND ISRAEL & THE PALESTINIAN TERRITORIES

Israel & the Palestinian Territories Today

Optimism about peace was widespread among both Israelis and Palestinians in the heyday of the Oslo peace process, back in the mid-1990s. But years of suicide bombings, rocket attacks from Hamas-controlled Gaza and Islamist calls for Israel's destruction have made many Israelis pessimistic about the chances for real peace and wary of new, potentially risky initiatives. A variety of factors have had a similar impact on the assessment of many Palestinians: continuing settlement construction, incidents of Israeli army brutality, daily humiliation at checkpoints and the right-wing, populist drift of Israeli politics.

Israeli Prime Minister Binyamin Netanyahu has publicly declared his support for a two-state solution to the Israeli-Palestinian conflict, but since his latest right-wing coalition government came to power in 2013, it has aggressively expanded Jewish settlements and offered only vague answers to Palestinian questions about eventual borders.

The leadership of the Palestinian Authority (PA) may be similarly hamstrung. Although PA President Mahmoud Abbas and his prime minister, Rami Hamdallah, have a long record of support for a two-state solution, they too have seemed reluctant to make any bold moves. Instead, Abbas has been putting efforts into having the State of Palestine recognised by international bodies such as the UN and demanding that the international community set a date for an end to Israel's occupation.

History

Ancient Times

Israel and the Palestinian Territories have been inhabited by human beings for some two million years. Between 10,000 and 8000 BC – a little later than in nearby Mesopotamia – people in places such as Jericho switched from hunting to the production of grain and the domestication of animals.

Around 1800 BC, Abraham is believed to have led his nomadic tribe from Mesopotamia (Iraq) to a land the Bible calls Canaan. His descendants were forced to relocate to Egypt because of drought and crop failure, but according to the Bible Moses led them out of slavery and back to the Land of Israel in about 1250 BC. Conflicts with the Canaanites and Philistines pushed the Israelites to abandon their loose tribal system and unify under King Saul (1050–1010 BC) and his successors, King David and King Solomon, builder of the First Temple in Jerusalem.

After Solomon's reign (965–928 BC), the Jews entered a period of division and periodic subjugation. Two rival entities came into being: the Kingdom of Israel, in what is now the northern West Bank and the Galilee; and the southern Kingdom of Judah, with its capital at Jerusalem. After Sargon II of Assyria (r 722–705 BC) destroyed the Kingdom of Israel in 720 BC, the 10 northern tribes disappeared from the historical record.

The Babylonians captured Jerusalem in 586 BC, destroying the First Temple and exiling the people of Judah to Babylonia (now Iraq). Fifty years later Cyrus II, king of Persia, defeated Babylon and allowed the Jews to return to the Land of Israel. They immediately set about constructing the Second Temple, consecrated in 516 BC.

Greeks & Maccabees, Romans & Christians

Greek rule over the Land of Israel began in the late 4th century BC. When the Seleucid king Antiochus IV Epiphanes (r 175–164 BC) banned temple sacrifices, Shabbat and circumcision, the Jews, led by Judah Maccabee, revolted. Using guerrilla tactics, they captured Jerusalem and rededicated the temple – an event celebrated by the Jewish holiday of Hanukkah.

The Maccabees also established the Hasmonean dynasty, but infighting made it easy for Rome to take over in 63 BC. At times the Romans ruled the Roman province of Judea (also spelled Judaea or Iudaea) directly through a procurator – the most famous of whom was Pontius Pilate – but they preferred a strong client ruler like Herod the Great (r 37–4 BC), whose major construction projects included expanding the Second Temple.

The 1st century AD was a time of tremendous upheaval in the Roman province of Judea, not least between approximately AD 26 and 29, when it is believed that Jesus of Nazareth carried out his ministry. The tension exploded in AD 66, when the Jews launched the Great Jewish Revolt against the Romans, also known as the First Jewish-Roman War. Four years later, Titus, the future emperor, crushed the rebels and laid waste to the Second Temple (Rome's Arch of Titus celebrates the victory). The mountaintop Jewish stronghold of Masada fell in AD 73, putting an end to even nominal Jewish sovereignty for almost 1900 years.

In the years following Jesus's crucifixion, which some experts believe took place in AD 33, Jews who believed him to be the Messiah and those who didn't often worshipped side by side. But around the time the Gospels were written (late 1st century AD), theological and political disagreements emerged and the two communities diverged.

With the Temple destroyed and the elaborate animal sacrifices prescribed in the Torah suspended, Jewish religious life was thrown into a state of limbo. In an effort to adapt to the new circumstances, Jewish sages set about reorienting Judaism towards prayer and synagogue worship.

After another failed Jewish revolt, the Bar Kochba Rebellion (AD 132–35), the triumphant Romans – in an attempt to erase Jews' connection to the country – renamed Jerusalem 'Aelia Capitolina' and the province of Judea 'Syria Palaestina'.

Muslims & Crusaders

Islam and the Arabs arrived in Palestine around AD 638 – just six years after the death of the Prophet Mohammed – when Caliph Omar (Umar), the second of the Prophet Mohammed's successors, accepted the surrender of Jerusalem. Jews were again permitted to settle in Jerusalem and Christian shrines, including those established by Helena (Constantine the Great's mother), were preserved.

Omar's successors built Al-Aqsa Mosque and the Dome of the Rock on the Temple Mount (known to Muslims as Al-Haram ash-Sharif), believed to be the site of Mohammed's Night Journey (Mi'raj) to behold the celestial glories of heaven.

Christian pilgrimage to the holy sites in Jerusalem was blocked in 1071 by the Seljuk Turks. In response, in 1095 Pope Urban II issued a call for a crusade to restore the site of Jesus's Passion to Christianity. By the time the Crusades began, the Seljuks had been displaced by the Fatimid dynasty, which was quite happy to allow the old pilgrimage routes to reopen. But it was too late. In 1099 the Crusaders overwhelmed Jerusalem's defences and massacred its Muslims and Jews.

In 1187 the celebrated Kurdish-Muslim general Saladin (Salah ad-Din) defeated a Crusader army at the Horns of Hattin in

Galilee (near Arbel) and took Jerusalem. The final Crusaders left the Middle East with the fall of Akko (Acre) in 1291.

Ottomans, Zionists & British

The Ottoman Turks captured Palestine in 1516, and two decades later Sultan Süleyman the Magnificent (r 1520–66) built the present massive walls around Jerusalem's Old City. For most of the 400 years of Ottoman rule, Palestine was a backwater run by pashas more concerned with tax collection than good governance.

While a small numbers of Jews had remained in Palestine continuously since Roman times, and pious Jews had been immigrating whenever political conditions permitted, organised Zionist immigration to agricultural settlements didn't begin until 1882, sparked by pogroms in Russia. For slightly different reasons, Jews from Yemen began arriving the same year. But until the 1920s, the vast majority of Palestine's Jews belonged to the old-line Orthodox community, most of it uninterested in Zionism (the movement to establish a Jewish state in Palestine), and lived in Judaism's four holy cities: Hebron, Tsfat (Safed), Tiberias and Jerusalem (which became Jewish-majority in about 1850).

In November 1917 the British government issued the Balfour Declaration, which stated that 'His Majesty's Government view with favour the establishment in Palestine of a National Home for the Jewish People'. The next month, British forces under General Edmund Allenby captured Jerusalem.

After the end of WWI Jews resumed immigration to Palestine, this time to territory controlled by a British mandate – approved by the League of Nations – that was friendly, modernising and competent. Among the Jewish immigrants were young, idealistic socialists, many of whom established kibbutzim (communal settlements) on marginal land purchased from absentee Arab landlords, sometimes displacing Arab peasant farmers. In the 1930s they were joined by refugees from Nazi Germany.

The Arab Revolt (1936–39), aimed both at the Zionists and British forces, was suppressed by the Mandatory government with considerable violence. However, it convinced the British – who, in case of war with Germany, would surely need Arab oil and political goodwill – to severely limit Jewish immigration to Palestine. Just as the Jews of Europe were becoming increasingly desperate to flee Hitler, the doors of Palestine slammed shut.

Independence & Catastrophe

By 1947 the British government, exhausted by WWII and tired of both Arab and Jewish violence in Palestine, turned the 'Palestine problem' over to the two-year-old UN. In a moment of rare agreement between the US and the Soviet Union, in 1947 the UN General Assembly voted in favour of partitioning Palestine into two independent states – one Jewish, the other Arab – with Jerusalem under a 'special international regime'. Palestinian Jews accepted the plan in principle, but Palestinian Arabs and nearby Arab countries rejected it. Arab bands immediately began attacking Jewish targets, beginning the 1948 Arab–Israeli War.

As soon as the British left, at midnight on 14 May 1948, two things happened: the Jews proclaimed the establishment of an independent Jewish state; and the armies of Egypt, Syria, Jordan, Lebanon and Iraq invaded Palestine. But to the Arab states' – and the world's – surprise the 650,000 Palestinian Jews were not defeated but rather took control of 77% of Mandatory Palestine (the Partition Plan had offered them 56%), though without Jerusalem's Old City. Jordan occupied (and annexed) the West Bank and East Jerusalem; Egypt took control of the Gaza Strip.

As a result of the 1948 Arab–Israeli War, Israel achieved independence. The establishment of a sovereign Jewish state guaranteed that Jews fleeing persecution would always have a country that would take them in.

But for the Palestinian Arabs, the war is remembered as Al-Naqba, the Catastrophe. Approximately 700,000 of the Arabs living in what was to become Israel fled or were expelled by the end of the year. While many fled their homes to escape fighting, others were forced out of their towns and villages by Israeli military units.

After Israel became independent, impoverished Jewish refugees began flooding in, including Holocaust survivors and refugees from Arab countries whose ancient Jewish communities had been targets of anti-Jewish violence. Within three years, Israel's Jewish population had more than doubled.

War, Terrorism & a Peace Treaty

In the spring of 1967, Arab capitals – especially Cairo – were seething with calls to liberate all of historic Palestine from what they saw as an illegitimate occupation by Israel. Egyptian President Gamal Abdel Nasser ordered UN peacekeeping forces to withdraw from Sinai and closed the Straits of Tiran to Israeli shipping.

On 6 June Israel launched a pre-emptive attack on Egypt, virtually wiping out its air force and, in less than a week, captured Sinai and Gaza from Egypt, the West Bank and East Jerusalem from Jordan, and the Golan from Syria. The conflict came to be known as the Six Day War (see www.sixdaywar.co.uk for the Israeli perspective).

In 1973 Egypt and Syria launched a surprise, two-front attack on Yom Kippur, the holiest day of the Jewish calendar. Unprepared because of intelligence failures, Israel was initially pushed back. Although in tactical and strategic terms Israel eventually achieved victory on the battlefield, it came away from the war feeling defeated, in part because the early Egyptian and Syrian advances, coming just six years after the stunning victory of 1967, were so bloody and traumatic.

Egyptian President Anwar Sadat stunned the world in 1977 by travelling to Jerusalem. He offered to make peace with Israel in return for an Israeli withdrawal from Sinai and promises (never fulfilled) of progress towards a Palestinian state. The Camp David Accords, the first peace treaty between Israel and an Arab state, were signed in 1978.

A popular uprising against Israeli rule broke out in the West Bank and Gaza in 1987. Known as the Intifada (Arabic for 'shaking off'), this spontaneous eruption of strikes, stones and Molotov cocktails gave Palestinians a renewed sense of hope and purpose.

In 1988 Yasser Arafat, then president of the PA, publicly renounced terrorism. Five years later, Israel and the Palestine Liberation Organization (PLO) signed the Oslo Accords, under which Israel handed over control of territory to the Palestinians in stages, beginning with the major towns of the West Bank and Gaza. The toughest issues – the future of Jerusalem and Palestinian refugees' 'Right of Return' – were to be negotiated at the end of a five-year interim period.

Renewed Violence & Stalemate

But the Oslo Accords didn't bring real peace. Rather, they drove those on both sides who opposed compromise to pursue their goals through violence. Hamas and Islamic Jihad launched suicide bombings against Israeli civilians; and in November 1995 a right-wing, Orthodox Jewish Israeli assassinated Prime Minister Yitzhak Rabin at a peace rally in Tel Aviv.

The Second Intifada (2000–05) brought an unprecedented wave of Palestinian suicide bombings against Israeli civilian targets, including buses, supermarkets, cafes and discos. Prime Minister Ariel Sharon, a tough-talking former general, sent tanks to occupy West Bank towns previously ceded to the PA and made frequent, bloody incursions into Gaza. Depressed and sick, Arafat's command of events and – according to some aides – reality weakened until his death in November 2004.

Over the course of the Second Intifada, over 1000 Israelis, 70% of them civilians, were killed by Palestinians and some 4700 Palestinians, more than 2000 of them civilians, were killed by Israelis, according to the Israeli human-rights group B'Tselem (www.btselem.org).

In 2005 Sharon – completely contradicting his reputation as an incorrigible hardliner – evacuated all 8600 Israeli settlers from the Gaza Strip and four settlements in the northern West Bank. Like many other hawkish Israeli leaders before and after, he had come to the conclusion that Israel's continued occupation of the territories captured in 1967 was against Israeli interests and, in the long run, geopolitically and demographically untenable.

Palestinian legislative elections were held in 2006 and Hamas – an Islamist political and militant group classified as a terrorist organisation by the United States, Canada, the UK and the European Union – won. The following year Hamas gunmen ran their Fatah counterparts out of the Gaza Strip after several days of bloody fighting, leaving the West Bank and Gaza under rival administrations. A reconciliation agreement was signed in 2014.

Israel and the Shiite Lebanese militia Hezbollah, backed by Iran, fought a brief war in the summer of 2006. Thousands of rockets rained down on Israeli cities, towns and villages, bringing life in northern Israel to a terrified halt. The scale of Israel's bombing attacks on Lebanese towns was widely condemned, but in late 2014 a tenuous ceasefire was still holding.

In response to years of rocket fire from Gaza, very late in 2008 Israel launched a major offensive, dubbed Operation Cast Lead, aimed at halting the attacks. Israel and Hamas again clashed in late 2012 and, even more violently, in the summer of 2014.

During the 50-day Hamas-Israel war, missiles and mortars were fired into Israel, many of which were intercepted by the pioneering Iron Dome antimissile defence system. Israeli air and ground attacks on Gaza killed over 2000 Gazans, most of them civilians, and left some 60,000 Palestinians homeless. The war ended with few real gains for either side.

People

Israel

As the only Jewish state, Israel and its society are unique in the Middle East – and the world. Three-quarters of Israelis are Jewish, but Israeli society is surprisingly diverse, encompassing communities of Muslim and Christian Arabs, Bedouins, Druze, Circassians and recently arrived asylum seekers from Africa (especially Eritrea and Sudan).

The ancestors of about half of Israeli Jews immigrated from Europe (especially Russia, Romania, Poland, Germany and Hungary) and the Americas, the other half from Africa (eg Morocco and Ethiopia) and Asia (especially Iraq, Iran, Yemen and India). Despite their diversity of background, Israeli Jews are bound together by a collective memory of exile and persecution, especially the Holocaust (1939–45), in which six million of the world's 18 million Jews perished.

The Israeli army, to which Jewish, Druze and Circassian men and most Jewish women are drafted at the age of 18 (men for three years, women for two), serves as a unifying force, although army-based bonds and social networks leave out groups that do not serve, including most Israeli Arabs and most ultra-Orthodox Jews. The country is always in a state of security vigilance, in recent times as a result of rocket attacks and attempted infiltrations from Gaza, Hezbollah's huge Iranian-supplied arsenal in Lebanon, instability in Sinai and Syria, and Iran's nuclear program.

In the economic sphere, Israel has forged strong links with Europe, the USA and South, Southeast and East Asia. It has the world's 25th-highest per-capita GDP, fuelled by a keen sense of entrepreneurism and world-class capacity in fields such as computers, chemistry and medical research.

Palestinian Territories

The perspectives and dreams of the residents of the Palestinian Territories have been forged by a century of loss, deprivation and violence. While Islam plays a major role in Palestinians' world view (only 8% of West Bankers and 0.3% of Gazans are Christians), the defining characteristic of Palestinian society is the desire for an independent homeland. For many Palestinians, years of unemployment, poverty and shortages have led to a collective sense of desperation and powerlessness, though some continue to work on building the institutions, infrastructure and economic structures of a future Palestinian state.

Government & Politics

Israel

Israel is a parliamentary democracy headed by a prime minister. Government decisions are made by the cabinet, presided over by the prime minister; its members (ministers) have executive responsibility for government ministries. The 120-member Knesset is elected by national proportional representation every four years (although elections are almost always called early). Israel also has a president – since 2014 the post has been held by Reuven Rivlin – whose role is largely ceremonial; he or she is elected by the Knesset for a term of seven years.

Since 2009 Israel's prime minister has been Binyamin Netanyahu, head of the right-wing Likud Party. The coalition he formed after the January 2013 elections is one of the most ideologically right-wing in Israeli history.

Palestinian Territories

The Palestinian Authority (Palestinian National Authority; PA or PNA) is an interim administrative body set up in 1994 under the Oslo Accords to rule parts of the West Bank and Gaza for five years, until the establishment of a Palestinian state. Final-status negotiations have dragged on – and so has the PA, now over 15 years past its envisioned replacement by a fully independent State of Palestine.

As part of the Oslo peace process, the PA assumed control of civil and security affairs in the major cities of the West Bank; covering about 3% of the land area of the West Bank, they are known collectively as Area A. A further 25% of the West Bank (most built-up villages), known as Area B, is under PA civil control; Israel retains responsibility for security affairs. The rest of the West Bank (some 72% of the land area) is designated as Area C, under full Israeli civil and security control.

The PA is headed by an executive president, directly elected – at least in theory – once every four years. Yasser Arafat held the post from 1994 until his death in 2004. In January 2005 Mahmoud Abbas (also known as Abu Mazen) was elected and has served as PA president ever since, despite the absence of subsequent elections.

The Palestinian Legislative Council (PLC), also known as the Palestinian parliament, has 132 members elected from 16 districts in the West Bank and Gaza. The last elections, won by Hamas, took place in 2006. A Fatah-Hamas unity government was sworn in in mid-2014.

In 2012, the United Nations General Assembly upgraded the status of the Palestinians to that of a nonmember observer state.

Religion

The largest religious groups in Israel are Jews (75%), Muslims (17.6%), Christians (1.7%) and Druze (1.6%).

Judaism

One of the oldest religions still practised, Judaism is based on a covenantal relationship between the Jewish people and God. The most succinct summary of Jewish theology and Judaism's strict monotheism is to be found in the Shema prayer, which reads, 'Hear O Israel, the Lord is your God, the Lord is One'.

Judaism is based on the Torah (the first five books of the Hebrew Bible, ie the Old Testament) and the Oral Law, as interpreted by rabbis and sages in works such as the

Mishna (edited in the 2nd and 3rd centuries AD) and the Talmud (edited from the 4th to 6th centuries AD).

Orthodox Judaism (the most conservative of the religion's streams) holds that the Oral Law, in its entirety, was given at Mt Sinai. The Reform, Conservative and Reconstructionist Movements believe that Judaism has always been dynamic and proactive, changing and developing over the generations as it faced new circumstances and ideas. All three accord equal status to women.

Islam

Islam was founded by the Prophet Mohammed (AD 570–632), who lived in what is now Saudi Arabia. It is based on belief in the absolute oneness of God (Allah) and in the revelations of his final prophet, Mohammed. The Arabic word *islam* means 'absolute submission' to God and his word. Islam's sacred scripture is the Quran (Koran), which was revealed to Mohammed and is believed to be God's infallible word.

Islam and Judaism share common roots, and Muslims consider Adam, Noah, Abraham, Isaac, Jacob, Joseph and Moses to be prophets. As a result, Jews and Muslims share a number of holy sites, including Al-Haram ash-Sharif/Temple Mount in Jerusalem and the Ibrahimi Mosque/Cave of Machpelah (Tomb of the Patriarchs) in Hebron. Because of their close scriptural links, Muslims consider both Jews and Christians to be an *ahl al-Kitab,* a 'people of the Book'. Judaism has always seen Islam as a fellow monotheistic faith (because of the Trinity, Jewish sages weren't always so sure about Christianity).

Christianity

Christianity is based on the life and teachings of Jesus of Nazareth, a Jew who lived in Judea and Galilee during the 1st century AD; on his crucifixion by the Romans; and on his resurrection three days later, as related in the New Testament. Christianity started out as a movement within Judaism, and Jesus's closest disciples, known as the Apostles, were all Jews. But after his death, the insistence of Jesus's followers that he was the Messiah caused Christianity to become increasingly distinct from Judaism.

The ownership of holy sites in Israel and the Palestinian Territories has long been a subject of contention among the country's various Christian denominations, which include Armenians, Assyrians, Copts and Ethiopians. At a number of sites in Jerusalem and Bethlehem, relations are still governed by a 'status quo' agreement drawn up in Ottoman times.

The Holy Land's largest denomination, the Greek Orthodox Church – almost all of whose local members are Arabic-speaking Palestinians – has jurisdiction over more than half of Jerusalem's Church of the Holy Sepulchre, and a large portion of Bethlehem's Church of the Nativity.

Other Belief Systems

The Druze religion is an 11th-century offshoot of Islam. Many Druze live in northern Israel (including Mt Carmel) as well as in Lebanon and Syria.

Haifa is the world centre of the Baha'i faith, founded in Persia in 1844.

Arts

Literature

Israelis are enormously proud of the revival of the Hebrew language and the creation of modern Hebrew literature, seeing them as the crowning cultural achievements of the Zionist movement. Some classic names to keep an eye out for (their major works are available in English translation) include Yehuda Amichai (1924–2000), Aharon Appelfeld (b 1932), AB Yehoshua (b 1936), Amos Oz (b 1939) and David Grossman (b 1954).

The most widespread form of literary expression among Palestinians has long been poetry, the leading voice of which remains Mahmoud Darwish (1941–2008; www.mahmouddarwish.com). Emile Habibi (1922–96) and Tawfiq Zayad (1929–94) – both of whom represented the Israeli Community Party in the Knesset – wrote highly regarded works of fiction. Habibi's *The Secret Life of Saeed the Pesoptimist* (1974) is a brilliant, tragicomic tale dealing with the difficulties facing Palestinian Arabs who became Israeli citizens after 1948. The stunning debut work of Ghassan Kanafani (1936–72), *Men in the Sun* (1963), delves into the lives, hopes and shattered dreams of its Palestinian characters.

Music

Israeli music mixes modes, scales and vocal styles from both East and West.

In the realms of classic Israeli pop and rock, names to listen for include Shlomo Artzi, Arik Einstein, Matti Caspi, Shalom Hanoch, Yehudit Ravitz, Assaf Amdursky and, more recently, Aviv Geffen. Idan Raichel introduced Ethiopian melodies to a mainstream audience.

Mizrahi (Oriental or Eastern) music, with its Middle Eastern and Mediterranean scales and rhythms, has its roots in the melodies of North Africa (especially Umm Kulthum-era Egypt and mid-century Morocco), Iraq and Yemen.

In recent years, mainstream performers such as Etti Ankri, Ehud Banai, David D'Or, Kobi Oz, Berry Sakharof and Gilad Segev have turned towards traditional – mainly Sephardic and Mizrahi – liturgical poetry and melodies, producing works with massive mainstream popularity.

Born in the *shtetls* (Jewish villages) of Eastern Europe, *klezmer* (Jewish soul) can take you swiftly from ecstasy to the depths of despair.

Israel also has a strong Western classical tradition thanks to Jewish refugees from Nazism and post-Soviet immigrants from Russia. The Israel Philharmonic Orchestra (www.ipo.co.il) – whose first concert, in 1936, was conducted by Arturo Toscanini – is world renowned.

Visitors to the West Bank and Arab areas of Israel may come across traditional Palestinian folk music featuring the sounds of the oud (a stringed instrument shaped like half a pear), the *daf* (tambourine) and the *ney* (flute). Palestinian rap, such as the works of DAM (www.damrap.com), frequently deals with the themes of occupation, the difficulties of daily life, and resistance.

Theatre & Dance

Many contemporary Israeli plays tackle the hot political and social issues of the day – in recent years, the West Bank occupation, suicide, homosexuality within Orthodox Judaism and the Holocaust have all been explored onstage. Tel Aviv, Jerusalem and Haifa have a profusion of companies, venues and festivals both large and small; some offer English supertitle translations.

Theatre has long been an important medium for expressing Palestinian national aspirations. Two of the main centres are the Palestinian National Theatre (www.pnt-pal.org) in East Jerusalem and Al-Kasaba Theatre & Cinematheque (www.alkasaba.org) in Ramallah.

Israel has several renowned contemporary dance troupes. Tel Aviv's Bat Sheva Dance Company (www.batsheva.co.il), founded by Martha Graham in 1964, is probably the best known; it is now led by celebrated choreographer Ohad Naharin (b 1952).

One of the best Palestinian dance groups is El-Funoun (www.el-funoun.org), based in Al-Bireh in the West Bank.

Cinema

In recent years, Israeli films – many of which take a highly critical look at Israeli society and policies – have been garnering prizes at major film festivals, including Cannes, Berlin, Toronto and Sundance. For a database of made-in-Israel movies, see the website of the Manhattan-based Israel Film Center (www.israelfilmcenter.org). There are film festivals and thriving cinematheques in Haifa (www.haifacin.co.il), Jerusalem (www.jer-cin.org.il) and Tel Aviv (www.cinema.co.il).

Most feature-length Palestinian movies are international co-productions. In 2014 *Omar,* a political thriller about trust and betrayal directed by Hany Abu-Assad, garnered an Oscar nomination.

The West Bank has a movie venue, Al-Kasaba Theatre & Cinematheque (p265) in Ramallah. In Gaza, Islamists have forced all the cinemas to close.

Food & Drink

Israelis and Palestinians disagree about many things, but food isn't one of them. Favourites among both peoples include hummus (chickpea paste), falafel (fried chickpea balls served with salad and hummus in a pita pocket), shwarma (chicken, turkey or lamb grilled on a giant spit and stuffed into a pita) and pita bread, both with and without the pocket.

Few countries offer a better selection of vegetarian options than Israel and the Palestinian Territories. Almost all restaurants serve giant – and often creative – salads, and in meat-heavy Arab and Levantine restaurants, the meze-style appetisers and salads can serve as a tasty, inexpensive meal.

Tel Aviv, Haifa, Nazareth and Ramallah are known for their excellent restaurants serving both Levantine classics and dishes from around the world. In both Israel and the Palestinian Territories, tipping 10% or 15% of the bill is as much of an established practice as it is in the English-speaking world.

Daily Life

Israeli society was founded on socialist principles, exemplified by the kibbutz (communal village). These days, though, the vast majority of Israelis have shifted to a decidedly bourgeois and individualistic outlook that embraces aspirations whose fulfillment depends on middle-class paychecks. Hiking, cycling, windsurfing, backpacking, camping and other outdoor activities are hugely popular.

Gaza is largely controlled by Islamic fundamentalists, but much of the West Bank retains a moderate outlook, and Ramallah in particular exhibits the trappings of modern, Western living, including shiny cars, health clubs and late-night bars.

Israeli women enjoy a freedom, opportunity and status on a par with their European counterparts and have historically played significant roles in the economy, politics and even the military. (Israel was one of the first countries to elect a female prime minister: Golda Meir, in 1969.) Though Palestinian women have traditionally assumed the role of home-based caregiver, recent years have seen more women encouraged to enter higher education and to work outside the home. However, as in Ottoman times, marriage and divorce in both Israel and the Palestinian Territories remain in the hands of a very conservative religious establishment, which tends to favour male prerogatives over women's rights. As there is no civil marriage in Israel, couples of mixed religious background wishing to wed must do so outside of Israel (eg in Cyprus).

The annual per-capita GDP in the West Bank is just US$2800, compared with Israel's US$34,000.

Language

Israel's two official languages are Hebrew and Arabic; the official language of the Palestinian Authority is Arabic. On the streets of Israel you'll also hear a lot of Russian, French, English and Amharic spoken by immigrants. Some ultra-Orthodox Jews and older Ashkenazim still speak Yiddish (the Germanic language of the Jews of Eastern Europe), and a small number of Sephardic Jews still use Ladino (Judeo-Espanyol), a blend of Hebrew and Spanish written – like Yiddish – using the Hebrew alphabet. Most Israelis and many Palestinians speak at least some English.

Israeli road signs generally appear in Hebrew, Arabic and English, but often with baffling transliterations. Caesarea, for example, may be rendered Qesariyya, Kesarya, Qasarya and so on; and Tsfat may appear as Zefat, Zfat or Safed. The sound V is often rendered, as in German, using a W.

Environment

Israel and the Palestinian Territories, which cover an area of 28,000 sq km, are bordered to the east by the 6000km-long Great Rift Valley (also known as the Syrian-African Rift), to which the Sea of Galilee, the Dead Sea and the Red Sea all belong. Between this mountain-fringed valley and the Mediterranean Sea lie the Judean Hills (up to 1000m high), which include Jerusalem and Hebron, and the fertile coastal plain, where the bulk of Israel's population and agriculture is concentrated. The arid, lightly populated Negev, the country's southern wedge, consists of plains, mountains, wadis and makhteshes (erosion craters).

Situated at the meeting point of two continents (Asia and Africa) and very near a third (Europe), Israel and the Palestinian Territories are home to a mix of habitats and ecologies found nowhere else on earth. Asian mammals such as the Indian porcupine live alongside African tropical mammals like the rock hyrax (dassie) and creatures more often found in European climes such as the stone marten. National parks and nature reserves encompass around 25% of Israel's total area.

Some 500 million birds from an incredible 283 species migrate through Israel and the Palestinian Territories each year – check out www.birds.org.il, www.israbirding.com and www.natureisrael.org/birdingcenters to find out more.

Environmental Issues

Israel is one of only two countries in the world to have entered the 21st century with more trees than it had at the beginning of the 20th (the other is the United States). But while afforestation programs re-created forest habitats, and innovative desert agriculture (using technologies such as drip irrigation, which was invented here) 'made the desert bloom', demands on the land from urbanisation have resulted in the same problems found in many parts of the world: air and water pollution, overuse of natural resources and poor waste management. Things are even worse on the coast of Gaza, where the problem of surface pollution is accompanied by seawater seepage into the aquifers.

Because of pumping from the Jordan River, its tributaries and the Sea of Galilee, the amount of water flowing into the Dead Sea each year is one billion cu metres (over 90%) less than it would be naturally. As a result, evaporation is causing the sea is shrink, with the water level dropping some 1.2m per year. In 2013 an agreement was signed by Israel, the Palestinian Authority and Jordan to build a 110km-long canal from Aqaba. Environmentalists are concerned about the impact on the Dead Sea of introducing seawater carrying living organisms and a different mix of minerals.

SURVIVAL GUIDE

ⓘ Directory A–Z

ACCOMMODATION

In Israel, expect prices – though not always standards – on a par with western Europe. The West Bank is quite a bit cheaper, with many of the best options clustered in Ramallah and Bethlehem.

Accommodation prices in Israel vary enormously depending on the day of the week and the season. Pricier weekend rates apply on Friday night and sometimes Thursday night (many Israelis don't work on Friday) and/or Saturday night. In the summer (especially July and August) and on Jewish and Israeli holidays (especially Rosh HaShana, Sukkot and Passover), prices can rise significantly and room availability plummets.

In the Palestinian Territories, room prices remain fairly constant year-round, the only exception being in Bethlehem, where rates rise around Christmas and Easter. Be sure to book well ahead if you're planning on travel at these times.

B&Bs (Tzimmers)

The most popular form of accommodation in the Galilee and Golan is the *tzimmer* (or *zimmer*), which we translate as B&B, though not all serve breakfast. For a double, count on paying 400NIS or 500NIS at the very least. To find a *tzimmer*, check out www.zimmeril.com or www.israel-tours-hotel.com.

Camping

Camping is forbidden inside nature reserves but various public and private bodies run inexpensive **camping sites** (www.campingil.org.il) at about 100 places around Israel, 22 of them next to nature reserves operated by the **Israel Nature & Parks Authority** (☑ 1222 3639; www.parks.org.il). Some are equipped with shade roofs (so you don't need a tent), lighting, toilets, showers and barbecue pits. In Hebrew, ask for a *chenyon laila* or an *orchan laila*.

Camping is particularly popular on the shores of the Sea of Galilee. Some organised beaches – offering toilets, showers and security – charge per-person admission fees, but others are free if you arrive on foot (visitors with wheels pay a per-car parking fee).

In the West Bank camping should be avoided because of general security concerns.

Hostels

Almost three dozen independent hostels and guesthouses belong to **Israel Hostels** (www.hostels-israel.com), the members of which offer dorm beds for 100NIS or less, good-value doubles and unmatched opportunities to meet other travellers.

Israel's 19 official hostels and guesthouses, run by the **Israel Youth Hostels Association** (www.iyha.org.il/eng) offer spotless, institutional rooms, many with four or more beds, that are ideal for families or groups of friends.

The **Society for the Protection of Nature in Israel** (SPNI; ☑ 057 200 3030; www.natureisrael.org) runs nine *beit sefer sadeh* (field schools) in areas of high ecological value. They offer simply furnished rooms, often with four or more beds, but most are accessible only by car. Book well ahead, especially during school vacation periods.

Hotels & Guesthouses

Israel's hotels and guesthouses range from grim to gorgeous. Generally speaking, prices are highest in Tel Aviv, Eilat and Jerusalem.

Most of the tourist-class hotels in the West Bank are in Ramallah and Bethlehem. **Palestine Hotels** (www.palestinehotels.com) is an excellent hotel booking website.

Kibbutz Guesthouses

Capitalising on their beautiful, usually rural locations, quite a few kibbutzim offer midrange guesthouse accommodation. Often constructed in the socialist era but significantly upgraded since, these establishments allow access to kibbutz facilities (including the swimming pool), have a laid-back vibe and serve deliciously fresh kibbutz-style breakfasts. For details and reservations, check out the **Kibbutz Hotels Chain** (☑ 03-560 8118; www.kibbutz.co.il).

ACTIVITIES

Cycling

Mountain biking has become hugely popular in Israel in recent years. **Shvil Net** (www.shvil.net) publishes Hebrew-language cycling guides that include detailed topographical maps.

Hiking

With its unbelievably diverse terrain – ranging from the alpine slopes of Mt Hermon to the parched makhteshes (erosion craters) of the Negev – and almost 10,000km of marked trails, Israel offers some truly superb hiking. Don't forget to bring a hat and plenty of water, and plan your day so you can make it back before dark. **Tiuli** (www.tiuli.com) has details in English on hiking options around the country.

At national parks and nature reserves run by the **Israel Nature and Parks Authority** (www.parks.org.il), walking maps with English text are usually handed out when you pay your admission fee. In other areas, the best maps to have – in part because they indicate the location of minefields and live-fire zones used for Israel Defense Forces training – are the 1:50,000-scale topographical maps produced by the Society for the Protection of Nature in Israel (SPNI), sold at bookshops and some nature reserves.

In the West Bank, it's generally not a good idea to wander around the countryside unaccompanied. Consult local organisations for up-to-date information on areas considered safe; Jericho and environs are usually a good bet.

Water Sports

The Red Sea has some of the world's most spectacular and species-rich coral reefs. Good-value dive packages and scuba courses are available in Eilat.

Israel's Mediterranean beaches, including those in Tel Aviv, are generally excellent, offering ample opportunities to swim, windsurf and sail. For freshwater swimming head to the Sea of Galilee. The supersaline Dead Sea offers that quintessential 'floating' experience.

CHILDREN

Travel with children in Israel and the Palestinian Territories is generally a breeze: the food's varied and tasty, the distances are short, there are child-friendly activities at every turn, and the locals absolutely love children.

Beaches are usually clean, well equipped with cafes and even playgrounds, and great for a paddle, a sandcastle or a swim. Most Israeli shopping malls have play areas. As wheelchair access to nature reserves has improved in recent years, so has the ease of getting around with a pram (stroller).

In the vast majority of hotels, guesthouses and B&Bs, babies and toddlers can sleep in their parents' room for free; older children (often from age three) are welcome for an extra charge. In hostels and SPNI field schools, rooms generally have at least four beds, making them ideal for families.

In the West Bank, getting through Israeli checkpoints can involve hassles and delays.

CUSTOMS REGULATIONS

Israel allows travellers aged 18 and over to import duty free up to 1L of spirits and 2L of wine, 250ml of perfume, 250g of tobacco products, and gifts worth no more than US$200. Bringing drugs, drug paraphenalia, mace (self-defence tear gas), laser jammers (to confuse police-operated laser speed guns), fresh meat and pornography is prohibited.

EMBASSIES & CONSULATES

Because of unresolved political issues, most countries' embassies in Israel are in or near Tel Aviv. A few countries maintain consulates in Jerusalem, Haifa and/or Eilat.

Most diplomatic missions are open in the morning from Monday to Thursday or Friday; some also open in the afternoon.

ℹ️ PRACTICALITIES

The security situation can change in a flash so staying up on the news can be extremely important.

Newspapers and magazines For daily news, try the English edition of left-of-centre *Haaretz* (www.haaretz.com); the right-of-centre *Jerusalem Post* (www.jpost.com); the online *Times of Israel* (www.timesofisrael.com); or the website affiliated with the Hebrew daily *Yediot Aharonot* (www.ynetnews.com).

Radio Regular English news bulletins can be heard on Israel Radio's IBA World (Reshet Reka; www.iba.org.il/world).

Smoking In Israel, smoking is prohibited in all indoor public spaces, including offices and restaurants, and on public transport.

TV Cable and satellite packages, including those in hotels, almost always include BBC World, CNN, Sky, Fox and other TV news channels.

Weights and measures Metric system.

Australian Embassy (Map p232; ☑ 03-693 5000; www.israel.embassy.gov.au; 28th fl, Discount Bank Tower, 23 Yehuda HaLevi St, 6513601 Tel Aviv)

Canadian Embassy (☑ 03-636 3300; www.canadainternational.gc.ca/israel; 3/5 Nirim St, 6706038 Tel Aviv)

Egyptian Embassy (www.egyptembassy.net) Eilat (Map p261; ☑ 08-637 6882; www.egyptembassy.net; 68 Afrouni St; ⊙9-11am Sun-Thu) Tel Aviv (Map p236; ☑ 03-546 4151; ⊙ 9-11am Sun-Tue) In Eilat, deliver your passport, application and one passport-size photo in the morning and pick up the visa around 2pm the same day. In Tel Aviv the process may take a few days.

French Embassy Jerusalem (Map p214; ☑ 02-629 8500; www.consulfrance-jerusalem.org; 5 Paul Émile Botta St, 9410905) Tel Aviv (Map p232; ☑ 03-520 8500; www.ambafrance-il.org; 112 Herbert Samuel Esplanade, 6357231)

German Embassy (Map p232; ☑ 03-693 1313; www.tel-aviv.diplo.de; 19th fl, 3 Daniel Frisch St, 6473104 Tel Aviv)

Irish Embassy (Map p232; ☑ 03-696 4166; www.embassyofireland.co.il; 17th fl, 3 Daniel Frisch St, 6473104 Tel Aviv)

Jordanian Embassy (☑ 03-751 7722; 10th fl, 14 Abba Hillel St, 5250607 Ramat Gan) You can apply in the morning and pick your visa up around 2pm the same day; bring one passport-size photo. Linked to adjacent Tel Aviv by various buses that serve Petach Tikva, including Dan bus 66.

Netherlands Embassy (☑ 03-754 0777; http://israel.nlembassy.org; 13th fl, 14 Abba Hillel St, 5250607 Ramat Gan)

New Zealand Embassy (Map p232; ☑ 03-695 1869; www.mfat.govt.nz; 3 Daniel Frisch St, 6473104 Tel Aviv)

Turkish Embassy (Map p236; ☑ 03-524 1101; 202 HaYarkon St, 6340507 Tel Aviv) Consulate in Jerusalem (☑ 02-591 0555; http://jerusalem.cg.mfa.gov.tr; 87 Nablus Rd, Sheikh Jerrah, 9720826).

UK Embassy Jerusalem (☑ 02-541 4100; www.ukinjerusalem.fco.gov.uk; 15 Nashashibi St, Sheikh Jarrah, 9720415) Tel Aviv (☑ 03-725 1222; www.ukinisrael.fco.gov.uk; 192 HaYarkon St, 6340502)

US Embassy Haifa (☑ 04-853 1470; 26 Ben-Gurion Ave, 350232) Jerusalem (☑ 02-630 4000; http://jerusalem.usconsulate.gov; 14 David Flusser, Arnona, 9378322) Tel Aviv (☑ 03-519 7475; http://israel.usembassy.gov; 71 HaYarkon St, 6343229)

GAY & LESBIAN TRAVELLERS

Israel has a very lively gay scene. Tel Aviv has plenty of rainbow-coloured flags, a huge Gay Pride Parade in early June and plenty of hangouts. Haifa and Jerusalem have smaller gay communities. The resort town of Eilat is gay friendly, although the scene is mostly Israeli tourists.

Gay culture is far less accepted in the Palestinian Territories. To better understand the difficult plight of gay and lesbian Palestinians, check out www.globalgayz.com/middle-east/palestine and www.aswatgroup.org/en.

INTERNET ACCESS

Wi-fi hot spots can be found all over Israel and in quite a few places in the Palestinian Territories. In Israel, wi-fi is also available on many intercity buses and trains and Tel Aviv-Jaffa (Yafo) offers free wi-fi in public spaces all over the city.

MONEY

ATMs

ATMs are widespread throughout Israel, but are less common in the Palestinian Territories so bring enough cash. Visa, MasterCard and, increasingly, American Express and Diners cards are accepted almost everywhere. Most, but not all, ATMs do Visa and MasterCard cash advances.

Travellers Cheques & Wire Transfers

Travellers cheques can be changed at most banks, but charges can be as high as 20NIS per cheque; instead use a no-commission exchange bureaux or the post office. Post offices offer Western Union international money transfer services.

OPENING HOURS

In Israel, shops, banks and offices are generally open from Sunday to Thursday and on Friday until sometime between 12.30pm and 3pm. Many restaurants, pubs and places of entertainment (cinemas and performance venues) remain open on Shabbat (Friday evening to Saturday night) and most Jewish holidays.

In predominantly Muslim areas (eg East Jerusalem, Akko's Old City, the West Bank and Gaza) businesses may be closed on Friday (but remain open on Saturday).

Christian-owned businesses (eg in Nazareth, Haifa's Wadi Nisnas, Bethlehem and the Armenian and Christian Quarters of Jerusalem's Old City) are closed on Sunday.

PUBLIC & RELIGIOUS HOLIDAYS

In addition to the main Islamic holidays, the following are observed in Israel and the Palestinian Territories:

New Year's Day Official holiday in the Palestinian Territories but not in Israel (1 January).

Christmas (Orthodox) Celebrated by Eastern Orthodox churches on 6–7 January and by Armenians in the Holy Land on 18–19 January.

Passover (Pesach) Weeklong celebration of the liberation of the Israelites from slavery in Egypt (23–29 April 2016, 10–17 April 2017, 30 March–6 April 2018).

Easter Sunday (Western) For Catholics and Protestants (27 March 2016, 16 April 2017, 1 April 2018).

Easter Sunday (Orthodox) For Eastern Orthodox and Armenians (1 May 2016, 16 April 2017, 8 April 2018).

Holocaust Memorial Day (Yom HaSho'ah) Places of entertainment closed. At 10am sirens sound and Israelis stand silently at attention (4–5 May 2016, 23–24 April 2017, 11–12 April 2018).

Memorial Day (Yom HaZikaron) Commemorates soldiers who fell defending Israel. Places of entertainment closed. At 8pm and 11am sirens sound and Israelis stand silently at attention (10–11 May 2016, 30 April–1 May 2017, 17–18 April 2018).

Israel Independence Day (Yom Ha'Atzma'ut) Celebrated on 11–12 May 2016, 1–2 May 2017, 18–19 April 2018.

International Labour Day Public holiday in both Israel and the Palestinian Territories (1 May).

Nakba Day Palestinian commemoration of the *nakba* (catastrophe) of 1948 (15 May).

Shavuot (Pentecost) Jews celebrate the giving of the Torah at Mt Sinai (11–12 June 2016, 30–31 May 2017, 19–20 May 2018).

Tish'a B'Av (Ninth of Av) Jews commemorate the destruction of the Temples in Jerusalem. Restaurants and places of entertainment closed (13–14 August 2016, 31 July–1 August 2017, 21–22 July 2018).

Rosh HaShanah (Jewish New Year) Celebrated 13–15 September 2015, 2–4 October 2016, 20–22 September 2017, 9–11 September 2018).

Yom Kippur (Jewish Day of Atonement) Solemn day of reflection and fasting. Israel's airports and land borders close, all transport ceases (22–23 September 2015, 11–12 October 2016, 29–30 September 2017, 18–19 September 2018).

Sukkot (Feast of the Tabernacles) Weeklong holiday that recollects the Israelites' 40 years of wandering in the desert (27 September–3 October 2015, 16–22 October 2016, 1–10 October 2017, 23–29 September 2018).

Hanukkah (Festival of Lights) Jews celebrate the rededication of the Temple after the Maccabean revolt; no closures (6–14 December 2015, 24 December 2016–1 January 2017, 12–20 December 2017).

Christmas (Western) Public holiday in the West Bank, but not in Israel or Gaza. Celebrated by Catholics and Protestants on 24–25 December.

SAFE TRAVEL

Airport & Border Security

If border officials suspect that you're coming to take part in pro-Palestinian political activities or if you have an Arab or Muslim name, they may ask some probing questions; on occasion they have even searched laptops. Sometimes they take an interest in passport stamps from places like Lebanon and Iran, but often they don't. The one sure way to get grilled is to sound evasive or

---

ⓘ EATING PRICE RANGES

Prices in reviews represent the cost of a restaurant's average main-course dish.

Israel

$ less than 35NIS (US$9)

$$ 35NIS to 70NIS (US$9 to US$18)

$$$ more than 70NIS (US$18)

Palestinian Territories

$ less than 35NIS (US$9)

$$ 35NIS to 55NIS (US$9 to US$14)

$$$ more than 55NIS (US$14)

to contradict yourself – the security screeners are trained to try to trip you up. Whatever happens, remain calm and polite.

Minefields

Some parts of Israel and the Palestinian Territories – particularly along the Jordanian border and around the periphery of the Golan Heights – are sown with antipersonnel mines. Known mined areas are fenced with barbed wire sporting dangling red (or rust) triangles and/or yellow and red 'Danger Mines!' signs. Flash floods sometimes wash away old mines, depositing them outside of marked minefields. Wherever you are, never, ever, touch anything that looks like it might be an old artillery shell, grenade or mine!

TELEPHONE

Mobile Phones

Israel's various mobile-phone operators, including old-timers **Orange** (www.orange.co.il), **Pelefone** (www.pelephone.co.il) and **Cellcom** (www.cellcom.co.il) and newcomers **Hot Mobile** (www.hotmobile.co.il) and **Golan Telecom** (www.golantelecom.co.il), offer pay-as-you-go SIM cards as well as cheap monthly plans with a variety of data options.

Phonecards

Prepaid local and international calls can be made using a variety of phonecards, sold at post offices, lottery kiosks and newsstands.

TRAVELLERS WITH DISABILITIES

In Israel, access for people in wheelchairs and with other disabilities is approaching the levels of western Europe and North America. Almost all hotels and HI hostels are required to have one or more rooms outfitted for wheelchair users, and many tourist attractions, including museums, archaeological sites and beaches, are wheelchair accessible to a significant degree. Quite a few nature reserves offer trails designed for wheelchairs (see www.parks.org.il and www.kkl.org.il). Restaurants are a mixed bag as few have fully wheelchair-accessible bathrooms. For details on accessibility in Israel, check out the website of **Access Israel** (www.aisrael.org).

The Palestinian Territories are less well equipped and getting around is made more difficult by IDF checkpoints, which often have to be crossed on foot and sometimes require moving over and around barriers.

VISAS

In general, Western visitors to Israel and the Palestinian Territories are issued free, on-arrival tourist (B/2) visas by Israel. For specifics on who qualifies, visit www.mfa.gov.il (click on 'Consular Services' and then 'Visas'). Your passport must be valid for at least six months from the date of entry. Officials can demand to see proof of sufficient funds and/or an onward or return ticket but rarely do so.

On-arrival visas are usually valid for 90 days. But some travellers, such as those entering by land from Egypt or Jordan, may be given just 30 days or even two weeks – it's up to the discretion of the border-control official. If there is any indication that you are coming to participate in pro-Palestinian protests, plan to engage in missionary activity or are seeking illegal employment, you may find yourself on the next flight home.

Israel no longer stamps tourists' passports (though it retains the right to do so). Instead, visitors are given a small loose-leaf entry card – try not to lose it as it's your only in-hand proof that you're in the country legally.

Students require a student (A/2) visa; kibbutz volunteers must arrange a volunteer's (B/4) visa through their host organisation.

Extensions

To extend a tourist (B/2) visa, you can either do a 'visa run' to Egypt, Jordan or overseas; or apply to extend your visa (90NIS). Extensions are granted by the **Population & Immigration Authority** (☑ 3450; www.piba.gov.il; ⊙ generally 8am-noon Sun-Tue & Thu), part of the **Ministry of the Interior** (for information dial ☑ 3450), the offices of which – generally open 8am to noon on Sunday, Monday, Tuesday and Thursday – include bureaux in **Jerusalem** (1 Shlomzion HaMalka St), **Tel Aviv** (Kiryat HaMamshala, 125 Menachem Begin Rd) and **Eilat** (2nd fl, HaKenyon HaAdom, HaTemarim Blvd).

Bring a passport valid for at least six months beyond the requested extension period, a recent photo, a letter explaining why you want/need an extension (plus documentation), and evidence of sufficient funds for the extended stay. Offices in smaller towns are often easier and faster to deal with than those in big cities.

VOLUNTEERING

Israel and the Palestinian Territories abound with volunteer opportunities. In Israel these are often on archaeological digs, at ILH hostels or environmental organisations, while in the Palestinian Territories they often involve helping the many NGOs working to improve everyday life for Palestinians. These websites list a selection of organisations that arrange volunteer placements: The National Council for Volunteering in Israel (www.ivolunteer.org.il), Israel Hostels (www.hostels-israel.com/volunteer-in-a-hostel) and Medical Aid for Palestinians (www.map-uk.org).

If you're between 18 and 35, it's also possible to volunteer on a traditional kibbutz in Israel. Volunteers interested in a taste of the lifestyle at these communal agricultural centres can expect

SECURITY SITUATION

There is no getting around the fact that the threat of terrorist attack and/or rocket fire is ever-present in Israel and the Palestinian Territories. When travelling here, you should regularly check the media for news about possible safety and security risks.

Israel has some of the most stringent security policies in the world. When entering all sorts of public venues, your bags are likely to be searched and in some cases X-rayed. Abandoned shopping bags, backpacks and parcels are picked up by bomb-squad robots and may be blown up.

Road passage between many Palestinian West Bank towns and Israel is regulated by Israeli army roadblocks, where you'll need to show a passport and may have to answer questions about your reason for travel. The situation in the West Bank and Gaza (which is effectively off limits) can change quickly so monitor the news. Some good rules of thumb:

➡ Always carry your passport.

➡ Travel during daylight hours.

➡ Use caution when approaching roadblocks and checkpoints. Remember: soldiers may have no idea that you're just a curious tourist.

➡ Don't wander into refugee camps on your own – go with a local guide.

➡ Avoid political demonstrations, which often get out of hand and can turn into violent confrontations.

to spend two to six months helping with manual labour, which could include anything from gardening to washing up or milking cows. Food and accommodation are provided and sometimes a small weekly allowance. For more information, visit www.kibbutz.org.il/eng or read about one Brit's personal experience at www.kibbutzvolunteer.com.

WOMEN TRAVELLERS

Female travellers will generally feel as safe and comfortable in Israel and the Palestinian Territories as they would in any Western country, though it's important to take the same sensible precautions you would back home.

When you plan your day, keep in mind local expectations regarding modest attire. While tight-fitting, revealing outfits are common in urban centres such as Tel Aviv, when visiting conservative areas and religious sites – Jewish, Muslim, Christian, Druze and Baha'i – you should wear clothing that covers your knees and shoulders. In Muslim and Christian areas, long trousers are OK, but in some Jewish areas – and at Jewish holy sites – only a long skirt is acceptable.

It's a good idea to carry a shawl or scarf with you at all times. You will need this to cover your head when visiting Muslim holy sites, and it can also come in handy to cover your shoulders, arms and/or legs, depending on the circumstances.

❶ Getting There & Away

ENTERING ISRAEL & THE PALESTINIAN TERRITORIES

Israel has peace treaties with Egypt and Jordan so it's easy to combine a visit to Israel and the Palestinian Territories with overland travel to Jordan and Egypt. (At press time, Western governments were recommending against travel to Sinai for security reasons.)

Flights and tours can be booked online at www.lonelyplanet.com/bookings.

AIR

Israeli airport security is very tight so international travellers should check in at least three hours prior to their flight – when flying both to and from Israel.

Airports

Israel's main gateway is **Ben-Gurion International Airport** (TLV; ✈ arrivals & departures 03-972 3333; www.iaa.gov.il), situated 52km northwest of Jerusalem and 18km southeast of central Tel Aviv. Ultramodern Terminal 3 handles about 14 million passengers a year. For up-to-the-minute details on arrivals and departures, go to the airport's English website and click 'On-Line Flights' at the top.

Airlines

Almost all the major European carriers have flights to Tel Aviv, and so do most Europe-based budget airlines.

Israel's privatised flag carrier, **El Al** (LY; ☎03-977 1111; www.elal.co.il), has direct flights to several dozen cities in western and eastern Europe, as well as long-haul services to North America, Johannesburg, Mumbai, Bangkok, Hong Kong and Beijing.

The only Middle Eastern cities with direct air links to Tel Aviv are Amman, served by **Royal Jordanian** (www.rj.com); Cairo, served by Air Sinai (a low-profile but astonishingly expensive subsidiary of Egyptair); and Istanbul, served by **Turkish Airlines** (www.turkishairlines.com).

The cheapest way to get to/from South, Southeast and East Asia is often via Istanbul on Turkish Airways; via Addis Ababa on **Ethiopian Airlines** (www.flyethiopian.com); or via Amman on carriers such as Royal Jordanian, Qatar Airways (with a stopover in Doha), Emirates (via Dubai) and Etihad (via Abu Dhabi). Tickets are available through **FLYeast** (☎09-970 0400; www.flyeast.co.il).

LAND

The borders between Israel and the two countries with which it has signed peace treaties, Egypt and Jordan, are open to both tourists and locals.

Egypt

Taba crossing This **crossing** (☎08-636 0999; www.iaa.gov.il; ⊗24hr), on the Red Sea 10km south of Eilat, is the only border post between Israel and Egypt that's open to tourists. However, because of recent attacks on tourists by Islamist militants, including an early-2014 attack at Taba itself that claimed four lives, we do not recommend that you travel along Sinai's Red Sea coast until the security situation improves. Both sides have exchange bureaux. Israel charges a departure tax of 107NIS; Egypt charges E£75 to enter and E£2 to exit. You can get a 14-day Sinai-only entry permit at the border, allowing you to visit Red Sea resorts stretching from Taba to Sharm el-Sheikh, plus St Katherine's. If you're planning on going further into Egypt, you'll need to arrange an Egyptian visa in advance, eg at the Egyptian consulate in Eilat or the embassy in Tel Aviv. Local bus 15 links Eilat's central bus station with the Taba crossing (4.90NIS, 30 minutes, hourly 8am to 9pm Sunday to Thursday, 8am to 3pm Friday and 9am to 7pm Saturday). On the way back to Eilat this line is known as bus 16. A taxi costs about 30NIS.

Rafah crossing With a few exceptions, Egypt has kept the Rafah crossing between Gaza and Sinai closed since 2013. When and if it reopens, it is unlikely to be usable by leisure travellers.

Jordan

While the two land crossings between Israel and Jordan are quick and efficient, the Allenby Bridge/King Hussein Bridge crossing between the Israeli-controlled West Bank and Jordan is not always as smooth.

Israel charges a departure tax of 107NIS (182NIS at Allenby Bridge/King Hussein Bridge), while Jordan charges JD5 to enter and J10 to exit. None of the crossings have ATMs but you should be able to get a cash advance at Israel-side currency-exchange windows, open whenever the terminal is.

Allenby Bridge (King Hussein Bridge) Linking the Israeli-controlled West Bank with Jordan, this busy **crossing** (☎02-548 2600; www.iaa.gov.il; ⊗8am-midnight Sun-Thu, 8am-3pm Fri & Sat, closed Yom Kippur & Eid al-Adha, hours subject to change) is just 46km east of Jerusalem, 8km east of Jericho and 60km west of Amman. It is the only crossing that people with Palestinian Authority travel documents, including West Bank Palestinians, can use to travel to and from Jordan and the outside world, so traffic can be heavy, especially on Sundays, around holidays and on weekdays from 11am to 3pm. Try to get to the border as early in the day as possible. Jordan does not issue on-arrival visas at the Allenby Bridge/King Hussein Bridge crossing; you'll have to arrange a visa in advance at a Jordanian embassy, such as the one in Ramat Gan, near Tel Aviv. However, if your visit to the Palestinian Territories and/or Israel started in Jordan, you won't need a new visa in order to cross back into Jordan through Allenby Bridge/King Hussein Bridge, provided you do so within the period of validity of your Jordanian visa – just show your stamped exit slip. The bus across the frontier costs JD7, plus JD1.500 per piece of luggage. Bring plenty of cash (Jordanian dinars are the most useful) and make sure you have small change. There are no ATMs but both sides have exchange bureaux. Shared taxis run by **Abdo** (☎02-628 3281) and **Al-Nijmeh** (☎02-627 7466), most frequent before 11am, link the blue and white bus station opposite Jerusalem's Damascus Gate with the border (30 minutes, 50NIS); the charge per suitcase is 5NIS. Private taxis can cost as much as 300NIS, with hotel pick-up as an option.

Yitzhak Rabin (Wadi Araba) Located just 3km northeast of Eilat, this **crossing** (☎08-630 0555, 08-630 0530; www.iaa.gov.il; ⊗6.30am-8pm Sun-Thu, 8am-8pm Fri & Sat) is handy for trips to Aqaba, Petra and Wadi Rum. A bonus: thanks to the Aqaba Special Economic Zone, Jordanian visas issued here are free. A taxi to/from Eilat (10 minutes) costs 45NIS.

Jordan River Bridge (Sheikh Hussein Bridge) Generally far less busy than Allenby Bridge/King Hussein Bridge, this **crossing** (☎04-609 3400; www.iaa.gov.il; ⊗6.30am-9pm Sun-Thu, 8am-7pm Fri & Sat, closed Yom Kippur & Al-Hijra/Muslim New Year) is in the Jordan Valley 8km east of Beit She'an, 30km south of the Sea of Galilee, 135km northeast of Tel Aviv and 90km northeast of Amman. Jordan issues on-arrival visas (JD40) for many nationalities. **Taxis** (%052-328 8977) wait at the border for travel to Beit She'an (50NIS, plus 5NIS per suitcase) and destinations around Israel, including Tiberias (240NIS), Jerusalem (550NIS) and Tel Aviv (580NIS). Kavim bus 16 connects Beit She'an with Kibbutz Ma'oz Haim (11 minutes, five or six daily Sunday to Friday), a walkable 1km west of the crossing. **Nazarene Tours** (☑ in Israel 04-601 0458, in Jordan 079-692 7455; Paulus VI St, Nazareth) links Nazareth with Amman (80NIS, 4½ to five hours), via the Jordan River/Sheikh Hussein crossing, on Sunday, Tuesday, Thursday and Saturday. Departures are at 8.30am from the company's Nazareth office, which is near the Bank of Jerusalem and the Nazareth Hotel (not to be confused with the office of Nazarene Transport & Tourism in the city centre); and at 2pm from Amman's Royal Hotel (University St). Reserve by phone at least two days ahead.

ℹ Getting Around

AIR

Air-ticket deals are available online, with tickets sometimes going for as little as US$25 one way to/from Ben-Gurion – the price of a bus ticket!

Seven days a week, flights to Eilat from Tel Aviv's Sde Dov airport (set to close in 2016), Ben-Gurion airport's domestic terminal and Haifa are handled by:

Arkia (www.arkia.com)

Israir (www.israirairlines.com)

BICYCLE

If you cycle between cities, bear in mind the hot climate, steep hills and erratic drivers; bicycles are not allowed on certain major highways.

Bicycles can be taken on intercity buses for no charge and are allowed on all trains – including those serving Ben Gurion airport – *except* during rush hour (6am to 9am and 3pm to 7pm) Sunday to Thursday and on Saturday evening.

One of the best places for leisure cycling is around the Sea of Galilee; bicycles can be hired in Tiberias.

BUS

Israel

Almost every town, village and kibbutz has bus service at least a few times a day – except, that is, on Shabbat (ie from mid-afternoon on Friday until the late afternoon or evening on Saturday) and some Jewish holidays.

Tickets are sold by bus drivers and, when available, at bus-station ticket windows; exact change is not needed. Return tickets, available on a few lines (eg to Eilat), cost 15% less than two one-way.

ℹ HITCHING

Although hitching was once a common way of getting around Israel, recent reports of violent crime, including kidnapping, make this a risky business and we do not recommend it. All travellers should be cautious about the cars they get into. The local method of soliciting a lift is simply to point an index finger at the road. Hitching is still most common in the Upper Galilee and Golan regions.

Most discounts are available only if you have a rechargeable Rav-Kav smartcard, which comes in two versions: personalised *(ishi)*, which has your picture on it and requires filling out an application; and anonymous *(anonimi)*, which is sold at stations (5NIS) and by drivers and is transferable but qualifies you for only limited discounts. The good news is that both get you 20% off all fares; the bad news is that at present, you need a separate Rav-Kav account for each bus company (a single card can hold up to eight).

Israel no longer has a bus duopoly, with the Egged and Dan cooperatives dividing the country between them. Rather, there are about 20 different companies, including Egged and Dan, that compete for routes in Ministry of Transport tenders. The **Public Transportation Info Center** (☑ 1 900 72 1111; www.bus.co.il) provides details in English on all bus companies' routes and times. Smartphone apps for Android and iPhones can be downloaded from the website.

The only bus tickets that need to be (or can be) ordered in advance are Egged tickets to/from Eilat, which can be reserved up to 14 days ahead via www.egged.co.il, by smartphone app or by phone (dial ☑ 2800 or ☑ 03-694 8888).

West Bank

In East Jerusalem and the West Bank, a number of Palestinian-owned bus companies provide public transport. Unlike their counterparts in Israel, they operate seven days a week.

CAR & MOTORCYCLE

To drive a vehicle in Israel and the Palestinian Territories, all you need is your regular driving licence (an international driving licence is not required).

Having your own wheels doesn't make much sense in Jerusalem or Tel Aviv – parking can be a huge hassle – but it's a great idea along the north coast and in the Galilee, Golan and Negev, where buses can be scarce. A car will also let you take advantage of cheap accommodation options, including hostels and free camping.

Car hire with insurance and unlimited kilometres costs as little as 140NIS per day, US$200 per week or US$600 per month. Most major international rental companies have offices in Israel.

Note that most Israeli rental agencies forbid you to take their cars into the Palestinian Territories; a notable exception is **Green Peace** (www.greenpeace.co.il).

LOCAL TRANSPORT

Bicycle

Bike paths have been going up in cities all over Israel but the most developed network is in Tel Aviv, which has a municipal bike-rental program, aimed at commuters, called **Tel-O-Fun** (www.tel-o-fun.co.il).

Taxi

In Israel, it's almost always to your advantage to use the meter (by law the driver has to put it on if you ask); make sure it was reset to the flagfall price after you get in. A trip across town in Jerusalem or Tel Aviv should cost about 30NIS to 50NIS. Taxi tariffs rise 25% between 9pm and 5.30am.

Palestinian yellow taxis rarely have meters. Negotiate your fare with the driver before you set out.

SHERUT

To Israelis it's a sherut (sheh-*root*) while the Palestinians call it a *servees* (ser-*vees*), but whatever name you use, shared taxis are a useful way to get around. These vehicles, often 13-seat minivans, operate on a fixed route for a fixed price, like a bus except that they don't have fixed stops and depart only when full. Some sheruts operate 24/7 and are the only means of public transport in Israel during Shabbat, when prices rise slightly.

TRAIN

Israel Railways (☏ 5770, 077-232 4000; www.rail.co.il) runs a comfortable, convenient and often-scenic network of passenger rail services linking destinations such as Ben-Gurion airport, Jerusalem, Tel Aviv, Haifa and Akko; details on departure times are also available from the Public Transportation Info Center (p289). Trains do not run from mid-afternoon Friday until after sundown on Saturday. Return tickets are 10% cheaper than two one-way tickets.

Jordan

Includes →

Best for Nature

→ Ajloun Forest Reserve
(p311)

→ Dana Biosphere Reserve
(p325)

→ Mujib Biosphere Reserve
(p316)

→ Wadi Rum Protected Area
(p337)

Best for Culture

→ Petra (p327)

→ Jerash (p307)

→ Umm Qais (Gadara; p312)

→ Madaba (p319)

Why Go?

Ahlan wa sahlan! – 'Welcome!' From the Bedouin of Wadi Rum to the taxi drivers of Amman, you'll be on the receiving end of this open-armed welcome every day. It's this, and a sense of stability amid a problematic neighbourhood, that makes travel in Jordan such a delight.

With heavyweight neighbours pulling big historical punches, Jordan easily holds its own. Amman, Jerash and Umm Qais were cities of the Roman Decapolis, while biblical sites include Bethany-Beyond-the-Jordan, where Jesus was baptised, and Mt Nebo, where Moses reputedly surveyed the Promised Land. Grandest of all is the impressive Nabataean capital of Petra, carved from vertical cliffs.

But Jordan is not just about antiquities – it also offers the great outdoors. Whether diving in Aqaba, trekking in the camel-prints of Lawrence of Arabia or hiking through stunning canyons, Jordan's eco-savvy nature reserves offer the best of adventures in the Middle East.

When to Go

Amman

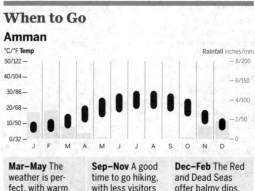

Mar–May The weather is perfect, with warm days, cool nights and spectacular wildflowers.

Sep–Nov A good time to go hiking, with less visitors and relief after intense summer heat.

Dec–Feb The Red and Dead Seas offer balmy dips, while upland Jordan shivers with winter chills.

Jordan Highlights

1 Admire the engineering precision of the **Roman Theatre** (p295) in Amman.

2 Wander the colonnaded streets of **Jerash** (p307), a well-preserved Roman provincial city.

3 Hike the trails of **Mujib** (p316) or **Dana Biosphere Reserves** (p325).

4 Descend to the depths for a bob in the **Dead Sea** (p313), the lowest point on earth.

5 Piece together early Christian history in the mosaics of **Madaba** (p319).

6 Listen to the thunder of ghostly hooves at **Karak Castle** (p324) and **Shobak Castle** (p326), Jordan's most impressive Crusader forts.

7 Tread the path of history through Petra's **Siq** (p331), the sheer-sided chasm leading to an ancient world.

8 Don mask and flippers and hover with the pipe fish over spectacular coral gardens in the **Red Sea** (p340).

9 Live a 'Lawrence moment' by riding through **Wadi Rum** (p337) on a camel.

10 Admire the risqué frescos in the bathhouse of **Qusayr Amra** (p319), a Unesco World Heritage site.

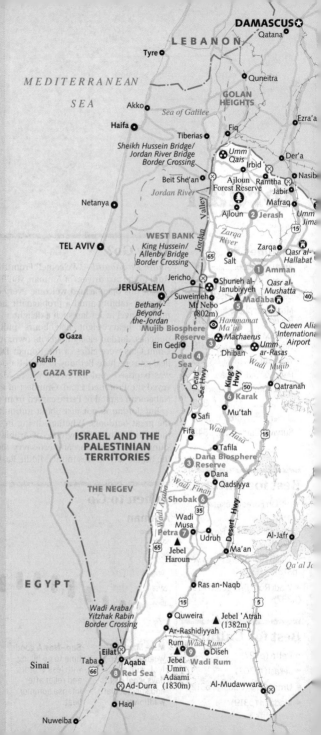

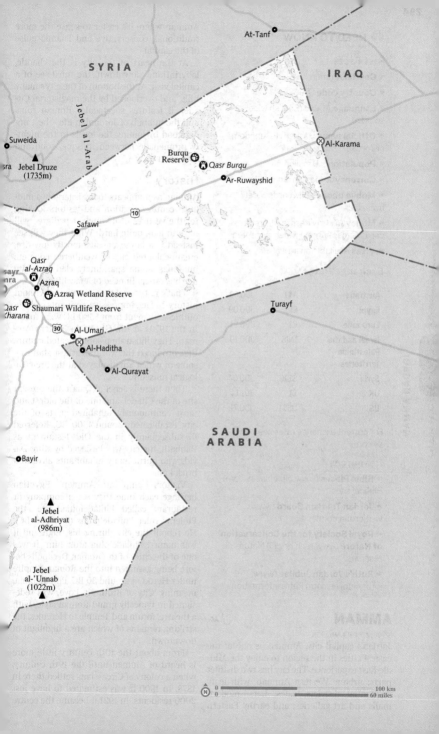

NEED TO KNOW

Fast Facts

➡ **Capital** Amman

➡ **Country code** ☑ 962

➡ **Language** Arabic (English widely spoken)

➡ **Official name** Hashemite Kingdom of Jordan

➡ **Population** 9.9 million

➡ **Currency** Jordanian dinar (JD)

➡ **Mobile phones** SIM cards widely available

➡ **Money** ATMs widespread; credit cards (except Amex) widely accepted

➡ **Visas** Available on arrival

Exchange Rates

Australia	A$1	JD0.62
Egypt	E£1	JD0.09
Euro zone	€1	JD0.91
Israel and the Palestinian Territories	1NIS	JD0.19
Syria	S£10	JD0.04
UK	£1	JD1.14
US	US$1	JD0.71

For current exchange rates see www.xe.com.

Resources

➡ **Bible Places** (www.bibleplaces.com) Biblical sites.

➡ **Jordan Tourism Board** (www.visitjordan.com)

➡ **Royal Society for the Conservation of Nature** (www.rscn.org.jo) Nature reserves.

➡ **Ruth's Jordan Jubilee** (www.jordanjubilee.com) Petra information.

AMMAN عمان

☑ 06 / POP 4 MILLION

Jordan's capital city, Amman, is one of the easiest cities in the region to enjoy the Middle East experience. The city has two distinct parts: urbane Western Amman, with leafy residential districts, cafes, bars, modern malls and art galleries; and earthy Eastern Amman where it's easier to sense the more traditional, conservative and Islamic pulse of the capital.

At the heart of the city is the chaotic, labyrinthine 'downtown', the must-see of a capital visit. At the bottom of the city's many hills, and overlooked by the magisterial Citadel, it features spectacular Roman ruins and the hubbub of Jordanian life – best understood by joining the locals in the nightly promenade between mosque, souq and coffeehouse.

History

Amman as it appears today is largely a mid-20th century creation and visitors looking for the vestiges of its ancient pedigree will have to look quite hard. What they will see instead is a homogeneous, mostly low-rise, cream-coloured city of weathered concrete buildings, some sparklingly clad in white marble, others in need of a facelift.

That's not to say that Amman is without history. In fact, impressive remnants of a Neolithic settlement from 8500 BC were found in the 1970s at Ain Ghazal in Eastern Amman. They illustrate a sophisticated culture that produced the world's earliest statues – some of which are displayed at the archaeological museum.

Then there is Jebel al-Qala'a, the present site of the Citadel, and one of the oldest and most continuously inhabited parts of the city, established around 1800 BC. Referred to subsequently in the Old Testament as Rabbath, the city was besieged by King David, who burnt many inhabitants alive in a brick kiln.

Visitors bump into Amman's Egyptian heritage each time they see a company or restaurant called Philadelphia, after the Ptolemy ruler Philadelphius (283–246 BC). He rebuilt the city during his reign and it was named Philadelphia after him. It was one of the cities of the Roman Decapolis before being assumed into the Roman Empire under Herod in around 30 BC. Philadelphia, meaning 'City of Brotherly Love', was redesigned in typically grand Roman style, with a theatre, forum and Temple to Hercules, the striking remains of which are a highlight of downtown.

From about the 10th century little more is heard of Amman until the 19th century, when a colony of Circassians settled there in 1878. In 1900 it was estimated to have just 2000 residents. In 1921 it became the centre of Transjordan when King Abdullah made it his headquarters. Following the formation of the state of Israel in 1948, Amman absorbed a flood of Palestinian refugees, and doubled its population in a mere two weeks. It continues to grow, swelled by Iraqi and Syrian refugees escaping the chaos across the border.

◉ Sights

Built originally on seven hills (like Rome), Amman now spreads across 19 hills and is therefore not a city to explore on foot. That said, the downtown area – known locally as *il-balad* – with its budget hotels and restaurants, banks, post offices and Amman's ancient sites, is compacted into a relatively small area in the heart of the great metropolis. All other areas of the city fan out from there.

◉ Downtown

★ Citadel   RUIN
(Map p298; ☑ 4638795; Jebel al-Qala'a; admission JD2; ☻ 8am-7pm Sat-Thu Apr-Sep, to 4pm Sat-Thu Oct-Mar) The area known as the Citadel sits on the highest hill in Amman, Jebel al-Qala'a (about 850m above sea level), and is the site of ancient Rabbath-Ammon. Occupied since the Bronze Age, it's surrounded by a 1700m-long wall, which were rebuilt many times during the Bronze and Iron Ages, as well as the Roman, Byzantine and Umayyad periods. There's plenty to see, but the Citadel's most striking sights are the Temple of Hercules and the Ummayad Palace.

★ Roman Theatre   THEATRE
(Map p298; admission incl Folklore Museum & Museum of Popular Traditions JD1; ☻ 8am-7pm Apr-Sep, 8am-4pm Sat-Thu & 9am-4pm Fri Oct-Mar) This magnificently restored theatre is the most obvious and impressive remnant of Roman Philadelphia, and is the highlight of Amman for most foreign visitors. The theatre itself is cut into the northern side of a hill, and has a seating capacity of 6000. The best time for photographs is the morning, when the light is soft – although the views from the top tiers just before sunset are also superb.

Nymphaeum   FOUNTAIN
(Map p298; Quraysh St; ☻ daylight Sat-Thu) FREE Built in AD 191, this elaborate public fountain was once a large, two-storey complex with water features, mosaics, stone carvings and possibly a 600-sq-metre swimming pool – all dedicated to the nymphs. Excavations started in earnest in 1993, and restoration will continue for many years. Except for a few columns, an elegant archway and a few alcoves, there is little to see, though the workers toiling away may yet reveal hidden treasures in the years to come.

Darat al-Funun   GALLERY
(House of Arts; Map p298; ☑ 4643251; www.daratalfunun.org; 13 Nadim al Mallah St, Weibdeh; ☻10am-7pm Sat-Thu) FREE On the hillside to the north of the downtown area, this cultural haven is dedicated to contemporary art. The main building features a small **art gallery** with works by Jordanian and other Arab artists, an art library, and workshops

JORDAN AMMAN

TOP JORDAN ITINERARIES

One Week
Arrive in **Aqaba** from Egypt, and party in Jordan's holiday town. On day two, take the early-morning bus to **Wadi Rum**, of Lawrence of Arabia fame. Hike or share the cost of a 4WD desert tour and return to Aqaba. On day three, take the early-morning bus to Wadi Musa and explore the rock-hewn wonders of **Petra**, a world-class site. On day four, catch the evening bus to **Amman** and spend day five exploring the capital. On day six, watch a chariot race in the Roman ruins of **Jerash** and leave the next day for Israel and the Palestinian Territories via the King Hussein crossing.

Two Weeks
Amplify the above by travelling the ancient **King's Highway** between Petra and Amman, by taxi, visiting the Crusader castles of **Shobak** and **Karak**, the escarpment village of **Dana**, and dramatic **Wadi Mujib** en route. Rest and relax in the travel-friendly town of **Madaba** from where you can tour the **Dead Sea** and **Bethany**, or romp round the **Eastern Desert** castles.

for both Jordanian and visiting sculptors and painters. A schedule of upcoming exhibitions, lectures, films and public discussion forums is available on the gallery's website as well as in the *Jordan Times* newspaper.

Al-Husseiny Mosque   MOSQUE
(Map p298; Hashemi St) Built by King Abdullah I in 1924, and restored in 1987, this compact mosque is in the heart of downtown on the site of an earlier mosque built in AD 640. The mosque is more interesting as a hive of activity than for any architectural splendour – the precinct is a popular local meeting place. Non-Muslims are not normally admitted.

Jebel Amman & Around

King Abdullah Mosque   MOSQUE
(Map p302; ☎5672155, ext 219; Suleiman al-Nabulsi St, Jebel Weibdeh; admission incl museum

JD2; ◷8-11am & 12.30-2pm Sat-Thu) Completed in 1989 as a memorial by the late King Hussein to his grandfather, this blue-domed landmark can house up to 7000 worshippers, with a further 3000 in the courtyard. There is also a small women's section for 500 worshippers, and a much smaller royal enclosure. The cavernous, octagonal prayer hall is capped by a magnificent blue dome 35m in diameter, decorated with Quranic inscriptions. This is the only mosque in Amman that openly welcomes non-Muslim visitors.

Jordan National
Gallery of Fine Arts   GALLERY
(Map p302; ☎4630128; www.nationalgallery.org; Hosni Fareez St, Jebel Weibdeh; admission JD5; ◷9am-5pm Wed-Mon) This small but impressive gallery is a wonderful place to gain an appreciation of contemporary Jordanian painting, sculpture and pottery. Renovated in 2005, the attractive space highlights contemporary art from around the Middle

Amman

East and the greater Muslim world. Temporary exhibitions here are of high quality, and serve as a valuable introduction (or refresher) to the world of Islamic art.

The gallery is signposted from Suleiman al-Nabulsi St, opposite the King Abdullah Mosque.

The gallery is housed in two buildings, separated by a small park: Building 1, on the north side of the park, is the smaller but holds an excellent gift shop; Building 2 opposite contains the bulk of the collection and a cafe.

🛌 Sleeping

Downtown Amman has many budget hotels. Places listed below all promise hot water and some even deliver. Unless otherwise stated, all of the midrange hotels are located in the Jebel Amman area. Top-end hotels are located in Jebel Amman and Shmeisani.

Downtown

★ **Jordan Tower Hotel**　　HOTEL $
(Map p298; ☎ 4614161; www.jordantoweramman.com; 50 Hashemi St; male & female dm JD13, s/d/tr JD28/39/46; ❄ @ 🛜) This warm and friendly hotel has a winning location: you couldn't be closer to the key sights without offering beds in the Forum. Rooms are bright and snug with flat-screen TVs, though the bathrooms are small; there's also a a big, bright and homely reception-cum-lounge area and rooftop restaurant. Offers day trips to the Dead Sea, Petra and other sites.

Palace Hotel　　HOTEL $
(Map p298; ☎ 4624326; Al-Malek Faisal St; s/d/tr with bathroom JD20/28/40, with bathroom JD18/26/30; ❄ @ 🛜) The Palace offers good-value budget accommodation and its location in the heart of King Faisal St can't be bettered (look for the entrance on the pedestrianised side street). Some of the basic, airy rooms have tiny balconies from which to enjoy the bustle of the street below. Guests can add their name to the lists for onward transport options and tours to top sites outside Amman

Farah Hotel　　HOTEL $
(Map p298; ☎ 4651443; www.farahhotel.com.jo; Cinema al-Hussein St; 4- to 6-bed dm JD6, s/d/tr JD22/30/39, without bathroom JD14/20/27; @ 🛜) A firm favourite with travellers, this

JORDAN AMMAN

JORDAN MUSEUM

Amman's downtown area of Ras Al-Ayn is enjoying a major redevelopment, and public gardens, panoramic vantage points and pedestrian trails linking the Citadel and the Roman Theatre are part of the ongoing project. The highlight of this project is the new international-standard Jordan Museum (Map p302; www.jordanmuseum.jo/en; btwn Omar Matar & Ali Bin Abi Taleb Sts; admission JD5; ⊙ 10am-2pm Sat-Mon, Wed & Thu), which is located next to the City Hall. Housed in a beautiful modern building, a series of beautifully presented and informative displays tell Jordan's historical epic from the first people through the Nabatean civilisation to the cusp of the modern era. Highlights include the oldest-known human statues (the spookily modern 8000-year-old mannequins of Ain Ghazal), Jordan's share of the Dead Sea scrolls, and a host of remains from Petra and surrounds.

Downtown Amman

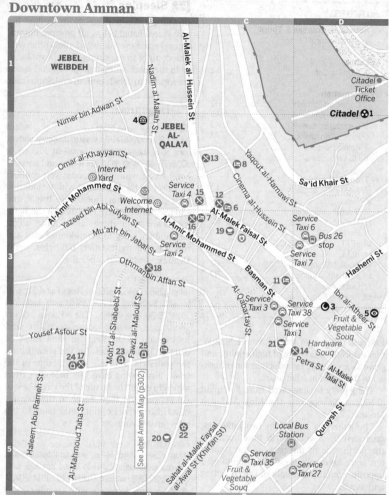

JORDAN AMMAN

this well-managed establishment downtown has a shady garden and a homely, tranquil atmosphere, unlike its neighbours off the high street. A roof terrace offers great views of downtown, and the hotel owners have many years of experience in onward transport and tours to the major tourist sites.

Cliff Hotel
HOTEL $

(Map p298; ☑4624273; Al-Malek Faisal St; s/d/tr/q without bathroom JD8/10/12/15, breakfast JD1.500; ☏) This long-standing shoestring favourite has basic and quite dark rooms, but there's a big bright lounge area that acts

as a sociable meeting place (don't be put off by the grungy hotel entrance). The shared bathrooms have hot water. A popular choice among younger travellers, the Cliff also offers a mattress on the roof in summer.

★ Art Hotel
HOTEL $$

(Map p298; ☑4638900; www.facebook.com/ArtHotelDowntown; 30 Al-Malek Faisal St; d around JD70; ☀❄☏) On the cusp of opening during research, this stylish new hotel looks to be a great addition to the downtown scene. Rooms are well finished in crisp white with good fittings. It has a deli-counter in the lob-

With 45 years' experience helping travellers, the Caravan also offers a comprehensive transport service with English-speaking drivers. It costs JD3 for a taxi to the North bus station.

Heritage House
HOTEL **$$**

(Map p298; ☑ 4643111; www.heritageamman.com; Rainbow St; r JD90; 🛜) It's taken a while for the hotel scene to catch up with what's happening around Rainbow St, but Heritage House has managed to take advantage of its location. Compact, subtle and modern, it's a useful getaway from city life, with a series of small rooms and studios.

Hisham Hotel
HOTEL **$$$**

(Map p302; ☑ 4644028; www.hishamhotel.com.jo; Mithqal al-Fayez St; s/d from JD80/102; ✳@🛜) This delightful hotel in a leafy embassy district of Jebel Amman is an excellent choice if you're looking for a hotel removed from the hustle and bustle of the city while still within easy reach of downtown. The rooms are comfortable with flat-screen TVs and minibars, and are brought to life with small, personal touches.

Jordan InterContinental Hotel
HOTEL **$$$**

(Map p302; ☑ 4641361; www.intercontinental. com; Al-Kulliyah al-Islamiyah St; r from JD190; ✳@🛜✳) The grandaddy of luxury hotels in Amman, the much-loved InterCon has been hosting foreign dignitaries since the early days of Jordan's founding. A great favourite for local weddings, complete with traditional drumming, and with excellent Jordanian and Lebanese restaurants, and quality craft and antique shops, this is as good a place as any for an introduction to local city culture.

✖ Eating

Budget eateries are concentrated downtown. Take a local approach to choosing a dinner venue: promenade Rainbow St in Jebel Amman, Culture St in Shmeisani or Waqalat St around the 7th Circle in Swafei, and pick the most appealing of the many restaurants.

✖ Downtown

★ Hashem Restaurant
FELAFEL **$**

(Map p298; Al-Malek Faisal St; the works JD3; ☺24hr) You haven't tried felafel until you've eaten here. This legendary eatery, run for half a century by a Turkish family, is so popular with locals and visitors alike that there's stiff competition for tables, many

by and a restaurant in the works. An informal atmosphere is encouraged, but it's the breezy roof terrace overlooking downtown that really seals the deal.

🛏 Jebel Amman

Caravan Hotel
HOTEL **$**

(Map p302; ☑ 5661195; caravan@go.com.jo; Al-Ma'moun St; s/d/tr/q JD22/28/33/38; @) On a quiet side-street location near the King Abdullah Mosque, this place is an excellent choice. The big, clean rooms have a bright aspect and en suite toilets and showers.

JORDAN AMMAN

Downtown Amman

of which overflow into the alleyway. Aim for an early lunch or supper if you want to avoid the queues, although it has to be said that Hashem does a fantastic job of feeding the multitude in record time. Mid-afternoon, it makes a great place to sup a mint tea and watch downtown slide towards siesta.

Afrah Restaurant & Coffeeshop
MIDDLE EASTERN $$
(Map p298; ☑ 4610046; Al-Malek Faisal St; mains from JD5; ⊙ 9am-1am) This popular restaurant in the heart of downtown is more about the ambience than the food. Squeezed into every nook and cranny of the renovated upper storeys of this typical townhouse, the tables fill up quickly in the evening, particularly those with a balcony view of Al-Malek Faisal St below. Live Arab pop entertainment is offered nightly from around 9pm.

Sara Seafood Restaurant
SEAFOOD $$
(Map p298; ☑ 4561115; Al-Malek Faisal St; fish dishes from JD5; ⊙ 10am-1am) This restaurant doesn't look much from the outside and looks positively uninviting from the street entrance (next to Cliff Hotel), but it turns out some of the best seafood in the neighbourhood. There's a tiny balcony overlooking busy Al-Malek al-Hussein St or quieter tables inside. The restaurant offers a decent choice of salads, whipped up at the microshop opposite the entrance downstairs.

Cairo Restaurant
MIDDLE EASTERN $
(Map p298; ☑ 4624527; Petra St; meals JD2-5; ⊙ 6am-10pm) Recommended by travellers, this simple restaurant serves good local food at budget prices. Most locals opt for the mutton stew and boiled goat's head, but you may prefer the *shish tawooq* (marinated chicken grilled on skewers) with portions of grilled chicken large enough for two.

Habibah
DESSERTS $
(Map p298; Al-Malek al-Hussein St; pastries from 500 fils) This legendary shop is a good bet for Middle Eastern sweets and pastries. Sweet tooths of all ages line up for honey-infused, pistachio-topped and filo-crusted variations on the region's most famous desserts. There is another branch on Al-Malek Faisal St.

🍴 Jebel Amman

Reem Cafeteria
MIDDLE EASTERN $
(Map p302; ☑ 4645725; 2nd Circle; shwarma from 850 fils) There are hundreds of shoebox-sized shwarma kiosks in Amman but few that have the customers queuing down the street at 3am. Having had one of Reem's delicious shwarmas (and a second and third), we know exactly why. Look for the red-and-white awning (with milling crowds) on 2nd Circle.

Al-Quds Restaurant
JORDANIAN $$

(Jerusalem Restaurant; Map p298; ☑4630168; Al-Malek al-Hussein St; pastries from 800 fils, mains from JD6; ☺7am-10pm) The Jerusalem Restaurant specialises in sweets and pastries, but it has a large, good-value restaurant at the back that provides a great opportunity to try typical Jordanian dishes. The house speciality is *mensaf*, a Bedouin dish of lamb on a bed of rice, and *maqlubbe* is frequently on the menu.

Ararat
ARMENIAN $$

(Map p302; ☑4601097; Rainbow St; mains JD6-12; ☺11am-11.45pm) Wondering what Armenian cuisine is like? Head to Ararat and leave with a belly full of great food. Try *sini kufta* (lamb and wheat casserole) and a variety of tasty cooked salads, or go for a selection of smaller starters (JD2.250 to JD4.500) – we were particularly taken with the *lemajoun* (Armenian 'pizza'), *mante* (baked dumplings), *buererg* (cheese pastries) and *makanek* (spiced sausages). The menu leans heavily towards the carnivorous.

Abu Ahmad Orient Restaurant
MIDDLE EASTERN $$

(Map p302; ☑3522520; 3rd Circle; mains JD5-11; ☺noon-midnight) This excellent midrange Lebanese place has a leafy outdoor terrace that bustles with life during the summer months. The standard fare comprises grilled meats, but the real highlights are the hot and cold mezze – try a *buraik* (meat or cheese pie) or the *yalenjeh* (stuffed vine leaves).

Romero Restaurant
ITALIAN $$$

(Map p302; ☑4644227; www.romero-jordan.com; Mohammed Hussein Haikal St; mains JD10-18) Established half a century ago in an elegant traditional townhouse, Romero comes complete with period furniture, Venetian chandeliers and a roaring fire in winter. With intimate tables tucked in unexpected corners, a fine wine list to savour and succulent homemade pasta, this venue is just the place to come for a celebration. Book in advance.

Fakhr El-Din Restaurant
MIDDLE EASTERN $$$

(Map p302; ☑4652399; 2nd Circle; mains JD8-15) Tastefully decorated and with crisp white-linen tablecloths, this fine-dining restaurant is located in a 1950s house with a beautiful little garden. Over 10 years, countless guests have visited this establishment in search of what the proprietor terms 'genuine Arabic cuisine and hospitality'. A range of raw-meat dishes, including lamb fillet, make an interesting addition to all the familiar Middle Eastern favourites.

★ Sufra
JORDANIAN $$$

(Map p298; ☑4611468; www.facebook.com/Sufra-Restaurant; 28 Rainbow St; starters from JD3.350, mains from JD10; ☺1-11.30pm Sun-Thu, 9.30am-11.30pm Fri & Sat) How good is Sufra when it comes to traditional Jordanian cuisine? Well, if the royal family are fans, we're hardly ones to argue. Housed in a lovely old villa with a terrace garden, this really is the place to eat well. The signature *mansaf* (lamb with rice and nuts, with a yoghurt sauce) is a delight.

JORDAN AMMAN

WORTH A TRIP

WILD JORDAN CENTRE

If visiting the Wild Jordan Centre, which doubles as the Royal Society for the Conservation of Nature (RSCN) booking office (p305), don't miss the cafe and nature store, and before you leave, pick up a downtown walking trail brochure for some backstreet revelations.

Wild Jordan Café (Map p298; ☑4633542; Othman Bin Affan St, downtown; mains JD7-12; ☺11am-midnight; ☎☑) At wonderful, ecofriendly Wild Jordan Café, the emphasis is on locally sourced produce, healthy wraps, organic salads and locally plucked herbs. Smoothies are a welcome change from the ubiquitous coffee of cafes elsewhere. The glass walls and open-air terrace offer vistas of the Citadel and the downtown area – a great way to gain a perspective of Amman's main sights. The weekend brunch is always popular.

Wild Jordan Centre (Map p298; ☑4633718; Othman bin Affan St, downtown; ☺10am-10pm) The nature store at the Wild Jordan Centre sells products made in Jordan's nature reserves, including silver jewellery, organic herbs and jams from Dana, and candles made by Bedouin women as part of an income-generating project in Feynan. Decorated ostrich eggs are another speciality. All profits are returned to the craftspeople and to nature-reserve projects.

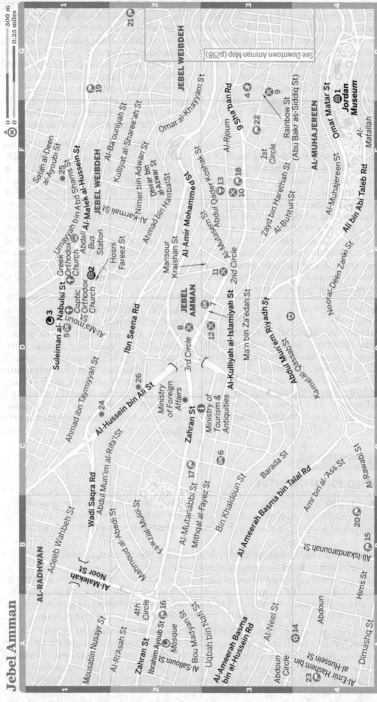

Jebel Amman

See Downtown Amman Map (p298)

JEBEL WEIBDEH

JEBEL WEIBDEH

JEBEL AMMAN

AL-RADHWAN

AL-MUHAJEREEN

0   500 m
0   0.25 miles

Jebel Amman

🍷 Drinking & Nightlife

Some of the cafes in downtown are perfect retreats from which to watch the world go by, write up your journal, tweet a friend, meet locals and play backgammon. A dozen or more cafes can be found around Hashemite Sq – a great place for people-watching in summer.

The place to be seen in Amman at night is Abdoun Circle, where there are dozens of popular cafes.

Downtown

Shaher's Penthouse Cafeteria   CAFE
(Map p298; Sahat al-Malek Faysal al-Awal St, downtown; coffee JD3; ⊙ 9.30am-11pm) This cosy cafe has a traditionally decorated indoor dining area as well as an outdoor terrace overlooking the street far below. Hussein, the resident musician, will happily play the oud (lute) or violin to provide a cultured counterpoint to the street noise below.

Al-Rashid Court Café   CAFE
(Map p298; ☑ 4652994; Al-Malek Faisal St, downtown; tea or coffee from JD3; ⊙ 10am-midnight Sat-Thu, 1-11pm Fri) The 1st-floor balcony here is *the* place to pass an afternoon and survey the chaos of the downtown area below, though competition for seats is fierce. Also known as the Eco-Tourism Café, this is one

of the best places for the uninitiated to try a nargileh (JD2). Although you won't see any local women here, it's well accustomed to foreign tourists. To find it, look for the flags of the world on the main facade; the entrance is down the side alley.

Jebel Amman

Living Room   COCKTAIL BAR
(Map p302; ☑ 4655988; Mohammed Hussein Haikal St, Jebel Amman; drinks JD4-8, mains JD8-20; ⊙ 1pm-1am) Part lounge, part sushi bar and part study (think high-backed chairs, a fireplace and the daily newspaper), the Living Room is so understated that it's easily missed. It offers quality bar meals, fine music and delicious iced tea with lemon grass and mint. Nonteetotallers can enjoy the full complement of expertly crafted cocktails on offer, which are served up deliciously strong. Book tables in advance at the weekend.

Grappa   BAR
(Map p302; ☑ 4651458; Abdul Qader Koshak St, Jebel Amman; beer JD4-5; ⊙ 6pm-1.30am) Stylish wooden benches and black-and-white photos on the wall give this rustic bar a hip feel, but it's the huge windows with views and the summer terrace seating that really draw the crowds.

JORDAN AMMAN

AMMAN FOR CHILDREN

While Amman is not the most exciting city for kids, they will feel welcome, even in a restaurant late at night.

Amman Waves (☑4121704; www.ammanwaves.com; Airport Rd; adult/child JD14/8; ⏱10am-7pm) This Western-style water park is about 15km south of town on the highway to the airport. Note that adults should respect local sensibilities and wear appropriate swimwear (no Speedos or bikinis).

Haya Cultural Centre (Map p296; ☑5665195; Ilya Abu Madhi St; ⏱9am-6pm Sat-Thu) Designed especially for children, this centre has a library, playground, an interactive eco-museum and an inflatable castle. It also organises regular activities and performances for kids.

⭐ Entertainment

Programs for these modern cinemas are advertised in the English-language newspapers. Ticket prices vary.

Royal Film Commission   CINEMA
(Map p298; ☑4642266; www.film.jo; 5 Omar bin al-Khattab Street) The home of the Jordanian film industry, the commission holds regular screenings and festivals featuring the best of local and international cinema. The outdoor theatre looking over downtown is a great place to see a film, while the stylish on-site Montage (Map p298; 5 Omar bin al-Khattab St; ⏱9am-11pm; ☎) cafe is worth a visit at any time of day.

Galleria   CINEMA
(Map p302; ☑5934793; Abdoun Circle, Jebel Amman) Western and Bollywood new releases.

🛍 Shopping

Amman is a good place to shop for souvenirs in Jordan, with everything from tourist kitsch to high-quality handicraft boutiques, many of which are run to benefit local communities.

The following are among the better places, and are generally open 9am to 6pm Saturday to Thursday. Prices are fixed. Rainbow St is good for a browse.

Jordan River Foundation   HANDICRAFTS
(Map p298; ☑5933211; www.jordanriver.jo; Bani Hamida House, Fawzi al-Malouf St, Jebel Amman; ⏱8.30am-7pm Sat-Thu, 10am-5pm Fri) Supporting top-notch worthy causes by selling equally top-notch crafted items, this shop has become an institution in Amman. The showroom supports handloomed rugs from Bani Hamida and exquisite Palestinian-style embroidery. Cushions, camel bags, embroidery, baskets and Dead Sea products make it an excellent place to buy items of stylish decor. Only the highest-quality pieces make it into the showroom (reflected in the prices).

Souk Jara   MARKET
(Map p298; www.facebook.com/soukjara; Rainbow St; ⏱10am-10pm Fri) A weekly open-air flea market run by the Jebel Amman Residents' Association (JARA), selling a variety of handicrafts. It's good fun to browse, and there are some great food and drink stalls and occasional live music to add to the atmosphere.

Mlabbas   CLOTHING
(Map p298; www.mlabbas.com; 28 Rainbow St) Want to look like a hip urban Jordanian? Head to this cool-as-you-like T-shirt shop on Rainbow St for an amazing array of screen-printed Ts by local artists. Styles range from big-brand pastiches through to graffiti art, manga and cartoons, as well as a witty line in Arabic puns (ask the staff for translations). Prints, postcards and stickers are also available.

ℹ Information

EMERGENCY

Tourist Police (Map p298; Hashemi St) Small booth near the Roman Theatre.

INTERNET ACCESS

Amman has plenty of internet cafes, particularly in downtown.

Internet Yard (Map p298; ☑5509569; dweib@joinnet.com.jo; Al-Amir Mohammed St, downtown; per hour JD1; ⏱9.30am-midnight)

Welcome Internet (Map p298; ☑4620206; Al-Amir Mohammed St, downtown; per hour JD1; ⏱10.30am-1am)

MEDIA

The *Jordan Times* and the *Star*, the two English-language newspapers, both print entertainment listings.

Jordan Today (www.jordantoday.com.jo) is a free monthly booklet that includes a yellow pages listing of embassies, airlines and the like. *Where to Go* is similar and includes a useful collection of Amman restaurant menus. Pick them up in the better hotels and restaurants.

BeAmman (www.beamman.com) Gives up-to-date listings of all that is fresh and happening in the capital.

MEDICAL SERVICES

The English-language *Jordan Times* and *Star* list the current telephone numbers of doctors and pharmacies on night duty throughout the capital.

Italian Hospital (Map p296; ☎4777101; Italian St, downtown)

MONEY

Changing money is easy, and the downtown area especially has many banks, ATMs and money changers.

POST

Central Post Office (Map p298; Al-Amir Mohammed St, downtown; ⏲7.30am-5pm Sat-Thu, 8am-1.30pm Fri)

TELEPHONE

SIM cards are available on arrival at the airport. Telephone cards for public booths can be purchased from corner shops.

TOURIST INFORMATION

Ministry of Tourism & Antiquities (Map p302; ☎4603360, ext 254; fax 4646264; Ground fl, Al-Mutanabbi St, Jebel Amman; ⏲8am-9pm) The most useful place for information is this office, southwest of the 3rd Circle, which is also the centre for the tourist police. The staff are friendly, and speak good English.

Wild Jordan Centre (Map p298; ☎4616523; www.rscn.org.jo; Othman Bin Affan St, downtown) Information and bookings for activities and accommodation in any of Jordan's nature reserves, including Dana and Wadi Mujib. The centre is run by the Royal Society for the Conservation of Nature (RSCN). There is also a small crafts shop and an organic cafe here (see p301).

Getting There & Away

AIR

The only domestic air route is between Amman and Aqaba.

BUS, MINIBUS & SERVICE TAXI

There are two main bus and minibus stations in Amman. In addition, there are smaller bus stations serving specific destinations such as the Dead Sea, as well as private coaches from the JETT and Trust offices.

Service taxis are generally faster, but they don't always follow fixed schedules. They depart from the same stations as the minibuses.

All departures are more frequent in the morning and most dry up completely after sunset.

Main Public Bus Stations

North bus station (Tabardour) Located in the northern suburbs, this station offers services to the north. A taxi to this station from downtown costs from JD3. Fairly regular minibuses and service taxis leave between 7am and 6.30pm for the following destinations: Ajloun (JD1, two hours, every 30 minutes), Jerash (900 fils, 1¼ hours, hourly) and Madaba (JD1, 45 minutes, every 10 minutes from 6am

JORDAN IN A HURRY? TAKE A TOUR!

Usually shy away from tours? Well Jordan is one place to make an exception, especially if you're short of time or on a tight budget. Tours run by budget hotels in Amman and Madaba have filled the public-transport gaps to destinations like the Eastern Desert, the Dead Sea and the King's Highway. The 'tours' are really just transport, so don't expect much from the guide-cum-driver. They do, however, offer a chance to meet fellow travellers and share costs.

The Cliff, Jordan Tower, Farah and Palace Hotels in Amman offer popular day trips to the Eastern Desert castles; another top trip is to Jerash, Ajloun and Umm Qais. Good-value trips along the King's Highway leave Amman at 8.30am and travel to Petra (9½ hours) via Madaba, Wadi Mujib, Karak, Shobak and Dana. The Black Iris Hotel (p320) and the Mariam Hotel (p321) in Madaba can arrange similar itineraries. A seat in a four-seater taxi or minibus costs from around JD15 to JD50, depending on the number of fellow passengers, stops, time and distance.

There are a few tour companies with a good reputation for comprehensive (but more expensive) tours around Jordan; try **Petra Moon** (Map p332; ☎07-96170666; www.petramoon.com) in Wadi Musa to get an idea of what's on offer.

to 8pm). Services are also available for Deir Alla (for Pella, one hour), Fuheis (45 minutes), Irbid (two hours), Ramtha (two hours), Salt (45 minutes) and Zarqa (for Azraq, 30 minutes); all these services cost under JD1.

South bus station (Wahadat) Almost all buses and service taxis heading south leave from this station in the southern suburbs by Middle East Circle (Duwaar Sharq al-Awsat). A taxi to this station from downtown costs from JD2.500. For Petra, minibuses and service taxis (JD7, four hours) depart for Wadi Musa when full from the far corner of the lot between around 6am and 4pm. Buses to Aqaba (JD5.500, five hours) leave every two hours or so until 9pm. There are regular buses to Karak (JD2, two hours) until 5pm, Shobak (JD5, 2½ hours) and Ma'an (JD2.750, three hours); most services stop running around 4pm. For Dana there are three buses a day from 11am for Qadsiyya (JD3, three hours); otherwise take a bus to Tafila (JD2.800, 2½ hours) and change. There are semiregular service taxis to Karak (JD3, 2½ hours), Ma'an (JD6, three hours) and also infrequently to Aqaba (JD10, five hours).

Other Public Bus Stations

Muhajireen bus station This small station is on Al-Ameerah Basma bin Talal St, opposite the Muhajireen police station. Minibuses to Wadi as-Seer (400 fils, 30 minutes) leave frequently from here during daylight hours. There are also services to Madaba and Mt Nebo (JD1, 45 minutes) between 6am and 5pm.

Abdali bus station (Map p302; Al-Malek al-Hussein St, Jebel Amman) This station is a 20-minute walk (2km uphill) from downtown; service taxi 6 or 7 from Cinema al-Hussein St goes right by. This is the station to use for air-conditioned buses and service taxis for international destinations. The bus station is transformed into a giant flea market on Fridays and there are plans to redevelop the entire site as part of an ambitious urban-regeneration project.

Private Coach Stations

JETT (Map p296; ✆ 5664146; www.jett.com.jo; Al-Malek al-Hussein St, Shmeisani) The domestic JETT office is about 500m northwest of the Abdali bus station. Passengers board the bus outside the office. There are six buses daily to Aqaba (JD7.500, five hours, 7am, 9am, 11am, 2pm, 4pm and 6pm), and one bus to King Hussein Bridge (JD7.250, one hour, 7am), for entry into Israel and the Palestinian Territories. There are daily services to Irbid (JD1.900, every 30 minutes from 6am to 7.30pm, two hours).

A daily JETT bus connects Amman with Petra, largely designed for those wanting to visit on a day trip. The service leaves at 6.30am (single/return JD9.500/19, four hours) and drops passengers off at Petra Visitor Centre in Wadi Musa

at 9.30am. The return bus leaves between 4pm and 5pm so bear in mind this option leaves very little time for visiting the sites of Petra.

A weekly Jett bus departs for Amman Beach at the Dead Sea (single JD8) on Fridays at 8am and returns at 4pm. If there are insufficient passengers, however, the service is cancelled.

Hijazi Travel & Tours (✆ 02-7240721) Hijazi Travel & Tours runs daily buses to Irbid (JD2, every 15 to 20 minutes from 6am to 7pm, 1½ hours). The buses leave from the North bus station.

CAR

All the major hotels have car-rental offices. The largest selection of rental companies is at King Abdullah Gardens.

🛈 Getting Around

TO/FROM THE AIRPORT

Queen Alia International Airport is 35km south of the city. The **Airport Express Bus** (✆ 4451531, 0880 022006) runs between the airport and the North bus station (Tabarbour), passing through the 4th, 5th, 6th and 7th Circles en route. This service (JD3, 45 minutes) runs hourly between 7am and 11pm, and at 1am and 3am, from the airport daily. From Amman, it starts at 6am to 10pm hourly and also runs at 2am and 4am.

A taxi costs JD20 to JD25 from the airport to Amman, slightly less in the opposite direction.

TAXI
Private Taxi

Private taxis are painted yellow. They are abundant, can be flagged from the side of the road and fares are cheap. A taxi from downtown to Shmeisani, for example, costs JD2.500 and it's JD3 to Tabarbour. For longer journeys around town, you're best off agreeing on a price per hour (JD10 was the going rate at the time of writing).

Service Taxi

Most fares in these white cabs cost from 400 fils per seat, and you usually pay the full amount regardless of where you get off. After 8pm, the price for all service taxis goes up by 25%. Following are some of the more useful routes:

Number 2 From Basman St, for 1st and 2nd Circles.

Number 3 From Basman St, for 3rd and 4th Circles.

Number 6 From Cinema al-Hussein St, for Abdali station and JETT offices.

Number 7 From Cinema al-Hussein St, past Abdali station and King Abdullah Mosque to Shmeisani.

Number 35 From Quraysh St for Al-Muhajireen Police Station.

JERASH & THE NORTH

You might expect that the far north of Jordan, with its exceptional Roman ruins, biblical associations, lively cities and complex terrain, would feature as a standard part of any visitor's trip to the country. This, however, is not the case and the region receives relatively few visitors compared with Petra and the south. For those in the know, this is excellent news as it means that it is quite possible to enjoy epic sites like Jerash without the epic crowds normally associated with a world-class destination.

Although many of the sites can be covered in a day trip from Amman, this ancient and populous region, dotted with olive groves and pine forests and liberally strewn with the ruins of Rome's great Decapolis cities, repays a longer visit. The availability of public transport and friendly accommodation facilitate this, and if the springtime flowers happen to be blooming, it will prove to be a hard region to leave.

Jerash جرش

📑 02 / POP 123,190

These beautifully preserved **Roman ruins** (admission JD8; ☉8am-4.30pm Oct-Apr, to 7pm May-Sep), located 51km north of Amman, are deservedly one of Jordan's major attractions. Archaeological digs have been ongoing for 85 years but it is estimated that 90% of the city is still unexcavated. In its heyday the ancient city, known in Roman times as Gerasa, had a population of around 15,000.

Allow at least three hours to do Jerash justice. The best times to visit are before 10am or after 4pm, but this is tricky if you are relying on public transport.

In July and August, Jerash hosts the **Jerash Festival** (www.jerashfestival.jo), featuring local and overseas artists, music and drama performances inside the ancient city, and displays of traditional handicrafts.

History

Although inhabited from Neolithic times, and settled as a town during the reign of Alexander the Great (333 BC), Jerash was largely a Roman creation and well-preserved remains of all the classic Roman structures – forum, cardo maximus, hippodrome, nymphaeum – are easily distinguishable among the ruins.

In the wake of Roman general Pompey's conquest of the region in 64 BC, Gerasa became part of the Roman province of Syria and, soon after, a city of the Decapolis. The city reached its peak at the beginning of the 3rd century AD, when it was bestowed with the rank of Colony, after which time it went into a slow decline as trade routes shifted.

By the middle of the 5th century AD, Christianity was the region's major religion and the construction of churches proceeded at a startling rate. With the Sassanian invasion from Persia in 614, the Muslim conquest in 636 and a devastating earthquake in 747, Jerash's heyday passed and its population shrank to about a quarter of its former size.

💿 Sights

The ruins at Jerash cover a huge area and can seem daunting at first, especially as there is virtually no signage. To help the ruins come alive, engage one of the knowledgable guides (JD20) at the ticket checkpoint to help you navigate the main complex. Walking at a leisurely pace and allowing time for sitting on a fallen column and enjoying the spectacular views, you can visit the main ruins in a minimum of three to four hours.

The entrance to the site is south of the ancient city, close to Hadrian's Arch. The **ticket office** (📑6351272) is in a modern souq with souvenir and antique shops, a post office and a semitraditional coffeehouse. Keep your ticket as you will have to show it at the South Gate.

At the extreme south of the site is the striking **Hadrian's Arch**, also known as the Triumphal Arch, which was built in AD 129 to honour the visit of Emperor Hadrian. Behind the arch is the **hippodrome**, which hosted chariot races watched by up to 15,000 spectators.

The **South Gate**, originally one of four along the city wall and built in AD 130, leads into the city proper. The Oval Plaza (forum) is one of the most distinctive sites of Jerash, unusual because of its shape and huge size (90m long and 80m at its widest point). Fifty-six Ionic columns surround the paved limestone plaza, linking the cardo maximus with the **Temple of Zeus**.

The elegant remains of the Temple of Zeus, built around AD 162, can be reached from the **forum** – a worthwhile climb if just for the view. Next door, the **South Theatre** was built in the 1st century AD with a capacity of 5000 spectators. From the upper stalls, the acoustics are still wonderful, as

Jerash

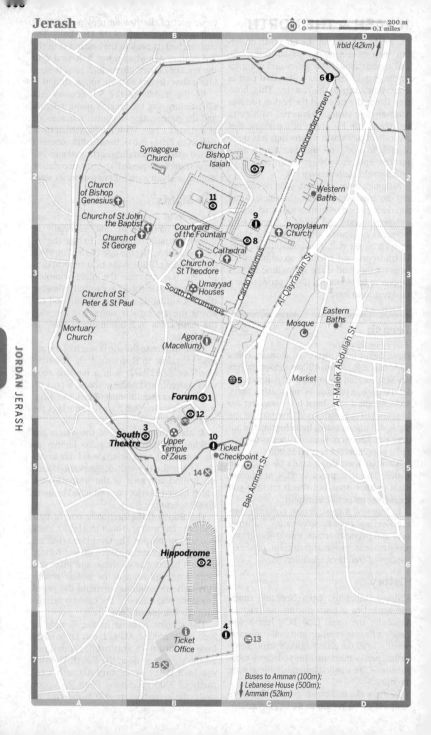

Irbid (42km)

Buses to Amman (100m);
Lebanese House (500m);
Amman (52km)

Jerash

demonstrated by the occasional roving minstrel or drummer.

To the northeast of the forum lies the cardo maximus, the city's main thoroughfare, also known as the colonnaded street. Stretching for 800m to the North Gate, the street is still paved with the original stones, rutted by the thousands of chariots that once jostled along its length.

The colonnaded street is punctuated by the nymphaeum, the main fountain of the city, before giving rise to a superb propylaeum (monumental gateway), and a staircase. The Temple of Artemis, towering over Jerash at the top of the stairs, was dedicated to the patron goddess of the city, but alas was dismantled to provide masonry for new churches under Theodorius in AD 386.

Further to the north is the North Theatre, built originally in AD 165 and now restored to former glory.

The small museum (☑ 6312267; ⊙ 8.30am-6pm Oct-Apr, to 5pm May-Sep) FREE contains a good collection of artefacts from the site.

🛏 Sleeping & Eating

Although Jerash can be visited as a day trip from Amman, an overnight stop is more rewarding and may be necessary if you're trying to visit by public transport. The modern town of Jerash, which encompasses the ruins of the Eastern Baths, comes to life after sunset and is a pleasant place to explore in the early evening. It's important to book ahead.

Hadrian Gate Hotel   HOTEL $$
(☑ 077 7793907; s/d/tr/penthouse from JD25/40/50/70; ✲) Run by the always friendly and accommodating Ismail Khasim and his son Walid, Jerash's only hotel boasts a spectacular location overlooking Hadrian's Gate. Breakfast is served on the rooftop ter-

races with a panoramic view of the Temple of Artemis to the west and Jerash's market gardens to the east.

Olive Branch Resort   HOTEL $$
(☑ 6340555; www.olivebranch.com.jo; s/d/tr incl breakfast from JD35/50/60, camping own tent/hired tent JD12/14; ✲) Around 7km from Jerash on the road to Ajloun, this hilltop countryside hotel is situated amid olive groves and pine trees. The spacious rooms have some oddities, such as a bathtub in the bedroom, but the balconies with rural views compensate. Country fare, including kebab suppers and *labneh* (yoghurt) breakfasts, are served in the poolside garden or in the modest restaurant.

Jerash Rest House   BUFFET $
(☑ 077 217584; buffet JD5; ⊙ noon-8pm) The only restaurant inside the ruins, this is a welcome stop for weary visitors. Located near the South Gate, it attracts large volumes of tourists, but service is quick and efficient and it serves alcohol. The lunch buffet and barbecue is more conducive to an afternoon nap than a jaunt round the ruins, but it's tasty nonetheless.

Jordan House Restaurant   BUFFET $$
(☑ 077217584; buffet JD6; ⊙ 8am-9pm; ☎) Serving a comprehensive buffet between 11am and 5pm, this friendly establishment at the entrance to the ruins is a good place for a Turkish coffee before starting out, and a fresh lemon and mint drink over lunch on your return.

★ Lebanese House   LEBANESE $$
(☑ 6353330; mains JD4-9; ⊙ noon-11pm; ☑) Nicknamed 'Umm Khalil', this rambling restaurant, which has served more than five million customers since 1977, is a national treasure. Try the fresh almonds while you

JORDAN JERASH

wait for sizzling mezze and fresh-baked bread. If you can't decide what to sample, try the regular meal (JD15) or the house special (JD22) for a selection of the best dishes.

🛈 Getting There & Away

BUS & MINIBUS

Buses and minibuses run frequently between Amman's North bus station and Jerash (800 fils, 1¼ hours), though they can take an hour to fill with enough passengers to warrant departure. From Jerash, minibuses travel regularly to Irbid (JD1, 45 minutes) and Ajloun (600 fils, 30 minutes) until mid-afternoon. Jerash's bus station is a 15-minute walk west of the site, at the second set of traffic lights. If you don't fancy the walk, you can often jump on buses headed to Amman from the junction southeast of the main ticket office. Transport drops off significantly after 5pm.

TAXI

Service taxis sometimes leave for Amman up to around 8pm (later during the Jerash Festival) from the bus station, but it's not guaranteed. A private taxi between Amman and Jerash should cost around JD18 to JD25 each way, with a bit of determined bargaining. From Jerash, a taxi to Irbid costs around JD14 to JD20.

Ajloun عجلون

📞 02 / POP 94,458

Ajloun (or Ajlun) is a popular and easy day trip from Amman, and can be combined with a trip to Jerash if you leave the capital early.

💿 Sights

Qala'at Ar-Rabad (Ajloun Castle)   CASTLE

This historic castle was built atop Mt 'Auf (1250m) between 1184 and 1188 by one of Saladin's generals (and nephew), 'Izz ad-Din Usama bin Munqidh. The castle commands views of the Jordan Valley and three wadis leading into it – making it an important strategic link in the defensive chain against the Crusaders, and a counterpoint to the Crusader Belvoir Fort on the Sea of Galilee (Lake Tiberias) in present-day Israel and the Palestinian Territories.

It was enlarged in 1214 with the addition of a new gate in the southeastern corner, and once boasted seven towers as well as a surrounding 15m-deep dry moat. With its hilltop position, Qala'at ar-Rabad was one in a chain of beacons and pigeon posts that enabled messages to be transmitted from Damascus to Cairo in a single day. The rearing of pigeons in the area is still a popular pastime.

After the Crusader threat subsided, the castle was largely destroyed by Mongol invaders in 1260, only to be almost immediately rebuilt by the Mamluks. In the 17th century an Ottoman garrison was stationed here, after which it was used by local villagers. The castle was 'rediscovered' by the well-travelled JL Burckhardt, who also just happened to stumble across Petra. Earthquakes in 1837 and 1927 badly damaged the castle, though slow and steady restoration is continuing.

Note that there is a useful explanation in English just inside the main gate, and a small museum containing pots, snatches of mosaic and some intriguing medieval hand grenades. Apart from this, nothing else in the castle is signposted, although not much explanation is needed to bring the place to life, especially given that the views from these lofty heights are nothing short of spectacular.

The castle is a tough (3km) uphill walk from the town centre, but minibuses very occasionally go to the top (about 100 fils). Alternatively, take a taxi from Ajloun (JD1 to JD2 each way). A return trip by taxi from Ajloun (JD7 to JD10), with about 30 minutes to look around, is money well spent. The visitors centre and ticket office is about 500m downhill from the castle entrance; there is a small scale model of the castle on display here and, perhaps more usefully, clean toilets.

🛏 Sleeping & Eating

There are a few places for a snack and a drink inside Ajloun Castle. For something more substantial, both **Abu-Alezz Restaurant** (meals JD2-3) and **Al-Raseed** (meals JD2-3) near the main roundabout in Ajloun offer standard Jordanian fare. Alternatively, head into the surrounding hills for a picnic.

Qalet al-Jabal Hotel   HOTEL $

(📞 6420202; www.jabal-hotel.com; s/d/tr from JD28/38/48) About 2km downhill from Ajloun Castle, this busy little hotel boasts a gorgeous garden of flowering jasmine, grapevines and roses. The decor is a tad tired and the furnishings on the minimal side but there are expansive views from many of the rooms. The highlight of the hotel is the outdoor terrace where meals are served.

Ajloun Hotel HOTEL **$**
(☑ 6420524; r incl breakfast from JD25) Located just 1km down the road from the castle, this is a handy option for an early-morning visit to the castle. There's a comfortable lounge area in the foyer, and the rooms were being re-done and improved when we visited. Choose a top-floor room for grand views of the countryside.

❶ Getting There & Away

From the centre of town, minibuses travel regularly to Jerash (600 fils, 30 minutes along a scenic road) and Irbid (JD1, 45 minutes). From Amman (900 fils, two hours), minibuses leave half-hourly from the North bus station.

Ajloun Forest Reserve   محمية عجلون الطبيعية

Located in the Ajloun Highlands, this small (13 sq km) but vitally important **nature reserve** (☑ 02-6475673; ⊘ year-round) **FREE** was established by the RSCN in 1988 to protect forests of oak, carob, pistachio and strawberry trees (look for the peeling, bright-orange bark) and provide sanctuary for the endangered roe deer.

To reach the reserve, charter a taxi for the 9km from Ajloun (around JD5 to JD7, one way).

❂ Sights & Activities

The Soap House CRAFT WORKSHOP
(Orjan Village; ⊘ 9am-4pm) 🅟 Ever wondered what pomegranate soap smells like? Local women demonstrate the art of making all kinds of health-promoting soaps using natural local ingredients and comprising 90% pure olive oil. Pomegranate is one of a dozen exotic fragrances.

Soap House Trail HIKING
(JD14; ⊘ year-round) This guided 7km trail (three hours) combines a visit to the reserve's oldest strawberry tree with a panoramic vista at Eagle's Viewpoint. Descending from the 1100m lookout, the trail leads through evergreen woodland to the soap house where enterprising women make natural olive-oil soap.

⊨ Sleeping & Eating

The Ajloun Forest Reserve operates **tented bungalows** (☑ 6475673; s/d/tr/q incl breakfast JD52/63/75/87) 🅟. The ablution block contains composting toilets and solar-heated

showers. There are also **cabins** (☑ 6475673; s/d/tr/q incl breakfast from JD81/92/104/116, luxe s/d/tr/q JD90/116/127/139; rooftop restaurant meals JD14) 🅟 available, equipped with private bathroom and terrace. Bring mosquito repellent in the summer. You can walk to the recommended **Biscuit House Bed & Breakfast** (☑ 6475673; s/d incl breakfast JD49/70) 🅟 within the reserve if you have time to spare.

In the tented rooftop restaurant (buffet JD14), there are lunchtime buffets with a good vegetarian selection. Outside, barbecue grills are available for public use.

Irbid   إربد
☑ 02 / POP 751,634
Jordan's second-largest city is a university town, and one of its more lively and progressive. Irbid is also a good base for exploring the historic sites of Umm Qais, Pella and even Jerash. The town comes alive at night, especially in the energetic area around the university, where the streets are lined with restaurants and internet cafes.

❂ Sights

Dar As Saraya Museum MUSEUM
(☑ 7245613; Al Baladia St; ⊘ 8am-6pm) **FREE** Located in a stunning old villa of basaltic rock, just behind the town hall, this museum is a real gem. Built in 1886 by the Ottomans, the building is typical of the caravanserai established along the Syrian pilgrimage route with rooms arranged around a paved internal courtyard. It was used as a prison until 1994 and now houses a delightful collection of local artefacts illustrating Irbid's long history.

Museum of Archaeology & Anthropology MUSEUM
(☑ 7211111; ⊘ 10am-1.45pm & 3-4.30pm Sun-Thu) **FREE** This recommended museum features exhibits from all eras of Jordanian history. The collection opens with 9000-year-old Neolithic statuettes found near present-day Amman, covers the Bronze and Iron Ages, continues through the Mamluk and Ottoman occupations, and closes with modern displays on rural Bedouin life. One of the highlights is a reconstruction of a traditional Arab pharmacy and smithy. The Numismatic Hall has some fascinating displays on the history of money over 2600 years. All displays are labelled in English.

🛏 Sleeping & Eating

It has to be said that the standard of hotels in Irbid is not great. The redeeming feature, especially among the budget options, is the great friendliness of the welcome.

Al-Joude Hotel
HOTEL $

(☎ 7275515; off University St; s/d/tr incl buffet breakfast from JD30/35/60; ✳@⧆) Located near the campus of Yarmouk University, this hotel has seen better days. Rooms are clean and spacious but sparse, noisy and tired. The good part is that you don't have to go looking for nightlife – in an evening, half of Irbid pours into the hotel's popular News Cafe or the Al-Joude Garden Restaurant.

Omayah Hotel
HOTEL $

(☎ 7245955; omayahhotel@yahoo.com; King Hussein St; s/d JD20/30; ✳) Fair value for money, this recently renovated budget hotel boasts satellite TV, as well as large picture windows overlooking the heart of the city. The friendly proprietor is kind and helpful and solo women will feel comfortable here.

Clock Tower Restaurant
JORDANIAN $

(Al Jaish St; meals JD3-5; ⏱ 8.30am-9.30pm) The name of this popular local is written in Arabic but as it's right next to the clock tower and has a huge spit of shwarma roasting in the window, it's hard to miss. There's a family seating area upstairs for a bit of peace and quiet, and the Jordanian staple dishes are cheap, cheerful and delicious.

Al-Joude Garden Restaurant
JORDANIAN $$

(off University St; mixed grill meals JD6-10) Students, visiting parents and local families crowd into the courtyard outside Al-Joude Hotel to sip fresh fruit juices and smoke a strawberry nargileh. The waiters are kept in a constant state of rush in this teeming venue as they are summoned for hot embers and top-ups of Turkish coffee – expect long waits for food orders.

ℹ Getting There & Away

Approximately 85km north of Amman, Irbid is home to three main minibus/taxi stations.

From the **North bus station**, there are minibuses to Umm Qais (45 minutes) for 800 fils.

Air-conditioned Hijazi buses (JD2, 90 minutes) leave from the **South bus station** (New Amman bus station) every 15 to 20 minutes between 6am and 7pm for Amman's North bus station. There are also less comfortable buses and minibuses from Amman's North bus station (less than JD1, about two hours) and plenty of service taxis (JD1). Minibuses also leave the South Bus Station for Ajloun (45 minutes), Jerash (45 minutes) and the Syrian border, for around 800 fils.

The **West bus station** (Mujamma al-Gharb al-Jadid) is about 1.5km west of the centre. Minibuses go from here to Sheikh Hussein Bridge for Israel and the Palestinian Territories (45 minutes) for JD1.200.

ℹ Getting Around

Service taxis (200 fils) and minibuses (100 fils) going to the South bus station can be picked up on Radna al-Hindawi St, three blocks east of Al-Ameen al-Kabir Hotel. For the North bus station head to Prince Nayef St. For the West bus station take a bus from Palestine St, just west of the roundabout.

A standard taxi fare from *al-Bilad* (the town) to *al-Jammiya* (the university) is 500 fils. A minibus from University St to the university gate costs 200 fils. Otherwise it's a 25-minute walk.

Umm Qais (Gadara) أم قيس

📞 02 / POP 5000

Tucked in the far northwest corner of Jordan, and about 25km from Irbid, are the ruins of Umm Qais, site of both the ancient Roman city of Gadara and an Ottoman-era village. The hilltop site offers spectacular views over the Golan Heights in Syria, the Sea of Galilee (Lake Tiberias) to the north, and the Jordan Valley to the south.

◎ Sights

★ West Theatre
AMPHITHEATRE

Entering Umm Qais from the south, the first structure of interest is the well-restored and brooding West Theatre. Constructed from black basalt, it once seated about 3000 people. This is one of two such theatres – the North Theatre is overgrown and missing the original black basalt rocks which were recycled by villagers in other constructions.

Decumanus Maximus
STREET

The main road passing through the site, and still paved to this day, once linked Gadara with other nearby ancient cities such as Abila and Pella. In its heyday, the road extended as far as the Mediterranean coast.

Museum
MUSEUM

(☎ 7500072; ⏱ 8am-6pm Sat-Thu, to 4pm Fri) FREE Housed in Beit Russan, a former residence of an Ottoman governor, this modest museum is set around an elegant and tranquil courtyard of fig trees. The main mosaic on display (dating from the 4th century and found in one of the tombs) illustrates the names of early Christian notables. Another highlight is the headless white marble statue of the Hellenic goddess Tyche, which was found sitting in the front row of the West Theatre.

🛏 Sleeping & Eating

Umm Qais Hotel   HOTEL **$**
(🖉 7500080; www.umqaishotel.com; s/d incl breakfast from JD15/20) With extremely modest rooms above a bakery (guess where bread for breakfast comes from) and a stone's throw from the ruins, this family-run hotel makes up for the lack of attractions with hearty hospitality. Home-cooked Jordanian food is available on request from the landlady. Half-day trips into the local countryside can be organised from here.

★ Umm Qais Resthouse   JORDANIAN **$$**
(🖉 7500555; meals JD3-8; ⏱ 10am-10pm Jun-Sep, to 7pm Oct-May; 🖉) Without doubt, one of the best parts of the Umm Qais site is pausing to take refreshment at the Umm Qais Resthouse, perched atop a small hill in the heart of the ruins. With stunning views over Galilee, the Golan and the peaks of Lebanon, it's the perfect venue for lunch or an early dinner.

ℹ Getting There & Away

Minibuses leave Irbid's North bus station for Umm Qais (800 fils; 45 minutes) on a regular basis. There's no direct transport from Amman. To continue to Pella on public transport, you'll have to backtrack to Irbid.

DEAD SEA & THE WEST

There are several excellent reasons to visit the Dead Sea region, not least for a float in the sea itself. Bethany-Beyond-the-Jordan is an important archaeological site that pinpoints a major event in the life of Jesus to a remarkably specific location on the banks of the Jordan River.

For something completely different, beautiful Mujib Biosphere Reserve offers some of Jordan's wettest and wildest adventure opportunities.

Public transport is unreliable on the Dead Sea Highway and this is one place to consider renting a car or taxi for the day. Most budget travellers visit the Dead Sea as part of an organised day trip from a hotel in Amman or Madaba.

Bethany-Beyond-the-Jordan (Al-Maghtas)   المغطس

This important site is claimed by Christians to be the place where Jesus was baptised by John the Baptist, where the first five apostles met, and where, at Tell Ellias, the prophet Elijah ascended to heaven in a chariot. It wasn't until the 1994 peace treaty with Israel that the remains of churches, caves and baptism pools were unearthed. Pope John Paul II authenticated the site in March 2000.

Entry to **Al-Maghtas (Baptism Site)** (www.baptismsite.com; JD12; ⏱ 8am-6pm Apr-Oct, to 4pm Nov-Mar) includes a mandatory guided tour, partly by shuttle bus, partly on foot. Tours often return via the **House of Mary the Egyptian** and a two-room **hermit cave**.

DEAD SEA FAST FACTS

➡ The Dead Sea is part of the Great Rift Valley; it is the lowest spot on earth at 429m below sea level and more than 390m deep.

➡ It is not actually a sea, but a lake filled with incoming water with no outlet.

➡ It is the second-saltiest body of water on earth (after Lake Aral in Djibouti) with a salt content of 31%.

➡ Egyptians used Dead Sea mud (bitumen) in their mummification process; the last lump of floating bitumen surfaced in 1936.

➡ The majority of Dead Sea minerals (including calcium and magnesium) occur naturally in our bodies and have health-giving properties.

➡ The Dead Sea is three million years old, but has shrunk by 30% in recent years (around a metre per year) due to evaporation and the demands of the potash industry, one of Jordan's most valuable commodities.

⊙ Sights

Site of Jesus' Baptism RUIN
The main archaeological site comprises the remains of three churches, one on top of the other. Steps lead down to the original water level and a building nearby marks the likely site of Jesus' baptism. Byzantine churches were built to mark the site during the 5th and 6th centuries, and rebuilt on the same site after they were destroyed by flooding. All that remains today are traces of original mosaic.

Jordan River RIVER
The walking trail passes a golden-roofed Greek Orthodox church and leads, under the watchful eye of border guards, to the river – little more than a stagnant ditch. It's not very inviting but you can be baptised in the Jordan if accompanied by a priest. Across the river (and the border) is a rival Israeli baptism complex. This is the only place where civilians can currently touch the Jordan River as the remainder runs through a military no man's land.

Tell Elias RUIN
Tell Elias is where Elijah is said to have ascended to heaven, although there is little to see here. The rebuilt arch marks the 5th- to 6th-century pilgrim chapel, where Pope John Paul II authenticated the site in March 2000. The nearby 3rd-century rectangular prayer hall is one of the earliest Christian places of worship ever discovered, dating from a period when Christianity was still illegal.

❶ Getting There & Away
Take any minibus to Suweimeh, en route to the Dead Sea. About 5km before the town, the road forks; the baptism site is signposted to the right. From here, you'll need to walk or hitch the 5km to the visitor centre.

A taxi from Madaba to the site, taking in the Dead Sea and Mt Nebo en route, costs around JD50 for a maximum of four people. Bethany is included in good-value tours of the Dead Sea through hotels in Madaba.

Dead Sea البحر الميت

⏱ 05 / POP 5000
The Dead Sea is at the lowest point on earth and has such high salinity (due to evaporation) that nothing but the most microscopic of life forms can survive in it. Indeed, the only things you're likely to see in the Dead Sea are a few overbuoyant tourists. A dip in the sea is one of those must-do experiences, but be warned: you'll discover cuts you didn't know you had, so don't shave before bathing! Sadly, the Dead Sea is under threat from shrinking water levels.

⊙ Sights & Activities
The most luxurious way to swim on the Jordanian side of the Dead Sea is at one of the upmarket resorts, which cost from JD25 (Sunday to Thursday at the Holiday Inn) to JD50 (at the Mövenpick Resort & Spa) for day access to their sumptuous grounds, private beaches and swimming pools. Access to the Mövenpick's renowned spa costs an extra JD50.

The resorts and public areas are very busy on Fridays – useful for finding a ride back to Amman if you missed the last bus. Take lots of water, as the humidity and heat is intense (over 40°C in summer) and there's little shade.

Dead Sea Panoramic Complex Lookout VIEWPOINT
(admission per person JD2; ⊙8am-10pm) Walk among the cacti to this lookout, high above the Dead Sea, then watch raptors wheel in the wadis below and you will have to pinch yourself to think that you are standing at sea level. This wonderful museum and restaurant complex offers breathtaking views, especially on a crisp day in winter when the Judaea Mountains across the water seem as if they are an arm's stretch away.

Amman Beach SWIMMING
(☑3560800; adult/child JD20/10, restaurant JD14 buffet; ⊙9am-8pm, restaurant 11am-5pm) This public facility goes under the full title of Amman Beach Tourism Resort, Restaurant & Pools. The beach, 2km south of the main resort strip gives affordable access to the Dead Sea. The grounds are attractively landscaped and the beach is clean, with sun umbrellas, freshwater showers and a vibrant local flavour.

Al-Wadi Resort SWIMMING
(adult/child JD25/18; ⊙9am-6pm Sat-Thu, to 7pm Fri) This privately run resort has a variety of water games, including a wave machine and slides, is pleasantly landscaped surroundings. There are two restaurants (open 10am to 5pm), one selling snacks and the other offering an Arabic menu. Children are measured on entry: those under 95cm

BRAVING LUXURY IN A DEAD SEA SPA

Even if you're a diehard, old-school traveller who feels that sleeping on a bed with a soft mattress is a sign of weakness, there's a certain gratification in succumbing to the spa experience. You'll be in good company: Herod the Great and Cleopatra, neither noted as wimpish types, both dipped a toe in spa waters. So ditch the hiking boots for a day, step into a fluffy bathrobe and brave the clinically white, marble entrance hall of a Dead Sea pleasure dome.

The spa experience (from around JD30) usually begins with a mint tea and a spa bag to stow your worldly goods – this isn't going to be a chlorinated swim in the municipal pool back home. You'll then be shown to the mirrored changing rooms, with Dead Sea soaps and shampoos and more towels than you'll have body to towel down. This marks the point of no-return: the silent-padding assistants waft you from here along marble corridors to the opulent bathhouses.

All the spas offer a range of cradling Dead Sea waters with different levels of salinity. There's usually a foot spa and a float in a Damascene-tiled jacuzzi. Outside pools assault visitors with a variety of bullying jet sprays. Best of all are the little pots that bubble when you sit in them and ought to be X-rated.

Luxury of this kind is an extreme sport and by the time you reach the spa's private infinity pool, you'll be so seduced by the ambience you won't have the energy to try the saunas, steam rooms or tropical sprays, let alone the gym. Lie instead under an oleander by the pool, sip a chilled carrot juice and wonder why you resisted the spa experience for so long.

are admitted free! The resort is about 500m north of the Convention Centre at the head of the resort strip.

O Beach
SWIMMING

(☏ 3492000; www.obeach.net; adult/child with lunch JD25/20, admission only JD15/10 ; ◷ 9am-6pm) This private beach, stepped down the hillside in a series of landscaped terraces and infinity pools, is a great way to enjoy the Dead Sea in comfort without paying for a night in the neighbouring hotels. If you're looking for an extrarestful experience, VIP areas are provided for an extra JD30 (couples only) with king-sized beds. A range of spa treatments and massages is also available. There are several restaurants and bars and a weekend buffet.

🛏 Sleeping & Eating

About 5km south of Suweimeh is a strip of opulent pleasure palaces that offer the latest in spa luxury. There are no budget or mid-range options.

Dead Sea Spa Hotel
RESORT $$$

(☏ 3561000; www.deadseaspahotel.com; r from JD120; ❄ ☀) Not as refined as its neighbours, this hotel is pleasant nonetheless. It has a medical/dermatological spa, private beach access, a big pool and a separate kids' pool with slides. Choose from rooms in the main block or bungalows. There's a restaurant

complex at the northern end of the hotel with some chain outlets and a sea view

Holiday Inn Resort Dead Sea
RESORT $$$

(☏ 3495555; www.ichotelsgroup.com; s/d from JD100/120; ❄ @ ☀) This excellent resort with plenty of pools will appeal to families, with its easier access to the Dead Sea. It is located at the far northern end of the hotel strip, well away from the current construction boom.

★ Mövenpick Resort & Spa
RESORT $$$

(☏ 3561111; www.moevenpick-hotels.com; r from JD215; ❄ @) This wonderfully planted haven boasts a river that ambles through the village-style complex of rustic two-storey apartments. Wooden screens and balconies allow guests to enjoy sea or garden views in private, while secluded seating areas around a superb infinity pool add to the ambience. The Zara Spa is renowned as one of the best in the Middle East.

ℹ Getting There & Away

Buses from Amman direct to Amman Beach leave on a demand-only basis from Muhajireen bus station between 7am and 9am; the journey takes an hour and a half, and the last bus returns to Amman around 5pm (4pm in winter).

JETT buses offer a Friday-only service from Amman (JD8) at 8am, returning at 4pm if there are sufficient passengers. The bus leaves from the JETT office near Abdali bus station. Check with the JETT office in Amman for the latest timetable.

Unreliable minibuses from Amman usually run only as far as Suweimeh, from where you must take a taxi – if you can find one.

The best way to reach the area without a car is to go on a day trip. The budget hotels in Amman and Madaba organise taxi tours, taking in various combinations of sites such as Bethany-Beyond-the-Jordan, Amman Beach and Hammamat Ma'in, with an hour's stop at each site. The cost (from JD35 to JD50) depends on the duration of the whole trip and the number of stops.

Mujib Biosphere Reserve محمية الموجب

The 215-sq-km **Mujib Biosphere Reserve** (07-77422125) was established by the RSCN for the captive breeding of the Nubian ibex, but it also forms the heart of an ambitious ecotourism project. It's a great place for hiking and canyoning, with water year-round.

There's no public transport to the reserve so you need to rent a car or take a taxi from Amman, Madaba or Karak.

◎ Sights & Activities

A trip to this reserve begins at the **visitor centre** (079 7203888), by the Dead Sea Highway. Bring a swimming costume, towel and a watertight bag for valuables as some of the trails are wet. Guides are compulsory for all but the Siq trail and should be booked in advance through the Wild Jordan Centre (p305) in Amman.

Siq Trail HIKING
(per person JD13) The easiest hike on offer, this exciting self-guided 2km wade and scramble into the gorge ends at a dramatic waterfall.

Malaqi Trail HIKING
(per person JD47) This wet trail is the reserve's most popular hike. It's a half-day trip involving a hot and unremitting climb into the wadi, a visit to the natural swimming pools of Wadi Hidan and a descent (often swimming) through the siq (gorge). The finale involves rappelling down the 18m waterfall (not suitable for nonswimmers or vertigo sufferers).

⊨ Sleeping & Eating

Mujib Chalets CHALET
(079 7203888; www.rscn.jo; s/d/tr JD55/65/75) The Mujib Biosphere Reserve operates 15 chalets on the windy shores of the Dead Sea. You need to book in advance, either by calling the chalet manager directly, or when booking your hike through the RSCN. The chalets have twin beds, a fridge and a shaded patio overlooking the Dead Sea in a plot that is still under development.

AZRAQ & THE EAST

The landscape east of Amman quickly turns into a featureless stone desert, known as the *badia*, cut by twin highways running to Iraq and Saudi Arabia. It has its own haunting, if barren, beauty, partly because it seems so limitless: indeed this is what 80% of Jordan looks like, while supporting only 5% of its population. If you stray into this territory, you'll be surprised to find you're not the first to do so. A whole assortment of ruined hunting lodges, bathhouses and pleasure palaces, known collectively as 'desert castles', have lured people into the wilderness for centuries. Most of these isolated outposts were either built or adapted by the Damascus-based Umayyad rulers, during the late 7th and early 8th centuries.

Accommodation and public transport is almost nonexistent out here so most travellers visit the region on a tour from budget hotels in Amman. Alternatively, hire a car and make a thorough job of it by staying overnight in Azraq.

Hallabat حلابات

Qasr al-Hallabat Fort CASTLE
(☉ daylight hours) **FREE** With a fair proportion of masonry still standing, some beautifully restored archways and a desolate perch on the edge of the Eastern Desert, this fort is a good introduction to the history of the region. Hallabat once boasted elaborate baths, intricate frescos and mosaics, a mosque and several reservoirs, and served as a focus for a thriving farming community. Restoration of a substantial part of the site under Spanish direction has restored an inkling of the castle's former stature.

Hammam as-Sarah RUIN
(☉ daylight hours) **FREE** Part of the neighbouring fort complex in Hallabat, this hammam (bathhouse) has been extensively

DESERT CASTLES

There are dozens of ruins belonging to the Umayyad dynasty scattered across the gravel plains of the Eastern Desert, so how do you choose which ones to visit?

Below is a list of the main castles and a guide to their accessibility. The castles fall into two convenient sets. The most famous ones lie on the so-called 'desert castle loop'. These are accessible on a day trip from Amman via Azraq, by tour or by car. Individual castles can be reached with more difficulty by a combination of minibus and taxi.

The other set lies on the so-called 'Eastern Desert Highway', or Hwy 10, which leads from the town of Mafraq to the Iraqi border. These are much more time-consuming to visit.

Each of the two sets takes a long, full day to cover. You can combine the two sets by staying the night in Azraq and using Hwy 5 to cut between the two.

Desert Castle Loop

CASTLE NAME	PUBLIC TRANSPORT	4WD	BY TOUR	WORTHWHILE?
Qasr al-Hallabat	Yes	No	Sometimes	✓✓
Qasr al-Azraq	Yes	No	Yes	✓✓✓
Qasr 'Uweinid	No	Yes	No	✓
Qusayr Amra	Taxi from Azraq	No	Yes	✓✓✓
Qasr Kharana	Taxi from Azraq	No	Yes	✓✓✓
Qasr Al-Mushatta	Taxi from Amman	No	No	✓✓

Eastern Desert Highway

CASTLE NAME	PUBLIC TRANSPORT	4WD	BY TOUR	WORTHWHILE?
Umm al-Jimal	Yes	No	Sometimes	✓✓
Qasr Deir al-Kahf	No	No	No	✓
Qasr Aseikhin	No	No	No	✓
Qasr Burqu	No	Yes	No	✓✓

restored, revealing the underfloor piping system that was used to heat the hot, cold and tepid bathing rooms. The hammam is located along the main road to Hallabat village, about 3km east of Qasr al-Hallabat and 5km from the main road. The minibus to Hallabat village drives past Hammam as-Sarah and can drop you off on request. The site is unlocked – just push open the gate.

Azraq   الأزرق

☑ 05 / POP 8000

The oasis town of Azraq (meaning 'blue' in Arabic) lies 80km east of Amman. For centuries an important meeting of trade routes, the town is still a junction of truck roads heading northeast to Iraq and south-east to Saudi Arabia. South Azraq was founded early last century by Chechens fleeing Russian persecution, while north Azraq is home to a minority of Druze, who fled French Syria in the 1920s. The edge of the town is dominated by the brooding black basalt castle that dates back to the Roman emperor Diocletian (AD 300), but owes its current form to the beginning of the 13th century. During WWI Sherif Hussein (father of King Hussein) and TE Lawrence made it their desert headquarters in the winter of 1917, during the Arab Revolt against the Ottomans. Lawrence, who famously wrote in the *Seven Pillars of Wisdom* of the 'Roman legionaries who languished here', stayed in the room directly above the southern entrance.

ℹ️ TOURING THE DESERT CASTLES

Jumping on an organised tour of the desert castles from Amman makes a lot of sense, especially if you're short of time or on a tight budget. Tours can be arranged at the Palace, Farah and Cliff Hotels (p297) in Amman, which charge about JD15 to JD20 per person for a full-day trip. You're unlikely to get a better deal by negotiating directly with the driver of a service taxi or private taxi in Amman, and regular taxi drivers are rarely keen on leaving the city. Tours, which can also be arranged from the Black Iris and Mariam Hotels (p320) in Madaba, usually encompass the big three – Al-Azraq, Amra and Kharana.

⊙ Sights & Activities

★ Azraq Wetland Reserve   NATURE RESERVE

(☏ 3835017; admission JD8.120; ⊙ 9am-6pm, to 4pm Sep-Feb) Administered by the RSCN, this small reserve is good for bird-watching. The Azraq Basin was originally 12,710 sq km (an area larger than Lebanon), but overpumping of groundwater sucked the wetlands dry in the '70s and '80s. In recent years, the RSCN has seized control of the wetlands and established a small nature reserve to help facilitate the recovery of the wetlands. Bird populations have returned but the wetlands remain a meagre reflection of their past glory.

★ Qasr al-Azraq   CASTLE

(admission JD1, ticket also valid for Qusayr Amra & Qasr Kharana; ⊙ daylight hours) Constructed out of black basalt stone, Qasr al-Azraq was originally three storeys high. Some paving stones in the main entrance have small indentations, carved by former gatekeepers who played a board game using pebbles to pass the time. By the courtyard entrance, look for the carvings of animals and various inscriptions.

Above the entrance is Lawrence's Room, strategically overlooking the entry and offset with arrow slits for defence. Opposite the entrance, and just to the left, are the remains of an altar, built in the 3rd century AD by the Romans. In the middle of the courtyard is a small mosque, angled as usual to face Mecca – it dates from the Ayyubid period (early 13th century), but was built on the ruins of a Byzantine church. In the northeast corner of the courtyard, a hole with stairs leads down to a well, full of water until about 20 years ago. In the northwest corner are the ruins of the prison.

The northern sections are residential areas with barely discernible ruins of a kitchen and dining room, and nearby storerooms and stables. The tower in the western wall is the most spectacular, and features a huge door made of a single massive slab of basalt. Lawrence describes in his book *Seven Pillars of Wisdom* how it 'went shut with a clang and crash that made tremble the west wall of the castle'.

Shaumari Wildlife Reserve   NATURE RESERVE

(Mahmiyyat ash-Shaumari; www.rscn.org.jo; ⊙ 8am-4pm) Established in 1975 by the RSCN, this 22-sq-km reserve was created with the aim of reintroducing wildlife that has disappeared from the region, most notably the highly endangered Arabian oryx, Persian onagers (wild ass), goitered and Dorcas gazelles, and blue-necked ostriches.

At the time of research, the Shaumari Wildlife Reserve remained closed to visitors while it continues to undergo a radical overhaul. A night safari may be possible to arrange with advanced booking with the Royal Society for the Conservation of Nature.

🍽️ Sleeping & Eating

A string of truck-stop restaurants lines the 1km stretch of road south of the main T-junction.

★ Azraq Lodge   HOTEL $$

(☏ 3835017; s/d incl breakfast from JD70/82; ❄️) This former British 1940s military hospital in south Azraq has been atmospherically renovated by the Royal Society for the Conservation of Nature as a base from which to explore the Eastern Desert. The RSCN has succeeded in preserving the historic building while incorporating modern facilities, so thankfully there's no need to rough it on bare stretchers.

Al-Azraq Resthouse   HOTEL $$

(☏ 3895215; s/d/tr incl breakfast from JD45/55/65; ❄️🛜🏊) This poorly maintained hotel features unkempt rooms in need of maintenance, but with minimal local alternatives it's an option if Azraq Lodge is full. The pool is available for day use (JD10 for four hours) and there is a restaurant serving standard international fare. It's about 2km north of the Azraq T-junction and 1.5km along a local track.

Azraq Palace Restaurant JORDANIAN **$$**
(☑079 935070; buffet JD10; ☺11am-4pm & 6-11pm) Apart from Azraq Lodge, this is the best place to eat in town, which is why it attracts tour groups on desert-castle excursions. The standard Jordanian fare of rice, grills, salads and dips is tasty and filling and the management helpful.

ⓘ Getting There & Away

Minibuses run up and down the road along northern and southern Azraq in search of passengers before joining the highway to Zarqa (JD1.200, 1½ hours). If you are driving, Azraq is a long and straight drive along Hwy 30 from Zarqa.

Around Azraq

The sights around Azraq are hard to access by public transport and the most feasible way to visit them is either with your own car or on a taxi tour from Amman or Madaba.

⊙ Sights

★**Qusayr Amra** CASTLE
(admission JD1, ticket also valid for Qasr al-Azraq & Qasr Kharana; ☺8am-6pm May-Sep, to 4pm Oct-Apr) One of the best-preserved desert buildings of the Umayyads, the Unesco World Heritage site of Qusayr Amra is the highlight of a trip into the Eastern Desert. Part of a much-greater complex that served as a caravanserai, bathhouse and hunting lodge, the *qusayr* (little castle) is renowned for its rather risqué 8th-century frescos of wine, women and wild times.

★**Qasr Kharana** CASTLE
(admission JD1, ticket also valid for Qusayr Amra & Qasr Al-Azraq; ☺8am-6pm May-Sep, to 4pm Oct-Apr) Located in the middle of a vast, treeless plain, this imposing thick-walled structure was the most likely inspiration for the 'desert castle' moniker and is arguably the most photogenic of all the desert castles. There is controversy about its function and purpose, but this important Umayyad structure remains an interesting sight for visitors, off the main Azraq–Amman road.

★**Umm al-Jimal Ruins** RUIN
(☺daylight hours) FREE The unpretentious urban architecture of Umm al-Jimal, near the Jordanian–Syrian border, encompasses over

150 buildings standing one to three stories above ground, including 128 houses and 15 churches. Together, these buildings provide a fascinating insight into rural life during the Roman, Byzantine and early Islamic periods. Compared to other archaeological sites in the region, Umm al-Jimal was rarely looted or vandalised, which has left much of the original layout intact.

ⓘ Getting There & Away

Qusayr Amra lies on the main road, 26km from Azraq, southwest of the junctions of Hwys 30 and 40, and Qasr Kharana on Hwy 40, nearer to Amman, making these two 'castles' accessible on the same day trip.

It's possible to reach Umm al-Jimal by public transport. Take a local minibus from Raghadan station to Zarqa (20 minutes), a minibus from there to Mafraq (45 minutes) and then another minibus for the final 20km to the ruins (20 minutes).

MADABA & THE KING'S HIGHWAY مأدبا & الطريق الملوكي

Of Jordan's three north–south highways (only one of which is a dual carriageway), the King's Highway is by far the most interesting and picturesque, with a host of attractions lying on the road or nearby. The highway connects the mosaic town of Madaba to the pink city of Petra via Crusader castles, Roman forts, biblical sites, a windswept Nabataean temple and some epic landscapes – including the majestic Wadi Mujib and a gem of a nature reserve at Dana.

Unfortunately, public transport along the King's Highway is patchy and stops altogether at Wadi Mujib, between Dhiban and Ariha, meaning that the only feasible travel along its length is by car or taxi. Helpfully, the Palace Hotel (p297) in Amman and budget hotels in Madaba organise daily transport for like-minded travellers.

Madaba مأدبا
☑05 / POP 156,300
The amiable market town of Madaba is best known for a collection of Byzantine-era mosaics. The most famous of these is the mosaic map on the floor of St George's Church, but there are many others carpeting different parts of the town, many of which are even more complete and vibrant in colour.

Look for the chicken – there's one in most mosaics, and trying to spot it may save 'mosaic-fatigue' syndrome.

One-third of Madaba's population is Christian (the other two-thirds are Muslim), making it one of the largest Christian communities in Jordan. The town's long tradition of religious tolerance is joyfully – and loudly – expressed on Friday. This is one day when you shouldn't expect a lie-in. The imam summons the faithful to pray before dawn, the carillon bells bid the Orthodox Christians to rise at first light, and finally Mammon gets a look in with the honks and groans of traffic.

Unlike most other towns along the highway, however, Madaba has a good choice of hotels and restaurants. Less than an hour by public transport from Amman, it makes an alternative base for exploring King's Highway and Dead Sea highlights. By taxi, you can even travel directly from Queen Alia International Airport in around 20 minutes, bypassing Amman altogether.

⊙ Sights

Admission for the Archaeological Park, the Church of the Apostles and Madaba Museum is a combination ticket (JD2) covering all three sites.

★ St George's Church & Mosaic Map
CHURCH

(Talal St; adult/child under 12yr JD1/free; ⊙ 8am-5pm Sat-Thu Nov-Mar, 8am-6pm Sat-Thu Apr-Oct, 9.30am-5pm Fri year-round) This rather modest 19th-century Greek Orthodox church houses a treasure of early Christianity. Imagine the excitement in 1884 when Christian builders came across the remnants of an old Byzantine church on their construction site. Among the rubble, having survived wilful destruction, fire and neglect, the flooring they discovered wasn't just another mosaic, it was one with extraordinary significance: to this day, it represents the oldest map of Palestine in existence and provides many historical insights into the region.

Madaba Archaeological Park I & Virgin Mary Church
MOSAIC

(☑ 3246681; Abu Bakr as-Seddiq St; combined ticket adult/child under 12yr JD2/free; ⊙ 8am-4pm Oct-Apr, to 5pm May-Sep) Some careful restoration and excavation in the early 1990s led to the creation of this open-air museum which houses a collection of ruins and fine mosaics

from the Madaba area. The Church of the Virgin Mary is also included in the site; built in the 6th century and unearthed beneath the floor of someone's house in 1887, the church boasts a central mosaic, thought to date from AD 767, that is a masterpiece of geometric design.

Church of the Apostles
MOSAIC

(King's Highway; combined ticket adult/child under 12yr JD2/free; ⊙ 9am-4pm Oct-Apr, 8am-5pm May-Sep) This insignificant-looking church contains a remarkable mosaic dedicated to the Twelve Apostles. The embroidery-like mosaic was created in AD 568 and is one of the few instances where the name of the craftsman (Salomios) is included. The central portion shows Thalassa, a female personification of the sea, surrounded by fish and slippery marine creatures. Native animals, birds, flowers, fruits and cherubic faces decorate the corners.

★ Shrine of the Beheading of John the Baptist (Latin Church)
MUSEUM

(☑ 3244065; Talal St; adult/child under 12yr JD1/free; ⊙ 9am-5pm Oct-Apr, to 7pm May-Sep) This operational early-20th-century Roman Catholic Church has been transformed into an intriguing destination for visitors and pilgrims by the restoration of the ancient sites upon which the church sits. The gem of the complex is the Acropolis Museum, housed in the ancient, vaulted underbelly of the church. Here, an ancient well dating to the Moabite era, 3000 years ago, is still operational.

Madaba Museum
MUSEUM

(☑ 3244189; Haya Bint Al-Hussin St; combined ticket adult/child under 12yr JD2/free; ⊙ 8am-5pm, to 7pm May-Sep) Housed in several old Madaba residences, highlights of this museum include a 6th-century mosaic depicting a naked satyr, a saucy (and partially damaged) mosaic of Ariadne dancing with cymbals on her hands and feet, and a mosaic in the courtyard depicting two rams tied to a tree – a popular image recalling Abraham's sacrifice. A small, dusty Folklore Museum is included in the admission price, featuring jewellery, traditional costumes and a copy of the Mesha Stele.

🛏 Sleeping

★ Black Iris Hotel
GUESTHOUSE $

(☑ 3241959; www.blackirishotel.com; near Al-Mouhafada Circle; s/d/tr JD25/30/40; 🛜)

CANYONING IN JORDAN

The central part of Jordan is riven with wadis and canyons, some of which only come alive during a flash flood and others which are home to permanent watercourses that push their way through the rocky landscape to the Dead Sea. Along the way the presence of water creates beautiful semitropical oases of palms, oleandar and ferns. Often hidden from the road, these secret gardens are among the treasures of Jordan.

While thankfully the most spectacular canyons (such as those of the lower Wadi Mujib) are protected and made safely accessible by the Royal Society for the Conservation of Nature, there is nothing to stop a visitor exploring other canyons off the beaten track.

It's worth bearing in mind with any veering off the beaten track in Jordan that canyoning is not as yet an established sport here and you're more likely to bump into shepherds than fellow adventurers.

To go it alone, the essential companion for canyoning is the widely available hikers' bible, called *Jordan: Walks, Treks, Caves, Climbs & Canyons*, by Di Taylor and Tony Howard (4th edition 2007). For escorted trips (recommended given the unpredictability of flash flooding), contact the RSCN (www.rscn.org.jo) at Wadi Mujib or Dana, Feynan Ecolodge (p326) or the Black Iris Hotel and Queen Ayola Hotel in Madaba.

For a 'home away from home' feeling, it's hard to beat this family-run hotel. The rooms are cosy and there's a spacious communal sitting area. The 'very special breakfast' includes date cake and homemade fig jam, and the owner (trained hotelier and former chef in Switzerland) makes homecooked Jordanian suppers on request, garnished with home-grown herbs from his garden.

Queen Ayola Hotel
HOTEL $

(☑ 3244087; www.queenayolahotel.com; Talal St; s/d JD25/30, s/d with shared bathroom JD10/18; ☎) With happy hour from 6pm to 10pm and good food, this is a popular travellers haunt. The rooms are simple but clean and two have balconies onto the street – fun for people-watching in the heart of town. The hotel facilitates local trips, such as half- and full-day hiking and canyoning.

St George's Church Pilgrim House
GUESTHOUSE $

(☑/fax 077 5364218; pilgrimshousemadaba@gmail.com; Talal St, entry via Prince Hassan St; s/d/tr JD25/35/45; ☎) Although it receives mainly Christian pilgrims, this guesthouse will give a warm welcome to all travellers. Rooms are ascetically simple. If you encounter the patron, the urbane and charming Father Innocent (self-confessedly 'Innocent by name, guilty by every other means'), then your stay will be extra blessed! Profits from the guesthouse are invested in the neighbouring church school.

★ Mariam Hotel
HOTEL $$

(☑ 3251529; www.mariamhotel.com; Aisha Umm al-Mumeneen St; s/d/tr/q JD30/40/50/60; ✦@☎✦) The Mariam has built a prodigious reputation over the years, offering good facilities including a bar, poolside restaurant and a cheerful communal area. A restaurant and bar on the 5th floor offers views across town. Reservations are recommended. The hotel arranges transport to/from the airport (around JD14) and to Petra (among other destinations) for hotel guests.

Mosaic City Hotel
HOTEL $$

(☑ 3251313; www.mosaiccityhotel.com; Yarmouk St; s/d JD44/53, extra bed JD15; ✦☎) This attractive family-run hotel has bright, spacious rooms. Some have balconies overlooking lively Yarmouk St but windows are double-glazed, keeping street noise to a minimum. The reception at this central hotel is ever-amiable and facilities include a cool new bar, pool table and handcrafted soap shop. A family room sleeps four, with a double-size bathroom (JD87).

✕ Eating

For freshly baked Arabic bread, head for the ovens opposite the Church of the Apostles. There are several grocery stores in town.

Abu Yousef
JORDANIAN $

(Ash Shuhada St; JD2; ☉8am-1pm; ☑) Little more than a hole in the wall, Abu Yousef's establishment is part of the fabric of the town, serving fresh hummus and felafel daily to those in the know. Found opposite the parking lot of Haret Jdouna, this modest restaurant has supported the owner Abu Yousef (now in his dotage) and his family for over 30 years.

Ayola Coffeeshop & Bar — CAFE $
(3251843; Talal St; snacks around JD2.500; 8am-11pm;) If you want a toasted sandwich, Turkish coffee, glass of arak with the locals, or simply a comfortable perch on which to while away some time with fellow travellers, then this is the place to come. There's free internet access if you have a laptop.

★Haret Jdoudna Complex — JORDANIAN $$
(3248650; Talal St; mains JD8-15; noon-midnight;) Popular with locals and discerning diners from Amman, and set in one of Madaba's restored old houses, this restaurant is a Madaba favourite. Sit indoors by a roaring fire in winter or in the shaded courtyard in summer and sample the traditional Jordanian dishes such as *mutaffi bethanjan* (fried eggplant with sesame).

Bowabit Restaurant — CAFE $$
(3240335; Talal St; mains JD7.500; 10am-midnight) With two tables overhanging the road opposite St George's Church, photographs of old Madaba on the wall and excellent Italian-style coffee, this is a number-one place to relax after strolling round town. Alternatively, make a night of it over a dish of Madaba chicken and a beer (JD4).

ⓘ Information

All the town's half-dozen banks can change money and have ATMs.

Tour.Net Internet (Talal St; per hour 500 fils; 9am-2am)

Visitors Centre (3253563; Abu Bakr as-Seddiq St; 8am-6pm Oct-Apr, to 7pm May-Sep) This helpful information office has a range of brochures and some informative displays. Ask to see the 10-minute film that sets Madaba in the context of the surrounding highlights. There are toilets and a handy car park.

ⓘ Getting There & Away

The bus station is about 15 minutes' walk east of the town centre, on the King's Highway. There is no public transport to Karak along the King's Highway.

Amman From the Muhajireen, South (Wahadat) and North (Tabarbour) bus stations in Amman, there are regular buses and minibuses (JD1, one hour) throughout the day for Madaba. Minibuses return to Amman until around 8pm

(earlier on Friday). Taxis cost JD15 during the day, JD20 at night.

Petra The Black Iris Hotel and the Mariam Hotel (for those staying at the hotel only) can arrange transport to Petra via the King's Highway (from around JD20 per person, minimum three people) and to the Dead Sea (JD28).

Mt Nebo — جبل نيبو

Mt Nebo, on the edge of the East Bank plateau and 9km from Madaba, is where Moses is said to have seen the Promised Land. He then died (aged 120!) and was buried in the area, although the exact location of the burial site is the subject of conjecture.

⊙ Sights

Moses Memorial Church — CHURCH
(Mt Nebo; admission JD1; 8am-4pm Oct-Apr, to 6pm May-Sep) On top of Mt Nebo, this modest church, or more accurately basilica, was built around 4th-century foundations in AD 597 and has just undergone a major reconstruction project. It houses important mosaics (from around AD 530), which rank as some of the best in Jordan. The masterpiece is a hunting and herding scene interspersed with an assortment of African fauna, including a zebu (humped ox), lions, tigers, bears, boars, zebras, an ostrich on a leash and a camel-shaped giraffe.

★Memorial Viewpoint — VIEWPOINT
(admission JD 1, or included in Moses Memorial Church admission; 8am-4pm Oct-Apr, to 6pm May-Sep) Moses' view of the Promised Land towards ancient Gilead, Judah, Jericho and the Negev is marked by an Italian-designed bronze memorial, next to the Moses Memorial Church. The ironwork, symbolising the suffering and death of Jesus on the cross and the serpent that 'Moses lifted up' in the desert, stands in the middle of an invariably windy viewing platform. Markers indicate notable points in the often-hazy distance, including the Golan Heights, Jerusalem (just 46km away) and the Dead Sea.

✕ Eating

★Nebo Restaurant & Terrace — BUFFET $$
(3242442; buffet JD10; 11.30am-6pm Sat-Thu, until late Fri) The spectacular view and warm welcome from the patrons makes this restaurant worth a trip to Mt Nebo in its own right. Panoramic windows and a roof terrace make the very best of the vista and the res-

taurant has its own ovens for fresh Arabic bread.

ⓘ Getting There & Away

From Madaba, shared taxis run to the village of Fasiliyeh, 3km before Mt Nebo (JD1.500). For an extra JD1 or so the driver will drop you at Mt Nebo. A return taxi, with about 30 minutes to look around, shouldn't cost more than JD8 per vehicle.

Machaerus (Mukawir)   مكاريوس (مكاور)

☑ 05 / POP 5000

Just beyond the village of Mukawir is the spectacular 700m-high hilltop perch of Machaerus, the castle of Herod the Great. The ruins themselves are only of moderate interest, but the setting is breathtaking and commands great views out over the surrounding hills and the Dead Sea.

◎ Sights

★ **Castle of Herod the Great**   CASTLE
(admission JD1.500; ◎ 8am-6pm) Machaerus is known locally as Qala'at al-Meshneq (Castle of the Gallows), a fitting name given that it is renowned as the place where John the Baptist was beheaded by Herod Antipas, the successor of Herod the Great. The castle is about 2km past Mukawir village and easy to spot. If you don't feel in the mood for a climb, it's worth coming this way just to see the hilltop fortress framed by sea and sky beyond.

🛍 Shopping

★ **Bani Hamida Weaving Centre & Gallery**   HANDICRAFTS
(☑ 3210155; www.jordanriver.jo; ◎ 8am-3pm Sun-Thu, 10am-6pm Fri, to 4pm winter) This women's cooperative in Mukawir village (by the side of the road leading to the castle) is run by the Bani Hamida Centre and is a good place to buy gorgeous, colourful kilims and cushions. The colour-ways are constantly updated to reflect contemporary tastes while traditional Bedouin patterns continue to inspire the weavers.

ⓘ Getting There & Away

From Madaba, minibuses (650 fils, one hour) go to the village of Mukawir four or five times a day (the last around 5pm). Unless you have chartered a taxi from Madaba, you'll probably need to walk the remaining 2km (downhill most of the way). However, your minibus driver may, if you ask nicely and sweeten the request with a tip, take you the extra distance.

Wadi Mujib   وادي الموجيب

Stretching across Jordan from the Desert Highway to the Dead Sea is the vast Wadi Mujib, proudly known as the 'Grand Canyon of Jordan'. This spectacular valley is about 1km deep and over 4km from one edge to the other. The canyon forms the upper portion of the Mujib Biosphere Reserve, which is normally accessed from the Dead Sea Highway.

DON'T MISS

MAKING MOSAIC HISTORY

In a bid to be registered in the Guinness World Records, the Madaba Tourism Development & Heritage Preservation Association has enlisted visitors to the region to participate in the creation of the largest mosaic in the world – appropriate for a region famed for its mosaic-making heritage. Included in the admission price to the La Storia complex (Ethnographic Diorama; ☑ 3241119; www.lastoria-nebo.com; admission JD2; ◎ 9am-5pm) on the road towards Mt Nebo, the activity involves placing one tile into a mosaic depiction of the King's Highway.

The finished 'portrait' will measure 6m by 30m long, with a total area of 180 sq meters. Around four million marble, granite and limestone tesserae, or tiles, each just 2cm in size, will be required to finish the project. Already, thanks to the help of Jordanian royalty, ambassadors, celebrities and 58,000 visitors, the mosaic is one-third complete. Charl Twal, one of the founders of this elaborate and engaging project, encourages all visitors to Madaba and Mt Nebo to participate: 'By placing a tile in the King's Highway,' he claims, 'you are not just visiting Madaba but becoming part of its future.'

Even if you are not intending to make the crossing, it's worth travelling to the canyon rim. Just after Dhiban, the road descends after 3km to a spectacular lookout. Some enterprising traders have set up a tea stall here, and fossils and minerals from the canyon walls are for sale. This is the easiest point on the road to stop to absorb the view, take a photograph and turn around if you're heading back to Madaba.

Dhiban is where almost all transport south of Madaba stops. The only reliable way to cross the mighty Mujib from Dhiban to Ariha (about 30km) is to charter a taxi from Madaba to Karak. Hitching is not advisable in the current climate.

Karak الكرك

📶 03 / POP 77,400

The evocative ancient Crusader castle of Karak became a place of legend during the 12th-century battles between the Crusaders and the Muslim armies of Saladin (Salah ad-Din). Although among the most famous, the castle at Karak was just one in a long line built by the Crusaders, stretching from Aqaba in the south to Turkey in the north. The fortifications still dominate the modern walled town of Karak.

At one point in its chequered history, the castle belonged to a particularly unsavoury knight of the cross, Renaud de Chatillon. Hated by Saladin for his treachery, de Chatillon arrived from France in 1148 to take part in the Crusades. He was renowned for his sadistic delight in torturing prisoners and throwing them off the walls into the valley 450m below; he even went to the trouble of having a wooden box fastened over their heads so they wouldn't lose consciousness before hitting the ground.

◉ Sights

The entrance to Karak Castle is at the southern end of Al Qala'a St through Ottoman's Gate. Informative display boards give detailed descriptions of the history and function of each structure. Beware touts at the entrance who will expect a JD5 to JD10 'guiding fee'.

★ Glacis & Upper Court   VIEWPOINT

Beyond the parapet at Karak Castle is the glacis, the dizzyingly steep rocky slope that prevented invaders from climbing up to the castle and prisoners from climbing down.

This is where Renauld de Châtillon delighted in expelling his enemies.

★ Crusader Gallery & Crusader's Gate   STABLES

The Crusader Gallery functioned as the stables of Karak Castle. Near the far end of the gallery, steps lead down to the Crusader's Gate. Those entering the castle did so via a narrow winding passage, separated from the Crusader Gallery by a wall. This restrictive access is typical of Crusader castles, ensuring the entrance could be easily defended.

★ Mamluk Palace and Mosque   PALACE

Built for Sultan al-Nasir Muhammad in 1311, the open-air reception hall of this palace is a variation of the classic Islamic design of four *iwans* (chambers) off the main hall; there are barrel-vaulted rooms on two sides. The mosque here, with a clearly visible *mihrab* (niche) indicating the direction of Mecca, was probably reserved for palace notables.

★ Islamic Museum   MUSEUM

(⊙8am-3pm Oct-Mar, to 6pm Apr-Sep) FREE
Down the hill by the Mamluk ruins is the excellent Islamic Museum. In a semisubterranean part of Karak Castle, with a vaulted ceiling, this evocatively lit collection houses some of the finds from the castle and excavations in the surrounding area.

🛏 Sleeping

Towers Castle Hotel   HOTEL $

(📶/fax 2354293; Al-Qala'a St; s/d/tr JD20/30/35) Near the castle, this friendly budget hotel is a good meeting place for younger travellers. Don't be put off by the dingy reception area: the rooms, with floral motifs, are clean and many open onto balconies with views across Wadi Karak. You can find help with onward travel from here.

Al-Mujeb Hotel   HOTEL $$

(📶2386090; almujeb_hotel@yahoo.com; King's Highway; s/d/tr incl breakfast JD30/45/60; ❄) This sprawling, three-storey hotel attracts an assortment of interesting guests who huddle round the gas heater in the foyer on a cold winter's evening. The hotel is around 5km from Karak, by the junction on the road to Ar-Rabba. If you are driving, consider parking here and taking a taxi (JD5 to JD6 one way) into town.

✗ Eating

Most restaurants are near the castle on Al-Mujamma St or near the statue of Saladin. Shwarma stands are clustered around Al-Jami St.

King's Restaurant JORDANIAN $
(☑ 2354293; Al-Mujamma St; mezze 500 fils, mains from JD4; ☺ 8am-10pm) Opposite an open area called Castle Plaza, this boulevard restaurant with tables on the pavement attracts travellers at all times of the day and night. It offers grills, pizzas and sandwiches, and local, home-cooked Jordanian dishes like *maqlubbeh*. The freshly squeezed orange juice is welcome after hot climbs up and down Al-Qala'a St. It's open for breakfast during Ramadan.

Al-Fid'a Restaurant JORDANIAN $
(☑ 079 5037622; Al-Mujamma St; mains JD5; ☺ 8am-10pm) This popular, unsophisticated eatery sells standard local fare of chicken, hummus and salad.

Kir Heres Restaurant JORDANIAN $$
(☑ 2355595; Al-Qala'a St; mains JD5-7; ☺ Noon-10pm; ☑) A popular meeting point for travellers, this restaurant serves ostrich steaks, chicken with local herbs, fried *haloumi* (salty cheese) and mushrooms with garlic and thyme – a welcome change from the usual grilled goat. Try the locally produced sweet white wine (not available during Ramadan) in the upper gallery at lunchtime and you can forget about visiting the castle afterwards!

❶ Getting There & Away

From the bus/minibus station at the bottom of the hill just south of town, reasonably regular minibuses go to Amman's South bus station (JD2, two hours) via the Desert Highway. Minibuses also run fairly frequently to Tafila (JD1.500, one hour) – the best place for connections to Qadsiyya (for Dana Biosphere Reserve) and Shobak. To Wadi Musa (for Petra), take a minibus to Ma'an (JD2.500, two hours) and change there. Minibuses to Aqaba (JD5, three hours) run about four times a day, mostly in the morning.

Tafila الطفيله

☑ 03 / POP 87,500

Tafila is a busy transport junction and you may have to change transport here. Minibuses run frequently from Karak (JD1.500,

one hour) across the dramatic gorge of Wadi Hasa. There are also direct minibuses to/from the South bus station in Amman (JD2.800, 2½ hours) via the Desert Highway; Aqaba (JD2.500, 2½ hours) via the Dead Sea Highway; Ma'an (JD1.500, one hour) via the Desert Highway; and Qadsiyya (for Dana Biosphere Reserve; JD1.300, 30 minutes) down the King's Highway.

Dana Biosphere Reserve محمية دانا الطبيعية

☑ 03

The RSCN-run Dana Biosphere Reserve (adult/student per day JD8.200/JD4.100, free with RSCN lodging) is one of Jordan's hidden gems and is its most impressive ecotourism project. The gateway to the reserve is the charming 15th-century stone village of Dana, which clings to a precipice overlooking the valley and commands exceptional views. It's a great place to spend a few days hiking and relaxing. Most of the reserve is accessible only on foot.

The reserve is the largest in Jordan and includes a variety of terrain – from sandstone cliffs over 1500m high near Dana to a low point of 50m below sea level in Wadi Araba. Sheltered within the red-rock escarpments are protected valleys that are home to a surprisingly diverse ecosystem. About 600 species of plant (ranging from citrus trees and juniper, to desert acacias and date palms), 180 species of bird, and over 45 species of mammal (of which 25 are endangered) – including ibexes, mountain gazelles, sand cats, red foxes and wolves – thrive in the reserve. Dana is also home to almost 100 archaeological sites, including the 6000-year-old copper mines of Khirbet Feynan.

✗ Activities

Rummana Mountain Trail HIKING
(☺ 15 Mar-31 Oct) From Rummana Campground to the nearby Rummana (Pomegranate) Peak, this 2.5km, one- to two-hour, self-guided trail gives great views over Wadi Araba. One Rummana receptionist, Mahmoun, described the trail as a good metaphor for life: lots of ups and downs, but greatly rewarding when you reach your goal.

⌂ Sleeping & Eating

Dana Tower Hotel GUESTHOUSE $
(☑ 077 7514804, 079 5688853; www.dana-tower-hotel.com; half board per person JD15, with shared

bathroom JD11, summer rooftop camping JD3) Free transfer to/from the main road, a quirky assembly of small, unheated rooms called 'Flying Carpet' and 'Crazy Camel', leafy courtyards, a *majlis* (Arab-style sitting area) draped in memorabilia and rooftop seating make this a winner with younger backpackers. Added perks: a dinner of 22 dishes, free tea, a washing machine and hot showers.

★ Al-Nawatef Camp
CAMP **$**

(☑ 079 6392079, 2270413; www.alnawatefcamp. com; half board in tented chalets with shared shower block JD15) Perched on the edge of an escarpment and surrounded by black iris, this wonderful camp is run by a hospitable local who knows the area 'because', he says, 'it runs in my blood'. The goat-hair chalets with beds, linen and blankets boast balconies with exceptional views. The camp is signposted 2km off the King's Highway, 5km south of the Dana turning in Qadsiyya.

★ Dana Guest House
ECOLODGE **$$**

(☑ 2270497; www.rscn.org.jo; s/d/tr/q with shared bathroom incl breakfast & park entry fee JD68/85/102/120, d with private bathroom JD96) With panoramic views across the reserve, a roaring fire in winter and enthusiastic park rangers, this ecolodge is run by the RSCN. The lodge has minimalist, stone-walled rooms, all but two of which have a balcony with exceptional views from which to shiver in the dawn. Heating and hot water are provided by solar panels.

Rummana Campground
CAMP **$$**

(s/d/tr/q tent incl breakfast & park-entry fee JD52/64/75/87; ⊙ 15 Mar-31 Oct) 🚶 Prices at this camp may seem steep given the minimal facilities, but waking up to the sound of Dana's wildlife, it's easy to see why reservations are necessary. With great hiking trails just beyond the tent pegs, you can step into the cloudscape as the mist rises from the valley floor. Tents come with mattresses and bedding. There's a 20% student discount.

Dana Hotel
BOUTIQUE HOTEL **$$**

(☑ 079 5597307, 2270537; www.suleimanjarad.webs. com; half board per person in villas JD25, s/d JD12/20, dinner JD5) A warm welcome is assured from the patrons of this hotel, run by the Sons of Dana, a cooperative that claims to provide social programs to around 150 local residents. It's the oldest established hotel in Dana and, thanks to the assistance of USAid, it has recently expanded into a number of attractively renovated old houses in the village.

★ Feynan Ecolodge
ECOLODGE **$$$**

(☑ +962 6 464 5580; www.ecohotels.me/feynan; Wadi Feynan; half board incl park-entry fee from s/d/tr JD101/127/170; ⊙ Sep-Jun; 🐾) 🚶 This one-of-a-kind ecolodge, owned by the RSCN, is accessible on foot from Dana (a day's hike) or by 4WD from the Dead Sea Highway. Powered entirely by solar energy, Feynan features mud-rendered architecture, and the candle-lit nights at the lodge, with its caravanserai ambiance, vegetarian suppers and guided star-gazing, are a real highlight.

ℹ Information

Visitor Centre (☑ 2270497; www.rscn.org. jo; ⊙ 8am-3pm) The visitor centre in the Dana Guest House complex is the place to obtain further information about the reserve and its hiking trails and to arrange a guide. Reservations for guides are advisable in spring and autumn as there is a daily maximum number of people permitted on certain trails. Admission fees are included in the price of RSCN accommodation.

ℹ Getting There & Away

Minibuses run every hour or so between Tafila and Qadsiyya (JD1.300, 30 minutes). The turn-off to Dana village is 1km north of Qadsiyya – ask to be dropped off at the crossroads. From here it's a 2.8km steep downhill walk to Dana village (the budget hotels may collect you). There are three daily buses to Amman (JD3, three hours); the first bus leaves Qadsiyya between 6am and 7am.

A taxi to Petra or Karak costs around JD36 to JD40.

Shobak
شوبك
☑ 03

The landscape around the small town of Shobak shifts from the fertility of the uplands to the semi-aridity that marks the upper reaches of mighty Wadi Araba. Hidden within the dazzlingly white, sheep-meandered hills is Shobak Castle, the Crusader gem at the end of the King's Highway. With some interesting cultural activities and beautiful hiking routes, it's worth overnighting to explore what the region has to offer.

⊙ Sights

★ Shobak Castle
CASTLE

(Mont Real, Montreal; ⊙ daylight hours) `FREE` Perched in a wild, remote landscape, Shobak Castle wins over even the most castle-weary, despite being less complete than its sister fortification at Karak. Formerly called Mons Realis (the Royal Mountain), it was built by the Crusader king Baldwin I in AD 1115. Restoration work is ongoing and hopefully this will include some explanatory signs. In the meantime, the caretaker shows visitors around for about JD10. Bring a torch for exploring the castle's many dark corners.

🛏 Sleeping & Eating

Jaya Tourist Camp   CAMP $
(☎079 5958958; www.jayatouristcamp.yolasite.com; half board per person JD20) 🅿 With 15 tents in a tranquil spot on high ground opposite Shobak Castle, this friendly campsite set in a garden of hollyhocks has a clean shower block and Bedouin goat-hair tents for relaxing. To reach the camp, follow the signs from the King's Highway. The road passes Montréal Hotel and ends after 1km at the camp, which also offers hiking.

Montréal Hotel   HOTEL $$
(☎077 6951714; www.jhrc.jo; r/ste JD50/90; 🖥) This hotel, with a spectacular view of the castle, has some lovely features including a stylish lounge around a central gas fire. The rooms are simple but comfortable. The hotel takes a sustainable approach and has solar panels for hot-water heating and electricity. Dinner is available (JD9).

ℹ Getting There & Away

Occasional buses link Shobak village with Amman's South bus station (JD5, 5.30am daily, 2½ hours), and there are irregular minibuses to Karak from Aqaba via the Shobak turn-off (ask the driver before setting out). Either way you'll still need a taxi for the last 3km or so to the fort.

PETRA & THE SOUTH

Travel along the King's Highway and you'll notice that somewhere after Dana the character of the countryside changes. As the fertile hilltop pastures of the north give way to the more arid landscapes of the south, you suddenly find you're in epic country – the country that formed the backdrop for *Lawrence of Arabia* and *Indiana Jones and the Last Crusade*.

To make the most of this exciting part of Jordan, with its unmissable world wonders at Petra and Wadi Rum, you need to spend a day or two more than the map might suggest. Find some time to hike and stay with

the Bedouin, and the experience is sure to become a highlight of your entire Middle Eastern trip.

Before catching the ferry to Egypt or crossing into Israel and the Palestinian Territories, spare an evening for Aqaba, a popular night out with travellers.

Petra & Wadi Musa   بترا & وادي موسى
☎ 03 / POP 30,050

The ancient Nabataean city of Petra, with its elaborate architecture chiselled out of the pink-hued cliffs, is not just the leading highlight of a country blessed with more than its fair share of top sites: it's a wonder of the world. It lay hidden for centuries, known only to the Bedouin who made it their home, until the great Swiss explorer, Jean Louis Burckhardt, happened upon it in 1812.

Built partly in honour of the dead, the Petra necropolis retains much of its sense of hidden mystery thanks to its inaccessible location in the heart of a windblown landscape. The site is reached via the Siq, a narrow rift in the land whose cliffs cast long shadows across the once-sacred way. The path suddenly slithers into sunlight in front of the Treasury – a spectacle that cannot fail to impress. Add to this the cheerfulness of the Bedouin, and it's easy to see what makes Petra a must.

History

Think of Petra and you will inevitably think of the Nabataeans, the nomadic tribe from western Arabia who built most of the monuments in the ancient city that are visible today. The Nabataeans arrived in the region around the 6th century BC. They were organised traders and over the next 500 years they used their wealth to build

Petra

WALKING TOUR

Splendid though it is, the Treasury is not the full stop of a visit to Petra that many people may imagine. In some ways, it's just the semicolon – a place to pause after the exertions of the Siq, before exploring the other remarkable sights and wonders just around the corner.

Even if you're on a tight schedule or worried the bus won't wait, try to find another two hours in your itinerary to complete this walking tour. Our illustration shows the key highlights of the route, as you wind through Wadi Musa from the **Siq ❶**, pause at the **Treasury ❷** and pass the tombs of the broader **Outer Siq ❸**. With energy and a stout pair of shoes, climb to the **High Place of Sacrifice ❹** for a magnificent eagle's-eye view of Petra. Return to the **Street of Facades ❺** and the **Theatre ❻**. Climb the steps opposite to the **Urn Tomb ❼** and neighbouring **Silk Tomb ❽**: these Royal Tombs are particularly magnificent in the golden light of sunset.

Is the thought of all that walking putting you off? Don't let it! There are donkeys to help you with the steep ascents and Bedouin stalls for a reviving herb tea. If you run out of steam, camels are on standby for a ride back to the Treasury.

Treasury

As you watch the sun cut across the facade, notice how it lights up the ladders on either side of Petra's most iconic building. These stone indents were most probably used for scaffolding.

Jebel Madba

Jebel al-Khubtha

To Entrance to Petra

Siq

This narrow cleft in the land forms the sublime approach to the ancient city of Petra. Most people walk through the corridor of stone but horse-carts are available for those who need them.

DOWN DIFFERENTLY

A superb walk leads from the High Place of Sacrifice, past the Garden Tomb to Petra City Centre.

TOP TIPS

» **Morning Glory** From around 7am in summer and 8am in winter, watch the early morning sun slide down the Treasury facade.

» **Pink City** Stand opposite the Royal Tombs at sunset (around 4pm in winter and 5pm in summer) to learn how Petra earned its nickname.

» **Floral Tribute** Petra's oleanders flower in May.

High Place of Sacrifice

Imagine the ancients treading the stone steps and it'll take your mind off the steep ascent. The hilltop platform was used for incense-burning and libation-pouring in honour of forgotten gods.

Outer Siq

Take time to inspect the tombs just past the Treasury. Some appear to have a basement but, in fact, they show how the floor of the wadi has risen over the centuries.

Street of Facades

Cast an eye at the upper storeys of some of these tombs and you'll see a small aperture. Burying the dead in attics was meant to deter robbers – the plan didn't work.

Stairs to High Place

Souvenir shops, teashops & toilets

Wadi Musa

⑤

⑥

Wadi Musa

To Petra City Centre →

⑦

⑧

Jebel Umm al'Amr (1066m)

Royal Tombs

Royal Tombs

HEAD FOR HEIGHTS

For a regal view of Petra, head for the heights above the Royal Tombs, via the staircase.

Urn Tomb

Earning its name from the urn-shaped finial crowning the pediment, this grand edifice with supporting arched vaults was perhaps built for the man represented by the toga-wearing bust in the central aperture.

Silk Tomb

Perhaps Nabataean builders were attracted to Wadi Musa because of the colourful beauty of the raw materials. Nowhere is this more apparent than in the weather-eroded, striated sandstone of the Silk Tomb.

Theatre

Most stone amphitheatres are freestanding, but this one is carved almost entirely from the solid rock. Above the back row are the remains of earlier tombs, their facades sacrificed in the name of entertainment.

Petra

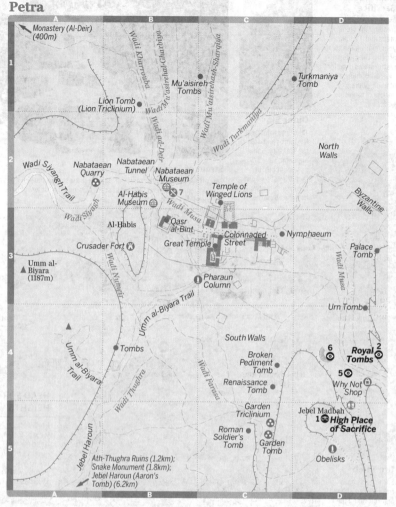

Monastery (Al-Deir)
(400m)

Wadi Kharroúba

Wadi Muʿaisireh ash-Sharqiya

Mu'aisireh
Tombs

Turkmaniya
Tomb

Lion Tomb
(Lion Triclinium)

Wadi ad-Deir

Wadi Turkmaniya

North
Walls

Wadi Siyagh Trail

Nabataean
Quarry

Nabataean
Tunnel

Nabataean
Museum

7

Temple of
Winged Lions

Al-Habis
Museum

Wadi Musa

Byzantine
Walls

Wadi Siyagh

Al-Habis

Qasr
al-Bint

Colonnaded
Street

Nymphaeum

Crusader Fort

Great Temple

Palace
Tomb

Umm al-
Biyara
(1187m)

Wadi Numer

Pharaun
Column

Umm al-Biyara Trail

Wadi Musa

Urn Tomb

South Walls

Tombs

Broken
Pediment
Tomb

6

Royal
Tombs

2

Umm al-Biyara Trail

Wadi Thughra

Wadi Farasa

Renaissance
Tomb

5

Why Not
Shop

Jebel Haroun

Garden
Triclinium

Roman
Soldier's
Tomb

Garden
Tomb

Jebel Madbah

1 High Place
of Sacrifice

Ath-Thughra Ruins (1.2km);
Snake Monument (1.8km);
Jebel Haroun (Aaron's
Tomb) (6.2km)

Obelisks

JORDAN PETRA & WADI MUSA

the city of Petra. In its heyday, under King
Aretas IV (8 BC–AD 40), the city was home
to around 30,000 people, including scribes
and expert hydraulic engineers who built
dams, cisterns and water channels to protect the site and its magnificent buildings.

By AD 106, as trade routes shifted from
Petra to Palmyra and new sea trade routes
via the Red Sea to Rome bypassed Petra
altogether, the Romans assumed control of
the weakened Nabataean empire. Far from
abandoning the city of Petra, however, the
invaders recast the ancient city with familiar Roman features, including a colonnaded
street and baths.

Earthquakes in 363 and 551 ruined much
of the city and Petra became a forgotten
outpost, a 'lost city' known only to local
Bedouin who preferred to keep its whereabouts secret. Part of the continuing allure
of the 'rose red city' is that despite many
years of scrutiny by archaeologists since
Burckhardt's visit in 1812, Petra still has
many secrets yet to be discovered.

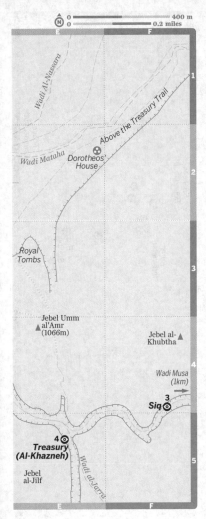

★ Treasury (Al-Khazneh)   TOMB

(Map p330) Known locally as the Treasury, this tomb is where most visitors fall in love with Petra. The Hellenistic facade is an astonishing piece of craftsmanship. Although carved out of iron-laden sandstone to serve as a tomb for the Nabataean King Aretas III (who reigned c 87 BC–62 BC), the Treasury derives its name from the story that an Egyptian pharaoh hid his treasure here (in the facade urn) while pursuing the Israelites.

Street of Facades   TOMBS

(Map p330) From the Treasury, the passage broadens into what is commonly referred to as the Outer Siq. Riddling the walls of the Outer Siq are over 40 tombs and houses built by the Nabataeans in a 'crow step' style reminiscent of Assyrian architecture. Colloquially known as the Street of Facades, they are easily accessible, unlike many tombs in Petra.

★ High Place of Sacrifice   VIEWPOINT

(Map p330) The most accessible of Petra's 'High Places', this well-preserved site was built atop Jebel Madbah with drains to channel the blood of sacrificial animals. A flight of steps signposted just before the Theatre leads to the site: turn right at the obelisks to reach the sacrificial platform. You can ascend by donkey (about JD10 one way), but you'll sacrifice both the sense of achievement on reaching the summit and the good humour of your poor old transport.

Theatre   THEATRE

(Map p330) Originally built by the Nabataeans (not the Romans) over 2000 years ago, the Theatre was chiselled out of rock, slicing through many caves and tombs in the process. It was enlarged by the Romans to hold about

⦿ Sights

★ Siq   CANYON

(Map p330) The 1.2km siq, or canyon, with its narrow, vertical walls, is undeniably one of the highlights of Petra. The walk through this magical corridor, as it snakes its way towards the hidden city, is one full of anticipation for the wonders ahead – a point not wasted on the Nabataeans who made the passage into a sacred way, punctuated with sites of spiritual significance.

JORDAN PETRA & WADI MUSA

Wadi Musa

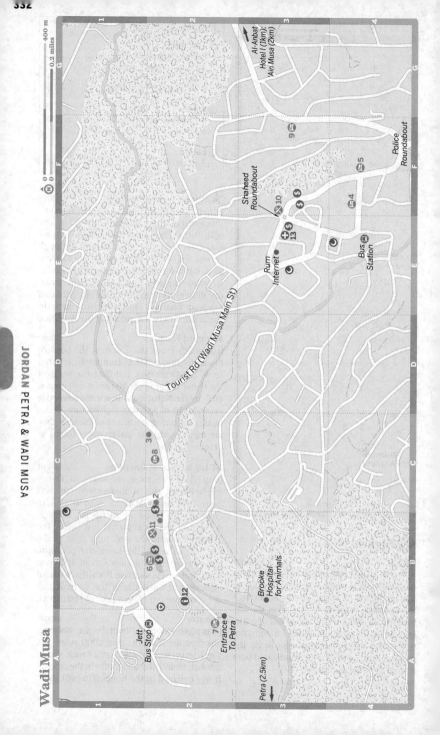

0 0 400 m
0 0 0.2 miles

Al-Anbat Hotel (1km); 'Ain Musa (2km)

Police Roundabout

Shaheed Roundabout

Rum Internet

Bus Station

Tourist Rd (Wadi Musa Main St)

Jett Bus Stop

Brooke Hospital for Animals

Entrance To Petra

Petra (2.5km)

Wadi Musa

8500 (around 30% of the population of Petra) soon after they arrived in AD 106. Badly damaged by an earthquake in AD 363, the Theatre was partially dismantled to build other structures but it remains a Petra highlight.

★ Royal Tombs TOMB
(Map p330) Downhill from the Theatre, the wadi widens to create a larger thoroughfare. To the right, the great massif of Jebel al-Khubtha looms over the valley. Within its west-facing cliffs are burrowed some of the most impressive burial places in Petra, known collectively as the 'Royal Tombs'. They look particularly stunning bathed in the golden light of sunset.

★ Monastery (Al-Deir) TOMB
Hidden high in the hills, the Monastery is one of the legendary monuments of Petra. Similar in design to the Treasury but far bigger (50m wide and 45m high), it was built in the 3rd century BC as a Nabataean tomb. It derives its name from the crosses carved on the inside walls, suggestive of its use as a church in Byzantine times. The ancient rock-cut path of more than 800 steps starts

from the Nabataean Museum and follows the old processional route.

✹ Activities

There are many rewarding hikes in Petra, perhaps the most popular of which is the one-hour hike from the High Place of Sacrifice to Petra City Centre. This unguided, moderately demanding route leads through Wadi Farasa past magnificent rock formations and wildflower gardens. Features of this walk also include the Lion Monument (an ingenious Nabataean fountain), the elegant Roman Soldier's Tomb and the Garden Triclinium (with unique interior decorations). The visitor centre is a good source of information for finding out which routes are accessible after the annual rains.

Wadi Muthlim to Royal Tombs HIKING
This adventurous 1½-hour canyon hike is an exciting alternative route into Petra if you've already taken the main Siq path. Flash floods are a serious issue in the area and a guide is mandatory (JD50). The hike is not difficult or too strenuous, but there are several boulder blockages and in winter you may need to wade through pools of water.

Jebel Haroun HIKING
This strenuous, six-hour-return hike via Snake Monument starts from Qasr al-Bint. Jebel Haroun (1350m) is thought to be the biblical Mt Hor – the burial site of Moses' brother Aaron; a white shrine built in the 14th century marks the site. The hike can be done with a guide (JD150) or self-guided.

⟳ Courses

★ Petra Kitchen COOKING COURSE
(Map p332; ☎ 2155700; www.petrakitchen.com; cookery course per person JD35; ◷ 6.30-9.30pm)
If you've always wanted to know how to whip up wonderful hummus or bake the perfect baklava, Petra Kitchen is for you. Located 100m up the main road from the Mövenpick Hotel, Petra Kitchen offers nightly cookery courses for those wanting to learn from locals how to cook Jordanian mezze, soup and main courses in a relaxed family-style atmosphere.

⌸ Sleeping

You can't overnight in Petra itself.

FINDING YOUR OWN PACE IN PETRA

Instead of trying to 'see it all' (the quickest way to monument-fatigue), make Petra your own by sparing time to amble among unnamed tombs or sip tea at a Bedouin stall.

Half Day (five hours) Stroll through the Siq, savouring the moment of revelation at the Treasury. Climb the steps to the High Place of Sacrifice and take the path through Wadi Farasa, passing a paintbox of rock formations.

One Day (eight hours) Complete the half-day itinerary, but pack a picnic. Visit the Royal Tombs, walk along to Qasr al-Bint and hike the wadi that leads to Jebel Haroun as far as Snake Monument – an ideal perch for a snack and a snooze. Save some energy for the climb to the Monastery, a fitting finale for any Petra visit.

Two Days Spend a second day scrambling through exciting Wadi Muthlim and restore your energies over a barbecue at the Basin Restaurant. Sit near the Theatre to watch the Royal Tombs at sunset – the best spectacle in Petra. Reward your efforts with a Turkish bath and a drink in the Cave Bar – the oldest pub in the world.

Lower Wadi Musa

The following hotels are located at the bottom end of town, within walking distance to the entrance to Petra.

⭐ **Petra Palace Hotel**   HOTEL $$
(Map p332; ☑ 2156723; www.petrapalace.com.jo; s/d/tr JD49/70/95; ❄@🛜☒) Located on the main street, 500m from the entrance to Petra, this attractive and well-established hotel – with its palm-tree entrance, big, bright foyer and helpful management – is an excellent choice. A whole suite of rooms open onto the outdoor swimming pool. The lively bar and restaurant are also drawcards.

⭐ **Petra Guest House Hotel**   HOTEL $$$
(Map p332; ☑ 2156266; www.guesthouse-petra. com; s/d/tr JD90/105/125; P❄🛜) You can't get closer to the entrance to Petra without sleeping in a cave – and indeed the hotel's bar (the famous Cave Bar) is located in one. Choose from spacious, motel-like chalets or sunny (if somewhat cramped) rooms in the main building. The staff are unfailingly delightful and the breakfast buffet is superior to most. Offers excellent value for money.

⭐ **Mövenpick Hotel**   LUXURY HOTEL $$$
(Map p332; ☑ 2157111; www.moevenpick-hotels. com; r from JD185; ❄@🛜☒) This beautifully crafted Arabian-style hotel, 100m from the entrance to Petra, is worth a visit simply to admire the inlaid furniture, marble fountains, wooden screens and brass salvers. As the hotel is in the bottom of the valley there are no views, but the large and superluxurious rooms all have huge windows regardless. The buffet breakfast and dinner are exceptional.

Wadi Musa Town Centre

The following hotels are near the bus station. Free transport to and from the entrance to Petra is usually offered once a day.

⭐ **Cleopetra Hotel**   HOTEL $
(Map p332; ☑ 2157090; www.cleopetrahotel.com; s/d/tr JD20/30/40; @🛜) This continues to be the friendliest and most efficiently run budget hotel in town. The hotel has bright, fresh rooms with private bathrooms and hot water. There's a communal sitting area in the lobby which is ideal for meeting fellow travellers, and rooftop developments are planned. Wi-fi is available for JD2.

⭐ **Amra Palace Hotel**   HOTEL $$
(Map p332; ☑ 2157070; www.amrapalace.com; s/d/tr JD44/64/84; ❄@🛜☒) This lovely hotel, with its pretty garden of roses and jasmine, marble-pillared lobby, giant brass coffeepots and homely furniture, offers a more Jordanian sense of hospitality than many of the rather bland hotels in town. The brothers who have run this establishment for many years take a personal interest in the details and it shows.

Upper Wadi Musa

Rocky Mountain Hotel   HOTEL $
(Map p332; ☑ 2155100; rockymountainhotel@yahoo.com; s/d/tr/q JD26/39/50/60, buffet dinner JD8; ❄@🛜) This backpacker-friendly hotel near the junction with the main road into town has caught just the right vibe to make

it a successful travellers' lodge. The hotel is 'big on cleanliness' and there's a cosy communal area with free tea and coffee. The *majlis*-style roof terrace makes the most of the impressive sweeping views.

Al-Anbat Hotel I
HOTEL $

(☏2156265; www.alanbat.com; s/d/tr JD20/35/45, buffet lunch or dinner JD10; ❄@🛰☷) Located some way out of town on the road between 'Ain Musa and Wadi Musa, this three-storey resort offers midrange quality for budget prices and features a beautiful, brand-new lobby with sofas spanning the magnificent view. The large rooms (many with gorgeous sunset views) have satellite TV and come with a balcony. The rooms in the extension are particularly attractive.

✖ Eating

Al-Wadi Restaurant
JORDANIAN $

(Map p332; ☏2157151; salads JD1, mains JD4-5; ⊙7am-late) Right on Shaheed roundabout, this lively spot offers pasta and a range of vegetarian dishes and local Bedouin specialities such as *gallaya* (meat, rice and onions in a spicy tomato sauce) and *mensaf* (lamb on a bed of rice topped with a lamb's head), most of which come with salad and rice.

★ Red Cave Restaurant
JORDANIAN $$

(Map p332; ☏2157799; starters JD1, mains from JD5; ⊙9am-10pm) Cavernous and friendly, this restaurant serves local Bedouin specialities including *mensaf* and *maqlubbeh*

(steamed rice with meat, grilled tomato and pine nuts). It's a popular travellers' meeting point and a cosy place to come on a chilly evening or to catch the breeze on a hot summer's day.

★ Basin Restaurant
BUFFET $$

(Map p330; lunch buffet JD17, fresh orange juice JD4; ⊙noon-4pm; 🖉) The Basin serves a wide spread of international dishes, including a healthy selection of salads, fresh felafel and barbecued spicy sausage. Lots of desserts are also on offer, including fruit and *umm ali* (a bread-pudding-like dessert). There's a fully air-conditioned interior seating area or groups sit by the ravine under canvas while independent travellers are given tables under the trees.

Al-Saraya Restaurant
INTERNATIONAL $$$

(Map p332; ☏2157111; lunch/dinner JD20/JD25; ❄🖉) Serving a top-notch international buffet in an elegant banquet hall, this fine-dining restaurant offers a quality of dishes that matches the general opulence of the Mövenpick Hotel in which it is located. Leave time for a nightcap in the grand, wood-panelled bar, which sports a roaring fire in the hearth in winter.

🍷 Drinking & Nightlife

★ Cave Bar
BAR

(Map p332; ☏2156266; ⊙4-11pm) You can't come to Petra and miss the oldest bar in the world. Occupying a 2000-year-old Nabataean

DON'T MISS

PETRA BY NIGHT

Like a grumbling camel caravan of snorting, coughing, laughing and farting miscreants, 200 people and one jubilantly crying baby make their way down the Siq 'in silence'. Asked to walk in single file behind the leader, breakaway contingents surge ahead to make sure they enjoy the experience 'on their own'. And eventually, sitting in 'reverential awe' outside the Treasury, the collected company shows its appreciation of Arabic classical music by lighting cigarettes from the paper-bag lanterns, chatting energetically, flashing cameras and audibly farting some more.

Welcome to public entertainment in the Middle East! If you really want the Siq to yourself, come in the winter, go at 2pm or take a virtual tour on the internet.

But despite the promotional literature to the contrary, silence and solitude is not what the **Petra by Night Tour** (Map p332; adult/child under 10yr JD17/free; ⊙8.30-10.30pm Mon, Wed & Thu) is all about. What this exceptional and highly memorable tour does give you is the fantastic opportunity to experience one of the most sublime spectacles on earth in the fever of other people's excitement. Huddles of whispering devotees stare up at the candlelit god blocks, elderly participants are helped over polished lozenges of paving stones, the sound of a flute wafts along the neck-hairs of fellow celebrants – this is surely much closer to the original experience of the ancient city of Petra than walking through the icy stone corridor alone.

JORDAN PETRA & WADI MUSA

ℹ WALKING TIMES TO KEY SIGHTS IN PETRA

The following table indicates one-way walking times at a leisurely pace. At a faster pace without stopping, you can hike from Petra Visitor Centre to the Treasury in 20 minutes and the museum in 40 minutes along the main thoroughfare. Don't forget to double the time for the uphill return journey.

DIRECT ROUTE	TIME (MIN)	DIFFICULTY
Visitor Centre to Siq entrance	15	Easy
Siq entrance to Treasury	20	Easy
Treasury to Royal Tombs	20	Easy
Treasury to Obelisk at High Place of Sacrifice	45	Moderate
Obelisk to museum (via main thoroughfare)	45	Easy
Treasury to museum	30	Easy
Museum to Monastery	40	Moderate

rock tomb, this blue-lit Petra hotspot has been known to stay open until 4am on busy summer nights. Sit among the spirits, alcoholic or otherwise, and you'll soon get a flavour of Petra you hadn't bargained on (not least the 26% tax and service charge!).

Wranglers Pub BAR
(Map p332; ☏ 2156723; ⊙ 2pm-midnight) The Petra Palace Hotel runs this sociable bar, decorated with assorted local memorabilia.

🛍 Shopping

Made in Jordan HANDICRAFTS
(Map p332; ☏ 2155700) This Wadi Musa shop sells quality crafts from local enterprises. Products include olive oil, soap, paper, ceramics, table runners, nature products from Wild Jordan in Amman, jewellery from Wadi Musa, embroidery from Safi, camel hair shawls, and bags from Aqaba as well as Jordan River Foundation goods. The fixed prices reflect the quality and uniqueness of each piece; credit cards are accepted.

ℹ Orientation

The village that has sprung up around Petra is Wadi Musa (Moses' Valley); a string of hotels, restaurants and shops stretching about 5km from Ain Musa, the head of the valley, down to the entrance to Petra. The village centre is at Shaheed roundabout, with shops, restaurants and budget hotels, while midrange hotels are strung out along the main road for the remaining 2km towards the entrance to Petra.

ℹ Information

The Housing Bank and Jordan Islamic, up from the Shaheed roundabout, are good places to change money and both have ATMs. There are a couple of banks (but no ATMs) at the lower end of town near Petra.

Petra Visitor Centre (Map p332; ☏ 2156020; www.visitpetra.jo; ⊙ 6am-6pm May-Sep, to 4pm Oct-Apr) Information is available at the Petra Visitor Centre, just before the entrance. It houses the ticket office (Map p332; ☏ /fax 2156044; JD50/55/60 for one-/two-/three-day passes, admission free for children under 15 years; ⊙ 6am-4pm, to 6pm in summer) and a helpful information counter and is surrounded by souvenir shops.

Rum Internet (Map p332; per hour JD1; ⊙ 10am-midnight)

Wadi Musa Pharmacy (Map p332) Located near the Shaheed roundabout.

ℹ Getting There & Around

Minibuses to and from other cities generally leave from the Wadi Musa bus station. The station is located in the town centre, a 10-minute walk uphill from the entrance to Petra. Private (yellow) unmetered taxis shuttle between the two (around JD3).

The following prices quoted for transport are current at press time but be ready to pay a little more or a little less, depending on the season, the number of other travellers waiting, the length of time you've already waited for the bus to fill, the amount of luggage and so forth. Your hotel manager will be used to giving travellers a current update for times and prices, or log on to **Jordan Jubilee** (www.jordanjubilee.com).

Amman A daily JETT bus connects Amman with Petra, largely designed for those wanting to visit on a day trip. The service leaves at 6.30am from the JETT office, near Abdali bus station (single/return JD9.500/19, four hours) and drops off passengers at the Petra visitor centre in Wadi Musa. The return bus leaves between

4pm and 5pm (check with the driver). Regular minibuses travel every day between Amman's South bus station (Wahadat) and Wadi Musa (JD7, four hours) via the Desert Highway. These buses leave Amman and Wadi Musa when full every hour or so between 6am and 4pm.

Aqaba Minibuses leave Wadi Musa for Aqaba (JD7, 2½ hours) at about 6am, 8.30am and 3pm; ask around the day before to confirm or check through your hotel.

Karak A minibus sometimes leaves at around 7am (JD7), but demand is low so it doesn't leave every day. Alternatively, travel via Ma'an.

Ma'an Minibuses leave Wadi Musa for Ma'an (JD1.500, 45 minutes) fairly frequently throughout the day (more often in the morning), stopping briefly at the university, about 10km from Ma'an. From Ma'an there are connections to Amman, Aqaba and (indirectly) Wadi Rum.

Wadi Rum There is a daily minibus (JD7, two hours) around 6am. It's a good idea to reserve a seat the day before; your hotel should be able to contact the driver. You may well be charged extra for 'luggage' (around JD3), especially if it takes up a seat that could be used for a paying customer. If you miss this bus, or the service isn't operating, take the minibus to Aqaba, get off at the Ar-Rashidiyyah junction and catch another minibus or hitch the remainder of the journey to Wadi Rum.

Wadi Rum وادي رم

♪03

Western visitors have been fascinated by the magnificent landscape of Wadi Rum (adult/child under 12yr JD5/free) ever since TE Lawrence wrote so evocatively about its sculpted rocks, dunes and Bedouin encampments in *Seven Pillars of Wisdom* in the early 20th century. David Lean's *Lawrence of Arabia*, which was party filmed here, not only contributed to the myth of the man who took part in the Arab Revolt, but also gave epic status to Wadi Rum itself.

Wadi Rum is everything you'd expect of a quintessential desert: extreme in summer heat and winter cold; violent and moody as the sun slices through chiselled siqs at dawn or melts the division between rock and sand at dusk; exacting on the Bedouin who live in it; and vengeful on those who ignore its dangers. For most visitors, on half- or full-day trips from Aqaba or Petra, Wadi Rum offers one of the easiest and safest glimpses of the desert afforded in the region. For the lucky few who can afford a day or two in their itinerary to sleep over at one of the desert camps, it can be an unforgettable way of stripping the soul to basics.

◉ Sights

Named in honour of Lawrence's book, the Seven Pillars of Wisdom is a large rock formation, with seven fluted turrets, easy to spot from the visitor centre. Further along Wadi Rum, the enormous, dramatic Jebel Rum (1754m) towers above Rum Village. Of the sites closest to Rum Village (distances from the Rest House in brackets), there's a 1st-century BC Nabataean temple (400m) and good views from Lawrence's Spring (3km), named after Lawrence because he wrote so invitingly of it in *Seven Pillars of Wisdom*.

🏃 Activities

There are several rewarding hikes in the area, though bear in mind that many of them require walking through soft sand – a tiring activity at the best of times and dangerously exhausting in the summer.

A camel ride offers one of the best ways to understand the rhythms of the desert. A two-hour trip costs JD10. Full-day camel hire costs JD60 per day; see the rates posted at the visitor centre. Beware that after one hour of camel riding, most people choose to get off and walk!

For ideas on more adventurous trips, see www.bedouinroads.com.

Makharas Canyon Hike HIKING
This worthwhile, moderate, unguided canyon hike includes open vistas, canyon hiking and grand dune views. It begins at the visitor centre and takes 2½ hours return.

Rakhabat Canyon SCRAMBLING
With a local guide or a copy of Tony Howard's *Walking in Jordan* you can navigate the labyrinthine siqs of Rakhabat Canyon for an exciting half-day trip through the heart of Jebel Umm al-Ishrin. The route starts at the western mouth of the canyon, just by Rum village.

Rum Horses HORSE RIDING
(☏079 5802108, 2033508; www.wadirumhorses. com) The highly recommended and long-established Rum Horses is the most professional camel- and horse-trekking agency. The stables are located on the approach road to the Wadi Rum visitor centre, about 10km from the Desert Highway. Look for a signboard beside the road.

HIGHLIGHTS OF WADI RUM

The main highlights of Wadi Rum are shown below (distances from the visitor centre in brackets):

Barrah Siq (14km) A long, picturesque canyon accessible on foot or by camel.

Burdah Rock Bridge (19km) This impressive 80m-high bridge can be viewed from the desert floor or, better still, you can scramble up to it with a guide (one hour).

Jebel Khazali (7km) Narrow siq with rock inscriptions.

Lawrence's House/Al-Qsair (9km) Legend has it that Lawrence stayed here during the Desert Revolt. The remote location and supreme views of the red sands are the main attractions.

Sand Dunes/Red Sands (6km) Superb red sand dunes on the slopes of Jebel Umm Ulaydiyya that seem to catch alight at sunset.

Sunset and Sunrise Points (11km) The places to be at dawn and dusk if you want to see the desert at its most colourful.

Umm Fruth Rock Bridge (13km) Smaller and more visited than Burdah, this bridge is tucked into an intimate corner of the desert.

Wadak Rock Bridge (9km) Easy to climb, this little rock bridge offers magnificent views across the valley.

🛏 Sleeping

There are no hotels in Wadi Rum, but camping can range from a goat-hair blanket under the stars at an isolated Bedouin camp to a mattress under partitioned canvas in a 'party tent'. Mattress, blankets and food are provided, but not always linen.

Some desert camps are located near the village of Diseh, clearly signposted off the Wadi Rum approach road, 16km from the Desert Highway. Hitch a ride near the police checkpoint to the village (8km – be prepared for a wait), or request someone from the camp come to meet you.

🛌 Rum Village & Around

⭐ **Rum Stars Camp**   CAMP $
(☑ 079 5127025; www.rumstars.com; half board in tent per person JD25) One of the camps situated deepest in the desert, it takes about 20 minutes by 4WD to reach. In a cosy location, tucked into the side of a mountain and overlooking quintessential Wadi Rum landscape, the camp is simple but well run by Bedouin brothers. The owner, Ahmed Ogla Al Zalabeyh, speaks excellent English and is passionate about his Bedouin heritage.

Bedouin Lifestyle Camp   CAMP $
(☑ 077 9131803; www.bedouinlifestyle.com; half board in tent per person JD25) In operation since 2011, Atalla Ablawi operates this popular and well-run camp. Born in the desert, he moved to the village at age 10 and studied English and French at university. 'I'm like the fish,' he says, 'if you take me out of the desert, it's like being taken out of the water'.

Rest House   CAMPGROUND $
(☑ 2018867; mattress & blankets per person in 2-person tent JD5) The frayed tents at the back of the Rest House offer the most accessible accommodation, but they're only recommended if you arrive in Wadi Rum too late to head into the desert. You can pitch your own tent for JD3, which includes use of toilets and shower block.

⭐ **Bait Ali Lodge**   CAMP $$
(☑ 079 5548133, 079 9257222; www.baitali.com; half board in tent per person from JD35, in small/medium/large cabin JD 45/52/58, in deluxe chalet JD68; 🖥🗑) 🖊 If you want to stay in the desert but are not wild about roughing it, then Bait Ali offers a highly recommended compromise. Tucked behind a hill, with a fine view of the wilderness, this ecofriendly camp is clearly signposted just off the road, 15km from the Desert Highway and 9km from the Wadi Rum visitor centre.

🛌 Diseh

Diseh camps include the secluded, upmarket **Rahayeb Camp** (☑ 079 6909030; www.rahayebcamp.com; half/full board per person

JD32/38); **Zawaideh Desert Camp** (☑079 5840664; zawaideh_camp@yahoo.com; half board per person JD20), close to the road and accessible by car; and **Captain's Camp** (☑079 5510432, 2016905; captains@jo.com.jo; half board per person JD35), a well-run midrange camp with hot showers, snug seating areas and good buffets.

✖ Eating

Rum Gate Restaurant BUFFET $$
(☑2015995; Wadi Rum visitor centre; snacks JD5, buffet lunch JD12; ☉8am-5pm; ❄☑) With 15 mixed salads and five hot dishes offered from noon to 3pm, the buffet at this restaurant is understandably popular. Outside lunchtime, the restaurant is a buzzing meeting place for guides, weary hikers and independent travellers who congregate over a nonalcoholic beer (JD2) and a chicken sandwich (JD5).

Rest House BUFFET $$
(☑/fax 2018867; breakfast JD5, lunch JD12, dinner buffet JD12; ☉7am-8.30pm) Dining here is open-air and buffet-style. Sipping a large Amstel beer (JD5) while watching the sun's rays light up Jebel Umm al-Ishrin is the perfect way to finish the day.

ℹ Information

Admission to Wadi Rum Protected Area (p337) is controlled through the visitor centre, 7km before reaching Rum village.

Most people visit the desert as part of a 4WD trip arranged on arrival at the visitor centre; half-/full-day excursions cost around JD67/80. Prices are regulated, but do not include overnight stays in a Bedouin camp (around JD30 extra).

Modest clothing is appreciated by the conservative Bedouin, especially out in the desert.

Visitor Centre (☑2090600; www.wadirum. jo; ☉7am-7pm) The visitor centre is situated at the entry to the protected area, about 30km east of the Desert Highway and 7km north of Rum village. This is where you buy your entry ticket, book a 4WD or camel excursion, organise accommodation at a camp and book a guide. There are no ATMs or credit-card payment facilities in Wadi Rum.

ℹ Getting There & Away

MINIBUS
Aqaba At the time of writing, there was at least one minibus a day to Aqaba (JD3, one hour) at around 7am. A second one may run at 8.30am.

Wadi Musa There is a fairly reliable daily minibus (JD7, 2 hours) at 8.30am. Check current departure times at the visitor centre or the Rest House when you arrive in Wadi Rum.
Ma'an, Karak or Amman The minibuses to either Aqaba or Wadi Musa can drop you off at the Ar-Rashidiyya crossroads with the Desert Highway (JD2, 20 minutes), where it is easy to hail onward transport.

TAXI
Occasionally taxis wait at the visitor centre (and sometimes the Rest House) for a fare back to wherever they came from – normally Aqaba, Wadi Musa or Ma'an. It costs about JD30 to JD35 to Aqaba, and JD50 to JD55 to Wadi Musa (Petra). A taxi jeep from Rum village to the Ar-Rashidiyya crossroads with the Desert Highway costs around JD10.

Aqaba العقبة
☑03 / POP 136,200

Aqaba is the most important city in southern Jordan and, with feverish development underway, is being groomed as the country's second city, if not in size at least in terms of status, revenue and tourism potential. Perched on the edge of the Gulf of Aqaba, ringed by high desert mountains and enjoying a pleasant climate for most of the year, Aqaba has what it takes to make a major resort. That's a fact not lost on hotel chains, which continue to expand along the coast.

Surprisingly, given this radical makeover, Aqaba retains the relaxed small-town atmosphere of a popular local holiday destination. For the visitor, although there's not much to 'do' as such, the town offers a sociable stopover en route to the diving and snorkelling clubs to the south, and the blockbuster destinations of Wadi Rum and Petra to the northeast. It's also an obvious place to break a journey to/from Israel and the Palestinian Territories or to/from Egypt.

◉ Sights

Aqaba is more about sea than sights but there are a couple of sights of interest, including the limited ruins of **Ayla** (Corniche; ☉24hr) **FREE**, the ancient **port of Aqaba** (next to the Mövenpick Resort) and **Aqaba Fort** (off King Hussein St; admission incl Aqaba Museum JD1; ☉8am-4pm Sat-Thu, 10am-4pm Fri). Built between 1510 and 1517, the fort was used as a khan (travellers' inn) for pilgrims on their way to Mecca. The Ottomans

Aqaba

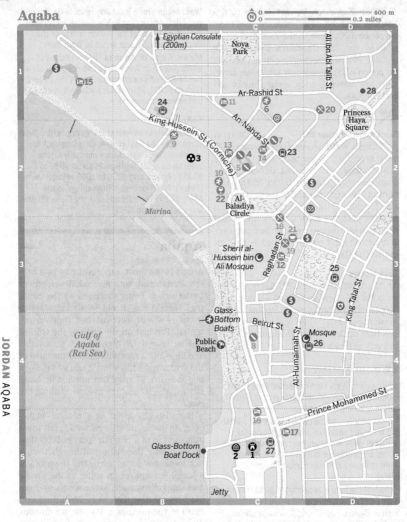

Egyptian Consulate
(200m)

Noya
Park

Ali Ibn Abi Talib St

Ar-Rashid St

An-Nahda St

King Hussein St (Corniche)

Princess
Haya
Square

Marina

Al-
Baladiya
Circle

Raghadan St

Sherif al-
Hussein bin
Ali Mosque

Gulf of
Aqaba
(Red Sea)

King Talal St

Glass-
Bottom
Boats

Beirut St

Al-Humaimah St

Mosque

Public
Beach

Prince Mohammed St

Glass-Bottom
Boat Dock

Jetty

JORDAN AQABA

---

occupied the castle until WWI when, in 1917, it was all but destroyed by shelling from the British Royal Navy. The neighbouring Museum of Aqaba Antiquities (West of King Hussein St; admission JD1; ☺8am-4pm Sat-Thu, 10am-4pm Fri) has a few interesting artefacts, including an old Roman milestone.

🏃 Activities

Diving & Snorkelling

According to the Jordan Royal Ecological Society (www.jreds.org) the Gulf of Aqaba has over 110 species of hard coral, 120 species of soft coral and about 1000 species of fish,

with some great sites for diving and snorkelling. Access is south of the town centre and ferry passenger terminal.

Aqaba's dive agencies are very professional. A typical two-dive trip from a boat (some sites have shore access) with tanks and weights costs around JD80 with an additional JD25 for full equipment rental. Night dives and PADI courses (from JD280) are available.

For snorkelling, all the following places rent out flippers, mask and snorkel for JD5 per day. Some offer whole boat trips for snorkelling for around JD45 per person.

Aqaba

Aqaba Adventure Divers Office DIVING
(☏ 079 5843724; www.aqaba-diving.com) Operates dives in conjunction with Bedouin Garden Village.

Aqaba International Dive Centre Office DIVING
(☏ 079 6949082; www.aqabadivingcenter.com) Popular, well equipped and one of Aqaba's best.

International Arab Divers Village Office DIVING
(☏ 03-2031808; www.aqabadive.com) Highly recommended year after year by Lonely Planet readers.

Dive Aqaba Office DIVING
(☏ 03-2108883; www.diveaqaba.com) A highly professional training centre known for its high-quality teaching staff.

Royal Diving Club DIVING
(☏ 03-2015555; www.coralbay.jo) Around 12km south of the city, the Royal Diving Club is one of Aqaba's most famous institutions. This is the place to come for the latest information on the condition of Jordan's key marine sites.

Swimming & Hammans

The cafe-lined public beaches of Aqaba are aimed at sunset strollers rather than swimmers. The Tala Bay complex, south of Aqaba, features a huge sandy bay in attractively landscaped gardens, surrounded by upmarket hotels.

★**Berenice Beach Club** WATER SPORTS
(www.berenice.com.jo; admission JD15; ☺ 9am-sunset) The only dedicated, private beach club on the south coast, Berenice has pools, a jetty giving access to a coral reef, a dive centre, watersports, restaurants and spotless changing rooms. It attracts record crowds on Fridays. It offers a 50% discount for guests of many Aqaba hotels and operates a regular free shuttle-bus service (check the website for current schedule).

Bab Al-Hara BATHHOUSE
(☏ 079 9663800; Ar-Rashid St; admission JD25; ☺ 9am-10pm) This spotlessly clean, friendly establishment offers steam bath, jacuzzi, foot and body massage, sauna and there's a separate pool for women and families. The masseur and owner, Mr Raid, has years of experience and trained in Dubai and China. He describes his establishment as 'very safe for ladies' and women tourists have recommended him.

Mövenpick Resort Hotel SWIMMING
(☏ /fax 2034020; www.moevenpick-hotels.com; King Hussein St; day use JD40; ☺ 8am-sunset) Day use of a clean beach, three pools, health club, sauna and jacuzzi; includes a JD5 drink voucher.

JORDAN AQABA

InterContinental Hotel
SWIMMING

(☎2092222; www.intercontinental.com; King Hussein St; day use JD25; ⊙8am-sunset) Day use of beautiful gardens, pools and beach.

Boat Trips

If you don't have time to go diving or snorkelling, the next best thing is a **glass-bottom boat**. Hire a boat for at least two to three hours to see the best fish.

Boats, which operate between 6am and sunset, congregate along the central public beach or at a jetty in front of Aqaba Castle. The cost is JD25 for 30 minutes, JD45 for an hour for a boat (holding about 10 people). Bring a swimsuit and snorkelling equipment.

Neptune Submarine Vision
BOAT TOUR

(☎9430969; www.aqababoat.com) A glass-bottom boat with a difference, the Neptune has a glass hull that is fully submersed allowing for a 360-degree view in what the company describes as a dry-dive experience. The self-styled 'underwater observatory' leaves daily from the Tala Bay marina, on the south coast.

Sindbad
CRUISE

(☎2050077; www.berenice.com.jo; Marina) Operates a number of popular cruises around the Gulf of Aqaba either from the marina or from Berenice Beach Club. Prices range from around JD20 to JD40 depending on choice of cruise. Most cruises operate daily and can be booked through any hotel.

🛏 Sleeping

Unless otherwise stated, budget places listed here offer (nonsatellite) TV, air-conditioning and private bathroom with hot water (not always reliable); they don't include breakfast. Midrange places have a fridge, satellite TV, telephone and hot water, and prices include breakfast.

Moon Beach Hotel
HOTEL $

(☎2013316; ashrafsaad77@yahoo.com; King Hussein St; s/d/tr with sea view JD18/30/35; ❄) Near the fort, this is undoubtedly the best budget option. The foyer is a welcoming mixture of heavy wooden furniture and photographs of old Aqaba. Most rooms have sea views, though the faded furnishings won't be to everyone's liking. The delightful family-run management easily makes up for the dodgy decor. Ask about the two-bedroom family suites for longer stays.

Al-Shula Hotel
HOTEL $

(☎2015153; alshulahotel@yahoo.com; Raghadan St; s/d/tr JD25/30/35; ❄) With its black-and-white marble reception desk and painted mirrors, the Al-Shula makes quite a statement. Most rooms have views to the sea across the mosque complex – good for a 4.30am wake-up call! The hotel is in the heart of one of Aqaba's busiest restaurant streets.

Captain's Hotel
BOUTIQUE HOTEL $$

(☎2060710; www.captains.jo; An-Nahda St; s/d JD75/85; ❄@🌐❄) Aqaba's version of a boutique hotel, the Captain's began life as a fish restaurant – still flourishing on the ground floor – and evolved, one storey at a time, into this stylish accommodation. With copper-tiled flooring and compact rooms featuring Arabian-style furniture, this is an upmarket choice for a midrange price. Other facilities include sauna and jacuzzi.

Aqaba Gulf Hotel
HOTEL $$

(☎2016636; www.aqabagulf.com; King Hussein St; r JD84; ❄@🌐❄) This tired old favourite (the only hotel in Aqaba with a tennis court) is just across the road from the Aqaba Gateway complex. The first hotel to be built in Aqaba, it has quite an honour roll of guests. The stained-wood, split-level dining room looks thoroughly dated, like the rest of the common-use areas, but this is not a criticism.

Yafko Hotel
HOTEL $$

(☎2042222; www.yafko.com; cnr Corniche & Prince Mohammed St; s/d JD25/45) Although not directly on the coast, in this newly opened hotel you can sit in bed and enjoy the sea views. Some rooms are an odd shape but the furnishings and stone trim make this an attractive choice. It is conveniently located near the fort, transport hubs and the road leading to the southern beaches.

Al-Cazar Hotel
HOTEL $$

(☎2014131; http://alcazarhotel.co; An-Nahda St; s/d/tr from JD35/40/50; ❄❄) If you're looking to stay somewhere with character, then book into this faded old grand dame of Aqaba, with its two dozen overgrown Washington palms in the front garden, an enormous, empty lobby and a bar with outrageous filigree plaster. The spacious rooms have bathrooms with multiple mirrors and marble surfaces that must have looked grand in their day.

★ InterContinental Hotel RESORT $$$

(☎ 2092222; www.intercontinental.com; King Hussein St; r from JD119; 🌐 @ 🏊) An imposing full stop at the end of the bay, the InterCon boasts less of an infinity pool than an infinity sea: on a calm day, the Gulf of Aqaba stretches in one seamless ripple all the way to Egypt. With exceptional landscape gardening, pools and a lazy river, the InterCon has stolen the top spot in Aqaba's luxury accommodation.

✗ Eating

Aqaba's speciality is fish, particularly *sayadieh*: it's the catch of the day, delicately spiced, served with rice in an onion and tomato (or tahini) sauce.

Al-Tarboosh Restaurant PASTRY $

(☎ 2018518; Raghadan St; pastries around 200 fils; ⊙ 7.30am-midnight) With the Arabic Moon, this is one of two neighbouring pastry shops that offer a great range of meat, cheese and vegetable *sambusas*. Order a bag to takeaway or sit and eat them straight from the oven at the tables outside.

★ Ali Baba Restaurant JORDANIAN $$

(☎ 2013901; Raghadan St; mains JD9; ⊙ 8am-midnight; 🌐 ✈) With its wooden awning, leafy cannas and potted palm trees, this favourite still draws the crowds. The outdoor seating area wrapped around the corner facade is a good vantage point for people-watching. In the evening the Ali Baba is more than just a restaurant – it's the amiable heart of old town Aqaba with alcohol served upstairs (available even during Ramadan).

Rakwet Kanaan Restaurant & Cafe JORDANIAN $$

(As-Sadah St; mains 7.500; ⊙ 10am-1am) Selling a delicious range of oriental pastries, cooked over firewood and liberally sprinkled with thyme, rosemary and sage, this restaurant is wrapped around the bend in the road where its pavement divans catch the breeze. The savoury dough platters are very filling so it's worth casting an eye at the size of your neighbour's portion before ordering your own!

★ Captain's Restaurant SEAFOOD $$$

(☎ 2016905; An-Nahda St; mains JD8-15; ⊙ 8am-midnight; 🌐) Serving consistently good quality seafood, including *sayadieh* (fish served with rice in an onion and tomato sauce) and seafood salad, this is a perennially popular choice for locals with something to celebrate. The stylish and amiable restaurant was so successful the owners built an entire hotel on the same site for those too full to make it home!

🍷 Drinking & Nightlife

Al-Fardos Coffee Shop COFFEEHOUSE

(⊙ 10am-midnight) Just off Zahran St, this is a traditional coffeehouse where local men sip *qahwa*, play backgammon and stare openmouthed at Arabic music videos. It has a pleasant outdoor setting, and foreign women are welcome.

Rovers Return PUB

(☎ 2032030; Aqaba Gateway; ⊙ 12.30pm-12.30am) An aerial version of the Amman expat favourite (it's located in a mock lighthouse), this pub attracts a young crowd. If you're British and feeling homesick, stay for fish and chips or roast beef (JD9.500) and watch three-screen football. The only downside is that the compact space can get oppressively smoky.

ℹ Information

Aqaba has a good sprinkling of internet cafes, particularly along As-Sadah St, most of which charge around JD1 to JD2 per hour. There are plenty of banks with ATMs and money changers around town.

10zll Internet Cafe (☎ 2022009; As-Sadah St; per hour JD2; ⊙ 24hr) Next to Days Inn, this large establishment offers a reliable, fast and continually updated service. In fact this is not your average net cafe: with fish, budgies and potted cacti, it lives up to the owner's vision of a 'beautiful net experience'.

General Post Office (⊙ 7.30am-7pm Sat-Thu, to 1.30pm Fri) Opposite Zahran St in the centre of town.

ℹ Getting There & Away

AIR

Royal Jordanian (☎ 2018633; www.rj.com; Ash-Sherif al-Hussein bin Ali St; ⊙ 9am-5pm Sun-Thu) Operates daily flights to Amman's Queen Alia International Airport. Its office at the airport is the place to buy, confirm or change Royal Jordanian or Royal Wings air tickets. Tickets to Amman cost from JD64 one way, JD139 return.

BOAT

There are boat services between Aqaba and Nuweiba in Egypt. Sindbad offers a 30-minute shuttle service by high-speed catamaran to Taba (political climate permitting) and Sharm el-Sheikh.

BUS

JETT Bus Office (☑ 2015222; King Hussein St) Buses run five times daily to Amman's north station (JD9, five hours), between 7am and 5pm. Book tickets for these buses at least a day in advance. Buses leave from outside the office, next to the Mövenpick Resort Hotel, a 10-minute walk from the centre of town.

JETT Bus Office (☑ 2032200; just off An-Nahda St) More of an office than a bus station, it operates one of two JETT bus services in Aqaba. There are five daily buses to Amman's south station (JD7, four hours) between 8am and 9pm. Book a day in advance.

MINIBUS

With the exception of those to Karak, minibuses leave from the main bus/minibus station on Ar-Reem St.

Wadi Musa For Petra, JD7, 2½ hours. Leaves when full between 6am and 7am, and between 11am and noon; you may have to wait up to an hour. Otherwise, get a connection in Ma'an (JD4, 80 minutes).

Wadi Rum JD3, one hour. Leaves at around 6.30am and, more reliably, 11am. At other times, catch a minibus towards Ma'an, get off at the turn-off to Wadi Rum at Ar-Rashidiyya and then hitch a ride to Rum Village.

Karak JD3.500, three hours. Via Safi and the Dead Sea Highway. Minibuses leave from the small station next to the mosque on Al-Humaimah St.

TAXI

Taxis can be chartered to Petra (one way JD60, 1½ hours) and Wadi Rum (one way JD50, one hour with two hours' waiting time).

❶ Getting Around

Minibuses (JD1) leave from near the entrance to Aqaba Fort, on King Hussein St, for the Royal Diving Club via the southern beach camps, dive sites and the ferry terminal (for boats heading to Egypt).

UNDERSTAND JORDAN

Jordan Today

In common with other parts of the Middle East, Jordan traditionally favours strong, centralised government under an autocratic leader – what might be called 'benign dictatorship'. This does not preclude voicing an opinion, however, and in November 1989 the first full parliamentary elections since 1967 were held, and women were allowed the vote. Four years later most political parties were legalised and able to participate in parliamentary and municipal elections. Despite these concessions, democracy in Jordan is still something of an alien concept – as illustrated by the brief and largely unremarkable demonstrations at the start of the decade that contrasted with the more urgent 'Arab Spring' uprisings in neighbouring countries. Perceived as promoting the interests of the individual over those of the community, the principles of democracy run against the grain of tribal traditions where respect for elders is paramount.

King Abdullah is widely regarded as a modernising monarch in touch with the sensibilities of a globalised world, supportive of social and economic reform and committed to stamping out corruption. Abdullah has proved adept at handling foreign affairs – imperative, considering the neighbourhood Jordan shares.

Occupying the calm eye of the storm in the Middle East, the country has a long tradition of absorbing the displaced peoples of its troubled neighbours. Currently coping with the fourth influx of refugees in 50 years (from the civil war in Syria), Jordan now has the region's second-largest population of Syrian refugees, and Za'atari camp, with its 120,000 residents, is equivalent in size to Jordan's largest cities. With each new flood of asylum seekers, Jordan's resources and the patience of its citizens are stretched to breaking point.

Despite the mixed origins of its population, the current political and economic difficulties, the insecurity of daily life in a volatile region, and the threat from Isis hovering just over the border, Jordanians largely remain united in pride for their country.

History

In Jordan history is not something that happened 'before'. It's a living, breathing part of everyday life, witnessed not just in the pragmatic treatment of ancient artefacts but also in the way people live. Jordanians value

BOOKS ON JORDAN

Lonely Planet offers a detailed *Jordan* guide. Other key reading includes the following:

➡ *Seven Pillars of Wisdom* (TE Lawrence; 1935) Describes Lawrence's epic adventures in Jordan and the part he played in the Arab Revolt (he wrote some of it in Amman).

➡ *Petra: Lost City of the Ancient World* (Christian Augé and Jean-Marie Dentzer; 2000) An excellent, portable background introduction to Petra.

➡ *Married to a Bedouin* (Marguerite van Geldermalsen; 2006) An idea of life with the Bedouin at Petra.

➡ *Walking in Jordan* (2001) and *Walks & Scrambles in Rum* (Tony Howard and Di Taylor; 1993) Describe dozens of hikes in Jordan, from wadi walks to climbing routes.

their heritage and are in no hurry to eschew ways of life that have proved successful for centuries. Each period of history thus features in the experiences of a visitor, not only through a pile of fallen columns, but in the taking of tea with old custodians of the desert or the bargaining for a kilim with designs inherited from the Byzantine era.

Early Settlements

Just step foot in Jordan and you begin your encounter with history. Visit the dolmens near Madaba, for example, and you'll be entering the cradle of civilisation; dating from 4000 BC, the dolmens embody the sophistication of the world's first villages.

The Copper and Bronze Ages helped bring wealth to the region (1200 BC). You can find forgings from Jordan's ancient copper mines in the Dana Biosphere Reserve. Trading in these metals had a cohesive impact – travel the King's Highway and not only will you walk on the path of royalty, but you'll also see how this route helped unify city-states into a recognisable Jordan between 1200 BC and 333 BC.

Great Empires

The Greeks, Nabataeans and Romans dominated Jordan's most illustrious historical period (333 BC to AD 333), leaving the magnificent legacies of Petra and Jerash. Located at the centre of the land bridge between Africa and Asia, the cities surrounding the King's Highway profited from the caravan routes that crossed the deserts from Arabia to the Euphrates, bringing shipments of African gold and South Arabian frankincense via the Red Sea ports in present-day Aqaba and Eilat.

By the 4th century BC, the growing wealth of Arab lands attracted the attention of Alexander the Great. The precocious 21-year-old stormed through the region in 334 BC, winning territories from Turkey to Palestine and bringing access to the great intellectual treasures of the classical era.

Trade was the key to Jordan's golden era (8 BC to AD 40), thanks to the growing importance of a nomadic Arab tribe from the south, known as the Nabataeans. The Nabataeans produced only copper and bitumen (for waterproofing boat hulls), but they knew how to trade in the commodities of neighbouring nations. They never possessed an 'empire' in the common military and administrative sense of the word; instead, from about 200 BC, they established a 'zone of influence' that stretched from Syria to Rome – one that inevitably attracted the conquering tendencies of the Roman Empire.

You only have to visit Jerash for five minutes, trip over a fallen column and notice the legions of other columns beside, to gain an immediate understanding of the importance of the Romans in Jordan. This magnificent set of ruins indicates the amount of wealth the Romans invested in this outpost of their empire. It's perhaps a fitting legacy of their rule that the Jordanian currency, the dinar, derives its name from the Latin *denarius* (ancient Roman silver coin).

Spirit of the Age

Under the influence of Rome, Christianity replaced the local gods of the Nabataeans, and several hundred years later Islam took its place. The arrival of Islamic dynasties is evident from the 7th century onwards, literally strewn over the deserts of eastern Jordan in the form of the intriguing Umayyad structures that dot the stark landscape. The

JORDAN HISTORY

conflict between Islam and Christianity, evident at Jordan's crusader castles in Ajloun, Karak and Shobak, is a defining feature of the next thousand years.

British imperialism dominates Jordan's history prior to the Arab Revolt of 1914; ride a camel through Wadi Rum and cries of 'To Aqaba!' hang in the wind. And so does the name of Lawrence, the British officer whose desert adventures have captured the imagination of visitors to such an extent that whole mountains are named after him. The Arab Revolt may not have immediately achieved its goal during peace negotiations, but it did lead directly to the birth of the modern state of Jordan. A series of treaties after 1928 led to full independence in 1946, when Abdullah was proclaimed king.

Modern State of Jordan

Jordan's modern history is about independence, modernisation (under the much-beloved King Hussein and his son and heir, the current King Abdullah). It's also marked by cohabitation with difficult neighbours. Much of the conflict stems from the creation of a Jewish national homeland in Palestine, where Arab Muslims accounted for about 90% of the population. Their resentment informed the dialogue of Arab–Israeli relations for the rest of the 20th century. Today, after the settlement of successive waves of refugees, the majority of the population of Jordan is made up of Palestinians.

On 26 October 1994, Jordan and Israel and the Palestinian Territories signed a momentous peace treaty, and for the past two decades Jordan has been preoccupied with its neighbours to the east rather the west – a shift in focus necessitated firstly by the Gulf War and subsequently by the US-led invasion of Iraq, which led to a further influx of refugees, this time from Iraq. Ironically, the refugees brought their relative prosperity with them – a windfall that has stimulated the economy throughout the past decade and helped turn Amman, in particular, into a cosmopolitan, modern city.

People & Society

Bedouin Roots

A strong tradition of hospitality and a lively sense of humour make it easy to connect with Jordanians. These are traits that belong to the Bedouin tradition. In fact, over 98% of Jordanians are Arab, descended from the original desert dwellers of Arabia. Living a traditional life of livestock rearing, the few remaining nomadic Bedouin are concentrated mainly in the Badia – the great desert plains of eastern Jordan. The majority of Jordan's indigenous population, however, now enjoy the benefits of settlement and education. While many are wistful about the stories of their grandparents, they are not nostalgic about the hardships they faced.

The most easily identifiable aspect of the Bedouin inheritance is an ingrained tribal respect for sheikhs (local elders). This characteristic is extended to the ultimate leaders of the country. Claiming unbroken descent from the Prophet Mohammed, Jordan's Hashemite royal family is a nationally beloved and regionally respected institution associated with benign and diplomatic governance and a history of charitable works. Despite protests against the government in the 2011 Arab Spring, there was no popular demand for a republic.

Importance of Family

Family ties are all-important to both modern and traditional Jordanians and paying respect to parents is where the sense of obeisance to elders is engendered. Socialising generally entails some kind of get-together with the extended family, with lines drawn loosely between the genders. This is reflected in terms of physical divisions within the house, where separate seating areas are reserved for men and women.

In Jordan, a woman's 'honour' is still valued in traditional society, and sex before marriage or adultery is often dealt with harshly by other members of the woman's family. Traditional concepts of *ird* (honour) run deep but sit uneasily with the freedoms many affluent Jordanian women have come to expect, largely thanks to universal access to one of the region's best education systems. A minimum of six women MPs is guaranteed by royal decree and while only 14% of the labour force was made up of women in 1991, today (according to UN data) this has risen to over one quarter.

Urbanisation

There is an increasing polarisation in Jordanian society between town and country. In Amman, modern Western-leaning middle-

and upper-class youths enjoy the fruits of a good education, shop in malls, drink lattes in Starbucks and and obsess over the latest fashions. In rural areas, meanwhile, unemployment is high and many populations struggle with making ends meet. For this reason, economic migration is common in Jordan, and many working-class families have at least one male who is temporarily working away from home – whether in Amman, the Gulf States or further abroad.

Religion

Over 92% of the population are Sunni Muslims. A further 6% are Christians living mainly in Amman, Salt, Madaba and Karak. There are tiny Shiite and Druze groups.

Most Christians belong to the Greek Orthodox Church, but there are also some Greek Catholics, a small Roman Catholic community, and Syrian, Coptic and Armenian Orthodox communities.

Arts & Crafts

Walk the streets of Madaba, with bright coloured kilims flapping in the wind, hike to the soap-making villages of Ajloun, or watch elderly Bedouin women threading beads at Petra, and it will become immediately apparent that the country has a strong handicraft tradition. The authorities have been quick to support this aspect of Jordan's heritage and now craft cooperatives are widespread, resulting in benefits for local communities and ensuring that Jordan's rich legacy endures for future generations. Taking an interest in Jordanian crafts, then, is not a remote aesthetic exercise – it represents sustainable tourism at its best.

Kilims

Jordan has a long-established rug-making industry dating back to the country's pre-Islamic, Christian communities. *Mafrash* (rugs) are usually of the flat, woven kind, compared with carpets that have a pile. To this day, especially in Madaba and Mukawir, it's possible to watch kilims based on early Byzantine designs being made.

Embroidery

This is an important skill among Jordanian women and most learn the craft at a young age. Teenagers traditionally embroider the clothes they will need as married women. Embroidery provides an occasion for women to socialise, often with a pot of tea spiced up with a pinch of local gossip.

Mosaics

With a noble and distinguished lineage in Jordan, mosaics are made from tiny squares of naturally coloured rock called tesserae – the more tesserae per centimetre, the finer and more valuable the mosaic. Portable pieces are available.

Food & Drink

Though little known outside the country, Jordan has a distinctive culinary tradition, largely thanks to the Bedouin influence.

The Bedouin speciality is *mensaf* – delicious spit-roasted lamb, basted with spices until it takes on a yellow appearance. It's served on a platter of rice and pine nuts, flavoured with the cooking fat, and often centrally garnished with the head of the lamb. Honoured guests are served the eyes

JORDAN ARTS & CRAFTS

ESSENTIAL JORDANIAN FOOD & DRINK

Fuul medames Fava-bean dish drizzled with fresh-pressed olive oil; served with unleavened Arabic bread, sour cream, local salty white cheese and a sprinkling of *zaatar* (thyme and other herbs).

Maqlubbeh Pyramid of steaming rice garnished with cardamom and sultanas; topped with slivers of onion, meat, cauliflower and fresh herbs.

Mensaf Bedouin dish of lamb, rice and pine nuts, combined with yoghurt and the liquid fat from the cooked meat.

Kunafa Addictive dessert of shredded dough and cream cheese, smothered in syrup.

Marrameeya Sage-based herbal tea, especially delicious at Dana.

You can also cook your own Jordanian specialty in Wadi Musa, at Petra Kitchen (p333).

(which have a slightly almond flavour); less honoured guests are offered the tongue (a rich-flavoured, succulent meat). The dish is served with a sauce of yoghurt, combined with the cooking fat.

In Wadi Rum you might be lucky enough to be offered a Bedouin barbecue from the *zarb*, a pit oven buried in the desert sand. Another Jordanian favourite is *maqlubbeh* (sometimes called 'upside down') – steamed rice pressed into a pudding basin, topped with meat, eggplant, tomato and pine nuts.

Dessert here, as in many parts of the Middle East, may be *kunafa* (vermicelli-like pastry over a vanilla base, soaked in syrup) or *muhalabiyya* (a milk custard containing pistachio nuts).

The universal drink of choice is sweet black tea (coffee comes a close second); most social exchanges, including haggling over a kilim, are punctuated with copious glasses that are usually too hot to handle. Other options include *yansoon* (aniseed herbal tea) and *zaatar* (thyme-flavoured tea).

Bottled mineral water is widely available, as are the usual soft drinks, Amstel beer and locally produced wines.

Environment

The Land

Jordan can be divided into three major geographic regions: the Jordan Valley, the East Bank plateau and the desert. The fertile valley of the Jordan River is the dominant physical feature of the country's western region, running from the Syrian border in the north, along the border with Israel and the Palestinian Territories and into the Dead Sea. Part of the larger African Rift Valley, the Jordan Valley continues under the name Wadi Araba and extends to the Gulf of Aqaba, where Jordan claims a sneeze-sized stretch of the Red Sea. The majority of the population lives in a hilly 70km-wide strip running the length of the country, known as the East Bank plateau. The remaining 80% of the country is desert, stretching into Syria, Iraq and Saudi Arabia.

Wildlife

Spring is the best time to see some of Jordan's 2000 flowers and plants, including the black iris, Jordan's redolent national flower.

Two of Jordan's most impressive wild animals are the Arabian oryx and Nubian ibex, resident at the Shaumari Wildlife Reserve and Mujib Biosphere Reserve respectively. Jordan is an important corridor for migratory birds en route to Africa and southern Arabia.

Nature Reserves

The **Royal Society for the Conservation of Nature** (RSCN; www.rscn.org.jo) operates six reserves in Jordan, of which Mujib and Dana Biosphere Reserves are the undoubted highlights. The Azraq Wetland Reserve, located in eastern Jordan, is a good place for bird-watching, and the Ajloun Forest Reserve protects a beautiful area of woodland, perfect for hiking.

Environmental Issues

The RSCN has pioneered models for sustainable development and tourism by working closely with local communities and making them stakeholders in conserving local reserves. The society has also been responsible for reintroducing several endemic animals in Jordan, including the endangered oryx.

Despite these welcome initiatives, there are still major problems, including a chronic lack of water, the pressure of tourism on fragile sites such as at Petra and in Wadi Rum, and increasing desertification through overgrazing.

Solutions to these problems are constantly under review and there are ambitious plans to build a pipeline, known as the 'Peace Conduit', connecting the Red and Dead Seas to provide desalinated water and to raise the diminishing level of the Dead Sea.

SURVIVAL GUIDE

ℹ️ Directory A–Z

ACCOMMODATION

Jordan has accommodation to suit most budgets. The Royal Society for the Conservation of Nature offers some of the country's most interesting accommodation options in nature reserves. These need to be booked in advance during peak season; see the Wild Jordan Centre (p305).

Holidays and weekends (Friday and Saturday) are extremely busy in Aqaba and the Dead Sea. Outside these periods, in nonpeak seasons, you can often negotiate discounts on published rates.

ACTIVITIES

Diving and snorkelling are popular pastimes in the Gulf of Aqaba.

Hiking is well organised in the Dana Biosphere Reserve, Wadi Rum Protected Area and Mujib Biosphere Reserve. Mujib in particular offers some great canyoning and rappelling. Wadi Rum is the Middle East's premier climbing destination.

For details of outdoor activities in Jordan's nature reserves, contact the **RSCN** (www.rscn.org.jo).

CHILDREN

Children are instant ice breakers in Jordan and you'll find people go out of their way to make families feel welcome.

Stick to bottled mineral water, and if travelling with infants, remember that disposable nappies are not readily available outside Amman and Aqaba.

See also Amman for Children (p304).

CUSTOMS REGULATIONS

➡ Up to 1L of alcohol and 200 cigarettes can be imported, duty free.

➡ Drugs, weapons and pornography are strictly prohibited.

➡ No restrictions on the import and export of Jordanian or foreign currencies.

EMBASSIES & CONSULATES

The following embassies and consulates are in Amman. Egypt also has a consulate in Aqaba. In general, offices are open 9am to 11am Sunday to Thursday for visa applications and 1pm to 3pm for collecting visas.

Australian Embassy (☑ 06-5807000; www.jordan.embassy.gov.au; 3 Youssef Abu Shahhout, Deir Ghbar)

Canadian Embassy (Map p296; ☑ 06-5901500; www.canadainternational.gc.ca/jordan-jordanie/; Abdul Hameed Shoman St, Shmeisani)

Egyptian Embassy & Consulate Aqaba Consulate (☑ 03-2016171; cnr Al-Isteglal & Al-Akhatal Sts, Aqaba; ⊙ 8am-3pm Sun-Thu)

Amman Embassy (Map p296; ☑ 06-5605175; fax 06-5604082; 22 Qortubah St, Jebel Amman; ⊙ 9am-noon Sun-Thu)

French Embassy (Map p302; ☑ 06-4604630; www.ambafrance-jo.org; Al-Mutanabbi St, Jebel Amman)

German Embassy (Map p296; ☑ 06-5930367; www.amman.diplo.de; 31 Bin Ghazi St, Jebel Amman) Between 4th and 5th Circles.

Iraqi Embassy (Map p302; ☑ 06-4623175; www.mofamission.gov.iq/amn; Al-Kulliyah al-Islamiyah St, Jebel Amman) Near the 1st Circle.

Irish Consulate (Map p302; ☑ 06-625632; King Hussein St, Jebel Amman)

Israeli Consulate (Map p296; ☑ 06-5503529; http://embassies.gov.il/amman-en; Maysaloon St, Shmeisani)

Lebanese Embassy (Map p302; ☑ 06-5929111; fax 06-5929113; Al-Neel St, Abdoun) Near the UK embassy.

New Zealand Consulate (Map p302; ☑ 06-4636720; fax 06-4634349; 99 Al-Malek al-Hussein St, downtown) On the 4th floor of the Khalaf Building.

Saudi Arabian Consulate (Map p302; ☑ 06-5924154; fax 06-5921154; 1st Circle, Jebel Amman)

UK Embassy (Map p302; ☑ 06-5909200; www.gov.uk/government/world/organisations/british-embassy-amman; Dimashq St, Wadi Abdoun, Abdoun)

US Embassy (Map p296; ☑ 06-5906000; http://jordan.usembassy.gov/; 20 Al-Umawiyeen St, Abdoun)

FOOD

A main dish is often accompanied by salad and various pickles, dips (such as hummus) and garnishes. These are offered free of charge and are invariably served with flat Arabic bread. This means that a main dish often doubles as a meal.

GAY & LESBIAN TRAVELLERS

In Jordan gay sex is legal and the age of consent is 16. Public displays of affection by heterosexuals are frowned upon and the same rules apply to gays and lesbians, although same-sex hand-holding is a common sign of friendship in Jordan.

ⓘ PRACTICALITIES

Discount cards International Student Identity Card (ISIC) offer discounts at some tourist sites; University ID cards are not accepted.

Newspapers and magazines

➡ *Jordan Times* (www.jordantimes.com)

➡ *Time* (www.time.com)

➡ *Newsweek* (www.newsweek.com)

Radio

➡ Radio Jordan (96.3 FM)

➡ BBC World Service (1323 AM)

➡ Popular hits (99.6 FM)

Smoking There are laws banning smoking in public places, but these are rarely enforced.

TV

➡ Jordan's Channel 2 (French and English)

➡ Satellite channels (BBC, CNN, MTV, Al-Jazeera) available in most midrange and top-end hotels

Weights and measures Jordan uses the metric system.

The legality of homosexuality shouldn't be confused with full societal acceptance, and discrimination and harassment is common. Gay-friendly venues that attract young, gay and straight crowds include the multi-purpose **Books@café** (Map p298; ☎ 06-4650457; Omar bin al-Khattab; mains JD5-12; ⏰ 10am-midnight; ⓐ) and the **Blue Fig Café** (Map p296; ☎ 06-5928800; Al-Emir Hashem bin al-Hussein St; mains JD4-8; ⏰ 8.30am-1am) in Amman.

INTERNET ACCESS

Almost every town in Jordan has at least one public internet centre, but wi-fi is becoming increasingly standard in hotels of most budgets, as well as many cafes and restaurants.

To keep connected on the move with your laptop, mobile providers Zain and Orange both offer USB modems, allowing you to get online for less than JD20.

MONEY

The currency in Jordan is the dinar (JD) – known as the *jay-dee* among hip young locals – and is made up of 1000 fils. A piastre refers to 10 fils. Often when a price is quoted, the ending will be omitted, so if you're told that something is 25, it's a matter of working out whether it's 25

fils, 25 piastre or 25 dinars! Although it sounds confusing, most Jordanians wouldn't dream of ripping off a foreigner, with the possible exception of taxi drivers.

ATMs

It is possible to travel in Jordan almost entirely on plastic. ATMs giving cash advances abound in all but the smaller towns. There are no local charges on credit-card cash advances.

Visa is the most widely accepted card at ATMs, followed by MasterCard. Other cards, such as Cirrus and Plus, are also accepted by many ATMs (eg Jordan National Bank and HSBC).

Credit Cards

Credit cards are widely accepted in midrange and top-end hotels and restaurants, and a few top-end shops. A commission (up to 5%) is often added.

Money Changers

It's easy to change money in Jordan. Most major currencies are accepted in cash. US dollars, UK pounds and euros are easier to change than Australian or New Zealand dollars. Travellers cheques are almost obsolete.

There are no restrictions on bringing dinars into Jordan. It's possible to change dinars back into some foreign currencies in Jordan.

Syrian, Lebanese, Egyptian, Israeli and Iraqi currency can all be changed in Amman. Egyptian and Israeli currency are also easily changed in Aqaba. Banks and moneychangers charge about the same for exchanging cash, but large hotels charge more. There are small branches of major banks at the borders and airports.

Tipping

Tips of 10% are generally expected in better restaurants. A service charge of 10% is automatically added at most midrange and top-end restaurants.

Travellers Cheques

Travellers cheques are not useful in Jordan.

OPENING HOURS

Opening times vary widely across the country. Many sights, government departments and banks close earlier in winter and during Ramadan. The following opening hours are therefore a rough guide only. The official weekend in Jordan is Friday and Saturday, so expect curtailed hours on these days.

Banks 8am to 3pm Sunday to Thursday

Bars and clubs 9pm to 1am daily

Cafes 9am to midnight daily

Restaurants Noon to midnight daily

Shops 9am to 8pm Saturday to Thursday; some close 2pm to 4pm

Souqs 9am to 8pm daily

PHOTOGRAPHY

Digital accessories and memory cards are widely available. Many camera shops can burn photos onto a CD and print digital pictures. A 1GB memory card costs around JD15.

Ask before taking taking shots of people, particularly women and the elderly, as some Jordanians object to being photographed.

POST

Postal rates from Jordan:

	LETTER/ POSTCARD	1KG PARCEL
AUSTRALIA	JD1	JD14.700
MIDDLE EAST	600 fils	JD9
UK/EUROPE	800 fils	JD18.600
USA/CANADA	JD1	JD15.300

PUBLIC HOLIDAYS

In addition to the main Islamic holidays, Jordan observes the following:

New Year's Day 1 January

Good Friday March/April

Labour Day 1 May

Independence Day 25 May

Army Day and Anniversary of the Great Arab Revolt 10 June

Christmas Day 25 December

SAFE TRAVEL

Jordan is very safe to visit and travel around – remarkably so considering the political turmoil surrounding it. However, given the security issues in neighbouring countries, and the quickly changing situation with regard to Isis, it is worth checking the latest travel advisories from your embassy or consulate. It is also worth asking for local information from your hotel before venturing too close to the borders with Syria and Iraq.

There is little crime or anti-Western sentiment in Jordan. The police keep a sharp eye on security, so carry your passport with you at all times, and expect to show it at checkpoints near the border with Israel and the Palestinian Territories and roads that approach the Dead Sea.

TELEPHONE

The telephone system in Jordan is privatised, so visitors can make a call from a private telephone agency, call from a hotel or shop, or buy a telephone card from one of the 1000 or more payphones throughout Jordan.

Local calls cost around 150 fils for three minutes. The easiest place to make a call is at your hotel, where local calls are often free. The cost of overseas calls from Jordan varies widely: check with your service provider.

Overseas calls can be made at any card payphone or from hotels, but are substantially more expensive. Reverse-charge telephone calls are not normally possible.

Mobile Phones

Mobile phones in Jordan use the GSM system. Two main service providers are **Zain** (www.zain.com) and **Orange** (www.orange.jo), both of which offer a full range of plans and prepaid SIM cards.

Phone Codes

☎ 962	Jordan country code
☎ 00	International access code
☎ 1212	Local directory assistance (Amman)
☎ 131	Local directory assistance (elsewhere)
☎ 132 or ☎ 133	International directory assistance

The following area codes precede six- or seven-digit landline, mobile and info numbers:

☎ 02	northern Jordan
☎ 03	southern Jordan
☎ 05	Jordan Valley, central and eastern districts
☎ 06	Amman district
☎ 07	Prefix for eight-digit mobile-phone numbers
☎ 0800	Prefix for toll-free numbers

TIME

Jordan is two hours ahead of GMT/UTC in winter and three hours ahead between 1 April and 1 October.

TOILETS

Most hotels and restaurants, except those in the budget category, now have Western-style toilets. Squat toilets come with either a hose or water bucket provided for cleaning and flushing. Toilet paper should be thrown in the bin provided, as the sewerage system is not designed for paper. Public toilets are generally best avoided except at Petra.

TOURIST INFORMATION

Jordan runs a good network of visitor centres inside the country, and the **Jordan Tourism Board** (www.visitjordan.com) has a comprehensive website. Contact the following offices for a package of brochures and maps:

JORDAN DIRECTORY A–Z

Visit Jordan France (📞 01 55 60 94 46; hala@visitjordan.com; 122 rue de Paris, 92100 Boulogne-Billancourt, France)

Visit Jordan Germany (📞 069-9231880; germany@visitjordan.com; Weser Strasse 4, 60329 Frankfurt)

Visit Jordan UK (📞 020 7223 1878; uk@visitjordan.com; 115 Hammersmith Rd, London, W14 0QH)

Visit Jordan USA (📞 877-733 5673, 703-243 7404; contactus@visitjordan.com; Suite 102, 6867 Elm St, McLean, VA 22101)

TRAVELLERS WITH DISABILITIES

Jordanians are quick to help those with disabilities, but cities are crowded and traffic is chaotic, and visiting most attractions, such as the vast archaeological sites of Petra and Jerash, involves long traverses over uneven ground. Horse and carriages are provided at Petra to help elderly travellers or those with disabilities.

The Royal Diving Club (p341), south of Aqaba, is a member of the **Access to Marine Conservation for All** (AMCA; www.amca-international.org), an initiative to enable people with disabilities to enjoy scuba diving and snorkelling.

VISAS

Visas are required by all foreigners entering Jordan (JD40) by land or by air and must be paid in dinars. Single-entry tourist visas (valid for three months and allowing stays for up to a month from date of entry) are issued at land borders and airports on arrival; multientry visas are obtainable from Jordanian embassies or consulates.

Exceptions

King Hussein Bridge (Allenby Bridge) This is the only border where visas are not issued; you must obtain them from Jordanian embassies or consulates outside the country (they are generally issued within 24 hours). If you want to re-enter Jordan here, you do not need to re-apply for a Jordanian visa, providing you return through King Hussein Bridge within the validity of your Jordanian visa or extension. Keep the stamped exit slip and present it on returning. This option does not apply at any of Jordan's other border crossings.

Aqaba If you arrive in Jordan's southern city of Aqaba, you are entitled to a free visa as part of the free-trade agreement with the Aqaba Special Economic Zone Area (Aseza). If you stay in Jordan for more than 15 days, you must register with the **Aqaba Special Economic Zone Authority** (ASEZA; 📞 03-2091000; www.aqabazone.com; Ash-Sherif al-Hussein bin Ali St-Amman Hwy) in Aqaba, opposite Safeway.

Extensions

Extensions for a stay of up to three months are available for free on registration with the police in Amman or Aqaba.

The process is simple but involves a little running around. Request your hotel to write a short letter confirming where you are staying. Your hotel will also need to fill out two copies of a small card, which states all their details (you fill in the details on the back). Take the form, the letter, a photocopy of the page in your passport with your personal details, your Jordanian visa page and your passport to the relevant police station. Plan to arrive between 10am and 3pm Saturday to Thursday (it's best to go early). Extensions are usually granted on the spot. Failure to register results in a fine of JD2 for each day overstayed.

Amman Start the process of lodging your paperwork at **Al-Madeenah Police Station** (Map p298; 📞 06-4657788; 1st fl, Al-Malek Faisal St, downtown), opposite the Arab Bank. Complete the process at **Muhajireen Police Station** (Markaz Amn Muhajireen; Map p302; Al-Ameerah Basma bin Talal Rd, downtown), west of the downtown area (from downtown, take a taxi or service taxi No 35 from along Quraysh St).

Aqaba The **police station** (📞 191, 2012411; Ar-Reem St) is opposite the bus station.

WOMEN TRAVELLERS

Most women who travel around Jordan experience no problems, and find they are welcomed with a mixture of warmth and friendly concern for their safety. That said, varying levels of sexual harassment do occur, especially in tourist areas where local men assume that 'anything goes'. Harassment can be somewhat mitigated by dressing modestly in baggy trousers or skirts, with loose shirts or blouses that cover the cleavage, shoulders and upper arms. It's not necessary to cover your head.

Women may feel uncomfortable on public beaches in Aqaba and may prefer to wear shorts and a loose T-shirt over swimwear at Dead Sea public beaches. Many restaurants usher female customers into their family areas, where single men are not permitted. Most women don't sit next to the driver in taxis.

Attitudes towards women vary greatly throughout the country. In the upmarket districts of Amman, women are treated the same as they would be in any Western country, whereas in rural areas more traditional attitudes prevail.

WORK

Work is not really an option for most foreigners passing through Jordan. Those hoping to work with Palestinian refugees might have luck with the public information office of the **UN Relief & Works Agency** (www.unrwa.org) contact them at least three months in advance.

ℹ Getting There & Away

Jordan is easily visited overland from neighbouring countries, with visas available on arrival at border crossings and Aqaba port. Arrival in Jordan is by boat (from Egypt), bus or service taxi; you can bring your own car or motorcycle (but not hire car). Leaving Jordan by land requires a little more planning and onward travel in the region can be problematic after visiting Israel and the Palestinian Territories. Check the latest situation in northern Sinai in Egypt, and around Jerusalem in Israel and the Palestinian Territories before venturing across the border.

AIR

The main international airport is **Queen Alia International Airport** (☑06-4010250; www.qaiairport.com), 35km south of Amman.

The excellent national carrier is Royal Jordanian (p354), but from the main European capitals you can generally get cheaper deals with other airlines. In Amman there are convenient offices in the Jordan InterContinental Hotel on Al-Kulliyah al-Isalamiyah St (☑06-4644267) and along Al-Malek al-Hussein St (☑06-5663525), uphill from the Abdali bus station.

The following other airlines fly to/from Jordan and have offices in Amman:

Air France (Map p296; ☑06-5100777; www.airfrance.com)

British Airways (☑06-5828801; www.ba.com)

Emirates (Map p302; ☑06-4615222; www.emirates.com)

Gulf Air (Map p302; ☑06-653613; www.gulfair.com)

KLM (Map p296; ☑06-655267; www.klm.com)

Kuwait Airways (Map p296; ☑06-5690144; www.kuwait-airways.com)

Lufthansa Airlines (Map p296; ☑06-5200180; www.lufthansa.com)

Qatar Airways (Map p296; ☑06-5679444; www.qatarairways.com)

Turkish Airlines (Map p302; ☑06-5548100; www.turkishairlines.com)

LAND

Saudi Arabia

Jordan has three borders with Saudi Arabia (at Al-Umari, Al-Mudawwara and Ad-Durra), but as visas for Saudi are not given for leisure travel, it's currently off limits for most people. Gulf Cooperation Council citizens don't need a visa.

Iraq

Travel to Iraq is not recommended at present. Minibuses and service taxis leave from Amman's

Abdali bus station for Baghdad, but the lack of security along the highway (via Fallujah) made this an extremely dangerous option at the time of writing.

If the situation improves, the easiest way to reach the capital is by air-conditioned Jordan Express Tourist Transport (p355) bus service to Baghdad on Saturdays and Wednesdays at 2.30pm (JD28.400).

Israel & the Palestinian Territories

Three border crossings are open to foreigners: Sheikh Hussein Bridge in the north, King Hussein Bridge near Amman, and Wadi Araba in the south. These border crossings are known respectively as Jordan River Bridge, Allenby Bridge, and Yitzhak Rabin in Israel and the Palestinian Territories; you should refer to them as such only when travelling on the Israeli side of the border.

At the Israeli border post, request officials to stamp the Jordanian exit slip rather than your passport if you intend to visit Syria and/or Lebanon. For entry to those countries, there must be no evidence in your passport of your trip to Israel, including use of any of Jordan's border crossings with Israel and the Palestinian Territories.

There may be reduced onward public transport on the Israeli side of the border from Friday at sundown to Saturday at sundown (the Shabbat).

Sheikh Hussein Bridge (Jordan River Bridge)
This border crossing (open 6.30am to 9pm Sunday to Thursday, 8am to 7pm Friday and Saturday) links northern Jordan with Beit She'an in Galilee. Regular service taxis travel between the West bus station at Irbid and the border (JD1, 45 minutes). From the bridge it's a 2km walk to the Israeli side. Taxis go to the Beit She'an bus station (10 minutes) for onward connections. Travelling in the other direction, take a bus to Tiberias, and change at Beit She'an (6km from the border). From there, take another bus to the Israeli border (7NIS; arrive early because there are few buses). Israeli exit tax is 102NIS at this border.

King Hussein Bridge (Allenby Bridge) This border crossing (open 8am to midnight Sunday to Thursday, 8am to 3pm Friday and Saturday, closed Yom Kippur and Eid al-Adha, hours subject to change) offers travellers the most direct route between Amman and Jerusalem or Tel Aviv. Take a service taxi from Amman's Abdali or South bus station to King Hussein Bridge (JD8, 45 minutes) or there's a single daily JETT bus (JD8.500, one hour, 7am). Buses (JD7 plus JD1.500 for each piece of luggage) shuttle between the two borders (expect long delays). It's not possible to walk, hitch or take a private vehicle across this border. To get to Jerusalem from the border, take a sherut (Israeli shared taxi; around 50NIS, 30 minutes) to Jerusalem's Damascus Gate. Travelling in the other direction, an Israeli exit tax of 177NIS (compared to around 102NIS at other borders) is payable. If you intend to return to Israel, keep the Jordanian entrance form safe – you will have to present it on exiting the border. You cannot take your own car or motorcycle through this border.

Wadi Araba (Yitzhak Rabin) This handy border crossing (open 6.30am to 8pm Sunday to Thursday, 8am to 8pm Friday and Saturday) in the south of the country links Aqaba to Eilat. Taxis run between Aqaba and the border (JD10, 15 minutes). You can walk the short distance across the border in a matter of minutes. Buses run to central Eilat, 2km away (five minutes). Travelling in the other direction, buses from Jerusalem to Eilat will stop at the turn-off for the border (five minutes), a short walk away. Israeli exit tax is 96NIS at this border. Jordanian exit tax is JD10.

Syria

The border crossings between Jordan and Syria are at Ramtha/Der'a and Jabir/Nasib. At the time of writing, travel to Syria was strictly to be avoided.

In the event of a resolution to the conflict, the enormous yellow *servees* (service taxis) are likely to resume service from the lower (eastern) end of Amman's Abdali bus station for Damascus, crossing at Jabir.

SEA

Visiting Egypt is both a popular side trip from Aqaba or feasible as part of your onward journey. Most nationalities can obtain Egyptian tourist visas on the boat or on arrival at Nuweiba (the Egyptian consulate in Aqaba also issues visas). Note that full visas are not issued in Taba, only the two-week Sinai Visitor Pass.

There are two main boat services to Egypt, which leave from the passenger terminal just south of Aqaba. Departure times are often subject to change so check with **Arab Bridge Maritime** (03-2092000; www.abmaritime.com.jo/en), which operates the service, before travelling.

The fast boat to Taba (US$95, 45 minutes) leaves daily at 6pm. Fares for children under eight are US$70. The return ferry leaves Taba at 6.30am. Check government advisories before using this crossing – at the time of writing there were warnings against travelling in this part of Sinai.

There is also a slower car-ferry service (US$95/75/65 in 1st/economy/3rd class, three to 12 hours!) departing twice daily at 2pm and midnight. It's notorious for being delayed. Fares for children under eight years are US$70/60/55. Services from Nuweiba leave at 6am and 3pm.

Departure tax (JD6) is not included in the ticket prices. You need to show your passport to buy tickets. Note that fares from Nuweiba must be paid for in US dollars, but there are currency-exchange facilities at the terminals at Aqaba and Nuweiba. Check safety advice before travelling the south Sinai.

🛈 Getting Around

Public transport is designed primarily for the locals and as it is notoriously difficult to reach many of the sights of interest (especially the Dead Sea, desert castles and King's Highway) consider hiring a car or using tours organised by hotels in Amman and Madaba.

AIR

There is only one domestic air route, between Amman and Aqaba. You can buy tickets at any travel agency or Royal Jordanian office.

Royal Jordanian (06-5100000; www.rj.com) Flights twice daily between Amman and Aqaba (one way around JD40, one hour).

Royal Wings (www.royalwings.com.jo) A subsidiary of Royal Jordanian, offering expensive charter flights.

BICYCLE

Cycling is not necessarily fun in Jordan. In summer it's prohibitively hot, and cyclists on the King's Highway have reported stone throwing by groups of young children. Cycling north or south can be hard work, as there is a strong prevailing western wind. Anywhere from the East Bank plateau down to the Dead Sea or Jordan Valley makes for exhilarating descents, but coming the other way will really test your calf muscles. Bring plenty of spare parts and contact **Bike Rush** (Map p302; 079-9454586; www.facebook.com/bikerush; ⊙noon-9pm Sat-Thu) in Amman for tips before departure, tours and/or bike hire in country.

BUS & MINIBUS

Just about all towns in Jordan are connected by 20-seat minibuses, although the King's Highway, Dead Sea area and eastern Jordan are less well served. Minibuses leave when full and it can take an hour or more for the seats to fill up. They may leave earlier if you're ready to pay extra for the empty seats.

JETT (☎ 06-5664141; www.jett.com.jo; Al-Malek al-Hussein St, Shmeisani, Amman) The national bus company JETT operates the most comfortable bus service from Amman to Aqaba. It also has services to King Hussein Bridge border crossing, Petra and Hammamat Ma'in.

CAR & MOTORCYCLE

Hiring a car is an ideal way to get the most out of Jordan. Distances are generally short and many prime destinations are difficult to get to by public transport. Road conditions are generally good outside Amman.

Driving Licence

International Driving Permits (IDPs) are not needed. If you're driving, keep your driving licence, rental or ownership papers and car registration in an easily accessible place.

Fuel & Spare Parts

Petrol is available along the Desert and King's Highways and in most sizeable towns. There are precious few mechanics in Jordan able to deal with the average modern motorcycle and its problems.

Hire

Charges, conditions, drop-off fees, insurance costs and waiver fees in case of accident vary considerably, so it's worth shopping around. Daily rates are JD40 to JD50; weekly rates JD140 to JD200. You can normally drop off the rental car in another city (eg Aqaba or Amman). Many hire companies require a minimum three-day hire, and all require a deposit of up to JD400, payable upon pick up and refunded upon return of the car.

The following hire companies are reliable:
Avis (Map p296; ☎ 06-5699420, 24hr 777-397405; www.avis.com.jo; King Abdullah Gardens, Amman) Offices at King Hussein Bridge and Aqaba; branches at the airport, Le Royal Hotel and Jordan InterContinental Hotel in Amman. The biggest car-hire company in Jordan.

Budget (Map p296; ☎ 06-5698131; www.budget.com; 125 Abdul Hameed Sharaf St, Amman)

Europcar (Map p296; ☎ 06-5655581; www.europcar.middleeast.com; Isam Al-Ajlouni St, Amman) Branches at Radisson SAS, King Abdullah Gardens and in Aqaba.

Hertz (Map p296; ☎ 06-5920926; www.hertz.com; King Abdullah Gardens, Amman) Offices at the airport, Grand Hyatt Amman, Sheraton and in Aqaba.

ℹ BEWARE THE TRICKS OF THE TRADE

Taken for a ride The taxi fare quoted on the meter is in fils, not in dinars, and visitors often misunderstand this when paying. Perhaps understandably, it is rare for a taxi driver to point out this mistake.

Crafty business Shop owners often claim something is genuinely locally crafted as part of a profit-share scheme, when in fact it is imported from abroad.

Money for old rope So-called 'antiques' are often merely last year's stock that has gathered an authentic-looking layer of dust. Similarly, 'ancient' oil lamps and coins are seldom what they are purported to be.

Reliable Rent-a-Car (Map p296; ☎ 06-5929676; www.rentareliablecar.com; 19 Fawzi al-Qawuqji St, Amman)

Insurance

All car rentals come with some kind of insurance, but you should find out how much your excess is (ie the maximum you will have to pay in case of an accident) – it may be as high as JD500. For JD7 to JD10 extra per day, you can buy Collision Damage Waiver (CDW), which takes your deductible down to JD100 or even zero.

Road Rules

Vehicles drive on the right-hand side of the road in Jordan – at least in theory. More often, they loiter in the middle. The general speed limit inside built-up areas is 50km/h or 70km/h on multilane highways in Amman, and 90km/h to 110km/h on the highways. Note that indicators are seldom used, rules are only occasionally obeyed, the ubiquitous horn is a useful warning signal and pedestrians must take their chances. Wearing a seat belt is now compulsory.

Keep your passport, driving licence, rental agreement and registration papers handy, especially along the Dead Sea Highway where check posts and traffic police are positioned at intervals.

HITCHING

In Wadi Rum you may need to wave down a ride; it's customary to give a few dinars to the driver. In the current political climate, with concerns surrounding the latest influx of refugees, it is not advisable to hitch elsewhere in Jordan.

LOCAL TRANSPORT

Bus

Local city buses are generally packed, routes are confusing and the chances of being pickpocketed are higher. Take a service taxi instead.

Taxi

Private taxis are good value in the cities. Note that metered fares are displayed in fils not dinars, and if you proffer the fare in dinars by mistake, the driver is unlikely to correct you.

White service taxis are a little more expensive than minibuses and don't cover as many routes, but they are generally faster and take less time to fill up (there are generally only four seats).

Lebanon

Best Places to Sleep

➡ Saifi Urban Gardens (p366)

➡ Hotel Albergo (p367)

➡ BEYt (p367)

➡ L'Auberge de la Mer (p379)

➡ Mir Amin Palace (p388)

Best Places to Eat

➡ Liza (p369)

➡ Mayrig (p369)

➡ Restaurant Mounir (p374)

➡ Chez Maguy (p379)

➡ Tawlet Ammiq (p388)

Why Go?

As contradictory and challenging as it is charming, this diminutive Mediterranean nation stands with one bejewelled slipper in the Arab world and one Manolo Blahnik planted firmly in the West. It's a place where culture, family and religion are all-important, but where sectarian violence can too often erupt – claiming lives and scarring both the landscape and the national pysche.

Home to a world-famous national cuisine, a string of sexy beach resorts and the Middle East's most glamorous city (Beirut), this is also a country where the fiery orators and fierce foot soldiers of Hezbollah are based, and where scores of Palestinian and Syrian refugees currently shelter. Scarred by decades of civil war, invasions and terrorist attacks, yet blessed with magnificent mountain vistas, majestic ancient ruins and a people who are resilient, indomitable and renowned for their hospitality, Lebanon rewards the traveller with food for thought and a feast for the senses and the stomach. Don't miss it.

When to Go
Beirut

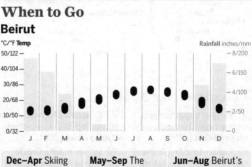

Dec–Apr Skiing and après-ski parties in the mountains.

May–Sep The perfect time to go hiking along wild trails and through cedar forests.

Jun–Aug Beirut's famous beach lounges and nightclubs beckon.

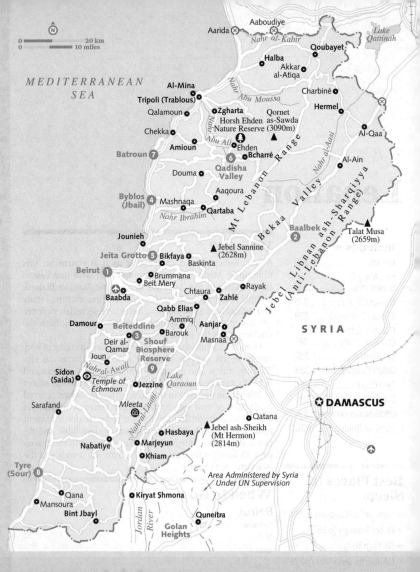

Lebanon Highlights

1 Party at beach lounges, rooftop nightclubs and hipster bars in **Beirut** (p359).

2 Explore haunting Roman-era ruins along the coastline and inland towards the ancient 'Sun City' of **Baalbek** (p390).

3 Admire Byzantine mosaics at **Beiteddine Palace** (p387).

4 Celebrate a Mediterranean sunset in pretty-as-a-picture **Byblos** (Jbail; p375).

5 Marvel at **Jeita Grotto** (p374) and its stalactites and stalagmites.

6 Hike past rock-cut monasteries and gushing waterfalls in the scenic **Qadisha Valley** (p382).

7 Visit a trio of up-and-coming organic wineries in the mountains above **Batroun** (p381).

8 Walk in the footsteps of the Romans at two archaeological sites by the sea in **Tyre** (Sour; p385).

9 Breathe crisp, cedar-scented air in the **Shouf Biosphere Reserve** (p389).

BEIRUT

بيروت

♪ 01 / POP 2.02 MILLION

If you're looking for the real East-meets-West so talked about in the Middle East, you need look no further than Beirut. Fast-paced, fashion-conscious and overwhelmingly friendly, it's not a relaxing city to spend time in – it's too crowded, polluted and chaotic for that – but its magnificent array of museums, restaurants, bars and clubs make it an essential stop on every Lebanese itinerary. In fact, the country is so small, and day trips to every city and major site so easy, that most travellers tend to base themselves here for their entire visit.

History

Though there's evidence of a large settlement on the site of modern Beirut dating back to at least ancient Egyptian times, it wasn't until the Roman era that the city really came into its own, both as a commercial port and military base. By the 3rd century AD it was the location of a world-renowned school of law, one of the first three in the world. The city's fame continued until AD 551, when a devastating earthquake and resultant tsunami caused massive death, destruction and decline. The law school was moved to Sidon, and Beirut didn't regain its importance as a trading centre and gateway to the Middle East until the 16th century, under local emir Fakhreddine.

In the 19th century Beirut enjoyed a commercial boom, but also experienced the first of much meddling by European powers when French troops arrived at the city's port. The early years of the 20th century saw citywide devastation and the loss of quarter of its population, the combined result of a WWI Allied blockade, famine, revolt and plague. Following WWII, however, Beirut slowly became a major business, banking and publishing centre, and remained so until the bloody, brutal civil war that ravaged the city's streets and citizens put paid to its supremacy.

Following the end of the war in 1990, rehabilitation of the city's infrastructure became the major focus of both the local and national governments. Initiatives such as the redevelopment of the city's Downtown area by The Lebanese Company for the Development & Reconstruction of Beirut Central District (Solidere) sought to restore its pre-war reputation as the 'Paris of the East'.

Beirut's battle scars, however, remain visible throughout the city to this day

◉ Sights & Activities

There are few headline sights in Beirut, but there are plenty of neighbourhoods worth exploring. The student district of Hamra is alive with cafes, restaurants and bars, and is a good place for people-watching. Directly north of Hamra runs the seafront Corniche, or Ave de Paris, along which Beirut's beach clubs and many of its top hotels are strung. To the south is affluent Verdun, home to designer clothes shops that line the Rue Verdun. East from Hamra you'll reach the beautifully restored Beirut Central District (BCD), at the centre of which is the landmark Place d'Étoile, also known as Nejmeh Sq. Just east again is Martyrs Sq (now pretty well a wasteland being redeveloped), where the huge demonstrations of 2005's Cedar Revolution were held. Nearby is the huge Mohammed Al-Amin Mosque (often called the Hariri Mosque, as it is where the slain former prime minister is buried).

ⓘ NEED TO KNOW

Fast Facts

➡ **Capital** Beirut

➡ **Country code** ♪ 961

➡ **Language** Arabic (English and French widely spoken)

➡ **Official name** Republic of Lebanon

➡ **Population** 4 million, plus 448,000 Palestinian refugees

➡ **Currency** Lebanese pound (LL)

Exchange rates

Australia	A$1	LL1122
Egypt	E£10	LL1929
Euro zone	€1	LL1565
Israel and the Palestinian Territories	10NIS	LL3707
Jordan	JD1	LL2077
UK	£1	LL2171
USA	US$1	LL1476

For current exchange rates see www.xe.com.

Greater Beirut

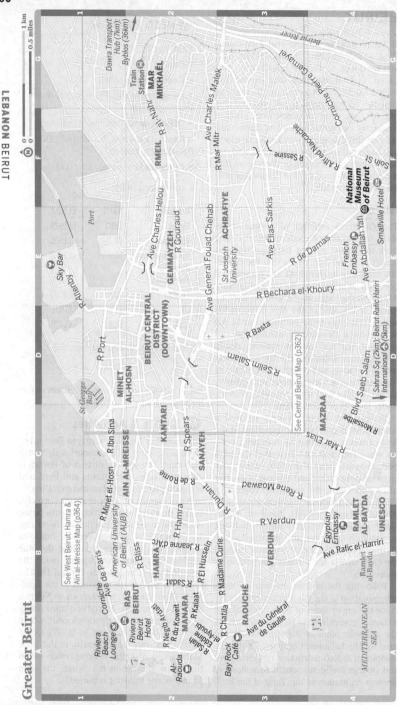

See West Beirut: Hamra &
Ain al-Mreisse Map (p364)

See Central Beirut Map (p362)

South of the Mohammed Al-Amin Mosque is the Rue de Damas (Damascus St), which was once the Green Line separating warring East and West Beirut. West of this are the hipster hangouts of Gemmayzeh and Mar Mikhaël, most of which are found on Rue Gouraud and its extension, Rue Armenia. South of these areas is Achrafiye, known for its upmarket apartments, restaurants and bars. South again is increasingly fashionable Badaro, where the National Museum is located.

★ **National Museum of Beirut**   MUSEUM
(Mathaf; Map p360; ☑ 426 703; www.beirutnationalmuseum.com; cnr Rue de Damas & Ave Abdallah Yafi; adult/student under 18 LL5000/1000; ☺ 9am-5pm Tue-Sun) Located on the former Green Line, this is Beirut's major cultural institution and is an essential stop for all visitors to the city. Its impressive, magnificently displayed collection of archaeological artefacts offers a great overview of Lebanon's history and the civilisations that made their home here. Highlights include the famous, much-photographed Phoenician gilded bronze figurines found buried near the Obelisk Temple at Byblos, and a moving group of Phoenician marble statues of baby boys (from Echmoun, 6th century BC).

At the start of your visit, leave your passport at the front desk and borrow one of the museum's complimentary iPads so that you can scan labels on significant pieces in the collection to receive a commentary about each (bring your own headphones if possible). You may also wish to view the 12-minute documentary that is screened in the audiovisual room off the foyer, which plays every hour on the hour between 9am and 4pm. This details how curators saved the museum's collection during the civil war and subsequently restored it to its former glory.

Entering the exhibition area, you will encounter a huge Byzantine mosaic depicting Calliope, the muse of philosophy, and two wonderful carved sarcophagi from Tyre dating from the 2nd century AD: one depicts drunken cupids and the other the legend of Achilles. In the hall to the right, there is a marble throne from Echmoun (350 BC) depicting an assembly of gods and a procession of dancers. Also here are the Phoenician statues of the baby boys; these were commissioned by Sidonian aristocrats as ex-votos to Echmoun, the Phoenican god of healing, to thank him for saving their children. In the next room, the exquisite statue of Hygeia, the goddess of health, came from Byblos and dates from the 2nd century AD.

The two rooms to the left of the entrance hall hold Egyptian and Phoenician artefacts. The most interesting of these is the sarcophagus of Ahirim, the 10th century BC king of Byblos, which displays the earliest known examples of the Phoenician alphabet.

Upstairs, you'll find pieces from the Bronze and Iron ages, as well as from the Hellenistic, Roman, Byzantine and Mamluk periods. Highlights include Egyptian gold pectorals encrusted with semiprecious stones (these were found in the royal necropolis at Byblos); an extraordinary Attic drinking vessel in the shape of a pig's head that dates somewhere between 6th and 4th centuries BC; a marble head of Dionysis from the Roman period; a magnificent collection of Phoenician glass; and the gilded bronze figurines from Byblos.

The museum is a 15-minute walk south of Sodeco Sq along Rue de Damas.

◉ Downtown

In its '60s heyday, a visit to the city's Downtown district, its streets filled with gorgeous Ottoman-era architectural gems, was akin to a leisurely stroll along Paris' Left Bank. By the 1980s, this part of the city had become the horrific, decimated centre of a protracted civil war; and during the 1990s, it proved the focus of prime minister Rafiq Hariri's colossally ambitious rebuilding program, which was undertaken by a land and real-estate developer called The Lebanese Company for the Development & Reconstruction of Beirut Central District, aka Solidere, that was founded by Hariri in 1994.

Today, the downtown streets are spotlessly clean and traffic-free, and the whole area is quite beautiful, though some locals suggest it lacks soul. Locals refer to it as Beirut Central District (BCD), Downtown or Solidere.

Robert Mouawad Private Museum MUSEUM
(Map p362; ☑ 980 970; www.rmpm.info; Rue de L'Armee, BCD; adult/student LL9000/5000) The world would be a poorer place if it didn't host idiosyncratic cultural institutions such as this one. Conceived and funded by jeweller and collector Robert Mouawad to showcase his magnificent and eclectic collection of art, furniture, carpets and antiquities, it is housed in the former home of the late

LEBANON BEIRUT

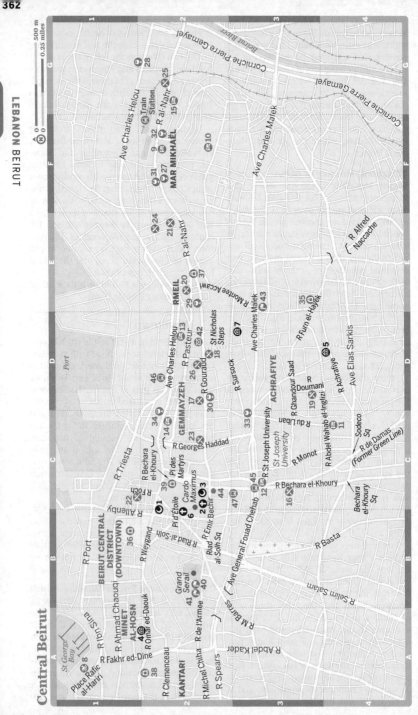

Central Beirut

0 ————— 500 m
0 ————— 0.25 miles

St George Bay

KANTARI

MINET AL-HOSN

BEIRUT CENTRAL DISTRICT (DOWNTOWN)

Place Rafic al-Hariri

R Clemenceau
R Michel Chiha
R Spears
R Abdel Kader
R Fakhr ed-Dine
R Omar ed-Daouk
R de l'Armee
R Ahmad Chaouqi
R Ibn Sina
R Port
R Trieste
R Foch
R Bechara el-Khoury
R Allenby
R Weygand
R Riad al-Solh
Pl d'Etoile
Riad al-Solh Sq
R Emir Bechir
Pl des Martyrs
Cardo Maximus
R Georges Haddad

GEMMAYZEH
R Gouraud
Ave Charles Helou
R Pasteur
St Nicholas Steps
R Sursock

RMEIL
R al-Nahr
R Montee Accawi

MAR MIKHAËL
Train Station
R al-Nahr

Ave Charles Helou
Corniche Pierre Gemayel
Beirut River

Ave Charles Malek

ACHRAFIYE
St Joseph University
R Monot
R du Liban
R Ghandour Saad
R Abdel Wahab el-Inglizi
R Doumani
R Achrafiye
Ave Elias Sarkis
R Furn el-Hayek
Sodeco Sq
R de Damas (Former Green Line)
R Bechara el-Khoury
Bechara el-Khoury Sq
R Basta
R Selim Salam
Ave General Fouad Chehab
R M Barres
Grand Serail
R Abel Naccache
R Alfred Naccache

Port

Central Beirut

Lebanese politician and art collector Henri Philippe Pharaoun, and set in lush gardens.

Built in the neo-Gothic style in 1911, the mansion was significantly rebuilt and totally redecorated by Pharaoun, and reflects his infatuation with Islamic art and architecture. Decorative wooden panels throughout the house date back to the 19th century and were largely sourced in Syria. Exhibits range from Byzantine icons, Mamluk ceramics and classical statuary to the Mouawad-produced 'Very Expensive Fantasy Bra', encrusted with precious stones, which is worth US$11 million (yes, really).

St George Greek Orthodox Cathedral   CHURCH
(Map p362; Place d'Étoile, BCD; museum adult/child LL5000/1000; ⊙museum 10am-6pm Tue-Sun) This church in the Place d'Étoile was built in 1767, and is one of the oldest buildings in the city. In 1975, during the civil war, a bomb fell here and unearthed the ruins of a Byzantine church. Now open as a muse-um, the ruins incorporate Byzantine mosaic floors and a number of tombs – one with a skeleton. A seven-minute documentary in English, French and Arabic gives an informative overview of the cathedral's history.

The chapel behind the cathedral has a number of religious frescos, some damaged during the war and still bearing bullet holes. The church itself was largely rebuilt after the bomb, and its early-20th century frescos were restored.

Mohammed al-Amin Mosque   MOSQUE
(Map p362) This unmistakable blue-domed mosque near Martyrs Sq was built between 2002 and 2007, and has four minarets standing 65m high. Slain former prime minister Rafiq Hariri is buried here.

Maronite Cathedral of St George   CHURCH
(Map p362; Rue Amir Bechir, BCD) The neoclassical facade of this late-19th-century cathedral, next to the Mohammed al-Amin mosque, was inspired by the Basilica of Santa Maria

West Beirut: Hamra & Ain al-Mreisse

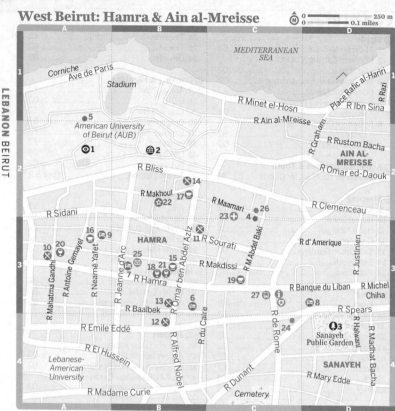

West Beirut: Hamra & Ain al-Mreisse

◉ Sights
1 American University of Beirut
   (AUB).. A2
2 AUB Museum... B2
3 Sanayeh Public Garden........................ D4

✚ Activities, Courses & Tours
4 American Language Center.................... C2
5 American University of Beirut A1

🛏 Sleeping
6 35 Rooms B3
7 Casa d'Or... B3
8 L'Hote Libanais D3
9 Mayflower Hotel.................................... A3

✕ Eating
10 Appetito Trattoria................................. A3
11 Aunty Salwa B3
12 Barbar.. B4
13 Kahwet Leila B3
   Paul .... (see 14)
14 Urbanista... B2

◉ Drinking & Nightlife
   Bricks .... (see 20)
15 Cafe de Prague B3
16 Café Younes A3
17 Café Younes B2
18 Dany's.. B3
19 Madame Om C3
20 Rabbit Hole A3
21 Walkman... B3

★ Entertainment
22 Blue Note B2

ℹ Information
23 American University of Beirut
   Hospital... C2
24 Helem.. C4
25 LibanPost Hamra................................... B3

ℹ Transport
26 Middle East Airlines C2
27 No 24 Hamra-National Museum........... C3

Maggiore in Rome. It's the base of the city's Maronite archdiocese.

Al-Omari Mosque
MOSQUE

(Map p362) Built in the 12th century as the Church of John the Baptist of the Knights Hospitaller, this attractive building was converted by the Mamluks into a mosque in 1291. It was the city's central Sunni mosque until construction of the nearby Mohammad Al-Amin Mosque, and still has a large and devoted congregation.

◉ Hamra & Ras Beirut

The university districts of Hamra and Ras Beirut, with their plethora of hotels, bookshops, cafes, bars and restaurants, are the preferred base for many travellers, especially as Hamra has a happening cafe and bar scene.

American University of Beirut
UNIVERSITY

(AUB; Map p364; www.aub.edu.lb; Rue Bliss) One of the Middle East's most prestigious and expensive universities, the AUB was founded in 1866 by American Protestant missionary Daniel Bliss. Spread over 28 tree-filled hectares, it is a true oasis in the heart of a fume-filled city. The on-site **archaeological museum** (Map p364; ☑ 340 549; www.aub.edu.lb/museum_archeo/Pages/index.aspx; AUB campus, Ras Beirut; ◉ 9am-5pm Mon-Fri) **FREE** was founded in 1868, and has a fine collection of Lebanese and Middle Eastern artefacts dating back to the early Stone Age.

Museum highlights include a Phoenician collection (glass, pottery, coins and steles), a display on the birth of writing and memorial portrait busts from Palmyra in Syria (2nd to 3rd century AD). The recently added mezzanine section displays jewellery, seals, weapons and oil lamps.

Note that the museum is closed during university holidays. Audioguides can be hired for LL3000.

◉ Corniche

Stretching roughly from Pigeon Rocks in the south to the St George Yacht Club downtown, the seafront Corniche is every Beiruti's favourite promenade spot, especially on warm summer evenings around sunset. Grab a cafe seat or a piece of sea wall and delight in some people-watching par excellence amid pole fishermen, families, courting couples and cavorting children. And if

it's something more serene you're looking for, walk on down to **Pigeon Rocks**, Beirut's famous natural offshore arches.

If you fancy a dip, several of Beirut's chic beach clubs are situated along this stretch (note that the word 'beach' is used loosely, since there's barely a grain of sand to be found in any of them and no local would ever swim in the heavily polluted waters, instead lazing by the club pools).

Riviera Beach Lounge
POOL

(Map p360; ☑ 373 210 ext 8300; www.rivierahotel.com.lb; Corniche El Manara; LL50,000; ◉ 9am-6pm) The pool/beach parties at Riviera resemble those held in Las Vegas or Ibiza, with international DJs and free-flowing alcohol. Families tend to congregate at 'Little Riviera', a kids pool and cafe serving kid-friendly food. You can hire jet skis, go diving or try out parasailing. Those with extra cash and lascivious desires tend to hire pool beds or private bungalows.

St George Yacht Motor Club
POOL

(Map p362; ☑ 356 065; http://stgeorges-yacht-club.com; Ain al-Mreisse; adult weekday/weekend US$23/27, child US$20/23; ◉ 9am-6pm) Under threat of closure at the time of research due to Solidere's planned forced acquisition of the hotel, this is one of the most family-friendly of the beach clubs. There's no party scene here, so it's a good choice if you're interested in relaxation rather than raunch.

◉ Achrafiye

Built on the site of the Roman City of the Dead, Achrafiye is an attractive and largely sedate area, historically one of the preserves of Beirut's Christian population and today dotted with upmarket galleries, boutiques, antiques shops, churches and restaurants. It's home to the popular ABC (p371) shopping mall and some of the city's best boutique hotels.

Sursock Museum
MUSEUM

(Map p362; ☑ 334 133; Rue Sursock) This privately owned contemporary art museum is housed in a 1902 mansion located in one of Achrafiye's most attractive streets. It originally opened its doors to the public in 1952 but at the time of research was closed for restoration. When it re-opens, expect to be impressed by the US$12 million extension, which has been designed by French architect Jean-Michel Wilmotte and Lebanese architect Jacques Aboukhaled.

BEIRUT FOR CHILDREN

Beirutis go gaga for children, and you'll have no problem finding family-friendly activities, restaurants and hotels throughout town. Good brands of baby supplies – nappies, powdered milk and the like – are widely available at pharmacies.

➡ **Planet Discovery** (Map p362; ☑ 980 650; www.solidere.com/beirut-souks/planet-discovery; Beirut Souks, Saad Zaghloul St, BCD; child LL10,000; ⊘ 8.30am-6pm Mon-Fri, 10.30am-7pm Sat & Sun) For something slightly cerebral, head to this fun and interactive science museum, for ages three to 15.

➡ **Sanayeh Public Garden** (Map p364; Rue Spears, Sanayeh) Though Beirut is hardly blessed with an abundance of open spaces, kids can let off steam somewhere green at the recently re-landscaped Sanayeh Public Garden, with bike and skate hire available.

➡ **St George Yacht Motor Club** (p365) The yacht club has a nice children's pool, a playground and grassy lawns to dash about on.

⊙ Gemmayzeh & Mar Mikhaël

Centred on attractive Rue Gouraud, Gemmayzeh is one of Beirut's major entertainment enclaves and is crammed with cafes, bars and restaurants. It's also home to arty boutiques and galleries. Further east, along Rue Armenia, is the neighbourhood of Mar Mikhaël, a haven for hipsters, foodies and those who aspire to live the bohemian life. This is where you should head to find the best bar scene in the city, and many of its most exciting restaurants.

✵ Festivals & Events

Beirut International Film Festival   FILM
(www.beirutfilmfestival.org) Held in October, this festival showcases films from Lebanon and the Middle East.

Beirut International Marathon   MARATHON
(www.beirutmarathon.org) Held each autumn, usually in November, and popular with international athletes. It starts and finishes Downtown.

🛏 Sleeping

Decent budget accommodation is thin on the ground in Beirut, and considering the fact that hotel occupancy rates have been extremely low since the Syrian conflict commenced, room prices are strangely high. High season is from June to August and over the Christmas/New Year period.

Most of Beirut's midrange options are located in and around Hamra, and the majority of boutique choices are in Achrafiye and Mar Mikhaël. Top-end hotels tend to be found on the Corniche. For upmarket homestays, check out **L'Hote Libanais** (Map p364; ☑ 03-513 766; www.hotelibanais.com).

★ **Saifi Urban Gardens**   HOSTEL $
(Map p362; ☑ 562 509; www.saifigardens.com; Pasteur St, Gemmayzeh; dm US$18, s/d US$46/50; ✵ 🛜) The best hostel in Lebanon, this hopping joint in the shadow of the Charles Helou motorway has a range of rooms and single-sex dorms, a communal lounge, a garden nargileh cafe that is a popular hangout for local arty types and a rooftop pub. The female dorm has a TV and fridge, and all beds have good mattresses and linen.

The hostel can be difficult to find – enter the laneway behind the Coral gas station on Rue Pasteur and then head down the stairs on the right (east) side of the blue building.

Hostel Beirut   HOSTEL $
(Map p362; ☑ 78 908 966; http://hostelbeirut.com; Akram al-3eed Bldg, 11 Rue 56, Geitawi, Achrafiye; dm US$18, s/d with shared bathroom US$25/35; 🛜) Close to the bar scene on Rue Armenia, this friendly hostel has been set up as an NGO with all profits going towards helping refugees go to university. Facilities are extremely basic, but so are the prices. It's difficult to find, so note the directions on the website.

Talal Hostel   HOTEL $
(Map p362; ☑ 562 567; www.talalhotel.com; Ave Charles Helou, Gemmayzeh; dm US$17, s/d/tr US$40/46/57; ✵ 🛜) The friendly owner will welcome you to this reliable budget option, which offers small and simple rooms (some with private bathroom, some with shared facilities). There's a communal kitchen and laundry facilities.

★**BEYt**   B&B $$

(Map p362; ☑ 444 110; www.beytguesthouse.com; Rue Armenia, Mar Mikhaël; s/d US$100/120, s with shared bathroom US$55-80, d with shared bathroom US$75-100; ✳ 🖥 🛜) For a taste of Beirut-style bohemia, you can't do any better than book a room at this atmospheric B&B operated by the Plan Bey Gallery in Mar Mikhaël. There are only four rooms (one with private bathroom, three with shared facilities) and all share a lounge, kitchen and secluded courtyard garden. Decor is thrift-shop chic and staff are very friendly.

35 Rooms   HOTEL $$

(Map p364; ☑ 345 676; www.35rooms.com; Rue Baalbek, Hamra; s/d/ste from US$145/165/200; ✳ 🛜) Claiming to be the 'trendiest hotel in town' may be a bit of a stretch, but this small hotel in the centre of Hamra provides its guests with a friendly welcome, clean and well-equipped rooms and exceptionally good value for money. The executive rooms and suites have kitchenettes with fridge, kettle and microwave.

Riviera Beirut Hotel   HOTEL $$

(Map p360; ☑ 373 210; www.rivierahotel.com. lb; Ave de Paris, the Corniche, Ras Beirut; r from US$150; ✳ @ 🛜 🛜) This four-star hotel is simply the best Beirut summer option, as it has the most impressive beach club in the city. It also has a history of offering excellent discounts via booking sites. Rooms are large and comfortable; some have balconies with sea views.

Mayflower Hotel   HOTEL $$

(Map p364; ☑ 340 680; www.mayflowerbeirut. com; Rue Neamé Yafet, Hamra; s/d US$90/120; ✳ 🖥 🛜 🛜) A Beirut institution, the Mayflower's rooms are looking worn, but they're clean, comfortable and well priced. We're not convinced that the place lives up to its motto of 'Exceeding our guest's expectations since 1957', but most seem happy (especially those who've attended the Friday happy hour between 7pm and 9pm at the hotel's venerable Duke of Wellington bar).

★**Hotel Albergo**   HOTEL $$$

(Map p362; ☑ 339 797; www.albergobeirut.com; 137 Rue Abdel Wahab el-Inglezi, Achrafiye; ste US$410-3600; ✳ @ 🛜 🛜) As classy as they come, the Albergo is undoubtedly Beirut's best hotel and is a wonderful choice for those who are willing to pay the hefty price tag. Guests enjoy decor rich in art and antiques, a rooftop pool, the city's best Italian restaurant and

highly professional service. Breakfast costs an extra US$25 to US$30.

Smallville Hotel   HOTEL $$$

(Map p360; ☑ 619 999; http://thesmallville.com; r US$180, ste US$300-430; ✳ 🖥 🛜 🛜) The hitherto nondescript suburb of Badaro has been gentrified over the past few years, and is now home to a crop of bars and cafes that are popular with the students at nearby St Joseph University. In the midst of this scene is this new and very swish high-rise hotel, which is known for its rooftop pool and bar.

Rooms are all generously sized, well appointed and comfortable. The hotel itself is close to the National Museum, and within walking distance of Achrafiye.

O Monot   BOUTIQUE HOTEL $$$

(Map p362; ☑ 338 777; www.omonot.com; Monot St, Saifi; r from US$300; ✳ 🛜 🛜) On first glance, the location of this recently opened boutique hotel doesn't look auspicious. But if you ignore the fact that a busy motorway is next door, the fact that Achrafiye, Gemmayzeh and Downtown are on the doorstep makes it extremely convenient. Rooms are wonderfully appointed and service is slick. The rooftop pool is a major draw.

Villa Clara   BOUTIQUE HOTEL $$$

(Map p362; ☑ 70 995 739; http://villaclara.fr; Rue Khenchara, Mar Mikhaël; s/d US$180/210; ✳ 🛜) Its French restaurant is well known, but the seven rooms in this boutique option remain a bit of a secret. On the 1st floor, they are chic and comfortable, albeit light on amenities. The location just off the Mar Mikhaël bar strip is excellent and the building, an elegant old villa, is a lovely place to spend a few days.

Casa d'Or   HOTEL $$$

(Map p364; ☑ 746 400; www.casadorhotel.com; Rue Jeanne d'Arc, Hamra; s US$180, d US$210-240; ✳ @ 🛜) The first three floors of this reliable three-star choice have recently been renovated – they're well worth the slight premium charged (check booking sites for good deals). All have tea/coffee-making facilities, a work desk and good-sized bathrooms. The unrenovated rooms have smaller bathrooms and don't have a kettle. Wi-fi officially costs US$11 for 24 hours but is usually free on request.

✖ Eating

There are eateries of every description in Beirut, from traditional restaurants specialising in mezzes and grills to glamorous brasseries serving exciting nouvelle Lebanese creations.

Every district is blessed with its own complement of juice stalls, fast-food outlets, and shwarma and felafel stands. Popular chains include **Barbar** (Map p364; Rue Spears, Hamra; ⊙ shwarmas LL4500)for quick and cheap mezze and shwarmas, and **Zataar w Zeit** (www.zaatarwzeit.net) for *manakeesh* (thyme and olive-oil pizza). The best felafel in town can be sourced at **Falafel Sayhoun** (Map p362; http://falafelsahyoun.com; Rue Bchara el Khoury, BCD; felafels LPB3500; ⊙ 9am-11pm Mon-Sat), which has been serving its tasty felafel rolls since 1933.

Every Saturday, the Beirut Souks hosts the **Souk El Tayeb Farmers Market** between 9am and 2pm. It's a great place to source organic farm produce.

Beirutis eat dinner late, with few arriving for dinner before 9pm or 10pm.

Mótto
INTERNATIONAL $

(Map p362; ☑ 70 954 057; http://mottorestaurant.wordpress.com; Rue de Madrid; ⊙ noon-3pm & 8-11pm Mon-Sat; ☑) Tucked into the small street behind Petrole Manar, this bohemian place has an English manager, a visiting cast of chefs from around the world and a clientele that loves the simple food and 'pay what you think is fair' pricing policy. There's a different cuisine each night (Indian, French, Mexican, Moroccan, Assyrian, Serbian and Ethiopian have all made an appearance).

Lunch is casual and doesn't stick to a formula; dinner is set and popular, so bookings are recommended. Check the Facebook page for the weekly menu.

Aunty Salwa
LEBANESE $

(Map p364; Baalbaki Bldg, off Rue Abdel Aziz, Hamra; salads LL4000-8000, mains LL12,000; ⊙ 8am-4.30pm Mon-Fri, to 4pm Sat; ☑) Though well-endowed with bars and cafes, Hamra isn't known for its restaurants. But if you're here during the day, this tiny place is worth considering for its cheap and tasty home-style cooking. There's always a plat du jour, as well as a daily spread of fresh mezze, salads and mains to choose from. Vegetarians are well catered for.

You'll find it in a laneway opposite the Cedarland Hotel.

Le Chef
LEBANESE $

(Map p362; ☑ 446 769; Rue Gouraud, Gemmayzeh; mezze LL4000, mains LL6000-10,000; ⊙ 11am-10pm Mon-Sat) Don't miss lunch at this beloved Beiruti institution where waiters dish up vast platefuls of 'workers' food' to all and sundry. There's little atmosphere, but the food is good value.

Paul
CAFE $

(Map p362; Rue Gouraud, Gemmayzeh; baguettes LL9000-16,000; ⊙ 7am-midnight) A favourite with the affluent Achrafiye set, this cafe at the start of Rue Gouraud is a fantastic spot to indulge in some people-watching. You'll need to fight for the waiter's attention if you're not overly made-up and artificially enhanced, but when you eventually order, your reward will be good coffee (or tea), freshly filled baguettes and delicious pastries.

There are other branches **Downtown** (Map p362; Rue Abdel Malek, BCD) and in **Hamra** (Map p364; Rue Bliss, Hamra).

★ Tawlet
LEBANESE $$

(Map p362; ☑ 448 129; www.tawlet.com; ground fl, Chalhoub Bldg, 12 Rue al-Nahr, Mar Mikhaël; buffet (incl arak) LL50,000; ⊙ 1-4pm Mon-Fri, noon-4pm Sat; ☑) There are loads of great restaurants in Beirut, but there's only one that commands the respect of every farmer, chef and foodie in the country – and that's Tawlet. Showcasing farm-fresh (often organic) produce and providing a venue where traditional recipes can be tested and sampled, this chic eatery offers a daily lunch buffet cooked by a visiting chef.

To find it, head east along Rue Armenia and into its extension Rue al-Nahr. Tawlet is the end of the lane behind the Anthurium flower shop, on the northern side of the road.

Enab
LEBANESE $$

(Map p362; ☑ 444 441; www.enab.me; Rue Armenia, Mar Mikhaël; mezze LL6000-16,000, grills LL15,000-28,000; ⊙ noon-midnight) Head up the wooden staircase to access this huge and ultra-popular restaurant, and then choose between a garden table or one in the attractively decorated front salons. The menu features all of the usual Levantine favourites, with a few wildcards (try the eggplant fatteh and you won't be disappointed).

Kahwet Leila
RESTAURANT, CAFE $$

(Map p362; ☑ 70 184 033; www.kahwetleila.com; Rue Gouraud, Gemmayzeh; mezze LL7000-13,500, platters LL14,500-26,000; ⊙ 10am-1am; ☎ ☑) Old Beirut lives on through clever recreations such as this chic coffeehouse, which is designed to evoke the city's 'Paris of the East' past. The menu features mezze and a choice of platters (burgers, shwarma, brochettes, felafel), but many head here for coffee and a nargileh, making good use of the cafe's backgammon sets and packs of cards.

There's a second branch in **Hamra** (Map p364; Rue Omar ben Abdel Aziz).

Tavolina ITALIAN $$
(Map p362; ☑442 244; Rue Kamille Yousef Chamoun, Mar Mikhaël; pizzas & pastas LL14,000-39,000, mains LL28,000-49,000; ☺12.30pm-11.30pm) Every suburb needs an Italian trattoria, and it would certainly be nice if all were as impressive as this one. Serving up handmade pasta, piping hot pizzas and well-executed classics such as *cotoletta alla Milanese* (crumbed veal cutlet), this place deserves its spot on the list of Beirut's best Italian eateries. Some of the pizzas and pastas are gluten-free.

Urbanista RESTAURANT, CAFE $$
(Map p362; ☑567 811; www.weare-urbanista. com; Rue Gouraud, Gemmeyzeh; burgers & sandwiches LL13,000-25,000, salads LL16,000-20,000; ☺8am-midnight; ☎) As international as its name would suggest, this industrial-chic cafe is as popular with expats as it is with locals. One of the few places in the city where lone diners aren't treated like pariahs, it has individual and communal tables, a courtyard, comfy armchairs and a laid-back vibe. The menu is strong on comfort food and salads.

There's another branch in **Hamra** (Map p364; Rue Bliss).

Appetito Trattoria ITALIAN $$
(Map p364; ☑347 346; www.appetitotrattoria.com; Rue Mahatma Ghandi, Hamra; pizzas LL16,000-28,500, pastas LL18,000-31,000; ☺noon-midnight) After indulging in a happy hour or two in Hamra, many locals head to this trattoria for a restorative bowl of pasta or a Roman-style (ie thin-crust) pizza. There's decent wine by the glass, a comfortable bar for solo diners and a menu that will please most tastes.

★**Liza** LEBANESE $$$
(Map p362; ☑208 108; www.lizabeirut.com; 1st fl, Metropolitan Club, Doumani St, Achrafiye; mezze LL9000-47,000, mains LL25,000-49,000; ☺12.30-3.30pm & 8-11.30pm Tue-Sat, 12.30-4pm Sun) Epitomising Beiruti chic, Liza serves expertly prepared nouvelle Lebanese food in surroundings that have graced the pages of many international design magazines. Prices are remarkably reasonable considering the quality – especially at lunch when the

plat du jour and a salad costs LL29,500 – and there's an expertly curated wine list by both the glass and bottle. Simply splendid.

★**Mayrig** ARMENIAN $$$
(Map p362; ☑572 121; www.mayrigbeirut.com; 282 Rue Pasteur, Gemmeyzeh; mezze LL7000-19,000, mains LL24,000-60,000; ☺1pm-11pm) Beirutis of Armenian descent tend to head to this elegant restaurant in Gemmeyzeh if they want to celebrate a special occasion, and once you've eaten here you'll understand why. The food is among the best in the city, and provides a nice change from the usual Levantine menu. The sour cherry kebab is particularly delicious.

Also on offer are pastry dishes, *kebbe, soujouk* (Armenian sausage) and *mante* (dumplings). Booking is recommended.

🍷 Drinking & Nightlife

For a drink in the afternoon, the coffee shops of the Corniche and Hamra are your best bets. The main bar strips are in Hamra, Gemmeyzeh and Mar Mikhaël, and there's a nascent bar and cafe scene emerging in Badaro behind the National Museum.

Bars

★**Torino Express** BAR, CAFE
(Map p362; Rue Gouraud, Gemmeyzeh; ☺10am-late) One of Beirut's longest-serving hipster hangouts, this neighbourhood place functions as a cafe during the day but hits its stride at night when the DJ spins a wildly eclectic collection of tracks and the barmen work their magic.

★**Dany's** BAR
(Map p364; www.danyslb.com; Street 78, off Rue Makdissi, Hamra; ☺10am-2.30am, from 5pm Sun) The original bar in Street 78 (aka The Alleyway), Dany's has been one of Hamra's favourite drinking dens since 1998, and retains our vote as the best in the area. There's indoor/outdoor seating, and a laid-back and inclusive vibe.

★**Junkyard** BAR, RESTAURANT
(Map p362; ☑448 632; Rue Qobaiyat, Mar Mikhaël; ☺6pm-2am) A stack of well-worn shipping containers converted into a fashionable bar/party venue hybrid, Junkyard has a huge glass atrium at its rear and a summer terrace that hosts one of the most fashionable drinking scenes in the city. The chef serves up his personal take on street-food

favourites, giving credence to the place's self-anointed gastropub tag.

Dragonfly
BAR

(Map p362; ☑ 561 112; Rue Gouraud, Gemmayzeh; ☺ 6pm-late) Attracting a 30s-something arty crowd, this long-standing bar has a Parisian-style decor and a reputation for spinning good jazz on its turntable.

Charlie's Bar
BAR

(Map p362; ☑ 442 019; Rue Gouraud Gemmayzeh; ☺ 11am-3am) A hipster haunt on Rue Gouraud, this place is so small that only one barman can fit behind the backlit bar and the loyal clientele is often pushed out onto the street.

Rabbit Hole
BAR

(Map p364; ☑ 70 151 328; Rue Makdissi, Hamra; ☺ 3pm-late) This unpretentious hole-in-the-wall bar is known for its herb-infused, fresh-fruit cocktails. Settle down at the wooden bar for happy hour (5pm to 8pm). DJs spin jazz, acid jazz and soft rock.

Abbey Road
BAR

(Map p362; ☑ 383 8472; Rue Armenia, Mar Mikhaël; ☺ 5pm-2am) Brits will feel at home in this pint-sized bar, which is decked out with Beatles memorabilia, London street signs and black-and-white photos of Old Blighty. In warm weather, the bar's front windows open up to the street and drinkers spill out in a convivial cascade.

Internazionale
BAR

(Map p362; ☑ 565 463; Rue Armenia, Mar Mikhaël; ☺ 4pm-late) Named after a Milanese football club, this bohemian place was one of the original bars in Mar Mikhaël. Be sure to check out the black-and-white photograph on the inside wall, which features the owner's super-cool grandfather. We're sure this is the type of bar he would have approved of.

Life Bar
GAY

(Map p362; ☑ 03 678 741; Liban St, Gemmayzeh; ☺ 7pm-3am Wed-Sun) A stalwart of Beirut's gay scene, Life Bar has a relatively restrained vibe. The DJs spin oriental tracks on Thursday, oriental and pop on Friday and Saturday and '80s flashbacks on Sunday. Karaoke reigns supreme on Wednesday.

Madame Om
CAFE, PUB

(Map p364; ☑ 03 870 459; ground fl, Estral Center, Hamra; ☺ 11am-late Mon-Sat) Named after the Egyptian diva Om Kulthoum, this gay-friendly cafe-pub hybrid is a popular choice in the afternoon and early evening

on weekdays, when drinks are discounted by 30%. Check its Facebook page for event info.

Bricks
PUB

(Map p364; ☑ 355 443; Makdissi St, Hamra; ☺ 11am-3pm) Spicy chicken wings with ice-cold beer is the combo of choice for the AUB students and staff who congregate here. The music won't be to all tastes ('70s and '80s ballads and rock), but that doesn't put the loyal clientele off.

Walkman
BAR

(Map p364; ☑ 76 885 887; Street 78, off Makdissi St, Hamra; ☺ 5pm-4am) The name gives a clue as to the theme at this newcomer to The Alleyway. It's all about the '80s here – Michael Jackson, Madonna and Bon Jovi dominate the soundtrack and the decor provides plenty of nostalgia-induced sniggers. Happy hour (5pm to 8pm) is popular.

Cafes

Café Younes
CAFE

(Map p364; ☑ 742 654; www.cafeyounes.com; Rue Abdel Aziz, Hamra; ☺ 7am-10pm; ☎) The aroma of freshly ground coffee beans has been enticing patrons into this friendly cafe near the American University of Beirut since 1935, rewarding them with the best coffee in Beirut (espresso, filter, decaf and traditional Middle Eastern styles). There's another branch nearby **Rue Neemat Yafet** (Map p364).

Cafe de Prague
CAFE

(Map p364; Rue Makdissi, Hamra; ☺ 9am-late) Popular with AUB students, intellectuals and artists, this cafe has comfy chairs and low-set tables, and feels like a large lounge room. Bring your laptop or you'll look out of place.

Bay Rock Café
CAFE

(Map p360; www.bayrockcafe-lb.com; Ave du Général de Gaulle, Raouché; ☺ 24hr) Grab a cold beer and watch the sun go down at this cafe spectacularly situated overlooking Pigeon Rocks – or wiggle with the belly dancers who usually perform around midnight at weekends.

Al-Raouda
CAFE

(Map p360; Corniche, Manara; ☺ 7.30am-midnight Jun-Sep, 8am-8pm Oct-May) Stop in for a hit of strong coffee or a languid nargileh at Al-Raouda, a waterfront favourite with local families. It's a little tricky to find: walk down the lane right next to the Luna Park entrance, then look for the misspelt 'El Rawda' sign.

Nightclubs

Beirut's clubbing scene is legendary, but it's predominantly limited to the summer months. The action starts around 10pm, hits its stride after midnight and continues until 4am or 5am. Thursday, Friday and Saturday are the big nights. Be warned that most venues charge a small fortune for tables and drinks, and that you are unlikely to be let through the door unless you're dressed to the nines.

B 018 CLUB
(Map p362; ☑03-810 618; Lot 317, La Quarantine; cover varies; ⊙9pm-late Thu-Sat) Easily the most famous club in town, this gay-friendly underground place a couple of kilometres east of Downtown is known for its mock-horror interior and sliding roof, which always opens at some point during the night. To get here, ask a cab driver to take you to the Forum de Beyrouth and follow the clubbers from there.

Posh GAY
(Map p362; Jamerek St, Saifi; ⊙10.30pm-4.30am Thu, Sat & Sun) In Saifi near Downtown, this club on top of a warehouse is party central for Beirut's gay community. A state-of-the-art lighting and sound system is used to great advantage, with patrons strutting their stuff to a pulsing background of house, RnB, rave, techno and electro-Arabic. Sunday is oriental night.

Sky Bar CLUB
(Map p360; ☑03-939 191; www.skybarbeirut. com; Biel Pavilion, BCD; minimum charge at tables US$100, no cover at bar; ⊙10.30pm-late Tue-Sun summer only) The sybaritic summer scene at this multiplatform rooftop loft is famous throughout the Middle East, and beautiful young things flock here to admire the view, drink expertly made cocktails, dance amid the LED display and marvel at occasional firework displays. Be sure to dress to impress.

White CLUB
(☑03-060 090; www.whitebeirut.com; Seaside Rd, Dawra; ⊙10pm-late summer only) An ultra-glam restaurant, lounge bar and club, this rooftop showpony brings in international DJs and dance acts and is a favourite with the bronzed and the beautiful. In winter the action moves to MAD Beirut (www.madbeirut. com), downstairs.

☆ Entertainment

Blue Note JAZZ
(Map p364; ☑743 857; www.bluenotecafe.com; Rue Makhoul, Hamra; ⊙noon-late) This is one of the very best places to hear jazz and blues in Lebanon. Local – and sometimes international – acts perform each Tuesday, Thursday, Friday and Saturday. Check the website for the program.

🛍 Shopping

The cheapest shops are found in Bourj Hammoud (near the Dawra transport hub) and in Hamra. Upmarket shopping can be found Downtown, in Verdun and in malls including **ABC** (Map p362; www.abc.com.lb/ site/ashrafieh; Rue Furn el-Hayek; ⊙10am-10pm) in Achrafiye and **City Mall** (☑905 555; www. citymall.com.lb; 14 Dawra Hwy, El Bauchrieh) near Dawra.

★Orient 499 HOMEWARES, FASHION
(499 East; Map p362; ☑369 499; www.orient499.com; 499 Omar Daouk Str, Mina El Hosn; ⊙10.30am-7pm Mon-Sat) Entranced by Middle Eastern design, Frank Luca and Aida Kawas decided to establish this atelier and boutique, where they design and make some objects (including Aida Kawas' wonderful clothing) and also sell products and artefacts sourced from other countries in the region. Exquisite homewares, handmade soaps, ceramics, metalwork, toys and furniture are on offer.

L'artisan du Liban HANDICRAFTS
(Map p362; ☑06-204 334; www.alyad.com; Centre Saint Antoine, Rue Gouraud, Gemmayzeh; ⊙9.30am-7pm Mon-Fri, to 5pm Sat) Head down the marble staircase in the Centre Saint Antoine to find this shop, which sells ceramics, silverware, traditional clothing, soap, embroidery, textiles and toys, all made by Lebanese artisans.

Beirut Souks SHOPPING MALL
(Map p362; ☑989 041; www.beirutsouks.com.lb; Saad Zaghloul St, BCD) Upmarket goods are available at this modern shopping complex and in shops in the surrounding streets.

Virgin Megastore MUSIC, BOOKS
(Map p362; ☑999 666; www.virginmegastore.com. lb; Opera Bldg, Place des Martyrs) A huge collection of books and maps (in Arabic, French and English) as well as local and regional music. Also sells tickets for Lebanon's summer arts festivals.

ⓘ SECURITY: BEIRUT

At the time of research, most foreign embassies were advising their citizens not to travel to the southern suburbs of Beirut due to the possibility of rocket attacks and car bombs. The southern suburbs are defined as the area south of the Camille Chamoun Sports Stadium to the airport and east of the main airport road, and include Chiyah, Ghobeire, Haret Hreik, Bir el Abed, Borj el Barajne, Mraije, Roueiss, Lailake, Hay el Sellom and Tahouitit el Ghadir. Also off limits were the suburbs west of the airport highway to the coast, and south from Adnon El Hakim Rd to Abbas El Mousawi Rd.

ⓘ Information

Though there are many landmarks that can be used as navigational markers (the towering, derelict former Holiday Inn being the most obvious), understanding the geography of Beirut can be tricky. The blue signs on street corners don't usually give the name of the street itself, instead displaying only the sector (suburb) name and rue (street) number. On top of this, numbered buildings are rare, and many streets don't have names at all, or are locally known by a different name from the one given on a map. That said, armed with a good street map, getting familiar with this compact city is actually rather easy.

DANGERS & ANNOYANCES

The biggest danger – and annoyance – in Beirut is the traffic. Rules both on and off the road are nonexistent, and pedestrians should take particular care when crossing the road.

EMERGENCY

Ambulance & Emergency ☑140
Fire ☑175
Police ☑112
Tourist Police ☑1735 (8am to 1pm Monday to Friday)

INTERNET ACCESS

Wi-fi is widely available in nearly every accommodation price range, as well as in most cafes – all you need is your laptop or smartphone. Note that Skype rarely works; Viber is more reliable.

MAPS

Geoprojects' *Beirut* fold-out map (1:10 000; US$5.50) is widely available.

MEDIA

Beirut's two foreign-language newspaper dailies are the French *L'Orient Le Jour* (www.lorientlejour.com) and the English *Daily Star* (www.daily-star.com). Online, the best source of independent news is *Ya Libnan* (www.yalibnan.com).

MEDICAL SERVICES

American University of Beirut Hospital (Map p364; ☑350 000, 354 911; Rue Sourati, Hamra) Considered one of the best hospitals in the Middle East, with English and French spoken.

MONEY

There are ATMs all over the city, most of which dispense both US dollars and Lebanese pounds. Moneychangers are dotted along Rue Hamra.

POST

Libanpost, the national post office, has plenty of branches scattered through town. Standard opening hours are 8am to 5pm Monday to Friday and 8am to 1.30pm Saturday. Two convenient branches:

LibanPost Hamra (Map p364; Matta Bldg, Rue Makdissi, Hamra)
LibanPost Gemmayzeh (Map p362; Zighbi Bldg, Rue Gouraud, Gemmayzeh)

TOURIST INFORMATION

Tourist Office (Map p364; ☑343 073; www.mot.gov.lb; ground fl, Ministry of Tourism Bldg, 550 Rue Banque du Liban, Hamra; ⊙9am-3pm Mon-Fri, to 1pm Sat) Enter by the back door through a covered car park (it's the second office on the left) to find helpful staff and some brochures. There's also an office in the arrivals hall at the airport (⊙10am to 6pm).
Tourist Police (Map p364; ☑1735; ⊙English hotline 8am-1pm Mon-Fri) For complaints or problems (including robbery), contact this office opposite the tourist office.

ⓘ Getting There & Away

Buses, minibuses and service taxis to destinations north of Beirut leave from Gemmayzeh's **Charles Helou bus station** (Map p362) and the **Dawra transport hub** in Dora, 7km northeast of town. To destinations south and southeast, they leave from the **Cola transport hub**, about 2km south of the BCD, or **Sahraa Square** between Cola and the airport.

Common destinations include:
Beit Mery LL1500, 50 minutes, every 30 minutes
Byblos LL1500, 50 minutes, every 15 minutes
Bcharré LL7000 to LL10,000, 2½ hours, 10 to 12 daily
Tyre LL5000, 1½ hours, regularly

ℹ Getting Around

TO/FROM THE AIRPORT

Beirut Rafic Hariri International Airport is approximately 9km south of Beirut's city centre. There are no scheduled buses servicing the airport but you can catch a minivan (LL1000) to get into the city. Go to the departures entrance (upstairs from arrivals) and wait for a minivan with an aeroplane sticker on the windscreen. One comes by every five to 10 minutes. It travels to the Dawra transport hub, stopping Downtown en route.

Taxis are available outside the arrivals area, but you'll need to negotiate your fare with the driver. The trip to Hamra, Downtown, Achrafiye or Gemmayzeh should cost around US$25 (LL40,000).

To get to the airport from Hamra, take CC bus No 4 (LL1000) from outside the tourist office to Bechara el-Khoury Sq, Downtown. Nearby, you can catch a minivan (there's no number – look for the aeroplane sticker on the windscreen; LL1000) directly to the airport entrance. These airport services pass by every five minutes or so. If you have excess luggage, expect to pay extra.

BUSES

Beirut is well serviced by its network of slow, crowded, but good-value buses. The red-and-white **Lebanese Commuting Company** (LCC; www.lccworld.com) buses operate on a 'hail-and-ride' system: just wave at the driver and, in theory at least, the bus will stop. There are no timetables, but buses generally run from around 5.30am to 7pm daily at intervals of 15 minutes or so.

The LCC bus routes that are most useful to travellers are listed below. A short trip will almost always cost LL1000, a longer ride will be LL1500.

No 1 Hamra-Khaldé Rue Sadat (Hamra), Rue Emile Eddé, Hotel Bristol, Rue Verdun, Cola roundabout, airport roundabout, Kafaat, Khaldé

No 2 Hamra-Antelias Rue Sadat (Hamra), Rue Emile Eddé, Radio Lebanon, Sassine Sq, Dawra transport hub, Antelias

No 4 AUB Medical Centre-Lebanese University (Map p362) AUB Medical Centre, Hamra, Bechara el-Khoury Sq (Downtown), Mazraa, Lebanese University

No 6 Cola-Byblos Antelias, Jounieh, Byblos (Jbail)

No 7 National Museum-Bharssaf National Museum, Beit Mery, Brummana, Baabdat, Bharssaf

No 24 Hamra-National Museum (Map p364) Hamra, Cola, National Museum (Mathaf)

CAR & MOTORCYCLE

If you have nerves of steel and a penchant for *Grand Theft Auto*, you may well enjoy driving in and around Beirut. The best local car rental company is **Advanced Car Rental** (Map p362; ☑ 999 884, 999 885; www.advancedcarrent. com; Azarieh Bldg, Rue Emir Bachir, Downtown), which offers great discounts on its published rates.

TAXI & SERVICE TAXI

Taxi drivers don't use meters, so you'll need to agree on a fare in advance. Within Beirut, taxis charge anywhere from LL10,000 to LL20,000, depending on your destination.

AROUND BEIRUT

Beit Mery & Brummana بيت مرعي & برومانا

☑ 04

Set in pine forests some 800m above and 17km east of Beirut, Beit Mery ('House of the Master' in Aramaic) is a lazy weekend getaway for Beirutis seeking respite from city pollution. The town dates back to Phoenician times and is home to some Roman and Byzantine ruins.

The town's **al-Bustan Festival** (www. albustanfestival.com) is held between mid-February and mid-March, with a varied program of chamber, choral and orchestral music. Many of the festival's performances take place at the Hotel al-Bustan.

About 4km northeast of Beit Mery is Brummana, a resort town connected to Beit Mery by a continuous strip of hotels, eateries, cafes, shops and nightclubs. In summer it's hugely popular with Beirutis escaping the city heat and has a carnival-like atmosphere, especially on weekends. There's nothing in particular to do here except to eat, drink and go clubbing; be aware that it's extremely quiet outside summer season and weekends.

⊙ Sights

Deir el-Qalaa MONASTERY
(Couvent St Jean Baptiste; ☑ 870 080; ⊙ grounds sunrise-sunset) Built over the remains of a Roman temple, this 17th-century Maronite monastery was extensively damaged during the civil war but has been fully restored. A few of the original Roman-era columns remain, one of which is built into the current

building's wall. A working monastery, it is surrounded by formal gardens and has a scenic terrace.

Just before the gates of the monastery, on the left-hand side of the road, are overgrown ruins dating from the Roman and Byzantine periods. The most interesting of these is a section of Byzantine mosaic flooring; you'll find this behind the house closest to the gate.

To reach the monastery, head towards St George's Church (signposted) at the lower end of Beit Mery's main street and then continue uphill and around the bend past the modern municipality building.

🛏 Sleeping & Eating

There are dozens of places to stay and eat in both Beit Mery and Brummana, but unless you're in Beit Mery for the festival, there's no compelling reason to stay here.

Hotel al-Bustan HOTEL **$$$**
(☑972 980; www.albustan-lb.com; Beit Mery; s/d US$308/352; ✸@🛜🏊) The grande dame of Beit Mery's hotels, this is an excellent choice during the popular al-Bustan Festival as many concerts are performed in the hotel itself. Though in need of a refurbishment, it is well maintained and offers extensive grounds with wonderful views over Beirut and the Mediterranean. Standard rooms are spacious, with enclosed balconies and work desks.

Common areas and facilities include an Italian restaurant, Oriental buffet, three bars, dining terrace, children's playground and fitness room. Breakfast costs an extra US$16.50.

Restaurant Mounir LEBANESE **$$**
(☑873 900; www.mounirs.com; Main St, Brummana; mezzes LL5750-15,750, grills LL6000-22,000; ⏱noon-late Tue-Sun) One of the country's most famous restaurants, this classy place just off the highway on the border of Beit Mery and Brummana boasts extensive gardens, a pleasant terrace (equipped with a children's playground) and spectacular views. Its Levantine menu is refined and totally delicious. Book in advance and request a table with a view.

ℹ Getting There & Away

LCC bus 7 (LL1500, 50 minutes) departs every 30 minutes or so from Mathaf (the National Museum junction) in Beirut and travels to both Beit Mery and Brummana. Flag the bus down on the southern side of ever-busy Abdallah el-Yafi

Ave, opposite the museum. In Beit Mery, buses stop at the roundabout near the Coral Petrol Station at the bottom end of the main street. In Brummana, they stop along the highway and the town's main street.

Minibuses leave from Dawra and also charge LL1500. A taxi costs around LL20,000.

Jeita Grotto مغارة جعيتا
📷 09

One of the Middle East's greatest natural wonders, the stunning Jeita Grotto Cave System (☑220 841; www.jeitagrotto.com; adult/child under 12yr LL18,150/10,175; ⏱9am-6pm Tue-Sun Jun-Sep, to 5pm Tue-Sun Oct-May, closed late Jan-early Feb) extends around 6km into the mountains 18km northeast of Beirut. Discovered in 1836 and opened as a tourist attraction in 1969, the caves were used as an ammunition store during the civil war despite the fact that their lower strata are flooded each winter due to the rising levels of the Nahr-el-Kalb (or Dog River) for which they form the source. These lower caves are always explored by small boat, and are closed when the flood levels rise too high; during these periods the ticket price drops to adult/child LL11,550/6875.

The simply extraordinary upper cavern stays open all year and is explored on foot. Accessed via a cable car from the ticket office, it has strategically positioned coloured lights that showcase the stalactites and stalagmites in all their crystalline glory. And despite all kinds of tatty side attractions – including a toy train ride between the ticket office and lower caves – the site remains a spectacular day trip from Beirut. Bear in mind that there's no photography allowed: you can stow your camera in lockers at the mouth of the caverns. The ticket price includes the toy train and cable-car rides, grotto entrance and a 20-minute video presentation about the caves (screened at different times of the day in English, French and Arabic). Allow 90 minutes to two hours for your visit.

To get to the grotto, take a minibus (LL1500) or LCC bus 6 (LL1500) from Dawra and ask the driver to drop you at the Jeita turn-off on the Beirut-Jounieh Hwy. From here, negotiate a return price with a waiting taxi for the 5km journey (around US$15 to US$20, according to demand), and make sure to figure in waiting time. Alternatively, a return taxi trip from Beirut should cost around US$60 including waiting time.

Jounieh جونيه

☑ 09

Once a sleepy fishing village, this satellite suburb 21km north of Beirut is now a pleasure playground hemmed in by the sea on one side and the mountains on the other. Famous as the home of the venerable Casino du Liban (www.cdl.com.lb), noisy bars, crowded restaurants and lurid 'super' nightclubs filled with bored exotic dancers, it certainly won't be to everyone's taste. Nevertheless, it does have one worthwhile distraction in its dizzying Teleferique.

◉ Sights & Activities

Jounieh Teleferique   CABLE CAR
(☑ 936 075; adult/child return Tue-Thu LL9000/5500, Fri & Sat LL11,000/6000; ⊙10.30am-5.30pm Tue-Thu, to 6.30pm Fri & Sat, open later in summer) Dubbed the Terorifique by some, this attraction runs cable cars from its base behind the St Louis Hospital to the mountaintop statue of Our Lady of Lebanon at Harissa. The views from the summit are spectacular. Note that it doesn't operate in windy weather.

✖ Eating

Jounieh has plenty of chain restaurants and glitzy, overpriced steak places. Most are located along the main street, Rue Mina al-Jadida, which runs next to, and parallel with, the coastline.

Chez Sami   SEAFOOD $$$
(☑ 910 520; www.chezsamirestaurant.com; Rue Maameltein; mezze & salads from LL8000, mains from LL30,000; ⊙noon-midnight) Considered one of the best seafood restaurants in Lebanon, Chez Sami offers great seaside views from its elegant glassed-in pavilion and magnificent outdoor deck, which is built over the water (book ahead for a table). There's no menu, so you'll need to choose your fish from the display near the front door and discuss salads and mezze with the waiter.

❶ Getting There & Away

From Beirut's Dawra transport hub, LCC bus 6 (LL1500, 30 minutes) travels to Jounieh and then on to Byblos. When returning to Beirut, flag the bus down on Rue Maameltein before the roundabout with the KFC, as this is where it turns left (east) to access the main highway.

A private taxi from Beirut to Jounieh costs around LL30,000.

Byblos (Jbail) بيبلوس

☑ 09

A pretty fishing port with an ancient harbour, medieval town centre, Crusader-era castle and atmospheric archaeological site, Byblos is a wonderful choice for those wanting a night or two out of Beirut, but it's also an easy and enjoyable day trip.

The town's tourist office (☑ 540 325; www.mot.gov.lb; ⊙9am-5pm Mon-Sat Mar-Nov) is located in the souq near the entrance to the archaeological site. Banks are found on Rue Jbail.

History

Excavations have shown that Byblos (the biblical Gebal) was probably inhabited as early as 7000 years ago; by the middle of the 3rd millennium BC it had become the busiest trading port on the eastern Mediterranean and an important religious centre, all under the direction of the maritime Phoenicians. Close links to Egypt fostered its cultural and religious development, and as the city flourished it developed its own distinct art and architecture, part Egyptian, part Mesopotamian. It was in Byblos, too, that our modern alphabet is said to have had its roots, developed by the Phoenicians as a way of accurately recording its healthy trade transactions.

The city was renamed Byblos by the Greeks, who ruled here from 333 BC; the name comes from the Greek word *bublos,* meaning papyrus, plenty of which was shipped from Egypt to Greece via Byblos' port. As the Greek empire fell into decline, the Romans, under Pompey, arrived in town, constructing temples, baths, colonnaded streets and public buildings. Later allied to the Byzantines and conquered in the 7th century by the Islamic invasion, it fell to the Crusaders in 1104. They swiftly set about building a castle and moat with stone and columns taken from the earlier Roman temples.

Subsequent centuries under Ottoman and Mamluk rule saw Byblos' international reputation as a trading port decline, just as Beirut's star was in the ascendancy. Byblos soon settled into a new incarnation as a sleepy fishing port, which it remains to this day. Excavations of its former glories began in 1860 and continue, albeit at a snail's pace, today.

Byblos (Jbail)

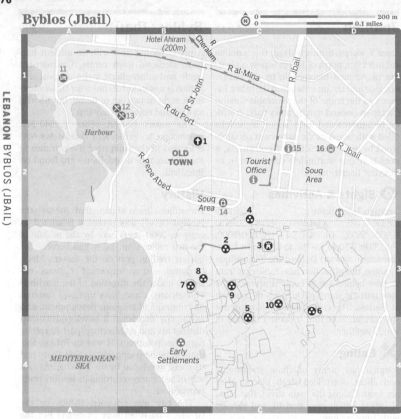

◉ Sights & Activities

Archaeological Site   HISTORIC SITE
(☏ 540 001; adult/child LL8000/2000; ⏱ 8am-
30min before sunset) A restored 12th-cen-
tury **Crusader castle** surrounded by a
10m-wide dry moat is located just inside
the entrance to Byblos' atmospheric archaeological site, which incorporates Neolithic, Chalcolithic, Greek and Roman
ruins. There are panoramic views over the
ruins and harbour from the castle's rooftop
and crenellated towers – be sure to climb
the stone staircases to the top of the donjon
(fortified central tower) to appreciate these.
Inside, there's a small museum and a room
with information panels outlining the city's
history.

After exploring the castle, backtrack to
the site **entrance** and turn left to explore
the ruins, which include the remains of
city ramparts dating from the 3rd and
2nd millennium BC, three temples, and a
Roman theatre overlooking the sea. In the
Roman period (64 BC–AD 395), the streets
here were lined with colonnades and sculptures adorned most public places. Interestingly, the layout wasn't according to the
usual Roman grid, instead being adapted
to the existing monuments on the site.

The L-shaped **Temple of Resheph**
dates from the 3rd millennium BC, and is
thought to have been burned down during
the Amorite invasions. More recent (early
2nd century BC) are the remains of the **Obelisk Temple**; the 1500 gold-covered votive
offerings in the shape of human figures
discovered here in the 20th century are
now displayed at Beirut's National Museum
(p361).

The site's oldest temple, the **Temple
of Baalat Gebal** (the Mistress of Byblos),
dates back to the 4th century BC. This was
the largest and most important temple constructed at Byblos, dedicated to Aphrodite

Byblos (Jbail)

👁 Sights
1 Church of St John the Baptist B2
2 City Ramparts C3
3 Crusader Castle C3
4 Entrance to Archaeological Site C2
5 King's Well C4
6 Obelisk Temple D3
7 Roman Theatre B3
8 Royal Tombs B3
9 Temple of Baalat Gebal C3
10 Temple of Resheph C3

😴 Sleeping
11 Byblos Sur Mer A1

🍴 Eating
12 Bab El Mina B1
13 Byblos Fishing Club B1

🛍 Shopping
14 Mémoire du Temps C2

ℹ Information
15 Byblos Festival Office C2

🚍 Transport
16 Taxi Stand D2

during the Roman period, and was rebuilt a number of times over its two-millennia long survival. Many temple findings, including alabaster vase fragments inscribed with the names of Old Kingdom pharaohs, are today also housed in the National Museum. The six standing columns approaching the temple are the vestiges of a Roman colonnaded street dating from c 300 AD.

West of the Temple of Baalat Gebal is the **Roman theatre**, a reconstruction that's one-third the size of the original. This is situated near the cliff edge and has great views across the sea. Behind this are nine **royal tombs**, cut in vertical shafts deep into the rock in the 2nd millennium BC. Some of the sarcophagi found here are now housed in the National Museum, including that of King Hiram, whose sarcophagus has one of the earliest Phoenician alphabet inscriptions in the world. His grave shaft is also inscribed, this time with the eerie phrase, 'Warning here. Thy death is below.'

Other remains include the **King's Well**, a spring that supplied the city with water until the end of the Hellenistic era (and where, according to legend, Isis sat weeping on her search for Osiris), and remnants of Neolithic (5th century BC) and Chalcolithic (4th century BC) enclosures, houses and huts.

Church of St John the Baptist   CHURCH
(Eglise St Jean Marc) Construction of this Romanesque-style church in the medieval streets above the harbour commenced in 1115 and the structure was extended and improved over subsequent centuries. It's thus an interesting mixture of Arab and Italian designs, with remains of Byzantine mosaics from an earlier structure scattered about the area. The unusual open-air baptistery sits against the north wall, its arches and four supporting pillars topped by a dome.

🎊 Festivals & Events

Byblos International Festival   MUSIC
(www.byblosfestival.org) Byblos hosts local and international performers at its popular annual summer festival. Check the website for events listings and ticketing details.

🛏 Sleeping

Hotel Ahiram   HOTEL $$
(☎540 440; www.ahiramhotel.com; Ahiram St; s/d/tr US$110/135/155; ❄🛜) A popular three-star choice, this unassuming place has friendly staff, direct access to a small, pebbly beach and a variety of room types (request one with a balcony and sea view). Ask about substantial off-season discounts.

Byblos Sur Mer   HOTEL $$$
(☎548 000; Rue du Port; s/d US$240/260; 🅿❄@🛜🏊) Hugely popular with young couples enjoying romantic breaks away from Beirut, this classy hotel overlooking the harbour has spacious, recently renovated rooms (many with balconies), a seafront pool and a sunny breakfast room where a lavish buffet is served. Public spaces include a waterside seafood restaurant, a summer-only sheesha lounge and a ground-floor restaurant with a glass-panelled floor floating above excavated ancient ruins.

🍴 Eating

For cheap eats, head to the many felafel and shwarma joints along Rue Jbail.

Byblos Fishing Club   LEBANESE $$
(Pepe's; ☎540 213; Rue Pepe Abed; mezze LL7000-22,000, mains LL22,500-40,000; ⊙11am-midnight) A Lebanese institution, the Fishing Club was founded in 1962 by the late Pépé Abed, who features on the photograph-covered wall dangling many a '60s film star on his knee. The quality of the food can be hit and miss, but

FABULOUS FOSSILS

Tucked away in an alleyway in the Byblos souq is the workshop of local palaeontologist Pierre Abi-Saad and his fascinating 100-million-year-old haul of fossils. Discovered in a quarry owned by his family for generations, now almost 1km above sea level, his glimpses into a prehistoric underwater world are today represented in almost every major international natural history museum, though he keeps his favourites for the long-awaited day when he, too, will open a museum of his own findings to the world.

More than 80% of the fossils Pierre has found represent species now extinct, and many haven't yet been studied or named. Those that are familiar include eels, stingrays, octopus, jellyfish and shrimp, and there are also plenty of coelacanths, one of the earliest fish ever to exist. His collection even includes such oddities as a fossil of a fish that had swallowed another fish before its ancient demise, and a 4m-long complete shark, the largest in the world.

It's possible to purchase fossils to take home from Pierre's shop **Mémoire du Temps** (⌨540 555; www.memoryoftime.com; Byblos souq; ◷9am-6pm, till 8pm Jun-Aug), the second fossil shop on the left as you enter the souq coming from the the the entrance to the archaeological site. Fossils are priced from US$5 and climb to as much as US$5000; all come with a certificate of authentication and can be legally taken out of the country.

the terrace is lovely – consider coming for a sunset drink instead of dinner.

In summer, the Fishing Club runs an alfresco Italian restaurant, Hacienda de Pépé, in a courtyard garden around the corner.

Bab El Mina　　　　　　SEAFOOD $$
(⌨540 475; www.babelmina.com; Rue Pepe Abed; seafood mezze LL17,000-22,000, mains LL25,500-34,500; ◷noon-midnight) Boasting a lovely location overlooking the port, this terrace restaurant next to the Byblos Fishing Club specialises in seafood and offers a well-priced set menu of fish, French fries, hummus, salad and beer for LL82,500 for two people.

❶ Getting There & Away

Northbound buses from Beirut's Charles Helou bus station stop on the highway at the entrance. LCC bus 6 (LL1500, 50 minutes) and private minibuses (LL1500, 50 minutes) travel from the Dawra transport hub in Beirut and stop on Rue Jbail. The **taxi stand** is across the road from the Banque Libanaise pour le Commerce on Rue Jbail. Private taxis charge LL35,000 to Dawra and LL15,000 to Batroun.

NORTH LEBANON

POP 860,000

Batroun

⌨06

It may lack sprawling medieval souqs and handsome ancient ruins, but this small town between Byblos and Tripoli has a semi-somnolent and highly atmospheric old neighbourhood near the water that rewards leisurely exploration.

Founded by the Phoenician king Ithobaal 1, Batroun was a busy port in ancient times but was levelled by an earthquake and mudslides in AD 551. Many historians believe that the town's large natural harbour was formed at this time.

The majority of the town's residents are Christian and there are many historic churches to visit in the old town's narrow cobbled streets. The **tourist office** (⌨741 522; www.mot.gov.lb; Old Souq; ◷8am-4pm Mon-Sat Jun-Sep, 8am-2pm Mon-Thu & Sat, to 11am Fri Oct-May) is in the pretty souq immediately southeast of the harbour.

◉ Sights

Our Lady of the Sea　　　　　CHURCH
(Sadiyat al-Bahr) Overlooking the remains of a Phoenician sea wall, this simple Greek Orthodox church is built right on the water's edge, and has a charming terrace with an arched belvedere framing sea views. The small church has a vaulted ceiling and stone walls.

St Stephen's Church　　　　　CHURCH
Batroun's main Maronite church is set on a square right next to the harbour. The stone building with its arched entrance, decorated facade and square crenellated towers is quietly imposing and usually packed with worshippers on a Sunday.

St George's Church
CHURCH

The oldest and most interesting of the town's places of worship, this Byzantine-style Greek Orthodox church was built in 1826 and features a dome, vaulted stone ceiling and icon screen.

🛏 Sleeping & Eating

The town is surrounded by citrus groves, and lemonade is a local speciality. The best places to sample this are **Limonade Tony Daou** or **Chez Hilmi**, where the lemonade is made by rubbing lemons against each other rather than being pressed. The juice is then mixed with sugar and orange blossom water and served in a long glass. Both shops can be found on the main street.

⭐ **L'Auberge de la Mer** BOUTIQUE HOTEL $$$
(📞 06-740 824; www.laubergedelamer.com; r US$170-200, ste US$350) Tucked between the churches of St Stephen and St George and commanding wonderful sea views from its upper floors, this recently opened hotel is a delightful option for a romantic break. The individually decorated rooms are comfortable and elegant; some have sea-facing balconies. There's a magnificent vaulted foyer lounge, a breakfast room overlooking the harbour and a rooftop Jacuzzi.

⭐ **Chez Maguy** SEAFOOD $
(Chez Magie; 📞 03-439 147; mains from LL28,000; ⊙ noon-midnight) Unsigned and without an official address, this simple but much-loved seafood restaurant is located in an old fisherman's shack behind a rock near the Phoenician sea wall and has an idyllic terrace overlooking the water. The fish and seafood here is so fresh it's almost writhing, and owner Maguy al-Mouhawas knows how to cook it to perfection.

ℹ Getting There & Away

Tripoli-bound buses from Beirut's Charles Helou bus station will drop passengers on the main highway at the Batroun exit; the fare should cost between LL2500 and LL6000. From here, it's a relatively short walk to the harbour. Private taxis charge LL15,000 for the trip to Byblos and LL50,000 to the Dawra transport hub in Beirut.

Tripoli (Trablous) طرابلس
📞 06

Lebanon's second largest city is famous for its medieval Mamluk architecture, including a bustling and labyrinthine souq that

is considered the best in the country. It's also blessed with handsome examples of Crusader- and Ottoman-era architecture. The largely Sunni population is known for its piety, so bar-hopping and clubbing aren't on offer; fortunately, the city's justly famous sweets provide compensation (the local speciality is *haliwat al-jibn*, a teeth-jarringly sweet confection made from curd cheese and served with syrup).

Tripoli comprises two main areas: the city proper, which includes modern Tripoli and the Old City; and Al-Mina, the rather down-and-out port area, 3km west along the seafront. The geographical centre of town is Saahat et-Tall (pronounced 'at-tahl'), a large square by the clock tower.

The old city sprawls east of Saahat et-Tall, while the modern centre is west of the square, along Rue Fouad Chehab. The **tourist office** (📞 433 590; www.mot.gov.lb; ⊙ 8am-5pm Mon-Sat) is located on Abdel Hamid Karami Sq.

History

Tripoli was a thriving trading post as early as the 8th century BC thanks to the constant comings and goings of traders from Tyre, Sidon and Arwad (the latter in present-day Syria). Each community settled in its own area, a fact reflected in the city's name, which derives from the Greek word *tripolis*, meaning 'three cities'.

Conquered in turn by the Seleucids, Romans, Umayyads, Byzantines and Fatimids, the city was invaded by the Crusaders in AD 1102, who held on to it for 180 years and built its imposing, and still-standing, hilltop fortress, the Citadel of Raymond de Saint-Gilles. In 1289 the Mamluk Sultan Qalaun took control of the city, and embarked upon an ambitious building program; many of the mosques, souqs, madrassas and khans that remain in the old city today date from either the Crusader period or subsequent Sultan Qalaun era. The Turkish Ottomans took over the city in 1516 and ruled in relative peace until 1920, when it became part of the French mandate of Greater Lebanon.

With a large influx of Palestinian refugees from 1948 onward, the city became the site of ferocious fighting during the civil war. Huge UN-administered refugee camps still hug Tripoli's outskirts, including the Nahr el-Bared camp, now infamous for its protracted Palestinian/Lebanese army deadlock

ℹ SECURITY: TRIPOLI

When this book was being researched, Tripoli was the location of frequent armed clashes between locally based supporters and opponents of the Syrian government. These clashes were predominantly in the neighborhoods of Bab al-Tabbaneh and Jabal Mohsen, and had resulted in deaths, injuries and the intervention of the Lebanese Armed Forces. The Islamic State of Iraq and the Levant (ISIL), the Abdullah Azzam Brigades (AAB) and the al-Nusrah Front (ANF) were also active here, so the threat of terrorist attacks and kidnappings was ever-present. As a result, most foreign embassies were counselling their citizens not to enter the city.

in 2007, during which nearly 400 Palestinians and Lebanese soldiers died.

◉ Sights

Tripoli's major sight is its Crusader fortress, but visitors should be sure not to miss the compact Old City to the citadel's northwest. Dating from the Mamluk era (14th and 15th centuries), this area is a maze of narrow alleys, colourful souqs, hammams, khans, mosques and madrassas. It's a lively and fascinating place where craftspeople, including tailors, jewellers, soap makers and coppersmiths, continue to work as they have done for centuries. The Souq al-Sayyaghin (the gold souq), Souq al-Attarin (for perfumes and spices), the medieval Souq al-Haraj (Plaque 21) and Souq an-Nahhassin (the brass souq) are highlights.

Women should dress modestly in the Old City, and check with the custodian before entering mosques.

Citadel of Raymond de Saint-Gilles CASTLE
(admission LL7500; ⊙8am-sunset) Towering above Tripoli, this Crusader fortress was originally built during the period from 1103 to 1104. Burned down in 1297, it was partly rebuilt the following century by a Mamluk emir. Today its most impressive element is the imposing entrance with its moat and three gateways (one Ottoman, one Mamluk, one Crusader).

Great Mosque MOSQUE
Built on the site of a 12th-century Crusader cathedral and incorporating some of its

features, this mosque has a magnificent entrance and an unusual minaret that was probably once the cathedral bell tower.

Madrassas HISTORIC BUILDING
Located near the Great Mosque are two madrassas (religious schools). Opposite the mosque's northern entrance is the **Madrassa al-Nouriyat**, which has distinctive black-and-white stonework and a beautiful inlaid mihrab, and is still in use today. Attached to the eastern side of the Grand Mosque is the **Madrassa al-Qartawiyya**, converted between 1316 and 1326 from the former St Mary's church. Its elegant black-and-white facade and honeycomb-patterned half-dome above the portal are well worth a look.

Al-Muallaq Mosque MOSQUE
(Hanging Mosque) You have to glance up to see this small and unusual 14th-century mosque, which is on the 2nd floor of a building. Located just opposite is the **Hammam al-Jadid**, the city's best-preserved bathhouse, in use from around 1740 well into the 1970s. It has some lovely coloured glass windows.

Khan as-Saboun HISTORIC BUILDING
In the centre of the souq, the Khan as-Saboun (Soap Caravansaray) was built in the 16th century and first used as an army barracks; since then it has for generations functioned as a point of sale for Tripoli's famous soaps.

Khan al-Khayyatin HISTORIC BUILDING
One of the most beautiful buildings in the Old City, this khan was formerly a Crusader hospital and is today a beautifully restored 14th-century tailors' souq lined with small workshops.

Khan al-Misriyyin HISTORIC BUILDING
Believed to date from the 14th century when it was used by Egyptian merchants, this dilapidated khan is home to one of the city's most famous businesses, **Sharkass**. Making olive-oil soap since 1803, this family-run company produces good-quality, authentic Tripoli soap; you're welcome to buy a bar of natural or perfumed soap, or simply look around. Note that the shop is on the 1st floor (not the one with the same name on the ground).

Taynal Mosque MOSQUE
Standing on its own to the south of the souqs on the outskirts of the Old City but well worth the walk is this restored mosque.

Dating from 1336, it represents probably the most outstanding example of Islamic religious architecture in Tripoli.

Bcharré & the Qadisha Valley

بشرى & وادي قاديشا

◨ 06

The trip up to the mountain village of Bcharré takes you through some of the most beautiful scenery in Lebanon. The road winds along mountainous slopes, continuously gaining in altitude and offering spectacular views of the Qadisha Valley, a Unesco World Heritage–listed site that is home to isolated rock-cut monasteries, wildflowers and plenty of wildlife. Red-roofed villages perch atop hills or cling precariously to the mountainsides; the Qadisha River, with its source just below the Cedars ski resort, runs along the valley bottom; and Lebanon's highest peak, Qornet as-Sawda (3090m), soars overhead. With plentiful opportunities for hiking quiet valley trails or scaling isolated mountain landscapes, this is the perfect antidote to the urban mayhem of Beirut.

Bcharré is the only settlement of any size in the area, and is particularly famous as the birthplace of the artist and poet Khalil Gibran. Outside the ski season (when the Cedars resort, further up the mountain road, should be your winter sports base), it's an excellent base for those hiking in the Qadisha Valley.

◉ Sights & Activities

Bcharré's little town centre is dominated by the St Saba Church in the main square, Place Mar Sea.

Gibran Museum   MUSEUM
(☑ 671 137; www.gibrankhalilgibran.org; adult/student LL8000/5000; ⊙ 10am-6pm Tue-Sun Mar-Nov, to 5pm Nov-Mar) According to his wishes, the body of poet and artist Khalil Gibran (1883–1931), author of the much-loved *The Prophet* (1923), was interred in the chapel of this 19th-century monastery built into the rocky slopes of a hill on the eastern outskirts of the town. Now a museum, the monastery building houses a large collection of Gibran's paintings, drawings and gouaches. It's popular with devotees of *The Prophet,* but of little interest for those who haven't read and admired his masterwork.

Stairs behind the museum lead to the site of some Phoenician tombs.

Qadisha Grotto   CAVE
(☑ 03-568   251;   admission   adult/child LL5000/2000; ⊙ 9.30am-sunset, closed mid-Dec–mid-May) Extending around 500m into the mountain, this small grotto contains some impressive limestone formations. Though not as spectacular as Jeita Grotto, its evocative setting makes it worth a visit. The grotto is a 7km walk or drive from Bcharré off the road to Cedars resort; follow the signs to L'Aiglon Hotel and then take the concrete footpath opposite (look for the 'Entree

---

BATROUN WINE REGION

There are two major winemaking regions in Lebanon: the Bekaa Valley, home to well-established names including Chateau Ksara, Chateau Kefraya and Domaine Wardy; and the up-and-coming Batroun region in the mountains above the coastal town of the same name. There are a number of organic wineries in this area, including three that welcome visitors.

Chateau Sanctus (www.chateausanctuslebanon.com) A boutique winery on 4 hectares in Marmama, this organic operation welcomes visitors to its vineyard and winery on weekends in spring and summer. Book ahead via email.

Coteaux de Botrys (☑ 03 238 937; www.coteauxdebotrys.com; Main Rd, Edde; ⊙ tastings 10am-noon Sat) Overlooking Batroun and the Mediterranean, this winery in Edde opens its 300-year-old farmhouse for tastings on Saturday. Bookings are essential (call between 9am and 3pm Monday to Friday).

IXSIR (☑ restaurant 71 773 770, tours 71 631 613; www.ixsir.com.lb; Basbina; ⊙ 9am-4pm Tue-Sun, to 1pm Wed) Producing a range of wines made with grapes from its three vineyards (one at Basbina in the hills above Batroun, one in Jezzine and another in the Bekaa Valley), IXSIR is rapidly developing a reputation as one of the country's most impressive wine operations. Its stylish and environmentally sustainable winery at Basbina is open for tours and tasting, or you can have lunch at its Nicolas Audi à la Maison d'IXSIR restaurant – call ahead to book a table or tour.

Grotte Kadicha' sign). It's then a 1.5km walk to the grotto. A simple restaurant operates here in summer.

🛏 Sleeping & Eating

Tiger House
HOSTEL **$**

(📞672 480; tigerhousepension@hotmail.com; Rue Cedre; dm US$10, d/tr US$40/50) On the high road out towards the Cedars ski resort, this is an extremely basic option offering little privacy but a warm welcome. You'll sleep in uncomfortable bunks or beds, or on a matress on the floor. No heating, cooling, wifi or communal kitchen, although simple meals are available. Breakfast costs LL6000.

Hotel Chbat
HOTEL **$$**

(📞03 292 494, 671 270; www.hotelchbat.net; Rue Gibran, Bcharré; s/d/tr US$95/115/145; P🛜) Genial owner Wadih Chbat loves helping his guests to take skiing lessons, trek through the valley and visit the local monasteries. Rooms at his sprawling and old-fashioned chalet-style hotel are clean but in need of refurbishment; public areas include a a welcoming lounge with pot-belly stove and a terrace restaurant. Wifi is in the lobby only.

La Montagnard
INTERNATIONAL **$$**

(📞672 222; Main St, Bcharré; meals LL6000-28,000; ⏰11am-last customer) Situated on the street directly below the Hotel Chbat, this bar and restaurant succeeds in channeling a rustic mountain theme, with wooden furniture and a fireplace being the decorative focus. The menu is dominated by snacks and comfort food (subs, pastas, burgers, pizzas).

❶ Getting There & Away

The **minibus office** (📞671 108) is located next to the St Saba Church. Buses travel from the Dawra transport hub in Beirut 10-12 times daily between 7.30am and 7.30pm, and from Bcharré to Dawra between 4.30am and 4.30pm. Tickets cost between LL7000 and LL10,000, depending on individual drivers. At Dawra, you'll need to go to the Abou Artine gas station near the Armenian statue to buy a ticket.

The Cedars
الأرز

📅06

One of Lebanon's most attractive ski resorts, the Cedars is also its oldest and most European in feel. The village takes its name from one of the country's few remaining groves of cedar

---

QADISHA VALLEY MONASTERIES

The soaring rocky hillsides and secluded floor of the Qadisha Valley are home to historic Maronite monasteries, grottoes, hermitages and chapels that are atmospheric stops when hiking through the area. The main route into the valley is via a winding road, and one of the most important monasteries, Deir Mar Elisha (St Élisée, St Eliseus; ⏰9am-sunset) FREE, can be accessed by car and now functions as a museum. Hewn out of the rock face, its centrepiece is a vaulted 19th-century church that houses an 8th-century icon of St Elisha. From here, it's a 5km (1½ to two-hour) walk to the serene still-working convent of Deir Qannoubin, probably the oldest religious community in the valley (some sources date the building to as early as the 4th century AD). The permanent residence of the Maronite Patriarchs between 1440 and 1790, its church features a fresco of the Coronation of the Virgin being witnessed by a group of patriarchs. Also here is the Chapel of Mar Marina, a hermit and patriarch who legend tells us was unmasked as a female after finding an abandoned baby and saving it by breast-feeding it herself. Mothers unable to produce breast milk sometimes make the pilgrimage here to plead for the saint's intervention.

Those who don't have the time and energy to walk between Deir Mar Elisha and Deir Qannoubin should be able to organise a ride in the all-terrain 4WD that are parked outside the restaurant next to the stream on the valley floor. The drivers usually charge around LL20,000 per person.

Other monasteries that can be visited include the 12th-century Deir Mar Semaan (St Simon's Hermitage) in the southern section of the valley; and the 13th-century Saydet Hawqa (Our Lady of Hawqa) and working monastery of Deir Mar Antonios Qozhaya near the village of Hawqa in the northern section of the valley. The latter was the Maronite see in the 12th century.

For a list of trekking guides working in the Qadisha Valley, see the 'Hike the LMT' section of the Lebanon Mountain Trail (www.lebanontrail.org) website.

---

trees, which stands on the right-hand side of the road as you head up towards the ski lifts. A few of these slow-growing trees are thought to be approaching 1500 years old, and fall under the protection of the Patriarch of Lebanon, who holds a festival here each August.

Since the trees are protected, the area can only be explored on marked trails (open 9am to 6pm between May and November; admission by donation).

The ski season takes place here from around December to April, depending on snow conditions, and there are currently six lifts in operation. Equipment can be rented from a number of small ski shops at the base of the lifts, coming in at between US$5 and US$15 per day. Snowmobile hire costs US$60 per hour. An adult day pass to the slopes costs US$30 on weekdays and US$40 at weekends. Beginners can use the baby slope and lift at Sami's Ski School & Shop for US$25 per day, including equipment; lessons cost US$20 per hour.

For more information about skiing in Lebanon, contact Ski Lebanon (☑09-231 611; www.skileb.com) for packages, trips and accommodation bookings.

🛏 Sleeping & Eating

There's a good sweep of accommodation for all budgets at the Cedars, with great off-season discounts if you're here in summer for hiking. Check, too, about midweek rates during winter, which are usually substantially cheaper than weekend prices. There aren't many dedicated restaurants in town, as most people eat at their hotels after a day on the slopes.

Hotel Cedrus HOTEL $$$
(☑678777; www.cedrushotel.com; s/d US$195/230, f US$255, ste US$310-470; P ❋ @ 🐱) If you plan to stay at the Cedars, this is the most comfortable option on offer. On the main street, and with the popular Le Pichet bar-restaurant on the ground floor, it offers 22 large, attractive and well-maintained rooms with mountain views. Prices are 20% cheaper on weekdays and even cheaper than that outside the ski season.

Le Pichet RESTAURANT, BAR $$
(☑678777; www.cedrushotel.com; mezze LL7000-13,000, mains LL15,000-40,000; ⊙9am-11pm) The restaurant at Hotel Cedrus is the best at The Cedars, offering everything from fondue (LL77,000 for two persons) to burgers, pas-

tas and Levantine mezze and grills. The bar tends to stay open later on weekends.

❶ Getting There & Away

The Cedars is 5km southeast of Bcharré. A taxi between Bcharré and the Cedars costs around LL20,000; during the ski season it is sometimes possible to take a servees (LL8000). Both leave from in front of St Saba Church.

SOUTH LEBANON
POP 768,000

Sidon (Saida) صيدا
☑07

Set amid thick citrus and banana groves, this port town 45km south of Beirut was once a rich and flourishing Phoenician city, with tight trade links to ancient Egypt and a globally renowned glass-making industry. These days it's best known for its fresh fruit and sweets (the local speciality is a crumbly cookie called *senioura*).

Traces of Sidon's rich history can still be found all over town, with many ancient remnants in the Old City. Unlike pretty Byblos to the north, Sidon makes few concessions to tourists: here, the history is very much part of everyday life, and while this means that options for accommodation and eating out are fairly limited, it also offers a stronger sense of DIY exploration than some of Lebanon's busier destinations. The small tourist office is open in the high season only.

The local Sunni population is conservative, so dress and behave accordingly.

⦿ Sights

Old Sidon, a fascinating labyrinth of vaulted souqs, tiny alleyways and medieval remnants, stretches out behind the buildings fronting the harbour. Officially, there are 60 listed historic sights here.

In the souqs you'll find craftspeople plying the same trades their ancestors have perfected over centuries. There are plenty of opportunities to pick up local produce such as fragrant orange-blossom water (good in both sweet and savoury cooking, or as a cordial for summer drinks).

With the exception of the Sea Castle, all of the city's sights are free to visit. However, opening hours can be a little erratic: if a place is closed, it pays to ask around since someone will probably be able to tell you where the key holder is to be found.

Sea Castle
CASTLE

(Qasr al-Bahr; adult/child under 10 LL4000/free; ⏲ 9am-sunset) Erected in 1228 by the Crusaders, this castle sits on a small island that was formerly the site of a temple dedicated to Melkart, the Phoenician version of Hercules, and is connected to the mainland by a fortified stone causeway. Largely destroyed by the Mamluks to prevent the Crusaders returning to the region, it was renovated by Fakhreddine in the 17th century. On calm days, you can see numerous broken rose granite columns lying on the surrounding sea floor.

Khan el-Franj
KHAN

(Inn of the Foreigners; ⏲ 8am-10pm) FREE A highlight of the souq area is the Khan el-Franj, the most beautiful and best preserved of all the limestone khans built by Fakhreddine (Fakhr ad-Din al-Maan II) in the 17th century. Wonderfully restored courtesy of the Hariri Foundation (www.hariri-foundation.org), it consists of vaulted arcades surrounding a large rectangular courtyard with a central fountain, and now houses Sidon's tourist office and the ateliers of some craftspeople.

Palace Debbané
HISTORIC BUILDING

(📋 720 110; www.museumsaida.org; Al-Moutran St; ⏲ 9am-6pm Sat-Thu) FREE Entered from the souq via a tall staircase marked with a sign, this former Ottoman aristocrat's building built in 1721 has intricate Mamluk decoration, including tile work and cedar wood ceilings, and various historical exhibits.

Omari Mosque
MOSQUE

(Port Rd) Facing the northern tip of the harbour, the Omari (Great) Mosque is said to be one of the finest examples of Islamic religious architecture of the 13th century, and was originally converted from a fortified Knights Hospitaller structure. It's open to non-Muslims outside prayer times.

Musée du Savon
MUSEUM

(Soap Museum; 📋 733 353; Rue al-Moutran; ⏲ 9am-5pm Sat-Thu) FREE Located in an old soap factory dating from the 17th century, this is Lebanon's only museum of that most humble yet indispensable of products. Well laid-out, with trilingual explanations (Arabic, English, French) on the art of 'saponification' (which we nonsaponifiers might simply call 'soap-making'), the museum also has a stylish cafe and a boutique with some lovely illustrated history and cookery books. Both entry and guides are free.

Bab as-Saray Mosque
MOSQUE

Just behind the Khan el-Franj, the Bab as-Saray Mosque is the oldest in Sidon, dating from 1201, and is filled with beautiful stonework. It may not always be open to non-Muslims, so check before entering.

ⓘ Getting There & Away

Minibuses (LL3000; 30 to 45 minutes) and service taxis (LL5000) from Beirut to Sidon sometimes leave from the Cola transport hub, but are more likely to travel to/from Sahraa Square, between Cola and the airport. There are also minibuses (LL2000, 50 minutes) and service taxis (LL5000) between Sidon and Tyre.

ⓘ SECURITY: SOUTH LEBANON

With a tragic history marred by frequent Israeli incursions and local sectarian fighting, South Lebanon has been subjected to more violence and disruption than any other region since the early days of the civil war. Unfortunately, this continues to the present day.

At the time of research (soon after the Israel-Hamas War of 2014), rocket attacks from southern Lebanon into Israel were occurring regularly and Israel was sometimes responding with artillery fire. These events can happen without warning. Tension in Sidon between Sunnis and Shiites had triggered violent confrontations, and most foreign embassies were advising their citizens to avoid both Sidon and all areas south of the Litani River, with the exception of the city of Tyre. Before heading this way, check with your embassy as to the current security situation.

While travelling here, don't venture too far off the main roads between Sidon and Tyre. The land itself is still littered with unexploded mines and cluster bombs, so it's definitely not the place to set off on any kind of hike. To date, more than 40 civilians have been killed and more than 300 injured by unexploded ordnance.

RESISTANCE TOURIST LANDMARK, MLEETA

An intriguing mix of memorial, museum and theme park, this **resistance monument** (📞70 076 060; www.mleeta.com; admission LL2000; ⊙9am-sunset) at Mleeta, on Mt A'mel near Nabatieh, has been established to celebrate Hezbollah's fight against the Israeli occupation of Lebanon from 1982 to 2000. This bleak but strategically important mountaintop, which is covered in oak trees and rocky caves, was one of the spots where Hezbollah resistance fighters were garrisoned during the occupation and visitors can follow paths that the fighters took through the forest, enter the tunnel system where they sheltered, and admire the views from their lookout points. There are two main exhibits: 'The Abyss', a huge pit filled with armoured vehicles and weapons abandoned by the Israelis; and a multipurpose space where a rousing film about the occupation and resistance is screened.

There's nothing balanced about the historical narrative being recounted here. Some visitors will find the whole set-up problematic, others will find the insight that it offers into the Hezbollah psyche fascinating. All are likely to agree that there's nothing else in Lebanon quite like it. Guides (free) speak Arabic, French, English, German and Farsi.

Mleeta is an 82km (approximately 90 minute) drive southeast of Beirut, via Sidon. Tyre is another 50km (one hour) south. You'll need a car to get here, as there is no public transport. Allow two hours for your visit.

Temple of Echmoun   معبد أشمون

About 3km northeast of Sidon, the **Temple of Echmoun** (Bustan al-Sheikh; ⊙8am-dusk) FREE is Lebanon's only Phoenician site boasting more than mere foundations. Today it contains the remains of temples and shops, as well as some interesting albeit damaged mosaics.

Begun in the 7th century BC, the temple complex was devoted to Echmoun, god of the city of Sidon, and other buildings were later added by the Persians, Romans and Byzantines. Today the highlight of the site is undoubtedly the throne of Astarte, flanked by two winged sphinxes.

From Sidon you can take a taxi (LL10,000) or minibus (LL1000) to the turn-off on the highway at the fun fair, then walk right (east) along the orchard-lined road to the ruins (approximately 1.5km). Although admission is free, it is polite to tip the volunteer caretaker LL5000.

Tyre (Sour)   صور

📞07

The fact that this predominantly Shiite town is the power base of Hezbollah's Secretary-General Hassan Nasrallah is only one of its claims to fame – it also boasts a proud Phoenician past, wonderful seaside location, Roman ruins and a medieval souq. Home to the UN Interim Force in Lebanon (UNIFIL), it also has good beaches and a decent array of hotels, making it a popular holiday destination for Beirutis.

Tyre's origins date back to its foundation in approximately 2750 BC, after which it was ruled by the Egyptians and then the famous King Hiram, under whom it prospered. Later colonised variously by the Assyrians, Neo-Babylonians, Greeks, Seleucids, Romans, Byzantines, Arabs, Crusaders, Mamluks and Ottomans, the settlement began to languish from the 13th century onwards and, despite many attempts, never quite recovered its former glory.

◉ Sights

The old part of Tyre lies on the peninsula jutting out into the sea. The modern town is on the left-hand side as you arrive from Beirut. Behind the port is the Christian quarter, with its tiny alleys and old houses with shaded courtyards.

In 1984 Tyre was declared a Unesco World Heritage site, and its archaeological remains are divided into three parts: Al-Mina (Areas 1 and 2) on the south side of the city, Al-Bass (Area 3) on the original mainland section, and a medieval site in the centre of town.

Al-Mina
Archaeological Site   ARCHAEOLOGICAL SITE

(📞740 115; Areas 1 & 2; adult/student/child LL6000/3000/1000; ⊙8.30am-30min before sunset) Dating to the 3rd millennium BC,

Tyre (Sour)

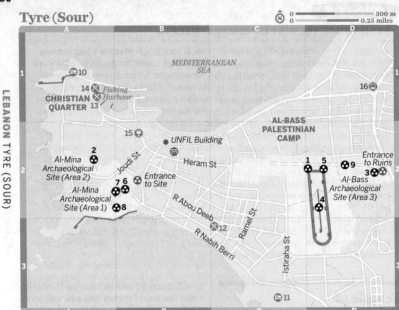

Tyre (Sour)

⊙ Sights

1 Aqueducts	D2
2 Crusader Cathedral	A2
3 Funerary Complex	D2
4 Hippodrome	D2
5 Monumental Archway	D2
6 Mosaic Street	B2
7 Rectangular Arena	B2
8 Roman Bathhouse	B2
9 Roman Road	D2

🛏 Sleeping

10 Hotel al-Fanar	A1

11 Rest House	C3

✖ Eating

12 Abou Deeb	C3
13 Chez Tony	A1
14 Le Phénicien	A1
Restaurant al-Fanar	(see 10)

🍷 Drinking & Nightlife

15 Diver's Inn	B2

ℹ Transport

16 Minibuses to Sidon & Beirut	D1

these atmospheric ruins cover a large area leading down to an ancient submerged harbour. Highlights include a street paved with geometrical Roman and Byzantine mosaics, on each side of which are rows of large columns. Look out also for the unusually large public Roman bathhouse from the 2nd or 3rd century AD and a 4th-century rectangular arena that would have held up to 2000 spectators, perhaps to watch some sort of ancient water sport.

A five-minute walk north of the main Al-Mina site brings you to the ruins of a 12th-century Crusader cathedral, along with a network of Roman and Byzantine roads.

Al-Bass
Archaeological Site ARCHAEOLOGICAL SITE
(☏740 530; Area 3; adult/student/child LL6000/3000/1000; ⊙8.30am-30min before sunset) This sprawling site lies 2km east of the Al-Mina site. Just past the entrance is a vast funerary complex, with hundreds of ornate stone and marble sarcophagi. Next to it, a well-preserved Roman road stretches for about 1.6km from an impressive 20m-high monumental archway that probably dates from the time of Emperor

Hadrian (2nd century AD). Beyond the archway is a large and well-preserved Roman **hippodrome** built in the 2nd century AD; this once held more than 20,000 spectators.

🛏 Sleeping

Hotel al-Fanar HOTEL **$$**
(☏741 111; www.alfanarresort.com; Rachid Nakle St; s/d US$70/100; ⚙🕏) With its toes almost in the water, this hotel's location next to Tyre's small white *fanar* (lighthouse) is its principal draw. Family run, it's in need of renovation but is clean and offers some rooms with excellent sea views. There's a gorgeous waterside terrace, as well as two restaurants.

Rest House HOTEL **$$$**
(☏742 000; www.resthouse-tyr.com.lb; Istiraha St; r US$155-190, ste US$210-220; ⚙@🕏🏊) A true resort, this huge place near the Al-Bass Archaeological Site has its own expansive stretch of sandy beach plus a huge pool, gym, restaurant, summer-only beach cafe and landscaped gardens. The tiled rooms have ochre-coloured walls, small patios or balconies, large beds, work desks and good bathrooms. Significant low-season discounts apply.

🍴 Eating & Drinking

There are a few fast-food places at the roundabout on Rue Abou Deeb, including the large and very popular **Abou Deeb** (⊘8am-late), which serves good felafels and shwarmas.

Chez Tony SEAFOOD **$$**
(☏70 108 641; salads LL6000, fish LL20000-25,000; ⊘9am-midnight) At first glance, this simple place opposite the port doesn't appear to offer much to the diner. But after sampling Tony's ultra-fresh fish and shrimps, you're sure to become an instant devotee. Dine on whatever is freshest, accompanied by a salad, bowl of hummus and ice-cold beer, and you'll leave happy and replete.

Restaurant al-Fanar RESTAURANT **$$**
(☏741 111; www.alfanarresort.com; Rachid Nakle St; pub mains LL10,000-35,000, sushi per piece LL1500-6000; ⊘pub 10am-late, sushi restaurant 4-11.30pm Tue-Thu, from 2pm Fri & Sat) The Hotel al-Fanar plays host to both a pub and a sushi restaurant. The terrace outside the pub is a great choice for a late-afternoon drink.

Le Phénicien SEAFOOD **$$$**
(☏740 564; Old Port; mezze LL5500-20,000, fish priced by kg; ⊘11am-11pm) Also known locally as 'Hadeed', this place is widely considered the best in town for its fresh fish, which is served fried or grilled. A pleasant outdoor terrace overlooks the fishing harbour – book ahead to score a seat here in summer or on weekends through the year.

Diver's Inn PUB, RESTAURANT
(☏03-359 687; Old Port; mains LL20,000-30,000; ⊘noon-late) A particularly good winter choice, this laid-back pub-restaurant in a vaulted space near the souq serves fish and steaks and is a great spot to meet up with locals, particularly if there's a football match on the TV.

ℹ Getting There & Away

Minibuses (LL5000, one to 1½ hours) travel between Tyre and Sahraa Square or the Cola transport hub in Beirut, stopping en route in Sidon (LL2000, 50 minutes). *Servees* charge LL10,000 to Beirut, LL5000 to Sidon.

CHOUF MOUNTAINS جبال الشوف

The southernmost part of the Mt Lebanon Range, this mountainous region southeast of Beirut is wild and isolated in some parts, covered with small villages and terraced agricultural plots in others. It's an easily reached and pleasant place for a day or two's exploration.

Beiteddine Palace (Beit ad-Din) بيت الدين

One of the highlights of the Chouf mountains is the early 19th-century **Beiteddine Palace** (Beit ad-Din; adult/student/child LL10,000/7000/3000; ⊘9am-5pm Tue-Sun Apr-Oct, to 3pm Nov-May), located in the otherwise unexceptional Beiteddine village around 50km southeast of Beirut.

Sitting majestically on a hill surrounded by terraced gardens and orchards, Beiteddine Palace was built over a period of 30 years in the early 19th century by Emir Bashir Chehab II, Ottoman-appointed governor of the region. Its name means 'House of Faith', acknowledging the older Druze hermitage that originally occupied the site. During the French mandate the palace was used for local administration, and after 1930 it was declared a historic monument. In 1943 Lebanon's first president after independence declared it his summer residence. The palace was extensively damaged during the Israeli invasion; it's estimated that up to 90% of the original contents were lost during this time. When fighting ended in 1984, the site was claimed by the Druze militia, and Walid Jumblatt, the Druze leader, ordered its restoration. In 1999 the Druze returned it to the government.

Although conceived by Italian architects, the palace incorporates many traditional forms of Arab architecture. The main gate opens onto a 60m-wide **outer courtyard** (Dar al-Baraniyyeh) that's walled on three sides only; the fourth side has views over the surrounding valleys and hills.

A double staircase on the outer courtyard's western side leads into a smaller **central courtyard** (Dar al-Wousta) with a fountain. Beyond this courtyard (accessed from its northern side) is the third – and last – **inner courtyard** (Dar al-Harim). This was the centre of the family quarters, and incorporates a beautiful **hammam** and huge kitchens.

Underneath the Dar al-Wousta (accessed via a doorway near the staircase) are the former stables, now home to an outstanding collection of 5th- and 6th-century **Byzantine mosaics**. Found at Jiyyeh, 30km south of Beirut, they were brought by Walid Jum-

blatt to Beiteddine in 1982. Whatever you do, don't miss them: they're truly stunning.

During June, July and August, the palace hosts a well-known annual **arts festival** (www.beiteddine.org). Check the festival website for full details.

🛏 Sleeping & Eating

The only food options in Beiteddine are a few snack bars. You'll need to eat at the nearby Mir Amin Palace or bring a picnic with you to eat in the palace garden beside the beautiful open-air mosaics.

Mir Amin Palace   HOTEL $$$
(☎ 05-501 315; www.miraminpalace.com; s/d from US$275/300; ❋ @ ⚅ ❄) Wealthy Beirutis in search of fresh air dominate the guest list at this elegant place. Built in the 19th century, it opened as a hotel in the 1970s and has been well maintained – though not noticeably refurbished – since then. All of the rooms are large, but the executive doubles and Imperial Suite are the pick of the bunch.

Common areas include an indoor restaurant, a lounge where you can enjoy a coffee and nargileh, a huge swimming pool and a summer-only terrace restaurant that is known for its Sunday lunch buffet (US$44). Note that the hotel is always fully booked over July and August – book well in advance if you are planning to visit at this time.

WORTH A TRIP

A FOODIE OUTING

Ask any Lebanese foodie to nominate their top choice for a weekend culinary adventure and they are likely to nominate **Tawlet Ammiq** (☎ 03 004 481; www.soukeltayeb.com; Ammiq Old Village, West Bekaa; set lunch US$40; ⊙1-4pm Sat & Sun Apr-Nov; P 🖉) 🍴, the Bekaa Valley branch of Souk el Tayeb, a Beirut-based outfit that runs a farmers market highlighting rural produce as well as a hugely popular restaurant where a constantly changing cast of cooks from across the country showcase their regional culinary traditions.

Set in the fertile Western Bekaa Valley bordering the Ammiq Wetlands (part of the Shouf Biosphere Reserve), Tawlet Ammiq gives local producers the opportunity to showcase their traditions, crops and techniques. It also acts as a test kitchen where local cooks are rediscovering and refining traditional recipes and customs.

Weekend lunches here are leisurely affairs, with diners choosing from a buffet piled high with delicacies. Those in the know arrive mid-morning to sample fresh manakeesh cooked on a saj (metal dome over coals) in the garden and then often zip off to enjoy a wine-tasting at nearby **Chateau Kefraya** (www.chateaukefraya.com; ⊙guided tours 10am-6pm) before returning for lunch. Seating is outside in warm weather, and around a pot-belly stove inside when the weather is cool.

The restaurant building is a model of sustainable design, and has sweeping views of the valley. You'll need a car to get here, as there is no public transport. It's 28km southwest of Chtaura.

ⓘ Getting There & Away

Minibuses ('Chouf Buses') from Beirut's Cola transport hub can drop passengers at Douwwar, which is within walking distance of Beiteddine (LL5000, two hours, every 30 minutes between 7.30am and 4pm). Taxis waiting there can take you to Deir al-Qamar, wait while you explore there and then bring you back to the palace (US$40). Alternatively, it's a picturesque but hilly one-hour walk between Deir al-Qamar and the palace.

A taxi will charge around US$125 to take you from Beirut to Deir al-Qamar and Beiteddine, wait while you explore both, and then return you to Beirut.

Deir al-Qamar دير القمر

📷 05

A pretty mountain village a few kilometres from Beiteddine, Deir al-Qamar ('Convent of the Moon') was the seat of Lebanon's emirates during the 17th and 18th centuries, and retains a number of handsome buildings from this time.

⊙ Sights

Main Square SQUARE
The main square is a showcase of fine Arab architecture, including the **Mosque of Emir Fakhreddine Maan**, built in 1493, and, behind it, a **cobbler's souq** housing shops and cafes. Above and behind the souq is a **silk khan** built in 1595 that now houses a French Cultural Centre. Nearby are handsome buildings that once housed a **Jesuit school** and a **synagogue**, as well as the **Palace of the poet Nicolas el-Turq**, which has a cafe on its ground floor.

Serail of Youssef Chehab HISTORIC BUILDING
(Palais de Justice; ⊙9am-5pm Mon-Fri) On the main street opposite the main square is this 18th-century palace, which now serves as the town hall (look for the two carved lions above the doorway, which represent justice). The entrance leads to an attractive courtyard off which there is an apartment with wooden panelling, domed ceiling and a window offering views over the valley.

Behind this building are steep and narrow cobbled streets, honey-hued stone houses and two churches: the 17th-century **Our Lady of the Rosary** and the 18th-century **Church of St Elie**.

🛏 Sleeping & Eating

La Bastide B&B $$
(📷505 320; s/d US$80/120; 🅿🛜) A large house around 1km from Deir al-Qamar on the road towards Beiteddine, this place has 15 old-fashioned rooms with small kitchenettes and mountain views. There's a small communal lounge with TV upstairs – the elderly French manager uses the formal lounge downstairs.

Al-Midane CAFE $
(Main Square; sandwiches & burgers LL9000-15,500, pizzas LL12,000; ⊙10am-10pm, closed Mon in winter & open to 3am in high summer) Popular with locals and tourists alike, this cafe in the cobbler's souq has an attractive outdoor terrace and is a great spot to linger over a light meal or coffee. The friendly Canadian-Lebanese owner is proud of his town and knowlegeable about its history – he'll happily supply sightseeing tips.

ⓘ Getting There & Away

There is no public transport to or from Deir al-Qamar.

Shouf Biosphere Reserve محميّة ارز الشوف

The largest of Lebanon's three natural protectorates, the **Shouf Biosphere Reserve** (📷05-350 250, 05-350 150; www.shoufcedar. org; admission LL7000; ⊙10am-6pm Jun-Sep, to 3.30pm Oct-May) comprises an incredible 5% of Lebanon's total land area, is the largest natural cedar reserve in the country, and has over 250km of hiking trails. Within it are ancient rock-cut fortress remains as well as six of the country's last remaining cedar forests, some with trees thought to be around 2000 years old. More than 200 species of birds and mammals (including wolves, gazelles and wild boar) inhabit or regularly pass through the area. The reserve incorporates the **Ammiq Wetland**, a remnant of the extensive marshes and lakes that once covered parts of the Bekaa Valley. The last significant wetland in Lebanon, it's an important staging and wintering area for migratory water birds en route between Europe and Africa.

There are four main entrances (Ain Zhalta, Barouk, Maasser and Niha) where you will find ranger huts with restrooms – you should be able to negotiate to hire a hiking guide at each of these, or obtain information about hiking trails. Those wanting to overnight in the reserve should check the website for details of the reserve's guesthouses.

You'll need private transport to get here.

BEKAA VALLEY وادي البقاع

POP 562,000

The fertile, pastoral Bekaa Valley is famous for its magnificent archaeological sites at Baalbek and Aanjar, and infamous for being the homeland of Hezbollah (Party of God), along with crops of 'Red Leb' (high-quality cannabis). Heavily cultivated over millennia (the valley was one of Rome's breadbaskets), it's actually a high plateau between the Mt Lebanon and Jebel Libnan ash-Sharqiyya (Anti-Lebanon) ranges. Though less agriculturally productive than in centuries past, due to a combination of deforestation and poor crop planning, its plentiful vineyards have gained an international reputation for their wines. Though you'll see Hezbollah's yellow flag fluttering around Baalbek, you'll find the locals (a mixture of Christians and Shiites) a welcoming lot and the attractions of the valley as intoxicating as its vintages.

Baalbek بعلبك

♪ 08

Known as the Heliopolis or 'Sun City' of the ancient world, Baalbek's ruins comprise the most impressive ancient site in Lebanon and are arguably the best preserved in the Middle East. The temples here, which were built on an extravagant scale, have enjoyed a stellar reputation throughout the centuries yet still manage to maintain the appealing air of an undiscovered wonder due to their semi-rural setting. The town itself, which is 86km northeast of Beirut, is the administrative headquarters for both the Bekaa Valley and the Hezbollah party. Whenever the political situation allows, it hosts the annual **Baalbek International Festival** (www.baalbek.org.lb).

◉ Sights

Baalbek Ruins ARCHAEOLOGICAL SITE
(♪370 645; adult/student/child under 8 LL15,000/5000/free; ⊙8.30am-30min before sunset) The highlights of this stupendous site are its three temples: the **Temple of Jupiter**, completed around 60 AD; the **Temple of Bacchus**, known in Roman times as the 'small temple' and completed around AD 150; and the much smaller **Temple of Venus**, opposite the main temple complex.

The Temple of Jupiter was built on an immense substructure over 90m long, and was approached by another monumental stair-

❶ SECURITY: BEKAA VALLEY & BAALBEK

The Bekaa Valley is Hezbollah's heartland, but at the time of research the Islamic State of Iraq and the Levant (ISIL) and al-Nusrah Front (ANF) were starting to be active around Baalbek and all along the border with Syria, making the threat of factional violence very real. There's also a long history of foreigners being kidnapped here. Before travelling, check the security situation with your embassy and in the Lebanese press.

case that rose high above the surrounding buildings. It consisted of a cellar in which the statue of the god was housed and a surrounding portico of 10 columns along the facade and 19 columns along the side, making for 54 columns in all. These columns are the largest in the world – 22.9m high with a girth of 2.2m. Today only six of these remain standing with the architrave still in position.

The Temple of Bacchus is often described as the most beautifully decorated temple in the Roman world, and is in an excellent state of preservation. The portico has eight columns along the facade and 15 along the sides, supporting a rich entablature and a ceiling of curved stone that is decorated with vivid scenes: Mars; a winged Victory; Diana taking an arrow from her quiver; Tyche with a cornucopia; Vulcan with his hammer; Bacchus; and Ceres holding a sheaf of corn.

Near the main ruins is the exquisite Temple of Venus, a circular building with fluted columns. During the early Christian era this was turned into a basilica and dedicated to St Barbara (who joined the saintly ranks when her pagan father tried to kill her for converting to Christianity – he got his comeuppance when a bolt of lightning reduced him to a smouldering heap).

Aanjar عنجر

♪ 08

The best-preserved Islamic archaeological site in Lebanon, Aanjar's 1300-year-old **Umayyad City** (adult/child LL6000/1500; ⊙8am-sunset) comprises the remains of a walled settlement, discovered by accident in the 1940s by archaeologists who were digging down for something else entirely.

The Umayyads ruled briefly but energetically from AD 660 to 750, and Aanjar is thought to have been built as a commercial centre or strategic outpost by their sixth Umayyad caliph, Walid I (r 705–15), meaning that the whole site might have been inhabited for as little as 50 years. The walled and fortified city was built along symmetrical Roman lines; the layout is in four equal quarters, separated by two 20m-wide avenues, the cardo maximus and the decumanus maximus. There is a tetrapylon, a four-column structure, where the two streets intersect, built in alternating layers of large blocks and narrow bricks, a Roman-type structure built in a typically Byzantine style.

In the city's heyday, its main streets were flanked by palaces, baths, mosques, shops (600 have been uncovered) and dwellings. Perhaps the most striking of all remains are those of the great palace, one wall and several arcades of which have been reconstructed.

UNDERSTAND LEBANON

Lebanon Today

Pity the poor Lebanese, who, after having lived through a bloody and protracted civil war and equally bloody and protracted invasions by Israel, were, at the time of research, being drawn into the sectarian violence unfolding in neighbouring Syria. With 1.3 million Syrian refugees joining the already significant number of Palestinian refugees

seeking refuge in Lebanon, the country's infrastructure and economy were breaking down, and the social fabric was being rent – the Lebanese are a deeply hospitable and generous people, but the sheer number of people needing support was draining their patience and pockets. Resentment was building, and was occasionally being manifested in sectarian violence.

The country's political system was also in disarray and machinery of government was often paralysed. The highly factionalised national parliament had been unable to agree on the appointment of a president after Michel Sulayman's term expired in May 2014, and despite making six attempts, the parliament had been unable to elect a replacement. Prime Minister Tammam Salam and his cabinet were temporarily taking over the duties of the president, and national elections, which had been due in 2014, had been postponed until 2017. Democracy in the country was well and truly under threat.

History

Prior to its independence, Lebanon formed a part of Greater Syria.

Early Years of Independence

On 22 November 1943, France – which had held its mandate in Lebanon since the end of WWI – gave in to local demands for in-

---

PALESTINIAN REFUGEES

Most Palestinians who fled to Lebanon in 1948 during the Arab-Israeli War were relegated to refugee camps administered by the UN Relief & Works Agency (UNRWA), and 12 of the original 16 camps still house most of Lebanon's Palestinian population today. The area of land allocated for these camps has not increased since their establishment, despite significant population growth, leading to situations whereby families of up to 10 members are forced to live in a single room.

According to UNRWA, there are now about 448,000 registered Palestinian refugees in Lebanon. Amnesty International estimates that there are another 3000 to 5000 second-generation unregistered refugees living illegally and without rights. Other UN agencies place the total number of registered and unregistered refugees at 655,000.

Palestinian refugees in Lebanon suffer from a lack of opportunities, being prohibited from joining many professions, largely barred from owning or improving property and having only limited access to public health care, education and welfare programs. Most are still provided for by the UNRWA, which runs the camps' schools, hospitals, women's centres and vocational training programs. At least 20,000 of them are internally displaced within Lebanon itself, having been forced out of the Nahr el-Bared camp north of Tripoli in 2007 when it was destroyed during fighting between the Lebanese army and the militant group Fatah al-Islam.

For more information, see www.unrwa.org.

SYRIAN REFUGEES

The civil war in neighbouring Syria has had a huge impact on Lebanon. In 2014, the fourth year of the conflict, the UN Refugee Agency (UNHCR) estimated that there were over three million Syrian refugees in the region, nearly 1.3 million of whom were in Lebanon. Added to these Syrian refugees were 4000 UNRWA-registered Palestine refugees from Syria who also fled across the border. This was an enormous burden for a country with a native population of only four million to shoulder, and though the UNHCR and other international aid organisations were in the country to assist, the task of housing, feeding, educating and providing health care for the refugees was placing a huge burden on Lebanon's weak economy and inadequate infrastructure.

At the time of writing there were no official Syrian refugee camps in Lebanon – the Lebanese wouldn't countenance the possibility of hosting more Palestinian-style permanent refugee settlements – so many of the Syrian refugees were living in appalling conditions without proper housing, heating, running water or electricity. None were able to work legally (even illegal jobs were scarce) and only a small percentage of Syrian children were attending school.

For more information, see www.unhcr.org.

dependent rule and officially declared the country independent. The last French troops withdrew in 1946 and a jubilant Lebanon was left to fend for itself.

Prior to full independence, the government (also known as the National Assembly) had already been uniquely divided along religious lines: Christians and Muslims held parliamentary seats at a ratio of 6:5, broadly representing the religious make-up of the country established by a 1932 census. The president, the constitution stated, must be a Maronite Christian and the prime minister a Sunni Muslim. The speaker was to be a Shiite Muslim and the chief of staff a Druze. Dividing the country along sectarian lines from the very start was to be a major source of strife for years to come.

The early years of independence for the fledgling government weren't easy. First came economic strife and next, on 14 May 1948, the declaration of Israeli independence in former Palestine. Immediately, Lebanese soldiers joined pan-Arab armies and Palestinian fighters in the struggle against Israel. During 1948 and 1949, while war raged, Palestinian refugees flooded north into Lebanon; Amnesty International claims that the tiny nation absorbed more Palestinians than any other country, over 100,000 by the end of 1949 alone. Though initially welcomed into Lebanon, the Maronite majority soon became uneasy about the refugees, mostly Sunni Muslims, who threatened to tilt their precarious balance of power. In 1949 Lebanon accepted an armistice with Israel, but although 1948's UN Resolution

194 stated that refugees should be allowed to return home if they wanted to, in most cases this didn't eventuate. The Palestinian refugees, largely against their own and locals' will, were in Lebanon to stay.

By the 1950s the National Assembly was once again struggling against economic crisis. In 1952 staunchly pro-Western president Camille Chamoun quickly garnered Muslim enemies by refusing all notions of pan-Arabism (the creation of a united Arab entity in the Middle East), and in 1958, when his term was about to end, the unpopular president tried to extend his presidency to a second term. Lebanon's first civil war soon erupted, with pro-Western Maronites pitted against largely Muslim, pro-pan-Arabism opponents. Chamoun panicked, turning to the US for help, and on 15 July 1958, 15,000 US troops landed in Beirut.

The presence of US troops quelled trouble and Chamoun was finally persuaded to resign, to be replaced by a new president, Fouad Chehab. With Chehab's talent for smoothing ruffled feathers, Lebanon soon prospered. Civil war, believed the optimistic Lebanese, was a thing of the past.

Swinging Sixties?

By the mid-'60s, Beirut, the newly crowned 'Paris of the East', was booming, but Palestinian refugees and the Shiites of the south remained in poverty. As Beirut basked in newfound riches, the less fortunate grew bitter and restive, and the good times were already numbered.

The outbreak of the 1967 Arab-Israeli Six Day War brought yet more Palestinian refugees into Lebanon. Refugee camps soon became centres of guerrilla resistance, and the government watched impotently as Palestinian attacks on Israel from Lebanese soil rapidly increased.

In May 1968, Israeli forces retaliated across the border. Meanwhile, with sectarian tensions growing, the Lebanese army clashed violently with Palestinian guerrillas. Palestinian forces proved too strong an opponent for the army, and in November 1969 Lebanon signed the Cairo Agreement with the Palestinian Liberation Organisation (PLO), agreeing to large-scale autonomy of its refugee camps and refugees' freedom 'to participate in the Palestinian revolution'.

Maronite opposition to the agreement was immediate. Many Muslims, on the other hand, felt an innate sympathy for their fellow Palestinians. In response, a group of Christians known as Phalangists began to arm and train young men, and by March 1970 fighting between Phalangists and Palestinians had erupted on Beirut's streets as southern Lebanon suffered under Israeli reprisals against relentless guerrilla attacks. Rapidly, the country factionalised and took up arms.

Civil War

It's widely agreed that Lebanon's civil war began on 13 April 1975 when Phalangist gunmen attacked a Beirut bus, killing 27 Palestinian passengers. Soon, there was outright chaos. In December, Phalangists stopped Beirut traffic and killed Muslim travellers. Muslims retaliated, prompting 'Black Saturday' during which around 300 people died.

The slaughter rapidly reached horrific proportions. In January 1976, Phalangists led a massacre of some 1000 Palestinians in Karantina, a Beirut slum. Two days later, Palestinians attacked the southern coastal town of Damour, and killed over 500 Christians. In August, Phalangists set their sights on the Tel al-Zaatar refugee camp in northeast Beirut, killing between 2000 and 3000 Palestinian civilians.

Soon Beirut was divided along the infamous Green Line, which split the city in two, with Christian enclaves to the east and Muslims to the west. Though allegiances and alliances along its border would shift many times in the coming strife, the Green Line would remain in place for 15 years.

Syria & Israel Intervene

In 1976 the civil war gave Syria a reason to send tens of thousands of troops into Lebanon. Though initially sympathetic to the Palestinians and the pan-Arab cause, it wasn't long before Syria switched allegiance to the Maronite side, occupying all but the far south and angering other Arab countries. Nevertheless, in October 1976 the Arab League brokered a deal with Syria, allowing it to keep 40,000 troops in Lebanon as part of a peace-keeping 'Arab Deterrent Force'. Syria was left in control of Lebanon, and the first of the civil war's 150 ceasefires was declared.

At the same time, Palestinian attacks on Israel continued, prompting Israel to launch 'Operation Litani' in 1978, swiftly occupying most of southern Lebanon. Immediately, the UN demanded Israel's withdrawal and formed the UN Interim Force in Lebanon (UNIFIL) to 'restore international peace'. Though Israel withdrew to a 19km 'security zone', it simultaneously installed the puppet South Lebanon Army (SLA) and proclaimed an 1800 sq km region south of Nahr al-Litani (the Litani River) 'Free Lebanon'. For the coming years, this area was mired in war.

In 1982 Israeli 'Operation Peace for Galilee' troops marched into Lebanon headed for Beirut, supported tacitly by Maronite and Phalangist leaders. By 15 June, Israeli forces had surrounded and besieged West Beirut, bombarding 16,000 PLO fighters entrenched there. Heavy fighting ensued, and in just two months the city was in ruins – 20,000 people, from both sides of the Green Line, were dead. On 21 August the PLO left Beirut, guaranteed safe passage by multinational forces. By now, however, battle was also raging in the Chouf Mountains, the historic preserve of Druze and Christians, and an area until now free from the ravages of war. The Lebanese army joined the Phalangists and Israelis against the Druze, who themselves were aided by the Shiite militia Amal, until the US intervened and another ceasefire was brokered.

By this time the US was becoming increasingly entrenched in the war, appearing to favour Israel and Lebanon's beleaguered government. In 1983 came the reprisals. In April, an Islamic Jihad–organised suicide attack on the US embassy in Beirut left 63 dead. In October, suicide bombers hit the US and French military headquarters in Beirut, killing over 300. In 1984 abductions and the

HEZBOLLAH

Often described as a 'State within a State', Hezbollah (aka the party of God, or Party of Allah) is a Lebanese Shiite Islamist political party and militant group with an armed wing known as the Jihad Council. It wields enormous influence in the country – particularly in the south – and currently holds 14 seats in the national parliament, including two cabinet positions. It also has its own radio station, TV network and countrywide network of social services

After the 1982 Israeli invasion of Lebanon, Iranian revolutionary guards began to preach to Lebanon's disaffected Shiites, who proved receptive to their message of over-throwing Western imperialism and the anti-Muslim Phalange. Hezbollah was formed at this time. Alongside suicide bombings, its ruthless armed wing also resorted to taking hostages, including CIA bureau chief William Buckley, who was kidnapped, tortured and killed in 1984–85. Other victims included Associated Press bureau chief Terry Anderson, kidnapped in 1985 and held until 1991; and UK envoy Terry Waite, kidnapped in 1987 and held until 1991.

Many in Lebanon and the Arab world credit Hezbollah with ending the Israeli occupation of Lebanon in 2000, an achievement celebrated at the Resistance Tourist Landmark in Mleeta near Nabitiyeh in the country's south.

Hezbollah's current leader and public face is Hassan Nasrallah (born 1960), whose base is in the village of Bazourieh, near Tyre. Nasrallah has studied Islamic theology in Lebanon, Iraq and Iran, and is known for his charismatic and evocative brand of rhetoric (in one of his best-known speeches he described Israel as being 'more fragile than a spiderweb').

Admired for its welfare and education projects, and feared for its military capability and terrorist activities, Hezbollah is branded a terrorist organisation by a number of Western governments and is known for its rocket attacks on Israel and kidnap missions against that country's soldiers. In May 2013, Nasrallah announced that Hezbollah soldiers would fight in Syria alongside the forces of President al-Assad against 'Islamic extremists' in that country. It is thought that as many as 5000 of its soldiers are now fighting over the border.

torture of foreigners – whose involvement in Lebanese affairs the abductors deeply resented – began. The following year, international forces hastily left Lebanon.

Battle of the Camps

In early 1985, the last Israeli troops finally withdrew to their self-proclaimed 'security zone', leaving their interests in the hands of the SLA and Christian militias, who immediately clashed with Druze and Shiite opponents around Sidon. In West Beirut fighting continued between Shiite, Sunni and Druze militias, all battling for the upper hand.

In the midst of the chaos, PLO forces began to return to Lebanon. Concerned, however, that this would lead to a renewed Israeli invasion of the south, the Shiite Amal fought to remove them. Heavy fighting battered the Palestinian refugee camps during 1986, causing many more thousands of casualties.

To add to the confusion, in 1987 the National Assembly finally fell apart and split in two, with a Muslim government to the west of Beirut and a Christian administration to the east. Fighting along the Green Line continued as Christian leaders attempted to drive Syria from Lebanon, angering Syria still more by accepting arms from Iraq. It wasn't until 1989 that a road to peace finally seemed viable, with the drafting of the Taif Accord.

Road to Peace

The Taif Accord, the product of a committee consisting of the Saudi and Moroccan kings and the Algerian president, proposed a ceasefire and a meeting of Lebanon's parliament to discuss a new government charter, which would redress the Christian–Muslim balance of power. The accord was ratified on 5 November 1989, and constitutional amendments included the expansion of the National Assembly from 99 to 128 seats, equally divided between Christians and Muslims.

Despite some in-fighting, in August 1990 the National Assembly voted to accept the terms of the Taif Accord. With the exception of the still-occupied south, the country saw peace for the first time in 15 years, and the civil war officially ended on 13 October 1990.

Syria's continued presence in Lebanon beyond the civil war was justified with reference to Lebanon's weak national army and the government's inability to carry out Taif Accord reforms, including dismantling militias, alone. In 1990 Syria formalised its dominance over Lebanon with the Treaty of Brotherhood, Co-operation & Coordination, followed in 1992 by a defence pact. In May 1991, most militias – except Hezbollah – were officially dissolved. In line with Taif Accord conditions, Syria began its military pull-out in March 1992, taking another 13 years to complete the job. The last Westerners kidnapped by Hezbollah were released in 1992.

Postwar Reconstruction

From 1993 onward, the Lebanese army and life were slowly rebuilt and Rafiq Hariri, a Lebanese-born multimillionaire and entrepreneur, became prime minister.

Meanwhile, the south remained impoverished and was the base for Israeli-Hezbollah skirmishes. In 1993 Israel launched 'Operation Accountability' and in 1996 'Operation Grapes of Wrath' in response to Hezbollah and Palestinian attacks; the latter was a land-sea-air offensive that devastated newly rebuilt structures, destroyed Beirut's power station and killed around 106 civilians in the beleaguered southern village of Qana.

In 1999 Israel launched further attacks, targeting Beirut's power stations, while Hezbollah continued its offensives. Sustained Israeli losses led to calls within that country for military withdrawal, and its army finally withdrew from southern Lebanon on 24 May 2000. However, Hezbollah stated that Israel would remain its target until Israeli troops were also withdrawn from Shebaa Farms, a 31 sq km area southeast of Lebanon that had been captured by Israel in the 1967 Six Day War. In the years since the civil war, this bone of contention has frequently been the alleged reason for Hezbollah violence and Israeli retaliation.

In Lebanon, discontent rumbled on. Maronite groups opposed Syria's refusal to withdraw from Lebanon while Shiites and Hezbollah continued to support its presence. On 2 September 2004, the UN issued Security Council Resolution 1559, which called 'upon all remaining foreign forces to withdraw from Lebanon'. Syria still did not comply, and on 20 October 2004, Prime Minister Hariri tendered his resignation, announcing that he would not be a candidate to head the next government.

Killing of Rafiq Hariri

On 14 February 2005, a massive Beirut car bomb killed the prime minister Rafiq Hariri and 21 others. Many Lebanese placed the blame firmly on Syria and attended demonstrations calling for Syrian withdrawal from Lebanon, for an independent commission to investigate the murder of Hariri, and for the organisation of free parliamentary elections. Together, these events became known as the Cedar Revolution. On 14 March, Lebanon's largest-ever public demonstration was held in Martyrs Sq, Beirut, with between 800,000 and one million attendees spanning sectarian divisions. The result was the March 14 Alliance, an anti-Syrian governmental alliance led by Hariri's son, Saad; Samir Geagea of the Lebanese Forces Party; and Walid Jumblatt of the Druze-led Progressive Socialist Party (PSP).

With the UN, the USA, Russia and Germany all backing Lebanese calls for withdrawal, Syria finally bowed to pressure, withdrawing its 14,000 remaining troops from Lebanon on 27 April 2005 after almost 30 years of occupation. For the first time in more than two decades, Lebanon was completely free from military forces other than its own.

The 2005 parliamentary elections, the first after Syria's withdrawal, saw a majority win for the March 14 Alliance led by Saad Hariri, with Fouad Siniora elected Lebanon's new prime minister. The elections also saw Hezbollah become a legitimate governmental force, winning 14 seats in parliament, while in the south its fighters continued to launch attacks on Israeli troops and towns. Though Siniora publicly denounced the attacks, it seemed that once again Lebanese authorities were powerless to stop them.

2009 Election & Beyond

The June 2009 election saw the March 14 Alliance winning 71 of 128 seats. The March 8 Alliance, made up of the Free Patriotic Movement, Amal, Hezbollah and five smaller parties, won 57. Saad Hariri became prime minister.

Hariri's government collapsed in January 2011 after March 8 Alliance ministers withdrew from the cabinet (PSP-aligned ministers had withdrawn even earlier in the picture).

Hariri has lived outside the country since this time, although he is still seen as a figurehead for the March 14 Alliance and the Sunni-dominated Movement of the Future party.

After Hariri's resignation a new March 8 Alliance government led by Najib Mikati was formed. This lasted until his resignation in March 2013, at which time new Tammam Salam, a March 14–backed consensus candidate, was installed as prime minister for the period leading up to the next election.

People

National Psyche

Though Lebanon's 18 official religions have fought quite consistently since the country's creation in 1943, one of the central paradoxes of the Lebanese psyche is the country's collective and overriding national pride in its tolerance of others. You're sure to hear this repeated, even when there's sectarian fighting going on just up the road.

You'll likely also experience the strange collective amnesia that seems to descend on the population if the country's civil war is brought up in conversation. A painful memory for most, reticence to talk about it (despite the physical scars that still pepper the landscape) is common. You usually won't encounter the same problem, however, if you mention current politics: everyone is keen to share an opinion on the political issue of the day or the dire state of the country's economy and infrastructure.

Daily Life

Though it's hard to generalise about such a factionalised country, family life, as in most Middle Eastern countries, is vitally important to every Lebanese. Extended families often live close together, and many children live at home until married, either to save money for their own home or simply because they prefer it that way. Social life, too, is both close-knit and gregarious: everyone within a small community tends to know everything there is to know about everyone else.

Marriage is a second crucial factor throughout Lebanon, and members of all religions tend to marry young. An unmarried woman in her thirties will raise eyebrows, though a man still single at 30, as in most parts of the Middle East, is usually thought to be simply waiting for the right girl. Though there has traditionally been an expectation that people will marry within their religion, this barrier is slowly being broken down.

The position of women in society is not as advanced as in most Western societies. Girls can be married (often against their will) as young as 12.5 years, polygamy is legal and violence against women is common. Voting is compulsory for all men, but is only authorised for women if they have an elementary education. In the 2009 parliamentary elections, only 3.1% of the seats were won by women and no women were given seats in cabinet.

A university education is highly valued in Lebanon but is becoming increasingly expensive. Many young people study with a view to emigrating overseas, lured by higher salaries and the promise of a safer, calmer lifestyle away from the unrest.

As you'll notice from the pace of Beirut nightlife, young Christians – both male and female – usually have far greater social freedom than Muslims or members of other religions. But while these freedoms may at first appear similar to their Western counterparts, there are definite limits to acceptable behaviour. Drinking heavily, relationships out of wedlock and taking drugs are generally frowned upon in Lebanese society – not that you'd necessarily know it on a night out at Beirut's nightclubs. And while party-central Beirut seems, on the surface, no different from any European capital city, venture just a few dozen kilometres north or south and you'll find people in traditional villages living and farming almost exactly as they did a century or more ago. Add to this a substantial population of refugees and migrant workers almost entirely cut off from the mainstream – and rarely referred to in conversation by the Lebanese themselves – and you'll find that daily life in this tiny country is incredibly complex, and often wildly contrasting.

Population

Lebanon's official population of just over four million people is boosted by its resident Palestinian refugees, officially numbered at around 448,000 but unofficially acknowledged to be nearly double this.

It's a largely urban population, with nearly 90% of people living in cities, of which Beirut is the most highly populated, followed by Tripoli, Sidon and Tyre. The population growth rate currently stands at around 9.37%, the highest in the world due to the huge influx of refugees in recent years. Just over a quarter of the population is under 14 years of age.

Religion

Lebanon hosts 18 'official' religious sects, which are Muslim (Shiite, Alawite, Ismaili and Sunni), Christian (Maronite, Greek Orthodox and Catholic, Armenian Catholic, Gregorian, Syrian Orthodox, Jacobite, Nestorian, Chaldean, Copt, Evangelical and Roman Catholic), Druze and Jewish. There are also small populations of Baha'is, Mormons, Buddhists and Hindus.

Muslims are estimated to comprise around 54% of the population; before the civil war unofficial statistics put the Muslim to Christian ratio closer to 50:50. The shift is attributed to the mass emigration of Christians during and since the civil war, and to higher birth rates among Muslims. Christians comprise 40.5% of the overall population and Druze 5.6%.

Traditionally, Muslim Shiites have largely inhabited the south of the country, the Bekaa Valley and southern suburbs of Beirut. Sunnis, meanwhile, have been concentrated in Beirut, Tripoli and Sidon; the Druze in the Chouf Mountains; and Maronite Christians (the largest Christian group) in the Mt Lebanon region. Though recent years have seen population shifts, particularly in Beirut, this still largely holds true today.

Arts

In summer, many towns and villages hold dance and music festivals, which are well worth looking out for. Those in Baalbek, Beiteddine and Byblos are particularly well known. The nation's capital hosts its own lively arts scene and is well equipped with theatres, cinemas and venues for the visual and performing arts.

Literature

Though it was the publishing powerhouse of the Middle East for much of the 20th century, Beirut suffered during the civil war and much of its recent literary output has been shaped by this long drawn-out and horrific event. Even today, a great deal of Lebanon's literary output remains concerned with themes drawn from these 15 years of hardship.

Of the writers who remained in Lebanon during the civil war, Emily Nasrallah (born 1931) is a leading figure who is best known for her award-winning debut novel *Birds of September*. Those who work overseas include Canada-based Rawi Hage (born 1964), whose Beirut-set debut novel *De Niro's Game* garnered strong international reviews; London-based Tony Hanania (born 1964), whose novel *Unreal City* is set in Beirut; and French-based Amin Maalouf (born 1949), two of whose novels are set in Lebanon: *Balthasar's Odyssey* in Jbail (Byblos), and *The Rock of Tanios* in a rural village. The latter was awarded the Prix Goncourt in 1993.

Of those authors most widely available in translation, Lebanon's two major figures are Elias Khoury (born 1948) and London-based feminist author Hanan al-Shaykh (born 1945). Al-Shayk's *Story of Zahra* is a harrowing account of the civil war, while her *Beirut Blues* is a series of long letters that contrast Beirut's cosmopolitan past with the book's war-torn present. Elias Khoury has published 10 novels, many available in translation: his 1998 novel *Gate of the Sun*

MUSTN'T-MISS MOVIES

If you get the chance, don't fail to watch some of these great Lebanese films.

➡ *Ghadi* (2013), directed by Amin Dora

➡ *The Attack* (2012), directed by Ziad Doueiri

➡ *Where Do We Go Now?* (2011), directed by Nadine Labaki

➡ *Caramel* (2007), directed by Nadine Labaki

➡ *Bosta* (2005), directed by Philippe Aractingi

➡ *The Kite* (2003), directed by Randa Chahel Sabag

➡ *In the Shadows of the City* (2000), directed by Jean Chamoun

➡ *Around the Pink House* (1999), directed by Joana Hadjithomas and Khalil Joreige

➡ *West Beirut* (1998), directed by Ziad Duweyri

➡ *The Little Wars* (1982), directed by Maroun Baghdadi

➡ *The Broken Wings* (1962), directed by Yousef Malouf

has achieved particular international acclaim.

Up-and-coming Lebanese novelists include Rabee Jaber (born 1972), author of *The Druze of Belgrade,* which was awarded the International Prize for Arabic Fiction in 2012.

Poet Khalil Gibran (1883–1931) remains the celestial light in Lebanon's poetry scene. Interestingly, today poetry is once again flourishing in the largely Shiite south, partly due to a movement known as Shu'ara al-Janub (Poets from the South), for whom poetry has become a means of expressing the frustrations and despair of life in that most war-ravaged of regions.

Cinema & TV

Lebanese cinema survived the civil war years and the industry is currently buoyant, despite frequently difficult circumstances.

Modern classics to look out for are Nadine Labaki's *Caramel* (2007), which focuses on the intersecting lives of five Beiruti women; *West Beirut* (1998), directed by Ziad Doueiri (a former Tarantino cameraman), which tells the semi-autobiographical story of a teenager living in West Beirut during the first year of the civil war; and the award-winning documentary *Children of Shatila,* of the same year, which looks at the history of the notorious refugee camp through children's eyes.

Music

With the 2014 death of the hugely popular singer and actress Sabah, Lebanon is left with two reigning divas: living legend Fairouz (born 1934) and Najwa Karam (born 1966), known as the 'Sun of Lebanese song'.

Fairouz has enjoyed star status since her first recordings in Damascus in the 1950s, and later became an icon for Lebanon during the civil war (which she sat out in Paris). Now in her eighties, her most recent album is 2010's *Eh Fi Amal* and her most recent live performances were in 2011.

Najwa Karam rose to stardom during the 1990s. With 19 albums, including the 2001 blockbuster *Nedmaneh,* she remains a driving force on the Lebanese music scene. Her most recent release is 2011's *Hal Leile...MaFi Noum* (Tonight, There's No Sleep).

Mainstream pop artists include Nancy Ajram and Haifa Wehbe, both producing catchy tunes and raunchy videos. More interesting are alt rock band Mashrou' Leila, which specialises in satirical lyrics and themes; and oud (lute) player and Marcel Khalife, who marries classical Arabic music with contemporary sounds.

In the bars and clubs of Beirut's Hamra, Gemmayzeh and Mar Mikhaël districts, contemporary fusions of oriental trip-hop, lounge, drum and bass, and traditional Arabic music are popular, alongside Western retro, mainstream and indie tracks.

Architecture

Ancient architecture in Lebanon can be found at Baalbek's spectacular remains; at the remnants of the Phoenician Temple of Echmoun; in the traces of the Phoenicians and Romans in Byblos (Jbail); at the Roman sites at Tyre (Sour); and at the Umayyad ruins at Aanjar. Crusader structures can be admired in Tripoli (Trablous), Sidon (Saida) and Byblos.

Much of Lebanon's more recent heritage architecture has been damaged or destroyed over the last century by the combined effects of war and redevelopment; this is particularly apparent in Beirut. To the north, Tripoli's old city souqs contain a wealth of medieval and Islamic architecture, while Deir al-Qamar, in the southern Chouf Mountains, is a well-preserved village with some beautiful 18th- and 19th-century villas and palaces. Beiteddine Palace, also in the Chouf Mountains, is a melange of Italian and traditional Arab architecture, more remarkable for its lavish interiors than any architectural innovation.

Interior designers are doing wonderful work in Lebanon these days, and Beirut's B 018 nightclub, designed by Bernard Khoury, is a top-notch example. Situated on the former Green Line, the club pays homage to the past at a site that was formerly a quarantine zone, a refugee camp and the site of an appalling massacre during the war – and is worth a visit as much for its appearance as for its DJs and crowd.

Visual Arts

Lebanon's first art school was established in 1937, and by the 1950s and '60s a number of galleries opened to showcase the country's art, while the private Sursock Museum, in Achrafiye, began to show new artists.

Though, like most of Lebanon's cultural output, the visual arts suffered during the civil war, the scene re-established itself with vigour soon afterwards. Famous 20th-century artists include the painters Hassan Jouni, Moustafa Farroukh and Mohammed Rawas. Better-known contemporary artists include Adnan Hakani, Mahmoud Amhaz, Marwan Rechmawi, Bassam Kahwaji, Amin al-Basha, Helen Khal, Salwa Zeidan, Etel Adnan, Hind Al Soufi and Salwa Raodash Shkheir.

Though she doesn't identify as Lebanese, the internationally acclaimed installation and video artist Mona Hatoum was born in Beirut in 1952 to Palestinian parents. She now lives and works in London. Other expatriate artists of note include Mireille Astore, a photomedia artist and filmmaker born in Beirut in 1961 but now living in Australia; and Palestinian-Lebanese painter Jeffar Khaldi, who is now based in Dubai.

The best places to investigate the current Lebanese visual arts scene are the numerous small galleries around Hamra, Gemmayzeh and Mar Mikhaël.

Food & Drink

Lebanese cuisine has a reputation as being one of the very best in the Middle East.

LEBANESE CUISINE

The equivalent of Italian antipasto or Spanish tapas, Lebanese mezze are the most famous elements of the Lebanese menu and are the perfect way to start a meal... or, with enough little dishes, to form a meal in themselves. The following form the nucleus of the Lebanese mezze menu and are almost always served with pita bread.

➸ **Hummus** Chickpea and tahini dip

➸ **Kibbeh** Croquettes of finely ground meat and minced onion encased in burghul (cracked wheat) and either fried or cooked in broth; a popular vegetarian version features spiced pumpkin

➸ **Kibbeh labaniyye** Kibbeh balls cooked in a warm yoghurt sauce

➸ **Kibbeh nayyeh** Raw spiced minced lamb topped with herbs and olive oil

➸ **Labneh** Thick yoghurt seasoned with olive oil and garlic

➸ **Moujaddara** Lentils cooked with rice and onions

➸ **Muttabal** Eggplant and tahini dip

➸ **Sambusas** Fried cheese or meat pastries, similar to samosas

➸ **Shanklish** Strong-tasting aged cow- or sheep-milk cheese, often rolled into balls and covered in dried zaatar or thyme

➸ **Warak arish** Stuffed vine leaves (also known as wara anaib)

Three popular salads are often ordered alongside mezze:

➸ **Fattoush** Toasted pita bread, cos lettuce, cucumbers, tomatoes and sumac

➸ **Tabbouleh** Parsley, tomato, spring onion, burghul salad and mint

➸ **Roca and wild thyme salad**

Main courses tend to be meat- or fish-dominated, and include:

➸ **Kofta** Mincemeat with parsley and spices grilled on a skewer

➸ **Sayadieh** Fish and rice topped with onion sauce

➸ **Shish taouk** Chicken marinated in olive oil, lemon, parsley and sumac and then grilled on skewers

There are also tasty fast-food options on offer:

➸ **Felafel** Deep-fried balls of spiced chickpeas and/or fava beans served on a platter or wrapped in pita bread

➸ **Lahma bi-ajeen** Spiced ground meat and tomato pizza

➸ **Manakeesh** Thyme and olive oil pizza

➸ **Shwarma** Thin slices of marinated meat garnished with fresh vegetables, pickles and tahini (sesame-seed paste), wrapped in pita bread

Fruit, vegetables and pulses are plentiful in Lebanon. Most meals start with a choice of salads and mezze (small dishes) and are a godsend for vegetarians. Seafood and grilled meats often feature as main dishes, and decadently sweet pastries are popular desserts. In Beirut, the diversity and quality of food on offer matches many international cities: want tapas at two in the morning, or sushi at six? You'll find it all here.

Arabic or Turkish coffee is particularly popular in Lebanon, while delicious freshly squeezed vegetable and fruit juices are on offer almost everywhere throughout the summer. Alcohol, too, is widely available in Lebanon; Beirut is awash with cocktails, but the most popular alcoholic old-timer is the potent aniseed-flavoured arak, mixed liberally with water and ice. The best local beer is Almaza, which lives up to its name ('diamond' in Arabic) when served ice-cold, and local wines are impressive – the best-known producers are Chateau Ksara and Château Kefraya in the Bekaa Valley and Chateau Musar in Ghazir, north of Beirut. The best of the boutique wineries are Domaine Wardy in Zahlé, Massaya near near Chtaura and IXSIR near Batroun.

Environment

The Land

Though Lebanon is one of the smallest countries in the world, its terrain is surprisingly diverse. Four main geographical areas run almost parallel to each other from north to south. They are (from west to east): the coastal plain, the Mt Lebanon Range, the Bekaa Valley and the Jebel Libnan ash-Sharqiyya (Anti-Lebanon) range.

The Mt Lebanon Range includes Lebanon's highest summit, Qornet as-Sawda (3090m). Jebel Libnan ash-Sharqiyya marks the border between Lebanon and Syria. Its highest summit is Jebel ash-Sheikh (Mt Hermon), at 2814m.

Environmental Issues

Ravaged by more than two decades of war, unfettered construction, endemic corruption and weak state control, Lebanon's environment remains very fragile, and some of the only areas to have escaped destruction are, ironically, the heavily landmined or cluster-bombed areas of the country still filled with unexploded ordnance.

LEBANON'S CEDARS

The most famous of the world's several species of cedar tree are the cedars of Lebanon, mentioned in the Old Testament, and once covering great swathes of the Mt Lebanon Range.

Jerusalem's original Temple of Solomon was made from this sort of cedar wood, and the ancient Phoenicians, attracted by its fragrance and durability, also used it in their buildings. Unfortunately, a long history of deforestation has meant that today just a few pockets of cedars remain in Lebanon – despite the tree appearing proudly on the nation's flag.

Of these remnants of a once-abundant arboreal past, the best places to view the remaining cedars of Lebanon are either at the Chouf Cedar Reserve, or at the small grove at the Cedars ski resort in the north of the country.

Generally the country's waste disposal systems are scandalously inadequate. In Beirut, for example, few locals swim in the local waters due to the high levels of untreated sewage that are pumped into the sea. Most other water sources are heavily polluted, leading to locals relying heavily on bottled water. Rubbish disposal is less than efficient and recycling is still not common, leading to major problems with uncollected rubbish (especially plastic bottles) in public areas. Air pollution is another serious and ongoing problem, particularly in Beirut, with a couple of million cars (many of them ancient, spluttering wrecks or petrol-guzzling SUVs) plying the crowded roads.

Fortunately, some local and international NGOs are working to secure a better future for Lebanon's environment. A good example is the Chouf Cedar Reserve (which makes up an incredible 5% of Lebanon's landmass) which, though underfunded and overstretched, is working hard to protect and regenerate its flora and fauna.

SURVIVAL GUIDE

❶ Directory A–Z

ACCOMMODATION

Prices are quoted for a room in high season (June to September and the Christmas–New Year period) except for the Cedars ski resort, where they are for a room between December and March. Prices are either in US dollars or in Lebanese lira (LL; also known as Lebanese pounds; LBP), depending on which is quoted by the establishment itself. Most midrange and top-end options have satellite TV and tea/coffee-making facilities.

Note that in low season discounts are sometimes available, so it's always worth checking. However, some smaller places may shut up shop if there seems to be no likelihood of travellers – call in advance if you have any doubts.

Hostelling International has nine affiliated hostels in Lebanon. Most are in small, rural villages, offering a taste of real local life, and offer dorm beds for between US$15 and US$25 per person per night. For upscale homestays across the country, look no further than L'Hote Libanais (p366), which can organise a single stay or an entire itinerary for reasonable prices.

Prices in reviews are for rooms in high season and include bathrooms, breakfast and taxes unless otherwise indicated.

$ less than LL121,000 (US$80)

$$ LL121,000 to LL273,000 (US$80 to US$180)

$$$ more than LL273,000 (US$180)

ACTIVITIES

The Lebanese passion for adventure translates into a wide variety of options for adventure activities.

Association Libanaise d'Etudes Speleologique (ALES; ☎ 03-666 469; www.alesliban. org) Caving trips for all levels of experience.

Atlantis Diving College (☎ 70 195 231) Based in Jounieh.

Lebanese Adventure (☎ 03-214 989; www. lebanese-adventure.com) Ecotourism operator organising rafting, hiking, trekking, caving, snowshoeing, climbing, abseiling and canyoning activities.

Liban Trek (☎ 01-329 975; www.libantrek. com) Specialises in hiking and trekking, but also offers speleology and cross-country skiing opportunities.

Ski Lebanon (☎ 70 103 222; www.skileb.com) The best place to access information on where and when to ski.

33 North (☎ 71 331 138, 03-454 996; www.33-north.com) Billing itself as an 'alternative tourism tour operator', this ecotourism outfit offers adventure tours (including hiking) and culinary tours.

EMBASSIES & CONSULATES

Nationals of New Zealand should contact the UK embassy for assistance.

Australian Embassy (Map p362; ☎ 01-960 600; www.lebanon.embassy.gov.au/birt/home; Serail Hill, BCD, Beirut)

British Embassy (Map p362; ☎ 01-960 800; www.gov.uk/government/world/organisations/british-embassy-beirut; Serail Hill, BCD, Beirut)

Canadian Embassy (☎ 04-726 700; www.canadainternational.gc.ca/lebanon-liban; 1st fl, Coolrite Bldg, Autostrade, 43 Jal ad-Dib Hwy, Beirut)

Egyptian Embassy (Map p360; ☎ 01-859 977; Dr Muhammed El-Bethri St, Be'er Hassan, Beirut)

French Embassy (Map p360; ☎ 01-420 000; www.ambafrance-lb.org; Rue de Damas, Beirut)

German Embassy (☎ 04-935 000; www.beirut.diplo.de; Maghzal Bldg, Rabieh, Beirut)

Italian Embassy (☎ 05-954 955; www.ambbeirut.esteri.it; Rue du Palais Presidentiel, Baabda, Beirut)

Jordanian Embassy (☎ 05-922 500; joremb@dm.net.lb; Rue Elias Helou, Baabda, Beirut)

Netherlands Embassy (Map p362; ☎ 01-211 150; http://lebanon.nlembassy.org; Netherlands Tower, Avenue Charles Malek, Achrafiye, Beirut)

Syrian Embassy (☎ 05-922 581; Yarzeh Area, Baabda, Beirut)

US Embassy (☎ 04-542 600; http://lebanon.usembassy.gov; Main St, Awkar, Antelias)

FOOD

Prices in reviews represent the cost of a standard main-course dish.

$ less than LL15,000 (US$10)

$$ LL15,000 to LL40,000 (US$10 to US$30)

$$$ more than LL40,000 (US$30)

LEBANON MOUNTAIN TRAIL

Running between Andqet in the north of the country to Marjaayoun in the south, this 470km self-guided hike passes through more than 75 towns and villages at altitudes ranging from 600 meters to 2000 meters above sea level. The trail was devised by the not-for-profit **Lebanon Mountain Trail Association** (☎ 05-955 302; www.lebanontrail.org; 1st Fl, Ghaleb Center, Sacré Coeur Hospital St, Baabda) to showcase the beauty and natural diversity of Lebanon's mountain regions, and to enhance economic opportunities in these regions by promoting responsible tourism. For information about the trail, including details about organised walks and links to local guides and ecotourism operators, see the association's website and Facebook page.

ℹ️ PRACTICALITIES

Electricity European two-round-pin plugs are needed to connect to Lebanon's electricity supply (220VAC, 50Hz).

Newspapers The *Daily Star* (www.dailystar.com.lb) provides coverage of local news in English and the daily *L'Orient Le Jour* (www.lorientlejour.com) does the same in French.

Radio The BBC World Service can be received on 1323kHz; Radio One (105.1 to 105.5 FM) is popular locally. The major local TV channels are the government-run broadcaster Tele-Liban and an array of commercial channels, many of which are politically aligned.

Weights and measures Lebanon uses the metric system for weights and measures.

GAY & LESBIAN TRAVELLERS

Homosexuality is illegal in Lebanon, but there's a thriving – if clandestine – gay scene in Beirut. Gay-friendly cafes, bars and clubs include B 018 (p371), Posh (p371), Life Bar (p370) and Madame Om (p370).

During 2012–14 there were a number of instances of police harassment of gay men in Beirut, with the arrests of patrons in some hammams and cinemas. There were also reports of invasive body searches being perpetrated on men in police custody. Before attending known gay venues, check the current situation with **Helem** (Map p364; ☑ 01-745 092; www.helem.net; 1st fl, Yamout Bldg, 174 Rue Spears, Beirut), an organisation whose name derives from the Arabic acronym for the Lebanese Protection for Lebanese Gays, Bisexuals and Transgenders. For lesbian-specific information, also check **Bint el Nas** (www.bintelnas.org).

LANGUAGE COURSES

The following centres in Beirut provide courses in Arabic for foreigners:

AMBergh Education (www.arabic-studies.com) Offers group and individual courses, and can help find accommodation.

American Language Center (Map p364; ☑ 01-741 262; www.alcbeirut.com; 1-2 Maamari Street, Hamra, Beirut) Offers three levels of colloquial Arabic courses (beginners, intermediate and advanced).

American University of Beirut (Map p364; ☑ 01-350 000 ext. 3845; www.aub.edu/lb) The American University's Centre for Arab and Middle Eastern Studies (CAMES) offers a seven-week intensive summer program in Modern Standard Arabic.

MONEY

➡ Lebanon's currency is the Lebanese lira (LL), also known locally as the Lebanese pound (LBP). Banknotes are of the following denominations: 1000, 5000, 10,000, 20,000, 50,000 and 100,000; there are also 25, 50, 100, 250 and 500 pound coins.

➡ US dollars are widely accepted countrywide, and higher-end establishments rarely quote prices in anything else.

➡ ATMs are reliable and available, and dispense cash in both Lebanese lira and US dollars.

➡ Tipping is widespread in Lebanon. For hotel porters and parking valets, tipping somewhere around LL4000, depending on the level of service, will be appreciated. Waiters are usually tipped around 10%, but check your bill before doing so, since some places automatically add a 15% service charge.

OPENING HOURS

Shops 10am to 7pm Monday to Friday, to mid-afternoon Saturday

Banks 8.30am to 2pm Monday to Friday, to noon Saturday

Post offices and government offices 8am to 5pm Monday to Friday, to 1.30pm Saturday

Restaurants Nonstandard opening hours; in Beirut they may stay open all night

PUBLIC HOLIDAYS

New Year's Day 1 January

Orthodox Christmas Day 6 January

Feast of Saint Maroun 9 February – feast of the patron saint of the Maronites

Easter March/April – Good Friday to Easter Monday

Labour Day 1 May

Martyrs' Day 6 May

Assumption 15 August

All Saints' Day 1 November

Independence Day 22 November

Christmas Day 25 December

Muslim holidays are also observed.

SAFE TRAVEL

At the time of research, many countries, including the UK, Australia and the USA, were counselling their citizens to reconsider their need to travel to Lebanon. Most specifically, foreign offices advised against travel to the southern suburbs of Beirut, Sidon, areas south of the

Litani River (with the exception of Tyre), the Bekaa Valley, all areas bordering Syria, Tripoli and northern Lebanon north of a line from Tripoli to Sir Ed Dinniyeh and Arsal.

Before travelling to Lebanon, register your travel plans with your country's foreign affairs department so that you can be sent security updates. When in the country, monitor the *Daily Star* or *L'Orient Le Jour* for up-to-the-minute news and regularly check the websites of foreign embassies for security updates. Be aware that the political and security situation in Syria can impact on Lebanon and compromise its stability, and that Israeli missiles are sometimes fired into southern Lebanon (usually in response to Hezbollah firing missiles into Israel). Also be aware that there are currently no safe land exits from the country, and that demonstrators and security forces sometimes block the primary road between downtown Beirut and Rafic Hariri International Airport, making it impossible to leave the country.

TELEPHONE

Mobile Phones

Mobile-phone coverage extends throughout most of the country (bar a few remote, mountainous areas). Your mobile phone from home will probably work on a local network, though of course you'll pay heavily for the privilege of making calls or sending text messages. Local Touch and Alfa SIM cards are widely available from phone stores, cost around US$35 (including some credit), are activated immediately and can be easily recharged.

Phone Codes

The country code for Lebanon is ✆ 961, followed by the local area code (minus the zero), then the subscriber number. The area code when dialling a mobile phone is ✆ 03 or ✆ 70. The international access code (to call abroad from Lebanon) is ✆ 00.

USEFUL WEBSITES

Agenda Culturel (www.agendaculturel.com) Arts, events and festival information and listings; in French.

Destination Lebanon (www.destinationlebanon.gov.lb) Chock-full of tourist information about the country.

VISAS

At the time of research, free one-month single-entry tourist visas renewable for three months were available at Rafic Hariri International Airport for citizens of many countries including Australia, Canada, China, France, Great Britain, Germany, Ireland, Italy, Japan, the Netherlands, New Zealand, Spain and the USA. For the most up-to-date information, visit the website of Lebanon's **General Security Office** (www.general-security.gov.lb).

Visa Extensions

To extend your one-month visa to a three-month visa, go to the General Directorate of General Security in Beirut a few days before your first month ends; you'll find the office across the road from the National Museum – head to the second floor. Take your passport, two passport photos, and two photocopies of your passport ID page and the page where your entry visa was stamped. Once your application is processed, you'll be given a receipt and told to return in seven days to collect your passport with its extended visa.

WOMEN TRAVELLERS

Lebanon is a relatively easy destination for solo female travellers. Western-style clothes are common in Beirut, and revealing beach wear is acceptable in the beach clubs that line the sands from Sidon up to Byblos. However, modest clothing is recommended for areas outside Beirut and the beach. In mosques or religious sites, women should cover their shoulders and heads, and avoid wearing shorts or short skirts. In taxis, it's best to sit in the back seat.

❶ Getting There & Away

At the time of research, travellers could enter Lebanon by air, or by sea from Turkey. Note, though, that the boat service from Turkey was to/from Tripoli, which was considered unsafe by many foreign embassies.

AIR

Beirut Rafic Hariri International Airport (p574) is Lebanon's only airport. The national carrier, **Middle East Airlines** (MEA; Map p364; ✆ 01-622 000; www.mea.com.lb; Beirut), has an extensive network including flights to and from Europe and to the Arab world.

The following international airlines, among others, currently service Beirut:

Air France (www.airfrance.com)

Cyprus Airways (✆ 01-629 872; http://cyprus-air.com; Beirut-RHIA)

EgyptAir (✆ 01-629 357; www.egyptair.com.eg; Beirut-RHIA)

Emirates (✆ 01-734 500; www.emirates.com)

Etihad Airways (✆ 01-989 393; www.etihad.com; Zein Bldg, ground Fl, Omar Daouk St, Bab Idriss, Beirut)

Qatar Airways (✆ 01-629 524; www.qatarairways.com; Beirut-RHIA)

Royal Jordanian (✆ 01-379 990; www.rj.com; Bliss St, Beirut)

Turkish Airlines (TK; ✆ 01-629 543; www.turkishairlines.com; Beirut-RHIA)

LAND

Border Crossings

The only land crossings from Lebanon are into Syria (the Israel–Lebanon land border has not been open for many years). The current conflict in that country means they are not usable by travellers.

Sea

At the time of research, Turkish company **Akgünler Deniz Cilik** (www.akgunlerdenizcilik. com) was operating a weekly ferry service between Tripoli and Taşucu, near Mersin in Turkey. The ferry left Taşucu at 6pm every Tuesday (adult/child one-way US$70/10, 12 hours), and Tripoli (adult/child one-way US$115/55, 12 hours) at 6pm every Thursday. Return tickets cost adult/child US$145/64. Note that ticket prices may rise over the summer months.

ℹ️ Getting Around

There are no air services or trains operating within Lebanon, but the country is so small that you don't really need them (you can drive from one end to the other in half a day). In and around Beirut and the coastal strip, the bus, minibus and taxi network is extensive, cheap and fairly reliable. To fully explore the hinterland of the country (especially around the Qadisha Valley, Bekaa Valley and the south), it's worth negotiating with a private taxi to avoid waiting for hours for irregular minibus services or *servees*.

BICYCLE

Lebanon's steep terrain, the state of many urban roads and the often erratic local driving style mean that cycling is not recommended.

BUS & MICROBUS

Minibuses travel between Beirut and all of Lebanon's major towns; the only route that has large, Pullman-style buses is Beirut–Tripoli. The best of the buses on that route are operated by **Connexion** (Connex; ☎ 06-626 969; www.connexion-transport.com) and will drop passengers off at any point along the Beirut–Tripoli highway on request. There are three main bus pick-up and drop-off points in Beirut:

➜ Charles Helou Bus Station
➜ Cola Transport Hub
➜ Dawra Transport Hub

Charles Helou is the only formal station and is divided into three signposted zones:

Zone A For buses to Syria.

Zone B For buses servicing Beirut (where the route starts or finishes at Charles Helou bus station).

Zone C For express buses to Jounieh, Byblos and Tripoli.

Zones A and C have ticket offices where you can buy tickets for your journey. In the other stations (Cola and Dawra transport hubs), ask any driver for your bus (if someone doesn't find you first). Buses usually have a route number and the destination displayed in the front window, but this is usually in Arabic only. Government-run buses have red number plates and there are a number of independently owned microbuses that cover the same routes; note that the embassies of foreign countries recommend using the government-run buses only. You pay for your ticket on board, either at the start or end of the journey.

CAR

You need to be a competent driver with very steady nerves to contemplate driving in Lebanon, since there are few rules of the road. A three-lane road, for example, can frequently become seven lanes. Hairpin bends and potholed roads are frequent in the mountains, and few roads are gritted after a snow fall. Beirut's traffic is often heavy, and road signs (where there are any at all) can be cryptic or misleading. In addition to being generally cautious, remember to stop at military checkpoints and have your passport and car rental papers ready for inspection.

LOCAL TRANSPORT

Bus

Some towns, including Beirut, have privately owned buses that operate a hail-and-ride system. Fares are generally LL1000 for intra-city destinations and LL1500 for inter-town destinations.

Taxi & Service Taxi

Most routes around Lebanese towns and cities are covered by service, or shared, taxis, which are usually elderly Mercedes with red licence plates and a taxi sign on the roof. You can hail them at any point on their route and also get out wherever you wish by saying '*anzil huun*' (drop me off here). Be sure to ask '*servees?*' before getting in (if it's an empty car), to ensure the driver doesn't try to charge you a private

---

ℹ️ ISRAELI PASSPORT STAMPS

Lebanon denies entry to all travellers with evidence of a visit to Israel in their passport. If asked at a border crossing or at the airport if you've ever been to Israel, bear in mind that saying 'yes' (if you have) will mean you won't be allowed into the country.

taxi fare. Going rates are generally LL1500 to LL2000 for trips within a town, and LL3000 to LL10,000 for trips to outlying areas. Note that at the time of research, the embassies of foreign nations were advising their citizens not to use service taxis due to the threat of kidnapping and robbery.

If you want to engage a private taxi, make sure the driver understands exactly where you want

to go and negotiate the fare clearly before you get in.

Reputable Beirut-based taxi companies that have English-speaking drivers and well-maintained cars include **Comfort Taxi** (☏ 70-697 666, 01-698 666; comfort.taxi@ymail.com) and Hamra-based **Lebanon Taxi** (☏ 01 353-153; www.lebanontaxi.com). Both charge around US$100 for half-day hire and US$150 for a full day.

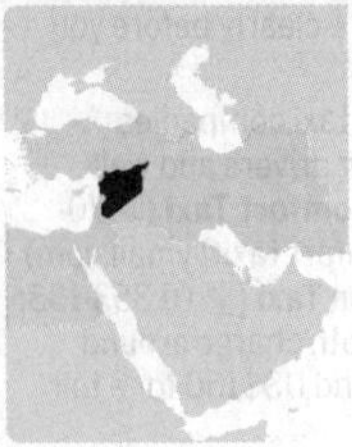

Syria

Fast Facts

➡ **Capital** Damascus

➡ **Area** 185,180 sq km

➡ **Population** 17.95 million

➡ **Life expectancy at birth**
68.41 years (before the war:
73.1 years)

➡ **Inflation** 59.1%

➡ **Casualties of war** 191,000
(August 2014)

➡ **Refugees within/outside
Syria** three/nine million

➡ **Percentage of refugees
who are children** 50%

Understand

At the time of writing, Syria is one of the most dangerous places on the planet. To put it simply, you can't go. And if you can, you shouldn't.

The uprising against the Assad regime that began in early 2011 long ago became a civil war. Syrians themselves have paid the heaviest price – an estimated 200,000 have died in the conflict and millions have been forced into exile. Most such tragedies happen far away from the international spotlight. But Westerners, including journalists and aid workers, have also been targeted, very publicly so, both for kidnapping and execution. By visiting Syria now, you would run the risk of both.

We have not, of course, visited Syria to update our coverage for this edition. For that reason, this chapter contains no information or advice for travellers to the country. Instead, we have shifted our focus to exploring what daily life is like for those still inside the country.

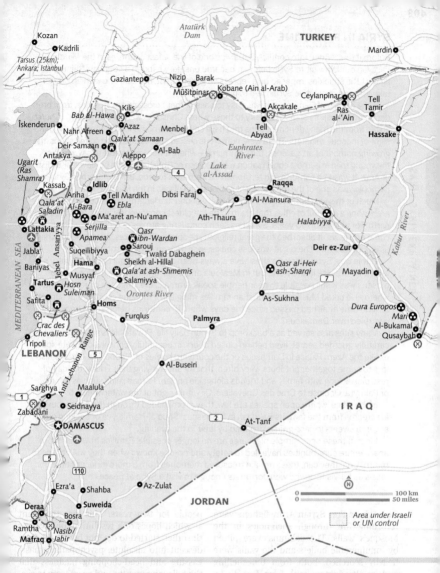

SYRIA EXPLAINED

By Richard Spencer, Middle East Correspondent of the Daily Telegraph *and Sunday Telegraph. He has reported regularly from Aleppo and other parts of Syria since the start of the civil war.*

One day in May 2013, I stood in the afternoon shadows of the courtyard of Aleppo's Great Umayyad Mosque, as gunfire rattled in the near distance, and took a photograph of a pile of rubble in the corner. This pile of ragged and forlorn stone was all that remained of the mosque's 11th century minaret, a symbol of Aleppo's Old City, a feature of countless postcards, the finest architectural monument of northern Syria.

It wasn't safe to walk in the centre of the courtyard, because it was in full view of government snipers on the upper floors of buildings a couple of hundred metres away; instead, my guides and I skirted the colonnades, rounding sandbagged positions

SYRIA IN PEACETIME

Before it descended into conflict, Syria was one of the safest countries in the Middle East. On our last visit to Syria before it became unsafe, we found a country straining against the shackles imposed by a repressive government, but also one with an unmistakeably and distinctive Syrian feel to it.

In the old city of Damascus, it was easy to pass, without crossing any frontline, from predominantly Muslims areas of the city to those where Christians were in the majority. Church spires from the many denominations that have called Syria home for millennia rose within sight of mosque minarets. There were numerous shared spaces, too – the coffee shops, the growing number of art galleries, the hammams – where it was impossible to say whether the young men in earnest conversation were Muslim or Christian, Sunni or Alawite, Kurdish or Arab. It wasn't a paradise and tension arose from time to time. But Syria, urban Syria in particular, was one of the most tolerant and peaceful places in the Middle East.

Much of this was born from a shared history of unusual length. Damascus and Aleppo are among a handful of cities that claim to be the oldest continuously inhabited cities on earth. For at least 5000 years, Syria has seen conquering armies and fleeing refugees come and leave. It absorbed the great religions, peoples and cultures, appropriating them as its own to form. The result was less coexistence than an intricate mosaic.

In this way, Syria's historic sites have always been an essential part of the country's fabric. Where else in the world but in Maaloula and other Christian towns close to Damascus was it still possible to hear people speak Aramaic, the language of Jesus? And where else could Muslim and Christian families mingle in a mosque courtyard at sunset as if no time at all had passed since the days when, 15 centuries before, the Umayyads had ruled over Damascus?

Many sites also served as a backdrop to Syrian daily life. Private life is most often a carefully guarded secret, lived behind closed doors, in beautifully conceived private spaces like the Azem Palace in Damascus or the courtyard homes of Aleppo. But Syrians also love to come together outdoors. Very often, that meant enjoying their Friday, the day of rest, picknicking with family and friends alongside ancient Roman ruins such as Apamea or Palmyra. Or close to Crac des Chevaliers. Or within sight of the waterwheels of Hama.

In the cities, where open spaces are few, they promenaded through the souqs, buying ice creams from the famous Bakdash in Damascus' Souq al-Hamidiyya or seeking out sugared sweets in case guests dropped by later in the evening.

Most of these once-simple pleasures are no longer possible. Families have been torn apart, entire communities have fled to safety and no-one knows when they will be able to return. Until they can, these remain treasured memories from a more innocent time, for locals as for visitors who were fortunate enough to visit a Syria at peace.

---

from where Free Syrian Army fighters were returning fire through shell-holes in the Mosque's walls. The columns were pitted by innumerable bullets and the walls were heavily scorched, both from the shelling and, so the fighters said, from fires lit by government soldiers before they had first retreated up the alleys of the Old City the previous September.

The mosque's library had gone up in flames then, as had parts of the adjoining souq, the market stalls disappearing into ash. The minaret had fallen under tank fire two weeks previously. It was a pitiful sight.

It was shocking, but hardly surprising, that Syria had begun to devour its monuments; it had already been devouring its people for two years. This was the point at which hopes of a resolution, one way or the other, started to die, but before the final descent into absolute, psychopathic, massgassing and head-chopping madness that the following months and years were to see.

From Revolution to War

In February 2011, at the time of the first stirrings of unrest, the Arab Spring was a moment of hope, and not a process of despair. When the first mass protests took place in Syria, the demonstrations were not even about removing the regime; at first the calls were for freedom and reform.

As with most civil wars, there was a process of escalation. The point of no return, though, was Tuesday, 15 March 2011, when a protest in the town of Deraa near the Jordanian border was fired on, resulting in scores of deaths. The *casus belli* was trivial: a group of teenagers accused of scrawling anti-regime graffiti on walls had been arrested and beaten up – nothing unusual in the Assads' Syria. But the scenes of death and mayhem outside Deraa's historic mosque, Skyped to the outside world, catalysed protests across the country, particularly in majority Sunni cities like Deraa – Homs and Hama, Deir al-Zour in the northeast.

These protests were also met with extreme force. As the year continued, so did the protests, so did the regime shootings, and so, gradually, did the armed resistance. There was a pattern: a surge of protests, followed by hints of reform by the regime, which went further than before each time but never anywhere near the protesters' rising demands. There was never a chance of the regime stepping down, or of serious glasnost.

Struggle for Control

Two years later, the revolt had become a revolution and then a war. By May 2013, armed rebels controlled swathes of northern and western Syria, particularly areas close to the Turkish and Lebanese borders, through which sympathetic individuals and, less often, governments poured in money and arms. The rebels had first seized patches of Homs, Idlib and Aleppo; every now and then, the government would muster the energy and intensity to reclaim areas with heavy use of force, most notably the Homs suburb of Baba Amr in February 2012, an assault preceded by an intense artillery bombardment – broadcast in real time by the BBC, Sky and other journalists smuggled inside. Some journalists, including Marie Colvin of the *Sunday Times,* were killed as they drew the world's attention to the slaughter of civilians.

These government attempts to reclaim the country were to little avail. As the rebels were driven out of one suburb, they just spread wider, until the Liwa Tawhid, a collection of militias from Sunni, former Muslim Brotherhood areas of Aleppo province, swept into the city itself in July 2012. The attack was the nadir of the war for the regime: at the same time, rebels came close to the centre of Damascus, while a bomb attack on a government security headquarters killed four of the regime's most senior cadres, including the defence minister.

A Proxy War

America and its allies gave the rebels their backing, but, nervous of the precedents of chaotic interventions in Iraq and now Libya, refused to send military support or authorise a no-fly zone without backing from the United Nations Security Council. That was never likely to be forthcoming, with Russia, a veto-holder, backing its old ally throughout.

As the regime wavered, Iran began to send in 'advisers', while Hezbollah, the Shia Iranian proxy based in Lebanon, also joined the fight on the regime's side. The war became a conflict of proxies: the Gulf-based funders of jihad, clerics, princes and businessmen among them, chose their own religiously inclined militias to support, and the whole country began to disintegrate into a patchwork of fiefdoms controlled by different armed gangs, often hard to distinguish from one another.

In the face of jihadi brutality and bombing of rebel areas, the Syrian people could do little but flee. Perhaps three million, more than a tenth of the population, are abroad; nine million more displaced internally.

The Emergence of Isis

The Western world, meanwhile, began to lose interest; it all seemed just too intractable. Even a chemical weapons attack, which killed more than 1000 people in Damascus in August 2013, did not trigger the long-awaited intervention. It took the rise of the Islamic State of Iraq and al-Sham (Isis), a splinter from Al-Qaeda's local franchise Jabhat al-Nusra, to reclaim attention. It carved out a 'Caliphate' in the east of the country, and only when it spread that Caliphate over the border into Iraq, threatening Baghdad, did it finally trigger the Western intervention so long denied to the rebels. The allied bombing, led by the United States, limited Isis' expansion, but did nothing to end the war, which many analysts fear could now continue for a decade. Isis, with its ability to spread terror, seems unstoppable.

The Future

Will Syria ever be put back together again? There is much talk of the end of the Sykes-Picot agreement, the boundaries the British and French drew up after the World War I. But no new territories could coherently divide Alawite from Sunni, Shia from Christian, without mass expulsions of citizens. No-one, apart from Isis, seems willing to contemplate such a result.

Whatever the flaws of Messrs Sykes' and Picot's settlement, Syria has existed for millennia, and survived wars before. Aleppo was conquered by Hittites, Assyrians, Greeks, Armenians, Romans and Persians in the centuries before the Rashidun arrived. It fell variously to the Byzantines, Mongols and Mamluks in the centuries after. It suffered earthquakes and massacres, and rebuilt itself. One hopes it will again.

CULTURE IN CONFLICT

By Issa Touma, Aleppo-based photographer, director of Le Pont Organization, which hosts art festivals and projects, and curator of photography gallery Le Pont.

As I write these lines, almost four years have passed since the civil war started in Syria, and my art organisation is still operating without financial support from any side. Here there is a lot of money and support around for killing and violence, but not for art and peace.

Culture suffers because for most sides in this war, it constitutes a threat that must be stopped. Years of conflict have effectively shut down Syria, which was once one of the most important cultural civilizations in the world. In Aleppo, I'm not sure that our cultural life can keep fiercely resisting for another four years but even though the city is hungry and unsafe, still we have hope.

Has the war put an end to culture? Of course not. Young artists have stayed active, forming a united society who stand together to save as much of our civil life as they can.

In December 2014, we hosted the annual Aleppo International Photography Festival, which showed works from artists around the world. It allowed the civilians of our city who live through the horrors of war to have a peaceful moment of normalcy, just to stand and enjoy photography. My gallery, Le Pont, which is the only gallery still operating in the region, regularly puts on other photography exhibitions and organises workshops with Western artists online to help young Syrian artists develop.

We also invite Aleppo citizens to take part in ongoing Art Camping projects. Art Camping is a communal activity which aims to give positive energy to people in a war zone through art. In one short video, 'Texture of the city we lost', people made pencil transfers of carved stone, coins and other traditional, everyday objects. In another, 'The Passageway', Aleppians described their journeys through a dangerous passageway between east and west Aleppo to get food and supplies.

This is how I understand our situation: traditional Arabic houses in Aleppo have high walls, with the windows so far up, they don't permit any contact with the outside world. Even though most of us now live in modern apartments, when we look into the mirror we still see the reflection of the traditional Arabic house in all aspects of our life, political, social and cultural. It runs in our blood.

I believe we suffer from the absence of trust in others, of contact with them in close society. But when cultural activities such as these projects are established, they depend entirely on dealing and communicating with each other. Syrians do have a chance – the first steps of freedom start from inside of each of us. We still believe art has to be the best way to build trust between countries, and our gallery's message is this: Art is Peace.

EVERYDAY LIFE IN DAMASCUS

By Karima Ward, journalist and editor at Syria Newsdesk, an agency covering the Syrian war.

Being the world's oldest continuously inhabited capital, Damascus has, throughout its long history, borne witness to perhaps every predicament imaginable.

Over the past four years, I have watched my country descend into indescribable chaos. Having been born and raised in Damascus, not long ago considered among the safest cities in the world, I find myself now living in one of the worst.

Walking the streets is a constant risk. Despite the fact that the actual fighting takes place at the city's outskirts, deafening sounds of fighter jets and violent clashes are always present in the background, replacing the hustle and bustle of a once cheerful life. Mor-

PRESERVING SYRIA'S HISTORIC SITES

The loss of human life during the Syrian conflict has been well-documented. Less is known about the damage caused to Syria's signature historic sites. As Unesco's Director-General, Irina Bokova, warned in 2014, 'we are reaching the point of no return where Syria's cultural heritage is concerned. The destruction of heritage represents a cultural haemorrhage in addition to the tragic humanitarian crisis and suffering experienced by the people of Syria'.

The State of Play

All of Syria's six Unesco World Heritage–listed sites – Aleppo's Old City, the Old City of Damascus, Palmyra, Bosra, the Crac des Chevaliers and a series of historic villages in northern Syria were added by Unesco to its list of World Heritage Sites in Danger in 2013.

In Aleppo, the Great Umayyad Mosque has been reduced to rubble and 121 historic buildings and 1500 shops have been destroyed in the covered souq. The citadel, surrounding buildings and many gates to the Old City have also been badly damaged, while the Yalbogha Hammam is, at the time of writing, occupied by military groups.

The Crac des Chevaliers, Syria's iconic Crusader-era castle, has been repeatedly hit in the fighting. Although its structure remains largely intact, the interior has been badly damaged. Looting has also occurred in the ancient cities of Palmyra, Bosra and Apamea.

The core of the Old City in Damascus has thus far largely escaped serious damage. Some mosaics on the facade of the Umayyad Mosque have been damaged by mortar rounds, although they have since been repaired by the government's General Directorate of Archeology and Museums. The national museum remains undamaged and, remarkably, open for visitors.

Beyond World Heritage Sites, Isis has repeatedly targeted Islamic shrines revered by locals, denouncing them as un-Islamic. They have also targeted Christian churches. The Armenian Genocide Martyrs' Memorial Church in Deir al-Zour, for example, was deliberately destroyed in mid-2014, along with its priceless library devoted to the Armenian Genocide.

What's Being Done

In 2014, UN Security Council Resolution 2139 called on all parties 'to immediately end all violence which has led to human suffering in Syria, save Syria's rich societal mosaic and cultural heritage, and take appropriate steps to ensure the protection of Syria's World Heritage Sites'.

Although unable to physically prevent or monitor attacks on most threatened sites within Syria, Unesco has put in place measures to stop illegal trafficking in looted antiquities, working closely with Interpol and customs authorities in neighbouring countries and around the world.

In a section on its website called 'Safeguarding Syrian Cultural Heritage', Unesco (www.unesco.org) also publishes comprehensive reports and photographic evidence of attacks on historic sites in a bid 'to monitor the situation of cultural heritage in Syria and help international cooperation to protect the country's heritage'.

For its part, the Syrian Government has launched a national campaign called 'Save Syria's History' and says that many of its workers have been killed trying to protect the country's ancient sites. The government's critics argue that indiscriminate bombing by the government itself has caused widespread damage to historic and cultural sites.

tar shells randomly shower the city, making the most mundane of chores a perilous task to accomplish.

Just getting around the city often takes longer than it used to, as innumerable security checkpoints dot many of its previously vibrant streets, and long lines of cars are a common sight.

I, along with most residents, now opt to run errands on foot, which allows us to save on much-needed gas money – diesel prices have more than quadrupled since the conflict began. Otherwise, the cost of living in Damascus is still cheap, especially for someone converting money from most foreign currencies.

Perhaps surprisingly, most of the city's attractions still stand, from the historic Umayyad Mosque to the iconic street vendors that past visitors have grown accustomed to seeing on every corner.

Hammams continue to welcome nostalgic folk who appreciate having a cup of tea after

SYRIA EVERYDAY LIFE IN DAMASCUS

THINGS THEY SAID ABOUT...
DAMASCUS

'...no recorded event has occurred in the world but Damascus was in existence to receive news of it. Go back as far as you will into the vague past, there was always a Damascus...She has looked upon the dry bones of a thousand empires and will see the tombs of a thousand more before she dies...To Damascus, years are only flitting trifles of time. She measures time, not by days and months and years, but by the empires she has seen rise, and prosper and crumble to ruin. She is a type of immortality.'

Mark Twain, The Innocents Abroad, *1869*

a long hot bath and maybe chat, discuss the latest events and smoke arghileh (sheesha). Both Hammam Al-Bakri and Nour al-Din are still functioning.

It's business as usual at the Souq al-Hamidiyya, except for the heavy security presence that can now be witnessed at every corner. The stores sell the usual merchandise and people frequent them just as often as they used to. Azem Palace remains open and undamaged, while the famous Al-Nawfara Coffee Shop remains steadfast too, still a place for customers to relax and unwind.

Nevertheless, a returning visitor would immediately notice that as a result of rampant inflation and the dwindling numbers of tourists, many shops, particularly those that sell souvenirs and antiques, have been forced to close their doors.

Damascus' nightlife scene is alive and well, if perhaps slightly altered, after adapting to the random surges of violence that sometimes erupt unannounced in different parts of the city. Bars, cafes and restaurants in the famed Bab Sharqi quarter of the Old City, while packed on any day of the week, now mostly close their doors at 9pm, and only a few remain open past midnight, defying hours of rationing of both electricity and water.

Many residents, particularly young people, have been forced to flee the country in search of job opportunities abroad, dissolving what was previously a tight-knit community. Inter-community relations have

undoubtedly been shaken by the conflict, however, residents of different religious backgrounds continue to coexist peacefully.

In spite of all those hardships, I try to remain hopeful and look forward to a brighter future. As uncertain as it is, I embrace a 'live-the-moment' attitude, because if Damascus has taught me anything, it's that life goes on.

FURTHER READING

Books

➡ *Syria: Descent Into The Abyss* (Patrick Cockburn, Robert Fisk & Kim Sengupta, 2014) Reportage by respected journalists.

➡ *Syria Speaks: Art and Culture from the Frontline* (edited by Malu Halasa, Zaher Omareen and Nawara Mahfoud, 2014) Work by more than fifty artists and writers.

➡ *My House in Damascus: An Inside View of the Syrian Revolution* (Diana Darke, 2014) Insider account of daily life.

➡ *Syria: Through Writers' Eyes* (edited by Marius Kociejowski, 2006) Writing about Syria down through the centuries.

Online

International Crisis Group (crisisgroup.org) Respected international NGO known for its objective, detailed coverage of conflicts worldwide.

Syrian Observatory for Human Rights (syriahr.com/en/) Tireless collating of deaths and battles from inside Syria.

Unesco (www.unesco.org) Go to the 'Safeguarding Syrian Cultural Heritage' section for the most comprehensive coverage of the threat to Syria's cultural heritage.

Documentaries

➡ *Ground Zero: Syria* (2012) A harrowing portrait of Aleppo at war.

➡ *Return to Homs* (2013) Follows young Syrian rebels through the rubble of Homs.

➡ *Rojava: Syria's Unknown War* (2014) The conflict as seen from Syria's Kurdish northeast.

Turkey

Why Go?

Turkey is where Asia and Europe meet and meld together. The 'bridge between continents' tag may be a cliché but this nation's juxtaposition of modern sophistication and ancient tradition is a surprising and heady brew that turns many travellers' first perceptions on their head. Steeped in age-old culture but imbued with a contemporary go-getting pulse, Turkey defies being pinned down and is the perfect introduction to the Middle East.

Every empire builder worth his salt has left their mark here. Stare in wonder at İstanbul's deluge of Byzantine and Ottoman finery or explore the rambling ruins of Ephesus – actually just trip over a rock in Turkey and it's probably going to be rubble from some long-gone empire's era of glory. Afterwards, hike the lunarscape of Cappadocia or sun-bake on a beach backed by lush Mediterranean coastline and you'll discover a countryside just as mesmerising as its monuments.

Best for Nature

➡ Cappadocia (p474)

➡ Lycian Way (p460)

➡ Blue Voyages (p459)

➡ Mt Ararat (p484)

Best for Culture

➡ İstanbul (p416)

➡ Konya (p473)

➡ Diyarbakır (p485)

➡ Mardin (p486)

➡ Ephesus (p450)

➡ Şanlıurfa (p487)

When to Go

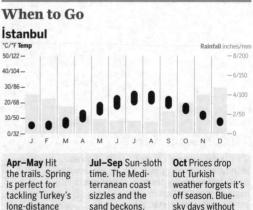

İstanbul

Apr–May Hit the trails. Spring is perfect for tackling Turkey's long-distance Lycian Way.

Jul–Sep Sun-sloth time. The Mediterranean coast sizzles and the sand beckons.

Oct Prices drop but Turkish weather forgets it's off season. Blue-sky days without the crowds.

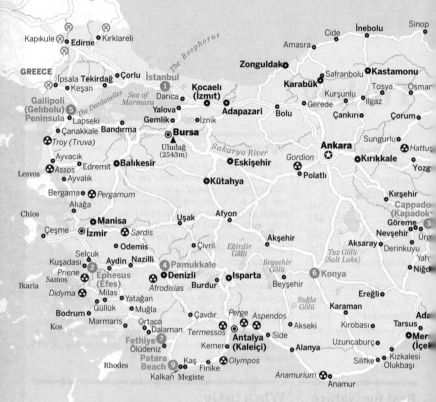

Turkey Highlights

❶ Craning your neck to gaze at Byzantine fresco frippery and Ottoman artistry before haggling your heart out in the Grand Bazaar, in **İstanbul** (p416).

❷ Channelling your inner Roman amid the ruins of **Ephesus** (p450).

❸ Scoping out the moonscape of **Cappadocia** (p474) from a hot-air balloon.

❹ Dipping your toes in thermal pools after scaling the hillside of **Pamukkale** (453).

❺ Remembering the fallen at the WWI battlefields on the **Gallipoli Peninsula** (p441).

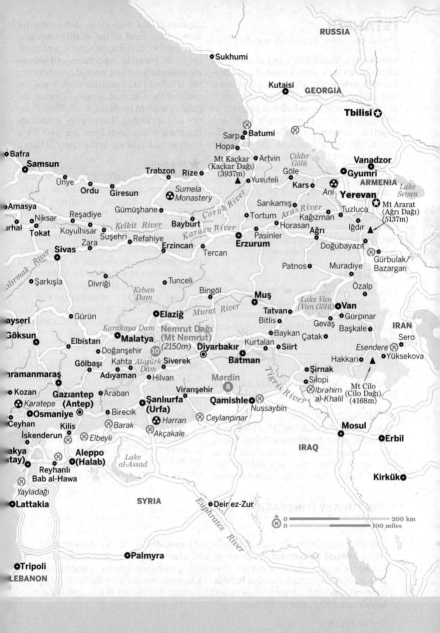

RUSSIA

Sukhumi

Kutaisi

GEORGIA

Tbilisi

Sarp
Batumi
Hopa

Bafra
Samsun

Ünye
Ordu
Giresun

Trabzon
Rize

Mt Kaçkar
(Kaçkar Dağı)
(3937m)

Artvin

Çıldır
Gölü

Yusufeli

Göle

Vanadzor
Gyumri

ARMENIA

Lake
Sevan

Kars

Ani

Yerevan

Amasya
Niksar
Reşadiye

Sumela
Monastery

Gümüşhane

Bayburt

Çoruh River

Karasu River

Sarıkamış

Tortum

Aras River

Kağızman

Tuzluca

Mt Ararat
(Ağrı Dağı)
(5137m)

rhal
Tokat
Koyulhisar

Kelkit River

Suşehri
Refahiye

Horasan

Iğdır

Zara
Sivas

Şarkışla

Divriği

Erzincan

Tercan

Pasinler

Erzurum

Ağrı

Doğubayazıt

Gürbulak/
Bazargan

Patnos
Muradiye

Özalp

Keban
Dam

Bingöl

Muş

Lake Van
(Van Gölü)

Van

Tunceli

Tatvan

ayseri
Gürün

Karakaya Dam

Elazığ

Nemrut Dağı
(Mt Nemrut)
(2150m)

Murat River

Bitlis

Gevaş
Baykan
Çatak

Gürpınar
Başkale

IRAN

Sero

Göksun
Elbistan
Malatya

Doğanşehir

Diyarbakır

Kurtalan
Siirt

Esendere
Yüksekova

Hakkari

Mt Cilo
(Cilo Dağı)
(4168m)

Gölbaşı

Kahta

Atatürk
Dam

Siverek

Batman

Şırnak
Silopi

hramanmaraş
Adıyaman

Hilvan

Mardin

İbrahim
al-Khalil

Kozan
Karatepe

Gaziantep
(Antep)

Araban

Viranşehir

Qamishle

Osmaniye

Birecik

Şanlıurfa
(Urfa)

Nussaybin

Ceyhan
İskenderun

Kilis

Harran

Ceylanpınar

Mosul

Erbil

akya
tay)

Aleppo
(Halab)

Barak

Akçakale

IRAQ

Reyhanlı
Bab al-Hawa

Elbeyli

Lake
al-Assad

Kirkük

Yayladağı

Lattakia

SYRIA

Euphrates River

Deir ez-Zur

N
0
0

200 km
100 miles

Tripoli

LEBANON

Palmyra

İSTANBUL

⊿ ASIAN SIDE 0216 / ⊿ EUROPEAN SIDE 0212 / POP 14 MILLION

İstanbul is a triumph of a city shaped first by the Byzantines, who decorated their capital with fresco-laden churches and palaces, and then by the Ottomans, who were quick to launch an ambitious building program to outbid them. The magnificently decorated imperial mosques that followed are architectural triumphs that have endowed the city with one of the world's great skylines.

İstanbul doesn't rest on its ancient laurels, though, and the street life is abuzz with innovative restaurants and fabulously cool bars. The wonders of old Constantinople may be what draw you here in the first place but the vitality of this energetic, sprawling metropolis will be your embracing memory of the city where east meets west.

⊙ Sights

Straddling the Bosphorus strait, İstanbul is broadly split into Asian and European 'sides'. European İstanbul is further divided by the Golden Horn (Haliç) into Old İstanbul in the south and Beyoğlu in the north.

⊙ Old İstanbul

Sultanahmet is the heart of Old İstanbul and boasts many of the city's famous sights.

★ **Topkapı Palace** PALACE
(Topkapı Sarayı; Map p426; ⊿ 212-512 0480; www.topkapisarayi.gov.tr; Babıhümayun Caddesi; palace adult/child under 12yr ₺30/free, Harem adult/child under 6yr ₺15/free; ⊙9am-6pm Wed-Mon mid-Apr–Oct, to 4pm Nov–mid-Apr; ⊡Sultanahmet)

Topkapı is the subject of more colourful stories than most of the world's museums put together. Libidinous sultans, ambitious courtiers, beautiful concubines and scheming eunuchs lived and worked here between the 15th and 19th centuries when it was the court of the Ottoman empire. Visiting the palace's opulent pavilions, jewel-filled Treasury and sprawling Harem gives a fascinating glimpse into their lives. See p418 for a glimpse into daily life in the Imperial Court.

★ **Aya Sofya** MUSEUM
(Hagia Sophia; Map p426; ⊿212-522 1750; www.ayasofyamuzesi.gov.tr; Aya Sofya Meydanı 1; adult/child under 12yr ₺30/free; ⊙9am-6pm Tue-Sun mid-Apr–Sep, to 4pm Oct–mid-Apr; ⊡Sultanahmet) There are many important monuments in İstanbul, but this venerable structure – commissioned by the great Byzantine emperor Justinian, consecrated as a church in 537, converted to a mosque by Mehmet the Conqueror in 1453 and declared a museum by Atatürk in 1935 – surpasses the rest due to its innovative architectural form, rich history, religious importance and extraordinary beauty. See p424 for more detail.

★ **Grand Bazaar** MARKET
(Kapalı Çarşı, Covered Market; Map p430; ⊙8.30am-7pm Mon-Sat; ✦; ⊠Veznecler, ⊡Beyazıt-Kapalı Çarşı) This colourful and chaotic bazaar is the heart of the Old City and has been so for centuries. Starting as a small vaulted *bedesten* (warehouse) built by order of Mehmet the Conqueror in 1461, it grew to cover a vast area as laneways between the *bedesten*, neighbouring shops and *hans* (caravanserais) were roofed and the market

---

TOP TURKEY ITINERARIES

Two Weeks

Lose yourself amid the empirical monuments of **İstanbul** then pay your respects at WWI's **Gallipoli battlefields**. Get your ruin-fix at ancient **Troy** and classical **Ephesus** followed by a quick inland trip to the bizarre blinding-white travertines of **Pamukkale**. Back on the coast, base yourself in **Fethiye** or **Kaş** to explore atmospheric Lycian city-remnants and the drop-dead gorgeous Mediterranean shore before finishing up in **Antalya's** beautifully restored old town.

Three Weeks

Follow the two-week itinerary to **Antalya**, then whirl northeast to **Konya**, Turkey's dervish centre. **Cappadocia's** other-worldly landscape then beckons for hiking amid fairy chimneys and hot-air ballooning. Watch sunrise atop **Nemrut Dağı (Mt Nemrut)**, surrounded by colossal stone heads, then head south to either stand on the city walls of **Diyarbakır** or stroll the mazy alleys of **Mardin** before munching the world's best baklava in **Gaziantep**.

assumed the sprawling, labyrinthine form that it retains today.

⭐ Museum of Turkish & Islamic Arts
MUSEUM

(Türk ve Islam Eserleri Müzesi; Map p426; www.tiem.gov.tr; Atmeydanı Caddesi 46; adult/child under 12yr ₺20/free; ⊙ refer to website; 🚇 Sultanahmet) This Ottoman palace on the western edge of the Hippodrome was built in 1524 for İbrahim Paşa, childhood friend, brother-in-law and grand vizier of Süleyman the Magnificent. Undergoing a major renovation at the time of research, it has a magnificent collection of artefacts, including exquisite examples of calligraphy and one of the world's most impressive collections of antique carpets.

⭐ İstanbul Archaeology Museums
MUSEUM

(İstanbul Arkeoloji Müzeleri; Map p426; 🗗 212-520 7740; www.istanbularkeoloji.gov.tr; Osman Hamdi Bey Yokuşu, Gülhane; adult/child under 12yr ₺15/free; ⊙ 9am-6pm Tue-Sun mid-Apr–Sep, to 4pm Oct–mid-Apr; 🚇 Gülhane) This superb museum showcases archaeological and artistic treasures from the Topkapı collections. Housed in three buildings, its exhibits include ancient artefacts, classical statuary and an exhibition tracing İstanbul's history. There are many highlights, but the sarcophagi from the Royal Necropolis of Sidon are particularly striking.

Basilica Cistern
CISTERN

(Yerebatan Sarnıçı; Map p426; 🗗 212-512 1570; www.yerebatan.com; Yerebatan Caddesi 13; admission for foreigners officially ₺20 but in reality ₺10; ⊙ 9am-6.30pm mid-Apr–Sep, to 5.30pm Nov–mid-Apr; 🚇 Sultanahmet) This subterranean structure was commissioned by Emperor Justinian and built in 532. The largest surviving Byzantine cistern in İstanbul, it was constructed using 336 columns, many of which were salvaged from ruined temples and feature fine carved capitals. Its symmetry and sheer grandeur of conception are quite breathtaking, and its cavernous depths make a great retreat on summer days.

Blue Mosque
MOSQUE

(Sultanahmet Camii; Map p426; Hippodrome; ⊙ closed to tourists during the 5 daily prayer times & Fri sermon; 🚇 Sultanahmet) İstanbul's most photogenic building was the grand project of Sultan Ahmet I (r 1603–17), whose tomb is located on the north side of the site facing Sultanahmet Park. The mosque's wonderfully curvaceous exterior features a cascade of

TURKEY İSTANBUL

domes and six slender minarets. Blue İznik tiles adorn the interior and give the building its unofficial but commonly used name.

⭐ Süleymaniye Mosque
MOSQUE

(Map p430; Professor Sıddık Sami Onar Caddesi; Ⓜ Vezneciler, 🚇 Laleli-Üniversite) The

Topkapı Palace

DAILY LIFE IN THE IMPERIAL COURT

A visit to this opulent palace compound, with its courtyards, harem and pavilions, offers a fascinating glimpse into the lives of the Ottoman sultans. During its heyday, royal wives and children, concubines, eunuchs and servants were among the 4000 people living within Topkapı's walls.

The sultans and their families rarely left the palace grounds, relying on courtiers and diplomats to bring them news of the outside world. Most visitors would go straight to the magnificent **Imperial Council Chamber ❶**, where the sultan's grand vizier and Dîvân (Council) regularly met to discuss affairs of state and receive foreign dignitaries. Many of these visitors brought lavish gifts and tributes to embellish the **Imperial Treasury ❷**.

After receiving any guests and meeting with the Dîvân, the grand vizier would make his way through the ornate **Gate of Felicity ❸** into the Third Court, the palace's residential quarter. Here, he would brief the sultan on the deliberations and decisions of the Dîvân in the ornate **Audience Chamber ❹**.

Meanwhile, day-to-day domestic chores and intrigues would be underway in the **Harem ❺** and servants would be preparing feasts in the massive **Palace Kitchens ❻**. Amid all this activity, the **Marble Terrace ❼** was a tranquil retreat where the sultan would come to relax, look out over the city and perhaps regret his sequestered lifestyle.

DON'T MISS

There are spectacular views from the terrace above the Konyalı Restaurant and also from the Marble Terrace in the Fourth Court.

Harem
The sultan, his mother and the crown prince had sumptuously decorated private apartments in the Harem. The most beautiful of these are the Twin Kiosks (pictured), which were used by the crown prince.

Harem Ticket Office

Middle Gate

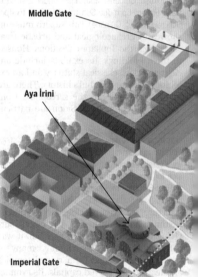

Aya İrini

Imperial Gate

Imperial Council Chamber
This is where the Dîvân (Council) made laws, citizens presente petitions and foreign dignitaries were presented to the court. The sultan sometimes eavesdropped on proceedings through the window with the golden grille.

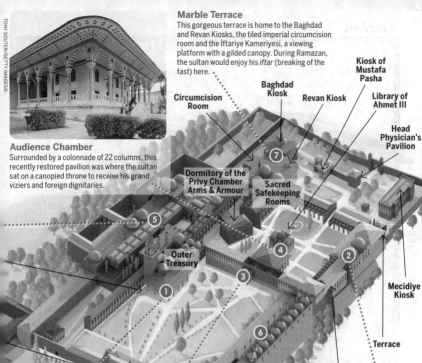

Marble Terrace
This gorgeous terrace is home to the Baghdad and Revan Kiosks, the tiled imperial circumcision room and the İftariye Kameriyesi, a viewing platform with a gilded canopy. During Ramazan, the sultan would enjoy his *iftar* (breaking of the fast) here.

Circumcision Room

Baghdad Kiosk

Revan Kiosk

Kiosk of Mustafa Pasha

Library of Ahmet III

Head Physician's Pavilion

Audience Chamber
Surrounded by a colonnade of 22 columns, this recently restored pavilion was where the sultan sat on a canopied throne to receive his grand viziers and foreign dignitaries.

Dormitory of the Privy Chamber Arms & Armour

Sacred Safekeeping Rooms

Outer Treasury

Mecidiye Kiosk

Terrace

Dormitory of the Expeditionary Force (Costume Collection)

Ticket Office

Gate of Felicity
This rococo-style gate was used for state ceremonies, including the sultan's accession and funeral. A 1789 work by court painter Kostantin Kapidagli records the enthronement ceremony of Sultan Selim III.

Palace Kitchens
Keeping the palace's 4000 residents fed was a huge task. Topkapı's kitchens occupied 10 domed buildings with 20 huge chimneys, and were workplace and home for 800 members of staff.

Imperial Treasury
One of the highlights here is the famous Topkapı Dagger, which was commissioned in 1747 by Sultan Mahmud I as a lavish gift for Nadir Shah of Persia. The shah was assassinated before it could be given to him.

İstanbul

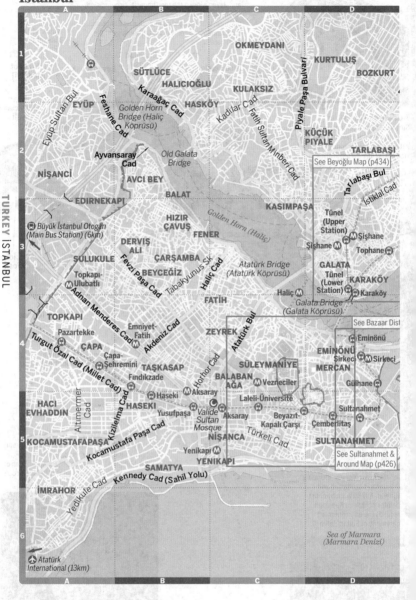

Süleymaniye crowns one of İstanbul's seven hills and dominates the Golden Horn, providing a landmark for the entire city. Though it's not the largest of the Ottoman mosques, it is certainly one of the grandest and most beautiful. It's also unusual in that many of its original *külliye* (mosque complex) buildings have been retained and sympathetically adapted for reuse.

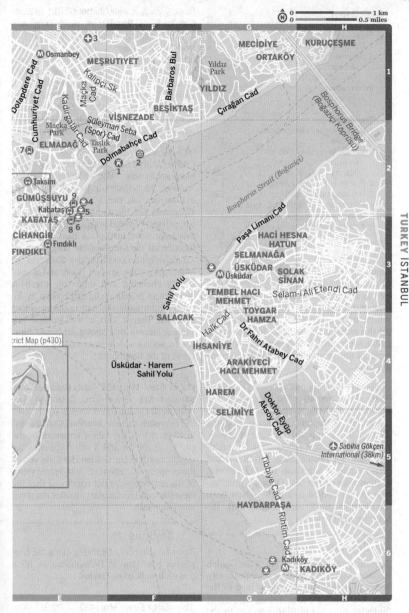

Map labels:

0 — 1 km
0 — 0.5 miles

MECİDİYE
KURUÇEŞME
ORTAKÖY
Osmanbey
MEŞRUTIYET
Yıldız Park
Dolapdere Cad
Kalipçi Sk
Maçka Cad
YILDIZ
Cumhuriyet Cad
Kadırgalar Cad
Barbaros Bul
BEŞİKTAŞ
Çırağan Cad
VİŞNEZADE
Bosphorus Bridge (Boğaziçi Köprüsü)
Maçka Park
Süleyman Seba (Spor) Cad
ELMADAĞ
Dolmabahçe Cad
Taşlık Park
1
2
Taksim
Bosphorus Strait (Boğaziçi)
GÜMÜŞSUYU
9
4
Kabataş
5
KABATAŞ
8 6
CİHANGİR
Paşa Limanı Cad
HACİ HESNA HATUN
FINDIKLI
Fındıklı
SELMANAĞA
ÜSKÜDAR
SOLAK SİNAN
Üsküdar
Selam-i Ali Efendi Cad
Sahil Yolu
TEMBEL HACI MEHMET
TOYGAR HAMZA
SALACAK
Halk Cad
Dr Fahri Atabey Cad
İHSANİYE
trict Map (p430)
Üsküdar - Harem Sahil Yolu
ARAKIYECİ HACI MEHMET
HAREM
Doktor Eyüp Aksoy Cad
SELİMİYE
Sabiha Gökçen International (38km)
Tıbbiye Cad
HAYDARPAŞA
Rıhtım Cad
Kadıköy
KADIKÖY

Eminönü

Eminönü is the gateway to Old İstanbul at the southern end of the Galata Bridge. At sunset there are glorious views of the Galata Tower across the Golden Horn in Beyoğlu.

Spice Bazaar

MARKET

(Mısır Çarşısı, Egyptian Market; Map p430; ☺8am-6pm Mon-Sat, to 7pm Sun; ⓐEminönü) Vividly coloured spices are displayed alongside jewel-like *lokum* (Turkish delight) at this Ottoman-era marketplace, providing eye

İstanbul

candy for the thousands of tourists and locals who make their way here every day. As well as spices, stalls sell caviar, dried herbs, nuts and dried fruits. The number of stalls selling tourist trinkets increases annually, yet this remains a great place to stock up on edible souvenirs, share a few jokes with the vendors and marvel at the well-preserved building.

Rüstem Paşa Mosque   MOSQUE
(Rüstem Paşa Camii; Map p430; Hasırcılar Caddesi, Rüstem Paşa; Ⓜ Haliç, ⓐ Eminönü) Nestled in the middle of the busy Tahtakale shopping district, this diminutive mosque is a gem. Dating from 1560, it was designed by architect Sinan for Rüstem Paşa, son-in-law and grand vizier of Süleyman the Magnificent. A showpiece of the best Ottoman architecture and tilework, it is thought to have been the prototype for Sinan's greatest work, the Selimiye in Edirne.

◎ Beyoğlu

Beyoğlu, on the northern side of the Golden Horn, was once the 'new', or 'European', city. Today this trendy district plays host to the city's best nightlife and dining. The Tünel funicular runs uphill from Karaköy to the southern end of Beyoğlu's pedestrianised main street, İstiklal Caddesi, which stretches up the hill to Taksim Meydanı (Taksim Sq).

★ Museum of Innocence   MUSEUM
(Masumiyet Müzesi; Map p434; ☏ 212 252 9738; www.masumiyetmuzesi.org; Çukurcuma Caddesi,

Dalgıç Çıkmazı, 2; adult/student ₺25/10; ⊙ 10am-6pm Tue-Sun, to 9pm Thu; Ⓜ Taksim, ⓐ Tophane) The painstaking attention to detail in this fascinating museum/piece of conceptual art will certainly provide every amateur psychologist with a theory or two about its creator, Nobel Prize–winning novelist Orhan Pamuk. Vitrines display a quirky collection of objects that evoke the minutiae of İstanbullu life in the mid-to-late 20th century, when Pamuk's novel of the same name is set.

★ İstanbul Modern   GALLERY
(İstanbul Modern Sanat Müzesi; Map p434; www.istanbulmodern.org; Meclis-i Mebusan Caddesi, Tophane; adult/student/under 12yr ₺17/9/free; ⊙ 10am-6pm Tue, Wed & Fri-Sun, to 8pm Thu; ⓐ Tophane) The big daddy of a slew of newish, privately funded art galleries in the city, this impressive institution has a stunning location on the shores of the Bosphorus, an extensive collection of Turkish 20th-century paintings on the ground floor, and a constantly changing and uniformly excellent program of mixed-media exhibitions by local and international artists in the basement galleries. There's also a well-stocked gift shop, a cinema that shows art-house films and a stylish cafe-restaurant with superb views of the Bosphorus.

Galata Tower   TOWER
(Galata Kulesi; Map p434; Galata Meydanı, Galata; admission ₺19; ⊙ 9am-8pm; ⓐ Karaköy) The cylindrical Galata Tower stands sentry over the approach to 'new' İstanbul. Constructed in 1348, it was the tallest structure in the city for centuries, and it still dominates the skyline north of the Golden Horn. Its vertiginous upper balcony offers 360-degree views of the city, but we're not convinced that the view (though spectacular) justifies the steep admission cost.

◎ Beşiktaş

Buses heading out of Karaköy along the Bosphorus road stop at Dolmabahçe, or it's a downhill walk from Taksim.

Dolmabahçe Palace   PALACE
(Dolmabahçe Sarayı; Map p420; ☏ 212-327 2626; www.millisaraylar.gov.tr; Dolmabahçe Caddesi, Beşiktaş; adult Selâmlık ₺30, Harem ₺20, joint ticket ₺40, student/child under 7yr ₺5/free; ⊙ 9am-3.30pm Tue-Wed & Fri-Sun Apr-Oct, to 2.30pm Nov-Mar; ⓐ Kabataş then walk) These days it's fashionable for architects and critics influenced by the less-is-more aesthetic of the

Bauhaus masters to sneer at buildings such as Dolmabahçe. The crowds that throng to this imperial pleasure palace with its neo-classical exterior and over-the-top interior fit-out clearly don't share their disdain, though, flocking here to visit its Selâmlık (Ceremonial Suites), Harem and Veliaht Dairesi (Apartments of the Crown Prince). The latter is home to the recently opened National Palaces Painting Museum (Milli Saraylar Resim Müzesi; Map p420; 212-236 9000; Dolmabahçe Caddesi; 9am-4pm Tue, Wed & Fri-Sun; Akaretler, Kabataş then walk).

Princes' Islands (Adalar)

With good beaches, open woodland, a couple of monasteries, Victorian villas and transport by horse-drawn carriages, this string of pretty islands, especially Büyükada, which is the biggest, makes an ideal escape from the noise and hustle of İstanbul. Ferries (p433) to the islands (₺10) leave from the Adalar İskelesi dock at Kabataş opposite the tram stop. Try to go midweek to avoid the crowds.

Tours

İstanbul Walks WALKING TOUR
(Map p426; 212-516 6300; www.istanbulwalks.com; 2nd fl, Şifa Hamamı Sokak 1; walking tours €30-80, child under 6yr free; Sultanahmet) Specialising in cultural tourism, this company is run by history buffs and offers a large range of guided walking tours conducted by knowledgable English-speaking guides.

Tours concentrate on İstanbul's various neighbourhoods, but there are also tours of major monuments, a Turkish Coffee Trail, and a tour of the Bosphorus and Golden Horn by private boat. Student discounts are available.

Courses

Cooking Alaturka COOKING COURSE
(Map p426; 0536-338 0896; www.cookingalaturka.com; Akbıyık Caddesi 72a, Cankurtaran; cooking class per person €65; Sultanahmet) Dutch-born Eveline Zoutendijk opened the first English-language Turkish cooking school in İstanbul in 2003 and since then has built a solid reputation for her convivial classes, which offer a great introduction to Turkish cuisine and are suitable for both novices and experienced cooks. The delicious results are enjoyed over a five-course meal in the school's restaurant (Map p426; 212-458 5919; www.cookingalaturka.com; Akbıyık Caddesi 72a, Cankurtaran; set lunch or dinner ₺55; lunch Mon-Sat, dinner by reservation Mon-Sat; ; Sultanahmet).

Sleeping

Accommodation prices are higher than in the rest of Turkey. The most convenient place to stay for visiting the attractions is Cankurtaran (in Sultanahmet), where a variety of options for all budgets is crammed into a small area. The other major accommodation district is Beyoğlu (around Taksim Meydanı).

TURKEY İSTANBUL

DON'T MISS

PLEASURES OF THE BATH

After a long day's sightseeing, few things could be better than relaxing in a hamam. Here are our top soapy-scrub experiences guaranteed to leave your skin rosy pink and silky soft:

Ayasofya Hürrem Sultan Hamamı (Map p426; 212-517 3535; www.ayasofyahamami.com; Aya Sofya Meydanı 2; bath treatments €85-170, massages €40-75; 8am-10pm; Sultanahmet) Reopened in 2011 after a meticulous restoration, this twin hamam is now offering the most luxurious traditional bath experience in the Old City. Designed by the great architect Sinan between 1556 and 1557, it was built just across the road from Aya Sofya by order of Süleyman the Magnificent and named in honour of his wife Hürrem Sultan, commonly known as Roxelana.

Çemberlitaş Hamamı (Map p430; 212-522 7974; www.cemberlitashamami.com; Vezir Han Caddesi 8; self-service TL60, bath, scrub & soap massage TL90; 6am-midnight; Çemberlitaş) There won't be too many times in your life when you'll get the opportunity to have a Turkish bath in a building dating back to 1584, so now might well be the time to do it – particularly as this twin hamam was designed by Sinan and is among the most beautiful in the city.

Aya Sofya

TIMELINE

537 Emperor Justinian, depicted in one of the church's famous **mosaics** ❶, presides over the consecration of Byzantium's new basilica, Hagia Sophia (Church of the Holy Wisdom).

557 The huge **dome** ❷, damaged during an earthquake, collapses and is rebuilt.

843 The second Byzantine Iconoclastic period ends and figurative **mosaics** ❸ begin to be added to the interior. These include a depiction of the Empress Zoe and her third husband, Emperor Constantine IX Monomachos.

1204 Soldiers of the Fourth Crusade led by the Doge of Venice, Enrico Dandolo, conquer and ransack Constantinople. Dandolo's **tomb** ❹ is eventually erected in the church whose desecration he presided over.

1453 The city falls to the Ottomans; Mehmet II orders that Hagia Sophia be converted to a mosque and renamed Aya Sofya.

1577 Sultan Selim II is buried in a specially designed tomb, which sits alongside the **tombs** ❺ of four other Ottoman Sultans in Aya Sofya's grounds.

1847–49 Sultan Abdül Mecit I orders that the building be restored and redecorated; the huge **Ottoman Medallions** ❻ in the nave are added.

1935 The mosque is converted into a museum by order of Mustafa Kemal Atatürk, president of the new Turkish Republic.

2009 The face of one of the four **seraphs** ❼ is uncovered during major restoration works in the nave.

2012 Restoration of the exterior walls and western upper gallery commences.

Ottoman Medallions
These huge medallions are inscribed with gilt Arabic letters giving the names of God (Allah), Mohammed and the early caliphs Ali and Abu Bakr.

Imperial Loge

Omphalion

Imperial Door

Seraph Figures
The four huge seraphs at the base of the dome were originally mosaics, but two (on the western side) were recreated as frescoe after being damaged during the Latin occupation (1204–61).

Dome

Soaring 56m from ground level, the dome was originally covered in gold mosaics but was decorated with calligraphy during the 1847–49 restoration works overseen by Swiss-born architects Gaspard and Giuseppe Fossati.

Christ Enthroned with Empress Zoe and Constantine IX Monomachos

This mosaic portrait in the upper gallery depicts Zoe, one of only three Byzantine women to rule as empress in their own right.

Ottoman Tombs

The tombs of five Ottoman sultans and their families are located in Aya Sofya's southern corner and can be accessed via Kabasakal Caddesi. One of these occupies the church's original Baptistry.

Aya Sofya Tombs

② ⑥ ③ ④ ① ⑤

Former Baptistry

Astronomer's House & Workshop

Exit

Ablutions Fountain

Primary School

Main Entrance

Constantine the Great, the Virgin Mary and the Emperor Justinian

This 11th-century mosaic shows Constantine (right) offering the Virgin Mary the city of Constantinople. Justinian (left) is offering her Hagia Sophia.

Grave of Enrico Dandolo

The Venetian doge died in 1205, only one year after he and his Crusaders had stormed the city. A 19th-century marker in the upper gallery indicates the probable location of his grave.

Sultanahmet & Around

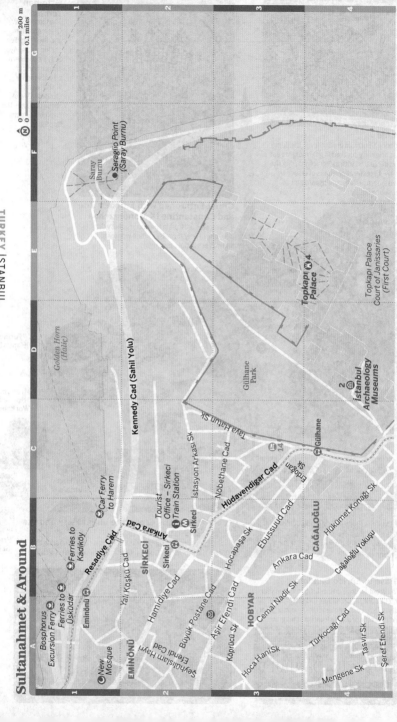

0 — 200 m
0 — 0.1 miles

A **B** **C** **D** **E** **F** **G**

Bosphorus Excursion Ferry
Ferries to Üsküdar
New Mosque
EMİNÖNÜ
Eminönü
Ferries to Kadiköy
Car Ferry to Harem
Reşadiye Cad
SİRKECİ
Sirkeci
Ankara Cad
Tourist Office – Sirkeci Train Station
Sirkeci
Golden Horn (Haliç)
Kennedy Cad (Sahil Yolu)
Saray Burnu
Seraglio Point (Saray Burnu)

Yalı Köşkü Cad
Hamidiye Cad
Büyük Postane Cad
Şeyhülislam Hayri Efendi Cad
Köprücü Sk
Aşir Efendi Cad
HOBYAR
Cemal Nadir Sk
Hoca Hani Sk
Ankara Cad
CAĞALOĞLU
Ebussuud Cad
Hükümet Konağı Sk
Cağaloğlu Yokuşu
Türkocağı Cad
Tasvir Sk
Şeref Efendi Sk
Mengene Sk
Hocapaşa Sk
Nobethane Cad
İstasyon Arkası Sk
Taya Hatun Sk
Hüdavendigar Cad
Erdoğan Sk
Gülhane
14
Gülhane Park
2 İstanbul Archaeology Museums
Topkapı Palace
4
Topkapı Palace Court of Janissaries (First Court)

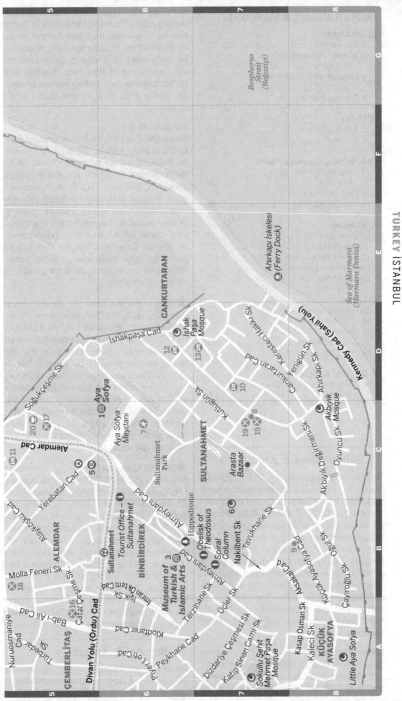

TURKEY İSTANBUL

Sultanahmet & Around

Sultanahmet & Around

★ **Marmara Guesthouse**　　PENSION $

(Map p426; ☑ 212-638 3638; www.marmaraguesthouse.com; Terbıyık Sokak 15, Cankurtaran; s €30-70, d €40-85, f €60-100; ❋ @ ☎; ⛢ Sultanahmet) There are plenty of family-run pensions in Sultanahmet, but few can claim the Marmara's levels of cleanliness and comfort. Manager Elif Aytekin and her family go out of their way to make guests feel welcome, offering plenty of advice and serving a delicious breakfast on the vine-covered, sea-facing roof terrace. Rooms have comfortable beds, good bathrooms and double-glazed windows.

Cheers Hostel　　HOSTEL $

(Map p426; ☑ 212-526 0200; www.cheershostel.com; Zeynep Sultan Camii Sokak 21, Cankurtaran; dm €16-22, d €60-80, tr €90-120; ❋ @ ☎; ⛢ Gül-

hane) The dorms here are worlds away from the impersonal barrackslike spaces in bigger hostels. Bright and airy, they feature wooden floorboards, rugs, lockers and comfortable beds; most have air-con. Bathrooms are clean and plentiful. It's a great choice in winter because the cosy rooftop bar has an open fire and a great view. Private rooms aren't as nice.

Bahaus Hostel　　HOSTEL $

(Map p426; ☑ 212-638 6534; www.bahausistanbul.com; Bayram Fırını Sokak 11, Cankurtaran; dm €11-24, d €60-70, without bathroom €50-60; @ ☎; ⛢ Sultanahmet) A small, clean and secure operation, Bahaus stands in stark and welcome contrast to the huge institutional-style hostels found on nearby Akbıyık Caddesi. Dorms (some female-only with bathroom) have curtained bunks with good mattresses, reading lights and lockers; they can be hot in summer. Top marks go to the plentiful bathrooms, entertainment program and rooftop terrace bar.

★ **Hotel Empress Zoe**　　BOUTIQUE HOTEL $$

(Map p426; ☑ 212-518 2504; www.emzoe.com; Akbıyık Caddesi 10, Cankurtaran; s €65-90, d €110-140, ste €160-275; ❋ ☎; ⛢ Sultanahmet) Named after the feisty Byzantine empress, this is one of the most impressive boutique hotels in the city. There's a range of room types but the garden suites are particularly enticing as they overlook a gorgeous flower-filled courtyard where breakfast is served in warm weather. You can enjoy an early-evening drink there, or while admiring the sea view from the terrace bar.

★ **Sirkeci Mansion**　　HOTEL $$

(Map p426; ☑ 212-528 4344; www.sirkecimansion.com; Taya Hatun Sokak 5, Sirkeci; standard r €120-215, superior & deluxe r €220-325, f €220-295; ❋ @ ☎ ⌘; ⛢ Gülhane) The owners of this terrific hotel overlooking Gülhane Park know what keeps guests happy – rooms are impeccably clean, well sized and loaded with amenities. It has a restaurant where a lavish breakfast is served, an indoor pool and a hamam. Top marks go to the incredibly helpful staff and the complimentary entertainment program, which includes walking tours and afternoon teas.

Beyoğlu & Around

World House Hostel　　HOSTEL $

(Map p434; ☑ 212-293 5520; www.worldhouseistanbul.com; Galipdede Caddesi 85, Galata; dm

€14-18, d/tr €68/78; @ 🛜; Ⓜ Şişhane, 🚋 Karaköy, then funicular to Tünel) Hostels in İstanbul are usually impersonal hulks with junglelike atmospheres, but World House is reasonably small and very friendly. Best of all is its location close to Beyoğlu's entertainment strips but not too far from the sights in Sultanahmet. There are large and small dorms (one shower for every six beds), but none are female-only.

★ Marmara Pera   HOTEL $$

(Map p434; 🖉 212-251 4646; www.themarmara hotels.com; Meşrutiyet Caddesi 1, Tepebaşı; s €109-160, d €135-199; ✳@🛜≋; Ⓜ Şişhane, 🚋 Karaköy, then funicular to Tünel) A great location in the midst of Beyoğlu's major entertainment enclave makes this high-rise modern hotel an excellent choice. Added extras include a health club, a tiny outdoor pool, a truly fabulous buffet breakfast spread and the Mikla (Map p434; www.miklarestaurant.com; Marmara Pera, Meşrutiyet Caddesi 15, Tepebaşı; ⊙ from 6pm Mon-Sat summer only; Ⓜ Şişhane, 🚋 Karaköy, then funicular to Tünel) rooftop bar and restaurant. Rooms with a sea view are approximately 30% more expensive.

Has Han Galata   BOUTIQUE HOTEL $$

(Map p434; 🖉 212-251 4218; www.hahsan.com.tr; Bankalar Caddesi 7, Galata; r €150-180, ste €180-215; ✳🛜; Ⓜ Şişhane, 🚋 Karaköy) Located on the cosmopolitan side of the Galata Bridge, this recently opened establishment has nine well-appointed and beautifully decorated rooms and an in-house cafe. The happening neighbourhood of Karaköy is close by, and the Old City is a relatively short walk away.

★ Witt İstanbul Hotel   BOUTIQUE HOTEL $$$

(Map p434; 🖉 212-293 1500; www.wittistanbul.com; Defterdar Yokuşu 26, Cihangir; ste €195-385, penthouse & superior king €385-450; ✳@🛜; Ⓜ Taksim, 🚋 Tophane) Showcasing nearly as many designer features as an issue of *Wallpaper* magazine, this stylish apartment hotel in the trendy suburb of Cihangir has 18 suites with kitchenette, seating area, CD/DVD player, iPod dock, espresso machine, king-sized bed and huge bathroom. Penthouse and superior king suites have fabulous views. It's a short but steep climb from the Tophane tram stop.

✖ Eating

Teeming with affordable fast-food joints, cafes and restaurants, İstanbul is a food-lover's paradise. Check out the possibilities online at İstanbul Eats (www.istanbuleats.com).

THE BOSPHORUS EXCURSION FERRY

İstanbul's vistas are at their most beautiful when seen from the water. Take the Bosphorus Excursion Ferry (Map p426; www.ido.com.tr; Boğaz İskelesi; long tour one way/return ₺15/25, short tour ₺10; ⊙ long tour 10.35am, plus 1.35pm Apr-Oct & noon summer; short tour 2.30pm Apr-Oct) and sit back on board and enjoy the view. Ferries depart from Eminönü and stop at various points before turning around at Anadolu Kavağı. The shores are sprinkled with monuments and various sights, including the monumental Dolmabahçe Palace, the majestic Bosphorus Bridge, the waterside suburbs of Arnavutköy, Bebek, Kanlıca, Emirgan and Sarıyer, as well as lavish *yalıs* (seafront mansions) and numerous mosques.

✖ Sultanahmet & Around

Sofa Cafe Restaurant   RESTAURANT $

(Map p426; 🖉 212-458 3630; Mimar Mehmet Ağa Caddesi 32, Cankurtaran; burgers ₺14, pastas ₺15-20, Turkish mains ₺17-35; ⊙ 11am-11pm; 🚋 Sultanahmet) Ten candlelit tables beckon patrons into this friendly cafe-bar just off Akbıyık Caddesi. There's a happy hour (in fact three) between 3.30pm and 6.30pm each day and a decidedly laid-back feel. The food is cheap but tasty, the glasses of wine are generous and the Efes is cold, meaning that there's plenty to like.

Sefa Restaurant   TURKISH $

(Map p426; 🖉 212-520 0670; www.sefarestaurant.com.tr; Nuruosmaniye Caddesi 17, Cağaloğlu; portions ₺8-14, kebaps ₺13-20; ⊙ 7am-5pm; 🖉; 🚋 Sultanahmet) This popular place near the Grand Bazaar describes its cuisine as Ottoman, but what's really on offer are *hazır yemek* (ready-made dishes) and kebaps at extremely reasonable prices. You can order from an English menu or choose daily specials from the bain-marie. Try to arrive early-ish for lunch because many of the dishes run out by 1.30pm. No alcohol.

Erol Lokantası   TURKISH $

(Map p426; 🖉 212-511 0322; Çatal Çeşme Sokak 3, Cağaloğlu; portions ₺6-14; ⊙ 11am-9pm Mon-Sat; 🖉; 🚋 Sultanahmet) One of the last *esnaf lokantası* (eateries serving ready-made

Bazaar District

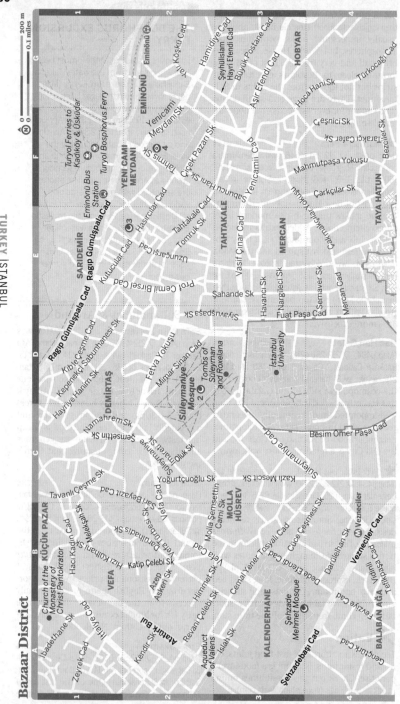

200 m
0.1 miles

G

Eminönü
Eminönü

Köşkü Cad
Yalı

Hamidiye Cad
Şeyhülislam
Hayri Efendi Cad
Büyük Postane Cad

HOBYAR

Turkocağı Cad

EMİNÖNÜ

Yenicami
Meydanı Sk

Aşir Efendi Cad

Hoca Hanı Sk

Çeşnici Sk

Tarakçı Cafer Sk

Bezciler Sk

Turyol Ferries to
Kadıköy & Üsküdar
Turyol Bosphorus Ferry

F

Tahmis Sk
4

Çiçek Pazar Sk

Sabuncu Hanı Sk

Yenicamii Cad

Mahmutpaşa Yokuşu

Çarkçılar Sk

TAYA HATUN

**YENİ CAMİ
MEYDANI**

TAHTAKALE

Çakmakçılar Yokuşu

Eminönü Bus
Station

Hasırcılar Cad

Tahtakale Cad

Tomruk Sk

MERCAN

SARIDEMİR

Ragıp Gümüşpala Cad

3

Kutucular Cad

Uzunçarşı Cad

Vasıf Çınar Cad

Semaver Sk

Mercan Cad

E

Prof. Cemil Birsel Cad

Şahande Sk

Havancı Sk

Nargileci Sk

Ragıp Gümüşpala Cad

Siyavuşpaşa Sk

Fuat Paşa Cad

D

Kıble Çeşme Cad
Kepenekçi Sabunhanesi Sk

Hayriye Hanım Sk

Fetva Yokuşu

Mimar Sinan Cad

Süleymaniye Cad

Süleymaniye Mosque
2

Tombs of
Süleyman
and Roxelana

**İstanbul
University**

DEMİRTAŞ

Namahrem Sk

Şemsettin Sk

Süleymaniye Tİcaret Sk

Siyoluk Sk

Besim Ömer Paşa Cad

C

Tavanlı Çeşme Sk

Sarı Beyazıt Cad

Yoğurtçuoğlu Sk

Kazıl Mescit Sk

Süleymaniye Cad

KÜÇÜK PAZAR

Church of the
Monastery of
Christ Pantokrator

Hızır Külhanı Sk

Haci Kadın Cad

Melekşah Sk

Darülhadis Sk

Vefa Türbesi Sk

Vefa Cad

Sarı Turbesi Cad

Vefa Cad

Molla Şemsettin
Cami Sk

Cüce Çeşmesi Sk

**MOLLA
HÜSREV**

Dede Efendi Cad

Dardelihan Sk

Vezneciler

Vezneciler Cad

Vidinli

Tetikpaşa Cad

B

İtalye Cad

İbadethane Sk

Zeyrek Cad

Katip Çelebi Sk

Azep
Askeri Sk

Himmet Sk

Revani Çelebi Sk

Cemal Yener Tosyalı Cad

VEFA

KALENDERHANE

Şehzade
Mehmet Mosque

Şehzadebaşı Cad

Fevziye Cad

BALABAN AĞA

Gençtürk Cad

A

Atatürk Bul

Kendir Sk

İslah Sk

Aqueduct
of Valens

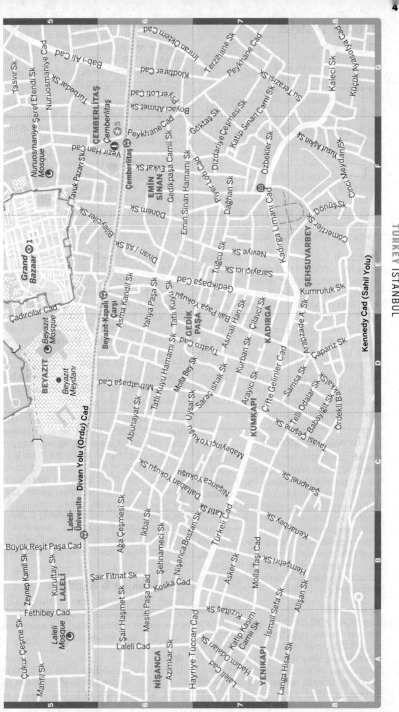

Bazaar District

◉ Top Sights

◎ Sights

✪ Activities, Courses & Tours

food) in Sultanahmet, Erol wouldn't win any awards for its interior design but might for its food – the dishes in the bain-marie are made fresh each day using seasonal ingredients and are really very good. Opt for a meat or vegetable stew served with buttery pilaf.

★ **Matbah**   OTTOMAN $$$
(Map p426; ☑ 212-514 6151; www.matbahrestaurant.com; Ottoman Imperial Hotel, Caferiye Sokak 6/1; mezes ₺10-19, mains ₺28-60; ⊙noon-11pm; ☑; 🚊Sultanahmet) One of a growing number of İstanbul restaurants specialising in so-called 'Ottoman Palace Cuisine', Matbah offers dishes that were first devised in the palace kitchens between the 13th and 19th centuries. The menu changes with the season and features unusual ingredients such as goose. Surrounds are attractive, the staff are attentive and there's live oud music on Friday and Saturday nights.

✗ Beyoğlu & Around

Asmalı Canım Ciğerim   ANATOLIAN $
(Map p434; Minare Sokak 1, Asmalımescit; portion ₺22, half portion ₺14; 🚊Karaköy, then funicular to Tünel) The name means 'my soul, my liver', and this small place behind the Ali Hoca Türbesi specialises in grilled liver served with herbs, *ezme* (spicy tomato sauce) and grilled vegetables. If you can't bring yourself to eat offal, fear not – you can substitute the liver with lamb if you so choose. No alcohol, but *ayran* (yoghurt drink) is the perfect accompaniment.

★ **Antiochia**   ANATOLIAN $$
(Map p434; ☑ 212-292 1100; www.antiochiaconcept.com; General Yazgan Sokak 3c, Asmalımescit; mezes ₺10-12, mains ₺18-28; ⊙lunch Mon-Fri, dinner Mon-Sat; 🚊Karaköy, then funicular to Tünel) Dishes from the southeastern city of Antakya (Hatay) are the speciality at this foodie destination. Meze are dominated by wild

thyme, pomegranate syrup, olives, walnuts and tangy homemade yoghurt, and the kebaps are equally flavoursome – try the succulent *şiş et* (grilled lamb) or *dürüm* (wrap filled with minced meat, onions and tomatoes). There's a discount at lunch.

★ **Zübeyir Ocakbaşı**   KEBAPS $$
(Map p434; ☑ 212-293 3951; Bekar Sokak 28; meze ₺7-9, kebaps ₺22-45; ⊙noon-1am; 🚊Kabataş, then funicular to Taksim) Every morning, the chefs at this popular *ocakbaşı* (grill house) prepare the fresh, top-quality meats to be grilled over their handsome copper-hooded barbecues that night: spicy chicken wings and Adana kebaps, flavoursome ribs, pungent liver kebaps and well-marinated lamb *şiş kebaps*. Their offerings are famous throughout the city, so booking a table is essential.

★ **Meze by Lemon Tree**   MODERN TURKISH $$$
(Map p434; ☑ 212-252 8302; www.mezze.com.tr; Meşrutiyet Caddesi 83b, Tepebaşı; meze ₺10-30, 4-course degustation menu for 2 persons ₺160; ⊙7-11pm; ☑; Ⓜ Şişhane, 🚊Karaköy, then funicular to Tünel) Chef Gençay Üçok creates some of the most interesting – and delicious – modern Turkish food seen in the city and serves it in an intimate restaurant opposite the Pera Palace Hotel. We suggest opting for the degustation menu or sticking to the wonderful meze here rather than ordering mains. Bookings essential.

Lokanta Maya   MODERN TURKISH $$$
(Map p434; ☑ 212-252 6884; www.lokantamaya.com; Kemankeş Caddesi 35a, Karaköy; starters ₺16-28, mains ₺34-52; ⊙noon-5pm & 7-11pm Mon-Sat; ☑; 🚊Karaköy) Critics and chowhounds alike adore the dishes created by chef Didem Şenol at her stylish restaurant near the Karaköy docks. The author of a successful cookbook focusing on Aegean cuisine, Didem's food is light, flavoursome, occasionally quirky and always assured. You'll need to book for dinner; lunch is cheaper and more casual.

🍷 Drinking & Nightlife

There's a thriving bar scene in Beyoğlu. Sultanahmet is not as happening, but there are a few decent watering holes, particularly on Akbıyık Caddesi in summer.

★ **360**   BAR
(Map p434; www.360istanbul.com; 8th fl, İstiklal Caddesi 163; ⊙noon-2am Sun-Thu, to 4am Fri & Sat; Ⓜ Şişhane, 🚊Karaköy, then funicular to

Tünel) İstanbul's most famous bar, and deservedly so. If you can score one of the bar stools on the terrace you'll be happy indeed – the view is truly extraordinary. It morphs into a club after midnight on Friday and Saturday, when a cover charge of around ₺40 applies.

★ **MiniMüzikHol** CLUB
(MMH; Map p434; ☑ 212-245 1718; www.minimuzikhol.com; Soğancı Sokak 7, Cihangir; ⊙10pm-late Wed-Sat; Ⓜ Taksim, Ⓖ Kabataş, then funicular to Taksim) The mother ship for innercity hipsters, MMH is a small, slightly grungy venue near Taksim that hosts the best dance party in town on weekends and live sets by local and international musicians midweek. It's best after 1am.

5 Kat BAR
(Map p434; www.5kat.com; 5th fl, Soğancı Sokak 7, Cihangir; ⊙5pm-1am Mon-Fri, 11am-1am Sat & Sun; Ⓜ Taksim, Ⓖ Kabataş) This İstanbul institution has been around for over two decades and is a great alternative for those who can't stomach the style overload at many of the high-profile Beyoğlu bars. In winter drinks are served in the boudoir-style bar on the 5th floor; in summer action moves to the outdoor roof terrace. Both have great Bosphorus views.

Caferağa Medresesi Çay Bahçesi TEA GARDEN
(Map p426; Soğukkuyu Çıkmazı 5, off Caferiye Sokak; ⊙8.30am-4pm; Ⓖ Sultanahmet) On a fine day, sipping a *çay* (tea) in the in the gorgeous courtyard of this Sinan-designed *medrese* near Topkapı Palace is a delight. Located close to both Aya Sofya and Topkapı Palace, it's a perfect pit stop between sights. There's simple food available at lunchtime.

ℹ Information

DANGERS & ANNOYANCES
Bag-snatching is a slight problem, especially on Galipdede Sokak in Tünel and İstiklal Caddesi's side streets. Most importantly, avoid so-called 'friends' who approach you and offer to buy you a drink; a scam (p496) is usually involved.

EMERGENCY
Police (☑155)
Tourist Police (Map p426; ☑ 212-527 4503; Yerebatan Caddesi 6) Across the street from the Basilica Cistern.

MEDICAL SERVICES
American Hospital (Amerikan Hastenesi; Map p420; ☑ 212-311 2000, 212-444 3777; www.

americanhospitalistanbul.org/ENG; Güzelbahçe Sokak 20, Nişantaşı; ⊙24hr emergency department; Ⓜ Osmanbey)

MONEY
Banks with ATMs are widespread, including in Sultanahmet's Aya Sofya Meydanı and all along İstiklal Caddesi in Beyoğlu.

POST
Central Post Office (Merkez Postane; Map p426; Büyük Postane Caddesi)

TOURIST INFORMATION
The website www.theguideistanbul.com is packed with great information on the city.
Tourist Office – Sultanahmet (Map p426; ☑ 212-518 8754; Hippodrome, Sultanhamet; ⊙9.30am-6pm mid-Apr–Sep, 9am-5.30pm Oct–mid-Apr; Ⓖ Sultanahmet)

ℹ Getting There & Away

AIR
İstanbul's **Atatürk International Airport** (IST, Atatürk Havalımanı; ☑ 212-463 3000; www.ataturkairport.com) is 23km west of Sultanahmet. **Sabiha Gökçen International Airport** (SAW, Sabiha Gökçen Havalımanı; ☑ 216-588 8888; www.sgairport.com) is some 50km east of Sultanahmet, on the Asian side of the city.

BOAT
Yenikapı, south of Aksaray Sq, is the dock for **ferries** (İDO; ☑ 444 4436; www.ido.com.tr) across the Sea of Marmara to Yalova and Bandırma (from where you can catch a train to İzmir).

BUS
Büyük İstanbul Otogarı (www.otogaristanbul.com) is the city's main otogar (bus station). It's in Esenler, about 10km northwest of Sultanahmet.

The Metro service stops here (₺4; Otogar stop) en route to/from the airport. From Taksim Sq, bus 830 (₺4, one hour) heads to the otogar every 15 minutes between 5.50am and 8.45pm. A taxi from Sultanahmet to the otogar costs around ₺35 (20 minutes). Many bus companies offer a free *servis* (shuttle bus) to or from the otogar.

TRAIN
The entire rail network in and out of İstanbul is undergoing a thorough upgrade which means there are only a few rail connections operating currently.

From Sirkeci train station the only international service operating is the daily 10pm *Bosfor Ekspresi* between İstanbul and Bucharest via Sofia (€39 to €59 plus couchette surcharge). Check **Turkish State Railways** (TCDD; www.tcdd.gov.tr) for details.

TURKEY İSTANBUL

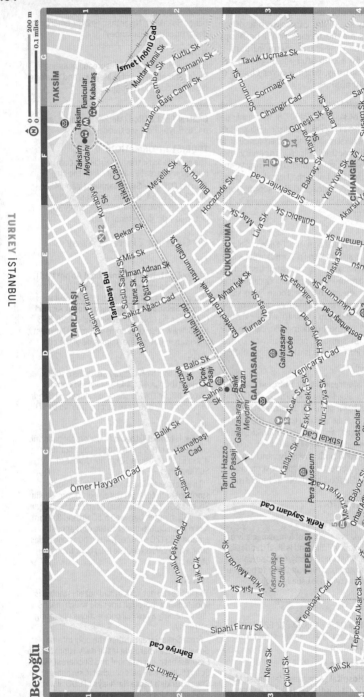

Beyoğlu

A **B** **C** **D** **E** **F** **G**

200 m
0.1 miles

TAKSİM

İsmet İnönü Cad

Muhtar Kamil Sk
Kutlu Sk
Osmanlı Sk
Kazancı Başı Camii Sk
Kazancı Pembe Sk

Tavuk Uçmaz Sk

Sormagir Sk

Cihangir Cad

Somuncu Sk

Güneşli Sk
Hayat Sk
Leşker Sk
Susam Sk
Samanyolu Sk
Kumrulu Sk

CİHANGİR

Oba Sk
Bakraç Sk
Sıraselviler Cad

Meşelik Sk

Hocazade Sk

Bilurcu Sk

İstiklal Cad

Kurabiye Sk

Bekar Sk

Gülabdici Sk
Liva Sk
Maç Sk

Yeni Yuva Sk
Akarsu Yokuşu
Anahtar Sk
Kadriler Yokuşu
Kasatura Sk
Şimşirci Sk
Findıklı

TARLABAŞI

Taksim Fırını Sk

Tarlabaşı Bul

Süslü Saksı Sk
Miş Sk
İman Adnan Sk
Nane Sk
Öğüt Sk

Haas Sk
Sakız Ağacı Cad
Hasnun Galip Sk
İstiklal Cad

Eğazete Sk
Ayhan Işık Sk
Gazeteci Erol Dernek Sk
Turnacıbaşı Sk

ÇUKURCUMA

Falıkbaşa Sk
Palaska Sk
Ağa Hamamı Sk

Çukurcuma Cad
Bostanbaşı Cad
Hayriye Cad
Museum of Innocence

TAKSİM
Taksim Meydanı
Funicular to Kabataş
Taksim

GALATASARAY

Nevizade Sk
Balo Sk
Çiçek Pasajı
Sahne Sk
Balık Pazarı
Galatasaray Meydanı

Galatasaray Lycée

Yeniçarşı Cad
Nuri Ziya Sk
Acar Sk
Eski Çiçekçi Sk
İstiklal Cad

Tomtom Kaptan Sk
Postacılar Sk

Ömer Hayyam Cad

Arslan Sk

Hamalbaşı Cad

Balık Sk

Tarihi Hazzo Pulo Pasajı

Kallavi Sk

Pera Museum

Meşrutiyet Cad
Balyoz Sk
Gönül Sk
Orhan Adli Apaydın Sk

ASMALIMESCİT

Kuyu Sk

TEPEBAŞI

Aynalı Çeşme Cad
Işık Çık
Işık Sk
Asmalı Mescit Sk

Kasımpaşa Stadium

Refik Saydam Cad

Tepebaşı Cad
Tepebaşı Akarca Sk

Bahriye Cad

Hakim Sk
Sipahi Fırını Sk
Neva Sk
Çivici Sk
Tali Sk

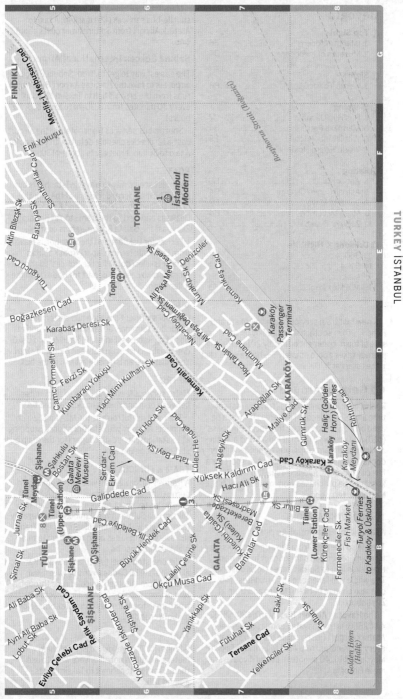

FINDIKLI

Meclis-i Mebusan Cad

Enli Yokuşu

Sanatkârlar Cad

Batarya Sk

Altın Bilezik Sk

Türkgücü Cad

Boğazkesen Cad

Karabaş Deresi Sk

TOPHANE

Tophane

İstanbul
Modern

Boşhorus Strait (Boğazic̣i)

Denizciler

Pasa Medresesi Sk

Murakıp Sk

Necatibey Cad

Ali Paşa Değirmeni Sk

Kemankeş Cad

Kemeraltı Cad

Camcı Ormealtı Sk

Fevzi Sk

Kumbaracı Yokuşu

Hacı Mimi Külhanı Sk

Ali Hoca Sk

İndek Cad

Hoca Tahsin Sk

Mumhane Cad

Karaköy
Passenger
Terminal

KARAKÖY

Arapoğlan Sk

Maliye Cad

Gümrük Cad

Haliç (Golden
Horn) Ferries

Rıhtım Cad

Şişhane

Şahkulu

Bostan Sk

Galata
Mevlevi
Museum

Serdar-ı
Ekrem Cad

Galipdede Cad

Tatar Beyi Sk

Lüleci Hendek Cad

Alageyik Sk

Yüksek Kaldırım Cad

Hacı Ali Sk

Karaköy
Meydanı

Karaköy Cad

Karaköy

TÜNEL

Jurnal Sk

Tünel
Meydanı

Tünel
(Upper Station)

Şişhane

Şişhane

İlk Belediye Cad

Büyük Hendek Cad

Galata
Kulesi (Galata
Tower)

Berekzade Sk

Madresesi Sk

Bilür Sk

Tünel
(Lower Station)

Fish Market

Fermeneciler Sk

Kürekçiler Cad

Turyol Ferries
to Kadıköy & Üsküdar

Şimal Sk

Ali Baba Sk

Ayni Ali Baba Sk

Lobut Sk

Evliya Çelebi Cad

Refik Saydam Cad

ŞİŞHANE

Yolcuzade İskender Cad

Şişhane Sk

Okçu Musa Cad

Laleli Çeşme Sk

Yanıkkapı Sk

GALATA

Bankalar Cad

Fütuhat Sk

Bakır Sk

Tersane Cad

Yelkenciler Sk

Tatan Sk

Golden Horn
(Haliç)

Beyoğlu

A new fast train service between Ankara and Pendik, 20km southeast of Kadıköy on the Asian side of town, commenced in July 2014. The journey takes approximately 3½ hours and ticket prices start at ₺70.

❶ Getting Around

Rechargeable İstanbulkarts (travelcards) save time and give a discount on fares. They can be used on all citywide public transport. Purchase (₺10) and recharge them at kiosks and machines at Metro and tram stops, bus terminals and ferry docks. If you're only using public transport for a few city journeys, *jetons* (single-trip travel tokens) can be purchased from machines at tram, Metro and ferry docks.

TO/FROM THE AIRPORT

Atatürk International Airport

The Metro line runs from the airport to Aksaray from where you you can connect to the tram that takes you to Sultanahmet (total cost ₺8). The whole trip takes about 50 minutes. You can also change between Metro and tram at Zeytinburnu.

The **Havataş Airport Bus** (Map p420; ☎212-444 2656; http://havatas.com) runs between Atatürk Airport (just outside the arrivals hall) every 30 minutes from 4am to 1am and Taksim Meydanı (₺10, 40 minutes); useful if you're staying in Beyoğlu.

Many İstanbul hotels can book airport shuttle-bus services (€5) if asked. A taxi to Atatürk Airport from Sultanahmet costs about ₺45.

Sabiha Gökçen International Airport

The easiest way to get to/from Sabiha Gökçen airport is to take the Havataş Airport Bus, which runs from the arrivals hall to Taksim Meydanı every 30 minutes from 3.30am to 1am (₺13, 1½ hours).

Shuttle-bus services from hotels to the airport cost €12; check schedule details with your hotel. A taxi to Sultanahmet costs about ₺130.

BOAT

The most scenic way to travel in İstanbul is by ferry. The main ferry docks are at the mouth of the Golden Horn (Eminönü and Karaköy), at Beşiktaş and next to the tram stop at Kabataş, 2km past the Galata Bridge. *Jetons* cost ₺4.

Ferries for Üsküdar and the Bosphorus leave from Eminönü; ferries depart from Kabataş (Adalar İskelesi dock) for the Princes' Islands. From Karaköy, ferries depart for Kadıköy on the Asian shore.

BUS

İstanbul's efficient citywide bus system has major bus terminals at Taksim Meydanı and at Beşiktaş, Kabataş, Eminönü, Kadıköy and Üsküdar; most services run between 6am and 11pm. You must have an İstanbulkart to use the bus.

METRO

Metro services leave every two to 10 minutes between 6am and midnight. *Jetons* cost ₺4.

The most useful route is the M1A Line, which connects Aksaray with Atatürk airport, stopping at 15 stations, including Otogar (for the main bus station), along the way.

TRAM & FUNICULAR

A *tramvay* (tramway) service runs from Zeytinburnu (where it connects with the M1A Metro) to Kabataş (connecting with the funicular to Taksim) via Sultanahmet, Eminönü and Karaköy (connecting with the funicular to Tünel). Trams run every five minutes or so from 6am to midnight. *Jetons* cost ₺4.

The one-stop Tünel funicular between Karaköy and İstiklal Caddesi runs between 7am and 10.45pm. Another funicular runs through a tunnel from Kabataş (where it connects with the tram) up to the Metro station at Taksim. *Jetons* for both cost ₺4.

TAXI

İstanbul is full of yellow taxis, all of them with meters, although not all drivers want to use them. From Sultanahmet to Taksim costs around ₺15.

AROUND İSTANBUL

Since İstanbul is such a vast city, few places are within easy reach on a day trip. However, if you make an early start it's just possible to see the sights of Edirne in Thrace (Trakya), the only bit of Turkey that is geographically within Europe. The fast ferry link means that you can also just make it to Bursa and back in a day, although it's much better to plan to stay overnight there.

Edirne

✆ 0284 / POP 150,260

Before the walls of Constantinople fell, Edirne was briefly the capital of the Ottoman Empire, and statement buildings of the imperial age still grace its centre. With the Greek and Bulgarian frontiers half an hour's drive away, the town has a distinct European feel and in summer locals and foreigners alike flock here for the famous oily **Kırpınar Wrestling Festival.**

☉ Sights

Selimiye Mosque   MOSQUE
(Selimiye Camii) Modern-day architects such as Zaha Hadid and Frank Gehry may be superstars of their profession, but neither is as prolific and revered as was the great Ottoman architect Mimar Koca Sinan (1497–1588). Sinan's best-known buildings adorn the İstanbul skyline and include the magnificent Süleymaniye Mosque, but many believe that his greatest achievement was this exquisite mosque, which is Edirne's major landmark.

Edirne Archaeology & Ethnography Museum   MUSEUM
(Edirne Arkeoloji ve Etnografya Müzesi; ✆ 225 1120; Kadır Paşa Mektep Sokak 7; admission ₺5; ☉ 9am-6.30pm Tue-Sun) Behind the Selimiye Mosque is this museum with two sections: one archaeological and the other ethnographic. Highlights of the archaeological section include Thracian funerary steles featuring horsemen. The ethnographic section showcases carpets, embroidery, textiles, calligraphy and jewellery; don't miss the wooden objects decorated in the Edirnekâri style, a lacquering technique developed locally during the Ottoman era.

🛏 Sleeping & Eating

Efe Hotel   HOTEL $$
(✆ 213 6080; www.efehotel.com; Maarif Caddesi 13; s/d ₺95/140; ❉❂@⊛) A time-warp feel dominates at this old-timer on busy (read: noisy) Maarif Caddesi. Rooms have nanna-esque decor with worn furniture and fittings, and the basement bar-restaurant where breakfast is served has tartan carpet that must have been ultrafashionable in the 1970s. It's clean, though, and the English-speaking manager goes out of his way to be helpful.

★**Hotel Edirne Palace**   HOTEL $$$
(✆ 214 7474; www.hoteledirnepalace.com; Vavlı Cami Sokak 4; s €45-80, d €60-90; ❂❉@⊛) Tucked into the backstreets below the Old Mosque, this modern business hotel offers comfortable, bright and impeccably clean rooms with a good range of amenities. Staff are extremely helpful and breakfast is slightly better than average. It's definitely the best sleeping option in the city centre.

Köfteci Osman   TURKISH $$
(✆ 214 1717; http://edirnelikofteciosman.com; Saraçlar Caddesi 3; ciğer or köfte ₺12; ☉ 11am-10pm) Widely recommended by locals for its tasty *tava ciğer* (thinly sliced calf's liver deep-fried and eaten with crispy fried red chillies) and *köfte* (meatballs), Osman has a prime location at the top of the city's main pedestrian drag so is easy to locate. Efficient waiters ensure that the indoor and outdoor tables turn over quickly.

ℹ Getting There & Away

The otogar is 9km southeast of the centre. There are frequent buses to İstanbul (₺30, 2¾ hours).

Dolmuşes (minibuses) run to the Bulgarian border crossing at Kapıkule (₺7, 25 minutes) and the Greek border at Pazarkule (₺3, 15 minutes) from the stops near the tourist office on Talat Paşa Caddesi.

Bursa

✆ 0224 / POP 1.7 MILLION

Sprawling at the base of Uludağ, Bursa was the first capital of the Ottoman Empire and today its core is still crammed full of the echoes of the past, with mosques, *medreses* (seminaries), *hans* (caravanserais) and hamams to explore. Fresh-air fiends are also in luck as Uludağ's tree-clad slopes are only a short jaunt from town.

☉ Sights & Activities

Whether it's winter or summer, it's worth taking a cable-car ride up the Great Mountain (2543m) to take advantage of the views and the cool, clear air of **Uludağ National Park.** As well as one of Turkey's most popular ski resorts (the season runs from December to early April), the park offers pine forests and the occasional snowy peak. Hiking to the summit of Uludağ takes three hours.

Ulu Camii
MOSQUE

(Atatürk Caddesi) This enormous Seljuk-style shrine (1399) is Bursa's most dominant and durable mosque. Sultan Beyazıt I built it in a monumental compromise – having pledged to build 20 mosques after defeating the Crusaders in the Battle of Nicopolis, he settled for one mosque, with 20 small domes. Two massive minarets augment the domes, while the giant square pillars and portals within are similarly impressive. The *mimber* (pulpit) boasts fine wood carvings, and the walls feature intricate calligraphy.

Muradiye Complex
HISTORIC SITE

(off Kaplıca Caddesi) This relaxing complex contains a shady park, a cemetery with historic tombs, and the Sultan Murat II (Muradiye) Camii (1426). Imitating Yeşil Camii's painted decorations, the mosque features an intricate *mihrab*.

The cemetery's 12 tombs (15th to 16th century) include that of Sultan Murat II (r 1421–51). Although his son, Mehmet II, would capture Constantinople, Murat did all the earlier hard work, annexing territories from enemy states during his reign.

Yeşil Camii
MOSQUE

(Green Mosque; Yeşil Caddesi) Built for Mehmet I between 1412 and 1419, Yeşil Camii represents a departure from the previous, Persian-influenced Seljuk architecture. Exemplifying Ottoman stylings, it contains a harmonious facade and beautiful carved marble work around the central doorway. The mosque was named for the interior wall's greenish-blue tiles.

🛏 Sleeping

Otel Çamlıbel
HOTEL $

(📞 221 2565; İnebey Caddesi 71; s ₺30-40, d & tw ₺60-80; 🛜) This central cheapie has seen better days but its en suite rooms with TV are clean and comfortable. The rooms with shared bathroom are basic, but the taps normally produce hot water, and renovations were underway when we visited. The blue-fronted building also contains triple and quadruple rooms.

Hotel Çeşmeli
HOTEL $$

(📞 224 1511; Gümüşçeken Caddesi 6; s/d ₺70/130; ❄🛜) Run by women, the Fountain is a good spot for female travellers near the market.

Although the rooms are slightly dated, they are spacious and spotlessly clean, the lobby is a pleasant environment for watching Bursa bustle past and the Çeşmeli remains a friendly central option.

★ Kitap Evi
BOUTIQUE HOTEL $$$

(📞 225 4160; www.kitapevi.com.tr; Burç Üstü 21; s ₺180-200, d ₺200-225; ❄🛜) The 'Book House', a former Ottoman residence and book bazaar, is a peaceful haven, tucked inside the citadel battlements far above Bursa's minarets and domes. The 12 eclectic rooms each have their own style (one boasts a marble-lined hamam) and the city seems far away when you're in the courtyard, with its fountain and resident tortoise.

🍽 Eating & Drinking

Hacıbey Lokantası
ESNAF LOKANTA $

(Çelebiler Caddesi 3; mains ₺6-9) Readers recommend this *lokanta* (eatery serving ready-made food) opposite the entrance to Tahtakale Çarşısı. It serves *köfte* and dishes from the bain-marie.

★ Kebapçı İskender
KEBAP $$$

(Ünlü Caddesi 7; İskender portion ₺22; ⏱ 11am-9pm) This refuge for serious carnivores is famous nationwide – it is where the legendary İskender kebap was created in 1867. The wood-panelled interior with tiled pillars and stained-glass windows is a refined environment for tasting the renowned dish. There is no menu; simply order *bir* (one) or *bir buçuk* (1½) portions.

Gren
CAFE

(www.grencafe.com; Sakarya Caddesi 46; mains ₺12) Bursa's 'photography cafe' hosts exhibitions and workshops matching its antique-camera decor and arty young clientele.

ℹ Information

The city centre, with banks, ATMs and post office, is along Atatürk Caddesi.

ℹ Getting There & Away

Bursa's otogar is 10km north of the centre. Bus 38 (₺2.50, 45 minutes) heads to the otogar from Atatürk Caddesi opposite the *eski belediye* (old town hall).

To İstanbul, take a bus to Yalova (₺12, 1¼ hours) and then catch the **ferry** (www.ido.com.tr), ₺16, 1¼ hours. There are also hourly buses around the Bay of İzmit (₺29, three hours).

Services to Çanakkale (₺40, five hours) and İzmir (₺40, 5½ hours) leave hourly.

AEGEAN COAST

The Aegean coast is studded with fantastic historic sites. Come here to see Troy, Ephesus and Pergamum, and more recent history at the battlefield sites on the Gallipoli Peninsula.

Çanakkale

📞 0286 / POP 116.078

Çanakkale is the springboard to the Gallipoli Peninsula, and to the ruined city of Troy, but this sprawling harbour town is more than just a base. Its university student

Aegean Coast

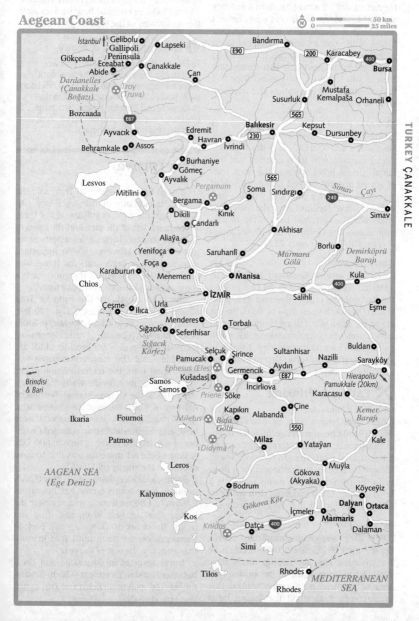

TURKEY ÇANAKKALE

population flavour the town with an upbeat, fun and youthful vibe, making it the liveliest settlement on the Dardanelles.

🛏 Sleeping

Anzac House Hostel HOSTEL $

(📞213 5969; www.anzachouse.com; Cumhuriyet Meydanı 59; dm/s/d without bathroom & excluding breakfast ₺25/45/70; 🛜) Recent years haven't been kind to Çanakkale's only backpacker hostel, with comfort and cleanliness levels plunging since the days when it was run by the Hassle Free Tours outfit. Fortunately, that crew is still based on the ground floor and is promising a full renovation and improvement in services.

★ Anzac Hotel HOTEL $$

(📞217 7777; www.anzachotels.com; Saat Kulesi Meydanı 8; s €30-40, d €40-55; ❄@) A professional management team ensures that this keenly priced hotel opposite the clock tower is well maintained and has high levels of service. Rooms are a good size, with tea- and coffee-making facilities and double-glazed windows. The convivial bar on the mezzanine shows the *Gallipoli* and *Troy* movies every night. Parking costs €2.50.

Hotel Limani HOTEL $$$

(📞217 2908; www.hotellimani.com; Yalı Caddesi 12; s ₺90-160, d ₺140-240; P❄@🛜) Overlooking the harbour, the Limani deserves its reputation as Çanakkale's best top-end hotel. Rooms are on the small side, but are comfortable and have a pretty, very feminine decor. It's worth paying extra for a land or sea view. The downstairs restaurant-bar serves decent meals and a mighty fine buffet breakfast.

🍴 Eating & Drinking

Cevahir Ev Yemekleri TURKISH $

(📞213 1600; Fetvane Sokak 15; meals from ₺8; ⊙11am-9pm) Cheap and cheerful is the motto at this popular *ev yemekleri* (eatery serving home-cooked food) close to the clock tower. Choose from bean, vegetable and meat dishes in the bain-marie. Set meals including a bowl of soup, salad and main dish with rice are available for less than ₺10. No alcohol.

★ Yalova SEAFOOD $$$

(📞217 1045; www.yalovarestaurant.com; Gümrük Sokak 7; meze ₺6-22, mains ₺20-40) Locals have been coming here for slap-up meals since 1940. A two-storey place on the *kordon* (waterfront promenade), it serves seafood that often comes straight off the fishing boats

moored out front. Head upstairs to choose from the meze and fish displays, and be sure to quaff some local Suvla wine with your meal.

Öküz Kültür Cafe Bar BAR

(📞214 1655; http://okuzkultur.com/tr/canakkale/; Fetvane Sokak 17; ⊙from noon) A busy program of live music (everything from electronica to Turkish folk) and regular happy hours make this a mainstay of the student party scene.

❶ Getting There & Away

To Eceabat there's an hourly ferry service (₺2.50, 25 minutes) from the harbour dock. There are regular buses to İzmir (₺40, 5¾ hours) via Ayvalık (₺30, 3¼ hours); and to İstanbul (₺45, six hours) from the otogar, 1km inland. Most bus companies run a free *servis* service from the otogar to the harbour.

Troy (Truva)

📞0286

'The wind brought wealth to Troy', said the ancient inhabitants of this legendary city. These days the wind is still there, but there is not much left of the city, and the ruins of Troy are among Turkey's least impressive historical sites. However, it's an important stop for history buffs; and for those who have read Homer's *Iliad*, the ruins have a romance few places on earth can match.

The ticket booth for the ruins of Troy (📞283 0536; adult/child under 12yr ₺20/free; ⊙8am-7pm Apr-Oct, to 4.30pm Nov-Mar) is 500m before the site. The site is rather confusing for nonexpert eyes – audioguides (₺10) are available – but the most conspicuous features, apart from the reconstruction of the Trojan Horse, include the walls from various periods; the Graeco-Roman Temple of Athena, of which traces of the altar remain; the Roman Odeon, where concerts were held; and the Bouleuterion (Council Chamber), built around Homer's time (c 800 BC). A state-of-the-art museum was due to have opened at the site by mid-2015.

From Çanakkale, dolmuşes to Troy (₺5, 35 minutes) leave hourly on the half hour from 9.30am to 4.30pm from a station under the bridge over the Sarı River, and drop you by the ticket booth. Dolmuşes run back to Çanakkale on the hour, until 7pm in summer and 5pm the rest of the year.

Travel agencies in Çanakkale and Eceabat offer half-day Troy tours (€25 to 32) and full-day Gallipoli battlefields and Troy excursions (around €75).

Eceabat (Maydos)

☑ 0286 / POP 5541

Easygoing Eceabat has the best access to the main Gallipoli battlefields and is a smaller though scruffier alternative to lively Çanakkale which faces it over the Dardanelles.

Ferries dock by the main square, Cumhuriyet Meydanı, which is ringed by hotels, restaurants, ATMs, a post office, bus company offices and dolmuş and taxi stands.

🛏 Sleeping & Eating

Hotel Crowded House   HOSTEL $

(☑ 814 1565; www.crowdedhousegallipoli.com; Hüseyin Avni Sokak 4; s/d/tr €23/30/39; ❄@🛜) The one decent budget hotel close to the battlefields, Crowded House has basic rooms with comfortable beds and clean bathrooms. The hotel's biggest draw is its association with the tour company of the same name – these guys can organise everything you will need when visiting Gallipoli, and do so in a friendly and professional fashion.

★ Kilye Suvla Lokanta   MODERN TURKISH $$$

(☑ 814 1000; www.suvla.com; Suvla Winery, Çınarlıdere 11; pizza ₺15-28, salads ₺12-18, mains ₺25; ⊙ lokanta noon-3pm, tasting room & concept store 8.30am-5.30pm) Since launching its first vintages in 2012, local outfit Suvla has taken Turkey's wine scene by storm. Its 60 hectares of certified organic vineyards are located near Kabatepe, but its winery, complete with restaurant, tasting room and produce store, is on Eceabat's outskirts. The food here is as impressive as the industrial-chic setting, and is worth a dedicated visit.

❶ Getting There & Away

Long-distance buses pass through Eceabat on the way from Çanakkale to İstanbul (₺45, five hours). The ferry service to Çanakkale (from ₺2.50, 25 minutes) runs hourly.

Gallipoli (Gelibolu) Peninsula

☑ 0286

Antipodeans and many Britons won't need an introduction to Gallipoli; it is the backbone of the 'Anzac legend' in which an Allied campaign in 1915 to knock Turkey out of WWI and open a relief route to Russia turned into one of the war's greatest fiascos. Some 130,000 men died, a third from Allied forces and the rest Turkish.

Today the battlefields are part of the Gallipoli Historical National Park (Gelibolu Yarımadası Tarihi Milli Parkı; http://gytmp.milliparklar.gov.tr) and tens of thousands of Turks and

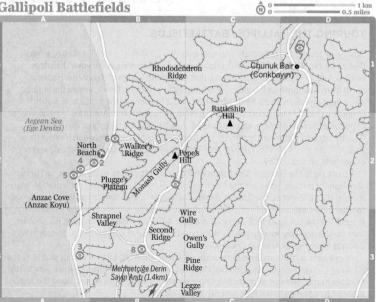

Gallipoli Battlefields

0 — 1 km
0 — 0.5 miles

Rhododendron Ridge

Chunuk Bair (Conkbayırı)

Battleship Hill

Aegean Sea (Ege Denizi)

North Beach / Walker's Ridge

Pope's Hill

Monash Gully

Plugge's Plateau

Anzac Cove (Anzac Koyu)

Shrapnel Valley

Wire Gully

Second Ridge

Owen's Gully

Pine Ridge

Mehmetçiğe Derin Saygı Anıtı (1.4km)

Legge Valley

Gallipoli Battlefields

foreigners alike come to pay their respects on pilgrimage each year. The Turkish officer responsible for the defence of Gallipoli was Mustafa Kemal (the future Atatürk); his victory is commemorated in Turkey on 18 March. On Anzac Day (25 April), a dawn service marks the anniversary of the Allied landings.

The easiest way to see the battlefields is with your own transport or on a tour from Çanakkale or Eceabat with Crowded House Tours (☑814 1565; www.crowdedhousegallipoli. com; Huseyin Avni Sokak 4, Eceabat), Hassle Free Tours (☑213 5969; www.anzachouse. com; Cumhuriyet Meydanı 59, Çanakkale), or tour guide Kenan Çelik (☑217 7468; www. kcelik.com; half-/full-day tours for small groups €120/150), one of Turkey's foremost experts on the Gallipoli campaign.

Ayvalık

☑0266 / POP 37,300

A few steps back from the palm trees and excursion-boat cluster on Ayvalık's waterfront, a squiggle of cobblestone lanes hide a tumbledown time-warp village brimming with picturesque shuttered houses falling into shabbily beautiful disrepair. Ayvalık may be best known as the jumping-off point for the Greek island of Lesvos but dally here a day to meander the alleyways full of bohemian craft shops and cutesy cafes and you'll soon fall under its spell.

🏃 Activities

In summer, cruises (per person including meal around ₺10 to ₺12) around the bay's islands leave Ayvalık at about 11am, stopping here and there for sunbathing and swimming.

🛏 Sleeping

Bonjour Pansiyon PENSION $$
(☑312 8085; www.bonjourpansiyon.com; Çeşme Sokak 5; s/d without bathroom ₺50/100; ❄) In a fine-looking old mansion that once belonged to an ambassador to the sultan, this place has a faded grandeur feel, with aged furniture and antique knick-knacks filling every corner. The 11 rooms are immaculately presented, and you receive a terrific welcome from the owners, Yalçin and Hatice.

TOURING THE GALLIPOLI BATTLEFIELDS

Start your tour at the extremely impressive Gallipoli Simulation Centre (Çannakale Destanı Tanıtım Merkezi; ☑810 0050; http://canakkaledestani.milliparklar.gov.tr; Kabatepe; admission ₺13; ◷9.30-11am & 1.30-5pm), 1km east of the village of Kabatepe. Heading north from Kabatepe on the coast road brings you to Anzac Cove, where the ill-fated Allied landing began on 25 April 1915. Another 300m along is the Arıburnu Sahil Anıtı (Arıburnu Coastal Memorial), a moving Turkish monument with Atatürk's famous words of peace and reconciliation, spoken in 1934. Just beyond the memorial is Arıburnu Cemetery and, 750m further north, Canterbury Cemetery. Between them is the Anzac Commemorative Site (Anzac Tören Alanı) at North Beach, where dawn services are held on Anzac Day.

Returning to the Gallipoli Simulation Centre, follow the signs to Lone Pine, just under 3km uphill. En route, you pass the Mehmetçiğe Derin Saygı Anıtı, dedicated to 'Mehmetçik' (Little Mehmet, the Turkish 'tommy' or 'digger'), that stands carried a Kiwi soldier to safety. Lone Pine (Kanlısırt), 400m uphill, is a moving Anzac cemetery stood on the grounds of the 6 August 1916 battle where over 4000 men died. From here, it's another 3km up the one-way road to the New Zealand Memorial Cemetery (Conkbayırı Yeni Zelanda Mezarlığı ve Anıtı) at Chunuk Bair.

About 1km uphill from Lone Pine, across the road from the Little Mehmet statue, is the 57 Alay Cemetery (57 Alay Şehitliği) for the Ottoman 57th Regiment, which was led by Mustafa Kemal and was almost completely wiped out on 25 April while halting the Anzac attempt to advance to the high ground of Chunuk Bair.

Taksiyarhis Pension
HOSTEL $$

(☑ 312 1494; www.taksiyarhispension.com; Mareşal Çakmak Caddesi 71; dm ₺30, s/d without bathroom ₺50/100; ❄ 🔊) This 120-year-old Greek house, behind the eponymous former cathedral, is one of the more stylish in Ayvalık. There's a vine-shaded terrace with sweeping views across the city, a communal kitchen and a decent book exchange. Rooms are rustic chic with exposed wooden beams; room 3 has a loft and 11 is a small dormitory. Breakfast costs ₺15 extra.

✖ Eating

Cafe Caramel
CAFE $

(☑ 312 8520; Barbaros Caddesi 8 Sokak; ⊙ 8am-10pm Mon-Sat) Lovely Yasemin fronts this nostalgic cafe in the old town. Jazz soundtracks, an extensive cake and dessert menu, homemade soda and simple meals like *mantı* and *menemem* (scrambled eggs with peppers and tomatoes) done well. Caramel hits the sweetest spot and has a loyal following.

Balıkçı
SEAFOOD $$$

(☑ 312 9099; Balıkhane Sokak 7; mains ₺17-25; ⊙ 8am-midnight) Run by a local association of fishermen and marine environmentalists, this is a fine place to sample local seafood and settle into the tiled terrace. Or sit inside for a better view of the Turkish troubadours, who get a singalong going from 8.30pm onwards daily in summer and on Wednesday, Friday and Sunday the rest of the year.

❶ Getting There & Away

Daily ferries operate to Lesvos (Greece) between May and September (one-way passenger/car €85/175, 1½ hours). There are three boats weekly from October to April. For information and tickets, contact **Jale Tour** (☑ 331 3170; www.jaletour.com; Yeni Liman Karşısı) or **Turyol** (☑ 331 67 00; www.turyolonline.com; Yeni Liman Karşısı).

The otogar is 1.5km north of the town centre. Frequent city bus services (₺2) link the otogar to the town centre.

There are hourly buses to İzmir (₺22, 2½ hours); and Bergama (₺8, 1½ hours); and three daily services to Çanakkale (₺30, 3¼ hours).

Bergama & Pergamum

☑ 0232 / POP 62,400

Bergama may be a workaday market town but its proximity to the remarkable ruins of Pergamum makes it a major stop on the tourist trail. During Pergamum's heyday (between Alexander the Great and the Roman domination of Asia Minor) it was one of the Middle East's richest and most powerful small kingdoms and the site of the preeminent medical centre of ancient Rome.

⊙ Sights

Bergama Acropolis
RUIN

(Bergama Akropol; www.muze.gov.tr/akropol; Akropol Caddesi 2; admission ₺25, audioguide ₺10; ⊙ 8am-7pm Apr-Sep, to 5pm Oct-Mar) The road up to the Acropolis, Bergama's richest archaeological site, wends 5km from the Red Hall to a car park at the top, with some souvenir and refreshment stands nearby. A much easier way to go is to follow the signposts along Akropol Caddesi to the lower station of the **Bergama Acropolis Cable Car** (Bergama Akropolis Teleferik; www.facebook.com/akropolisteleferik; Akropol Caddesi; return ₺6; ⊙ 8am-7pm Apr-Sep, to 5pm Oct-Mar). The ride up takes five minutes and is worth it for the views alone. You can easily explore as you make your way down.

Asclepion
RUIN

(Asklepion; www.muze.gov.tr/asklepion; Prof Dr Frieldhelm Korte Caddesi 1; admission/parking ₺20/5; ⊙ 8am-7pm Apr-Sep, to 5pm Oct-Mar) An ancient medical centre, the Asclepion was founded by Archias, a local who had been cured at the Asclepion of Epidaurus (Greece). Treatments included mud baths, the use of herbs and ointments, enemas and sunbathing. Diagnosis was often by dream analysis. The Asclepion may not be as dramatic as the Acropolis, but in many ways it is complete and evocative of the times and how ancient people lived.

The uphill road to the Asclepion is signposted from Cumhuriyet Caddesi.

Red Hall
RUIN

(Kızıl Avlu; Kınık Caddesi; admission ₺5; ⊙ 8am-7pm Apr-Sep, to 5pm Oct-Mar) The cathedral-sized Red Hall, sometimes called the Red Basilica, was originally built as a giant temple to the Egyptian gods Serapis and Isis in the 2nd century AD. It's still an imposing-looking place, though rather scattered and battered. At the time of research, the structure was closed for renovation, which will see some of the hall's severely damaged high walls repaired.

⨼ Sleeping

Odyssey Guesthouse
PENSION $

(☑ 631 3501; www.odysseyguesthouse.com; Abacıhan Sokak 13; dm ₺25, s/d from ₺50/85, without bathroom ₺40/70; 🌐@🛜) The pension in this grand old house is excellent, with superb views of all three archaeological sites from the upstairs terrace lounge. The main building has six basic doubles, with excellent showers; the other building has three rooms. Self-caterers enjoy the small kitchenette and separate sleeping area. There's a book exchange, and a copy of Homer's *Odyssey* in every room.

Hera Hotel   BOUTIQUE HOTEL **$$$**
(📞631 0634; www.hotelhera.com; Tabak Köprü Caddesi 38; s/d €60/80; 🌐🛜) A pair of 200-year-old Greek houses have been cobbled into most sophisticated accommodation. Each of the 10 rooms, named after mythological Greek deities, features timber ceilings, parquet floors, kilims and curios hand-picked by the erudite couple in charge. Zeus (€120) is a beautiful suite with two balconies, while Nike, in the second building, just does it.

✖ Eating

Bergama Sofrası   TURKISH **$**
(📞631 5131; Bankalar Caddesi 44; mains ₺8-12; ◷10am-5am) Sit outside next to the hamam or inside the diner-like interior, with its clean surfaces and open kitchen under bright lights. The spicy *köfte* (₺8) is the specialty. It's best to eat here at lunch when the food is still fresh.

Kervan   PIDE, KEBAP **$$**
(📞633 2632; Atatürk Caddesi 16; mains ₺6-10; ◷8am-11pm; 🌐) Kervan is popular among locals for its large outdoor terrace and good dishes. The menu features a good range of kebaps, pide, *çorba* (soup) and, for dessert, *künefe* (syrup-soaked dough and sweet cheese sprinkled with pistachios).

ℹ Information

İzmir Caddesi (the main street) is where you'll find ATMs, the post office and pretty much everything else you are likely to need.

ℹ Getting There & Around

Bergama's new otogar lies 7km from the centre on the İzmir–Çanakkale highway. Free *servis* buses shuttle between here and the town centre between 6am and 7pm.

There are buses every 45 minutes to İzmir (₺12, two hours), and hourly services to Ayvalık (₺10, 1¼ hours).

İzmir

📞0232 / POP 2.8 MILLION

This bustling commercial hub is rightly proud of its past when it was the grand port city of Smyrna and one of the Mediterranean's vibrant trade centres, with large Greek, Levantine and Jewish communities adding to the cosmopolitan buzz. Today, İzmir still beats to a distinctly liberal and laid-back drum that sets it apart from other Turkish cities.

Thanks to the fire that destroyed much of the old town during Turkey's War of Independence after WWI there's not many actual 'sights' to see, but hang out, seafront, on the *kordon* (promenade) to feel the city's pulse, or explore İzmir's burgeoning cultural scene.

◉ Sights

Ethnography Museum   MUSEUM
(Etnografya Müzesi; 📞483 7254; Halil Rifat Paşa Caddesi 3, Bahri Baba Parkı; ◷8.30am-5.30pm Tue-Sun) FREE The Ethnography Museum occupies the former St Roche Hospital just beside the Archaeology Museum. The lovely, old four-storey stone building houses colourful displays (including dioramas, photos and information panels) of local arts, crafts and customs. You'll learn about everything from camel wrestling, pottery and tin-plating to felt-making, embroidery and weaponry.

Agora   RUIN
(Agora Caddesi; admission ₺5; ◷8.30am-7pm Apr-Sep, to 5.30pm Oct-Mar; 🅿) The ancient Agora, built for Alexander the Great, was ruined in an earthquake in AD 178, but rebuilt soon after by the Roman emperor Marcus Aurelius. Reconstructed Corinthian colonnades, vaulted chambers and arches give you a good idea of what a Roman bazaar looked like. A Muslim cemetery was later built on the site and many of the old tombstones can be seen around the perimeter. The site is entered on the south side, just off Gazi Osmanpaşa Bulvarı.

Kadifekale   FORTRESS
(Velvet Castle; Rakım Elkutlu Caddesi) In the 4th century BC, Alexander the Great chose a secure site for Smyrna's acropolis on Mt Pagos, southeast of the modern city centre, erecting the fortifications that still crown the hill. The view from 'Velvet Fortress' is magnificent, especially just before sunset. Bus 33 from Konak will carry you up the hill.

🛏 Sleeping

Most of the budget and midrange accommodation is in Basmane (near the train station).

Güzel İzmir Oteli   HOTEL $

(☑483 5069; www.guzelizmirhotel.com; 1368 Sokak 8; s/d from ₺65/80; 🆘@🛜) It's all change at the 'Pretty', making this budget option in Basmane even more attractive. The 30 rooms, though small, have been given a thorough facelift, there are lovely old photos of Smyrna, a sunny, sunny breakfast room and even a small fitness centre. Room 307 is larger than most and 501 opens on to the terrace.

Hotel Baylan Basmane   HOTEL $$

(☑483 0152; www.hotelbaylan.com; 1299 Sokak 8; s/d ₺75/120; 🆘@🛜) The 30-room Baylan is among Basmane's best options. The entrance via the huge car park is a little disconcerting, but inside is a spacious and attractive hotel with a welcoming terrace-cum-garden in back. All rooms have polished floorboards and large bathrooms.

⭐ Otel Kilim   HOTEL $$$

(☑484 5340; www.kilimotel.com.tr; Atatürk Caddesi; s ₺145, d ₺210-260; 🆘🛜) This extremely well-run hotel in the Pasaport section of the *kordon* attracts a swath of return visitors – including us. The 70 rooms are generous (both in dimensions and minibar contents) with lovely showers and vintage photos of İzmir. Some seven rooms face the sea – room 703 is the choicest – though the others have good side views.

🍴 Eating

Yengeç Restaurant   SEAFOOD $$

(☑464 5757; Atatürk Caddesi 314a; mains ₺12-25, meze ₺6; ⊘10am-midnight) Our favourite seafood restaurant on the *kordon*, the 'Crab' serves some of the best fish dishes in coastal Turkey. Even better, the price is always right and the staff are both welcoming and very helpful.

⭐ Sakız   MODERN TURKISH $$$

(☑464 1103; www.sakizalsancak.com; Şehıt Nevresbey Bulvarı 9a; mains ₺18-38, meze ₺6-16; ⊘11am-11pm Mon-Sat) Sakız, specialising in Aegean and Cretan cuisine, is the most inventive restaurant in İzmir. Its fresh meze include shrimps wrapped in filo pasty and *köz patlıcan* (smoked aubergine with tomatoes and peppers), while some of the

unusual mains are sea bass with milk thistle and haddock with Aegean herbs.

ℹ Information

Banks, ATMs and the post office can be found on and around Cumhuriyet Bulvarı, known locally as İkinci (second) Kordon, a block inland from the waterfront. The **tourist office** (☑483 5117; 1344 Sokak 2; ⊘8.30am-7.30pm May-Sep, 8am-5pm Oct-Apr) is just off Atatürk Caddesi.

ℹ Getting There & Away

AIR

İzmir's **Adnan Menderes Airport** (☑455 0000; www.adnanmenderesairport.com) is 18km south of the city and has flights to all major Turkish cities, and some European destinations. The **Havaş Airport Bus** (www.havas.net) runs from Gazi Osman Paşa Bulvarı to the airport for ₺15 between 3.30am and 11.30pm.

BUS

The otogar is 6.5km northeast of the centre and has frequent buses to Bergama (₺13, two hours); Kuşadası (₺15, 1¼ hours); and Selçuk (₺9, one hour); as well as regular services to destinations nationwide. Although buses to the Çeşme Peninsula (₺15, 1½ hours) depart from a different bus terminal in Üçkuyular, they pick up and drop off at the otogar as well.

TRAIN

Most intercity trains arrive at and depart from Alsancak Garı (Train Station), including services to Ankara (₺37, 14 hours). There are seven express trains daily to Selçuk (₺6, 1½ hours) that arrive at/depart from Basmane Garı.

Selçuk

☑0232 / POP 28,213

Cute-as-a-button Selçuk is a budget-traveller favourite. With Ephesus right on its doorstep, a swag of great monuments and a stork nest–studded aqueduct in the centre, and back lanes chock-a-block with red-tile-roof and cobblestone loveliness, Selçuk is prime territory for chucking your bag down for a few days to explore.

◉ Sights

Ephesus Museum   MUSEUM

(Map p451; Uğur Mumcu Sevgi Yolu Caddesi; admission ₺10; ⊘8.30am-6.30pm Apr-Oct, to 4.30pm Nov-Mar) This museum holds artefacts from Ephesus' Terraced Houses, including scales, jewellery and cosmetic boxes, plus coins, funerary goods and

Ephesus

A DAY IN THE LIFE OF THE ANCIENT CITY

Visiting Ephesus might seem disorienting, but meandering through the city that was once second only to Rome is a highlight of any trip to Turkey. The illustration shows Ephesus in its heyday – but since barely 18% of Ephesus has been excavated, there's much more lurking underfoot than is possible to depict here. Keep an eye out for archaeologists digging away – exciting new discoveries continue to be made every year.

A typical Ephesian day might begin with a municipal debate at the Odeon **1**. These deliberations could then be pondered further while strolling the Curetes Way **2** to the Latrines **3**, perhaps marvelling on the way at imperial greatness in the sculpted form of Emperor Trajan standing atop a globe, by the Trajan fountain. The Ephesian might then have a look at the merchandise on offer down at the Lower Agora, before heading back to the Terraced Houses **4** for a leisurely lunch at home. Afterwards, they might read the classics at the Library of Celsus **5**, or engage in other sorts of activities at the Brothel **6**. The good citizen might then supplicate the gods at the Temple of Hadrian **7**, before settling in for a dramatic performance at Ephesus' magnificent Great Theatre **8**.

FACT FILE

» Ephesus was famous for its female artists, such as Timarata, who painted images of the city's patron goddess, Artemis.

» The Great Theatre could hold up to 25,000 spectators.

» According to ancient Greek legend, Ephesus was founded by Amazons, the mythical female warriors.

» Among Ephesus' 'native sons' was the great pre-Socratic philosopher, Heraclitus.

Brothel
As in other places in the ancient Mediterranean, a visit to the brothel was considered rather normal for men. Visitors would undertake progressive stages of cleansing after entering, and finally arrive in the marble interior, which was decorated with statues of Venus, the goddess of love. A foot imprint on the pavement outside the rubble indicates the way in.

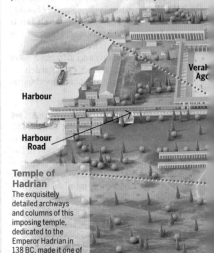

Verah Ago

Harbour

Harbour Road

Temple of Hadrian
The exquisitely detailed archways and columns of this imposing temple, dedicated to the Emperor Hadrian in 138 BC, made it one of the most impressive structures in the city.

Library of Celsus
Generations of great thinkers studied at this architecturally advanced library, built in the 2nd century AD. The third-larges library in the ancient world (after Alexandria and Pergamum) it was designed to guard its 12,000 scrolls from extremes of temperature and moisture.

Latrines
A fixture of any ancient Greco-Roman city, the latrines employed a complex drainage system. Some wealthier Ephesians possessed a 'membership', which allowed them to reserve their own seat.

Great Theatre
Built into what is today known as Mt Panayır, the Great Theatre was where Ephesians went to enjoy works of classical drama and comedy. Its three storeys of seating, decorated with ornate sculpture, were often packed with crowds.

Odeon
The 5000-seat Odeon, with its great acoustics, was used for municipal meetings. Here, debates and deliberations were carried out by masters of oratory – a skill much prized by ancient Greeks and Romans.

Lower Agora

Trajan Fountain

Hercules Gate

Upper Agora

Curetes Way

Terraced Houses
These homes of wealthy locals provide the most intimate glimpse into the lives of ancient Ephesians. Hewn of marble and adorned with mosaics and frescoes, they were places of luxury and comfort.

Curetes Way
Ephesus' grandest street, the long marble length of the Curetes Way, was once lined with buzzing shops and statues of local luminaries, emperors and deities.

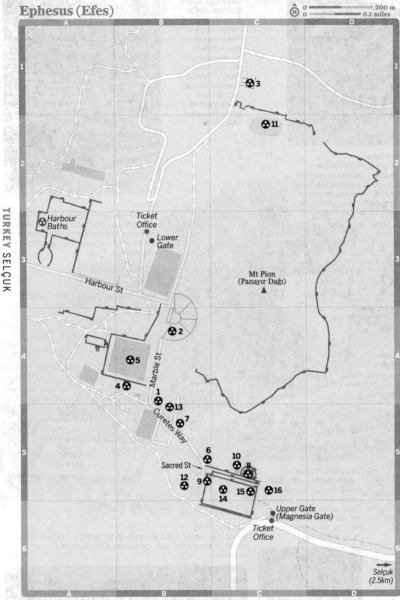

0   200 m
0   0.1 miles

TURKEY SELÇUK

Harbour Baths

Ticket Office

Lower Gate

Harbour St

Mt Pion (Panayır Dağı)

Marble St

Curetes Way

Sacred St

Upper Gate (Magnesia Gate)

Ticket Office

Selçuk (2.5km)

ancient statuary. The famous effigy of Phallic god Priapus, visible by pressing a button, draws giggles, and a whole room is dedicated to Eros in sculpted form. The punters also get a rise out of the multi-breasted marble Artemis statue, which is a very fine work indeed.

Basilica of St John   RUIN, HISTORIC SITE
(Map p451; St Jean Caddesi; admission incl Ayasuluk Fortress ₺10; ☺8am-6.30pm Apr-Oct, to

Ephesus (Efes)

4.30pm Nov-Mar) Despite a century of restoration, the once-great basilica built by Byzantine emperor Justinian (r 527–65) is still but a skeleton of its former self. Nonetheless, it is an atmospheric site with excellent hilltop views, and the best place in the area for a sunset photo. The information panels and scale model highlight the building's original grandeur, as do the marble steps and monumental gate.

Temple of Artemis   RUIN

(Artemis Tapınağı; Map p451; off Dr Sabrı Yayla Bulvarı; admission free; ⊙8am-7pm Apr-Oct, 8.30am-6pm Nov-Mar) FREE In an empty field on Selçuk's western extremities, this solitary reconstructed pillar is all that remains of the massive Temple of Artemis, one of the seven wonders of the ancient world. At its zenith, the structure had 127 columns; today, the only way to get any sense of this grandeur is to see Didyma's better-preserved Temple of Apollo (which had 122 columns; see p453).

🛏 Sleeping

Barım Pension   PENSION $

(Map p451; ☑892 6923; info@barimpension.com; 1045 Sokak 34; s ₺45-50, d ₺80-90; 🕸🗐) This long-running pension stands out for its unusual and winding wire art, crafted by two friendly metalworking brothers who run Barım with their wives. The pension occupies a characterful 140-year-old stone house, with a leafy back garden for breakfast. The 10 rooms are reasonably modern;

two and five are good doubles, the latter up its own private staircase.

★ Boomerang   GUESTHOUSE, HOSTEL $$

(Map p451; ☑892 4879; www.boomerang guesthouse.com; 1047 Sokak 10; dm/s/d/tw/tr/f from €10/30/40/40/60/70; 🕸🗐) 🖋 People do indeed keep coming back to this Turkish-Chinese operation, to spend chilled-out evenings among the trees in the stone courtyard, where the recommended bar-restaurant (mains ₺12 to ₺20) serves dishes including kebaps, Chinese food and cheesy köfte. Some rooms have balconies, while budget options are also available (single/double/twin/triple €20/30/30/45) along with extras such as a travel desk and bike hire.

Homeros Pension   PENSION $$

(Map p451; ☑892 3995; www.homerospension. com; 1048 Sokak 3; s/d ₺50/100; 🕸🗐) Recommended by readers, this long-time favourite offers a dozen rooms in two buildings, unique for their colourful hanging textiles and handcrafted furniture made by owner Derviş, a carpenter and antiques collector. Enjoy good views and dinners on the roof terraces. There are also budget rooms with shared bathroom.

Nazar Hotel   HOTEL $$

(Map p451; ☑892 2222; www.nazarhotel.com; S.P. Metin Tavaslıoğlu Caddesi 34; s/d/tr/f from €35/40/60/80; 🕸@🗐🕸) In a rustic residential area beneath Ayasuluk Fortress, the Turkish-French Nazar stands out for its excellent service. Nothing is too much trouble for owner İlker, and the breakfasts and dinners (€10) on the roof terrace are home-cooked feasts with views of the Basilica of St John. Rooms are plain with small bathroom and some with balcony.

🍴 Eating

Sişçi Yaşar'ın Yeri   KÖFTE, KEBAP $

(Map p451; Atatürk Caddesi; mains from ₺8; ⊙lunch & dinner) Under overhanging leaves next to a 14th-century mosque, Yaşar's place is good for a simple lunch of köfte (meatballs), çöp şiş (şiş kebap served rolled in a thin pita with onions and parsley) and ayran (yoghurt drink).

Tat Restaurant   TURKISH $$

(Map p451; Cengiz Topel Caddesi 19; mains ₺12; ⊙lunch & dinner) Touristy Tat's food won't set the world on fire – although the güveç (stew) and other fiercely sizzling dishes

TURKEY SELÇUK

DON'T MISS

EPHESUS (EFES)

Even if you're not an architecture buff, you can't help but be dazzled by the sheer beauty of the ruins of **Ephesus** (adult/student/parking ₺30/20/7.50; ⊙8am-7.30pm May-Oct, to 5pm Nov-Apr, last admission one hour before closing), the best-preserved classical city in the eastern Mediterranean. Note that there are two entry points, roughly 3km apart. A taxi from Selçuk to the main entrance costs about ₺15, but it's also a pleasant 2.5km walk from town. There's a wealth of sights to explore, but the following are major highlights not to miss:

Curetes Way Named for the demigods who helped Lena give birth to Artemis and Apollo, the Curetes Way was Ephesus' main thoroughfare, lined with statuary, great buildings, and rows of shops selling incense, silk and other goods. Walking this street is the best way to understand Ephesian daily life.

Temple of Hadrian (Map p448) One of Ephesus' star attractions, this ornate, Corinthian-style temple honours Trajan's successor, and originally had a wooden roof and doors. Note its main arch; supported by a central keystone, this architectural marvel remains perfectly balanced, with no need for cement or mortar. The temple's designers also covered it with intricate decorative details and patterns; Tyche, goddess of chance, adorns the first arch, while Medusa wards off evil spirits on the second.

Library of Celsus (Map p448) The early-2nd-century AD governor of Asia Minor, Celsus Polemaeanus, was commemorated in this magnificent library. Originally built as part of a complex, the library looks bigger than it actually is: the convex facade base heightens the central elements, while the central columns and capitals are larger than those at the ends. Facade niches hold replica statues of the Greek Virtues: Arete (Goodness), Ennoia (Thought), Episteme (Knowledge) and Sophia (Wisdom).

Great Theatre (Map p448) Originally built under Hellenistic King Lysimachus, the Great Theatre was reconstructed by the Romans between AD 41 and AD 117. However, they incorporated original design elements, including the ingenious shape of the *cavea* (seating area). Seating rows are pitched slightly steeper as they ascend, meaning that upper-row spectators still enjoyed good views and acoustics – useful, considering that the theatre could hold 25,000 people.

could start a blaze – but it is a pleasant spot with seating among lanterns on a pedestrianised walkway. Multilingual waiters chat to diners and humour their children, between delivering kebaps, seafood, and meze such as fried zucchini and hummus.

Ejder Restaurant TURKISH, KEBAP $$
(Map p451; Cengiz Topel Caddesi 9/E; mezes ₺6-8, mains ₺9-25; ⊙lunch & dinner) Next to the Byzantine Aqueduct, this outdoor restaurant on a pedestrianised walkway is good for lunch on a sunny day, with lots of choices including the generous *tavuk şiş* (roast skewered chicken). The kind owners, Mehmet, Rahime and their son Arkan, are proud to show off their guestbooks and memorabilia, which include photos from the Clinton family's visit in 1999.

Selçuk Köftecisi KÖFTE $$
(Map p451; Şahabettin Dede Caddesi; meze ₺8, köfte ₺12; ⊙lunch & dinner) In a modern building by the fish market, this long-running local favourite serves excellent *köfte*, cooked to perfection and accompanied by salad, rice and fried onions. The good selection of side salads includes a spicy walnut option.

❶ Information

Banks, ATMs and exchange offices are along Cengiz Topel Caddesi and Namık Kemal Caddesi.

Tourist Office (Map p451; www.selcuk.gov.tr; Agora Caddesi 35; ⊙8am-noon & 1-5.30pm daily May-Sep, Mon-Fri Oct-Apr)

❶ Getting There & Away

Selçuk's otogar is directly across Atatürk Caddesi from the tourist office. There are at least two departures daily to İstanbul (₺80, 10 hours); services every 40 minutes to İzmir (₺9, one hour); and buses to Kuşadası (₺5, 25 minutes) every half hour. For Pamukkale, and destinations on the Mediterranean coast, you

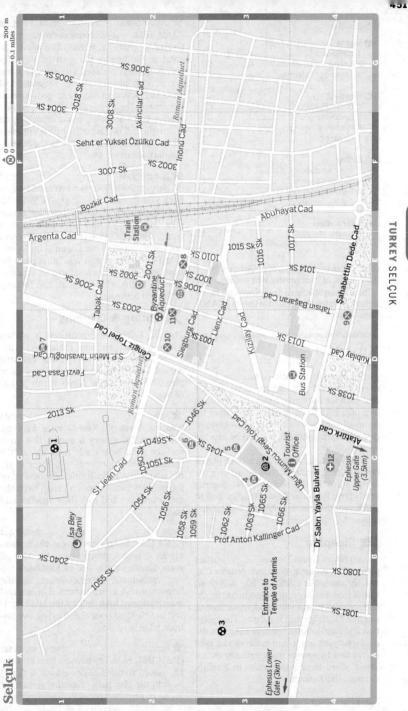

451

Selçuk

TURKEY SELÇUK

200 m
0.1 miles

3005 Sk
3018 Sk
3004 Sk
3005 Sk
3006 Sk
Akıncılar Cad
Roman Aqueduct
3008 Sk
Şehit er Yüksel Özülkü Cad
İnönü Cad
3007 Sk
3002 Sk
Bozkir Cad
Argenta Cad
Abuhayat Cad
Train Station
2001 Sk
2002 Sk
Byzantine Aqueduct
2003 Sk
2006 Sk
Tabak Cad
1010 Sk
1007 Sk
1006 Sk
1015 Sk
1016 Sk
1017 Sk
1014 Sk
Şahabettin Dede Cad
Tahsin Başaran Cad
Cengiz Topel Cad
S.P. Metin Tavasiioğlu Cad
Fevzi Paşa Cad
Roman Aqueduct
Siegburg Cad
Lienz Cad
Kızılay Cad
1003 Sk
1013 Sk
Bus Station
1038 Sk
Kublay Cad
2013 Sk
St Jean Cad
1046 Sk
1049 Sk
1050 Sk
1051 Sk
1045 Sk
Uğur Mumcu Sevgi Yolu Cad
Tourist Office
Atatürk Cad
Dr Sabri Yayla Bulvari
Ephesus Upper Gate (3.5km)
İsa Bey Camii
2040 Sk
1054 Sk
1056 Sk
1058 Sk
1059 Sk
1062 Sk
1063 Sk
1065 Sk
1066 Sk
1055 Sk
Prof Anton Kallinger Cad
1080 Sk
1081 Sk
Entrance to Temple of Artemis
Ephesus Lower Gate (3km)

Selçuk

usually have to change buses at Denizli (₺30, three hours, at least two departures daily).

There are eight trains a day to İzmir (₺5.75, 1½ hours) via the airport; and to Denizli (₺14.50, three hours).

Kuşadası

📞 0256 / POP 70,143

Aimed squarely at package tourism, Kuşadası's fast-food restaurants, brash bazaar and karaoke bars aren't exactly everyone's cup of tea. If you're looking to temper an Ephesus visit with a spot of let-your-hair-down partying, though, it could be just the ticket.

A dinky stone castle, which once played home to local pirates, stands guard over the cruise ships in the harbour, and popular sandy strip Kadınlar Denizi (Ladies Beach) is 2.5m south of town, served by regular dol-muşes (₺5, 30 minutes).

🛏 Sleeping

Sezgin Hotel Guest House   HOSTEL $
(📞 614 4225; www.sezginhotel.com; Arslanlar Caddesi 68; dm/s/d/tr €15/25/35/50; ✲@🅰✉) Uphill from the bar action, Sezgin has bright and spacious rooms with modern bathroom, satellite TV, fridge and hairdryer. The reception and corridors are less appealing, but the rear courtyard has a chill-out area and pool overlooked by orange trees. Friendly owner Deniz offers local information in English, German and Japanese.

★ Villa Konak   BOUTIQUE HOTEL $$
(📞 614 6318; www.villakonakhotel.com; Yıldırım Caddesi 55; r €55-70; ✲🅰✉) Far above the coast in the quieter old quarter, Villa Konak occupies a restored 140-year-old stone house, with pictures of old Kuşadası and Ottoman knick-knacks scattered around the rooms. The alcove seats in the poolside garden and bookcases of paperbacks both create the feel of a relaxing haven, completed by the homemade cookies in the complimentary afternoon tea.

★ Liman Hotel   HOTEL $$
(Mr Happy's; 📞 614 7770; www.limanhotel.com; cnr Kıbrıs & Güvercinada Caddesis; s/d/tr €30/50/60; ✲@🅰) Run by seasoned traveller Hasan (aka 'Mr Happy') and an equally upbeat team, 'Harbour' Hotel's name references not just its location but Hasan's aim to provide a safe harbour and 'a solution place for travellers'. Rooms are comfortable, straightforward affairs with balconies and recently renovated bathrooms.

✕ Eating & Drinking

The old Kaleiçi neighbourhood is packed with restaurants and bars. Barlar Sokak (Bar St) is chock-a-block with rowdy drinking dens. It's a scruffy-around-the-edges kind of place, but after a few drinks it can be lots of fun.

★ Avlu   TURKISH $
(Cephane Sokak 15, Kaleiçi; meze from ₺5, mains from ₺8; ⊙lunch & dinner) The great and the good have made their way to the glass-fronted 'Courtyard' restaurant to try the traditional Turkish cuisine produced by its open kitchen. Choose a kebap from the menu or point and pick daily specials and meze.

Kazım Usta   SEAFOOD $$$
(📞 614 1226; Balıkçı Limanı; meze ₺8-25, mains ₺16-35; ⊙lunch & dinner) Going for over 40 years, Kazım Usta is one of Kuşadası's top fish restaurants, serving dishes ranging from swordfish kebap to farmed bream and meat options. Order fish by the kilo (1kg is ₺80 to ₺120) and book ahead to bag a waterfront table in summer.

★ Ferah   SEAFOOD, AEGEAN $$$
(📞 614 1281; İskele Yanı Güvercin Parkı İçi; meze ₺6, seafood portion ₺20-22; ⊙lunch & dinner) Next to the play park, 'Pleasure' restaurant is one of Kuşadası's classier waterfront fish

eateries, with great sunset sea views and good-quality seafood and meze.

ℹ Getting There & Away

Ferries to Samos in Greece (one-way/return €35/40, 1¼ hours) operate daily from April to October. Tickets are available from **Meander Travel** (☑ 612 8888; www.meandertravel.com; Güvercinada Caddesi; ☉7am-11pm summer, 9am-6pm Mon-Sat winter).

From the otogar, on the bypass highway, there are three departures daily to Bodrum (₺33, 3½ hours) and services every half hour to İzmir (₺17, two hours). Most bus companies provide free *servis* shuttles between the otogar and the centre.

Dolmuşes to Selçuk (₺5, 25 minutes) via Ephesus; and Söke (₺5, 30 minutes) leave every half hour from the central dolmuş stop on Candan Tarhan Bulvarı in town.

Pamukkale

☑ 0258 / POP 2630

The gleaming white travertines of Pamukkale are among Turkey's most famous natural wonders. The bizarre calcite hill is speckled with shallow pools of mineral-rich water while the magnificent ruins of the Roman spa-city of Hierapolis lie on the hill summit, making the sight a supreme two-for-one special. Unsurprisingly it's daytripper central. Stay the night to beat the crowds and stroll the travertines at sunset to see Pamukkale at its best.

◉ Sights

Travertines   NATURE RESERVE
(₺25; ☉9am-7pm summer) The saucer-shaped travertines (or terraces, as they are also called) wind sideways down the powder-white mountain, providing stunning contrast to the clear blue sky and green plains below. To protect the unique calcite surface, guards oblige you to go barefoot, so if planning to walk down to the village via the travertines, be prepared to carry your shoes with you.

Hierapolis   RUIN
The ruins of this Roman and Byzantine spa city evoke life in a bygone era, in which Greeks, Romans and Jews, pagans and Christians, and spa tourists peacefully coexisted. It became a curative centre when founded around 190 BC by Eumenes II of Pergamum, before prospering under the Romans and, even more so, the Byzantines,

when large Jewish and Orthodox Christian communities comprised most of the population. Recurrent earthquakes brought disaster, and Hierapolis was finally abandoned after a 1334 tremor.

🛏 Sleeping

Most hotels provide good, cheap, home-cooked meals.

Beyaz Kale Pension   PENSION $
(☑272 2064; www.beyazkalepension.com; Oguzkaan Caddesi 4; s/d/q/f ₺60/80/130/150; ❋➹➘) On a quiet street just outside the village centre, the cheery yellow 'White Castle' has 10 spotless rooms on two floors, some more modern than others. The friendly lady of the house, Hacer, serves some of the best local pension fare (dinner menu ₺20) on the relaxing rooftop terrace with travertine views. A cot is available for junior travellers.

★Melrose House   HOTEL $$
(☑272 2250; www.melrosehousehotel.com; Vali Vekfi Ertürk Caddesi 8; s €35-55, d €40-55; ❋➹➘) The closest thing to a boutique hotel in Pamukkale, Melrose House has 17 spacious modern rooms, including a family room and suites with circular beds worthy of a Blaxploitation movie. Decor throughout mixes handmade Kütahya tiles and pillars, wallpaper and exposed stonework, and the poolside restaurant is an agreeable place to linger.

WORTH A TRIP

PRIENE, MILETUS & DIDYMA

Selçuk and Kuşadası are good bases for visits to the superb ancient cities of Priene (admission ₺5; ☉8.30am-7pm May-Sep, to 5pm Oct-Apr), Miletus (admission free, parking ₺3, audio guide ₺10; ☉24hr) FREE and Didyma (admission ₺10, audio guide ₺10; ☉8.30am-7pm mid-May–mid-Sep, to 5pm mid-Sep–mid-May), all to the south. If you're pushed for time, a 'PMD' tour from Selçuk or Kuşadası tour operators costs around €35. Perched high on the craggy slopes of Mt Mykale, Priene has a beautiful, windswept setting; Miletus boasts a spectacular theatre; and Didyma hosts the stupendous Temple of Apollo.

ℹ️ Getting There & Away

Pamukkale doesn't have an otogar. Buses drop off passengers in the village centre at Cumhuriyet Meydanı, next to the bus-company ticket offices.

Most services to/from Pamukkale involve changing in Denizli. If your destination states Pamukkale on your ticket, bus companies should provide a free *servis* from Denizli otogar. Otherwise, there are frequent dolmuşes (₺5, 40 minutes) between Pamukkale and Denizli otogar.

Bodrum

📞 0252 / POP 36,401

This once-sleepy fishing village rules the roost as Turkey's primo summer resort. The back lanes brim with uniformly white-washed cottages all sporting natty blue trims while the waterfront's palm-tree promenade and bobbing, shiny yachts provide the chief strolling territory for droves of holidaymakers each summer.

◉ Sights & Activities

Castle of St Peter   CASTLE, MUSEUM
(📞316 2516; www.bodrum-museum.com; İskele Meydanı; admission ₺25, audio guide ₺10; ⊙8.30am-6.30pm, to 4.30pm winter, exhibition halls closed noon-1pm) There are splendid views from the battlements of Bodrum's magnificent castle, built by the Knights Hospitaller in the early 15th century. The castle houses the Museum of Underwater Archaeology, displaying the underwater archaeology treasures amassed during the building's renovation.

The Knights, based on Rhodes, built the castle during Tamerlane's Mongol invasion of Anatolia (1402), which weakened the Ottomans and gave the order an opportunity to establish this foothold in Anatolia. They used marble and stones from Mausolus' famed mausoleum and changed the city's name from Halicarnassus to Petronium (hence the Turkicised 'Bodrum').

Mausoleum   RUIN
(Turgutreis Caddesi; admission ₺10; ⊙8am-7pm Tue-Sun, to 5pm winter) One of the seven wonders of the ancient world, the Mausoleum was the greatest achievement of Carian King Mausolus (r 376–353 BC), who also moved the Carian capital from Mylasa (Milas) to Halicarnassus. Today, the only ancient elements to survive are the pre-Mausolean stairways and tomb chambers, the Mausolean drainage system, the entry to Mausolus' tomb chamber, precinct wall bits and some large fluted marble column drums.

Boat Trips   BOAT TOUR
Excursion boats moored in both bays offer day trips around the peninsula's beaches and bays daily between April and October, typically charging about ₺35 including five or so stops and lunch. **Karaada** (Black Island), with hot-spring waters gushing from a cave, is a popular destination where you can swim and loll in supposedly healthful orange mud.

🛏️ Sleeping

Kaya Pension   PENSION $
(📞316 5745; www.kayapansiyon.com.tr; Eski Hükümet Sokak; s/d ₺130/160; ⊙Apr-Oct; ❀🔊) One of Bodrum's better pensions, Kaya has 13 clean, simple rooms with hairdryer, safe and TV, seven with balcony. There is a roof terrace for breakfast, a flower-filled courtyard and comfy reception for lounging, and helpful owner Mustafa can arrange activities.

★Su Otel   BOUTIQUE HOTEL $$
(📞316 6906; www.bodrumsuhotel.com; off Turgutreis Caddesi; s/d/ste from €65/95/135; ❀@🔊) Epitomising Bodrum's white-and-sky-blue aesthetic, the relaxing 'Water Hotel' has 25 rooms and suites around a pool glinting with silver tiles, an Ottoman restaurant and a bar scattered with red sofas. Owner Zafer's zingy artwork decorates the premises along with hand-painted İznik tiles, Ottoman candlesticks and antiques.

Antique Theatre Hotel   BOUTIQUE HOTEL $$
(📞316 6053; www.antiquetheatrehotel.com; Kıbrıs Şehitler Caddesi 169; r €120-140, ste €160-180; ❀🔊) Taking its name from the ancient theatre across the road, this opulent place enjoys great castle and sea views, and has a big outdoor pool and one of Bodrum's best hotel restaurants. Original artwork and antiques adorn the rooms, which each have an individual character and offer better value than the suites.

El Vino Hotel   BOUTIQUE HOTEL $$$
(📞313 8770; www.elvinobodrum.com; Pamili Sokak; r €170-220, ste €230; ❀🔊) This rustic place behind a stone wall in the backstreets has large and well-appointed rooms with wooden floors. Try for a room with views of the pool and garden area (where breakfast is served). The rooftop restaurant also affords nice views.

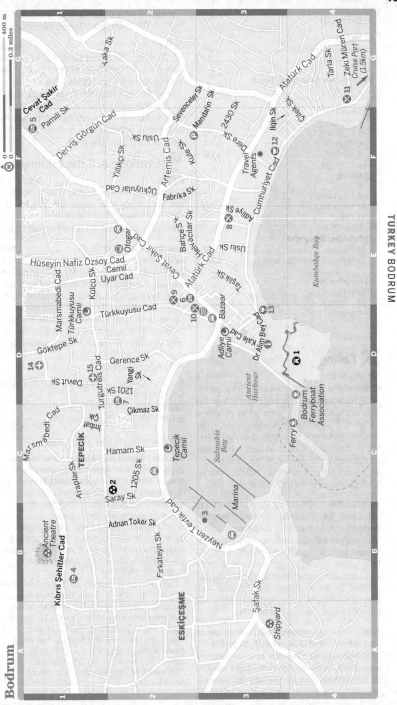

455

TURKEY BODRUM

Bodrum

400 m
0.2 miles

G **F** **E** **D** **C** **B**

ESKIÇEŞME

TEPECİK

Ancient Theatre
Kıbrıs Şehitler Cad

Marsmabedi Cad
Araplar Sk

Adnan Toker Sk
Fırkateyn Sk

Şafak Sk
Shipyard

Neyzen Tevfik Cad

Saray Sk
1205 Sk
Hamam Sk

Çikmaz Sk
1201 Sk
Yangı Sk

Gerence Sk
Turgutreis Cad
Davut Sk

Göktepe Sk
Marsmabedi Cad
Kılcı Sk

Hüseyin Nafiz Özsoy Cad
Cemil Uyar Cad

Türkkuyusu Cad
Türkkuyusu Camii

Derviş Görgün Cad
Üçkuyular Cad

Cevat Şakir Cad
Pamili Sk

Yaka Sk

Uslu Sk
Yıllıkçı Sk
Artemis Cad
Fabrika Sk

Sevenceler Sk
Mandalın Sk
2430 Sk
Dere Sk

Atatürk Cad
Çiçek Sk
Tarla Sk
Zeki Müren Cad

Cumhuriyet Cad
Ilgın Sk

Bahçe Sk
Henacılar Sk
Cevat Şakir Cad
Atatürk Cad

Taşlık Sk
Uslu Sk
Adliye Sk

Kumbahçe Bay

Ancient Harbour
Adliye Camii
Dr Alim Bey Cad
Kale Cad
Bazaar
Ferry
Bodrum Ferryboat Association

Salmakis Bay
Marina
Tepecik Camii

Imbat Çık
Kule Sk

Travel Agents

Ferry

5
2
3
4
14
15
7
9
6
10
8
13
12
11
1

Bodrum

✕ Eating

★ Nazik Ana
TURKISH $

(Eski Hükümet Sokak 5; dishes from ₺6, kebaps ₺8-15; ☺breakfast, lunch & dinner, closed Sun winter) This simple back-alley place offers prepared dishes hot and cold (viewable at the front counter), letting you sample different Turkish traditional dishes at shared tables. You can also order kebaps and *köfte*. It gets busy with workers at lunchtime, offering one of Bodrum's most authentic eating experiences.

Fish Market
SEAFOOD $$

(off Cevat Şakir Caddesi; ☺dinner Mon-Sat) Bodrum's fish market (sometimes called *'manavlar'* for the fruit stands at the entrance to this small network of back alleys) offers a unique sort of direct dining: you choose between myriad fresh fish and seafood on ice at fishmongers' tables and, having paid there, have them cooked at any adjoining restaurant for about ₺10.

Avlu
MODERN TURKISH, INTERNATIONAL $$

(☑316 3694; Sanat Okulu Sokak 14; mains ₺18-38) This bistro in an old stone house decorated with black-and-white photos offers seating in its courtyard or on the cobbled lane. It has a good wine selection and serves mostly Turkish food with a few burgers thrown in.

Orfoz
SEAFOOD $$$

(☑316 4285; Cumhuriyet Caddesi 177/B; meals from ₺120, incl wine from ₺150; ☺dinner daily Jun-Sep, dinner Tue-Sun Oct-May) Often listed as one of Turkey's best fish restaurants, Orfoz serves delectable seafood such as oysters with parmesan, baby calamari with onions and garlic, scallops, sea urchins and blue crab. Reservations essential.

🍷 Drinking & Entertainment

Dr. No
NARGILE CAFE

(Cumhuriyet Caddesi 145; nargile ₺25; ☺10am-late) With white sofas on the water's edge, Dr. No offers several flavours of Arabic tobacco and coffee, cocktails, wine and draught Efes.

Marine Club Catamaran
CLUB

(☑313 3600; www.clubcatamaran.com; Dr Alim Bey Caddesi; admission ₺60-80; ☺10pm-4.30am Jun-Sep) Europe's biggest floating disco, this party boat sails at 1.30am, keeping the licentiousness offshore for a good three hours. Its transparent dance floor can pack in 2000 clubbers plus attendant DJs. A free shuttle operates every 10 minutes to the eastern bay.

ⓘ Information

There are plenty of ATMs and banks along Cevat Şakir Caddesi.

Tourist Office (☑316 1091; Kale Meydanı; ☺8am-6pm Mon-Fri, daily Jun-Oct)

ⓘ Getting There & Away

Bodrum International Airport (www.bodrum-airport.com), 36km from town, receives flights from all over Europe. **Havaş Airport Buses** (www.havas.net) shuttle between the airport and Bodrum otogar (₺15).

Bodrum otogar is on Cevat Şakir Caddesi, 500m inland from the harbour. There are two buses daily to Antalya (₺70, eight hours); eight services per day to Denizli (₺36, five hours); and İstanbul (₺90, 13 hours); and hourly buses to İzmir (₺40, 3½ hours).

Daily ferries link Bodrum with Kos in Greece (one way/return €17/19, one hour) from April to October. There are also twice-weekly ferries to Rhodes (one way/return €50/60, 2½ hours) during July to September. For information and tickets check with the **Bodrum Ferryboat Association** (Bodrum Feribot İşletmeciliği; ☑316 0882; www.bodrumferryboat.com; Kale Caddesi 22; ☺8am-9pm May-Sep, reduced hours winter).

MEDITERRANEAN COAST

The western Mediterranean, also known as the 'Turquoise Coast', is blessed with sand-lined coves, backed by dramatically craggy mountain slopes and home to more ancient ruins than you can shake a stick at.

Meanwhile, the eastern Mediterranean with its fertile fields and Arab-spiced cities continues to stay firmly off the traveller radar despite the pretty beaches here being a favoured haunt for summer-holidaying Turks.

Whether you're here to explore the atmospheric Lycian ruins that litter the hillsides, get some sandcastle action in Patara or the twin villages of Olympos and Çıralı, or head out onto the azure blue Med to see this coastline at its best, you really can't go wrong.

Marmaris

☑ 0252 / POP 34,047

Loud and proud; Marmaris is a brash, party-it-up town firmly stamped on the package-tourist trail. Despite the deluge (and we're talking serious flood) of sun-and-sand resort goers during July and August, the stunning natural harbour and surrounding countryside is drop-dead gorgeous. With your own wheels, head out to the deeply indented Reşadiye and Hisarönü Peninsulas nearby, which hide snoozy fishing villages and teensy white-sand coves backed by pine-covered mountains.

◉ Sights & Activities

Marmaris Castle & Museum   FORTRESS, MUSEUM
(Marmaris Kalesi ve Müzesi; admission ₺8; ☺ 8am-7pm Tue-Sun) Marmaris' hilltop castle (1522) was Süleyman the Magnificent's assembly point for 200,000 troops, used to capture Hospitaller-held Rhodes. The castle hosts small **Marmaris Museum**, which exhibits amphorae, tombstones, figurines, oil lamps and other finds, including from Knidos and Datça. Saunter the castle's **walls** and gaze down on the bustling marina.

Boat Trips   BOAT TOUR
(Atatürk & Yeni Kordon Caddesi; ☺ May-Oct) Marmaris Bay **day trips** (₺35 to ₺50 including lunch, soft drinks, pick-up and drop-off) offer eye-opening views and inviting swimming holes. So many old salts advertise tours that their boats are practically bumping and grinding into one another on the

docks. Before signing up, confirm all details (exact boat, itinerary, lunch etc).

🛏 Sleeping

Barış Motel & Pansiyon   PENSION $
(☑ 413 0652; www.barismotel.com; 66 Sokak 16; s/d without breakfast €20/25, breakfast €3; ❈ 🛜) The popular 'Peace' has spartan but clean rooms and a front patio. If you're planning to stay out after midnight, ask for a key to get back in. Not to be confused with Barış Hotel & Apart, located in a different part of town.

Maltepe Pansiyon   PENSION $
(☑ 412 1629; www.maltepepansiyon.com; 66 Sokak 9; s/d/tr/q ₺35/75/90/120; ❈ 🛜) This slightly ramshackle family-run pension has a shady courtyard where guests can drink *elma çay* (apple tea) under vine trellises. A self-catering kitchen is available, as are cheaper rooms with shared bathroom.

Marina Apart   APARTMENT, HOTEL $$
(☑ 412 2030; www.marinaapartotel.com; Mustafa Kemal Paşa Sokak 24; s/d/apt €30/40/50; 🅿 ❈ @ 🛜 ❄) These four-person self-catering apartments are quite bare but good value, each with the full complement of cooking implements, cutlery, sofa and balcony. There's a cafe-bar in reception and a neighbouring bakery for provisions. Rates include breakfast, and hotel services such as Dalaman Airport transfers (€50) are offered.

🍴 Eating

Meryemana   TURKISH $
(35 Sokak 5/B; mains ₺5-9) In addition to *mantı* and *gözleme,* this friendly local eatery serves delicious pre-prepared *etli yemek* (meat dishes) and *sebze yemek* (vegetable dishes). A good place to try some Turkish classics.

★ Ney   TURKISH $$$
(☑ 412 0217; 26 Sokak 24; meze ₺8, mains ₺20-27; ☺ lunch Mon-Sat, dinner daily Mar-Nov) Perched on a winding lane above the waterfront, with views of yacht masts between the stone houses, little Ney occupies a whitewashed 250-year-old Greek house. The home-cooked dishes include some wonderful meze and house specials *mantı* and *köfte* with yoghurt and garlic.

Aquarium   INTERNATIONAL $$$
(☑ 413 1522; Barbaros Caddesi; mains ₺15-40) One of the cooler and more creative

waterfront eateries, Aquarium is scattered with books, magazines and a chess set (its pieces made of piping). Large grills and steaks are offered, while the lunch menu features lighter meals including fish and chips, wraps and pizzas.

🍷 Drinking & Nightlife

Drinkers and hedonists should stagger straight to Barlar Sokak (also called 39 Sokak) which runs parallel to the harbour, behind the castle, where there is no shortage of bars and clubs to choose from. Action here keeps going until the early hours.

ℹ️ Information

İskele Meydanı (the main square) and the **tourist office** (📞 412 1035; İskele Meydanı 2; ⊙ 8am-noon & 1-5pm Mon-Fri mid-Sep–May, daily Jun–mid-Sep) are by the harbour, north of the castle. The **post office** (PTT; 51 Sokak; ⊙ 8.30am-midnight) is just to the east.

ℹ️ Getting There & Away

The nearest airports are at **Dalaman** (📞 0252 792 5555; www.atmairport.aero/Dalaman_en/index.php), which is 98km southeast, and Bodrum (135km northwest). **Havaş Airport Buses** (www.havas.net) run between Dalaman Airport and Marmaris (₺15).

The otogar is 3km north of town. Regular buses leave to Bodrum (₺25, three hours); Fethiye (₺23, three hours); and İzmir (₺25, 4¼ hours). Bus companies provide free *servis* to the otogar from their offices along Gral Mustafa Muğliali Caddesi.

Catamarans to Rhodes sail daily from June to October (one way/return €40/42, one hour). Buy your ticket at any Marmaris travel agency.

Fethiye

📞 0252 / POP 82,000

The 1958 earthquake levelled much of what remained of ancient Telmessos, but today Fethiye is a prosperous, low-key town that makes an excellent base for delving into the sights of the surrounding region. Its natural harbour, in a broad bay scattered with dinky islands, is one of Turkey's finest and is crowded with bobbing *gülets* (Turkish yachts) ready to whisk you out onto the sea.

⭕ Sights & Activities

Tomb of Amyntas   TOMB
(⊙ 8am-7pm) **FREE** Fethiye's most recognisable sight is the mammoth Tomb of Amyntas, an Ionic temple facade carved into the sheer rock face in 350 BC, in honour of 'Amyntas son of Hermapias'. Located south of the centre, it is best visited at sunset. Other, smaller rock tombs lie about 500m to the east.

Fethiye Museum   MUSEUM
(www.lycianturkey.com/fethiye-museum.htm; 505 Sokak; admission ₺5; ⊙ 8am-5pm Tue-Sun) Focusing on Lycian finds from Telmessos as well as the ancient settlements of Tlos and Kaunos, this museum exhibits pottery, jewellery, small statuary and votive stones (including the important Grave Stelae and the Stelae of Promise). Its most prized significant possession, however, is the so-called Trilingual Stele from Letoön, dating from 358 BC, which was used partly to decipher the Lycian language with the help of ancient Greek and Aramaic.

12-Island Tour Excursion Boats   BOAT TOUR
(per person incl lunch ₺30-35, on sailboat ₺50; ⊙ 10.30am-6pm mid-Apr–Oct) Many travellers sign up for the 12-Island Tour, a boat trip around Fethiye Bay. The boats usually stop at six islands and cruise by the rest. Some are booze-cruise-style tours so check you're getting what you want. Hotels and agencies sell tickets or you can negotiate a price with the boat companies at the marina.

🛏️ Sleeping

Most accommodation is west of the marina or up the hill behind it.

⭐ Yildirim Guest House   PENSION $
(📞 0543-779 4732, 614 4627; www.yildirimguesthouse.com; Fevzi Çakmak Caddesi 21; dm/s/d/tr ₺25/50/80/120; ✳️🛜) This shipshape hostel-pension just opposite the marina is Fethiye's top pit stop for budget travellers, with a selection of dorms (with four to six beds) and simple, spotless rooms. Well-travelled host Omer Yapıs is a mine of local information. There are free bikes for guests, free tea and coffee, and pick-ups and excursions are all easily arranged.

Ferah Pension   PENSION $
(📞 0532-265 0772, 614 2816; www.ferahpension.com; Ordu Caddesi 23; dm/s/d €15/25/38; ✳️🛜🏊) If you're looking for character you can't bypass the Ferah. The inner terrace, dripping in vines and bedecked by flower pots, has a teensy pool. The 10 simple rooms are kept spick and span; grab one at the very top of the house for harbour views to die for. Don't leave without sampling owner Monica's superb home cooking (dinner ₺20).

BLUE VOYAGES

For many travellers a four-day cruise on a *gület* (Turkish yacht) – known as a 'blue voyage' *(mavi yolculuk)* – is the highlight of their trip. Usually advertised as travelling between Fethiye and Olympos, the boats actually stop (or start) at Kale and the trip to/from Olympos (1¼ hours) is by bus. From Fethiye, boats call in at Ölüdeniz and Butterfly Valley and stop at Kaş, Kalkan and/or Kekova, with the final night at Gökkaya Bay.

Food is usually included in the price, but you sometimes have to pay for water and soft drinks and always for alcohol. All boats are equipped with showers, toilets and smallish double cabins. In practice, most people sleep on mattresses on deck.

Depending on the season the price is €165 to €250 per person. While it makes sense to shop around, note that cheaper companies may skimp on food. Make sure the crew speak English, and don't be swayed by gimmicks such as free water sports. Most of all, steer clear of street touts selling voyages and avoid buying your ticket in İstanbul.

We recommend the following owner-operated outfits for running a tight ship:

Before Lunch Cruises (📞0535-636 0076; www.beforelunch.com; Fethiye; 3-night cruise per person €250-325)

Ocean Yachting (📞612 7798; www.bluecruise.com; Fethiye Marina; 3-night cruise per person from €225)

Olympos Yachting (📞0242-892 1145; www.olymposyachting.com; Olympos; 3-night cruise from €185)

Villa Daffodil
HOTEL **$$**

(📞614 9595; www.villadaffodil.com; Fevzi Çakmak Caddesi 139; s €37-49, d €50-75, ste €100; ❄🛜🏊) This Ottoman-styled guesthouse has rooms bedecked with dark wood furnishings, old carpets and quirky details (such as Ottoman-meets-Serengeti touches in some of the suites). Grab one with a sea view for the best experience. The classy pool area, at the back, is perfect for glamour-puss lounging after a long day's sightseeing.

🍴 Eating & Drinking

Nefis Pide
PIDE **$**

(📞614 5504; Eski Cami Sokak 9; pide ₺5-12; ⏱9am-midnight) Tucked away in an alleyway next to the Old Mosque, Nefis serves up Fethiye's best pide, along with good-value kebap and *dürüm* (kebap sandwich) plates. It's friendly, sparkling clean and has lovely outdoor seating. Order the *karaşık* (mixed) pide for a satisfying feast.

★ Meğri Lokantasi
TURKISH **$$**

(📞614 4047; Çarşı Caddesi 26; plates ₺6-14; 📞) Looking for us at lunchtime in Fethiye? We're usually here. Packed with locals who spill onto the streets, the Meğri offers excellent and hearty homestyle cooking at very palatable prices. Mix and match your meal by choosing from the huge glass display window of vegetarian and meat dishes. It's pretty much all delicious.

Cem & Can
SEAFOOD **$$$**

(Hal ve Pazar Yeri 67) One way to taste Fethiye's fish is to buy your own (per kilo ₺18 to ₺30) from the circle of fishmongers in the fish market, then take it to one of the restaurants opposite to have them cook it. Our favourite is Cem & Can, which charges ₺8 per head for cooking the fish, plus salad and bread.

Kum Saati Bar
BAR

(Haman Sokak 31) What looks like just another joint along what is Fethiye's most raucous street after dark, the 'Hour Glass' keeps good time throughout the day as a bar and turns into a club with music and dancing at the bewitching hour.

ℹ Information

Atatürk Caddesi, the main street, has banks with ATMs and exchange offices. The **tourist office** (📞614 1527; İskele Meydanı; ⏱8am-7pm Mon-Fri, 10am-5pm Sat & Sun) is opposite the marina, just past the Roman theatre.

ℹ Getting There & Away

Fethiye's otogar is 2.5km east of the centre. Buses head to Antalya (₺30, six hours) via Kalkan (₺13, 1½ hours) and Kaş (₺16, two hours) at least hourly.

Local dolmuşes for Ölüdeniz (₺5, 25 minutes), Kayaköy (₺4.50, 20 minutes) and surrounding villages leave from the dolmuş stop near the mosque just off Atatürk Caddesi in the centre.

WALKING THE LYCIAN WAY

Acclaimed as one of the top 10 long-distance walks in the world, Turkey's **Lycian Way** follows waymarked trails down the Mediterranean coast from Fethiye to Antalya. The route leads through pine and cedar forests in the shadow of mountains rising almost 3000m, past villages, stunning coastal views and an embarrassment of ruins at ancient Lycian cities.

For keen walkers who don't have time to add in a longer trek, the Kayaköy to Ölüdeniz section is easily doable as a half-day hike from Fethiye. Take a dolmuş to Kayaköy and look for the signposted trailhead within Kayaköy's abandoned village ruins. The walk is waymarked the entire length and takes two to 2½ hours (8km).

Get information on walking all, or some of the sections, of the Lycian Way at www.cultureroutesinturkey.com.

Ölüdeniz

📞 0252 / POP 4708

Over the mountains to the south of Fethiye, Ölüdeniz's too-perfect-to-be-true **lagoon** (Ölüdeniz Caddesi; lagoon admission adult/child ₺4.50/2), backed by the jagged shadow of Baba Dağ (Mt Baba), Turkey's main **paragliding** (tandem flight ₺150-175, plus ₺25 entrance fee to Baba Dağ) centre, brings in the crowds every summer. The setting has serious wow-factor but don't expect a tranquil beach break. Ölüdeniz has long since given its soul to the package-holiday resorts that back up behind the sand.

🛏 Sleeping & Eating

Sugar Beach Club   CAMPGROUND $
(📞617 0048; www.thesugarbeachclub.com; Ölüdeniz Caddesi 20; campsite per person ₺15, caravan incl electricity ₺25, bungalow s/d from ₺100/110; ❄@🖥) This ultrachilled spot, run by affable Erkin, is the pick of the crop in Ölüdeniz for backpackers. The design is first class – a strip of beach shaded by palms and lounging areas, with a waterfront bar and restaurant and backed by two-dozen colourful bungalows with bathrooms and air-conditioning. It's 500m north of the lagoon entrance.

Oba Motel Restaurant   INTERNATIONAL $$
(📞617 0158; www.obamotel.com.tr/Erestaurant.asp; Mimar Sinan Caddesi; mains ₺15-25; ⊙8am-midnight; 🖥) Partly housed in a wooden cabin, the restaurant of the leafy Oba Motel has a great reputation for homestyle food at palatable prices. It also does great Turkish/European breakfasts, including homemade muesli with mountain yoghurt and local pine honey. The menu offers everything from snacks to full-on mains, including a half-dozen vegie options.

❶ Getting There & Away

Frequent minibuses run between Ölüdeniz and Fethiye (₺5, 25 minutes).

Patara

📞 0242 / POP 950

With 20-odd kilometres of uninterrupted sand, Patara takes the crown for Turkey's longest beach. But if beach-bliss isn't enough the ruins of **Ancient Patara** (admission incl Patara Beach ₺5, long-stay ticket allowing 10 entries over 10 days ₺7.50; ⊙9am-7pm), scattered along the main beach-access road, have a swag of Lycian splendour to explore. The teensy village of Gelemiş is a charmingly rural place despite the beach's fame and is a great spot to chill out for a few days.

🛏 Sleeping

All the accommodation is in Gelemiş village, 1.5km inland from the beach. Most hotels serve food.

★Akay Pension   PENSION $
(📞843 5055, 0532-410 2195; www.pataraakaypension.com; s/d/tr/apt ₺60/90/120/160; ❄@🖥🏊) Run by keen-to-please Kazım and his wife, Ayşe, the Akay has a comfy Ottoman-style lounge to hang out and meet other travellers, and 13 very well-maintained, sweetly decorated rooms all with gleaming-new bathrooms and balconies overlooking citrus groves. There's an apartment for self-catering families too. Ayşe's cooking is legendary; sample at least one set meal (from ₺20) while here.

★ **Flower Pension**   PENSION $
(☑843 5164, 0530 511 0206; www.pataraflowerpension.com; d/tr ₺90/120, studio ₺120, apt ₺150; ❄@🛜❄) The Flower has nine bright and airy rooms with balconies overlooking the garden as well as five kitchen-equipped studios and three apartments well set up for families. Manager Bekir is a fount of local information. His mum presides over the kitchen, so guests who choose to dine in are guaranteed Turkish soul food at its best.

ℹ Getting There & Away

Buses on the Fethiye–Kaş route drop you on the highway 3.5km from Gelemiş village. From here, dolmuşes run to the village hourly between mid-April and October. Otherwise, there are dolmuşes from Kalkan (₺5, 25 minutes) hourly that you can hail from the turn-off.

Kalkan

☑ 0242 / POP 3349

Once the Ottoman-Greek backwater fishing village of Kalamaki, Kalkan today is an upmarket resort favoured by yachties and the hobnobbing holiday-villa set. While its outskirts are rimmed by rental apartment blocks which encroach up the steep hill, the central old town, hugging a turquoise-blue bay, has hung on to its cobbled-alley and stone-cut-cottage character. It's a good base from which to explore the coast, just be aware Kalkan's chichi status means it tends to be more expensive than neighbouring coastal towns like Kaş.

🛏 Sleeping

Holiday Pansiyon   PENSION $
(☑844 3154; Süleyman Yılmaz Caddesi 2; s/d ₺70/90; ❄🛜) Though the seven rooms here are simple, they're spotless and charming. The three in the older Ottoman section are particularly atmospheric, with wooden beams, lacy curtains and delightful balconies with good views. It's run by the charming Ahmet and Şefika, who make delicious breakfast jams.

★ **Türk Evi**   PENSION $$
(☑0533 335 3569, 844 3129; www.kalkanturkevi.com; Şehitler Caddesi 19; s €40, d €50-60; ❄🛜) Full of character and old-world Ottoman style, this old stone house (dating from the 1950s) is one of Kalkan's most charming hotels. It houses nine larger-then-average rooms individually decorated with period

furniture and colourful kilims. Some of the rooms upstairs have wonderful sea views.

Courtyard Hotel   BOUTIQUE HOTEL $$$
(☑0532-443 0012, 844 3738; www.courtyardkalkan.com; Süleyman Yilmaz Caddesi 24-26; r from €120) Cobbled out of a couple of 19th-century village houses, with rooms retaining their original fireplaces, wooden ceilings and floors, the Courtyard has lashings of Ottoman old world character. Check out room number one with its 'cave bathroom' converted from a 400-year-old water cistern. Halil and Marion are delightful hosts.

🍴 Eating & Drinking

Zeytinlik   MODERN TURKISH $$$
(Olive Garden; ☑844 3408; Hasan Altan Caddesi; mains ₺23-36; ☑) This British-Turkish joint venture, under the guidance of Fathi and Rebecca, serves some of the most adventurous Turkish food around: try the fish *dolmas*, the samosa-like minced lamb in filo pastry triangles, or any of the several vegetarian options.

Aubergine   MODERN TURKISH $$$
(Patlıcan; ☑844 3332; www.kalkanaubergine.com; İskele Sokak; mains ₺19-36; ⊙8am-3am; 🛜) With a shaded terrace bang on the marina, as well as cosy seats inside, this restaurant is a magnet for its location alone. But add to that specialities like its slow-roasted wild boar, and swordfish fillet served in a creamy vegetable sauce, and you have a winner. Caffeine fiends should note that they also make a damn fine cappuccino.

Moonlight Bar   BAR
(☑844 3043; Hasan Altan Caddesi; ⊙9am-4am) Just down from the post office, Kalkan's oldest boozer is still its most 'happening'.

ℹ Getting There & Away

From the otogar on Şehitler Caddesi, regular buses (half-hourly from April to October) connect Kalkan with Fethiye (₺13, 1½ hours) and Kaş (₺5, 35 minutes). Dolmuşes also run hourly to Patara (₺5, 25 minutes).

Kaş

☑ 0242 / POP 7558

While other coastal towns anchor their popularity in sandy beach fun, Kaş is all about adventure activities. For divers this is Turkey's hub for underwater exploits, while a plethora of boat trips, kayaking tours and hikes are all easily arranged from here. It's a mellow place with a postage-stamp-sized old town, a handful of ruins and the bulky silhouette of the Greek island of Meis standing sentinel just offshore.

◎ Sights

★ Antiphellos Theatre
RUIN

(Hastane Caddesi) FREE Antiphellos was a small settlement and the port for Phellos, the much larger Lycian town further north in the hills. The small Hellenistic theatre, 500m west of Kaş' main square, could seat some 4000 spectators and is in very good condition.

Liman Ağzı
BEACH

If you're after a full day on the beach, the best idea is to hop on one of the water taxis (return fare ₺12; ☉ Jun-Aug services every 20 minutes, fewer services in spring and autumn) in Kaş harbour and head for one of three beaches on the peninsula opposite at Liman Ağzı. All three have cafes and you can rent sunloungers and sunshades. You can also hike here along a nice trail that begins at Büyük Çakıl Beach.

☞ Tours

The nearby Kekova area, with its underwater ruins, pretty coastal scenery and charming hamlets of Üçağız and Kaleköy, is ideal for day trips by sea or scooter and Kaş travel operators specialise in tours here.

Dragoman
OUTDOOR ACTIVITIES

(☑ 836 3614; www.dragoman-turkey.com; Uzun Çarşı Sokak) Dragoman is Kaş' diving specialist, with a variety of dive packages offered (€26 for one dive, including equipment). It also organises the full gamut of outdoor activities with some interesting options other tour companies don't offer. There's sea kayaking (€25 to €50), a range of day-hike options (€26 to €40) and, for the more adventurous, coasteering (from €45).

Xanthos Travel
OUTDOOR ACTIVITIES

(☑ 836 3292; www.xanthostravel.com; İbrahim Serin Caddesi 5/A) Xanthos runs extremely popular and recommendable boat day tours in the Kekova area (€25 to €35) as well as a variety of different sea-kayaking tours that get you up close with the sunken city ruins (€30 to €45). For landlubbers there are jeep safaris (€30 to €35) and a variety of different mountain-biking and trekking options.

⊨ Sleeping

Anı Pension
PENSION $

(☑ 0533 326 4201, 836 1791; www.motelani.com; Süleyman Çavuş Caddesi 12; dm/s/d ₺25/40/90; ❉ @ 🛜) The Anı leads the way for budget digs in Kaş, mostly thanks to on-the-ball host Ömer who continues to improve his pension. The decent-sized rooms all have balconies and the roof terrace is a hub where you can kick back, cool off with a beer and swap travel stories with fellow guests.

★ Hideaway Hotel
HOTEL $$

(☑ 0532 261 0170, 836 1887; www.hotelhideaway.com; Anfitiyatro Sokak; s €40, d €50-70, ste €80; ❉ @ 🛜 ⛱) The Hideaway just keeps getting better. Run by the unstoppable Ahmet, a fount of local information, this lovely hotel has large, airy rooms (six have sea views) with a fresh white-on-white minimalist feel and gleaming modern bathrooms. There's a pool for cooling off and a chilled-out roof terrace with an honour-system bar and superb views.

Ateş Pension
PENSION $$

(☑ 0532 492 0680, 836 1393; www.atespension.com; Anfitiyatro Sokak 3; dm/s/d/tr/f ₺40/70/110/150/160; ❉ @ 🛜) A cut above the other pensions in Kaş, the Ateş has rooms with snugly duvets on the beds and modern bathrooms, while black-and-white photographs grace the walls. Owners Recep and Ayşe are superfriendly hosts and also arrange barbecue feasts on the pleasant roof terrace (₺25). Guests get to use the pool at the nearby Hideaway Hotel.

Nur Hotel
HOTEL $$$

(☑ 836 1203; www.nurotel.com; Hükümet Caddesi; d/f/ste €80/100/170; ❉ 🛜 ⛱) There's a contemporary beachy feel to the light-filled rooms here, which feature painted wood features and lashings of white. The suites ooze luxuriant modern decadence with mammoth jacuzzis and oversized beds. One room has been fully fitted out for wheelchair access.

✖ Eating

Havana Balık Evi
SEAFOOD $

(☑ 836 4111; Öztürk Sokak 7; mains ₺6-15; ☉ 9am-midnight; ☑) Head here for cheap and cheerful *balık ekmek* (₺6) – the simple fish sandwich that is a staple in coastal Turkey. Keeping up with the fishy theme, there are also hearty bowls of *balık guveç* (fish casserole, ₺15) and *hamsı tava* (pan-fried Turkish anchovies; ₺10). You can bring your own alcohol.

Bi Lokma
ANATOLIAN $$

(☑836 3942; Hükümet Caddesi 2; mains ₺13-21; ⊙9am-midnight; ☑) Also known as 'Mama's Kitchen', this place has tables meandering around a terraced garden overlooking the harbour. Sabo – the 'mama' in question – turns out great traditional Turkish soul-food including excellent meze, and her famous *mantı* (Turkish ravioli; ₺13) and *börek* (filled pastry; ₺13).

Köşk
ANATOLIAN $$

(☑836 3857; Gürsoy Sokak 13; mains ₺14-25) In a lovely little square off a cobbled street just up from the water, Köşk occupies a rustic, 150-year-old house with two terraces and seating in the open courtyard. Forgo the mains and feast instead on the gorgeous meze dishes, which draw from both Mediterranean and Anatolian influence. Delicious.

★ İkbal
MODERN TURKISH $$$

(☑836 3193; Sandıkçı Sokak 6; mains ₺20-34; ⊙9am-midnight) Arguably Kaş' best restaurant, run by Vecdi and his German wife, Barbara, İkbal serves excellent seafood and the house speciality, slow-cooked leg of lamb, from a small but well-chosen menu. The wine list has a good selection of Turkish wines from Mediterranean vineyards.

ⓘ Getting There & Away

The otogar is along Atatürk Bulvarı 350m north of the centre. Dolmuşes leave half-hourly to Kalkan (₺5, 35 minutes); and to Antalya (₺24, 3½ hours) via Olympos (₺18, 2½ hours). Buses to Fethiye (₺16, 2½ hours) leave hourly.

Olympos & Çıralı

☑0242

Beach bums unite. The twin hamlets of Olympos and Çıralı are all about sunbathing, lounging and generally getting in some serious hammock time. Saying that, the Olympos side of the beach is backed by the vine-draped remnants of **Ancient Olympos** (admission incl Olympos Beach ₺5, long-stay ticket allowing 10 entries over 10 days ₺7.50; ⊙9am-7.30pm) – which had its Lycian heyday in the 2nd century BC – while the enigmatic eternal flame of the **Chimaera** (admission ₺5) is a one-hour walk from Çıralı.

The big attraction though is lolling on the sand and practicing the fine art of *keyif* (relaxation). Olympos is a budget traveller centre with a slight bohemian vibe (and a reputation for hard partying in the height of summer) while Çıralı is more laid-back and family-friendly.

🛏 Sleeping

🛏 Olympos

The famed Olympos 'tree houses' are something of a misnomer. The 'tree houses' are actually rustic bungalows slightly raised off the ground that share bathrooms. Most camps also offer bungalows with en suite and air-conditioning. Prices for accommodation listed here are per person and include half board (ie breakfast and dinner) with all drinks extra.

Şaban Pansion
BUNGALOW $

(☑892 1265, 0507 007 6600; www.sabanpansion. com; dm ₺40, tree house ₺45, bungalow with bathroom & air-con ₺70; ❉ 🛜) Our personal favourite, this is the place to come if you want to snooze in a hammock or on cushions in the shade of orange trees. In the words of the charming manager Meral: 'It's not a party place'. Instead it sells itself on tranquillity, space and great home cooking, plus room 7 really is a tree house.

Bayrams
BUNGALOW $

(☑892 1243, 0532 494 7454; www.bayrams.com; dm ₺40, tree house ₺50, bungalow with bathroom & air-con ₺75; ❉ 🛜) We love the lively communal feel here. Guests relax on cushioned platforms, playing backgammon or reading in the garden or puffing away on a nargile (water pipe) at the bar. Come here if you want to socialise but not necessarily party. The camp can fit 150 guests.

🛏 Çıralı

Çıralı is basically just two dirt roads lined with pensions that has become hugely popular with nature lovers, post-backpackers and those looking for a chill out with a blissful to-do list of nothing.

Hotel Canada
HOTEL $$

(☑0532 431 3414, 825 7233; www.canadahotel.net; d €60, 4-person bungalow €90; ❉ 🛜 ▨) This is a beautiful place offering the quintessential Çıralı experience: warmth, friendliness and house-made honey. The main-house rooms are comfortable and the garden is filled with hammocks, citrus trees, and 11 bungalows. Canadian Carrie and foodie husband Şaban also offer excellent set meals (€10). It's 750m from the beach; grab a free bike and pedal on down.

★ **Myland Nature** BUNGALOW $$$

(☑0532 488 2653, 825 7044; www.mylandnature. com; s/d/tr €69/93/115; ❄🐾) 🍃 This is an artsy, holistic and very green place that is sure to rub you up the right way (massage, free yoga and meditation workshops available). The 13 spotless and spacious wooden bungalows, with skylight features, are set around a pretty garden with hammocks strung between the orange trees. The food (vegetarian set meal ₺20) garners high praise.

❶ Getting There & Away

Buses plying the Fethiye–Antalya road will drop you at a roadside restaurant from where hourly dolmuşes from 8am to 8pm go to Olympos (₺5) between May and October (every two hours November to April) and Çıralı (₺5) between June and September (two services per day October to May).

Antalya

☑0242 / POP 1 MILLION

This vibrant modern hub has an ancient trick up its sleeve. Right in the city's core is the preserved Kaleiçi (old town) district where grand Ottoman houses rub shoulders with chunky remnants of Roman and Byzantine wall and the alleyways wind their way down to a Roman harbour packed with sailboats. Many of the mansions have been restored to become boutique hotels, making Kaleiçi a favourite stop for culture vultures. Outside of the centre, Antalya's museum is world class, while the hinterland, stuffed full of ruins, is just one more reason to linger here.

◉ Sights

★ **Antalya Museum** MUSEUM

(☑236 5688; www.antalyamuzesi.gov.tr/en; Konyaaltı Caddesi 1; admission ₺20; ⊙9am-6.30pm) On no account should you miss this comprehensive museum with exhibitions covering everything from the Stone and Bronze Ages to Byzantium. The Hall of Regional Excavations exhibits finds from ancient cities in Lycia (such as Patara and Xanthos) and Pam-

phylia while the Hall of Gods displays beautiful and evocative statues of some 15 Olympian gods, many of them in near-perfect condition. Most of the statues, including the sublime Three Graces, were found at Perge.

★ **Suna & İnan Kıraç Kaleiçi Museum** MUSEUM

(☑243 4274; www.kaleicimuzesi.org; Kocatepe Sokak 25; adult/child ₺3/2; ⊙9am-noon & 1-6pm Thu-Tue) This small ethnography museum is housed in a lovingly restored Antalya mansion. The 2nd floor contains a series of life-size dioramas depicting some of the most important rituals and customs of Ottoman Antalya. Much more impressive is the collection of Çanakkale and Kütahya ceramics housed in the former Greek Orthodox church of Aya Yorgi (St George), just behind the main house, which has been fully restored and is worth a look in itself.

Yivli Minare HISTORIC SITE

(Fluted Minaret; Cumhuriyet Caddesi) Antalya's symbol is the Yivli Minare, a handsome and distinctive 'fluted' minaret erected by the Seljuk Sultan Aladdin Keykubad I in the early 13th century. The adjacent mosque (1373) is still in use. Within the Yivli Minare complex is the heavily restored Mevlevi Tekke (Whirling Dervish Monastery), which probably dates from the 13th century). Nearby to the west are two türbe (tombs), one from the late 14th century and the other from 1502.

Kesik Minare HISTORIC SITE

(Truncated Minaret; Hesapçı Sokak) This stump of a tower marks the ruins of a substantial building that has played a major role in Antalya's religious life over the centuries. Built originally as a 2nd-century Roman temple, it was converted into the Byzantine Church of the Virgin Mary in the 6th century and then a mosque three centuries later. It became a church again in 1361 but fire destroyed most of it in the 19th century.

★ **Hadrian's Gate** GATE

(Hadriyanüs Kapısı; Atatürk Caddesi) Commonly known as Üçkapılar (the 'Three Gates') in Antalya, the monumental Hadrian's Gate was erected for the Roman emperor's visit to Antalya in 130 AD.

🏃 Activities

Boat Excursions BOAT TOUR

(Roman Harbour) Excursion yachts tie up in the Roman harbour in Kaleiçi. Some trips go

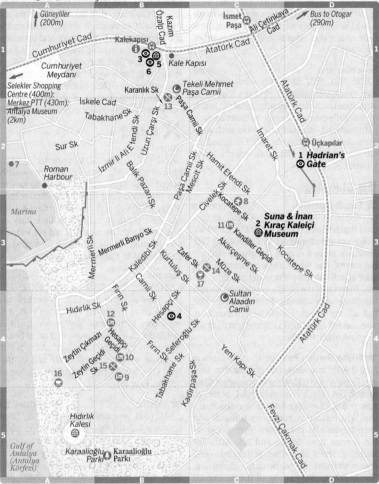

Antalya (Kaleiçi)

as far as Kemer, Phaselis, Olympos, Demre and even Kaş. You can take one-/two-hour trips (₺20/35) or a six-hour voyage (₺80 with lunch) which visits Kemer and Phaselis, the Gulf of Antalya islands and some beaches for a swim.

Sefa Hamamı
HAMAM

(☑ 241 2321, 0532 526 9407; www.sefahamam. com; Kocatepe Sokak 32; ☺10am-9pm) The atmospheric Sefa Hamamı retains much of its 13th-century Seljuk architecture. A bath costs ₺25 and the full works with soap massage and scrub costs ₺45. Oil massages are an extra ₺30. Men and women bathe separately.

🛏 Sleeping

★ Sabah Pansiyon
PENSION $

(☑ 0555 365 8376, 247 5345; www.sabahpansiyon. com; Hesapçı Sokak 60; dm/s/d/tr €13/25/30/45, 2-bedroom self-catering apt €100; ❈ 🕏 ⚏) Our favourite budget digs in Antalya is still going strong. The Sabah has long been the first port of call for travellers watching their kuruş, thanks to the Sabah brothers who run the place with aplomb. Rooms vary in size but all are sweet, simple and superclean. The shaded courtyard is prime territory for meeting other travellers.

★ White Garden Pansiyon
PENSION $$

(☑ 241 9115; www.whitegardenpansion.com; Hesapçı Geçidi 9; s/d €32/40, self-catering apt €110; ❈ 🕏 ⚏) A positively delightful place to stay – full of quirky Ottoman character – the White Garden combines tidiness and class beyond its price level, with impeccable service from Metin and his staff. The building itself is a fine restoration and the courtyard is particularly charming. The breakfast here is one of the best you'll see in Turkey.

Mavi & Anı Pansiyon
PENSION $$

(☑ 247 0056; www.maviani.com; Tabakhane Sokak 26; s/d/tr €30/45/57, self-catering apt €72-100; ❈ 🕏) This restored Ottoman house has a fabulously peaceful garden; common areas decorated with old Anatolian furniture and bric-a-brac; and rooms brimming with old-world character, some of which are Turkish style (beds on the floor). It's a wonderfully atmospheric place to stay. If you want something more contemporary, it also has four newly renovated apartments, all with kitchen facilities, nearby.

Villa Perla
BOUTIQUE HOTEL $$$

(☑ 248 4341; www.villaperla.com; Hesapçı Sokak 26; s/d €100/120; ❈ 🕏 ⚏) We love this authentic Ottoman place snuggled around a courtyard complete with pool and tortoises. The seven comfortable rooms are at the top of a staircase that starts with a 12th-century stone step, the wooden ceilings are the real deal and some of the rooms have four-post beds and folk-painted cupboards. The in-house restaurant makes excellent meze.

🍴 Eating

Güneyliler
KEBAP $

(☑ 241 1117; 4 Sokak 12/A; meals ₺9-12) With its cafeteria-style interior, this reasonably priced locals-only joint isn't much to look at. But the wood-fired *lahmacun* (Arabic-style pizza; ₺3 to ₺6) and expertly grilled kebaps are served with so many complimentary extras, you'll want to return. If you get lost, ask for directions at the landmark Best Western Khan Hotel at Kazım Özalp Caddesi 55.

Yemenli
TURKISH $$

(☑ 247 5346; Zeytin Sokak 16; mains ₺14.50-17.50; ☑) Tried-and-true Turkish favourites are served up at this lovely restaurant with dining either in the leafy garden courtyard or inside the charmingly renovated stone house. It's run by the same team behind the Sabah Pansiyon, so service is friendly and on-the-ball. There's a couple of excellent vegetarian options here too.

★ Vanilla
INTERNATIONAL $$$

(☑ 247 6013; www.vanillaantalya.com; Zafer Sokak 13; mains ₺22-40) One indicator of Antalya's rising stock is this outstanding, ultramodern restaurant led by British chef Wayne and his Turkish wife, Emel. Banquettes, glass surfaces and cheery orange bucket chairs provide a streamlined and unfussy atmosphere, allowing you to concentrate on the menu: Mediterranean-inspired international dishes like roasted courgette and leek risotto, duck confit and chicken livers with smoked pancetta.

Seraser
MEDITERRANEAN $$$

(☑ 247 6015; www.seraserrestaurant.com; Tuvana Hotel, Karanlık Sokak 18; mains ₺25-50; ☺1pm-midnight) The signature restaurant at the Tuvana Hotel and among Antalya's best, Seraser offers international dishes with a Mediterranean twist – try the sea bass wrapped in vine leaves or the Santorini-style octopus – in especially fine Ottoman sur-

ASPENDOS & PERGE

Between Antalya and Side there are several magnificent Graeco-Roman ruins to explore. Rent a car or join a tour from Antalya (from €45 per person).

Aspendos (admission ₺20, parking ₺5; ☺9am-7pm) People come in droves to this ancient site near the modern-day village of Belkıs for one reason: to view the awesome **theatre**, considered the best-preserved Roman theatre of the ancient world. It was built during Aspendos' golden age in the reign of Emperor Marcus Aurelius (AD 161–80), and used as a caravanserai by the Seljuks during the 13th century. The history of the city, though, goes all the way back to as far as the Hittite Empire (800 BC).

Perge (admission ₺20; ☺9am-7pm) Some 17km east of Antalya and 2km north of Aksu on highway D400, Perge was one of the most important towns of ancient Pamphylia. Inside the site, walk through the massive **Roman Gate** with its four arches; to the left is the southern **nymphaeum** and well-preserved **baths**, and to the right the large square-shaped **agora**. Beyond the **Hellenistic Gate**, with its two huge towers, is the fine **colonnaded street**, where an impressive collection of columns still stands.

rounds. (We love the pasha-style chairs and the glass-bead chandelier.) The Turkish coffee crème brûlée is legendary.

🍷 Drinking & Nightlife

Dem-Lik　　　　　　　　　　　　　BAR
(☑247 1930; Zafer Sokak 6; beer ₺6, coffee ₺4; ☺noon-midnight) This chilled-out garden bar-cafe, with tables scattered under shady fruit trees, is where Antalya's university crowd reshapes the world between ice-cold beers while listening to (mostly) jazz, reggae and blues (live at the weekend). There's a menu of cheap pasta and other international dishes on offer as well.

Castle Café　　　　　　　　　　　CAFE
(☑248 6594; Hıdırlık Sokak 48/1; ☺8am-11pm) Our favourite place along the cliff's edge is this lively cafe and bar which attracts a good crowd of young Turks with its affordable drinks. Service can be slow but the jaw-dropping views from the terrace more than make up for it.

The Lounge　　　　　　　　　　　BAR
(☑247 6013; Hesapçı Sokak; ice cream ₺3.50, cakes ₺10; ☺9am-1am; 🛜) Under the same management as (and next door to) the outstanding Vanilla Restaurant, this very slick cafe-bar offers imported Mövenpick ice cream and a genuine Lavazza espresso machine for those weary of Turkish coffee. Panini and pizza (₺10 to ₺18) are available, and there's live music on Friday and Saturday nights.

ℹ️ Information

Atatürk Caddesi is lined with banks and ATMs. The **tourist office** (☑241 1747; Cumhuriyet Meydanı; ☺8am-6pm) is west of the Yivli Minare.

ℹ️ Getting There & Away

Antalya International Airport (Antalya Havalimanı; ☑444 7423; www.aytport.com) is 10km east of the city centre. There are frequent flights to/from İstanbul and Ankara. A taxi from the airport to the central city costs about ₺35.

The otogar is 4km north of the centre on the D650 highway. A tram (₺1.50) runs from here to the city centre (İsmetpaşa tram stop). From the otogar, services include two overnight buses to Göreme (₺50, nine hours); several daily to Alanya (₺18, three hours); and Konya (₺45, five hours); and frequent dolmuşes and buses to Fethiye (₺30, 7½ hours) via the coastal towns; and Side (₺12, 1½ hours).

Side

☑0242 / POP 11,993

Down at the harbour the re-created colonnade of the Temple of Athena marches towards the blue sea. At the top of the old town's gentle hill, Side's theatre still lords it up over the surrounding countryside. Between the two, the lanes of this once-docile fishing village have long since given themselves over to souvenir peddlers and restaurant touts intent on hustling for business. Side is a shameless tourist trap but its grand Roman ruins still make it a worthwhile stopover.

◎ Sights

★ **Theatre**   RUIN
(Çağla Caddesi; admission ₺15; ⊙9am-7pm) Built in the 2nd century AD, Side's spectacular theatre seats up to 20,000 spectators and rivals the nearby theatre of Aspendos for sheer drama. Look to the wall of the *skene* (stage building) for reliefs of figures and faces, including those of Comedy and Tragedy.

★ **Temples of Apollo & Athena**   RUIN
This compact site is one of the most romantic on the Mediterranean coast. Dating from the 2nd century BC, a half-dozen columns from the Temple of Athena have been placed upright in their original spots, and after dark a spotlight dramatically outlines their form.

The site was cordoned off due to restoration work when we last came through town but work should hopefully be finished by the time you visit.

⊨ Sleeping & Eating

★ **Onur Pansiyon**   PENSION $
(⊉753 2328; www.onur-pansiyon.com; Karanfil Sokak 3; s/d ₺60/90; ❄🛜) With oodles of character at wallet-saving prices, this family-run pension oozes traditional pension style right down to the Turkish lace curtains. Rooms are charmingly cosy and there's a relaxing garden full of potted plants and climbing vines to chill out in. The friendly manager is helpful with advice and local lore.

Beach House Hotel   HOTEL $$
(⊉753 1607; www.beachhouse-hotel.com; Barbaros Caddesi; s/d/tr/f ₺60/120/150/180; ❄🛜🏊) Once the celebrated Pamphylia Hotel, a magnet for celebrities in the 1960s, the Beach House's prime seafront location and welcoming owners lures a loyal band of regulars. Most rooms face the sea and all have balconies. We love the roof terrace (with teensy pool), the library full of beach-reads and the garden which comes complete with Byzantine ruins.

Ocakbaşı   TURKISH $$$
(⊉753 1810; Zambak Sokak; mains ₺20-35; 🍴) With friendly service and a huge menu of tasty Turkish grills and meze, Ocakbaşı is a hugely popular Side dinner spot. Vegetarians can breath a sigh of relief; there's a decent choice of dishes here. It can get noisy and crowded so dine early (before 7.30pm)

if you don't fancy being squeezed between tables of large tour groups.

❶ Getting There & Away

In summer, Side otogar, 300m east of the old town, has direct bus services to İzmir (₺40, 8½ hours) and İstanbul (₺60, 13 hours). Otherwise, frequent dolmuşes connect Side with Manavgat otogar (₺2.50), from where regular buses go to Antalya (₺12, 1½ hours) and Alanya (₺12, 1½ hours).

Alanya

🕿 0242 / POP 107,486

Alanya is a tale of two halves. Alongside the silky-sand beach, bars, tattoo parlours and tourist T-shirt shops jostle for place all the way along to the harbour where captains tout for party-boat excursions. But looming above the harbour is a brilliant **fortress district**, with trappings of a fine Seljuk castle, a wonderful mess of ruins and active remnants of village life.

◎ Sights & Activities

★ **Alanya Castle**   CASTLE
(Alanya Kalesı; Kaleyolu Caddesi; admission ₺15; ⊙9am-7pm) Presiding with stately grace over the clutter of bars and souvenir shops below is Alanya's awesome Seljuk-era castle with views across the city and out to the Pamphylian plain and Cilician mountains.

Right at the top of the castle area is the İç Kale (Inner Fortress). Within are plentiful (though poorly preserved) ruins including a half-dozen cisterns and the shell of an 11th-century Byzantine church.

Red Tower   HISTORIC BUILDING
(Kızılkule; İskele Caddesi; admission ₺4, combined ticket with Tersane & guardhouse ₺10; ⊙9am-7pm) This five-storey octagonal defence tower, measuring nearly 30m in diameter, more than 30m in height and with a central cistern within for water storage, looms over the harbour at the lower end of İskele Caddesi. Constructed in 1226 by Seljuk Sultan Alaeddin Keykubad I (who also built Alanya Castle), it was the first structure erected after the Armenian-controlled town surrendered to the sultan.

Excursion Boats   BOAT TOUR
(per person incl lunch ₺35) Every day at around 10.30am, boats leave from near Rıhtım Caddesi for a six-hour voyage around the promontory, visiting several caves, as well as

Cleopatra's Beach. Other cruises include sunset jaunts around the harbour (from ₺20).

🛏 Sleeping

Alanya is low on budget accommodation. İskele Caddesi is your best bet if you are on a budget.

Temiz Otel HOTEL $
(☑ 513 1016; http://temizotel.com.tr; İskele Caddesi 12; s/d ₺60/90; ❄🖤) If you want to be slam in the centre of the downtown action, the Temiz has 32 decently sized, if bland, rooms. Rooms at the front have balconies, but light sleepers should steer clear and ask for a room at the back as the thumping noise from the bars goes on into the wee hours.

★Centauera BOUTIQUE HOTEL $$$
(☑ 519 0016; www.centauera.com; Andızlı Camii Sokak 4, Tophane; r €60-120; 🅿❄🖤) A 10-minute stroll from the harbour, the romantic Centauera is a world away from downtown Alanya, with views across the elegant sweep of bay and birdsong the only sound you hear most mornings. This restored Ottoman house is packed full of old world elegance and ably run by friendly owner Koray. With just five rooms it's an intimate choice.

🍴 Eating & Drinking

★İskele Sofrası TURKISH $$
(Tophane Caddesi 2b; meze ₺6-8, mains ₺15-35) Eschew the glitzier harbour restaurants and head for this intimate option, run by the friendly Öz family. The menu includes more than 70 meze, including *girit ezmesi*, an unforgettable mash of feta, walnuts and olive oil. All the usual grills and loads of seafood headline the menu, but there are also pasta and vegie options.

Lokanta Su MEDITERRANEAN $$$
(☑ 512 1500; www.lokantasualanya.com; Damlataş Caddesi 14a; mains ₺23-45) From Italy to the Middle East, Lokanta Su's menu covers the best of the Mediterranean, but the beautiful courtyard of this Ottoman house (originally the residence of the governor of Alanya) is also a lovely spot to come for a drink, with one of the best wine lists in town. The pizza menu (₺23 to ₺30) showcases some innovative touches.

Red Tower
Brewery Restaurant BAR, RESTAURANT
(www.redtowerbrewery.com; İskele Caddesi 80) It's fusion confusion at this multistorey pleasure palace with harbour views. The ground-floor brew pub serves two decent beers, there's an international restaurant on the 1st floor, Turkish dishes on the 3rd floor, and sushi and live guitar music in the 6th-floor Sky Lounge. Our pick is a pint of the authentically hoppy pilsner on Red Tower's alfresco deck.

❶ Getting There & Away

The otogar is on Atatürk Caddesi, 3km west of the centre. Buses leave hourly to Antalya (₺18, two hours) and eight times daily to Adana (₺60, 10 hours). Frequent dolmuşes (₺1.50) zip between the otogar and the Grand Bazaar downtown.

Antakya (Hatay)
☑ 0326 / POP 217,072

Biblical Antioch, where both St Paul and St Peter dropped by to preach, is a fascinating melding of Turkish and Arab culture. Check out the creaky old-town district, sandwiched in between Hürriyet Caddesi and Kurtuluş Caddesi, then feast your eyes on the magnificent Roman mosaic collection inside **Hatay Archaeology Museum** (Hatay Arkeoloji Müzesi; Gündüz Caddesi 1; admission ₺10; ⊗ 9am-6.30pm Tue-Sun). Afterwards visit the ancient **Church of St Peter** (St Pierre Kilisesi; admission ₺10; ⊗ 9am-noon & 1-6pm), one of the earliest Christian places of worship in the world.

🛏 Sleeping & Eating

Antik Beyazıt Hotel BOUTIQUE HOTEL $$
(☑ 216 2900; www.antikbeyazitoteli.com; Hükümet Caddesi 4; s/d/tr 110/150/200; ❄🖤) Housed in a pretty French Levantine colonial house (1903), Antakya's first boutique hotel is looking a bit frayed, though it's as friendly as ever and the antique furnishings, oriental carpets and ornate chandelier in the lobby still evoke a more elegant past. The 27 rooms are fairly basic; the ones on the 1st floor have the most character.

★Liwan Hotel BOUTIQUE HOTEL $$$
(☑ 215 7777; www.theliwanhotel.com; Silahlı Kuvvetler Caddesi 5; s/d ₺130/200; ❄🖤) This 1920s eclectic-style building was once owned by the president of Syria, and contains two dozen tastefully furnished rooms across four floors. The restaurant is in an open courtyard (once an internal garden with ogee arches) that is covered in chillier months.

For those who adore old-timer hotels, there is bucketloads of atmosphere to lap up here.

★ **Hatay Sultan Sofrası** ANATOLIAN $$
(www.sultansofrasi.com; İstiklal Caddesi 20a; mains ₺10-16) Antakya's premier spot for affordable tasty meals, this bustling place is just the ticket to dive into Hatay's fusion of Middle Eastern and Turkish cuisine. The articulate manager loves to guide diners through the menu, and will help you pick from the diverse array of meze and spicy local kebap options. Leave room to order *künefe* for dessert.

ⓘ Getting There & Away

The otogar is 7km northwest of the centre. There are frequent services to Gaziantep (₺25, four hours) and Şanlıurfa (₺30, seven hours) along with decent connections to destinations across Turkey.

Most big bus companies run free *servis* shuttles from the otogar to the town centre. Otherwise catch bus 5, 9, 16 or 17 (₺1.50) from just outside the otogar into town.

CENTRAL ANATOLIA

This is the region where every historical heavyweight from the Hittites to Atatürk established their capital. Here Alexander the Great cut the Gordian knot and King Midas turned everything to gold. Julius Caesar uttered his famous line '*Veni, vidi, vici*' ('I came, I saw, I conquered'), the whirling dervishes first whirled, and Atatürk began the revolution that would create modern Turkey.

Most travellers bypass this region in the rush to journey between the coast and Cappadocia, but if you've got time up your sleeve don't miss stopping off at the time-warp town of Safranbolu, fuelling your history-bug at Turkey's best museum in Ankara, and paying pilgrimage at Mevlâna's tomb in Konya. The rolling Anatolian plains offer an opportunity to immerse yourself in everyday Turkish life.

Ankara

☑ 0312 / POP 4.7 MILLION

İstanbullus may quip that the best view in Ankara is on the ride home, but the Turkish capital is seriously underrated. Ankara offers a more manageable vignette of urban Turkey than İstanbul, and two of the country's most important sights: the Anıt Kabir, Atatürk's hilltop mausoleum, and the Museum of Anatolian Civilisations are both here. Stroll the hilltop citadel neighbourhood in the afternoon and after sunset hit the hip student haunt of Kızılay district to join young Turks on cafe-and-bar-hopping forays.

◉ Sights

★ **Museum of Anatolian Civilisations** MUSEUM
(Anadolu Medeniyetleri Müzesi; ☑ 0312-324 3160; Gözcü Sokak 2; admission ₺15; ☺ 8.30am-6.15pm Apr-Oct, to 5pm Nov-Mar; ⓜ Ulus) The superb Museum of Anatolian Civilisations is the perfect introduction to the complex weave of Turkey's ancient past, housing artefacts cherry-picked from just about every significant archaeological site in Anatolia.

The museum is housed in a 15th-century *bedesten* (covered market). The central room houses reliefs and statues, while the surrounding hall displays exhibits from Palaeolithic, Neolithic, Chalcolithic, Bronze Age, Assyrian, Hittite, Phrygian, Urartian and Lydian periods. Downstairs are classical Greek and Roman artefacts and a display on Ankara's history.

Anıt Kabir MONUMENT
(Atatürk Mausoleum & Museum; www.anitkabir. org; Gençlik Caddesi; audio guide ₺10; ☺ 9am-5pm May-Oct, to 4pm Nov-Apr; ⓜ Tandoğan) **FREE** The monumental mausoleum of Mustafa Kemal Atatürk (1881–1938), the founder of modern Turkey, sits high above the city with its abundance of marble and air of veneration. The tomb itself actually makes up only a small part of this fascinating complex, which consists of museums and a ceremonial courtyard. For many Turks a visit is virtually a pilgrimage, and it's not unusual to see people visibly moved. Allow at least two hours in order to visit the whole site.

Citadel NEIGHBOURHOOD
(Ankara Kalesi; ⓜ Ulus) The imposing *hisar* is the most interesting part of Ankara to poke about in. This well-preserved quarter of thick walls and intriguing winding streets took its present shape in the 9th century AD, when the Byzantine emperor Michael II constructed the outer ramparts. The inner walls date from the 7th century.

🛏 Sleeping

★ Deeps Hostel
HOSTEL $

(📞 0312-213 6338; www.deepshostelankara.com; Ataç Sokak 46; dm/s/d without breakfast ₺30/50/75; 🛜; Ⓜ Kızılay) At Ankara's best budget choice, friendly Şeyda, the owner of Deeps, has created a colourful, light-filled hostel with spacious dorms and rooms, and squeaky-clean, modern shared bathrooms. It's all topped off by masses of advice and information, a fully equipped kitchen and a cute communal area downstairs where you can swap your Turkish travel tales.

Angora House Hotel
HISTORIC HOTEL $$

(📞 0312-309 8380; www.angorahouse.com.tr; Kale Kapısı Sokak 16; s/d €70/100; 🛜; Ⓜ Ulus) Be utterly charmed by this restored Ottoman house, which oozes subtle elegance at every turn. The six spacious rooms are infused with loads of old-world atmosphere, featuring dark wood accents, creamy 19th-century design textiles and colourful Turkish carpets, while the walled courtyard garden is the perfect retreat from the citadel streets. Delightfully helpful staff add to the appeal.

And Butik Hotel
HISTORIC HOTEL $$

(📞 310 2303, 0312-310 2304; www.andbutikhotel.com; İstek Sokak 2; s/d from ₺100/125; 🛜; Ⓜ Ulus) Right in the heart of the citadel, this place, which is so cheap you might wonder if you heard the price right, is housed inside a pleasingly renovated Ottoman-era building. The small rooms are crammed with character, there's a warm welcome from your hosts, and a little courtyard garden. The only small niggle is that wi-fi doesn't generally reach the rooms.

Divan Çukurhan
HISTORIC HOTEL $$$

(📞 0312-306 6400; www.divan.com.tr; Depo Sokak 3, Ankara Kalesi; s/d €130/150, ste €180-400; ❄🛜; Ⓜ Ulus) This fabulous upmarket hotel offers guests a chance to soak up the historic ambience of staying in the 16th-century Çukurhan caravanserai. Set around a dramatic glass-ceilinged interior courtyard, each individually themed room blends ornate decadence with sassy contemporary style. Ankara's best bet for those who want to be dazzled by oodles of sumptuous luxury and sleek service.

🍴 Eating

Leman Kültür
INTERNATIONAL $

(📞 0312-310 8617; www.lmk.com.tr; Konur Sokak 8; mains ₺8-20; Ⓜ Kızılay) Named after a cult Turkish comic strip – and decorated accordingly – this is still the pre-party pick for a substantial feed and for spotting beautiful, young, educated things. The food is generally of the meatballs, burgers and grilled meats variety. Drinks are reasonably priced and the speakers crank everything from indie-electro to Türk pop.

Zenger Paşa Konağı
ANATOLIAN $$

(📞 0312-311 7070; www.zengerpasa.com; Doyran Sokak 13; mains ₺15-25; Ⓜ Ulus) Crammed with Ottoman ephemera, the Zenger Paşa at first looks like a deserted ethnographic museum, but climb up the rickety stairs and you'll find views of the city that are worth a visit alone. Wealthy locals love the pide, meze and grills, still cooked in the original Ottoman oven.

★ Balıkçıköy
SEAFOOD $$$

(📞 0312-466 0450; Abay Kunanbay Caddesi 4/1; mains ₺18-25; ⏱ noon-midnight) This is the third instalment of Ankara's favourite seafood restaurant. Take the waiter's recommendations for the cold meze, then take your pick of the fried and grilled fish – the fried whitebait (₺13) is a favourite – which are all perfectly cooked and brought to the table quickly. Book ahead to avoid disappointment.

ⓘ Orientation

Ankara's citadel crowns a hill 1km east of Ulus Meydanı (Ulus Sq), near most of the inexpensive hotels. The newer Ankara with the districts of Kızılay and Kavaklıdere lies further south, connected by Atatürk Caddesi, which has the post office and plenty of banks and ATMs.

ⓘ Getting There & Away

AIR

Ankara's **Esenboğa Airport** (📞 0312-590 4000; www.esenbogaairport.com; Özal Bulvarı, Esenboğa), 33km north of the city centre, has daily flights to most Turkish cities.

BUS

Ankara's mammoth **Ankara Şehirlerarası Terminali İşletmesi otogar** (AŞTİ; Mevlâna Bulvarı) is 5.5km southwest of Ulus and 4.5km west of Kızılay. Buses depart to all corners of Turkey day and night. Services to İstanbul (₺19 to ₺45, six hours) leave half-hourly.

The AŞTİ is at the western end of Ankara's Ankaray Metro line (fare ₺1.75), and is by far the easiest way to travel between the otogar and the centre.

TURKEY ANKARA

TRAIN

Ankara Train Station (Ankara Garı; Talat Paşa Bulvarı), 1km west of Ulus Meydanı, has six high-speed services daily to Pendik, a suburb 25km east of İstanbul (₺75, 3½ hours). High-speed trains also run to Konya (economy/business class ₺27.50/35, two hours, eight daily).

There are also plenty of slow trains heading to destinations across the country. The Trans-Asia train to Iran leaves at 10.25am every Wednesday.

Safranbolu

✏ 0370 / POP 42,800

Safranbolu is so perfectly pretty it looks like it's fallen off a chocolate-box lid. The old town (known as Çarşı) is Turkey's best-preserved Ottoman quarter and meandering through the lanes is like stepping back in time. The town rose to prominence as a spice-route hub and many of the fine merchant mansions gracing the streets have been converted into boutique hotels. This is the place to play out pasha daydreams and kip down for the night amid historic finery.

◉ Sights & Activities

Cinci Hanı   HISTORIC BUILDING
(Eski Çarşı Çeşme Mahalessi; admission ₺1) Çarşı's most famous and imposing structure is this brooding 17th-century caravanserai that's now a hotel. Nonguests are welcome to come and explore: climb up to the rooftop for red-tiled-roof panoramas over the town. On Saturdays a market takes place in the square behind it.

Kaymakamlar Müze Evi   MUSEUM
(Hıdırlık Yokuşu Sokak; adult/student ₺4/3; ☺ 9am-5.30pm) This typical Safranbolu home has all the classic features of Ottoman houses. It was owned by a lieutenant colonel and still feels like an address of note as you climb the stairs towards the wooden ceiling decoration. Tableaux (featuring some rather weary mannequins) re-create scenes such as bathing in a cupboard and a wedding feast.

Cinci Hamam   HAMAM
(✏ 0370-712 2103; Kazdağlıoğulu Meydanı; full treatment ₺35; ☺ men 6am-11pm, women 9am-10pm) One of the most renowned bathhouses in all of Turkey, with separate baths for men and women.

⌂ Sleeping

All the good accommodation is in Çarşı.

Efe Backpackers Pension   PENSION $
(✏ 0370-725 2688; www.backpackerspension.com; Kayadibi Sokak 8; dm/s/d ₺25/70/90; 🛜) This place dishes up all of Safranbolu's Ottoman charm at a smidgen of the cost of other hotels. Efe is the kind of hostel where being on a budget doesn't mean scrimping on quality, cleanliness or efficiency. There's a basic dorm for those really saving their lira and the snug private rooms are packed full of local character.

⭐**Imren Lokum Konak**   HISTORIC HOTEL $$
(✏ 0370-725 2324; www.imrenkonak.com; Kayyim Ali Sokak; s/d ₺160/230; 🛜) This old Ottoman building houses a fine hotel with rooms that, though keeping all their old Safranbolu flavour, have enough modern touches to make them truly user friendly. There's a large open courtyard and restaurant that attract many an overnighting tourist from Ankara at weekends and this ensures a holiday vibe.

✕ Eating

Hanım Sultan   ANATOLIAN $
(Akın Sokak 6, Çeşme Mahallesi; mains ₺5-10) Squirreled away down a little alleyway, this place rustles up rustic, wholesome cooking. Try the divine pot of *etli dolma* (vine leaves stuffed with meat) for a hearty, delicious lunch.

Kadıoğlu Şehzade Sofrası   TURKISH $$
(✏ 0370-712 5657; Arasta Arkası Sokak 8; mains ₺11-23; ☺ 11.30am-10.30pm) It's all traditional Ottoman-style seating at this converted mansion restaurant. The huge, steaming hot pide, *çorba,* grills and *zerde* (saffron dessert) are all recommended.

❶ Information

In Çarşı, the bank and ATM and the **tourist office** (✏ 0370-712 3863; www.safranbolu.gov.tr; Kazdağlıoğulu Meydanı; ☺ 9am-5.30pm) are on the main square.

❶ Getting There & Away

Most buses finish at Kıranköy otogar (upper Safranbolu), from where a *servis* or local dolmuş will deposit you in central Kıranköy, near the dolmuş stand for Çarşı. Dolmuşes (₺1.25) ply the route from central Kıranköy to Çarşı's main square, every 15 minutes.

From Kıranköy otogar there are regular services to Ankara (₺25, three hours) and İstanbul (₺45, seven hours).

Konya

0332 / POP 1.1 MILLION

Konya treads a delicate path between its historical significance as the home of the whirling-dervish orders and a bastion of Seljuk culture, and its modern importance as an economic boom town. Lose your way amid the mazelike market and crane your neck at tile-laden ceilings in *medreses* that are now museums, before paying your respects at the Mevlâna shrine to discover Konya's true soul.

◎ Sights & Activities

Tile Museum   MUSEUM
(Karatay Medresesi Çini Müzesi; ☑ 0332-351 1914; Alaaddin Meydanı; admission ₺5; ☺ 9am-6.40pm) Gorgeously restored, the interior central dome and walls of this former Seljuk theological school (1251) showcase some finely preserved blue-and-white Seljuk tilework. There is also an outstanding collection of ceramics on display, including exhibits of the octagonal Seljuk tiles unearthed during excavations at Kubad Abad Palace on Lake Beyşehir. Emir Celaleddin Karatay, a Seljuk general, vizier and statesman who built the *medrese,* is buried in one of the corner rooms.

Museum of Wooden
Artefacts and Stone Carving   MUSEUM
(Tas ve Ahsap Eserler Müzesi; ☑ 0332-351 3204; Adliye Bulvarı; admission ₺5; ☺ 9am-12.30pm & 1.30-6.40pm Tue-Sun) The İnce Minare Medresesi (Seminary of the Slender Minaret), now the Museum of Wooden Artefacts and Stone Carving, was built in 1264 for Seljuk vizier

Sahip Ata. Inside, many of the carvings feature motifs similar to those used in tiles and ceramics. The Seljuks didn't heed Islam's traditional prohibition of human and animal images: there are images of birds (the Seljuk double-headed eagle, for example), humans, lions and leopards.

🛏 Sleeping

Ulusan Otel   HOTEL $
(☑ 0332-351 5004; Çarşi PTT Arkasi 4; s/d without bathroom ₺35/70; 🛜) This is the pick of the Konya cheapies. The rooms may be totally basic, but they're bright and spotlessly clean. Shared bathrooms are immaculately kept (some rooms have private bathrooms) and the communal area is full of homely knick-knacks.

★ Derviş Otel   BOUTIQUE HOTEL $$
(☑ 0332-350 0842; www.dervishotel.com; Güngör Sokak 7; r €55-80; 🅿🛜) This airy, light-filled 200-year-old house has been converted into a rather wonderful boutique hotel. All of the seven spacious rooms have lovely soft colour schemes, with local carpets covering the wooden floors, comfortable beds and modern bathrooms to boot. With enthusiastic management providing truly personal service, this is a top-notch alternative to Konya's more anonymous hotels.

Hotel Rumi   HOTEL $$
(☑ 0332-353 1121; www.rumihotel.com; Durakfakih Sokak 5; d ₺100-180; 🅿🛜) Rooms at the Rumi are a tad on the small side, but are elegantly styled in soft mauves and sage green. Staff

TURKEY KONYA

DON'T MISS

KONYA'S WHIRLING DERVISH SIGHTS

Mevlâna Museum (☑ 0332-351 1215; admission ₺5, audio guide ₺10; ☺ 10am-5pm Mon, 9am-5pm Tue-Sun) For Muslims and non-Muslims alike, the main reason to come to Konya is to visit the Mevlâna Museum, the former lodge of the whirling dervishes. It's Celaleddin Rumi (later known as Mevlâna) that we have to thank for giving the world the whirling dervishes and, indirectly, the Mevlâna Museum. Calling it a mere museum, however, makes it sound dead and stale, but the truth couldn't be more different. As one of the biggest pilgrimage centres in Turkey, the museum constantly buzzes with energy.

Mevlâna Culture Centre (Whirling Dervish Performance; Aslanlı Kışla Caddesi; ☺ 9pm Sat) The *sema* (Mevlevi worship ceremony) is a ritual dance representing union with God; it's what gives the dervishes their famous whirl, and appears on Unesco's third Proclamation of Masterpieces of the Oral and Intangible Heritage of Humanity. Watching a *sema* can be an evocative, romantic, unforgettable experience. There are many dervish orders worldwide that perform similar rituals, but the original Turkish version is the smoothest and purest, more of an elegant, trancelike dance than the raw energy seen elsewhere.

appear to delight in offering genuinely good service and the top-level breakfast room has killer views over to the Mevlâna Museum. An oasis of calm in central Konya.

✖ Eating

★ **Konak Konya Mutfağı** ANATOLIAN **$$**
(☑ 0332-352 8547; Piriesat Caddesi 5; mains ₺15-20; ☉ 11am-10pm) This excellent traditional restaurant is run by well-known food writer Nevin Halıcı, who puts her personal twist on Turkish classics. Grab an outside table and dine beside vine-draped pillars and a fragrant rose garden. Aubergine aficionados shouldn't miss the *sebzeli közleme* (a grill of smoked aubergine and lamb) and sweet-tooths should definitely save room to try the unusual desserts.

Gülbahçesı Konya Mutfağı TURKISH **$$**
(☑ 0332-351 0768; Gülbahçe Sokak 3; mains ₺9-18; ☉ 8am-10pm) One of Konya's best restaurants, predominantly because of its upstairs terrace which has great views of the Mevlâna Museum. Dishes include *yaprak sarma* (stuffed vine leaves), Adana kebap and *etli ekmek*. It's a little hidden away in a mainly pedestrianised zone behind the tourist office.

❶ Information

You'll find numerous banks with ATMs and internet cafes around Alaaddin Tepesi. The **tourist office** (☑ 0332-353 4020; Aslanı Kışla Caddesi; ☉ 9am-5pm Mon-Sat) is behind the Mevlâna Museum.

❶ Getting There & Away

Konya Airport, 13km northeast of the city, has regular flights to İstanbul. Expect to pay ₺40 for a taxi into the centre.

Konya's otogar is 7km north of the centre and connected by tram. There are frequent buses to all major destinations, including Ankara (₺25, 3½ hours); İstanbul (₺68, 11½ hours); and Göreme (₺30, three hours). Bus companies have ticket offices in the centre.

Express trains link Konya with Ankara (adult/child ₺27.50/13, 1¾ hours) eight times daily.

CAPPADOCIA (KAPADOKYA)

As if plucked from a whimsical fairy tale and set down upon the stark Anatolian plains, Cappadocia is a geological oddity of honeycombed hills and towering boulders of other-worldly beauty. The fantastical topography is matched by the human history here. People have long utilised the region's soft stone, seeking shelter underground and leaving the countryside scattered with fascinating troglodyte-style architecture. The fresco-adorned rock-cut churches of Göreme Open-Air Museum and the subterranean refuges of Derinkuyu and Kaymaklı are the most famous sights, while simply bedding down in one of Cappadocia's cave hotels is an experience in 21st-century cavern dwelling.

❶ Getting There & Away

Two airports serve central Cappadocia: **Kayseri Airport** (Kayseri Erkilet Havalimanı ; ☑ 0352-337 5494; www.kayseri.dhmi.gov.tr; Kayseri Caddesi) and **Nevşehir Airport** (Nevşehir Kapadokya Havalimanı ; ☑ 0384-421 4451; www. kapadokya.dhmi.gov.tr; Nevşehir Kapadokya Havaalanı Yolu, Gülşehir). Both have several flights daily to/from İstanbul.

Most long-distance buses from western Turkey key destinations travel to Cappadocia overnight and terminate in Nevşehir, where a bus-company *servis* takes you on to Uçhisar, Göreme, Avanos or Ürgüp. Make sure your ticket states your final destination, not Nevşehir. Beware of touts at Nevşehir otogar and only use the bus company's official *servis* shuttle.

For onward travel, the major bus companies all have offices at Göreme, Ürgüp and Avanos otogars and service destinations nationwide. Heading out, most journeys involve a *servis* to Nevşehir and transferring there.

❶ Getting Around

Airport shuttle-bus services operate between both Cappadocia airports and the various villages. They must be prebooked before arrival. All hotels can arrange this for you or book directly through **Helios Transfer** (☑ 0384-271 2257; www.heliostransfer.com; Adnan Menderes Caddesi 24/A, Göreme; per passenger to/from either airport €10).

Cappadocia's villages have excellent public transport links. Dolmuşes (₺2.50 to ₺3.50) travel between Ürgüp and Avanos, via Göreme, hourly between 8am and 7pm. There's a half-hourly dolmuş between Göreme and Nevşehir, via Uçhisar, and several other routes.

Göreme

☑ 0384 / POP 2101
Surrounded by epic sweeps of moonscape valley, this remarkable honey-coloured village hollowed out of the hills may have long

since grown beyond its farming-hamlet roots, but its charm has not diminished. Nearby, the Göreme Open-Air Museum is an all-in-one testament to Byzantine life, while if you wander out of town you'll find storybook landscapes and little-visited rock-cut churches at every turn. With its easygoing allure and stunning setting, it's no wonder Göreme continues to send travellers giddy.

◎ Sights

★ **Göreme Open-Air Museum**　　　MUSEUM
(Göreme Açık Hava Müzesi; ☑ 271 2167; Müze Caddesi; admission ₺20; ⊙ 8am-6.30pm) One of Turkey's Unesco World Heritage sites, the Göreme Open-Air Museum is an essential stop on any Cappadocian itinerary and deserves a two-hour visit. First an important Byzantine monastic settlement that housed some 20 monks, then a pilgrimage site from the 17th century, this splendid cluster of monastic Byzantine artistry with its rock-cut churches, chapels and monasteries is 1km uphill from Göreme's centre.

Note that the museum's highlight – the Karanlık Kilise – has an additional ₺10 entrance fee.

Güllüdere Valley　　　PARK
The trails that loop around Güllüdere (Rose) Valley are easily accessible to all levels of walkers and provide some of the finest fairy-chimney-strewn vistas in Cappadocia. As well as this, though, they hide fabulous, little-visited rock-cut churches boasting vibrant fresco fragments and intricate carvings hewn into the stone.

If you only have time to hike through one valley in Cappadocia, this is the one to choose.

El Nazar Kilise　　　CHURCH
(Church of the Evil Eye; admission ₺5; ⊙ 8am-5pm) Carved from a ubiquitous conelike rock formation, the 10th-century El Nazar Kilise has been well restored with its snug interior a riot of colourful frescos. To find it, take the signposted Zemi Valley trailhead off Müze Caddesi.

☞ Tours

Most Göreme tour companies offer two standard full-day tours, referred to locally as the Red Tour (including visits to Göreme Open-Air Museum, Uçhisar rock castle, Paşabağı and Devrent Valleys, and Avanos), and the Green Tour (including a hike in

Central Cappadocia

Ihlara Valley and a trip to an underground city).

Heritage Travel　　　GUIDED TOUR
(☑ 271 2687; www.turkishheritagetravel.com; Uzundere Caddesi) This highly recommended local agency specialises in tailor-made Turkey packages but also runs three popular guided day tours (€60 per person) including an excellent 'Undiscovered Cappadocia' trip to Soğanlı. A range of more offbeat activities, from photography safaris (€125 per person) to cooking classes (€50 per person) and daytrips to Hacıbektaş, are also offered.

Yama Tours　　　GUIDED TOUR
(☑ 271 2508; www.yamatours.com; Müze Caddesi 2) This popular backpacker-friendly travel agency runs daily Red (regional highlights; ₺110) and Green (Ihlara Valley; ₺120) tours and can book a bagful of other Cappadocia adventures and activities for you.

🛏 Sleeping

Köse Pension　　　HOSTEL **$**
(☑ 271 2294; www.kosepension.com; Ragıp Üner Caddesi; dm/d/tr ₺15/100/120, s/tr without bathroom ₺30/90; 🐾 ⊠) It may have no cave character, but travellers' favourite Köse is still the pick of Göreme's budget digs. Ably managed by Sabina, this friendly place provides

CAPPADOCIA FROM ABOVE

If you've never taken a flight in a hot-air balloon, Cappadocia is one of the best places in the world to try it. Flight conditions are especially favourable here, with balloons operating most mornings throughout the year. Seeing this area's remarkable landscape from above is a truly magical experience and many travellers judge it to be the highlight of their trip. It's your responsibility to check the credentials of your chosen operator carefully. Don't pick just based on price as cheaper operators may take short cuts on safety or overfill the balloon baskets.

The following agencies have good credentials.

Butterfly Balloons (☑271 3010; www.butterflyballoons.com; Uzundere Caddesi 29)

Royal Balloon (☑271 3300; www.royalballoon.com; Dutlu Sokak 9)

a range of spotless rooms featuring brilliant bathrooms, bright linens and comfortable beds, more basic rooms, and a spacious rooftop dorm. The swimming pool is a bonus after a long, hot hike.

★**Kelebek Hotel & Cave Pension** HOTEL $$
(☑271 2531; www.kelebekhotel.com; Yavuz Sokak 31; fairy chimney s/d €44/55, deluxe s/d €56/70, ste €85-130; 🛜🌊) It's reassuring to know the oldie is still the goodie. Local guru Ali Yavuz leads a charming team at one of Göreme's original boutique hotels that has seen a travel industry virtually spring from beneath its stunning terrace. Exuding Anatolian inspiration at every turn, the rooms are spread over two gorgeous stone houses, each with a fairy chimney protruding skyward.

Taşkonak HOTEL $$
(☑270 2680; www.taskonak.com; Güngör Sokak 23; s/d/ste/f €35/40/80/110; 🛜) Angela and Yilmaz provide huge helpings of hospitality at this friendly and highly relaxed hideaway. Standard rooms are snug but sweet, while the spacious cave suites are among the best-value deals in town. Killer views from the terrace and a breakfast feast of homemade spreads, freshly baked delights and proper coffee will leave you grinning at your good fortune.

Kismet Cave House HOTEL $$
(☑271 2416; www.kismetcavehouse.com; Kağnı Yolu 9; s €52, d €65-95, f €130; 🛜) Kismet's fate is assured. Guests consistently rave about the intimate experience here, created by welcoming, well-travelled host Faruk. The rooms are full of local antiques, carved wood features, colourful rugs and quirky artwork, while communal areas are home to cosy cushion-scattered nooks. This honest-to-impending-greatness Anatolian cave house is delightfully homey in every way.

✕ Eating

Fırın Express PIDE $
(☑271 2266; Eski Belediye Yanı Sokak; pide ₺6-10; 🛜☑) Simply the best pide (Turkish-style pizza) in town is found in this local haunt. The cavernous wood oven fires up meat and vegetarian options and anything doused with egg. We suggest adding an *ayran* (yoghurt drink) and a *çoban salatası* (shepherd's salad) for a delicious bargain feed.

Pumpkin Cafe ANATOLIAN $$
(☑0542-808 5050; İçeridere Sokak 7; set menu ₺35; ⊙6-11pm) With its dinky balcony decorated with whimsically carved-out pumpkins (what else), this cute-as-a-button cafe is one of the cosiest dining picks in Göreme. The daily-changing four-course set menu is a fresh feast of simple Anatolian dishes, all presented with delightful flourishes.

★**Topdeck Cave Restaurant** ANATOLIAN $$$
(☑271 2474; Hafız Abdullah Efendi Sokak 15; mains ₺18-30; ⊙6-10pm Wed-Mon; 🖉) If it feels as though you're dining in a family home, it's because you are. Talented chef Mustafa (aka Topdeck) and his clan have transformed an atmospheric cave room in their house into a cosy restaurant where the kids pitch in with the serving and diners dig into hearty helpings of Anatolian favourites with a spicy twist.

★**Seten Restaurant** MODERN TURKISH $$$
(☑271 3025; www.setenrestaurant.com; Aydınlı Sokak; mains ₺16-40; 🖉) Brimming with an artful Anatolian aesthetic, Seten is a feast for the eye as well as for the stomach. Named after the old millstones used to grind bulgur wheat, this restaurant is an education for newcomers to Turkish cuisine and a treat for well-travelled palates. Attentive service complements classic main dishes and myriad luscious and unusual meze.

Around Göreme

From Göreme, an easy 3km walk through **Pigeon (Güvercinlik) Valley** – or take the Göreme–Nevşehir dolmuş – brings you to **Uçhisar Castle** (Uçhisar Kalesi; admission ₺3; ⊙8am-8.15pm), with awesome views of the lunarscape below.

Hike through **Rose (Güllüdere)** and **Red (Kızılçukur) Valleys** to **Çavasın** village to visit the **Church of St John the Baptist** `FREE`, high up in the cliff overlooking the old village ruins.

Between Göreme and Avanos (hop on the Ürgüp–Avanos dolmuş) is the valley of **Paşabağı**, with some of Cappadocia's most famous fairy-chimney formations. Further along the road, is the old monastic settlement of **Zelve Open-Air Museum** (Zelve Açık Hava Müzesi; admission ₺10; ⊙8am-7pm).

Southwest of Göreme is a series of ancient underground cities first carved out by the Hittites and once occupied by Byzantine Christians taking refuge from Persian and Arab armies. The largest of these is **Derinkuyu** (admission ₺20; ⊙8am-6.30pm), which, unbelievably, once sheltered 10,000 people and their livestock. Another at **Kaymaklı** (admission ₺20; ⊙8am-6.30pm) is located 10km to the north. There is little in the way of information at either site so it's worthwhile hiring a guide.

Continuing southwest you reach **Ihlara Valley** (Ihlara Vadısı; admission incl Selime Monastery ₺10; ⊙8am-6.30pm), a beautiful canyon full of rock-cut churches dating back to Byzantine times. A hiking trail threads the length of the gorge following the course of the river, Melendiz Suyu, which flows for 13km from Selime village and its rock-hewn **monastery** (admission incl Ihlara Valley ₺10; ⊙dawn-dusk) to Ihlara village.

To get there by bus, you must change in Nevşehir and Aksaray, making it tricky to do a day return from Göreme and have time to walk. The Green Tour (p475) is by far the best way to see Ihlara Valley in a day if you don't have your own transport.

Avanos

🖉 0384 / POP 13,250

The Kızılırmak (Red River) is the slow-paced pulse of this provincial town and the unusual source of its livelihood; the river's distinctive red clay is used to produce Avanos' famed pottery. Up from the river an old quarter of gently decaying grand Greek houses snakes up the hillside, while riverside is the place to ponder the sunset as you sip your umpteenth *çay* (tea).

🛏 Sleeping & Eating

★**Kirkit Pension**   PENSION $$
(🖉511 3148; www.kirkitpension.com; Genç Ağa Sokak; s/d/tr/f €40/55/70/90; 🛜) This Avanos institution, right in the centre of town, is a rambling stone house with rooms full of kilims (pileless woven rugs), old black-and-white photographs, intricately carved cupboards and *suzanis* (Uzbek bedspreads), all set around a courtyard brimming with plants and quirky antiques. Looked after by incredibly knowledgable and helpful management, Kirkit is the perfect base for trips around Cappadocia.

★**Dayının Yeri**   KEBAP $$$
(🖉511 6840; Atatürk Caddesi; mains ₺13-25) Locals grumble that it's not as cheap as it used to be, but this modern grill restaurant is one of Cappadocia's best. Steer clear of the meze and it's still good value too. Don't leave without sampling the *künefe* – layers of *kadayıf* dough cemented together with sweet cheese, doused in syrup and served hot with a sprinkling of pistachio.

Ürgüp

🖉 0384 / POP 20,061

Ürgüp is the rural retreat for those who don't fancy being too rural, with its bustling downtown a direct foil to the old village back lanes clinging to the hillside rim. There's not a lot to do in town itself. Instead, Ürgüp has positioned itself as the connoisseur's base for exploring Cappadocia, with boutique-hotel frippery and fine dining at your fingertips.

🛏 Sleeping

Hotel Elvan   PENSION $$
(🖉341 4191; www.hotelelvan.com; Barbaros Hayrettin Sokak 11; s/d/tr ₺70/120/180; 🛜) Bah! – who needs boutique-style when you have pensions like the Elvan, where Hasan and family dish out oodles of homespun hospitality? Set around an internal courtyard brimming with colourful pot plants, the 20 neat rooms feature daisy bedspreads, pinewood floors and tiny bathrooms, all kept sparkling clean.

★ **Esbelli Evi** BOUTIQUE HOTEL $$$
(☑341 3395; www.esbelli.com; Esbelli Sokak 8; d €110, ste €160-220; ☎) Jazz in the bathroom, whisky by the tub, secret tunnels to secluded walled gardens draped in vines – this is one of Cappadocia's most individual boutique hotels. A lawyer who never practised, Süha Ersöz instead (thank God) purchased the 12 surrounding properties over two decades and created a highly cultured yet decidedly unpretentious hotel that stands out on exclusive Esbelli Hill.

Serinn House BOUTIQUE HOTEL $$$
(☑341 6076; www.serinnhouse.com; Esbelli Sokak 36; d €120-145; ☎) Charming hostess Eren Serpen has truly set a new standard for hotel design in Cappadocia with this contemporary effort that seamlessly merges İstanbul's European aesthetic with Turkish provincial life. The six minimally furnished rooms employ dashes of colour and feature Archimedes lamps, signature chairs, hip floor rugs and tables too cool for coffee.

✖ Eating

Zeytin Cafe TURKISH $$
(☑341 7399; Atatürk Bulvarı; dishes ₺6-15; ✐) Our top lunchtime spot in Ürgüp is this thoroughly welcoming, modern *lokanta* (eatery serving ready-made food) dishing up wholesome homemade stews, *mantı* (ravioli) and Turkish staples. Head inside to the counter and choose from the daily-changing selection.

Cafe In INTERNATIONAL $$
(Cumhuriyet Meydanı; mains ₺13-17; ✐) If you're hankering after a decent plate of pasta, this dinky cafe should be your first port of call. Servings are on the generous side, the coffee is the best in town and it also does some excellent, inventive salads.

★ **Ziggy's** MODERN TURKISH $$$
(☑341 7107; Yunak Mahallesi, Tevfik Fikret Caddesi 24; meze set menus ₺55-60, mains ₺20-45; ✐) This tribute to the adored pet dog of charismatic hosts Nuray and Selim is a luscious success. The two-tiered terrace fills day and night with a hip clientele enjoying strong cocktails and feasting on the finest meze menu in Cappadocia, created by chef Ali Ozkan. Ziggy's has nailed the essence of casual-yet-classy Cappadocian dining.

Kayseri
☑0352 / POP 1 MILLION

Mixing Seljuk tombs, mosques and modern developments, Kayseri is Turkey's most Islamic city after Konya and one of the country's economic powerhouses. An afternoon pottering within the huge bazaar and poking about the Seljuk and Ottoman monuments of this Turkish boom town – all loomed over by mighty Erciyes Dağı (Mt Erciyes) – is an interesting contrast to exploring the more famous fairy-chimney vistas to the city's west.

◉ Sights

★ **Museum of Seljuk Civilisation** MUSEUM
(Selçuklu Uygarlığı Müzesi; Mimar Sinan Parkı; admission ₺2; ◷9am-7pm) This excellent museum is set in the restored Çifte Medrese, a 13th-century twin hospital and seminary built at the bequest of Seljuk sultan Keyhüsrev I and his sister Gevher Nesibe Sultan and thought to be one of the world's first medical-training schools. The strikingly serene architecture is offset by beautiful exhibits of Seljuk artistry, culture and history, complemented by up-to-the-minute multimedia displays. Our one grumble is that not enough of the information panels have English translations.

★ **Güpgüpoğlu Konağı** MUSEUM
(Ethnography Museum; Tennuri Sokak; ◷8am-5pm Tue-Sun) **FREE** Ignore the scruffy mannequin-inhabited dioramas acting out Ottoman daily life and instead feast your eyes on the glorious interior of this grand mansion's painted wooden wall panels and ceilings. The building dates from the 15th century and Mamluk architectural influence is obvious in its regal black-and-white stone façade. During the 19th century the house's multicoloured beams and intricately carved woodwork were home to composer and lyricist Ahmet Mithat Güpgüpoğlu.

⌂ Sleeping & Eating

İmamoğlu Paşa Hotel HOTEL $$
(☑336 9090; www.imamoglupasaotel.com.tr; Kocasinan Bulvarı 24; s/d ₺90/140; ✖☎) Near the train station, only a short jaunt from Kayseri centre, is this jazzy place with modern rooms decked out in neutral beige and grey tones and probably the most comfortable beds in town. Unlike most Kayseri hotels, it has some designated nonsmoking rooms, so

you don't have to wake up to the lingering smell of stale tobacco.

Hotel Çapari
HOTEL **$$**

(☑222 5278; Donanma Caddesi 12; s/d ₺70/110; ✳🛜) Enthusiastic staff, a great, central but quiet location and tidy rooms make the Çapari a decent place to rest your head for the night in Kayseri.

★ Alamet-i Farika
ANATOLIAN **$$**

(☑232 1080; Deliklitaş Caddesi 8; mains ₺10-24) The interior is all European-style elegance, but the food is top-notch Anatolian. Tuck into the *mantı* (ravioli), devour the meaty speciality *çentik kebap* (grilled meat served atop potatoes with a yoghurt and tomato sauce) and save room for the naughtily sweet desserts. Finish up with a Turkish coffee, served in a dainty teacup and complete with a shot glass of lemonade on the side.

Elmacioğlu İskander Merkez
KEBAP **$$**

(☑222 6965; 1st & 2nd fl, Millet Caddesi 5; mains ₺10-22) Bring on the calories. Skip the diet for the day and ascend the lift to the top-floor dining hall, with views over the citadel, to order the *İskender kebap* (döner kebap on fresh pide and topped with savoury tomato sauce and browned butter) house speciality. Your waistline won't thank us, but your tastebuds will.

ℹ Information

You'll find banks with ATMs and a helpful **tourist office** (☑222 3903; Cumhuriyet Meydanı; ⊘8am-5pm Mon-Fri) in the centre.

ℹ Getting There & Away

Kayseri Airport (p474) is 9km north of the centre. A taxi from the central city to the airport costs around ₺15, or hop on a city bus for ₺1.25.

The otogar is is 9km west of the centre. Bus companies provide a free *servis* into the central city. There are hourly buses to Ankara (₺35, five hours) via Nevşehir (₺15, 1½ hours); and regular evening departures to Erzurum (₺55, 10 hours); Trabzon (₺60, 11½ hours); and Van (₺60, 13 hours). Dolmuşes to Ürgüp (₺5, one hour, nine services daily) leave from the smaller terminal across the car park from the main otogar.

Kayseri train station is 500m north of the centre. There are slow services to Ankara, and eastern destinations from here.

BLACK SEA & NORTHEASTERN ANATOLIA

The craggy and spectacular coastline of the Black Sea is scattered with the legacy of the civilisations and empires that have ebbed and flowed in this historic region. The local castles, churches and monasteries remember the kings of Pontus, the Genoese and the Ottomans while pint-size fishing villages and inland alpine *yaylalar* (mountain pastures) provide some of Turkey's most stunning scenery.

The far-flung northeastern Anatolia region is ruggedly beautiful and remote – all the more reason to go exploring. Here the flavours of central Asia, the Caucasus and Iran intermingle on the steppes while the archaeological sites and historic monuments are devoid of other travellers.

Trabzon

☑0462 / POP 244,000

The Black Sea's most cosmopolitan city has a somewhat louche, seaside-town feel. The modern buzz and bustle shines the brightest around Atatürk Alanı, Trabzon's busy main square. Most travellers stop here to see Sumela Monastery, 46km to the south, but don't miss visiting the picturesque old neighbourhood of Ortahisar, straddling a ravine, past the bazaar to the west of the centre.

◉ Sights

Sumela Monastery
MONASTERY

(Sümela Manastırı; www.sumela.com; admission ₺15; ⊘9am-7pm Jun-Sep, to 5pm Apr, to 6pm May, to 4pm Oct-Mar) The Greek Orthodox Monastery of the Virgin Mary, better known as Sumela Monastery, 46km south of Trabzon, is one of the historical highlights of the Black Sea coast. The monastery was founded in the 4th century AD and abandoned in 1923 after the creation of the Turkish Republic and the so-called exchange of populations. The highlight of the complex is the main church, with damaged but stunningly coloured frescos both inside and out.

Aya Sofya Mosque & Museum
MOSQUE, MUSEUM

(Aya Sofya Müzesi ve Camii; ☑223 3043; www.trabzonmuzesi.gov.tr; Aya Sofya Sokak; ⊘9am-7pm Jun-Aug, 9am-6pm Apr-May & Sep-Oct, 8am-5pm

DRIVING THE BLACK SEA COAST

To see the best of the Black Sea, travel the glorious, vertigo-inducing curves on the coastal road from **Amasra**, with its Roman and Byzantine ruins, to the fortified town of **Sinop**. Carry on east – passing through the busy port of Samsun – to **Ünye**, with an old town of preserved Ottoman houses that is ripe for wandering. Finish up in **Ordu** for breathtaking Black Sea vistas from the cable car that trundles up the hill behind town.

Nov-Mar) FREE Originally called Hagia Sophia (Church of Divine Wisdom), Aya Sofya sits 4km west of Trabzon's centre on a terrace close to the sea. Built between 1238 and 1263, it was influenced by Georgian and Seljuk design, although the wall paintings and mosaic floors follow the prevailing Constantinople style of the time. It was converted to a mosque after Ottoman conquest in 1461, and later used as an ammunition-storage depot and hospital by the Russians, before restoration in the 1960s.

🛏 Sleeping

Hotel Can HOTEL **$**
(☑ 326 8281; Güzelhisar Caddesi 2; s/d ₺30/50; ✱🕸🛜) There isn't much difference between the tall, thin 18-room 'Hotel Soul' and some of its neighbours – except for the price and the friendly staff. This is probably Trabzon's top budget choice and the best place to meet fellow travellers.

★ Hotel Nur HOTEL **$$**
(☑ 323 0445; www.nurotel.net; Cami Sokak 15; s/d ₺70/140, without bathroom ₺45/90; ✱🛜) A long-standing travellers' favourite, with a fabulous lounge/bar on the rooftop and very helpful staff, the Nur has 10 rooms with bathrooms and five with shared facilities. Some rooms are pint-sized but the views across Atatürk Alanı make up for the squeeze. The nearby mosque doesn't skimp on the 5am call to prayer.

🍴 Eating & Drinking

★ Kalender TURKISH **$$**
(☑ 323 1011; Zeytinlik Caddesi 16/B; mains ₺13, salads ₺4-9; ⊙ 8.30am-9pm) This welcoming cafe-restaurant just south of the museum has a cosmopolitan vibe. It's perfect for a postmuseum coffee and brunch of *menemen* (scrambled eggs with peppers and tomatoes) or *gözleme* (stuffed savoury crepe). The front tables overlook a side street and, on weekdays, you can choose a mixed plate of three/four of the seven or eight hot (₺13/15) and cold (₺7/9.50) daily dishes.

Reis'in Yeri TURKISH, TEAHOUSE **$$**
(Reis' Place; Liman Mukli İdare; mains ₺15-22; ⊙ 8am-11pm) Head down Gazipaşa Caddesi from Atatürk Alanı and across the footbridge to this sprawling fish/chicken/*köfte* grill house, which doubles as a tea garden. It's guaranteed dolmuş free, and you can even hire rowing boats to steer around the tiny cove.

ℹ Information

Banks with ATMs, exchange offices and the post office are along Maraş Caddesi. The **tourist office** (☑ 326 4760; Atatürk Alanı; ⊙ 8am-5.30pm Jun-Sep, 8am-5pm Mon-Fri Oct-May) is in the centre.

ℹ Getting There & Away

Trabzon otogar is 3km east of the centre. Regular dolmuşes shoot between the otogar and Atatürk Alanı. There are five daily services to Ankara (₺50, 12 hours); and Erzurum (₺30, five hours); and at least one bus daily to Kars (₺40, 10 hours); and Kayseri (₺60, 12 hours). An 8pm bus heads to Tbilisi (₺80, 10 hours) in Georgia.

To Sumela Monastery, Ulusoy and Metro run buses from the otogar (₺25 return, one hour), leaving at 10am and departing from Sumela at 1pm/2pm in winter/summer.

Ferries to Sochi in Russia (about US$150) have no regular timetable. Check information with **Sarı Denizcilik** (www.saridenizcilik.com) or **Port of Trabzon** (www.al-port.com).

Erzurum

☑ 0442 / POP 395,000
Lovers of architecture will be in paradise in Erzurum, where fantastic Seljuk and Mongol monuments line the main street. Take it all in from atop the citadel, with mountains and steppe forming a heavenly backdrop to the jumble of billboards and minarets.

⦿ Sights

★ Çifte Minareli Medrese MEDRESE
(Twin Minaret Seminary; Cumhuriyet Caddesi) East of the city centre, this building dates from the 1200s when Erzurum was a wealthy Sel-

Erzurum

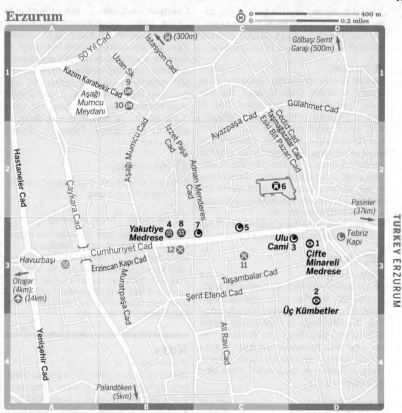

Erzurum

juk city, before suffering attack and devastation by the Mongols in 1242. The twin brick minarets are decorated with eye-catching small blue tiles. Walk to the back of the building to see the grand, 12-sided domed hall at the far end of the main courtyard from the entrance. It served as the Hatuniye Türbesi, or Tomb of Huand Hatun, the *medrese's* founder.

★**Yakutiye Medrese**   MUSEUM, MEDRESE
(Yakutiye Seminary; Cumhuriyet Caddesi) Rising above a central square, this imposing Mongol theological seminary dates from 1310. The Mongols borrowed the basics of Seljuk architecture and developed their own variations, as seen in the entrance with its geometric, plant and animal motifs. Of the two

original minarets, only the base of one and the lower part of the other have survived. The one sporting superb mosaic tilework wouldn't look out of place in central Asia.

★ Ulu Cami
MOSQUE

(Mosque; Cumhuriyet Caddesi) Unlike the elaborately decorated Çifte Minareli, the Ulu Cami, built in 1179 by the Saltuk Turkish emir of Erzurum, is restrained but elegant, with seven aisles running north to south and six running east to west, resulting in a forest of columns. You enter from the north along the central aisle. Above the third east–west aisle, a striking stalactite dome opens to the heavens. At the southern end of the central aisle are a curious wooden dome and a pair of bull's-eye windows.

A short hop from the Ulu Cami, you'll notice the small Ottoman Caferiye Camii.

🛏 Sleeping

Hekimoğlu Hotel HOTEL **$**

(🖉 234 3049; Kazım Karabekir Caddesi 66; s/d/tr ₺60/90/120; 🛜) With halls bedecked with colourful carpets and a jovial team at reception, the Hekimoğlu is a good-value option in Erzurum's main hotel area. Rooms are on the small side, but simple and clean. There's a busy *lokanta* (casual restaurant) downstairs, so that's everything sorted after a long Anatolian bus ride.

Grand Hotel Hitit HOTEL **$$**

(🖉 233 5001; grandhitit@gmail.com; Kazım Karabekir Caddesi 26; s/d/tr ₺90/150/180; 🛜) On a street with budget and lower midrange hotels, the Hitit has pleasant rooms with TV, dark wood decor, well-sprung mattresses, big showers, minibars and safes. It's professionally managed and a good choice for solo women travellers.

✕ Eating

★ Erzurum Evleri CAFE **$$**

(Yüzbaşı Sokak 5; entry ₺2, mains ₺10-20; ⏱10am-11pm) This old wooden house, signposted from Cumhuriyet Caddesi, is filled with Ottoman paraphernalia. Dishes include soup, *börek* (filled pastry) and *tandır kebap* (stew), served in private alcoves with cushions and low tables. Overlooking the courtyard, Şahane offers *çay*, Turkish coffee and, from 6pm, traditional live music. Round the back, Daşhane has nargiles (water pipes) and beanbags. There is a small entry fee for all this heritage ambience.

Güzelyurt Restorant MEZE, INTERNATIONAL **$$**

(🖉 234 5001; www.guzelyurtrestaurant.com.tr; Cumhuriyet Caddesi 42; mains ₺11-23; ⏱11am-10pm; ✔) Erzurum's smartest restaurant, in business since 1928, is quaintly anachronistic, with shrouded windows, thick carpets and bow-tied waiters creating an old-fashioned charm. It's licensed, and a good place to splurge on a great meal. The meze (₺4 to ₺8) are the headliner, with about 20 different specialities, including lots of vegetarian options.

ℹ Information

Banks and ATMs cluster on or around Cumhuriyet Caddesi, the main drag.

ℹ Getting There & Away

The airport is 14km west of town and has regular flights to İstanbul and Ankara. Frequent city buses (₺3) run to the central city.

From Erzurum otogar, 4km from the centre, there are regular services to Kars (₺20, three hours) and Trabzon (₺30, six hours); and five buses daily to Diyarbakır (₺35, eight hours) and Doğubayazıt (₺25, 4½ hours).

Kars

🖉 0474 / POP 76,700

With its stately, pastel-coloured stone buildings dating from the Russian occupation, and a mix of influences – Azeri, Turkmen, Kurdish, Turkish and Russian – Kars has a distinctly different feel to other eastern cities. It's usually regarded as a base for Ani, but it's worth spending a day exploring Kars' sights and soaking up the eclectic vibe.

🛏 Sleeping

Hotel Temel HOTEL **$**

(🖉 223 1376; www.hoteltemel.com; Yenipazar Caddesi 9; s/d ₺60/80; 🛜) Hotel Base offers neat rooms with immaculate sheets and a soothing blue-and-yellow colour scheme, but its wood-panelled interiors are dated and gloomy. Thankfully it's near the minibus terminal and has a lift and satellite TV. Nearby, the rooms at Hotel Temel 2 (🖉 223 1376; Yenipazar Caddesi; s/d/tr ₺25/40/60 ; 🛜) are small and old but clean.

Güngören Otel HOTEL **$$**

(🖉 212 6767; www.gungorenhotel.com; Millet Sokak; s/d/tr ₺90/160/210; 🛜) The Güngören is a stalwart on the travelling circuit with smart rooms with flat-screen TVs and tiled bathrooms. The staff speak some English, and the location on a quiet street is convenient. Some upper-floor rooms have not been renovated, so be sure to check when you book.

★ **Hotel Cheltikov**   BOUTIQUE HOTEL **$$$**
(☑ 212 0035; www.hotelcheltikov.com; Şehit Hulusi Aytekin Caddesi 63; s/d ₺180/250; 🛜) In a sleepy residential neighbourhood 10 minutes' walk from central Kars, this boutique hotel fills a stately 19th-century building that was formerly a maternity hospital. Rooms are spacious and elegant, many with carved wooden ceilings and chandeliers. Accommodation in the 'Store Room' section at the building's front incorporates dramatic stone walls, and the bathrooms are most likely eastern Turkey's best.

✖ Eating

★ **Hanimeli Kars Mutfağı**   ANATOLIAN **$$**
(www.karshanimeli.com; Faik Bey Caddesi 156; mains ₺10-15; 🕙 11am-9pm) With a rustic, country-kitchen vibe, Hanimeli specialises in homestyle cooking influenced by the broader Caucasian region. Dishes include Armemian-style *Erivan köfte* (meatballs), a silkily smooth pasta soup called *eriste aşi*, and the ravioli-like *hangel*. Roast duck is on offer, delicious Kars honey for sale, and a refreshing local drink is *reyhane*, made from purple-coloured red basil.

Ocakbaşı Restoran   TURKISH **$$**
(☑ 212 0056; www.kaygisizocakbasi.com; Atatürk Caddesi 276; mains ₺10-15; 🍴) This 40-year-old favourite serves unusual Turkish dishes, such as its house specialities *ali nazık* (aubergine purée with yoghurt and beef tenderloin; ask for *et siz* for the vegetarian version) and *ejder kebap* (sesame bread stuffed with meat, cheese, parsley, nuts and eggs).

ℹ Information

Banks and ATMs congregate on Atatürk Caddesi.
Tourist Office (☑ 212 1705; cnr Faik Bey & Gazi Ahmet Muhtar Paşa Caddesis; 🕙 8am-5pm Mon-Fri)

ℹ Getting There & Away

Daily flights to Ankara and İstanbul leave from the airport 6km outside of town.

Long-distance buses depart from the otogar, 2km southeast of the centre. Buses run to Ankara (₺50, 16 hours), Trabzon (₺35, nine hours), and Van (₺35, six hours) a couple of times daily.

WORTH A TRIP

ANI

Set amid spectacular scenery 45km east of Kars, **Ani** (admission ₺8; 🕗 8.30am-6pm May-Sep, to 3pm Oct-Apr) exudes an eerie ambience. The site was completely deserted in 1239 after a Mongol invasion, but before that it was a stately Armenian capital, rivalling Constantinople in power and glory. Fronted by a hefty wall, the ghost city now lies in fields overlooking the Arpa Çayi gorge, which forms the border with Armenia. The ruins include several notable churches and a cathedral built between AD 987 and 1010.

From the central city dolmuş terminal there are hourly services to Erzurum (₺20, three hours) and Iğdır (₺20, for Doğubayazıt).

Doğubayazıt

☑ 0472 / POP 73,505
On one side, the talismanic Mt Ararat (Ağrı Dağı, 5137m), Turkey's highest mountain, hovers majestically over the horizon. On the other side, İshak Paşa Palace, a breathtakingly beautiful fortress-palace-mosque complex, surveys town from its rocky perch. Doğubayazıt itself doesn't have many attractions, but it's an obvious base for climbing Mt Ararat and exploring Kurdish heritage. It's also the main kicking-off point for the overland trail through Iran (the border is 35km away).

◎ Sights

İshak Paşa Palace   PALACE
(İshak Paşa Sarayı; admission ₺5; 🕗 8am-7pm) Located 6km southeast of town, İshak Paşa Palace is perched on a small plateau abutting stark cliffs. Combining Seljuk, Ottoman, Georgian, Persian and Armenian architecture, the palace was begun in 1685 and completed in 1784. Minibuses (₺1.50) rattle between the centre and the palace. Taxis charge about ₺15 to ₺20 one way; ₺25 to ₺30 return, including a one-hour wait. The protective glass roofing means you can visit on a rainy day.

🛏 Sleeping & Eating

Hotel Tahran   HOTEL **$**
(☑ 312 0195; www.hoteltahran.com; Büyük Ağrı Caddesi 124; s/d/tr ₺35/60/80; 🛜) The well-managed Tahran exudes mellow vibes.

MT ARARAT

Hikers with a sense of adventure will surely be itching to climb the country's highest peak, Mt Ararat (5137m) – but you need a permit (US$50), a guide and a healthy bank balance to do so. Various tour companies based in Doğubayazıt offer similar four- to seven-day treks, but usually require a group of at least four (four-day climb around €500). You can apply for a permit through any reputable travel agency in Turkey but should do so well in advance. Permit regulations have changed several times over the last few years, so we recommend you seek current advice when planning your trip. At the time of writing you were required to send a scan of your passport and confirmed trekking dates at least a month in advance.

Although small and old, rooms have crisp white sheets, and the top-floor kitchen and dining room have glimpses of Mt Ararat and İshak Paşa Palace. There's a laundry service, book exchange, and reception with inviting chairs and offers of çay. Affable, English-speaking manager Bilal is clued up on subjects such as getting to Iran.

Butik Ertur Hotel HOTEL $$

(☑ 312 7866; www.butikerturhotel.com; Güburlak Çevreyolu Üzeri; s/d ₺100/160) 'Butik (boutique)' is stretching it, but this recently refurbished hotel near the otogar is the most comfortable place in town. Bathrooms are spacious and spotless, and the licensed restaurant downstairs is a good spot for a beer and decent food. Kurdish weddings are sometimes held in an adjacent reception hall, and curious hotel guests are usually welcome to join the fun.

Beyazit ANATOLIAN $$

(Dr İsmail Beşikçi Caddesi; mains ₺8-13) Look for the big colourful photos of Doğubayazıt's two most famous attractions – Ararat and İshak Paşa Palace – and ascend to the 2nd floor for good main drag views. Beyazit's combo of pide, kebaps and local dishes is popular with families.

ⓘ Information

There are lots of banks, ATMs and exchange offices (which can swap lira for Iranian rials) in the centre.

ⓘ Getting There & Away

The otogar is 2km west of town. For long-distance destinations, you need to head to Erzurum (₺25, four hours). To Van (₺15, three hours) there are five daily dolmuşes.

Dolmuşes to Iğdır (₺7, 45 minutes), to change for Kars and to the Iranian border at Gürbulak (₺7, 30 minutes), leave from separate dolmuş stands in the central city.

SOUTHEASTERN ANATOLIA

Turkey's wild child, southeastern Anatolia feels different from the rest of the country, and that's part of its appeal. Apart from a few Arabic and Christian pockets, this huge chunk of territory is predominantly Kurdish. Choose from a menu of historical cities, including honey-toned, hilltop Mardin and the old city of Diyarbakır, ensnared in mighty basalt walls. Move on to Nemrut Dağı (Mt Nemrut), topped with colossal ancient statues, or Lake Van, edged with snowcapped mountains. Be aware that a few places could be off limits to foreigners when you visit – mainly near the borders with Iraq and Syria – but most of southeastern Anatolia is safe and accessible to independent travellers.

Van

☑ 0432 / POP 353,500

Vibrant Van with its casual, liberal vibe is something of an anomaly in conservative southeastern Anatolia. Young couples walk hand in hand on the main drag, live bands knock out Kurdish tunes in pubs, and a resilient population coping with the impact of recent earthquakes creates a satisfying urban buzz.

Van boasts a brilliant location near the eponymous lake. Focus your sightseeing on the monuments around it and spend a few days exploring the nearby historic sites of Çavuştepe and Hoşap.

◎ Sights

Van Castle CASTLE

(Rock of Van; admission ₺5; ⊙9am-dusk) Nothing is quite so impressive in Van as the Van Castle, which dominates the view of the city. About 3km west of the city centre, it's a wonderful place to come for a picnic.

🏛 Akdamar Kilisesi
CHURCH

(Church of the Holy Cross; admission ₺5; ⊘8am-6pm) One of the marvels of Armenian architecture is the carefully restored Akdamar Kilisesi. It's perched on an island 3km out in Lake Van. In 921, Gagik Artzruni, King of Vaspurkan, built a palace, church and monastery on the island. Little remains of the palace and monastery, but the church walls are in superb condition and the wonderful relief carvings are among the masterworks of Armenian art.

🛏 Sleeping

Royal Berk Hotel
HOTEL $$

(📞215 0050; www.royalberkhotel.com; Bankası Bitişiği Sokak 5; s/d from ₺90/130) Built after the 2011 earthquakes, the Royal Berk combines spacious and very comfortable rooms with a brilliant location in a quiet laneway just metres from Van's main street. Decor stays just the right side of OTT, the crew at reception are easygoing and friendly, and the huge breakfast spread closely replicates what's on offer in the city's famed *kahvaltı* restaurants.

Elite World Hotel
HOTEL $$$

(📞0212-444 0883; www.eliteworldhotels.com. tr; Kazım Karabekir Caddesi 54; s/d €65/85; ⊜❄@🛜🏊) Van's most comfortable hotel overflows with business-traveller-friendly features including a bar, nonsmoking rooms, and a spa, sauna and swimming pool. Combined with luxury decor, it's easily Van's top place to stay.

🍴 Eating

Aişe
ANATOLIAN $

(Özok is Merkezi Karşi 5; mains ₺7-10; ⊘10am-4pm; 📞) Run by an enterprising group of local women, this restaurant presents around six different Turkish and Kurdish dishes each day. Count on around ₺10 to ₺12 for a full meal including bread and soup, all best enjoyed in the restaurant's colourful outdoor patio.

Kervansaray
ANATOLIAN $$

(Cumhuriyet Caddesi; mains ₺12-16) Upstairs from the bustle of Cumhuriyet Caddesi, Kervansaray is Van's go-to spot for a more elegant and refined dining experience. Dive into a few shared plates of excellent meze as you peruse a menu containing a few local specialities. Fans of lamb should try the tender *kağıt kebap* (paper kebab), wrapped and cooked in paper.

ℹ Getting There & Away

The otogar is on the northwestern outskirts of town. Bus companies provide free *servis* transport into the city. There are frequent buses to Diyarbakır (₺40, seven hours) and Erzurum (₺40, seven hours) and decent connections to Şanlıurfa (₺60, 11 hours), along with plenty of dolmuşes heading to the surrounding villages.

Diyarbakır
📞0412 / POP 963,300

Full of heart, soul and character, Diyar is finally tapping into its fantastic potential as a destination for travellers. While it's proud of remaining the symbol of Kurdish identity and tenacity, thanks to increasing promotion and restoration programs Turkish and foreign tourists are beginning to come back. Behind the grim basalt walls, the old city's twisting alleyways are crammed full of historical buildings and Arab-style mosques. As well as the monuments, though, this is the number-one place in Turkey to delve into Kurdish culture.

⊙ Sights

⭐Dengbêj Evi
CULTURAL CENTRE

(http://turizm.diyarbakir.bel.tr/en/s/Dengbej_House; Kılıççı Sokak, near Behram Paşa Camii; ⊘9am-6pm Tue-Sun) The Dengbêj Evi (House of Dengbêj) showcases the Kurdish tradition of Dengbêj, storytelling by song. Kurdish elders gather together in informal groups and take turns to sing and chant in an ethereal and mesmerising style. Their associates add bold affirmations to underpin the melancholy and yearning melodies, and it's a compelling way to spend an hour or so in Turkey's most important Kurdish city. The complex also houses a tea garden.

⭐City Walls & Gates
FORTRESS

Diyarbakır's single most conspicuous feature is its great circuit of basalt walls, probably dating from Roman times, although the present walls, around 6km in total length, date from early Byzantine times (AD 330–500). Be prudent when walking on and along the walls as there have been reports of attempted robberies. Try to go in a group and keep personal items and cameras safe.

⭐Ulu Cami
MOSQUE

Diyarbakır's most impressive mosque is the Ulu Cami, built in 1091 by a Seljuk sultan. Incorporating elements from an earlier Byzantine church on the site, it was restored in 1155 after a fire. The rectangular layout is Arabic, rather than Ottoman. The entrance portal, adorned with two medallions figuring a lion and a bull, leads to a huge courtyard with two-storey arcades, two cone-shaped *şadırvans* (ritual ablutions fountains), elaborate pillars, and friezes featuring fruits and vegetables.

🛏 Sleeping

Hotel Surkent   HOTEL $
(📞 228 1014; www.hotelsurkent.com; İzzet Paşa Caddesi; s/d ₺35/70; ✳️ 🛜) In a quiet centrally-located street, the colourful Surkent is a popular choice for overland travellers. Top-floor rooms boast good views – for singles, rooms 501, 502 and 503 are the best. Avoid the downstairs rooms near reception as they can be noisy. Breakfast is an additional ₺5 and there's no lift.

New Tigris Hotel   HOTEL $$
(📞 224 9696; www.newtigrishotel.com; Kıbrıs Caddesi 3; s/d ₺90/130; ✳️ 🛜) In close proximity to good restaurants, the New Tigris has lifted the game for competing hotels along bustling Kıbrıs Caddesi. Wooden floors, neutral decor, and sparkling and spacious bathrooms make the New Tigris one of the best midrange deals in town.

Otel Ertem   HOTEL $$
(📞 223 4047; İzzet Paşa Caddesi; s/d ₺70/120) Compact rooms, modern decor and gleaming bathrooms all combine at one of Diyarbakır's newest hotels. Reception is particularly snazzy and the rooms upstairs are just as trendy.

🍴 Eating

Şafak Kahvaltı & Yemek Salonu   TURKISH $
(Kıbrıs Caddesi; mains ₺8-12; ⏲24hr) Nosh on freshly prepared meat dishes, hearty casseroles and stuffed vegetables in this brisk Diyarbakır institution. It also does superb crisp wood-fired pide and is open around the clock if you arrive on a late bus.

★ Diyarbakır Kahvaltı Evi   CAFE $$
(www.diyarbakirevi.com; Dicle Sokak 20; breakfast ₺15, snacks & mains ₺7-15; 🛜) Kick off another fascinating Diyabakır day with a leisurely breakfast in the leafy courtyard of this heritage mansion. A posse of cats occasionally mooches in from nearby laneways, and there's live music with jazz, rock and Kurdish tunes most Saturday nights from 8pm.

Drop by and see what's scheduled. From the Şeyh Mutahhar Camii, turn left.

Selim Amca'nın Sofra Salonu   TURKISH $$
(Ali Emiri Caddesi; set menu for two people ₺65) This bright eatery outside the city walls is famous for its *kaburga dolması* (lamb stuffed with rice and almonds). Round it off with a devilish *İrmik helvası* (a gooey dessert).

ℹ Information

You'll find ATMs and the post office in Old Diyarbakır.

ℹ Getting There & Away

There are several daily flights between Diyarbakır Airport and İstanbul and Ankara. A taxi costs ₺15 into the centre.

The otogar is 14km out of town. Most bus companies, though, have offices on Kıbrıs Caddesi or Gazi Caddesi. Frequent buses run to Şanlıurfa (₺20, three hours) among others. There are also three daily buses to Dohuk (₺50, six hours) and Erbil (₺60, nine hours) in Iraqi Kurdistan.

Hourly dolmuşes to Mardin (₺15, 1¼ hours) leave from the dolmuş terminal (called İlçe Garajı) 1.5km southwest of the city.

Mardin
📞 0482 / POP 88,000

Minarets emerge from a baked brown labyrinth of meandering lanes, a castle dominates the old city, and stone houses cascade down the hillside above the Mesopotamian plains. As a melting pot of Kurdish, Yezidi, Christian and Syrian cultures, Mardin also has a fascinating heritage. The honey-coloured collage of old buildings has been truly discovered, though, so don't expect to have the place to yourself.

⦿ Sights

★ Sakıp Sabancı
Mardin City Museum   MUSEUM
(Sakıp Sabancı Mardin Kent Müzesi; www.sabanci-muzesimardin.gov.tr; Eski Hükümet Caddesi; admission ₺2; ⏲8am-5pm Tue-Sun) Housed in former army barracks, this superb museum showcases the fascinating history and culture of Mardin. Excellent English-language translations and effective use of audio and video reinforce how cosmopolitan and multicultural the city's past was. Downstairs is used as an art gallery for a rotating series of exhibitions, often including images by iconic Turkish photographers.

Kasımiye Medresesi
MOSQUE

Built in 1469, two domes stand over the tombs of Kasım Paşa and his sister, but the highlights are the courtyard with arched colonnades and a magnificent carved doorway. Upstairs, see the students' quarters, before ascending for great Mardin rooftop panorama. It's signposted 800m south of Yeni Yol.

★ Sultan İsa (Zinciriye) Medresesi
MOSQUE

(Cumhuriyet Caddesi) FREE Dating from 1385, the complex's highlight is the imposing recessed doorway, but make sure you wander through the pretty courtyards, lovingly tended by the caretaker, and onto the roof to enjoy the cityscape. The tea garden is a top spot to sit and survey Mardin's beauty.

🛏 Sleeping & Eating

Şahmeran Otanik Pansiyon
PENSION $

(☑ 213 2300; www.sahmeranpansiyon.com; Cumhuriyet Caddesi, 246 Sokak 10; dm ₺30, r per person ₺70, without bathroom ₺50; ☜) This rustic pension is arrayed around a honey-coloured stone courtyard just a short uphill meander from Mardin's main thoroughfare. Kilims and heritage features decorate the simply furnished rooms and shared dorms. Breakfast is an additional ₺5.

Ipek Yolu Guesthouse
GUESTHOUSE $$

(☑ 212 1477; www.ipekyolukadinkoop.com; Cumhuriyet Caddesi, Sokak 7; s/d ₺80/160; ❄☜) Antique radios add a quirky touch to this restored heritage guesthouse a short stroll from Mardin's main street, and flowers brighten up the (mainly) spacious rooms. Head to the top floor for excellent views of Mardin's honey-coloured architectural jumble, or get your travel diary up to date in the lovely shared courtyard.

★ Seyr-İ-Mardin
ANATOLIAN $$

(Cumhuriyet Caddesi 249; meze & mains ₺6-25; ☺9am-10pm) Translating to 'Mardin's Eye', this multilevel cafe, teahouse and restaurant has superb views. Settle in to one of the colourful couches and feast on excellent grills or the *meze tabagi* (mixed meze). Look forward to good service courtesy of the owner who speaks very good English.

Cercis Murat Konağı
ANATOLIAN $$$

(☑ 213 6841; Cumhuriyet Caddesi; mains ₺25; ☺noon-11pm) The Cercis occupies a traditional Syrian Christian home with two finely decorated rooms and a terrace with stunning views. *Mekbuss* (aubergine pickles

with walnut), *kitel raha* (Syrian-style meatballs) and *dobo* (lamb with garlic, spices and black pepper) rank among the highlights. Dive into the meze platters (₺30 to ₺50) for a taste of everything that's good.

ℹ Getting There & Away

Mardin airport is 20km south of town and receives daily flights from Ankara and İstanbul. Dolmuşes heading to Kızıltepe can drop you there (₺2.50).

There are hourly dolmuşes to Diyarbakır (₺12, 1¼ hours); and regular services to Şanlıurfa (₺30, three hours); and Cizre (for Iraqi Kurdistan, ₺25, 2½ hours) from the İlçe Otogar east of the centre.

Şanlıurfa (Urfa)

📋 0414 / POP 585,000

Şanlıurfa (the Prophets' City; also known as Urfa) is a pilgrimage town and spiritual centre where the prophets Job and Abraham left their marks, and the Dergah complex of mosques and the holy Gölbaşı area imbued with a compelling atmosphere redolent of the Middle East. The city's streets hum with an energetic buzz, the traditional bazaar is bundles of fun to potter about in and the nearby temple of Göbekli Tepe is one of eastern Turkey's unmissable destinations.

◎ Sights

Göbekli Tepe
RUIN

(www.gobeklitepe.info; admission ₺5; ☺daylight hours) Around 11km northeast of Urfa, 'Pot Belly Hill' was first unearthed in 1995, and its circle of Neolithic megaliths is estimated to date from 9500 BC, around 6500 years before Stonehenge. A wooden walkway circles the site, making it easy to study the centuries-old stone pillars with exquisitely stylised carvings of lions, foxes and vultures. Previously the site was thought to be a medieval cemetery, but is now thought to be the world's first place of worship

Edessa Mosaic Museum
MUSEUM

(Haleplibaçhe Caddesi; admission incl Şanlıurfa Archeology Museum ₺8; ☺8am-5pm Tue-Sat) This modern domed structure protects the excellent Haleplibaçhe (Aleppo Gardens) mosaics, part of a Roman villa complex only discovered in 2006 when construction started on a planned theme park. Highlights include wonderfully detailed mosaics showing Amazon warrior queens and the life of

WORTH A TRIP

HARRAN

About 50km to the southeast of Urfa, Harran is one of the oldest continuously occupied settlements in the world. Its ruined walls, **Ulu Cami**, crumbling **fortress** and beehive houses are powerful, evocative sights. Minibuses for Harran (₺5, one hour) leave hourly from the regional terminal below the Urfa otogar.

Achilles. The theme park has been usurped by Şanlıurfa's sprawling Archeopark, also taking in the city's massive new archaeology museum.

Dergah
PARK

Southeast of Gölbaşı is the Dergah complex of mosques and parks surrounding the colonnaded courtyard of the **Hazreti İbrahim Halilullah** (Prophet Abraham's Birth Cave; admission ₺1), built and rebuilt over the centuries as a place of pilgrimage. To visit these important places of worship you should be modestly dressed. Its western side is marked by the **Mevlid-i Halil Camii**, a large Ottoman-style mosque. At its southern side is the entrance to the cave where Abraham was reputedly born.

★ Gölbaşı
HISTORIC SITE

Legend claims that Abraham (İbrahim), the Islamic prophet, was in old Urfa destroying pagan gods when Nimrod, the local Assyrian king, took offence. Nimrod had Abraham immolated on a funeral pyre, but God turned the fire into water and the burning coals into fish. Abraham was hurled into the air from where the fortress stands, landing safely in a bed of roses. Urfa's picturesque Gölbaşı area of fish-filled pools and rose gardens is a symbolic re-creation of this story.

🛏 Sleeping

Hotel Uğur
HOTEL $

(☑ 313 1340, 0532-685 2942; musma63@yahoo. com; Köprübaşı Caddesi 3; per person without bathroom ₺30; ❋ ⬦) Rooms are sparsely decorated and relatively compact, but clean and spotless. There's a great travellers' vibe, enhanced by a few cold beers on the hotel's terrace as you watch Urfa's cinematic buzz unfold before you. Rates exclude breakfast, but there's a good *kahvaltı salonu* (breakfast restaurant) downstairs.

Otel Urhay
HISTORIC HOTEL $$

(☑ 216 2222, 0544-215 7201; www.otelurhay. com; Sarayönü Caddesi, Beyaz Sokak; s/d/tr ₺70/100/120; ❋ ⬦) A cool kilim-decorated lounge/restaurant combines with simple whitewashed rooms that feature both aircon – essential during an Urfa summer – and private bathrooms. The quiet inner courtyard is perfect for drinking tea. Note that weddings and parties are sometimes hosted on weekends.

Manici Hotel
HISTORIC HOTEL $$$

(☑ 215 9911; www.manici.com.tr; Balıklı Göl Mevkii; r ₺160-200; ❋ ⬦) The opulent Manici has restored and romantic rooms. The luxe furnishings stop just short of being OTT, and there's more of a contemporary vibe than at other heritage accommodation around town. The attached restaurant serves beer and wine.

✖ Eating

Beyaz Köşk
KEBAP $

(Akarbaşı Göl Cadessi 20; mains ₺7-10; ⊙ 10am-10pm) Turkey's best *lahmacun* (Arabic-style pizza) restaurants reputedly huddle in Gölbaşı's labyrinth of lanes, and the 'White House' is a great place to try plate-covering pizza sprinkled with spicy *ızot*. Head upstairs to the breezy terrace and observe Urfa's gentle mayhem down below.

Çift Mağara
TURKISH $$

(Çift Kubbe Altı Balıklıgöl; mains ₺10-20; ⊙ 10am-11pm) The dining room is carved into a rocky bluff overlooking Gölbaşı, but the lovely terrace for dining alfresco beats the cavernous interior. Try the *içli köfte* (ground lamb and onion with a bulgur coating).

Gülhan Restaurant
TURKISH $$

(Atatürk Caddesi; mains ₺10-15; ⊙ 11am-10pm) Razor-sharp waiters and salubrious surroundings combine with a pictorial menu of grills and local dishes with English translations. For dessert, try the *şıllık*.

ⓘ Information

Banks, ATMs and the post office can all be found along Divan Yolu Caddesi.

ⓘ Getting There & Away

Şanlıurfa GAP Airport, 45km from town, has daily connections to/from Ankara and İstanbul. **Havaş Airport Buses** (www.havas.net) run between the airport and the centre (₺10) with departures coordinated with flight arrivals.

The otogar is 5km north of the centre. Regular buses connect Şanlıurfa with Gaziantep (₺20, 2½ hours); and Diyarbakır (₺16, three hours). There are several dolmuşes daily to Kahta (for Karadut and Nemrut Dağı, ₺15) from the regional terminal below the main otogar.

Nemrut Dağı (Mt Nemrut)

Two thousand years ago, on the summit of Nemrut Dağı (2150m) an obscure megalomanic Commagene king erected a fabulous funerary mound in his own honour. Toppled by earthquakes, the fallen heads of the once-gigantic statues of gods and kings, that now lie scattered on the mountaintop, form one of Turkey's most enduring images.

The mountain is part of **Nemrut Dağı Milli Parkı** (admission ₺8; ⊘ dawn-dusk) and most people arrive on a sunset or sunrise tour either booked in Malatya or Kahta (tours from ₺120) or in Karadut, the closest base only 12km from the summit (tours from ₺60). Cappadocia travel agencies also offer rather exhausting two-day tours to Nemrut. Be aware that Kahta is notorious for hassles and rip-offs. The best time to visit is between late May and October. The summit road often becomes impassable with snow the rest of the year.

🛏 Sleeping

🛏 Malatya

Malatya Büyük Otel   HOTEL **$$**
(☎ 0422-325 2828; www.malatyabuyukotel.com; Halep Caddesi, Yeni Cami Karşısı; s/d ₺80/120; ❄) Behind the Yeni Cami, this older hotel has recently renovated rooms with modern wooden decor, sparkling bathrooms and lots of English-language local knowledge at reception. The location near the bazaar is very handy.

🛏 Kahta

Kommagene Hotel   HOTEL **$**
(☎ 0416-725 5548, 0532-200 3856; www.kommagenehotel.com; Mustafa Kemal Caddesi 1; s/d ₺50/90; ❄ @ 🗐) This place has cosy wood-lined rooms, private bathrooms, a guest kitchen and laundry, and free pick-ups are available from the Kahta otogar or Adıyaman airport. During summer, the hotel will shuttle guests out to a nearby lake for swimming. Packages incorporating accommodation and a tour to Nemrut Dağı are

₺155 per person. Daily departures are guaranteed from April to November.

🛏 Karadut

Karadut Pension   PENSION **$**
(☎ 0416-737 2169, 0533-616 4564; www.karadutpansiyon.net; Karadut; per person ₺40, campsite ₺10; ❄ @) This pension in Karadut has 14 neat, compact rooms (some with air-con), cleanish bathrooms and a shared kitchen. Meals are available along with wine, beer or rakı in the alfresco terrace bar. Campers can pitch their tent in a partially shaded plot at the back. Staff will pick you up from Kahta for ₺30.

Nemrut Kervansaray Hotel   HOTEL **$$**
(☎ 0416-737 2190; www.nemrutkervansaray.com; Karadut; s/d from €35/45; ❄ 🗐 🏊) One of Karadut's established hotels now has new rooms with mountain views and private balconies. Good English is spoken, there is a decent on-site restaurant with wine and cold beer, and the whole operation is friendly and very well run. The swimming pool is a welcome addition on summer days, and minibus transport to the summit is ₺100.

Gaziantep (Antep)

📞 0342 / POP 1.5 MILLION

Gaziantep is home to the superb Gaziantep Zeugma Mosaic Museum – worth travelling across Turkey for. The old-city district is being lovingly restored and the lively bazaar area of **Bakırcılar Çarşısı** is perfect for an afternoon's fosicking. Better yet, Gaziantep calls dibs on producing the best baklava in the world and boasts a staggering 180 pastry shops.

⦿ Sights

★ **Gaziantep Zeugma Mosaic Museum**   MUSEUM
(www.gaziantepmuzesi.gov.tr; Sehitkamil Caddesi; admission ₺10; ⊘ 8.30am-5.30pm Tue-Sun) This modern museum showcases superb mosaics unearthed at the Roman site of Belkıs-Zeugma before the Birecik Dam flooded most of the site forever. The 2nd floor has excellent views of virtually complete floor mosaics retrieved from Roman villas, providing a detailed insight into past centuries. Other incredibly well-preserved highlights include the poignant Gypsy Girl and the Birth of Venus mosaics, and modern

Gaziantep (Antep)

interactive technology also brings history to life in a compelling way.

★ Kale
FORTRESS

(Citadel; ⊙ 8.30am-5.30pm) FREE Thought to have been constructed by the Romans, the citadel was restored by Emperor Justinian in the 6th century AD, and rebuilt extensively by the Seljuks in the 12th and 13th centuries. The interior of the castle contains the **Gaziantep Defence and Heroism Panoramic Museum** (admission ₺1; ⊙ 8.30am-5.30pm), a tribute to the fighters who bravely defended the city against the French in 1920.

Emine Göğüş Culinary Museum
MUSEUM

(Köprübaşı Sokak; admission ₺1; ⊙ 8am-5pm) This interesting museum provides both information and inspiration for exploring Gaziantep's terrific eateries. English-language translations are key ingredients in the museum's successful recipe of explaining what dishes to try in local restaurants.

🛏 Sleeping

Güzel Otel
HOTEL $

(☑ 221 3216; Gaziler Caddesi 7; s/d ₺35/60; 🅰 🛜) A convenient location near the market and clean rooms make this one of Gaziantep's best-value budget hotels.

Hıdıroğlu Konak
BOUTIQUE HOTEL $$

(☑ 230 4555; www.hidiroglukonak.com; Hıdır Sokak 19; r ₺130-200; 🅰 🛜) Six rooms fill a restored century-old mansion in Gaziantep's former Armenian neighbourhood. Vaulted wooden ceilings and antique furniture instill a heritage ambience, and the stone construction and spacious courtyard create a cooling haven during a Gaziantep summer.

★ Asude Konak
BOUTIQUE HOTEL $$$

(☑ 0532-577 8792, 230 4104; www.asudekonak.com; Arkası Millet Sokak 20; s €35-45, d €70-85; 🅰 @ 🛜) You'll feel like you're staying with friends or family at this lovingly restored

Gaziantep (Antep)

courtyard house. Meals are prepared by host Jale Özaslan, and can include gossamer-light *katmer* (flatbread layered with nuts and clotted cream) for breakfast, and the local speciality of *yuvarlama* (soup made with rice, meat, chickpeas and yoghurt) for dinner. Evening meals are often lingering alfresco affairs.

Eating

★**Orkide**   BAKERY $
(www.orkidepastanesi.com; Gazimuhtarpaşa Bulvarı 17; cakes ₺4-6) Renowned as the city's finest *pastane* (patisserie), Orkide also serves the best brunch (₺30) in town. Look forward to *katmer*, local cheeses, jams, honey and salads, all partnered with warm and fluffy flatbread. Turn north along Gazimuhtarpaşa Bulvarı 400m west of the tourist information office.

İmam Çağdaş   TURKISH $$
(Kale Civarı Uzun Çarşı; mains ₺10-20; ◷10am-10pm) The Çağdaş family's pistachio baklava is delivered daily to customers throughout Turkey. The secret of their success is fresh, carefully chosen ingredients; also good are the creamy, chargrilled aubergine flavours of the *ali nazik* kebap. The restaurant is popular with Turkish tourists.

★**Şirvan**   KEPAB $$$
(Ali Fuat Cebesoy Bulvarı; mains ₺16-22; ◷11am-10pm) Lauded as home of the city's finest kebaps, Şirvan is definitely worth the short taxi ride from central Gaziantep for seasonal specialties such as kebaps with *keme mantari* (local truffles), or *Malta eriği* (loquats). Zingy salads, house-made *ayran* (salted

yoghurt drink), and superlative baklava are other reasons to seek out Şirvan.

❶ Information

The main square (at the intersection Atatürk Bulvarı and Hürriyet Caddesi) has a clutch of banks with ATMs and the post office.

The **tourist office** (☑230 5969; www.gaziantepcity.info; 100 Yıl Atatürk Kültür Parkı İçi; ◷8am-noon & 1-5pm Mon-Fri) is in the city park.

❶ Getting There & Away

Gaziantep's Oğuzeli Airport is 20km from the centre. The **Havaş Airport Bus** (www.havas.net) meets all flights and head into town (₺10).

The otogar is 6.5km from the centre. City buses (₺2.50) zip between the otogar and Hürriyet Caddesi. From the otogar frequent buses leave to Ankara (₺50, 10 hours); Antakya (₺25, four hours); Mardin (₺40, six hours); and Şanlıurfa (₺20, 2½ hours).

UNDERSTAND TURKEY

Turkey Today

A loyal Western ally in a troubled neighbourhood, Turkey remains pivotal on the world stage.

The Adalet ve Kalkınma Partisi (AKP; Justice and Development Party) headed by Recep Tayyip Erdoğan has been in power since 2002 and has overseen an extended period of economic growth. The standard of living and infrastructure across the country have improved markedly, but critics allege the government is increasingly authoritarian. Criticism of the AKP came to a head during the Gezi Park protests of 2013 which spread across the country, with up to eight civilians, and two policemen, killed.

In December 2013 allegations of extensive corruption were levelled at senior members of the AKP. Many predicted that the AKP would suffer a loss in popularity, but in the municipal elections of early 2014 the AKP emerged as victors. This clearly demonstrated that despite having many vocal detractors its message still resonates with many Turks. Erdoğan then campaigned for the first direct presidential elections in Turkey's history. He won, ensuring a five-year stay in the presidential palace.

TURKEY TURKEY TURKEY TODAY

One area where the AKP has made clear gains in recent years is in attempts to solve the Kurdish question. The government recently pushed forward with discussions with Abdullah Öçalan, the imprisoned leader of the Partiya Karkerên Kurdistan (PKK; Kurdistan Workers' Party), resulting in a ceasefire in early 2013 and the evacuation of PKK military units from Turkish soil.

Overall these days, Turkey holds much less tenaciously to the nationalist idea that ethnic diversity is a threat to the nation-state. There is much more acknowledgement of the contributions of Armenians, Greeks, Syriacs and others, and as a consequence Turkey's diverse ethnic communities are more visible and confident in day-to-day life.

Turkey's goal to become a regional leader though remains unfulfilled at best. The conflict in Syria and the rise of Isis has set off alarm bells in Turkey and left Turkey hosting up to one million Syrian refugees within its borders.

History

Few countries can claim to have played such a significant role in the history of human civilisation as Turkey, and the country's location on the major trade routes between Europe and Asia identified it as a strategic target for empire builders across the ages.

Early Anatolian Civilisations

The Hittites, the greatest early civilisation in Anatolia, were a force to be reckoned with from 2000 to 1200 BC, ruling their empire from their capital, Hattuşa (east of present-day Ankara).

After the collapse of the Hittite empire, Anatolia splintered into small states and it wasn't until the Graeco-Roman period that parts of the country were reunited. Christianity later spread through the region, preached by the apostle Paul, who crossed Anatolia on the new Roman roads.

Rome, then Byzantium

In AD 330 the Roman emperor, Constantine, founded a new imperial city at Byzantium (İstanbul). Renamed Constantinople, it became the capital of the Eastern Roman Empire and was the centre of the Byzantine Empire for 1000 years. During the European Dark Ages, the Byzantine Empire kept alive the flame of Roman culture, although it was intermittently threatened from the east (Persians, Arabs, Turks) and west (European powers such as the Goths and Lombards).

Coming of the Turks: Seljuks & Ottomans

The Byzantine Empire began to decline from 1071, when the Seljuk Turks defeated its forces at Manzikert, north of Lake Van. The Seljuks overran most of Anatolia, establishing a provincial capital at Konya.

The Byzantines endeavoured to protect Constantinople and reclaim Anatolia, but during the Fourth Crusade (1202–04), which was supposedly instigated to save Eastern Christendom from the Muslims, an unruly Crusader force sacked Constantinople.

The Seljuks, meanwhile, were defeated by the Mongols at Köse Dağ in 1243. The region fractured into a mosaic of Turkish *beyliks* (principalities) and Mongol fiefdoms, but by 1300, a single Turkish bey, Osman, established the Ottoman dynasty.

Having captured Constantinople in 1453, the Ottoman Empire reached its zenith a century later under Süleyman the Magnificent. It expanded deep into Europe, Asia and North Africa, but when its march westward stalled at Vienna in 1683, the rot set in. By the 19th century, European powers had begun to covet the Ottomans' domains.

Nationalism swept Europe after the French Revolution, and Greece, Romania, Montenegro, Serbia and Bosnia all won independence from the Ottomans. The First Balkan War removed Bulgaria and Macedonia from the Ottoman map, while Bulgarian, Greek and Serbian troops advanced on İstanbul. The empire was now known as the 'sick man of Europe'.

Republic

WWI stripped the Turks of Syria, Palestine, Mesopotamia (Iraq) and Arabia, and the victorious Europeans intended to share most of Anatolia among themselves, leaving the Turks virtually nothing.

Enter Mustafa Kemal Atatürk, the father of modern Turkey. Atatürk made his name by repelling the British and Anzac forces in their attempt to capture Gallipoli. Rallying the tattered Turkish army, he outmanoeuvred the Allied forces in the War of Independence and, in 1923, pushed the invading Greeks into the sea at Smyrna (İzmir).

After renegotiation of the WWI treaties, a new Turkish Republic, reduced to Anatolia and part of Thrace, was born. Atatürk embarked on a modernisation program, introducing a secular democracy, the Roman script, European dress and equal rights for women. The capital shifted from İstanbul to Ankara. Many of the sweeping changes did not come easily and their reverberations can still be felt today. In population exchanges with Greece, around 1.5 million Greeks left Turkey and nearly half a million Turks moved in.

Since Atatürk's death in 1938, Turkey has experienced three military coups and, during the 1980s and '90s, the government and the PKK waged a viscious conflict in the southeast over the PKK's aims to create a Kurdish state.

After a wobbly decade of weak coalition governments in the 1990s, Recep Tayyip Erdoğan's AKP won government in 2002, heralding an era of societal reforms and economic recovery.

People

Turkey has a population of just over 80 million, the great majority of whom are Muslim and Turkish. Kurds form the largest minority (numbering approximately 15 million), but there is an assortment of other groups – both Muslim and non-Muslim. Since the 1950s there has been a steady movement of people into urban areas, so today 70% of the population lives in cities. Whether urban or rural, Muslim or Christian, Turkish, Kurdish or otherwise, the peoples of Turkey tend to be family-focused, easygoing, hospitable, gregarious and welcoming.

Language

Turkish is the official language, but in southeastern Anatolia, you may hear Kurmancı and Zazakı, the two Kurdish dialects, spoken as well. Around Antakya, Gaziantep and Şanlıurfa Arabic is used as well as Turkish.

Religion

Roughly 80% of the population are Sunni Muslim; however, many Turks take a relaxed approach to religious duties and practices. Islam's holy days and festivals are observed but for many Turks Islamic holidays are the only times they'll visit a mosque. An additional 19.8% of the population are Alevi Muslims, living mainly in the east of the country.

Of the remaining 0.2%, the two most significant Christian minorities are the Armenians (formerly from Anatolia) and the Greeks (formerly spread throughout the country) though both groups now live mainly in İstanbul.

A small Jewish community of around 25,000 also lives mostly in İstanbul, while a declining community of Nestorian and Assyrian Orthodox Christians are based in the southeast of the country.

Food

Kebaps and *köfte* (meatballs) in all their variations may be the mainstay of restaurant meals but Turkish food is more complex than just grilled meat (as succulent as that grilled meat may be). The national

ESSENTIAL TURKISH FOOD & DRINK

Ayran Refreshing salty yoghurt drink that Turks swear is the perfect companion for a tasty kebap.

Baklava Syrupy pistachio pastries sent to tempt the weak.

Gözleme Thin savoury pancakes typically stuffed with cheese, spinach or potato.

Mantı Teensy pasta parcels of cheese or meat smothered with tomato sauce and yoghurt.

Rakı Aniseed-flavoured clear spirit that turns white when mixed and is not for the faint of heart.

İmam bayıldı Slow-cooked aubergines stuffed with tomato, onion and garlic.

İskender kebap Döner meat served on yoghurt-doused pide bread and drowned in a rich tomato and butter sauce. Not for calorie counters.

cuisine is made memorable by the use of seasonal ingredients, ensuring freshness and flavour.

The king of cheap eats is a döner kebap (spit-roasted lamb slices) sandwich – called a *dürüm* – but pide (Turkish pizza) with both vegetarian and meat toppings, and *lahmacun* (Arabic-style pizza) which has a paper-thin base spread with a meat-and-tomato topping, come a close second. The humble *simit* (sesame-encrusted bread ring) is everyone's food-on-the-run favourite.

Meze is where Turkish cuisine really comes into its own, and for vegetarians is an excellent way to ensure a varied diet. *Acılı ezme* (spicy tomato-and-onion paste), *fasulye pilaki* (white beans cooked with tomato paste and garlic) and *yaprak sarma* (vine leaves stuffed with rice, herbs and pine nuts) are just a few of the myriad meze dishes on offer.

Main dishes are usually meat-based. The most famous of these is the kebap – *şiş* (shish kebab; skewered meat) and döner – but *saç kavurma* (stir-fried cubed meat dishes) and *güveç* (meat and vegetable stews cooked in a terracotta pot) are just as common.

Those with a sweet tooth are in luck as Turkey outdoes itself on syrupy treats. Baklava and *lokum* (Turkish delight) are well worth chucking away your calorie-counter for.

SURVIVAL GUIDE

ℹ Directory A–Z

ACCOMMODATION

Turkey has accommodation options to suit all budgets. Rooms are often discounted by about 20% during winter. Hotels in more popular tourist destinations often quote their rates in euros.

Outside tourist areas, solo travellers of both sexes should be cautious about the cheapest hotel options. Suss out the staff and atmosphere in reception; theft and even sexual assaults have occurred in budget establishments (albeit very rarely).

CUSTOMS REGULATIONS

➡ Buying and exporting genuine antiquities is illegal.

➡ Carpet shops should be able to provide a form certifying that your purchase is not an antiquity.

EMBASSIES & CONSULATES

➡ Most embassies are in Ankara.

➡ Many countries also have consulates in İstanbul.

➡ Most embassies and consulates in Turkey open from 8am or 9am to noon Monday to Friday, then after lunch until 5pm or 6pm for people to pick up visas.

➡ There are consulates in other Turkish cities (check the websites following in the embassies list for their locations).

Embassies in Ankara

Australian Embassy (☑ 0312-459 9500; www. turkey.embassy.gov.au; 7th fl, MNG Building, Uğur Mumcu Caddesi 88, Gaziosmanpaşa)

Azerbaijani Embassy (☑ 0312-491 1681; www. azembassy.org.tr; Diplomatik Site, Bakü Sokak 1, Oran)

Bulgarian Embassy (☑ 0312-467 2071; www. mfa.bg/embassies/turkey; Atatürk Bulvarı 124, Kavaklıdere)

Canadian Embassy (☑ 0312-409 2700; www. canadainternational.gc.ca; Cinnah Caddesi 58, Çankaya)

Dutch Embassy (☑ 0312-409 1800; turkije. nlambassade.org; Hollanda Caddesi 5, Hilal Mahallesi)

French Embassy (☑ 0312-455 4545; www.ambafrance-tr.org; Paris Caddesi 70, Kavaklıdere)

Georgian Embassy (☑ 0312-491 8030; www. turkey.mfa.gov.ge; Diplomatik Site, Kılıç Ali Sokak 12, Oran)

German Embassy (☑ 0312-455 5100; www.ankara.diplo.de; Atatürk Bulvarı 114, Kavaklıdere)

Greek Embassy (☑ 0312-448 0647; www.mfa. gr/ankara; Zia Ür Rahman Caddesi 9-11, Gaziosmanpaşa)

ℹ SLEEPING PRICE RANGES

The following price ranges are based on the cost of a double room in high season (June to August; apart from İstanbul, where high season is April, May, September, October, Christmas and Easter) and include breakfast, en suite bathroom and taxes unless otherwise stated.

İstanbul & Bodrum

$ less than €90

$$ €90 to €200

$$$ more than €200

Rest of Turkey

$ less than ₺90

$$ ₺90 to ₺180

$$$ more than ₺180

Iranian Embassy (☑ 0312-468 2821; http://
en.mfa.ir; Tehran Caddesi 10, Kavaklıdere)

Iraqi Embassy (☑ 0312-468 7421; www.
mofamission.gov.iq; Turan Emeksiz Sokak 11,
Gaziosmanpaşa)

Irish Embassy (☑ 0312-459 1000; www.
embassyofireland.org.tr; 3rd fl, MNG Building,
Uğur Mumcu Caddesi 88, Gaziosmanpaşa)

New Zealand Embassy (☑ 0312-446 3333;
www.nzembassy.com/turkey; Kizkulesi Sokak
11, Gaziosmanpaşa)

Russian Embassy (☑ 0312-439 2122; www.
turkey.mid.ru; Karyağdı Sokak 5, Çankaya)

UK Embassy (☑ 0312-455 3344; ukinturkey.
fco.gov.uk; Şehit Ersan Caddesi 46a, Çankaya)

USA Embassy (☑ 0312-455 5555; tur-
key.usembassy.gov; Atatürk Bulvarı 110,
Kavaklıdere)

GAY & LESBIAN TRAVELLERS

➡ Homosexuality is not a criminal offence in
Turkey, but prejudice remains strong and there
are sporadic reports of violence towards gay
people – the message is discretion.

➡ İstanbul has a flourishing gay scene, as does
Ankara.

➡ For more on the challenges facing LGBT
people in Turkey, visit the websites iglhrc.org/
region/turkey and www.ilga-europe.org.

MONEY

The Turkish lira (₺) comes in notes of five, 10, 20,
50, 100 and 200, and coins of one, five, 10, 25
and 50 kuruş, and one lira.

ATMs

ATMs dispense Turkish lira, and occasionally euros and US dollars, to Visa, MasterCard, Cirrus
and Maestro cardholders. Look for these logos
on machines, which are found in most towns.

Credit Cards

Visa and MasterCard are widely accepted by
hotels, shops and restaurants, although often
not by pensions and local restaurants outside
the main tourist areas. You can also get cash
advances on these cards. Amex is less commonly accepted.

Money Changers

US dollars and euros are the easiest currencies
to change. You'll get better rates at exchange
offices than at banks.

Shops, hotels and restaurants in many tourist
areas often accept foreign currencies.

Tipping

Turkey is fairly European in its approach to
tipping and you won't be pestered by demands
for baksheesh, as elsewhere in the Middle East.
Leave waiters and hamam attendants around

> ### ⓘ EATING PRICE RANGES
>
> Prices in listings are based on the cost of
> a main course.
>
> **İstanbul & Bodrum**
>
> $ less than ₺20
>
> $$ ₺20 to ₺30
>
> $$$ more than ₺30
>
> **Rest of Turkey**
>
> $ less than ₺9
>
> $$ ₺9 to ₺17.50
>
> $$$ more than ₺17.50

10% of the bill. It's normal to round up taxi fares
to the nearest 50 kuruş.

OPENING HOURS

The working day shortens during the holy month
of Ramazan (Ramadan). More Islamic cities such
as Konya and Kayseri virtually shut down during
noon prayers on Friday; apart from that, Friday
is a normal working day in Turkey. Opening hours
of tourist attractions and tourist-information
offices may shorten in the low season.

Listings include opening hours only when they
differ significantly from these standard hours.

Bars 4pm to late

Clubs 11pm to late

Government departments, offices and banks
8.30am to noon and 1.30pm to 5pm Monday
to Friday

Information 8.30am to noon and 1.30pm to
5pm Monday to Friday

Restaurants Breakfast 7.30am to 10am, lunch
noon to 2.30pm, dinner 6.30pm to 10pm

Shops 9am to 6pm Monday to Friday (longer in
tourist areas and big cities – including weekend
opening)

POST

Turkish *postanes* (post offices) are indicated
by black-on-yellow 'PTT' signs. Postcards sent
abroad cost about ₺2.50.

PUBLIC HOLIDAYS

Turkey observes the following national holidays
in addition to the traditional Islamic holidays:

New Year's Day 1 January

Children's Day 23 April

International Workers' Day 1 May

Youth & Sports Day 19 May

Victory Day 30 August

Republic Day 28 to 29 October

ⓘ PRACTICALITIES

Electricity Current is 220V AC, 50Hz. Wall sockets are the round, two-pin European type.

Newspapers For the news in English, pick up *Today's Zaman* (www.to-dayszaman.com).

Smoking Illegal in hotels, restaurants and public buildings though outside of İstanbul and major tourist areas this isn't strictly enforced.

Weights and measures Turkey uses the metric system.

SAFE TRAVEL

Although Turkey is one of the safest countries in the region, you should take all the usual precautions and watch out for the following:

➡ The 30-year conflict between the Turkish state and the PKK ended in 2013. Peace talks subsequently stalled, and the conflict in neighbouring Syria and Iraq has complicated the situation, but both sides are committed to finding a solution. If fighting resumes, PKK attacks generally happen far from travellers' routes in remote parts of mountainous southeastern Anatolia, but check the latest situation if visiting the area.

➡ Following on from this, the border area facing Syria is currently a no-travel zone on most official travel-advisory websites. Check your government's latest travel advisories for up-to-date information.

➡ Protests are not unheard of in major cities. Keep well away from demonstrations as tear gas and water cannons are often used.

➡ In İstanbul, single men are sometimes approached and lured to a bar by new 'friends'. The victim is then made to pay an outrageous bill, regardless of what he drank. Drugging is sometimes a problem, especially for lone men. It pays to be a tad wary of who you befriend, especially when you're new to the country.

TELEPHONE

Payphones can be found in many major public buildings, public squares and transportation terminals. They require cards that can be bought at telephone centres or, for a small mark-up, at some shops.

Country code ☑ 90

International access code ☑ 00

Mobile Phones

➡ Mobile phone numbers start with a four-digit code beginning with ☑ 05.

➡ If you set up a roaming facility with your home phone provider, you should be able to connect your mobile to a network.

➡ Major networks are **Turkcell** (www.turkcell.com.tr), the most comprehensive, **Vodafone** (www.vodafone.com.tr) and **Avea** (www.avea.com.tr).

➡ If you buy a local SIM card and use it in your home mobile, the network detects and bars foreign phones within a month.

➡ To avoid barring, register your phone when you buy your Turkish SIM. At a certified mobile-phone shop, show your passport and fill in a short form declaring your phone is in Turkey. The process costs about ₺100.

➡ *Kontör* (credit) is widely available – at streetside kiosks and shops as well as mobile-phone outlets.

VISAS

➡ Nationals of countries including Denmark, Finland, France, Germany, Israel, Italy, Japan, New Zealand, Sweden and Switzerland don't need a visa to visit Turkey for up to 90 days.

➡ Nationals of countries including Australia, Austria, Belgium, Canada, Ireland, the Netherlands, Norway, Portugal, Spain, the UK and USA need a visa, which must be purchased online at www.evisa.gov.tr before travelling.

➡ Most nationalities, including the above, are given a 90-day multiple-entry visa.

➡ At the time of writing, the e-visa charge was US$20 for most nationalities, with a few exceptions including Australians and Canadians, who paid US$60, and South Africans, who received it free.

➡ In most cases, the 90-day visa stipulates 'per period 180 days'. This means you can spend three months in Turkey within a six-month period; when you leave after three months, you can't re-enter for three months.

➡ Your passport should be valid for at least six months from the date you enter Turkey.

WOMEN TRAVELLERS

Travelling in Turkey is straightforward for women, provided you follow some simple guidelines.

➡ Tailor your behaviour and dress to your surroundings. Outside of İstanbul and heavily touristed destinations you should dress modestly.

➡ Cover your hair when visiting mosques or religious buildings.

➡ In more conservative areas (particularly out east) your contact with men should be polite and formal, not chatty and friendly or they are likely to get the wrong idea about your intentions.

➡ Outside of tourist areas some restaurants and tea gardens aiming to attract women and families set aside a separate section. Look for the term *aile salonu* (family room).

➡ Very cheap hotels are not recommended for single women travellers. If a place has a bad vibe, find somewhere else.

ℹ Getting There & Away

Turkey occupies the same important position on the travellers trail today that it once occupied on the trade routes. Land borders with Bulgaria and Greece funnel visitors through to Asia via İstanbul, while ferry services link the Mediterranean's coastal cities and resorts with nearby Greek islands. In the east, Hopa is the gateway to Georgia and the rest of the Caucasus, Doğubayazıt is the last major centre before the Gürbulak crossing into Iran and Diyarbakır has regular bus services to Iraqi Kurdistan. Due to the current conflict, attempting to cross into Syria cannot be recommended – and is downright dangerous – and travellers heading to Iraqi Kurdistan should keep themselves up to date with the current security situation. There are frequent, and well-priced, flights to Lebanon and Egypt (and not so well-priced ones to Jordan) from İstanbul.

AIR

The main international airports are in western Turkey. **Turkish Airlines** (☑ 0850-333 0849; www.thy.com), the national carrier, has an extensive international network.

Antalya International Airport (p467)
Bodrum International Airport (p456)
Dalaman International Airport (p458)
İstanbul Atatürk International Airport (p433)
İstanbul Sabiha Gökçen (p433)
İzmir Adnan Menderes Airport (p445)

LAND
Iraq

Between Silopi (Turkey) and Zahko (Iraqi Kurdistan), there's no town or village at the Habur–Ibrahim al-Khalil crossing. A taxi from Silopi to Zakho costs between US$50 and US$70 or there are direct daily buses from Diyarbakır to Dohuk (₺50, six hours) and Erbil (₺60, nine hours) in Iraqi Kurdistan.

Citizens of most countries, including the USA, Australia, New Zealand, as well as EU nations, are automatically issued a free 15-day tourist visa at the Habur–Ibrahim al-Khalil border. Be aware that this visa is issued by the Kurdish Regional Government and is good for travelling within Iraqi Kurdistan only.

The security situation in Iraq (including Iraqi Kurdistan) remains unstable and you should inform yourself properly before considering visiting. At the time of writing, Iraqi Kurdish forces were engaged in fighting Isis insurgents in towns to the southwest of Erbil and most government

travel advisories were warning against travel to some or all of Iraqi Kurdistan.

Syria

Turkey shares eight border posts with Syria. At the time of writing, advisories warned against all travel to Syria – and all travel to border areas – due to Syria's civil war. Check your government's travel advice for updates.

SEA

Turkey has passenger-ship connections with Greece and northern Cyprus.

ℹ Getting Around

AIR

Internal flights are reasonably priced, and, given the distances involved in traversing the country, are well worth the investment if time is an issue.

Turkey's main domestic airlines:

AnadoluJet (☑ 444 2538; www.anadolujet. com)

Pegasus Airlines (☑ 0850-250 0737; www. pegasusairlines.com)

Sun Express (☑ 444 0797; www.sunexpress. com)

Turkish Airlines (☑ 0850-333 0849; www. thy.com)

BUS

Turkey's intercity bus system is as good as any you'll find, with modern, comfortable coaches crossing the country at all hours and for very reasonable prices.

A town's otogar (bus station) is often on the outskirts, but the bigger bus companies often have a free *servis* (shuttle bus) to ferry you into the centre and back again. In addition to intercity buses, the otogar often handles dolmuşes

---

ℹ BORDER CROSSINGS

Turkey shares borders with Armenia, Azerbaijan, Bulgaria, Georgia, Greece, Iran, Iraq and Syria. The land border with Armenia remains closed. Turkey's relationships with most of its neighbours tend to be tense, which can affect when and where you can cross. Check for the most up-to-date information – **Lonely Planet's Thorn Tree forum** (www.lonelyplanet.com/thorntree) and the Turkish embassy in your country are two sources of information.

Border procedures can often be long and frustrating with baggage checks on both sides of the border regardless of the country.

(minibuses) that operate local routes, although some locations have a separate station for such services.

Major bus companies with extensive route networks include **Kamil Koç** (☑ 444 0562; www.kamilkoc.com.tr), **Metro Turizm** (☑ 444 3455; www.metroturizm.com.tr) and **Ulusoy** (☑ 444 1888; www.ulusoy.com.tr).

CAR & MOTORCYCLE

Driving Licence

An international driving permit (IDP) may be handy if your driving licence is from a country likely to seem obscure to a Turkish police officer.

Fuel

Turkey has the world's second-highest petrol prices. Petrol/diesel cost about ₺5 per litre.

Hire

You must be at least 21 years old to hire a car in Turkey. Most car-hire companies require a credit card. Most hire cars have standard (manual) transmission; you'll pay more for automatic. The majority of the big-name companies charge hefty one-way fees. Stick to hiring from the big international companies as the local agencies often do not have insurance.

Insurance

You must have third-party insurance if you are bringing your own car into the country. Buying it at the border is a straightforward process (one month €80).

Road Rules & Safety

In theory, Turks drive on the right and yield to traffic approaching from the right. In practice,

they often drive in the middle and yield to no one. Maximum speed limits, unless otherwise posted, are 50km/h in towns, 90km/h on highways and 120km/h on *otoyols* (motorways).

Road accidents claim about 10,000 lives each year. To survive on Turkey's roads:

➡ Drive cautiously and defensively.

➡ Do not expect your fellow motorists to obey road signs or use indicators.

➡ Avoid driving at night, when you won't be able to see potholes, animals, or vehicles driving without lights, with lights missing, or stopped in the middle of the road.

TRAIN

The **Turkish State Railways** (TCDD; www.tcdd.gov.tr) network covers the country fairly well, with the notable exception of the coastlines. At the time of writing trains to Ankara from İstanbul were operating from Pendik (25km southeast of the centre near Sabiha Gökçen International Airport, reached via Metro to Kartal and bus or taxi from there). For updates visit www.seat61.com/Turkey2.

High-speed routes:

➡ Ankara–Konya

➡ Eskişehir–Konya

➡ İstanbul Pendik–Eskişehir–Ankara

Long-haul routes are often painfully slow although this slow style can be part of the appeal. The following trains depart from Ankara:

➡ Diyarbakır via Kayseri, Sivas and Malatya

➡ Kars via Kayseri, Sivas and Erzurum

➡ Tatvan (Lake Van) via Kayseri, Sivas and Malatya

Understand
the Middle
East

The Middle East Today

The more things change, the more they stay the same. Syria and most of Iraq remain at war. The Palestinians and Israelis seem further apart than ever. Egypt and Lebanon appear one step away from crisis. And the stakes keep getting higher in the struggle between secular and extremist world views. Behind this larger picture, however, there are many nuances, not to mention hopeful signs that peace and/or stability can triumph amid all the gloom.

Best Books

From the Holy Mountain (William Dalrymple) Well-told journey through the region's landscape of sacred and profane.

The Innocents Abroad (Mark Twain) Still many people's favourite travel book about the region, 140 years later.

The Thousand and One Nights Resonates with all the allure and magic of the Middle East.

Nine Parts of Desire (Geraldine Brooks) Fascinating look at the lives of Middle Eastern women.

The Arab Awakening: Islam and the new Middle East (Tariq Ramadan) A field guide to the hopes and disappointments of the Arab Spring.

Best on Film

Lawrence of Arabia (1962) Evokes the complicated, early-20th-century Middle East.

Caramel (2007) Women in war-ravaged Beirut.

Once Upon a Time in Anatolia (2011) Acclaimed evocation of the Turkish soul and steppe.

A Separation (2011) Oscar-winning Iranian film portraying the angst of modern Iran.

Omar (2014) Oscar-nominated film about the fatal entwining of Palestinians and Israelis.

What Happened to the Arab Spring?

When a young, unemployed man named Mohammed Bouazizi set fire to himself in the central Tunisian town of Sidi Bouzid in December 2010, few imagined the firestorm of change his desperate suicide would ignite across the region. Within months, the 30-year dictatorship of Egyptian president Hosni Mubarak had been overthrown in a popular uprising. Soon, leaders of similarly long standing had been swept from power in Libya and Yemen. Power had, it seemed, been returned to the people, ushering in a brief interlude of hope in a region desperately in need of good news.

But as Iraqis had long ago learned, getting rid of despotic governments was to prove far easier – except in Syria – than building the open, democratic societies which many of those who had demonstrated for freedom craved. With the dictators gone, most countries faced a profound political vacuum. In the heady days that followed the revolution in Egypt, for example, it became clear that those who had led the push for change had neither the unity, experience nor political program needed to build what came next. The well-organised Muslim Brotherhood swept to power, then the army threw the Brotherhood out and seized power for itself. Egyptians still don't have a voice but now have grave uncertainty and disappointment to go with the other struggles of daily life.

Syria & Iraq

It is difficult to quantify the catastrophe that has befallen Syria. Perhaps the simplest statistic is this: as of the end of 2014, an estimated 200,000 people had died in six years of conflict. The troubles began as a peaceful uprising by those aspiring to a democratic Syria. All that remains of that ideal is a vicious war fought between government forces and a fractured rebel movement increasingly dominated by Isis (also referred to as 'Islamic State', 'ISIL' and 'Daesh'), an organisation so radical as to have sidelined even al-Qaeda. In this land once renowned for its tolerance, where Christians lived peacefully alongside Muslims, where Kurds, Arabs and Armenians shared the same plate, all voices of moderation have been silenced.

It is a fate that Syria now shares with much of northern and western Iraq. It was from Iraq that Isis, formerly Al-Qaeda in Iraq, grew, feeding off the country's weak political institutions, insecurity and growing Sunni disillusionment with the new Iraq. From Raqqa in Syria to Mosul in Iraq, Isis is wiping out all forms of opposition, forcing minorities into exile and tearing the region's social fabric to shreds. Even by Middle Eastern standards, it represents one of the darkest periods in the region's history.

The Arab-Israeli Conflict

We'd like to take a more optimistic line, but peace between Arabs and Israelis appears further away than ever. Hardliners hold the ascendancy on both sides, militants have learned that a single attack can scuttle months of cautious optimism and the prospect of meaningful and comprehensive peace talks appears, on the surface at least, to be a forlorn hope. When the short but devastating war in Gaza ended in mid-2014, more than 2200 people had died and little of value had been achieved. All that the war managed to accomplish was a deepening of the gloom that surrounds a conflict already well into its seventh decade.

The Good News

The clamour of war and repression tend to drown out the good news, but it's certainly there if you know where to look.

Jordan, for example, remains at peace, reprising its role as a haven for massive numbers of refugees from neighbouring conflicts while managing to keep everything calm on the home front. While not without its problems, Turkey, too, offers hope, an example of a country moving rapidly forwards, deftly maintaining a balance of sorts between the country's secular and Islamist streams within a solid democratic framework. Lebanon, though pushed closer to conflict by the war in Syria, remains relatively peaceful (compared to recent Lebanese history), while Iran was nudging closer (by inches, it must be said, rather than in great strides) to a detente with the West at the time of writing. And most remarkably of all, Iraqi Kurdistan has become a stable country-within-a-country. It may not sound like much, but it means everything to the people who live there.

LIFE EXPECTANCY (YEARS):
HIGHEST/LOWEST 81.28 (ISRAEL)/68.41 (SYRIA)

ADULT LITERACY RATE (%):
HIGHEST/LOWEST 97.1 (ISRAEL)/73.9 (EGYPT)

GDP PER CAPITA (US$):
HIGHEST/LOWEST 36,200 (ISRAEL)/2900 (WEST BANK & GAZA STRIP)

if Middle East were 100 people

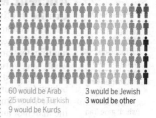

60 would be Arab
25 would be Turkish
9 would be Kurds
3 would be Jewish
3 would be other

belief systems
(% of population)

91 Muslim   6 Christian

3 Jewish

population per sq km

EGYPT   ISRAEL   TURKEY

≈ 65 people

History

The Middle East *is* history, home to a roll call of some of the most important landmarks ever built. Mesopotamia (now Iraq) was the undisputed cradle of civilisation. Damascus (Syria), Aleppo (Syria), Byblos (Lebanon), Jericho (Israel and the Palestinian Territories) and Erbil (Iraq) all stake compelling claims to be the oldest continuously inhabited cities on earth. And it was here in the Middle East that the three great monotheistic religions – Judaism, Christianity and Islam – were born.

Ancient Middle East

Cradle of Civilisation

The Epic of Gilgamesh, written in 2700 BC and one of the first works of world literature, tells the story of a Sumerian king from the ancient city of Uruk (which gave Iraq its name).

The first human beings to walk the earth did just that: they walked. In their endless search for sustenance and shelter, they roamed the earth, hunting, foraging plants for food and erecting makeshift shelters as they went. The world's first nomads, they carried what they needed; most likely they lived in perfect harmony with nature and left next to nothing behind for future generations to write their story.

The first signs of agriculture, arguably the first major signpost along the march of human history, grew from the soils surrounding Jericho in what is now the West Bank, around 8500 BC. Forced by a drying climate and the need to cluster around known water sources, these early Middle Easterners added wild cereals to their diet and learned to farm them. In the centuries that followed, these and other farming communities spread east into Mesopotamia (a name later given by the Greeks, meaning 'Between Two Rivers'), where the fertile soils of the Tigris and Euphrates floodplains were ideally suited to the new endeavour. For some historians, this was a homecoming of sorts for humankind: these two rivers are among the four that, according to the Bible, flowed into the Garden of Eden.

In around the 5th century BC, the Sumerians became the first to build cities and to support them with year-round agriculture and river-borne trade. In the blink of a historical eye, although almost 2000 years later in reality, the Sumerians invented the first known form of writing: cuneiform, which consisted primarily of pictographs and would later evolve

TIMELINE	250,000 BC	5000 BC	4000 BC
	The earliest traces of human presence appear in the Nile Valley. Little is known about them, but they are thought to have been nomadic hunter-gatherers.	Al-Ubaid culture, the forerunner to the great civilisations that would earn Mesopotamia (now Iraq) the sobriquet of the cradle of civilisation, rises between the Tigris and Euphrates Rivers.	The Sumerian civilisation takes hold in Mesopotamia. They would rule the region until the 24th century BC and invent cuneiform, the world's first writing.

PHOENICIANS

The ancient Phoenician Empire (1500–300 BC), which thrived along the Lebanese coast, may have been the world's first rulers of the sea. Their empire was the Mediterranean Sea and its ports, and their lasting legacy was to spread the early gains of Middle Eastern civilisation to the rest of the world.

An offshoot of the Canaanites in the Levant, the Phoenicians first established themselves in the (now Lebanese) ports of Tyre and Sidon. Quick to realise that there was money to be made across the waters, they cast off in their galleys, launching in the process the first era of true globalisation. From the unlikely success of selling purple dye and sea snails to the Greeks, they expanded their repertoire to include copper from Cyprus, silver from Iberia and even tin from Great Britain.

As their reach expanded, so too did the Phoenicians' need for safe ports around the Mediterranean rim. Thus it was that Carthage, one of the greatest cities of the ancient world, was founded in what is now Tunisia in 814 BC. Long politically dependent on the mother culture in Tyre, Carthage eventually emerged as an independent, commercial empire. By 517 BC, the powerful city-state was the leading city of North Africa, and by the 4th century BC, Carthage controlled the North African coast from Libya to the Atlantic.

But the nascent Roman Empire didn't take kindly to these Lebanese upstarts effectively controlling the waters of the Mediterranean Sea, and challenged them both militarily and with economic blockades. With Tyre and Sidon themselves severely weakened and unable to send help, Carthage took on Rome and lost, badly. The Punic Wars (Phoenician civilisation in North Africa was called 'Punic') between Carthage and Rome (264–241 BC, 218–201 BC and 149–146 BC) reduced Carthage, the last outpost of Phoenician power, to a small, vulnerable African state. It was razed by the Romans in 146 BC, the site symbolically sprinkled with salt and damned forever.

into alphabets on which modern writing is based. With agriculture and writing mastered, the world's first civilisation had been born.

Elsewhere across the region, in around 3100 BC, the kingdoms of Upper and Lower Egypt were unified under Menes, ushering in 3000 years of Pharaonic rule in the Nile Valley.

Birth of Empire

The moment in history when civilisations evolved into empires is unclear, but by the 3rd century BC, the kings of what we now know as the Middle East had heard the fragmented news brought by traders of fabulous riches just beyond the horizon.

The Sumerians, who were no doubt rather pleased with themselves for having tamed agriculture and invented writing, never saw the Akkadians coming. One of many city-states that fell within the Sumerian realm,

3100 BC	2400 BC	1800 BC	1750 BC
Menes unites the kingdoms of Upper and Lower Egypt. Thus begins one of the great civilisations of antiquity, the ancient Egypt of the pharaohs, who would rule for almost 3000 years.	Sargon of Akkad, ruler of the city-state of Akkad in Sumerian Mesopotamia, conquers the region, taking much of what we now know as the Levant.	According to the Book of Genesis, Abraham, the great patriarch of the Jewish faith and prophet in both Christianity and Islam, is born in Ur of the Chaldees in Mesopotamia.	The Babylonian kingdoms are first united under Hammurabi, creating the capital, the Hanging Gardens of Babylon. They would rule the Tigris-Euphrates region for over 500 years.

Akkad, on the banks of the Euphrates southwest of modern Baghdad, had grown in power, and, in the late 24th and early 23rd centuries BC, Sargon of Akkad conquered Mesopotamia and then extended his rule over much of the Levant. The era of empire, which would convulse the region almost until the present day, had begun.

Although the Akkadian Empire would last no more than a century, Sargon's idea caught on. The at-once sophisticated and war-like Assyrians, whose empire would, from their capital at Nineveh (Iraq), later encompass the entire Middle East, were the most enduring power. Along with their perennial Mesopotamian rivals, the Babylonians, the Assyrians would dominate the human history of the region for almost 1000 years.

The 7th century BC saw the conquest of Egypt by Assyria and, far to the east, the rise of the Medes, the first of many great Persian empires. In 550 BC, the Medes were conquered by Cyrus the Great, widely regarded as the first Persian shah (king). In the 7th century BC the king of one of the Persian tribes, Achaemenes, created a unified state in southern Iran, giving his name to what would become the First Persian Empire, the Achaemenids. His 21-year-old great-grandson Cyrus II ascended the throne in 559 BC, and within 20 years it would be the greatest empire the world had known up until that time.

Having rapidly built a mighty military force, Cyrus the Great (as he came to be known) ended the Median Empire in 550 BC. Within 11 years, Cyrus had campaigned his way across much of what is now Turkey, east into modern Pakistan, and finally defeated the Babylonians. It was in the aftermath of this victory in 539 BC that Cyrus established a reputation as a benevolent conqueror. Over the next 60 years, Cyrus and his successors, Cambyses (r 525–522 BC) and Darius I (r 521–486 BC), battled with the Greeks for control over Babylon, Egypt, Asia Minor and parts of Greece.

Egypt won independence from the Persians in 401 BC, only to be reconquered 60 years later. The second Persian occupation of Egypt was brief: little more than a decade after they arrived, the Persians were again driven out of Egypt, this time by the Greeks. Europe had arrived on the scene and would hold sway in some form for almost 1000 years until the birth of Islam.

Greeks

The definition of which territories constitute 'the Middle East' has always been a fluid concept. Some cultural geographers claim that the Middle East includes all countries of the Arab world as far west as Morocco. But most historians agree that the Middle East's eastern boundaries were determined by the Greeks in the 4th century BC.

In 336 BC, Philip II of Macedonia, a warlord who had conquered much of mainland Greece, was murdered. His son Alexander assumed the

The Great Pyramid of Khufu (built in 2570 BC) remained the tallest human-built structure in the world until the building of the Eiffel Tower in 1889.

In 333 BC, Persian Emperor Darius, facing defeat by Alexander, abandoned his wife, children and mother on the battlefield. His mother was so disgusted she disowned him and adopted Alexander as her son.

1600–609 BC	1500 BC	15th century BC	814 BC
The Assyrian Empire rules from its capital at Nineveh (present-day Iraq) over a territory that reaches as far as Egypt. Its heyday is around 900 BC.	The Phoenicians set out to conquer the waters of the Mediterranean from their base in Tyre and Sidon (modern-day Lebanon). They rule the seas for 1200 years.	Hieroglyphic tablets make reference to a city called 'Dimashqa', conquered by the Egyptians. It's the first written record of a city and may date back to 3000 BC.	At the height of their power, the Phoenicians from the eastern Mediterranean found Carthage in what is now Tunisia. The city would become one of the greatest cities of the ancient world.

ALEXANDER THE GREAT

One of the greatest figures to ever stride the Middle Eastern stage, Alexander (356–323 BC) was born into greatness. His father was King Philip II of Macedonia, who many people believed was a descendant of the god Hercules, and his mother was Princess Olympias of Epirus, who counted the legendary Achilles among her ancestors. For his part, the precocious young Alexander sometimes claimed that Zeus was his real father.

Alexander was the ultimate alpha male, as well versed in poetry as in the ways of war. At the age of 12, the young Alexander tamed Bucephalus, a horse that the most accomplished horsemen of Macedonia dared not ride. By 13, he had Aristotle as his personal tutor. His interests were diverse: he could play the lyre, learned Homer's *Iliad* by heart and admired the Persian ruler Cyrus the Great for the respect he granted to the cultures he conquered.

He rode out of Macedonia in 334 BC to embark on a decade-long campaign of conquest and exploration. His first great victory was against the Persians at Issus in what is now southeast Turkey. He swept south, conquering Phoenician seaports and thence into Egypt where he founded the Mediterranean city that still bears his name. In 331 BC, the armies of Alexander the Great made a triumphant entrance into Cyrenaica. After the Oracle of Ammon in Siwa promised Alexander that he would indeed conquer the world, he returned north, heading for Babylon. Crossing the Tigris and the Euphrates Rivers, he defeated another Persian army before driving his troops up into Central Asia and northern India. Eventually fatigue and disease brought the drive to a halt and the Greeks turned around and headed back home. En route, Alexander succumbed to illness (some say he was poisoned) and died at the tender age of 33 in Babylon. The whereabouts of his body and tomb remain unknown.

throne and began a series of conquests that would eventually encompass most of Asia Minor, the Middle East, Persia and northern India. Under Alexander, the Greeks were the first to impose any kind of order on the Middle East as a whole.

In 331 BC, just five years after taking control, Alexander the Great's armies swept into what is now Libya. Greek rule extended as far east as what is now the Libyan city of Benghazi, beyond which the Romans would hold sway. Ever since, the unofficial but widely agreed place where the Middle East begins and ends has been held to be Cyrenaica in Libya.

Upon Alexander's death in 323 BC, his empire was promptly carved up among his generals. This resulted in the founding of three new ruling dynasties: the Antigonids in Greece and Asia Minor; the Ptolemaic dynasty in Egypt; and the Seleucids. The Seleucids controlled the swath of land running from modern Israel and Lebanon through Mesopotamia to Persia.

Under Ptolemaic patronage and with access to a library of 700,000 written works, scholars in Alexandria calculated the earth's circumference, discovered it circles the sun and wrote the definitive edition of Homer's work.

663 BC	586 BC	550 BC	536 BC
After a series of military and diplomatic confrontations, Ashurbanipal, King of the Assyrians, attacks Egypt, sacks Thebes and loots the Temple of Amun.	Babylonia's King Nebuchadnezzar marches on Jerusalem, destroys the Jewish temple and carries the Jewish elite and many of their subjects into Mesopotamian exile.	Cyrus the Great forms one of the ancient world's most enlightened empires in Persia, known for its tolerance and the freedoms granted to subject peoples.	Cyrus the Great overruns Babylon, frees the Jewish exiles and helps them to return home to Jerusalem, complete with funds to rebuild the temple.

But, this being the Middle East, peace remained elusive. Having finished off a host of lesser competitors, the heirs to Alexander's empire then proceeded to fight each other. It took an army arriving from the west to again reunite the lands of the east – this time in the shape of the legions of Rome.

Pax Romana

Even for a region accustomed to living under occupation, the news of massed, disciplined ranks of Roman legions marching down across the plains of central Anatolia must have struck fear into the hearts of people across the Middle East. But this was a region in disarray and the Romans chose their historical moment perfectly.

Rome's legionaries conquered most of Asia Minor (most of Turkey) in 188 BC. Syria and Palestine soon fell, if not without a fight then without too much difficulty. When Cleopatra of Egypt, the last of the Ptolemaic dynasty, was defeated in 31 BC, the Romans controlled the entire Mediterranean world. Only the Sassanids in Persia held Rome at bay.

Foreign occupiers they may have been, but the Romans brought much-needed stability and even a degree of prosperity to the region. Roman goods flooded into Middle Eastern markets, improving living standards in a region that had long ago lost its title as the centre of the world's sophistication. New methods of agriculture increased productivity across the region and the largely peaceful Roman territories allowed the export of local products to the great markets of Rome. Olive trees, with their origins in Turkey and the Levant, were, like the oilfields of today, a lucrative product, with insatiable demand in Rome driving previously unimaginable growth for local Middle Eastern economies.

What the Mesopotamians began with their city-states, the Romans perfected in the extravagant cities that they built to glorify the empire but which also provided new levels of comfort for local inhabitants. Their construction or development of earlier Phoenician and Greek settlements at Ephesus, Palmyra, Baalbek and Jerash announced that the Romans intended to stay.

Jewish Revolt

So was the Roman Middle East a utopia? Well, not exactly. As just about any foreign power has failed to learn right up to the 21st century, Middle Easterners don't take kindly to promises of wealth in exchange for sovereignty. The Jews living in Palestine in particular found themselves stripped of political power and operating in an ever-diminishing space of religious and economic freedom. By the middle of the 1st century AD, Jews across the Roman Empire had had enough. Primary among their grievances were punitive taxes, the Roman decision to appoint Jewish

Five out of the Seven Wonders of the Ancient World were within the boundaries of the modern Middle East: the Temple of Artemis (Turkey), the Mausoleum of Halicarnassus (Turkey), the Hanging Gardens of Babylon (Iraq), Pharos of Alexandria (Egypt) and the Pyramids of Giza (Egypt).

525 BC	334 BC	323 BC	3rd century BC
The Persian king Cambyses conquers Egypt, rules as pharaoh, then disappears with his army in the Saharan sands as he marches on Siwa.	A youthful Alexander the Great of Macedonia marches out of Greece and doesn't stop until a vast empire stretching from Libya to India is within his grasp.	Alexander the Great dies aged just 33. His empire is carved up among his generals: the Antigonids (Greece and Asia Minor); the Ptolemaic dynasty (Egypt); and the Seleucids (everywhere else).	The Nabataeans build their rock-hewn fortress of Petra and hold out against the Romans until AD 106, through entrepreneurial guile, military might and carefully negotiated treaties.

ZIONISM: A PRIMER

Contrary to popular belief, Zionism, the largely secular movement to create a Jewish homeland in Palestine, began decades before the Holocaust. In the late 19th century, pogroms against Jews in the Russian Empire and the 1894 Dreyfus Affair (in which a French Jewish officer was wrongly accused of treason) shone uncomfortable light on racism against the Jews in Europe. Two years later, Theodor Herzl, a Hungarian Jew, published *Der Judenstaat (The Jewish State)*, which called for the setting up of a Jewish state in Palestine. In 1897, Herzl founded the World Zionist Organization (WZO) at the First Zionist Congress in Basel. At the conclusion of the Congress, Herzl is said to have written in his diary: 'At Basel I founded the Jewish State. If I said this out loud today I would be greeted by universal laughter. In five years perhaps, and certainly in 50 years, everyone will perceive it.' Another leading Zionist, Chaim Weizmann, who would later become the first president of Israel, was instrumental in lobbying the British government for what became the 1917 Balfour Declaration, whose text assured Jews that the British government would 'view with favour' the creation of 'a national home for the Jewish people' in Palestine, provided that 'nothing shall be done which may prejudice the civil and religious rights of existing non-Jewish communities in Palestine'. Over the years that followed, the WZO funded and otherwise supported the emigration of Jews to Palestine under the catch cry 'A land without people for a people without land'. The Jews were indeed a people without land, but the rallying cry ignored the presence in Palestine of hundreds of thousands of Arabs who had lived on the land for generations. The WZO also set up numerous quasi-state institutions that were transplanted to the new Israeli state upon independence.

high priests and the not-inconsiderable blasphemy of Emperor Caligula's decision in AD 39 to declare himself a deity. Anti-Roman sentiment had been bubbling away for three decades, in part due to one rebellious orator – Jesus of Nazareth – and to a Jewish sect called the Zealots, whose creed stated that all means were justified to liberate the Jews.

Led by the Zealots, the Jews of Jerusalem destroyed a small Roman garrison in the Holy City in AD 66. Infighting within the revolt and the burning of food stockpiles in order to force wavering Jews to participate had disastrous consequences. Jerusalem was razed to the ground and up to 100,000 Jews were killed in retaliation; some Jewish historians claim that the number of dead over the four years of the revolt reached a million.

The failed uprising and the brutal Roman response (which came to be known as the First Jewish-Roman War) would have consequences that have rippled down through the centuries. Jerusalem was rebuilt as a Roman city and the Jews were sent into exile (which, for many Jews, ended only with the creation of the State of Israel in 1948). Few people in the Middle East dared to challenge the Romans after that.

188 BC	146 BC	64 BC	31 BC
The massed ranks of the Roman legionnaires conquer Asia Minor (Turkey), then continue south sweeping all before them. The Romans would rule the Middle East in some form for over six centuries.	The destruction of Carthage (in present-day Tunisia) by the Romans signals the end of more than a millennium of Phoenician/Punic dominance of the Mediterranean.	Pompey the Great abolishes the Seleucid kingdom, annexes Syria and transforms it into a province of the Roman Empire. Rome sets its sights on Egypt.	The Romans defeat Cleopatra, bringing to an end the era of the pharaohs and drawing Egypt under their control. Unable to bear the ignominy, Cleopatra commits suicide.

Byzantines

In AD 331, the newly converted Emperor Constantine declared Christianity the official religion of the 'Holy Roman Empire', with its capital not jaded, cynical Rome but the newly renamed city of Constantinople (formerly Byzantium, later to become İstanbul). Constantinople reached its apogee during the reign of Justinian (AD 527-65), when the Byzantine Empire consolidated its hold on the eastern Mediterranean.

But the Byzantine (or Eastern Roman) Empire, as it became known, would soon learn a harsh lesson that the Ottomans (ruling from the same city) would later fail to heed. Spread too thinly by controlling vast reaches of the earth and riven with divisions at home, they were vulnerable to the single most enduring historic power in Middle Eastern history, stirring in the deserts of Arabia: Islam.

The Cyrus Cylinder, which is housed at the British Museum with a replica at the UN, is a clay tablet with cuneiform inscriptions, and is widely considered to be the world's first charter of human rights.

Islamic Middle East

Arrival & Spread of Islam

No one in sophisticated Constantinople, an opulent city accustomed to the trappings of world power, could have imagined that the greatest threat to their rule would come from a small oasis community in the desert wastes of Arabia. The Byzantines, it is true, were besieged in their coastal forts of the southern Mediterranean, their power extending scarcely at all into the hinterland. And the Sassanid empire to the east was constantly chipping away at poorly defended Byzantine holdings. But there was little to suggest to the heirs of the Roman domain that these were anything more than minor skirmishes on the outer reaches of their empire.

In the 7th century AD, southern Arabia lay beyond the reach of both the Byzantines and the Sassanids. The cost and difficulty of occupying the Arabian Peninsula simply wasn't worth the effort, home as it was only to troublesome nomads and isolated oases. Thus it was that when, far from the great centres of power, in the nondescript town of Mecca (now in Saudi Arabia), a merchant named Mohammed (b AD 570) began preaching against the pagan religion of his fellow Meccans, no one in Constantinople paid the slightest attention.

Mohammed died in 632, but within a few short decades the entire Middle East would be under the control of his followers. Under Mohammed's successors, known as caliphs (from the Arabic word for 'follower'), the new religion spread rapidly, reaching all of Arabia by 634. By 646, Syria, Palestine and Egypt were all in Muslim hands, while most of Iraq, Iran and Afghanistan were wrested from the Sassanids by 656. By 682, Islam had reached the shores of the Atlantic in Morocco.

AD 0	AD 33	AD 39	AD 66–70
Jesus of Nazareth is born in Bethlehem (in the present-day Palestinian Territories), which was, at the time, fully incorporated into the Roman Empire.	Jesus is crucified by the Romans in Jerusalem. According to Christian tradition, he rises from the dead three days later, then ascends to heaven. His followers spread out across the world.	The Roman emperor Caligula, not content with ruling much of the world, declares himself a deity, adding to the resentment already felt by Jews and Christians living across the Roman Empire.	The Jews in Jerusalem and elsewhere revolt against oppressive Roman rule. The uprising is brutally put down, the Jewish temple destroyed and, within four years, over 100,000 Jews are killed.

WHO ARE THE ARABS?

The question of who the Arabs are exactly is still widely debated. Fourteen centuries ago, only the nomadic tribes wandering between the Euphrates River and the central Arabian Peninsula were considered Arabs, distinguished by their language. However, with the rapid expansion of Islam, the language of the Quran spread to vast areas. Although the Arabs were relatively few in number in most of the countries they conquered, their culture quickly became established through language, religion and intermarriage. In addition to the original nomads, the settled inhabitants of these newly conquered provinces also became known as Arabs. In the 20th century, rising Arab nationalism legitimised the current blanket usage of the term to apply to all the peoples of the Middle East – except the Persians, Kurds, Israelis and Turks.

The most romanticised group of Arabs is no doubt the Bedouin (Bedu in Arabic). While not an ethnic group, they are the archetypal Arabs – the camel-herding nomads who roam all over the deserts and semideserts in search of food for their cattle. From among their ranks came the warriors who spread Islam to North Africa and Persia 14 centuries ago. Today, the Bedouin are found mainly in Jordan, Iraq, Egypt's Sinai Peninsula and the Gulf States.

Umayyads

Having won the battle for supremacy over the Muslim world, Mu'awiyah, the Muslim military governor of Syria and a distant relative of Mohammed, became the fifth caliph, moved the capital from Medina to Damascus and established the first great Muslim dynasty – the Umayyads. Thanks to the unrelenting success of his armies, Mu'awiyah and his successors found themselves ruling an empire that held sway over almost a third of the world's population.

The decision to make Damascus the capital meant that, for the first time in the Middle East's turbulent history, the region was ruled from its Levantine heartland. The Umayyads gave the Islamic world some of its greatest architectural treasures, including the Dome of the Rock in Jerusalem and the Umayyad Mosque in Damascus – lavish monuments to the new faith, if a far cry from Islam's simple desert origins.

History, however, has not been kind to the Umayyads. Perhaps seduced by Damascus' charms, they are remembered as a decadent lot, known for the high living, corruption, nepotism and tyranny that eventually proved to be their undoing. News of Umayyad excesses never sat well with the foot soldiers of Islam and even confirmed their long-held suspicions about their adherence to Islamic tenets.

224	267–71	331	527–65
The Sassanids commence almost four decades of rule in Persian. For most of their rule, Zoroastrianism is the dominant faith.	Queen Zenobia seizes power in Palmyra, defeats the Roman legion sent to dethrone her, briefly occupies Syria, Palestine and Egypt, and declares herself independent of Rome. Rome is not amused.	Emperor Constantine declares Christianity the official religion of the Roman Empire and moves his capital to Constantinople (previously known as Byzantium). This event marks the birth of the Byzantine Empire.	Emperor Justinian reigns over the Byzantine Empire whose realm extends through the Mediterranean, including coastal North Africa and most of the Middle East.

Abbasids

In 750, the Umayyads were toppled in a revolt fuelled, predictably, by accusations of impiety. Their successors, and the strong arm behind the revolt, were the Abbasids. The Abbasid caliphate created a new capital in Baghdad, and the early centuries of its rule constituted what's often regarded as the golden age of Islamic culture in the Middle East. The most famous of the Abbasid caliphs was Haroun ar-Rashid (r 786–809) of *The Thousand and One Nights* fame. Warrior-king Haroun ar-Rashid led one of the most successful early Muslim invasions of Byzantium, almost reaching Constantinople. But his name will forever be associated with Baghdad, which he transformed into a world centre of learning and sophistication.

After Haroun ar-Rashid's death, the cycle that had already scarred Islam's early years – a strong, enlightened ruler giving way upon his death to anarchy and squandering many of the hard-won territorial and cultural gains of his reign – was repeated.

There is no finer work in English on the history of the Arabs, from the Prophet Mohammed to modern times, than *A History of the Arab Peoples* by Albert Hourani – it's definitive, encyclopedic and highly readable.

Seljuks

By the middle of the 10th century, the Abbasid caliphs were the prisoners of their Turkish guards, who spawned a dynasty of their own, known as the Seljuks (1038–1194). The Seljuks extended their reach throughout Persia, Central Asia, Afghanistan and Anatolia, where the Seljuk Sultanate of Rum made its capital at Konya. The pressure on the Byzantine Empire was intense enough to cause the emperor and the Greek Orthodox Church to swallow their pride and appeal to the Roman Catholic Church for help.

What happened next would plant the seeds for a clash of civilisations, whose bitterness would reverberate throughout the region long after the swords of Islam and Christianity had been sheathed.

Genghis Khan & the Mongol Invasion

In the early 13th century, the Seljuk Empire came to a final and bloody end when the rampaging Mongols swept across the Persian plateau on their horses, leaving a trail of cold-blooded devastation and thousands of dismembered heads in their wake.

Under the leadership first of Genghis Khan, and then his grandsons, including Hulagu, the Mongol rulers managed to seize all of Persia, as well as an empire stretching from Beijing (China) to İstanbul (Turkey). Eventually they established a capital at Tabriz. The Mongols destroyed many of the Persian cities they conquered, obliterating much of Persia's documented history. But they also became great arts patrons, leaving many fine monuments.

The empire fragmented when Abu Said died without a successor, and soon succumbed to invading forces from the east led by Tamerlane (Lame Timur).

570	622	632	642
The Prophet Mohammed is born in Mecca (present-day Saudi Arabia). Despite his humble origins, he will become the 25th and most revered prophet of the world's second-largest religion.	When his message from Allah is rejected by powerful Meccans, the Prophet flees to Medina. In the Islamic calendar, this flight is known as the Hejira and marks Year Zero.	After returning to Mecca at the head of Islam's first army in 630, the Prophet Mohammed dies in Mecca. Despite squabbles over succession, his followers carry the new religion across the world.	Islam's battle for succession reaches its critical moment with the death of Hussein, the son of Ali. Ever since this date, the Muslim world has been divided into two strains – Sunni and Shiite.

The Crusades & Their Aftermath

Preparing for War

With the Muslim armies gathering at the gates of Europe, and already occupying large swaths of Iberia, Pope Urban II in 1095, in response to the eastern empire's alarm, called for a Western Christian military expedition – a 'Crusade' – to liberate the holy places of Jerusalem. Rome's motives were not entirely benevolent: Urban was eager to assert Rome's primacy in the east over Constantinople. The monarchs and clerics of Europe attempted to portray the Crusades as a 'just war'. The battle cry attracted zealous support.

Bitterly fought on the battlefield, the Crusades remain one of the region's most divisive historical moments. For the Muslims, the Christian call to arms was a vicious attack on Islam itself, and the tactics used by the Crusaders confirmed the Muslim suspicion that Christianity's primary concern was imperial conquest. So deep does the sense of grievance run in the region that President Bush's invasion of Iraq in 2003 was widely portrayed as the next Christian crusade. In the Christian world view, the Crusades were a necessary defensive strategy, lest Islam sweep across Europe and place Christianity's very existence under threat.

Christian Invasion

Whatever the rights and wrongs, the crusading rabble enjoyed considerable success. After linking up with the Byzantine army in 1097, the Crusaders successfully besieged Antioch (modern Antakya, in Turkey), then marched south along the coast before turning inland, towards Jerusalem, leaving devastation in their wake. A thousand Muslim troops held Jerusalem for six weeks against 15,000 Crusaders before the city fell on 15 July 1099. The victorious Crusaders then massacred the local population – Muslims, Jews and Christians alike – sacked the non-Christian religious sites and turned the Dome of the Rock into a church.

Curiously, even after the gratuitous violence of the Crusades, Christians and Muslims assimilated in the Holy Land. European visitors to Palestine recorded with dismay that the original Crusaders who remained in the Holy Land had abandoned their European ways. They had become Arabised, taking on eastern habits and dress – perhaps it was not an unwise move to abandon chain mail and jerkins for flowing robes in the Levantine heat. Even with their semi-transformation into locals, the Crusaders were never equipped to govern the massive, newly resentful Middle East. A series of Crusader 'statelets' arose through the region during this period.

Muslim Backlash

These statelets aside, the Middle East remained predominantly Muslim, and within 50 years the tide had begun to turn against the Crusaders. The

The Crusades Through Arab Eyes by Amin Maalouf is brilliantly written and captures perfectly why the mere mention of the Crusades still arouses the anger of many Arabs today.

646	656	660	711
Barely a decade after the death of Mohammed, Syria, Palestine and Egypt have all been conquered by the followers of Islam. Modern Israel aside, they have been predominantly Muslim ever since.	Islam takes hold in Iraq, Persia and Afghanistan, defeating the ruling Sassanids and building on the expansion of Islam, which had been born just a few decades before.	Mu'awiyah moves the capital of the Muslim world from Arabia to Damascus, shifting Islam's balance of power. The Umayyad caliphate rules over an empire that encompasses almost the entire Middle East.	The armies of Islam cross from North Africa into Europe and the Iberian Peninsula is soon under their control. Al-Andalus, in southern Iberia, becomes a beacon for tolerance and the arts.

BAGHDAD THE BEAUTIFUL

When Haroun ar-Rashid came to power in AD 786, Baghdad, on the western bank of the Tigris, had only been in existence for 24 years. By the time he died, it had become one of the world's pre-eminent cities. Haroun ar-Rashid tried to rename the city Medinat as-Salaam (City of Peace). Although the name never caught on, everything else that Haroun ar-Rashid and his immediate successors did was an unqualified success. Baghdad was remade into a city of expansive pleasure gardens, vast libraries and distinguished seats of learning, where the arts, medicine, literature and sciences all flourished. It was soon the richest city in the world. The crossroads of important trade routes to the east and west, it rapidly supplanted Damascus as the seat of power in the Islamic world, which stretched from Spain to India. Al-Maamun, Haroun's son and successor, founded the Beit al-Hikmah (House of Wisdom), a Baghdad-based academy dedicated to translating Greek and Roman works of science and philosophy into Arabic. It was only through these translations that most of the classical literature we know today was saved for posterity.

Muslim leader responsible for removing the Crusaders from Jerusalem (in 1187) was Salah ad-Din al-Ayyoub, better known in the West as Saladin.

Saladin and his successors (a fleeting dynasty known as the Ayyubids) battled the Crusaders for 60 years until they were unceremoniously removed by their own army, a strange soldier-slave caste, the Mamluks, who ran what would today be called a military dictatorship. The only way to join their army was to be press-ganged into it – non-Muslim boys were captured or bought outside the empire, converted to Islam and raised in the service of a single military commander. They were expected to give this commander total loyalty, in exchange for which their fortunes would rise (or fall) with his. Sultans were chosen from among the most senior Mamluk commanders, but it was a system that engendered vicious, bloody rivalries, and rare was the sultan who died of natural causes.

The Mamluks were to rule Egypt, Syria, Palestine and western Arabia for nearly 300 years (1250–1517), and it was they who finally succeeded in ejecting the Crusaders from the Near East, prising them out of their last stronghold of Acre (modern-day Akko in Israel) in 1291.

The Ottoman Middle East

Rise of the Ottomans

Turkey, saved for now from an Islamic fate by the Crusaders, had remained largely above the fray. But the Byzantine rulers in Constantinople felt anything but secure. The armies of Islam may have been occupied fighting the Crusaders (and each other) in the so-called Holy Lands, but

750	786–809	969	1038–1194
The first Arab dynasty, the Umayyad caliphate in Damascus, falls amid accusations of impiety, and power shifts to Baghdad, the base for the Abbasids.	Haroun ar-Rashid rules the Abbasid world from his capital of Baghdad. This was the Abbasid heyday and provides the setting for tales in *The Thousand and One Nights*.	The Shiite general Jawhar lays the foundations for a new palace city, Al-Qahira (Cairo). Two years later, a new university and mosque complex, al-Azhar, is founded.	The Seljuks, the former Turkish guards of the Abbasids, seize power, effectively ruling the Abbasid Empire. In addition to Turkey, they take Afghanistan, Persia and much of Central Asia.

the Byzantines nervously looked towards the south, keeping their armies in a state of high readiness. Little did they know that their undoing would come from within.

In 1258, just eight years after the Mamluks seized power in Cairo and began their bloody dynasty, a boy named Osman (Othman) was born to the chief of a Turkish tribe in western Anatolia. He converted to Islam in his youth and later began a military career by hiring out his tribe's army as mercenaries in the civil wars, then besetting what was left of the Byzantine Empire. Payment came in the form of land.

Rather than taking on the Byzantines directly, Osman's successors (the Ottomans) deliberately picked off the bits and pieces of the empire that Constantinople could no longer control. By the end of the 14th century, the Ottomans had conquered Bulgaria, Serbia, Bosnia, Hungary and most of present-day Turkey. They had also moved their capital across the Dardanelles to Adrianople, today the Turkish city of Edirne. In 1453 came their greatest victory, when Sultan Mehmet II took Constantinople, the hitherto unachievable object of innumerable Muslim wars almost since the 7th century.

Sixty-four years later, on a battlefield near Aleppo, an army under the gloriously named sultan Selim the Grim routed the Mamluks and assumed sovereignty over the Hejaz. At a stroke, the whole of the eastern Mediterranean, including Egypt and much of Arabia, was absorbed into the Ottoman Empire. By capturing Mecca and Medina, Selim the Grim claimed for the Ottomans the coveted title of the guardians of Islam's holiest places. For the first time in centuries, the Middle East was ruled in its entirety by a single Islamic entity.

The Court of the Caliphs by Hugh Kennedy is the definitive account of Abbasid Baghdad in its prime, blending careful scholarship and Arab sources with a lively and compelling style.

HISTORY THE OTTOMAN MIDDLE EAST

Golden Age

The Ottoman Empire reached its peak, both politically and culturally, under Süleyman the Magnificent (r 1520–66), who led the Ottoman armies west to the gates of Vienna, east into Persia, and south through the holy cities of Mecca and Medina and into Yemen. His control also extended throughout North Africa. A remarkable figure, Süleyman was noted as much for codifying Ottoman law (he is known in Turkish as Süleyman Kanunı – law bringer) as for his military prowess. Süleyman's legal code was a visionary amalgam of secular and Islamic law, and his patronage of the arts saw the Ottomans reach their cultural zenith.

Another hallmark of Ottoman rule, especially in its early centuries, was its tolerance. In general, Christian and Jewish communities were accorded the respect the Quran outlines for them as 'People of the Book' and were given special status. The Ottoman state was a truly multicultural and multilingual one, and Christians and Muslims rose to positions of great power within the Ottoman hierarchy. In a move unthinkable for a

1097	1099	1171	1187
In response to a cry for help from the besieged Byzantines in Constantinople, the Christian Crusaders sweep down across the Middle East, trying to end Muslim rule in the Holy Land.	After a withering siege, the Crusaders enter Jerusalem, massacre thousands regardless of their religion and claim the city for Christianity. The Dome of the Rock is turned into a church.	The Kurdish-born general Salah ad-Din al-Ayyub (aka Saladin) seizes power from the Fatimid Shiite caliph in Egypt, restores Sunni rule and establishes the Ayyubid dynasty.	Saladin retakes Jerusalem from the Crusaders and forever after becomes a hero to Muslims around the world. Fighting elsewhere between Saladin's forces and the Crusaders continues.

SALADIN – THE KURDISH HERO OF ARAB HISTORY

Saladin – or Salah ad-Din (Restorer of the Faith) al-Ayyoub – was born to Kurdish parents in 1138 in what is modern-day Tikrit in Iraq. He joined other members of his family in the service of Nureddin (Nur ad-Din) of the ruling Zangi dynasty. By the time Nureddin died in 1174, Saladin had risen to the rank of general and had already taken possession of Egypt. He quickly took control of Syria and, over the next 10 years, extended his authority into parts of Mesopotamia. In 1187, Saladin crushed the Crusaders at the Battle of Hittin and captured Jerusalem, precipitating the Third Crusade and pitting himself against Richard I (the Lionheart) of England. After countless clashes, the two rival warriors signed a peace treaty in 1192, giving the coastal territories to the Crusaders and the interior to the Muslims. Saladin died three months later in Damascus, where he is buried.

Muslim ruler today, Sultan Beyazit II even invited the Jews expelled from Iberia by the Spanish Inquisition to İstanbul in 1492.

But as so often happened in Middle Eastern history upon the death of a charismatic leader, things began to unravel soon after Süleyman died fighting on the Danube. The Ottomans may have held nominal power throughout their empire for centuries to come, but the growing decadence of the Ottoman court and unrest elsewhere in the countries that fell within the Ottoman sphere of influence ensured that, after Süleyman, the empire went into a long, slow period of decline.

Saladin in his Time by PH Newby reads like a novel, except that it's all true, with surprising plot twists, epic events and picaresque characters brought to life.

Under Attack

Five years after Süleyman's death, Spain and Venice destroyed virtually the entire Ottoman navy at the Battle of Lepanto (in the Aegean Sea), thereby costing the Ottomans control over the western Mediterranean. North Africa soon fell under the sway of local dynasties. Conflict with the Safavids – Persia's rulers between the 16th and 18th centuries – was almost constant.

To make matters worse, within a century of Süleyman's death, the concept of enlightened Ottoman sultans had all but evaporated. Assassinations, mutinies and fratricide were increasingly the norm among Constantinople's royals, and the opulent lifestyle was taking its toll. Süleyman was the last sultan to lead his army into the field, and those who came after him were generally coddled and sequestered in the fineries of the palace, having minimal experience of everyday life and little inclination to administer or expand the empire. The Ottomans remained moribund, inward looking and generally unaware of the advances that were happening in Europe – the Ottoman clergy did not allow the use of the printing press until the 18th century, a century and a half after it had been introduced into Europe.

1192	1250	1258	1291
Saladin signs a peace treaty with his long-time enemy, Richard the Lionheart. The Crusaders get the coast, the Muslims get the interior and Saladin dies three months later.	The Mamluks, a military empire forged from the ranks of the Muslim armies, seize power for themselves and begin a 300-year rule over Egypt, Syria and Palestine.	Baghdad is sacked by the Mongol hordes sweeping down out of Central Asia, destroying the city and officially ending the Abbasid Cailphate. Osman (founder of the Ottomans) is born.	With energy drained from the Crusader cause, the Mamluks drive the last Crusaders from their coastal fortress of Acre (now Akko in Israel) and from the Middle East.

Just as it had under the similarly out-of-touch Umayyads in the 8th century, the perceived impiety of the sultans and their representatives gave power to local uprisings. The Ottoman Empire lumbered along until the 20th century, but the empire was in a sorry state and its control over its territories grew more tenuous with each passing year.

European Incursions

Europe had begun to wake from its medieval slumber and the monarchs of France and Great Britain, in particular, were eager to bolster their growing prosperity by expanding their zones of economic influence. More than that, the prestige that would accompany colonial possessions in lands that had held an important place in the European imagination was undeniable. The reflected glory of 'owning' the Holy Lands or becoming the rulers over what was once the cradle of civilisation was too much for these emerging world powers to resist, and fitted perfectly within their blueprint for world domination. They may have talked of a 'civilising mission'. They may even have believed in it. But it was prestige and greed that ultimately drove them as they cast their eye towards the Middle East.

In 1798, Napoleon invaded Egypt. It was not by accident that he chose the Middle East's most populous country as his first conquest in the region. By conquering the one-time land of the pharaohs, this ruler with visions of grandeur and an eye on his place in history announced to the world that France was the world power of the day. The French occupation of Egypt lasted only three years, but left a lasting mark – even today, Egypt's legal system is based on a French model.

The British, of course, had other ideas. Under the cover of protecting their own interests in India, they forced the French out of Egypt in 1801.

Decline

Four years later, Mohammed Ali, an Albanian soldier in the Ottoman army, emerged as the country's strongman and he set about modernising the country. As time passed, it became increasingly obvious that Constantinople was becoming ever more dependent on Egypt for military backing rather than the reverse. Mohammed Ali's ambitions grew. In the 1830s, he invaded and conquered Syria, and by 1839 he had effective control of most of the Ottoman Empire.

While it might have appeared to have been in Europe's interests to consign the Ottoman Empire to history, they were already stretched by their other colonial conquests and holdings (the British in India, the French in Africa) and had no interest, at least not yet, in administering the entire region. As a consequence, the Europeans prevailed upon Mohammed Ali to withdraw to Egypt. In return, the Ottoman sultan gave long-overdue acknowledgment of Mohammed Ali's status as ruler of a

Süleyman the Magnificent was responsible for achievements as diverse as building the gates of Jerusalem and introducing to Europe, via Constantinople, the joys of coffee.

At the Battle of the Pyramids, Napoleon's forces took just 45 minutes to rout the Mamluk army, killing 1000 for the loss of just 29 of their own men.

1453	1492	1520–66	1571
After encircling the city during his Eastern European conquests, Sultan Mehmet II of the Ottoman Empire captures Constantinople, which had never before been in Muslim hands.	Muslim Al-Andalus falls to the Christian armies of the Spanish Reconquista, ending seven centuries of enlightened but increasingly divided rule. Jewish people begin arriving across the Middle East.	Süleyman the Magnificent rules over the golden age of the Ottoman Empire, expanding the boundaries of the empire down into Arabia (including the holy cities of Mecca and Medina), Persia and North Africa.	Five years after the death of Süleyman the Magnificent, Spain and Venice defeat the Ottomans at the Battle of Lepanto in the Aegean. Ottoman power has peaked and will never be as strong again.

OTTOMAN CONQUEST OF EUROPE

Just as the forces of Christian Europe were on the verge of expelling Al-Andalus, the Islamic civilisation that ruled southern Spain from Christian soil, the Ottoman Turks, gathering in the east, opened a new front.

Horse-borne, and firing arrows from the saddle, the Ottoman Turks emerged from the Anatolian steppe in the 14th century, eager to gain a foothold on European soil. It was the boldest of moves, considering that the Abbasid advance on Constantinople had prompted the fierce European backlash of the Crusades. But the Ottomans were better equipped to take on war-weary Europe and advanced so swiftly – so seemingly miraculously – into Eastern Europe that Martin Luther openly wondered whether they should be opposed at all. The Ottoman Empire, at its greatest extent, reached from western Libya to the steppes of Hungary.

The end of Ottoman expansion is variously pinpointed as the failed Vienna campaign in 1683 or the treaty of Karlowitz (in which the Ottomans lost the Peloponnese, Transylvania and Hungary) in 1699 when the Ottomans sued for peace for the first time.

virtually independent Egypt, and bestowed the right of hereditary rule on his heirs (who continued to rule Egypt until 1952). In some quarters, the Ottoman move was viewed as a wise strategy in keeping with their loose administration of their empire. In truth, they had little choice.

The emboldened Europeans were always at the ready to expand their influence in the region. In 1860, the French sent troops to Lebanon after a massacre of Christians by the local Druze. Before withdrawing, the French forced the Ottomans to set up a new administrative system for the area guaranteeing the appointment of Christian governors, over whom the French came to have great influence.

While all of this was happening, another import from the West – nationalism – was making its presence felt. The people of the Middle East watched with growing optimism as Greece and the Ottomans' Balkan possessions wriggled free, marking the death knell of Ottoman omniscience and prompting Middle Easterners to dream of their own independence. In this, they were encouraged by the European powers, who may have paid lip service to the goals of independence, but were actually laying detailed plans for occupation. Mistaking (or, more likely, deliberately misinterpreting or ignoring) the nationalist movement as a cry for help, the European powers quickly set about filling the vacuum of power left by the Ottomans.

The Ottoman regime, once feared and respected, was now universally known as the 'sick man of Europe'. European diplomats and politicians condescendingly pondered the 'eastern question', which in practice

Ottoman Centuries by Lord Kinross is perhaps the definitive history of the Ottoman Empire, covering everything from the key events of Ottoman rule to the extravagances of its royal court.

1683	1760s	1798	1839
The Ottoman armies march on Vienna, but their defeat marks the end of Ottoman expansion and furthers the centuries-long period of Ottoman decline.	The Wahhabi movement in central Arabia calls for a return to Islam's roots. Wahhabi Islam still prevails in Saudi Arabia and forms the basis for Al-Qaeda thought.	Napoleon invades Egypt, ushering in the period of colonial rivalry between France and Britain (who force the French out in 1801) that would ultimately redraw the map of the Middle East.	Mohammed Ali of Egypt, an Albanian Ottoman soldier, establishes de facto control over the declining Ottoman Empire from his base in Egypt. The dynasty he founded would rule Egypt until 1952.

meant deciding how to dismember the empire and cherry-pick its choicest parts. In 1869, Mohammed Ali's grandson Ismail opened the Suez Canal. But within a few years, his government was so deeply in debt that in 1882, the British, who already were playing a large role in Egyptian affairs, occupied the country. It was a sign of things to come.

Colonial Middle East

Broken Promises

With the exception of Napoleon's stunning march into Egypt, Britain and France had slowly come to occupy the Middle East less by conquest than by stealth. European advisers, backed by armed reinforcements when necessary, were increasingly charting the region's future and it would not be long before their efforts were rewarded.

With the outbreak of WWI in 1914, the Ottoman Empire made its last serious (and ultimately fatal) error by throwing its lot in with Germany. Sultan Mohammed V declared a jihad (holy war), calling on Muslims everywhere to rise up against Britain, France and Russia (who were encroaching on Eastern Anatolia). When the British heard the Ottoman call to jihad, they performed a masterstroke – they negotiated an alliance with Hussein bin Ali, the grand sherif (Islamic custodian and descendant of the Prophet Mohammed) of Mecca, who agreed to lead an Arab revolt against the Turks in return for a British promise to make him 'King of the Arabs' once the conflict was over. This alliance worked well in defeating the Ottomans.

Lords of the Horizons: A History of the Ottoman Empire by Jason Goodwin is anecdotal and picaresque but still manages to illuminate the grand themes of Ottoman history.

There was just one problem. With the Ottomans out of the way, the British never had any serious intention of keeping their promise. Even as they were negotiating with Sherif Hussein, the British were talking with the French how to carve up the Ottoman Empire. These talks yielded the 1916 Sykes-Picot Agreement – the secret Anglo-French accord that divided the Ottoman Empire into British and French spheres of influence. With a few adjustments, the Sykes-Picot Agreement determined the post-WWI map of the Middle East. Not surprisingly, this remains one of the most reviled 'peace agreements' in 20th-century Middle Eastern history.

European Occupation

In the closing year of the war, the British occupied Palestine, Transjordan, Damascus and Iraq. After the war, France took control of Syria and Lebanon, while Britain retained Egypt in addition to its holdings elsewhere. The Arabs, who'd done so much to free themselves from Ottoman rule, suddenly found themselves under British or French colonial administration, with the prospect of a Jewish state in their midst not far over the horizon thanks to the 1917 Balfour Declaration.

When the newly minted League of Nations initiated its system of mandates in 1922, thereby legitimising the French and British occupations,

1860	1869	1882	1896
The massacre of Christians by the Druze in Lebanon's mountains prompts the French to send troops to restore order. The Ottomans remain nominal sovereigns, but the French never really leave.	Ismail, the grandson of Mohammed Ali and ruler of Egypt, formally opens the landmark engineering feat that is the Suez Canal. Britain is heavily involved in Egyptian affairs.	Weary of the Egyptian government's alleged financial ineptitude, the British formalise their control over the country, making it their first full-blown colonial possession in the Middle East.	Theodor Herzl publishes *Der Judenstaat (The Jewish State)*, in which he makes a call for a Jewish state in Palestine. This book is often described as the moment when Zionism was born.

the sense of betrayal across the region was palpable. As was the colonial way, no one had thought to ask the people of the region what they wanted. As the Europeans set about programs of legal and administrative reform, their occupying forces faced almost continual unrest. The Syrians and Lebanese harried the French, while the predominantly Arab population of Palestine battled the British.

The problems in Palestine were particularly acute. Since taking control of Palestine in 1918, the British had been under pressure to allow unrestricted Jewish immigration to the territory. With tensions rising between Palestine's Arab and Jewish residents, they refused to do this and, in the late 1930s, placed strict limits on the number of new Jewish immigrants. It was, of course, a crisis of Britain's own making, having promised to 'view with favour' the establishment of a Jewish state in Palestine in the Balfour Declaration.

> In 1922, there were around 486,000 Palestinian Arabs and 84,000 Jews in Palestine. By 1946, the Palestinian population had doubled to 1.1 million, whereas Jews had increased 550% to around 610,000.

Turkish Independence

As Iraq, Syria, Lebanon and Palestine simmered, Turkey was going its own way, mercifully free of both the Ottoman sultans and their European successors. Stripped of its Arab provinces, the Ottoman monarchy was overthrown and a Turkish republic was declared under the leadership of Mustafa Kemal 'Atatürk', a soldier who became Turkey's first president in 1923.

His drive towards secularism (which he saw as synonymous with the modernisation necessary to drag Turkey into the 20th century) found an echo in Persia, where, in 1923, Reza Khan, the commander of a Cossack brigade who had risen to become war minister, overthrew the decrepit Ghajar dynasty. After changing his name from Khan to the more Persian-sounding Pahlavi (the language spoken in pre-Islamic Persia), he moved to set up a secular republic on the Turkish model. Protests from the country's religious establishment caused a change of heart and he had himself crowned shah instead. In 1934, Reza Shah changed the country's name from Persia to Iran.

Looking back now at the turbulent years between the two world wars, it's easy to discern the seeds of the major conflicts that would come to define the Middle East in the late 20th and early 21st centuries: the Arab-Israeli conflict, Iran's Islamic Revolution and Turkey's struggle to forge an identity as a modernising Muslim country.

Israel's Independence

For the past 60 years, no issue has divided the Middle East quite like Israeli independence. Four major conflicts, numerous skirmishes and an unrelenting war of words and attrition have cast a long shadow over everything that happens in the region. If a way could be found to forge peace between Israel and the Palestinians, the Middle East would be a very different place.

1914	1915	1916–18	1916
WWI breaks out. The Ottomans side with Germany, while the Allies persuade the Grand Sherif of Mecca to support them in return for promises of postwar independence for the Arabs.	In the last years of the Ottoman Empire, Turkey's Armenian population is driven from the country. More than a million Armenians are killed in what Armenians claim was a genocide.	TE Lawrence assists in the Arab Revolt against the Ottoman Empire, raising hopes among Arabs that they would be rewarded with independence after World War II.	The French and British conclude the secret Sykes-Picot Agreement, which divides the region between the two European powers in the event of an Allied victory.

THE SILK ROAD

Silk first began moving westward from China more than 2000 years ago when the Parthians became enamoured with the soft, fine fabric. By about 100 BC the Parthians and Chinese had exchanged embassies, and silk, along with myriad other goods, was being traded along the route. Trade grew after the Romans developed a fixation with the fabric and eventually silk would become more valuable than gold to the Romans.

It took many months to traverse the 8000km Silk Road route, which was not a single road but rather a web of caravan tracks dotted with caravanserais a day's travel apart – roughly 30km. These were fortified rest stops with accommodation for traders, their camels and goods. The network had its main eastern terminus at the Chinese capital Ch'ang-an (now Xian). Caravans entered present-day Iran anywhere between Merv (modern Turkmenistan) and Herat (Afghanistan), and passed through Mashhad and Tabriz (among other stops) en route to Constantinople (now İstanbul).

Unlike the Silk Road's most famous journeyman, Marco Polo, caravanners were mostly short- and medium-distance hauliers who marketed and took on freight along a given beat. Goods heading east included gold, silver, ivory, jade and other precious stones, wool, Mediterranean coloured glass, grapes, wine, spices and – early Parthian crazes – acrobats and ostriches. Going west were silk, porcelain, spices, gems and perfumes. In the middle lay Central Asia and Iran, great clearing houses that provided the horses and Bactrian camels that kept the goods flowing.

The Silk Road was eventually abandoned when the new European powers discovered alternative sea routes in the 15th century.

There is very little on which the two sides agree, although the following historical chronology is *probably* among them: in early 1947 the British announced that they were turning the entire problem over to the newly created UN. The UN voted to partition Palestine, but this was rejected by the Arabs. Britain pulled out and the very next day the Jews declared the founding of the State of Israel. War broke out immediately, with Egypt, Jordan and Syria weighing in on the side of the Palestinian Arabs. Israel won.

Beyond that, the issue has become a forum for claim and counter-claim, to the extent that for the casual observer truth has become as elusive as the peace that all sides claim to want. What follows is our summary of the main bodies of opinion about Israeli independence among Israelis and Palestinians as they stood in 1948.

The Israeli View

For many Jews in 1948, the founding of the State of Israel represented a homecoming for a persecuted people who had spent almost 2000 years

1917	1922	1923	1920s & '30s
The British government's Balfour Declaration promises 'a national home for the Jewish people' in Palestine. The declaration gives unstoppable momentum to the Zionist movement.	The League of Nations grants Syria and Lebanon to the French, and Palestine, Iraq and Transjordan to the British. Egypt becomes independent but Britain remains in control.	Kemal Atatürk, becomes the first president of Turkey on a mission to modernise the country and create a secular state. Reza Khan seizes power in Iran.	Jewish immigration to Palestine gathers pace. The arrival of the immigrants prompts anger among Palestinian Arabs and the British impose restrictions on the number of arrivals.

WHAT HAPPENED TO THE ARMENIANS?

The final years of the Ottoman Empire saw human misery on an epic scale, but nothing has proved as enduringly controversial as the fate of the Armenians. For millennia, this large but disparate community had lived in eastern Anatolia. In the early 20th century, the Orthodox Christian Armenians made the error of siding with the Russians against the Muslim Turk majority. It was an error for which they paid dearly.

The tale begins with eyewitness accounts, in autumn 1915, of Ottoman army units rounding up Armenian populations and marching them towards the Syrian desert. It ends with an Anatolian hinterland virtually devoid of Armenians. What happened in between remains one of the most controversial episodes in the 20th-century Middle East.

The Armenians maintain, compellingly it must be said, that they were subject to the 20th century's first orchestrated 'genocide'. They claim that over a million Armenians were summarily executed or killed on death marches and that Ottoman authorities issued a deportation order with the intention of removing the Armenian presence from Anatolia. To this day, Armenians demand an acknowledgement of this 'genocide'. Very few Armenians remain in Turkey, although there are significant Armenian communities in Syria, Iran and Israel and the Palestinian Territories.

Less compellingly, although with equal conviction, Turkey refutes any claims that such 'genocide' occurred. It does admit that thousands of Armenians died, but claims the Ottoman order had been to 'relocate' Armenians with no intention to eradicate them. The deaths, according to Turkish officials, were the result of disease and starvation, direct consequences of the tumultuous state of affairs during a time of war.

in exile. Coming so soon as it did after the horrors of the Holocaust, in which more than six million Jews were killed, Israel, a state of their own, was the least the world could do after perpetrating the Holocaust or at the very least letting it happen. The Holocaust was the culmination of decades, perhaps even centuries of racism in European countries. In short, the Jewish people had ample reason to believe that their fate should never again be placed in the hands of others.

Although the Jews were offered a range of alternative sites for their state, it could never be anywhere but on the southeastern shores of the Mediterranean. By founding a Jewish state in Palestine, the Jews were returning to a land rich in biblical reference points and promises – one of the most enduring foundations of Judaism is that God promised this land to the Jews. Indeed, it is difficult to overestimate the significance of this land for a people whose traditions and sacred places all lay in Palestine, especially Jerusalem. This may have been the driving force for many observant religious Jews. But the dream of a return had deeper cultural roots, maintained down through the generations during an often difficult

1939–45	1947	1948	1951
After decades of anti-Semitism in Europe, more than six million Jews are killed by the Nazis and their allies during WWII, giving fresh urgency to the call for a Jewish state.	Britain hands the issue over to the newly formed UN, which decides to partition Palestine into two states, one Jewish, the other Palestinian. Arabs reject the plan.	The British withdraw from Palestine, Israel declares independence and the Arab armies of neighbouring countries invade. The new State of Israel wins the war, and increases its territory.	King Abdullah I, the founder of modern Jordan, is assassinated as recriminations ripple out across the Arab world in the wake of its devastating defeat by Israel.

exile and shared by many secular Jews. This latter branch of Jewish society hoped to create an enlightened utopia, an egalitarian society in which a strong and just Israel finally took its rightful place among the modern company of nations.

The Palestinian View

For many Palestinians in 1948, the founding of the State of Israel was 'Al-Naqba' – the Catastrophe. Through no fault of their own, and thanks to decisions made in Europe and elsewhere, and on which they were never consulted, the Palestinians were driven from their land. While the British were promising Palestine to the Jews in 1917, the Palestinians were fighting alongside the British to oust the Ottomans. Later, subject to British occupation, Palestinians suffered at the hands of Jewish extremist groups and found themselves confronted by an influx of Jews who had never before set foot in Palestine but who claimed equal rights over the land. Many Palestinians who had lived on the land for generations could do nothing without international assistance. No one came to their aid. In short, when they were offered half of their ancestral homelands by the UN, they had ample reason to reject the plan out of hand.

As with the Israelis, it is difficult to overestimate the significance of this land for Palestinians, many of whose traditions and sacred places lay in Palestine. Jerusalem (Al-Quds) is the third-holiest city for Palestinian Muslims after Mecca and Medina (the Prophet Mohammed is believed to have ascended to heaven from the Al-Aqsa Mosque), and the holiest city on earth for Palestinian Christians. But this was never really about religion. Had they not lived alongside the Jews for centuries, many Palestinians asked, considered them equals and given them the respect that their religion deserved? For the Palestinians forced to flee, it was about the right to the homes in which people had lived and to the fields that they had farmed. As they fled into their own exile, they longed for a Palestinian homeland taking its rightful place among the modern company of nations.

Orientalism, by Edward Said, is dense and academic but is *the* seminal work on the history of Western misconceptions and stereotypes about the Middle East from colonial times to the present.

Arab Middle East
Arab (Dis)unity

The Arab countries that waged war against Israel were in disarray, even before they went to war. Newly independent themselves, they were governed for the most part by hereditary rulers whose legitimacy was tenuous at best. They ruled over countries whose boundaries had only recently been established and they did so thanks to centuries of foreign rule, ill prepared to tackle the most pressing problems of poverty, illiteracy and the lack of a clear national vision for the future. Although united in the common cause of opposing Israel, they were divided over just about everything else.

1952	1956	1958–61	1961
Gamal Abdel Nasser leads a coup against the monarchy in Egypt and becomes the first Egyptian ruler over Egypt since the days of the pharaohs.	Shortly after becoming Egyptian president, Nasser nationalises the Suez Canal, then stares down Israel, Britain and France who are forced to retreat. Nasser's popularity soars.	Egypt and Syria unite to form the United Arab Republic, a short-lived union that Nasser hopes will spark a pan-Arab mega-state that brings together all the Arab countries of the region.	Kurds in northern Iraq launch a short-lived military campaign for an independent Kurdistan. The move fails and will become an important justification for later campaigns against the Kurds.

ISRAELI INDEPENDENCE: A PRIMER

In addition to the books listed below, *The War for Palestine: Rewriting the History of 1948*, edited by Eugene L Rogan and Avi Shlaim, brings together both Israeli and Palestinian scholars.

History by Israelis

➡ *1948: A History of the First Arab-Israeli War* by Benny Morris – Israel's most prominent historian has drawn criticism from both sides.

➡ *The Birth of the Palestinian Refugee Problem Revisited* by Benny Morris – An attempt to explain why 700,000 Palestinians ended up in exile.

➡ *The Arab-Israeli Wars: War and Peace in the Middle East* by Chaim Herzog and Shlomo Gazit – Although it covers more recent events, Herzog takes a long look at 1948.

➡ *The Ethnic Cleansing of Palestine* by Ilan Pappe – A controversial text that challenges many of Israel's founding myths.

➡ *The Invention of the Jewish People* by Shlomo Sand – A polemical book that revisits the question of Jewish identity.

History by Palestinians

➡ *The Question of Palestine* by Edward W Said – An eloquent, passionate, but fair-minded study of the issue by the late, leading Palestinian intellectual.

➡ *Expulsion of the Palestinians: The Concept of 'Transfer' in Zionist Political Thought, 1882–1948* by Nur Masalha – Revealing insights from Zionist archives.

➡ *The Iron Cage: The Story of the Palestinian Struggle for Statehood* by Rashid Khalidi – Looks at 1948 and the decades that preceded it.

The disastrous performance of the combined Arab armies in the 1948 Arab-Israeli War had far-reaching consequences for the region. People across the Middle East blamed their leaders for the defeat, a mood fuelled by the mass arrival of Palestinian refugees in Lebanon, Syria, Egypt and, most of all, Jordan, whose population doubled almost overnight. Recriminations over the humiliating defeat and the refugee problem it created laid the groundwork for the 1951 assassination of King Abdullah of Jordan. Syria, which had gained its independence from France in 1946, became the field for a seemingly endless series of military coups.

Rise of Nasser

It was in Egypt, where the army blamed the loss of the war on the country's corrupt and ineffective politicians, that the most interesting developments were taking shape. In July 1952, a group of young officers

1964	1967	1968–69	1970
Against the objections of Jordan and Israel, the Palestine Liberation Organisation (PLO), an umbrella group of Palestinian resistance groups, is formed.	Israel launches a pre-emptive strike and destroys Egypt's air force. Israel emerges from the resulting Six Day War with much of the West Bank, Sinai, the Golan Heights and the Gaza Strip.	Saddam Hussein emerges as the key powerbroker in Iraq after a coup brings the Ba'ath Party to power. A year later, Yasser Arafat becomes leader of the PLO.	Hafez al-Assad assumes power in Syria after what he called 'The Corrective Revolution'. At the head of the Syrian Ba'ath Party, he ruled Syria until his death in 2000.

toppled the monarchy, with the real power residing with one of the coup plotters: Gamal Abdel Nasser. King Farouk, descendant of the Albanian Mohammed Ali, departed from Alexandria harbour on the royal yacht, and Colonel Nasser – the first Egyptian to rule Egypt since the pharaohs – became president in elections held in 1956. His aim of returning some of Egypt's wealth to its much-exploited peasantry struck a chord with Egypt's masses. He became an instant hero across the Arab world.

Nasser's iconic status reached new heights in the year of his inauguration, when he successfully faced down Britain and France in a confrontation over the Suez Canal, which was mostly owned by British and French investors. On 26 July, the fourth anniversary of King Farouk's departure, Nasser announced that he had nationalised the Suez Canal to finance the building of a great dam that would control the flooding of the Nile and boost Egyptian agriculture. A combined British, French and Israeli invasion force, which intended to take possession of the canal, was, to great diplomatic embarrassment, forced to make an undignified retreat after the UN and US applied pressure. Nasser emerged from the conflict the most popular Arab leader in history.

Israel was the last country in the region to achieve independence, following in the wake of Egypt (1922), Iraq (1932), Lebanon (1941), Jordan and Syria (both 1946); Iran was never ruled by a colonial power in the modern era.

Attempts at Unity

Such was Nasser's popularity that the Syrians joined Egypt in what would prove to be an ultimately unworkable union, the United Arab Republic, in 1958. At the time, it seemed as if Nasser's dream of pan-Arab unity was one step closer to reality. But behind the staged photo opportunities in which the region's presidents and monarchs lined up to bask in Nasser's reflected glory, the region was as divided as ever. With the United Arab Republic at Jordan's borders to the north and south, King Hussein feared for his own position and tried a federation of his own with his Hashemite cousins in Iraq; it lasted less than a year before the Iraqi Hashemite monarchy was overthrown, and British troops were sent in to Jordan to protect Hussein. Egypt and Syria went their separate ways in 1961.

Meanwhile, Lebanon was taking an entirely different course, exposing the fault lines that would later tear the country apart. The Western-oriented Maronite Christian government that held sway in Beirut had been, in 1956, the only Arab government to support the US and UK during the Suez Canal crisis, a deeply unpopular decision among Lebanon's Muslim community.

And yet, for all the division and gathering storm clouds, there was a palpable sense of hope across the Arab world. Driven by Nasser's 'victory' over the European powers in the 1956 Suez crisis, there was a growing belief that the Arab world's time was now. While this manifested itself in the hope that the region had acquired the means and self-belief to finally defeat Israel when the time came, it was also to be found on the streets of cities across the region.

A Peace to End All Peace: Creating the Modern Middle East, 1914–1922 by David Fromkin is an intriguing account of how the map of the modern Middle East was drawn arbitrarily by European colonial governments.

1973	1975	1977	1978
Egypt launches a surprise attack on Israel. After initial gains, Israel recovers to seize yet more territory. Despite the defeat, the war is hailed as a victory in the Arab world.	After years of tension, war breaks out in Lebanon between Palestinians and Christian militias. The fighting, which draws in other militant groups, will last until 1990.	Egyptian president Anwar Sadat's landmark visit to Jerusalem reverberates around the region. Egypt is expelled from the Arab League and Sadat is hailed around the world.	Anwar Sadat and Israel's Menachem Begin sign the Camp David peace treaty. Egypt gets Sinai and recognises Israel's right to exist.

Rise of the PLO

All too often, the Arab-Israeli conflict, as with so many other events in the Middle East, has been explained away as a religious war between Jews and Muslims. There has at times indeed been a religious dimension, especially in recent years with the rise of Hamas in the Palestinian Territories and the religious right in Israel. But this has always been fundamentally a conflict over land, as was shown in the years following Israel's independence. Governments – from the Ba'ath parties of Syria and Iraq to Nasser's Egypt – invariably framed their demands in purely secular terms.

This again became clear after the formation in 1964 of the Palestine Liberation Organisation (PLO). Although opposed by Jordan, which was itself keen to carry the banner of Palestinian leadership, the PLO enjoyed the support of the newly formed Arab League. The Palestine National Council (PNC) was established within the PLO as its executive body – the closest thing to a Palestinian government in exile. The PLO served as an umbrella organisation for an extraordinary roll call of groups that ranged from purely military wings to communist ideologues. Militant Islamic factions were, at the time, small and drew only limited support.

Just as the PLO was at risk of dissolving into an acrimony born from its singular lack of a united policy, an organisation called the Palestine National Liberation Movement (also known as Al-Fatah) was established. One of the stated aims of both the PLO and Al-Fatah was to train guerrillas for raids on Israel. Al-Fatah emerged as the dominant force within the PLO, and its leader, Yasser Arafat, would become chair of the executive committee of the PLO in 1969 and, later, the PLO's most recognisable face.

At the same time, Islam as a political force *was* starting to stir. Nasser may have been all-powerful, but there was a small group of clerics who saw him, Egyptian or not, as the latest in a long line of godless leaders ruling the country. Sayyid Qutb, an Egyptian radical and intellectual, was the most influential, espousing a return to the purity of grassroots Islam. He also prompted the creation of the Muslim Brotherhood, who would withdraw from society and prepare for violence and martyrdom in pursuit of a universal Muslim society. Qutb was executed by Nasser in 1966, but the genie could not be put back in the bottle, returning to haunt the region, and the rest of the world, decades later.

When Zionist and British policy makers were looking for a homeland for the Jewish people, sites they considered included Uganda, northeastern Australia and the Jebel Akhdar in the Cyrenaica region of Libya.

Arab-Israeli Wars

1967 War

With the Arab world growing in confidence, war seemed inevitable. In May 1967, the Egyptian army moved into key points in Sinai and announced a blockade of the Straits of Tiran, effectively closing the southern Israeli port of Eilat. The Egyptian army was mobilised and the country put on a

1979	1980	1981	1982
After brutal repression of opposition protests, the Shah of Iran, Reza Pahlavi, leaves Iran. The Islamic Revolution brings Āyatollāh Ruhollāh Khomeini to power.	Counting on a weakened Iran in the wake of the Islamic Revolution, Saddam Hussein launches a surprise attack on Iran. The war, in which millions died and neither country gained any territory, would last until 1988.	Anwar Sadat is assassinated in Cairo during a military parade, by a member of his armed forces (and also a secret member of an Islamist group) as the parade passes the presidential box.	Israel invades Lebanon. In September, Israeli forces surround the Palestinian refugee camps, Sabra and Shatila, while Phalangists massacre thousands. Israel withdraws in 1983.

war footing. On 5 June, Israel responded with a devastating pre-emptive strike that wiped out virtually the entire Egyptian air force in a single day. The war lasted only six days (hence the 'Six Day War'), and when it was over, Israel controlled the Sinai Peninsula, the Gaza Strip, the West Bank (including Jerusalem's Old City) and the Golan Heights.

After more than a decade of swaggering between Cairo and Damascus, and empty promises to the Palestinians that they would soon be returning home, the Six Day War was viewed as an unmitigated disaster throughout the Arab world and sent shockwaves across the region. Not only were leaders like Nasser no match for the Israelis, despite the posturing, but also tens of thousands more Palestinian refugees were now in exile. The mood across the region was grim. A humiliated Nasser offered to resign, but in a spontaneous outpouring of support, the Egyptian people wouldn't accept the move and he remained in office. In November 1970 the president died of a heart attack, reportedly a broken man.

1973 War

With Palestinian militancy on the rise, the year 1970 saw the ascension of new leaders in both Egypt (Anwar Sadat) and Syria (Hafez al-Assad). Preparations were also well under way for the next Middle Eastern war, with these radical new leaders under constant pressure from their citizens to reclaim the land lost in 1967. On 6 October 1973, Egyptian troops crossed the Suez Canal, taking Israel (at a standstill, observing the holy day of Yom Kippur) almost entirely by surprise. After advancing a short distance into Sinai, however, the Egyptian army stopped, giving Israel the opportunity to concentrate its forces against the Syrians on the Golan Heights and then turn back towards Egypt. Although the war preserved the military status quo, it was widely portrayed throughout the region as an Arab victory.

When the war ended in late 1973, months of shuttle diplomacy by the US secretary of state, Henry Kissinger, followed. Pressure on the USA to broker a deal was fuelled when the Gulf States embargoed oil supplies to the West 10 days after the war began. The embargo's implications were massive, achieving nothing less than a shift in the balance of power in the Middle East. The oil states, rich but underpopulated and militarily weak, gained at the expense of poorer, more populous countries. Huge shifts of population followed the two oil booms of the 1970s, as millions of Egyptians, Syrians, Jordanians, Palestinians and Yemenis went off to seek their fortunes in the oil states.

Peace & Revolution

By the mid 1970s, the Middle East had reached a temporary stalemate. On one side, Israel knew that it had the wherewithal to hold off the armed forces of its neighbours. But Israel also lived in a state of siege and on

A Modern History of the Kurds by David McDowall has been updated to 2004 (although the body of the work finishes in 1996), and it remains an excellent primer on the social and political history of the Kurds, focusing on Turkey and Iraq.

HISTORY PEACE & REVOLUTION

1983	1984	1987	1988
Turkey returns to democratic rule after a succession of coups. The new constitution that forbids prior political participation suggests that the Turkish military remains the real power in the country.	Abdullah Öcalan forms the Kurdistan Workers Party (PKK) and launches a brutal insurgency that paralyses Turkey's southeast. The 'war' lasts until Öcalan is captured in 1999.	A grassroots uprising known as the intifada breaks out in the Palestinian Territories. Although the PLO later tries to claim credit, the intifada is a spontaneous national rebellion.	Egypt's Naguib Mahfouz becomes the first Arab to win the Nobel Prize for Literature. His win is the cause of great national pride.

maximum alert, all the time facing escalating attacks at home and abroad on its citizens from Palestinian terrorist groups aligned to the PLO. On the other side, Arab governments continued with their rhetoric but knew, although none admitted it, that Israel was here to stay. To the north, Lebanon was sliding into a civil war that was threatening to engulf the region.

Camp David

On 7 November 1977, Egyptian president Anwar Sadat made a dramatic visit to Israel to address the Israeli Knesset with a call for peace. The Arab world was in shock. That the leader of the Arab world's most populous nation, a nation that had produced Gamal Abdel Nasser, could visit Israeli-occupied Jerusalem had hitherto been inconceivable. The shock turned to anger the following year when Sadat and the hardline Israeli prime minister, Menachem Begin, shepherded by US president Jimmy Carter, signed the Camp David Agreement. In return for Egypt's long-coveted recognition of Israel's right to exist, Egypt received back the Sinai Peninsula. Egypt did rather well out of the deal, but was widely accused of breaking ranks and betrayal for one simple reason: the Palestinians received nothing. Arab leaders meeting in Baghdad voted to expel Egypt from the Arab League and moved the group's headquarters out of Cairo in protest. The peace treaty won Sadat (and Begin) a Nobel Peace Prize, but it would ultimately cost the Egyptian leader his life: he was assassinated in Cairo on 6 October 1981.

Although the 1973 war is painted as a victory and re-assertion of Arab pride by many historians, by the time it ended, the Israelis actually occupied more land than when it began.

Iran's Islamic Revolution

Before his death, and with Sadat basking in the acclaim of the international community, one of the few friends he had left in the region was facing troubles of his own. Discontent with the Shah of Iran's autocratic rule and his personal disregard for the country's Shiite Muslim religious traditions had been simmering for years. Political violence slowly increased throughout 1978. The turning point came in September of that year, when Iranian police fired on anti-shah demonstrators in Tehran, killing at least 300. The momentum of the protests quickly became unstoppable.

On 16 January 1979, the shah left Iran, never to return (he died in Egypt a year later). The interim government set up after his departure was swept aside the following month when the revolution's leader, the hitherto obscure Āyatollāh Ruhollāh Khomeini, returned to Tehran from his exile in France and was greeted by adoring millions. His fiery brew of nationalism and Muslim fundamentalism had been at the forefront of the revolt, and Khomeini achieved his goal of establishing a clergy-dominated Islamic Republic (the first true Islamic state in modern times) with brutal efficiency. Opposition disappeared, executions took place after meaningless trials and minor officials took the law into their own hands.

1990	1991	1993	1994
Saddam Hussein's Iraq invades Kuwait and remains there until the US-led coalition (operating from its bases in Saudi Arabia) drives him out in early 1991. Saddam turns on Iraqi Shiites and Kurds.	Israel and its Arab neighbours sit down for the first time to discuss a comprehensive peace plan in Madrid. Talks dissolve in recrimination, but the fact that they do so face to face is seen as progress.	After a year and a half of secret negotiations between Israel and the Palestinians, Yasser Arafat and Yitzhak Rabin sign the Oslo Accords setting out a framework for future peace.	Building on the goodwill generated by the Oslo Accords, Jordan under King Hussein becomes the second Arab country (after Egypt in 1979) to sign a peace treaty with Israel.

Bloody Aftermath

For decades, the Middle East's reputation for brutal conflict and Islamic extremism owed much to the late 1970s and early 1980s. It was the worst of times in the Middle East, a seemingly relentless succession of blood-letting by all sides. The religious fervour that surrounded Khomeini's Iran and the images of the masses chanting *'Marg bar amrika!'* ('Death to America!') also marked the moment when militant Islam became a political force and announced to the world that the West was in its sights. While this development applied to only a small proportion of the region's Muslims, the reputation has stuck.

The events that flowed from, or otherwise followed, the Iranian Revolution read like a snapshot of a region sliding out of control. In 1979, militants seized the Grand Mosque in Mecca. They were ejected several weeks later only after bloody gun battles inside the mosque itself, leaving more than 250 people dead inside Islam's holiest shrine. In November of that year, student militants in Tehran overran the US embassy, taking the staff hostage. They would be released only after 444 days in captivity. Away to the north, in 1980, Turkey's government was overthrown in a military coup, capping weeks of violence between left- and right-wing extremists. The same year, Saddam Hussein, supported by the US, invaded Khuzestan in southwestern Iran, on the pretext that the oil-rich province was historically part of Iraq. The resulting war lasted until 1988 and claimed millions of lives as trench warfare and poison gas were used for the first time since WWI.

Covering Islam by Edward Said is a classic, exploring how the Iranian Revolution and Palestinian terrorism changed forever the way we view the Middle East.

Lebanon Falls Apart

In June 1982, Israel marched into Lebanon, joining Syria, the PLO and a host of Lebanese militias in a vicious regional conflict from which no side emerged with clean hands. The PLO had long been using the anarchy at large in Lebanon to set up a state within a state, from where it launched hundreds of rocket attacks across the Israeli-Lebanese frontier. Led by Defence Minister Ariel Sharon, Israel entered the war claiming self-defence. But these claims lost considerable credibility when, weeks after the PLO leadership had already left Beirut for Tunis, Israeli soldiers surrounded the Palestinian refugee camps of Sabra and Shatila in Beirut and stood by as their Phalangist allies went on a killing rampage. Hundreds, possibly thousands, of civilians were killed. Israel withdrew from most of Lebanon in 1983, but continued to occupy what it called a self-declared security zone in southern Lebanon.

The Lebanese Civil War rumbled on until 1990, but even when peace came, Israel controlled the south and Syria's 30,000 troops in Lebanon had become the kingmakers in the fractured Lebanese polity. In the 15 years of war, more than a million Lebanese are believed to have died.

1995	1999	2000	2003
Israeli prime minister Yitzhak Rabin is assassinated by a Jewish extremist who hoped to end the process Rabin had begun with the Oslo Accords. A year later, the right-wing Binyamin Netanyahu is voted into power.	Jordan's King Hussein dies of cancer, having ruled since 1952. He is seen as one of the architects of peace in the region and more than 50 heads of state attend his funeral.	The second Palestinian intifada breaks out in the Palestinian Territories. In Damascus, Hafez al-Assad dies after 30 years in power and his son, Bashar, becomes president.	The US and the UK, with a much smaller coalition and less international support than in 1990–91, invade Iraq, winning the war, but Iraq descends into open rebellion.

Intifada

Down in the Palestinian Territories, violence flared in 1987 in what became known as the 'First Intifada' (the grassroots Palestinian uprising). Weary of ineffectual Palestinian politicians having achieved nothing of value for their people in the four decades since Israeli independence, ordinary Palestinians took matters into their own hands. Campaigns of civil disobedience, general strikes and stone-throwing youths were the hallmarks of the intifada, which ran until 1993.

War & Peace

While all of this was going on, elsewhere in the region there were a few bright spots. Turkey had returned to democratic rule in 1983, albeit with a new constitution barring from public office anyone who had been involved in politics prior to the 1980 coup. In 1988, Iran and Iraq grudgingly agreed to a ceasefire. A year later, Egypt was quietly readmitted to the Arab League and Jordan held its first elections in more than 20 years. But these important landmarks were overshadowed by events in Lebanon, which had led many people to wonder whether the region would ever be at peace.

Arafat by the Palestinian writer Said K Aburish is a highly critical look at one of the Middle East's most intriguing yet flawed personalities. *Arafat: The Biography* by Tony Walker and Andrew Gowers is also good.

Iraq, Kuwait & the West

Just as the region was breathing a collective sigh of relief at the end of the Lebanese Civil War and the cessation of hostilities between Iraq and Iran, Iraq invaded Kuwait in August 1990. The 1990s were, it seemed, destined to repeat the cycle of violence that had so scarred the previous decade.

Fearful that Iraqi president Saddam Hussein had Saudi Arabia in his sights, King Fahd requested help from the USA. The result was a US-led coalition whose air and ground offensive drove Iraq out of Kuwait. In the process, Saddam Hussein (previously supported by the West in his war against Iran) became world public enemy number one. When the US-led coalition stopped short of marching on Baghdad, the Iraqi leader used his reprieve to attack the country's Shiite population in the south and the Kurds in the north with levels of brutality remarkable even by his standards. Not willing to wait around for Saddam's response to the Kurds' perceived support for the US-led coalition, hundreds of thousands of Kurds streamed across the border into Turkey in one of the largest refugee exoduses in modern history.

There was another, less immediately obvious consequence of the war. The presence of US troops on Saudi soil enraged many in a country known for its strict (some would say puritanical) adherence to Wahhabi Islamic orthodoxy. To have the uniformed soldiers of what many considered to be Islam's enemy operating freely from the same soil as the holy cities of Mecca and Medina was considered an outrage. From this anger, many respected analysts argue, would come Al-Qaeda.

2004	2005	2006	2006
Evidence of the torture of Iraqi prisoners emerges from the US-controlled Abu Ghraib prison in Baghdad. The United States' reputation in the region sinks to an all-time low.	Yasser Arafat, chairman of the PLO and leader of the Palestinian Authority, dies in Paris and is later buried in Ramallah, ending four eventful decades at the frontline of Middle Eastern politics.	After Hezbollah captures two Israeli soldiers, Israel launches a sustained air attack on Lebanon. The resulting war produces a stalemate and is widely portrayed throughout the region as a victory for Hezbollah.	The height of the insurgency against the US military and administrative presence in Iraq. According to the UN, more than 100 civilians die every day, with suicide bombings a near-daily occurrence.

Israeli-Palestinian Peace?

From the ashes of war came an unlikely movement towards peace. While attempting to solicit Arab support for the anti-Iraq coalition, then-US president George Bush promised to make Arab-Israeli peace a priority once the Iraqis were out of Kuwait. Endless shuttling between Middle Eastern capitals culminated in a US-sponsored peace conference in Madrid in October 1991. It achieved little, but by late summer 1993 it was revealed that Israel and the Palestinians had been holding secret talks in Norway for 18 months. The 'Oslo Accords' were cemented with one of the most famous handshakes in history, between Yasser Arafat and Israeli prime minister Yitzhak Rabin on the White House lawn in September 1993.

An unprecedented era of hope for peace in the Middle East seemed on the horizon. Lebanon had just held its first democratic elections for 20 years and the mutually destructive fighting seemed well and truly at an end. In 1994, Jordan became the second Arab country to sign a formal peace treaty with Israel.

But, sadly, it was not to last. The peace process was derailed by the November 1995 assassination of Rabin and the subsequent election of hardline candidate Binyamin Netanyahu. A blip of hope re-emerged when Netanyahu lost office to Ehud Barak, a prime minister who pulled his troops out of occupied south Lebanon and promised to open negotiations with the Syrians and the Palestinians. But critical momentum had been lost. When these talks came to nothing at two high-stakes summits at Camp David and in the Egyptian resort of Sharm el-Sheikh during the last months of the Clinton presidency, everyone knew that an opportunity had been lost.

In September 2000, after Ariel Sharon, by then the leader of the right-wing Likud Party, visited the Al-Aqsa Mosque in Jerusalem, riots broke out among Palestinians. This was the trigger, if not the ultimate cause, for the second Palestinian intifada that has continued in one form or another in the years since. The election of that same Ariel Sharon – a politician as reviled by Palestinians as Yasser Arafat was by Israelis – as Israeli prime minister in 2001 was another nail in the coffin of the already much-buried peace process. Although the death of Yasser Arafat in November 2004 offered some signs for hope, the violent occupation of Palestinian land and bloody suicide bombings targeting Israeli citizens continued. By then, the hope that had spread like a wave across the Middle East in the early 1990s had come to seem like a distant memory.

Prelude to the Arab Spring

Some things don't change in the Middle East. Israel and the Palestinians still trade accusations of bad faith and no solution has been found to the Arab-Israeli conflict. Hundreds of thousands of Palestinian refugees

Pity the Nation: Lebanon at War by Robert Fisk ranges far beyond Lebanon's borders and is a classic account of the issues that resonate throughout the region. Fisk's polemical style has made him a controversial figure, especially among right-wing Israelis.

HISTORY PRELUDE TO THE ARAB SPRING

2008	2010	2011	2011
Civil war threatens again in Lebanon after Hezbollah besieges the government. Syria admits to indirect talks with Israel through Turkish mediators.	A young Tunisian man sets himself ablaze in the town of Sidi Bouzid, the trigger for a popular uprising that would lead to the demise of leaders in Tunisia, Libya and Egypt.	Hosni Mubarak is driven from power after having ruled Egypt since succeeding Anwar Sadat in 1981. He is later put on trial, while Egyptians attempt to build a democracy from scratch.	Syria descends into civil war, a popular and largely peaceful uprising giving way to an armed insurrection in which army defectors battle government loyalists with civilians caught in between.

WHO ARE THE KURDS?

The Kurds, the descendants of the Medes who ruled an empire over much of the Middle East in 600 BC from what is now northwestern Iran, are the Middle East's largest minority group. Kurds (who are predominantly Sunni Muslims) constitute significant minorities in Turkey (18% of the population), Iraq (15% to 20%), Iran (10%) and Syria (7% to 8%). The Kurdish homeland is a largely contiguous area split between southeastern Turkey, northeastern Syria, northern Iraq and northwestern Iran.

Turkey

Turkey's sparsely populated eastern and southeastern regions are home to perhaps seven million Kurds, while seven million more live elsewhere in the country, more or less integrated into mainstream Turkish society. Relations between Turks and Kurds soured after the formation of the republic, in which Atatürk's reforms left little room for anything other than Turkishness. Until relatively recently the Turkish government refused to even recognise the existence of the Kurds, insisting they be called 'Mountain Turks'.

Since 1984, when Abdullah Öcalan formed the Kurdistan Workers Party (PKK), a separatist conflict raged in Turkey's Kurdish areas, prompting Turkey's government to declare a permanent state of emergency. After 15 years and the deaths of some 30,000 people, Öcalan was captured in 1999. The insurgency died out.

In 2002, the Turkish government finally gave some ground on the issue of Kurdish rights, approving broadcasts in Kurdish and giving the go-ahead for Kurdish to be taught in language schools. Emergency rule was lifted in the southeast. Life for Kurds in the southeast has since become considerably easier, although worrying but low-level fighting has recently resumed.

Iraq

Iraq is home to over four million Kurds, who live in the northern provinces of the country. The 1961 Kurdish campaign to secure independence from Iraq laid the foundations for an uneasy relationship between the Kurds and the Iraqi state. After the 1991 Gulf War, when an estimated two million Kurds fled across the mountains to Turkey and Iran, the Kurdish Autonomous Region was set up in northern Iraq under UN protection and Kurdish Iraq became a model for a future federal Iraqi system.

After the fall of Saddam, the Kurds won 17% of the vote in the 2005 elections and Kurdish leaders restated their commitment to a federal but unified Iraq.

Iran

An estimated five million Kurds live in Iran, particularly in the country's northwest which borders Kurdish areas across the borders in Turkey and Iraq. A low-level insurgency against the Islamic Republic by militant Kurdish groups has simmered since the 1979 revolution.

2011	2012	2012	2013
More than eight years after the US-led invasion of Iraq, the last US troops leave the country. Iraqi security forces are now responsible for security and the government is by elected parliament.	The impact of the fighting in Syria ripples across the region with large numbers of Syrian refugees in neighbouring countries, and Turkey accusing Syria of following rebels across the border.	The Muslim Brotherhood emerges from Egypt's first democratic parliamentary elections with 235 of the 508 seats. The biggest surprise is the 121 seats won by the extreme Islamist Salafi party, Nour.	The Brotherhood's Mohammed Morsi is overthrown after only a year as Egyptian president following mass demonstrations across the country.

(including second- and third-generation exiles) languish in refugee camps, many still holding on to the keys of homes they left in 1948 or 1967. And wars great and small continue to flare around the region.

Iraq War

In 2003, US and UK forces, with support from a small band of allies, invaded Iraq. Their military victory was swift, driving Saddam Hussein from power, but the aftermath has proved to be infinitely more complicated. With large communities of Shiites, Kurds and the hitherto all-powerful Sunnis vying for power, the country descended into a sectarian conflict with strong echoes of Lebanon's civil war. Hundreds of thousands, perhaps millions of Iraqis fled the fighting, placing huge pressure on the resources of neighbouring countries. Iraqis have paid a terrible price for their freedom.

Seeds of Change

In 2006, Israel and Hezbollah fought a bitter month-long war that shattered the Lebanese peace, while fighting broke out between Hezbollah and the Lebanese government in 2008. The power of Hezbollah, and the shifting of Palestinian power from Al-Fatah to Hamas in the Palestinian Territories, has confirmed a process that had begun with the PLO in the 1960s: the rise of nonstate actors as powerful players in the Middle East.

Governments of Arab countries have singularly failed to meet the aspirations of their people, from bringing about a lasting peace between Israel and the Palestinians to providing the basic services necessary to lift them out of poverty. Little wonder, then, that many Middle Easterners have turned to organisations such as Hezbollah and Hamas who, in the eyes of many Arabs, have matched their words with actions. Both groups have built up extensive networks of social safety nets and, with limited success, taken on Israel on the battlefield. That these groups are avowedly Islamic in focus and enjoy the support of arch-enemy Iran has only served to widen the gulf between Israel (and the US) and its neighbours.

By 2010, the region had reached something of an impasse with the issues of the past 60 years frozen into seemingly perpetual division that sometimes spilled over into open warfare, but more often festered like an open wound. The Palestinians still dream of returning home. The Israelis still dream of a world free from fear. In the meantime, the two sides came no closer to a resolution. These are real issues that make life a daily struggle for ordinary people and the sad fact remains that, for many Middle Easterners, life is no easier than it was 60 years ago. If a scrap of consolation can be found amid the ashes of failed peace processes, it is that such a time frame is the mere blink of an historical eye for this part of the world.

Of the almost 11 million Palestinians, only five million live in Israel (1.3 million) or the Palestinian Territories (3.7 million). Palestinians comprise around 60% of Jordan's population, with around 400,000 in each of Lebanon and Syria.

In 1997, Israeli agents poisoned Hamas activist Khaled Meshaal in Amman. Jordan's King Hussein insisted Israel hand over the antidote. Meshaal, who lives in Syria, later became leader of Hamas. For more on this strange episode, read *Kill Khalid: The Failed Mossad Assassination of Khalid Mishal and the Rise of Hamas* by Paul Mcgeough.

HISTORY PRELUDE TO THE ARAB SPRING

2013	2014	2014	2014
Isis emerges as the most powerful and brutal of the radical Islamist military forces, and declares a caliphate in the areas of northern Iraq and Syria under its control.	Field Marshal Abdel Fatah al-Sisi is sworn in as Egypt's president after a landslide victory in an election where less than half of the electorate turned out to vote.	Egypt jails three Al-Jazeera journalists prompting an international outcry. At the same time, the Egyptian army fights Islamic militants in the Sinai Peninsula.	By the end of the year, close to 200,000 people have been killed in Syria's ongoing conflict with no end in sight to the bloodletting.

Religion

The Middle East is where it all began for the three big monotheistic world religions: Judaism, Christianity and Islam. Infusing almost every aspect of daily life in the region, from the five-times-daily call to prayer and cultural norms to architecture and disputes over historical claims to land, these three religions provide an important backstory to your travels in the Middle East.

Islam: A Short History by Karen Armstrong is almost like Islam 101, a readable journey through Islam's birth and subsequent growth with easy-to-follow coverage of the schism between Sunnis and Shiites.

Islam

Birth of Islam

Abdul Qasim Mohammed ibn Abdullah ibn Abd al-Muttalib ibn Hashim (the Prophet Mohammed) was born in 570 AD. Mohammed's family belonged to the Quraysh tribe, a trading family with links to Syria and Yemen. By the age of six, Mohammed's parents had both died and he came into the care of his grandfather, the custodian of the Kaaba in Mecca.

At the age of 40, in 610, Mohammed retreated into the desert and Muslims believe that he began to receive divine revelations from Allah via the voice of the archangel Gabriel; the revelations would continue throughout Mohammed's life. Three years later, Mohammed began imparting Allah's message to Meccans, gathering a significant following in his campaign against idolaters. His movement appealed especially to the poorer, disenfranchised sections of society.

Islam provided a simpler alternative to the established faiths, which had become complicated by hierarchical orders, sects and complex rituals, offering instead a direct relationship with God based only on the believer's submission to God (Islam means 'submission').

By 622, Mecca's powerful ruling families had forced Mohammed and his followers to flee north to Medina where Mohammed's supporters rapidly grew. In 630 Mohammed returned triumphantly to Mecca at the head of a 10,000-strong army to seize control of the city. Many of the surrounding tribes quickly swore allegiance to him and the new faith.

When Mohammed died in 632, the Arab tribes spread quickly across the Middle East, in very little time conquering what now constitutes Jordan, Syria, Iraq, Lebanon and Israel and the Palestinian Territories. To the east, Persia and India soon found themselves confronted by the

SHARED TRADITIONS

As most Muslims will attest, the God invoked in Friday prayers across the Middle East is the same God worshipped in synagogues and churches around the globe. The Quran never attempts to deny the debt it owes to the holy books that came before it. Indeed the Quran itself was revealed to Mohammed by the archangel Gabriel. The suras contain many references to the earlier prophets – Adam, Abraham (Ibrahim), Noah, Moses (Moussa) and Jesus (although Muslims strictly deny his divinity) are all recognised as prophets in a line that ends definitively with the greatest of them all, Mohammed. Not surprisingly, given the shared heritage, Muslims traditionally attribute a place of great respect to Christians and Jews as *ahl al-kitab* (the people of the book; sura 2:100-15).

> **RELIGIONS IN THE MIDDLE EAST**
> ....
> Jews make up around 80% of Israel's and around 15% of the Palestinian Territories' pop-
> ulations. Christians make up less than 10% of most Middle Eastern populations, except in
> Lebanon, where 39% of the population is Christian.

new army of believers. To the west, the unrelenting conquest swept
across North Africa. By the end of the 7th century, the Muslim armies
had reached the Atlantic and marched on Spain in 710, an astonishing
achievement given the religion's humble desert roots.

Shiite & Sunni

Despite the Prophet Mohammed's original intentions, Islam did not remain simple. The Prophet died leaving no sons and no instructions as to
who should succeed him. Competing for power were Abu Bakr, the father
of Mohammed's second wife Aisha, and Ali, Mohammed's cousin and the
husband of his daughter Fatima. Initially, power was transferred to Abu
Bakr, who became the first caliph, or ruler, with Ali reluctantly agreeing.

Abu Bakr's lineage came to an abrupt halt when his successor was
murdered. Ali reasserted his right to power and emerged victorious in
the ensuing power struggle, moving his capital to Kufa (later renamed
Najaf, in Iraq), only to be assassinated himself in 661. After defeating Ali's
successor, Hussein, in 680 at Karbala, the Umayyad dynasty rose to rule
the majority of the Muslim world, marking the start of the Sunni sect.
Those who continued to support the claims of the descendants of Ali
became known as Shiites.

Beyond this early dynastic rivalry, there's little doctrinal difference
between Shiite Islam and Sunni Islam, but the division remains to this
day. Sunnis comprise some 90% of the world's Muslims, but Shiites are
believed to form a majority of the population in Iraq, Lebanon and Iran.
There are also Shiite minorities in almost all Arab countries.

The Quran

For Muslims the Quran is the word of God, directly communicated to
Mohammed. It comprises 114 suras, or chapters, which govern all aspects
of a Muslim's life.

It's not known whether the revelations were written down during Mohammed's lifetime, although Muslims believe the Quran to be the direct
word of Allah as told to Mohammed. The third caliph, Uthman (644–56),
gathered together everything written by the scribes (parchments, stone
tablets, the memories of Mohammed's followers) and gave them to a pan-
el of editors under the caliph's aegis. A Quran printed today is identical to
that agreed upon by Uthman's compilers 14 centuries ago.

Another important aspect of the Quran is the language in which it
is written. Some Muslims believe that the Quran must be studied in its
original classical Arabic form ('an Arabic Quran, wherein there is no
crookedness'; sura 39:25) and that translations dilute the holiness of its
sacred texts. For Muslims, the language of the Quran is known as *sihr
halal* (lawful magic).

Five Pillars of Islam

In order to live a devout life, Muslims are expected to observe, as a minimum, the five pillars of Islam.

Shahada This is the profession of faith, Islam's basic tenet: 'There is no god but
Allah, and Mohammed is the Prophet of Allah'. This phrase forms an integral part of
the call to prayer and is used at all important events in a Muslim's life.

*The Story of
the Qur'an: Its
History and Place
in Muslim Life* by
Ingrid Mattson is
a landmark 2007
text that's filled
with insights into
what it means to
be a Muslim in
the 21st century.

MUSLIM PRAYER

Allahu akbar, Allahu akbar	God is great, God is great
Ashhadu an la Ilah ila Allah	I testify that there is no God but Allah
Ashhadu an Mohammed rasul Allah	I testify that Mohammed is his Prophet
Haya ala as-sala	Hurry towards prayer
Haya ala af-fala	Hurry towards success
Allahu akbar, Allahu akbar	God is great, God is great
La Ilah ila Allah	There is no God but Allah

Sala (sura 11:115) This is the obligation of prayer, ideally five times a day: at sunrise, noon, mid-afternoon, sunset and night. It's acceptable to pray at home or elsewhere, except for Friday noon prayers, which are performed at a mosque.

Zakat (sura 107) Muslims must give alms to the poor to the value of one-fortieth of a believer's annual income.

Sawm (sura 2:180-5) Ramadan, the ninth month of the Muslim calendar, commemorates the revelation of the Quran to Mohammed. As Ramadan represents a Muslim's renewal of faith, nothing may pass their lips (food, cigarettes, drinks) and they must refrain from sex from dawn until dusk.

Hajj (sura 2:190-200) Every physically and financially able Muslim should perform the hajj (pilgrimage) to the holiest of cities, Mecca, at least once in their lifetime. The reward is considerable: the forgiving of all past sins.

Call to Prayer

Five times a day, Muslims are called, if not actually to enter a mosque to pray, at least to take the time to do so where they are; the call to prayer is made by the muezzin. The midday prayers on Friday, when the imam of the mosque delivers his weekly khutba, or sermon, are considered the most important. For Muslims, prayer is less a petition to Allah (in the Christian sense) than a ritual reaffirmation of Allah's power and a reassertion of the brotherhood and equality of all believers.

The act of praying consists of a series of predefined movements of the body and recitals of prayers and passages of the Quran, all designed to express the believer's absolute humility and Allah's sovereignty.

> The flight of Mohammed and his followers from Mecca to Medina (the Hejira) marks the birth of Islam and the first year of the Islamic calendar – 1 AH (AD 622).

Islamic Customs

In everyday life, Muslims are prohibited from drinking alcohol (sura 5:90-5) and eating carrion, blood products or pork, which are considered unclean (sura 2:165), the meat of animals not killed in the prescribed manner (sura 5:1-5) and food over which the name of Allah has not been said (sura 6:115). Adultery (sura 18:30-5), theft (sura 5:40-5) and gambling (sura 5:90-5) are also prohibited.

Islam is not just about prohibitions but also marks the important events of a Muslim's life. When a baby is born, the first words uttered to it are the call to prayer. A week later follows a ceremony in which the baby's head is shaved and an animal sacrificed in remembrance of Abraham's willingness to sacrifice his son to Allah. The major event of a boy's childhood is circumcision, which normally takes place between the ages of seven and 12. When a person dies, a burial service is held at the mosque and the body is buried with the feet facing Mecca.

Judaism

Judaism is the first recorded monotheistic faith and one of the oldest religions still practised. Its major tenet is that there is one God who created the universe and remains omnipresent. Judaism's power is held not in a central authority or person, but rather in its teachings and the Holy Scriptures.

Until the foundation of the State of Israel in 1948, Jewish communities lived peacefully alongside their Muslim neighbours in the countries of the Middle East; Iraq was home to a particularly large Jewish community. Tiny Jewish communities may remain in some Muslim countries, but most fled or were expelled in the years following 1948.

Foundations of Judaism

The patriarch of the Jewish faith was Abraham who, according to the calculations of the Hebrew Torah, was born 1948 years after Creation and lived to the ripe old age of 175. According to Jewish belief he preached the existence of one God and in return God promised him the land of Canaan (the Promised Land in Jewish tradition), but only after his descendants would be exiled and redeemed. Accordingly, his grandson Jacob set off for Egypt, where later generations found themselves bound in slavery. Moses led them out of Egypt and received the Ten Commandments on Mt Sinai.

It was Rambam, the 12th-century Jewish rabbi, who laid out the 13 core principles of Jewish belief. These principles include the belief in one unique God to whom prayer must be directed; the belief that God rewards the good and punishes the wicked; and the belief in the coming of the Messiah and the resurrection of the dead. Having said this, Judaism doesn't focus on abstract cosmological beliefs and rather than a strict adherence to dogmatic ideas, actions such as prayer, study and performing mitzvah, which means adherence to the commandments, are of greater importance.

The Torah & Talmud

The basis for the Jewish religion is the Torah, the first five books of the Old Testament. The Torah contains the revelation from God via Moses more than 3000 years ago, including, most importantly, God's commandments (613 commandments in total). The Torah is supplemented by the rest of the books of the Old Testament, of which the most important are the prophetic books.

These books are, in turn, complemented by the Talmud, a collection of another 63 books. The Talmud was written largely in exile after the Romans crushed the Jewish state and destroyed the Temple in Jerusalem in AD 70, and within its pages is most of what separates Judaism from other religions. Included are plenty of rabbinical interpretations of the earlier scriptures, with a wealth of instructions and rulings for Jewish daily life.

Jewish Customs

The most obvious Jewish custom you'll experience in Israel is Shabbat, the day of rest. It begins on Friday night with sundown and ends at nightfall on Saturday. No work of any kind is allowed on Shabbat, unless someone's health is at stake. Tasks such as writing or handling money are forbidden. Starting a fire is also prohibited and in modern terms this means no use of electricity is allowed (lights can be turned on before Shabbat starts but must stay on until it ends). Permitted activities include visiting with friends and family, reading and discussing the Torah, and prayer at a synagogue. Sex is also allowed; in fact, it's a double mitzvah on Shabbat.

God's laws, as recorded in the Torah, govern every facet of an observant Jew's life, including issues like the prohibition of theft, murder and idolatry. There are other commandments to which Jews must adhere,

A Brief Guide to Judaism: Theology, History and Practice by Naftali Brawer is one of the better introductions to what is often a complex faith, focusing on major ideas and historical events rather than the minutiae of Jewish doctrine.

RELIGION JUDAISM

Reeva Simon's *The Jews of the Middle East and North Africa in Modern Times* looks at the Jewish presence in the region during the last two centuries, with half of the book taken up with country-by-country sections that include Turkey, Syria, Iraq, Lebanon, Egypt and Israel and the Palestinian Territories.

such as eating kosher foods and reciting the shema (affirmation of Judaism) twice daily.

Some Jewish sects are easily recognised by their clothing, although most Jews wear Western street clothes. The most religious Jews, the Hasidim (or *haredim*), are identified by their black hats, long black coats, collared white shirts, beards and *peyot* (side curls). *Haredi* women, like Muslim women, act and dress modestly, covering up exposed hair and skin (except the hands and face). Many Jews, both secular and orthodox, wear a kippa (skullcap).

Christianity is the world's largest religion, with an estimated 2.2 billion followers. Islam comes next with at least 1.6 billion adherents. Judaism has an estimated 14 to 18 million followers.

Christianity

Jesus preached in what is present-day Israel and the Palestinian Territories, but Christians form only minority groups in all Middle Eastern countries. Lebanon's one million Maronites have followers all over the world, but by far the biggest Christian sect in the region is formed by the Copts of Egypt, who make up most of that country's Christian population. Originally it was the apostle Mark who established Christianity in Egypt, and by the 4th century it was the state religion. The Coptic Church split from the Byzantine Orthodox Church in the 5th century after a dispute about the human nature of Jesus.

Otherwise, the Arab Christians of the Middle East belong to many churches in all main branches of the religion – Orthodox, Catholic and Protestant. The number of Christians in the Middle East is, however, in decline thanks largely to falling birth rates and high rates of emigration among the region's Christians.

Foundations of Christianity

From the Holy Mountain: A Journey in the Shadow of Byzantium by William Dalrymple takes the reader through the heart of the Middle East and pays homage to the survival of Eastern Christianity.

Jesus of Nazareth was born in Bethlehem in what is now the Palestinian Territories in the year zero (or AD 1, depending on who you believe) of the Christian calendar. After baptism by John the Baptist, Jesus was said to have been led by God into the desert, where he remained for 40 days and nights, during which time he refuted the temptations of the Devil. Christians believe that his ministry was marked by numerous miracles, such as healings, walking on water and the resuscitation of the dead (Lazarus). At the age of 33, Jesus was accused of sedition and condemned to death by Jerusalem's Roman governor Pontius Pilate. After being crucified, Christians believe, Jesus was resurrected and ascended to heaven. Christians believe that God's divine nature is expressed in the Trinity: God, Jesus Christ and the Holy Spirit.

The followers of Jesus came to be known as Christians (Christ is a Greek-derived title meaning 'Anointed One'), believing him to be the son of God and the Messiah. Within a few decades of Jesus' death, having interpreted and spread his teachings, his followers had formed a faith distinct from Judaism. A Greek-speaking Christian community emerged in Jerusalem in the mid-2nd century and the Greek Orthodox Church is now the largest denomination in Israel and the Palestinian Territories.

Architecture

Middle Eastern architecture ranges from the sublime to the downright ugly. On one hand, the graceful lines and elaborate tilework of Islamic architecture draw on the rich historical legacy left by the great empires that once ruled the region. On the other, the perennially unfinished cinder-block architecture of grim functionality blights many city outskirts and smaller towns. We prefer to concentrate on the former.

Ancient World

Ancient Egyptian Architecture

The tombs and temples of ancient Egypt rank among the Middle East's most impressive architectural forms. Whereas private homes have disappeared – most were built of sun-dried mud-brick and occurred along now-flooded stretches of the Nile Valley – ancient Egypt's public architecture has stood the test of time, in part because most structures were built on higher ground than the residential areas. In most cases, Pharaonic tombs and temples (including the Pyramids of Giza) were built of locally quarried sandstone and sturdy granite.

The tombs of ancient Egypt were designed at once to impress with their grandeur and to deter tomb raiders from plundering the treasures contained within. As a result, most were almost fortress-like, with thick sloping walls, very few openings and labyrinthine passageways in the interior. Tomb decoration was often elaborate, adorned with hieroglyphics and frescos, and it is from such imagery that archaeologists have been able to piece together so much of what we know about the period, from religious beliefs and the afterlife to questions of dynastic succession.

Such paintings also adorned the facades of temples, and temple hieroglyphics, once decoded, have also become another rich source of information about historical events and even everyday life. Egyptian temples, each dedicated to one among many Egyptian gods, are most often characterised by the use of flat roofs, massive stone blocks and tightly spaced columns. Most were also aligned with important astronomical occurrences, their measurements and design carefully calculated by royal astronomers and, in some cases, the pharaohs themselves.

Greek & Roman Architecture

Although it is Roman architecture that dominates the ruined cities that are such a feature of travelling in the Middle East, the Romans drew heavily on the architecture of the ancient Greeks. Indeed, it was from the Greeks that the Romans acquired their prototypes for temples, theatres, monumental gateways, public squares (agora to the Greeks, forum to the Romans) and colonnaded thoroughfares.

But in the Middle East at least it was the Romans who perfected these forms and it is the Roman version that endures, at once monumental in scale and extremely intricate in detail. The Romans also added their own innovations, many of them to do with water – perhaps the most enduring of these are aqueducts and the concept of richly decorated public baths, the forerunner to the hammam.

Most of the buildings that survive played critical roles in public Roman life: the temples were the focus of religious devotion, the theatres and amphitheatres were the centrepieces of public entertainment and the monumental arched gateways reinforced the cult that surrounded the emperors of ancient Rome. Private homes, often belonging to wealthy noble families, were often paved in intricate mosaics.

Aside from individual elements of public Roman architecture, the whole was also extremely important and it was in town planning that the Romans really made their mark. In the cities of the ancient Roman Empire, city life revolved around a public square (forum), which was a meeting place (and sometimes a market) and surrounded by imposing temples and administrative buildings. A well-ordered grid of streets, paved with flagstones and sometimes lined with porticoes, surrounded the forum, with two main streets – the north–south *cardo* and the east–west *decumanus,* which usually intersected at the forum, providing the main thoroughfares. An outer defensive wall, beyond which lay farmland, usually encircled the core of the city.

**Greek &
Roman
Architecture**
Ephesus (Efes),
Turkey
Baalbek, Lebanon
Caesarea, Israel
Jerash, Jordan
Temple of Amun,
Egypt

Ancient Persian Architecture

Iran is home to some of the oldest extant structures in the Middle East, among them the remarkable Elamite ziggurat at Choqa Zanbil, which predates the 7th century BC. But the most stirring examples of ancient Persian architecture come from the Achaemenid era (550–330 BC), among them the magnificent ceremonial palace complexes and royal tombs at Pasargadae, Naqsh-e Rostam, Shush and awesome Persepolis. These are decorated with bas-reliefs of kings, soldiers, suppliants, animals and the winged figure of the Zoroastrian deity Ahura Mazda.

The Achaemenids typically built with sun-dried brick and stone and there are links with the old ziggurats in both shape and decoration. The Achaemenid style also incorporated features taken from Egyptian and Greek architecture. They built colossal halls supported by stone and wooden columns with typically Persian bull's-head capitals.

Places of Worship

Mosques

Embodying the Islamic faith and representing its most predominant architectural feature throughout the region is the masjid (mosque, also called a *jamaa*).

Islam: Art & Architecture, edited by
Markus Hattstein
and Peter Delius,
is comprehensive,
lavishly illustrated
and one of those
coffee-table
books that you'll
treasure and dip
into time and
again.

Prayer Hall

The house belonging to the Prophet Mohammed is said to have provided the prototype of the mosque. It had an enclosed oblong courtyard with huts (housing Mohammed's wives) along one wall and a rough portico providing shade. This plan developed with the courtyard becoming the *sahn*, the portico the arcaded *riwaq* and the house the *haram* (prayer hall).

The prayer hall is typically divided into a series of aisles. The central aisle is wider than the rest and leads to a vaulted niche in the wall called the mihrab; this indicates the direction of Mecca, towards which Muslims must face when they pray. Also in the prayer hall is usually a minbar (a wooden pulpit that stands beside the mihrab), from where the imam delivers his khutba (sermon) at the main Friday noon prayers.

Before entering the prayer hall, Muslims must perform a ritual washing of the hands, forearms, neck and face (by washing themselves before prayer, the believer indicates a willingness to be purified). For this purpose mosques have traditionally had a large ablutions fountain at the centre of the courtyard, often fashioned from marble and worn by centuries of use. These days, modern mosques just have rows of taps.

Rising above the main mosque structure is at least one (but often numerous) minarets, some of which were adapted from former church steeples. In ancient times, the minaret was where the muezzin climbed to call the faithful to prayer – these days, a loudspeaker performs a similar function.

Arab & Turkish Styles

When it came to mosque design, each region developed its own local flourishes. The Umayyads of Damascus favoured square minarets, the Abbasid dynasty in Iraq built spiral minarets echoing the ziggurats of the Babylonians, and the Fatimids of Egypt made much use of decorative stucco work. The Mamluks (1250–1517), a military dynasty of former slaves ruling out of Egypt, brought a new level of sophistication to mosque architecture – their buildings are characterised by the banding of different coloured stone (a technique known as *ablaq*) and by the elaborate carvings and patterning around windows and in the recessed portals. The best examples of their patronage are found in Cairo but impressive Mamluk monuments also grace the old cities of Damascus, Tripoli and Jerusalem. Tripoli's Taynal Mosque and Cairo's Mosque of Qaitbey, with its exquisitely carved dome, are perhaps the high points of Mamluk style.

It was the Ottoman Turks who left some of the most recognisable (and, given the reach of the Ottoman Empire, widespread) landmarks. Ottoman mosques were designed on the basic principle of a dome on a square, and are instantly recognisable by their slim, pencil-shaped minarets. The Süleymaniye Camii in İstanbul and the Selimiye Mosque in Edirne, both the work of the Turkish master architect Sinan, represent the apogee of the style.

AGA KHAN: ISLAMIC ARCHITECTURE'S SAVIOUR

If there's one figure who has been responsible above all others for reviving Islamic architecture worldwide, it's the Aga Khan IV, the imam (religious teacher) of the largest branch of the Ismaili Shia Muslims since 1957. Through the Aga Khan Development Network (www.akdn.org), one of the largest private development organisations in the world, the Aga Khan funds programs encompassing public health, education, microfinance, rural development and architecture.

One focus of his efforts has been the Historic Cities Program, which aims to rescue, restore and bring back to life public buildings across the Islamic world. Cairo in Egypt and, prior to the war, Syria's Damascus and Aleppo were the main beneficiaries in the Middle East. Rather than focusing solely on bricks and mortar, the projects prioritise improvements in social infrastructure and living conditions in surrounding areas, thereby transforming architectural restoration into wider projects for social renewal.

In Cairo, a city with one of the lowest ratios of green space to urban population on earth, the first stage of the US$30 million project has involved creating the 30-hectare Al-Azhar Park on land reclaimed from what had been a rubbish dump for 500 years. The project also involved restoring 1.5km of the 12th-century Ayyubid Wall, rescuing a number of dilapidated mosques and an integrated plan for improving housing, infrastructure and living conditions in the adjacent Darb al-Ahmar, one of Cairo's poorest districts and home to more than 90,000 people; many of the rooftops were fitted with solar heating systems, water cisterns and vegetable gardens.

A further pillar in the Aga Khan's master plan has been the triennial Aga Khan Award for Architecture (www.akdn.org/architecture), one of the world's most prestigious architecture awards. Winning projects since the award was announced in 1977 have included the restorations of İstanbul's Topkapı Palace, Cairo's Citadel of Saladin and the rehabilitation of Iran's Tabriz Bazaar.

Persian Styles

The defining aspects of Persian architecture are its monumental simplicity and its lavish use of surface ornamentation and colour. The ground plans of ordinary Persian buildings mix only a few standard elements: a courtyard and arcades, lofty entrance porticoes and four *iwan* (barrel-vaulted halls opening onto the courtyard). These basic features are often so densely covered with decoration that observers are led to imagine the architecture is far more complex than it actually is. The decorations are normally geometric, floral or calligraphic.

Even in ancient times, minarets in Persia were far more decorative than practical. Since someone standing atop a minaret could look into the private family areas of nearby houses, Shiite mosques often have a separate hutlike structure on the roof from where the muezzin makes the call to prayer.

The development of the dome was one of the greatest achievements of Persian architecture. The Sassanians (AD 224–642) were the first to discover a satisfactory way of building a dome on top of a square chamber by using two intermediate levels, or squinches – the lower octagonal and the higher 16-sided – on which the dome could rest. Later domes became progressively more sophisticated, incorporating an inner semicircular dome sheathed by an outer conical or even onion-shaped dome. Externally the domes were often encased in tiles, with patterns so elaborate they had to be worked out on models at ground level first.

Under a succession of enlightened and cultivated Safavid rulers (1502–1736), most notably Shah Abbas I, came the final refinement of styles that marked the culmination of the Persian Islamic school of architecture. Its greatest expression was Abbas' royal capital of Esfahan, a supreme example of town planning with one of the most magnificent collections of buildings from one period anywhere in the world – the vast and unforgettable Naqsh-e Jahan (Imam) Square.

Synagogues

Although many synagogues follow a similar style, there is also great variety in their architectural forms. This is partly because Jewish tradition dictates that God can be present wherever there are 10 adults gathered together.

There are, however, some elements common to all synagogues. The first of these is the presence of an ark (in some cases simply a cupboard, or a chest), which contains the scrolls of the Torah. All synagogues also have a table (or in some cases a platform or pulpit) from which the Torah can be read, and from where some services are conducted. In most synagogues, a light is also illuminated at all times to symbolise the menorah (candelabra) in the Temple in Jerusalem. The synagogue, or at the very least its prayer room, should also be aligned to face towards Jerusalem.

Synagogues

Hurva Synagogue, Jerusalem

Western Wall, Jerusalem

Hamat Tveriya National Park

Beit Alpha

Synagogue Quarter, Tsfat

Tzipori

Hisham's Palace, Jericho

There are also a number of Talmudic instructions that synagogues should take – they must have windows and be taller than other buildings in town – although these were often ignored or simply not possible.

Other features of Jewish religious architecture vary from one synagogue to the next – some are simple prayer rooms, others are adorned with inscriptions in Hebrew and otherwise richly decorated. In many cases, there are also separate sections of the synagogue for men and women.

Churches

After the first three centuries of Christianity (during which time the faith was illegal and worshippers most often gathered in private homes), the church evolved from a one-room meeting place to one that contained a space for the congregation and a separate space where the priest could perform the rites of Mass. Over time, church architecture became more sophisticated with aisles (which became necessary as churches grew in size), a steeple (which usually housed the bells), chapels and a baptistery.

Early church architecture, and indeed many of its most enduring forms, owes much to the Romans. It was not the temples that provided the greatest inspiration, because these had little space for the congregation. Rather, inspiration (and indeed the name) came from the Roman basilicas which were not places of worship but places for meetings, markets and administrative functions such as courts. More specifically, many Roman basilicas had a semi-circular apse covered with a half-dome roof, which became an essential element in later church architecture. Roman mausoleums, with their square or circular domed structures, also filtered into Christian architecture – Jerusalem's Church of the Holy Sepulchre is an example of this.

Another crucial and oft-observed element of church architecture is a floor plan in the shape of a cross. Although the exact shape of this cross may vary depending on the region and date of construction, the two main forms mimic the Latin and Greek crosses – the former has a rectangular form and has a long nave crossed by a shorter transept, while the Greek cross design was usually square with the four 'arms' of equal length.

Mosaics were also a stunning feature of churches, particularly in Byzantine times. The best examples are in Madaba in Jordan.

Secular Architecture

Urban Buildings

The Middle East's cities are where the failure of architecture and urban planning to keep pace with burgeoning populations is most distressingly on show. Take Cairo, for example. In 1950, Cairo had a population of around 2.3 million. Now as many as 18 million people live cheek-by-jowl within greater Cairo's ever-expanding boundaries. The result is an undistinguished sprawl of grime-coated, Soviet-style apartment blocks and unplanned shanty towns, often without even the most basic amenities.

Palaces & Private Homes

Usually built around a courtyard and hidden behind high walls, the Middle East's private homes and palaces were perfectly adapted to the dictates of climate and communal living. The homes often housed up to a dozen families, each with their own space opening onto the shared patio. The palaces worked on the same principle, containing the royal living quarters with separate rooms for women and domestic staff. Most such residences included a cooling central fountain and an *iwan* (arched alcove that served as a summer retreat), and were adorned with tilework, woodcarved lintels and elegant arches. Comfortable and stylish, private and largely self-contained, these homes were ideally suited to a region with long, hot summers and where complicated rules of engagement existed between the public and private spheres.

Rural Buildings

Architecture in rural areas of the Middle East has always been a highly localised tradition, determined primarily by the dictates of climate. In the oases, particularly the Saharan towns of Egypt's Western Oases, mud-brick was easy to manufacture and ensured cool interiors under the baking desert sun. Although perfectly adapted to ordinary climatic conditions, these homes also proved extremely vulnerable to erosion and rains, which explains why so few examples remain across the region. The best examples are in Siwa (Egypt) and Yazd (Iran).

But the undoubted star when it comes to unique traditional architecture is Cappadocia (Kapadokya), Turkey, where homes and churches were hewn from the weird and wonderful landscape of caves, rock walls and soft volcanic tuff.

Most forms of vernacular rural architecture face an uncertain future. Rural poverty and unrelenting urbanisation have caused the widespread abandonment of traditional forms of architecture. The simple truth about the future of rural architecture in the Middle East is this: unless places become established as tourist attractions, their traditional architecture will disappear within a generation, if it hasn't done so already.

Churches

Church of the Holy Sepulchre, Jerusalem

Church of the Nativity, Bethlehem

Basilica of the Annunciation, Nazareth

St George's Orthodox Cathedral, Beirut

Church of St John the Baptist, Byblos

Kelisa-ye Vank, Esfahan

St George's Church, Madaba

Moses Memorial Church, Mt Nebo

St Katherine's Monastery, Sinai

ARCHITECTURE SECULAR ARCHITECTURE

Middle Eastern Cuisine

For all the religious, political and social issues that divide the region, an emphatic belief in the importance of good food is one thing on which all the people of the Middle East agree. And little wonder given what's on offer. Middle Easterners see eating as a social event to be shared between family and friends, a means of marking the most important moments in life, and a pastime that's worth spending hours over. In short, life revolves around food.

The Complete Middle East Cookbook by Tess Mallos is full of easy-to-follow recipes, and devotes individual chapters to national cuisines, including those of Turkey, Iraq, Iran, Egypt and Israel.

Staples & Specialities

Middle Eastern cooking draws on a range of influences, from sophisticated Ottoman and Persian sensibilities, or the improvisation of the desert cooking pot, to a Mediterranean belief in letting fresh ingredients speak for themselves. Where the excitement really lies is in the astonishing variety in its feasts of colour and complementary tastes.

Mezze

Mezze (meze in Turkish) ranks alongside Spanish tapas and Italian antipasto as one of the world's greatest culinary inventions. A collection of appetisers or small plates of food, mezze allows you to sample a variety of often complementary tastes and takes the difficulty out of choosing what to order – choose everything! Mezze mirrors the time-honoured practice of hosts throwing a party, offering up for their guests a banquet of choice. Largely vegetable-based and bursting with colour and flavour, it's the region's most compelling culinary flourish.

Although it's usually perfectly acceptable for diners to construct an entire meal from the mezze list and forgo the mains on offer, there are subtle differences from country to country in just how far you can take this mezze obsession. Mezze is the headline act when it comes to Levantine cuisine, but it's the understudy to kebaps in Turkey and the trusted warm-up to the region's other cuisines.

Breads

For all the variety of the Middle Eastern table, bread (khobz or a'aish, which means 'life') is the guaranteed constant, considered a gift from God and the essential accompaniment to any Middle Eastern meal. In fact, it's considered such a necessity that few Middle Eastern restaurants dare charge a cent for it. If you're wandering through the streets of an Arab city in the morning and you see a large queue forming at an otherwise innocuous hole in the wall, you've almost certainly stumbled upon the local bakery.

The staple Middle Eastern bread follows a 2000-year-old recipe. Unleavened and cooked over an open flame, it's used in lieu of cutlery to scoop dips and ripped into pieces to wrap around morsels of meat. Dinner is always served with baskets of bread to mop up mezze, while kebabs (kebaps in Turkey) are often served with a tasty bread canopy coated in tomato, parsley and spices.

Almost every meal in Iran is accompanied by *nun* (bread). The four main types of *nun* are *barbari* (crisp, salty and often covered with sesame seeds), *lavash* (flat and thin breakfast bread), *sangak* (long and thick and baked on a bed of stones to give it its characteristic dimpled appearance), and *taftun* (crisp with a ribbed surface).

A New Book of Middle Eastern Food by Claudia Roden brought the cuisines of the region to the attention of Western cooks when it was released in 1968. It's still an essential reference, as fascinating for its cultural insights as for its great recipes.

Salads

It's inconceivable for most people in the region to eat a meal without salad, which forms a zesty, fresh complement to a piping-hot kebab. Middle Easterners are loyal to their basic salads and don't mind eating them meal after meal. Elaborations or creative flourishes are rare and simplicity is the key: crunchy fresh ingredients (including herbs), often caressed by a shake of oil and vinegar at the table. Salads are eaten with relish as a mezze or as an accompaniment to a meat or fish main course. Three salads, found throughout the region, form an integral part of the local diet:

fattoosh – toasted *khobz,* tomatoes, onions and mint leaves, sometimes served with a smattering of tangy pomegranate syrup

shepherd's salad – a colourful mix of chopped tomatoes, cucumber, onion and pepper; extremely popular in Turkey, where it's known as *çoban salatası*

tabbouleh – the region's signature salad combines burghul wheat, parsley and tomato, with a tangy sprinkling of sesame seeds, lemon and garlic

Street Foods

The regional stars of the snack-food line-up are shwarma and felafel, and they're both things of joy when served and eaten fresh. Shwarma is the Arabic equivalent of the Greek *gyros* sandwich or the Turkish döner

POPULAR MEZZE SPECIALITIES

Among the seemingly endless candidates, we've narrowed the typical mezze offering down to the following dishes (spellings and names may differ from country to country):

baba ghanoosh – purée of grilled aubergines (eggplants) with tahini and olive oil

basturma – cold, sliced meat cured with fenugreek

borek – pastry stuffed with salty white cheese or spicy minced meat with pine nuts; also known as *sambousek*

fatayer – triangular deep-fried pastries stuffed with spinach, meat or cheese

hummus bi tahina – cooked chickpeas ground into a paste and mixed with tahini, lemon, olive oil and garlic

kibbeh – minced lamb, burghul wheat and pine nuts made into a lemon-shaped patty and deep-fried

labneh – thick yoghurt flavoured with garlic and sometimes with mint

loobieh – French-bean salad with tomatoes, onions and garlic

mouhamarra – walnut and pomegranate syrup dip

muttabal – purée of aubergine mixed with tahini, yoghurt and olive oil; similar to but creamier than baba ghanoosh

shanklish – tangy, eye-wateringly strong goat's cheese served with onions, oil and tomatoes

tahini – paste made of sesame seeds and served as a dip

wara ainab – stuffed vine leaves, served both hot and cold; in Egypt also called mahshi

VEGETARIANS & VEGANS

Although it's quite normal for the people of the Middle East to eat a vegetarian meal, the concept of vegetarianism is quite foreign. Say you're a vegan and they will either look mystified or assume that you're 'fessing up to some strain of socially aberrant behaviour.

Fortunately, it's not that difficult to find vegetable-based dishes. You'll find yourself eating loads of mezze and salads, *fuul* (fava-bean paste), tasty cheese and spinach pastries, the occasional omelette or oven-baked vegetable *tagens* (stew baked in a terracotta pot) featuring okra and aubergine (eggplant).

Watch out also for those vegetables that are particular to Middle Eastern cuisine, including *molokhiyya* (aka *moolookhiye* or *melokhia*), a slimy but surprisingly tasty green leafy vegetable known in the West as mallow. In Egypt it's made into an earthy garlic-flavoured soup that has a glutinous texture and inspires an almost religious devotion among the locals. In Syria and Lebanon *molokhiyya* is used to make strongly spiced lamb and chicken stews.

The main source of inadvertent meat eating is meat stock, which is often used to make otherwise vegetarian pilafs, soups and vegetable dishes. Your hosts may not even consider such stock to be meat, so may assure you that the dish is vegetarian. Chicken and mutton often lurk in vegetable dishes and mezze.

The best country for vegetarians is Israel, where kosher laws don't permit the mixing of meat and dairy products, resulting in a lot of 'dairy' restaurants where no meat is served.

kebap – strips are sliced from a vertical spit of compressed lamb or chicken, sizzled on a hot plate with chopped tomatoes and garnish, then stuffed into a pocket of bread. Felafel is mashed chickpeas and spices rolled into balls and deep-fried; a variation known as ta'amiyya, made with dried fava beans, is served in Egypt.

In Egypt look out for shops sporting large metal tureens in the window: these specialise in the vegetarian delight *kushari,* a delicate mix of noodles, rice, black lentils and dried onions, served with an accompanying tomato sauce that's sometimes fiery with chilli. An alternative more often seen at Israeli sandwich stands is *shakshuka,* a dish of eggs poached in tangy stewed tomatoes, which makes a good breakfast but is eaten any time.

In Lebanon, nothing beats grabbing a freshly baked *fatayer bi sbanikh* (spinach pastry) from one of the hole-in-the-wall bakeries that dot city streets. In Turkey, visitors inevitably fall deeply in love with melt-in-the-mouth *su böreği,* a noodle-like pastry oozing cheese and butter.

Variations on the pizza abound, one of the most delicious being Egypt's *fiteer,* featuring a base of thin, filo-style pastry. In Turkey, the best cheap snack is pide, the Turkish version of pizza, a canoe-shaped dough topped with *peynirli* (cheese), *yumurtalı* (egg) or *kıymalı* (mince). A *karaşık pide* has a mixture of toppings.

The most unassuming of all Middle Eastern fast foods is also one of the most popular. *Fuul* (fava-bean paste) is mopped up by bread for breakfast and ladled into a pocket of bread for a snack on the run. You'll find it in Egypt (where it's the national dish), Syria, Jordan, Lebanon and Iraq.

In Iran, simple kababis tend to be found around major *meydans* (squares) and serve, yes, kababs.

Arabesque: Modern Middle Eastern Food by Greg and Lucy Malouf lists the 42 essential ingredients from the region and offers insights into how they can be used to create authentic dishes.

Kebabs & Other Meats

There are more variations on the kebab in this part of the world than you could poke a skewer at. Every country has its specialities – Turkey is understandably proud of its luscious İskender kebap (döner kebap on a bed of pide bread with a side serving of yoghurt) and Lebanon has an unswerving devotion to *shish tawooq* (grilled chicken kebab, often served with a garlic sauce).

In Iran, even in a restaurant with a long menu, most main-dish options will be kabab. These are served either on bread or as *chelo kabab* (on a vast mound of rice), and, in contrast with the greasy kebabs inhaled after rough nights in the West, Iranian kababs are tasty, healthy and cooked shish-style over hot charcoals. They are usually sprinkled with spicy *sumaq* (sumac) and accompanied by raw onion, grilled tomatoes and, for an extra fee, a bowl of *mast* (yoghurt).

The kebab might be king in most Middel Eastern countries, but when it comes to meat dishes there are courtiers waiting in the wings. Primary among these is *kibbeh*, a strong candidate for the title of Lebanon's national dish. Indeed, these croquettes of ground lamb, cracked wheat, onion and spices are considered the ultimate test of a Lebanese cook's skills. In Beirut they're served raw like a steak tartare, accompanied with fresh mint leaves, olive oil and spring onions. Raw *kibbeh (kibbeh nayye)* has many variations. In northern Lebanon you often find mint and fresh chillies mixed through the meat. *Kibbeh saniye* is *kibbeh* flattened out on a tray with a layer of spiced lamb and pine nuts in between.

Another culinary star is *kofta* (spiced ground meat formed into balls; *köfte* in Turkey), which is served in innumerable ways and is the signature element of the Egyptian favourite *daood basha* (meatballs cooked in a *tagen* pot with pine nuts and tomato sauce).

Rice Dishes

Although not native to the Middle East, rice is a region-wide staple that's ever-present in home cooking but far less common on restaurant menus. Usually cooked with lamb or chicken, a subtle blend of spices and sometimes saffron, its arrival as the centrepiece of an already groaning table is often a high point of the meal. It's also the point at which you wish you hadn't eaten so much mezze.

If your average Middle Easterner loves rice, it's the Bedouins who revere it. Easy to store, transport and cook, rice was perfectly suited to the once-nomadic lifestyle of many Bedouin. For this hardy desert people, *mensaf* (lamb served on a bed of rice and pine nuts and accompanied by a tangy yoghurt sauce) is what it's all about. Such is the popularity of *mensaf* that you'll find it on menus in the Palestinian Territories and Jordan.

Another regional rice speciality that won't disappoint is *makhlooba* (literally 'upside-down') rice. It's cooked in stock and spices with chickpeas, onions and off-the-bone lamb shanks, then pressed in a deep bowl and turned upside down to reveal a delicious work of art. The vegetarian version incorporates eggplants with almonds and pine nuts.

Desserts & Sweets

All Middle Easterners love their sweets but desserts are arguably most worshipped in Turkey. The prince of the regional desserts is undoubtedly *muhalabiyya* (also known as *mahallabiye*), a blancmange-like concoction made of ground rice, milk, sugar, and rose or orange water, topped with chopped pistachios and almonds. Almost as popular is *ruz bi laban* (rice pudding, known as *fırın sütlaç* in Turkey).

But best of all are the pastries. Although these are sometimes served in restaurants for dessert, they're just as often enjoyed as an any-time-of-the-day snack. Old favourites include *kunafa*, a vermicelli-like pastry over a vanilla base soaked in syrup; and the famous baklava, made from delicate filo drenched in honey or syrup. Variations on baklava (called *baghlava* in Iran) are flavoured with fresh nuts or stuffed with wickedly rich clotted cream (called *kaymak* in Turkey, *eishta* elsewhere).

The Turkish dish *imam bayıldı* ('the imam fainted') is aubergine stuffed with onion and garlic, slow-cooked in olive oil and served cold. Legend has it that an imam fainted with pleasure on first tasting it.

To ask, 'Do you have any vegetarian dishes?' in Egypt say, '*Andak akla nabateeyya?*' In Turkey ask, '*Etsiz yemekler var mı?*' (Is there something to eat that has no meat?). In other countries ask for dishes that are '*bidoon lahem*' (without meat).

MIDDLE EASTERN CUISINE STAPLES & SPECIALITIES

Drinks

Tea & Coffee

Drinking tea *(shai, chai* or *çay)* is the signature pastime of the region and it is seen as strange and decidedly antisocial not to swig the tannin-laden beverage at regular intervals throughout the day. The tea will either come in the form of a tea bag plonked in a cup or glass of hot water (Lipton is the usual brand) or a strong brew of the local leaves. Sometimes it's served with *na'ana* (mint), and it always comes with sugar. Be warned that you'll risk severe embarrassment if you ask for milk, unless you're in a tourist hotel or restaurant.

Surprisingly, Turkish or Arabic coffee *(qahwa)* is not widely consumed in the region, with instant coffee (always called Nescafé) being far more common. If you do find the real stuff, it's likely to be a thick and powerful Turkish-style brew that's served in small cups and drunk in a couple of short sips. In private homes, a good guest will accept a minimum of three cups but when you've had enough, gently tilt the cup from side to side (in Arabic, 'dancing' the cup).

Damascus: Tastes of a City by Rafik Schami is one of the most engaging books written about Middle Eastern food, introducing you to the kitchens and characters of Old Damascus.

Alcoholic Drinks

Though the region is predominantly Muslim and hence abstemious, most countries have a local beer. The best are Turkey's Efes, Egypt's Stella and Sakkara, Lebanon's famous Almaza and Jordan's Amstel, a light brew made under licence from the popular Dutch brewer Amstel. Less impressive is Israel's Maccabee, the dark-draught Gold Star and light Nesher. The most interesting ale is the preservative-free Taybeh, the product of the Arab world's first microbrewery, in Ramallah; it comes in light and malt-heavy dark varieties.

Wine is growing in popularity in the Middle East, thanks largely to the wines being produced in Lebanon. Lebanon's winemaking, which is based on the 'old-world' style, began with the French winemaker Gaston Hochar who took over an 18th-century castle, Château Musar in Ghazir, 24km north of Beirut, in 1930. Together with his sons, Hochar created a wine that, despite the civil war, was able to win important awards in France, including the prestigious Winemaker's Award for Excellence. Ninety per cent of their produce is exported. The main wine-growing areas are Kefraya and Ksara in the Bekaa Valley, and we particularly recommend the products of Château Musar and Ksara's Reserve du Couvent. Turkey and Israel also have small wine-producing areas.

Cooking courses are few and far between in the Middle East, but Petra Kitchen (www.petra-kitchen.com) in Wadi Musa, near Petra in Jordan, is worth the wait, with local Bedouin teachers, and plenty to learn and sample.

If there is a regional drink, it would have to be the grape-and-aniseed firewater known as rakı in Turkey and as arak (lion's milk) in the rest of the region. The aniseed taste of these two powerful tipples perfectly complements mezze. You'll find many Middle Easterners for whom mezze without arak (combined with water and served in small glasses) is just not taking your mezze seriously.

Nonalcoholic Drinks

Juice stalls selling cheap and delicious freshly squeezed *asiir* (juices) are common throughout the region. Popular juices include lemon (which is often blended with sugar syrup and ice, and sometimes with mint), orange, pomegranate, mango, carrot and sugar cane, and you can order combinations of any or all of these. For health reasons, steer clear of stalls that add milk to their drinks.

Other traditional drinks include *aryan,* a refreshing yoghurt drink made by whipping yoghurt with water and salt to the consistency of pouring cream. Another favourite is the delicious and unusual *sahlab* (*sahlep* in Turkey), a drink made from crushed tapioca-root extract and served with milk, coconut, sugar, raisins, chopped nuts and rosewater.

Famed for its aphrodisiacal properties, it is served hot in winter and cold in summer.

In the baking heat of an Egyptian summer, coffee and tea drinkers forgo their regular fix for cooler drinks such as the crimson-hued, iced *karkadai*, a wonderfully refreshing drink boiled up from hibiscus leaves, or *zabaady* (yoghurt beaten with cold water and salt).

Celebrations

Food plays an important part in the religious calendar of the region and holy days usually involve a flurry of baking and hours of preparation in the kitchen.

Ramadan & Other Islamic Celebrations

The region's most important religious feasts occur during Ramadan (Ramazan in Turkish), the Muslim holy month. There are two substantial meals a day during this period. The first, *imsak* (or *sahur*), is a breakfast eaten before daylight. Tea, bread, dates, olives and pastries are scoffed to give energy for the day ahead. *Iftar*, the evening meal prepared to break the fast, is a special feast calling for substantial soups, rice dishes topped with almond-scattered grilled meats and other delicacies. *Iftar* is often enjoyed communally in the street or in large, specially erected tents. In Turkey, a special round flat pide is baked in the afternoon and collected in time for the evening feast.

The end of Ramadan (Eid al-Fitr) is also celebrated in great culinary style. In Turkey, locals mark this important time with Şeker Bayramı (Sugar Festival), a three-day feast in which sweet foods (especially baklava) occupy centre stage.

Jewish Celebrations

The Shabbat (Sabbath) meal is an article of faith for most Jews and central to that weekly celebration is the bread known as *challah* (Sabbath bread), which is baked each week by Jewish householders in Israel and

The Arab Table: Recipes and Culinary Traditions by May Bsisu takes a holistic approach that blends practical recipes with discursive sections on Arab culinary philosophy, with a special focus on celebratory meals.

MIDDLE EASTERN CUISINE CELEBRATIONS

THE CAFE & COFFEEHOUSE EXPERIENCE

There's nothing more authentically Middle Eastern than spending an hour (or an afternoon) soaking up the ambience and fragrant nargileh smoke at a *qahwa* (coffeehouse; *ahwa* in Egypt); in Turkey they're called *çay bahçesi* (tea gardens). Most serve up more tea than coffee and all have loyal, predominantly male, clients who enjoy nothing more than a daily natter and a game of dominoes or *towla* (backgammon). Adding to the atmosphere is the smoke from countless water pipes, a fragrant cloud of lightly scented tobacco that's one of the Middle East's most distinctive sensory experiences.

Called a nargileh in Turkey, Lebanon, Jordan and Syria and a sheesha in Egypt, the water pipe is a tradition, an indulgence and a slightly naughty habit all wrapped into the one gloriously relaxing package. A feature of coffeehouses from Ankara to Aswan, it's as addictive as it is magical. Consider yourselves warned.

When you order a water pipe you'll need to specify the type of tobacco and molasses mix you'd like. Most people opt for tobacco soaked in apple juice (known as *elma* in Turkey and *tufah* in Egypt), but it's also possible to order strawberry, melon, cherry or mixed-fruit flavours. Some purists order their tobacco unadulterated, but in doing this they miss out on the wonderfully sweet aroma that makes the experience so memorable. Once you've specified your flavour, a decorated bulbous glass pipe filled with water will be brought to your table, hot coals will be placed in it to get it started and you'll be given a disposable plastic mouthpiece to slip over the pipe's stem. Just draw back and you're off. The only secret to a good smoke is to take a puff every now and again to keep the coals hot; when they start to lose their heat the waiter (or dedicated water-pipe minder) will replace them. Bliss!

FOOD & RITES OF PASSAGE

In the Middle East, food is always associated with different milestones in an individual's and a family's life. When a baby is born, Egyptians mark the birth of a son by serving an aromatic rice pudding with aniseed called *meghlie;* in Lebanon it's called *mighlay* and is made of rice flour and cinnamon. The same dish is called *mughly* in the Palestinian Territories, where it is believed to aid lactation.

In Lebanon, chickpeas and tooth-destroying sugar-coated almonds are the celebratory treats when the baby's first tooth pushes through. In Egypt, *ataïf* (pancakes dipped in syrup) are eaten on the day of a betrothal and biscuits known as *kahk bi loz* (almond bracelets) are favourites at wedding parties. Guests at Turkish engagement parties and weddings, are invariably served baklava.

Mourning carries with it a whole different set of eating rituals. A loved one is always remembered with a banquet. This takes place after the burial in Christian communities, and one week later in Muslim communities. The only beverages offered are water and bitter, unsweetened coffee. In Israel and the Palestinian Territories, Muslims may serve dates as well, while Christians bake *rahmeh,* a type of bun commemorating the soul of the departed. Muted varieties of much-loved sweets, such as *helva* and *lokum* (Turkish delight), are commonly part of the mourning period in Turkey: a bereaved family will make *irmik helvası* (semolina *helva*) for visiting friends and relatives.

When observant Jews mourn the dead, religious dictates urge them to sit around the deceased for seven days and then have a solemn meal of bread, to signify sustenance, and boiled eggs and lentils, whose circular forms invoke the continuation of life.

the Palestinian Territories. A slowly cooked heavy stew called *cholent* is another Shabbat tradition widely enjoyed in Israel. Fatty meat, beans, grains, potatoes, herbs and spices stewed for hours in a big pot will heartily serve the family as well as guests.

The Pesah (Jewish Passover) is celebrated even by the nondevout, the majority of Israelis. Unleavened bread is the best-known ingredient. During Hanukkah, potato pancakes and special jam doughnuts *(soofganiot)* are traditional dishes, while Rosh Hashanah means eating sweet foods like apples, carrots or braided *challah* bread dipped in honey.

Easter

Easter heralds another round of feasting, with Good Friday's abstinence from meat bringing out dishes such as *m'jaddara* (spiced lentils and rice) or *shoraba zingool* (sour soup with small balls of cracked wheat, flour and split peas) in Lebanon. *Selak,* rolls of silver beet (Swiss chard) stuffed with rice, tomato, chickpeas and spices, are also served. The fast is broken on Easter Sunday with round semolina cakes called *maamoul* stuffed with either walnuts or dates. The Armenian Christmas, the Epiphany (6 January), has the women busy making *owamaut* (small, deep-fried honey balls).

The Arts

The Middle East's artistic heritage is a rich one. Under often extremely difficult circumstances, and often from exile, the Middle East's film-makers, writers and musicians of the modern era continue to produce some remarkable work. If you're looking to step beyond the stereotypes and discover new insights into the Middle East's stunning creative diversity, the arts are an ideal place to begin your search.

Cinema

The region's film industries stand at a crossroads. On one level, a small, elite company of directors is gaining critical acclaim, picking up awards at international festivals and inching its way into the consciousness of audiences around the world. But many of these live in exile, and the industry as a whole has spent much of the last two decades in crisis, plagued by a critical lack of government funding, straining under the taboos maintained by repressive governments or fundamentalist religious movements, and facing unprecedented competition from Middle Easterners' unfettered access to satellite TV. Amid the upheaval of the Arab Spring, film-makers have at times been prominent voices for reform, but funding for film-making remains a marginal priority for many of the region's governments.

The way most Middle Eastern directors survive under such conditions is to produce films that either overtly support the government line and stray dangerously close to propaganda, or to focus on the microscopic details of daily life, using individual stories to make veiled commentaries on wider social and political issues. It is in this latter body of work, schooled in subtlety and nuanced references to the daily struggles faced by many in the region, that Middle Eastern film truly shines.

> Arab Film Distribution (www.arabfilm.com) is the Amazon of Arab cinema, with a large portfolio of DVDs that you just won't find on the shelves of your local rental store or mainstream online sources.

Egypt: Coming of Age

In its halcyon years of the 1970s, Cairo's film studios turned out more than 100 movies a year, filling cinemas throughout the Arab world. These days the annual figure is closer to 20 and most are soap-opera-style movies, usually with a little belly dancing thrown in for (rather mild) spice.

One Egyptian director who consistently stood apart from the mainstream was Youssef Chahine (1926–2008). He directed over 35 films, has been called Egypt's Fellini and was honoured at Cannes in 1997 with a lifetime achievement award. His later and more well-known works are 1999's *Al-Akhar* (The Other), 1997's *Al-Masir* (Destiny) and 1994's *Al-Muhagir* (The Emigrant). Others to look out for are *Al-Widaa Bonaparte* (Adieu Bonaparte), a historical drama about the French occupation, and *Iskandariyya Ley?* (Alexandria Why?), an autobiographical meditation on the city of Chahine's birth.

Since the 2011 revolution a new wave of film-makers has entered the Egyptian cinema scene and are taking Egyptian cinema into exciting and uncharted territory. In early 2014 Zawya, a new cinema in downtown Cairo, opened, showing art-house movies and work by young Egyptian filmmakers.

> **Middle East Film Festivals**
>
> *Fajr Film Festival, Iran (Feb)*
>
> *Antalya Golden Orange Film Festival, Turkey (Oct)*
>
> *Beirut International Film Festival, Lebanon (Oct)*
>
> *Cairo International Film Festival, Egypt (Dec)*

MUST-SEE MOVIES

➡ *Lawrence of Arabia* (1962) David Lean's masterpiece captures all the hopes and subsequent frustrations for Arabs in the aftermath of WWI.

➡ *Sallah Shabati* (1964) Ephraim Kishon's enduringly popular comedy about a family of new immigrants to Israel.

➡ *Yol* (The Way; 1982) By Yilmaz Güney and epic in scale, it follows five finely rendered Turkish prisoners on parole around their country.

➡ *A Moment of Innocence* (1996) Semi-autobiographical film by Iran's Mohsen Makhmalbaf about his stabbing of a policeman at a rally as a youth before trying to make amends two decades later.

➡ *West Beirut* (1998) Begins on 13 April 1975, the first day of the Lebanese Civil War, and is Ziad Doueiri's powerful meditation on Lebanon's scars and hopes.

➡ *Paradise Now* (2005) Palestinian director Hany Abu-Assad's disturbing but finely rendered study of the last hours of two suicide bombers. It was nominated for the Best Foreign Language Film Oscar in 2005.

➡ *Caramel* (2007) A stunning debut for Lebanese director Nadine Labaki. It follows the lives of five Lebanese women struggling against social taboos in war-ravaged Beirut.

➡ *Once Upon a Time in Anatolia* (2011) Runner-up at the 2011 Cannes Film Festival, this Nuri Bilge Ceylan film broods across the Anatolian steppe.

➡ *A Separation* (2011) Directed by Iranian Ashgar Farhadi and winner of the 2012 Oscar for Best Foreign Language Film, it portrays a couple torn between seeking a better life for their son and staying in Iran to care for an elderly parent with Alzheimers.

➡ *Omar* (2014) The second Palestinian film to be nominated for the Best Foreign Language Film Oscar, it touches on questions of Palestinian and Israeli revenge and the question of who can be trusted.

Israel

Film directors from elsewhere in the Middle East must look with envy at the level of government funding and freedom of speech enjoyed by Israeli film-makers. It's a freedom that Israeli directors have used to produce high-quality films that have been praised for their even-handedness by juries and audiences alike at international film festivals.

A readiness to confront uncomfortable truths about Israel's recent history has long been a hallmark of Amos Gitai (b 1950) who has won plaudits for his sensitive and balanced portrayal of half a century of conflict. He became a superstar almost overnight with *Kadosh* (1998), which seriously questioned the role of religion in Israeli society and politics. He followed it up with *Kippur* (1999), a wholly unsentimental portrayal of the 1973 war, and *Kedma* (2001), which caused a stir by questioning many of the country's founding myths through the lens of the Israeli War of Independence. Avi Mograbi (b 1956) goes a step further than Gitai with no-holds-barred depictions of the difficulties of life for the Palestinians under Israeli occupation.

Beyond the politically charged films that are causing a stir, there's also a feeling within Israel that the country's film industry is entering something of a golden age. Highlighting the sense of excitement, Shira Geffen and Etgar Keret won the Caméra d'Or for best film by debut directors at the 2007 Cannes Film Festival for *Meduzot* (Jellyfish). At the same festival, Eran Kolirin's *The Band's Visit* won the Jury Prize of the International Federation of Film Critics. Joseph Cedar (b 1968) has been nominated twice for an Academy Award for Best Foreign Language Film with *Beaufort* (2007) and *Footnote* (2011).

Israeli films have received more Oscar nominations (10) for Best Foreign Language Film than films from any other Middle Eastern country (including in 2007, 2008, 2009 and 2011), although they've yet to win the prize.

Palestinian Territories

Starved of funding, faced with the barriers erected by Israeli censors and living in occupation or exile, Palestinian film-makers have done it tough, but have nonetheless turned out some extraordinary movies.

One Palestinian director who has made an international impact is Nazareth-born Michael Khaleifi (b 1950), whose excellent *Images from Rich Memories* (1980), *The Anthem of the Stone* (1990) and *Wedding in Galilee* (1987) were all shot covertly inside the Palestinian Territories. Gaza-born Rasheed Masharawi (b 1962) has been rejected in some Palestinian circles for working with Israeli production companies, but the quality of his work is undeniable. The work of Elia Suleiman (b 1960) is a wonderful corpus of quietly angry and intensely powerful films – *Chronicle of a Disappearance* won Best Film Prize at the 1996 Venice Film Festival, while *Divine Intervention* won the Jury Prize at Cannes in 2002.

Iran

It was in the 1970s that the first 'new wave' of Iranian cinema captured the attention of art-house movie fans around the world: Abbas Kiarostami, Dariush Mehrjui, Bahram Beiza'i, Khosrow Haritash and Bahram Farmanara. The second 'new wave' was made up of post-revolutionary directors such as Mohsen Makhmalbaf, Rakhshan Bani Etemad, Majid Majidi and Jafar Panahi. It helped develop a reputation for Iranian cinema as art house, neorealist and poetic. The newest generation's most notable exponents are Asghar Farhadi, Bahman Ghobadi and Mani Haghighi.

Whatever the number, Iranian new wave is consistent in looking at everyday life through a poetic prism that is part fictional feature, part real-life documentary. The strict censorship of the post-revolutionary state has encouraged the use of children, nonprofessional actors and stories that are fixated on the nitty-gritty of life.

As well as the works of these directors, other films worth seeking out include Majid Majidi's film *Children of Heaven,* which was nominated for the Best Foreign Language Film Oscar in 1998. It is a delicate tale focusing on two poor children losing a pair of shoes. *The White Balloon* (1995), written by Abbas Kiarostami and directed by Jafar Panahi, tells the story of a young girl who loses her money while on the way to buy a goldfish.

Young Lebanese director Ziad Doueiri, whose slick debut *West Beyrouth* (1998) is considered one of the best films about the Lebanese Civil War, was Quentin Tarantino's lead cameraman for *Pulp Fiction* and *Reservoir Dogs*.

Literature

The telling of tales that are both mischievous and reveal the social and political times from which they arise has always occupied centre stage in Middle Eastern life, from the epic tales from the 8th-century Baghdad court of Haroun ar-Rashid, so wonderfully brought to life in *The Thousand and One Nights,* to the wandering storytellers who once entertained crowds in the coffeehouses and theatres of the region. It's a heritage with two tightly interwoven strands: entertainment through suspense and comedy, and thinly veiled commentaries on the issues of the day.

But the writers of the region face many challenges, including government repression and the lack of a book-buying culture in Arabic-speaking countries. Storytelling in the Middle East, including poetry, was always a predominantly oral tradition and it was not until the 20th century that the first Arabic-language novels appeared.

Poetry

The Lebanese-born poet Khalil Gibran (1883–1931) is, by some estimates, the third biggest-selling poet in history behind Shakespeare and Lao Tse. Born in Bcharré in Lebanon, he spent most of his working life in the US, but it didn't stop him from becoming a flag bearer for Arabic poetry. His masterpiece, *The Prophet* (1923), which consists of 26 poetic essays, became, after the Bible, America's second biggest-selling book of the 20th century.

Mahmoud Darwish (1941–2008) has become one of the most eloquent spokesmen for Palestinian rights, his more than 30 volumes of poetry reading like a beautifully composed love letter to the lost land of his childhood.

Another leading Arab poet and one of the great celebrities of the Arab literary scene is Syria's Nizar Qabbani (1923–98), who was unusual in that he was able to balance closeness to successive Syrian regimes with subject matter (love, eroticism and feminism) that challenged many prevailing opinions within conservative Syrian society. His funeral in Damascus – a city that he described in his will as 'the womb that taught me poetry, taught me creativity and granted me the alphabet of jasmine' – was broadcast live around the Arab world.

In Iran, poetry is overwhelmingly the most important form of writing. Familiarity with famous poets and their works is universal: almost anyone on the street can quote lines from Hafez or Rumi.

To learn more about how the stories of *The Thousand and One Nights* came together, read the excellent introduction by Husain Haddawy in *The Arabian Nights*.

Novels

The novel as a literary form may have come late to the Middle East, but that didn't stop the region producing three winners of the Nobel Prize for Literature: Shmuel Yosef Agnon (1966), a Zionist Israeli writer whose works are published in English under the name SY Agnon; Naguib Mahfouz (1988); and Orhan Pamuk (2006).

Much of the credit for the maturing of Arabic literature can be given to Naguib Mahfouz (1911–2006), who was unquestionably the single-most important writer of fiction in Arabic in the 20th century. A lifelong native of Cairo, Mahfouz began writing in the 1930s. From Western-copyist origins he went on to develop a voice that is uniquely of the Arab world and draws its inspiration from storytelling in the coffeehouses and the dialect and slang of the streets. He repeatedly fell foul of Egypt's fundamentalist Islamists, first for his 1959 novel *Children of Gebelawi* (which was banned for blasphemy in Egypt) and later for defending Salman Rushdie; Mahfouz was seriously injured in an assassination attempt in 1994. His best-known works are collectively known as *The Cairo Trilogy*, consisting of *Palace Walk, Palace of Desire* and *Sugar Street*.

Orhan Pamuk (b 1952) is Turkey's foremost literary celebrity. His works include an impressive corpus of novels and an acclaimed memoir of İstanbul, *Istanbul: Memories of a City*. His work has been translated into more

BEST MIDDLE EASTERN LITERATURE

➡ *The Prophet* by Khalil Gibran somehow expounds in poetic form on the great philosophical questions while speaking to the dilemmas of everyday life.

➡ Choose anything by Orhan Pamuk and you won't be disappointed, but it was with *The Black Book* that he leapt onto the international stage.

➡ Naguib Mahfouz rarely sounds a wrong note. Choose anything from *The Cairo Trilogy*, but if you have to choose just one title, *The Harafish* would be our desert-island choice.

➡ *The Map of Love* by Ahdaf Soueif is the Booker-nominated historical novel by this Anglo-Egyptian writer. *In the Eye of the Sun* is simply marvellous.

➡ *Memed My Hawk* by Yaşar Kemal deals with near-feudal life in the villages of eastern Turkey and is considered perhaps the greatest Turkish novel of the 20th century.

➡ *The Stone of Laughter* by Hoda Barakat is a lyrical work by a young Lebanese writer that beautifully charts Lebanon's civil war.

➡ *The Dark Side of Love* by Syria's Rafik Schami could just be the first 'Great Arab Novel' of the 21st century, with its follow-up *The Calligrapher's Secret* also brilliant.

➡ *The Yacoubian Building* by Egypt's Alaa Al Aswany is a populist yet finely crafted portrayal of the late Mubarak period.

THE THOUSAND AND ONE NIGHTS

After the Bible, *The Thousand and One Nights* (in Arabic, *Alf Layla w'Layla*, also known as *The Arabian Nights*) must be one of the best-known, least-read books in the English language.

That few people have read the actual text is unsurprising considering that its most famous English-language edition (translated by the Victorian adventurer Sir Richard Burton) runs to 16 volumes; an old Middle Eastern superstition holds that nobody can read the entire text of *The Thousand and One Nights* without dying.

With origins that range from pre-Islamic Persia, India and Arabia, the stories as we now know them were first gathered together in written form in the 14th century. *The Thousand and One Nights* is a portmanteau title for a mixed bag of colourful and fantastic tales (there are 271 core stories). The stories are mainly set in the semi-fabled Baghdad of Haroun ar-Rashid (r AD 786–809), and in Mamluk-era (1250–1517) Cairo and Damascus.

All versions of *The Thousand and One Nights* begin with the same premise: the misogynist King Shahriyar discovers that his wife has been unfaithful, whereafter he murders her and takes a new wife every night before killing each in turn before sunrise. The wily Sheherezade, the daughter of the king's vizier, insists that she will be next, only to nightly postpone her death with a string of stories that leaves the king in such suspense that he spares her life so as to hear the next instalment.

---

than 50 languages and, like Mahfouz, Pamuk has never shirked from the difficult issues; in *Snow* (2004), Pamuk unflinchingly explores the fraught relationship between two of the great themes of modern Turkish life: Islamic extremism and the pull of the West. Also like Mahfouz, Pamuk is known as a staunch defender of freedom of speech.

Among the region's other best-known writers are Turkey's Yaşar Kemal (b 1923) and the Israeli writer Amos Oz (b 1939); Oz's work includes essays and award-winning novels with themes that speak to the pride and angst at the centre of modern Israeli life. Of the native Lebanese writers, the most famous is Hanan al-Shaykh (b 1945), who writes poignant but humorous novels that resonate beyond the bounds of the Middle East. Also worth tracking down are the works of Jordan's Abdelrahman Munif (1933–2004), Egypt's prolific Nawal el-Saadawi (b 1931) and Lebanese-born Amin Maalouf (b 1949).

Sadeq Hedayat (1903–51) is the best-known Iranian novelist outside Iran, and one whose influence has been most pervasive in shaping modern Persian fiction. *The Blind Owl,* published in 1937, is a dark and powerful portrayal of the decadence of a society failing to achieve its own modernity. Hedayat's uncensored works have been banned in Iran since 2005.

According to one UN estimate, Spain translates more books each year than have been translated into Arabic in the past 1000 years.

Music

If you're a music lover, you'll adore the Middle East, which has home-grown music as diverse as the region itself. This is one part of the world where local artists dominate air time and you're likely to hear Umm Kolthum, soulful Iraqi oud (Middle Eastern lute) or the latest Lebanese pop sensation.

Arab

Classical

If one instrument has come to represent the enduring appeal of classical Arabic music, it's the oud, an instrument that has made the transition from backing instrument to musical superstar in its own right. The oud is a pear-shaped, stringed instrument and is distinguished from its successor, the Western lute, by its lack of frets, 11 strings (five pairs and a single string) and a neck bent at a 45- to 90-degree angle. Oud players are to be found throughout the region, but its undisputed masters are in Iraq, where the sound of the oud is revered as a reflection of the Iraqi soul.

Even so, Syria produced the Arab world's so-called 'King of the Oud', Farid al-Atrache (1915–74). Sometimes called the 'Arab Sinatra', he was a highly accomplished oud player and composer, who succeeded in updating Arabic music by blending it with Western scales and rhythms and the orchestration of the tango and waltz. His melodic improvisations on the oud and his *mawal* (a vocal improvisation) were the highlights of his live performances, and recordings of these are treasured. By the time of his death, he was considered – and still is by many – to be the premier male Arabic music performer of the 20th century.

The other defining feature of classical Arabic music is the highly complicated melodic system known as *maqam*. The foundation for most traditional music in the Arab world, *maqam* is based on a tonal system of scales and intervals and is wholly different from Western musical traditions. Master *maqam* and you've mastered the centuries-old sound of the region.

Naguib Mahfouz: His Life & Times by Rasheed El-Elnany is the first (and, it must be said, long-overdue) English-language biography of the Arab world's most accomplished and prolific novelist.

Contemporary Arab Music

Seemingly a world away from classical Arabic music, and characterised by a clattering, hand-clapping rhythm overlaid with synthesised twirlings and a catchy, repetitive vocal, the first true Arabic pop came out of Cairo in the 1970s. The blueprint for the new youth sound (which became known as *al-jeel,* from the word for generation) was set by Egyptian Ahmed Adawiyya (b 1945), the Arab world's first 'pop star'.

During the 1990s there was a calculated attempt to create a more up-market sound, with many musicians mimicking Western dance music. Tacky electronics were replaced with moody pianos, Spanish guitars and thunderous drums. Check out the Egyptian singer Amr Diab (b 1961), whose heavily produced songs have made him the best-selling artist ever in the Arab world (achieved with his 1996 album *Nour al-Ain*).

Heading the current crop of megastar singers (the Arabic music scene is totally dominated by solo vocalists, there are no groups) are Majida al-Rumi (b 1956) of Lebanon, Iraqi-born Kazem (Kadim) al-Saher (b 1957) and Iraq's Ilham al-Madfai (b 1942), who founded the Middle East's first rock band back in the 1960s. Syria's prolific Omar Suleyman (b 1966), who emerged from that quintessential Middle Eastern genre of wedding performances, has produced over 500 albums, appeared at the 2011 Glastonbury Festival and has collaborated with everyone from Björk to Damon Albarn.

Turkish

Traditional Turkish music is enjoying something of a revival with Sufi music, dominated by traditional instrumentation, leading the way. Sufi music's spiritual home is Konya and the sound is bewitchingly hypnotic – a simple repeated melody usually played on the *nai* (reed pipe), accompanied by recitations of Sufi poetry.

Sufi music's growing popularity beyond Turkey's borders owes much to the work of artists like Mercan Dede (www.mercandede.com; b 1966), whose blend of Sufism with electronica has taken the genre beyond its traditional boundaries and into a mainstream audience. He even doubles as a DJ with the stage name Arkin Allen, spinning hardcore house and techno beats at rave festivals in the US and Canada. Not surprisingly, one Turkish newspaper described him as a 'dervish for the modern world'.

But Turkey's most pervasive soundtrack of choice is Turkish pop, with its skittish rhythms and strident vocals. Sezen Aksu (b 1954), known as 'the Queen of Turkish music', launched the country's love affair with the genre with her first single in 1976. Combining Western influences and local folk music to create a thoroughly contemporary sound, she's also an independent spirit not afraid to speak out on environmental issues and Turkey's treatment of its minorities.

MIDDLE EASTERN MUSIC – OUR TOP 10 ALBUMS

➡ *The Lady & the Legend*, Fairouz (Lebanon)

➡ *Al-Atlaal*, Umm Kolthum (Egypt)

➡ *Awedony*, Amr Diab (Egypt)

➡ *Le Luth de Baghdad*, Nasseer Shamma (Iraq)

➡ *Asmar*, Yeir Dalal (Israel)

➡ *The Idan Raichel Project*, The Idan Raichel Project (Israel)

➡ *Nar with Secret Tribe*, Mercan Dede (Turkey)

➡ *Deli Kızın Türküsü*, Sezen Aksu (Turkey)

➡ *Les Plus Grands Classiques de la Musique Arabe*, various artists

➡ *Drab zeen*, Toufic Faroukh (Lebanon)

Other super-popular stars include Tarkan, Serdat Ortaç and Mustafa Sandal. Notable rock bands include Duman and Mor ve Ötesi. maNga create a mix of metal, rock and Anatolian folk. Their 2012 album *e-akustik* is worth seeking out.

Israeli

In recent decades there has been a drive to excavate Jewish rhythms from broader European traditions. The result is a deep, distinctive Israeli sound.

Perhaps the most successful example of this latter phenomenon is *klezmer*. With its foundations laid by the Jewish communities of Eastern Europe, *klezmer*'s fast-paced, instrumental form was ideally suited to Jewish celebrations and it has sometimes been branded as Jewish jazz, in recognition of its divergence from established musical styles. The modern version has added vocals – almost always in Yiddish.

If *klezmer* takes its inspiration from Jewish diaspora roots in Europe, the Idan Raichel Project (www.idanraichelproject.com), arguably Israel's most popular group, casts its net more widely. Israeli love songs are its forte, but it's the Ethiopian instruments, Jamaican rhythms and Yemeni vocals that mark the group out as something special. Although originally rejected by leading local record labels for being 'too ethnic', the Idan Raichel Project's building of bridges between Israel's now-multicultural musical traditions struck a chord with audiences at home and abroad.

Mizrahi (Oriental or Eastern) music, with its Middle Eastern and Mediterranean scales and rhythms, has its roots in the melodies of North Africa, Iraq and Yemen, and may be Israel's most popular genre. Shlomo Bar (www.shlomobar.com), inspired by the traditional Jewish music of Morocco, is still performing, joined more recently by superstars Sarit Hadad (www.sarit-hadad.com), who has been described as Israel's Britney Spears, and Amir Benayoun, whose genre-defying concerts mix love songs and medieval Jewish liturgical poems. Moshe Peretz enjoys crossing the line from Mizrahi to mainstream and back again.

Another artist to have adapted ancient musical traditions for a modern audience is Yasmin Levy (b 1975), who sings in Ladino, the language of Sephardic Jews, who lived in Andalusia for centuries until 1492. The flamenco inflections in her music speak strongly of what she calls 'the musical memories of the old Moorish and Jewish-Spanish world'. Crossing frontiers of a different kind, Yair Dalal (b 1955; www.yairdalal.com) is an outstanding Israeli oud player who has collaborated with Palestinian and other Arab musicians.

Landscape & Environment

The Middle East faces some of the most pressing environmental issues of our time and there are few regions of the world where the human impact upon the environment has been quite so devastating. Further, as one of the world's largest oil-producing regions, the Middle East's contribution to the gathering global environmental crisis far outweighs its size. There *are* pockets of good news, but, it must be said, there aren't many.

In the 178-country 2014 Environmental Performance Index, Israel ranked highest among Middle Eastern countries at 39th, followed by Egypt (50th), Jordan (60th), Turkey (66th), Syria (68th), Iran (83rd), Lebanon (91st) and Iraq (149th).

Land

Deserts

Deserts consume the countries of the Middle East, covering 93% of Egypt, 77% of Jordanian and Iraqi territory, and 60% of Israel and the Palestinian Territories. Although deserts dominate much of the region, they're rarely home to the sandy landscapes of childhood imaginings. Apart from the Saharan sand seas in parts of Egypt, sand dunes worthy of the name are rare and stony gravel plains are the defining feature. Desert oases – such as Palmyra in Syria or Siwa in Egypt – have played an important role in the history of the region, serving as crucial watering points for caravans travelling the Silk Road and the Sahara.

Mountains

More than half of Iran is covered by mountains. The majestic Alborz Mountains skirt the Caspian Sea from the border of Azerbaijan as far as Turkmenistan, and are home to ski fields and the snowcapped Mt Damavand (5671m), the Middle East's tallest mountain. The immense Zagros Mountains stretch about 1500km from Turkey to the Persian Gulf, rising and falling like the ridged back of a great crocodile.

Eastern Turkey is similarly glorious with seriously high mountains rising above 5000m – the 5137m-high Mt Ararat (Ağrı Dağı) is the highest mountain in the country. Southeastern Anatolia offers windswept rolling steppe, jagged outcrops of rock that spill over into far-north Iraq and northwestern Iran. The vast, high plateau of rolling steppe and mountain ranges of Central Anatolia are similarly dramatic.

In Lebanon, the Mt Lebanon Range forms the backbone of the country: the highest peak, Qornet as-Sawda (3019m) rises southeast of Tripoli. Other Lebanese ranges include the beautiful Chouf Mountains, the Mt Lebanon Range and Bekaa Valley, and the Anti-Lebanon Range, a sheer arid massif averaging 2000m in height, which forms a natural border with Syria.

Rivers

The Nile, which runs for 6695km, 22% of it in Egypt, is the longest river on earth and along its banks flourished the glorious civilisation of ancient Egypt. Other Middle Eastern rivers resonate just as strongly with legends and empires past. According to the Bible, the Euphrates and Tigris are among the four rivers that flowed into the Garden of Eden and they would later provide the means for the cradle of civilisation in Mesopotamia. The Jordan River, the lowest river on earth, also features prominently in biblical texts. Even today, were it not for the rivers that run through these lands – hence providing a water source and narrow fertile agricultural zones close to the riverbanks – it's difficult to see how these regions could support life at all.

Wildlife

Animals

Occupying the junction of three natural zones, the Middle East was once a sanctuary for an amazing variety of mammals. Hardly any are left. Worse still, official government policies to protect wildlife are as rare as many of the animals. Casual wildlife sightings are extremely rare in the Middle East, although desert expeditions in Egypt's Sinai or Sahara offer the chance to see gazelle, rock hyraxes, fennec fox and even the graceful Nubian ibex. Otherwise, if you see anything more exciting than domesticated camels, donkeys and water buffaloes, you'll belong to a very small group of privileged Middle Eastern travellers.

Israel

The Israeli initiative known as Hai Bar (literally 'wildlife') is a small beacon of hope amid an otherwise gloomy outlook. Begun more than 45 years ago, the Hai Bar program set itself the most ambitious of aims: to reintroduce animals that roamed the Holy Land during biblical times by collecting a small pool of rare animals, breeding them, then reintroducing them to the wild. Consequently, the wild ass, beloved by the Prophet Isaiah, has turned the corner in Israel, though it's not likely to come off the endangered list any time soon. But the story of the Persian fallow deer is the one that really captured the public imagination. A small flock of the species was secretly flown in from Iran in 1978 on the last El Al flight to leave Tehran before the Islamic revolution. These shy animals have taken hold in the Galilee reserve of Akhziv and around the hills west of Jerusalem.

Jordan

It's in Jordan where you've the best chance of spotting charismatic fauna. Oryx, ostrich, gazelle and Persian onager are all being reared for reintroduction to the wild and are on show at Jordan's Shaumari Wildlife Reserve in eastern Jordan. Jordan's striking caracal (Persian lynx), a feline with outrageous tufts of black hair on the tips of its outsized, pointy ears, is occasionally seen in Wadi Mujib and Dana Nature Reserves.

Iran

Iran is home to 158 species of mammal, about one-fifth of which are endemic. Large cats, including the Persian leopard and Asiatic cheetah, are the standout species. The latter, down to between 70 and 110 in the wild, is the focus of intense conservation efforts and represents the only cheetah population outside of Africa. Those that remain inhabit the thinly populated salt deserts and remote mountains of Iran's interior.

Notable other species include the spectacular Persian wild ass, goitered and Jebeer gazelles, maral, Asian black bear, brown bear and seven species of wild sheep. Most larger mammals are found in the forests of the Alborz Mountains.

Birds

In contrast to the region's dwindling number of high-profile mammals, the variety of bird life in the Middle East is exceptionally rich. As

At the disappearing wetlands of Azraq Wetland Reserve (p318) in Jordan, 347,000 birds were present on 2 February 1967. On the same date 33 years later there were just 1200.

The cedars for which Lebanon is famous are now confined to a few mountain-top sites, most notably at the small grove at the Cedars ski resort and the Chouf Cedar Reserve in the Chouf Mountains.

well as being home to numerous indigenous species, the Middle East, despite the critical loss of wetlands in Jordan and Iraq, continues to serve as a way station on migration routes between Asia, Europe and Africa. Twice a year, half a billion birds of every conceivable variety soar along the Syro-African rift, the largest avian fly way in the world, which is compressed into a narrow corridor along the eastern edge of Israel and the Palestinian Territories; indeed, Israel claims to be the world's second-largest flyway (after South America) for migratory birds.

At least one highly endangered bird species, the northern bald ibis, is not being allowed to migrate for its own safety.

Egypt's Sinai Peninsula and Al-Fayoum Oasis, and Wadi Araba in Jordan also receive an enormous and varied amount of ornithological traffic. Egypt alone has recorded sightings of over 430 different species, while the species count for Iran exceeds 500. Some useful resources:

Birdlife International (www.birdlife.org/middle-east)

International Birdwatching Center of the Jordan Valley (www.birdwatching.org.il)

International Center for the Study of Bird Migration (www.birds.org.il)

Society for the Protection of the Nature of Israel (SPNI; natureisrael.org)

Marine Life

The Red Sea teems with more than 1000 species of marine life, an amazing spectacle of colour and form. Fish, sharks, turtles, stingrays, dolphins, corals, sponges, sea cucumbers and molluscs all thrive in these waters. The rare loggerhead turtle nests on some of Turkey's Mediterranean beaches.

Most of the bewildering variety of fish species in the Red Sea – including many that are found nowhere else – are closely associated with the coral reef, and live and breed in the reefs or nearby sea-grass beds. Threats to the coral reefs – from both global warming and more localised causes – therefore threaten a large number of species.

In the Red Sea waters off Hurghada, for example, conservationists estimate that more than 1000 pleasure boats and almost as many fishing boats ply the waters. For decades, there was nothing to stop captains from anchoring to the coral, or snorkellers and divers breaking off a colourful chunk to take home. But in 1992, 12 of Hurghada's more reputable

Notable National Parks & Reserves

Ras Mohammed National Park, Egypt

Shaumari Wildlife Reserve, Jordan

Dana Biosphere Reserve, Jordan

Azraq Wetland Reserve, Jordan

Mujib Biosphere Reserve, Jordan

Chouf Cedar Reserve, Lebanon

Ein Gedi, Israel

SAVING THE ARABIAN ORYX

The Arabian oryx – sometimes said to be the unicorn of historical legend – is a majestic creature that stands about 1m high at the shoulder and has enormous horns that project over 50cm into the air. Adapted well to their desert environment, wild oryx once had an uncanny ability to sense rain on the wind. One herd is recorded as having travelled up to 155km, led by a dominant female, to rain. In times of drought, oryxes have been known to survive 22 months without water, obtaining moisture from plants and leaves.

Their white coats offered camouflage in the searing heat of the desert, providing a measure of protection from both heat and hunters, but the oryxes and their long, curved horns were highly prized. In 1972, the last wild Arabian oryx was killed by hunters in Oman, which led officials to declare the oryx extinct in the wild. Nine oryxes left in captivity around the world were pooled and taken to the Arizona Zoo for a breeding program. They became known as the 'World Oryx Herd' and eventually grew to over 200 in number. As a result of programs to reintroduce the Arabian oryx into the wild across the region, an estimated 1000 oryxes were thought to survive in the wild in 2011, with populations in Saudi Arabia (around 600), United Arab Emirates (200), Israel (100), Jordan (50) and Oman (50). There are also between 6000 and 7000 oryxes in captivity around the world.

The most accessible place to see an Arabian oryx (in captivity, but partly free-ranging) should be in Jordan's Shaumari Wildlife Reserve (p318) once it reopens.

dive companies formed the Hurghada Environmental Protection & Conservation Association (www.hepca.com). Working with the Egyptian National Parks Office, Hepca works to conserve the Red Sea's reefs through public-awareness campaigns, direct community action and lobbying of the Egyptian government to introduce appropriate laws. Thanks to these efforts, the whole coast south of Suez Governorate is now known as the Red Sea Protectorate. One of its earliest successes was to establish over 570 mooring buoys at popular dive sites around Hurghada. In 2009 the NGO also took over responsibility for waste management in the region, implementing door-to-door rubbish collection and recycling in Marsa Alam and Hurghada.

National Parks & Wildlife Reserves

Although there are exceptions, most of the Middle East's officially protected areas exist in name only, and are poorly patrolled and poorly funded. There are, however, exceptions.

Nearly 25 years ago the Jordanian government established 12 protected areas, totalling about 1200 sq km, amounting, in total, to just 1% of Jordan's territory. Some were abandoned, but the rest survive thanks to the impressive **Royal Society for the Conservation of Nature** (RSCN; www.rscn.org.jo), Jordan's major environmental agency.

In recent years, thanks to EU aspirations, Turkey has stepped up its environmental protection practices. The growing number of protected areas includes 33 national parks, 16 nature parks and 35 nature reserves. It also includes 58 curiously named 'nature monuments', which are mostly protected trees, some as old as 1500 years. Sometimes the parks' regulations are carefully enforced, but at other times a blind eye is turned to such problems as litter-dropping picnickers. Visitor facilities are rare.

The Middle East's star environmental performer is undoubtedly Israel due to its strong regulation of hunting and a system of nature reserves comprising some 25% of the land. However, the parks are not without their problems. Many are minuscule in size and isolated, providing only limited protection for local species. Moreover, many of the reserves in the south are also used as military firing zones.

Environmental Issues

Water

It's often said that the next great Middle Eastern war will be fought not over land but over water. Syria and Iraq have protested to Turkey because it is building dams at the headwaters of the Tigris and Euphrates. Egypt has threatened military action against Sudan and Ethiopia or any other upstream country endangering its access to the waters of the Nile. And Jordan and Israel regularly spar over the waters of the shared Jordan River, which has now been reduced to a trickle, half of which is 50% raw sewage and effluent from fish farms.

To understand the extent of the Middle East's water-scarcity problem, consider Jordan, which has just 106 cu metres of renewable water per capita per year, compared to the UK's 2262. Jordan's figure is expected to fall below 90 cu metres by 2025. Anything less than 500 cu metres is considered to be a scarcity of water. Another study suggests that Jordan currently uses about 60% more water than is replenished from natural sources. By some estimates, Jordan will simply run out of water within 20 years. Dams on the Yarmouk River, water pipelines, plans to tap underground fossil water and desalination plants are all part of the projected (and extremely expensive) solution.

The Middle East is home to 4.5% of the world's population and around half of the world's oil supplies, but only receives 2% of the world's rainfall and possesses just 0.4% of the world's recoverable water supplies.

Columbia University's Water in the Middle East (library.columbia.edu/locations/global/virtual-libraries/middle_east_studies/water) hosts numerous links to articles on the Middle East's most pressing environmental issue.

THE DEAD SEA IS DYING – DR ALON TAL

The Dead Sea is the lowest place on earth and probably one of the hottest. The high resulting evaporation produces an astonishing salinity of 31%, about nine times higher than the oceans. The water's oily minerals also contain salubrious properties. German health insurance covers periodic visits to the Dead Sea for psoriasis patients to luxuriate in the healing waters.

Sadly, no natural resource in the Middle East shows more signs of impact from relentless population growth and economic development than the Dead Sea. Technically, the sea is a 'terminal lake' into which the Jordan River, along with other more arid watersheds, deposits its flow. In 1900, the river discharged 1.2 trillion litres a year into the Dead Sea. When Israeli and Jordanian farmers began to divert its water to produce a new agricultural economy in the 1950s, the flow was reduced to a putrid trickle and the Dead Sea began to dry up. Water levels in the river today are barely 10% of the natural flow. The Jordanian and Israeli potash industries in the southern, largely industrial Dead Sea region exacerbate the water loss by accelerating evaporation in their production processes. The impact is manifested in sinkholes, created when underground salt gets washed away by the infiltrating subsurface freshwater flow. Perhaps the most acute environmental consequence, though, is the 27m drop in the sea's water level and the long and discouraging walks now required to reach the edge of the retreating beach.

Among the suggested solutions to bring water back to the Dead Sea is a pipeline from the Gulf of Aqaba (Red Sea) to the Dead Sea's southern shore, producing hydroelectricity as well as a desalination plant that would provide water to Amman. The US$5 billion project, dubbed the 'Peace Conduit', took a big step forward with the signing of an agreement between Israel, the Palestinian Territories and Jordan to let the project proceed.

Dr Alon Tal is a professor in the Desert Ecology Department at Israel's Ben-Gurion University.

Desertification

Desertification, which is caused by overgrazing, deforestation, the overuse of off-road vehicles, wind erosion and drought, is a significant problem faced by all Middle Eastern countries, with the possible exception of Lebanon. The seemingly unstoppable encroachment of the desert onto previously fertile, inhabited and environmentally sensitive areas is resulting in millions of hectares of fertile land becoming infertile and, ultimately, uninhabitable. Jordan, Syria, Egypt, Iran and Iraq are on the frontline, but even largely desert-free Turkey is casting a worried eye on the future. Environmentalists fear that much of Turkey could be desert by 2025.

Pollution

Levels of waste – whether industrial outflow, sewage discharge or everyday rubbish – have reached critical levels across the region; recycling is almost nonexistent. At one level, the impact is devastating for local fishing industries, agricultural output, freshwater supplies and marine environments – Lebanon did not have functioning waste-water treatment plants until the mid-1990s, while up to 75% of Turkey's industrial waste is discharged without any treatment whatsoever. At another level, the great mounds of rubbish and airborne plastic bags provide an aesthetic assault on the senses for traveller and local alike.

The related issue of air pollution is also threatening to overwhelm in a region where the motor vehicle is king. In Cairo, for example, airborne smoke, soot, dust and liquid droplets from fuel combustion constantly exceed World Health Organization (WHO) standards (up to 275 micrograms per cu metre of air, when the international standard is 50), leading to skyrocketing instances of emphysema, asthma and cancer among the city's population. Cairo may be an extreme case, but it's a problem facing urban areas everywhere in the Middle East.

Survival Guide

Traveller Etiquette

Like anywhere else in the world, the people of the Middle East have particular ways of doing things and these customs can seem strange to first-time visitors. While you should always try to follow local customs, most people in the Middle East will be too polite to say anything if you break one of the region's taboos. In most cases, an apology and obvious goodwill will earn instant forgiveness.

Eating Etiquette

Middle Easterners can be a hospitable lot and it's not unusual for visitors to receive at least one invitation to eat in someone's home while travelling through the region. While each invitation needs to be assessed on its merits, our general advice would be that eating in a family home can be one of your most memorable travel experiences in the Middle East.

Homes

To avoid making your hosts feel uncomfortable, there are a few simple guidelines to follow.

➡ Bring a small gift of flowers, chocolates, pastries, fruit or honey.

➡ It's polite to be seen to wash your hands before a meal.

➡ Always remove your shoes before sitting down on a rug to eat or drink tea.

➡ Don't sit with your legs stretched out – it's considered rude during a meal.

➡ Always sit next to a person of the same sex at the dinner table unless your host(ess) suggests otherwise.

➡ Use only your right hand for eating or accepting food.

➡ When the meal begins, accept as much food as is offered to you. If you say 'no thanks' continually, it can offend the host.

➡ It's good manners to leave a little food on your plate at the end of the meal: traditionally, a clean plate was thought to invite famine. It can also suggest to your host that they haven't fed you sufficiently.

➡ Your host will often lay the tastiest morsels in front of you; it's polite to accept them.

➡ The best part – such as the meat – is usually saved until last, so don't take it until offered.

Restaurants

There are fewer etiquette rules to observe in restaurants, but it's still worth trying to do so, particularly if you're eating as the guest of a local or sharing a table with locals.

➡ Picking teeth after a meal is quite acceptable and toothpicks are often provided.

➡ Be sure to leave the dining area and go outside or to the toilet before blowing your nose.

➡ Take food from your side of the table; stretching to the other side is considered impolite.

➡ It's polite to accept a cup of coffee after a meal and impolite to leave before it's served.

Religion

At some point during your travels in the Middle East, the conversation is likely to turn to religion. More specifically, you'll probably be asked, 'What's your religion?' Given that most foreign travellers come from secular Western traditions where religion is a private matter, the level of frankness in some of these discussions can come as a surprise. At the same time, there's no better way of getting under the skin of a nation than talking about the things that matter most in life. So how do you go about answering this question?

It's usually easy to explain that you are Christian or, in some circumstances, Jewish, although these rules, of course, go out the window when in the company of Hamas or Islamic State militants or on the unfamiliar streets of Baghdad. The overwhelming majority of Muslims won't bat an eyelid and may even welcome the opportunity to talk about the common origins and doctrines that Christianity, Judaism and Islam share. Traditionally, Christians and Jews were respected as 'people of the book' who share the same God. In fact, many a Bedouin encounter begins with a celebration of that fact, with greetings such as 'Your God, my God same – *Salaam* (Peace)!'

The question of religion gets complicated when it comes to atheists. 'I don't believe in God' can call into question the very foundation of a Muslim's existence. If you are concerned your atheism will cause offence, perhaps say, 'I'm a seeker', suggesting you haven't quite made up your mind but may do so in the future. Be aware that Muslims may respond by explaining the merits of Islam to you. If that's not how you planned to spend your afternoon, try saying, 'I'm not religious'. This will likely lead to understanding nods and then, perhaps on subsequent meetings, an earnest attempt at conversion. Phrases like 'You'll find God soon, God-willing' are a measure of someone's affection for you and a reasonable response would be *shukran* (thank you).

General Etiquette

Tourism has the potential to improve the relationship between the Middle East and the West, but the gradual erosion of traditional life is the flipside of mass tourism. Sexual promiscuity, public drunkenness among tourists and the wearing of unsuitable clothing are all concerns to be aware of.

Try to have minimal impact on your surroundings. Create a positive precedent for those who follow you by keeping in mind the following:

➡ Don't hand out sweets or pens to children on the streets, since it encourages begging. Similarly, doling out medicines can encourage people not to seek proper medical advice and you have no control over whether the medicines are taken appropriately. A donation to a project, health centre or school is a far more constructive way to help.

➡ Buy your snacks, cigarettes, bubble gum etc from the enterprising grannies trying to make ends meet, rather than from state-run stores. Also, use locally owned hotels and restaurants and buy locally made products.

➡ Try to give people a balanced perspective of life in the West. Try also to point out the strong points of the local culture, such as strong family ties and comparatively low crime.

➡ Make yourself aware of the human-rights situation, history and current affairs in the countries you travel through.

➡ If you're in a frustrating situation, be patient, friendly and considerate. Never lose your temper as a confrontational attitude won't go down well. For many Arabs, a loss of face is a serious and sensitive issue.

➡ Try to learn some of the standard greetings – it will make a very good first impression.

➡ Always ask before taking photos of people. Don't worry if you don't speak the language – a smile and gesture will be appreciated. Never photograph someone if they don't want you to. If you agree to send someone a photo, make sure you follow through on it.

➡ Be respectful of Islamic traditions and don't wear revealing clothing; loose lightweight clothing is preferable.

➡ Men should shake hands when formally meeting other men, but not women, unless the woman extends her hand first. If you are a woman and uncomfortable with men extending their hand to you (they don't do this with local women), just put your hand over your heart and say hello.

➡ Public displays of physical affection are almost always likely to be misunderstood. Be discreet.

Safe Travel

Don't believe everything you read about the Middle East. Yes, there are regions that are dangerous to visit and you should, of course, always be careful while travelling in the region. But alongside the sometimes disturbing hard facts is more often a vast corpus of exaggeration, stereotyping and downright misrepresentation. We'll try and put this as simply as possible: there's every chance that you'll be safer in many parts of the Middle East than you would be back home.

Is it Safe?

Imagine somebody whose image of the USA was built solely on the 9/11 attacks, or who refused to visit Spain or the UK as a result of the terrorist attacks in Madrid and London in recent years. Just as the USA, the UK and Spain are rarely considered to be dangerous destinations, so too, day-to-day life in the Middle East very rarely involves shootings or explosions. There are trouble spots where violence is serious and widespread, such as Syria and many regions of Iraq, and there are places where violence flares from time to time (such as in the Palestinian Territories or Lebanon). But such outbreaks of violence usually receive widespread media coverage, making it relatively easy to avoid these places until things settle down.

Terrorist incidents also do occur, and there have been attacks in Israel and the Palestinian Territories and the Red Sea resorts of Egypt's Sinai Peninsula in recent years. While such incidents are clearly major causes for concern, they are definitely the exception rather than the norm. The sad fact about modern terrorism is that you may face similar dangers anywhere in the world and you're probably no more at risk in much of the Middle East than you may be in your home country. As one holidaymaker was reported saying in the wake of the 2005 Sharm el-Sheikh bombings: 'Actually, I live in central London. I don't really want to go home!'

As a foreigner, you may receive the occasional question ('Why does the West support Israel?'), but you'll rarely be held personally accountable for the policies of Western governments. Once in Tehran we stood, obviously Westerners, with cameras and pasty complexions, and watched a crowd march by chanting 'Death to America! Death to Britain!' Several marchers grinned, waved and broke off to come over and ask how we liked Iran.

So, while right now we advise against visits to Gaza, Hebron, Mosul or anywhere in Syria, don't let problems in some areas tar your image of the entire region. Keep abreast of current affairs, and if you need to phone your embassy for travel advice, then do so. Otherwise, just go.

Common Dangers

Road Accidents

Perhaps the most widespread threat to your safety comes from travelling on the region's roads. Road conditions vary, but driving standards are often poor and high speeds are common. Tips for minimising the risk of becoming a road statistic:

➡ Try to avoid night travel.

➡ A full-sized bus is usually safer than a minibus.

➡ If travelling in a shared taxi or minibus, avoid taking the seat next to the driver.

Political Unrest

The recent popular uprisings against regimes from Cairo to Damascus has added a layer of uncertainty to travel in the region, although with the exception of Syria and, for a time, Egypt, the impact upon travellers has been minimal. Trouble spots in the region are usually well defined, and as long as you keep track of political developments, you're unlikely to come to any harm. Avoid political demonstrations or large gatherings and always ask the advice of locals if unsure.

Theft & Petty Crime

Crime rates are extremely low in most countries in the Middle East – theft is rarely a problem and robbery (mugging) even less of one. Even so, take the standard precautions. Always keep valuables with you or locked in a safe – never leave them in your room or in a car or bus. Use a money belt, a pouch under your clothes, a leather wallet attached to your belt, or internal pockets in your clothing. Keep a separate record of your passport, credit card and travellers cheque numbers; it won't cure problems, but it will make them easier to bear. We're sorry to say this, but beware of your fellow travellers; there are more than a few backpackers who make their money go further by helping themselves to other people's.

Country by Country

What follows is a high-level overview of the safety situation in the area.

Egypt

Egypt remains a relatively safe country to visit, although the political turmoil since 2011 has seen security become a concern in some areas, particularly as it relates to women travellers and/or petty theft. Avoid political demonstrations (especially those in Cairo's Tahrir Sq) and be particularly wary in areas with mixed Muslim-Coptic Christian populations.

Iran

Iran is one of the safest countries of the Middle East in which to travel. Violent crime against foreigners is extremely rare, although areas close to the borders with Iraq and Afghanistan should generally be avoided. Western embassies advise their nationals to register on arrival.

GOVERNMENT TRAVEL ADVICE

The following government websites offer travel advisory services and information for travellers:

Australian Department of Foreign Affairs & Trade (www.smartraveller.gov.au)

Canadian Department of Foreign Affairs & International Trade (www.voyage.gc.ca)

French Ministère des Affaires et Étrangères Européennes (www.diplomatie.gouv.fr/fr/conseils-aux-voyageurs_909)

Italian Ministero degli Affari Esteri (www.viaggiaresicuri.mae.aci.it)

UK Foreign & Commonwealth Office (www.gov.uk/foreign-travel-advice)

US Department of State (www.travel.state.gov)

Iraq

Most of Iraq remains off-limits to travellers, including Baghdad, southern, northern and central Iraq. Most of Iraqi Kurdistan, however, is considered reasonably safe and was increasingly attracting both independent travellers and organised tours, prior to the rise of Isis elsewhere in the country.

Israel & the Palestinian Territories

Although the security situation has greatly improved in recent years, travellers should continue to exercise caution in Israel and the Palestinian Territories. You're unlikely to experience difficulties in most areas, although we strongly recommend against travel to the Gaza Strip. You should always keep your ear to the ground in Jerusalem, Hebron and other potential flashpoints.

Jordan

Jordan has largely escaped the unrest arising from the Arab Spring and it remains one of the safest countries in the region to visit.

Lebanon

Although it hasn't happened often and the country remains generally safe to visit, the conflict in Syria has spilled over into Lebanon often enough for us to advise caution. Border areas with Syria and the northern city of Tripoli have been particularly affected. Beyond that, the potential for political unrest and attendant violence remains a constant of Lebanese life and care should be taken in southern Lebanon and Hezbollah's stronghold in the Bekaa Valley.

Syria

Syria was, at the time of research and writing, one of the most dangerous countries on earth for travellers to visit. Don't go there – it's as simple as that.

Turkey

Turkey is one of the safest countries in the Middle East for travellers, with a stable and democratic political system and well-developed transport infrastructure. Always check the security situation, however, before you travel in areas close to the borders with Syria and Iraq.

Women Travellers

Despite the Middle East's reputation as difficult terrain for women travellers, there's no reason why women can't enjoy the region as much as their male counterparts. In fact, some seasoned women travellers to the Middle East consider their gender to be a help, not a hindrance.

Attitudes towards Women

For many people in the region, both men and women, the role of a woman is specifically defined: she is mother and matron of the household, while the man is the provider. Generalisations can, however, be misleading and the reality is often far more nuanced.

There are thousands of middle- and upper-middle-class professional women in the Arab world who, like their counterparts in the West, juggle work and family responsibilities. Among the working classes or in conservative rural areas where adherence to tradition is strongest, the ideal may be for women to concentrate on home and family, but economic reality means that millions of women are forced to work (but are still responsible for all domestic chores).

Contrary to stereotypes, the treatment of foreign women can be at its best in more conservative societies, providing, of course, you adhere to the prevailing social mores.

The treatment of women can also be due to age: older women will find they are greatly respected. One seasoned Middle Eastern expat and traveller told us she was so traumatised after travelling in Israel as a 21-year-old that she took up karate. Now in her forties, she's been going back to the region ever since. 'I realise the older I get, the less harassment I receive,' she said. She finds this a wonderful relief – 'I've reached that age where I can have a meaningful conversation with men without inviting other expectations. Having a husband is also immensely useful!'

LET'S TALK ABOUT SEX

When it comes to sex, the differences between Western and Middle Eastern women become most apparent. Premarital sex (or, indeed, any sex outside marriage) is taboo in most of the region. With occasional exceptions among the upper classes, women are expected to be virgins when they marry and a family's reputation can rest upon this.

The presence of foreign women presents, in the eyes of some Middle Eastern men, a chance to get around these norms with ease and without consequences, a perception reinforced by distorted impressions gained from Western TV and the behaviour of a small number of women travellers. As one hopeful young man in Egypt remarked, when asked why he persisted in harassing every Western woman he saw: 'For every 10 that say no, there's one that says yes.'

Pros & Cons

Advantages

Women travellers are no different from their male counterparts in that meeting local people is a highlight of travelling in the Middle East. And unlike male travellers, they can meet Middle Eastern women without social restrictions, opening up a whole Middle Eastern world that men can never hope to experience. Local women are as curious about life for women beyond the Middle East as you are about their lives, and they love to chat to women visitors. That said, local women are less likely than men to have had an education that included learning English – you'll find this to be the only major barrier to getting to meet and talk with them.

One other advantage, and one you should exploit to the full, is that in some countries it's often perfectly acceptable for a woman to go straight to the front of a queue or ask to be served first. This is less likely to occur in Lebanon, Turkey, Israel and Iran.

Disadvantages

Sexual harassment is a problem worldwide and the Middle East is no exception. Harassment can come in many forms: from stares, muttered comments and uncomfortably close contact on crowded public transport, to the difficulty of eating in public on your own, where you may receive endless unwanted guests – even the wandering hands of waiters can be a problem. Women also report being followed and hissed at by unwanted male admirers on a fairly regular basis.

That said, although 'mild' harassment can be common in some countries, reports of serious physical harassment are rare. Whether that's because it rarely occurs or because it's rarely reported varies greatly from country to country. Significant social stigma attaches to sexual harassment in many Middle Eastern countries.

What to Wear

Fair or not, how women travellers dress will, considering the stereotypes at large in the region, go a long way towards determining how they're treated. To you, short pants and a tight top might be an appropriate reaction to the desert temperatures, but to many local men, your dress choice will send an entirely different message,

SURVIVAL STRATEGIES

Your experience of travelling in the region may depend partly on situations beyond your control, but there are some things you can try so as to minimise problems:

➡ Retain your self-confidence and sense of humour.

➡ Balance alertness with a certain detachment: ignoring stares and refusing to dignify suggestive remarks with a response generally stops unwanted advances in their tracks.

➡ Eat in a restaurant's family section, where one exists, or at places more used to tourists.

➡ If necessary, invent or borrow a husband, wear a wedding ring, even carry a photo of your 'kids'. While this may cause some consternation – what sort of mother/wife are you to have left your family to travel alone? – it will deter many suitors.

➡ Avoid direct eye contact with local men (dark sunglasses help), although a cold glare can also be an effective riposte if deployed at the right moment.

➡ Maximise your interaction with local women.

➡ In taxis, avoid sitting in the front seat unless the driver is female.

➡ On all forms of public transport, sit next to another woman whenever possible.

➡ You're lost? Try asking a local woman for directions.

➡ If nothing else works and you can't shake off a hanger-on, go to the nearest public place, such as a hotel lobby. If he persists, asking the receptionist to call the police will usually frighten him off.

confirming the worst views held of Western women.

The best way to tackle the stereotypes is to visibly debunk them: in other words, do as the locals do, dress and behave more modestly than you might at home and always err on the side of caution. As with anywhere, take your cues from those around you.

Dressing 'modestly' really means covering your upper legs and arms, shoulders and cleavage. A scarf is also useful, both to cover your neckline and to slip over your head when you want to look even more inconspicuous or when the occasion requires it (such as when visiting a mosque).

For all the inconvenience, dressing conservatively means you'll get a much warmer reception from the locals, you'll attract less unwanted attention, and you may feel more comfortable (long baggy clothes will keep you cooler under the fierce Middle Eastern sun).

In Iran – and there's no use beating about the bush – most female travellers will find dress rules to be both an imposition and an inconvenience. Since the revolution of 1979 all women in Iran, including foreigners, have been required by law to wear loose-fitting clothes to disguise their figures and must also cover their hair.

Directory A–Z

Accommodation

In most countries of the Middle East, you'll find accommodation that ranges from cheap and nasty to plush and palatial; most places sit comfortably somewhere in between. In reviews, accommodation is divided into price categories (budget, midrange and top end); within each category prices are listed in order of author preference.

Generally Iran and Egypt have the cheapest accommodation, while Turkey, Jordan, Israel and the Palestinian Territories and Lebanon will cost a little more. However, travelling through the Middle East is now such a well-worn path that in most major destinations you'll find at least one high-quality place to suit your budget, whether you're travelling on a shoestring or an expense account.

Camping

Camping in the Middle East is possible, but stick to officially sanctioned campsites – many areas that are military or restricted zones aren't always marked as such and erecting a tent on an army firing range won't be a highlight of your trip. There are official camping grounds in Egypt, Lebanon, Turkey and Israel and the Palestinian Territories.

Hostels

There are youth hostels in Egypt, Israel and the Palestinian Territories. It's not usually necessary to hold a Hostelling International card to stay at these places, but it will usually get you a small discount.

Hotels

BUDGET

In hotels at the bottom end of the price scale, rooms are not always clean. In fact, let's be honest: they can be downright filthy. Very cheap hotels are just dormitories where you're crammed into a room with whoever else fronts up. The cheapest places are rarely suitable for women travelling alone.

That said, there are some places that stand out and while they may have no frills, nor do their shared bathrooms give any indication of the good health or otherwise of previous occupants. Some places treat you like a king even as you pay the price of a pauper. The happy (and most common) medium is usually a room devoid of character, but containing basic, well-maintained facilities.

MIDRANGE

In the midrange, rooms have private bathrooms, usually with hot water, fans to stir the air, a bit more space to swing a backpack and (sometimes) TVs promising international satellite channels.

TOP END

Hotels at the top end of the range have clean, self-contained rooms with hot showers and toilets that work all the time, not to mention satellite TV, shampoo and regularly washed towels in the bathrooms, air-con to provide refuge from the Middle Eastern sun and a few luxuries to lift the spirits.

An increasing (and entirely welcome) trend is the proliferation of tastefully designed boutique hotels that make a feature of traditional design.

Customs Regulations

Customs regulations vary from country to country, but in most cases they aren't that different from what

---

BOOK YOUR STAY ONLINE

For more accommodation reviews by Lonely Planet authors, check out http://lonelyplanet.com/hotels/. You'll find independent reviews, as well as recommendations on the best places to stay. Best of all, you can book online.

you'd expect in the West – a couple of hundred cigarettes and a couple of bottles of booze.

There was a time when electronics used to arouse interest when entering or leaving Egypt, but it's becoming increasingly rare. If they do pull you up, items such as laptop computers and especially video cameras may be written into your passport to ensure that they leave the country with you and are not sold. If you're carrying printed material that could be interpreted as being critical of the government, be discreet, although customs officials at major entry/departure points rarely search the bags of tourists.

Iran is a notable exception to some of these rules – alcohol is illegal in the Islamic Republic of Iran, and any publications showing (even modestly exposed) female flesh will be confiscated.

Discount Cards

An International Student Identity Card (ISIC) can be useful in the Middle East. Egypt, Israel and the Palestinian Territories and Turkey have various (and often considerable) student discounts for admission to museums, archaeological sites and monuments. In Israel, cardholders also qualify for 10% reductions on some bus fares and 20% on rail tickets. Bear in mind that a student card issued by your own university or college may not be recognised elsewhere; it really should be an ISIC (www.isic.org).

Embassies & Consulates

It's important to realise what your own embassy can and can't do to help you if you get into trouble. Generally speaking, it won't be much help in emergencies if the trouble you're in is remotely

GRAND OLD HOTELS OF THE MIDDLE EAST

If you're hankering after the Middle East of TE Lawrence and other stiff-upper-lipped colonial types, a few grand old hotels from the era still exist. Some have been tarted up with only hints remaining of their former glories, but a few are fraying around the edges a little, perhaps adding to the appeal for nostalgia buffs.

Windsor Hotel (Map p62; ☑2591 5810; www.windsorcairo. com; 19 Sharia Alfy, Cairo, Egypt; s/d from US$46/59, with shower & hand basin US$37/47; ✵🛜)

Winter Palace Hotel (Map p86; ☑237 1197; www.sofitel. com; Corniche an-Nil, Luxor, Egypt; old wing r from $160, ste from $450; ☻✵@🛜🏊)

Abbasi Hotel (Map p158; ☑031-3222 6010; www.abbasiho-tel.ir; Shahid Medani St, Esfahan, Iran; s/d US$64/98, deluxe d US$117-147, ste US$165-258; 🅿✵@🛜🏊)

King David Hotel (Map p214; ☑02-620 8888; www.danho-tels.com; 23 King David St, Jerusalem, Israel and the Palestinian Territories; r US$470-600, ste $960; ✵@🛜🏊)

your own fault. Remember that you are bound by the laws of the country you're in. Your embassy will not be sympathetic if you end up in jail after committing a crime locally, even if such actions are legal in your own country.

In genuine emergencies, you might get some limited assistance, but only if other channels have been exhausted. For example, if you need to get home urgently, a free ticket home is exceedingly unlikely – the embassy would expect you to have insurance. If all your money and documents are stolen, it might assist with getting a new passport, but a loan for onward travel is out of the question.

Gay & Lesbian Travellers

The situation for gay and lesbian travellers in the Middle East is more diverse than you might imagine. Israel is the best place in the region to be gay – homosexuality is legal, and Tel Aviv in particular has a thriving gay and lesbian

scene. Elsewhere, especially in conservative Jerusalem, the gay and lesbian scene is well and truly underground. The same doesn't apply to the Palestinian Territories, and hundreds of Palestinian gays have been forced to seek refuge in Israel.

Homosexuality inhabits a legal black hole in Turkey – while not illegal, nor is it officially legal. On one hand, İstanbul and Ankara are both home to a small but thriving gay community. Turkey is, however, a Muslim country and homophobia is on the rise; the local authorities have from time to time used morality laws to close down gay advocacy groups. As always, discretion is key.

It is slightly more complicated in Egypt and Jordan, where, although the criminal code doesn't expressly forbid homosexual acts, laws regarding public decency have been used to prosecute gays, especially in Egypt; the Jordanian capital Amman nonetheless has a couple of gay-friendly spots. Homosexuality is illegal in Lebanon, Syria, Iran and Iraq, although

Beirut takes a fairly liberal approach with a small but vibrant gay scene. In March 2014, a Lebanese court ruled that same-sex relations are not 'contradicting the laws of nature' and cannot therefore be considered a crime.

In those countries where homosexuality is illegal or ambiguous in a legal sense, penalties include fines and/or imprisonment. That does not mean that gays aren't active, but it does mean that gay identity is generally expressed only in certain trusted, private spheres.

Useful Resources

Gay Middle East (www.facebook.com/pages/Gay-Middle-East/133301836703856) Links to the prevailing situation, including news updates, with postings by locals and gay visitors.

Global Gayz (www.globalgayz.com) An excellent country-by-country rundown on the situation for gays and lesbians in all countries of the Middle East.

Spartacus International Gay Guide (www.spartacusworld.com/gayguide) Good for information on gay-friendly bars and hotels.

Insurance

Travel insurance covering theft, loss and medical problems is highly recommended. Some policies offer travellers lower and higher medical-expense options; the higher ones are chiefly for countries such as the USA which have extremely high medical costs. Watch particularly for the small print as some policies specifically exclude 'dangerous activities', which can include scuba diving, motorcycling and even trekking.

Internet Access

You're never too far from an internet cafe in all major cities and larger towns across the Middle East, although ones that last the distance are pretty rare. If you need to track one down, ask your hotel reception or head to the university district (if there is one) and ask around.

If you're travelling with a laptop, smartphone, iPad or other device, wireless internet access is increasingly the norm in most top-end hotels as well as many in the midrange categories. It's also getting easier to connect in upmarket cafes and restaurants.

Given its reputation for political censorship, there are surprisingly few websites that are blocked by governments in the region, although Iran is a significant exception; in the latter everything from news sites to Skype can fall foul of the censors.

Money

If we had to choose our preferred way of carrying our money to the Middle East, it would be a combination of withdrawing money from ATMs and carrying a supply of US dollars or euro cash, although remember that cash is king if you're travelling to Iran and Iraq.

ATMs

ATMs are now a way of life in most Middle Eastern countries and, with a few exceptions, it's possible to survive on cash advances. This is certainly the case in Turkey, Lebanon, Israel and the Palestinian Territories, Jordan and Egypt, where ATMs are everywhere and they're usually linked to one of the international networks (eg MasterCard, Maestro, Cirrus, Visa, Visa Electron or Global-Access systems). ATMs are appearing in Iraq, but they're still unreliable – bring US dollars cash. The same applies to Iran, where ATMs are widespread, but none accept international cards.

Another thing to consider is whether the convenience of withdrawing money as you go is outweighed by the bank fees you'll be charged for doing so. It's a good idea to check the transaction fees both with your own bank back home and, if possible, with the banks whose machines you'll be using while you travel.

Cash

Although credit cards are increasingly accepted, cash remains the most reliable way to carry your money in the Middle East. And not just any cash. US dollars and, increasingly, euros are the currency of choice in most countries of the Middle East, and not just for changing money – many midrange and top-end hotels prefer their bills to be settled in either currency.

If your funds have run dry and you've no means of withdrawing money, Western Union (www.westernunion.com) has representatives in every country in the region except Iran.

The only danger in relying solely on travelling with cash is that if you lose it, it's lost forever – insurance companies simply won't believe that you had US$1000 in cash.

Credit Cards

Credit cards (especially Visa and MasterCard) are accepted by an ever-growing number of Middle Eastern hotels, top-end restaurants and handicraft shops, but the situation is still a long way from one where you could pay your way solely by flashing a card. Israel and the Palestinian Territories, Lebanon and Turkey are the most credit-card-friendly countries in the region. You should always be wary of surcharges for paying by card – many Egyptian and Jordanian businesses also sting for commissions over and above the purchase price. Credit cards are still useless in Iraq and Iran.

Tipping

Tipping is expected to varying degrees in all Middle Eastern countries. Called baksheesh, it's more than just a reward for having rendered a service. Salaries and wages are much lower than in Western countries, so baksheesh is often regarded as an essential means of supplementing income. To a cleaner in a one- or two-star hotel, who may earn the equivalent of US$50 per month, the accumulated daily dollar tips given by guests can constitute the mainstay of his or her salary.

For Western travellers who aren't used to continual tipping, demands for baksheesh for doing anything from opening doors to pointing out the obvious in museums can be quite irritating. But it is the accepted way. Don't be intimidated into paying baksheesh when you don't think the service warrants it, but remember that more things warrant baksheesh here than anywhere in the West. One hint: carry lots of small change with you, but keep it separate from bigger bills, so that baksheesh demands don't increase when they see that you can afford more.

Tipping is increasingly expected in midrange and top-end restaurants in Israel and the Palestinian Territories, Lebanon and Turkey. Check your bill closely, however, as many such restaurants include an additional charge for service, in which case a further tip is not necessary. One country where baksheesh or tipping isn't as prevalent is Jordan, where many locals feel irritated when tourists throw their money around, not least because some employers are known to deduct anticipated tips from their employees, resulting in even lower wages!

Other circumstances in which a tip is expected is where you've taken a tour with a guide or a taxi driver, or both. How much to leave depends on the length of the expedition and the helpfulness of the guide.

Travellers Cheques

If you're among the dwindling ranks of travellers still using travellers cheques, perhaps you should reconsider. Yes, they're secure and replaceable, but so too are most credit and other bank cards. However, the main reason for not using travellers cheques is that only a limited number of banks will change them, they'll always charge a commission for doing so, and it always means you'll spend longer in the bank. Travellers cheques are useless in Iran.

If you do take travellers cheques, carry a mix of high- and low-denomination notes, as well as cheques, so that if you're about to leave a country, you can change just enough for a few days and not end up with too much local currency to get rid of.

Photography
Equipment

Memory cards are widely available in most countries of the Middle East, although you'll have a wider choice of brands in major cities. Expect prices to be broadly similar to what you'd pay back home. The situation for batteries is also similar, although for more professional cameras, you'd be better off bringing your own supply.

When it comes to burning photos onto CDs, many internet cafes will do so without batting an eyelid.

Cameras and lenses collect dust quickly in desert areas. Lens paper, a dust brush and cleaners can be difficult to find in some countries, so bring your own.

Photographing People

As a matter of courtesy, never photograph people without first asking their permission. While that's a general rule for photography anywhere, it's especially important in the Middle East. In more conservative areas, including many rural areas, men should never photograph women and in most circumstances should never even ask. In countries where you can photograph women, show them the camera and make it clear that you want to take their picture. Digital cameras have the advantage of being able to show people their photo immediately after you've taken it, which is usually temptation enough for most people to say yes.

Restrictions

In most Middle Eastern countries, it is forbidden to photograph anything even vaguely military in nature (including bridges, train stations, airports, border crossings and other public works). The definition of what is 'strategic' differs from one country

TIME

COUNTRY	TIME ZONE	DAYLIGHT SAVING
Egypt	GMT/UTC + two hours	yes
Iraq	GMT/UTC + three hours	yes
Israel & the Palestinian Territories	GMT/UTC + two hours	yes
Jordan	GMT/UTC + two hours	yes
Lebanon	GMT/UTC + two hours	yes
Syria	GMT/UTC + two hours	yes
Turkey	GMT/UTC + two hours	yes

to the next, and signs are not always posted, so err on the side of caution and, if in doubt, ask your friendly neighbouring police officer for permission.

Photography is usually allowed inside religious and archaeological sites, unless signs indicate otherwise. As a rule, do not photograph inside mosques during a service. Many Middle Easterners are sensitive about the negative aspects of their country, so exercise discretion when taking photos in poorer areas.

Public Holidays

All Middle Eastern countries, save Israel, observe the main Islamic holidays listed below. Countries with a major Shiite population also observe Ashura, the anniversary of the martyrdom of Hussein, the third imam of the Shiites. Most of the countries in the area also observe both the Gregorian and the Islamic New Year holidays. Every country also has its own national days and other public holidays.

Eid al-Adha (Kurban Bayramı in Turkey) This feast marks the time that Muslims make the pilgrimage to Mecca.

Eid al-Fitr (Şeker Bayramı in Turkey) Another feast, this time to herald the end of Ramadan

fasting; the celebrations last for three days.

Islamic New Year Also known as Ras as-Sana, it literally means 'the head of the year'.

Lailat al-Mi'raj This is the celebration of the Ascension of the Prophet Mohammed.

Prophet's Birthday This is also known as Moulid an-Nabi, 'the feast of the Prophet'.

Ramadan (Ramazan in Turkey and Iran) This is the ninth month of the Muslim calendar, when Muslims fast during daylight hours. Foreigners are not expected to follow suit, but it's considered impolite to smoke, drink or eat in public during Ramadan. As the sun sets each day, the fast is broken with *iftar* (the evening meal prepared to break the fast).

Ashura The anniversary of the martyrdom of Hossein, the third Shiite imam, in the battle at Karbala in October AD 680. This is celebrated with religious theatre and sombre parades in Shiite areas, especially in Iran, Iraq and Lebanon.

Islamic Calendar

All Islamic holidays fall according to the Muslim calendar, while secular activities are planned according to the Christian system.

The Muslim year is based on the lunar cycle and is divided into 12 lunar months, each with 29 or 30 days. Consequently, the Muslim year is 10 or 11 days shorter

than the Christian solar year, and the Muslim festivals gradually move around our year, completing the cycle in roughly 33 years. Actual dates may occur a day or so later, but probably not earlier, depending on western hemisphere moon sightings.

Telephone

In most countries of the Middle East, the cheapest way to make international calls is at your friendly local internet cafe for a fraction of the cost of calling on a normal landline. Staff at these cafes (most of which are equipped with webcams, microphones and headsets) are generally pretty tech-savvy, and can sell you the relevant card (there are usually a number of brands to choose from) and show you how to use it. Most internet cafes will also let you use operators such as Skype (www.skype.com) – remember to take your sign-in details – although Skype is one of those websites routinely blocked by Iranian censors.

If you're a traditionalist, or if internet-connected phone calls aren't possible, head for the public telephone office, which usually sits adjacent to the post office. Here, you can generally make operator-connected calls or buy cards for use in phone booths around the city;

ISLAMIC HOLIDAYS

HEJIRA YEAR	NEW YEAR	PROPHET'S BIRTHDAY	LAILAT AL-MI'RAJ	RAMADAN BEGINS	EID AL-FITR	EID AL-ADHA	ASHURA
1437	15 Oct 2015	23 Dec 2015	5 Apr 2016	5 Jun 2016	8 Jul 2016	14 Sep 2016	24 Oct 2015
1438	4 Oct 2016	12 Dec 2016	25 Mar 2016	25 May 2017	27 Jun 2017	3 Sep 2017	13 Oct 2016
1439	24 Sep 2017	1 Dec 2017	14 Mar 2017	14 May 2018	18 Jun 2018	23 Aug 2018	2 Oct 2017
1440	13 Sep 2018	20 Nov 2018	3 Mar 2018	3 May 2019	7 Jun 2019	12 Aug 2019	21 Sep 2018
1441	2 Sep 2019	9 Nov 2019	20 Feb 2019	22 Apr 2020	28 May 2020	1 Aug 2020	10 Sep 2019

kiosks dotted around most major cities generally sell the same cards. There are also privately run call centres (although many of these have three-minute call minimums), where you can make international calls and send faxes. Costs for international calls start at about US$3 per minute, and a few countries offer reduced rates at night.

Mobile Phones

Mobile networks in Middle Eastern countries all work on the GSM system, and it's rare that your mobile brought from home won't automatically link up with a local operator. That's fine for receiving calls, but roaming charges can make for a nasty surprise back home if you've made a few calls on your trip. If you plan to be in a country for a while, your best option is to buy a local SIM card, an easy process in every country of the region except Turkey, where it can be complex and time-consuming.

Toilets

Outside the midrange and top-end hotels and restaurants (where Western-style loos are the norm), visitors will encounter their fair share of Arab-style squat toilets (which, incidentally, according to physiologists, encourage a far more natural position than the Western-style invention!).

It's a good idea to carry an emergency stash of toilet paper with you for the times when you're caught short outside the hotel as most of these toilets have a water hose and bucket for the same purpose.

Tourist Information

Most countries in the region have tourist offices with branches in big towns and at tourist sights. That said, don't expect much. Usually, the most the offices can produce is a free map; help with booking accommodation or any other service is typically beyond the resources of the often-nonetheless-amiable staff. The exceptions to this rule are some of the offices in Israel and the Palestinian Territories, which are in fact very useful. Elsewhere, you'll usually get better results relying on the knowledge and resourcefulness of your hotel reception or a local guide.

Travellers with Disabilities

Generally speaking, scant regard is paid to the needs of disabled travellers in the Middle East. Steps, high kerbs and other assorted obstacles are everywhere, streets are often badly rutted and uneven, roads are made virtually uncrossable by heavy traffic, and many doorways are low and narrow. Ramps and specially equipped lodgings and toilets are an extreme rarity. The exception is Israel and the Palestinian Territories. Elsewhere, you'll have to plan your trip carefully and will probably be obliged to restrict yourself to luxury-level hotels and private, hired transport.

If it all sounds difficult, remember that where Middle Eastern governments have singularly failed to provide the necessary infrastructure, local officials, guides and hotel staff almost invariably do their best to help in any way they can.

Useful Resources

Access-Able Travel Source (www.access-able. com) Has lists of tour operators offering tours for travellers with disabilities. There are listings for Egypt, Israel and Jordan.

Accessible Travel & Leisure (☑0145-272 9739; www.accessibletravel.co.uk) Claims to be the biggest UK travel agent dealing with travel for the disabled, including some options for Egypt. The company encourages the disabled to travel independently.

Society for Accessible Travel and Hospitality (www.sath.org) A good resource which gives advice on how to travel with a wheelchair, kidney disease, sight impairment or deafness.

Tourism for All (www. tourismforall.org.uk) Advice for disabled and less-mobile senior travellers.

Volunteering

There aren't many opportunities for volunteering in the Middle East but some international organisations (including some of the following) have projects in the region:

Earthwatch (www.earth-watch.org) Volunteering trips with an environmental focus.

Idealist.org (www.idealist. org) Numerous options in the region.

International Volunteer Programs Association (www.volunteerinternational. org) Possibilities in some Middle Eastern countries.

Transport

GETTING THERE & AWAY

Flights, tours and rail tickets can be booked online at www. lonelyplanet.com/bookings.

Entering the Middle East

Entry requirements vary from country to country although most border crossings are generally hassle-free. There are, of course, a wide range of possible experiences – you're far more likely to find heightened security and immigration checks if you're crossing Iran's land border with Afghanistan than you will flying into İstanbul from Europe.

Passports

Please note that neither Israeli citizens nor anyone who has an Israeli stamp in their passport will be allowed to enter Iran, Iraq, Lebanon or Syria.

Air

Airports

The Middle East's main international airports are as follows. Please note that both Egypt and Turkey have additional airports that receive international flights.

Atatürk International Airport (Atatürk Havalimanı; www.ataturkairport.com) İstanbul, Turkey

Beirut–Rafic Hariri International Airport (Beirut–RHIA; ☑628 000; www. beirutairport.gov.lb)

Ben-Gurion International Airport (www.iaa.gov.il) Tel Aviv, Israel

Cairo International Airport (www.cairo-airport.com) Cairo, Egypt

Erbil Airport (www.erbilairport.net) Erbil, Iraq

Imam Khomeini International Airport (www.ikia.ir) Tehran, Iran

Queen Alia International Airport (www.qaiairport.com) Amman, Jordan

Airlines

Airlines that serve destinations in the Middle East include the following:

Air Arabia (www.airarabia.com)

Arkia (www.arkia.co.il)

EgyptAir (www.egyptair.com.eg)

El Al (www.elal.co.il)

Emirates (www.emirates.com)

Gulf Air (www.gulfair.com)

Iran Air (www.iranair.com)

Iraqi Airways (www.iraqiairways.com.iq)

Jazeera Airways (www.jazeeraairways.com)

Middle East Airlines (www.mea.com.lb)

Qatar Airways (www.qatarairways.com)

Royal Jordanian (www.rj.com)

Turkish Airlines (www.turkishairlines.com)

CLIMATE CHANGE & TRAVEL

Every form of transport that relies on carbon-based fuel generates CO_2, the main cause of human-induced climate change. Modern travel is dependent on aeroplanes, which might use less fuel per kilometre per person than most cars but travel much greater distances. The altitude at which aircraft emit gases (including CO_2) and particles also contributes to their climate change impact. Many websites offer 'carbon calculators' that allow people to estimate the carbon emissions generated by their journey and, for those who wish to do so, to offset the impact of the greenhouse gases emitted with contributions to portfolios of climate-friendly initiatives throughout the world. Lonely Planet offsets the carbon footprint of all staff and author travel.

Land

Border Crossings

AFRICA

Libya

Service taxis and occasional Cairo-Benghazi buses cross the border at Amsaad, 12km west of Sallum. Check the security situation before travelling into Libya.

Sudan

The **Nile River Valley Transport Corporation** (☑Aswan 097-303 348, Cairo 02-575 9058) runs one passenger ferry per week between Aswan in Egypt and Wadi Halfa in Sudan (16 to 24 hours). Options include 1st class with bed in a cabin, an airline seat and deck class. To board the ferry, you must have a valid Sudanese visa in your passport.

CAUCASUS

Armenia

The Turkish-Armenian border has been closed to travellers for years – travel via Georgia. Around three weekly buses depart from Trabzon's otogar heading for Yerevan.

Georgia

At least two daily buses depart from Trabzon's otogar for Tbilisi (19 hours).

EUROPE

It's fairly easy to get to İstanbul by direct bus from many points in Europe via Bulgaria. Several Turkish bus lines offer reliable and quite comfortable services between İstanbul and Germany, Italy, Austria and Greece. Due to infrastructure upgrades, the only train service in operation at the time of writing was between İstanbul and Bucharest.

Bulgaria & Eastern Europe

There are several bus departures daily to Sofia, and the coastal cities of Varna and Burgas in Bulgaria from İstanbul's otogar. There are also daily departures to Skopje, Tetovo and Gostivar in Macedonia, and to Constanta and Bucharest (Romania).

The daily *Bosphorus Express (Bosfor Ekspresi)* train runs from İstanbul to Bucharest, from where you can travel onwards by train to Moldova and Hungary. You can also catch the *Bosphorus Express* as far as Dimitrovgrad (Bulgaria) from where you can travel onwards to Sofia (Bulgaria) and on to Belgrade (Serbia). You'll need to take your own food and drinks as there are no restaurant cars on these trains.

Greece

At least six weekly buses travel from Athens' Peloponnese train station to İstanbul. You can also pick up the bus in Thessaloniki and at Alexandroupolis. Alternatively, you can make your own way to Alexandroupolis and take a service from the intercity bus station to the border town of Kipi. You can't walk across the border, but it's easy enough to hitch. Otherwise, take a bus to İpsala (5km east beyond the border) or Keşan (30km east beyond the border), from where there are many buses to the capital.

There were no train services operating between Greece and Turkey at the time of writing due to infrastructure work. For updates, see the websites of Turkish State Railways (www.tcdd.gov.tr) or the Hellenic Railways Organisation (www.ose.gr).

Sea

Ferries shuttle reasonably regularly between southern Europe and Israel, Turkey and Egypt. There are other less-frequented routes connecting Egypt with Sudan and the Arabian Peninsula.

Although vehicles can be shipped on most routes, bookings may have to be made some time in advance. The charge usually depends on the length or volume of the vehicle and should be checked with the carrier. As a rule, motorcycles cost almost nothing to ship while bicycles are free.

You're unlikely to regret taking an adequate supply of food and drink with you on any of these ships; even if it's available on board, you're pretty stuck if it doesn't agree with you or your budget.

Ferry Lines (www.ferrylines.com) is a good place to get started when looking at possible routes into the region.

Cyprus

If you have a multiple-entry visa for Turkey, you should be able to cross over to Northern Cyprus and back again without buying a new one. However, if your visa has expired, you should anticipate long queues at immigration.

Akgünler (www.akgunler.com.tr) Girne (Northern Cyprus) to Taşucu in Turkey (1½ hours, daily).

Salamis Cruise Lines (www.varianostravel.com) From Limassol (Cyprus) to Haifa in Israel (10 to 12 hours, weekly).

Greece

Private ferries link Turkey's Aegean coast and the Greek islands. Services are usually daily in summer, several times a week in spring and autumn, and perhaps just once a week in winter. Please note that all the information that follows covers travelling to Turkey from Greek cities and towns.

Car-ferry services operate between Greek ports and several Turkish ports, but not to İstanbul. Among the most important routes are Chios-Çeşme, Kastellorizo-Kaş, Kos-Bodrum, Lesvos-Ayvalık, Rhodes (Rhodos)-Bodrum, Rhodes (Rhodos)-Datça, Rhodes (Rhodos)-Marmaris and Samos-Kuşadası.

Salamis Cruise Lines (www.varianostravel.com) also operates a weekly Haifa-Lavrio (Greece) service that takes five days.

Russia & Ukraine

The main routes out of Turkey are Trabzon-Sochi (for Russia) and İstanbul-Illichivsk (for Ukraine). Other seasonal routes may include: Samsun-Batumi (Georgia), Samsun-Novorossiysk (Russia) and İstanbul-Sevastopol.

Sari Denizcilik (www.saridenizcilik.com) Weekly ferry between Sochi, in Russia, and Trabzon (12 hours).

Stena Sea Line (www.stena-sealine.com) Twice-weekly service between İstanbul and Illichivsk in Ukraine (27 to 31 hours).

UKR Ferry (www.ukrferry.com) Twice-weekly İstanbul-Illichivsk (27 to 31 hours).

Tours

For a clearing house of sustainable tour options, visit www.responsibletravel.com.

Australia

Intrepid (www.intrepidtravel.com) Tours to every Middle Eastern country except Iraq and (for the time being) Syria.

Passport Travel (www.travelcentre.com.au) Tours to Turkey, Egypt, Iran, Jordan and Israel.

Italy, France & Germany

Antichi Splendori Viaggi (www.antichisplendori.it) Experienced Italian operator.

Dabuka Expeditions (www.dabuka.de) German expeditions into the Egyptian Sahara.

Terres d'Aventure (www.terdav.com) French operator that visits most countries in the region.

Zig-Zag (www.zigzag-randonnees.com) Experienced French company that gets off the beaten track.

UK

Ancient World Tours (www.ancient.co.uk) Ancient Egypt specialists.

Andante Travels (www.andantetravels.co.uk) Archaeology

tours, including to southeastern Turkey.

Crusader Travel (www.crusadertravel.com) Sinai treks and Red Sea diving.

USA

Bestway Tours & Safaris (www.bestway.com) All the usual tours plus Iraqi Kurdistan.

Yalla Tours (www.yallatours.com) Middle East specialists.

GETTING AROUND

Air

With no regional rail network to speak of, and distances that make the bus a discomforting test of endurance, flying is certainly the most user-friendly method of transport in the Middle East if your time is tight.

Flying isn't possible between Israel and the Palestinian Territories and other Middle Eastern countries, except for Egypt, Jordan and Turkey. But, these exceptions aside, almost every Middle Eastern capital is linked to each of the others.

Airlines

Until recently, most flights were operated by state airlines. Of these, when it comes to service, punctuality and safety, El Al (Israel), Royal Jordanian, Turkish Airlines and Middle East Airlines (Lebanon) are probably the pick of the bunch, with Egypt Air solid and *usually* reliable.

The growth of private (usually low-cost) airlines, especially in Turkey and Israel, means that flying domestic routes within these countries has become a lot more feasible.

Pegasus Airlines (www.flypgs.com)

Sun Express (www.sunexpress.com)

Air Passes

Emirates (www.emirates.com) offers the 'Arabian Airpass' that allows cut-price travel around the Middle East. To qualify, you need to buy a flight to Dubai. Onward flight 'coupons' (a minimum of two, maximum of six) are then available to cities such as Cairo, Amman or Beirut. Prices are based upon zones, with the above cities coming within Zone C.

Bicycle

Although the numbers doing it are small, cycling round

CYCLING TIPS

➡ Carry a couple of extra chain links, a chain breaker, spokes, a spoke key, two inner tubes, tyre levers and a repair kit, a flat-head and Phillips-head screwdriver, and Allen keys and spanners to fit all the bolts on your bike.

➡ Check the bolts daily and carry spares.

➡ Fit as many water bottles to your bike as you can.

➡ Confine your panniers to a maximum weight of 15kg.

➡ Carrying the following equipment in your panniers is recommended: a two-person tent (weighing about 1.8kg) that can also accommodate the bike where security is a concern; a sleeping bag rated to 0°C and an inflatable mattress; a small camping stove; cooking pot; utensils; a water filter (two microns) and a compact torch.

the Middle East is a viable proposition, provided that cyclists are self-sufficient and able to carry litres of extra water.

Most of the people we spoke to reckoned that the most enjoyable cycling was in Turkey. Although hilly, the scenery in Turkey is particularly fine and accommodation is fairly easy to come by, even in the smallest villages. This is definitely not the case elsewhere. In Turkey, if you get tired of pedalling, it's also no problem to have your bike transported in the luggage hold of the big modern buses.

One big plus about cycling through the region is the fact that cyclists are usually given warm welcomes (a trademark of the Middle East in any case) and are showered with food and drinks. There have been, however, reports of kids throwing stones at cyclists along Jordan's King's Highway.

By far the major difficulty cited by all cyclists is the heat which is at its peak from June to August. May to mid-June and September through October are the best times. Even then, you're advised to make an early morning start and call it a day by early afternoon.

There are bicycle-repair shops in most major towns and the locals are excellent 'bush mechanics', with all but the most modern or sophisticated equipment.

Boat

The most popular boat services are the two ferry services between Nuweiba in Egypt and Aqaba in Jordan. The fast-ferry service takes 45 minutes, while the slow (and cheaper) ferry makes the journey in 2½ to three hours. Vehicles can usually be shipped on these routes, but advance arrangements may have to be made.

Bus

Buses are the workhorses of the Middle East, and in most places they're probably your only option for getting from A to B. Thankfully, most buses are reliable and comfortable.

The cost and comfort of bus travel varies enormously throughout the region. One typical nuisance is bus drivers' fondness (presumably shared by local passengers) for loud videos; sleep is almost always impossible. Another potential source of discomfort is that in most Middle Eastern countries, the concept of a 'nonsmoking bus' is not always observed.

Reservations

It's always advisable to book bus seats in advance at the bus station, which is usually the only ticket outlet and source of reliable information about current services. Reservations are a must over the Muslim weekend (Friday) as well as during major public holidays.

Car & Motorcycle

Bringing your own car to the Middle East will give you a lot more freedom, but it's certainly not for everyone. For all the positives, it's difficult to imagine a route through the Middle East that would justify the expense and hassle of bringing a car and getting it out again.

Throughout the Middle East, motorcycles are fairly popular as a means of racing around in urban areas, but little used as long-distance transport. If you do decide to ride a motorcycle through the region, try to take one of the more popular Japanese models if you want to stand any chance of finding spare parts. Even then, make sure your bike is in very good shape before setting out. Motorcycles can be shipped

or, often, loaded as luggage onto trains.

Bringing Your Own Vehicle

Anyone planning to take their own vehicle with them needs to check in advance what spare parts and petrol are likely to be available.

A number of documents are also required (if you're unsure what to take, check with the automobile association in your home country):

➡ **Carnet de passage** Like a passport for your car and ensures you don't sell your car along the way; can be expensive. Ask your home automobile association for details.

➡ **Green card** Issued by insurers. Insurance for some countries is only obtainable at the border.

➡ **International Driving Permit (IDP)** Obtainable from your local automobile association.

➡ **Vehicle registration documents** In addition to carrying all ownership papers, check with your insurer whether you're covered for the countries you intend to visit and whether third-party cover is included.

Driving Licences

If you plan to drive, get an IDP from your home automobile association. An IDP is compulsory for foreign drivers and motorcyclists in Egypt, Iran, Iraq and Syria. Most foreign (or national) licences are acceptable in Israel and the Palestinian Territories, Lebanon and Turkey, and for foreign-registered vehicles in Jordan. However, even in these places an IDP is recommended. IDPs are valid for one year only.

Fuel & Spare Parts

Mechanical failure can be a problem as spare parts – at least official ones – are often unobtainable. Fear not, ingenuity often compensates for factory parts; your mechanic back home will either have a heart attack or learn new techniques when you show them what's gone on under your hood in the Middle East.

Generally, Land Rovers, Volkswagens, Range Rovers, Mercedes and Chevrolets are the cars for which spare parts are most likely to be available, although in recent years Japan has been a particularly vigorous exporter of vehicles to the region. One tip is to ask your vehicle manufacturer for a list of any authorised service centres it has in the countries you plan to visit. The length of this list is likely to be a pretty good reflection of how easy it is to get parts on your travels.

Usually two grades of petrol are available; if in doubt get the more expensive one. Petrol stations are few and far between on many desert roads. Away from the main towns, it's advisable to fill up whenever you get the chance. Diesel isn't readily available in every Middle Eastern country, nor is unleaded petrol.

Car Hire

International hire companies such as **Hertz** (www.hertz. com), **Avis** (www.avis.com) and **Europcar** (www.europcar.com) are represented in many large towns. Local companies are usually cheaper, but the cars of international companies are often better maintained and come with a better back-up service if problems arise. Local companies sometimes carry the advantage of including a driver for a similar cost to hiring the car alone. A good place to find competitive rates is **Imakoo Cars** (www. imakoocars.co.uk), a clearing house for cheap rates from international companies with services in most countries in the area.

To hire a car, you'll need any or all of the following: a photocopy of your passport and visa; deposit or credit-card imprint; and your driving licence or IDP. The minimum age varies between 21 and 25 – the latter is most common, particularly with international companies.

Always make sure that insurance is included in the hire price and familiarise yourself with the policy – don't hire a car unless it's insured for every eventuality.

Insurance

Insurance is compulsory in most Middle Eastern countries, not to mention highly advisable. Given the large number of minor accidents, not to mention major ones, fully comprehensive insurance (as opposed to third-party) is strongly advised, both for your own and any hire vehicle.

Make certain you're covered for off-piste travel, as well as travel between Middle Eastern countries (if you're planning cross-border excursions).

In the event of an accident, make sure you submit the accident report as soon as possible to the insurance company or, if hiring, the car-hire company, and do so before getting the car repaired.

Road Conditions

Conditions across the Middle East vary enormously, but in almost all cases, they'll be worse than you're used to back home. The main roads are generally good, or at least reasonable, but there are plenty of unsurfaced examples, and the international roads are generally narrow and crowded. Turkey, Jordan and Israel and the Palestinian Territories probably have the best roads, but those in Lebanon, Iran and Syria adhere to the following rule: worse than they should be but probably better than you'd expect. Some of Egypt's roads are fine, others are bone-jarringly bad.

Road Hazards

Driving in the Middle East can be appalling by Western norms. Fatalism and high speed rule supreme. Car horns, used at the slightest provocation, take the place of caution and courtesy. Except in well-lit urban areas, try to avoid driving at night, as you may find your vehicle is the only thing on the road with lights.

In desert regions, particularly in Egypt, beware of wind-blown sand and wandering, free-range camels – the latter can be deadly at night.

Road Rules

You're unlikely even to know what the speed limit is on a particular road, let alone be forced to keep to it – the rules exist more in theory than they are enforced in reality.

A warning triangle is required for vehicles (except motorcycles) in most Middle Eastern countries; in Turkey two triangles and a first-aid kit are compulsory.

In all countries, driving is on the right-hand side of the road and the rules of when to give way (at least officially) are those that apply in continental Europe.

Hitching

Although many travellers hitchhike, it's never an entirely safe way of getting around and those who do so should understand that they are taking a small but potentially serious risk. There is no part of the Middle East where hitching can be recommended for unaccompanied women travellers. Just because we explain how hitching works, doesn't mean we recommend you do it.

Hitching as commonly understood in the West hardly exists in the Middle East (except in Israel and the Palestinian Territories). Although in most countries you'll often see people standing by the road hoping for a lift, they will nearly always expect (and be expected) to offer to pay. Hitching in the Middle Eastern sense is not so much an alternative to the public transport system as an extension of it, particularly in areas where there's no regular public transport. The going rate is often roughly the equivalent of the bus or shared taxi fare, but may be more if a driver takes you to an address or place off their route. You may well be offered free lifts from time to time, but you won't get very far if you set out deliberately to avoid paying for transport.

Throughout the Middle East a raised thumb is a vaguely obscene gesture. A common way of signalling that you want a lift is to extend your right hand, palm down.

Local Transport

Bus

In most cities and towns, a minibus or bus service operates. Fares are very cheap, and services are fast, regular and run on fixed routes with, in some cases, fixed stops. However, unless you're very familiar with the town, they can be difficult to get to grips with (few display their destinations, fewer still do so in English, and they are often very crowded). Unless you can find a local who speaks your language to help you out, your best bet is to stand along the footpath (preferably at a bus stop if one exists) of a major thoroughfare heading in the direction you want to go, and call out the local name (or the name of a landmark close to where you're heading) into the drivers' windows when they slow down.

Taxi

In the West, taxis are usually considered a luxury. In the Middle East they're often unavoidable. Some cities have no other form of urban public transport, while there are also many rural routes that are only feasible in a taxi or private vehicle.

Taxis are seemingly everywhere you look and, if you can't see one, try lingering on the footpath next to a major road and, within no time, plenty of taxis will appear as if from nowhere and will soon toot their horns at you just in case you missed them, even if you're just trying to cross the street.

If you want to save money, it's important to be able to differentiate between the various kinds of taxis.

REGULAR TAXI

Regular taxis (variously known as 'agency taxis', 'telephone taxis', 'private taxis' or 'special taxis') are found in almost every Middle Eastern town or city. Unlike shared taxis, you pay to have the taxi to yourself, either to take you to a pre-agreed destination or for a specified period of time. They are primarily of use for transport within towns or on short rural trips, but in some countries hiring them for excursions of several hours is still cheap. They are also often the only way of reaching airports or seaports.

SHARED TAXI

A compromise between the convenience of a regular taxi and the economy of a bus, the shared taxi picks up and drops off passengers at points along its (generally fixed) route and runs to no particular schedule. It's known by different names – collect, collective or service taxi in English, *servees* in Arabic, *sherut* in Hebrew and *dolmuş* in Turkish. Most shared taxis will take up to four or five passengers, but some seat up to about 12 and are indistinguishable for most purposes from minibuses.

TIPS FOR CATCHING TAXIS

On the whole, taxi drivers in the Middle East are helpful, honest and often humorous. Others – as in countries all over the world – find new arrivals too tempting a target for minor scams or a spot of overcharging. Here are a few tips:

➡ Not all taxi drivers speak English. Generally, in cities used to international travellers, they will (or know enough to get by), but not otherwise. If you're having trouble, ask a local for help.

➡ Always negotiate a fare (or insist that the meter is used if it works) before jumping in. If in doubt about local rates, inquire at your point of departure.

➡ Don't rely on street names (there are often several versions and the driver may recognise your pronunciation of none of them). If you're going to a well-known destination (such as a big hotel), find out if it's close to a local landmark and give the driver the local name for the landmark. Even better, get someone to write down the name in Arabic or whatever the local language is.

➡ Avoid using unlicensed cab drivers at airports or bus stations.

➡ Note that at the time of writing, travellers to Lebanon were being advised not to use shared taxis due to the increased security risk.

Shared taxis are much cheaper than private taxis and, once you get the hang of them, can be just as convenient. They are dearer than buses, but more frequent and usually faster, because they don't stop so often or for so long. They also tend to operate for longer hours than buses. They can be used for urban, intercity or rural transport.

Fixed-route taxis wait at the point of departure until full or nearly full. Usually they pick up or drop off passengers anywhere en route, but in some places they have fixed halts or stations. Sometimes each service is allocated a number, which may be indicated on the vehicle. Generally, a flat fare applies for each route, but sometimes it's possible to pay a partial fare.

Fares depend largely on time and distance, but can also vary slightly according to demand.

Beware of boarding an empty taxi, as the driver may assume you want to hire the vehicle for your exclusive use and charge you accordingly. It's advisable to watch what other passengers pay and to hand over your fare in front of them. Passengers are expected to know where they are getting off. 'Thank you' in the local language is the usual cue for the driver to stop. Make it clear to the driver or other passengers if you want to be told when you reach your destination.

Train

There are train networks in Egypt, Israel and the Palestinian Territories, Iran and Turkey and these can represent the best transport option on some routes, such as between Cairo and Luxor in Egypt. Levels of comfort vary from country to country – you'll find that many of Egypt's trains are badly in need of an overhaul, Iran's are OK, while Israel and the Palestinian Territories and Turkey use brand-new trains on some routes.

In general, trains are less frequent and usually slower than buses, while many stations are some distance out of the town centres they serve.

In general, tickets are only sold at the station and reservations are either compulsory or highly recommended.

Health

Prevention is the key to staying healthy while travelling in the Middle East. Infectious diseases can and do occur in the Middle East, but these are usually associated with poor living conditions and poverty and can be avoided with a few precautions. The most common reason for travellers needing medical help is as a result of accidents – cars are not always well maintained, seatbelts are rare and poorly lit roads are littered with potholes. Medical facilities can be excellent in large cities, but in remote areas may be more basic.

BEFORE YOU GO

A little planning before departure can save you a lot of trouble later. See your dentist before a long trip; carry a spare pair of contact lenses and glasses (and take your optical prescription); and carry a first-aid kit with you.

It's tempting to leave it all to the last minute – don't! Many vaccines don't ensure immunity until two weeks after treatment, so visit a doctor four to eight weeks before departure. Ask your doctor for an International Certificate of Vaccination (otherwise known as the yellow booklet), which will list all the vaccinations you've received. This is mandatory for countries that require proof of yellow fever vaccination upon entry (and you'll need

this if you're flying in from sub-Saharan Africa), but it's a good idea to carry it wherever you travel.

Travellers can register with the **International Association for Medical Advice to Travellers** (IMAT; www. iamat.org). Its website can help travellers to find a doctor with recognised training. Those heading off to very remote areas may like to do a first-aid course (Red Cross and St John Ambulance can help).

Bring medications in their original, clearly labelled containers. A signed and dated letter from your physician describing your medical conditions and medications, including generic names, is also a good idea. If carrying syringes or needles, be sure to have a physician's letter documenting their medical necessity.

Insurance

Find out in advance if your insurance plan will make payments directly to providers or reimburse you later for overseas health expenditures (in many Middle Eastern countries doctors expect payment in cash). It's also worth making sure that your travel insurance will cover repatriation home or to better medical facilities elsewhere. Your insurance company may be able to locate the nearest source of medical help, or

you can ask at your hotel. In an emergency, contact your embassy or consulate. Your travel insurance will not usually cover you for anything other than emergency dental treatment. Not all insurance covers emergency aeromedical evacuation home or to a hospital in a major city, which may be the only way to get medical attention for a serious emergency.

Recommended Vaccinations

The World Health Organization (WHO) recommends that all travellers, regardless of the region they are travelling in, should be covered for diphtheria, tetanus, measles, mumps, rubella and polio, as well as hepatitis B. While making preparations to travel, take the opportunity to ensure that all of your routine vaccination cover is complete. The consequences of these diseases can be severe and outbreaks do occur in the Middle East.

IN THE MIDDLE EAST

Availability & Cost of Health Care

The health care systems in the Middle East are varied. Medical care can be excellent in Israel and Turkey, with well-trained doctors and nurses, but can be patchier elsewhere. Reciprocal health arrangements with countries rarely exist and you should be prepared to pay for all medical and dental treatment.

Medical care is not always readily available outside major cities. Medicine, and even sterile dressings or intravenous fluids, may need to be bought from a local pharmacy. Nursing care may be limited or rudimentary as this is something families and friends are expected to provide.

Standards of dental care are variable throughout the region, and there is an increased risk of hepatitis B and HIV transmission via poorly sterilised equipment.

For minor illnesses such as diarrhoea, pharmacists can often provide valuable advice and sell over-the-counter medication. They can also advise as to whether more specialised help is needed.

Infectious Diseases

Diphtheria

Diphtheria is spread through close respiratory contact. It causes a high temperature and severe sore throat. Sometimes a membrane forms across the throat requiring a tracheotomy to prevent suffocation. Vaccination is recommended for those likely to be in close contact with the local population in infected areas. The vaccine is given as an injection alone, or with tetanus, and lasts 10 years.

Hepatitis A

Hepatitis A is spread through contaminated food (particularly shellfish) and water. It causes jaundice, and although it is rarely fatal, can cause prolonged lethargy and delayed recovery. Symptoms include dark urine, a yellow colour to the whites of the eyes, fever and abdominal pain. Hepatitis A vaccine (Avaxim, VAQTA, Havrix) is given as an injection: a single dose will give protection for up to a year, while a booster 12 months later will provide a subsequent 10 years of protection.

Hepatitis B

Infected blood, contaminated needles and sexual intercourse can all transmit hepatitis B. It can cause jaundice, and affects the liver, occasionally causing liver failure. All travellers should make this a routine vaccination. (Many countries now give hepatitis B vaccination as part of routine childhood vaccination.) A course will give protection for at least five years, and can be given over four weeks or six months.

Leishmaniasis

Spread through the bite of an infected sand fly, leishmaniasis can cause a slowly growing skin lump or ulcer. It may develop into a serious life-threatening fever usually accompanied by anaemia and weight loss. Sand fly bites should be avoided whenever possible. Infected dogs are also carriers. Leishmaniasis is present in Iran, Iraq, Israel and the Palestinian Territories, Jordan, Lebanon, Syria and Turkey.

Malaria

The prevalence of malaria varies throughout the Middle East. Many areas are considered to be malaria free, while others have seasonal risks. The risk of malaria is minimal in most cities; however,

---

MEDICAL CHECKLIST

Following is a list of other items you should consider packing in your medical kit.

⇒ acetaminophen/paracetamol (eg Tylenol) or aspirin

⇒ adhesive or paper tape

⇒ antibacterial ointment (eg Bactroban) for cuts and abrasions

⇒ antibiotics (if travelling off the beaten track)

⇒ antidiarrhoeal drugs (eg containing loperamide)

⇒ antihistamines (for hay fever and allergic reactions)

⇒ anti-inflammatory drugs (eg containing ibuprofen)

⇒ bandages, gauze, gauze rolls

⇒ insect repellent that contains DEET (for skin)

⇒ insect spray that contains permethrin (for clothing, tents and bed nets)

⇒ iodine tablets (for water purification)

⇒ oral-rehydration salts

⇒ pocket knife

⇒ scissors, safety pins, tweezers

⇒ steroid cream or cortisone (for allergic rashes)

⇒ sunscreen

⇒ syringes and sterile needles (if travelling to remote areas)

⇒ thermometer

check with your doctor if you are considering travelling to any rural areas. It is important to take antimalarial tablets if the risk is significant. For up-to-date information about the risk of contracting malaria in a specific country, contact your local travel health clinic.

Poliomyelitis

Generally spread through contaminated food and water, polio is present, though rare, throughout the Middle East. It is one of the vaccines given in childhood and should be boosted every 10 years, either orally (a drop on the tongue), or as an injection. Polio may be carried asymptomatically, although it can cause a transient fever and, in rare cases, potentially permanent muscle weakness or paralysis.

Rabies

Spread through bites or licks on broken skin from an infected animal, rabies (present in all countries of the Middle East) is fatal. Animal handlers should be vaccinated, as should those travelling to remote areas where a reliable source of postbite vaccine is not available within 24 hours. Three injections are needed over a month. If you have not been vaccinated you will need a course of five injections starting 24 hours or as soon as possible after the injury. Vaccination does not provide you with immunity, it merely buys you more time to seek appropriate medical treatment.

Rift Valley Fever

This haemorrhagic fever, which is found in Egypt, is spread through blood or blood products, including those from infected animals. It causes a flu-like illness with fever, joint pains and occasionally more serious complications. Complete recovery is possible.

WATER WARNING

Many locals don't drink the tap water and we recommend that you follow their lead. If you do decide to risk the local water, the safest places to do so are in Israel, Syria and Turkey. Don't even *think* of drinking from the tap in Egypt, Iran, Iraq, the Palestinian Territories or Lebanon. Cheap bottled water is readily available throughout the region.

Schistosomiasis

Otherwise known as bilharzia, this is spread through the freshwater snail. It causes infection of the bowel and bladder, often with bleeding. It is caused by a fluke and is contracted through the skin from water contaminated with human urine or faeces. Paddling or swimming in suspect freshwater lakes or slow-running rivers should be avoided. There may be no symptoms. Possible symptoms include a transient fever and rash, and advanced cases of bilharzia may cause blood in the stool or in the urine. A blood test can detect antibodies if you have been exposed and treatment is then possible in specialist travel or infectious-disease clinics. Be especially careful in Egypt, Iran, Iraq and Syria.

Tuberculosis (TB)

Tuberculosis is spread through close respiratory contact and occasionally through infected milk or milk products. BCG vaccine is recommended for those likely to be mixing closely with the local population. It is more important for those visiting family or planning on a long stay, and those employed as teachers and milk- or health-care workers. TB can be asymptomatic, although symptoms can include coughing, weight loss or fever months or even years after exposure. An X-ray is the best way to confirm if you have TB. BCG gives a moderate degree of protection against TB. It causes a small permanent

scar at the site of injection, and is usually only given in specialised chest clinics. As it's a live vaccine it should not be given to pregnant women or immunocompromised individuals. The BCG vaccine is not available in all countries.

Typhoid

Typhoid is spread through food or water that has been contaminated by infected human faeces. The first symptom is usually fever or a pink rash on the abdomen. Septicaemia (blood poisoning) may also occur. Typhoid vaccine (typhim Vi, typherix) will give protection for three years. In some countries, the vaccine Vivotif is also available.

Yellow Fever

Yellow fever vaccination is not required for any areas of the Middle East. However, the mosquito that spreads yellow fever has been known to be present in some parts of the region. It is important to consult your local travel health clinic as part of your predeparture plans for the latest details. Any travellers from a yellow fever endemic area (eg parts of sub-Saharan Africa) will need to show proof of vaccination against yellow fever before entry.

Environmental Hazards

Heat Illness

Heat exhaustion occurs after heavy sweating and excessive fluid loss with

TRAVEL HEALTH WEBSITES

Lonely Planet (www.lonelyplanet.com) A good place to start.

Centers for Disease Control & Prevention (wwwnc. cdc.gov) A useful source of traveller health information.

MD Travel Health (www.mdtravelhealth.com) Complete travel health recommendations for every country, updated daily.

Travel Doctor (www.traveldoctor.co.uk) Another good source of travel health information.

WHO (www.who.int/ith/en) Publishes a good book, *International Travel and Health*.

It's also usually a good idea to consult your government's travel health website before departure.

Australia (www.smartraveller.gov.au)

UK (www.nhs.uk/Healthcareabroad)

USA (wwwnc.cdc.gov/travel)

inadequate replacement of fluids and salt. It is particularly common in hot climates when taking unaccustomed exercise before full acclimatisation. Symptoms include headache, dizziness and tiredness. Dehydration is already happening by the time you feel thirsty – aim to drink sufficient water so that you produce pale, diluted urine. The treatment of heat exhaustion consists of fluid replacement with water or fruit juice or both, and cooling by cold water and fans. The treatment of the salt-loss component consists of taking in salty fluids (such as soup or broth), and adding a little more table salt to foods than usual.

Heat stroke is much more serious. This occurs when the heat-regulating mechanism in the body breaks down. An excessive rise in body temperature leads to sweating ceasing, irrational and hyperactive behaviour, and eventually loss of consciousness and death. Rapid cooling by spraying the body with water and fanning is an ideal treatment. Emergency fluid and electrolyte replacement by intravenous drip is usually also required.

Insect Bites & Stings

Mosquitoes may not carry malaria but can cause irritation and infected bites. Using DEET-based insect repellents will prevent bites. Mosquitoes also spread dengue fever.

Bees and wasps only cause real problems to those with a severe allergy (anaphylaxis). If you have a severe allergy to bee or wasp stings you should carry an adrenaline injection or similar.

Scorpions are frequently found in arid or dry climates. They can cause a painful sting, which is rarely life threatening.

Bed bugs are often found in hostels and cheap hotels. They lead to very itchy lumpy bites. Spraying the mattress with an appropriate insect killer will do a good job of getting rid of them.

Scabies are also frequently found in cheap accommodation. These tiny mites live in the skin, particularly between the fingers. They cause an intensely itchy rash. Scabies is easily treated with lotion available from pharmacies.

Snake Bites

Do not walk barefoot or stick your hand into holes or cracks. Half of those bitten by venomous snakes are not actually injected with poison (envenomed). If bitten by a snake, do not panic. Immobilise the bitten limb with a splint (eg a stick) and apply a bandage over the site using firm pressure, similar to a bandage over a sprain. Do not apply a tourniquet, or cut or suck the bite. Get the victim to medical help as soon as possible so that antivenene can be given if necessary.

Traveller's Diarrhoea

To prevent diarrhoea, avoid tap water unless it has been boiled, filtered or chemically disinfected (with iodine tablets). Eat only fresh fruits or vegetables if cooked or if you have peeled them yourself, and avoid dairy products that may contain unpasteurised milk. Buffet meals are risky, as food should be piping hot; meals freshly cooked in front of you in a busy restaurant are more likely to be safe.

If you develop diarrhoea, be sure to drink plenty of fluids, preferably an oral rehydration solution containing salt and sugar. A few loose stools don't require treatment but, if you start having more than four or five stools a day, you should start taking an antibiotic (usually a quinolone drug) and an antidiarrhoeal agent (such as loperamide). If diarrhoea is bloody, persists for more than 72 hours, or is accompanied by fever, shaking chills or severe abdominal pain you should seek medical attention.

Travelling with Children

All travellers with children should know how to treat minor ailments and when to seek medical treatment. Make sure children are up to date with the routine vaccinations, and discuss possible travel vaccinations well before departure as some are not suitable for children aged under one year old.

In hot, moist climates any wound or break in the skin may lead to infection. The area should be cleaned and then kept dry and clean. Remember to avoid potentially contaminated food and water. If your child is vomiting or experiencing diarrhoea, lost fluid and salts must be replaced. It may be helpful to take rehydration powders for reconstituting with boiled water. Ask your doctor about this.

Children should be encouraged to avoid dogs or other mammals because of the risk of rabies and other diseases. Any bite, scratch or lick from a warm blooded, furry animal should immediately be thoroughly cleaned. If there is any possibility that the animal is infected with rabies, immediate medical assistance should be sought.

Women's Health

Emotional stress, exhaustion and travelling through different time zones can all contribute to an upset in the menstrual pattern. If using oral contraceptives, remember some antibiotics, diarrhoea and vomiting can stop the pill from working and lead to the risk of pregnancy – it's safest to take other forms of contraception with you.

Emergency contraception is most effective if taken within 24 hours after unprotected sex. The **International Planned Parent Federation** (www.ippf.org) can advise about the availability of contraception in different countries.

Tampons and sanitary towels are not always available outside of major cities in the Middle East.

Travelling during pregnancy is usually possible, but there are important things to consider. Have a medical check-up before embarking on your trip. The most risky times for travel are during the first 12 weeks of pregnancy, when miscarriage is most likely, and after 30 weeks, when complications such as high blood pressure and premature delivery can occur. Most airlines will not accept a traveller after 28 to 32 weeks of pregnancy, and long-haul flights in the later stages can be very uncomfortable. Antenatal facilities vary greatly between countries in the Middle East and you should think carefully before travelling to a country with poor medical facilities or where there are major cultural and language differences compared with home. Taking written records of the pregnancy, including details of your blood group, is likely to be helpful if you need medical attention while away. Ensure your insurance policy covers pregnancy, delivery and postnatal care, but remember insurance policies are only as good as the facilities available.

Language

ARABIC

The following phrases are in MSA (Modern Standard Arabic), which is the official language of the Arab world. There are significant differences between MSA and the colloquial Arabic varieties spoken. Egyptian, Gulf, Levantine and Tunisian Arabic are the most commonly spoken, sometimes mutually unintelligible and with no official written form. Arabic is written from right to left in Arabic script. Read our coloured pronunciation guides as if they were English and you should be understood. Note that a is pronounced as in 'act', aa as the 'a' in 'father', aw as in 'law', ay as in 'say', ee as in 'see', i as in 'hit', oo as in 'zoo', u as in 'put', gh is a throaty sound (like the Parisian French 'r'), r is rolled, dh is pronounced as in 'that', th as in 'thin' and kh as the 'ch' in the Scottish *loch*. The apostrophe (') indicates the glottal stop (like the pause in the middle of 'uh-oh'). The stressed syllables are indicated with italics. Masculine and feminine options are indicated with 'm' and 'f' respectively.

WANT MORE?

For in-depth language information and handy phrases, check out Lonely Planet's *Middle East Phrasebook*. You'll find it at **shop.lonelyplanet.com**, or you can buy Lonely Planet's iPhone phrasebooks at the Apple App Store.

Basics

Hello.	السلام عليكم.	as·sa·*laa*·mu 'a·*lay*·kum
Goodbye.	إلى اللقاء.	*i*·laa al·li·*kaa*'
Yes.	نعم.	*na*·'am
No.	لا.	laa
Excuse me.	عفواً.	*'af*·wan
Sorry.	آسف.	*'aa*·sif (m)
	آسفة.	*'aa*·si·fa (f)
Please.	لو سمحتَ.	law sa·*mah*·ta (m)
	لو سمحتِ.	law sa·*mah*·ti (f)

Thank you.	شكراً.	*shuk*·ran

How are you?

كيف حالُكَ؟	*kay*·fa *haa*·lu·ka (m)
كيف حالُكِ؟	*kay*·fa *haa*·lu·ki (f)

Fine, thanks. And you?

بخير شكراً	bi·*khay*·rin *shuk*·ran
وأنتَ/أنتِ؟	wa·'*an*·ta/wa·'*an*·ti (m/f)

What's your name?

ما اسمُكَ؟	maa '*is*·mu·ka (m)
ما اسمُكِ؟	maa '*is*·mu·ki (f)

My name is ...

اسمي ...	'*is*·mee ...

Do you speak English?

هل تتكلّمُ/	hal ta·ta·*kal*·la·mu/
تتكلّمين الإنجليزية؟	ta·ta·kal·la·*mee*·na al·'inj·lee·*zee*·ya (m/f)

I don't understand.

أنا لا أفهم.	*'a*·naa laa '*af*·ham

Signs – Arabic	
Entrance	مدخل
Exit	مخرج
Open	مفتوح
Closed	مغلق
Information	معلومات
Prohibited	ممنوع
Toilets	دورات المياه
Men	الرجال
Women	النساء

Accommodation

Where's a ...?	أين أجدُ ...؟	'ay·na 'a·ji·du ...
guesthouse	بيت للضيوف	bayt li·du·yoof
hotel	فندق	fun·duk
Do you have a ... room?	هل عندكم غرفة ...؟	hal 'in·da·kum ghur·fa·tun ...
single	بسرير منفردٍ	bi·sa·ree·rin mun·fa·rid
double	بسرير مزدوّجٍ	bi·sa·ree·rin muz·daw·waj
How much is it per ...?	كم ثمنه لِ ...؟	kam tha·ma·nu·hu li ...
night	ليلةٍ واحدة	lay·la·tin waa·hid

Eating & Drinking

Can you recommend a ...?	هل يمكنك أن توصي ...؟	hal yum·ki·nu·ka 'an too·see·ya ... (m)
	هل يمكنك أن توصي ...؟	hal yum·ki·nu·ki 'an too·see ... (f)
cafe	مقهىً	mak·han
restaurant	مطعمٌ	mat·'am

What's the local speciality?
ما الوجبة الخاصّة لهذه المنطقة؟ — maa al·waj·ba·tul khaa·sa li·haa·dhi·hil man·ta·ka

Do you have vegetarian food?
هل لديكم طعام نباتيٍّ — hal la·day·ku·mu ta·'aa·mun na·baa·tee

I'd like the ..., please.	أريد ...، لو سمحتُ.	u·ree·du ... law sa·mah·ta
bill	الحساب	hi·saab
menu	قائمة الطعام	kaa·'i·ma·tu at·ta·'aam

Emergencies

Help!	ساعدني!	saa·'id·nee (m)
	ساعديني!	saa·'i·dee·nee (f)
Go away!	اتركني!	'it·ruk·nee (m)
	اتركيني!	'it·ru·kee·nee (f)
Call ...!	اتّصل بـ ...!	'it·ta·sil bi ... (m)
	اتّصلي بـ ...!	'it·ta·si·lee bi ... (f)
a doctor	طبيب	ta·beeb
the police	الشرطة	ash·shur·ta

I'm lost.
أنا ضائع. — 'a·naa daa·'i' (m)
أنا ضائعة. — 'a·naa daa·'i·'a (f)

Where are the toilets?
أين دورات المياه؟ — 'ay·na daw·raa·tul mee·yaah

Numbers – Arabic

1	١	واحد	waa·hid
2	٢	اثنان	'ith·naan
3	٣	ثلاثة	tha·laa·tha
4	٤	أربعة	'ar·ba·a
5	٥	خمسة	kham·sa
6	٦	ستة	sit·ta
7	٧	سبعة	sab·'a
8	٨	ثمانية	tha·maa·ni·ya
9	٩	تسعة	tis·'a
10	١٠	عشرة	'a·sha·ra
100	١٠٠	مائة	mi·'a
1000	١٠٠٠	ألف	'alf

Note that Arabic numerals, unlike letters, are written from left to right.

I'm sick.
أنا مريض. — 'a·naa ma·reed

Shopping & Services

I'm looking for ...
أبحثُ عن ... — 'ab·ha·thu 'an ...

Can I look at it?
هل يمكنني أن أراه؟ — hal yum·ki·nu·nee 'an 'a·raa·hu

How much is it?
قديش ههذا؟ — 'ad·deesh ha·'·u

Where's an ATM?
أين جهاز الصرافة؟ — 'ay·na ji·haaz as·sar·raa·fa

Transport & Directions

Is this the ... to (Beirut)?	هل هذا الـ ... إلى (دبي)؟	hal haa·dhaa al ... 'i·laa (Beirut)
boat	سفينة	sa·fee·na
bus	باص	baas
plane	طائرة	taa·'i·ra
train	قطار	ki·taar
What time's the ... bus?	في أيّ ساعةٍ يغادر الباص الـ ...؟	fee 'ay·yee saa·'a·tin yu·ghaa·di·ru al·baas al ...
first	أوّل	'aw·wal
last	آخر	'aa·khir
One ... ticket, please.	تذكرة ... واحدة، لو سمحت.	tadh·ka·ra·tu ... waa·hi·da law sa·mah·ta
one-way	ذهاب فقط	dha·haa·bu fa·kat
return	ذهاب	dha·haa·bu

وإياب   wa·'ee·yaab

How much is it to ...?

كم الأجرة إلى ...؟   kam al·'uj·ra·ti 'i·laa ...

Please take me to (this address).

أوصلني عند   'aw·sal·nee 'ind
(هذا العنوان)   (haa·dhaa al·'un·waan)
لو سمحت.   law sa·mah·ta

Can you show me (on the map)?

هل يمكنك أن   hal yum·ki·nu·ka 'an
توضح لي   tu·wad·da·ha lee
(على الخريطة)؟   ('a·laa al·kha·ree·ta) (m)
هل يمكنك أن   hal yum·ki·nu·ki 'an
توضحي لي   tu·wad·da·hee lee
(على الخريطة)؟   ('a·laa al·kha·ree·ta) (f)

What's the address?

ما هو العنوان؟   maa hu·wa al·'un·waan

FARSI

The official language of Iran is called Farsi by its native speakers; in the West it's commonly referred to as Persian. Farsi is written and read from right to left in the Perso-Arabic script. If you read our coloured pronunciation guides as if they were English, you'll be understood. Note that a is pronounced as in 'act', aa as the 'a' in 'father', e as in 'bet', ee as in 'see', o as in 'tone' and oo as in 'zoo'. Both gh (like the French 'r') and kh (like the 'ch' in the Scottish *loch*) are guttural sounds, pronounced in the back of the throat, r is rolled and zh is pronounced as the 's' in 'pleasure'. The apostrophe (') indicates the glottal stop (like the pause in the middle of 'uh-oh'). The stressed syllables are indicated with italics.

Basics

Hello.	سلام	sa·*laam*
Goodbye.	خدا حافظ	kho·daa·haa·*fez*
Yes.	بله	ba·*le*
No.	نه	na
Please.	لطفا	lot·*fan*
Thank you.	متشکرم	mo·te·shak·*ke*·ram

Excuse me. ببخشید   be·bakh·*sheed*

Sorry. متأسفم   mo·ta·as·se·fam

How are you? حالتون چطور هست؟   haa·le·toon che·to·re

Fine, thanks. And you?

خوبم خیلی ممنون   khoo·bam khey·lee mam·noon
شما چطور هستید؟   sho·maa che·to·reen

What's your name?

اسمتون چی هست؟   es·me·toon chee·ye

My name is ...

اسم من ... هست   es·me man ... hast

Do you speak English?

شما انگلیسی حرف   sho·maa een·gee·lee·see
می زنید؟   harf mee·za·need

I don't understand. من نمی فهم   man ne·*mee*·fah·mam

Accommodation

Where's a ...? ... کجاست؟   ... ko·jaast

guesthouse	مهمان	meh·*maan*·
	پذیر	pa·*zeer*
hotel	هتل	ho·*tel*

Do you have a ... room? شما اتاق ... دارید؟   sho·maa o·taa·ghe ...daa·reen

| single | یک خوابه | yek khaa·*be* |
| double | دو خوابه | do khaa·*be* |

How much is it per ...? برای هر ... چقدر هست؟   ba·raa·ye har ... *che*·ghadr hast

| night | شب | shab |

Eating & Drinking

Can you recommend a ...? می توانید یک ... پیشنهاد کنین؟   *mee*·too·neen yek ... peesh·na·*haad* ko·neen

| cafe | کافه | kaaf·*fe* |
| restaurant | رستوران | res·too·*raan* |

What's the local speciality?

غذای مخصوص   gha·zaa·ye makh·soo·se
محلی چی هست؟   ma·hal·lee chee·ye

Do you have vegetarian food?

شما غذای   sho·maa gha·zaa·ye
گیاه خواری دارید؟   gee·yaah·khaa·ree daa·reen

I'd like (the) ..., please. لطفا من ... را می خواهم   lot·*fan* man ... ro mee·*khaam*

| bill | صورت حساب | soo·*rat* he·*saab* |
| menu | منو | me·*noo* |

Emergencies

Help!	كمك!	ko·*mak*
Go away!	برو كنار!	bo·ro ke·*naar*
Call ...!	... صدا كنيد!	... se·*daa* ko·*neen*
a doctor	يك دكتر	yek dok·*tor*
the police	پليس	po·*lees*

I'm lost.

من گم شده ام   man gom sho·*dam*

Where are the toilets?

توالت كجاست؟   too·vaa·*let* ko·*jaast*

I'm sick.

من مريض هستم   man ma·*reez* has·*tam*

Shopping & Services

I'm looking for ...

... من دنبال   man don·baa·*le* ...
می گردم   *mee*·gar·dam

Can I look at it?

می توانم به آن   *mee*·too·nam be oon
نگاه كنم؟   ne·*ghaah* ko·nam

How much is it?

آن چقدر هست؟   oon che·ghadr hast

What's your lowest price?

پايين ترين   paa·yeen·ta·*reen*
قيمت تون چند هست؟   ghey·ma·te·*toon chan*·de

Where's an ATM?

خود پرداز كجاست؟   khod·par·*daaz* ko·*jaast*

Transport & Directions

Is this the ... to (Tehran)?	این ... برای (رشت) هست؟	een ... ba·raa·ye (Tehran) hast
boat	كشتی	kesh·tee
bus	اتوبوس	oo·too·*boos*
plane	هواپيما	ha·vaa·pey·*maa*
train	قطار	gha·*taar*

What time's the ... bus?	... اتوبوس کی هست؟	oo·too·boo·se ... key hast
first	اول	av·*val*
last	آخر	aa·*khar*

One ... ticket, please.	... يك بليط لطفا	yek be·*leet* ... lot·*fan*
one-way	يك سره	yek sa·*re*
return	دو سره	do sa·*re*

Numbers – Farsi

1	١	يك	yek
2	٢	دو	do
3	٣	سه	se
4	٤	چهار	chaa·*haar*
5	٥	پنج	panj
6	٦	شش	shesh
7	٧	هفت	haft
8	٨	هشت	hasht
9	٩	نه	noh
10	١٠	ده	dah
100	١٠٠	صد	sad
1000	١٠٠٠	هزار	he·*zaar*

Arabic numerals, used in Farsi, are written from left to right (unlike script).

How much is it to ...?

... برای   ba·raa·ye ...
چقدر می شود؟   che·ghadr *mee*·she

Please take me to (this address).

لطفا من را   lot·*fan* man ro
(به اين آدرس) ببر   (be een aad·res) be·bar

Can you show me (on the map)?

می توانید   *mee*·too·neen
(در نقشه) به   (dar nagh·she) be
من نشان بدهيد؟   man ne·*shun* be·deen

What's the address?

آدرس اش چی هست؟   aad·re·sesh chee hast

HEBREW

Hebrew is the national language of Israel, with seven to eight million speakers world-wide. It's written from right to left in its own alphabet. Most Hebrew sounds have equivalents in English; follow our pronunciation guides and you'll be understood. Note that a is pronounced as 'ah', ai as in 'aisle', e as in 'bet', i as the 'ea' in 'heat', o as 'oh' and u as the 'oo' in 'boot'. Both kh (like the 'ch' in the Scottish *loch*) and r (similar to the French 'r') are throaty sounds, pronounced at the back of the throat. Apostrophes (') indicate the glottal stop (like the pause in the middle of 'uh-oh'). The stressed syllables are indicated with italics. Masculine and feminine options are indicated by 'm' and 'f' respectively.

Basics

Hello.	שלום.	sha·*lom*
Goodbye.	להתראות.	le·hit·ra·ot

Yes.	כן.	ken
No.	לא.	lo
Please.	בבקשה.	be·va·ka·sha
Thank you.	תודה.	to·da
Excuse me./Sorry.	סליחה.	sli·kha

How are you?

מה נשמע? ma nish·ma

Fine, thanks. And you?

טוב, תודה. tov to·da
ואתה/ואת? ve·a·ta/ve·at (m/f)

What's your name?

איך קוראים לך? ekh kor·im le·kha/lakh (m/f)

My name is ...

שמי ... shmi ...

Do you speak English?

אתה מדבר אנגלית? a·ta me·da·ber ang·lit (m)
את מדברת אנגלית? at me·da·be·ret ang·lit (f)

I don't understand.

אני לא מבין/מבינה. a·ni lo me·vin/me·vi·na (m/f)

Accommodation

Where's a ...?	איפה ...?	e·fo ...
guesthouse	בית	bet
	ההראחה	ha·'a·ra·kha
hotel	בית המלון	bet ma·lon

Do you have	יש לך	yesh le·kha/lakh
a ... room?	חדר ...?	khe·der ... (m/f)
single	ליחיד	le·ya·khid
double	זוגי	zu·gi
How much is	כמה זה	ka·ma ze
it per ...?	עולה ל ...?	o·le le ...
night	לילה	lai·la

Eating & Drinking

Can you	אתה יכול	a·ta ya·khol
recommend	להמליץ על ...?	le·ham·lits al ... (m)
a ...?	את יכולה	at ye·cho·la
	להמליץ על ...?	le·ham·lits al ... (f)

Signs – Hebrew	
Entrance	כניסה
Exit	יציאה
Open	פתוח
Closed	סגור
Information	מודיעין
Prohibited	אסור
Toilets	שירותים
Men	גברים
Women	נשים

| cafe | בית קפה | bet ka·fe |
| restaurant | מסעדה | mis·a·da |

What's the local speciality?

מה המאכל ma ha·ma·'a·khal
המקומי? ha·me·ko·mi

Do you have vegetarian food?

יש לכם אוכל yesh la·khem o·khel
צמחוני? tsim·kho·ni

I'd like the	אני צריך/	a·ni tsa·rikh/
..., please.	צריכה את ...,	tsri·kha et ...
	בבקשה.	be·va·ka·sha (m/f)
bill	החשבון	ha·khesh·bon
menu	התפריט	ha·taf·rit

Emergencies

| Help! | הצילו! | ha·tsi·lu |
| Go away! | לך מפה! | lekh mi·po |

Call ...!	תתקשר ל ...!	tit·ka·sher le ...
a doctor	רופא	ro·fe/ro·fa (m/f)
the police	משטרה	mish·ta·ra

I'm lost.

אני אבוד. a·ni a·vud (m)
אני אבודה. a·ni a·vu·da (f)

Where are the toilets?

איפה השירותים? e·fo ha·she·ru·tim

I'm sick.

אני חולה. a·ni kho·le/kho·la (m/f)

Shopping & Services

I'm looking for ...

אני מחפש ... a·ni me·kha·pes ... (m)
אני מחפשת ... a·ni me·kha·pe·set ... (f)

Can I look at it?

אפשר להסתכל ef·shar le·his·ta·kel
על זה? al ze

How much is it?

כמה זה עולה? ka·ma ze o·le

Where's an ATM?

איפה יש כספומט? e·fo yesh kas·po·mat

Transport & Directions

Is this the ...	האם זה/זאת	ha·im ze/zot
to (Haifa)?	ה ... ל	ha ... le·
	(חיפה)?	(khai·fa) (m/f)
boat	אוניה	o·ni·ya (f)
bus	אוטובוס	o·to·bus (m)
plane	מטוס	ma·tos (m)
train	רכבת	ra·ke·vet (f)

Numbers – Hebrew

1	אחת	a·khat
2	שתיים	shta·yim
3	שלוש	sha·losh
4	ארבע	ar·ba
5	חמש	kha·mesh
6	שש	shesh
7	שבע	she·va
8	שמונה	shmo·ne
9	תשע	te·sha
10	עשר	e·ser
100	מאה	me·a
1000	אלף	e·lef

Note that English numerals are used in modern Hebrew text.

What time's   באיזו שעה   be·e·ze sha·a
the ... bus?   האוטובוס   ha·o·to·bus
  ...? ה   ha ...
  first   ראשון   ri·shon
  last   אחרון   a·kha·ron

One ... ticket,   כרטיס   kar·tis
please.   ... אחד   e·khad ...
  בבקשה.   be·va·ka·sha
  one-way   לכיוון אחד   le·ki·vun e·khad
  return   הלוך ושוב   ha·lokh va·shov

How much is it to ...?
  ?... כמה זה ל   ka·ma ze le ...

Please take me to (this address).
תיקח/תיקחי אותי   ti·kakh/tik·khi o·ti
(כתובת הזאת)ל   (lak·to·vet ha·zot)
בבקשה.   be·va·ka·sha (m/f)

Can you show me (on the map)?
אתה/את יכול   a·ta/at ya·khol/ye·kho·la
להראות   le·har·ot
?(על המפה) לי   (li al ha·ma·pa) (m/f)

What's the address?
?מה הכתובת   ma hak·to·vet

TURKISH

Turkish is the official language of Turkey and co-official language of Cyprus (alongside Greek). Turkish vowels are generally shorter and slightly harsher than in English. When you see a double vowel in our pronunciation guides, eg sa·at, you need to pronounce it twice. Note also that a is pronounced as the 'u' in 'run', ai as in 'aisle', ay as in 'say', e as in 'bet', ee as in 'see', eu as the 'u' in 'nurse', ew as ee with rounded lips, o as in 'pot', oo as in 'zoo', uh as the 'a' in 'ago', zh as the 's' in 'pleasure', r is always rolled and v is softer than in English (pronounced between a 'v'

and a 'w'). The stressed syllables are indicated with italics. Polite and informal options are indicated by 'pol' and 'inf' respectively.

Basics

Hello.   Merhaba.   mer·ha·ba
Goodbye.   Hoşçakalın.   hosh·cha·ka·luhn (pol)
(when leaving)   Hoşçakal.   hosh·cha·kal (inf)
Goodbye.   Güle güle.   gew·le gew·le
(when staying)
Yes.   Evet.   e·vet
No.   Hayır.   ha·yuhr
Please.   Lütfen.   lewt·fen
Thank you.   Teşekkür.   te·shek·kewr
Excuse me.   Bakar   ba·kar
  mısınız?   muh·suh·nuhz
Sorry.   Özür   er·zewr
  dilerim.   dee·le·reem

How are you?
Nasılsınız? (pol)   na·suhl·suh·nuhz
Nasılsın? (inf)   na·suhl·suhn
Fine. And you?
İyiyim.   ee·yee·yeem
Ya siz/sen? (pol/inf)   ya seez/sen
What's your name?
Adınız nedir?   a·duh·nuhz ne·deer (pol)
Adınız ne?   a·duh·nuhz ne (inf)
My name is ...
Benim adım ...   be·neem a·duhm ...
Do you speak English?
İngilizce   een·gee·leez·je
konuşuyor   ko·noo·shoo·yor
musunuz?   moo·soo·nooz
I don't understand.
Anlamıyorum.   an·la·muh·yo·room

Accommodation

Where's a ...?   Buralarda   boo·ra·lar·da
  nerede ... var?   ne·re·de ... var
  guesthouse   misafirhane   mee·sa·feer·ha·ne
  hotel   otel   o·tel

Signs – Turkish	
Giriş	Entrance
Çıkış	Exit
Açık	Open
Kapalı	Closed
Danışma	Information
Yasak	Prohibited
Tuvaletler	Toilets
Erkek	Men
Kadın	Women

Numbers – Turkish

1	*bir*	beer
2	*iki*	ee·*kee*
3	*üç*	ewch
4	*dört*	dert
5	*beş*	besh
6	*altı*	al·*tuh*
7	*yedi*	ye·*dee*
8	*sekiz*	se·*keez*
9	*dokuz*	do·*kooz*
10	*on*	on
100	*yüz*	yewz
1000	*bin*	been

Do you have a ... room?	*... odanız var mı?*	... o·da·*nuhz* var muh
single	*Tek kişilik*	tek kee·shee·*leek*
double	*İki kişilik*	ee·*kee* kee·shee·*leek*

How much is it per ...?	*... ne kadar?*	... ne ka·*dar*
night	*Geceliği*	ge·je·lee·*ee*

Eating & Drinking

Can you recommend a ...?	*İyi bir ... tavsiye edebilir misiniz?*	ee·*yee* beer ... tav·see·*ye* e·de·bee·*leer* mee·see·*neez*
cafe	*kafe*	ka·*fe*
restaurant	*restoran*	res·to·*ran*

What's the local speciality?
Bu yöreye has yiyecekler neler?
boo yeu·re·*ye* has yee·ye·jek·*ler* ne·*ler*

Do you have vegetarian food?
Vejeteryan yiyecekleriniz var mı?
ve·zhe·ter·*yan* yee·ye·jek·le·ree·*neez* var muh

I'd like the ..., please.	*... istiyorum.*	... ees·*tee*·yo·room
bill	*Hesabı*	he·sa·*buh*
menu	*Menüyü*	me·new·*yew*

Emergencies

Help!	*İmdat!*	eem·*dat*
Go away!	*Git burdan!*	geet boor·*dan*
Call ...!	*... çağırın!*	... cha·*uh*·ruhn

a doctor	*Doktor*	dok·*tor*
the police	*Polis*	po·*lees*

I'm lost.
Kayboldum.   kai·bol·*doom*

Where are the toilets?
Tuvaletler nerede?   too·va·let·*ler* ne·re·de

I'm sick.
Hastayım.   has·*ta*·yuhm

Shopping & Services

I'm looking for ...
... istiyorum.   ... ees·*tee*·yo·room

Can I look at it?
Bakabilir miyim?   ba·ka·bee·*leer* mee·*yeem*

How much is it?
Ne kadar?   ne ka·*dar*

Where's an ATM?
Bankamatik nerede var?   ban·ka·ma·*teek* ne·re·de var

Transport & Directions

Is this the ... to (Sirkeci)?	*(Sirkeci'ye) giden ... bu mu?*	(seer·ke·jee·ye) gee·*den* ... boo moo
boat	*vapur*	va·*poor*
bus	*otobüs*	o·to·*bews*
plane	*uçak*	oo·*chak*
train	*tren*	tren

What time's the ... bus?	*... otobüs ne zaman?*	... o·to·*bews* ne za·*man*
first	*İlk*	eelk
next	*Sonraki*	son·ra·*kee*

One ... ticket, please.	*..., lütfen.*	... lewt·fen
one-way	*Bir gidiş bileti*	beer gee·*deesh* bee·le·*tee*
return	*Gidiş-dönüş bir bilet*	gee·deesh-deu·*newsh* beer bee·*let*

How much is it to ...?
... ne kadar?   ... ne ka·*dar*

Please take me to (this address).
Lütfen beni (bu adrese) götürün.
lewt·fen be·*nee* (boo ad·re·se) geu·*tew*·rewn

Can you show me (on the map)?
Bana (haritada) gösterebilir misiniz?
ba·*na* (ha·ree·ta·da) geus·te·re·bee·*leer* mee·seen·*neez*

What's the address?
Adresi nedir?   ad·re·see ne·*deer*

GLOSSARY

This glossary contains some English, Arabic (Ar), Egyptian (E), Farsi (Far), Hebrew (Heb), Jordanian (J), Lebanese (Leb) and Turkish (T) words and abbreviations you may encounter in this book. For other useful words and phrases, see Language (p586).

Abbasid dynasty – Baghdad-based successor dynasty to the *Umayyad dynasty*; ruled from AD 750 until the sacking of Baghdad by the Mongols in 1258

abu (Ar) – father or saint

acropolis – high city; hilltop citadel of a classic Hellenic city

agora – open space for commerce and politics in a classic Hellenic city, such as a marketplace or forum

ahwa (E) – see *qahwa*

Ashkenazi – a Jew of German or Eastern European descent

Ayyubid dynasty – Egyptian-based dynasty (AD 1169–1250) founded by *Saladin*

badia (J) – stone or basalt desert

bait – see *beit*

baksheesh – alms or tip

balad (Ar) – land or city

beit (Ar) – house; also *bait*

calèche (E) – horse-drawn carriage

cami(i) (T) – mosque

caravanserai – see *khan*

cardo – road running north–south through a Roman city

carnet de passage – permit allowing entry of a vehicle to a country without incurring taxes

çarşı (T) – market or bazaar

çay (T) – see *shai*

centrale – telephone office

chador (Ar) – black, one-piece, head-to-toe covering garment; worn by many Muslim women

decumanus – road running east–west through a Roman city

deir (Ar) – monastery or convent

dervish – Muslim mystic; see also *Sufi*

diaspora – community in dispersion or exile from its homeland

dolmuş (T) – minibus that sometimes runs to a timetable but more often sets off when it's full

Eid al-Adha – Feast of Sacrifice marking the pilgrimage to Mecca

Eid al-Fitr – Festival of Breaking the Fast celebrated at the end of *Ramadan*

emir – literally 'prince'; Islamic ruler, military commander or governor

evi (T) – house

Fatimid dynasty – Shiite dynasty (AD 908–1171) from North Africa, later based in Cairo, claiming descent from Mohammed's daughter Fatima

felafel – deep-fried balls of chickpea paste with spices; ta'amiyya in Egypt

felucca – traditional wooden sailboat used on the Nile in Egypt

fuul – paste made from fava beans

gebel (E) – see *jebel*

gület (T) – traditional wooden yacht

hajj – annual Muslim pilgrimage to Mecca; one of the five pillars of Islam

hamam (T) – see *hammam*

Hamas – militant Islamic organisation that aims to create an Islamic state in the pre-1948 territory of Palestine; the word is an acronym (in Arabic) for Islamic Resistance Movement

hammam (Ar) – bathhouse; *hamam* in Turkish

haram – anything that is forbidden by Islamic law; also refers to the prayer hall of a mosque

hasid – (plural *hasidim*) member of an ultra-orthodox Jewish sect; also *hared*

Hejira – Mohammed's flight from Mecca to Medina in AD 622; the starting point of the Muslim era and the start of the Islamic calendar

Hezbollah – 'Party of God'; Lebanon-based organ of militant *Shiite* Muslims

imam – prayer leader or Muslim cleric

intifada – Palestinian uprising against Israeli authorities in the West Bank, Gaza and East Jerusalem; literally 'shaking off'

jamaa – see *masjid*

jebel (Ar) – hill, mountain; *gebel* in Egypt

jihad – literally 'striving in the way of the faith'; holy war

keffiyeh (Ar) – chequered scarf worn by Arabs

khan – travellers' inn, usually constructed on main trade routes, with accommodation on the 1st floor and stables and storage on the ground floor; also *caravanserai, han, wikala* in Egypt

kibbutz – (plural kibbutzim) Jewish communal settlement run cooperatively by its members

kilim – woven rug

kippa – skullcap

Knesset – Israeli parliament

Koran – see *Quran*

kosher – food prepared according to Jewish dietary law

Likud – Israeli right-wing political party

lokanta (T) – restaurant

madrassa – Muslim seminary; modern Arabic word for school; *medrese(si)* in Turkey

mahalle(si) (T) – neighbourhood, district of a city

masjid (Ar) – mosque; also *jamaa*

medina – city or town, especially the old quarter of a city

medrese(si) (T) – see *madrassa*

Mesopotamia – ancient name for Iraq from the Greek meaning 'between two rivers'

meydan(ı) – see *midan*

meyhane (T) – (plural meyhaneler) tavern

mezze – a collection of appetisers or small plates of food; *meze* in Turkish

midan (Ar) – town or city square; *meydan(ı)* in Turkish (plural *meydanlar*)

midrahov (Heb) – pedestrian mall

mihrab – niche in a mosque indicating direction of Mecca

minbar – pulpit used for sermons in a mosque

mitzvah (Heb) – adherence to Jewish commandments

muezzin – cantor who sings the call to prayer

mullah – Muslim scholar, teacher or religious leader

nargileh (Ar) – water pipe used to smoke tobacco; *sheesha* in Egypt

obelisk – monolithic stone pillar with square sides tapering to a pyramidal top; used as a monument in ancient Egypt

otogar (T) – bus station

pansiyon – pension, B&B or guesthouse

pasha – Ottoman governor appointed by the sultan in Constantinople

Peshmerga – Kurdish

soldiers, literally 'those who face death'

PKK – Kurdistan Workers Party

PLO – Palestine Liberation Organisation

PTT (T) – Posta, Telefon, Telğraf; post, telephone and telegraph office

pylon – monumental gateway at the entrance to a temple

qahwa (Ar) – coffee, coffeehouse; *ahwa* in Egypt

qasr – castle or palace

Quran – the holy book of Islam; also *Koran*

Ramadan – ninth month of the lunar Islamic calendar during which Muslims fast from sunrise to sunset; Ramazan in Turkish

ras (Ar) – cape, headland or head

sahn (Ar) – courtyard of a mosque

Sala – the Muslim obligation of prayer, ideally to be performed five times a day; one of the five pillars of Islam

Saladin – (Salah ad-Din in Arabic) Kurdish warlord who retook Jerusalem from the Crusaders; founder of the *Ayyubid dynasty*

Sawm – the Muslim month of *Ramadan;* one of the five pillars of Islam

servees – shared taxi with a fixed route

settler – term used to describe Israelis who have created new communities on Arab territory, usually land captured from the Arabs during the 1967 war

Shabbat – Jewish Sabbath observed from sundown on Friday to one hour after sundown on Saturday

Shahada – Islam's basic tenet and profession of faith: 'There is no god but Allah, and Mohammed is the Prophet of Allah'; one of the five pillars of Islam

shai (Ar) – tea; çay in Turkish

sheesha (E) – see *nargileh*

sheikh – venerated religious scholar; also shaikh

sherut (Heb) – shared taxi with a fixed route

Shiite – one of the two main branches of Islam

shwarma – grilled meat sliced from a spit and served in pita-type bread with salad; also döner kebap in Turkish

siq (Ar) – narrow passageway or defile such as the one at Petra

souq – market or bazaar

Sufi – follower of any of the Islamic mystical orders that emphasise dancing, chanting and trances in order to attain unity with God; see also *dervish*

sultan – absolute ruler of a Muslim state

Sunni – one of the two main branches of Islam

ta'amiyya (E) – see *felafel*

Talmud – a collection of 63 Jewish holy books that complement the *Torah*

tell – ancient mound created by centuries of urban rebuilding

Torah – five books of Moses, the first five Old Testament books; also called the Pentateuch

Umayyad dynasty – first great dynasty of Arab Muslim rulers, based in Damascus (AD 661–750); also Omayyad dynasty

wikala (E) – see *khan*

willayat – village

Zakat – the Muslim obligation to give alms to the poor; one of the five pillars of Islam

ziggurat (Far) – rectangular temple tower or tiered mound built in *Mesopotamia* by the Akkadians, Babylonians and Sumerians

Behind the Scenes

SEND US YOUR FEEDBACK

We love to hear from travellers – your comments keep us on our toes and help make our books better. Our well-travelled team reads every word on what you loved or loathed about this book. Although we cannot reply individually to your submissions, we always guarantee that your feedback goes straight to the appropriate authors, in time for the next edition. Each person who sends us information is thanked in the next edition – the most useful submissions are rewarded with a selection of digital PDF chapters.

Visit **lonelyplanet.com/contact** to submit your updates and suggestions or to ask for help. Our award-winning website also features inspirational travel stories, news and discussions.

Note: We may edit, reproduce and incorporate your comments in Lonely Planet products such as guidebooks, websites and digital products, so let us know if you don't want your comments reproduced or your name acknowledged. For a copy of our privacy policy visit lonelyplanet.com/privacy.

AUTHOR THANKS

Anthony Ham

Shukran to all of those from Cairo to İstanbul and most places in between who have, on every visit, reinforced my love affair with the region. A heartfelt thanks to my editor Helen Elfer, my coauthors, and to Marina, Carlota and Valentina, my three girls who make coming home the greatest gift in the world. My work on this book is dedicated to Ron, whose visit to Damascus all those years ago made it a true place of the soul.

Sofia Barbarani

Thank you to the many local men and women who helped me get my bearings and pointed me towards the region's more beautiful sights. To all the welcoming families that took me into their homes during my travels, making the Kurdish experience all the more genuine and meaningful. To my Kurdish friends, who gave up their best-kept secrets and took me to their favourite spots for the benefit of the guide. Most of all thank you to Michael Stephens, who was always patient and supportive.

Jessica Lee

Big thanks to fellow authors on the *Turkey* guide: James Bainbridge, Brett Atkinson,

Stuart Butler, Steve Fallon, Will Gourlay, and Virginia Maxwell, and to Jo Cooke for her patience with my acronym queries. And a huge *çok teşekkürler* to Ömer Yapıs; Kazım and Ayşe Akay and Bekir Kırca; Ömer and Ahmet in Kaş; Meral; and Yakup Kahveci.

Virginia Maxwell

Many thanks to Lynne Miller, Lou-Ellen Martin, Dana Nasr, Hala Mansour, Olivier Gougeon, Paul Newson and Ruth Young.

Daniel Robinson

Special thanks to Irit Steinberg (Hula Nature Reserve), Riki & Dov Ruckenstein and Moshe Tov Kreps (Tzfat); Etha & Erwin Frenkel (Korazim); Mariana Bravo (Magdala); Moshe Ohz (Tiberias); Nissim Mazig (Kursi); Ayala & Ofer Markman and Roni Barziv (Haifa); Maoz Yinon, Linda Hallel, Sami Jabali & Silke, Emile Emran, Abed and Abu Ayyad of the White Mosque, and Tariq Bsoul of Nazarene Transport & Tourism (Nazareth); Michal and Sivan (Ein Gedi Nature Reserve); Sarinah, Leo, Bella and Shoshana Kalb (Ein Bokek); Asaf Madmony (Ne'ot HaKikar); and, most especially, my wife Rachel and son Yair for their unceasing support, understanding and patience.

Anthony Sattin

Among the many people who have provided assistance, information, advice and gossip during the research and writing of this book, I would particularly like to thank HE Hisham Zaazou, Minister of Tourism to the Egyptian Tourist Authority, and Mrs Omayma El Husseini, director of the Egyptian State Tourist Office London; to the experts Ali and Elisabeth at the International Travel Bureau of Egypt; Dr Mounir Neamatalla; Heba Bakri; Christopher Tutty; Rafic Khairallah; Christoph Schleissing; Linda Wheeler; Zeina Abou Kheir; Marwa and Mohammed Abdel Rehim; Tim Baily; Aiman Zaki; and Dr Haitham Ibrahim and Mohamed Ezat of the Egyptian Environmental Affairs Agency.

Andy Symington

Kind help was provided by numerous Iranians but I owe especial thanks to Rosa Khishdoust, Nasser Khan, Hassan Kandovani, Najafi Mehran, Shary Zarrin Panjeh, Amir Abedinpour, Lourdes Villa Diez, Jo Cooke, Mustafa Hocaoglu, Yousef Shariyat, David Thomson, Mohsen Asadi, Hassan Khakbaz, Massoun Khani, Mary Northmore, Helen Carmichael, YuanYuan Huang, Miguel García, editor Helen Elfer and expert coordinator Anthony Ham. Thanks to my family for their support and to José Eliseo Vázquez González, Michael

Burren and Eduardo Cuadrado Diogo for keeping things going at home while I'm away.

Jenny Walker

Returning to Jordan is always a great pleasure, not just on account of the spectacular scenery and 'wondrous sights', but also because the people of Jordan are so unfailingly welcoming and optimistic in the face of great challenges. Thanks as ever to all Jordanian friends who have helped over the years of engagement with this chapter and to my beloved husband, Sam Owen, who continues to accompany and support beyond the call of duty during research and write-up.

ACKNOWLEDGEMENTS

Climate map data adapted from Peel MC, Finlayson BL & McMahon TA (2007) 'Updated World Map of the Köppen-Geiger Climate Classification', Hydrology and Earth System Sciences, 11, 163344.

Illustrations pp60–1, pp84–5, pp124–5, pp220–1, pp418–9, pp424–5 and pp446–7 by Javier Zarracina; pp328–9 by Michael Weldon.

Cover photograph: Wadi Rum and Jebel Qatar, Jordan; Michele Falzone/AWL.

THIS BOOK

This 8th edition of Lonely Planet's *Middle East* guidebook was researched and written by coordinating author Anthony Ham, and Sofia Barbarani, Jessica Lee, Virginia Maxwell, Daniel Robinson, Anthony Sattin, Andy Symington and Jenny Walker.

Destination Editor
Helen Elfer

Product Editor
Katie O'Connell

Senior Cartographer
Valentina Kremenchutskaya

Book Designer
Jennifer Mullins

Assisting Editors
Kate Chapman, Samantha Forge, Gabrielle Innes, Kate James, Anne Mulvaney, Charlotte Orr, Monique Perrin

Assisting Cartographers
Corey Hutchison

Cover Researcher
Naomi Parker

Thanks to Shahara Ahmed, Angie Mills-Smith, Ilana Myers, Claire Naylor, Karyn Noble, Denis O'Connor, Ellie Simpson, Lauren Wellicome, Kristina West

Index

Map Legend

Sights

- Beach
- Bird Sanctuary
- Buddhist
- Castle/Palace
- Christian
- Confucian
- Hindu
- Islamic
- Jain
- Jewish
- Monument
- Museum/Gallery/Historic Building
- Ruin
- Shinto
- Sikh
- Taoist
- Winery/Vineyard
- Zoo/Wildlife Sanctuary
- Other Sight

Activities, Courses & Tours

- Bodysurfing
- Diving
- Canoeing/Kayaking
- Course/Tour
- Sento Hot Baths/Onsen
- Skiing
- Snorkelling
- Surfing
- Swimming/Pool
- Walking
- Windsurfing
- Other Activity

Sleeping

- Sleeping
- Camping

Eating

- Eating

Drinking & Nightlife

- Drinking & Nightlife
- Cafe

Entertainment

- Entertainment

Shopping

- Shopping

Information

- Bank
- Embassy/Consulate
- Hospital/Medical
- Internet
- Police
- Post Office
- Telephone
- Toilet
- Tourist Information
- Other Information

Geographic

- Beach
- Hut/Shelter
- Lighthouse
- Lookout
- Mountain/Volcano
- Oasis
- Park
- Pass
- Picnic Area
- Waterfall

Population

- Capital (National)
- Capital (State/Province)
- City/Large Town
- Town/Village

Transport

- Airport
- Border crossing
- Bus
- Cable car/Funicular
- Cycling
- Ferry
- Metro station
- Monorail
- Parking
- Petrol station
- S-Bahn/S-train/Subway station
- Taxi
- T-bane/Tunnelbana station
- Train station/Railway
- Tram
- Tube station
- U-Bahn/Underground station
- Other Transport

Note: Not all symbols displayed above appear on the maps in this book

Routes

- Tollway
- Freeway
- Primary
- Secondary
- Tertiary
- Lane
- Unsealed road
- Road under construction
- Plaza/Mall
- Steps
- Tunnel
- Pedestrian overpass
- Walking Tour
- Walking Tour detour
- Path/Walking Trail

Boundaries

- International
- State/Province
- Disputed
- Regional/Suburb
- Marine Park
- Cliff
- Wall

Hydrography

- River, Creek
- Intermittent River
- Canal
- Water
- Dry/Salt/Intermittent Lake
- Reef

Areas

- Airport/Runway
- Beach/Desert
- Cemetery (Christian)
- Cemetery (Other)
- Glacier
- Mudflat
- Park/Forest
- Sight (Building)
- Sportsground
- Swamp/Mangrove

Daniel Robinson

Israel & the Palestinian Territories Brought up near San Francisco and Chicago, Daniel spent part of his childhood in Jerusalem, a bit of his youth at Kibbutz Lotan and many years in Tel Aviv, where he worked on a PhD in late Ottoman history, covered suicide bombings for the AP, and helped lead the local Critical Mass campaign for bike paths. A Lonely Planet author since 1989, he holds a BA in Near Eastern Studies from Princeton and an MA in Jewish History from Tel Aviv University.

Anthony Sattin

Egypt Anthony has been travelling around the Middle East for several decades and has lived in Cairo, as well as other cities in the region. His highly-acclaimed books include *Lifting the Veil*, *A Winter on the Nile* and *The Gates of Africa*. His latest, *Young Lawrence*, looks at the five years TE Lawrence spent in the Middle East leading up to 1914. He happily spends several months each year along the Nile and is still looking for a plot where he can tread mud-bricks and build himself a house. He tweets about Egypt and travel @anthonysattin.

Andy Symington

Iran Andy is an experienced Lonely Planet author based in Spain who has contributed to numerous guidebooks, articles and other products on countries across the world. He has a degree in Iranian archaeology and has long had a fascination with this beautiful land. On this trip he baked in desert heat, shivered in northern blizzards and marvelled at the country's fabulous culture, landscapes and people.

Jenny Walker

Jordan For over a decade Jenny has written extensively on the Middle East for many Lonely Planet guides, and is a member of the British Guild of Travel Writers. She has a long academic engagement in the region (she did her dissertation on Doughty and Lawrence, her MPhil thesis from Oxford University on the perception of the Arabic Orient, and is currently studying for her PhD at NTU). Associate Dean at Caledonian University College of Engineering in Oman since 2008, she has travelled in 110 countries from Panama to Mongolia.

OUR STORY

A beat-up old car, a few dollars in the pocket and a sense of adventure. In 1972 that's all Tony and Maureen Wheeler needed for the trip of a lifetime – across Europe and Asia overland to Australia. It took several months, and at the end – broke but inspired – they sat at their kitchen table writing and stapling together their first travel guide, *Across Asia on the Cheap*. Within a week they'd sold 1500 copies. Lonely Planet was born.

Today, Lonely Planet has offices in Franklin, London, Melbourne, Oakland, Beijing and Delhi, with more than 600 staff and writers. We share Tony's belief that 'a great guidebook should do three things: inform, educate and amuse'.

OUR WRITERS

Anthony Ham

Coordinating Author, Syria Anthony first landed in Damascus in 1998 and couldn't bear to leave. His first job for Lonely Planet was the Iraq chapter of this guide back in 1999, and he has since written or contributed to Lonely Planet guides to Jordan, Iran, Saudi Arabia and Libya, and five editions of this *Middle East* guide. He has also worked in Australia as a refugee lawyer with clients from the Middle East and has a Masters degree in Middle Eastern politics. Anthony now divides his time between Melbourne and Madrid and writes for magazines and newspapers around the world. Read more about Anthony at www.anthonyham.com.

Sofia Barbarani

Iraq Sofia is Italian but has lived in Iraq's Kurdish region for over a year. She was drawn to Iraq and Kurdistan following a Masters degree in Middle East studies and moved to the region to pursue a career in journalism. Despite her previous knowledge of Kurdistan, travelling the region gave her a better understanding of the enclave and its people. Her favourite trip was undoubtedly to Akre, where the hospitality of the Kurds really shone through.

Jessica Lee

Turkey Jessica first went to Turkey in 2005 and ended up leading adventure tours across the breadth of Anatolia for four years. In 2011 she moved there to live and now calls Turkey home. As a co-author on the last two editions of Lonely Planet's *Turkey* guide, she's travelled to most of Turkey's far-flung corners but especially loves the wild landscapes of the southeast, the ruin-strewn trails of the Lycian Way and the wacky rock formations of Cappadocia. She tweets @jessofarabia.

Read more about Jess at:
lonelyplanet.com/members/jessicalee1

Virginia Maxwell

Lebanon Although based in Australia, Virginia spends much of her year travelling in the Middle East, Mediterranean Europe and North Africa. She has written Lonely Planet guidebooks to Turkey, Egypt, Syria, Iran and the United Arab Emirates, and this is the second time she has worked on the Lebanon chapter of Lonely Planet's *Middle East* book.

OVER PAGE
MORE WRITERS

Published by Lonely Planet Publications Pty Ltd
ABN 36 005 607 983
8th edition – September 2015
ISBN 978 1 74220 800 8
© Lonely Planet 2015   Photographs © as indicated 2015
10 9 8 7 6 5 4 3 2 1
Printed in China